Microsoft FOUNDATION CLASS 4 BIBLE

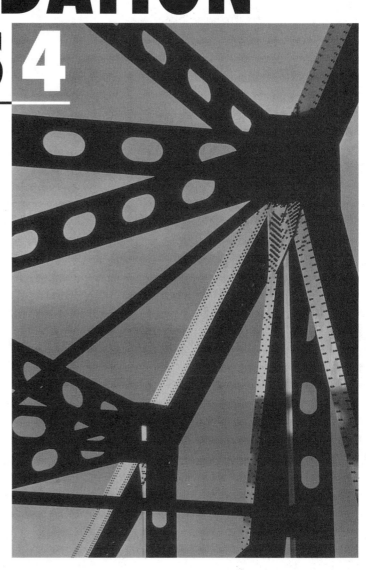

FRED PANDOLFI

MIKE OLIVER

MICHAEL WOLSKI

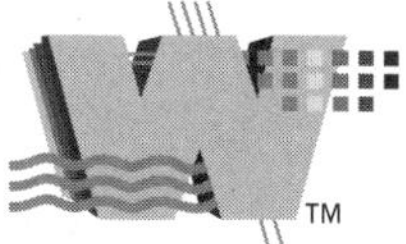

Waite Group Press™
A Division of Sams Publishing
Corte Madera, CA

Publisher Mitchell Waite
Associate Publisher Charles Drucker

Acquisitions Manager Jill Pisoni
Acquisitions Editor Joanne Miller

Editorial Director John Crudo
Project Editor Lisa Goldstein
Content Editor Harry Henderson
Copy Editor Marc Polonsky
Technical Reviewer David Calhoun

Production Director Julianne Ososke
Production Manager Cecile Kaufman
Production Editor Mark Nigara
Cover Design Sestina Quarequio
Interior Design Sestina Quarequio, Michele Cuneo
Production LeeAnn Nelson
Illustrations Hans & Cassidy, Inc.
Cover Image © Kay Chernush/Image Bank

Published by Waite Group Press™, 200 Tamal Plaza, Corte Madera, CA 94925.
Waite Group Press™ is a division of Sams Publishing.

Printed in the United States of America
96 97 98 99 • 10 9 8 7 6 5 4 3 2 1

Library of Congress Cataloging-in-Publication Data
Pandolfi, Fred
Microsoft Foundation Class 4 bible / Fred Pandolfi, Mike Oliver, Michael Wolski.
p. cm.
Includes index.
ISBN 1-57169-021-2
1. Microsoft Windows (Computer file) 2. C++ (computer program language)
I. Oliver, Mike. II. Wolski, Michael. III. Title.
QA76.76.W56P35 1996
005.26'2--dc20

96-14120
CIP

Dedication

I dedicate this book to my wife, Andrea. Andrea has patiently put up with and supported me while I worked (and work) almost every waking moment of my life.

—Fred Pandolfi

To the memories of C.S. and R.S., and to K.B. (S.B.), who was (almost) always understanding

—Mike Oliver

There is no way I could have written this book without the support and understanding of my family and friends. Without them, I would certainly have self-destructed over the course of the last year. But most of all, I have to credit my drive and determination to my Mom and Dad. This one is for you!

—Michael Wolski

Message from the **Publisher**

Welcome to Our Nervous System

Some people say that the World Wide Web is a graphical extension of the information superhighway, just a network of humans and machines sending each other long lists of the equivalent of digital junk mail.

I think it is much more than that. To me, the Web is nothing less than the nervous system of the entire planet—not just a collection of computer brains connected together, but more like a billion silicon neurons entangled and recirculating electro-chemical signals of information and data, each contributing to the birth of another CPU and another Web site.

Think of each person's hard disk connected at once to every other hard disk on earth, driven by human navigators searching like Columbus for the New World. Seen this way the Web is more of a super entity, a growing, living thing, controlled by the universal human will to expand, to be more. Yet, unlike a purposeful business plan with rigid rules, the Web expands in a nonlinear, unpredictable, creative way that echoes natural evolution.

We created our Web site not just to extend the reach of our computer book products but to be part of this synaptic neural network, to experience, like a nerve in the body, the flow of ideas and then to pass those ideas up the food chain of the mind. Your mind. Even more, we wanted to pump some of our own creative juices into this rich wine of technology.

Taste Our Digital Wine

And so we ask you to taste our wine by visiting the body of our business. Begin by understanding the metaphor we have created for our Web site—a universal learning center, situated in outer space in the form of a space station. A place where you can journey to study any topic from the convenience of your own screen. Right now we are focusing on computer topics, but the stars are the limit on the Web.

If you are interested in discussing this Web site or finding out more about the Waite Group, please send me e-mail with your comments, and I will be happy to respond. Being a programmer myself, I love to talk about technology and find out what our readers are looking for.

Sincerely,

Mitchell Waite

Mitchell Waite, C.E.O. and Publisher

200 Tamal Plaza
Corte Madera, CA 94925
415-924-2575
415-924-2576 fax

Website:
http://www.waite.com/waite

Creating the Highest Quality Computer Books in the Industry

Waite Group Press
Waite Group New Media

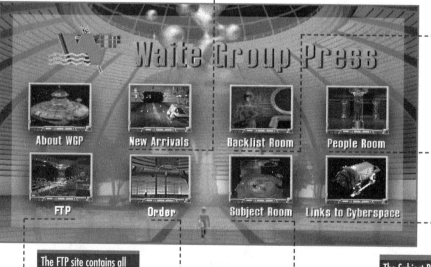

About the Authors

Fred Pandolfi is a product manager at CheckFree Corporation, and holds a B.S. degree in Computer Engineering from Pennsylvania State University. He has been developing software since age 13 and has worked with MFC for many years. In his spare time, Fred enjoys playing racquetball, listening to music, and a variety of outdoor activities. Fred and his wife live in Sterling, Virginia. Fred can be reached at 102761.1546@compuserve.com.

Mike Oliver is a product manager with CheckFree Corporation, and holds a B.S. degree in Aerospace Engineering and English from the University of Virginia. He has been playing with computers ever since the early days of the Atari 800, working with MFC since Visual C++ 1.0. Mike can be reached at msoliver@aol.com.

Michael Wolski is a product manager with CheckFree Corporation, and holds a B.S. degree in Electrical Engineering from the University of Virginia. He has been actively writing software for the past 14 years on several different platforms. In his copious free time he can be found reading, rollerblading, or dabbling in the kitchen. Michael can be reached at 102761.1550@compuserve.com.

Table of Contents

Contents

Acknowledgment

Thanks to Lisa Goldstein for her tireless efforts to keep us novices in line. Thanks to Ken Benvenuto, who unknowingly was "on board" from the very beginning.

"Best" regards, Ken!

—Fred, Mike, and Michael

Introduction

The popularity of a programming language is a transient thing. From the very early days of computing, as the first practitioners of the gentle art of programming began applying their craft, there have been raging debates over which programming language is best and for what reasons. Some have, for example, always held the position that a programming language should be high-level, as close to a natural language like English as possible. Others have believed that a language should be low-level, byte-oriented, giving the programmer ultimate control over the machine. For forty years now, one or another programming language has taken center stage, declared with great fanfare to be "the" language only to be replaced a couple of years later. Often, this change has been brought about by the evolution of one language to another (e.g. PL/1 leading to C in turn leading to C++). Other times, enhancements in computer hardware or compiler technology have been the driving forces behind this transformation. Although there is no guarantee that this trend will not continue, there has been a new development with C++, the reigning champion. Whereas the underlying language has not only retained but increased its acceptability and widespread usage over the past 10 years, different supersets known as class libraries, have seen their popularity wax and wane.

In the mid '90s, the usage of a particular class library, MFC (Microsoft Foundation Classes), has grown exponentially. For years, APIs (Application Programmer's Interface), accessed from procedure-based languages like Pascal and C, have been the primary way programmers have been able to command modern day operating systems like Windows and Macintosh's System 7. MFC represents an evolution of these APIs by replacing the procedural language interface with an object-oriented C++ one. Written by Microsoft and supported by their Visual C++ compiler as well as several other competing compilers, MFC has become the de facto standard with which Windows applications are developed and, as hinted by the title on the front cover, the subject of this book. There is a lot to cover, but before getting to the good stuff, this introductory chapter will go over the outline and structure of the book as well as some of the major conventions used.

What's Included

Discussing the whole of MFC is a major undertaking. There have been four separate major versions of MFC (the current one being version 4.0), and the product now consists of thousands of lines of source code. Furthermore, MFC can exist on five separate platforms (Windows/Windows for Workgroups 3.x, Win32s on 16-bit Windows, Windows 95, Windows NT, and Macintosh). It's simply not possible to cover everything in sufficient detail with a bound paperback book such as this. In order to keep the page count to a reasonable limit, the authors were compelled to leave out discussions of ancillary topics, specifically the portions of MFC covering WOSA extensions (MAPI and ODBC), Sockets, and OLE. The book concentrates on version 4.0 of MFC; implementation details of earlier versions that are now obsolete have not been included. There are, however, more than one thousand pages discussing the core "foundation" of the Microsoft Foundation Classes. There is also a companion CD-ROM that not only contains an on-line help version of the book, but also has many MFC example programs, demos of MFC utilities, and even the semi-official MFC FAQ.

This book should appeal both to the beginner MFC programmer and the advanced MFC guru. No matter how long you have been using it, there is always something new to be learned about MFC. The authors are experienced MFC programmers and have written this book with an eye towards concentrating on topics generally misunderstood or unknown by MFC programmers. This book does assume, however, a working knowledge both of Windows itself and of the C++ language. There are several excellent books that deal with these important topics (*Master C++ for Windows* is such a book from Waite Group Press). The following is a breakdown of each chapter of the book and an overview of what each covers.

Chapter 1—Overview of Windows Programming

Welcome to the wonderful world of Windows programming. We'll be introducing some basic Windows programming concepts and traditional methods and hint as to how MFC does things in its own unique (and better!) way.

Chapter 2 - The MFC Framework

Here we will be introducing the MFC framework and including some general guidelines to follow when programming with MFC. There is also a discussion of some of the core MFC classes such as CObject and CRuntimeClass, a listing of MFC's many helper functions, and an overview of how MFC uses resources and provides for context-sensitive help. This is an especially important chapter to programmers new to MFC.

Chapter 3—The Application Classes

Say goodbye to WinMain. This chapter covers the MFC application and thread classes, CWinApp and CWinThread, which contain the beating heart of any Windows application, the message loop.

Chapter 4—Windows Messaging

If you've been programming with the Windows SDK, you know all about the lengthy switch statements and the cumbersome message-handling system. Now you will learn how to handle messages the MFC way with C++ class member functions—an easy, object-oriented approach that will make it much easier to keep track of your program structure. You'll also learn about the related CCmdTarget and CCmdUI classes.

Chapter 5—The MFC Window

One of the founding principles of MFC is a thin-layer philosophy that provides for programmers an object-oriented interface to the Windows API. This principle is most prominent and most important in the CWnd class, the MFC interface class that encapsulates the ubiquitous HWND found in Windows programming. You'll learn about this all-important class in this chapter.

Chapter 6—Documents/Views

There are many different architectures popular in object-oriented design for encapsulating and presenting information. Model/View/Controller and Document/View are two such possibilities. MFC promotes the Document/View architecture with the CDocument and CView classes. Here you will be presented with an overview of the principle concepts and learn about the individual classes involved in MFC's inplementation of Document/View.

Chapter 7—Frame Windows

MFC contains special CWnd-derived classes dedicated to frame windows, the main top-level windows found in a Windows application. In this chapter, you will learn about the MDI (Multiple Document Interface) parent, MDI child, and SDI (Single Document Interface) frame windows of MFC.

Chapter 8—Dialog Boxes

MFC also contains special CWnd-derived classes for dialogs, including support for new interface concepts such as property pages, property sheets, and wizards. We'll be getting into the guts of these classes here, exploring the tricks of the trade for using them.

Chapter 9—Windows Controls

For every Windows control (list box, edit box, combo box, etc.), there is an MFC wrapper class. In this chapter, we'll be discussing each one of them, including the new common controls introduced with Windows 95.

Chapter 10—Menus and Control Bars

Other MFC classes exist for additional interface concepts such as menus, toolbars, and status bars. If you want your MFC application to include these elements, take a look at this chapter, which covers the CMenu, CControlBar, CStatusBar, and CToolBar classes.

Chapter 11—Device Contexts

The MFC class that encapsulates the Windows device context deserves a chapter of its own. A device context is the interface through which the programmer can draw something on the screen or print something to the printer. Wrapper classes for the device context portion of the Windows API, the CDC class, and classes derived from it (as the fundamental tools for interacting with a display or printer), are very useful to the MFC programmer.

Chapter 12—The MFC GDI

Another source for very useful wrapper classes is the MFC classes dedicated to the Windows GDI (Graphic Device Interface). Here, we'll be going over the classes that interact with the device context CDC class: fonts, brushes, pens, bitmaps, etc. If used properly, these classes will ensure that you'll never need to worry about not freeing your system resources.

Chapter 13—Collection Classes

Most object-oriented frameworks include classes for holding a dynamic amount of information in memory. MFC is no different. MFC includes collection classes discussed in this chapter: arrays, lists, and maps, as well as a special CString class for implementing a dynamic character buffer. As soon as you begin writing MFC applications, you'll wonder how you were ever able to program without them.

Chapter 14—Files and Serialization

One of the nicest built-in benefits of MFC is the support for object serialization. In this chapter, we'll be talking about the classes involved in executing this process. Discussed are the CFile-based file I/O classes, used to read from and write to the actual file, and the higher level CArchive class, used for tracking and archiving the objects stored to and loaded from the CFile-based object.

Chapter 15—Debugging and Exception Handling

Maybe you're the one programmer that makes no mistakes. The code is perfect from day one. Maybe you're not, though, so you might want to know about some of the very useful debugging features provided by MFC. There is also a discussion of MFC exception handling support.

Appendix A—MFC Class Hierarchy Cross-Reference

Appendix A provides a MFC class hierarchy diagram and a cross-reference indicating in which parts of the book each class is discussed.

Conventions

The structure of every chapter, with just one or two exceptions, is the same. Each chapter covers a related group of MFC classes by first giving an overview of the context of their usage and then discussing each class and its member functions individually. In the listing of each member function, several conventions have been used. To explain these conventions, let's take a look at an example entry:

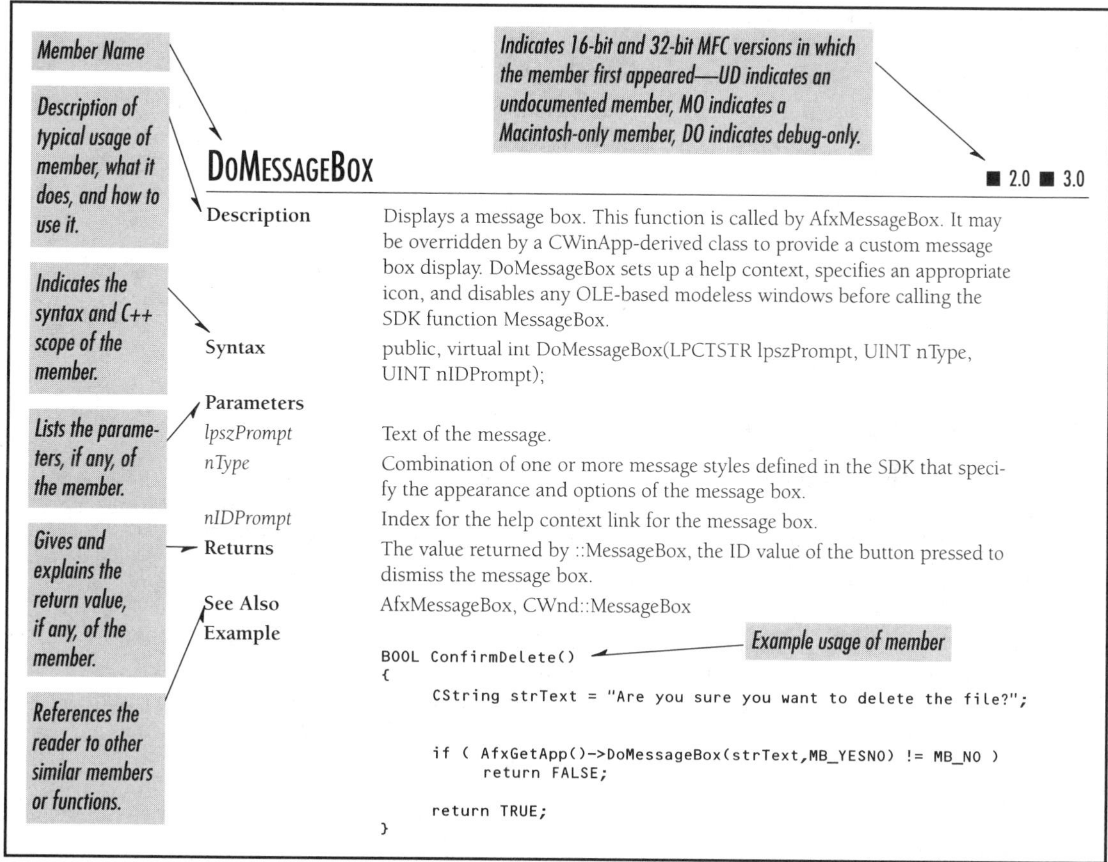

Member Name
Description of typical usage of member, what it does, and how to use it.
Indicates the syntax and C++ scope of the member.
Lists the parameters, if any, of the member.
Gives and explains the return value, if any, of the member.
References the reader to other similar members or functions.
Indicates 16-bit and 32-bit MFC versions in which the member first appeared—UD indicates an undocumented member, MO indicates a Macintosh-only member, DO indicates debug-only.
DoMessageBox
■ 2.0 ■ 3.0
Description
Displays a message box. This function is called by AfxMessageBox. It may be overridden by a CWinApp-derived class to provide a custom message box display. DoMessageBox sets up a help context, specifies an appropriate icon, and disables any OLE-based modeless windows before calling the SDK function MessageBox.
Syntax
public, virtual int DoMessageBox(LPCTSTR lpszPrompt, UINT nType, UINT nIDPrompt);
Parameters
lpszPrompt
Text of the message.
nType
Combination of one or more message styles defined in the SDK that specify the appearance and options of the message box.
nIDPrompt
Index for the help context link for the message box.
Returns
The value returned by ::MessageBox, the ID value of the button pressed to dismiss the message box.
See Also
AfxMessageBox, CWnd::MessageBox
Example
Example usage of member
BOOL ConfirmDelete()
{
CString strText = "Are you sure you want to delete the file?";
if (AfxGetApp()->DoMessageBox(strText,MB_YESNO) != MB_NO)
return FALSE;
return TRUE;
}

Figure 0-1 Member Listing Example

On the top line of the listing, the name of the member function is given. To the right of the name are the version numbers in which the member function first appeared in the 16-bit and 32-bit versions of MFC. There are many functions in this book that do not have a 16-bit version and are thus only available in the 32-bit versions of MFC. There may also be a "NM" indicator, indicating that the member function is not available in the Macintosh version of MFC, or a "MO" indicator, indicating that the member function is a Macintosh-only function. These two conditions are rare. "UD" indicates that the member is undocumented in the Visual C++ documentation as of Visual C++ 4.0. "DO" indicates that the member is only available in the debug build of MFC.

Next is a description of the member function, giving its typical usage, some helpful hints, and, if appropriate, a description of how and when to override the function in derived classes. The syntax of the function follows, including several different versions for overloaded members. The syntax appears with the correct C++ scope indicator (public, protected, or private). Next, the parameters and return value of the function are enumerated and described, as well as any related member functions, macros, etc. Finally, when appropriate, there is an example of the usage of the member function or a reference to another entry that contains an example that includes the function. For space reasons, we've concentrated on providing examples for the more important, useful, or hard to understand functions. We've omitted examples for functions that are intended for MFC internal use only, for most constructors and destructors, and for functions that are straightforward. Where useful, we have also provided reference entries for some class data members. These, too, generally don't require examples. Note that we provide many additional and more substantial example programs on the accompanying CD.

How to Use This Book

This book can be used in two distinct ways: It can be read cover-to-cover, linearly, or treated as a reference book. Whichever manner is more useful will depend upon the reader. Reading through each chapter provides in-depth coverage of a group of related classes as well as an understanding of the context of each class member. This is recommended particularly for the beginner MFC programmer, who can readily appreciate a formal introduction to MFC and its classes. The experienced MFC reader might choose instead to dive right in and take a look at specific parts of MFC. For this purpose, the class hierarchy cross-reference appendix and the index can be used to help the reader quickly find individual classes and member function entries. The on-line help version found on the companion CD-ROM adds to the reference value of this book.

About the CD-ROM

This book comes with a companion CD-ROM. Its purpose is to provide supplemental information that the reader can use to get better acquainted with MFC programming. The CD-ROM contents can be broken down into four categories:

- Chapter Source Code—contains source code written by the authors of sample applications that illustrate concepts discussed in the different chapters of this book.
- MFC Primer Excerpts—contains selected excerpts from *The MFC Primer* from Waite Group Press, another great source of MFC information.
- Online Help Version of Book—contains the online help version of this book.
- MFC Samples—contains sample programs written by MFC programmers around the world. Also included is some miscellaneous MFC-related neat stuff that the reader might find interesting.

To install the contents of the CD-ROM, simply copy the files you wish onto your hard drive, ensuring that the same directory structure is maintained for the source code projects.

1

WINDOWS PROGRAMMING

1

WINDOWS PROGRAMMING

When the Windows operating system was first introduced, it consisted of a handful of library functions that allowed the application developer access to a simple user interface. Windows programming today has evolved into something much more than a simple user interface. It has grown to provide a powerful graphics engine, a rich set of reusable controls, efficient event processing, multitasking, and a means for cross-application communication. With the introduction of Windows NT and Windows 95, Windows supports new features such as a 32-bit programming model, multi-threaded applications, and structured exception handling.

But, to be able to efficiently use Windows, it is necessary that developers have a basic understanding of how these components relate to one another. This chapter provides a very brief overview of working within Windows, since it is assumed that the developer already has some previous experience programming for the Windows operating system. Later chapters will explore each aspect of Windows in much greater detail as it relates to the corresponding MFC classes.

Graphical User Interface

One of the most obvious benefits of working with Windows is being able to take advantage of the graphical user interface (GUI). Windows provides a standard graphics Application Programming Interface (API) and a set of user controls that allows the programmer to display and manipulate data easily, without having to resort to a proprietary third party solution that is not common across many applications. A benefit of these standards is a common look and feel among Windows applications.

At the core of the Windows GUI is the basic window. In its purest form, a window is simply a means to receive messages and, optionally, a space in which to display

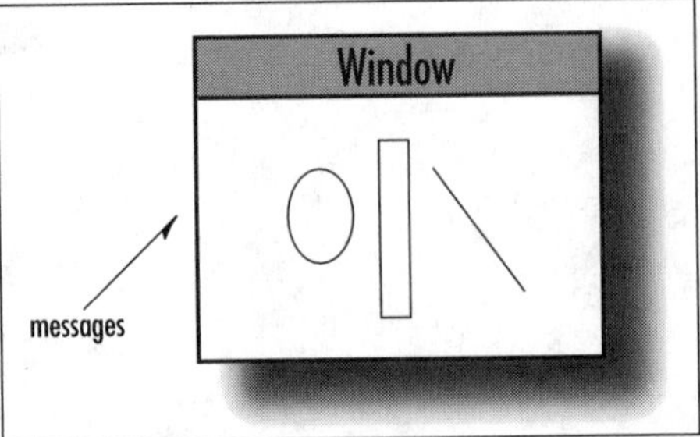

Figure 1-1 Basic window

data. Messages are generated by system, application, or user events. In Figure 1-1, the window is notified that an event has occurred, and can display data to indicate that an action has taken place.

A window can be used to display a document, picture, or any other piece of graphical information. Also, it can be used to only receive messages and never be seen by the user. This is the case in the 16-bit Windows serial I/O support where a window is used to receive messages when data has arrived at the communications port for processing. Most of the time, however, a window will be used to interact with the user by displaying information in some sort of graphical context.

Windows also have a hierarchy associated with them. A dialog box, for example, is a *parent* window to all of the controls within it, which are the *children*. This hierarchy allows actions to be propagated among the family. For example, when a dialog window is destroyed, each child window of the dialog is destroyed as well. Also, the developer can enumerate through the hierarchy to pass messages to all windows under a given parent.

Resources

Graphical applications require an efficient means of producing and optimizing the display of information. Windows accomplishes this through the use of resources. Some of the most common resources are pens, brushes, bitmaps, icons, dialog boxes, menus, and text strings. Pens and brushes are resources created by the application to draw lines and boxes within a window. Bitmaps and icons are reusable pictures that can be stored within the application executable file and displayed within a window. Dialog boxes are used to query the user for input. Menus are used to display a list of choices. Finally, text string resources are a way to collect all text strings within an application into the resource file, and allow the application to access these strings given a unique identifier. (Having all text strings stored as a separate resource also makes it easier to, for example, create foreign-language versions of an application.)

All of the resources mentioned above are reusable objects and their use is optimized by the operating system. For example, a dialog box can be displayed many times during the execution of the application, and the same dialog can be used for different purposes. A dialog might be created to query the user for an employee's name that will be stored in a database. The same dialog can be reused for a wide variety of applications that need employee names. The developer does not need to manage the controls or perform the actual drawing of the dialog; this is handled by the operating system. The only things the developer needs to manage are the messages generated by the dialog.

Similar in concept to the employee name dialog mentioned above, Windows provides several reusable dialog resources called *common dialogs*. These dialogs perform specific, routine functions and are supplied so that the developer can rely on the common dialog instead of developing a new one. Also, if developers use these dialogs then their applications will have a common look and feel with other applications using the same dialogs. Some of the common dialogs are the File Open, File Save, Choose Font, and Choose Color dialogs.

Controls

Another set of reusable components is called *controls*. Windows supplies a host of controls that accomplish most of the common user interface tasks found in applications. Controls are just like any other window: They can send and receive messages and display data. The extra value that they provide is a specialized way of interacting with the user.

Some of the most used visual controls are *buttons*, *list boxes*, and *combo boxes*. Standard buttons are used to execute an action. *Radio buttons* are used to select a single choice from among multiple options, while *check boxes* (which are really buttons) are used to select multiple choices. List boxes display multiple items in a scrollable list, allowing the user to select among them. Combo boxes display only a single item, unless the list is "dropped down" to display other selections.

With the introduction of Windows 95, many new controls were added. One of these controls is the tree view, which displays hierarchical relationships of data such as parent/child relationships. Another control that was added to provide more flexibility when displaying a list of items is the list view. Other controls include the toolbar, image list, and progress bar. Refer to Chapter 9, *Windows Controls,* for a complete reference on these controls.

The behavior of all these controls is customizable through styles and messages. When each control is created, certain styles are chosen that reflect the behavior of the control. These styles include whether or not a list box allows the user to select multiple items, or whether a combo box allows the user to type a custom value or is limited to predefined values. Also, every control generates messages that the developer can use to customize the control. For example, messages are generated when a selection changes in a list box or when a button is pressed.

Messages

Due to the event-driven nature of Windows, nothing really happens until an event occurs. This is quite a change from traditional procedural programming where execution proceeds down a well-defined path to a conclusion. In Windows, the application waits for an event, processes the event, then waits for the next event. This allows for much more dynamic execution of an application where the user can do basically anything at any time. Of course, developers can create procedural Windows applications and in some cases this makes sense, but to work well with Windows an application should take advantage of events. All events fall into three basic categories: user interaction, system, and programmer-defined.

Every window receives messages generated by these events and can act upon them. For example, when the user presses the left mouse button over a window, that particular window will receive a WM_LBUTTONDOWN message along with the coordinates of the current mouse position. The application developer can respond to this event by drawing a point on the window at the specified coordinate, or can ignore the message entirely. When the user then releases the left mouse button, the window will receive a WM_LBUTTONUP message that can also be acted upon. Every action that a user can take is passed to the corresponding window as a message.

Messages are also generated at the system level. A window will be notified with a WM_SYSCOLORCHANGE message when a system color has been changed. This will allow any windows that depend on these colors to update themselves with any necessary changes. As another example, the system sends a WM_TIMER message to a window that has previously requested a notification after a certain period of time has elapsed.

The application developer can create his or her own types of events to affect other windows on the system. For example, a developer could define a message named WM__USER_DISPLAYHELLO. This message could be sent to any other window on the system that can interpret this message. When the window receives this event, it might display the text "Hello". The developer can create custom messages that can be sent to other windows to affect program execution.

With all these messages passing back and forth, it is necessary for some sort of arbitrator to ensure that the correct message is sent to the correct window. This arbitrator is known as the main message pump, and its sole purpose is to maintain a queue of events for the application and pass them to the proper window at the proper time. The reason for the queue of events is that in an event-driven operating system such as Windows, events tend to arrive in clusters and the handling of each event might not be complete before the next one arrives. The queue ensures that each event will be handled in turn.

To handle these messages, every window contains a function that accepts messages and acts upon them. This function is commonly referred to as a WNDPROC (Window Procedure) function that receives messages and optional message-specific data. For example, when the user presses the left mouse button, a WM_LBUTTONDOWN message is generated (along with the current mouse coordinates and window handle) and is entered into the main message pump's queue of events. When the message pump gets to this message, it dispatches the message to the specified window. At this point, the window's WNDPROC will receive and process the message.

Between events and when the main message pump has no more events to pass on, Windows uses the free time to yield execution to other applications and processes. This allows multiple applications to execute and process data on the system at the same time.

Windows 95 and Windows NT

In Windows 95 and Windows NT, the operating system does not rely solely upon the message pump for multitasking processes. This is due to their ability to preemptively multitask processes, which means that even while an application is responding to a message, control can be passed to another application (process) running on the system. The main difference between the pre-emptive multitasking on Windows NT and Windows 95 is their multitasking of 16-bit applications. Windows NT can preemptively multitask 16-bit applications if they are executed in separate protected memory spaces called Virtual DOS Machines (VDM). In Windows 95, however, all 16-bit applications are executed within the same VDM and are dependent on the message pump to yield execution.

MFC provides a very useful encapsulation of process creation through the CWinThread object. This object hides the complexities of creating, blocking, and terminating individual processes. In fact, the CWinApp object, which all MFC applications are derived from, is itself derived from the CWinThread object. Application programmers can easily take advantage of the multi-threaded execution of Windows NT and Windows 95 by using the MFC class library.

Windows API

Program execution and events in a Windows application are handled through calls to the Windows Application Programming Interface (or API for short). At its most native level, this interface is a series of function calls that allow the programmer to manipulate windows, resources, and events. Until the past few years, when MFC and other third-party Windows API encapsulations became available, the developer relied solely upon the Windows Software Development Kit (SDK). This kit, distributed by Microsoft, contains the libraries necessary for a programmer to create an application using the Windows API.

The Windows API is nothing more than a set of standardized functions and data types used to interact with the operating system. For example, to create a list box control, the programmer would make a call like the one in Listing 1-1.

Listing 1-1 CreateWindow API function

```
HWND hwndParent;
HINSTANCE hInst;
...
HWND hMyWindow;
hMyWindow = CreateWindow("LISTBOX","My Window Title",
                        WS_CHILD|WS_VISIBLE,
                        0,0,100,200,
                        hwndParent,NULL,hInst,NULL);
```

In this code fragment, the CreateWindow function and the parameters it takes are part of the Windows API. This API function returns a handle to the newly created window represented by the HWND variable. An HWND is a handle to a window object and is just a unique identifier for that particular window. All interaction with this window is done by specifying a handle in the API calls. For example, the word "hello" can be added into the list box after it has been created by making the API call shown in Listing 1-2.

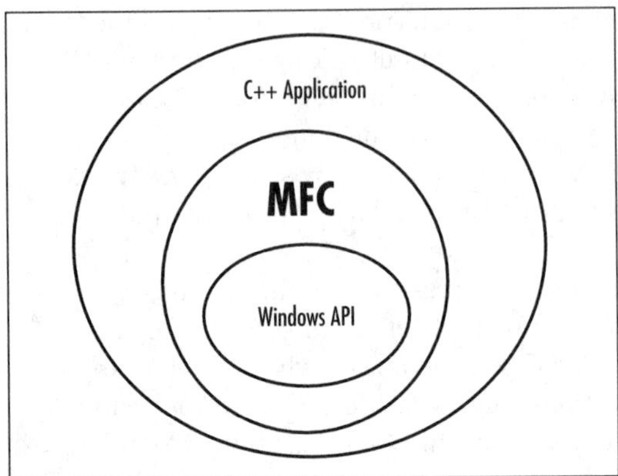

Figure 1-2 MFC encapsulation of Windows API

Listing 1-2 SendMessage API function

```
LRESULT lRes;
lRes = SendMessage(hMyWindow,LB_ADDSTRING,0,"hello");
```

The SendMessage API function shown above will send a message to the specified window. Here, the window is identified by hMyWindow. The message that is sent is the predefined API message LB_ADDSTRING. The list box will receive this message in its WNDPROC procedure, and insert the supplied data into the list. The SendMessage function is used to pass messages to any window, not just list boxes. The messages it sends, however, are interpreted by different windows in different ways.

MFC and Windows

The subject of this book is the Microsoft Foundation Classes (MFC) and how they relate to Windows programming. MFC, as Figure 1-2 shows, is an object-oriented encapsulation of the Windows API that Microsoft started shipping with its C++ compiler to assist developers in creating Windows applications. MFC is a fully reusable C++ class library that hides the fundamental Windows API in easy-to-use class hierarchies. It provides an abstraction layer on which a developer can write a Windows application without needing to know the details of the native Windows API.

By using MFC as the foundation for a Windows application, a developer can create a powerful program with very little effort. For example, MFC already provides a model for displaying Multiple Document Windows (MDI) called the Document/View architecture. By deriving from the CDocument and CView classes, the developer can concentrate on writing the code that manages the document data rather than having to also develop a data display model. These base classes also provide much of the support for the saving, retrieval, printing, and print previewing of documents. And since MFC is a C++ object-oriented class library, the default behavior of any of its classes can simply be overridden in the derived classes. A more in-depth explanation of the Document/View architecture can be found in Chapter 6.

A much overlooked benefit of MFC is that it wraps the API in an easy-to-use class hierarchy that still resembles the native API. This might not seem to be a benefit at first since the idea of wrapping the API is to encapsulate many of the core functions so that developers need not concern themselves with much of the API drudgery. But MFC is a thin wrapper. It takes the basic Windows API, adds structure, and syntactically mirrors many of the API functions in its class methods.

A good example of this syntactical mirroring can be seen by comparing an API function call to its equivalent in MFC. The following code sets the title of a window using the API:

```
HWND hMyWindow;
...
SetWindowText(hMyWindow,"My Window Title");
```

In MFC, the equivalent would read

```
Cwnd * pWindow;
...
pWindow->SetWindowText("My Window Title");
```

Notice how the function calls use a similar syntax. This might seem like a minor point, but it really is not. Those developers already familiar with the native Windows API will find that they will learn MFC quickly because it is very similar to what they already know. They do not need to learn an abstraction schema that is far removed from the fundamental API. Also, since it is possible to mix the native API calls and MFC calls within an MFC application, the resulting code maintains a consistency that increases readability.

MFC also provides for a much easier way to handle window messaging. Instead of having to use the generic SendMessage function and supply a message code, MFC wraps messages into class methods. For example, sending a message to a list box using the API would read

```
LRESULT lRes;
lRes = SendMessage(hMyWindow,LB_ADDSTRING,0,"hello");
```

The equivalent operation under MFC would read

```
CListBox * pListBox;
...
int nRes;
nRes = pListBox->AddString("hello");
```

Another benefit of MFC is that it routes incoming messages to virtual functions that can be overridden by the developer. In the Windows API, every message enters the WNDPROC function and then enters a series of tests to determine which message it is and how it is to be handled. In MFC, this is handled by the base window class and the messages are parsed out to virtual member functions of the class. The developer can then override the default behavior of the messages of interest by supplying a new method. This vastly increases the readability of the source code and decreases the time it takes to write handlers for messages.

MFC also provides structure for an application through its class hierarchy. The CWinApp object provides the basic encapsulation of the code necessary to run a Windows application. All windows are derived from the CWnd class. These include the

CDialog, CComboBox, CListBox, CMDIChildWnd, CScrollBar, and the CView. There are all sorts of classes to handle graphics output such as CPen, CBrush, CFont, and CDC.

Another important aspect of developing for Windows that MFC handles is the transition from 16- to 32-bit applications. The original Windows API targeted a 16-bit operating system, but with the introduction of Windows NT and Windows 95, a new 32-bit API was created. This API, called Win32, is handled transparently by using MFC. Of course, not all Win32 functions are available under the Windows API and some API functions no longer exist under Win32. But by using MFC, an application can be written that targets both platforms. MFC handles portability between processors because it can be compiled to run on the Macintosh and DEC Alpha machines.

OLE and Inter-Application Communications

Another very important aspect of working with Windows is Object Linking and Embedding (OLE). Unfortunately, a full-blown discussion of OLE is outside the scope of this book. But it is important to note that OLE is an essential part of Windows programming because it allows much tighter integration of applications than was previously possible. Through OLE, information from one application can be embedded into another with neither application having specific information about the other. OLE also allows for the automation of an application. Automation is the term used when a scripting language or another application can command an application to perform certain tasks. In all, OLE promises to be just as important as any other component in creating an application that works well in Windows.

Working Well with Windows

Ironically enough, with all the power and reusability of the Windows GUI, application developers do not take enough advantage of the graphics capabilities. Many developers content themselves with porting their legacy source code to Windows or creating a new application with little thought of how the user expects a Windows application to behave. Working with Windows does not mean merely developing an application that executes under Windows; it also implies user expectations about behavior. For example, the user expects to be able to Cut, Copy, or Paste information from one area to another. Also, an evolving standard is the use of right mouse button menus when the user clicks on an object (this is even more important for Windows 95 applications and its use of property sheets). Another expected behavior of a Windows application is the ability to resize a window to display as little or as much information as the user desires. For some applications these methods do not apply, but for the majority they do.

MFC provides an excellent foundation for creating an application that works well in Windows. It is a fully extensible object-oriented class library that developers can tailor to meet their specific needs through derivation. MFC also provides much built-in support for common Windows behavior, which takes much of the drudgery out of Windows development. As the following chapters illustrate, MFC is a robust library that hides much of the complexity of programming in Windows through easy-to-use classes.

2

THE MFC FRAMEWORK

2

THE MFC FRAMEWORK

For millions of years, prehistoric programmers created Windows applications with such brute-force: rudimentary tools such as the crude but effective message loop; Stroustrup's best friend, the static window procedure; and the gargantuan, ever-expanding, kudzu-like message-processing switch statement. With every new program, these tools needed to be redeveloped time and time again. True code reuse and object-oriented development were something only managers talked about. With pressing development milestones always on the horizon, there was never any time to do things the "right" way. Then, like the black obelisk of *2001: A Space Odyssey*, application frameworks came upon the world, leading the masses to a better way, freeing them from the limitations of their primitive tools.

In all seriousness, application frameworks, along with accompanying prototyping "wizards" and "experts," represent such a leap of technology that it is hard to even imagine going back to the old ways. They have truly become a solid foundation from which virtually any application can be built more efficiently. With an application framework, among many other advantages, productivity can be increased tenfold, bugs can be located and fixed with greater ease, and new technologies (e.g., ODBC and OLE) can be integrated more seamlessly.

So what is an application framework? In short, it is a library of code that contains general functionality (such as elements of the user interface) found in almost all applications of a similar nature (e.g., all Windows applications), rather than being devoted to a specific purpose or functionality (a word processing program vs. a finite element analysis program, for example). An application framework may also contain helper code for performing traditionally necessary tasks such as string manipulation and array and list management, as well as code that implements standard optional features of an application such as status bars. The driving philosophy behind application frameworks

The Old Way
1. Create a WinMain function.
2. Register your window classes.
3. Create window procedures for your windows.
4. Write big switch statements to process messages for your windows.
5. Call Windows API to draw interface elements and use controls.
6. Call C run-time functions for file I/O; call ODBC API for database I/O.
7. Roll your own code for dynamic arrays, strings, and other storage needs.
The New (MFC) Way
1. Use AppWizard to create a new CWinApp-derived application class.
2. Create new CWnd-derived classes and override virtual functions to handle messages.
3. Use GDI, window, and control classes to create user interface.
4. Use ClassWizard to add members to CCmdTarget or CWnd-based classes to handle user input.
5. Use file and ODBC classes for I/O.
6. Use MFC collection classes for strings, arrays, lists, and maps.

Figure 2-1 The old way and new (MFC) way of Windows development

is that it is not necessary for a programmer to be constantly "reinventing the wheel." The programmer should not be the millionth person to write a linked-list implementation or a menu class. Rather, the programmer should be able to concentrate on the application-specific coding required.

Although not mandatory, an application framework is usually written in C++ or some other object-oriented language. In C++, an application framework is implemented as a library of classes that proceed by inheritance from general to more specific objects that contain the desired functionality. Currently, there are many competing Windows application frameworks. Chief among them are the Microsoft Foundation Classes (MFC) from Microsoft, and Object Windows Library (OWL) from Borland. As with most things, each framework has its advantages and disadvantages. Since this book covers MFC exclusively, however, we'll stick to the discussion of the Foundation Classes.

What's in the MFC?

The first question posed by a programmer looking to use MFC is a basic one: What can it do? The short answer is that MFC provides the application developer with all of the main ingredients of a Windows application, supplying hooks to be used for adding everything that is application-specific. The long answer is what the rest of this book is about. In general, though, MFC provides a new and better way of creating Windows applications. In Figure 2-1, you can see the differences between some of the old ways of creating a simple new program and the new MFC way for doing the same tasks.

An overview of MFC's general capabilities, however, are as follows:

Foundation for a Windows Application or Process

MFC has classes that encapsulate a Windows task. These include the generic CWinThread and CWinApp classes. The CWinThread class is the one containing the message-processing pump. CWinApp is derived from CWinThread.

Object Serialization and Run-Time Type-checking

CObject, MFC's base class for almost all other classes, includes object-oriented serialization and run-time type-checking mechanisms.

Document/View Data Representation Model

MFC includes optional CDocument and CView classes that can be used to represent the contents, storage, and representation of information.

Object-Oriented Approach for Handling Windows, Dialogs, and Their Messages

MFC liberates the programmer from the necessity of static window procedures and large message-processing switch statements with the CWnd class, which encapsulates the Windows HWND-based window handle. Programmers can handle messages by defining virtual functions for their own CWnd-derived classes. Sensible default behavior for system messages is part of MFC, though, so programmers typically only need to define handlers for messages that implement functionality specific to their applications.

"Thin" Object-Oriented Wrapper of the Windows 3.x and Win32 APIs

MFC wraps almost all of the most common Windows API functions as member functions of its classes. In many cases, the syntax is identical, minus one parameter indicating the associated handle (window, brush, device context, etc.). The associated handle then becomes part of the particular class (m_hWnd for the CWnd class, m_hObject for the CGdiObject class, m_hDC for the CDC class, etc.). This is, arguably, one of MFC's great advantages because programmers who know the API can begin MFC programming from day one.

Enhanced Memory Allocation, Debugging, and Exception-Handling

MFC integrates with Microsoft's C run-time library to provide for enhanced memory allocation, debugging, and exception-handling. MFC has many different assertion-based macros that are used by MFC and should be used by the MFC programmer to test the integrity of the application while running. MFC also performs task-oriented exception-handling to create a robust, stable platform from which an application can be built.

Implementation for Standard Collections Such as Arrays, Lists, and Maps, as Well as Strings

The programmer can use MFC's template-based or non-template-based collection classes for holding collections of data, including strings, in memory. The collection classes take over where the streamlined data types supplied by C++ leave off.

State-of-the-Art Interface Elements Such as Property Sheets and Tree Controls

If you see some neat interface concept in one of Microsoft's applications, the odds are that sooner or later, MFC will have a class to implement it. Moreover, MFC has classes that encapsulate the standard Windows controls, including the relatively new Windows 95 common controls.

Support for Application Extensions Such as OLE, ODBC, DAO, MAPI, and WINSOCK

MFC has had a good history of encapsulating rather complex emerging technologies, such as OLE, so that MFC programmers can seamlessly include them in their applications.

Miscellaneous Useful Functionality like File I/O and Time/Date Manipulations

MFC also includes some generically useful classes for such things as file I/O and time/date manipulations. These include the CFile, CTime, and CTimeSpan classes.

MFC Versions and Compatibility Issues

There have now been four major versions of MFC. Following each major release, there have always been one or more minor releases that have contained bug fixes and small enhancements. The initial version, MFC 1.0, was released in the early part of 1992 with the Microsoft C/C++ 7.0 compiler. Many of the major architectural components in MFC today were first introduced in this version, with the notable exception of the document and view classes, which showed up in MFC 2.0. MFC 2.x was released with Visual C++ 1.0 in February, 1993. It was the last major 16-bit version (MFC 2.52c was actually the last 16-bit maintenance release). MFC 3.x arrived with Visual C++ 2.0 in September, 1994 and included a substantial number of new classes to support the new Windows 95 interface. MFC 4.0 arrived with Visual C++ 4.0 (Microsoft chose to sync up the versioning of MFC and Visual C++ with this release) in November, 1995.

So far, Microsoft has made good on its commitment to keep MFC backwards compatible. Code written for MFC 1.0 will still compile today. It is important to note, however, that this is not true for code that relies upon the internals of the MFC implementation. When changes have been made, because of design reasons or advances in compiler technology, Microsoft has kept the published syntax intact. However, the implementation can, and, in most cases, most likely will change over time. Many first-time MFC programmers ask whether it is allowed to use undocumented members of classes. In most cases, MFC uses the C++ access specifiers (the public, protected, and private keywords) to define what can and cannot be accessed by the MFC programmer. This alone is not enough because many public members of MFC are considered implementation-related by Microsoft and may change over time. Here are some general rules of thumb when contemplating this issue:

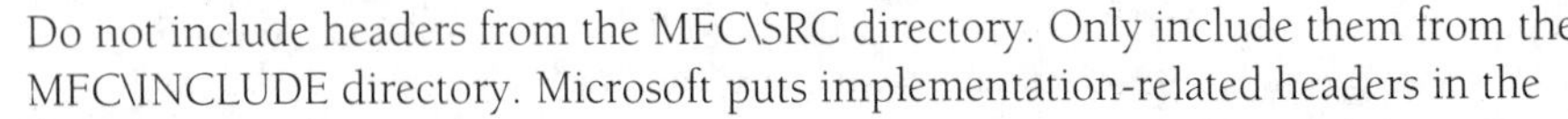

- Do not include headers from the MFC\SRC directory. Only include them from the MFC\INCLUDE directory. Microsoft puts implementation-related headers in the

MFC\SRC directory and puts the published interface headers in the MFC\INCLUDE directory. Any #INCLUDEs inserted by AppWizard will always be from this directory.

- Do not call or access any members of a class declared below the "// Implementation" comment in the header file of the class. These members are intended for internal use, and may change in subsequent versions of MFC.

- If you do have to disregard the above rule, write a wrapper function that breaks the rule and call that function instead. This way, if the syntax of the implementation does change, you will hopefully only need to change your code in one place.

For example, in MFC 2.x – 3.x, there was a public member of the CWinApp class, m_templateList, that was used to store all document templates in the application. This member, however, was defined after the "// Implementation" comment in the header file. Many MFC applications used m_templateList to iterate through the document templates. In MFC 4.0, this member was replaced by the public member, m_pDocManager, a pointer to an object of the new CDocManager class which encapsulates the functionality of the old m_templateList member. This new member is located above the "// Implementation" comment, indicating that it is here to stay.

In the chapters that follow, the predominant class components of MFC will be discussed. As mentioned in the introduction, space limits of this book preclude discussion of the entire MFC; classes covering ODBC and WINSOCK, for example, have been left out. A complete depiction of the class hierarchy with a cross-reference to where each class appears in the book can be found in Appendix A. To start things off, the rest of this chapter will deal with the fundamental building blocks of MFC, the base class of almost all classes in the hierarchy; CObject, including the CRuntimeClass class which is used for run-time type-checking; a listing of MFC's helper functions; and a brief discussion of how MFC uses resources and how it implements on-line help. Table 2-1, below, summarizes the contents of this chapter.

Table 2-1 Chapter 2 class summary

Class Name	Description
CObject	Base class for MFC
CRuntimeClass	Contains run-time type-checking information for MFC classes
Afx_ functions	MFC helper functions

The CObject Class

The CObject class is the base class for almost all of the other classes of MFC. Microsoft suggests that this class be used as the base class for any new classes added by the programmer. Whether or not the programmer should heed this advice depends in general upon the circumstances and uses of the new class. Although there is little overhead in deriving a class from CObject, it is certainly valid for the programmer to choose not to use CObject as a base class in all situations, especially when there is no foreseeable need for its services. Be aware that there is one significant drawback to CObject, in that there are problems when multiply inheriting from two or more CObject-derived classes. First, only the left-most parent class declared when deriving a new class will be reported by the MFC-specific run-time type information mechanism. Second, to avoid ambiguities, the programmer will need to declare explicitly which parent a derived CObject member is referencing.

CObject Services

The three major services provided by CObject are run-time type information, dynamic object creation, and serialization. Run-time type information, something that is inherent in other object-oriented languages like Smalltalk, allows the programmer to ask an object what type it is when its type is ambiguous at compile time. An example of how this can be done in MFC is shown in Listing 2-1.

Listing 2-1 Checking run-time type information of a CObject-derived class

```
void CMyApp::DoSomething(CObject* pAnObject)
{
        if ( pAnObject->IsKindOf(RUNTIME_CLASS(CMyClass)) )
        {
                // do something special with a CMyClass object
        }
        else if ( pAnObject->IsKindOf(RUNTIME_CLASS(CMyOtherClass)) )
        {
                // do something special with a CMyOtherClass object
        }
}
```

There are conflicting philosophies as to how useful run-time information is or even if it should be used at all. Many believe that relying on run-time type information promotes lazy C++ coding. A general rule of thumb, though, is to shy away from instinctively using run-time information without first determining whether or not built-in features of C++, like polymorphism (virtual functions), can provide the same functionality.

Dynamic creation of an object involves cleverly constructing an object when its type is unknown at compile time. One way of looking at this is that dynamic creation simulates a virtual class constructor, something that is outside the bounds of the C++ standard. MFC accomplishes this through the CRuntimeClass structure. A CRuntimeClass structure is associated with every CObject-derived class which has at least the run-time information service. Among other things, the CRuntimeClass structure has a CreateObject() member which, when called, constructs an object of the associated CObject-derived class's type.

An example of how MFC uses this mechanism can be seen in how a document template creates new documents of the right data type. Listing 2-2 shows the

CDocTemplate::CreateNewDocument member function. CDocTemplate has a data member, m_pDocClass, set when the object is constructed, that stores the CRuntimeClass structure for the associated CDocument-derived class. CDocTemplate::CreateNewDocument uses this member to create the right document by calling CRuntimeClass:CreateObject. For more information about documents and document templates, see Chapter 6, *Document/View*.

Listing 2-2 CDocTemplate usage of dynamic creation

```
CDocument* CDocTemplate::CreateNewDocument()
{
      // default implementation constructs one from CRuntimeClass
      if (m_pDocClass == NULL)
      {
            TRACE0("Error: you must override CDocTemplate::CreateNewDocument\n");
            ASSERT(FALSE);
            return NULL;
      }
      CDocument* pDocument = (CDocument*)m_pDocClass->CreateObject();
      if (pDocument == NULL)
      {
            TRACE1("Warning: Dynamic create of document type %Fs failed\n",
                  m_pDocClass->m_lpszClassName);
            return NULL;
      }
      ASSERT(pDocument->IsKindOf(RUNTIME_CLASS(CDocument)));
      AddDocument(pDocument);
      return pDocument;
}
```

CObject serialization is a C++ implementation of the concept of object persistence. Similar to the maintenance of run-time information discussed earlier, persistence is also an intrinsic feature present in other object-oriented languages. An object is persistent if the values of its data members are preserved independently of its creation or destruction. This usually means that the data is stored on separate media (like a hard drive) just before the object is destroyed, and restored automatically when the object is next constructed. MFC serialization even supports versioning of objects through the use of a schema parameter. CObject serialization is discussed in detail in Chapter 14, *Files and Serialization*.

Deriving Classes from CObject

Deriving a class from CObject is no different from any other class derivation except for the inclusion of macros in both the declaration (DECLARE_ macros) and the implementation (IMPLEMENT_ macros) of the class when CObject run-time information, dynamic creation, and/or serialization services are desired.

Table 2-2 Macros for CObject-Derived classes

Macro	Purpose	Location
DECLARE_DYNAMIC	run-time information	class declaration
IMPLEMENT_DYNAMIC	run-time information	class implementation
DECLARE_DYNCREATE	run-time information and dynamic creation	class declaration
IMPLEMENT_DYNCREATE	run-time information and dynamic creation	class implementation
DECLARE_SERIAL	run-time information, dynamic creation, and serialization	class declaration
IMPLEMENT_SERIAL	run-time information, dynamic creation, and serialization	class implementation

As Table 2-2 illustrates, the CObject services are cumulative; each service builds upon a previous one, beginning with run-time information. Depending upon which services are desired for your derived class, you should choose one pair of these macros (i.e. one DECLARE_ and one IMPLEMENT_) and place them as appropriate. The DECLARE_ macro should be placed directly within the class declaration as in Listing 2-3:

Listing 2-3 CObject macro in class declaration

```
class CMyClass : public CObject
{
     DECLARE_DYNCREATE(CMyClass)
public:
     CMyClass();
};
```

The IMPLEMENT_DYNAMIC macro can be placed anywhere within the class implementation file. In versions of MFC prior to MFC 4.0, the IMPLEMENT_DYNCREATE and IMPLEMENT_SERIAL macros had to be placed in the implementation file before inclusion of the debugging line, #define new DEBUG_NEW, in order to avoid compilation errors. In MFC 4.0, however, this is no longer the case because the inner workings of the CRuntimeClass were changed to prevent this arcane problem.

CObject Macro Reference

DECLARE_DYNAMIC

■ 1.0 ■ 3.0

Description This macro should be part of the declaration of a CObject-derived class that uses run-time information. When expanded, this macro adds the appropriate CRuntimeClass data member to the class. This structure is a static member of the class in order to minimize the overhead necessary in providing this information. The macro also includes a GetRuntimeClass() member function that is used to retrieve the static CRuntimeClass structure.

Syntax DECLARE_DYNAMIC(class)

Parameters

class Class name (no quotes needed).

Returns Nothing is returned.

See Also IMPLEMENT_DYNAMIC, DECLARE_DYNCREATE, IMPLEMENT_DYNCREATE, DECLARE_SERIAL, IMPLEMENT_SERIAL, CRuntimeClass

Example

```
class CMyObject : public CObject
{
     DECLARE_DYNAMIC(CMyObject)
public:
     CMyObject();
}
```

IMPLEMENT_DYNAMIC

■ 1.0 ■ 3.0

Description This macro should be part of the implementation of a CObject-derived class that uses run-time information. When expanded, this macro initializes the static CRuntimeClass structure for the class. It also implements the GetRuntimeClass() member function.

Syntax IMPLEMENT_DYNAMIC(class, base_class)

Parameters

class Class name (no quotes needed).

base_class Base class name (no quotes needed).

Returns Nothing is returned.

See Also DECLARE_DYNAMIC, DECLARE_DYNCREATE, IMPLEMENT_DYNCREATE, DECLARE_SERIAL, IMPLEMENT_SERIAL

Example

```
IMPLEMENT_DYNAMIC(CMyObject,CObject)
```

DECLARE_DYNCREATE

■ 1.0 ■ 3.0

Description This macro should be part of the declaration of a CObject-derived class that uses dynamic creation. This macro expands to the DECLARE_DYNAMIC macro and adds a static CreateObject() member function used internally by MFC for dynamic creation of objects of this class.

Syntax DECLARE_DYNCREATE(class)

Parameters

class Class name (no quotes needed).

Returns Nothing is returned.

See Also DECLARE_DYNAMIC, IMPLEMENT_DYNAMIC, IMPLEMENT_DYNCREATE, DECLARE_SERIAL, IMPLEMENT_SERIAL

Example

```
class CMyObject : public CObject
{
     DECLARE_DYNCREATE(CMyObject)
public:
     CMyObject();
};
```

IMPLEMENT_DYNCREATE

■ 1.0 ■ 3.0

Description
This macro should be part of the implementation of a CObject-derived class that uses dynamic creation. This macro expands to the IMPLEMENT_DYNAMIC macro and implements the static CreateObject() member function used internally by MFC for dynamic creation of objects of this class.

Syntax
IMPLEMENT_DYNCREATE(class, base_class)

Parameters

class — Class name (no quotes needed).

base_class — Base class name (no quotes needed).

Returns
Nothing is returned.

See Also
DECLARE_DYNAMIC, IMPLEMENT_DYNAMIC, DECLARE_DYNCREATE, DECLARE_SERIAL, IMPLEMENT_SERIAL

Example

```
IMPLEMENT_DYNCREATE(CMyObject,CObject)
```

DECLARE_SERIAL

■ 1.0 ■ 3.0

Description
This macro should be part of the declaration of a CObject-derived class that uses serialization. This macro expands to the the DECLARE_DYNCREATE macro and adds an operator>> member function used internally by MFC for serialization.

Syntax
DECLARE_SERIAL(class)

Parameters

class — Class name (no quotes needed).

Returns
Nothing is returned.

See Also
DECLARE_DYNAMIC, IMPLEMENT_DYNAMIC, DECLARE_DYNCREATE, IMPLEMENT_DYNCREATE, IMPLEMENT_SERIAL

Example

```
class CMyObject : public CObject
{
	DECLARE_SERIAL(CMyObject)
public:
	CMyObject();
};
```

IMPLEMENT_SERIAL

■ 1.0 ■ 3.0

Description
This macro should be part of the implementation of a CObject-derived class that uses serialization. This macro expands to the IMPLEMENT_DYNCREATE macro and implements the operator>> member function used internally by MFC for serialization. The schema parameter can be used to distinguish between different versions of the same object. If an application needs to support different versions of

objects, changes in the schema for an object should be also reflected in the Serialize() member of the class.

Syntax IMPLEMENT_SERIAL(class, base_class, schema)

Parameters

class Class name (no quotes needed).

base_class Base class name (no quotes needed).

schema "Version number" of class, a UINT.

Returns Nothing is returned.

See Also DECLARE_DYNAMIC, IMPLEMENT_DYNAMIC, DECLARE_DYNCREATE, IMPLEMENT_DYNCREATE, DECLARE_SERIAL

Example

```
IMPLEMENT_SERIAL(CMyObject,CObject,1)
```

CObject Class Reference

COBJECT

■ 2.0 ■ 3.0

Description The constructor of the CObject class, can only be called by derived objects. The private copy constructor forces the programmer to explictly provide a copy constructor for CObject-derived classes when desired. If the programmer tries to use a copy constructor without defining one, the default bitwise copy constructor will not be called; instead, a compile error will occur.

Syntax protected, CObject();

private, CObject(const CObject& objectSrc);

Parameters

objectSrc Object to be copied, theoretically (this version of the constructor cannot be used).

Returns Nothing is returned.

See Also CObject::~CObject

Example

```
      CObject* CreateAccount(BOOL bChecking)
{
      CObject* pAccount;

      // both CCheckAccount & CAccount derived from CObject
      if ( bChecking )
      {
      // will call CCheckAccount::CCheckAccount() & CObject::CObject()
           pAccount = new CCheckAccount();
      }
      else
      {
      // will call CAccount::CAccount() & CObject::CObject()
           pAccount = new CAccount();
      }

      return pAccount;
}
```

~COBJECT

■ 2.0 ■ 3.0

Description The virtual destructor of the object. Each derived object should use a destructor to clean up (usually involves memory de-allocation).

Syntax public, virtual ~CObject();

Parameters None.

Returns Nothing is returned.

See Also CObject::CObject

Example

```
CObject* CreateAccount(BOOL bChecking)
{
      CObject* pAccount;

      // both CCheckAccount & CAccount derived from CObject
      if ( bChecking )
      {
      // will call CCheckAccount::CCheckAccount() & CObject::CObject()
            pAccount = new CCheckAccount();
      }
      else
      {
      // will call CAccount::CAccount() & CObject::CObject()
            pAccount = new CAccount();
      }

      return pAccount;
}

void DoSomething()
{
      // creates a CCheckAccount object
      CObject* pAccount = CreateAccount(TRUE);

      // do something with account

      delete pAccount;
      // will call CCheckAccount::~CCheckAccount & CObject::~CObject
}
```

_GETBASECLASS

–. ■ 3.0 ■ UD

Description Returns NULL, indicating no base class for CObject (CObject is the base class). This function exists only when using the DLL version of MFC. Similar functions exist for each CObject-derived class that uses run-time type information. Normally, the run-time type information mechanism accesses the base class of an object directly as a member of its associated CRuntimeClass.

Syntax public, CRuntimeClass* _GetBaseClass();

Parameters None.

Returns Pointer to the static CRuntimeClass object for the base class of the object.

SeeAlso GetRuntimeClass, CRuntimeClass::m_pBaseClass

AssertValid

■ 2.0 ■ 3.0 ■ DO

Description Validates the object. Each CObject-derived class should override this function to perform specific validation. This function typically is only implemented for derived classes when in debug mode (conditionally included by checking the _DEBUG define). The base CObject version of AssertValid exists in release mode as well to avoid compile errors. All it does is test that the *this* pointer is not equal to NULL. See Chapter 15, *Debugging and Exception Handling,* for more details. The ASSERT_VALID macro provides a quick and easy way to test as well the value of the pointer to the object itself. In debug mode, ASSERT_VALID will first check the memory pointed to by a CObject-derived pointer, then call the AssertValid member. In release mode, ASSERT_VALID does nothing.

Syntax public, virtual void AssertValid() const;

Parameters None.

Returns Nothing is returned.

See Also CObject::Dump

Example

```
void CheckDocument(CDocument* pDocument)
{
      // will call CDocument-derived implementation of AssertValid in
      // debug mode, will call CObject::AssertValid in release mode
      pDocument->AssertValid();
}
```

Dump

■ 2.0 ■ 3.0 ■ DO

Description Dumps the contents of the object to a dump context. Each CObject-derived class should override this function to perform specific dumping. This function typically is only implemented for derived classes when in debug mode (conditionally included by checking the _DEBUG define). The base CObject version of Dump exists in release mode as well to avoid compile errors. All it does is dump the class name and the value of the *this* pointer. See Chapter 15, *Debugging and Exception Handling,* for more details.

Returns Nothing is returned.

See Also CObject::AssertValid

Example

```
void DumpDocument(CDocument* pDocument)
{
      // will call CDocument-derived implementation of Dump in
      // debug mode, will call CObject::Dump in release mode
      pDocument->Dump();
}
```

GetRuntimeClass ■ 2.0 ■ 3.0

Description Returns a pointer to the static CRuntimeClass object for the object. Each CObject-derived class that uses run-time type information overrides this function. Automatically, the DECLARE_ and IMPLEMENT_ series of macros insert into a CObject-derived class the appropriate CRuntimeClass class as a static member and an implementation of GetRuntimeClass. The CObject version of this function always exists and returns the CRuntimeClass object for CObject.

Syntax public, virtual CRuntimeClass* GetRuntimeClass() const;

Parameters None.

Returns Pointer to CRuntimeClass object.

See Also CObject::IsKindOf

Example

```
CDocument* pMyDocument;
CRuntimeClass* pRuntimeClass;

pMyDocument = new CMyDocument();

// will return CRuntimeClass for CObject if CMyDocument does not use
// run-time type information
pRuntimeClass = pMyDocument->GetRuntimeClass();
```

IsKindOf ■ 2.0 ■ 3.0

Description Determines whether an object is an instance of or is derived from some other CObject-derived class.

Syntax public, BOOL IsKindOf(const CRuntimeClass* pClass) const;

Parameters

pClass Pointer to CRuntimeClass for specified class; can be easily obtained using the RUNTIME_CLASS macro.

Returns TRUE if object is the specified class or derived from the specifed class; FALSE otherwise.

See Also CObject::GetRuntimeClass

Example

```
BOOL IsMyDocument(CDocument* pDocument)
{
	return pDocument->IsKindOf(RUNTIME_CLASS(CMyDocument));
}
```

IsSerializable ■ 2.0 ■ 3.0

Description Determines whether an object can be serialized. This function checks the m_wSchema member of the CRuntimeClass of the object to make sure it is not equal to 0xFFFF. When a CObject-derived class is defined without

the DECLARE_SERIAL and IMPLEMENT_SERIAL macros, the value of this member is set to 0xFFFF by default.

Syntax public, BOOL IsSerializable() const;

Parameters None.

Returns TRUE if object can be serialized; FALSE otherwise.

See Also CObject::Serialize

Example See CObject::Serialize

OPERATOR=

■ 2.0 ■ 3.0

Description The assignment operator for CObject is declared private in the header. This means that if the programmer tries to assign one CObject-derived object to another without explictly overloading operator = for the specific class, the default bit-wise copy will not be called. Instead, a compile error will occur.

Syntax private, void operator=(const CObject& objectSrc);

Parameters N/A

Returns N/A

OPERATOR DELETE

■ 2.0 ■ 3.0

Description Special delete operator used by MFC to keep track of memory allocation. See Chapter 15, *Debugging and Exception Handling,* for more details.

Syntax public, void AFX_CDECL operator delete(void* p);

Parameters

p Pointer of object to delete.

Returns Nothing is returned.

See Also CObject::operator new

Example

```
CObject* pAccount;

pAccount = new CAccount();
delete pAccount; // will use special CObject delete operator
```

OPERATOR NEW

■ 2.0 ■ 3.0

Description Special new operator used by MFC to keep track of memory allocation. Inserting the line #define new DEBUG_NEW will cause the new operator with the file and line information to be called always. See Chapter 15, *Debugging and Exception Handling,* for more details.

Syntax public, void* PASCAL operator new(size_t nSize);

public, void* PASCAL operator new(size_t, void* p)

public, void* PASCAL operator new (size_t nSize, LPCSTR lpszFileName, int nLine);

Parameters

nSize Size in bytes of object to create.

p Pointer to memory already allocated, used when you only want to call the correct constructor without doing any memory allocation.

lpszFileName File name of object creation, automatically set to __FILE__ (current compiling file) when using DEBUG_NEW.

nLine Line number of object creation, automatically set to __LINE__ (current compiling line) when using DEBUG_NEW.

Returns Nothing is returned.

See Also CObject::operator delete

Example

```
CObject* pAccount;

pAccount = new CAccount(); // will use special CObject new operator
delete pAccount;
```

SERIALIZE

■ 2.0 ■ 3.0

Description Serializes an object to or from an archive. This function should be overridden by all CObject-derived classes that use serialization. See Chapter 14, *Files and Serialization*, for more details.

Syntax public, virtual void Serialize(CArchive& ar);

Parameters

ar Archive.

Returns Nothing is returned.

See Also CObject::IsSerializable

Example

```
void SerializeDocument(CDocument* pDocument,CArchive& ar)
{
	if ( pDocument->IsSerializable() )
		pDocument->Serialize(ar);
}
```

The CRuntimeClass Class

The CRuntimeClass class is used in conjunction with CObject-derived classes. It stores type information that can be accessed at run-time by the programmer. For each class defined with the DECLARE_ and IMPLEMENT_ series of macros, a static CRuntimeClass member is included. The CRuntimeClass class also has one static member used to keep track of, in a singly-linked list, the CRuntimeClass classes for all the CObject-derived classes in the application that have specified run-time type information.

In MFC programming, it is rarely necessary to access the members of the CRuntimeClass class directly. Normally this is done through calls to functions like

CObject::IsKindOf(). MFC even includes a RUNTIME_CLASS macro that automatically returns a pointer to the CRuntimeClass member of the desired class. For example

pDocument->IsKindof(RUNTIME_CLASS(CMyDocument));

The run-time type information architecture implemented by MFC was established long before the Visual C++ compiler included native C++ run-time type information (RTTI). MFC has not changed its implementation to use RTTI, partly because RTTI does not include all information that MFC relies upon, and partly in order to allow MFC to be continually supported by compilers that have yet to implement RTTI.

CRuntimeClass Class Reference

CreateObject

■ 2.0 ■ 3.0

Description Creates a new object of the associated CObject-derived class. This function was modified somewhat from MFC 3.x to MFC 4.0 to avoid previous conflicts with DEBUG_NEW. It will catch exceptions thrown during construction.

Syntax public, CObject* CreateObject();

Parameters None.

Returns Pointer to object created.

See Also CRuntimeClass::m_pfnCreateObject

Example

```
CObject* pObject;

// essentially the same as calling pObject = new CMyObject
pObject = RUNTIME_CLASS(CMyObject)->CreateObject();
```

IsDerivedFrom

■ 2.0 ■ 3.0 ■ UD

Description Determines whether the associated CObject-derived class is derived from another CObject-derived class.

Syntax public, BOOL IsDerivedFrom(const CRuntimeClass* pBaseClass) const;

Parameters

pBaseClass Pointer to CRuntimeClass of base class to check.

Returns TRUE if the associated CObject-derived class is derived from the base class or if the CObject-derived class is the base class; FALSE otherwise.

See Also CObject::IsKindOf

Example

```
BOOL IsMyDocument(CDocument* pDocument)
{
	CRuntimeClass* pClass;

	pClass = pDocument->GetRuntimeClass();

	return pClass->IsDerivedFrom(RUNTIME_CLASS(CMyDocument));
}
```

Load ■ 2.0 ■ 3.0 ■ UD

Description Loads CRuntimeClass information from an archive. After determining the class name and schema value, this function will then search through all the CRuntimeClass objects of the application and linked DLLs to find the appropriate object. This function is called automatically during object serialization. See Chapter 14, *Files and Serialization,* for more details.

Syntax public, static CRuntimeClass* PASCAL Load(CArchive& ar, UINT* pwSchemaNum);

Parameters

ar Archive.

pwSchemaNum Set to the schema value of the CRuntimeClass loaded from the archive.

Returns Pointer to CRuntimeClass object found. NULL indicates that MFC could not find the object (could be caused by removing obsolete class definitions from the application).

See Also CRuntimeClass::Store

m_lpszClassName ■ 2.0 ■ 3.0

Description The class name of the associated CObject-derived class.

Syntax public, LPCSTR m_lpszClassName;

m_nObjectSize ■ 2.0 ■ 3.0

Description Size of the associated CObject-derived class.

Syntax public, int m_nObjectSize;

m_pBaseClass ■ 2.0 ■ 3.0

Description Pointer to the CRuntimeClass object of the parent class of the associated CObject-derived class. When in a DLL (when _AFXDLL is defined), this member is not present. Instead, there is a function called (m_pfnGetBaseClass) to access this value.

Syntax public, CRuntimeClass* m_pBaseClass;

See Also CRuntimeClass::m_pfnGetBaseClass

m_pfnCreateObject –. ■ 4.0

Description Pointer to a function used to create an object of the associated CObject-derived class. This is always set to the CreateObject() member of the CObject-derived class automatically created by the DECLARE/IMPLEMENT_DYNCREATE and

DECLARE/IMPLEMENT_SERIAL macros. The value of this member should be NULL for abstract classes. This member replaced the old m_pfnConstruct member as of MFC 4.0.

Syntax public, CObject* (PASCAL* m_pfnCreateObject)();

M_PFNGETBASECLASS

■ 2.0 ■ 3.0 ■ UD

Description Pointer to a function used only in a DLL (when _AFXDLL is defined), that returns the CRuntimeClass object of the parent class of the associated CObject-derived class.

Syntax public, CRuntimeClass* (PASCAL* m_pfnGetBaseClass)();

M_PNEXTCLASS

■ 2.0 ■ 3.0 ■ UD

Description Pointer to the next object in MFC's singly-linked list of all the CRuntimeClass objects in the application.

Syntax public, CRuntimeClass* m_pNextClass;

M_WSCHEMA

■ 2.0 ■ 3.0

Description The schema (version) of the associated CObject-derived class. For classes that cannot be serialized, this value is set to 0xFFFF.

Syntax public, UINT m_wSchema;

STORE

■ 2.0 ■ 3.0 ■ UD

Description Stores the CRuntimeClass information of the associated CObject-derived class to an archive. This function is called automatically during object serialization. See Chapter 14, *Files and Serialization,* for more details.

Syntax public, void Store(CArchive& ar) const;

Parameters

ar Archive.

Returns Nothing is returned.

See Also CRuntimeClass::Load

Afx_ Helper Functions

One of the numerous benefits of MFC is the large number of helper functions available for performing important recurring tasks. These functions are designated by an "Afx" prefix. The average MFC application uses these functions liberally. Some of these functions implement MFC's prescribed way of doing certain things, whereas other functions simply represent a quick and dirty way of performing a rudimentary job. Also included are sophisticated diagnostics and debugging functions which are available only in debug mode.

AfxAbort

■ 2.0 ■ 3.0

Description Aborts an MFC program. This function should only be called when an unrecoverable error has occurred.

Syntax void AfxAbort();

Parameters None.

Returns Nothing is returned.

AfxBeginThread

■ 2.0 ■ 3.0

Description Dynamically constructs a CWinThread object and begins a thread. This function can create both worker threads and user interface threads.

Syntax CWinThread* AfxBeginThread(AFX_THREADPROC pfnThreadProc, LPVOID pParam, int nPriority = THREAD_PRIORITY_NORMAL, UINT nStackSize = 0,DWORD dwCreateFlags = 0, LPSECURITY_ATTRIBUTES lpSecurityAttrs = NULL);

CWinThread* AfxBeginThread(CRuntimeClass* pThreadClass,int nPriority = THREAD_PRIORITY_NORMAL, UINT nStackSize = 0,DWORD dwCreateFlags = 0, LPSECURITY_ATTRIBUTES lpSecurityAttrs = NULL);

Parameters

pfnThreadProc Pointer to controlling function of the thread, only valid for worker threads. The syntax of this function should be as follows: UINT DoProcess(LPVOID pParam);

pParam Pointer to data passed to controlling function.

nPriority Thread priority—either 0, meaning that the priority of the primary thread will be used or one of the following values:
THREAD_PRIORITY_TIME_CRITICAL
THREAD_PRIORITY_HIGHEST
THREAD_PRIORITY_ABOVE_NORMAL
THREAD_PRIORITY_NORMAL
THREAD_PRIORITY_BELOW_NORMAL
THREAD_PRIORITY_LOWEST
THREAD_PRIORITY_IDLE

nStackSize Stack size, in bytes, of the thread. If 0, the stack size for the process's primary thread will be used.

dwCreateFlags Creation flag, one of two values: CREATE_SUSPENDED creates the thread in a suspended state—use ResumeThread to begin thread execution; 0 indicates that the thread should be executed immediately.

lpSecurityAttrs Pointer to a SECURITY_ATTRIBUTES structure that indicates the thread's security.

pThreadClass Pointer to CRuntimeClass for CWinThread-derived class to use for the thread.

Returns Pointer to CWinThread-derived object created; NULL if unsuccessful.

See Also AfxGetThread, AfxEndThread

Example

```
CMyThread* pThread;

pThread = AfxBeginThread(RUNTIME_CLASS(CMyThread), THREAD_PRIORITY_IDLE);
```

AfxCheckMemory

■ 2.0 ■ 3.0 ■ DO

Description Checks the integrity of the memory blocks allocated on the heap. This function is only available in the debug version of MFC. For more information about debugging see Chapter 15, *Debugging and Exception Handling*.

Syntax BOOL AfxCheckMemory();

Parameters None.

Returns TRUE if no errors are found; FALSE otherwise.

See Also AfxIsMemoryBlock, AfxIsValidAddress

Example

```
CMyObject* pObject = new CMyObject();
delete pObject;
delete pObject; // corrupt the heap
AfxCheckMemory(); // will report error
```

AfxDoForAllClasses

■ 2.0 ■ 3.0 ■ DO

Description Iterates through the CRuntimeClass objects for all CObject-derived classes in the application that have run-time information and calls the specified function for each. This is possible because MFC automatically keeps track of every CRuntimeClass object created in a singly-linked list. AfxDoForAllClasses is only available in the debug version of MFC.

Syntax void AfxDoForAllClasses(void (*pfn)(const CRuntimeClass* pClass,void* pContext), void* pContext);

Parameters

pfn Function to call for each CRuntimeClass object. The syntax for this function should be as follows: void DoForClass(const CRuntimeClass* pClass, void* pContext); pClass provides the class information and pContext references the pointer passed in to AfxDoForAllClasses.

pContext Void pointer to structure to pass to iterating function for each CRuntimeClass object.

Returns Nothing is returned.

See Also AfxDoForAllObjects

Example

```
// iterating function
void DoForClass(CRuntimeClass* pClass,void* pContext)
{
     CString strOutput = pClass->m_lpszClassName;

     // output each class
     OutputDebugString(strOutput + "\r\n");
}

AfxDoForAllClasses(DoForClass,NULL);
```

AfxDoForAllObjects

■ 2.0 ■ 3.0 ■ DO

Description Iterates through all dynamically allocated CObject-derived objects and calls the specified function for each. AfxDoForAllObjects is only available in the debug version of MFC.

Syntax void AfxDoForAllObjects(void (*pfn)(CObject* pObject, void* pContext),void* pContext);

Parameters

pfn Function to call for each object. The syntax for this function should be as follows: void DoForObject(const CObject* pObject, void* pContext);

pContext Void pointer to structure to pass to iterating function for each object.

Returns Nothing is returned.

See Also AfxDoForAllClasses

Example

```
int nObjects = 0;

// iterating function
void DoForObject(CObject* pObject,void* pContext)
{
     nObjects++; // count objects
}

AfxDoForAllObjects(DoForObject,NULL);

CString str;
str.Format("Number of objects: %I\r\n",nObjects);
OutputDebugString(str);
```

AfxDump

■ 2.0 ■ 3.0 ■ DO

Description Dumps an object to the CodeView debugger. This function should only be called in the debugger, not in source code. For more information about debugging, see Chapter 15, *Debugging and Exception Handling*.

Syntax void AfxDump(const CObject* pOb);

Parameters

pOb Pointer to CObject-based object to dump.

Returns Nothing is returned.

SeeAlso CObject::Dump

AfxEnableMemoryTracking ■ 2.0 ■ 3.0 ■ DO

Description Enables/Disables MFC's memory tracking and leak detection. By default, memory tracking is enabled while debugging. This function can be used in situations in which the programmer does not want MFC to report a memory allocation as leaked even if it is. AfxEnableMemoryTracking is only available in the debug version of MFC. For more information about debugging see Chapter 15, *Debugging and Exception Handling*.

Syntax BOOL AfxEnableMemoryTracking(BOOL bTrack);

Parameters

bTrack TRUE to enable memory tracking; FALSE to disable memory tracking.

Returns TRUE if memory tracking was previously enabled; FALSE otherwise.

See Also CMemoryState class

Example

```
CMyObject* pObject1;
CMyObject* pObject2;

pObject1 = new CMyObject(); // reported as leaked if not deleted

BOOL bEnable = AfxEnableMemoryTracking(FALSE);
pObject2 = new CMyObject(); // not reported as leaked
AfxEnableMemoryTracking(bEnable);
```

AfxEndThread ■ 2.0 ■ 3.0

Description Terminates the current thread.

Syntax void AfxEndThread(UINT nExitCode, BOOL bDelete = TRUE);

Parameters

nExitCode Exit code of the thread.

bDelete If bDelete is TRUE, the associated CWinThread-derived object for the thread will be deleted. This parameter should never be set to TRUE for CWinThread-derived objects created on the stack.

Returns Nothing is returned.

See Also AfxBeginThread, AfxGetThread

Example

```
void CMyThread::DoWork()
{
     try
     {
          DoFunc1();
          DoFunc2();
          DoFunc3();
```

continued on next page

continued from previous page

```
        }
        catch(...)
        {
                AfxEndThread(-1,FALSE);
        }

        AfxEndThread(0,FALSE);
}
```

AfxFormatString1

■ 2.0 ■ 3.0

Description Inserts a string into a string stored as a resource, replacing any occurrences of the string "%1".

Syntax void AfxFormatString1(CString& rString, UINT nIDS, LPCTSTR lpsz1);

Parameters

rString Resultant string.

nIDS String resource ID.

lpsz1 String to insert.

Returns Nothing is returned.

See Also AfxFormatString2

Example

```
void ShowErrorMessage(CString& strError)
{
        CString strMessage;

        // IDS_ERROR = "An error has occurred: %1"
        AfxFormatString1(strMessage,IDS_ERROR,strError);
        AfxMessageBox(strMessage);
}
```

AfxFormatString2

■ 2.0 ■ 3.0

Description Inserts two strings into a string stored as a resource, replacing any occurrences of the string "%1" and the string "%2".

Syntax void AfxFormatString2(CString& rString, UINT nIDS,LPCTSTR lpsz1, LPCTSTR lpsz2);

Parameters

rString Resultant string.

nIDS String resource ID.

lpsz1 String to insert in replace of "%1".

lpsz2 String to insert in replace of "%2".

Returns Nothing is returned.

See Also AfxFormatString1

Example

```
void ShowErrorMessage(CString& strError,CString& strCause)
{
```

```
        CString strMessage;

        // IDS_ERROR = "An error has occurred: %1 caused by %2"
        AfxFormatString2(strMessage,IDS_ERROR,strError,strCause);
        AfxMessageBox(strMessage);
}
```

AfxGetApp

■ 2.0 ■ 3.0

Description Gets the pointer to the CWinApp-derived application object. This function can be used anywhere in a program to retrieve the application object. Type-cast the returned value to call new members of your CWinApp-derived class.

Syntax CWinApp* AfxGetApp();

Parameters None.

Returns Pointer to CWinApp-derived object.

See Also AfxGetThread

Example

```
AfxGetApp()->DoWaitCursor(1);
((CMyApp*)AfxGetApp())->DoMyCommand();
AfxGetApp()->DoWaitCursor(-1);
```

AfxGetAppName

■ 2.0 ■ 3.0

Description Gets the application name. The application name can be stored as a string resource with an ID of AFX_IDS_APP_TITLE . Otherwise, MFC will use the name of the executable.

Syntax LPCTSTR AfxGetAppName();

Parameters None.

Returns Application name as a NULL-terminated string.

Example

```
void CMyApp::OnUpdateFileExit(CCmdUI* pCmdUI)
{
        CString strText = AfxGetAppName();

        // set File Exit menu command to Exit MyApp
        strText = "E&xit " + strText;
        pCmdUI->SetText(strText);
}
```

AfxGetInstanceHandle

■ 2.0 ■ 3.0

Description Gets the instance handle of the application. This will always be for the executable unless called from a DLL which uses the USRDLL version of MFC (as opposed to the more usual AFXDLL DLL version of MFC). AfxGetInstanceHandle is especially useful when having to call SDK functions or third party API functions that need as a parameter the HINSTANCE of the application.

Syntax HINSTANCE AfxGetInstanceHandle();

Parameters None.

Returns Instance handle of the application.

Example

```
::LoadCursor(AfxGetInstanceHandle(),"MYCURSOR");
```

AfxGetMainWnd

■ 2.0 ■ 3.0

Description Gets the main window of the application. For an OLE server application, this function returns the container of an in-place object if it is active; otherwise it returns the m_pMainWnd member of the application. For a non-OLE server application, AfxGetMainWnd always returns the m_pMainWnd member of the application.

Syntax CWnd* AfxGetMainWnd();

Parameters None.

Returns Main window of the application.

Example

```
AfxGetMainWnd()->ShowWindow(SW_MAXIMIZE);
```

AfxGetResourceHandle

■ 2.0 ■ 3.0

Description Gets the default resource instance handle used by Windows when finding resources. Using AfxGetResourceHandle() and AfxSetResourceHandle() in tandem is sometimes necessary when loading resources from DLLs in cases where MFC does not walk the chain of DLLs when trying to load the resource.

Syntax HINSTANCE AfxGetResourceHandle();

Parameters None.

Returns Resource instance handle.

See Also AfxSetResourceHandle();

Example

```
HINSTANCE hDLLInstance = ::GetModuleHandle("MYDLL.DLL");
HINSTANCE hSaveInstance;

hSaveInstance = AfxGetResourceHandle();
AfxSetResourceHandle(hDLLInstance);

m_BitmapButton.LoadBitmaps(IDB_MYBITMAPBUTTON);

AfxSetResourceHandle(hSaveInstance);
```

AfxGetThread

■ 2.0 ■ 3.0

Description Gets the pointer to the CWinThread-derived object for the current thread. This will always be for the thread from which AfxGetThread is called.

Syntax CWinThread* AfxGetThread();

Parameters None.

Returns Pointer to CWinThread-derived object.

See Also AfxBeginThread, AfxEndThread

Example

```
AfxGetThread()->SetThreadPriority(THREAD_PRIORITY_IDLE);
```

AfxIsMemoryBlock

■ 2.0 ■ 3.0 ■ DO

Description Checks a memory block to make sure it has been properly allocated and is of a certain size. The allocation sequence number can be requested as well. This function is only available in the debug version of MFC. For more information about debugging see Chapter 15, *Debugging and Exception Handling*.

Syntax BOOL AfxIsMemoryBlock(const void* p, UINT nBytes, LONG* plRequestNumber = NULL);

Parameters

p Pointer to memory block.

nBytes Number of bytes memory block should be.

plRequestNumber Pointer to LONG reserved for allocation sequence number. This value is set only if the memory block is valid.

Returns TRUE if the memory block is valid and is the specified size; FALSE otherwise.

See Also AfxIsValidAddress

Example

```
CMyObject* pObject = new CMyObject;
BOOL bValid;

// look at memory one byte before p pointer
bValid = AfxIsMemoryBlock(p,sizeof(CMyObject) - 1); // returns FALSE
```

AfxIsValidAddress

■ 2.0 ■ 3.0

Description Checks a memory block to verify that it is within the memory space of an application. It also checks if it is both readable and writable or just readable.

Syntax BOOL AfxIsValidAddress(const void* lp, UINT nBytes, BOOL bReadWrite = TRUE);

Parameters

lp Pointer to memory block.

nBytes Size that memory block should be.

bReadWrite TRUE if memory block should be both readable and writable; FALSE if the memory block should only be readable.

Returns TRUE if address if valid; FALSE otherwise.

See Also AfxIsMemoryBlock

Example

```
CMyObject object;

// can test objects on stack
ASSERT(AfxIsValidAddress(&object,sizeof(CMyObject),TRUE));
```

AfxIsValidString ■ 2.0 ■ 3.0

Description Checks a string to verify that it is within the memory space of an application and readable.

Syntax BOOL AfxIsValidString(LPCWSTR lpsz, int nLength = -1);

BOOL AfxIsValidString(LPCSTR lpsz, int nLength = -1);

Parameters

lpsz Pointer to string.

nLength Number of bytes to check, if -1, MFC assumes that the string is NULL-terminated.

Returns TRUE if the pointer is a valid address and the bytes up to the NULL-terminated byte are within the memory space of the calling application; FALSE otherwise.

Example

```
CString strTest = "Hello World";

ASSERT(AfxIsValidString(strText)); // validates string
```

AfxMessageBox ■ 2.0 ■ 3.0

Description Helper function for calling the DoMessageBox function of the CWinApp-derived class.

Syntax int AfxMessageBox(LPCTSTR lpszText, UINT nType = MB_OK,UINT nIDHelp = 0);

int AfxMessageBox(UINT nIDPrompt, UINT nType = MB_OK,UINT nIDHelp = (UINT)-1);

Parameters

lpszText Text of the message.

nIDPrompt String resource ID for text of the message.

nType Combination of one or more message styles defined in the SDK that specify the appearance and options of the message box.

nIDHelp Index for help context. 0 if not used; -1 if the value of the string resource ID should be used.

Returns The value returned by ::MessageBox, the ID value of the button pressed to dismiss the message box.

See Also CWinApp::DoMessageBox

Example

```
BOOL ConfirmDelete()
{
     CString strMessage = "Are you sure you want to delete the file?";

     if ( AfxMessageBox(strMessage,MB_YESNO) != MB_YES )
          return FALSE;

     return TRUE;
}
```

AfxRegisterClass

■ 2.0 ■ 3.0

Description Registers a window class with Windows. This function can be used from a DLL to ensure that the class is unregistered when the DLL unloads. Use this function to create your own window class that circumvents the MFC message-map mechanism and has its own window procedure.

Syntax BOOL AfxRegisterClass(WNDCLASS* lpWndClass);

Parameters

lpWndClass Pointer to WNDCLASS structure; see the Windows SDK for details.

Returns TRUE if successful; FALSE otherwise.

See Also AfxRegisterWndClass

Example

```
WNDCLASS wndclass;
HINSTANCE hDLLInstance = ::GetModuleHandle("mydll.dll");

wndclass.style = CS_HREDRAW | CS_VREDRAW;
wndclass.lpfnWndProc = CMyWnd::CMyWndProc; // static wnd procedure
wndclass.cbClsExtra = 8;
wndclass.cbWndExtra = 8;
wndclass.hInstance = hDLLInstance;
wndclass.hIcon = NULL;
wndclass.hCursor = NULL;
wndclass.hbrBackground = COLOR_WINDOW + 1;
wndclass.lpszMenuName = NULL;
wndclass.lpszClassName = "MyClass";

AfxRegisterClass(&wndclass);
```

AfxRegisterWndClass

■ 2.0 ■ 3.0

Description Registers a custom window class. This function is used to register a new window class that will use the MFC message-map mechanism and window procedure.

Syntax LPCTSTR AfxRegisterWndClass(UINT nClassStyle,HCURSOR hCursor = 0, HBRUSH hbrBackground = 0, HICON hIcon = 0);

Parameters:

nClassStyle Class style; see the Windows SDK for details.

hCursor Cursor used for the window class; see the Windows SDK for details.

hbrBackground Background brush for the window class; see the Windows SDK for details.

hIcon Icon for the window class; see the Windows SDK for details.

Returns Unique class name generated by MFC.

See Also AfxRegisterClass

Example

```
// get my own class
CString strMyClass = AfxRegisterWndClass(CS_HREDRAW | CS_VREDRAW);
CMyWnd* pMyWnd = new CMyWnd();
CRect rect;

AfxGetMainWnd()->GetClientRect(rect);

pMyWnd->Create(strMyClass,"MyWindow",WS_CHILD | WS_VISIBLE,rect,
           AfxGetMainWnd(),1);
```

AfxSetAllocHook

■ 2.0 ■ 3.0

Description Sets a hook function to be called by MFC when each memory block is allocated.

Syntax AFX_ALLOC_HOOK AfxSetAllocHook(AFX_ALLOC_HOOK pfnAllocHook);

Parameters

pfnAllocHook Hook function to call. The syntax of this function should be BOOL AllocHook(size_t nSize, BOOL bObject, LONG lRequestNumber); where nSize is the size of the allocation, bObject indicates whether or not the object is CObject-based, and lRequestNumber is the allocation sequence number. This function should return TRUE if the allocation should be performed, FALSE otherwise.

Returns Previous allocation hook function.

AfxSetResourceHandle

■ 2.0 ■ 3.0

Description Sets the default resource instance handle used by Windows when finding resources. Using AfxGetResourceHandle() and AfxSetResourceHandle() in tandem is sometimes necessary when loading resources from DLLs in cases where MFC does not walk the chain of DLLs when trying to load the resource.

Syntax void AfxSetResourceHandle(HINSTANCE hInstResource);

Parameters

hInstResource Resource instance handle.

Returns Nothing is returned.

See Also AfxGetResourceHandle

Example See AfxGetResourceHandle

AfxThrowArchiveException ■ 2.0 ■ 3.0

Description Throws an archive exception. For more information about exception-handling, see Chapter 15, *Debugging and Exception Handling*.

Syntax void AfxThrowArchiveException(int cause, LPCTSTR lpszArchiveName = NULL);

Parameters

cause Integer value indicating cause of exception.

lpszArchiveName archive name.

Returns Nothing is returned.

See Also CArchiveException

AfxThrowFileException ■ 2.0 ■ 3.0

Description Throws a file exception. For more information about exception-handling, see Chapter 15, *Debugging and Exception Handling*.

Syntax void AfxThrowFileException(int cause, LONG lOsError = -1,LPCTSTR lpszFileName = NULL);

Parameters

cause Cause of error.

lOsError I/O error reported.

lpszFileName Name of file involved.

Returns Nothing is returned.

See Also CFileException

AfxThrowMemoryException ■ 2.0 ■ 3.0

Description Throws a memory exception. For more information about exception-handling, see Chapter 15, *Debugging and Exception Handling*.

Syntax public, AfxThrowMemoryException();

Parameters	None.
Returns	Nothing is returned.
See Also	CMemoryException

AfxThrowNotSupportedException ■ 2.0 ■ 3.0

Description	Throws a not-supported exception. For more information about exception-handling, see Chapter 15, *Debugging and Exception Handling*.
Syntax	void AfxThrowMemoryException();
Parameters	None.
Returns	Nothing is returned.
See Also	CNotSupportedException

AfxThrowResourceException ■ 2.0 ■ 3.0

Description	Throws a resource exception. For more information about exception-handling, see Chapter 15, *Debugging and Exception Handling*.
Syntax	void AfxThrowResourceException();
Parameters	None.
Returns	Nothing is returned.
See Also	CResourceException

AfxThrowUserException ■ 2.0 ■ 3.0

Description	Throws a user exception. For more information about exception-handling, see Chapter 15, *Debugging and Exception Handling*.
Syntax	void AfxThrowUserException();
Parameters	None.
Returns	Nothing is returned.
See Also	CUserException

Resources and Context-Sensitive Help

Resources are the heart of the interface of almost all Windows applications. Created either dynamically at run-time, or through resource design programs like AppStudio (the much-preferred method), dialogs, menus, bitmaps, and the like are the building blocks of the GUI of Windows. For the typical Windows application, the Visual C++ developers will spend almost as much time using AppStudio to generate, modify, and code the integration of resources as they spend in coding other areas of the program.

Whereas this chapter does not endeavor to explore the many different formats and types of resources supported by the Windows API—there are many good sources for this information—it does attempt to discuss various important aspects of using resources that are specific to MFC.

RC Files

When AppWizard is used to create a new project in the Visual C++ environment, an .RC file is generated that contains all of the default resources for the application. As the programmer adds resources to the project using AppStudio, this .RC file is updated automatically with each new change. For resources that are not editable by AppStudio, third-party controls for example, there is an .RC2 file as well that is included by the .RC file when Visual C++ compiles the resources for the application. The #defines for the identifiers used in this .RC (and subsequently used in the code) are found in a RESOURCE.H file with every project. For the default resources, the #defines are found in the AFXRES.H file which is part of the MFC source code.

MFC suggests but does not enforce a naming convention for the prefixes of identifiers used for standard resources found in a Windows program. Table 2-3 lists these prefixes:

Table 2-3 Standard prefixes for resource identifiers

Prefix	Use
IDD_	Dialog templates
IDC_	Dialog controls and cursors (except for IDOK, IDCANCEL, and the like)
ID_	Menu item commands (and commands in general), also used for the string resources associated with the prompts for the menu commands
IDS_	Strings not related to menu commands (this is used for the actual ID, no relation to the actual string segments, which combine 16-string resources in one group)
IDI_	Icons
IDB_	Bitmaps
IDR_	Shared identifier (used when one identifier is used for many resources, as is the case for documents that have one resource identifier for their menus, accelerators, strings, and icons)
IDP_	Formatted strings (for example, strings that contain "%1" or "%2" as place-holders for run-time values)

The values for these identifiers are limited by Windows itself as well as the MFC framework. It is a good idea when using third-party libraries to make sure that their identifiers do not fall outside of the ranges prescribed in Table 2-4 below. It is also a good idea to check the user-defined window messages for conflicts as well.

Table 2-4 Valid ranges for resource identifiers

Prefix	Range	Reason
IDD_	1 - 0x6FFF	0x7000 - 0xFFFF are reserved by MFC
IDC_	8 - 0xDFFF	1 - 7 reserved for standard controls (IDOK, IDCANCEL etc.)
ID_	0x8000 - 0xDFFF	MFC framework only recognizes values greater than 0x8000
IDS_, IDP_	1 - 0x7FFF	0x8000 - 0xFFFF are reserved by MFC for menu prompts
IDR_	1 - 0x6FFF	0x7000 - 0xFFFF are reserved by MFC
IDC_, IDI_, IDB_	1 - 0x6FFF	0x7000 - 0xFFFF are reserved by MFC

When the programmer creates new controls and resources in AppStudio, increasing valid values for identifiers are automatically assigned. AppStudio tracks the values last given through the use of #defines in the RESOURCE.H file. The _APS_NEXT_RESOURCE_VALUE #define keeps track of the next identifier value for dialog template resources. The _APS_NEXT_COMMAND_VALUE #define keeps track of the next identifier value for commands. The _APS_NEXT_CONTROL_VALUE define keeps track of the next identifier value for dialog controls. It is important for the programmer to update these #defines whenever manually editing the identifiers for the resources of the project so that AppStudio will not generate duplicate identifiers.

It is sometimes necessary to include other resource files and header files in the project. To do this, choose the Set Includes command from the File menu in AppStudio. In the "Read-Only Symbol Directives" section, add the additional header files you need. In the "Compile-Time Directives" section, add the additional .RC files you need. This generates TEXTINCLUDE "resources" in your primary .RC file. AppStudio uses these "resources" when it regenerates the .RC file whenever the project resources are saved. Alternatively, you could just manually create these "resources." An example .RC file that includes another header file and another .RC file is shown in Listing 2-4.

Listing 2-4 Typical .RC file for project with multiple resource files

```
//Microsoft App Studio generated resource script.
//
#include "resource.h"

#define APSTUDIO_READONLY_SYMBOLS
/////////////////////////////////////////////////////////////////////////////
//
// Generated from the TEXTINCLUDE 2 resource.
//
#include "afxres.h"
#include "c:\myapp\include\widget.h"
/////////////////////////////////////////////////////////////////////////////
#undef APSTUDIO_READONLY_SYMBOLS

#ifdef APSTUDIO_INVOKED
/////////////////////////////////////////////////////////////////////////////
//
// TEXTINCLUDE
```

```
//

1 TEXTINCLUDE DISCARDABLE
BEGIN
    "resource.h\0"
END

2 TEXTINCLUDE DISCARDABLE
BEGIN
    "#include ""afxres.h""\r\n"
    "#include ""c:\\myapp\\widget\\widget.h""\0"
END

3 TEXTINCLUDE DISCARDABLE
BEGIN
    "#include ""res\\myapp.rc2""  // non-App Studio edited resources\r\n"
    "#include ""c:\\myapp\\widget\\widget.rc"" // widget resources\r\n"
    "#include ""afxres.rc""  \011// Standard components\r\n"
    "#include ""afxprint.rc""\011// printing/print preview resources\r\n"
    "#include ""afxolecl.rc""\011// OLE container resources\r\n"
    "#include ""afxdb.rc""\011\011// Database resources\r\n"
    "\0"
END

/////////////////////////////////////////////////////////////////////////////
#endif    // APSTUDIO_INVOKED

// RESOURCE DEFINED HERE

#ifndef APSTUDIO_INVOKED
/////////////////////////////////////////////////////////////////////////////
//
// Generated from the TEXTINCLUDE 3 resource.
//
#include "res\myapp.rc2"  // non-App Studio edited resources
#include "c:\myapp\widget\widget.rc" // widget resources
#include "afxres.rc"    // Standard components
#include "afxprint.rc"  // printing/print preview resources
#include "afxolecl.rc"  // OLE container resources
#include "afxdb.rc"          // Database resources

/////////////////////////////////////////////////////////////////////////////
#endif    // not APSTUDIO_INVOKED
```

Using Resources

For the most part, using resources in MFC code is fairly straightforward. There are wrapper classes for almost all of the standard Windows resources. Each class allows the programmer to specify the identifier for the resource either in the constructor:

```
CDialog(LPCSTR lpszTemplateName, CWnd* pParentWnd = NULL);
CDialog(UINT nIDTemplate, CWnd* pParentWnd = NULL);
```

or in member functions:

```
BOOL CBitmap::LoadBitmap(LPCSTR lpszResourceName);
BOOL CBitmap::LoadBitmap(UINT nIDResource);
```

The SDK functions that do the actual loading are eventually called by these classes.

The major complication that can arise when loading resources occurs if the resources are being loaded by a DLL and/or they are located in a DLL. For most of MFC, whenever a resource needs to be loaded, there is code that will search all of the registered DLLs (CDynLinkLibrary objects) and the application itself before failing. This means that the programmer needs to write no special coding in these cases. However, there are some functions, like CBitmapButton::LoadBitmaps, that only search for the resource in the application's resource file. In these situations, the helper functions AfxSetResourceHandle and AfxGetResourceHandle are used to set and reset which module Windows uses when loading resources. Listing 2-5 is an example of code used to initialize a bitmap button in a DLL that contains the bitmap resources.

Listing 2-5 Example of AfxGetResourceHandle and AfxSetResourceHandle

```
int CMyView::OnCreate(LPCREATESTRUCT lpCreateStruct)
{
   // store previous handle
   HINSTANCE hResPrev = AfxGetResourceHandle();

   // set resource handle to my DLL
   AfxSetResourceHandle(::GetModuleHandle("mydll.dll"));

   // safe to load my bitmaps here...
   m_MyBitmapButton.LoadBitmaps(IDB_PICTURE);


   // reset resource handle to application
   AfxSetResourceHandle(hResPrev);

   return 0;
}
```

Context-Sensitive Help

The MFC framework supports two types of context-sensitive help for applications. Direct context-sensitive help launches the help file immediately, jumping to the topic specified by the current dialog or frame window. It is activated by pressing the F1 key or clicking on the Help button of a dialog. Interactive context-sensitive help allows the user to choose to receive help on a particular interface element by clicking on it. It is activated by pressing the F1 key while holding down the SHIFT key; this causes the cursor to change to an arrow and a question mark, indicating interactive context-sensitive help. Once a choice has been made, the cursor changes back to what it was previously.

Context-sensitive help is activated through the use of accelerator keys. When creating a new project with AppWizard with context-sensitive help enabled, accelerators are added for each CDocument document for both the F1 key and the SHIFT-F1 key combination. The command ID_HELP is used for direct context-sensitive help; the command ID_CONTEXT_HELP is used for interactive context-sensitive help. When adding a Help button to a dialog, MFC requires that this button be given an identifier of ID_HELP. If there are no handlers for the ID_HELP command,

CDialog::OnInitDialog will automatically hide all Help buttons on dialogs. MFC includes default handlers for these two commands both at the CWinApp (CWinThread) level and at the CFrameWnd level. To link in these handlers, you must declare message map entries for the classes desired.

Direct Context-Sensitive Help

Direct context-sensitive help for dialogs uses the resource identifier of the dialog template as the basis for the context value of the help. MFC takes this value and adds the constant HID_BASE_RESOURCE to calculate the context value sent to WinHelp. Similarly, for frame windows, MFC takes the resource identifier of the frame and adds the constant HID_BASE_RESOURCE to it, unless there is a menu command being selected, in which case MFC uses that resource indentifier and adds the constant HID_BASE_COMMAND to it. Don't worry about having to convert the resource identifiers in order to create the correct content mappings for the help file. Visual C++ comes with a utility program, MAKEHM.EXE, that will take a header file and translate it into a .HM file, offsetting the identifier values as necessary, which then can be used by such help-generating programs as Doc-To-Help(TM) or RoboHelp(TM). When AppWizard is used to create a project and context-sensitive help is enabled, a MAKEHELP.BAT batch file is produced that will envoke the MAKEHM.EXE utility to convert a RESOURCE.H file to a contextually accurate .HM file. If you need to include the resource identifiers for default MFC resources (like the common dialogs), it is a good idea to first temporarily copy over the values from the AFXRES.H file to the RESOURCE.H file so that these identifiers will be included in the translation. Listing 2-6 contains the batch file for the Courses application on the CD:

Listing 2-6 Example MAKEHELP.BAT file

```
@echo off
REM -- First make map file from App Studio generated resource.h
echo // MAKEHELP.BAT generated Help Map file.  Used by COURSES.HPJ. >hlp\courses.hm
echo. >>hlp\courses.hm
echo // Commands (ID_* and IDM_*) >>hlp\courses.hm
makehm ID_,HID_,0x10000 IDM_,HIDM_,0x10000 resource.h >>hlp\courses.hm
echo. >>hlp\courses.hm
echo // Prompts (IDP_*) >>hlp\courses.hm
makehm IDP_,HIDP_,0x30000 resource.h >>hlp\courses.hm
echo. >>hlp\courses.hm
echo // Resources (IDR_*) >>hlp\courses.hm
makehm IDR_,HIDR_,0x20000 resource.h >>hlp\courses.hm
echo. >>hlp\courses.hm
echo // Dialogs (IDD_*) >>hlp\courses.hm
makehm IDD_,HIDD_,0x20000 resource.h >>hlp\courses.hm
echo. >>hlp\courses.hm
echo // Frame Controls (IDW_*) >>hlp\courses.hm
makehm IDW_,HIDW_,0x50000 resource.h >>hlp\courses.hm
REM -- Make help for Project COURSES
call hc31 courses.hpj
echo.
```

The MFC handler for the ID_HELP command will in almost all cases eventually call the CWnd::OnHelp member function. As seen in Listing 2-7, this function will first determine which is the active window and send a WM_COMMANDHELP (MFC-defined user messsage) message to it. If this window processes this message (returning a non-zero value), the handling of the command will terminate. Otherwise, the function will traverse up the parent window tree until a window is found that processes the message. If no window processes the message, the ID_DEFAULT_HELP command is sent to the main window of the application.

Listing 2-7 CWnd::OnHelp

```
void CWnd::OnHelp()  // use context to derive help context
{
   // attempt to map current context to help topic
   CWnd* pWnd = GetTopLevelParent();
   HWND hWnd = ::GetLastActivePopup(pWnd->GetSafeHwnd());
   while (hWnd != NULL)
   {
      // attempt to process help
      if (::SendMessage(hWnd, WM_COMMANDHELP, 0, 0))
         break;

      // try next parent/owner in the parent/owner chain
      hWnd = _AfxGetParentOwner(hWnd);
   }
   if (hWnd == NULL)
   {
      // No context available, bring up default.
      SendMessage(WM_COMMAND, ID_DEFAULT_HELP);
   }
}
```

The WM_COMMANDHELP message is, by default, always handled by a CDialog. Its implementation is found in Listing 2-8; it simply calls WinHelp with the appropriate context identifier.

Listing 2-8 CDialog::OnCommandHelp

```
LRESULT CDialog::OnCommandHelp(WPARAM, LPARAM lParam)
{
   if (lParam == 0 && m_nIDHelp != 0)
      lParam = HID_BASE_RESOURCE + m_nIDHelp;
   if (lParam != 0)
   {
      AfxGetApp()->WinHelp(lParam);
         return TRUE;
   }
   return FALSE;
}
```

Interactive Context-Sensitive Help

Interactive context-sensitive help always works through the main frame window. The MFC handler for the ID_CONTEXT_HELP command should always call the

CFrameWnd::OnContextHelp handler. This function changes the cursor, captures the mouse, and sets up its own message loop. With each message generated while in this loop, MFC checks to see if either the user has requested to escape from this help mode or if the left mouse button has been pressed. On a user click in the client area of a window, MFC calls the MapClientArea function. This function sends a WM_HELPHITTEST message (MFC-defined message) to the window on top of which the user has clicked, requesting the context value for the help. As seen in Listing 2-9, this function, similar to CWnd::OnHelp, will traverse the parent tree looking for a window to process the WM_HELPHITTEST message. If the message is never processed, the ID_DEFAULT_HELP command will be sent to the main window.

Listing 2-9 MapClientArea function

```
static DWORD NEAR PASCAL MapClientArea(HWND hWnd, POINT point)
{
   DWORD dwContext;

   do
   {
      ASSERT(::IsWindow(hWnd));

      // try current window
      ::ScreenToClient(hWnd, &point);
      dwContext = ::SendMessage(hWnd, WM_HELPHITTEST, 0,
         MAKELONG(point.x, point.y));
      ::ClientToScreen(hWnd, &point);

      // don't use owners of popup windows, just child/parent relationship
      if ((GetWindowLong(hWnd, GWL_STYLE) & WS_CHILD) == 0)
         break;
      // try parent window
      hWnd = ::GetParent(hWnd);
   }
   while (hWnd && dwContext == 0);

   return dwContext == 0 ? -1 : dwContext;
}
```

The handler for the WM_HELPHITTEST message has the following syntax:

afx_msg LRESULT CWnd::OnHelpHittest(WPARAM wParam, LPARAM lParam);

The wParam is unused. The LOWORD of the lParam contains the horizontal mouse position relative to the client area. The HIWORD of the lParam contains the vertical mouse position relative to the client area. A return value of zero indicates that the message was not processed. Any non-zero value will be used as the help context value.

3

APPLICATION CLASSES

3

APPLICATION CLASSES

The very first thing to do when creating an application framework is to create a class for the application itself. This way, C++ programmers can have the antiquated, procedure-bound main or WinMain functions forever hidden within the application class itself. Global variables then are almost never needed because they become data members of the application object which, by definition, should be around as long as the application is running. Also, all functionality common to applications of a similar type can be encapsulated to be used over and over again by the programmer. This is exactly what the Microsoft engineers have done with CWinThread and CWinApp, the process and application classes of MFC. The CWinThread class encapsulates a Windows thread handle and ID, whereas CWinApp specifically encapsulates an application's HINSTANCE instance handle, including as well a lot of useful code for managing application-level functionality such as on-line help, profile/registry entries and printer settings.

This chapter covers these all-important classes. The CCommandLineInfo class, abstracting the shell launching instructions passed in through the command line, is discussed as well. CWinThread is a class derived from the generic CCmdTarget class. CWinApp is a class derived from CWinThread. This chapter does not delve into the CCmdTarget aspects of CWinThread and CWinApp; see Chapter 4, *Windows Messaging,* for information regarding command targets.

Each 32-bit MFC application makes use of CWinThread and CWinApp and contains one and only one CWinApp-derived class that represents the desired application object. In 16-bit versions of MFC, there is no CWinThread class (distinguishing between a thread and an application task has no meaning in Windows 3.x). Instead, CWinApp is directly derived from CCmdTarget for Windows 3.x. We will be discussing the parent CWinThread class first. Keep in mind that the CWinApp class has all of the properties and members of the CWinThread class in addition to characteristics unique to a

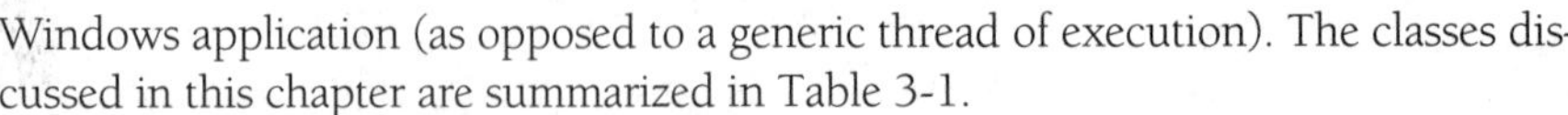

Windows application (as opposed to a generic thread of execution). The classes discussed in this chapter are summarized in Table 3-1.

Table 3-1 Chapter 3 class summary

Class Name	Description
CWinThread	Encapsulates Windows process.
CCommandLineInfo	Helper class for OLE, DDE, and shell-based command line options.
CWinApp	Encapsulates Windows application; includes code for managing application-level functionality.

The CWinThread Class

The CWinThread class serves as an abstraction of a Windows process. This class was not present in versions of MFC before 3.0. Most of its members, however, did exist in the CWinApp class, described later in this chapter. When MFC left the 16-bit, non-preemptive tasking world, all parts of the CWinApp class that were process-specific were pulled out to form the CWinThread class. What was application-specific was left in the CWinApp class. Like CWinApp in earlier versions of MFC, the CWinThread class is derived from the CCmdTarget class.

The CWinThread class supports two kinds of threads: user-interface threads and worker threads. A user-interface thread is a Windows process that includes a message loop. A worker thread does not include a message loop. Instead, worker threads represent well-defined background-processing tasks that require no user input. MFC worker threads operate through controlling functions. The thread begins by executing the controlling function; once this function terminates, the thread ends as well.

For the most part, this chapter will be talking about user-interface threads. The Run member encapsulates the message loop for user-interface threads. It consists of a repetitive loop in which messages are polled and then processed until receiving a WM_QUIT message, causing the thread to terminate. It is called automatically by the framework when an application begins. There are two major advantages to the way in which MFC processes messages. One is that the virtual member OnIdle gets called conditionally whenever there are no messages in the queue. MFC uses the OnIdle member to do many cleanup-type activities such as deletion of temporary handles and user interface command updating. This allows the programmer greater flexibility in determining how an application will take advantage of idle time. If the programmer overrides this member, however, the default must be called to ensure that MFC can perform its maintenance tasks. Another benefit is that the virtual member PreTranslateMessage gets called before a message is actually dispatched. This gives the programmer a first-chance opportunity to handle a message of any type. The message can then either be swallowed up or be translated and dispatched to the appropriate window. A depiction of how messages are processed by CWinThread::Run is shown in Figure 3-1.

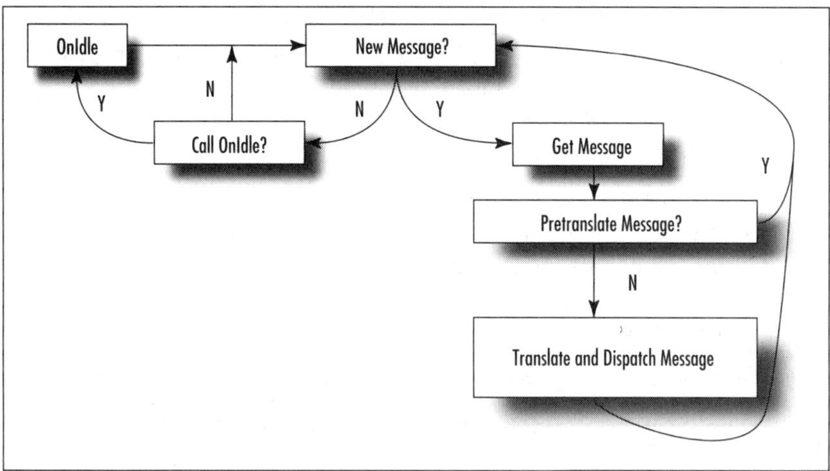

Figure 3-1 MFC Message Loop

In the documentation of the CWinThread class that follows, the members of CWinThread which include a 16-bit MFC version indicator actually were part of the CWinApp class in that version.

CWinThread Class Reference

CWinThread ■ 2.0 ■ 3.0

Description The constructor of the CWinThread class. There are two ways to create a thread. One way is to instantiate a CWinThread object and then call the CreateThread method to create the actual thread. This method is best when the CWinThread object needs to stay around for the creation and termination of multiple threads. Another way is to use the AfxBeginThread helper function discussed in Chapter 2 *The MFC Framework*. This function will create the CWinThread object, using the second overloaded constructor shown below. It will then call CreateThread itself to create the Windows thread process. By default, CWinThread-derived objects of this type will delete themselves when AfxEndThread (see Chapter 2, *The MFC Framework*) is called to terminate the thread. To change this functionality, set the m_bAutoDelete member to FALSE; it is set to TRUE by the constructor. AfxBeginThread is usually used for one-time-only threads.

Syntax public, CWinThread();

public, CWinThread(AFX_THREADPROC pfnThreadProc, LPVOID pParam);

Parameters

pfnThreadProc Pointer to controlling function of the thread, only valid for worker threads. The syntax of this function should be as follows: UINT DoProcess(LPVOID pParam);

pParam Pointer to data passed to controlling function.

Returns Nothing is returned.

See Also CWinThread::~CWinThread, CWinThread::CommonConstruct, AfxBeginThread, AfxEndThread

Example

```
CWinThread* pThread;

pThread = new CWinThread(); // use simple constructor
pThread->m_bAutoDelete = FALSE; // do not auto delete
pThread->CreateThread(); // create the actual thread
```

~CWinThread

■ 2.0 ■ 3.0

Description The destructor for the CWinThread class. The destructor frees the Windows handle for the actual thread.

Syntax public, ~CWinThread();

Parameters None.

Returns Nothing is returned.

See Also CWinThread::CWinThread

Example

```
void DeleteThread(CWinThread*& pThread)
{
     // only necessary when m_bAutoDelete = FALSE
delete pThread;
     pThread = NULL;
}
```

AssertValid

■ 2.0 ■ 3.0

Description Validates the object. This function simply calls the inherited version of AssertValid from the CCmdTarget class. For more information regarding object validation, see Chapter 15, *Debugging and Exception Handling*.

Syntax public, virtual void AssertValid() const;

Parameters None.

Returns Nothing is returned.

See Also CWinThread::Dump, CCmdTarget::AssertValid

Example

```
void CheckThread(CWinThread* pThread)
{
     pThread->AssertValid();
}
```

CommonConstruct

–. ■ 3.0 ■ UD

Description Serves as a common initializer for the two CWinThread class constructors. This function rarely needs to be called outside of MFC.

Syntax public, void CommonConstruct();

Parameters None.

Returns Nothing is returned.

See Also CWinThread::CWinThread

CreateThread

–. ■ 3.0

Description Creates the actual thread. This function is called either by the programmer directly for already existing CWinThread objects, or by AfxBeginThread that first creates a CWinThread object and then calls CreateThread to create the Windows thread process.

Syntax public, BOOL CreateThread(DWORD dwCreateFlags = 0, UINT nStackSize = 0, LPSECURITY_ATTRIBUTES lpSecurityAttrs = NULL);

Parameters

dwCreateFlags Creation flag, one of two values: CREATE_SUSPENDED creates the thread in a suspended state—use ResumeThread to begin thread execution; 0 indicates that the thread should be executed immediately.

nStackSize Stack size, in bytes, of the thread. If 0, the stack size for the process's primary thread will be used.

lpSecurityAttrs Pointer to a SECURITY_ATTRIBUTES structure that indicates the thread's security. See the Windows SDK for information about the SECURITY_ATTRIBUTES structure.

Returns TRUE if thread is created successfully; FALSE otherwise.

See Also CWinThread::CWinThread, AfxBeginThread, AfxEndThread

Example

```
CWinThread* pThread;

pThread = new CWinThread();
pThread->CreateThread(CREATE_SUSPENDED);

// do something here

pThread->ResumeThread();
```

Delete

■ 2.0 ■ 3.0 ■ UD

Description Deletes the *this* pointer to the CWinThread object if m_bAutoDelete = TRUE. This member is called by the helper function, AfxEndThread, when a thread terminates or by AfxBeginThread when the thread creation process fails. This function should not be called by the programmer directly.

Syntax public, virtual void Delete();

Parameters None.

Returns Nothing is returned.

See Also CWinThread::~CWinThread

DUMP ■ 2.0 ■ 3.0

Description Diagnostics function for the CWinThread object. Dumps the contents of all member variables to the dump context. For more information, see Chapter 15, *Debugging and Exception Handling*.

Syntax public, virtual void Dump(CDumpContext& dc) const;

Parameters

dc Dump context.

Returns Nothing is returned.

See Also CWinThread::AssertValid

Example

```
void DumpThread(CWinThread* pThread)
{
     Cfile file;


     if ( file.Open("log.txt",CFile::modeCreate | CFile::modeWrite) )
     {
     CDumpContext dc(&file);
     pThread->Dump(dc);
     }
}
```

EXITINSTANCE ■ 2.0 ■ 3.0

Description Performs cleanup for the thread. This function is typically overridden by derived classes. It is called by MFC when a thread terminates. It should be called by the programmer only in an overridden version of the Run() member.

Syntax public, virtual int ExitInstance();

Parameters None.

Returns The exit code for the thread.

See Also CWinThread::InitInstance

Example

```
int CMyThread::ExitInstance()
{
     // delete objects created for the instance
     delete m_pMyObject1;
     delete m_pMyObject2;

     // always call default
return CWinThread::ExitInstance();
}
```

GetMainWnd

■ 2.0 ■ 3.0

Description Returns the main window for the thread. This is typically the SDI or MDI frame window for the application.

Syntax public, virtual CWnd* GetMainWnd();

Parameters None.

Returns Pointer to the main window.

Example

```
void DisplayDialog()
{
     CWinThread* pThread;

     pThread = AfxGetThread(); // get active thread
     CMyDialog dlg(pThread->GetMainWnd()); // parent = main window
     dlg.DoModal();
}
```

GetThreadPriority

–. ■ 3.0

Description Gets the priority of the thread.

Syntax public, int GetThreadPriority();

Parameters None.

Returns Thread priority — one of the following values:

THREAD_PRIORITY_TIME_CRITICAL
THREAD_PRIORITY_HIGHEST
THREAD_PRIORITY_ABOVE_NORMAL
THREAD_PRIORITY_NORMAL
THREAD_PRIORITY_BELOW_NORMAL
THREAD_PRIORITY_LOWEST
THREAD_PRIORITY_IDLE

See Also CWinThread::SetThreadPriority

Example

```
int nPriority = pThread->GetThreadPriority(); // store old priority

// give thread highest priority
pThread->SetThreadPriority(THREAD_PRIORITY_TIME_CRITICAL);

// do something here

// restore thread to previous priority
pThread->SetThreadPriority(nPriority);
```

InitInstance

■ 2.0 ■ 3.0

Description Performs initialization for the thread. This function must be overridden by derived classes. Do not call the default version of this function; it will always return FALSE.

Syntax public, virtual BOOL InitInstance();

Parameters None.

Returns TRUE, if successfully initialized; FALSE otherwise.

See Also CWinThread::ExitInstance

Example:

```
BOOL CMyThread::InitInstance()
{
m_pMyObject1 = new CMyObject1();
     m_pMyObject2 = new CMyObject2();

// default will just return FALSE, do not call
return TRUE;
}
```

IsIdleMessage

■ 2.0 ■ 3.0

Description Called by the Run member to see if OnIdle should be called. The default version returns FALSE for redundant mouse messages and caret blinks. This function may be overridden by the programmer to perform additional checking.

Syntax public, virtual BOOL IsIdleMessage(MSG* pMsg);

Parameters

pMsg Pointer to message to check.

Returns TRUE if OnIdle() should be called; FALSE otherwise.

See Also CWinThread::OnIdle

Example

```
BOOL CMyThread::IsIdleMessage(MSG* pMsg)
{
      if ( !CWinThread::IsIdleMessage(pMsg) || m_bNoIdle )
           return FALSE;
      else
           return TRUE;
}
```

OnIdle

■ 2.0 ■ 3.0

Description Called by the Run member for idle processing when no messages are in the message queue. The default version deletes temporary handles and performs command UI updating. If the programmer overrides this function, the default should be called.

Syntax public, virtual BOOL OnIdle(LONG lCount);

Parameters

lCount Counter indicating how many times OnIdle has been called since the thread has been in an idle state. This counter is set to 0 when a new message has been processed and IsIdleMessage returns TRUE.

Returns TRUE if more idle processing time is required (should OnIdle be called again); FALSE otherwise. If FALSE is returned, OnIdle will not be called again until IsIdleMessage returns TRUE.

See Also CWinThread::IsIdleMessage

Example

```
BOOL CMyThread::OnIdle(LONG lCount)
{
     // perform idle tasks...

return CWinThread::OnIdle(lCount);
}
```

OPERATOR HANDLE

■ 3.0 ■ UD

Description Type-casting operator which returns the handle to the thread. This operator is used when calling Win32 SDK functions that require a thread handle.

Syntax public, operator HANDLE() const;

Parameters None.

Returns Handle to the thread.

Example

```
void Resume(CWinThread& thread)
{
     // compiler inserts call to operator HANDLE to convert
     // CWinThread to HANDLE
     ::ResumeThread(thread);
}
```

PRETRANSLATEMESSAGE

■ 2.0 ■ 3.0

Description Performs first-chance processing of messages before they are dispatched. This function can be overridden by derived classes.

Syntax public, virtual BOOL PreTranslateMessage(MSG* pMsg);

Parameters

pMsg Message to process.

Returns TRUE if message has been fully processed; it will not be dispatched. Returning FALSE means that the message should be dispatched.

See Also CWinThread::ProcessMessageFilter

Example

```
BOOL CMyThread::PreTranslateMessage(MSG* pMsg)
{
     if ( pMsg->message == WM_LBUTTONUP )
          return TRUE; // steal left-button-up messages
     else
          return CWinThread::PreTranslateMessage(pMsg);
}
```

ProcessMessageFilter ■ 2.0 ■ 3.0

Description Hook filter function for menu, scrollbar, message box, or dialog box messages. This function is called during modal states when the main message loop is not processing messages. Derived classes that override this function should call the default version. The default version performs standard translations such as generating an ID_HELP command when the F1 key is pressed by the user in a dialog.

Syntax public, virtual BOOL ProcessMessageFilter(int code, LPMSG lpMsg);

Parameters

code Code indicating message origin, one of the following values:
MSGF_DDEMGR—DDE-related message
MSGF_DIALOGBOX—dialog box-related message
MSGF_MENU—menu-related message
MSGF_NEXTWINDOW—message generated when the user presses Alt-Tab to activate the next window
MSGF_SCROLLBAR—scroll bar-related message

lpMsg pointer to message.

Returns TRUE if the message is processed; FALSE otherwise.

See Also CWinThread::PreTranslateMessage

Example

```
BOOL CMyThread::ProcessMessageFilter(int code,LPMGS lpMsg)
{
	if ( !CWinThread::ProcessMessageFilter(code,lpMsg) )
	{
		// MFC didn't process the message
		if ( IsMyMessage(code,lpMsg) )
			return TRUE;
	}

	return FALSE;
}
```

ProcessWndProcException ■ 2.0 ■ 3.0

Description Last-chance handler for exceptions thrown by command and message handlers. The default version handles exceptions thrown by WM_CREATE and WM_PAINT messages. This function can be overridden by derived classes to handle exceptions for other messages. For more information about exceptions, see Chapter 15, *Debugging and Exception Handling*.

Syntax public, virtual LRESULT ProcessWndProcException(CException* e, const MSG* pMsg);

Parameters

e Exception thrown.

pMsg Pointer to message whose handler caused the exception to be thrown.

Returns Return code for message reported to Windows.

Example

```
LRESULT CMyThread::ProcessWndProcException(CException* e, const MSG* pMsg)
{
     OutputDebugString("Exception thrown during message processing");

     return CWinThread::ProcessWndProcException(e,pMsg);
     }
```

PUMPMESSAGE

■ 2.0 ■ 3.0 ■ UD

Description Internal MFC function called by the Run member to call PreTranslateMessage() and dispatch the message. This function should not be directly called by the programmer.

Syntax public, virtual BOOL PumpMessage();

Parameters None.

Returns FALSE if WM_QUIT message is detected; ExitInstance will then be called. Returns TRUE for every other message.

See Also CWinThread::Run

RESUMETHREAD

■ 3.0

Description Resumes execution of a thread that has been suspended. It reduces the suspend count for the thread by one. If the suspend count equals 0, the thread resumes execution

Syntax public, DWORD ResumeThread();

Parameters None.

Returns Previous suspend count if successful; 0xFFFFFFFF otherwise.

See Also CWinThread::SuspendThread

Example

```
pThread->SuspendThread();

// do something here

pThread->ResumeThread();
```

RUN

■ 2.0 ■ 3.0

Description The message loop for the thread. This function should not be called directly. It is called automatically when the application is loaded.

Syntax public, virtual int Run();

Parameters None.

Returns Exit code for thread.

See Also CWinThread::OnIdle, CWinThread::PreTranslateMessage, CWinThread::IsIdleMessage, CWinThread::PumpMessage

SetThreadPriority ■ 3.0

Description Sets the priority of the thread.

Syntax public, BOOL SetThreadPriority(int nPriority);

Parameters

nPriority Thread priority — one of the following values:
THREAD_PRIORITY_TIME_CRITICAL
THREAD_PRIORITY_HIGHEST
THREAD_PRIORITY_ABOVE_NORMAL
THREAD_PRIORITY_NORMAL
THREAD_PRIORITY_BELOW_NORMAL
THREAD_PRIORITY_LOWEST
THREAD_PRIORITY_IDLE

Returns TRUE, if successful; FALSE otherwise.

See Also CWinThread::GetThreadPriority

Example

```
int nPriority = pThread->GetThreadPriority(); // store old priority

// give thread highest priority
pThread->SetThreadPriority(THREAD_PRIORITY_TIME_CRITICAL);

// do something here

// restore thread to previous priority
pThread->SetThreadPriority(nPriority);
```

SuspendThread ■ 3.0

Description Suspends the execution of the thread. It increments the suspend count of the thread. If the suspend count is greater than 0, the thread does not execute. Call ResumeThread to resume execution.

Syntax public, DWORD SuspendThread();

Parameters None.

Returns Previous suspend count if successful; 0xFFFFFFFF otherwise.

See Also CWinThread::ResumeThread

Example

```
pThread->SuspendThread();

// do something here

pThread->ResumeThread();
```

The CCommandLineInfo Class

Before discussing the CWinApp class, let's first talk briefly about the CCommandLineInfo class, a helper class added in MFC 4.0 to assist in the parsing of command line parameters passed in when an application starts. With the advent of Windows 95 and OLE technology, there are now many more different situations in which an application can be launched. According to Windows convention, the context of the initialization of an instance is specified in the command line, whether the command has been issued as a result of OLE automation or embedding, shell commands (File New, File Open, and File Print), DDE, or user execution. The purpose of the CCommandLineInfo class, then, is to perform the grunt work in determining this context.

The CCommandLineInfo class operates in conjunction with the ParseCommandLine and ProcessShellCommand members of the CWinApp class. By default, in the InitInstance member of the AppWizard-created CWinApp-derived class, a CComandLineInfo object is instantiated, a call to ParseCommandLine is made to parse through the command line, looking for the special keywords indicating the initialization context, and a call to ProcessShellCommand is made to perform the desired actions. This is shown in Listing 3-1.

Listing 3-1 AppWizard-Generated Code for Command Line Processing

```
BOOL CMyApp::InitInstance()
{
	// code...

	// Parse command line for standard shell commands, DDE, file open
	CCommandLineInfo cmdInfo;
	ParseCommandLine(cmdInfo);

	// Dispatch commands specified on the command line
	if (!ProcessShellCommand(cmdInfo))
		return FALSE;

	// code...
}
```

When a CCommandLineInfo object is instantiated, the default shell command is set to be "File New." What this means is that if your application's InitInstance member is structured like the one in Listing 3-1, the call to ProcessShellCommand will perform a "File New" (create a default document) in the general case that there are no shell commands passed in through the command line. If this is not the desired behavior for your application, you will need to modify the code generated by AppWizard by setting the m_nShellCommand member of the CCommandLineInfo object to CCommandLineInfo::FileNothing after it has been constructed.

CCommandLineInfo Class Reference

CCommandLineInfo — ■ 4.0

Description The constructor of the CCommandLineInfo class. The constructor initializes the launching context variable members to the default values.

Syntax public, CCommandLineInfo();

Parameters None.

Returns Nothing is returned.

See Also CCommandLineInfo::~CCommandLineInfo

~CCommandLineInfo — ■ 4.0

Description The destructor of the CCommandLineInfo class. This destructor does nothing.

Syntax public, ~CCommandLineInfo();

Parameters None.

Returns Nothing is returned.

See Also CCommandLineInfo::~CCommandLineInfo

ParseParam — ■ 4.0

Description Parses a given parameter from the command line to determine the launching context. This function is called by the CWinApp member, ParseCommandLine, for each parameter of the command line. This function can be overridden by derived classes of CCommandLineInfo in order to perform additional command line interpretations.

Syntax public, virtual void ParseParam(const char* pszParam, BOOL bFlag, BOOL bLast);

Parameters

pszParam Parameter to examine.

bFlag OLE flag.

bLast TRUE if last parameter; FALSE otherwise.

Returns Nothing is returned.

See Also CWinApp::ParseCommandLine

m_bRunAutomated — ■ 4.0

Description Indicates that the instance is running by OLE automation.

Syntax public, BOOL m_bRunAutomated;

m_bRunEmbedded

–. ■ 4.0

Description Indicates that the instance is running by OLE embedding.

Syntax public, BOOL m_bRunEmbedded;

m_bShowSplash

–. ■ 4.0

Description Indicates whether or not the splash screen should be displayed. Normally, splash screens are not displayed during OLE embedding or automation.

Syntax public, BOOL m_bShowSplash;

m_nShellCommand

–. ■ 4.0

Description Indicates which shell command caused the instance to be launched.

Syntax public, enum { FileNew, FileOpen, FilePrint, FilePrintTo, FileDDE, FileNothing = -1 } m_nShellCommand;

m_strDriverName

–. ■ 4.0

Description Device driver name for printing.

Syntax public, CString m_strDeviceName;

m_strFileName

–. ■ 4.0

Description File name for opening and printing.

Syntax public, CString m_strFileName;

m_strPortName

–. ■ 4.0

Description Port name for printing.

Syntax public, CString m_strPortName;

m_strPrinterName

–. ■ 4.0

Description Printer name for printing.

Syntax public, CString m_strPrinterName;

The CWinApp Class

The CWinApp class is at the core of the MFC framework. Put simply, it encapsulates a Windows .EXE executable. Each MFC application consists of one CWinApp-derived class. AppWizard creates one by default. Typically, the CWinApp-derived class of an MFC application consists of such things as global data, application-level command handlers, and application initialization and termination code. Some of the roles performed by the CWinApp class members include wrappers for SDK functions which take an HINSTANCE parameter, supporting functions for MFC's Document/View architecture, and helper functions for using the system registry. Many of these members are rarely called by the programmer directly. Instead, they are called by MFC as an inherent part of the implementation of the application framework.

One of the major changes made to the CWinApp class in MFC 4.0 was caused by the introduction of the CDocManager class, discussed in Chapter 6, *Document/View*. In previous versions of MFC, the CWinApp class itself took care of maintaining all of the document templates for the application, storing them in a list kept by the m_templateList member. With MFC 4.0, the CWinApp class now has a CDocManager member which encapsulates this list and the operations performed on it. As a result, a lot of functionality that once resided in the CWinApp class now is present in this new class. For backwards compatibility reasons, MFC retained the syntax by providing wrapper functions which simply call equivalent members of the CDocManager class.

CWinApp Class Reference

CWinApp ■ 2.0 ■ 3.0

Description	The constructor of the CWinApp class. The constructor initializes the CWinApp object and attaches it to the MFC framework. Rarely does the programmer need to construct a CWinApp-derived object other than the one generated by AppWizard.
Syntax	public, CWinApp();
Parameters	None.
Returns	Nothing is returned.
See Also	CWinApp::~CWinApp

~CWinApp ■ 2.0 ■ 3.0

Description	The destructor of the CWinApp class. The destructor frees structures allocated for the CWinApp-derived object.
Syntax	public, ~CWinApp();
Parameters	None.
Returns	Nothing is returned.
See Also	CWinApp::CWinApp

AddDocTemplate

■ 2.0 ■ 3.0

Description Adds a document template to the global list kept by the CDocManager member of the CWinApp class for MFC 4.0 and above, and by the CWinApp class itself for earlier versions of MFC. Document templates are stored in a CPtrList list. As a result, document templates should not be created on the stack, but rather dynamically. This list is used to access all of the current documents and document templates for the application.

Syntax public, void AddDocTemplate(CDocTemplate* pTemplate);

Parameters

pTemplate Pointer to a document template—MFC will delete this object automatically.

Returns Nothing is returned.

See Also CDocManager class

Example

```
CMultiDocTemplate* pDocTemplate;
pDocTemplate = new CMultiDocTemplate(
    IDR_TESTTYPE,
    RUNTIME_CLASS(CTestDoc),
    RUNTIME_CLASS(CChildFrame), // custom MDI child frame
    RUNTIME_CLASS(CTestView));
AddDocTemplate(pDocTemplate);
```

AddToRecentFileList

■ 2.0 ■ 3.0

Description Adds a file name to the MRU (Most Recently Used) file list maintained by MFC. This member is called whenever a document is saved. The file names of the most recently opened documents appear as menu commands on the application's menu. The list is stored either in the registry or in the application's .INI file. MFC uses the ID_FILE_MRU_FILE1 command as the marker for the beginning of this list. AppWizard puts this command on the File menu, right above the Exit command. When the user selects one of these commands, the associated file is loaded by the appropriate document. The number of files tracked by the MRU list is specified when calling the LoadStdProfileSettings member. This number is 4 by default and can be as high as 16, if desired. The OnUpdateRecentFileMenu member is the command UI handler for the MRU list. The OnOpenRecentFile member is the command handler for the MRU list.

Syntax public, virtual void AddToRecentFileList(LPCTSTR lpszPathName);

Parameters

lpszPathName File name which is to be added to the MRU list.

Returns Nothing is returned.

See Also CWinApp::LoadStdProfileSettings, CWinApp::OnUpdateRecentFileMenu, CWinApp::OnOpenRecentFile

Example

```
void SaveFile(CMyDocument* pDocument)
{
     ASSERT(pDocument);
     CString strFileName = pDocument->GetPathName();

     pDocument->DoMySave(); // perform custom save

     if ( !strFileName.IsEmpty() )
     {
                    // add to MRU
                    AfxGetApp()->AddToRecentFileList(strFileName);
}
}
```

AssertValid

■ 2.0 ■ 3.0

Description Validates the object. This function calls the inherited version from CWinThread and checks the validity of internal members of the CWinApp object. For more information regarding object validation, see Chapter 15, *Debugging and Exception Handling*.

Syntax public, virtual void AssertValid() const;

Parameters None.

Returns Nothing is returned.

See Also CWinApp::Dump, CWinThead::AssertValid

Example

```
void CheckApplication()
{
     AfxGetApp()->AssertValid();
}
```

CloseAllDocuments

■ 2.0 ■ 3.0

Description Closes all documents for the application. A call to this function in turn calls the CloseAllDocuments member of each document template of the application. The CloseAllDocuments member of the document template calls OnCloseDocument for each currently opened document. This function is called by MFC when the main frame window closes.

Syntax public, void CloseAllDocuments(BOOL bEndSession);

Parameters

bEndSession TRUE if Windows is terminating; FALSE otherwise.

Returns Nothing is returned.

See Also CDocManager::CloseAllDocuments

CreateInitialDocument

–. ■ 3.0 ■ MO ■ UD

Description Creates an initial document in response to an Apple launching event. This member is only present for Macintosh applications.

Syntax public, virtual BOOL CreateInitialDocument();

Parameters None.

Returns TRUE if successful; FALSE otherwise.

See Also CWinApp::OnFileNew

CreatePrinterDC

–. ■ 4.0

Description Creates a compatible DC for the currently selected printer.

Syntax public, BOOL CreatePrinterDC(CDC& dc);

Parameters

dc Reference to device context.

Returns TRUE if successful; FALSE otherwise.

See Also CWinApp::SelectPrinter, CWinApp::GetPrinterDeviceDefaults

Example

```
CDC dc;
if ( AfxGetApp()->CreatePrinterDC(dc) )
{
      DOCINFO docinfo;

      strcpy(docinfo.lpszDocName,"test");
      dc.StartDoc(&docinfo);
      dc.StartPage();
      dc.TextOut(10,10,"Test",4);
      dc.EndPage();
      dc.EndDoc();
}
```

DevModeChange

■ 2.0 ■ 3.0 ■ UD

Description Processes changes to devices like printers. This function is called by CWnd::OnDevModeChange, which is the default handler for the WM_DEVMODECHANGE message. The CWinApp class caches the device parameters of the current printer. The DevModeChange function updates this cache.

Syntax public, void DevModeChange(LPTSTR lpDeviceName);

Parameters

lpDeviceName Name for device changed.

Returns Nothing is returned.

See Also CWinApp::UpdatePrinterSelection

DoMessageBox

■ 2.0 ■ 3.0

Description Displays a message box. This function is called by AfxMessageBox. It may be overridden by a CWinApp-derived class to provide a custom message box display. DoMessageBox sets up a help context, specifies an appropriate icon, and disables any OLE-based modeless windows before calling the SDK function MessageBox.

Syntax public, virtual int DoMessageBox(LPCTSTR lpszPrompt, UINT nType, UINT nIDPrompt);

Parameters

lpszPrompt Text of the message.

nType Combination of one or more message styles defined in the SDK that specify the appearance and options of the message box.

nIDPrompt Index for the help context link for the message box.

Returns The value returned by ::MessageBox, the ID value of the button pressed to dismiss the message box.

See Also AfxMessageBox, CWnd::MessageBox

Example

```
BOOL ConfirmDelete()
{
	CString strText = "Are you sure you want to delete the file?";


	if ( AfxGetApp()->DoMessageBox(strText,MB_YESNO) != MB_NO )
		return FALSE;

	return TRUE;
}
```

DoPrintDialog

■ 2.0 ■ 3.0 ■ UD

Description Internal MFC function for displaying a CPrintDialog dialog and caching the printer values selected. This function is called by OnFilePrintSetup. It is rarely called by the programmer directly.

Syntax public, int DoPrintDialog(CPrintDialog* pPD);

Parameters

pPD Pointer to the CPrintDialog object.

Returns Response from the call to DoModal() made for the CPrintDialog object. See the CPrintDialog class for details.

See Also CWinApp::OnFilePrintSetup, CWinApp::UpdatePrinterSelection

DoPromptFileName

■ 2.0 ■ 3.0 ■ UD

Description Requests a file name from the user, used for opening and saving a document. This is a helper function for using the CFileDialog class, discussed in Chapter 8, *Dialog Boxes*. This function is called by MFC when opening and saving documents.

Syntax public, BOOL DoPromptFileName(CString& fileName, UINT nIDSTitle, DWORD lFlags, BOOL bOpenFileDialog, CDocTemplate* pTemplate);

Parameters

fileName Reference to file name specified by the user.

nIDSTitle String resource ID for title of dialog.

lFlags Flags for dialog; see CFileDialog for details.

bOpenFileDialog TRUE if for File Open; FALSE for Save As.

pTemplate Pointer to document template associated with file; NULL indicates all document templates are available. MFC will fill up the File Type list in the dialog with the file types associated with each document template, including the default "*.*".

Returns TRUE if CFileDialog dialog dismissed by OK button (IDOK); FALSE otherwise.

See Also CFileDialog class

Example

```
// MFC code
void CDocManager::OnFileOpen()
{
      // prompt the user (with all document templates)
      CString newName;
      if (!DoPromptFileName(newName, AFX_IDS_OPENFILE,
        OFN_HIDEREADONLY | OFN_FILEMUSTEXIST, TRUE, NULL))
          return; // open cancelled

      AfxGetApp()->OpenDocumentFile(newName);
          // if returns NULL, the user has already been alerted
}
```

DoWaitCursor

■ 2.0 ■ 3.0

Description Displays or restores from the wait (hour glass) cursor. MFC keeps a counter for the wait cursor. When it is positive, the wait cursor is displayed; otherwise the old cursor is restored. With MFC 4.0, there is now a CWaitCursor class that calls DoWaitCursor in a more object-oriented manner. This function can be overridden by CWinApp-derived classes to modify default behavior. When DoWaitCursor is called to set the wait cursor, MFC keeps track of the old cursor. Be careful not to call DoWaitCursor to decrement the wait cursor counter when there is no old cursor; the cursor will disappear!

Syntax public, virtual void DoWaitCursor(int nCode);

Parameters

nCode 1—increment the wait cursor counter, display the wait cursor.

0—display the wait cursor, but do not increment the counter (will only display if the counter is positive).

-1—decrement the wait cursor counter.

Returns Nothing is returned.

See Also CWaitCursor class

Example

```
AfxGetApp()->DoWaitCursor(1);

// do some long process

AfxGetApp()->DoWaitCursor(-1);
```

DUMP ■ 2.0 ■ 3.0

Description Diagnostics function for the CWinApp object. Dumps the contents of all member variables to the dump context. For more information, see Chapter 15, *Debugging and Exception Handling*.

Syntax public, virtual void Dump(CDumpContext& dc) const;

Parameters

dc Dump context.

Returns Nothing is returned.

See Also CWinApp::AssertValid

Example

```
void DumpApplication()
{
      Cfile file;


      if ( file.Open("log.txt",CFile::modeCreate | CFile::modeWrite) )
      {
            CDumpContext dc(&file);
            AfxGetApp()->Dump(dc);
      }
}
```

ENABLE3DCONTROLS ■ 2.0 ■ 3.0

Description Enables the 3D controls implemented in the CTL3D-based DLL (either CTL3DV2.DLL, 16-bit, or CTL3D32.DLL, 32-bit). Enable3DControlsStatic (discussed in the next entry) is for enabling the static library version. For Windows 95, this function does nothing; 3D appearance of controls is now built into the operating system.

Syntax protected, BOOL Enable3dControls();

Parameters None.

Returns TRUE if successful, FALSE otherwise.

See Also CWinApp::Enable3DControlsStatic

Example

```
BOOL CTestApp::InitInstance()
{
   // default AppWizard-added code

 #ifdef _AFXDLL
   Enable3dControls(); // Call this when using MFC in a shared DLL
 #else
   Enable3dControlsStatic(); // Call this when linking to MFC statically
 #endif

   // more code...

   return TRUE;
}
```

Enable3DControlsStatic ■ 2.0 ■ 3.0

Description Enables the 3D controls implemented in the CTL3D-based static library. For Windows 95, this function does nothing; 3D appearance of controls is now built into the operating system.

Syntax protected, BOOL Enable3dControlsStatic();

Parameters None.

Returns TRUE if successful; FALSE otherwise.

See Also CWinApp::Enable3DControls

Example See Enable3DControls

EnableModeless ■ 2.0 ■ 3.0 ■ UD

Description Enables or disables modeless windows for OLE-based objects. This is an OLE requirement when an application displays a modal dialog. It is called internally by MFC when necessary. It is rarely called by the programmer directly.

Syntax public, void EnableModeless(BOOL bEnable);

Parameters

bEnable TRUE to enable the modeless windows; FALSE to disable.

Returns Nothing is returned.

EnableShellOpen ■ 2.0 ■ 3.0

Description In conjunction with RegisterShellFileTypes, allows the application to be launched by the Windows File Manager with an associated file to open or print. EnableShellOpen initializes the unique identifiers for the application used in the DDE link with File Manager when launching the program.

Syntax protected, void EnableShellOpen();

Parameters None.

Returns Nothing is returned.

See Also CWinApp::RegisterShellFileTypesCompat

Example

```
BOOL CTestApp::InitInstance()
{
     // initialization code...

     EnableShellOpen();
     RegisterShellFileTypes();

     // additional initialization code...

     return TRUE;
}
```

ExitInstance ■ 2.0 ■ 3.0

Description Performs cleanup for the Windows instance. This function is called by MFC when the instance is about to exit. Although it is rarely called directly by the programmer, it is often overridden by CWinApp-derived classes. The CWinApp implementation does little, except for calling SaveStdProfileSettings.

Syntax public, virtual int ExitInstance();

Parameters None.

Returns Exit code for the instance.

See Also CWinApp::InitInstance, CWinThread::ExitInstance

GetAppRegistryKey –. ■ 3.0 ■ UD

Description Gets the base registry key for the application. The key is for HKEY_CURRENT_USER\"Software"\RegistryKey\ProfileName, where RegistryKey is typically the company name and ProfileName is typically the application name. The key will be created if it does not already exist. The caller is responsible for calling RegCloseKey() to close the key returned. The SetRegistryKey member must be called first before this function may be used. GetAppRegistryKey is a helper function for GetSectionKey, which is

in turn a helper function for all of the registry-based profile access members (e.g., GetProfileInt, WriteProfileString) discussed later in this chapter.

Syntax public, HKEY GetAppRegistryKey();

Parameters None.

Returns Registry key.

See Also CWinApp::SetRegistryKey

Example

```
SetRegistryKey("MyCompany");

HKEY hKey = GetAppRegistryKey();

// do something with key
RegCloseKey(hKey);
```

GetFirstDocTemplatePosition ■ 2.0 ■ 3.0

Description Gets the position of the first document template in the application-level template list. The position is then used with the GetNextDocTemplate member to iterate through all of the document templates. With MFC 4.0 and above, this function now simply calls the equivalent member found in the CDocManager class.

Syntax public, POSITION GetFirstDocTemplatePosition() const;

Parameters None.

Returns Position of the first document template, passed to GetNextDocTemplate to retrieve the actual pointer; NULL indicates that there are no templates.

See Also CWinApp::GetNextDocTemplate, CDocManager class

Example

```
void CTestApp::DoMyCommand()
{
      CDocumentTemplate* pTemplate;
      POSITION pos;

      pos = GetFirstDocTemplatePosition();
      while ( pos != NULL )
      {
            pTemplate = GetNextDocTemplate(pos);
            if ( pTemplate->IsKindOf(RUNTIME_CLASS(CMyTemplate)) )
                  ((CMyTemplate*)pTemplate)->DoMyCommand();
      }
}
```

GetNextDocTemplate ■ 2.0 ■ 3.0

Description Gets the next document template in the application-level template list. This function is used in conjunction with GetFirstDocTemplatePosition to iterate through all of the document templates. With MFC 4.0 and above, this function now simply calls the equivalent member found in the CDocManager class.

Syntax public, CDocTemplate* GetNextDocTemplate(POSITION& pos) const;

Parameters

pos Position of the next document template, this value is modified with each call to GetNextDocTemplate; will be equal to NULL when the list has been exhausted.

Returns Pointer to the document template.

See Also CWinApp::GetFirstDocTemplatePosition, CDocManager class

Example See GetFirstDocTemplatePosition

GetOpenDocumentCount ■ 2.0 ■ 3.0 ■ UD

Description Gets the number of open documents. With MFC 4.0 and above, this function now simply calls the equivalent member found in the CDocManager class.

Syntax public, int GetOpenDocumentCount();

Parameters None.

Returns The number of currently opened documents.

See Also CDocManager class

Example

```
void CTestApp::OnUpdateClose(CCmdUI* pCmdUI)
{
	pCmdUI->Enable(GetOpenDocumentCount() > 1);
}
```

GetPrinterDeviceDefaults ■ 2.0 ■ 3.0

Description Gets the device values for the selected printer. The function fills in the PRINTDLG structure with the cached printer values kept by MFC: m_hDevMode, the device mode structure for the selected printer and m_hDevNames, the device, driver, and port names for the selected printer. GetPrinterDeviceDefaults is called from within CView::DoPreparePrinting() and is rarely called by the programmer directly.

Syntax public, BOOL GetPrinterDeviceDefaults(PRINTDLG* pPrintDlg);

Parameters

pPrintDlg Pointer to PRINTDLG structure.

Returns TRUE if successful; FALSE if there is no default printer.

See Also CWinApp::DoPrintDialog, CWinApp::UpdatePrinterSelection

GetProfileBinary –. ■ 4.0 ■ UD

Description Gets a binary value from either the registry or the application's .INI file. GetProfileBinary will only use the registry if the programmer has called

SetRegistryKey() first. The registry option is not available on the Macintosh. When using the .INI file option, MFC stores the binary data as a string, converting each byte into two equivalent character values so that .INI entry is composed solely of printable characters.

Syntax public, BOOL GetProfileBinary(LPCTSTR lpszSection, LPCTSTR lpszEntry, LPBYTE* ppData, UINT* pBytes);

Parameters

lpszSection Section name.

lpszEntry Entry name.

ppData Pointer to buffer array that will be allocated by GetProfileBinary; the buffer array must be deleted by the programmer.

pBytes Number of bytes retrieved.

Returns TRUE if successful; FALSE otherwise.

See Also CWinApp::SetRegistryKey, CWinApp::GetProfileInt, CWinApp::GetProfileString, CWinApp::WriteProfileBinary, CWinApp::WriteProfileInt, CWinApp::WriteProfileString

Example

```
BOOL GetParameters(CMyParameters& parameters)
{
     LPBYTE pData;
     UINT nBytes;

     if ( !GetProfileBinary("Global","Parameters",&pData,&nBytes) ||
          nBytes != sizeof(CMyParameters) )
          return FALSE;

     // copy parameters
     memcpy(&parameters,pData,sizeof(CMyParameters));

     // delete buffer
     delete pData;

     return TRUE;
}
```

GetProfileInt

■ 2.0 ■ 3.0

Description Gets an integer value from either the registry or the application's .INI file. GetProfileInt will only use the registry if the programmer first calls SetRegistryKey(). The registry option is not available on the Macintosh.

Syntax public, UINT GetProfileInt(LPCTSTR lpszSection, LPCTSTR lpszEntry, int nDefault);

Parameters

lpszSection Section name.

lpszEntry Entry name.

nDefault Value returned if there is no entry.

Returns Integer value of the entry.

See Also CWinApp::SetRegistryKey, CWinApp::GetProfileBinary, CWinApp::GetProfileString, CWinApp::WriteProfileInt, CWinApp::WriteProfileBinary, CWinApp::WriteProfileString

Example

```
CRect CTestApp::GetWindowPosition()
{
     CRect rect;

     rect.left = GetProfileInt("WindowPosition","Left",0);
     rect.top = GetProfileInt("WindowPosition","Top",0);
     rect.right = GetProfileInt("WindowPosition","Right",100);
     rect.bottom = GetProfileInt("WindowPosition","Botton",100);

     return rect;
}
```

GetProfileString ■ 2.0 ■ 3.0

Description Gets a string value from either the registry or the application's .INI file. GetProfileString will only use the registry if the programmer has called SetRegistryKey() first. The registry option is not available on the Macintosh.

Syntax public, CString GetProfileString(LPCTSTR lpszSection, LPCTSTR lpszEntry, LPCTSTR lpszDefault = NULL);

Parameters

lpszSection Section name.

lpszEntry Entry name.

lpszDefault Value returned when there is no entry; NULL indicates that an empty string will be returned.

Returns String value of the entry.

See Also CWinApp::SetRegistryKey, CWinApp::GetProfileBinary, CWinApp::GetProfileInt, CWinApp::WriteProfileString, CWinApp::WriteProfileBinary, CWinApp::WriteProfileInt

Example

```
CString CTestApp::GetDefaultFile()
{
     CString strFile;

     strFile = GetProfileString("Global","FileName");

     return strFile;
}
```

GetSectionKey –. ■ 3.0 ■ UD

Description Gets the registry key for a given section. The key is for HKEY_CURRENT_USER\"Software"\RegistryKey\AppName\lpszSection, where RegistryKey is typically the company name, AppName is typically the application name, and lpszSection is the section name. The key will be created if it does not already exist. The caller is responsible for calling RegCloseKey() to close the key returned. The SetRegistryKey() member must be called first. This function is used by the registry-based profile access members (e.g., GetProfileInt, WriteProfileString) to obtain the key from which the entry keys are based. Generally, there is no need to call this function directly instead of using the profile access members when dealing with the registry.

Syntax public, HKEY GetSectionKey(LPCTSTR lpszSection);

Parameters

lpszSection Section name.

Returns Key for the section; NULL indicates that the key could not be created, typically because SetRegistryKey has yet to be called.

See Also CWinApp::GetAppRegistryKey, CWinApp::SetRegistryKey

HideApplication ■ 2.0 ■ 3.0

Description Hides the application. This function hides the main window and puts it at the bottom of the Windows window Z-order list so that it is not activated.

Syntax public, void HideApplication();

Parameters None.

Returns Nothing is returned.

Example

```
void CTestApp::HideShowApplication(BOOL bHide)
{
     if ( bHide )
          HideApplication(); // hide
     else
          AfxGetMainWnd()->ActivateFrame(SW_SHOW);
}
```

InitApplication ■ 2.0 ■ 3.0

Description One-time initialization of the application. This function is called the first time a program is run, when there are no other instances of the program currently running. InitInstance, however, is called when each instance begins. InitApplication may be overridden by CWinApp-derived classes when needed. It is a good place for an application to register its own Windows window classes.

Syntax public, virtual BOOL InitApplication();

Parameters None.

Returns TRUE if successful; FALSE otherwise.

See Also CWinApp::InitInstance

Example

```
BOOL CTestApp::InitApplication()
{
      CTime tTime = CTime::GetCurrentTime();
      CString strTimeDateStamp;

      // record when program is first run
      strTimeDateStamp = tTime.Format("%M-%D-%y");

WriteProfileString("Global","TimeDateStamp",strTimeDateStamp);

      return TRUE;
}
```

InitInstance

■ 2.0 ■ 3.0

Description Initializes instance. This function is called when each instance of an application starts. InitInstance is almost always overridden by CWinApp-derived classes. It is called from within the MFC framework; rarely is it called by the programmer directly. InitInstance is where AppWizard puts a lot of its standard application startup code.

Syntax public, virtual BOOL InitInstance();

Parameters None.

Returns TRUE if successful; FALSE otherwise.

See Also CWinApp::InitApplication

Example

```
// InitInstance generated by AppWizard
BOOL CTestApp::InitInstance()
{
   // Standard initialization
   // If you are not using these features and wish to reduce the size
   //  of your final executable, you should remove from the following
   //  the specific initialization routines you do not need.

#ifdef _AFXDLL
   Enable3dControls();      // Call this when using MFC in a shared DLL
#else
   Enable3dControlsStatic();  // Call this when linking to MFC statically
#endif

LoadStdProfileSettings();// Load standard INI file options (including MRU)

   // Register the application's document templates.  Document templates
   //  serve as the connection between documents, frame windows, and views.

   CMultiDocTemplate* pDocTemplate;
   pDocTemplate = new CMultiDocTemplate(
      IDR_TESTTYPE,
      RUNTIME_CLASS(CTestDoc),
      RUNTIME_CLASS(CChildFrame), // custom MDI child frame
      RUNTIME_CLASS(CTestView));
```

```
    AddDocTemplate(pDocTemplate);

    // create main MDI Frame window
    CMainFrame* pMainFrame = new CMainFrame;
    if (!pMainFrame->LoadFrame(IDR_MAINFRAME))
        return FALSE;
    m_pMainWnd = pMainFrame;

    // Parse command line for standard shell commands, DDE, file open
    CCommandLineInfo cmdInfo;
    ParseCommandLine(cmdInfo);

    // Dispatch commands specified on the command line
    if (!ProcessShellCommand(cmdInfo))
        return FALSE;

    // The main window has been initialized, so show and update it.
    pMainFrame->ShowWindow(m_nCmdShow);
    pMainFrame->UpdateWindow();

    return TRUE;
}
```

LoadCursor

■ 2.0 ■ 3.0

Description Loads a cursor resource. This function is a wrapper for the ::LoadCursor SDK function. MFC uses AfxFindResourceHandle() to specify the instance for the load. For some unknown reason, MFC does not include a CCursor class. To use cursors in MFC, the programmer must still deal with the HCURSOR handles from the SDK.

Syntax public, HCURSOR LoadCursor(LPCTSTR lpszResourceName) const;
HCURSOR LoadCursor(UINT nIDResource) const;

Parameters

lpszResourceName Resource name for cursor; can be generated using the MAKEINTRESOURCE macro.

nIDResource Resource ID for cursor.

Returns Handle to cursor; NULL indicates that the load failed .

See Also CWinApp::LoadOEMCursor, CWinApp::LoadStandardCursor

Example

```
HCURSOR hCursor, hOldCursor;

hCursor = AfxGetApp()->LoadCursor(IDC_MYCURSOR);
if ( hCursor )
{
     hOldCursor = ::SetCursor(hCursor);

     // do something...

     ::SetCursor(hOldCursor);
}
```

LoadIcon

■ 2.0 ■ 3.0

Description Loads an icon resource. This function is a wrapper for the ::LoadIcon SDK function. MFC uses AfxFindResourceHandle() to specify the instance for the load. For some unknown reason, MFC does not include a CIcon class. To use icons in MFC, the programmer must still deal with the HICON handles from the SDK.

Syntax public, HICON LoadIcon(LPCTSTR lpszResourceName) const;
HICON LoadIcon(UINT nIDResource) const;

Parameters

lpszResourceName Resource name for icon; can be generated using the MAKEINTRESOURCE macro.

nIDResource Resource ID for icon.

Returns Handle to icon; NULL indicates that the load failed.

See Also CWinApp::LoadStandardIcon, CWinApp::LoadOEMIcon

Example

```
HICON hMyIcon = AfxGetApp()->LoadIcon(IDC_MYICON);
CClientDC dc(AfxGetMainWnd());

if ( hMyIcon )
     dc.DrawIcon(10,10,hMyIcon);
```

LoadOEMCursor

■ 2.0 ■ 3.0

Description Loads an OEM-based predefined cursor. The programmer must include a #define OEMRESOURCE line before including "afxwin.h".

Syntax public, HCURSOR LoadOEMCursor(UINT nIDCursor) const;

Parameters

nIDCursor Cursor ID, must be one of the OCR_-based control IDs found in "WINUSER.H"

Returns Handle to cursor; NULL indicates that the load failed.

See Also CWinApp::LoadCursor, CWinApp::LoadStandardCursor

Example

```
HCURSOR hCursor, hOldCursor;

hCursor = AfxGetApp()->LoadOEMCursor(OCR_WAIT);
if ( hCursor )
{
     hOldCursor = ::SetCursor(hCursor);

     // do something...

     ::SetCursor(hOldCursor);
}
```

LoadOEMIcon

■ 2.0 ■ 3.0

Description Loads an OEM-based predefined icon. The programmer must include a #define OEMRESOURCE line before including "AFXWIN.H".

Syntax public, HICON LoadOEMIcon(UINT nIDIcon) const;

Parameters

nIDIcon Icon ID, must be one of the OIC-based control IDs found in "WINUSER.H".

Returns Handle to icon; NULL indicates that the load failed.

See Also CWinApp::LoadIcon, CWinApp::LoadStandardIcon

Example

```
HICON hOEMIcon = AfxGetApp()->LoadOEMIcon(OIC_QUES);
CClientDC dc(AfxGetMainWnd());

if ( hOEMIcon )
     dc.DrawIcon(10,10,hOEMIcon);
```

LoadStandardCursor

■ 2.0 ■ 3.0

Description Loads a standard predefined Windows cursor.

Syntax public, HCURSOR LoadStandardCursor(LPCTSTR lpszCursorName) const;

Parameters

lpszCursorName One of the predefined IDC_-based cursor IDs found in "WINUSER.H".

Returns Handle to cursor; NULL indicates that the load failed.

See Also CWinApp::LoadCursor, CWinApp::LoadOEMCursor

Example

```
HCURSOR hCursor, hOldCursor;

hCursor = AfxGetApp()->LoadStandardCursor(IDC_ARROW);
if ( hCursor )
{
     hOldCursor = ::SetCursor(hCursor);

     // do something...

     ::SetCursor(hOldCursor);
}
```

LoadStandardIcon

■ 2.0 ■ 3.0

Description Loads a standard predefined Window icon.

Syntax public, HICON LoadStandardIcon(LPCTSTR lpszIconName) const;

Parameters

lpszIconName One of the predefined IDI_-based icon IDs found in "WINUSER.H".

Returns Handle to icon; NULL indicates that the load failed.

See Also CWinApp::LoadIcon, CWinApp::LoadOEMIcon

Example

```
HICON hAsterisk = AfxGetApp()->LoadStandardIcon(IDI_ASTERISK);
CClientDC dc(AfxGetMainWnd());

if ( hAsterisk )
     dc.DrawIcon(10,10,hAsterisk);
```

LoadStdProfileSettings ■ 2.0 ■ 3.0

Description Loads the standard MFC application settings, which includes the MRU list and the default number of preview pages during print preview, from either the registry or the application .INI file. If LoadStdProfileSettings is not called, the MRU list will not be used. This function is typically called by the InitInstance member of the CWinApp-derived class.

Syntax protected, void LoadStdProfileSettings(UINT nMaxMRU = _AFX_MRU_COUNT);

Parameters

nMaxMRU Maximum number of files in the MRU list; the default is 4. This number should not be greater than 16; MFC can track no more than 16 files. If nMaxMRU equals 0, the MRU list will not be used.

Returns Nothing is returned.

See Also CWinApp::SaveStdProfileSettings

Example

```
BOOL CTestApp::InitInstance()
{
     // initialization code...

     LoadStdProfileSettings(6); // up to 6 entries in the MRU list

     // initialization code...

     return TRUE;
}
```

OnAppExit ■ 2.0 ■ 3.0 ■ UD

Description Default handler for the ID_APP_EXIT command. ID_APP_EXIT is the AppWizard-generated command for the File Exit menu command. OnAppExit() simply sends a WM_CLOSE message to the main window. The programmer can add a custom ID_APP_EXIT command handler to provide additional functionality. A command handler is present for this command in the CWinApp message map.

Syntax protected, afx_msg void OnAppExit();

Parameters None.

Returns Nothing is returned.

Example

```
void CTestApp::OnAppExit()
{
     CString strMessage = "Are you sure you want to quit?";

if ( AfxMessageBox(strMessage,MB_YESNO) == MB_YES )
          CWinApp::OnAppExit();
}
```

OnContextHelp

■ 2.0 ■ 3.0

Description Default handler for the ID_CONTEXT_HELP command. When context-sensitive help is requested, AppWizard makes SHIFT-F1 an accelerator key for ID_CONTEXT_HELP for the main window. Context help allows the user to select with the mouse an area of the screen on which to get help. For more information about context help, see Chapter 2, *The MFC Framework*. OnContextHelp simply calls the OnContextHelp handler for the main window, which is where all the work for context help gets done. A command handler such as this:

ON_COMMAND(ID_CONTEXT_HELP, CWinApp::OnContextHelp)

must be present in the application's message map for this function to be called.

Syntax public, afx_msg void OnContextHelp();

Parameters None.

Returns Nothing is returned.

See Also CFrameWnd::OnContextHelp

OnDDECommand

■ 2.0 ■ 3.0

Description Called by the main window while handling the WM_DDE_EXECUTE message to execute a DDE command sent to the application. The Windows File Manager uses DDE to open or print a file double-clicked by the user. This handler can be overridden by CWinApp-derived classes to also process application-specific DDE commands. With MFC 4.0 and above, this function now simply calls the equivalent member found in the CDocManager class.

Syntax public, virtual BOOL OnDDECommand(LPTSTR lpszCommand);

Parameters

lpszCommand Command sent through DDE.

Returns TRUE if command is handled; FALSE otherwise.

See Also CFrameWnd::OnDDEExecute

Example

```
BOOL CTestApp::OnDDECommand(LPTSTR lpszCommand)
{
     if ( CWinApp::OnDDECommand(lpszCommand) )
          return TRUE;

     if ( strcmp(lpszCommand,"RunReport") == 0 )
     {
          RunReport(); // run report
          return TRUE;
     }

     return FALSE;
}
```

OnFileNew

■ 2.0 ■ 3.0

Description

Default handler for the ID_FILE_NEW command. ID_FILE_NEW is the AppWizard-generated command for the File New menu command. OnFileNew() creates a blank document by passing NULL to the specific OpenDocumentFile member of the appropriate document template. When there is only one document template for the application, OnFileNew() will use it. Otherwise, OnFileNew() will prompt the user to select a specific document type. OnFileNew() is sometimes called when an application initializes so that the user can start out with a blank document. With MFC 4.0 and above, this function now simply calls the equivalent member found in the CDocManager class. A command handler such as this:

ON_COMMAND(ID_FILE_NEW, CWinApp::OnFileNew)

must be present in the application's message map for this function to be called.

Syntax public, afx_msg void OnFileNew();

Parameters None.

Returns Nothing is returned.

See Also CDocManager class, CWinApp::OnFileOpen, CDocTemplate::OpenDocumentFile

Example

```
BOOL CTestApp::InitInstance()
{
     // initialization code...

     OnFileNew(); // start out with blank document

     // initialization code...

     return TRUE;
}
```

OnFileOpen

■ 2.0 ■ 3.0

Description Default handler for the ID_FILE_OPEN command. ID_FILE_OPEN is the AppWizard-generated command for the File Open menu command. OnFileOpen() prompts the user to specify a file to open, calling DoPromptFileName(), then opens the file by calling OpenDocumentFile(). With MFC 4.0 and above, this function now simply calls the equivalent member found in the CDocManager class. A command handler such as this

```
ON_COMMAND(ID_FILE_OPEN, CWinApp::OnFileOpen)
```

must be present in the application's message map for this function to be called.

Syntax public, afx_msg void OnFileOpen();

Parameters None

Returns Nothing is returned

See Also CDocManager class, CWinApp::DoPromptFileName, CWinApp::OpenDocumentFile

Example See DoPromptFileName

OnFilePrintSetup

■ 2.0 ■ 3.0

Description Default handler for the ID_FILE_PRINT_SETUP command. ID_FILE_PRINT_SETUP is the AppWizard-generated comand for the File Print Setup menu command. OnFilePrintSetup() instantiates a CPrintDialog for print setup, then calls DoPrintDialog to process the dialog. A command handler such as this

```
ON_COMMAND(ID_FILE_PRINT_SETUP, CWinApp::OnFilePrintSetup)
```

must be present in the application's message map for this function to be called.

Syntax public, afx_msg void OnFilePrintSetup();

Parameters None.

Returns Nothing is returned.

See Also CPrintDialog class, CWinApp::DoPrintDialog

OnHelp

■ 2.0 ■ 3.0

Description Default handler for the ID_HELP command. ID_HELP is the MFC-defined command for launching context-sensitive help. When context-sensitive help is requested, AppWizard makes F1 an accelerator key for ID_CONTEXT_HELP for the main window. For more information about context help, see Chapter 2, *The MFC Framework.* A command handler such as this:

ON_COMMAND(ID_HELP, CWinApp::OnHelp)

must be present in the application's message map for this function to be called.

Syntax public, afx_msg void OnHelp();

Parameters None.

Returns Nothing is returned.

See Also CWinApp::OnHelpFinder, CWinApp::OnHelpIndex, CWinApp::OnHelpUsing

OnHelpFinder ■ 2.0 ■ 3.0

Description Default handler for the ID_HELP_FINDER command. ID_HELP_FINDER is the MFC-defined command for jumping to the contents of the application help file. The ID_DEFAULT_HELP command, the command sent by MFC when no help context can be determined, is typically linked to the OnHelpFinder handler as well. For more information about help, see Chapter 2, *The MFC Framework.* A command handler such as this:

ON_COMMAND(ID_HELP_FINDER, CWinApp::OnHelpFinder)

must be present in the application's message map for this function to be called.

Syntax public, afx_msg void OnHelpFinder();

Parameters None.

Returns Nothing is returned.

See Also CWinApp::OnHelp, CWinApp::OnHelpIndex, CWinApp::OnHelpUsing

OnHelpIndex ■ 2.0 ■ 3.0

Description Default handler for the ID_HELP_INDEX command. ID_HELP_INDEX is the MFC-defined command for jumping to the index of the application help file. For more information about help, see Chapter 2, *The MFC Framework.* A command handler such as this:

ON_COMMAND(ID_HELP_INDEX, CWinApp::OnHelpIndex)

must be present in the application's message map for this function to be called.

Syntax public, afx_msg void OnHelpIndex();

Parameters None.

Returns Nothing is returned.

See Also CWinApp::OnHelp, CWinApp::OnHelpFinder, CWinApp::OnHelpUsing

OnHelpUsing

■ 2.0 ■ 3.0

Description Default handler for the ID_HELP_USING command. ID_HELP_USING is the MFC-defined command for loading the help file for the Windows help engine itself. For more information about help, see Chapter 2, *The MFC Framework*. A command handler such as this:

ON_COMMAND(ID_HELP_USING, CWinApp::OnHelpUsing)

must be present in the application's message map for this function to be called.

Syntax public, afx_msg void OnHelpUsing();

Parameters None.

Returns Nothing is returned.

See Also CWinApp::OnHelp, CWinApp::OnHelpFinder, CWinApp::OnHelpIndex

OnIdle

■ 2.0 ■ 3.0

Description Performs idle processing. This function is called by MFC's message pump when there are no messages to process. It can be overridden by CWinApp-derived classes to perform application-specific idle processing.

Syntax public, virtual BOOL OnIdle(LONG lCount);

Parameters

lCount Counter indicating how many times OnIdle has been called since the application has been in an idle state. This counter is set to 0 when a new message has been processed and IsIdleMessage returns TRUE.

Returns TRUE if more idle processing time is required (should OnIdle() be called again); FALSE otherwise. If FALSE is returned, OnIdle() will not be called again until IsIdleMessage returns TRUE.

See Also CWinThread::OnIdle

Example

```
BOOL CTestApp::OnIdle(LONG lCount)
{
	POSITION pos;
	CDocTemplate* pTemplate;

	// call OnIdle for my document templates
	pos = GetFirstDocTemplatePosition();
	while ( pos != NULL )
	{
		pTemplate = GetNextDocTemplate(pos);
		if ( pTemplate->IsKindOf(RUNTIME_CLASS(CMyDocTemplate)) )
			((CMyDocTemplate*)pTemplate)->OnIdle(lCount);
	}

	// perform application-level idle (CMDUI stuff)
	CWinApp::OnIdle(lCount);

	return TRUE; // always want idle called
}
```

OnOpenRecentFile

■ 2.0 ■ 3.0 ■ UD

Description Command handler for the MRU (Most Recently Used) file list menu commands. OnOpenRecentFile() opens the specified file by calling OpenDocumentFile(). This function is rarely called directly by the programmer. Instead, it is called by the MFC framework on account of the following command handler included in the CWinApp message map:

ON_COMMAND_EX_RANGE(ID_FILE_MRU_FILE1, ID_FILE_MRU_FILE16, OnOpenRecentFile)

Syntax protected, afx_msg BOOL OnOpenRecentFile(UINT nID);

Parameters

nID Command ID of the chosen file in the MRU list, in the range ID_FILE_MRU_FILE1 through ID_FILE_MRUI_FILE16

Returns TRUE if successful; FALSE otherwise.

See Also CWinApp::AddToRecentFileList, CWinApp::OnUpdateRecentFileMenu

OnUpdateRecentFileMenu

■ 2.0 ■ 3.0 ■ UD

Description Command UI handler for the MRU list. This is the function that adds a menu command for each file in the MRU list. OnUpdateRecentFileMenu is hooked to the ID_FILE_MRU_FILE1 command, the command that specifies the start of the MRU list. If there are no files in the list, OnUpdateRecentFileMenu() disables the ID_FILE_MRU_FILE1 command. This function is rarely called directly by the programmer. Instead, it is called by the MFC framework on account of the following command handler included in the CWinApp message map:

ON_UPDATE_COMMAND_UI(ID_FILE_MRU_FILE1, OnUpdateRecentFileMenu)

Syntax protected, afx_msg void OnUpdateRecentFileMenu(CCmdUI* pCmdUI);

Parameters

pCmdUI Pointer to command UI interface object.

Returns Nothing is returned.

See Also CWinApp::AddToRecentFileList, CWinApp::OnOpenRecentFile

OpenDocumentFile

■ 2.0 ■ 3.0

Description Opens a document specified by a file. This function examines the file extension of the file and tries to determine which document template should be used to create the document to be opened. If the file name is NULL, a blank document is created by the first document template of the application. If a document with the file name already exists, it is activated. This function may be overridden by CWinApp-derived classes. With MFC 4.0 and above, this function now simply calls the equivalent member found in the CDocManager class.

Syntax public, virtual CDocument* OpenDocumentFile(LPCTSTR lpszFileName);

Parameters

lpszFileName File name; a blank document is created if NULL.

Returns Pointer to the document created if successful; NULL otherwise.

See Also CDocManager class, CWinApp::OnFileNew, CWinApp::OnFileOpen

Example

```
BOOL OpenFile(CString strFileName)
{
      CDocument* pDocument;

      pDocument = AfxGetApp()->OpenDocumentFile(strFileName);
      if ( pDocument == NULL )
      {
           CString strMessage = "The file cannot be opened.";
           AfxMessageBox(strMessage);
           return FALSE;
      }

      return TRUE;
}
```

ParseCommandLine

–. ■ 4.0

Description Parses the command line. This function fills in a CCommandLineInfo object by parsing the command line. This function is typically called by the InitInstance member of a CWinApp-derived class. It is usually followed by a call to ProcessShellCommand(). See the discussion above concerning the CommandLineInfo class for more information.

Syntax public, void ParseCommandLine(CCommandLineInfo& rCmdInfo);

Parameters

rCmdInfo Reference to CCommandLineInfo object to be filled in.

Returns Nothing is returned.

See Also CCommandLineInfo class, CWinApp::ProcessShellCommand

Example

```
// AppWizard-generated code
BOOL CTestApp::InitInstance()
{
      // initialization code...

      CCommandLineInfo cmdInfo;
      ParseCommandLine(cmdInfo);

      // Dispatch commands specified on the command line
      if (!ProcessShellCommand(cmdInfo))
```

continued on next page

continued from previous page

```
                return FALSE;

        // initialization code...

        return TRUE;
}
```

ProcessShellCommand

–. ■ 4.0

Description Processes the shell command (e.g., File Open, File Print) sent through the command line. See the discussion above concerning the CCommandLineInfo class for more information.

Syntax public, BOOL ProcessShellCommand(CCommandLineInfo& rCmdInfo);

Parameters

rCmdInfo Reference to CCommandLineInfo object that specifies the command.

Returns TRUE if successful; FALSE otherwise.

See Also CCommandLineInfo class, CWinApp::ParseCommandLine

Example See ParseCommandLine

ProcessWndProcException

■ 2.0 ■ 3.0

Description Last-chance handler for exceptions thrown by command and message handlers. CWinApp::ProcessWndProcException displays a message box notifying the user. "Command failed" is the text for command messages, whereas "Internal Application Error" is the text for all others. This function can be overridden by CWinApp-derived classes to handle exceptions for other messages. For more information about exceptions, see Chapter 15, *Debugging and Exception Handling*.

Syntax public, virtual LRESULT ProcessWndProcException(CException* e, const MSG* pMsg);

Parameters

e Exception thrown.

pMsg Pointer to message whose handler caused the exception to be thrown.

Returns Return code for message reported to Windows.

RegisterShellFileTypes

■ 2.0 ■ 3.0

Description Registers the file types with the operating system for all of the application's documents. This function is typically called by the CWinApp-derived InitInstance member. It should be called only after all document templates have been added to the application.

Syntax protected, void RegisterShellFileTypes(BOOL bWin95=FALSE);

Parameters

bWin95	TRUE if running on Windows 95, FALSE otherwise.
Returns	Nothing is returned.
See Also	CWinApp::EnableShellOpen
Example	See EnableShellOpen

RegisterShellFileTypesCompat

–. ■ 4.0 ■ UD

Description	Backwards compatible, pre-Windows 95 version of RegisterShellFileTypes().
Syntax	protected, void RegisterShellFileTypesCompat();
Parameters	None.
Returns	Nothing is returned.
See Also	CWinApp::RegisterShellFileTypes
Example	See RegisterShellFileTypes

Run

■ 2.0 ■ 3.0

Description	Runs the application, called by MFC's version of the WinMain application entry point. It is the main function containing the message loop that executes until the application is terminated. CWinApp::Run() checks to make sure that the main window is not NULL and then calls the CWinThread version. Run() should not be called directly by the programmer. See the CWinThread class for more information regarding the MFC message loop.
Syntax	public, virtual int Run();
Parameters	None.
Returns	Exit code for application.
See Also	CWinThread::Run
Example	See CWinThread::Run

RunAutomated

■ 2.0 ■ 3.0

Description	Determines if the appplication is executing through OLE automation. This function was made obsolete by the CCommandLineInfo class but is still included for backward compatibility.
Syntax	public, BOOL RunAutomated();
Parameters	None.
Returns	TRUE if executed through OLE automation; FALSE otherwise.
See Also	CWinApp::RunEmbedded, CCommandLineInfo class

RunEmbedded

■ 2.0 ■ 3.0

Description Determines if the appplication is executing through OLE embedding. This function was made obsolete by the CCommandLineInfo class but is still included for backward compatibility.

Syntax public, BOOL RunEmbedded();

Parameters None.

Returns TRUE if executed through OLE embedding; FALSE otherwise.

See Also CWinApp::RunAutomated, CCommandLineInfo class

SaveAllModified

■ 2.0 ■ 3.0

Description Attempts to save all modified documents. Called by MFC (in response to a WM_QUERYENDSESSION message) before the application terminates or before the main window closes. SaveAllModified() calls the SaveAllModified member of all document templates of the application. It is not usually called by the programmer directly. With MFC 4.0 and above, this function now simply calls the equivalent member found in the CDocManager class.

Syntax public, virtual BOOL SaveAllModified();

Parameters None.

Returns TRUE if it is OK to exit; FALSE otherwise.

See Also CDocManager class, CDocTemplate::SaveAllModified

SaveStdProfileSettings

■ 2.0 ■ 3.0 ■ UD

Description Saves the standard MFC application settings that include the MRU list and the default number of preview pages during print preview, from either the registry or the application .INI file. This function is called by the CWinApp::ExitInstance member, meaning that it does not need to be called by the programmer directly.

Syntax protected, void SaveStdProfileSettings();

Parameters None.

Returns Nothing is returned.

See Also CWinApp::LoadStdProfileSettings

SelectPrinter

■ 2.0 ■ 3.0

Description Selects a printer, tells MFC which printer should be used. This function updates the cached printer values maintained by MFC and frees the previous values.

Syntax public, void SelectPrinter(HANDLE hDevNames, HANDLE hDevMode, BOOL bFreeOld = TRUE);

Parameters

hDevNames Handle to DEVNAMES structure, containing the device name, driver name, and printer name.

hDevMode Handle to DEVMODE structure, containing the device characteristics of the printer.

bFreeOld TRUE if previous values should be freed; FALSE otherwise.

Returns Nothing is returned.

See Also CWinApp::GetPrinterDeviceDefaults, CWinApp::DoPrintDialog

SetCurrentHandles ■ 2.0 ■ 3.0 ■ UD

Description Internal MFC function for initializing framework variables. This function should not be called by the programmer.

Syntax public, void SetCurrentHandles();

Parameters None.

Returns Nothing is returned.

SetDialogBkColor ■ 2.0 ■ 3.0

Description Sets the background and text color for dialogs. The default colors are gray and black.

Syntax protected, void SetDialogBkColor(COLORREF clrCtlBk = RGB(192, 192, 192), COLORREF clrCtlText = RGB(0, 0, 0));

Parameters

clrCtlBk Background color.

clrCtlText Text color.

Returns Nothing is returned.

Example

```
BOOL CTestApp::InitInstance()
{
	// initialization code...

	// background to white, text to grey
	SetDialogBkColor(RGB(255,255,255),RGB(192,192,192));

	// initialization code...

	return TRUE;
}
```

SetRegistryKey

–. ■ 3.0

Description Sets the registry key and tells MFC to use the registry when the profile access members (e.g., WriteProfileInt, GetProfileString) are called. The registry key is typically the company name. This function must be called before any of the other registry members are called. SetRegistryKey() does nothing on the Macintosh.

Syntax protected, void SetRegistryKey(LPCTSTR lpszRegistryKey); void SetRegistryKey(UINT nIDRegistryKey);

Parameters

lpszRegistryKey Registry key.

nIDRegistryKey String resource ID that specifies the registry key.

Returns Nothing is returned.

See Also CWinApp::GetAppRegistryKey, CWinApp::SetSection Key

Example

```
AfxGetApp()->SetRegistryKey("MyCompany");
```

UpdatePrinterSelection

■ 2.0 ■ 3.0 ■ UD

Description Updates MFC's cached printer values of the current printer. This function is called internally by MFC and should rarely be called by the programmer directly.

Syntax protected, void UpdatePrinterSelection(BOOL bForceDefaults);

Parameters

bForceDefaults TRUE if MFC should set its printer values to those of the default printer; FALSE otherwise.

Returns Nothing is returned.

See Also CWinApp::DoPrintDialog, CWinApp::GetPrinterDeviceDefaults, CWinApp::SelectPrinter

WinHelp

■ 2.0 ■ 3.0

Description Launches the Windows help engine with the application's help file. This function serves as a wrapper for the ::WinHelp SDK function. For more information about help, see Chapter 2, *The MFC Framework*.

Syntax public, virtual void WinHelp(DWORD dwData, UINT nCmd = HELP_CONTEXT);

Parameters

dwData Data parameter used in conjunction with nCmd parameter to determine where to jump in the help file.

nCmd Command parameter for the WinHelp engine, see the SDK documentation of ::WinHelp for more information.

Returns Nothing is returned.

See Also CWinApp::OnHelp, CWinApp::OnHelpFinder, CWinApp::OnContextHelp, CWinApp::OnHelpUsing, CWinApp::OnHelpIndex

Example

```
AfxGetApp()->WinHelp(0,HELP_HELPONHELP);
```

WRITEPROFILEBINARY

–. ■ 4.0 ■ UD

Description Writes a binary value to either the registry or the application's .INI file. WriteProfileBinary will only use the registry if the programmer has called SetRegistryKey() first. The registry option is not available on the Macintosh. When using the .INI file option, MFC stores the binary data as a string, converting each byte into two equivalent character values so that the .INI entry is composed solely of printable characters.

Syntax public, BOOL WriteProfileBinary(LPCTSTR lpszSection, LPCTSTR lpszEntry, LPBYTE pData, UINT nBytes);

Parameters

lpszSection Section name.

lpszEntry Entry name.

pData Binary buffer array.

nBytes Number of bytes to write.

Returns TRUE if successful; FALSE otherwise.

See Also CWinApp::SetRegistryKey, CWinApp::GetProfileInt, CWinApp::GetProfileString, CWinApp::GetProfileBinary, CWinApp::WriteProfileInt, CWinApp::WriteProfileString

Example

```
BOOL SetParameters(CMyParameters& parameters)
{
      return WriteProfileBinary("Global","Parameters",
           (LPBYTE)&parameters,sizeof(CMyParameters);

}
```

WRITEPROFILEINT

■ 2.0 ■ 3.0

Description Writes an integer value to either the registry or the application's .INI file. WriteProfileInt only uses the registry if the programmer first calls SetRegistryKey(). The registry option is not available on the Macintosh.

Syntax public, BOOL WriteProfileInt(LPCTSTR lpszSection, LPCTSTR lpszEntry, int nValue);

Parameters

lpszSection Section name.

lpszEntry Entry name.

nValue Integer value to write.

Returns TRUE if successful; FALSE otherwise.

See Also CWinApp::SetRegistryKey, CWinApp::GetProfileBinary, CWinApp::GetProfileString, CWinApp::GetProfileInt, CWinApp::WriteProfileBinary, CWinApp::WriteProfileString

Example

```
void CTestApp::SaveWindowPosition()
{
	CRect rect;

	AfxGetMainWnd()->GetClientRect(&rect);
	WriteProfileInt("WindowPosition","Left",rect.left);
	WriteProfileInt("WindowPosition","Top",rect.top);
	WriteProfileInt("WindowPosition","Right",rect.right);
	WriteProfileInt("WindowPosition","Bottom",rect.bottom);
}
```

WriteProfileString ■ 2.0 ■ 3.0

Description Writes a string value to either the registry or the application's .INI file. WriteProfileString only uses the registry if the programmer has called SetRegistryKey() first. The registry option is not available on the Macintosh. If the string value is NULL, the entry is removed. Use this function to remove entries not only for string values, but for binary and integer values too.

Syntax public, BOOL WriteProfileString(LPCTSTR lpszSection, LPCTSTR lpszEntry, LPCTSTR lpszValue);

Parameters

lpszSection Section name.

lpszEntry Entry name.

lpszValue String value; entry is removed if NULL.

Returns TRUE if successful; FALSE otherwise.

See Also CWinApp::SetRegistryKey, CWinApp::GetProfileBinary, CWinApp::GetProfileInt, CWinApp::GetProfileString, CWinApp::WriteProfileBinary, CWinApp::WriteProfileInt

Example

```
void CTestApp::SaveFile(CString& strFile)
{
	WriteProfileString("Global","FileName",strFile);
}
```

4

WINDOWS MESSAGING

4

WINDOWS MESSAGING

As reviewed in Chapter 1, *Windows Programming,* Microsoft Windows is an event-driven system. Windows applications, including those built with MFC, respond to a menagerie of messages generated from a variety of sources. These sources may include the Windows system, users, other applications, and the receiving application itself. In the old SDK days the call-back procedure WndProc and its giant switch statement handled the myriad of messages received by an application. An application framework such as MFC provides a more object-oriented method of dealing with these messages. MFC provides a clean encapsulation of these messages and their associated handler functions. This encapsulation is provided by a set of macros as well as several classes. The classes and macros covered in this chapter are shown below in Table 4-1.

Table 4-1 Chapter 4 class summary

Class Name	Description
Message Map Macros	A series of macros that map specified messages to specified member functions.
CCmdTarget	Base class for all objects which will receive command messages.
CCmdUI	Aids in the update of user-interface objects, i.e., enabling and disabling.

The Windows message pump is hidden within the Run member function of the CWinApp class. This message pump retrieves messages and then sends them on to the proper window for handling. Each message is then handled by its own function, eliminating the need for the large switch statement used to process messages in most Windows SDK applications. The vast majority of MFC applications need not be concerned with the mechanics of message routing at all. MFC not only handles standard message routing, but in fact enhances it. This is discussed in detail in the Message Routing in MFC section of this chapter.

MFC uses a dedicated handler function to process each message. These handler functions are member functions of various classes. MFC provides many default handlers, but the developer can override the various handlers in order to perform application-specific operations in response to a message. While you can edit the handler functions by hand (which was the only recourse in MFC 1.0), Microsoft Visual C++ (MSVC) provides the ability to add and modify message handler functions with the ClassWizard tool. In the vast majority of cases you will not need to modify the handler templates created with the ClassWizard tool. You will simply fill in the content of the shell that was automatically created.

Types of Messages

Beginning with MFC 2.0, Microsoft stated that there are three main categories of messages needing handlers: window messages, control notifications, and command messages. Window messages include most of the WM_XXX messages, such as the WM_LBUTTONDOWN, WM_MOUSEMOVE, and WM_CHAR messages. Control notifications include the WM_COMMAND messages sent by Windows controls to their parents. This would include, for example, the CBN_SELCHANGE combo-box notification and the EN_CHANGE edit box notification. Finally, command messages include WM_COMMAND messages sent by user interface objects such as menu items and accelerators.

Message Handling in MFC

Under MFC 1.0, the only kind of messages dealt with by classes were command messages that were handled by windows (the CWnd class), and those objects derived from CWnd. With MFC 2.0+, window and control notification messages are now handled by objects of classes derived from CWnd (e.g., CFrameWnd, CDialog). The MFC framework allows a wider range of non-CWnd derived classes to also support command messages. Any object derived from the CCmdTarget class can, as the name implies, respond to a command message. Objects derived from the CCmdTarget class include the CWnd class (and therefore all CWnd derived objects), the application object (CWinApp), and the document object (CDocument).

Window messages, as mentioned above, include most of the WM_ messages defined in windows.h with the exception of the WM_COMMAND and WM_NOTIFY messages. Window messages are handled by CWnd-derived classes and typically have parameters associated with them. These parameters are the same as the ones passed in the wParam and lParam values in an SDK application, except now the framework parses the wParam and lParam information into more meaningful message-specific parameters. Note that because MFC parses the wParam and lParam for the application, MFC applications tend to port between 16-bit Windows and 32-bit Windows more easily than SDK-based applications.

Expanded Use of Control Messages

The control notification type of messages are the WM_COMMAND messages sent from Windows controls such as edit controls, list boxes, and other child windows to their parent windows. It also includes the new WM_NOTIFY message introduced with Windows 95 and included in MFC beginning with version 3.1. WM_NOTIFY is used for notifications sent by the Windows 95 common controls and was introduced in order to take some of the load off of the WM_COMMAND message, which was already overused. MFC 2.0+ also provides support for Visual Basic control (VBXs) messages which have the VBN_ prefix rather than the WM_ prefix.

Anatomy of Command Messages

The command message type includes all the WM_COMMAND messages from user interface objects like menus and accelerator keys. In MFC, it also includes the button-clicked messages from buttons. Even though buttons are controls, MFC handles button events as if they were command messages from a menu item. MFC does this because the pressing of a button often indicates that the user is requesting that some command be carried out, just like when a menu item is chosen. In actual fact, MFC routes all control notifications through the special command routing scheme discussed in the next section of this chapter. Most MFC literature does not mention this fact because it would be very rare that you would want to use it. However, there is always that one situation in which the obscure becomes necessary. For example, you may want your application to recognize when the text in a particular edit box on a dialog has changed. Normally, you would probably detect this in the dialog itself, but if you wanted your application to be automatically notified, you could use MFC's command routing scheme. Note that in order for MFC to consider a user interface object (menu item, button, etc.) a command-generating item, you should assign it a resource ID greater than or equal to 0x8000. Resource IDs above 0x8000 are within MFC's official command ID range. Currently, MFC only requires this for controls inside a dialog but it is a good idea to obey this rule in all cases. If you are using an MFC-aware resource editor like AppStudio, this is taken care of for you.

On top of all this, MFC Version 4.0 adds a new concept called "message reflection." Message reflection is a mechanism by which a particular message sent by a control (like an edit box) to its parent window can be "reflected" back to the control itself. See the section titled Message Reflection later in this chapter for a more in-depth discussion of message reflection.

A sample program called MSGSMPL, which shows how to use many of the functions and concepts documented in this chapter, is included on the CD-ROM packaged with this book. MSGSMPL demonstrates how each type of message is routed in an MFC program. It also shows how to use the command update UI mechanism to control the state of various user interface elements. MSGSMPL is a Visual C++ 4.0 (32-bit) project.

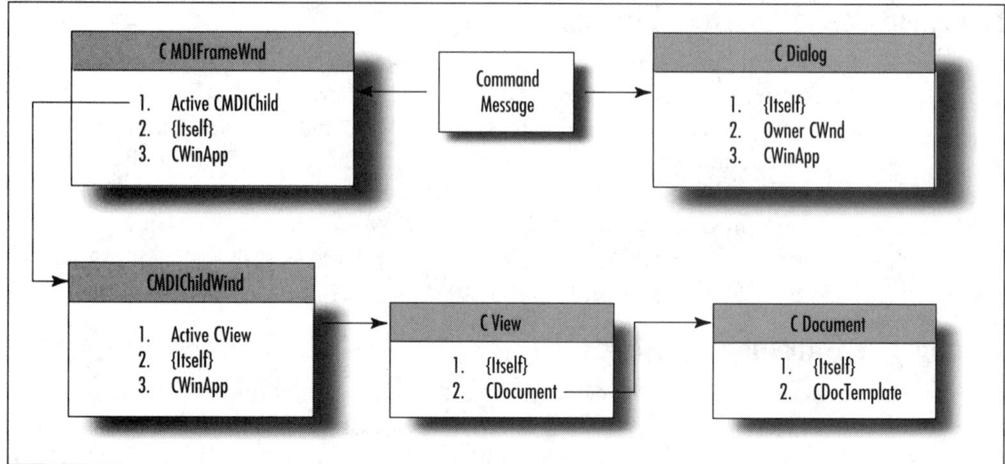

Figure 4-1 MFC Command Message Routing

Message Routing in MFC

MFC routes different types of messages differently. All types of messages are first received by the window to which the message was sent (dispatched by the message pump in the CWinApp::Run function). MFC uses a single, "universal" window procedure (CWnd::WindowProc) to receive these messages. Window messages and most control messages are handled directly by the WindowProc function—each message being dispatched to an MFC or user-defined function designated to handle that message. If no function has been designated to handle a particular message, then the message is passed to the default window procedure (CWnd:: DefWndProc) just like in an SDK application.

Command Message Routing

Unlike window messages, command messages are routed through a series of command targets (CCmdTarget-derived classes). Each target in the chain has the option to handle the message and/or pass it on to the next target in the chain. The standard target chain through which command messages are routed is shown in Figure 4-1. All of the classes depicted in the figure are derived from CCmdTarget, either directly or indirectly, and therefore, any class derived from any of these classes may handle command messages. MFC routes command messages by calling the OnCmdMsg member function of the destination command target object. This routing begins when the OnCmdMsg function is called by the WindowProc function of the window that originally received a message. The OnCmdMsg function then decides whether it will handle the message or pass it along to other, associated command target objects. As you can see from Figure 4-1, the command target will often give other command targets a chance to handle the message before it tries to handle it itself. If no command target handles a particular message, then

MFC passes it to its default window procedure (DefWndProc). As an example, let's assume that the user selects a menu item called "Delete Item" in an MDI application. Assuming that the user has an MFC "view" (which is composed of a frame window, the view itself, and an underlying document) on the screen, the message will be routed like this: 1) The main MDI frame window receives the message and passes it the active MDI child; 2) The active MDI child passes the command to its associated view; 3) If the view has a handler for the message, routing stops; otherwise, the view passes the message to its associated document; 4) If a handler for the message exists in the document, routing stops; otherwise, the message is passed to the document template associated with the document and view; 5) If the document template has a handler for the message, routing stops; otherwise, the routing unravels back to the MDI child window; 6) If the MDI child window has a handler for the message, routing stops; otherwise, the message is passed to the main application class; 7) If the main application class has a handler for the message, routing stops; otherwise, things unravel again back to the main MDI frame window; 8) If the main frame window has a handler for the message, routing stops; otherwise, the application is given one more shot at it. If no handler exists at the application level, the message is passed to the default window procedure. For more information regarding general message routing and command message routing, see Technical Note 21 included with MSVC.

Message Reflection

As mentioned above, MFC Version 4.0 introduces a concept called "message reflection." Message reflection is a mechanism by which a particular message sent by a control (like an edit control) to its parent window can be "reflected" back to the control itself. MFC automatically "reflects" all control notification messages. Those of you who have worked with Windows in the past will probably recall the WM_CTLCOLOR message which is sent by dialog controls to the dialog that contains them in order to get a brush to be used for painting the background of the control. Depending on the parent, such things can be problematic in the object-oriented world. Message reflection allows you to create a self-contained control which can be reused without the user having to worry about responding to messages. Of course, you can still override the reflection and handle the message at the parent, if desired. Also, message reflection is fully backward compatible—if you write code to handle control notifications, it will still work. Reflected messages in MFC are handled just like any other message—via a message map macro that associates a particular function with a reflected message. All message map macros associated with reflected messages end with "REFLECT."

Message Maps

The programmer, of course, needs to somehow tell MFC whether or not a particular CCmdTarget-based object will handle a message and which function in the object will handle it. This is accomplished through an entity known as a "message map." As is implied by the name, a message map "maps" a particular message or messages to a member function which will handle that message.

A message map is defined by a series of macros that let the framework efficiently attach a function to a specified message. This could be accomplished with virtual functions, but this would create massive virtual pointer tables (v-tables) in the various base classes and thus waste both code space and run-time (especially considering that most objects in an application will only respond to a few different messages).

With MFC 1.0, these message maps were tied to CWnd-derived objects and were thus limited to window objects. Beginning with MFC 2.0, Microsoft moved the message maps into the CCmdTarget object which now serves as the parent for the CWnd object (as well as several other objects). A typical message map generated by the MSVC AppWizard is shown below in Listing 4-1. A message map is placed in the implementation file for the class which, in the example shown in Listing 4-1, is the main application class. The message map is delimited by two macros, BEGIN_MESSAGE_MAP and END_MESSAGE_MAP. Between these two macros are placed other macros which map commands and other window messages to their handler functions.

BEGIN_MESSAGE_MAP takes two parameters: the name of the current class and the name of its parent's class. MFC uses these two items to implement inheritance for message maps. In other words, a derived class "inherits" all of the message map entries from its parent. When MFC searches for a matching entry for a message, it starts at the bottom and works its way up this inheritance chain. For more information regarding the implementation of message maps in MFC, see Technical Note 6 included with MSVC.

Listing 4-1 Message map for CMsgSmplApp

```
BEGIN_MESSAGE_MAP(CMsgSmplApp, CWinApp)
      //{{AFX_MSG_MAP(CMsgSmplApp)
      ON_COMMAND(ID_APP_ABOUT, OnAppAbout)
      ON_COMMAND(ID_MESSAGES_SENDCOMMANDMESSAGEHANDLEDBYAPPLICATION,
                  OnMessagesSendcommandmessagehandledbyapplication)
      ON_UPDATE_COMMAND_UI(ID_UIUPDATE_UIENABLEDBYAPPLICATION,
                  OnUpdateUiupdateUienabledbyapplication)
      ON_UPDATE_COMMAND_UI(ID_UIUPDATE_UIENABLEDBYAPPLICATIONCHECKEDBYVIEW,
                  OnUpdateUiupdateUienabledbyapplicationcheckedbyview)
      ON_COMMAND(ID_UIUPDATE_UIENABLEDBYAPPLICATION,
                  OnUiupdateUienabledbyapplication)
      ON_COMMAND(ID_UIUPDATE_UIENABLEDBYAPPLICATIONCHECKEDBYVIEW,
                  OnUiupdateUienabledbyapplicationcheckedbyview)
      ON_COMMAND(ID_UIUPDATE_UIENABLEDBYDOCUMENT,
                  OnUiupdateUienabledbydocument)
      ON_COMMAND(ID_UIUPDATE_UIENABLEDBYVIEW, OnUiupdateUienabledbyview)
      ON_COMMAND(ID_WAITING_INTERRUPTEDLENGTHYPROCESS,
                  OnWaitingInterruptedlengthyprocess)
      ON_COMMAND(ID_WAITING_LENGTHYPROCESS, OnWaitingLengthyprocess)
      //}}AFX_MSG_MAP
      // Standard file based document commands
      ON_COMMAND(ID_FILE_NEW, CWinApp::OnFileNew)
      ON_COMMAND(ID_FILE_OPEN, CWinApp::OnFileOpen)
END_MESSAGE_MAP()
```

Listing 4-2, below, shows the three steps required to implement a message map for a particular message. Each message map requires a handler function declaration in the declaration of the class, a message map macro entry within the message map block in the implementation file, and finally the handler function definition itself. The message map macros are converted into arrays of function pointers which MFC uses to look up the relevant handler functions for particular messages. Note that if you are using a compiler which supports MFC, it will probably provide a tool for creating the message map entries as well as the function declarations and shell definitions. MSVC provides the ClassWizard tool for this purpose.

Listing 4-2 Typical steps to implement a message map

```
// handler declaration
class CMsgSmplView : public CView
{
...
protected:
	//{{AFX_MSG(CMsgSmplView)
	afx_msg void OnMessagesSendwindowmessage();
	afx_msg LONG OnTestUserMessage2( UINT, LONG );
	afx_msg void OnRButtonDown(UINT nFlags, CPoint point);
	afx_msg void OnRButtonUp(UINT nFlags, CPoint point);
	afx_msg void OnRangemacrosCommands(UINT nCmd);
	afx_msg void OnUpdateRangemacrosCommands(CCmdUI* pCmdUI);
	//}}AFX_MSG
	DECLARE_MESSAGE_MAP()
};

// message map entry
BEGIN_MESSAGE_MAP(CMsgSmplView, CView)
	//{{AFX_MSG_MAP(CMsgSmplView)
	ON_COMMAND(ID_MESSAGES_SENDWINDOWMESSAGE, OnMessagesSendwindowmessage)
	ON_MESSAGE(WM_USER_TESTMESSAGE2,OnTestUserMessage2)
	ON_WM_RBUTTONDOWN()
	ON_WM_RBUTTONUP()
	ON_COMMAND_RANGE(ID_RANGEMACROS_COMMAND1, ID_RANGEMACROS_COMMAND3,
		OnRangemacrosCommands)
	ON_UPDATE_COMMAND_UI_RANGE(ID_RANGEMACROS_COMMAND1,
		ID_RANGEMACROS_COMMAND3, OnUpdateRangemacrosCommands)
	//}}AFX_MSG_MAP
END_MESSAGE_MAP()

// handler definition
LONG CMsgSmplView::OnTestUserMessage2( UINT, LONG )
{
	AfxMessageBox("User message WM_USER_TESTMESSAGE2 received by view.");
	return 0;
}
```

Message Map Macros

As discussed above, a message map is basically a series of macros. Below is a discussion of each of these macros.

DECLARE_MESSAGE_MAP

■ 2.0 ■ 3.0

Description The DECLARE_MESSAGE_MAP macro indicates that the CCmdTarget-derived class will supply a message map. If used, this macro must appear in the object's class declaration.

Syntax DECLARE_MESSAGE_MAP()

See Also BEGIN_MESSAGE_MAP, END_MESSAGE_MAP

BEGIN_MESSAGE_MAP

■ 2.0 ■ 3.0

Description The BEGIN_MESSAGE_MAP macro indicates the beginning of a message map definition. The message map must be concluded with the END_MESSAGE_MAP macro.

Syntax BEGIN_MESSAGE_MAP(*class*, *base class*)

Parameters

class The name of the class for which this message map is being defined. Do not place quote marks around the class name.

base class The name of the immediate parent class for this class. Make sure that this is correct or you may not inherit message map entries correctly. "Cut-and-paste" message map building often causes this parameter to be incorrect.

Example See Listing 4-1.

END_MESSAGE_MAP

■ 2.0 ■ 3.0

Description The END_MESSAGE_MAP macro marks the end of a message map definition.

Syntax END_MESSAGE_MAP()

Parameters None.

Example See Listing 4-1.

ON_COMMAND

■ 2.0 ■ 3.0

Description The ON_COMMAND macro is inserted in a message map to indicate which function will handle a command message from a command user-interface object such as a menu item or toolbar button. When an object derived from CCmdTarget receives a Windows WM_COMMAND message with the specified *id*, the member function indicated by the *memberFxn* parameter is invoked to handle the message. There should be only one ON_COMMAND macro in the class's message map for each menu or accelerator command which needs to be mapped to a message-handler function.

Syntax ON_COMMAND(*id*, *memberFxn*)

Parameters

id The command ID, usually defined in a dialog resource or header file.

memberFxn The name of the message-handler function to which the command is mapped. The declaration for this function is as follows: afx_msg void memberFxn( );

See Also ON_COMMAND_RANGE, ON_UPDATE_COMMAND_UI

ON_COMMAND_RANGE

■ 2.0 ■ 3.0

Description MFC 3.0 introduced this macro to map a contiguous range of command IDs to a single message handler function. The range of IDs starts with *startid* and ends with *endid*. This macro is most useful when a series of commands are very similar. Using ON_COMMAND_RANGE, you can map all of the similar commands to one handler which first performs the tasks common to all of the commands and then, based on the *uCmd* parameter passed to the handler, performs command-specific tasks. ClassWizard does not support message map ranges, so you must place the macro yourself. Be sure to put it outside the message map //{{AFX_MSG_MAP delimiters.

Syntax ON_COMMAND_RANGE(*startid*, *endid*, *memberFxn*)

Parameters

startid Beginning command ID for contiguous set of ids.

endid Ending command ID.

memberFxn The name of the message-handler function to which the commands are mapped. The declaration for this function is as follows: afx_msg void memberFxn(UINT uCmd);

See Also ON_UPDATE_COMMAND_UI_RANGE, ON_CONTROL_RANGE

Example

```
// handler declaration
afx_msg void OnRangemacrosCommands(UINT nCmd);

// message map for handler
BEGIN_MESSAGE_MAP(CMsgSmplView, Cview)
...
      ON_COMMAND_RANGE(ID_RANGEMACROS_COMMAND1,
            ID_RANGEMACROS_COMMAND3, OnRangemacrosCommands)
...
END_MESSAGE_MAP()

// handler implementation
void CMsgSmplView::OnRangemacrosCommands(UINT nCmd)
{
      DoCommonStuff();
      if (nCmd == ID_RANGEMACROS_COMMAND1)
            DoCommand1Stuff();
```

continued on next page

continued from previous page

```
        else if (nCmd == ID_RANGEMACROS_COMMAND2)
             DoCommand2Stuff();
        else if (nCmd == ID_RANGEMACROS_COMMAND3)
             DoCommand3Stuff();
}
```

ON_CONTROL

■ 2.0 ■ 3.0

Description Indicates which function will handle a control notification message. Note that MFC provides special message map macros for most standard notifications. This macro is most often used for custom controls.

Syntax ON_CONTROL(*codeId*, *id*, *memberFn*)

Parameters

codeId The event notification code.

id The resource ID of the control.

memberFn The name of the message-handler function to which the event is mapped. The declaration for this function is as follows: afx_msg void memberFxn( );

Example

```
// handler declaration
afx_msg void OnEditChanged();

// handler message map entry
ON_CONTROL (HGN_SOMENOTIFICATION,IDC_CUSTOMCONTROL,OnControlNotif)

// handler function definition
void CRangeDlg:: OnControlNotif()
{
     // notification handling code here
}
```

ON_CONTROL_RANGE

■ 2.0 ■ 3.0

Description Use this macro to map a contiguous range of control IDs to a single message handler function for a specified Windows notification message, such as EN_CHANGED. The range of IDs starts with *id1* and ends with *id2*. The handler is called for the specified notification coming from any of the mapped controls. One particularly useful application for this is to detect when the text in any of several edit controls changes. ClassWizard does not support message map ranges, so you must place the macro yourself. Be sure to put it outside the message map //{{AFX_MSG_MAP delimiters.

Syntax ON_CONTROL_RANGE(*wNotifyCode*, *id1*, *id2*, *memberFn*)

Parameters

wNotifyCode The notification code to which your handler is responding.

id1 Command ID at the beginning of a contiguous range of control IDs.

id2 Command ID at the end of a contiguous range of control IDs.

memberFn The name of the message-handler function to which the controls are mapped. The declaration for this function is as follows: afx_msg void memberFxn(UINT nCtl);

See Also ON_UPDATE_COMMAND_UI_RANGE, ON_COMMAND_RANGE

Example

```
// handler declaration
afx_msg void OnEditChanged(UINT nCtl);

// handler message map entry
ON_CONTROL_RANGE(EN_CHANGE,IDC_EDIT1,IDC_EDIT4,OnEditChanged)

// handler function definition
void CRangeDlg::OnEditChanged(UINT nCtl)
{
     // contents of dialog have changed
     m_ctMessage.SetWindowText("The contents have changed.");
}
```

ON_CONTROL_REFLECT

–. ■ 4.0

Description Indicates which function will handle a control notification message reflected back to the control from the parent. This macro allows you to write a control that handles some, or all, of its notification messages itself. Any control notification you would typically associate with the parent (for example BN_CLICKED for a button click) is reflected back to the control and can be handled with this macro.

Syntax ON_CONTROL_REFLECT(*wNotifyCode*, *memberFn*)

Parameters

wNotifyCode The control notification code (for example, BN_CLICKED).

memberFn The name of the message-handler function to which the notification is mapped. The declaration for this function is as follows: afx_msg void memberFxn( );

See Also ON_CONTROL, ON_CONTROL_REFLECT_EX

Example

```
// handler declaration
afx_msg void OnClicked();

// handler message map entry
ON_CONTROL_REFLECT(BN_CLICKED,OnClicked)

// handler function definition
void CMyButton::OnClicked()
{
     // notification handling code here
}
```

ON_CONTROL_REFLECT_EX

–. ■ 4.0

Description

Indicates which function will handle a control notification message reflected back to the control from the parent. This macro allows you to write a control that handles some, or all, of its notification messages itself. Any control notification you would typically associate with the parent (for example BN_CLICKED for a button click) is reflected back to the control and can be handled with this macro. This macro is different from the ON_CONTROL_REFLECT macro because it also allows you to optionally pass the message on to the parent after you have processed it at the control.

Syntax

ON_CONTROL_REFLECT_EX(*wNotifyCode*, *memberFn*)

Parameters

wNotifyCode The control notification code (for example, BN_CLICKED).

memberFn The name of the message-handler function to which the notification is mapped. The declaration for this function is as follows: afx_msg BOOL memberFxn( );. Return TRUE from this function if you want the message to go back to the parent.

See Also

N_CONTROL, ON_CONTROL_REFLECT

Example

```
// handler declaration
afx_msg void OnClicked();

// handler message map entry
ON_CONTROL_REFLECT_EX(BN_CLICKED,OnClicked)

// handler function definition
BOOL CMyButton::OnClicked()
{
     // notification handling code here
     return TRUE; // allow parent a crack at it too
}
```

ON_MESSAGE

■ 2.0 ■ 3.0

Description

Indicates which function will handle a user-defined message. User-defined messages are usually defined in the range WM_USER to 0x7FFF. User-defined messages are any messages that are not standard Windows WM_XXXX messages. There should be exactly one ON_MESSAGE macro statement in your message map for every user-defined message that must be mapped to a message-handler function.

Syntax

ON_MESSAGE(*message*, *memberFxn*)

Parameters

message The message ID.

memberFxn The name of the message handler function to which the message is mapped. The declaration for this function is as follows: afx_msg LONG memberFxn(UINT, LONG);

Example

```
// handler declaration
afx_msg LONG OnMyMessage(UINT wParam, LONG lParam);

// handler message map entry
ON_MESSAGE(WM_USERMESSAGE,OnMyMessage)

// handler function definition
LONG CRangeDlg::OnMyMessage(UINT wParam, LONG lParam)
{
      // message received
      return 1;
}
```

ON_NOTIFY

–. ■ 3.1

Description Indicates which function will handle a control notification message. When Windows 95 was designed, Microsoft decided that the WM_COMMAND message was overloaded with control notification variations. Also, there is no way to pass additional information regarding the message with the WM_COMMAND message. To solve this problem, the Microsoft engineers added a new message, WM_NOTIFY, which allows for more complex notifications.

Syntax ON_NOTIFY(*wNotifyCode*, *id*, *memberFn*)

Parameters

wNotifyCode The event notification code.

id The resource ID of the control.

memberFn The name of the message-handler function to which the event is mapped. The declaration for this function is as follows: afx_msg void memberFxn(NMHDR *, LRESULT *);. The NMHDR parameter may actually point to an NMHDR structure or it may point to a notification-dependent structure which contains a NMHDR structure as its first member. In this way, each control can pass additional information as needed and, at the same time, you can always use the pointer as a plain NMHDR (since it is always the first member of any more advanced structures which might be passed). If the particular notification you are handling requires a return code, you should place it in the buffer pointed to by the second parameter.

Example

```
// handler declaration
afx_msg void OnToolInfoNeeded();

// handler message map entry
ON_NOTIFY(TBN_GETBUTTONINFO,IDC_MYTOOLBAR, OnToolInfoNeeded)

// handler function def. - Win95 toolbar control will call this
```

continued on next page

continued from previous page

```
// function when it needs info about a custom tool on the toolbar
void CMyParentWnd:: OnToolInfoNeeded(NMHDR *pNmHdr, LRESULT *pRes)
{
      // structure is actual a TBNOTIFY
      TBNOTIFY *pTb = (TBNOTIFY *)pNmHdr;

      // notification handling code here
      *pRes = 0;
}
```

ON_NOTIFY_REFLECT

■ 4.0

Description

Indicates which function will handle a control notification message reflected back from the parent of the control. When Windows 95 was designed, Microsoft decided that the WM_COMMAND message was overloaded with control notification variations. Also, there is no way to pass additional information regarding the message with the WM_COMMAND message. To solve this problem, the Microsoft engineers added a new message, WM_NOTIFY, which allows for more complex notifications. The ON_NOTIFY_REFLECT macro allows you to handle one of these notifications at the control level.

Syntax

ON_NOTIFY_REFLECT(*wNotifyCode*, *memberFn*)

Parameters

wNotifyCode — The event notification code.

memberFn — The name of the message-handler function to which the event is mapped. The declaration for this function is as follows: afx_msg void memberFxn(NMHDR *, LRESULT *);. The NMHDR parameter may actually point to an NMHDR structure or it may point to a notification-dependent structure which contains a NMHDR structure as its first member. In this way, each control can pass additional information as needed and, at the same time, you can always use the pointer as a plain NMHDR (since it is always the first member of any more advanced structures which might be passed). If the particular notification you are handling requires a return code, you should place it in the buffer pointed to by the second parameter.

Example

```
// handler declaration
afx_msg void OnToolInfoNeeded();

// handler message map entry
ON_NOTIFY_REFLECT(TBN_GETBUTTONINFO, OnToolInfoNeeded)

// handler function def. - Win95 toolbar control will call this
// function when it needs info about a custom tool on the toolbar
void CMyToolbar:: OnToolInfoNeeded(NMHDR *pNmHdr, LRESULT *pRes)
{
      // structure is actual a TBNOTIFY
      TBNOTIFY *pTb = (TBNOTIFY *)pNmHdr;

      // notification handling code here
      *pRes = 0;
}
```

ON_NOTIFY_REFLECT_EX

–. ■ 4.0

Description Indicates which function will handle a control notification message reflected back from the parent of the control. When Windows 95 was designed, Microsoft decided that the WM_COMMAND message was overloaded with control notification variations. Also, there is no way to pass additional information regarding the message with the WM_COMMAND message. To solve this problem, the Microsoft engineers added a new message, WM_NOTIFY, which allows for more complex notifications. This macro allows you to handle one of these notifications at the control level. This macro is different from the ON_NOTIFY_REFLECT macro because it also allows you to optionally pass the message on to the parent after you have processed it at the control.

Syntax ON_NOTIFY_REFLECT_EX(*wNotifyCode*, *memberFn*)

Parameters

wNotifyCode The event notification code.

memberFn The name of the message-handler function to which the event is mapped. The declaration for this function is as follows: afx_msg BOOL memberFxn(NMHDR *, LRESULT *);. The NMHDR parameter may actually point to an NMHDR structure or it may point to a notification dependant structure which contains a NMHDR structure as its first member. In this way, each control can pass additional information as needed and, at the same time, you can always use the pointer as a plain NMHDR (since it is always the first member of any more advanced structures which might be passed). If the particular notification you are handling requires a return code, you should place it in the buffer pointed to by the second parameter. You should return TRUE from the function if you process the message and don't want it passed on to the parent; otherwise, return FALSE.

Example

```
// handler declaration
afx_msg void OnToolInfoNeeded();

// handler message map entry
ON_NOTIFY_REFLECT_EX(TBN_GETBUTTONINFO, OnToolInfoNeeded)

// handler function def. - Win95 toolbar control will call this
// function when it needs info about a custom tool on the toolbar
void CMyToolbar:: OnToolInfoNeeded(NMHDR *pNmHdr, LRESULT *pRes)
{
     // structure is actual a TBNOTIFY
     TBNOTIFY *pTb = (TBNOTIFY *)pNmHdr;

     // notification handling code here
     *pRes = 0;

     return TRUE;
}
```

ON_REGISTERED_MESSAGE

■ 2.0 ■ 3.0

Description The Windows RegisterWindowMessage function is used to define a new window message that is guaranteed to be unique throughout the system. This macro indicates which function will handle the registered message. The variable *nMessageVariable* should be declared with the near modifier.

Syntax ON_REGISTERED_MESSAGE(*nMessageVariable*, *memberFxn*)

Parameters

nMessageVariable The registered window-message ID variable.

memberFxn The name of the message-handler function to which the message is mapped. The declaration for this function is as follows: afx_msg LONG memberFxn(UINT, LONG);

Example

```
// handler declaration
afx_msg LONG OnFindReplace(UINT wParam, LONG lParam);

// registering the message
static UINT WM_FINDREPLACE = RegisterWindowMessage(FINDMSGSTRING);

// handler message map entry
ON_REGISTERED_MESSAGE(WM_FINDREPLACE, OnFindReplace)

// handler function definition
LONG CRangeDlg:: OnFindReplace(UINT wParam, LONG lParam)
{
     // message received from find/replace common dialog
     ...
     return 1;
}
```

ON_UPDATE_COMMAND_UI

■ 2.0 ■ 3.0

Description This macro is usually inserted in a message map by ClassWizard to indicate which function will handle a user-interface update command message. For more information about user interface objects and the process of updating the state of these objects, see the following section of this chapter entitled User Interface Objects.

Syntax ON_UPDATE_COMMAND_UI(*id*, *memberFxn*)

Parameters

id The message ID.

memberFxn The name of the message-handler function to which the message is mapped. The declaration for this function is as follows: afx_msg void memberFxn(CCmdUI *pCmdUI);

See Also ON_UPDATE_COMMAND_UI_RANGE

Example

```
// handler declaration
afx_msg void OnUpdateMyMenuItem(CCmdUI* pCmdUI);

// message map entry
ON_UPDATE_COMMAND_UI (ID_EDIT_MYMENUITEM,OnUpdateMyMenuItem)

// handler definition
void CMsgSmplView:: OnUpdateMyMenuItem(CCmdUI* pCmdUI)
{
      pCmdUI->Enable(TRUE);
      pCmdUI->SetRadio(TRUE);
}
```

ON_UPDATE_COMMAND_UI_RANGE ■ 2.0 ■ 3.0

Description Use this macro to map a contiguous range of command IDs to a single update message handler function. ClassWizard does not support message map ranges, so you must place the macro yourself. Be sure to put it outside the message map //{{AFX_MSG_MAP delimiters. This macro is very useful when the state of several commands is determined by a single event. For example, you may have an edit command and a delete command, both of which should only be enabled if an item in a list is selected.

Syntax ON_UPDATE_COMMAND_UI_RANGE(*id1*, *id2*, *memberFxn*)

Parameters

id1 Command ID at the beginning of a contiguous range of command IDs.

id2 Command ID at the end of a contiguous range of command IDs.

memberFxn The name of the update message-handler function to which the commands are mapped. The declaration for this function is as follows: afx_msg void memberFxn(CCmdUI *pCmdUI);

See Also ON_UPDATE_COMMAND_UI, ON_COMMAND_RANGE, ON_CONTROL_RANGE

Example

```
// handler declaration
class CMsgSmplView : public CView
{
...
protected:
      //{{AFX_MSG(CMsgSmplView)
      //}}AFX_MSG
      afx_msg void OnUpdateRangemacrosCommands(CCmdUI* pCmdUI);
      DECLARE_MESSAGE_MAP()
};

// message map entry
BEGIN_MESSAGE_MAP(CMsgSmplView, CView)
      //{{AFX_MSG_MAP(CMsgSmplView)
```

continued on next page

continued from previous page

```
      //}}AFX_MSG_MAP
      ON_UPDATE_COMMAND_UI_RANGE(ID_RANGEMACROS_COMMAND1,
            ID_RANGEMACROS_COMMAND3, OnUpdateRangemacrosCommands)
END_MESSAGE_MAP()

// handler definition
void CMsgSmplView::OnUpdateRangemacrosCommands(CCmdUI* pCmdUI)
{
      pCmdUI->Enable(TRUE);
      pCmdUI->SetRadio(TRUE);
}
```

ON_UPDATE_COMMAND_UI _REFLECT

–. ■ 4.0

Description This macro allows a control to handle its own user-interface updates. Usually, these updates are handled by the parent of the control. For more information about user interface objects and the process of updating the state of these objects see the following section of this chapter entitled User Interface Objects.

Syntax ON_UPDATE_COMMAND_UI_REFLECT(*memberFxn*)

Parameters

memberFxn The name of the message-handler function to which the message is mapped. The declaration for this function is as follows: afx_msg void memberFxn(CCmdUI *pCmdUI);

See Also ON_UPDATE_COMMAND_UI

Example

```
// handler declaration
afx_msg void OnUpdateMyself(CCmdUI* pCmdUI);

// message map entry
ON_UPDATE_COMMAND_UI_REFLECT(OnUpdateMyself)

// handler definition
void CMyEditBox:: OnUpdateMyself(CCmdUI* pCmdUI)
{
      // I always want to be enabled
      pCmdUI->Enable(TRUE);
}
```

ON_VBXEVENT

■ 2.0 ■ 3.0

Description This macro is usually inserted in a message map by ClassWizard. It indicates which function will handle a message from a Visual Basic control.

Syntax ON_VBXEVENT(*wNotifyCode*, *id*, *memberFxn*)

Parameters

wNotifyCode The notification code of the VBX event.

id The message ID.

memberFxn The name of the message-handler function to which the message is mapped.

ON_WM_XXXX

■ 2.0 ■ 3.0

Description This macro is usually inserted in a message map by ClassWizard. MFC provides a ON_WM_XXXX macro for almost every Windows message (i.e., ON_WM_CREATE, ON_WM_SIZE). Curiously, until MFC Version 4.0, a few were missing—for example there was no ON_WM_TIMER for the WM_TIMER message, although there is now. The signature of the function that is mapped with this macro varies with the message that it will handle. MFC parses the wParam and lParam into more meaningful, message-specific parameters and then passes them to your handler.

Syntax ON_WM_XXXX( )

Parameters None.

Example

```
// handler declaration
class CMsgSmplView : public CView
{
...
// Generated message map functions
protected:
	//{{AFX_MSG(CMsgSmplView)
	afx_msg void OnRButtonDown(UINT nFlags, CPoint point);
	//}}AFX_MSG
	DECLARE_MESSAGE_MAP()
};

// message map entry
BEGIN_MESSAGE_MAP(CMsgSmplView, CView)
	//{{AFX_MSG_MAP(CMsgSmplView)
	ON_WM_RBUTTONDOWN()
	//}}AFX_MSG_MAP
END_MESSAGE_MAP()

// handler definition
void CMsgSmplView::OnRButtonDown(UINT nFlags, CPoint point)
{
	// output coordinates of cursor when right mouse button was
	// pressed
	CClientDC dc(this);
	CString strText;
	strText.Format("WM_RBUTTONDOWN received with coordinates: \
	    %d, %d dc.TextOut(5,5,strText);
	CView::OnRButtonDown(nFlags, point);
}
```

ON_WM_CHARTOITEM_REFLECT

–. ■ 4.0

Description This macro allows a control to handle the WM_CHARTOITEM message reflected back from the control's parent. The WM_CHARTOITEM message is sent by an owner-draw combo box or list box to determine how it should respond to a key stroke.You can use this message map macro to handle the message at the control itself. The function which will handle the message should have the following form (including the name): afx_msg void CharToItem(UINT, UINT);. For more information about this function, see CWnd::OnCharToItem.

Syntax ON_WM_CHARTOITEM_REFLECT( )

Parameters None

See Also CWnd::OnCharToItem

Example See ON_WM_CTLCOLOR_REFLECT for a related example.

ON_WM_COMPAREITEM_REFLECT

–. ■ 4.0

Description This macro allows a control to handle the WM_COMPAREITEM message reflected back from the control's parent. The WM_COMPAREITEM message is sent by an owner-draw sorted combo box or list box when it needs to know where to place a particular item in the sort order. You can use this message map macro to handle the message at the control itself. The function which will handle the message should have the following form (including the name): afx_msg int CompareItem(LPCOMPAREITEMSTRUCT);. For more information about this function, see CWnd::OnCompareItem.

Syntax ON_WM_COMPAREITEM_REFLECT( )

Parameters None.

See Also CWnd::OnCompareItem

Example See ON_WM_CTLCOLOR_REFLECT for a related example.

ON_WM_CTLCOLOR_REFLECT

–. ■ 4.0

Description This macro allows a control to handle the WM_CTLCOLOR message reflected back from the control's parent. The WM_CTLCOLOR message is sent by a control to its parent to determine what brush should be used to paint the background of the control. You can use this message map macro to handle the message at the control itself. The function which will handle the message should have the following form (including the name): afx_msg HBRUSH CtlColor(CDC *, UINT);

Syntax ON_WM_CTLCOLOR_REFLECT( )

Parameters None.

Example

```
// handler declaration
afx_msg HBRUSH CtlColor(CDC *pDc, UINT nCtlColor);

// handler message map entry
ON_WM_CTLCOLOR_REFLECT()

// handler function definition
void CMyControl::CtlColor(CDC *pDc, UINT nCtlColor)
{
```

```
        // I want the control to be red
        return CreateSolidBrush(RGB(255,0,0));
    }
```

ON_WM_DELETEITEM_REFLECT

–. ■ 4.0

Description This macro allows a control to handle the WM_DELETEITEM message reflected back from the control's parent. The WM_DELETEITEM message is sent by an owner-draw combo box or list box when the control or one of the items in it is deleted.You can use this message map macro to handle the message at the control itself. The function which will handle the message should have the following form (including the name): afx_msg void DeleteItem(LPDELETEITEMSTRUCT);. For more information about this function, see CWnd::OnDeleteItem.

Syntax ON_WM_DELETEITEM_REFLECT( )

Parameters None.

See Also CWnd::OnDeleteItem

Example See ON_WM_CTLCOLOR_REFLECT for a related example.

ON_WM_DRAWITEM_REFLECT

–. ■ 4.0

Description This macro allows a control to handle the WM_DRAWITEM message reflected back from the control's parent. The WM_DRAWITEM message is sent by an owner-draw button, combo box, list box, or menu when a part of the control needs to be drawn. You can use this message map macro to handle the message at the control itself. The function which will handle the message should have the following form (including the name): afx_msg void DrawItem(LPDRAWITEMSTRUCT);. For more information about this function, see CWnd::OnDrawItem.

Syntax ON_WM_DRAWITEM_REFLECT( )

Parameters None.

See Also CWnd::OnDrawItem

Example See ON_WM_CTLCOLOR_REFLECT for a related example.

ON_WM_HSCROLL_REFLECT

–. ■ 4.0

Description This macro allows a control to handle the WM_HSCROLL message reflected back from the control's parent.You can use this message map macro to handle the message at the control itself. The function which will handle the message should have the following form (including the name): afx_msg void HScroll(UINT, UINT);. For more information about this function, see CWnd::OnHScroll.

Syntax	ON_WM_HSCROLL_REFLECT( )
Parameters	None.
See Also	CWnd::OnHScroll
Example	See ON_WM_CTLCOLOR_REFLECT for a related example.

ON_WM_MEASUREITEM_REFLECT

–. ■ 4.0

Description This macro allows a control to handle the WM_MEASUREITEM message reflected back from the control's parent. The WM_MEASUREITEM message is sent by an owner-draw button, combo box, list box, or menu when the control is created in order to obtain the desired dimensions of the control. You can use this message map macro to handle the message at the control itself. The function which will handle the message should have the following form (including the name): afx_msg void MeasureItem(LPMEASUREITEMSTRUCT);. For more information about this function, see CWnd::OnMeasureItem.

Syntax	ON_WM_MEASUREITEM_REFLECT( )
Parameters	None.
See Also	CWnd::OnMeasureItem
Example	See ON_WM_CTLCOLOR_REFLECT for a related example.

ON_WM_PARENTNOTIFY_REFLECT

–. ■ 4.0

Description This macro allows a control to handle the WM_PARENTNOTIFY message reflected back from the control's parent. The WM_PARENTNOTIFY message is sent by a child control to notify its parent of one of several events.You can use this message map macro to handle the message at the control itself. The function which will handle the message should have the following form (including the name): afx_msg void ParentNotify(UINT, LPARAM);. For more information about this function, see CWnd::OnParentNotify.

Syntax	ON_WM_PARENTNOTIFY_REFLECT( )
Parameters	None.
See Also	CWnd::OnParentNotify
Example	See ON_WM_CTLCOLOR_REFLECT for a related example.

ON_WM_VKEYTOITEM_REFLECT

–. ■ 4.0

Description This macro allows a control to handle the WM_VKEYTOITEM message reflected back from the control's parent. The WM_VKEYTOITEM message is sent by an owner-draw combo box or list box to determine how it should respond to a virtual key stroke.You can use this message map macro to handle the message at the control itself. The function that will handle the message should have the following form (including the name): afx_msg int VKeyToItem(UINT, UINT);. For more information about this function, see CWnd::OnVKeyToItem.

Syntax ON_WM_VKEYTOITEM_REFLECT( )

Parameters None.

See Also CWnd::OnVKeyToItem

Example See ON_WM_CTLCOLOR_REFLECT for a related example.

ON_WM_VSCROLL_REFLECT

–. ■ 4.0

Description This macro allows a control to handle the WM_VSCROLL message reflected back from the control's parent. You can use this message map macro to handle the message at the control itself. The function that will handle the message should have the following form (including the name): afx_msg void VScroll(UINT, UINT);. For more information about this function, see CWnd::OnVScroll.

Syntax ON_WM_VSCROLL_REFLECT( )

Parameters None.

See Also CWnd::OnVScroll

Example See ON_WM_CTLCOLOR_REFLECT for a related example.

ON_XXXX

■ 2.0 ■ 3.0

Description This macro is usually inserted in a message map by ClassWizard. It indicates which function will handle one of the standard control notification messages. For example, the ON_BN_CLICKED macro is used to map a function to the BN_CLICKED notification from a button control. All message map functions mapped with this macro have a signature as follows: afx_msg void memberFxn( ).

Syntax ON_XXXX(*id*, *memberFxn*)

Parameters

id The control's resource ID.

memberFxn The name of the message-handler function to which the control notification is mapped.

Example

```
// handler declaration
afx_msg void OnButtonPressed();

// handler message map entry
ON_BN_CLICKED(IDC_MYBUTTON,OnButtonPressed)
```

continued on next page

continued from previous page

```
// handler function definition
void CRangeDlg::OnButtonPressed
{
     // button was pressed
}
```

User Interface Objects

Command messages are generated by what MFC calls "user interface objects." A user interface object can be a menu item, accelerator key, toolbar button, etc. Each user interface object which can generate a command is assigned a command ID. This ID is really just the resource ID of the user interface object. The IDs for objects that you created should be in the range of 0x8000 to 0xDFFF. MFC defines its command IDs in the range 0xE000 to 0xEFFF.

Standard Command Implementation

MFC defines many standard command messages in the file afxres.h, some of which are shown in Table 4-2. The framework generally names the IDs after their functionality in the form :

ID_Menu-Name_Menu-Item

Microsoft suggests developers do the same for application-specific command IDs except that for menu items the command ID should begin with IDM_. As mentioned above, the values for the pre-defined commands are in the range of 0xE000 to 0xEFFF.

Table 4-2 Some standard command IDs supported by MFC

Command ID	Description
ID_FILE_NEW	Command generated by the File I New menu item.
ID_FILE_OPEN	Command generated by the File I Open menu item.
ID_FILE_CLOSE	Command generated by the File I Close menu item.
ID_FILE_SAVE	Command generated by the File I Save menu item.
ID_FILE_SAVE_AS	Command generated by the File I Save As menu item.
ID_APP_EXIT	Command generated by the File I Exit menu item.
ID_EDIT_CLEAR	Command generated by the Edit I Clear menu item.
ID_EDIT_COPY	Command generated by the Edit I Copy menu item.
ID_EDIT_CUT	Command generated by the Edit I Cut menu item.
ID_WINDOW_CASCADE	Command generated by the Window I Cascade menu item.
ID_APP_ABOUT	Command generated by the Help I About menu item.
ID_HELP_INDEX	Command generated by the Help I Index menu item.

The Framework provides a complete implementation for some of the pre-defined command IDs, but leaves the implementation for others to the developer. You can also override the default implementations provided by MFC. Technical Notes 20 and 22, which are included with Microsoft Visual C++ beginning with version 1.0, provide more information on the standard command IDs, naming conventions, and their level of implementation in MFC.

User Interface Update

MFC provides a mechanism for updating the state of an application's user interface objects depending on whether or not the command represented by that user interface object is currently available. MFC accomplishes this by routing a special message called ON_UPDATE_COMMAND_UI. This message is routed through the same command target chain that is used for actual command messages. The message map macro ON_UPDATE_COMMAND_UI is used to indicate that a particular command target will handle the update procedure for a particular user interface object. A typical user interface update function declaration is shown below:

```
afx_msg void OnUpdateEditCut(CCmdUI* pCmdUI);
```

The CCmdUI object is passed to all user interface update functions and provides several functions that you can use to set the state of whatever user interface object it represents. The example shown above is used to update the state of the Cut menu item on the Edit menu. Therefore, the CCmdUI object passed to the function represents the Cut menu item and any CCmdUI functions called by the update function will affect the state of that menu item. By default, if MFC cannot find a user interface update function for a particular command, it will enable or disable the user interface object depending on the existence of a function which would handle the command. In other words, MFC searches the current command target chain looking for the function that would handle the command. If one exists, it assumes the command is currently available and enables the user interface object; otherwise, it disables it. By the way, you can disable this feature by setting the m_bAutoMenuEnable member of your main frame window to FALSE in the constructor for the frame.

MFC initiates the update of various user interface objects at different times. For menu items, it calls for their update right before the menu which contains them will be shown. This is accomplished by the CFrameWnd default message handler for the WM_INITMENUPOPUP message. This handler performs ON_UPDATE_COMMAND_UI processing for each item on the popup menu as well as for the popup menu itself. For submenus, which have no ID, MFC uses the ID of the first item in the submenu and sets the m_pSubMenu member variable of the CCmdUI object to point to the submenu. This means that one update handler handles the submenu as well as the first item on the submenu—deciding what to do by inspecting the value of m_pSubMenu. For non-menu items such as toolbar buttons, MFC initiates the update process from within the application's idle loop (when nothing else is going on). If you have mapped dialog controls in a modal dialog to commands, you must call for their update manually; usually in response to an event you know may have changed the state of one or more controls on your dialog. You do this by calling the UpdateDialogControls CWnd member function.

The CCmdTarget Class

CCmdTarget forms the base class for the MFC Library message-map architecture, as described above. The message map entries route commands and messages to the appropriate member functions. The CCmdTarget class is derived from the CObject class. It serves as a parent class for the CWnd, CDocument, CDocTemplate, and CWinApp classes. The reference descriptions for the class members follow.

CCmdTarget ■ 2.0 ■ 3.0

Description	The constructor for the CCmdTarget class. The constructor does nothing of any real interest.
Syntax	public, CCmdTarget();
Parameters	None.
Returns	Nothing is returned.
See Also	~CCmdTarget

~CCmdTarget ■ 2.0 ■ 3.0

Description	The destructor for the CCmdTarget class. The destructor does nothing of any real interest.
Syntax	public, ~CCmdTarget( );
Parameters	None.
Returns	Nothing is returned.
See Also	CCmdTarget

AssertValid ■ 2.0 ■ 3.0 ■ DO

Description	AssertValid is a diagnostic function used to test the validity of a CCmdTarget object. The CCmdTarget version of this function does nothing but call the CObject version. See Chapter 2, *The MFC Framework*, for a description of CObject.
Syntax	public, virtual void AssertValid() const;
Parameters	None.
Returns	Nothing is returned.
See Also	CObject::AssertValid

Example

```
void SomeFunc(CCmdTarget *pTarget)
{
     // make sure target is valid before using
     pTarget->AssertValid();
     ...
```

BeginWaitCursor ■ 2.0 ■ 3.0

Description Use this function to display the cursor as an hourglass when a command or operation is expected to take a noticeable amount of time.

Syntax public, void BeginWaitCursor( );

Parameters None.

Returns Nothing is returned.

See Also CCmdTarget::EndWaitCursor, CCmdTarget::RestoreWaitCursor, CWinApp::DoWaitCursor

Example

```
      // header file

#ifndef __CWAIT_H
#define __CWAIT_H

class CWaitClass : public CCmdTarget
{
public:
      CWaitClass();
      ~CWaitClass();
      void Restore();
};

#endif

// implementation file

// this class aids in setting and removing a wait cursor without
// having to worry about remembering to set or reset the cursor
// manually - it is done in the constructor and destructor for
// the class
CWaitClass::CWaitClass()
{
      BeginWaitCursor();
}

CWaitClass::~CWaitClass()
{
      EndWaitCursor();
}

void CWaitClass::Restore()
{
      RestoreWaitCursor();
}
```

Dump ■ 2.0 ■ 3.0 ■ DO

Description Dump is a diagnostic function that outputs the current state of a CCmdTarget object to the specified dump context.

Syntax public, virtual void Dump(CDumpContext& *dc*) const;

Parameters

dc A reference to the dump context to which the status information should be sent. Usually this will be the MFC default debug dump context *afxDump*. *afxDump* sends its output to the debugger and only exists in the debug build of MFC.

Returns Nothing is returned.

See Also CObject::Dump, CDumpContext, afxDump

EndWaitCursor ■ 2.0 ■ 3.0

Description This function is the reverse of the BeginWaitCursor function and should be called after that member function to return from the hourglass cursor to the previous cursor.

Syntax public, void EndWaitCursor( );

Parameters None.

Returns Nothing is returned.

See Also CCmdTarget::BeginWaitCursor, CCmdTarget::RestoreWaitCursor, CWinApp::DoWaitCursor

Example See CCmdTarget::BeginWaitCursor

GetRoutingView ■ 2.0 ■ 3.0 ■ UD

Description GetRoutingView returns the CView object through which the current command was routed. The value returned could be NULL and is only valid while handling a command message within a CDocument-derived class or a CDocTemplate-derived class. This is because the OnCmdMsg function in the CView object sets the value returned by this function before routing the command message to its document.

Syntax protected, CView *GetRoutingView();

Parameters None.

Returns A pointer to the view (CView object) that routed the command.

See Also CView::OnCmdMsg

OnCmdMsg

■ 2.0 ■ 3.0

Description

The framework calls this function to route and dispatch command messages and handle the update of command user-interface objects. OnCmdMsg is the main implementation routine for the MFC framework command architecture.

Syntax

public, virtual BOOL OnCmdMsg(UINT *nID*, int *nCode*, void* *pExtra*, AFX_CMDHANDLERINFO* *pHandlerInfo*);

Parameters

nID Contains the command ID.

nCode Identifies the command notification code.

pExtra Used according to the value of nCode.

pHandlerInfo If not NULL, OnCmdMsg fills in the pHandlerInfo structure with the pTarget and pmf members of the AFX_CMDHANDLERINFO structure instead of dispatching the command. Typically, this parameter should be NULL. MFC passes a non-NULL value to determine if a command would be handled without actually executing the command. This, in turn, is used to implement the default user-interface updating features of MFC. The AFX_CMDHANDLERINFO structure is defined in afxpriv.h.

Returns

Non-zero if the message is handled; otherwise 0.

See Also

Technical Note 21 and the MSDN article INF: Dynamic Processing of WM_COMMAND Messages , PSS ID Number: Q97693.

Example

The following example shows how to override the default OnCmdMsg for a document object. You will rarely want to do this, but in some cases, as is done in the example below, you may want to directly handle some command messages. If you do override this function, make sure you call the base class implementation if you do not directly handle the command.

```
// Override of the standard OnCmdMsg function used by MFC to route command
// messages. This allows us to filter out any messages we don't want MFC to
// see and process them ourselves
BOOL CMsgDlg::OnCmdMsg(UINT nID, int nCode, void* pExtra,
AFX_CMDHANDLERINFO* pHandlerInfo)
{
      // if pHandlerInfo is NULL, then handle the message
      if (pHandlerInfo == NULL)
      {
            // only handle our special button IDC_ONCMDMSG
            if (nID == IDC_ONCMDMSG)
            {
                  // actual command (button pushed)
                  if (nCode == CN_COMMAND)
                  {
                        DoCmdButtonPushed();
                  }
                  //command ui update request(pExtra is actually CCmdUI)
                  else if (nCode == CN_UPDATE_COMMAND_UI)
                  {
```

continued on next page

continued from previous page

```
                    DoCmdButtonUIUpdate((CCmdUI *)pExtra);
                }
                return TRUE;
            }
        }

        return CDialog::OnCmdMsg(nID, nCode, pExtra, pHandlerInfo);
}
```

RestoreWaitCursor ■ 2.0 ■ 3.0

Description This function restores the appropriate hourglass cursor after the system cursor has changed. This function is often called to restore the wait cursor after a message box has been displayed while the wait cursor was displayed.

Scope public

Syntax void RestoreWaitCursor( );

Parameters None.

Returns Nothing is returned.

See Also CCmdTarget::BeginWaitCursor, CCmdTarget::EndWaitCursor, CWinApp::DoWaitCursor

Example

```
BeginWaitCursor();

while (!done)
{
        // do some lengthy stuff here
        done = some_leng_calc();

        if (  (generic_app *)AfxGetApp()->TimedOut )
        {
                result = AfxMessageBox( "Continue?", MB_YESNO );

                if ( result == IDYES )
                        RestoreWaitCursor();
                else
                        done = TRUE;
        }

} // end while

EndWaitCursor();
```

The CCmdUI Class

The CCmdUI class is used to represent various user-interface objects such as menu items and toolbar buttons for the purpose of updating the state of those items. CCmdUI is not derived from any other class.

CCmdUI

■ 2.0 ■ 3.0

Description The constructor for the CCmdUI class. CCmdUI does nothing of real interest.

Syntax public, CCmdUI();

Parameters None.

Returns Nothing is returned.

ContinueRouting

■ 2.0 ■ 3.0

Description Call this function from within an update handler function if you want MFC to continue routing the command even though you have handled it. Normally, once it finds a handler function, MFC will assume that the update has been taken care of.

Syntax public, void ContinueRouting();

Parameters None.

Returns Nothing is returned.

DoUpdate

■ 2.0 ■ 3.0 ■ UD

Description DoUpdate is called by the framework to perform the actual update of the user-interface object. First, it attempts to allow the application to handle the update by routing the update message through the current command target chain. If an applicable ON_UPDATE_COMMAND_UI message map is found, it is called. If the update is not handled by the application and bDisableIfNoHndler is TRUE, MFC searches the current command target chain for the existence of a message map entry that would handle the command generated from the user-interface object (if one was generated). If a handler is found, the user-interface object is enabled; otherwise it is disabled.

Syntax public, void DoUpdate(CCmdTarget* *pTarget*, BOOL *bDisableIfNoHndler*);

Parameters

pTarget A pointer to the command target through which the update command should be routed.

bDisableIfNoHndler TRUE if MFC should perform its default enable/disable behavior if the application does not handle the update.

Returns Nothing is returned.

Enable

■ 2.0 ■ 3.0

Description This function enables or disables the user-interface object. The default implementation will enable or disable a menu item or control; otherwise it is ignored.

Syntax public, virtual void Enable(BOOL *bOn* = TRUE);

Parameters

bOn TRUE will enable the user-interface object. FALSE will disable it.

Returns Nothing is returned.

Example

```
void CMyWnd:: OnUpdateMyMenuItem(CCmdUI* pCmdUI)
{
     // enable menu item at all times
     pCmdUI->Enable(TRUE);
}
```

SetCheck

■ 2.0 ■ 3.0

Description This function will check or uncheck a user-interface object. The default implementation will check or uncheck a menu item or a button control; otherwise it is ignored.

Syntax public, virtual void SetCheck(int *nCheck* = 1);

Parameters

nCheck 0 for unchecked, 1 for checked, or 2 for indeterminate.

Returns Nothing is returned.

See Also CCmdUI::SetRadio

Example

```
void CMyWnd:: OnUpdateMyMenuItem(CCmdUI* pCmdUI)
{
     static int nCheck = 1;

     // toggle check mark each time menu opened
     pCmdUI->SetCheck(nCheck);
     nCheck = !nCheck;
}
```

SetRadio

■ 2.0 ■ 3.0

Description For menu items, this function will place or remove a "dot" from the menu item (instead of a check). For everything else, it simply calls SetCheck.

Syntax public, virtual void SetRadio(BOOL *bOn* = TRUE);

Parameters

bOn 0 for unchecked, 1 for checked.

Returns Nothing is returned.

See Also CCmdUI::SetCheck

Example

```
void CMyWnd:: OnUpdateMyMenuItem(CCmdUI* pCmdUI)
{
     static BOOL bRadio = FALSE;

     // toggle button mark each time menu opened
     pCmdUI->SetRadio(bRadio);
     bRadio = !bRadio;
}
```

SetText

■ 2.0 ■ 3.0

Description For menu items, this function will change the menu item text to the specified string. In all other cases, it sets the window text of the user-interface object to the specified string.

Syntax public, virtual void SetText(LPCTSTR *lpszText*);

Parameters

lpszText A pointer to a NULL-terminated character buffer.

Returns Nothing is returned.

Example

```
void CMyWnd:: OnUpdateMyMenuItem(CCmdUI* pCmdUI)
{
      static BOOL bText = FALSE;

      // change text back and forth
      if (bText)
            pCmdUI->SetText("Turn Item On");
      else
            pCmdUI->SetText("Turn Item Off");
      bText = ! bText;
}
```

5

THE MFC WINDOW

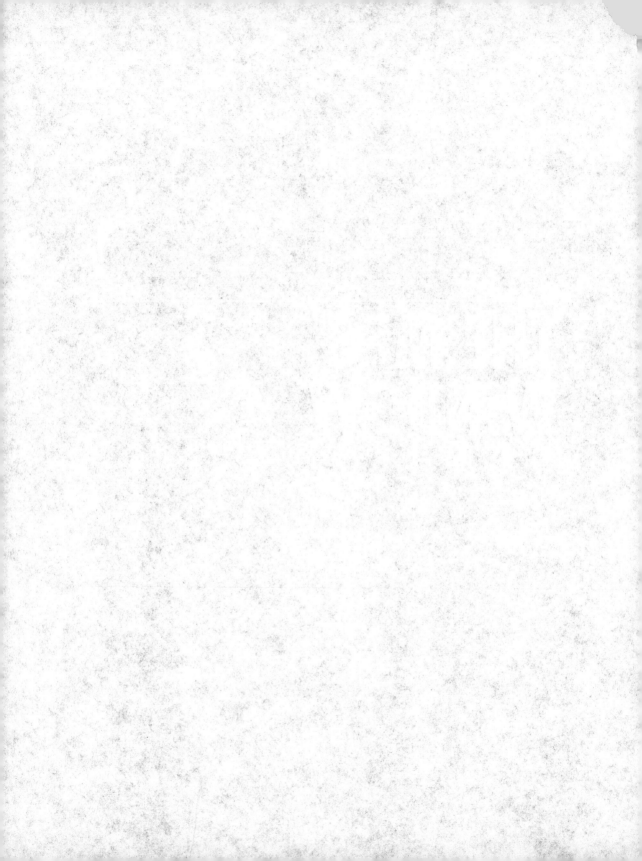

5

THE MFC WINDOW

This chapter is devoted solely to the CWnd class—the MFC class that encapsulates the Windows window. Obviously, it is the CWnd class that provides the foundation for any MFC-based Windows application. Many of the member functions of the CWnd class are simple wrappers around Windows SDK functions while others provide a significant value-add. One interesting thing you will note about the member functions of the CWnd class is that many of them include the word "Window" in them—something that seems, at first, to be redundant. If the function is a CWnd member function then of course it operates on a "window." The reason that the designers of MFC did this was to be consistent with the Windows SDK. To set the text of a window using the SDK, you call SetWindowText. If MFC were developed in a vacuum, this function would probably have been called SetText, instead of SetWindowText, since it would always be called in the context of a CWnd object. But for the sake of consistency—and so that SDK developers didn't have to relearn all the function names—MFC uses the same function names as the SDK. This, of course, only applies to those CWnd member functions which wrap an SDK function.

Much of the message routing and mapping scheme discussed in Chapter 3, *Application Classes,* is implemented by members of the CWnd class (which is derived from the CCmdTarget class which provides the rest of the implementation). The CWnd class also provides default handler functions for a large number of Windows messages. In most cases, if you provide a handler for a particular message, you will want to call the base CWnd implementation from your override. This is not always the case, however. If you are using MSVC, the ClassWizard will provide guidance on the subject (as will other compiler's "wizards"). If you write the functions in a completely manual fashion, you will have to figure it out for yourself.

A couple of final notes about the CWnd class. You will notice that the CWnd class contains many functions that are normally associated only with dialogs (see Chapter 8, *Dialog Boxes*) and, in fact, many of them have the word "dialog" in their name. This fact is actually a very revealing one. The reason these functions are here—instead of in the CDialog object—is that they are not restricted to dialogs. For example, the CWnd::GetDlgItem (in the SDK, simply GetDlgItem), retrieves a pointer to a CWnd object which has the specified ID and is a child window of the CWnd object for which you call GetDlgItem. Normally, this child window is a control in a dialog. However, all child windows have "IDs" (it is the next-to-last parameter of the Create function used to create a window), and you can always retrieve one using the GetDlgItem function—dialog or not. Finally, you will also notice that MFC provides default message handler functions for many Windows messages. Most of these functions do nothing but call the default window procedure. They exist simply because if you override them and call the base implementation from your derived implementation the default window procedure gets called. An interesting fact is that if you call these base class implementations from your implementation, the parameters you pass will not be used—MFC uses the original values sent by Windows in the window message.

The declarations of all of the functions contained in this chapter can be found in the MFC header file *afxwin.h*. Example uses of the CWnd class and its member functions can be found in all of the sample programs on the CD-ROM included with this book.

The CWnd Class

In addition to all of the normal CWnd member functions, the CWnd class contains a long list of default handler functions for many Windows messages. As discussed at the beginning of the chapter, most of these functions do nothing but call the default window procedure. Table 5-1, below, lists these message handler functions along with the messages they respond to. For a complete description of the parameters associated with each message, see the Windows SDK documentation.

Table 5-1 Windows message handler functions

Message	Handler Function
WM_ACTIVATE	void OnActivate(UINT nState, CWnd* pWndOther, BOOL bMinimized);
WM_ACTIVATEAPP	void OnActivateApp(BOOL bActive, HTASK hTask);
WM_ACTIVATETOPLEVEL	LRESULT OnActivateTopLevel(WPARAM, LPARAM);
WM_ASKCBFORMATNAME	void OnAskCbFormatName(UINT nMaxCount, LPTSTR lpszString);
WM_CANCELMODE	void OnCancelMode();
WM_CAPTURECHANGED	void OnCaptureChanged(CWnd* pWnd);
WM_CHANGECBCHAIN	void OnChangeCbChain(HWND hWndRemove, HWND hWndAfter);
WM_CHAR	void OnChar(UINT nChar, UINT nRepCnt, UINT nFlags);
WM_CHARTOITEM	int OnCharToItem(UINT nChar, CListBox* pListBox, UINT nIndex);
WM_CHILDACTIVATE	void OnChildActivate();
WM_CLOSE	void OnClose();
WM_COMPACTING	void OnCompacting(UINT nCpuTime);
WM_COMPAREITEM	int OnCompareItem(int nIDCtl, LPCOMPAREITEMSTRUCT lpCompareItemStruct);
WM_CONTEXTMENU	void OnContextMenu(CWnd* pWnd, CPoint pos);
WM_CREATE	int OnCreate(LPCREATESTRUCT lpCreateStruct);

Message	Handler Function
WM_DEADCHAR	void OnDeadChar(UINT nChar, UINT nRepCnt, UINT nFlags);
WM_DELETEITEM	void OnDeleteItem(int nIDCtl, LPDELETEITEMSTRUCT lpDeleteItemStruct);
WM_DESTROY	void OnDestroy();
WM_DESTROYCLIPBOARD	void OnDestroyClipboard();
WM_DEVICECHANGE	BOOL OnDeviceChange(UINT nEventType, DWORD dwData);
WM_DEVMODECHANGE	void OnDevModeChange(LPTSTR lpDeviceName);
WM_DISPLAYCHANGE	LRESULT OnDisplayChange(WPARAM, LPARAM);
WM_DRAGLIST	LRESULT OnDragList(WPARAM, LPARAM);
WM_DRAWCLIPBOARD	void OnDrawClipboard();
WM_DRAWITEM	void OnDrawItem(int nIDCtl, LPDRAWITEMSTRUCT lpDrawItemStruct);
WM_DROPFILES	void OnDropFiles(HDROP hDropInfo);
WM_ENABLE	void OnEnable(BOOL bEnable);
WM_ENDSESSION	void OnEndSession(BOOL bEnding);
WM_ENTERIDLE	void OnEnterIdle(UINT nWhy, CWnd* pWho);
WM_ENTERMENULOOP	void OnEnterMenuLoop(BOOL bIsTrackPopupMenu);
WM_EXITMENULOOP	void OnExitMenuLoop(BOOL bIsTrackPopupMenu);
WM_ERASEBKGND	BOOL OnEraseBkgnd(CDC* pDC);
WM_FONTCHANGE	void OnFontChange();
WM_GETDLGCODE	UINT OnGetDlgCode();
WM_GETMINMAXINFO	void OnGetMinMaxInfo(MINMAXINFO* lpMMI);
WM_COMMAND	void OnHelp(); (ID_HELP)
WM_COMMAND	void OnHelpFinder(); (ID_HELP_FINDER)
WM_COMMAND	void OnHelpIndex(); (ID_HELP_INDEX)
WM_COMMAND	BOOL OnHelpInfo(HELPINFO* lpHelpInfo); (ID_HELP_INFO)
WM_HSCROLL	void OnHScroll(UINT nSBCode, UINT nPos, CScrollBar* pScrollBar);
WM_HSCROLLCLIPBOARD	void OnHScrollClipboard(CWnd* pClipAppWnd, UINT nSBCode, UINT nPos);
WM_ICONERASEBKGND	void OnIconEraseBkgnd(CDC* pDC);
WM_INITMENU	void OnInitMenu(CMenu* pMenu);
WM_INITMENUPOPUP	void OnInitMenuPopup(CMenu* pPopupMenu, UINT nIndex, BOOL bSysMenu);
WM_KEYDOWN	void OnKeyDown(UINT nChar, UINT nRepCnt, UINT nFlags);
WM_KEYUP	void OnKeyUp(UINT nChar, UINT nRepCnt, UINT nFlags);
WM_KILLFOCUS	void OnKillFocus(CWnd* pNewWnd);
WM_LBUTTONDBLCLK	void OnLButtonDblClk(UINT nFlags, CPoint point);
WM_LBUTTONDOWN	void OnLButtonDown(UINT nFlags, CPoint point);
WM_LBUTTONUP	void OnLButtonUp(UINT nFlags, CPoint point);
WM_MACINTOSH	LRESULT OnMacintosh(WPARAM wParam, LPARAM lParam);
WM_MBUTTONDBLCLK	void OnMButtonDblClk(UINT nFlags, CPoint point);
WM_MBUTTONDOWN	void OnMButtonDown(UINT nFlags, CPoint point);
WM_MBUTTONUP	void OnMButtonUp(UINT nFlags, CPoint point);

continued on next page

continued from previous page

Message	Handler Function
WM_MDIACTIVATE	void OnMDIActivate(BOOL bActivate, CWnd* pActivateWnd, CWnd* pDeactivateWnd);
WM_MEASUREITEM	void OnMeasureItem(int nIDCtl, LPMEASUREITEMSTRUCT lpMeasureItemStruct);
WM_MENUCHAR	LRESULT OnMenuChar(UINT nChar, UINT nFlags, CMenu* pMenu);
WM_MENUSELECT	void OnMenuSelect(UINT nItemID, UINT nFlags, HMENU hSysMenu);
WM_MOUSEACTIVATE	int OnMouseActivate(CWnd* pDesktopWnd, UINT nHitTest, UINT message);
WM_MOUSEMOVE	void OnMouseMove(UINT nFlags, CPoint point);
WM_MOVE	void OnMove(int x, int y);
WM_MOVING	void OnMoving(UINT nSide, LPRECT lpRect);
WM_NCACTIVATE	BOOL OnNcActivate(BOOL bActive);
WM_NCCALCSIZE	void OnNcCalcSize(BOOL bCalcValidRects, NCCALCSIZE_PARAMS* lpncsp);
WM_NCCREATE	BOOL OnNcCreate(LPCREATESTRUCT lpCreateStruct);
WM_NCDESTROY	void OnNcDestroy();
WM_NCHITTEST	UINT OnNcHitTest(CPoint point);
WM_NCLBUTTONDBLCLK	void OnNcLButtonDblClk(UINT nHitTest, CPoint point);
WM_NCLBUTTONDOWN	void OnNcLButtonDown(UINT nHitTest, CPoint point);
WM_NCLBUTTONUP	void OnNcLButtonUp(UINT nHitTest, CPoint point);
WM_NCMBUTTONDBLCLK	void OnNcMButtonDblClk(UINT nHitTest, CPoint point);
WM_NCMBUTTONDOWN	void OnNcMButtonDown(UINT nHitTest, CPoint point);
WM_NCMBUTTONUP	void OnNcMButtonUp(UINT nHitTest, CPoint point);
WM_NCMOUSEMOVE	void OnNcMouseMove(UINT nHitTest, CPoint point);
WM_NCPAINT	void OnNcPaint();
WM_NCRBUTTONDBLCLK	void OnNcRButtonDblClk(UINT nHitTest, CPoint point);
WM_NCRBUTTONDOWN	void OnNcRButtonDown(UINT nHitTest, CPoint point);
WM_NCRBUTTONUP	void OnNcRButtonUp(UINT nHitTest, CPoint point);
WM_NTCTLCOLOR	LRESULT OnNTCtlColor(WPARAM wParam, LPARAM lParam);
WM_PAINT	void OnPaint();
WM_PAINTCLIPBOARD	void OnPaintClipboard(CWnd* pClipAppWnd, HGLOBAL hPaintStruct);
WM_PALETTECHANGED	void OnPaletteChanged(CWnd* pFocusWnd);
WM_PALETTEISCHANGING	void OnPaletteIsChanging(CWnd* pRealizeWnd);
WM_PARENTNOTIFY	void OnParentNotify(UINT message, LPARAM lParam);
WM_QUERY3DCONTROLS	LRESULT OnQuery3dControls(WPARAM, LPARAM);
WM_QUERYDRAGICON	HCURSOR OnQueryDragIcon();
WM_QUERYENDSESSION	BOOL OnQueryEndSession();
WM_QUERYNEWPALETTE	BOOL OnQueryNewPalette();
WM_QUERYOPEN	BOOL OnQueryOpen();
WM_RBUTTONDBLCLK	void OnRButtonDblClk(UINT nFlags, CPoint point);
WM_RBUTTONDOWN	void OnRButtonDown(UINT nFlags, CPoint point);
WM_RBUTTONUP	void OnRButtonUp(UINT nFlags, CPoint point);
WM_RENDERALLFORMATS	void OnRenderAllFormats();

Message	Handler Function
WM_RENDERFORMAT	void OnRenderFormat(UINT nFormat);
WM_SETCURSOR	BOOL OnSetCursor(CWnd* pWnd, UINT nHitTest, UINT message);
WM_SETFOCUS	void OnSetFocus(CWnd* pOldWnd);
WM_SHOWWINDOW	void OnShowWindow(BOOL bShow, UINT nStatus);
WM_SIZE	void OnSize(UINT nType, int cx, int cy);
WM_SIZECLIPBOARD	void OnSizeClipboard(CWnd* pClipAppWnd, HGLOBAL hRect);
WM_SIZING	void OnSizing(UINT nSide, LPRECT lpRect);
WM_SPOOLERSTATUS	void OnSpoolerStatus(UINT nStatus, UINT nJobs);
WM_STYLECHANGED	void OnStyleChanged(int nStyleType, LPSTYLESTRUCT lpStyleStruct);
WM_STYLECHANGING	void OnStyleChanging(int nStyleType, LPSTYLESTRUCT lpStyleStruct);
WM_SYSCHAR	void OnSysChar(UINT nChar, UINT nRepCnt, UINT nFlags);
WM_SYSCOLORCHANGE	void OnSysColorChange();
WM_SYSCOMMAND	void OnSysCommand(UINT nID, LPARAM lParam);
WM_SYSDEADCHAR	void OnSysDeadChar(UINT nChar, UINT nRepCnt, UINT nFlags);
WM_SYSKEYDOWN	void OnSysKeyDown(UINT nChar, UINT nRepCnt, UINT nFlags);
WM_SYSKEYUP	void OnSysKeyUp(UINT nChar, UINT nRepCnt, UINT nFlags);
WM_TCARD	void OnTCard(UINT idAction, DWORD dwActionData);
WM_TIMECHANGE	void OnTimeChange();
WM_TIMER	void OnTimer(UINT nIDEvent);
WM_VKEYTOITME	int OnVKeyToItem(UINT nKey, CListBox* pListBox, UINT nIndex);
WM_VSCROLL	void OnVScroll(UINT nSBCode, UINT nPos, CScrollBar* pScrollBar);
WM_VSCROLLCLIPBOARD	void OnVScrollClipboard(CWnd* pClipAppWnd, UINT nSBCode, UINT nPos);
WM_WINDOWPOSCHANGED	void OnWindowPosChanged(WINDOWPOS* lpwndpos);
WM_WINDOWPOSCHANGING	void OnWindowPosChanging(WINDOWPOS* lpwndpos);
WM_WININITCHANGE	void OnWinIniChange(LPCTSTR lpszSection);

CWnd

■ 2.0 ■ 3.0

Description Constructor for the CWnd class. The constructor does absolutely nothing. You must use one of the window creation functions to create the window associated with the window object. The second form of this function is used internally by MFC to create windows objects and immediately associate them with a particular window. You should not use the second form directly.

Syntax public, CWnd(); private, UD, CWnd(HWND hWnd);

Parameters

hWnd The handle of the window to associate with the CWnd object.

Returns Nothing is returned.

See Also ~CWnd, CWnd::Create, CWnd::CreateEx

~CWnd

■ 2.0 ■ 3.0 ■ UD

Description Destructor for the CWnd class. If a window is currently attached to the CWnd object, the window is destroyed by a call to the CWnd::DestroyWindow function. The debug version of the destructor will warn you that destroying the window via the CWnd destructor means that the OnDestroy and OnNcDestroy handler functions in the derived class will not be called as they normally would when DestroyWindow is called.

Syntax public, ~CWnd();

Parameters None.

Returns Nothing is returned.

See Also CWnd::CWnd, CWnd::OnDestroy, CWnd::OnNcDestroy

ActivateTopParent

■ 2.0 ■ 3.0 ■ UD

Description Used internally by MFC to activate the parent of a floating toolbar (instead of the toolbar itself) when the user clicks the toolbar.

Syntax public, void ActivateTopParent();

Parameters None.

Returns Nothing is returned.

See Also CWnd::SetForegroundWindow

ArrangeIconicWindows

■ 2.0 ■ 3.0

Description Arranges all minimized (iconic) child windows of this window. Note that if this window is the desktop window, then all icons on the desktop are arranged. You can retrieve a pointer to the desktop window by calling the CWnd::GetDesktopWindow function. Do not use this function to arrange MDI children within an MDI frame window—use the CMDIFrameWnd::MDIIconArrange function instead.

Syntax public, UINT ArrangeIconicWindows();

Parameters None.

Returns The height, in pixels, of one row of icons if successful; otherwise, zero.

See Also CWnd::GetDesktopWindow, CMDIFrameWnd::MDIIconArrange, ::ArrangeIconicWindows

Example

```
// arrange icons on the desktop
CWnd *pDeskTopWnd = CWnd::GetDeskTopWindow();
pDeskTopWnd->ArrangeIconicWindows();
```

AssertValid

■ 2.0 ■ 3.0 ■ DO

Description Tests the validity of the CWnd object. The CWnd version of AssertValid checks to make sure that the window handle associated with the CWnd object is either NULL or a valid window handle by calling ::IsWindow. If the CWnd is associated with a window handle, then it checks to make sure that the CWnd object is in either the permanent window map or the temporary window map. MFC maintains these two maps in order to track all CWnd objects. A CWnd object that is attached to a window handle should always be in one of these maps. For this reason, if you are doing multi-threaded programming, you must be careful when passing CWnd objects between threads.

Syntax public, void CWnd::AssertValid() const;

Parameters None.

Returns Nothing is returned.

See Also CCmdTarget::AssertValid

Example

```
void SomeFunc(CWnd *pWnd)
{
     // make sure passed window is valid
     pWnd->AssertValid();
```

Attach

■ 2.0 ■ 3.0

Description Attaches a Windows window (HWND) to the CWnd object. Once a window has been attached to the CWnd object, CWnd member function can be used to manipulate the window. Use this function if you want to manipulate a window that was created outside of MFC (without the CWnd::Create or CWnd::CreateEx functions). This may be a window that was created by the system itself or by a third-party software library. Note that attaching a window to a CWnd object does not allow you to automatically receive messages sent to the window. See the CWnd::SubclassWindow function for more information on receiving messages.

Syntax public, BOOL Attach(HWND hWndNew);

Parameters

hWndNew The handle of the window which should be attached to this CWnd object.

Returns Non-zero if successful; otherwise, zero.

See Also CWnd::SubclassWindow, CWnd::Detach

Example

```
void SomeFunc(HWND hWnd)
{
     // attach to window
     CWnd wnd;
     wnd.Attach(hWnd);
```

continued on next page

continued from previous page

```
// use window

// detach from the window
wnd.Detach();
```

BeginModalState

■ 2.0 ■ 4.0

Description Disables the window by calling ::EnableWindow. Child class implementations of this function (see CFrameWnd::BeginModalState) perform more involved operations.

Syntax public, virtual void BeginModalState();

Parameters None.

Returns Nothing is returned.

See Also CWnd::EndModalState, CFrameWnd::BeginModalState

BeginPaint

■ 2.0 ■ 3.0

Description Prepares the window for painting, creates and returns a device context for painting, and fills a PAINTSTRUCT structure with information about the painting. Typically, you would only call this function in response to a WM_PAINT message. If you call this function, make sure you call CWnd::EndPaint when you are done painting. Usually, you will not need to call this function because the MFC CPaintDC class encapsulates window painting. See Chapter 11, *Device Contexts,* for a discussion on the CPaintDC class. If the update region in the window is marked for erasing, BeginPaint sends a WM_ERASEBKGND message to the window. If the area to be painted contains the caret, BeginPaint automatically hides it so that it is not erased by the painting.

Syntax public, CDC *BeginPaint(LPPAINTSTRUCT lpPaint);

Parameters

lpPaint A pointer to a PAINTSTRUCT. For more information about the PAINTSTRUCT structure, see the Windows SDK documentation.

Returns A pointer to a CDC object to be used for painting.

See Also CWnd::EndPaint, CPaintDC, ::BeginPaint

Example

```
void CMyWnd::OnPaint(LPPAINTSTRUCT ps)
{
      CDC *pDc = BeginPaint(&ps);

      // do painting

      EndPaint(&ps);
}
```

BringWindowToTop

■ 2.0 ■ 3.0

Description Brings the window to the top of the stack of overlapping windows. Use this function to ensure that a window is completely visible. This function does not make the style of the window "always on top." To make a window always on top, use the CWnd::SetWindowPos function. If the window is a popup, top level, or MDI child window, this function will also activate the window.

Syntax public, void BringWindowToTop();

Parameters None.

Returns Nothing is returned.

See Also ::BringWindowToTop

Example

```
// bring window to top of all other windows
pWnd->BringWindowToTop();
```

CalcWindowRect

■ 2.0 ■ 3.0

Description Calculates the rectangle necessary to contain a window with the specified client area. You can use this function to create or size a window that has the desired client rectangle.

Syntax public, virtual void CalcWindowRect(LPRECT lpClientRect, UINT nAdjustType = adjustBorder);

Parameters

lpClientRect On input, a pointer to a RECT structure or a CRect object containing the coordinates of the desired client rectangle. After the function completes, this rectangle is filled with the coordinates of the resulting window rectangle.

nAdjustType adjustBorder if scrollbars should be ignored in the calculation or adjustOutside if scrollbars should be factored in.

Returns Nothing is returned.

See Also ::AdjustWindowRect

Example

```
CRect rc(0,0,100,200);

// want a window with client area 100x200
pWnd->CalcWindowRect(rc);
pWnd->MoveWindow(10,10,rc.right-rc.left,rc.bottom-rc.top,TRUE);
```

CancelToolTips

■ 4.0

Description Removes the currently displayed tooltip window. You can enable tooltips by calling CWnd::EnableToolTips. Tooltips are the little windows that pop up when the user, for example, hesitates on a toolbar button. A tooltip usually provides a brief explanation of what the object beneath the cursor does. See Chapter 10, *Menus and Control Bars,* for further discussion about tooltips.

Syntax public, static void PASCAL CancelToolTips(BOOL bKeys = FALSE);

Parameters

bKeys If FALSE, the tooltip is removed immediately. If TRUE, the tooltip is removed the next time a key is pressed.

Returns Nothing is returned.

See Also CWnd::EnableToolTips, CWnd:: FilterToolTipMessage, CWnd:: OnToolHitTest

Example

```
// don't want tooltips for this window
pWnd->CancelToopTips();
```

CenterWindow ■ 2.0 ■ 3.0

Description Centers the window on its parent, or alternatively, on the specified window. This function is very useful for centering dialogs on their parent window.

Syntax public, void CenterWindow(CWnd *pAltOwner = NULL);

Parameters

pAltOwner The window on which this window should be centered. If NULL and the window is a child window, it is centered on its parent. If NULL and the window is a popup window, the window is centered on its owner. If the popup window does not have an owner, it is centered on the desktop. You can force centering of a window on the desktop by passing the desktop window handle returned from CWnd::GetDesktopWindow for this parameter.

Returns Nothing is returned.

See Also CWnd::GetDesktopWindow

Example

```
void CMyDialog::OnInitDialog()
{
     // center dialog on its parent
     CenterWindow();
     ...
```

ChangeClipboardChain ■ 2.0 ■ 3.0

Description Call this function to remove this CWnd from the Clipboard viewer chain. Windows sends various messages to all windows that are in the Clipboard chain to notify them when, for example, the contents of the Clipboard change. Call the CWnd::SetClipboardViewer function to add a CWnd to the current Clipboard chain.

Syntax public, BOOL ChangeClipboardChain(HWND hWndNext);

Parameters

hWndNext The window handle of the window that follows the CWnd in the Clipboard viewer chain. This handle is supplied by Windows when the CWnd joins the Clipboard viewer chain using the CWnd::SetClipboardViewer function.

Returns Non-zero if successful; otherwise, zero.

See Also CWnd::SetClipboardViewer, ::ChangeClipboardChain

Example See CWnd::SetClipboardViewer

CheckAutoCenter ■ 2.0 ■ 3.0 ■ UD

Description The CWnd-level implementation of this function always returns TRUE. MFC calls this function to determine if a window should automatically be centered on its parent or owner. Classes derived from CWnd may implement this function differently. See CDialog::CheckAutoCenter for an example.

Syntax public, virtual BOOL CheckAutoCenter();

Parameters None.

Returns TRUE if the window should be centered; FALSE otherwise.

See Also CDialog::CheckAutoCenter

CheckDlgButton ■ 2.0 ■ 3.0

Description Check or unchecks a button by sending the button window a BM_SETCHECK message. Also sets the state of tri-state buttons (checked, unchecked, indeterminate).

Syntax public, void CheckDlgButton(int nIDButton, UINT nCheck);

Parameters

nIDButton The resource ID of the button.

nCheck Zero if the button should be unchecked, non-zero if it should be checked, or, for tri-state buttons, two if the state of the button should be indeterminate.

Returns Nothing is returned.

See Also CButton::SetCheck, CWnd::IsDlgButtonChecked, CWnd::CheckRadioButton, ::CheckDlgButton

Example

```
void CMyDialog::OnInitDialog()
{
      // want to initially check a button
      CheckDlgButton(IDC_MYBUTTON, 1);
```

CheckRadioButton ■ 2.0 ■ 3.0

Description Sets the selection in a group of radio buttons to the specified button. This function removes the "check" from each button in the group except for the specified button that it "checks."

Syntax public, void CheckRadioButton(int nIDFirstButton, int nIDLastButton, int nIDCheckButton);

Parameters

nIDFirstButton The resource ID of the first button in the group. Note that the first button in the group must have the resource ID with the smallest numeric value.

nIDLastButton The resource ID of the last button in the group. Note that the last button in the group must have the resource ID with the largest numeric value.

nIDCheckButton The resource ID of the button that should be selected, or checked.

Returns Nothing is returned.

See Also CWnd::GetCheckedRadioButton, CWnd::CheckDlgButton, ::CheckRadioButton

Example

```
void CMyDialog::OnInitDialog()
{
	// want to initially check a button
	CheckRadioButton(IDC_FIRSTBUTTON, IDC_LASTBUTTON, IDC_MYBUTTON);
```

ChildWindowFromPoint ■ 2.0 ■ 3.0

Description Determines which child window, if any, of the CWnd contains the given point. If the given point is not within a child window, but is within the client area of the CWnd, then CWnd is returned. If the given point is outside the client area of the CWnd, then NULL is returned. Although the given point may be within more than one child of the CWnd, only the first child found is returned. The second version of this function is new for Windows 95 and allows filtering of which types of windows qualify for the search. Invisible, disabled, and/or transparent windows may be excluded.

Syntax public, CWnd *ChildWindowFromPoint(POINT pt) const;

public, CWnd *ChildWindowFromPoint(POINT pt, UINT uFlags) const;

Parameters

pt The point, in client coordinates, for which the containing child window should be determined.

uFlags A combination of the following values which describe which types of windows qualify for the search:

CWP_ALL Include all child windows in the search.

CWP_SKIPINVISIBLE Do not include invisible windows in the search.

CWP_SKIPDISABLED Do not include disabled windows in the search.

CWP_SKIPTRANSPARENT Do not include transparent windows in the search.

Returns A pointer to a CWnd identifying the child window which contains the specified point. If the specified point is not within the client area of the CWnd, NULL is returned. If the specified point is within the client area but not within a child of the CWnd, then a pointer to the CWnd itself is returned.

See Also CWnd::WindowFromPoint, ::ChildWindowFromPoint

Example

```
// get the child window at a specific location
CWnd *pChild;
CPoint pt(10,50);
pChild = pWnd->GetWindowFromPoint(pt);
```

ClientToScreen ■ 2.0 ■ 3.0

Description Converts a given point or rectangle from client coordinates to screen coordinates. Client coordinates are relative to the top-left corner of the client area of the CWnd. Screen coordinates are relative to the top-left corner of the display screen.

Syntax public, void ClientToScreen(LPPOINT lpPoint) const;

public, void ClientToScreen(LPRECT lpRect) const;

Parameters

lpPoint A pointer to a POINT structure or CPoint object that contains a point in client coordinates. The contents of this point will be replaced with the calculated screen coordinates.

lpRect A pointer to a RECT structure or a CRect object that contains a rectangle in client coordinates. The contents of this rectangle will be replaced with the calculated screen coordinates.

Returns Nothing is returned.

See Also CWnd::ScreenToClient, ::ClientToScreen

Example

```
void CWnd::OnLButtonDown(UINT nFlags, CPoint pt)
{
      // convert mouse click to screen coordinates
      ClientToScreen(&pt);
```

CloseWindow ■ 4.0 ■ NM

Description Strangely enough, minimizes the window. The window is not destroyed.

Syntax public, void CloseWindow();

Parameters None.

Returns Nothing is returned.

Example

```
// minimize a window
pWnd->CloseWindow();
```

ContinueModal

■ 2.0 ■ 3.0

Description Determines whether the modal state of the window, begun with CWnd::BeginModalState should end. This function simply returns the state of a flag within the CWnd object. Basically, ContinueModal returns TRUE until CWnd::EndModalState is called.

Syntax public, virtual BOOL ContinueModal();

Parameters None.

Returns TRUE if the modal state should continue; FALSE otherwise.

See Also CWnd::BeginModalState, CWnd::EndModalState

Create

■ 2.0 ■ 3.0

Description Creates a window with the given characteristics and style and associates the window with the CWnd object.

Syntax public, virtual BOOL Create(LPCTSTR lpszClassName, LPCTSTR lpszWindowName, DWORD dwStyle, const RECT& rect, CWnd* pParentWnd, UINT nID, CCreateContext* pContext = NULL);

Parameters

lpszClassName A pointer to a NULL-terminated string that contains the name of the window class to use for the window. If NULL, MFC will use a default window class that is good enough in most cases. You can use the AfxRegisterWndClass function to register your own window classes.

lpszWindowName A pointer to a NULL-terminated string that contains the name of the window. The name of the window is what is displayed as its caption.

dwStyle Window styles to be used when creating the window. For a list of valid window styles, see the Windows SDK documentation. Note that the WS_POPUP style cannot be used. To create a popup window, use the CWnd::CreateEx function.

rect A reference to a RECT structure or a CRect object that contains the coordinates of the window. These coordinates should be expressed in the parent window's client coordinates (the parent window is specified by the *pParentWnd* parameter).

pParentWnd A pointer to a CWnd that identifies the parent window of this window. Can be NULL, in which case the parent will be the desktop window.

nID An ID to assign to the window. You can reference the window via its parent using this ID. For example, the CWnd::GetDlgItem function retrieves a pointer to a child window given its ID.

pContext A pointer to a CCreateContext structure that is used to describe the context in which the window is being created. Unless you are replacing parts of MFC's document/view/frame architecture, you will want to set this parameter to NULL (or simply omit it).

Returns Non-zero if the window was created; otherwise, zero.

See Also CWnd::CWnd, CWnd::CreateEx, AfxRegisterWndClass

Example

```
CWnd wnd;

// create a window
CRect rect(1,1,500,300);
wnd. Create( NULL, "Test Window", WS_CHILD|WS_VISIBLE, rect, pParentWnd,
1);
```

CreateCaret

■ 2.0 ■ 3.0

Description Creates a caret of a specified shape and associates it with the CWnd. The caret is a system resource (there is only one), so you should only create a caret for a particular window when that window has the input focus or is the active window. The caret is initially hidden—call the CWnd::ShowCaret function to make it visible. Although Windows automatically destroys a window's caret if another window calls CreateCaret, you should destroy it yourself when the window loses focus or becomes inactive.

Syntax public, void CreateCaret(CBitmap* pBitmap);

Parameters

pBitmap A pointer to the bitmap that will be used for the caret.

Returns Nothing is returned.

See Also CWnd::ShowCaret, CBitmap::LoadBitmap, CBitmap::CreateBitmap, ::CreateCaret, ::DestroyCaret

Example

```
void CMyWnd::OnSetFocus(CWnd *pOldWnd)
{
     // load the caret shape
     CBitmap bmp;
     bmp.LoadBitmap(IDB_MYCARET);
     CreateCaret(&bmp);   // create the caret
     ShowCaret();         // show the caret
     CWnd::OnSetFocus(pOldWnd);
}

void CMyWnd::OnKillFocus(CWnd *pNewWnd)
{
     // destroy the caret
     ::DestroyCaret();
     CWnd::OnKillFocus(pNewWnd);
}
```

CreateDlg

■ 4.0 ■ UD

Description Loads the dialog resource with the specified name and calls CWnd::CreateDlgIndirect to create the dialog. This function, along with its CreateDlgIndirect partner are used internally by MFC wherever a dialog or dialog-like window needs to be created. For example, the CDialog::DoModal function uses CWnd::CreateDlgIndirect to actually create the dialog.

Syntax protected, BOOL CreateDlg(LPCTSTR lpszTemplateName, CWnd* pParentWnd);

Parameters

lpszTemplateName A pointer to a NULL-terminated string that contains the name of the dialog resource. Alternatively, can be the value returned by MAKEINTRESOURCE.

pParentWnd Pointer to the parent window of the dialog.

Returns Non-zero if the function is successful; otherwise, zero.

See Also CWnd::CreateDlgIndirect, CDialog::DoModal

Example

```
// create a dialog
AfxGetMainWnd()->CreateDlg(MAKEINTRESOURCE(IDD_MYDIALOG), pParentWnd);
```

CreateDlgIndirect

■ 4.0 ■ UD

Description Creates a dialog given a DLGTEMPLATE structure. CreateDlgIndirect does this by simply calling the Windows SDK ::CreateDlgIndirect function. Before creating the dialog it does some work to set up for OLE controls (if there are any) and then, if the dialog does not specify a font, selects the system font for the dialog. MFC uses this function internally whenever it needs to create a dialog or dialog-like window. For example, the CDialog::DoModal function uses CWnd::CreateDlgIndirect to actually create the dialog.

Syntax protected, BOOL CreateDlgIndirect(LPCDLGTEMPLATE lpDialogTemplate, CWnd* pParentWnd);

Parameters

lpDialogTemplate A pointer to a DLGTEMPLATE structure that describes the dialog. For a full description of the DLGTEMPLATE structure, see the Windows SDK documentation.

pParentWnd A pointer to the parent window of the dialog.

Returns Nothing is returned.

See Also CWnd::CreateDlg, CDialog::DoModal

CreateEx

■ 2.0 ■ 3.0

Description Creates a window with the given characteristics and extended styles and associates the window with the CWnd object. Use this function instead of the CWnd::Create function if you need to create a window with an extended style—for example, a transparent window.

Syntax public, BOOL CreateEx(DWORD dwExStyle, LPCTSTR lpszClassName, LPCTSTR lpszWindowName, DWORD dwStyle, int x, int y, int nWidth, int nHeight, HWND hwndParent, HMENU nIDorHMenu, LPVOID lpParam = NULL);

Parameters

dwExStyle Extended window styles. For a list of extended styles, see the Windows SDK documentation.

lpszClassName A pointer to a NULL-terminated string that contains the name of the window class to use for the window. If NULL, MFC will use a default window class that is good enough in most cases. You can use the AfxRegisterWndClass function to register your own window classes.

lpszWindowName A pointer to a NULL-terminated string that contains the name of the window. The name of the window is what is displayed as its caption.

dwStyle Window styles to be used when creating the window. For a list of valid window styles, see the Windows SDK documentation.

x The x-coordinate of the upper-left corner of the window, expressed in the parent's client coordinates.

y The y-coordinate of the upper-left corner of the window, expressed in the parent's client coordinates.

nWidth The width of the window.

nHeight The height of the window.

hwndParent The window handle of the window's parent window.

nIDorHMenu An ID to assign to the window or the ID of the menu, depending on the window style. You can reference the window via its parent using this ID. For example, the CWnd::GetDlgItem function retrieves a pointer to a child window given its ID.

lpParam A pointer to user data. You can pass any pointer for this parameter. This pointer is passed to the CWnd::OnCreate handler as the lpCreateParams parameter of the CREATESTRUCT structure.

Returns Non-zero if the function is successful; otherwise, zero.

See Also CWnd::Create, ::CreateWindowEx

Example

```
CWnd wnd;

// create a window that accepts dropped files from File Manager
wnd. Create( WS_EX_ACCEPTFILES, NULL, "Test Window", WS_CHILD|WS_VISIBLE, ø
        1,1,500,300, pParentWnd, 1);
```

CreateGrayCaret ■ 2.0 ■ 3.0

Description Creates a gray, rectangular caret of the specified width and height and associates it with the CWnd. The caret is a system resource (there is only one), so you should only create a caret for a particular window when that window has the input focus or is the active window. The caret is initially hidden—call the CWnd::ShowCaret function to make it visible. Although Windows automatically destroys a window's caret if another window calls CreateCaret, you should destroy it yourself when the window loses focus or becomes inactive.

Syntax public, void CreateGrayCaret(int nWidth, int nHeight);

Parameters

nWidth The width of the caret in logical units. If this parameter is zero, Windows will use the window border width.

nHeight The height of the caret in logical units. If this parameter is zero, Windows will use the window border height.

Returns Nothing is returned.

See Also CWnd::CreateCaret, CWnd::CreateSolidCaret, CWnd::ShowCaret, ::DestroyCaret

Example

```
void CMyWnd::OnSetFocus(CWnd *pOldWnd)
{
      CreateGrayCaret(2,10);           // create gray "line" caret
      ShowCaret();                     // show the caret
      CWnd::OnSetFocus(pOldWnd);
}
```

CreateSolidCaret ■ 2.0 ■ 3.0

Description Creates a solid, rectangular caret of the specified width and height and associates it with the CWnd. The caret is a system resource (there is only one), so you should only create a caret for a particular window when that window has the input focus or is the active window. The caret is initially hidden—call the CWnd::ShowCaret function to make it visible. Although Windows automatically destroys a window's caret if another window calls CreateCaret, you should destroy it yourself when the window loses focus or becomes inactive.

Syntax public, void CreateSolidCaret(int nWidth, int nHeight);

Parameters

nWidth The width of the caret in logical units. If this parameter is zero, Windows will use the window border width.

nHeight The height of the caret in logical units. If this parameter is zero, Windows will use the window border height.

Returns Nothing is returned.

See Also CWnd::ShowCaret, CBitmap::LoadBitmap, CBitmap::CreateBitmap, ::CreateCaret, ::DestroyCaret

Example

```
void CMyWnd::OnSetFocus(CWnd *pOldWnd)
{
	CreateSolidCaret(2,10);		// create solid "line" caret
	ShowCaret();			// show the caret
	CWnd::OnSetFocus(pOldWnd);
}
```

Default

■ 2.0 ■ 3.0

Description Calls the CWnd::DefWindowProc function.

Syntax protected, LRESULT Default();

Parameters None.

Returns The result returned for the call to DefWindowProc.

See Also CWnd::DefWindowProc

DefWindowProc

■ 2.0 ■ 3.0

Description The default window procedure. Any message that an application does not process is passed to the default window procedure for processing.

Syntax protected, virtual LRESULT DefWindowProc(UINT message, WPARAM wParam, LPARAM lParam);

Parameters

message The window message ID.

wParam Additional information that is message dependent.

lParam Additional information that is message dependent.

Returns Message-dependent.

See Also CWnd::Default, ::DefWindowProc

DeleteTempMap

■ 2.0 ■ 3.0

Description Deletes any temporary CWnds created using the CWnd::FromHandle function or any other function which returns a temporary CWnd. MFC automatically calls this function as part of its idle-time processing (in the CWinApp idle handler). The windows associated with the temporary CWnds are detached from the CWnds before the CWnds are deleted. The windows are not destroyed. This function is an MFC utility function that you would rarely want to call yourself.

Syntax public, static void PASCAL DeleteTempMap();

Parameters None.

Returns Nothing is returned.

See Also CWnd::Detach, CWnd::FromHandle, CWinApp::OnIdle

DestroyWindow ■ 2.0 ■ 3.0

Description Destroys the window associated with the CWnd object. This function does not delete the CWnd object itself. In addition to destroying the window, this function destroys any menus or timers associated with the window. It also flushes the message queue of any messages associated with the window. DestroyWindow also sends WM_DESTROY and WM_NCDESTROY messages to the window which, in turn, deactivate the window and remove keyboard focus from the window. Finally, any child windows of the window are automatically destroyed. Child windows are destroyed before the window itself is destroyed. Use DestroyWindow to destroy windows created with the Create or CreateEx CWnd member functions as well as modeless dialogs created using the CDialog::Create function.

Syntax public, virtual BOOL DestroyWindow();

Parameters None.

Returns Non-zero if the window is destroyed; otherwise, zero.

See Also CWnd::Create, CWnd::CreateEx, CDialog::Create, CWnd::OnDestroy, CWnd::OnNcDestroy, ::DestroyWindow

Example

```
// destroy window
pWnd->DestroyWindow();
delete pWnd;
```

Detach ■ 2.0 ■ 3.0

Description Detaches the CWnd object from the currently attached window (HWND). Once a CWnd object is attached to an HWND the CWnd can be used to manipulate the window. Detaching the window renders the CWnd object useless until it is re-attached to a window.

Syntax public, HWND Detach();

Parameters None.

Returns The HWND that was attached to the CWnd object.

See Also CWnd::Attach

Example

```
void SomeFunc(HWND hWnd)
{
      // attach to window
      CWnd wnd;
      wnd.Attach(hWnd);
```

```
// use window

// detach from the window
wnd.Detach();
```

DlgDirList

■ 2.0 ■ 3.0 ■ NM

Description Fills a specified list box with a listing of files that match a given path and file specification and given location and a given type.

Syntax public, int DlgDirList(LPTSTR lpPathSpec, int nIDListBox, int nIDStaticPath, UINT nFileType);

Parameters

lpPathSpec Points to a NULL-terminated string buffer that contains the directory and file specifications for the files to be listed. If the string pointed to by this parameter does not contain a file specification, "*.*" is assumed. After this function executes, the drive and path part of the specified string are removed.

nIDListBox The resource ID of the list box into which the files will be listed. If this parameter is zero, DlgDirList assumes that no list box should be filled with the file listing.

nIDStaticPath The resource ID of the static control that will be set to the current drive and directory. If this parameter is zero, DlgDirList assumes that no control should contain this information.

nFileType A set of flags that indicate the type(s) of files that should be listed. The available flags are shown below:

Flag	Description
DDL_READWRITE	Read-write data files with no additional attributes.
DDL_READONLY	Read-only files.
DDL_HIDDEN	Hidden files.
DDL_SYSTEM	System files.
DDL_DIRECTORY	Directories.
DDL_ARCHIVE	Archives.
DDL_POSTMSGS	If this flag is set, Windows places the messages generated by DlgDirList in the application's queue; otherwise, they are sent directly to the dialog box procedure.
DDL_DRIVES	Drives. If the DDL_DRIVES flag is set, the DDL_EXCLUSIVE flag is set automatically.
DDL_EXCLUSIVE	If this flag is set, only files of the specified type are listed; otherwise normal files and files of the specified type are listed.

Returns Non-zero if successful; otherwise, zero.

See Also CWnd::DlgDirListComboBox, CWnd::DlgDirSelect, ::DlgDirList

Example

```
void CMyDialog::OnInitDialog()
{
     DlgDirList("c:\\temp\\*.*", IDC_FILELIST, IDC_DIR, DDL_READONLY);
     ...
     CDialog::OnInitDialog();
}

void CMyDialog::OnOK()
{
     // retrieve the selected file name from the box
     char sFileName[256];
     DlgDirSelect(sFileName,IDC_FILELIST);
}
```

DlgDirListComboBox

■ 2.0 ■ 3.0 ■ NM

Description Fills a specified combo box with a listing of files that match a given path and file specification and given location and of a given type.

Syntax public, int DlgDirListComboBox(LPTSTR lpPathSpec, int nIDComboBox, int nIDStaticPath, UINT nFileType);

Parameters

lpPathSpec Points to a NULL-terminated string buffer that contains the directory and file specifications for the files to be listed. If the string pointed to by this parameter does not contain a file specification, "*.*" is assumed. After this function executes, the drive and path part of the specified string are removed.

nIDComboBox The resource ID of the combo box into which the files will be listed. If this parameter is zero, DlgDirListComboBox assumes that no combo box should be filled with the file listing.

nIDStaticPath The resource ID of the static control that will be set to the current drive and directory. If this parameter is zero, DlgDirList assumes that no control should contain this information.

nFileType A set of flags that indicate the type(s) of files that should be listed. See CWnd::DlgDirList for a listing of valid flags.

Returns Non-zero if successful; otherwise, zero.

See Also CWnd::DlgDirList, CWnd:DlgDirSelectComboBox, ::DlgDirListComboBox

Example

```
void CMyDialog::OnInitDialog()
{
     DlgDirListComboBox("c:\\temp\\*.*", IDC_FILELIST, IDC_DIR,DDL_READONLY);
     ...
     CDialog::OnInitDialog();
}

void CMyDialog::OnOK()
```

```
{
     // retrieve the selected file name from the box
     char sFileName[256];
     DlgDirSelectComboBox(sFileName,IDC_FILELIST);
}
```

DlgDirSelect

■ 2.0 ■ 3.0

Description Retrieves the current selection from a list box. This function is provided as a companion to the CWnd::DlgDirList function which lists files, directories, and/or drive names in a list box. Make sure that the buffer you provide is big enough to hold the selection.

Syntax public, BOOL DlgDirSelect(LPTSTR lpString, int nIDListBox);

Parameters

lpString A pointer to a NULL-terminated buffer that will receive the selected list box string. You must ensure that the buffer is large enough to contain the retrieved selection.

nIDListBox The resource ID of the list box from which the selection will be retrieved.

Returns Non-zero if successful; otherwise, zero.

See Also CWnd::DlgDirList, CWnd::DlgDirSelectComboBox, ::DlgDirSelect

Example See CWnd::DlgDirList

DlgDirSelectComboBox

■ 2.0 ■ 3.0

Description Retrieves the current selection from a combo box. This function is provided as a companion to the CWnd::DlgDirListComboBox function which lists files, directories, and/or drive names in a combo box. Make sure that the buffer you provide is big enough to hold the selection.

Syntax public, BOOL DlgDirSelectComboBox(LPTSTR lpString, int nIDComboBox);

Parameters

lpString A pointer to a NULL-terminated buffer that will receive the selected combo box string. You must ensure that the buffer is large enough to contain the retrieved selection.

nIDComboBox The resource ID of the combo box from which the selection will be retrieved.

Returns Non-zero if successful; otherwise, zero.

See Also CWnd::DlgDirListComboBox, CWnd::DlgDirSelect, ::DlgDirSelectComboBox

Example See CWnd::DlgDirListComboBox

DoDataExchange

■ 2.0 ■ 3.0

Description Called by MFC from the CWnd::UpdateData function to exchange data with the controls in a dialog (or any window) and optionally validate that data. The default implementation of this function does nothing. You should override this function for any dialog box you create if you want to use MFC's data exchange and validation. If you create a dialog class using MSVC's ClassWizard or some other tool, this function will be stubbed out for you with the appropriate exchange and validation calls. For more information about dialog data exchange and validation, see Chapter 8, *Dialog Boxes*.

Syntax protected, virtual void DoDataExchange(CDataExchange* pDX);

Parameters

pDX A pointer to a CDataExchange object. For a description of the member functions of this class, see Chapter 8, *Dialog Boxes*. The m_bSaveAndValidate member of CDataExchange is TRUE if data is being retrieved from the dialog and FALSE if data is being sent to the dialog.

Returns Nothing is returned.

See Also CDataExchange

Example

```
void CTestDlg::DoDataExchange(CDataExchange* pDX)
{
	CDialog::DoDataExchange(pDX);
	//{{AFX_DATA_MAP(CTestDlg)
	DDX_Control(pDX, IDC_LIST1, m_ctListBox);
	DDX_Control(pDX, IDC_COMBO1, m_ctComboBox);
	DDX_Control(pDX, IDC_CUSTOM, m_ctCustom);
	DDX_Check(pDX, IDC_CHECK1, m_bCheck);
	DDX_CBString(pDX, IDC_COMBO1, m_strComboSelect);
	DDX_LBString(pDX, IDC_LIST1, m_strListSelect);
	DDX_Text(pDX, IDC_EDIT1, m_nEditVal);
	DDV_MinMaxInt(pDX, m_nEditVal, 1, 10);
	DDX_Text(pDX, IDC_CUSTOM, m_strCustom);
	DDV_MaxChars(pDX, m_strCustom, 3);
	//}}AFX_DATA_MAP
}
```

DragAcceptFiles

■ 2.0 ■ 3.0

Description Call this function to indicate whether a window will accept files dragged from File Manager. When acceptance is enabled, the window will receive WM_DROPFILES messages. Typically, you would call this function for your application's main window at the beginning of your application.

Syntax public, void DragAcceptFiles(BOOL bAccept = TRUE);

Parameters

bAccept TRUE if the window will accept dragged files; FALSE otherwise.

Returns Nothing is returned.

See Also ::DragAcceptFiles, WM_DROPFILES

Example

```
BOOL CMyApp::OnInitInstance()
{
      ...
      m_pMainWnd->DragAcceptFiles(TRUE);
```

DrawMenuBar

■ 2.0 ■ 3.0

Description Redraws the menu bar at the top of the window. When you make changes to the menu bar, Windows does not automatically redraw the menu.

Syntax public, void DrawMenuBar();

Parameters None.

Returns Nothing is returned.

See Also ::DrawMenuBar

Example

```
void CMyWnd::ChangeMenu()
{
      GetMenu()->DeleteMenu(1,MF_BYPOSITION);

      // now that it is changed, must update
      DrawMenuBar();
}
```

Dump

■ 2.0 ■ 3.0 ■ DO

Description Dump is a diagnostic function that outputs the current state of a CWnd object to the specified dump context. See the example section below to see what information is dumped.

Syntax public, virtual void Dump(CDumpContext& dc) const;

Parameters:

dc A reference to the dump context to that the status information should be sent. Usually this will be the MFC default debug dump context *afxDump*. *afxDump* sends its output to the debugger and only exists in the debug build of MFC.

Returns Nothing is returned.

See Also CObject::Dump, CDumpContext, afxDump

Example Example output from the Dump function.

```
// call to Dump
void CTestWnd::OnDump()
{
      // dump window data to debug context
      Dump(afxDump);
}

// output from Dump function
a CWnd at $12FB58
```

EnableScrollBar

■ 2.0 ■ 3.0

Description Enables or disables one or both arrows on the specified scroll bars.

Syntax public, BOOL EnableScrollBar(int nSBFlags, UINT nArrowFlags = ESB_ENABLE_BOTH);

Parameters

nSBFlags SB_BOTH if the operation performed should affect both scroll bars, SB_VERT if only the vertical scroll bar should be affected, or SB_HORZ if only the horizontal scroll bar should be affected.

nArrowFlags ESB_ENABLE_BOTH to enable both arrows on the scroll bar(s), ESB_DISABLE_LTUP to disable the left/up arrow, ESB_DISABLE_RTDN to disable the right/down arrow, or ESB_DISABLE_BOTH to disable both buttons.

Returns Non-zero if successful or zero if an error occurs or if the scroll bar buttons were already in the desired state.

See Also CWnd::ShowScrollBar, CScrollBar::EnableScrollBar, ::EnableScrollBar

Example

```
// make only the down arrow available on the vertical scroll bar
pWnd->EnableScrollBar(SB_VERT, ESB_DISABLE_LTUP);
```

EnableScrollBarCtrl

■ 2.0 ■ 3.0

Description Enables or disables the specified scroll bar. If this window has a sibling scroll bar then that scroll bar is used; otherwise, the window's scroll bar is used.

Syntax public, void EnableScrollBarCtrl(int nBar, BOOL bEnable = TRUE);

Parameters

nBar SB_VERT if the vertical scroll bar should be enabled/disabled or SB_HORZ if the horizontal scroll bar should be enabled/disabled.

bEnable TRUE to enable the scroll bar or FALSE to disable it.

Returns Nothing is returned.

See Also CWnd::EnableScrollBar, ::EnableScrollBarCtrl

Example

```
// enable the horizontal scroll bar
pWnd->EnableScrollBarCtrl(SB_HORZ,TRUE);
```

EnableToolTips

■ 2.0 ■ 3.0

Description Enables "tooltips" for this window. Tooltips are the little windows that pop up when the user, for example, hesitates on a toolbar button. An example of a tooltip is show in Figure 5-1. A tooltip usually provides a brief explanation of what the object beneath the cursor does. This function installs or

Figure 5-1 Example Tooltip

removes a hook function that filters messages and decides when tooltips should be displayed and removed. When tooltips are enabled, MFC calls the OnToolHitTest handler function to display the tools. You should override the OnToolHitTest function if you want to implement tooltips for a particular window. See Chapter 10, *Menus and Control Bars*, for further discussion about tooltips.

Syntax public, BOOL EnableToolTips(BOOL bEnable = TRUE);

Parameters

bEnable TRUE to enable tooltips and FALSE to disable them.

Returns TRUE if tooltips are enabled; FALSE if they are disabled.

See Also CWnd::CancelToolTips, CWnd::OnToolHitTest

Example

```
// enable tooltips for the application main window
AfxGetMainWnd()->EnableToolTips(TRUE);

// process tooltip message
int CMyMainWnd::OnToolHitTest(CPoint point, TOOLINFO* pTI)
{
      if (CWnd::OnToolHitTest(point,pTI))
      {
            pTI->lpszText = "No Tool-Tip";
            return 1;
      }
      return 0;
}
```

EnableWindow ■ 2.0 ■ 3.0

Description Enables or disables the window. A disabled window cannot become active and does not accept input of any kind. This function sends a WM_ENABLE message to the window before returning. All children of the window are also disabled, but they are not sent the WM_ENABLE message.

Syntax public, BOOL EnableWindow(BOOL bEnable = TRUE);

Parameters

bEnable TRUE if the window should be enabled and FALSE if it should be disabled.

Returns TRUE if the window was previously disabled or FALSE if the window was previously enabled.

See Also CWnd::OnEnable, ::EnableWindow

Example

```
// enable the main window
AfxGetMainWnd()->EnableWindow(TRUE);
```

EndModalLoop

■ 2.0 ■ 3.0

Description Called by the framework to end a modal loop that was started with the CWnd::RunModalLoop function. See the CWnd::RunModalLoop function for a discussion of how MFC uses these functions.

Syntax public, virtual void EndModalLoop(int nResult);

Parameters

nResult An integer result that will be returned from the call to RunModalLoop, which this call to EndModalLoop is terminating.

Returns Nothing is returned.

See Also CWnd::RunModalLoop, CWnd::ContinueModal

EndModalState

■ 2.0 ■ 3.0

Description Enables the window by calling ::EnableWindow. Child class implementations of this function (see CFrameWnd::EndModalState) perform more involved operations.

Syntax public, virtual void EndModalState();

Parameters None.

Returns Nothing is returned.

See Also CWnd::BeginModalState, CFrameWnd::EndModalState

EndPaint

■ 2.0 ■ 3.0

Description Call this function when you are done painting a window that you are painting in response to a WM_PAINT message (the CWnd::OnPaint message handler). This function frees the device context allocated by a call to the CWnd::BeginPaint function. It is often easier to use the CPaintDC, which encapsulates the calls to BeginPaint and EndPaint within its constructor and destructor.

Syntax public, void EndPaint(LPPAINTSTRUCT lpPaint);

Parameters

lpPaint A pointer to the PAINTSTRUCT structure that was supplied by the corresponding call to CWnd::BeginPaint.

Returns Nothing is returned.

See Also CWnd::BeginPaint, CWnd::OnPaint, CPaintDC

Example

```
void CMyWnd::OnPaint(LPPAINTSTRUCT ps)
{
      CDC *pDc = BeginPaint(&ps);
      // do painting
      EndPaint(&ps);
}
```

ExecuteDlgInit

■ 2.0 ■ 3.0

Description Called by the framework to perform dialog initialization. The first form of the function loads the dialog template resource from the program's executable or from a DLL linked to the executable and then calls the second form. The second form of the function assumes the resource is already loaded. It parses the resource in order to implement a feature provided by the MSVC ClassWizard. The ClassWizard allows the developer to associate strings with combo boxes and list boxes at the time the dialog is developed. These strings are then automatically loaded into the list or combo box when the dialog is displayed. ExecuteDlgInit performs this function.

Syntax public, BOOL ExecuteDlgInit(LPCTSTR lpszResourceName);
public, BOOL ExecuteDlgInit(LPVOID lpResource);

Parameters

lpszResourceName A pointer to a NULL-terminated string containing the name of the dialog template resource. Alternatively, can be an integer resource ID created using the MAKEINTRESOURCE macro.

lpResource A pointer to a dialog resource.

Returns TRUE if initialization succeeds; FALSE otherwise.

See Also CDialog::OnInitDialog

FilterToolTipMessage

■ 2.0 ■ 3.0

Description Handles the display and destruction of tooltips as well as routing messages to an existing tooltip. MFC calls this function from the CWnd::PreTranslateMessage function.

Syntax public, void FilterToolTipMessage(MSG *pMsg);

Parameters

pMsg — A pointer to an MSG structure that defines the current message. For a complete description of the MSG structure, see the Windows SDK documentation.

Returns — Nothing is returned.

See Also — CWnd::OnToolHitTest, CWnd::PreTranslateMessage

FindWindow

■ 2.0 ■ 3.0

Description — Finds the top-level window with the specified class name and window name. FindWindow will not locate child windows.

Syntax — public, static CWnd* PASCAL FindWindow(LPCTSTR lpszClassName, LPCTSTR lpszWindowName);

Parameters

lpszClassName — A pointer to a NULL-terminated string buffer containing the class name of the desired window. Can be NULL, in which case any class name will match.

lpszWindowName — A pointer to a NULL-terminated string buffer containing the window name of the desired window. Can be NULL, in which case any window name will match.

Returns — A pointer to the matching CWnd object or NULL if one is not found. This pointer may be temporary so it should not be stored for later use. Temporary CWnds are automatically destroyed during idle-time processing so you can only depend on the validity of the CWnd returned by FindWindow until your application enters its idle loop, which can occur any time you return control to Windows (i.e., returning from a message map).

See Also — ::FindWindow

Example

```
// find application window and change title
CWnd *pWnd = FindWindow("MYWNDCLS","My Application");
if (pWnd)
     pWnd->SetWindowText("My New Application");
```

FlashWindow

■ 2.0 ■ 3.0

Description — Flashes the window. Flashing the window causes the title bar to change between the inactive color and the active color. Each call to FlashWindow (with bInvert = FALSE) changes from one state to the other. To truly implement the flashing effect, you will need to repeatedly call FlashWindow by setting up a timer and calling it on each timer message. Calling FlashWindow with bInvert = TRUE returns the window title bar to its initial state.

Syntax public, BOOL FlashWindow(BOOL bInvert);

Parameters

bInvert TRUE to flash the window; FALSE to return the window to its original state.

Returns Non-zero if the window was active before the call; otherwise, zero.

See Also CWnd::SetTimer, ::FlashWindow

Example See CWnd::SetTimer

FromHandle ■ 2.0 ■ 3.0

Description Returns a pointer to a CWnd given a window handle. If MFC does not already have a permanent CWnd associated with the specified handle, it creates a temporary one and attaches it to the handle. Temporary CWnds are automatically destroyed during idle-time processing so you can only depend on the validity of the CWnd returned by FromHandle until your application enters its idle loop which can occur any time you return control to Windows (i.e., returning from a message map).

Syntax public, static CWnd* PASCAL FromHandle(HWND hWnd);

Parameters

hWnd A window handle that will be associated with a CWnd object.

Returns A pointer to the new CWnd, which may be temporary.

See Also CWnd::DeleteTempMap, CWnd::FromHandlePermanent

Example

```
void SomeFunc(HWND hWnd)
{
	CWnd *pWnd = CWnd::FromHandle(hWnd);
```

FromHandlePermanent ■ 2.0 ■ 3.0

Description Returns a pointer to a CWnd given a window handle. Unlike the CWnd::FromHandle function, this function will not create a temporary CWnd object. Therefore, if MFC does not already have a permanent CWnd object for the specified window handle, it returns NULL.

Syntax public, static CWnd* PASCAL FromHandlePermanent(HWND hWnd);

Parameters

hWnd The handle of the window for which a CWnd should be found.

Returns A pointer to a permanent CWnd for the window handle or NULL if one does not exist.

See Also CWnd::FromHandle

GetActiveWindow

■ 2.0 ■ 3.0

Description Retrieves a pointer to the currently active window. The active window is the window with input focus or the window made active by a call to the CWnd::SetActiveWindow function.

Syntax public, static CWnd* PASCAL GetActiveWindow();

Parameters None.

Returns A pointer to the window that is active or NULL if no window is currently active. The returned pointer may be temporary and should not be stored for later use. Temporary CWnds are automatically destroyed during idle-time processing so you can only depend on the validity of the CWnd returned by GetActiveWindow until your application enters its idle loop, which can occur any time you return control to Windows (i.e., returning from a message map).

See Also CWnd::GetFocus(), ::GetActiveWindow

Example

```
// retrieve active window and change its title
CWnd *pActiveWnd = CWnd::GetActiveWindow();
if (pActiveWnd)
        pActiveWnd->SetWindowText("Active Window Title");
```

GetCapture

■ 2.0 ■ 3.0

Description Retrieves a pointer to the window that has the mouse capture. Only one window can have mouse capture at a time. A window captures the mouse by calling the CWnd::SetCapture function. When a window has the mouse captured, it receives mouse messages even if the cursor position is not within the window.

Syntax public, static CWnd* PASCAL GetCapture();

Parameters None.

Returns A pointer to the window with the mouse capture or NULL if there is none. The returned pointer may be temporary and should not be stored for later use. Temporary CWnds are automatically destroyed during idle-time processing so you can only depend on the validity of the CWnd returned by GetCapture until your application enters its idle loop, which can occur any time you return control to Windows (i.e., returning from a message map).

See Also CWnd::SetCapture, ::GetCapture

Example See CWnd::SetCapture

GetCaretPos

■ 2.0 ■ 3.0

Description Retrieves the client coordinates of the caret.

Syntax public, static CPoint PASCAL GetCaretPos();

Parameters None.

Returns A CPoint object containing the coordinates of the caret, in client coordinates.

See Also CWnd::SetCaretPos, ::GetCaretPos

Example

```
CPoint pt = pWnd->GetCaretPos();
```

GetCheckedRadioButton

■ 2.0 ■ 3.0

Description Determines which radio button, in a group of radio buttons, is checked.

Syntax public, int GetCheckedRadioButton(int nIDFirstButton, int nIDLastButton);

Parameters

nIDFirstButton The resource ID of the first button in the group.

nIDLastButton The resource ID of the last button in the group.

Returns The resource ID of the selected button in the group or zero if no button is selected.

See Also CWnd::CheckRadioButton

Example

```
void CMyDialog::OnClickMyButton1()
{
	int nButton = GetCheckedRadioButton(IDB_FIRST, IDB_LAST);
```

GetClientRect

■ 2.0 ■ 3.0

Description Retrieves the rectangle that defines the client area of the window. The rectangle is expressed in client coordinates. Therefore, the top-left corner is always 0,0.

Syntax public, void GetClientRect(LPRECT lpRect) const;

Parameters

lpRect A pointer to a RECT structure or a CRect object that will be filled with the coordinates of the window's client area.

Returns Nothing is returned.

See Also CWnd::GetWindowRect, CWnd::ClientToScreen

Example

```
CRect rc;
pWnd->GetClientRect(rc);
```

GetClipboardOwner ■ 2.0 ■ 3.0

Description Retrieves a pointer to the window that currently "owns" the Clipboard or NULL if there is none. Typically, the last window to place data in the Clipboard is the owner. The ::EmptyClipboard function assigns Clipboard ownership.

Syntax public, static CWnd* PASCAL GetClipboardOwner();

Parameters None.

Returns A pointer to the window that owns the clipboard or NULL if the Clipboard is not owned. The returned pointer may be temporary and should not be stored for later use. Temporary CWnds are automatically destroyed during idle-time processing so you can only depend on the validity of the CWnd returned by GetClipboardOwner until your application enters its idle loop, which can occur any time you return control to Windows (i.e., returning from a message map).

See Also CWnd::GetClipboardViewer, ::GetClipboardOwner, ::EmptyClipboard

Example

```
CWnd *pClipOwner = CWnd::GetClipboardOwner();
```

GetClipboardViewer ■ 2.0 ■ 3.0

Description Retrieves a pointer to the first window in the Clipboard viewer chain.

Syntax public, static CWnd* PASCAL GetClipboardViewer();

Parameters None.

Returns A pointer to the first window in the Clipboard viewer chain. The returned pointer may be temporary and should not be stored for later use. Temporary CWnds are automatically destroyed during idle-time processing so you can only depend on the validity of the CWnd returned by GetClipboardViewer until your application enters its idle loop, which can occur any time you return control to Windows (i.e., returning from a message map).

See Also CWnd::GetClipboardOwner, ::GetClipboardViewer

Example

```
CWnd *pClipOwner = CWnd::GetClipboardViewer();
```

GetCurrentMessage ■ 2.0 ■ 3.0

Description Retrieves a pointer to the message that is currently being processed. You can call this function when responding to a message to determine the exact message that was sent.

Syntax protected, static const MSG* PASCAL GetCurrentMessage();

Parameters None.

Returns A pointer to an MSG structure which defines the current message. For a complete description of the MSG structure, see the Windows SDK documentation.

Example

```
MSG *pMsg;
pMsg = CWnd::GetCurrentMessage();
if (pMsg->message == WM_RBUTTONDOWN)
     // do something if message is right mouse button click
```

GetDC

■ 2.0 ■ 3.0

Description Retrieves a device context for the client area of the window. Usually, the device context returned is a common device context. However, depending on the style flags used for the window's class, a private or class device context may be returned. The CS_OWNDC, CS_PARENTDC, and CS_CLASSDC flags control this feature. Common device contexts are reinitialized to the Windows defaults each time you get one. Private device contexts are not reset. Common device contexts must be freed when you are done using them by calling the CWnd::ReleaseDC function. It is very important to do this promptly in 16-bit Windows (and Win32s) because the system is limited to a total of five common device contexts.

Syntax public, CDC* GetDC();

Parameters None.

Returns A pointer to the device context. This pointer may be temporary and should not be stored for later use. Temporary CDCs are automatically destroyed during idle-time processing so you can only depend on the validity of the CDC returned by GetDC until your application enters its idle loop, which can occur any time you return control to Windows (i.e., returning from a message map).

See Also CWnd::GetDCEx, CWnd::ReleaseDC

Example

```
...
CDC *pDc = pWnd->GetDC();
pDc->Rectangle(1,1,100,100);
pWnd->ReleaseDC(pDc);
```

GetDCEx

■ 2.0 ■ 3.0

Description Retrieves a device context for the client area of the window. GetDCEx differs from GetDC in that it allows you to control the initial clipping region of the device context. GetDC automatically returns a device context with a clipping region of the entire rectangle. Usually, the device context returned is a common device context. However, depending on the style flags used for the window's class, a private or class device context may be returned. The CS_OWNDC, CS_PARENTDC, and CS_CLASSDC flags control this feature. Common device contexts are reinitialized to the Windows defaults each time you get one. Private device contexts are not reset. Common device contexts must be freed when you are done using them by calling the CWnd::ReleaseDC function. It is very important to do this promptly in 16-bit Windows (and Win32s) because the system is limited to a total of five common device contexts.

Syntax public, CDC* GetDCEx(CRgn* prgnClip, DWORD flags);

Parameters

prgnClip Points to a CRgn that can be combined with the default clipping region of the device context. See the *flags* parameter for how this region will be combined.

flags Controls the clipping region of the device context. Can be one of the following values:

DCX_CACHE Returns a device context from the cache (a common device context) rather than a private or class device context, even if the CS_OWNDC or CS_CLASSDC class styles were specified.

DCX_CLIPCHILDREN Excludes the visible regions of all child windows below the CWnd window.

DCX_CLIPSIBLINGS Excludes the visible regions of all sibling windows above the CWnd window.

DCX_EXCLUDERGN Excludes the clipping region identified by prgnClip from the visible region of the returned device context.

DCX_INTERSECTRGN Intersects the clipping region identified by prgnClip within the visible region of the returned device context.

DCX_LOCKWINDOWUPDATE Allows drawing even if there is a LockWindowUpdate call in effect that would otherwise exclude this window. This value is used for drawing during tracking.

DCX_PARENTCLIP Uses the visible region of the parent window and ignores the parent window's WS_CLIPCHILDREN and WS_PARENTDC style bits. This value sets the device context's origin to the upper-left corner of the CWnd window.

DCX_WINDOW Returns a device context that corresponds to the window rectangle rather than the client rectangle.

Returns A pointer to the device context. This pointer may be temporary and should not be stored for later use. Temporary CDCs are automatically destroyed during idle-time processing so you can only depend on the validity of the CDC returned by GetDCEx until your application enters its idle loop, which can occur any time you return control to Windows (i.e., returning from a message map).

See Also CWnd::GetDC, CWnd::ReleaseDC

Example See CWnd::GetDC

GetDescendantWindow

■ 2.0 ■ 3.0

Description

Retrieves the child window of this window, or a specified window, with the specified ID. This function differs from CWnd::GetDlgItem because it searches all descendants of this window—not just immediate children.

Syntax

public CWnd* GetDescendantWindow(int nID, BOOL bOnlyPerm = FALSE) const;
public, static CWnd* PASCAL GetDescendantWindow(HWND hWnd, int nID, BOOL bOnlyPerm);

Parameters

hWnd The parent window of the child to find.

nID The ID of the child window to find.

bOnlyPerm TRUE if the function should only return the child window if it is currently in the permanent window map or FALSE if this function is allowed to create a temporary CWnd object for the window.

Returns

A pointer to the child window with the specified ID. If *bOnlyPerm* is FALSE, this pointer may be temporary and should not be stored for later use. Temporary CWnds are automatically destroyed during idle-time processing so you can only depend on the validity of the CWnd returned by GetDescendantWindow until your application enters its idle loop, which can occur any time you return control to Windows (i.e., returning from a message map).

See Also

CWnd::GetDlgItem, CWnd::IsChild

Example

```
// same as using GetDlgItem
void CMyDialog::OnInitDialog()
{
      CDialog::OnInitDialog();
      CListBox *pList = (CListBox *)GetDescendantWindow(IDC_LIST,FALSE);
      pList->AddString("hello");
}
```

GetDesktopWindow

■ 2.0 ■ 3.0

Description

Retrieves a pointer to the desktop window. The desktop window is the window that covers the entire screen and upon which all other windows are drawn. This pointer may be temporary so it should not be stored for later use. Temporary CWnds are automatically destroyed during idle-time processing so you can only depend on the validity of the CWnd returned by GetDesktopWindow until your application enters its idle loop, which can occur any time you return control to Windows (i.e., returning from a message map).

Syntax

public, static CWnd* PASCAL GetDesktopWindow();

Parameters None.

Returns A pointer to the desktop window.

Example

```
// arrange icons on the desktop
CWnd *pDeskTopWnd = CWnd::GetDeskTopWindow();
pDeskTopWnd->ArrangeIconicWindows();
```

GetDlgCtrlID ■ 2.0 ■ 3.0

Description Returns the child window ID for this window. If this window is not a child window, the return value is undefined. Note that every child window has an ID, not just controls in a dialog.

Syntax public, int GetDlgCtrlID() const;

Parameters None.

Returns The ID of this child window.

See Also ::GetDlgCtrlID

Example

```
int nId = pWnd->GetDlgCtrlID(); // get the ID of pWnd
```

GetDlgItem ■ 2.0 ■ 3.0

Description Retrieves a pointer to, or the handle of, a specified child window. Typically, this function is used to retrieve a control in a dialog. This pointer may be temporary so it should not be stored for later use. Temporary CWnds are automatically destroyed during idle-time processing so you can only depend on the validity of the CWnd returned by GetDlgItem until your application enters its idle loop, which can occur any time you return control to Windows (i.e., returning from a message map).

Syntax public, CWnd* GetDlgItem(int nID) const;
public, void GetDlgItem(int nID, HWND* phWnd) const;

Parameters

nID The ID of the child window to retrieve.

phWnd A pointer to an HWND which will be filled with the handle of the specified child window.

Returns The first form of this function returns a pointer to the specified child window or NULL if the child window does not exist.

Example

```
void CMyDialog::OnInitDialog()
{     // get a temporary object for the specified list box
      CListBox *pBox = (CListBox *)GetDlgItem(IDC_MYLIST);
```

GetDlgItemInt

■ 2.0 ■ 3.0

Description Retrieves the contents of a specified child window as a signed or unsigned integer. This function will fail if non-numeric characters are found in the window text or if the translated value is greater than 65535 for unsigned numbers or 32767 for signed numbers.

Syntax public, UINT GetDlgItemInt(int nID, BOOL* lpTrans = NULL, BOOL bSigned = TRUE) const;

Parameters

nID The ID of the child window.

lpTrans If supplied, the location pointed to by this parameter will be filled with non-zero if the function is successful and zero if it fails. If you do not care about error reporting, this parameter can be NULL.

bSigned TRUE if the value can be negative or FALSE if it can not. If TRUE, GetDlgItemInt allows a - sign at the front of the number. If you use GetDlgItemInt for signed numbers, you will need to cast the return value to a signed value.

Returns The translated numeric value.

See Also CWnd::GetDlgItemText, CWnd::GetWindowText, ::GetDlgItemInt

Example

```
void CMyDialog::OnOK()
{
	// retrieve signed integer
	BOOL bTrans;
	int nVal = (int)GetDlgItemInt(IDC_EDITBOX,&bTrans,TRUE);
```

GetDlgItemText

■ 2.0 ■ 3.0

Description Retrieves the window text associated with the specified child window that is usually a control in a dialog.

Syntax public, int GetDlgItemText(int nID, LPTSTR lpStr, int nMaxCount) const;
public, int GetDlgItemText(int nID, CString &strBuf) const;

Parameters

nID The ID of the child window.

lpStr A pointer to a buffer that will be filled with the window text.

nMaxCount The maximum number of characters to transfer to the buffer pointed to by *lpStr*.

strBuf A reference to a CString that will be filled with the window text.

Returns Nothing is returned.

See Also CWnd::GetWindowText, CWnd::GetDlgItemInt, ::GetDlgItemText

Example

```
void CMyDialog::OnOK()
{
	// retrieve edit box text
	CString strText;
	GetDlgItemText(IDC_EDITBOX,strText);
```

GetExStyle

■ 2.0 ■ 3.0

Description Retrieves the extended style flags for the window. This function simply calls the SDK function ::GetWindowLong with the GWL_EXSTYLE flag.

Syntax public, DWORD GetExStyle() const;

Parameters None.

Returns Nothing is returned.

See Also CWnd::GetStyle, ::GetWindowLong

GetFocus

■ 2.0 ■ 3.0

Description Retrieves a pointer to the window that currently has the input focus.

Syntax public, static CWnd* PASCAL GetFocus();

Parameters None.

Returns A pointer to the CWnd that currently has focus. This pointer may be temporary so it should not be stored for later use. Temporary CWnds are automatically destroyed during idle-time processing so you can only depend on the validity of the CWnd returned by GetFocus until your application enters its idle loop, which can occur any time you return control to Windows (i.e., returning from a message map).

See Also CWnd::SetFocus, CWnd::GetActiveWindow, ::GetFocus

Example

```
CWnd *pFocusWnd = CWnd::GetFocus();
```

GetFont

■ 2.0 ■ 3.0

Description Retrieves a pointer to the current font for this window.

Syntax public, CFont* GetFont() const;

Parameters None.

Returns A pointer to the font used by the window. This pointer may be temporary so it should not be stored for later use. Temporary CFonts are automatically destroyed during idle-time processing so you can only depend on the validity of the CFont returned by GetFont until your application enters its idle loop, which can occur any time you return control to Windows (i.e., returning from a message map).

See Also CWnd::SetFont, ::GetFont

Example

```
CFont *pFont = pWnd->GetFont();
```

GetForegroundWindow

■ 2.0 ■ 3.0

Description Retrieves a pointer to the current foreground window. The foreground window is the window in which the user is currently working. Only top-level windows can be the foreground window.

Syntax public, static CWnd* PASCAL GetForegroundWindow();

Parameters None.

Returns A pointer to the current foreground window. This pointer may be temporary so it should not be stored for later use. Temporary CWnds are automatically destroyed during idle-time processing so you can only depend on the validity of the CWnd returned by GetForegroundWindow until your application enters its idle loop, which can occur any time you return control to Windows (i.e., returning from a message map).

See Also CWnd::SetForegroundWindow, ::GetForegroundWindow

Example

```
CWnd *pFgWindow = CWnd::GetForegroundWindow();
```

GetIcon

■ 2.0 ■ 3.0

Description Retrieves either the 32x32 ("big") icon associated with the window or the 16x16 ("small") icon associated with the window.

Syntax public, HICON GetIcon(BOOL bBigIcon) const;

Parameters

bBigIcon TRUE to retrieve a handle to the 32x32 icon associated with the window; FALSE to retrieve the 16x16 icon associated with the window.

Returns Handle to the icon or NULL is unsuccessful.

See Also CWnd::SetIcon

Example

```
HICON hIcon = pWnd->GetIcon(TRUE);
```

GetLastActivePopup

■ 2.0 ■ 3.0

Description Retrieves a pointer to the popup window, owned by this window, which was most recently active. This function will return a pointer to this window itself if this window was most recently active, this window does not own any popup windows, or this window is not a top-level window or is owned by another window.

Syntax public, CWnd* GetLastActivePopup() const;

Parameters None.

Returns A pointer to the last active popup window owned by this window. This pointer may be temporary so it should not be stored for later use. Temporary CWnds are automatically destroyed during idle-time processing so you can only depend on the validity of the CWnd returned by GetLastActivePopup until your application enters its idle loop, which can occur any time you return control to Windows (i.e., returning from a message map).

Example

```
CWnd *pPopup = pWnd->GetLastActivePopup();
```

GetMenu ■ 2.0 ■ 3.0

Description Retrieves a pointer to the menu associated with the window. Since child windows do not have menus, you should not call this function for a child window.

Syntax public, CMenu* GetMenu() const;

Parameters None.

Returns A pointer to the menu associated with the window. This pointer may be temporary so it should not be stored for later use. Temporary CMenus are automatically destroyed during idle-time processing so you can only depend on the validity of the CMenu returned by GetMenu until your application enters its idle loop, which can occur any time you return control to Windows (i.e., returning from a message map).

See Also ::GetMenu

Example See CWnd::SetMenu

GetNextDlgGroupItem ■ 2.0 ■ 3.0

Description Retrieves a pointer to the window that is next or previous in a group relative to a specified window. A "group" is begun by a window that has the WS_GROUP style and ends with the last control that does not have the WS_GROUP style (the first one before the next WS_GROUP window).

Syntax public, CWnd* GetNextDlgGroupItem(CWnd* pWndCtl, BOOL bPrevious = FALSE) const;

Parameters

pWndCtl A pointer to the window to start searching from.

bPrevious TRUE if the window previous in the group should be found or FALSE if the one next in the group should be found.

Returns A pointer to the window next or previous in the group. This pointer may be temporary so it should not be stored for later use. Temporary CWnds are automatically destroyed during idle-time processing so you can only depend on the validity of the CWnd returned by GetNextDlgGroupItem until your application enters its idle loop, which can occur any time you return control to Windows (i.e., returning from a message map).

See Also CWnd::GetNextDlgTabItem, ::GetNextDlgGroupItem

GetNextDlgTabItem ■ 2.0 ■ 3.0

Description Retrieves a pointer to the window which is next or previous in the tab order (has the WS_TABSTOP style) relative to a specified window. Typically, this function is used in regard to tabbing between controls in a dialog.

Syntax public, CWnd* GetNextDlgTabItem(CWnd* pWndCtl, BOOL bPrevious = FALSE) const;

Parameters

pWndCtl A pointer to the window to start searching from.

bPrevious TRUE if the window previous in the tab order should be found or FALSE if the one next in the tab order should be found.

Returns A pointer to the window next or previous in the tab order or NULL if there is none. This pointer may be temporary so it should not be stored for later use. Temporary CWnds are automatically destroyed during idle-time processing so you can only depend on the validity of the CWnd returned by GetNextDlgTabItem until your application enters its idle loop, which can occur any time you return control to Windows (i.e., returning from a message map).

See Also CWnd::GetNextDlgGroupItem, ::GetNextDlgTabItem

Example

```
CWnd *pNextCtrl = pDialog->GetNextDlgTabItem(GetDlgItem(IDC_EDIT),TRUE);
```

GetNextWindow ■ 2.0 ■ 3.0

Description Retrieves a pointer to the next or previous window (compared to this window) in the window manager's list of windows. The window manager maintains a list of all windows. If this window is a top-level window, then this function finds the next or previous top-level window. Likewise, if this window is a child window then this function finds the next or previous child window.

Syntax public, CWnd* GetNextWindow(UINT nFlag = GW_HWNDNEXT) const;

Parameters

nFlag GW_HWNDNEXT to get the next window or GW_HWNDPREV to get the previous window.

Returns Nothing is returned.

See Also CWnd::GetWindow, ::GetNextWindow

Example

```
CWnd *pNextWnd = pWnd->GetNextWindow();
```

GetOpenClipboardWindow

■ 2.0 ■ 3.0

Description Retrieves the window that currently has the Clipboard open or NULL if one does not exist. A window opens the Clipboard by calling the CWnd::OpenClipboard function.

Syntax public, static CWnd* PASCAL GetOpenClipboardWindow();

Parameters None.

Returns A pointer to the window that has the Clipboard open. This pointer may be temporary so it should not be stored for later use. Temporary CWnds are automatically destroyed during idle-time processing so you can only depend on the validity of the CWnd returned by GetOpenClipboardWindow until your application enters its idle loop, which can occur any time you return control to Windows (i.e., returning from a message map).

See Also CWnd::GetClipboardOwner, CWnd::GetClipboardViewer, CWnd::OpenClipboard, ::GetOpenClipboardWindow

GetOwner

■ 2.0 ■ 3.0

Description Retrieves a pointer to the window's owner window or the parent window if this window has no owner. The owner of a window is not necessarily the same as its parent.

Syntax public, CWnd* GetOwner() const;

Parameters None.

Returns A pointer to the owner window of this window. This pointer may be temporary so it should not be stored for later use. Temporary CWnds are automatically destroyed during idle-time processing so you can only depend on the validity of the CWnd returned by GetOwner until your application enters its idle loop, which can occur any time you return control to Windows (i.e., returning from a message map).

See Also CWnd::GetParent, CWnd::GetParentFrame, CWnd::GetParentOwner, CWnd::SetOwner, ::GetOwner

Example

```
CWnd *pOwner = pWnd->GetOwner();
```

GetParent

■ 2.0 ■ 3.0

Description Retrieves the parent window of this window.

Syntax public, CWnd* GetParent() const;

Parameters None.

Returns A pointer to the parent window of this window. This pointer may be temporary so it should not be stored for later use. Temporary CWnds are automatically destroyed during idle-time processing so you can only depend on the validity of the CWnd returned by GetParent until your application enters its idle loop, which can occur any time you return control to Windows (i.e., returning from a message map). This function may return NULL if the CWnd object is not attached to a window or if the window has no parent.

See Also CWnd::GetParentFrame, CWnd::GetParentOwner, ::GetParent

Example

```
CWnd *pParent = pWnd->GetParent();
```

GetParentFrame ■ 2.0 ■ 3.0

Description Retrieves a pointer to the parent frame of this window. If no parent of this window is a frame window, GetParentFrame returns NULL.

Syntax public, CFrameWnd* GetParentFrame() const;

Parameters None.

Returns A pointer to the parent frame window of this window. This pointer may be temporary so it should not be stored for later use. Temporary CFrameWnds are automatically destroyed during idle-time processing so you can only depend on the validity of the CFrameWnds returned by GetParentFrame until your application enters its idle loop, which can occur any time you return control to Windows (i.e., returning from a message map). This function may return NULL if the CWnd object is not attached to a window or if the window's parent is not a frame window.

See Also CWnd::GetParent, CWnd::GetParentOwner, CWnd::GetOwner

Example

```
CWnd *pParent = pWnd->GetParentFrame();
```

GetParentOwner ■ 2.0 ■ 3.0

Description Retrieves a pointer to this window's first non-child parent window.

Syntax public, CWnd* GetParentOwner() const;

Parameters None.

Returns A pointer to this window's first non-child parent window. This pointer may be temporary so it should not be stored for later use. Temporary CWnds are automatically destroyed during idle-time processing so you can only depend on the validity of the CWnd returned by GetParentOwner until your application enters its idle loop, which can occur any time you return control to Windows (i.e., returning from a message map). This function may return NULL if the CWnd object is not attached to a window or if the window has no parent.

See Also CWnd::GetParent, CWnd::GetParentFrame, CWnd::GetOwner

Example

```
CWnd *pParent = pWnd->GetParentOwner();
```

GetSafeHwnd ■ 2.0 ■ 3.0

Description Returns the window handle currently associated with the CWnd object. The function is called "safe" because even if called for a NULL CWnd, this function will operate correctly (returning NULL).

Syntax public, HWND GetSafeHwnd() const;

Parameters None.

Returns The window handle associated with the CWnd object or NULL if the CWnd is NULL or not associated with a window.

Example

```
HWND hWnd = pWnd->GetSafeHwnd();
```

GetSafeOwner ■ 2.0 ■ 3.0

Description An internal MFC function that does a bit more than its name implies. GetSafeOwner retrieves the first non-child parent window of the specified window. If the second parameter is supplied, it also disables the top-level window and returns the handle of that window. MFC uses this function to determine the owner window for dialogs and property sheets when one is not supplied and to disable that owner window along with the top-level window.

Syntax public, static CWnd* PASCAL GetSafeOwner(CWnd* pParent = NULL, HWND* pWndTop = NULL);

Parameters

pParent A pointer to the parent window whose owner is to be found or NULL in which case the application's main window is used.

pWndTop A pointer to a window handle which will be filled with the handle of the top-level window. If this parameter is supplied, the top-level window is found and disabled.

Returns A pointer to the owner window or NULL if there is none.

See Also AfxGetMainWnd

Example See CWnd::GetSafeHwnd

GetScrollBarCtrl

■ 2.0 ■ 3.0

Description Retrieves a pointer to the specified sibling scrollbar control. If the window does not have a sibling scrollbar, this function returns NULL. Note that the scrollbars created for a window with the WS_HSCROLL and/or WS_VSCROLL styles are not sibling scrollbars. The CWnd-level implementation of this function always returns NULL. Other MFC classes derived from CWnd (see CView) implement this function differently.

Syntax public, virtual CScrollBar* GetScrollBarCtrl(int nBar) const;

Parameters

nBar SB_HORZ to retrieve the horizontal scrollbar or SB_VERT to retrieve the vertical scrollbar.

Returns A pointer to the specified scrollbar.

Example

```
void CMyWnd::SomeFunc()
{ // get the horizontal scrollbar control and disable it
CScrollBar *pBar = GetScrollBarCtrl(SB_HORZ);
if (pBar)
     pBar->EnableWindow(FALSE);
}
```

GetScrollInfo

■ 4.0

Description Retrieves detailed information about the positioning of the specified scrollbar. GetScrollInfo and SetScrollInfo allow you to do full 32-bit scrollbar positioning. It also supports the proportional scrollbars introduced with Windows 95. You can call this function while processing the OnHScroll or OnVScroll handlers in order to retrieve the true 32-bit position of a scrollbar. The parameters passed to these handler functions are only 16 bits.

Syntax public, BOOL GetScrollInfo(int nBar, LPSCROLLINFO lpScrollInfo, UINT nMask = SIF_ALL);

Parameters

nBar SB_HORZ to get information about the horizontal scrollbar associated with the window, SB_VERT to retrieve information about the vertical scrollbar associated with the window, or SB_CTL if the window itself is a scrollbar.

lpScrollInfo A pointer to a SCROLLINFO structure. For more information about this structure, see the Windows SDK documentation.

nMask A combination of the following flags that determine what types of information will be retrieved:

SIF_ALL Combination of SIF_PAGE, SIF_POS, and SIF_RANGE, SIF_TRACKPOS.

SIF_PAGE The nPage member contains the page size for a proportional scrollbar.

SIF_POS — The nPos parameter contains the scroll box position.

SIF_RANGE — The nMin and nMax members contain the minimum and maximum values for the scrolling range.

SIF_TRACKPOS — The nPos parameter contains the current scroll box position while the user is dragging it.

Returns — Non-zero if any information is retrieved; otherwise, zero.

See Also — CWnd::SetScrollInfo, CWnd::OnHScroll, CWnd::OnVScroll

Example

```
SCROLLINFO si;
pWnd-> GetScrollInfo(SB_VERT, &si, SIF_ALL);
```

GetScrollLimit ■ 4.0

Description — Retrieves the maximum value of the specified scrollbar.

Syntax — public, int GetScrollLimit(int nBar);

Parameters

nBar — SB_HORZ to retrieve the maximum value of the horizontal scrollbar or SB_VERT to retrieve the maximum value of the vertical scrollbar.

Returns — The maximum value of the selected scrollbar.

See Also — CScrollBar::GetScrollRange, CWnd::GetScrollPos, CWnd::GetScrollRange, ::GetScrollRange

Example

```
int nScrollMax = pWnd->GetScrollLimit(SB_VERT);
```

GetScrollPos ■ 2.0 ■ 3.0

Description — Retrieves the current position of the thumb for a specified scrollbar. The current position is a relative value that depends on the current scroll range of the scrollbar.

Syntax — public, int GetScrollPos(int nBar) const;

Parameters

nBar — SB_HORZ to retrieve the current position of the horizontal scrollbar or SB_VERT to retrieve the current position of the vertical scrollbar.

Returns — The current position of the scrollbar.

See Also — CWnd::SetScrollPos, CWnd::GetScrollRange, CWnd::GetScrollLimit, CScrollBar::GetScrollPos, ::GetScrollPos

Example

```
int nPos = pWnd->GetScrollPos(SB_HORZ);
```

GetScrollRange ■ 2.0 ■ 3.0

Description Retrieves the current minimum and maximum values for the specified scrollbar.

Syntax public, void GetScrollRange(int nBar, LPINT lpMinPos, LPINT lpMaxPos) const;

Parameters

nBar SB_HORZ to retrieve the range of the horizontal scrollbar or SB_VERT to retrieve the range of the vertical scrollbar.

lpMinPos The address of an integer that will be set to the minimum possible value of the scrollbar.

lpMaxPos The address of an integer that will be set to the maximum possible value of the scrollbar.

Returns Nothing is returned.

See Also CWnd::SetScrollRange, CWnd::GetScrollPos, CWnd::GetScrollLimit, CScrollBar::GetScrollRange, ::GetScrollRange

Example

```
int nMinPos, nMaxPos;
pWnd->GetScrollRange(SB_HORZ,&nMinPos,&nMaxPos);
```

GetStyle ■ 2.0 ■ 3.0

Description Returns the window's style flags. For a list of these flags, see the Windows SDK documentation. GetStyle is simply a call to the SDK function ::GetWindowLong with the GWL_STYLE flag.

Syntax public, DWORD GetStyle() const;

Parameters None.

Returns The window's style flags.

See Also ::GetWindowLong

Example

```
DWORD dwStyle = pWnd->GetStyle();
if (dwStyle & WS_VISIBLE)
     ; // window is visible
```

GetSuperWndProcAddr ■ 2.0 ■ 3.0

Description This function is obsolete for 32-bit versions of MFC. In the 16-bit version, MFC calls this function to retrieve a pointer to a location in which it will place the old window procedure whenever the window is subclassed by a call to SubclassWindow. 32-bit versions of MFC store this pointer automatically in a member variable of the CWnd class. If you subclass a window in 16-bit MFC, you must override this function to supply the address in which the old window procedure address should be placed.

Syntax public, virtual WNDPROC* GetSuperWndProcAddr();

Parameters None.

Returns A pointer to a WNDPROC. MFC will fill in this location with the address of the old window procedure.

See Also CWnd::SubclassWindow

GetSystemMenu ■ 2.0 ■ 3.0

Description Retrieves a pointer to a copy of the system menu for this window or returns the system menu to the default. You can use this function to provide a custom system menu for a window. By default, all windows receive the default Windows system menu. To customize the system menu, call GetSystemMenu to get a copy of the system menu (bRevert = FALSE). Then, modify this menu using the menu functions (i.e., AppendMenu, ModifyMenu). Windows will use this modified system menu until GetSystemMenu is called with bRevert = TRUE. When the menu is reverted back to the default, Windows will automatically destroy the copy.

Syntax public, CMenu* GetSystemMenu(BOOL bRevert) const;

Parameters

bRevert FALSE to retrieve a copy of the system menu for modification; TRUE to revert the menu back to the system menu. This pointer may be temporary so it should not be stored for later use. Temporary CMenus are automatically destroyed during idle-time processing so you can only depend on the validity of the CMenu returned by GetSystemMenu until your application enters its idle loop, which can occur any time you return control to Windows (i.e., returning from a message map).

Returns A pointer to a copy of the system menu for this window.

See Also CMenu::AppendMenu, CMenu::ModifyMenu, ::GetSystemMenu

Example

```
CMenu *pMenu = AfxGetMainWnd()->GetSystemMenu(FALSE);
pMenu->DeleteMenu(MF_BYCOMMAND,SC_CLOSE); // remove close from menu
```

GetTopLevelFrame ■ 2.0 ■ 3.0

Description Retrieves a pointer to the top-level parent frame window of this window. If the top-level parent of this window is not a frame window, this function returns NULL.

Syntax public, CFrameWnd* GetTopLevelFrame() const;

Parameters None.

Returns A pointer to this window's top-level owner window. This pointer may be temporary so it should not be stored for later use. Temporary CFrameWnds are automatically destroyed during idle-time processing so

	you can only depend on the validity of the CFrameWnd returned by GetTopLevelFrame until your application enters its idle loop, which can occur any time you return control to Windows (i.e., returning from a message map). This function may return NULL if the CWnd object is not attached to a window or if the top-level parent of the window is not a frame window.
See Also	CWnd::GetTopLevelParentWnd, CWnd::GetTopLevelOwner

GetTopLevelOwner ■ 2.0 ■ 3.0

Description	Retrieves a pointer to this window's top-level owner window. The top-level owner window is the window that is a direct child of the desktop window and an owner (either directly or indirectly) of this window.
Syntax	public, CWnd* GetTopLevelOwner() const;
Parameters	None.
Returns	A pointer to this window's top-level owner window. This pointer may be temporary so it should not be stored for later use. Temporary CWnds are automatically destroyed during idle-time processing so you can only depend on the validity of the CWnd returned by GetTopLevelOwner until your application enters its idle loop, which can occur any time you return control to Windows (i.e., returning from a message map).
See Also	CWnd::GetTopLevelParent, CWnd::GetTopLevelFrame

GetTopLevelParent ■ 2.0 ■ 3.0

Description	Retrieves a pointer to this window's top-level parent window.
Syntax	public, CWnd* GetTopLevelParent() const;
Parameters	None.
Returns	A pointer to this window's top-level parent window. This pointer may be temporary so it should not be stored for later use. Temporary CWnds are automatically destroyed during idle-time processing so you can only depend on the validity of the CWnd returned by GetTopLevelParent until your application enters its idle loop, which can occur any time you return control to Windows (i.e., returning from a message map).
See Also	CWnd::GetTopLevelOwner, CWnd::GetTopLevelFrame

GetTopWindow ■ 2.0 ■ 3.0

Description	Retrieves the top-level child window of this window. If this window has no children, the function returns NULL.
Syntax	public, CWnd* GetTopWindow() const;

Parameters None.

Returns A pointer to the top-level child of this window or NULL if this window has no children. This pointer may be temporary so it should not be stored for later use. Temporary CWnds are automatically destroyed during idle-time processing so you can only depend on the validity of the CWnd returned by GetTopWindow until your application enters its idle loop, which can occur any time you return control to Windows (i.e., returning from a message map).

See Also CWnd::GetWindow, ::GetTopWindow

GetUpdateRect

■ 2.0 ■ 3.0

Description Retrieves the bounding rectangle of the current update region. The bounding rectangle is the smallest rectangle that can completely contain the update region. Also, note that Windows validates the update region before sending a WM_PAINT message so any call to this function while processing WM_PAINT will return an empty rectangle.

Syntax public, BOOL GetUpdateRect(LPRECT lpRect, BOOL bErase = FALSE);

Parameters

lpRect A pointer to a RECT structure or a CRect object that will be filled with the coordinates of the update region bounding rectangle. If the window class for this window has the CS_OWNDC style and the mapping mode is not MM_TEXT, the coordinates are in logical units; otherwise, the coordinates are in client coordinates. In Win32, you can pass NULL for this parameter (the function still returns non-zero if the update region is not empty and zero if it is).

bErase TRUE if the update region should be erased before it is painted. If any part of the update region is marked for erasure, the entire update region is erased. The region is erased by sending a WM_ERASEBKGND message to the window.

Returns Non-zero if the update region is not empty; otherwise, zero.

See Also CWnd::GetUpdateRgn, ::GetUpdateRect

Example

```
CRect rectUpdate;
pWnd->GetUpdateRect(rectUpdate,FALSE);
```

GetUpdateRgn

■ 2.0 ■ 3.0

Description Retrieves the current update region. The update region is the area of the window marked for painting. Note that the region you pass in must already contain a valid region; that is, you can't just create a CRgn object and pass it to this function—you must create some type of region and associate it with the CRgn object (by calling CRgn::CreateRectRgn, for example). Finally, note that Windows validates the update region before sending a WM_PAINT message so any call to this function while processing WM_PAINT will return an empty region.

Syntax public, int GetUpdateRgn(CRgn* pRgn, BOOL bErase = FALSE);

Parameters

pRgn Pointer to a CRgn object that will be set to the update region.

bErase TRUE if the update region should be erased before it is painted. If any part of the update region is marked for erasure, the entire update region is erased. The region is erased by sending a WM_ERASEBKGND message to the window.

Returns One of the following values:

SIMPLEREGION The region has no overlapping borders.

COMPLEXREGION The region has overlapping borders.

NULLREGION The region is empty.

ERROR No region was created.

See Also CWnd::GetUpdateRect, ::GetUpdateRgn

Example

```
CRgn rgn;
rgn.CreateRectRegion(0,0,0,0);
pWnd->GetUpdateRect(&rgn,FALSE);
```

GetWindow

■ 2.0 ■ 3.0

Description Retrieves a pointer to a window which has the specified relationship to this window.

Syntax public, CWnd* GetWindow(UINT nCmd) const;

Parameters

nCmd A constant that identifies the relationship between this window and the desired window. Can be one of the following values:

GW_CHILD Retrieves the window's first child window.

GW_HWNDFIRST If this window is a child window, retrieves the first sibling window; otherwise, it retrieves the first top-level window.

GW_HWNDLAST If this window is a child window, retrieves the last sibling window; otherwise, it returns the last top-level window.

GW_HWNDNEXT Retrieves the next window on the window manager's list.

GW_HWNDPREV Retrieves the previous window on the window manager's list.

GW_OWNER Retrieves the window's owner.

Returns Pointer to the requested window.

See Also CWnd::GetParent, CWnd::GetOwner, CWnd::GetNextWindow, ::GetWindow

GetWindowContextHelpId

■ 2.0 ■ 3.0 ■ NM

Description Returns the current help ID associated with the window. This can be used to look up the appropriate help topic in a Windows help file. GetWindowContextHelpId simply returns the value that was previously set using the SetWindowContextHelpId function.

Syntax public, DWORD GetWindowContextHelpId() const;

Parameters None.

Returns The help context ID.

See Also CWnd::SetWindowContextHelpId

Example

```
DWORD dwId = pWnd->GetWindowContextHelpId();
```

GetWindowDC

■ 2.0 ■ 3.0

Description Retrieves a pointer to a device context object that can be used to paint anywhere within the windows bounding rectangle, including the non-client areas. You must call CWnd::ReleaseDC to free the device context once you are done with it. Instead of using this function, you may want to use the CWindowDC object which encapsulates the creation and release of the device context in its constructor and destructor.

Syntax public, CDC* GetWindowDC();

Parameters None.

Returns A pointer to a device context for the entire window area.

See Also CWnd::ReleaseDC, CWindowDC

Example See CWnd::GetDC

GetWindowPlacement

■ 2.0 ■ 3.0

Description Fills a WINDOWPLACEMENT structure with show state and placement information about the window.

Syntax public, BOOL GetWindowPlacement(WINDOWPLACEMENT* lpwndpl) const;

Parameters

lpwndpl A pointer to a WINDOWPLACEMENT structure that will be filled with show state (visible, hidden, maximized, minimized, etc.) and placement information about the window. The flag's member of this structure is always set to zero by this function. For a complete description of the WINDOWPLACEMENT structure, see the Windows SDK documentation.

Returns Non-zero if the function is successful; otherwise, zero.

See Also CWnd::SetWindowPlacement

Example

```
WINDOWPLACEMENT place;
pWnd->GetWindowPlacement(&place);
```

GetWindowRect

■ 2.0 ■ 3.0

Description Retrieves the coordinates of the bounding rectangle of the window. The coordinates are retrieved in screen coordinates.

Syntax public, void GetWindowRect(LPRECT lpRect) const;

Parameters

lpRect A pointer to a RECT structure or a CRect object that will be filled with the window's coordinates.

Returns Nothing is returned.

See Also CWnd::GetClientRect, ::GetWindowRect

Example

```
CRect windowRect;
pWnd->GetWindowRect(windowRect);
```

GetWindowText

■ 2.0 ■ 3.0

Description Retrieves the current window caption text. The caption text is used in different ways by different types of windows. For a normal window, the caption text is usually displayed in the caption bar at the top of the window. For an edit box, the caption text is the text contained in the edit control itself.

Syntax public, int GetWindowText(LPTSTR lpszStringBuf, int nMaxCount) const;
public, void GetWindowText(CString& rString) const;

Parameters

lpszStringBuf A pointer to a character buffer in which the NULL-terminated window text will be placed.

nMaxCount The size of the buffer pointed to by *lpszStringBuf*.

rString A reference to a CString that will be filled with the window text.

Returns The first form of the function returns the number of characters actually copied to the supplied buffer. Nothing is returned by the second form.

See Also CWnd::GetWindowTextLength, CWnd::SetWindowText, ::GetWindowText

GetWindowTextLength

■ 2.0 ■ 3.0

Description Retrieves the length of the current window caption text. Call this function before calling the form of the GetWindowText function that takes a character buffer pointer in order to determine the size of the buffer required to hold the window caption text.

Syntax public, int GetWindowTextLength() const;

Parameters None.

Returns The number of characters in the current window caption.

See Also CWnd::GetWindowText

GrayCtlColor ■ 2.0 ■ 3.0 ■ UD

Description Helper function called by the CWnd::OnGrayCtlColor handler to handle the default gray background dialog look. CWnd::OnGrayCtlColor is, in turn, called by CDialog::OnCtlColor.

Syntax public, static BOOL PASCAL GrayCtlColor(HDC hDC, HWND hWnd, UINT nCtlColor, HBRUSH hbrGray, COLORREF clrText);

Parameters

hDC Device context where the gray background colors are set up. This device context is passed to the OnCtlColor handler by Windows and is forwarded to this function by MFC.

hWnd The window for which the colors are being set.

nCtlColor Specifies the type of control for which the color is being set. For a list of values for this parameter, see the CWnd::OnCtlColor function.

hbrGray The brush to use for the dialog background.

clrText The color to use as the text color.

Returns TRUE if the specified colors were used; FALSE if the caller should call the default window procedure to set the colors.

See Also CDialog::OnCtlColor, CWnd::OnGrayCtlColor

HandleFloatingSysCommand ■ 2.0 ■ 3.0 ■ UD

Description Performs special system menu processing for floating toolbars. Its location at the CWnd level is suspect, considering it is only used to filter system menu commands for a CMiniFrameWnd window. The CMiniFrameWnd object is used to contain a floating toolbar.

Syntax public, BOOL HandleFloatingSysCommand(UINT nID, LPARAM lParam);

Parameters

nID The ID of the selected system command. For a list of these commands, see the CWnd::OnSysCommand function.

lParam If the system menu command was selected with the mouse, this parameter contains the cursor coordinates. The low word contains the x coordinate and the high word contains the y coordinate. Use the LOWORD and HIWORD macros to obtain these values. If the command was selected with the keyboard, this parameter is not used.

Returns Nothing is returned.

See Also CWnd::OnSysCommand

HideCaret

■ 2.0 ■ 3.0

Description Hides the caret. HideCaret does not destroy the caret; it simply removes it from the display. Call CWnd::ShowCaret to show the caret. If you call HideCaret multiple times, you will have to call ShowCaret an equivalent number of times before the caret will actually be shown.

Syntax public, void HideCaret();

Parameters None.

Returns Nothing is returned.

See Also CWnd::ShowCaret, ::HideCaret

HiliteMenuItem

■ 2.0 ■ 3.0

Description Highlights or un-highlights a specified menu item on a top-level menu. A top-level menu is a menu bar, not a popup menu.

Syntax public, BOOL HiliteMenuItem(CMenu* pMenu, UINT nIDHiliteItem, UINT nHilite);

Parameters

pMenu A pointer to the CMenu object containing the item to be highlighted.

nIDHiliteItem Specifies the menu item to highlight. Depending on the value of *nHilite*, this should be the resource ID of the item or the ordinal position of the item in the menu.

nHilite Flags that indicate whether the menu item should be highlighted or unhighlighted and whether the *nIDHiliteItem* contains a menu item ID or an ordinal position value. The flags and their meanings are listed below:

MF_BYCOMMAND *nIDHiliteItem* contains the menu-item ID (the default).

MF_BYPOSITION *nIDHiliteItem* contains the zero-based ordinal position of the menu item.

MF_HILITE Highlights the item.

MF_UNHILITE Removes the highlight from the item (the default).

Returns Non-zero if the menu item was highlighted; otherwise, zero.

See Also CWnd::ModifyMenu, ::HiliteMenuItem

Example

```
pWnd->HiliteMenuItem(pWnd->GetMenu(),1,MF_BYPOSITION|MF_HILITE);
```

Invalidate

■ 2.0 ■ 3.0

Description Marks the entire client area of the window as invalid. Calling this function is equivalent to calling CWnd::InvalidateRect with a NULL rectangle pointer. Invalid areas of a window are accumulated into the current update region. The update region is the area of the window that will be repainted the next time Windows sends a WM_PAINT message to the window. Windows sends a paint message to the window only when the update region is not empty and there are no other messages waiting for the application. You can remove parts of the update region by calling the CWnd::ValidateRgn or CWnd::ValidateRect function.

Syntax public, void Invalidate(BOOL bErase = TRUE);

Parameters

bErase TRUE if the update region should be erased before it is painted. If any part of the update region is marked for erasure, the entire update region is erased. The region is erased by sending a WM_ERASEBKGND message to the window.

Returns Nothing is returned.

See Also CWnd::InvalidateRect, CWnd::InvalidateRgn, CWnd::ValidateRect, CWnd::ValidateRgn, CWnd::OnPaint, CWnd::OnEraseBkgnd

Example

```
pWnd->Invalidate();
```

InvalidateRect

■ 2.0 ■ 3.0

Description Marks the specified rectangle as invalid. Invalid areas of a window are accumulated into the current update region. The update region is the area of the window that will be repainted the next time Windows sends a WM_PAINT message to the window. Windows sends a paint message to the window only when the update region is not empty and there are no other messages waiting for the application. You can remove parts of the update region by calling the CWnd::ValidateRgn or CWnd::ValidateRect function.

Syntax public, void InvalidateRect(LPCRECT lpRect, BOOL bErase = TRUE);

Parameters

lpRect A pointer to a RECT structure or a CRect object containing the rectangle to invalidate, in client coordinates. If NULL, Windows invalidates the entire client area of the window.

bErase TRUE if the update region should be erased before it is painted. If any part of the update region is marked for erasure, the entire update region is erased. The region is erased by sending a WM_ERASEBKGND message to the window.

Returns Nothing is returned.

See Also CWnd::InvalidateRgn, CWnd::ValidateRect, CWnd::ValidateRgn, CWnd::OnPaint, CWnd::OnEraseBkgnd, ::InvalidateRect

Example

```
CRect rect(1,1,200,100);
pWnd->InvalidateRect(rect,TRUE);
```

InvalidateRgn

■ 2.0 ■ 3.0

Description Marks the specified region as invalid. Invalid areas of a window are accumulated into the current update region. The update region is the area of the window that will be repainted the next time Windows sends a WM_PAINT message to the window. Windows sends a paint message to the window only when the update region is not empty and there are no other messages waiting for the application. You can remove parts of the update region by calling the CWnd::ValidateRgn or CWnd::ValidateRect function.

Syntax public, void InvalidateRgn(CRgn* pRgn, BOOL bErase = TRUE);

Parameters

pRgn A pointer to a CRgn object identifying the region to invalidate. The region should be in client coordinates. If NULL, Windows invalidates the entire client area of the window.

bErase TRUE if the update region should be erased before it is painted. If any part of the update region is marked for erasure, the entire update region is erased. The region is erased by sending a WM_ERASEBKGND message to the window.

Returns Nothing is returned.

See Also CWnd::InvalidateRect, CWnd::ValidateRect, CWnd::ValidateRgn, CWnd::OnPaint, CWnd::OnEraseBkgnd, ::InvalidateRgn

Example

```
CRgn rgn;
rgn.CreateRectRgn(1,1,200,100);
pWnd->InvalidateRgn(&rgn,TRUE);
```

IsChild

■ 2.0 ■ 3.0

Description Determines whether a specified window is a child or other direct descendant of this window.

Syntax public, BOOL IsChild(const CWnd* pWnd) const;

Parameters

pWnd A pointer to the window to check.

Returns Non-zero if the window is a child or direct descendant of this window; otherwise, zero.

See Also ::IsChild

Example

```
// repaint window if it is a child
void CMyWnd::RepaintIfChild(CWnd *pPossibleChild)
{
     if (IsChild(pPossibleChild))
           pPossibleChild->InvalidateRect(NULL);
}
```

IsDialogMessage ■ 2.0 ■ 3.0

Description Called by the framework to determine if a message is meant for a modeless dialog or dialog-like window. If MFC is built without support for OCXs, it simply calls the SDK ::IsDialogMessage function. If OCXs are being supported, it also parses out messages meant for those controls.

Syntax public, BOOL IsDialogMessage(LPMSG lpMsg);

Parameters

lpMsg A pointer to an MSG structure. For a full description of this structure, see the Windows SDK documentation. The contents of this structure are typically filled in by Windows via a call to the ::GetMessage or ::PeekMessage structures.

Returns Nothing is returned.

See Also ::IsDialogMessage

IsDlgButtonChecked ■ 2.0 ■ 3.0

Description Determines if a button is checked, unchecked, or in the case of a three-state button, if it is indeterminate.

Syntax public, UINT IsDlgButtonChecked(int nIDButton) const;

Parameters

nIDButton Resource ID of the button whose state should be queried.

Returns Zero if the button is unchecked, non-zero if it is checked. If the button is a tri-state button, a return value of two indicates that the button is in the indeterminate (dimmed) state. If the button is a push button, this function always returns zero.

See Also CWnd::CheckDlgButton, CWnd::CheckRadioButton, CButton::GetChecked, ::IsDlgButtonChecked

Example

```
// handler for button click
void CMyDialog::OnClickButton1()
{ // enable another button based on state of this one
        CWnd *pWnd = GetDlgItem(IDC_BUTTON2);
        if (pWnd)
                  pWnd->EnableWindow(IsDlgButtonChecked(IDC_BUTTON1));
}
```

IsFrameWnd

■ 2.0 ■ 3.0

Description Determines if the window is a frame window—that is, if it is derived from the CFrameWnd class. IsFrameWnd does this by simply calling IsKindOf(RUNTIME_CLASS(CFrameWnd)).

Syntax public, virtual BOOL IsFrameWnd() const;

Parameters None.

Returns Non-zero if the window is a frame window; otherwise, zero.

See Also CObject::IsKindOf

IsIconic

■ 2.0 ■ 3.0

Description Determines whether the window is minimized.

Syntax public, BOOL IsIconic() const;

Parameters None.

Returns Non-zero if the window is minimized; otherwise, zero.

See Also ::IsIconic

Example

```
// if iconic, draw icon; otherwise, paint normal
void CWnd::OnPaint()
{
      CPaintDC dc(this); // device context for painting
      if (IsIconic())
      {
            HICON hIcon = AfxGetApp()->LoadIcon(IDI_MYICON);
            dc.DrawIcon(0,0,hIcon);
      }
      else
            // paint normal
```

IsTopParentActive

■ 2.0 ■ 3.0

Description Determines whether the current foreground window is the last active popup of the top-level parent of this window.

Syntax public, BOOL IsTopParentActive() const;

Parameters None.

Returns TRUE if the current foreground window is the last active popup of the top-level parent of this window; otherwise, FALSE.

See Also CWnd::GetForegroundWindow, CWnd::GetTopLevelParent, CWnd::GetLastActivePopup

IsWindowEnabled

■ 2.0 ■ 3.0

Description Determines whether the window is enabled or disabled.

Syntax public, BOOL IsWindowEnabled() const;

Parameters None.

Returns Non-zero if the window is enabled; otherwise, zero.

See Also CWnd::EnableWindow, ::IsWindowEnabled

IsWindowVisible

■ 2.0 ■ 3.0

Description Determines whether the window is visible or not. This function returns TRUE if the WS_VISIBLE style is set for the window and its parent window is also visible. IsWindowVisible does not actually determine if the window is visible on the display screen—it may be covered by other windows.

Syntax public, BOOL IsWindowVisible() const;

Parameters None.

Returns Non-zero if the window is visible; otherwise, zero.

See Also CWnd::ShowWindow, ::IsWindowVisible

IsZoomed

■ 2.0 ■ 3.0

Description Determines whether the window is maximized or not.

Syntax public, BOOL IsZoomed() const;

Parameters None.

Returns Non-zero if the window is maximized; otherwise, zero.

Example See CWnd::IsIconic

KillTimer

■ 2.0 ■ 3.0

Description Destroys a timer that was created with the SetTimer function.

Syntax public, BOOL KillTimer(int nIDEvent);

Parameters

nIDEvent The ID of the timer that should be destroyed. This ID is returned from the call to CWnd::SetTimer that created the timer.

Returns Non-zero if the timer was destroyed or zero if the specified timer could not be found.

See Also CWnd::SetTimer, ::KillTimer

Example See CWnd::SetTimer

LockWindowUpdate ■ 2.0 ■ 3.0 ■ NM

Description Prevents drawing in the window. A window that has been locked is not updated and cannot be moved. If you draw into a locked window, Windows keeps track of the bounding rectangle of the drawing operations but does not actually draw. When the window is later unlocked (using the CWnd::UnlockWindowUpdate function), this area is invalidated and will eventually be repainted. Only one window can be locked at any given time.

Syntax public, BOOL LockWindowUpdate();

Parameters None.

Returns Non-zero if successful; otherwise, zero.

See Also CWnd::UnlockWindowUpdate, ::LockWindowUpdate

MapWindowPoints ■ 2.0 ■ 3.0

Description Converts points expressed in client coordinates of this window to client coordinates of a specified window.

Syntax public, void MapWindowPoints(CWnd* pWndTo, LPPOINT lpPoint, UINT nCount) const; public, void MapWindowPoints(CWnd* pWndTo, LPRECT lpRect) const;

Parameters

pWndTo A pointer to the window to which the coordinates will be converted. If this parameter is NULL, the coordinates are converted to screen coordinates.

lpPoint A pointer to an array of POINT structures or CPoint objects that will be converted.

nCount The number of points pointed to by *lpPoint.*

lpRect A pointer to a RECT structure or a CRect object that will be converted.

Returns Nothing is returned.

See Also ::MapWindowPoints

MessageBox ■ 2.0 ■ 3.0

Description Displays a message along with an icon and one or more action buttons. The icon displayed and the buttons available depend on the type of flags that are specified. An example message box is shown in Figure 5-2. Typically, you would use the global MFC function AfxMessageBox instead of this function. AfxMessageBox automatically provides the application's main window as the parent window for the message box.

Syntax public, int MessageBox(LPCTSTR lpszText, LPCTSTR lpszCaption = NULL, UINT nType = MB_OK);

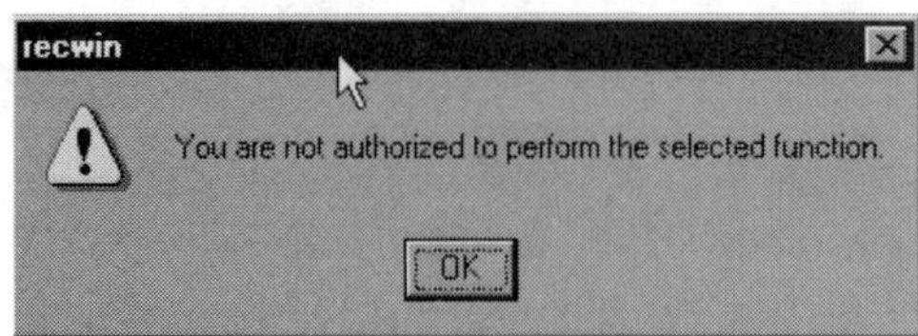

Figure 5-2 Example Message Box

Parameters

lpszText	A pointer to a NULL-terminated string that contains the text to display in the message box.
lpszCaption	A pointer to a NULL-terminated string that contains the text to display as the caption of the message box.
nType	A combination of flags. Possible flags are listed below. Only one flag from each group should be used:

Button Flags:

MB_ABORTRETRYIGNORE	Abort, Retry, and Ignore buttons.
MB_OK	OK button only.
MB_OKCANCEL	OK and Cancel buttons.
MB_RETRYCANCEL	Retry and Cancel buttons.
MB_YESNO	Yes and No buttons.
MB_YESNOCANCEL	Yes, No, and Cancel buttons.

Icon Flags:

MB_ICONEXCLAMATION	Exclamation-point icon.
MB_ICONINFORMATION	An icon consisting of an "i" in a circle.
MB_ICONQUESTION	A question-mark icon.
MB_ICONSTOP	A stop-sign icon.

Default Button Flags:

MB_DEFBUTTON1	The first button is the default button. This is the default.
MB_DEFBUTTON2	The second button is the default button.
MB_DEFBUTTON3	The third button is the default button.

Modality Flags:

MB_APPLMODAL	The user must respond to the message box before continuing work in the current window. However, the user can move to the windows of other applications and work in those windows. The default is MB_APPLMODAL if neither MB_SYSTEMMODAL nor MB_TASKMODAL is specified.

MB_SYSTEMMODAL	All applications are suspended until the user responds to the message box. System-modal message boxes are used to notify the user of serious, potentially damaging errors that require immediate attention and should be used sparingly.
MB_TASKMODAL	Similar to MB_APPLMODAL, but not useful within a Microsoft Foundation Class application. This flag is reserved for a calling application or library that does not have a window handle available.

Returns Zero if the function fails or a value that indicates which button the user pressed (IDABORT, IDCANCEL, IDIGNORE, IDNO, IDOK, IDRETRY, or IDYES).

See Also AfxMessageBox, ::MessageBox

Example

```
void CMyWnd::DisplayErrorMessage(LPCSTR sMsg)
{
     MessageBox(sMsg,"Error",MB_OK|MB_ICONSTOP);
}
```

ModifyStyle ■ 2.0 ■ 3.0

Description Modifies the window styles associated with this window by adding the specified style flags and removing other specified style flags. ModifyStyle will also optionally call the ::SetWindowPos function with a set of specified flags.

Syntax public, BOOL ModifyStyle(DWORD dwRemove, DWORD dwAdd, UINT nFlags = 0); public, static BOOL PASCAL ModifyStyle(HWND hWnd, DWORD dwRemove, DWORD dwAdd, UINT nFlags);

Parameters

dwRemove Combination of window style flags that should be removed from the window. For a listing of these styles, see the Windows SDK documentation.

dwAdd Combination of window style flags that should be added to the window. For a listing of these styles, see the Windows SDK documentation.

nFlags SetWindowPos flags that will be passed to a call to SetWindowPos. The flags SWP_NOSIZE, SWP_NOMOVE, SWP_NOZORDER, SWP_NOACTIVATE are automatically used because there is no way to specify the required parameters to ModifyStyle. If this parameter is zero, SetWindowPos will not be called.

hWnd Window handle of the window to modify.

Returns Non-zero if successful; zero otherwise.

See Also CWnd::ModifyStyleEx, CWnd::SetWindowPos, ::SetWindowPos

ModifyStyleEx ■ 2.0 ■ 3.0

Description Modifies the extended window styles associated with this window by adding the specified style flags and removing other specified style flags. ModifyStyleEx will also optionally call the ::SetWindowPos function with a set of specified flags.

Syntax public, BOOL ModifyStyleEx(DWORD dwRemove, DWORD dwAdd, UINT nFlags = 0); public, static BOOL PASCAL ModifyStyleEx(HWND hWnd, DWORD dwRemove, DWORD dwAdd, UINT nFlags);

Parameters

dwRemove Combination of extended window style flags that should be removed from the window. For a listing of these styles, see the Windows SDK documentation.

dwAdd Combination of extended window style flags that should be added to the window. For a listing of these styles, see the Windows SDK documentation.

nFlags SetWindowPos flags that will be passed to a call to SetWindowPos. The flags SWP_NOSIZE, SWP_NOMOVE, SWP_NOZORDER, SWP_NOACTIVATE are automatically used because there is no way to specify the required parameters to ModifyStyleEx. If this parameter is zero, SetWindowPos will not be called.

hWnd Window handle of the window to modify.

Returns Non-zero if successful; zero otherwise.

See Also CWnd::ModifyStyle, CWnd::SetWindowPos, ::SetWindowPos

MoveWindow ■ 2.0 ■ 3.0

Description Moves the window to the specified location and resizes it to the specified size. When you move a window with this function, Windows sends a WM_GETMINMAXINFO message to the window. This message gives the window an opportunity to control the size and position of the window.

Syntax public, void MoveWindow(int x, int y, int nWidth, int nHeight, BOOL bRepaint = TRUE); public, void MoveWindow(LPCRECT lpRect, BOOL bRepaint = TRUE);

Parameters

x The new x coordinate of the top-left corner of the window. If this window is a top-level window, x is relative to the top-left corner of the screen. If this window is a child window, x is relative to the top-left corner of the client area of the parent.

y The new y coordinate of the top-left corner of the window. If this window is a top-level window, y is relative to the top-left corner of the screen. If this window is a child window, y is relative to the top-left corner of the client area of the parent.

nWidth The new width of the window.

nHeight The new height of the window.

bRepaint TRUE if the window should be repainted or FALSE if not. If you pass FALSE for this parameter, no repainting will occur—this includes the area of the parent window which is uncovered by the move.

lpRect Pointer to a RECT structure or a CRect object that contains the new position and size of the window.

Returns Nothing is returned.

See Also CWnd::SetWindowPos, ::MoveWindow

Example

```
void CMyWnd::MoveChild()
{     // move child window to upper-left corner and make it half the
      // size of its parent
      CRect rc;
      GetClientRect(rc);
      m_pChildWnd->MoveWindow(0,0,rc.right/2,rc.bottom/2,TRUE);
}
```

OnChildNotify

■ 2.0 ■ 3.0

Description This function is called by MFC from this window's parent window whenever it receives a message that applies to this window. Normally, this window is a control and the parent is the control's container, often a dialog. The default implementation of this function simply returns zero, indicating that the parent should handle the message.

Syntax public, OnChildNotify(UINT message, WPARAM wParam, LPARAM lParam, LRESULT *plResult);

Parameters

message The message sent to the parent.

wParam Message-specific additional information.

lParam Message-specific additional information.

pResult A pointer to the result generated by the child window which will be returned to the parent window.

Returns Non-zero if the message was handled by this window; zero if the parent window should handle the message.

See Also CWnd::ReflectChildNotify, CWnd::SendChildNotifyLastMessage, CWnd::ReflectLastMsg

OnCommand

■ 2.0 ■ 3.0

Description Responds to the WM_COMMAND message sent when a menu item is selected, a child control sends a notification, or an accelerator keystroke is translated. MFC routes the message through its command-routing scheme. See Chapter 4, *Windows Messaging,* for a detailed description of message routing. You can override this function if you want to alter the way in which MFC routes command messages or if you want to handle certain command messages yourself prior to routing.

Syntax public, virtual BOOL OnCommand(WPARAM wParam, LPARAM lParam);

Parameters

wParam The low-order word contains the ID of the menu item or control associated with the WM_COMMAND message. The high-order word contains the notification code if the message is from a control: one if the message is from a translated accelerator keystroke, or zero if the message is from a menu item.

lParam If the message is from a control, this parameter contains a pointer to the control that sent the message; otherwise, the parameter is zero.

Returns Non-zero if the message is processed; otherwise, zero.

OnCtlColor ■ 2.0 ■ 3.0

Description Handler function for the WM_CTLCOLOR message. This message is usually sent by a child control to its parent just before it is about to be drawn in order to obtain the brush to be used when painting the background of the control. You can also set the color used to draw text in the control by calling the CDC::SetTextColor function with the desired color. For edit controls, you must return the desired brush in response to both the CTLCOLOR_EDIT and CTLCOLOR_MSGBOX codes as well as call CDC::SetBkColor. Note that for drop-down combo boxes, the drop-down list box is actually a child of the combo box and, therefore, the OnCtlColor message is sent to the combo box itself.

Syntax public, afx_msg HBRUSH OnCtlColor(CDC *pDC, CWnd * pWnd, UINT nCtlColor);

Parameters

pDC A pointer to the device context that will be used to draw the control.

pWnd A pointer to the control.

nCtlColor One of the following constants identifying the type of control:

CTLCOLOR_BTN Button control.

CTLCOLOR_DLG Dialog box.

CTLCOLOR_EDIT Edit control.

CTLCOLOR_LISTBOX List box control.

CTLCOLOR_MSGBOX Message box.

CTLCOLOR_SCROLLBAR Scrollbar control.

CTLCOLOR_STATIC Static control.

Returns A handle to the brush that will be used to paint the background of the control.

See Also CWnd::OnGrayControlColor

OnGrayCtlColor ■ 2.5 ■ 4.0 ■ UD

Description Called by MFC from the CDialog::OnCtlColor function in order to implement the standard gray background dialogs.

Syntax public, BOOL OnGrayCtlColor;

Parameters None.

Returns Non-zero if the window is restored; otherwise, zero.

See Also CDialog::OnCtlColor, CWnd::OnCtlColor, CWnd::GrayCtlColor

OnToolHitTest ■ 2.0 ■ 3.0

Description Called by MFC to determine if a tooltip should be displayed and, if so, which one. The CWnd version of OnToolHitTest simply searches for the child window containing the specified point and registers a callback that will actually supply the tooltip text for that child window (if any).

Syntax public, virtual int OnToolHitTest(CPoint point, TOOLINFO *pTI) const;

Parameters

point The coordinates, relative to the upper-left corner of the containing window, of the cursor.

pTI A pointer to a TOOLINFO structure that is filled with information regarding the tooltip to be displayed. If the specified point is within a child window, this structure is modified as follows:

pTI->hwnd Set to the handle of this window.

pTI->uId Set to the handle of the child window containing the point.

pTI->uFlags The TTF_IDISHWND flag is OR'd with the current contents.

pTI->lpszText Set to LPSTR_TEXTCALLBACK.

Returns One if an appropriate tooltip was found; otherwise, negative one.

OnWndMsg ■ 2.0 ■ 3.0 ■ NM ■ UD

Description Called by the default window procedure, CWnd::WindowProc, or during the process of message reflection. This function basically handles routing of all window messages.

Syntax public, virtual BOOL OnWndMsg(UINT message, WPARAM wParam, LPARAM lParam, LRESULT *plResult);

Parameters

message	The message to handle.
wParam	Message-specific additional information.
lParam	Message-specific additional information.
pResult	A pointer to the result generated by processing the message. Used for WM_NOTIFY messages.
Returns	Non-zero if the message was handled; otherwise, zero.
See Also	CWnd::WindowProc

OpenClipboard ■ 2.0 ■ 3.0

Description	Opens the Clipboard if another window does not currently have it open. When a window has the Clipboard open, no other application can write to the Clipboard. Note that the Clipboard is not owned by this window until the CWnd::EmptyClipboard function is called.
Syntax	public, BOOL OpenClipboard();
Parameters	None.
Returns	Non-zero if the Clipboard is opened; zero if the Clipboard is already open.
See Also	CWnd::EmptyClipboard, CWnd::CloseClipboard, ::OpenClipboard

OpenIcon ■ 2.0 ■ 3.0 ■ NM ■ UD

Description	Restores the window from the iconic state to the normal state and activates the window.
Syntax	public, BOOL OpenIcon();
Parameters	None.
Returns	Non-zero if the window is restored; otherwise, zero.
See Also	CWnd::IsIconic, CWnd::ShowWindow, ::OpenIcon

operator HWND ■ 2.0 ■ 3.0

Description	Returns the HWND handle associated with the CWnd object. This operator allows you to pass a CWnd object wherever an HWND is required. This is handy if you need to call an SDK function directly.
Syntax	public, operator HWND() const;
Parameters	None.
Returns	The HWND associated with this CWnd.

PostMessage

■ 2.0 ■ 3.0

Description Posts a message to the application's message queue. Posting a message is different from sending a message. When a message is sent it is immediately received. When a message is posted, it is put in the queue behind any other messages already in the queue and will be received by the application at some point in the future. PostMessage does not wait for the message to be processed.

Syntax public, BOOL PostMessage(UINT message, WPARAM wParam = 0, LPARAM lParam = 0);

Parameters

message The message to post.

wParam Message-specific additional information.

lParam Message-specific additional information.

Returns Non-zero if the message was posted; otherwise, zero.

See Also CWnd::SendMessage, ::PostMessage

Example

```
void CMyDialog::OnInitDialog()
{
      // post message to dialog so that dialog can be displayed
      // before the work is done
      PostMessage(WM_USER_MYMSG);
      CDialog::OnInitDialog();
}
```

PostNcDestroy

■ 2.0 ■ 3.0

Description Called by the framework after a window is destroyed. The default implementation does nothing. You can override this function to perform cleanup when the window is destroyed.

Syntax protected, virtual void PostNcDestroy();

Parameters None.

Returns Nothing is returned.

See Also CWnd::OnDestroy, CWnd::DestroyWindow

PreCreateWindow

■ 2.0 ■ 3.0

Description Called by the framework immediately before a window is created. The default implementation of this function takes care of assigning MFC's default window class to the window if a class was not supplied. You can override this function in order to modify the window creation variables before the window is created.

Syntax public, virtual BOOL PreCreateWindow(CREATESTRUCT& cs);

Parameters

cs — A pointer to a CREATESTRUCT that describes the window to be created. See the Windows SDK documentation for a complete descripion of this structure.

Returns — Non-zero if the window should be created or zero if creation should be aborted.

See Also — CWnd::Create, CWnd::CreateEx

Example

```
BOOL CMyWnd::PreCreateWindow(CREATESTRUCT& cs)
{ // remove scroll bar styles before window is created
cs.style &= ~(WS_HSCROLL | WS_VSCROLL);
return CWnd::PreCreateWindow(cs);
}
```

PreSubclassWindow ■ 2.0 ■ 3.0

Description — Called by the framework immediately prior to the subclassing of a window. The default implementation of this function does nothing. Override this function if you want to do something before the window is subclassed—such as subclassing the window yourself.

Syntax — public, virtual void PreSubclassWindow();

Parameters — None.

Returns — Nothing is returned.

See Also — CWnd::SubclassWindow

PreTranslateInput ■ 2.0 ■ 3.0 ■ UD

Description — Internal MFC function that first checks to see if a message is an input message (keyboard input or mouse input) and then calls CWnd::IsDialogMessage to process dialog messages.

Syntax — public, BOOL PreTranslateInput(LPMSG lpMsg);

Parameters

lpMsg — A pointer to an MSG structure containing the message to process. For a description of the MSG structure, see the Windows SDK documentation.

Returns — The result of a call to IsDialogMessage that returns non-zero if the message is processed and zero if it is not.

See Also — CWnd::IsDialogMessage

PreTranslateMessage ■ 2.0 ■ 3.0

Description — Called by MFC to filter and dispatch tooltip messages. If tooltips are not enabled, this function does nothing. If tooltips are enabled, it simply calls the CWnd::FilterToolTipMessage function.

Syntax public, virtual BOOL PreTranslateMessage(MSG* pMsg);

Parameters

pMsg A pointer to an MSG structure containing the current message. For a complete description of the MSG structure, see the Windows SDK documentation.

Returns TRUE if the message is processed; FALSE otherwise.

See Also CWnd::FilterToolTipMessage

PRINT ■ 4.0

Description Call this function to draw a window in a specified device context that is usually a printer device context.

Syntax public, void Print(CDC* pDC, DWORD dwFlags) const;

Parameters

pDC A pointer to the device context into which the window should paint itself. Usually, this would be a printer device context.

dwFlags Flags that describe exactly that the window should do. Can be a combination of any of the following values:

PRF_CHECKVISIBLE Draw the window only if it is visible.

PRF_CHILDREN Draw all visible children windows.

PRF_CLIENT Draw the client area of the window.

PRF_ERASEBKGND Erase the background before drawing the window.

PRF_NONCLIENT Draw the nonclient area of the window.

PRF_OWNED Draw all owned windows.

Returns Nothing is returned.

See Also CWnd::PrintClient

PRINTCLIENT ■ 4.0

Description Call this function to draw the client area of a window in a specified device context that is usually a printer device context.

Syntax public, void PrintClient(CDC* pDC, DWORD dwFlags) const;

Parameters

pDC A pointer to the device context into which the window should paint itself. Usually, this would be a printer device context.

dwFlags Flags that describe exactly what the window should do. See the CWnd::Print function for a list of valid flags.

Returns Nothing is returned.

See Also CWnd::Print

RedrawWindow

■ 2.0 ■ 3.0

Description Updates a specified region of the window.

Syntax public, BOOL RedrawWindow(LPCRECT lpRectUpdate = NULL, CRgn* prgnUpdate = NULL, UINT flags = RDW_INVALIDATE | RDW_UPDATENOW | RDW_ERASE);

Parameters

lpRectUpdate A pointer to a RECT structure or a CRect object that contains the coordinates of the rectangle within the window that should be updated. If the *prgnUpdate* parameter is non-NULL, this parameter is ignored.

prgnUpdate A pointer to a CRgn containing the region of the window that should be invalidated. If this parameter is NULL, the *lpRectUpdate* parameter is used. If both parameters are NULL then the entire client area is updated.

flags A series of flags that describe exactly how to do the repainting:

RDW_ERASE Sends a WM_ERASEBKGND message to the window when it is repainted. If RDW_INVALIDATE is not specified, RDW_ERASE has no effect.

RDW_FRAME Causes any part of the nonclient area of the window that intersects the update region to receive a WM_NCPAINT message. If RDW_INVALIDATE is not specified, RDW_FRAME has no effect.

RDW_INTERNALPAINT Posts a WM_PAINT message to the window regardless of whether the window contains an invalid region.

RDW_INVALIDATE Invalidate *lpRectUpdate* or *prgnUpdate*.

RDW_NOERASE Suppresses any pending WM_ERASEBKGND messages.

RDW_NOFRAME Suppresses any pending WM_NCPAINT messages. If the RDW_VALIDATE flag is not specified, this flag has no effect.

RDW_NOINTERNALPAINT Suppresses any pending internal WM_PAINT messages. This flag does not affect WM_PAINT messages resulting from invalid areas.

RDW_VALIDATE Validates *lpRectUpdate* or *prgnUpdate*

RDW_ERASENOW Causes the affected windows, as specified by the RDW_ALLCHILDREN and RDW_NOCHILDREN flags, to receive WM_NCPAINT and WM_ERASEBKGND messages.

RDW_UPDATENOW Causes the affected windows, as specified by the RDW_ALLCHILDREN and RDW_NOCHILDREN flags, to receive WM_NCPAINT, WM_ERASEBKGND, and WM_PAINT messages.

RDW_ALLCHILDREN Includes child windows, if any, in the repainting operation.

RDW_NOCHILDREN Excludes child windows, if any, from the repainting operation.

Returns Non-zero if the window was redrawn; otherwise, zero.

See Also CWnd::InvalidateRect, CWnd::ValidateRect, CWnd::InvalidateRgn, CWnd::ValidateRgn

ReflectChildNotify ■ 2.0 ■ 3.0

Description Internal MFC function that is called by the OnChildNotify handler in order to reflect messages back to their source window. For more information about message reflection, see the discussion in Chapter 4, *Windows Messaging*.

Syntax public, BOOL ReflectChildNotify(UINT message, WPARAM wParam, LPARAM lParam, LRESULT* pResult);

Parameters

message The message to reflect.

wParam Message-specific additional information.

lParam Message-specific additional information.

pResult A pointer to the result generated by the child window that will be returned to the parent window.

Returns TRUE if the message is reflected; otherwise, FALSE.

See Also CWnd::OnChildNotify, CWnd::SendChildNotifyLastMessage, CWnd::ReflectLastMsg

ReflectLastMsg ■ 2.0 ■ 3.0

Description Called by the framework to reflect the last message to a child window. MFC only reflects the message if the child is an OLE control or if the child is in the permanent window map. It does this because if neither of these conditions are true, then the reflected message could not be handled anyway.

Syntax public, static BOOL PASCAL ReflectLastMsg(HWND hWndChild, LRESULT* pResult = NULL);

Parameters

hWndChild The window to reflect the message to.

pResult Holds the result returned by the child to the parent.

Returns Non-zero if the message is handled; otherwise, zero.

See Also CWnd::OnChildNotify, CWnd::SendChildNotifyLastMessage, CWnd::ReflectChildNotify

ReleaseDC ■ 2.0 ■ 3.0

Description Releases a device context that was obtained using the CWnd::GetDC or CWnd::GetDCEx functions. You must release any device contexts obtained by these functions.

Syntax public, int ReleaseDC(CDC* pDC);

Parameters

pDC A pointer to the device context that should be released.

Returns Non-zero if successful; otherwise, zero.

See Also CWnd::GetDC, CWnd::GetDCEx, ::ReleaseDC

Example See CWnd::GetDC

RepositionBars

■ 2.0 ■ 3.0

Description Called by the framework to lay out the client area of a window that contains one or more control bars (toolbar, dialog bar, etc.).

Syntax public, void RepositionBars(UINT nIDFirst, UINT nIDLast, UINT nIDLeftOver, UINT nFlag = reposDefault, LPRECT lpRectParam = NULL, LPCRECT lpRectClient = NULL, BOOL bStretch = TRUE);

Parameters

nIDFirst The child ID of the first control bar to reposition.

nIDLast The child ID of the last control bar to reposition.

nIDLeftOver The child ID of the control bar that should be sized to fit the area left over after all other children are repositioned.

reposDefault One of the following flags:

CWnd::reposDefault	Performs the layout of the control bars.
CWnd::reposExtra	Adds the contents of *lpRectParam* to the client area of *nIDLast* and performs the layout.
CWnd::reposQuery	The control bars are not actually repositioned. *lpRectParam* is filled with the size of the client area, as if the layout had actually been done.

lpRectParam A pointer to a RECT structure or a CRect object that, if the CWnd::reposQuery flag is used, will be filled with the client area left after the control bars are repositioned. If the CWnd::reposQuery flag is not specified, this parameter can be NULL.

lpRectClient A pointer to a RECT structure or a CRect object containing the available client area. If NULL, the entire client area is used.

bStretch TRUE to stretch the last bar to fill the available space.

Returns Nothing is returned.

See Also CFrameWnd::RecalcLayout, CControlBar::OnSizeParent

RunModalLoop

■ 2.0 ■ 3.0

Description MFC uses this function to implement “modal” behavior. One key use of this function is that when you display a dialog in modal form by calling the CDialog::DoModal function, MFC does not actually rely on Windows to implement the modal behavior. MFC actually creates the dialog as modeless and then calls RunModalLoop to implement modal behavior. This allows MFC to perform other operations while the modal behavior is

in effect, such as idle-time processing. RunModalLoop retrieves, translates, and dispatches messages until CWnd::ContinueModal returns FALSE, which, by default, it does after a call to CWnd::EndModalLoop.

Syntax public, int RunModalLoop(DWORD dwFlags = 0);

Parameters

dwFlags A combination of the following flags or zero.

MLF_NOIDLEMSG Don't send WM_ENTERIDLE messages to the parent.

MLF_NOKICKIDLE Don't send WM_KICKIDLE messages to the window.

MLF_SHOWONIDLE Show the window when message queue goes idle.

Returns The value passed to EndModalLoop, which ended the modal loop.

See Also CWnd::ContinueModal, CWnd::EndModalLoop

ScreenToClient ■ 2.0 ■ 3.0

Description Converts coordinates from screen coordinates to client coordinates for this window. Screen coordinates are relative to the upper-left corner of the screen. Client coordinates are relative to the upper-left corner of the client area of the window.

Syntax public, void ScreenToClient(LPPOINT lpPoint) const;
public, void ScreenToClient(LPRECT lpRect) const;

Parameters

lpPoint A pointer to a POINT structure or a CPoint object containing the point to convert.

lpRect A pointer to a RECT structure or a CRect object containing the points to convert.

Returns Nothing is returned.

See Also CWnd::ClientToScreen, ::ScreenToClient

Example

```
CPoint pt;
::GetCursorPos(&pt);
pWnd->ScreenToClient(&pt); // convert to client coordinates of pWnd
```

ScrollWindow ■ 2.0 ■ 3.0

Description Scrolls the contents of all or part of the client area of the window. ScrollWindow automatically invalidates the area of the window that is uncovered and needs updating. It does not immediately update this area, however. Call UpdateWindow if you want this area to be immediately updated.

Syntax public, void ScrollWindow(int xAmount, int yAmount, LPCRECT lpRect = NULL, LPCRECT lpClipRect = NULL);

Parameters

xAmount The amount to scroll horizontally (in device units). Positive values scroll to the right; negative values scroll to the left.

yAmount The amount to scroll vertically (in device units). Positive values scroll down; negative values scroll up.

lpRect A pointer to a RECT structure or a CRect object that contains the coordinates of the portion of the client area that should be scrolled. This parameter can be NULL, in which case the entire client area is scrolled. Also, if this parameter is NULL, child windows in the window will be scrolled. If this parameter is not NULL, child windows will not be scrolled.

lpClipRect A pointer to a RECT structure or a CRect object that contains the coordinates of the clipping rectangle to use for the scroll operation. Only the area within the clipping rectangle will be scrolled. This parameter can be NULL.

Returns Nothing is returned.

See Also CWnd::ScrollWindowEx, CDC::ScrollDC, ::ScrollWindow

Example

```
// scroll bottom half of window up to top half
CRect rc;
pWnd->GetClientRect(rc);
pWnd->ScrollWindow(0,rc.bottom/2,rc,rc);
```

ScrollWindowEx ■ 2.0 ■ 3.0

Description Scrolls the contents of all or part of the client area of the window. ScrollWindowEx will optionally automatically invalidate the area of the window that is uncovered and needs updating. It does not immediately update this area, however. Call UpdateWindow if you want this area to be immediately updated. ScrollWindowEx is different from CWnd::ScrollWindow in that it allows greater control of the scrolling and provides information regarding the invalidated region caused by the scrolling.

Syntax public, int ScrollWindowEx(int xAmount, int yAmount, LPCRECT lpRect, LPCRECT lpRectClip, CRgn* prgnUpdate, LPRECT lpRectUpdate, UINT flags);

Parameters

xAmount The amount to scroll horizontally (in device units). Positive values scroll to the right; negative values scroll to the left.

yAmount The amount to scroll vertically (in device units). Positive values scroll down; negative values scroll up.

lpRect A pointer to a RECT structure or a CRect object that contains the coordinates of the portion of the client area that should be scrolled. This parameter can be NULL, in which case the entire client area is scrolled. Also, if this parameter is NULL, child windows in the window will be scrolled. If this parameter is not NULL, child windows will not be scrolled.

lpClipRect	A pointer to a RECT structure or a CRect object that contains the coordinates of the clipping rectangle to use for the scroll operation. Only the area within the clipping rectangle will be scrolled. This parameter can be NULL.
prgnUpdate	Points to a region that, after the function executes, will contain the region invalidated by the scrolling. Can be NULL.
lpRectUpdate	Points to a RECT structure or a CRect object that, after the function executes, will be filled with the bounding rectangle of the area invalidated by the scrolling. Can be NULL.
flags	A combination of the following flags:
SW_ERASE	When specified with SW_INVALIDATE, erases the invalidated region by sending a WM_ERASEBKGND message to the window.
SW_INVALIDATE	Invalidates the region pointed to by *prgnUpdate* after scrolling.
SW_SCROLLCHILDREN	Scrolls all child windows that intersect the rectangle pointed to by *lpRectScroll* by the number of pixels specified in *xAmount* and *yAmount*. Windows sends a WM_MOVE message to all child windows that intersect *lpRectScroll*, even if they do not move.
Returns	SIMPLEREGION, COMPLEXREGION, or NULLREGION if the function is successful; otherwise, ERROR.
See Also	CWnd::ScrollWindow, CDC::ScrollDC, ::ScrollWindowEx
Example	See CWnd::ScrollWindow

SendChildNotifyLastMsg ■ 2.0 ■ 3.0

Description	Internal function used by MFC to reflect the current message back from the parent to the child that was its original source. This function is part of the new message reflection in MFC 4.0. See Chapter 4, *Windows Messaging*, for a discussion on message reflection.
Syntax	public, BOOL SendChildNotifyLastMsg(LRESULT* pResult = NULL);
Parameters	
pResult	Pointer to a buffer that contains the result sent back from the child.
Returns	Non-zero if the message was reflected back to the child; otherwise, zero.
See Also	CWnd::ReflectLastMsg

SendDlgItemMessage ■ 2.0 ■ 3.0

Description	Similar to CWnd::SendMessage except that it takes a child window ID to identify the destination for the message. See CWnd::SendMessage for further discussion.
Syntax	public, LRESULT SendDlgItemMessage(int nID, UINT message, WPARAM wParam = 0, LPARAM lParam = 0);

Parameters

nID The ID of the child window to which the message will be sent.

message The message to be sent.

wParam Message-specific additional information.

lParam Message-specific additional information.

Returns The result of the message processing. Varies depending on the message.

See Also CWnd::PostMessage, ::SendMessage

Example

```
void CMyDialog::OnInitDialog()
{
     SendDlgItemMessage(IDC_MYEDIT,WM_CLEAR,0,0);
```

SendMessage ■ 2.0 ■ 3.0

Description Sends a message to the specified window. Sent messages differ from posted messages because they are sent immediately. SendMessage does not return until the message is processed.

Syntax public, LRESULT SendMessage(UINT message, WPARAM wParam = 0, LPARAM lParam = 0);

Parameters

message The message to be sent.

wParam Message-specific additional information.

lParam Message-specific additional information.

Returns The result of the message processing. Varies depending on the message.

See Also CWnd::PostMessage, ::SendMessage

Example

```
// close the window
pWnd->SendMessage(WM_CLOSE);
```

SendMessageToDescendants ■ 2.0 ■ 3.0

Description Sends a specified message to all of the children of a specified window (the first version of the function) or this window (the second version of the function). You can control whether the message is sent to all children or just immediate children and whether the message should be sent to permanent and temporary windows or just permanent windows.

Syntax public, static void PASCAL SendMessageToDescendants(HWND hWnd, UINT message, WPARAM wParam, LPARAM lParam, BOOL bDeep, BOOL bOnlyPerm);

public, void PASCAL SendMessageToDescendants(UINT message, WPARAM wParam, LPARAM lParam, BOOL bDeep, BOOL bOnlyPerm);

Parameters

hWnd	The parent window whose children will be sent the message.
message	The message to send to the children.
wParam	Message-specific additional data.
lParam	Message-specific additional data.
bDeep	TRUE if all children should be sent the message; FALSE if only immediate children should be sent the message.
bOnlyPerm	TRUE if the message should only be sent to child windows in the permanent window map; FALSE if the message should also be sent to temporary windows.

Returns Nothing is returned.

See Also CWnd::SendMessage

Example

```
void CMyWnd::SendMyChildrenAMessage()
{
     SendMessageToDescendants(GetSafeHwnd(), WM_USER_MYMESSAGE, 0, 0,
                              TRUE, TRUE);
}
```

SendNotifyMessage

■ 2.0 ■ 3.0 ■ NM

Description Sends a message to the window. If the window was created in the current thread, the message is sent directly and this function waits for the result. If the window was created in another thread, the message is posted and this function does not wait for the message to be processed.

Syntax public, BOOL SendNotifyMessage(UINT message, WPARAM wParam, LPARAM lParam);

Parameters

message	The message to be sent.
wParam	Message-specific additional data.
lParam	Message-specific additional data.

Returns Non-zero if successful; otherwise, zero.

See Also CWnd::SendMessage, CWnd::PostMessage, ::SendNotifyMessage

Example

```
pWnd->SendNotifyMessage(WM_CLOSE);
```

SetActiveWindow

■ 2.0 ■ 3.0

Description Makes this window the active window.

Syntax public, CWnd* SetActiveWindow();

Parameters None.

Returns A pointer to the previously active window. The returned pointer may be temporary and should not be stored for later use. Temporary CWnds are automatically destroyed during idle-time processing so you can only depend on the validity of the CWnd returned by SetActiveWindow until your application enters its idle loop, which can occur any time you return control to Windows (i.e., returning from a message map).

See Also CWnd::GetActiveWindow, CWnd::SetFocus, ::SetActiveWindow

Example

```
void CMyWnd::OnSomeEvent()
{
	SetActiveWindow();
}
```

SetCapture

■ 2.0 ■ 3.0

Description Causes all mouse messages to be sent to this window regardless of whether the cursor is over this window. Mouse messages are "captured" until the CWnd::ReleaseCapture function is called. Often, you may want to call this funtion when the user presses the left mouse button and release the capture when the button is released.

Syntax public, CWnd* SetCapture();

Parameters None.

Returns A pointer to the window that had the capture before or NULL if there is none. The returned pointer may be temporary and should not be stored for later use. Temporary CWnds are automatically destroyed during idle-time processing so you can only depend on the validity of the CWnd returned by SetCapture until your application enters its idle loop, which can occur any time you return control to Windows (i.e., returning from a message map).

See Also CWnd;:ReleaseCapture, ::SetCapture

Example

```
void CMyWnd::OnLButtonDown(UINT nFlags, CPoint pt)
{ // if we don't already have it,  get it
	if (GetCapture() != this)
		SetCapture();
	CWnd::OnLButtonDown();
}

void CMyWnd::OnLButtonUp(UINT nFlags, CPoint pt)
{
	ReleaseCapture();
	CWnd::OnLButtonUp();
}
```

SetCaretPos

■ 2.0 ■ 3.0

Description Moves the caret position to the specified coordinates. The caret is moved only if it is currently owned by a window within the current task.

Syntax public, static void PASCAL SetCaretPos(POINT point);

Parameters

point A POINT structure or CPoint object containing the new coordinates of the caret.

Returns Nothing is returned.

See Also CWnd::GetCaretPos, ::SetCaretPos

SetClipboardViewer

■ 2.0 ■ 3.0

Description Adds this window to the list of windows that are notified whenever the contents of the Clipboard change. Windows notifies windows in the Clipboard viewer chain by sending them a WM_DRAWCLIPBOARD message. A window in the Clipboard viewer chain must respond to this message as well as the WM_CHANGECBCHAIN and WM_DESTROY messages. This window should pass each of these messages on to the next window in the chain. The next window in the chain is returned by the call to the SetClipboardViewer function.

Syntax public, HWND SetClipboardViewer();

Parameters None.

Returns The window handle of the next window in the Clipboard viewer chain. You should save this window handle so that you can pass Clipboard messages on to it.

See Also CWnd::ChangeClipboardChain, CWnd::OnDrawClipboard, CWnd::OnChangeCBViewer, ::SetClipboardViewer

Example

```
void CMyWnd::AddToClipboard()
{
	m_hPrivCBWnd = pWnd->SetClipboardViewer();
}

void CMyWnd::RemoveFromClipboard()
{
	if (m_hPrivCBWnd)
	{
		ChangeClipboardChain(m_hPrivCBWnd);
		m_hPrivCBWnd = NULL;
	}
}

void CMyWnd::OnDrawClipboard()
{
	if (m_hPrivCBWnd)
	{ // do our clipboard stuff and pass the message on
	::SendMessage(m_hPrivCBWnd,WM_DRAWCLIPBOARD,0,0);
	}
}
```

SetDlgCtrlID

■ 2.0 ■ 3.0

Description Changes the ID of this child window to the specified ID. The ID of a child window can be used to reference the window in many functions—for example, the CWnd::GetDlgItem function. Typically, child window IDs are thought of in the context of dialog controls, but they actually apply to any child window.

Syntax public, int SetDlgCtrlID(int nID);

Parameters

nID The new ID of the child window.

Returns The old ID of the child window.

See Also CWnd::GetDlgCtrlID, ::SetDlgCtrlID

Example

```
pComboBoxControl->SetDlgCtrlID(IDC_MYCOMBOBOX);
```

SetDlgItemInt

■ 2.0 ■ 3.0

Description Converts an integer to text and sets the window text of the specified child window (usually a control in a dialog) to the converted text.

Syntax public, void SetDlgItemInt(int nID, UINT nValue, BOOL bSigned = TRUE);

Parameters

nID ID of the child window.

nValue The integer value to convert to text.

bSigned TRUE if the value in *nValue* is signed; otherwise, FALSE.

Returns Nothing is returned.

See Also CWnd::GetDlgItemInt, CWnd::SetDlgItemText, ::SetDlgItemInt

Example

```
void CMyDlg::OnInitDialog()
{
	SetDlgItemInt(IDC_NUMAPPLES,10,FALSE);
```

SetDlgItemText

■ 2.0 ■ 3.0

Description Sets the window text of a specified child window (usually a dialog control) to the specified text string. This function is basically a short-cut to retrieving the child window and using the CWnd::SetWindowText function.

Syntax public, void SetDlgItemText(int nID, LPCTSTR lpszString);

Parameters

nID The ID of the child window whose window text should be set.

lpszString A pointer to a NULL-terminated string buffer containing the new window text.

Returns Nothing is returned.

See Also CWnd::SetWindowText, CWnd::SetDlgItemInt, ::SetDlgItemText

Example

```
void CMyDlg::OnInitDialog()
{
	SetDlgItemText(IDC_NAME,"Fred Pandolfi");
```

SetFocus

■ 2.0 ■ 3.0

Description Makes this window have the current input focus. The window with input focus receives all keyboard and mouse input. If another window has the input focus when this function is called, that window will receive a WM_KILLFOCUS message. This window will receive a WM_SETFOCUS message. SetFocus also makes this window, or its parent, the active window.

Syntax public, CWnd* SetFocus();

Parameters None.

Returns A pointer to the window that previously had the input focus or NULL if there was none. The returned pointer may be temporary and should not be stored for later use. Temporary CWnds are automatically destroyed during idle-time processing so you can only depend on the validity of the CWnd returned by SetFocus until your application enters its idle loop, which can occur any time you return control to Windows (i.e., returning from a message map).

See Also CWnd::GetFocus, CWnd::SetActiveWindow, ::SetFocus

Example

```
pWnd->SetFocus();
```

SetFont

■ 2.0 ■ 3.0

Description Sets the font to be used by the window and optionally forces a redraw of the window. Most windows use their font simply to draw their caption text.

Syntax public, void SetFont(CFont* pFont, BOOL bRedraw = TRUE);

Parameters

pFont A pointer to the new window font.

bRedraw TRUE forces an immediate update of the window; FALSE does not repaint the window.

Returns Nothing is returned.

See Also CWnd::GetFont, ::SetFont

Example

```
CFont font;

// create a font
font.CreateFont(14,0,0,0,FW_NORMAL,0,0,0,DEFAULT_CHARSET,
                OUT_DEFAULT_PRECIS,CLIP_DEFAULT_PRICIS,DRAFT_QUALITY,
                VARIABLE_PITCH|FF_SWISS,"MS Sans Serif");

// set the window font
AfxGetMainWnd()->SetFont(&font);
```

SetForegroundWindow

■ 2.0 ■ 3.0

Description Makes this window the foreground window and brings the thread that owns this window to the foreground. This window is made active and given the input focus. The foreground window is the one that the user is working with.

Syntax public, BOOL SetForegroundWindow();

Parameters None.

Returns Non-zero if successful; otherwise, zero.

See Also CWnd::GetForegroundWindow, CWnd::SetActiveWindow, CWnd::SetFocus

Example

```
// bring our application to the front
AfxGetMainWnd()->SetForegroundWindow();
```

SetIcon

■ 2.0 ■ 3.0

Description Sets the small or big icon associated with the window. Normally, all windows in a window class share the same icon, but you can use this function to supply an icon for a specific window. If a small icon is not associated with a window, Windows will synthesize it from the large icon.

Syntax public, HICON SetIcon(HICON hIcon, BOOL bBigIcon);

Parameters

hIcon A handle to the new window icon.

bBigIcon TRUE indicates that *hIcon* refers to the 32x32 icon for the window; FALSE indicates that *hIcon* refers to a 16x16 icon for the window.

Returns A handle to the window's previous icon.

See Also CWnd::GetIcon

Example

```
HICON hBigIcon;

hBigIcon = AfxGetApp()->LoadIcon(IDI_MYWINDOWICON);
pWnd->SetIcon(hBigIcon,TRUE);
```

SetMenu

■ 2.0 ■ 3.0

Description Changes the menu for this window to a specified menu. SetMenu will automatically redraw the window to reflect the new menu. Note that SetMenu will not, however, destroy the old menu associated with the window. Therefore, you should retrieve the old menu with the CWnd::GetMenu function and destroy it with the CMenu::DestroyMenu function.

Syntax public, BOOL SetMenu(CMenu* pMenu);

Parameters

pMenu A pointer to the new menu. This parameter can be NULL, in which case the current menu will be removed from the window.

Returns Non-zero if the function is successful; otherwise, zero.

See Also CWnd::GetMenu, CMenu::DestroyMenu, ::SetMenu

Example

```
CMenu *pMenu = new CMenu;

// make very basic menu
pMenu->AppendMenu(MF_STRING,1,"&File");
pMenu->AppendMenu(MF_STRING,2,"&View");

// get the old menu and kill it
CMenu *pOldMenu = pWnd->GetMenu();
if (pOldMenu)
      pOldMenu->DestroyMenu();

// install new menu
pWnd->SetMenu(pMenu);
```

SetOwner

■ 2.0 ■ 3.0

Description Changes the owner of this window to the specified window. By default, the owner of a window is its parent. Setting the owner to a different window allows notifications to be sent from a child window to a window other than its parent. This feature is used heavily in the MFC OLE implementation where a child window's parent is in a container application but the owner is back in the server application.

Syntax public, void SetOwner(CWnd* pOwnerWnd);

Parameters

pOwnerWnd The new owner of the window. Can be NULL, in which case the window has no owner.

Returns Nothing is returned.

See Also CWnd::GetOwner, CWnd::SetParent, ::SetOwner

Example

```
pChildWnd->SetOwner(pOwnerWnd);
```

SetParent

■ 2.0 ■ 3.0

Description Changes the parent of this window to the specified window. If this child window is visible, the required redrawing will automatically be done.

Syntax public, CWnd* SetParent(CWnd* pWndNewParent);

Parameters

pWndNewParent A pointer to the new parent window.

Returns A pointer to the previous parent window. The returned pointer may be temporary and should not be stored for later use. Temporary CWnds are automatically destroyed during idle-time processing so you can only depend on the validity of the CWnd returned by SetParent until your application enters its idle loop, which can occur any time you return control to Windows (i.e., returning from a message map).

See Also CWnd::GetParent, CWnd::SetOwner, ::SetParent

Example

```
pChildWnd->SetParent(pNewParent);
```

SetRedraw

■ 2.0 ■ 3.0

Description Sets or clears the redraw flag associated with the window. If the redraw flag is cleared, Windows will not repaint the window. This function is useful if you need to perform several updates on a window and don't want it to repaint until all updates have been performed.

Syntax public, void SetRedraw(BOOL bRedraw = TRUE);

Parameters

bRedraw TRUE to set the redraw flag; FALSE to clear the redraw flag.

Returns Nothing is returned.

Example

```
void CMyDialog::AddItemsToListBox()
{
	CListBox *pList = (CListBox *)GetDlgItem(IDC_MYLIST);
	pList->SetRedraw(FALSE);
	pList->AddString("String 1");
	pList->AddString("String 2");
	pList->AddString("String 3");
	pList->SetRedraw(TRUE);
}
```

SetScrollInfo

■ 2.0 ■ 3.0

Description Initializes various characteristics of a scrollbar. SetScrollInfo allows you to set the range, page size, and current position of the scrollbar. This function also allows you to set these values as full 32-bit quantities. This differs from the SetScrollPos and SetScrollRange functions that only use 16-bit values.

Syntax public, BOOL SetScrollInfo(int nBar, LPSCROLLINFO lpScrollInfo, BOOL bRedraw = TRUE);

Parameters

nBar Indicates which scrollbar should be affected; SB_HORZ for the horizontal scrollbar, SB_VERT for the vertical scrollbar, or SB_BOTH for both scrollbars.

lpScrollInfo Pointer to a SCROLLINFO structure. For a complete description of this structure, see the Windows SDK documentation.

bRedraw TRUE if scrollbar should be redrawn; FALSE, otherwise.

Returns Non-zero if successful; otherwise, zero.

See Also CScrollBar::SetScrollInfo, CWnd::GetScrollInfo, CWnd::SetScrollPos, CWnd::OnHScroll, CWnd::OnVScroll, ::SetScrollInfo

Example

```
// initialize vertical scroll bar
SCROLLINFO sinfo;
sinfo.cbsize = sizeof(sinfo);
sinfo.fMask = SIF_POS|SIF_RANGE;
sinfo.nMin = 0;
sinfo.nMax = 100;
sinfo.nPos = 50;
pWnd->SetScrollInfo(SB_VERT,&sinfo);
```

SetScrollPos ■ 2.0 ■ 3.0

Description Sets the current position of the specified scrollbar.

Syntax public, int SetScrollPos(int nBar, int nPos, BOOL bRedraw = TRUE);

Parameters

nBar SB_HORZ to change the horizontal scrollbar or SB_VERT to change the vertical scrollbar.

nPos The new position of the scrollbar.

bRedraw TRUE if the scrollbar should be redrawn; FALSE if not.

Returns The previous position of the scrollbar.

See Also CWnd::SetScrollRange, CWnd::GetScrollPos, ::SetScrollPos

Example

```
pWnd->SetScrollPos(SB_VERT,20);
```

SetScrollRange ■ 2.0 ■ 3.0

Description Sets the scroll range of the specified scrollbar.

Syntax public, void SetScrollRange(int nBar, int nMinPos, int nMaxPos, BOOL bRedraw = TRUE);

Parameters

nBar SB_HORZ to change the horizontal scrollbar or SB_VERT to change the vertical scrollbar.

nMinPos The minimum possible scroll value.

nMaxPos The maximum possible scroll value.

bRedraw TRUE to redraw the scrollbar; FALSE otherwise.

Returns Nothing is returned.

See Also CWnd::SetScrollPos, CWnd::GetScrollRange, ::SetScrollRange

Example

```
pWnd->SetScrollRange(SB_HORZ,0,100,TRUE);
```

SetTimer

■ 2.0 ■ 3.0

Description Sets a timer that calls a callback procedure or sends a WM_TIMER message to the window at a specified interval. Timer messages are actually always posted as WM_TIMER messages even if a callback is supplied, so timer messages may not be received at exactly the specified interval.

Syntax public, UINT SetTimer(UINT nIDEvent, UINT nElapse, void (CALLBACK* lpfnTimer)(HWND, UINT, UINT, DWORD));

Parameters

nIDEvent Timer identifier.

nElapse The interval, in milliseconds, at which to send the timer messages.

lpfnTimer A pointer to a timer callback function that will be called at the specified interval. If this parameter is NULL, WM_TIMER messages will be posted to the application's message queue and received by this window. The callback function has the following form:

```
void CALLBACK EXPORT TimerProc(
    HWND hWnd,       //handle of CWnd that called SetTimer
    UINT nMsg,       //WM_TIMER
    UINT nIDEvent    //timer identification
    DWORD dwTime     //system time
    );
```

Returns A timer identifier that should identify the timer. This value is passed with the WM_TIMER message and to the callback procedure and should be passed to the CWnd::KillTimer function when the timer is being destroyed.

See Also CWnd::KillTimer, ::SetTimer

Example

```
// set a timer that will post a WM_TIMER message every second
void CMyWnd::OnCreate(LPCREATESTRUCT lpCreate)
{
      m_nTimerId = SetTimer(1,1000,NULL);
}

void CMyWnd::OnDestroy()
{
```

```
        if (m_nTimerId)
                KillTimer(m_nTimerId);
}

void CMyWnd::OnTimer(UINT uEventId)
{ // make the window flash
        if (uEventId == m_nTimerId)
            FlashWindow(TRUE);
}
```

SetWindowContextHelpId

■ 2.0 ■ 3.0 ■ NM

Description Associates a help context ID with the window. MFC passes this ID to the WinHelp application when the user requests help. By default, child windows inherit the help ID of their parent. This is most useful for dialogs where each control inherits the help context of the dialog itself.

Syntax public, BOOL SetWindowContextHelpId(DWORD dwContextHelpId);

Parameters

dwContextHelpId The help context ID for this window.

Returns Non-zero if successful; otherwise, zero.

See Also CWnd::GetWindowContextHelpId, CWnd::WinHelp

Example

```
pWnd->SetWindowContextHelpId(22000);
```

SetWindowPlacement

■ 2.0 ■ 3.0

Description Sets the show state and positions of the window. This function can be used to set the positions of the window in its normal and minimized states.

Syntax public, BOOL SetWindowPlacement(const WINDOWPLACEMENT* lpwndpl);

Parameters

lpwndpl A pointer to a WINDOWPLACEMENT structure that describes the show state and positions of the window. For a full description of this structure, see the Windows SDK documentation.

Returns Non-zero if successful; otherwise, zero.

See Also CWnd::GetWindowPlacement, ::SetWindowPlacement

SetWindowPos

■ 2.0 ■ 3.0

Description Controls the size, position, and Z-order positioning of the window.

Syntax public, BOOL SetWindowPos(const CWnd* pWndInsertAfter, int x, int y, int cx, int cy, UINT nFlags);

Parameters

pWndInsertAfter The window after which this window will be placed in the z-order. Can also be one of the following constants: wndBottom, wndTop, wndNoTopMost, or wndTopMost.

x The new x coordinate of the upper-left corner of the window.

y The new y coordinate of the upper-left corner of the window.

cx The new width of the window.

cy The new height of the window.

nFlags A combination of the following flags:

SWP_DRAWFRAME Draws a frame (defined when the window was created) around the window.

SWP_HIDEWINDOW Hides the window.

SWP_NOACTIVATE Does not activate the window. If this flag is not set, the window is activated and moved to the top of either the topmost or the nontopmost group (depending on the setting of the *pWndInsertAfter* parameter).

SWP_NOMOVE Retains current position (ignores the x and y parameters).

SWP_NOREDRAW Does not redraw changes. If this flag is set, no repainting of any kind occurs. This applies to the client area, the nonclient area (including the title and scrollbars), and any part of the parent window uncovered as a result of the moved window. When this flag is set, the application must explicitly invalidate or redraw any parts of the window and parent window that must be redrawn.

SWP_NOSIZE Retains current size (ignores the cx and cy parameters).

SWP_NOZORDER Retains current ordering (ignores pWndInsertAfter).

SWP_SHOWWINDOW Displays the window.

Returns Non-zero if successful; otherwise, zero.

See Also ::SetWindowPos

Example

```
// make sure our window always stays on top
pWnd->SetWindowPos(CWnd::wndTopMost,0,0,0,0,SWP_NOMOVE|SWP_NOSIZE);
```

SetWindowText ■ 2.0 ■ 3.0

Description Sets the text associated with the window. Most windows display their window text in the caption bar of the window although other windows, such as dialog controls, use the text differently. For example, the window text for an edit box is the text that is actually contained in the edit control.

Syntax public, void SetWindowText(LPCTSTR lpszString);

Parameters

lpszString A pointer to a NULL-terminated string that will be used as the new window text.

Returns Nothing is returned.

See Also CWnd::GetWindowText, CWnd::SetDlgItemText, ::SetWindowText

Example

```
void CMyDialog::OnInitDialog()
{
     m_ctEditBox.SetWindowText("Some edit text");
```

ShowCaret ■ 2.0 ■ 3.0

Description If the caret is owned by this window, ShowCaret shows the caret. Once the caret is showing, it flashes automatically. Note that Windows maintains a count of the number of times CWnd::ShowCaret and CWnd::HideCaret are called. The caret is only shown if ShowCaret has been called more times than HideCaret.

Syntax public, void ShowCaret();

Parameters None.

Returns Nothing is returned.

See Also CWnd::HideCaret, ::ShowCaret

Example See CWnd::CreateCaret

ShowOwnedPopups ■ 2.0 ■ 3.0

Description Shows or hides all popup windows owned by this window.

Syntax public, void ShowOwnedPopups(BOOL bShow = TRUE);

Parameters

bShow TRUE if the popup windows should be shown; FALSE if they should be hidden.

Returns Nothing is returned.

See Also CWnd::ShowWindow, ::ShowOwnedPopups

Example

```
pWnd->ShowOwnedPopups(TRUE);
```

ShowScrollBar ■ 2.0 ■ 3.0

Description Shows or hides the specified scrollbar. You should not call this function while processing a scrollbar notification message.

Syntax public, void ShowScrollBar(UINT nBar, BOOL bShow = TRUE);

Parameters

nBar SB_HORZ to show/hide the horizontal scrollbar; SB_VERT to show/hide the vertical scrollbar; SB_BOTH to show/hide both scrollbars.

bShow TRUE to show the scrollbar(s) or FALSE to hide the scrollbar(s).

Returns Nothing is returned.

See Also CScrollBar::ShowScrollBar, ::ShowScrollBar

Example

```
// show both scrollbars
pWnd->ShowScrollBar(SB_BOTH,TRUE);
```

SHOWWINDOW

■ 2.0 ■ 3.0

Description Controls the visibility and state of the window.

Syntax public, BOOL ShowWindow(int nCmdShow);

Parameters

nCmdShow One of the following flags:

SW_HIDE Hides this window and passes activation to another window.

SW_MINIMIZE Minimizes this window and activates the top-level window in the window manager's list.

SW_RESTORE Activates and displays this window. If this window is minimized or maximized, it is restored to its original size and position.

SW_SHOW Activates this window and displays it in its current size and position.

SW_SHOWMAXIMIZED Activates this window and displays it as a maximized window.

SW_SHOWMINIMIZED Activates this window and displays it as an icon.

SW_SHOWMINNOACTIVE Displays this window as an icon. The window that is currently active remains active.

SW_SHOWNA Displays this window in its current state. The window that is currently active remains active.

SW_SHOWNOACTIVATE Displays this window in its most recent size and position. The window that is currently active remains active.

SW_SHOWNORMAL Activates and displays this window. If this window is minimized or maximized, Windows restores it to its original size and position.

Returns Non-zero if the window was previously visible; otherwise, zero.

See Also CWnd::OnShowWindow, CWnd::ShowOwnedPopups

Example

```
void CMyDialog::OnInitDialog()
{
      // hide a couple of controls
      m_ctMyEdit.ShowWindow(SW_HIDE);
      m_ctMyCombo.ShowWindow(SW_HIDE);
```

SUBCLASSCTL3D

■ 2.0 ■ 3.0

Description Subclasses a particular control using the CTL3D.DLL library. CTL3D.DLL adds a 3-dimensional look to dialogs and their controls. This function is no longer necessary in Windows 95. This function does nothing on the Macintosh. SubclassCtl3d is an internal MFC function that you will rarely need to call yourself. The MFC global function AfxEnable3dControls takes care of this for you.

Syntax public, BOOL SubclassCtl3d(int nControlType = -1);

Parameters

nControlType Usually -1, can be an identifier which indicates which type of control is being subclassed (e.g. combo box, edit box, etc.).

Returns Non-zero if the control is subclassed; otherwise, zero.

See Also CWnd::SubclassDlg3d

SubclassDlg3d ■ 2.0 ■ 3.0 ■ UD

Description Causes all controls in the dialog to be automatically subclassed by the CTL3D.DLL library. CTL3D.DLL adds a 3-dimensional look to dialogs and their controls. This function is no longer necessary in Windows 95. This function does nothing on the Macintosh. SubclassDlg3d is an internal MFC function that you will rarely need to call yourself. The MFC global function AfxEnable3dControls takes care of this for you.

Syntax public, BOOL SubclassDlg3d(DWORD dwMask = 0xFFFF);

Parameters

dwMask Mask passed to the CTL3D.DLL library that describes exactly what parts of the dialog should be sublassed. Usually, this parameter is CTL3D_ALL, which causes all controls and the dialog itself to be subclassed.

Returns Non-zero if successful; otherwise, zero.

See Also CWnd::SubclassCtl3d

SubclassDlgItem ■ 2.0 ■ 3.0

Description Subclasses a dialog control window. This function is basically a shortcut for the CWnd::SubclassWindow function. See the description for that function for a discussion on subclassing.

Syntax public, BOOL SubclassDlgItem(UINT nID, CWnd* pParent);

Parameters

nID The control ID of the dialog item to subclass.

pParent A pointer to the parent of the control—usually a dialog.

Returns Non-zero if the window is subclassed; otherwise, zero.

See Also CWnd::SubclassWindow, CWnd::UnsubclassWindow, CWnd::GetSuperWndProcAddress

SubclassWindow ■ 2.0 ■ 3.0

Description Subclasses the specified window and attaches it to the CWnd object. Messages from a subclassed window are routed through the message map of the derived CWnd class. This gives the derived class first crack at all messages. In 16-bit MFC you must override the CWnd::GetSuperWndProcAddress function to supply a place for MFC to store the address of the window's old window procedure (which it replaces in order to route the messages correctly). 32-bit MFC takes care of this bit of ugliness automatically.

Syntax public, BOOL SubclassWindow(HWND hWnd);

Parameters

hWnd The handle of the window that should be subclassed.

Returns Non-zero if successful; otherwise, zero.

See Also CWnd::UnsubclassWindow, CWnd::GetSuperWndProcAddress

Example

```
void CMyDialog::OnInitDialog()
{
      // subclass an edit control
      m_MyEditBox.SubclassWindow(::GetDlgItem(this,IDC_EDITBOX));
```

UnlockWindowUpdate ■ 2.0 ■ 3.0 ■ NM

Description Unlocks a window that was locked with the CWnd::LockWindowUpdate function. Only one window can be locked at a time. A locked window is not repainted and cannot be moved.

Syntax public, void UnlockWindowUpdate();

Parameters None.

Returns Nothing is returned.

See Also CWnd::LockWindowUpdate

UnsubclassWindow ■ 2.0 ■ 3.0

Description Removes a window subclass that was established with the CWnd::SubclassWindow function. Subclassing a window allows you to receive all window messages first—that is, messages are routed through the derived CWnd class's message map. Calling this function also automatically detaches the window from this CWnd object.

Syntax public, HWND UnsubclassWindow();

Parameters None.

Returns A handle to the unsubclassed and detached window.

See Also CWnd::SubclassWindow

UpdateData

■ 2.0 ■ 3.0

Description Initiates dialog data exchange and validation. This function performs some initialization and then calls the CWnd::DoDataExchange member of the CWnd to perform the actual data exchange and validation. For a complete discussion of dialog data exchange and validation, see Chapter 8, *Dialog Boxes*. Usually, you will not have to call this function yourself because MFC automatically calls it to initialize dialog controls in the CDialog::OnInitDialog function and again to retrieve data from a dialog in the default implementation of CDialog::OnOK.

Syntax public, BOOL UpdateData(BOOL bSaveAndValidate = TRUE);

Parameters

bSaveAndValidate TRUE indicates that data should be retrieved from the window and optionally validated; FALSE indicates that data should be sent to the window.

Returns Non-zero if successful; otherwise, zero.

See Also CWnd::DoDataExchange, CDialog::OnInitDialog, CDialog::OnOK

Example

```
pDialog->UpdateData(TRUE);
```

UpdateDialogControls

■ 2.0 ■ 3.0

Description Called by MFC to update the controls in control bars such as toolbars or dialog bars. You can call this function directly if you are using the command-ui update mechanism to update controls in a normal dialog. See Chapter 4, *Windows Messaging*, for details regarding the command-ui update mechanism.

Syntax public, void UpdateDialogControls(CCmdTarget* pTarget, BOOL bDisableIfNoHandler);

Parameters

pTarget Pointer to the command target (usually, the main window) through which the update messages will be routed.

bDisableIfNoHandler If TRUE, then child windows that do not have an update handler will be automatically disabled.

Returns Nothing is returned.

UpdateWindow

■ 2.0 ■ 3.0

Description Forces the window to be updated immediately. Normally, invalid areas of a window are accumulated and the window is repainted only when no messages are waiting for the application in its application queue. UpdateWindow sends the window a WM_PAINTmessage immediately.

Syntax public, void UpdateWindow();

Parameters None.

Returns Nothing is returned.

See Also CWnd::OnPaint, CWnd::RedrawWindow, ::UpdateWindow

Example

```
pWnd->UpdateWindow();
```

ValidateRect

■ 2.0 ■ 3.0

Description Validates a rectangular area of a window by removing it from the current update region. The update region is the area of the window marked for repainting. Call this function if you want to prevent an area of the window from being repainted with the next WM_PAINT message.

Syntax public, void ValidateRect(LPCRECT lpRect);

Parameters

lpRect A pointer to a RECT structure or a CRect object containing the coordinates of the area to validate.

Returns Nothing is returned.

See Also CWnd::ValidateRgn, CWnd::InvalidateRect, CWnd::InvalidateRgn

Example

```
CRect rect(1,1,300,200);
pWnd->ValidateRect(rect);
```

ValidateRgn

■ 2.0 ■ 3.0

Description Validates a region of a window by removing it from the current update region. The update region is the area of the window marked for repainting. Call this function if you want to prevent an area of the window from being repainted with the next WM_PAINT message.

Syntax public, void ValidateRgn(CRgn* pRgn);

Parameters

pRgn A pointer to the region that should be removed from the update region.

Returns Nothing is returned.

See Also CWnd::ValidateRect, CWnd::InvalidateRgn, CWnd::InvalidateRect, ::ValidateRgn

Example

```
CRegion rgn;
rgn.CreateRectRgn(1,1,300,200);
pWnd->ValidateRgn(&rgn);
```

WalkPreTranslateTree

■ 2.0 ■ 3.0

Description Internal MFC function that walks up the window chain (from parent to parent) from this window to the specified window, giving each window a chance to translate the message by calling the CWnd::PreTranslateMessage function of the window.

Syntax public, static BOOL PASCAL WalkPreTranslateTree(HWND hWndStop, MSG* pMsg);

Parameters

hWndStop The handle of the window where MFC should stop walking the window tree.

pMsg A pointer to an MSG structure containing the current message. For a complete description of the MSG structure, see the Windows SDK documentation.

Returns TRUE if any window in the tree translated the message; otherwise, FALSE.

See Also CWnd::PreTranslateMessage

WindowFromPoint

■ 2.0 ■ 3.0

Description Retrieves a pointer to the window that contains the specified point. WindowFromPoint will not consider a hidden, disabled, or transparent window.

Syntax public, static CWnd* PASCAL WindowFromPoint(POINT point);

Parameters

point The point for which a window should be found, expressed in screen coordinates.

Returns A pointer to the window containing the specified point or NULL if the point is not within a window. The returned pointer may be temporary and should not be stored for later use. Temporary CWnds are automatically destroyed during idle-time processing so you can only depend on the validity of the CWnd returned by WindowFromPoint until your application enters its idle loop, which can occur any time you return control to Windows (i.e., returning from a message map).

See Also CWnd::ChildWindowFromPoint, ::WindowFromPoint

Example

```
CWnd *pWnd = CWnd::WindowFromPoint(CPoint(20,50));
```

WindowProc

■ 2.0 ■ 3.0

Description The window procedure for all CWnd objects. This function actually does very little. Most of the work is actually done in the CWnd::OnWndMsg helper function. If the CWnd::OnWndMsg function does not process a message, this function calls CWnd::DefWindowProc, which invokes the Windows default window procedure.

Syntax protected, virtual LRESULT WindowProc(UINT message, WPARAM wParam, LPARAM lParam);

Parameters

message The message received.

wParam Message-specific additional data.

lParam Message-specific additional data.

Returns The result of the message processing that depends on the message.

See Also CWnd::OnWndMsg, CWnd::DefWindowProc

WinHelp

■ 2.0 ■ 3.0

Description Runs the WinHelp application and initializes the help topic as specified.

Syntax public, virtual void WinHelp(DWORD dwData,
UINT nCmd = HELP_CONTEXT);

Parameters

dwData Value and meaning depend on the value of the *nCmd* parameter.

nCmd Specifies the type of help to display and/or how to search for the specified help topic. For a complete list of values and their meanings, see the ::WinHelp function in the Windows SDK documentation.

Returns Nothing is returned.

See Also ::WinHelp

Example

```
// display the help contents
AfxGetMainWnd()->WinHelp(0,HELP_CONTENTS);
```

6

DOCUMENT / VIEW

6

DOCUMENT/VIEW

One of the most common application development tasks is to display a set of data in a way that the user can manipulate and render in various formats. For example, a financial program might allow entry of a list of stock quotes that the user may want to display as a list of text values or as a graph. Or, a weather program might access a database of temperature readings that the user may want to display as columned data or as a trend chart.

MFC provides a simple mechanism for developing applications like those described above. It is called the Document/View architecture. The document contains the data, such as the stock quotes or the temperature readings. The view displays the data that is contained in the document. For applications like those above that require different displays (like textual or graphical), documents can have multiple views. MFC also provides a built-in mechanism for updating views when the data in the document changes, as well as for saving and loading of the document data.

This chapter details the classes that implement the Document/View architecture that MFC provides. In MFC, there are three main classes that make up the Document/View architecture: The CDocument class that provides an encapsulation of data, the CView class that provides an encapsulation of the physical representation or display of the data in the document, and the CFrameWnd class which provides an object that manages one or more CView classes. Since these three classes are integral to the architecture, they are associated by using one of the CDocTemplate classes.

When using these classes, there are a few relationships of which you should be aware. A Single Document Interface (SDI) application can have only one document and uses the main frame window for display. A Multiple Document Interface (MDI) application can have many documents. Each document can have multiple views. Each frame window can have only one view, however, unless it has a splitter window that will allow it to manage multiple views (as in Figures 6-1 and 6-2).

One of the benefits of this architecture is efficiency. For example, if you have a large amount of statistical data and wish to display two different graphs, then you would not want to keep two copies of the same data in memory. The statistical data can be kept in a CDocument class. The user could then bring up multiple views that display the

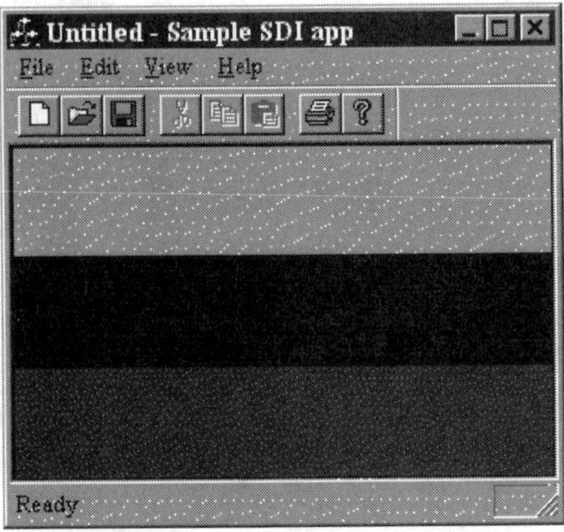

Figure 6-1 Sample SDI application is limited to one view

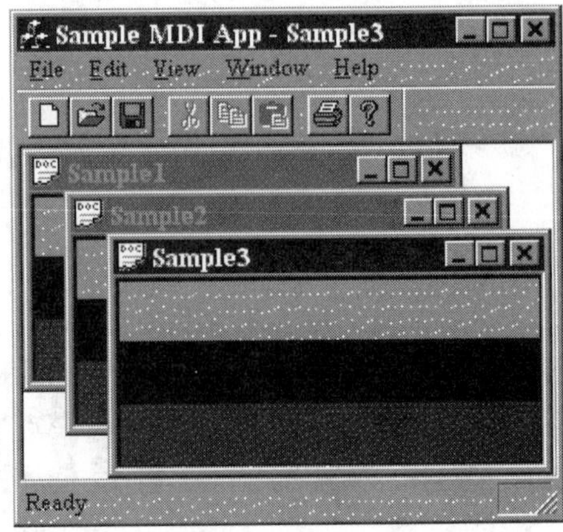

Figure 6-2 Sample MDI application can display multiple views at once

data in a graph. Since each view is a separate instance of a CView object, the views can have different display attributes. Also, if there is a change to the data, then this architecture provides a means of notifying all the associated views.

Table 6-1 summarizes the classes covered in this chapter.

Table 6-1 Chapter 6 class summary

Class Name	Description
CCtrlView	Base class used to derive a view from a window control.
CDocManager	Undocumented helper class used by the CWinApp object to manage documents.
CDocTemplate	The abstract base class that defines the relationship between the CDocument, CView, and CFrameWnd classes.
CDocument	The base class used to contain the data in the document/view relationship.
CEditView	Implementation of a simple text editor view based on a CEdit control.
CFormView	Base implementation of a view based on a dialog template.
CListView	A view object that manages a CListCtrl common control.
CMultiDocTemplate	A document template used for Multiple Document Interface applications where multiple documents can be opened simultaneously.
CRichEditView	Implementation of a rich edit view, with extensive support for formatting.
CScrollView	Base class used to implement a view with a virtual display space.
CSingleDocTemplate	The document template base class used for Single Document Interface applications where only one document may be opened at a time.
CTreeView	A view object that manages a CTreeCtrl common control.
CView	The base class used to display a particular aspect of the data contained in the document.

The CCtrlView Class

The CCtrlView class is a base class used to create a view based on any window control. This view is the base class of the CEditView, CListView, and CTreeView classes discussed later in this chapter. You can easily create a view from any other window control by overriding the constructor and supplying the control's class name. See the CEditView, CListView, or CTreeView classes for good examples of how to use the CCtrlView as a base class and also see the samples included on the CD-ROM.

CCtrlView

■ 4.0

Description The constructor for the CCtrlView class. This member intializes the internal member variables for the frame object. Also, MFC keeps track of the CFrameWnds created in the application by adding the new CFrameWnd to the CFrameWnd list stored in the AFX_THREAD_STATE structure.

Syntax public, CCtrlView(LPCTSTR lpszClass, DWORD dwStyle);

Parameters

lpszClass The Windows class name of the control to use for this view.

dwStyle Default window style.

Returns Nothing is returned.

Example The sample below shows how a view can be created from a simple list box control.

```
class CListBoxVView : public CCtrlView
{
protected:
      CListBoxVView();
      DECLARE_DYNCREATE(CListBoxVView)

      // other members listed here
...
};

CListBoxVView::CListBoxVView()
: CCtrlView(_T("LISTBOX"),  AFX_WS_DEFAULT_VIEW|WS_HSCROLL | WS_VSCROLL
| LBS_NOINTEGRALHEIGHT | LBS_NOTIFY)
{
      // add your own custom construction code here
}
```

AssertValid

■ 4.0 ■ DO

Description Determines whether the CCtrlView is in a valid state and if it is not, throws an assertion. This member is only compiled into the debug version of the application.

Syntax public, virtual void AssertValid() const;

Parameters None.

Returns Nothing is returned.

See Also CWnd::AssertValid

DUMP

■ 4.0 ■ DO

Description This member is an MFC diagnostic function that is only compiled into the debug version of the application. This member is used to output the state of the CCtrlView object, and can be called directly by the programmer.

Syntax public, virtual void Dump(CDumpContext& dc) const;

Parameters

dc A streamable object that accepts the diagnostic text.

Returns Nothing is returned.

ONDRAW

■ 4.0

Description This member is called by the application framework when an image of the view needs to be drawn. The given CDC object is used to represent the context in which the view should render itself. There is no default implementation of this member.

Syntax protected, virtual void OnDraw(CDC * pDC) const;

Parameters

pDC A pointer to a CDC object that represents the particular display context the view should render into.

Returns Nothing is returned.

ONPAINT

■ 4.0 ■ UD

Description This member is called to repaint a portion of the control view window. The CCtrlView implementation simply circumvents the calling of the base CView::OnPaint member.

Syntax protected, afx_msg void OnPaint() const;

Parameters None.

Returns Nothing is returned.

PRECREATEWINDOW

■ 4.0

Description This member is overriden to modify the attributes of the CCtrlView before the window is created. This member can be used to set the initial size, position, and style of the view.

Syntax	protected, virtual BOOL PreCreateWindow(CREATESTRUCT & cs);
Parameters	
cs	A reference to a CREATESTRUCT that will receive the modified attributes.
Returns	TRUE to continue with creation of the window; FALSE to halt creation.

The CDocManager Class

The CDocManager class is used internally by the CWinApp object to manage document templates. A document template relates a document to a particular view so that MFC can handle most of the automatic opening, closing, saving, and loading of the document. Using the financial application mentioned at the beginning of the chapter as an example, a document template would be created that relates the stock data to the graphical view. If a textual view is also required, then another template would be created to relate the stock data to the text view.

The CDocManager handles all of the document templates that are initialized for the application. Through this class, you can retrieve each registered document template. But, this member is mainly used by the internals of MFC to handle most of the work in managing documents and views.

CDocManager

■ 4.0 ■ UD

Description	The constructor for the CDocManager class.
Syntax	public, CDocManager();
Parameters	None.
Returns	Nothing is returned.
See Also	~CDocManager()

~CDocManager

■ 4.0 ■ UD

Description	The destructor for the CDocManager class. All registered document templates are deleted during destruction.
Syntax	public, virtual ~CDocManager();
Parameters	None.
Returns	Nothing is returned.
See Also	CDocManager()

AddDocTemplate

■ 4.0 ■ UD

Description	This member will register a new document template with the CDocManager. This object keeps an internal list of all templates added. Each template should be registered only once.

Syntax public, virtual void AddDocTemplate(CDocTemplate * pTemplate);

Parameters

pTemplate A pointer to a CDocTemplate object to be added. If *pTemplate* is NULL, then all of the static templates are registered with the CDocManager.

Returns Nothing is returned.

AssertValid

■ 4.0 ■ UD ■ DO

Description Determines whether the CDocManager is in a valid state and if it is not, throws an assertion. This member is only compiled into the debug version of the application.

Syntax public, virtual void AssertValid() const;

Parameters None.

Returns Nothing is returned.

CloseAllDocuments

■ 4.0 ■ UD

Description This member iterates through all of the document templates registered and closes all the documents associated with each template.

Syntax public, virtual void CloseAllDocuments(BOOL bEndSession);

Parameters

bEndSession TRUE indicates that the session is ending; otherwise FALSE.

Returns Nothing is returned.

DoPromptFileName

■ 4.0 ■ UD

Description This member is called from CDocManager::OnFileOpen and is used to prompt the user with document choices. The File Open dialog that this member displays is loaded with the extensions for the registered documents.

Syntax public, virtual BOOL DoPromptFileName(CString & filename, UINT nIDSTitle, DWORD dwFlags, BOOL bOpenFileDialog, CDocTemplate* pTemplate);

Parameters

filename A file name used to initially display in the File Open dialog.

nIDSTitle The title for the File Open dialog.

dwFlags The File Open dialog box creation flags. These can be found in the Windows SDK.

bOpenFileDialog TRUE will display the File Open dialog; FALSE indicates the File Save As dialog.

pTemplate A pointer to a specific document template. If this parameter is not NULL, then only the file extension associated with this template will appear in the dialog. Otherwise, the extensions for all documents are displayed in the dialog.

Returns TRUE if the user selected IDOK from the dialog; otherwise FALSE.

See Also CFileDialog()

DUMP

■ 4.0 ■ UD ■ DO

Description This member is an MFC diagnostic function that is only compiled into the debug version of the application. This member is used to output the state of the CDocManager object, and can be called directly by the programmer.

Syntax public, virtual void Dump(CDumpContext& dc) const;

Parameters

dc A streamable object that accepts the diagnostic text.

Returns Nothing is returned.

GETFIRSTDOCTEMPLATEPOSITION

■ 4.0 ■ UD

Description This member allows access to the CDocManager's internal list of registered document templates. Usually this member is called in conjunction with CDocManager::GetNextDocTemplate() to iterate through the registered templates.

Syntax public, virtual POSITION GetFirstDocTemplatePosition() const;

Parameters None.

Returns A POSITION referencing the first document template.

See Also CDocManager::GetNextDocTemplate()

GETNEXTDOCTEMPLATE

■ 4.0 ■ UD

Description When used with CDocManager::GetFirstDocTemplate(), this member will allow iteration of the internal document templates.

Syntax public, CDocTemplate * GetNextDocTemplate(POSITION & pos) const;

Parameters

pos A POSITION that indicates the current template position and is updated with the next template position.

Returns A pointer to the next CDocTemplate.

See Also CDocManager::GetFirstDocTemplatePosition()

GetOpenDocumentCount

■ 4.0 ■ UD

Description This member returns the total number of open documents. This is determined by iterating through the document templates, then counting the number of documents based on each template.

Syntax public, virtual int GetOpenDocumentCount();

Parameters None.

Returns The total number of open documents for the document templates added into this object.

OnDDECommand

■ 4.0 ■ UD ■ NM

Description This member is called to process a DDE execute command. The default implementation will attempt to interpret the file open and print DDE commands for a registered document type.

Syntax public, virtual BOOL OnDDECommand(LPTSTR lpszCommand);

Parameters

lpszCommand The DDE command string received.

Returns TRUE if the command was handled; otherwise FALSE.

OnFileNew

■ 4.0 ■ UD

Description This member is called to create a new document. If only one document template has been registered, then a new document of that type is created. If more than one document template has been registered, then a dialog displaying the registered document types is displayed. After the user selects a document type, then a new document of that type is created.

Syntax public, virtual void OnFileNew();

Parameters None.

Returns Nothing is returned.

OnFileOpen

■ 4.0 ■ UD

Description This member is called to open an existing document. The default behavior is to call CDocManager::DoPromptFileName to let the user select a document to open.

Syntax public, virtual void OnFileOpen();

Parameters None.

Returns Nothing is returned.

See Also CDocManager::DoPromptFileName()

OpenDocumentFile

■ 4.0 ■ UD

Description	This member is called to open a document file from a given name. The default implementation attempts to determine if the document is already open and if not, loads the document. This member may fail if there is no document template loaded that matches the file given.
Syntax	public, virtual CDocument * OpenDocumentFile(LPCSTR lpszFileName);
Parameters	
lpszFileName	The name of the file to open.
Returns	A pointer to a CDocument if successful, or NULL if no matching template was found or if the document is already open.

RegisterShellFileTypes

■ 4.0 ■ UD ■ NM

Description	This member registers all of the document types with the Windows File Manager. This allows the user to double-click on a document type and automatically execute its associated application. For Windows 95 application, this member will also register a small icon for the document type.
Syntax	public, virtual void RegisterShellFileTypes(BOOL bWin95);
Parameters	
bWin95	TRUE indicates that the registration should use Windows 95 extensions to the File Manager.
Returns	Nothing is returned.

SaveAllModified

■ 4.0 ■ UD

Description	This member will iterate through all of the document templates and save all associated documents that have been modified.
Syntax	public, virtual BOOL SaveAllModified();
Parameters	None.
Returns	TRUE if successful; otherwise FALSE.
See Also	CDocTemplate::SaveAllModified()

The CDocTemplate Class

The CDocTemplate is an abstract base class used to define a template relationship. This relationship defines the document, view, and frame objects used to display information in the Document/View architecture. By defining the template, the application framework will handle most of the associated processing in creating, opening, and saving documents.

CDocTemplate ■ 2.0 ■ 3.0

Description The constructor for the CDocTemplate class. Upon construction, the document template will load all associated resources including the menu and accelerators.

Syntax protected, CDocTemplate(UINT nIDResource, CRuntimeClass* pDocClass,CRuntimeClass* pFrameClass, CRuntimeClass* pViewClass);

Parameters

nIDResource The resource ID of the menu and accelerators associated with the template.

pDocClass A pointer to the run-time class for the document type.

pFrameClass A pointer to the run-time class for the frame type.

pViewClass A pointer to the run-time class for the view type.

Returns Nothing is returned.

See Also ~CDocTemplate()

~CDocTemplate ■ 2.0 ■ 3.0

Description The destructor for the CDocTemplate class. This member frees any system resources associated with the template.

Syntax public, virtual ~CDocTemplate();

Parameters None.

Returns Nothing is returned.

See Also CDocTemplate()

AddDocument ■ 2.0 ■ 3.0

Description This member associates a document with the template.

Syntax public, virtual void AddDocument(CDocument * pDoc);

Parameters

pDoc A pointer to the document.

Returns Nothing is returned.

AssertValid ■ 2.0 ■ 3.0 ■ DO

Description Determines whether the CDocTemplate is in a valid state and if it is not, throws an assertion. This member is only compiled into the debug version of the application.

Syntax public, virtual void AssertValid() const;

Parameters None.

Returns Nothing is returned.

CloseAllDocuments

■ 2.0 ■ 3.0

Description	This member iterates through all of the documents associated with this template and closes them. If this member is called and the session is ending, then all views are disconnected from their documents before the documents are closed.
Syntax	public, virtual void CloseAllDocuments(BOOL bEndSession);
Parameters	
bEndSession	TRUE indicates that the application session is ending; otherwise FALSE.
Returns	Nothing is returned.
See Also	CDocument::OnCloseDocument, CDocument::DisconnectViews
Example	See CDocTemplate::GetFirstDocPosition()

CreateNewDocument

■ 2.0 ■ 3.0

Description	This member creates a new document from its stored document run-time class and adds it to the template.
Syntax	public, virtual CDocument * CreateNewDocument();
Parameters	None.
Returns	A pointer to the new CDocument if successful; otherwise NULL.

CreateNewFrame

■ 2.0 ■ 3.0

Description	This member creates a new frame window from its stored frame run-time class. If successful, the frame's resources are loaded into memory. The frame is used to contain the views associated with the document.
Syntax	public, virtual CFrameWnd * CreateNewFrame(CDocument * pDoc, CFrameWnd * pOther);
Parameters	
pDoc	A pointer to a document that will be associated with the new frame; otherwise NULL.
pOther	A pointer to a frame that the new frame will be based upon, or NULL to use the frame associated with the template.
Returns	A pointer to the new CFrameWnd if successful; otherwise NULL.
See Also	CFrameWnd::LoadFrame()

Dump

■ 2.0 ■ 3.0 ■ DO

Description	This member is an MFC diagnostic function that is only compiled into the debug version of the application. This member is used to output the state of the CDocTemplate object and can be called directly by the programmer.

Syntax public, virtual void Dump(CDumpContext& dc) const;

Parameters

dc A streamable object that accepts the diagnostic text.

Returns Nothing is returned.

GetDocString ■ 2.0 ■ 3.0

Description This member is used to retrieve one of the many strings used to describe a document type. These strings are stored as part of the application resources.

Syntax public, virtual BOOL GetDocString(CString & rString, enum DocStringIndex index) const;

Parameters

rString A reference to a CString that will receive the retrieved text.

index The particular document string to be retrieved. This value can be one of the following:

CDocTemplate::docName The default base document name. This is the default name used when the user selects the New command.

CDocTemplate::fileNewName The name of the file displayed in the File New dialog box.

CDocTemplate::filterExt The default extension used for documents of this type.

CDocTemplate::filterName The description and wildcard filter representing documents of this type.

CDocTemplate::regFileTypeId The document ID used internally with the Windows registry.

CDocTemplate::regFileTypeName The name of the document type stored in the registry. This name is often used by other applications that list available document types by querying the system registry.

CDocTemplate::windowTitle Used for Single Document Interface applications to retrieve the text in the application's title bar.

Returns TRUE if the string was found; otherwise FALSE.

GetFirstDocPosition ■ 2.0 ■ 3.0

Description This member retrieves the position of the first document in the template's list of open documents. This member is often used in conjunction with CDocTemplate::GetNextDoc to iterate through all the documents associated with this template. This is a purely abstract member and therefore must be supplied in any object derived from CDocManager.

Syntax public, virtual POSITION GetFirstDocPosition() const = 0;

Parameters None.

Returns The POSITION of the first document associated with this template.

Example

The following example shows how to use the GetFirstDocPosition member to retrieve and count all the documents for the given document template. Note that the CObject::IsKindOf member is used to determine if the retrieved document is of a specific type. This step is important when the exact type of document needs to be determined; otherwise it may be left out.

```
void CMainFrame::OnCountDocuments()
{
      CDocument* pDoc = NULL;
      POSITION posDoc;
      int nNumDocs = 0;

      // get the application since it holds the document template
      CDocTempApp * pApp = (CDocTempApp *)AfxGetApp();
      ASSERT_VALID(pApp);
      CMultiDocTemplate * pDocTemplate = pApp->m_pCustDocTemplate;
      ASSERT_VALID(pDocTemplate);

      if( pDocTemplate )
      {
            // traverse all documents for the template
            posDoc = pDocTemplate->GetFirstDocPosition();
            while (posDoc != NULL)
            {     // for every document in template
                  pDoc = pDocTemplate->GetNextDoc(posDoc);
                  if( pDoc && pDoc->IsKindOf(RUNTIME_CLASS(CDocTemplDoc)))
                        nNumDocs++;
            } // end while template has documents
      } // end if template ok

      // display the document count
      CString strMsg;
      strMsg.Format("There are currently %ld open documents.",nNumDocs);
      AfxMessageBox(strMsg,MB_ICONINFORMATION|MB_OK);
}
```

GetNextDoc

■ 2.0 ■ 3.0

Description

This member retrieves the next document in the associated list of documents for the template. This is a purely abstract member and therefore must be supplied in any object derived from CDocManager.

Syntax

public, virtual CDocument * GetNextDoc(POSITION & rPos) const = 0;

Parameters

rPos

Holds the POSITION of the document to retrieve and receives the position of the next document in the document list.

Returns

A pointer to the associated CDocument if successful; otherwise NULL.

See Also

CDocTemplate::GetFirstDocPosition()

Example

See CDocTemplate::GetFirstDocPosition()

InitialUpdateFrame

■ 2.0 ■ 3.0

Description This member is called to allow all the views of a document to receive an OnInitialUpdate notification. This member simply passes control to the CFrameWnd::OnInitialUpdateFrame function.

Syntax public, virtual void InitialUpdateFrame(CFrameWnd * pFrame, CDocument * pDoc, BOOL bMakeVisible = TRUE);

Parameters

pFrame The frame window containing the document to receive notification.

pDoc The document whose views are to be notified. This value may be NULL.

bMakeVisible TRUE will make the frame window visible; FALSE will not.

Returns Nothing is returned.

See Also CFrameWnd::OnInitialUpdateFrame()

LoadTemplate

■ 2.0 ■ 3.0

Description This member is used to load the resources associated with the document template. The document strings associated with the template are loaded, as are various OLE resources.

Syntax public, virtual void LoadTemplate();

Parameters None.

Returns Nothing is returned.

MatchDocType

■ 2.0 ■ 3.0 ■ NM

Description This member can be used to determine which CDocTemplate should be used to open a given document. Iterate through each template and call this function to determine which template is the best match.

Syntax public, virtual Confidence MatchDocType(LPCTSTR lpszPathName, CDocument *& rpDocMatch); public, virtual Confidence MatchDocType(LPCTSTR lpszPathName, DWORD dwFileType, CDocument *& rpDocMatch);

Parameters

lpszPathName The path name of the file to open.

rpDocMatch A pointer to a CDocument reference that will return the existing document if the file is currently open.

lpszPathName The path name of the file to open. (Macintosh only)

dwFileType The type of document. (Macintosh only)

Returns The confidence level of the match for this template. This value can be any one of the following:

```
enum Confidence {noAttempt,maybeAttemptForeign,maybeAttemptNative,
yesAttemptForeign,yesAttemptNative,yesAlreadyOpen};
```

OnIdle

■ 2.0 ■ 3.0

Description This member is called when the application message queue is empty and can be used to perform tasks when the application is not currently processing data. The default behavior of this member is to call the OnIdle member of all documents associated with this template.

Syntax public, virtual void OnIdle();

Parameters None.

Returns Nothing is returned.

OpenDocumentFile

■ 2.0 ■ 3.0

Description This member can either open an existing document file or create a new document for this template. This purely virtual member must be supplied in classes derived from CDocTemplate.

Syntax public, virtual CDocument * OpenDocumentFile(LPCTSTR lpszPathName, BOOL bMakeVisible = TRUE) = 0;

Parameters

lpszPathName The path name of the document file to open. If NULL, then a new CDocument will be created.

bMakeVisible If TRUE, then the window containing the document is made visible; otherwise it is not.

Returns A pointer to the new CDocument.

Example The following is an example of how to use the CDocTemplate::OpenDocumentFile member to create and display a new document. Usually the application framework will handle the creation of a new document, but there may be some instances where special initialization of the document is necessary.

```
void CMainFrame::OnManuallyCreateDocument()
{
	// get the application since it holds the document template
	CDocTempApp * pApp = (CDocTempApp *)AfxGetApp();
	ASSERT_VALID(pApp);
	CMultiDocTemplate * pDocTemplate = pApp->m_pCustDocTemplate;
	ASSERT_VALID(pDocTemplate);

	if(pDocTemplate)
	{
		CDocTemplDoc * pDoc = (CDocTemplDoc*)pDocTemplate-⇒
		                      >OpenDocumentFile(NULL);
		ASSERT_VALID(pDoc);
		// can call any CDocTemplDoc member for initialization here
		// NOTE: do not delete this pointer, the framework handles it
		// from here...
	}
}
```

RemoveDocument ■ 2.0 ■ 3.0

Description This member is used to disassociate the document from the document template.

Syntax public, virtual void RemoveDocument(CDocument * pDoc);

Parameters

pDoc The document to remove.

Returns Nothing is returned.

SaveAllModified ■ 2.0 ■ 3.0

Description This member is used to iterate through all of the associated documents and invoke each document's SaveModified member.

Syntax public, virtual BOOL SaveAllModified();

Parameters None.

Returns TRUE if successful; otherwise FALSE.

SetDefaultTitle ■ 2.0 ■ 3.0

Description This member is used to set the title for the given document. This purely virtual member must be supplied in classes derived from CDocTemplate.

Syntax public, virtual void SetDefaultTitle(CDocument * pDocument) = 0;

Parameters

pDocument The document whose title is to be set.

Returns Nothing is returned.

The CDocument Class

The CDocument class contains the data in the Document/View data model. This object also manages the creation of a new document, the loading of an existing document, and the saving of a modified document. The CDocument class has members that allow management of CView objects that are used to display the document's data. Each document can have multiple views of the data in an MDI application, or is limited to one view in an SDI application. See the samples included on the CD-ROM for examples of how to use documents.

CDocument ■ 2.0 ■ 3.0

Description The constructor for the CDocument class. This member initializes various internal class members.

Syntax public, CDocument();

Parameters None.

Returns Nothing is returned.

See Also ~CDocument()

~CDocument ■ 2.0 ■ 3.0

Description The destructor for the CDocument class. This member asserts that there are no current views associated with the document and detaches itself from the document template.

Syntax public, virtual ~CDocument();

Parameters None.

Returns Nothing is returned.

See Also CDocument()

AddView ■ 2.0 ■ 3.0

Description This member adds the given view to the list of views associated with this document. The given view should not be currently attached to another document or currently attached to this document.

Syntax public, void AddView(CView * pView);

Parameters

pView A pointer to the CView object to add to the document.

Returns Nothing is returned.

AssertValid ■ 2.0 ■ 3.0 ■ DO

Description Determines whether the CDocument is in a valid state and if it is not, throws an assertion. By calling this member, each view associated with this document will have its AssertValid member called. This member is only compiled into the debug version of the application.

Syntax public, virtual void AssertValid() const;

Parameters None.

Returns Nothing is returned.

CanCloseFrame ■ 2.0 ■ 3.0

Description This member is called by the framework before a frame window displaying the document is about to be closed. The default behavior is to allow closing of all frame windows except if it is the last frame window displaying the document. If it is the last frame window, then the document's SaveModified member is called, allowing the contents of the document to be saved.

Syntax public, virtual BOOL CanCloseFrame(CFrameWnd * pFrame);

Parameters

pFrame A pointer to the frame window displaying the document.

Returns TRUE if the frame can be closed; otherwise FALSE.

See Also CDocument:: SaveModified()

DeleteContents ■ 2.0 ■ 3.0

Description This member is called to allow the document to destroy any data it might have. This member is invoked before the document is destroyed or (in an SDI application) before the document object is reused. By default, this member does nothing.

Syntax public, virtual void DeleteContents();

Parameters None.

Returns Nothing is returned.

Example The example below illustrates how a document that holds an array of strings should destroy its data by overriding this member.

```
class CListBoxVDoc : public CDocument
{
protected: // create from serialization only
	CListBoxVDoc();
	DECLARE_DYNCREATE(CListBoxVDoc)

// Attributes
public:
	CStringArray	m_straInfo;

	void	AddString(const CString & str) { m_straInfo.Add(str);
}

//other attributes go here
...
}

void CListBoxVDoc::DeleteContents()
{
	// remove the contents of the string array
	m_straInfo.RemoveAll();

	CDocument::DeleteContents();
}
```

DisconnectViews ■ 2.0 ■ 3.0 ■ UD

Description This member is called to detach any views that are currently associated with this document.

Syntax public, void DisconnectViews();

Parameters None.

Returns Nothing is returned.

DoFileSave

■ 2.0 ■ 3.0 ■ UD

Description This member is invoked to save the contents of the document, usually in response to the user selecting the FILE SAVE menu option. If the current document is read-only then the CDocument::DoSave is invoked with a file name of NULL to prompt the user for a file name. Otherwise, the CDocument::DoSave member is called with the current document name.

Syntax public, virtual BOOL DoFileSave();

Parameters None.

Returns TRUE if successful; otherwise FALSE.

See Also CDocument::DoSave()

DoSave

■ 2.0 ■ 3.0 ■ UD

Description This member is called to perform the actual work of saving the contents of the document to a file. If the file name passed is NULL, then the user will be prompted for a new file name using the default extension supplied with the document template.

Syntax public, virtual BOOL DoSave(LPCTSTR lpszPathName, BOOL bReplace = TRUE);

Parameters

lpszPathName The file name to save the contents under. Passing NULL is the same as doing a "Save As..." on the document.

bReplace If TRUE, then a new file name will be given to the document. If FALSE, then the contents will be saved under the new name, but the document will not reflect this (like "Save Copy As...").

Returns TRUE if the document was saved; otherwise FALSE.

See Also CDocument::DoFileSave()

Dump

■ 2.0 ■ 3.0 ■ DO

Description This member is an MFC diagnostic function that is only compiled into the debug version of the application. This member is used to output the state of the CDocument object, and can be called directly by the programmer.

Syntax public, virtual void Dump(CDumpContext& dc) const;

Parameters

dc A streamable object that accepts the diagnostic text.

Returns Nothing is returned.

GetDefaultAccelerator

■ 2.0 ■ 3.0 ■ UD

Description This member is used to retrieve the default accelerators for this document. The default implementation returns NULL. Override to supply custom accelerators.

Syntax public, virtual HACCEL GetDefaultAccelerator();

Parameters None.

Returns HACCEL handle to the default accelerators.

GetDefaultMenu

■ 2.0 ■ 3.0 ■ UD

Description This member is used to retrieve the default menu for the document. The default implementation returns NULL. Override to supply a custom menu for the document.

Syntax public, virtual HMENU GetDefaultMenu();

Parameters None.

Returns HMENU handle to the default menu.

GetDocTemplate

■ 2.0 ■ 3.0

Description This member retrieves the document template associated with this document.

Syntax public, CDocTemplate * GetDocTemplate() const;

Parameters None.

Returns A pointer to the associated document template, or NULL if none currently exists.

GetFile

■ 2.0 ■ 3.0

Description This member is used to retrieve a pointer to a CFile object. The CFile object returned is not necessarily associated with the document; this is simply a helper function.

Syntax public, virtual CFile * GetFile(LPCTSTR lpszFileName, UINT nOpenFlags, CFileException * pError);

Parameters

lpszFileName The file name.

nOpenFlags File open flags. See CFile for a Description.

pError A pointer to a CFileException that will receive the status of the open file operation.

Returns A pointer to the new CFile object if successful; otherwise NULL.

See Also CDocument::ReleaseFile()

GetFirstViewPosition ■ 2.0 ■ 3.0

Description This member is used to retrieve the first view associated with this document. Use this member in conjunction with GetNextView to iterate through all views of this document.

Syntax public, virtual POSITION GetFirstViewPosition() const;

Parameters None.

Returns A POSITION reference to the first view associated with this document.

See Also CDocument::GetNextView()

Example The following example shows how to use CDocument::GetFirstViewPosition to retrieve the number of views currently associated with this document. This same method can be used to iterate through all of the document's views, and to call an internal view member function.

```
void CListBoxView::OnItemsCountDocumentViews()
{
      POSITION posView;
      CView * pView = NULL;
      int nNumViews = 0;

      // traverse all views for this document
      posView = GetDocument()->GetFirstViewPosition();
      while (posView != NULL)
      {     // for every view in document
            pView = GetDocument()->GetNextView(posView);
            if( pView && pView->IsKindOf(RUNTIME_CLASS(CListBoxView)))
                  nNumViews++;
      } // end while document has views

      // display the view count
      CString strMsg;
      strMsg.Format("There are currently %ld open views for this
document.",nNumViews);
      AfxMessageBox(strMsg,MB_ICONINFORMATION|MB_OK);
}
```

GetNextView ■ 2.0 ■ 3.0

Description Use this member to retrieve the next view associated with this document. This member should be used after an initial call to GetFirstViewPosition.

Syntax public, virtual CView * GetNextView(POSITION & rPosition) const;

Parameters

rPosition A reference to the view to retrieve. *rPosition* is also updated with the position of the next associated view.

Returns A pointer to the next CView if successful; otherwise NULL.

See Also CDocument::GetFirstViewPosition()

Example See CDocument::GetFirstViewPosition()

GetPathName

■ 2.0 ■ 3.0

Description This member is used to retrieve the fully qualified path name of the document.

Syntax public, const CString & GetPathName() const;

Parameters None.

Returns The fully qualified path name of the document.

See Also CDocument::SetPathName()

GetTitle

■ 2.0 ■ 3.0

Description This member retrieves the title of the document. By default, the title is based on the document file name.

Syntax public, const CString & GetTitle() const;

Parameters None.

Returns The document title.

See Also CDocument::SetTitle()

IsModified

■ 2.0 ■ 3.0

Description This member tells whether or not the contents of the document have changed since it was last saved or created. Call this member to determine whether or not the document needs to be saved.

Syntax public, virtual BOOL IsModified();

Parameters None.

Returns TRUE if the document was modified; otherwise FALSE.

See Also CDocument::SetModifiedFlag()

OnChangedViewList

■ 2.0 ■ 3.0

Description This member is called whenever a view is added or removed from the document. The default behavior updates the current view titles and closes the document if there are no current views.

Syntax public, virtual void OnChangedViewList();

Parameters None.

Returns Nothing is returned.

OnCloseDocument

■ 2.0 ■ 3.0

Description This member will destroy the document and all of its associated views. This member does not allow for any prompting or saving of the document's contents

(See OnFileClose). First, all associated views are closed. Second, a call is made to CDocument::DeleteContents. And, optionally, the document itself is destroyed.

Syntax public, virtual void OnCloseDocument();

Parameters None.

Returns Nothing is returned.

See Also CDocument::OnFileClose()

OnCmdMsg ■ 2.0 ■ 3.0 ■ UD

Description This member is used to pass command messages to the document. The default behavior passes the messages to either the base class CCmdTarget or the associated document template.

Syntax public, virtual BOOL OnCmdMsg(UINT nID, int nCode, void * pExtra, AFX_CMDHANDLERINFO * pHandlerInfo);

Parameters

nID Command ID.

nCode Notification code.

pExtra Dependent on *nCode*.

pHandlerInfo Typically NULL. If not NULL, then it is filled with handler information.

Returns TRUE if the command message is handled; otherwise FALSE.

OnFileClose ■ 2.0 ■ 3.0 ■ UD

Description This member is called to close the document, prompting the user to save the contents if the document has been modified.

Syntax protected, afx_msg void OnFileClose();

Parameters None.

Returns Nothing is returned.

See Also CDocument::SaveModified(), CDocument::OnCloseDocument()

OnFileSave ■ 2.0 ■ 3.0 ■ UD

Description This member is invoked when the user selects to save the contents of the document. The default behavior simply calls CDocument::DoFileSave.

Syntax protected, afx_msg void OnFileSave();

Parameters None.

Returns Nothing is returned.

See Also CDocument::DoFileSave()

OnFileSaveAs

■ 2.0 ■ 3.0 ■ UD

Description	This member is invoked when the user selects to save the contents of the document under a new file name. The default behavior simply calls CDocument::DoSave.
Syntax	protected, afx_msg void OnFileSaveAs();
Parameters	None.
Returns	Nothing is returned.
See Also	CDocument::DoSave()

OnFileSendMail

■ 2.0 ■ 3.0

Description	This member is used to send the contents of this document as a mail attachment. This member will only work if there is a current mail host and MAPI is installed.
Syntax	protected, afx_msg void OnFileSendMail();
Parameters	None.
Returns	Nothing is returned.

OnIdle

■ 2.0 ■ 3.0

Description	This member is called when the application message queue is empty and can be used to perform tasks when the application is not currently processing data. The default behavior of this member does nothing but can be overridden to perform document-specific tasks.
Syntax	public, virtual void OnIdle();
Parameters	None.
Returns	Nothing is returned.

OnNewDocument

■ 2.0 ■ 3.0

Description	This member is called by the application framework when the user creates a new document. The default behavior calls DeleteContents and clears the document modification flag. Override this member to perform document-specific initialization.
Syntax	public, virtual BOOL OnNewDocument();
Parameters	None.
Returns	TRUE if successful; otherwise FALSE.

OnOpenDocument ■ 2.0 ■ 3.0

Description This member is invoked by the framework when the user selects to open a document. SDI applications use this member to initialize the document. This member calls DeleteContents to clear the current document, loads the document information from an archive, then clears the document modification flag.

Syntax public, virtual BOOL OnOpenDocument(LPCTSTR lpszPathName);

Parameters

lpszPathName The name of the document to open.

Returns TRUE if successful; otherwise FALSE.

OnSaveDocument ■ 2.0 ■ 3.0

Description The application framework calls this function when the user selects to save the document. The file is opened, the document is then serialized to the file, then the document's modification flag is cleared.

Syntax public, virtual BOOL OnSaveDocument(LPCTSTR lpszPathName);

Parameters

lpszPathName The file name to save the document under.

Returns TRUE is successful; otherwise FALSE.

OnUpdateFileSendMail ■ 2.0 ■ 3.0

Description This member is used to enable or disable the command interface depending on whether or not the system has a mail host.

Syntax protected, afx_msg void OnUpdateSendMail(CCmdUI* pCmdUI);

Parameters

pCmdUI The user interface device to update.

Returns Nothing is returned.

PreCloseFrame ■ 2.0 ■ 3.0

Description This member is called prior to destroying the frame window of each view associated with this document. The default implementation of this member does nothing, but it can be overridden to provide custom behaviour.

Syntax public, virtual void PreCloseFrame(CFrameWnd * pFrame);

Parameters

pFrame The frame window that is about to be destroyed.

Returns Nothing is returned.

RecordDataFileOwner ■ 2.0 ■ 3.0 ■ UD ■ MO

Description This Macintosh-only member is used to record the owner of the saved document. This member is called directly from CDocument::OnSaveDocument.

Syntax public, virtual void RecordDataFileOwner(LPCTSTR lpszPathName, LPCTSTR lpszAppName);

Parameters

lpszPathName The name of the data file.

lpszAppName The name of the owner application.

Returns Nothing is returned.

ReleaseFile ■ 2.0 ■ 3.0

Description This member is used to close a previously opened CFile object. This member may be used in conjunction with the CDocument::GetFile, but the *pFile* parameter can be any valid CFile object.

Syntax public, virtual void ReleaseFile(CFile * pFile, BOOL bAbort);

Parameters

pFile A CFile object to close.

bAbort If TRUE, then the file is closed without the possibility of throwing an exception; otherwise FALSE will allow file exceptions to be thrown.

Returns Nothing is returned.

See Also CDocument::GetFile()

RemoveView ■ 2.0 ■ 3.0

Description This member is used to disassociate a view from this document. After the view is removed, then the document's OnChangedViewList member is called.

Syntax public, void RemoveView(CView * pView);

Parameters

pView The view to remove.

Returns Nothing is returned.

ReportSaveLoadException ■ 2.0 ■ 3.0

Description This member is invoked when an exception occurs when loading or saving the document. The default behavior displays any error message given by the exception, but can be overridden to display document-specific error messages.

Syntax public, virtual void ReportSaveLoadException(LPCTSTR lpszPathName, CException * e, BOOL bSaving, UINT nIDPDefault);

Parameters

lpszPathName The file name used.

e The exception that occurred.

bSaving If TRUE, then the exception happened during a save; otherwise the error occurred during a load operation.

nIDPDefault If no error message is found, this message specifies the default message to be displayed.

Returns Nothing is returned.

SaveModified

■ 2.0 ■ 3.0

Description This member is invoked by the framework before the document is to be closed. By default, the member will only attempt to save the contents of the document if its modified flag has been set. The user is prompted whether the document should be saved; then the DoFileSave member is invoked.

Syntax public, virtual BOOL SaveModified();

Parameters None.

Returns TRUE if the document was saved or the user selected not to save the document; otherwise FALSE.

SendInitialUpdate

■ 2.0 ■ 3.0 ■ UD

Description This member is used to iterate through all of the views associated with the document and invoke their OnInitialUpdate method.

Syntax public, void SendIntialUpdate();

Parameters None.

Returns Nothing is returned.

SetModifiedFlag

■ 2.0 ■ 3.0

Description This member is used to set whether the contents of the document have changed and need to be saved. This member should be called when a user changes the data associated with the document, so that the changes will be saved when the document is closed.

Syntax public, virtual void SetModifiedFlag(BOOL bModified = TRUE);

Parameters

bModified TRUE indicates the document should be saved; FALSE indicates the contents do not need to be saved.

Returns Nothing is returned.

Example The following example illustrates marking the document as modified when its contents have changed.

```
void CListBoxVDoc::RemoveString(const CString & str)
{
      CString strTemp;

      for(int nI=0;nI<m_straInfo.GetSize();nI++)
      {
            strTemp = m_straInfo[nI];
            if( strTemp == str )
            {
                  m_straInfo.RemoveAt(nI);
                  // mark as modified so we will be prompted to save
                  SetModifiedFlag();
                  break;
            }
      }
}
```

SetPathName

■ 2.0 ■ 3.0

Description This member sets the document's fully qualified path name. This is the name of the disk file that is associated with saving and loading this document.

Syntax public, virtual void SetPathName(LPCTSTR lpszPathName, BOOL bAddToMRU = TRUE);

Parameters

lpszPathName The fully qualified file path name.

bAddToMRU TRUE will add the document name to the application's Most Recently Used list; FALSE will not.

Returns Nothing is returned.

SetTitle

■ 2.0 ■ 3.0

Description This member is used to set the document title.

Syntax public, virtual void SetTitle(LPCTSTR lpszTitle);

Parameters

lpszTitle The new document title.

Returns Nothing is returned.

UpdateAllViews

■ 2.0 ■ 3.0

Description This member is used to update all views associated with this document. This member will call each CView::OnUpdate member with the given parameters.

Syntax public, void UpdateAllViews(CView * pSender, LPARAM lHint = 0L, CObject * pHint = NULL);

Parameters

pSender The CView object that originated the update. This member may be NULL.

lHint A programmer-supplied hint value that can provide information about the content of the data that has changed.

pObject A CObject-derived class that can contain information more specific to the hint specified by *lHint*.

Returns Nothing is returned.

Example The following example illustrates how to invoke the CDocument::UpdateAllViews member to send refresh hints to the individual views owned by the document. In this example, an individual view becomes dirty, so it notifies its parent document to update all the other views.

```
void CListBoxView::OnItemsDeleteselecteditem()
{
        CLBHint lbHint;
        // retrieve the index of the selected item
        int nSelIdx = GetListBoxCtrl().GetCurSel();
        ASSERT(nSelIdx != LB_ERR);
        GetListBoxCtrl().GetText(nSelIdx,lbHint.m_strString);
        // remove the item from the document
        GetDocument()->RemoveString(lbHint.m_strString);
        // update all views
        GetDocument()
->UpdateAllViews(NULL,LBV_HINT_REMOVE_STRING,&lbHint);
}
```

UpdateFrameCounts

■ 2.0 ■ 3.0 ■ UD

Description This member is used to update the titles of the frames associated with this document. If there is more than 1 frame associated with this document, then each frame's title will be appended with the frame number (such as 1, 2, 3, etc...). Only visible frames associated with this document are considered.

Syntax public, virtual void UpdateFrameCounts();

Parameters None.

Returns Nothing is returned.

The CEditView Class

The CEditView is derived from the CCtrlView object described above. This view is based on the standard Windows edit control. Use this view to allow the user to display, edit, save, and load simple text. For text that needs extensive formatting, see the CRichEditView.

CEditView

■ 2.0 ■ 3.0

Description The constructor for the CEditView class.

Syntax public, CEditView();

Parameters None.

Returns Nothing is returned.

~CEditView ■ 2.0 ■ 3.0

Description	The destructor for the CEditView class.
Syntax	public, virtual ~CEditView();
Parameters	None.
Returns	Nothing is returned.

AssertValid ■ 2.0 ■ 3.0 ■ DO

Description	Determines whether the CEditView is in a valid state and if it is not, throws an assertion. This member is only compiled into the debug version of the application.
Syntax	public, virtual void AssertValid() const;
Parameters	None.
Returns	Nothing is returned.
See Also	CWnd::AssertValid

CalcWindowRect ■ 2.0 ■ 3.0

Description	This member is called to determine the smallest rectangle necessary to enclose the CEditView window that has the given size for its client area.
Syntax	protected, virtual void CalcWindowRect(LPRECT lpClientRect,UINT nAdjustType = adjustBorder);
Parameters	
lpClientRect	Contains the client rectangle size, and is filled with the calculated window rectangle.
nAdjustType	Used for OLE in-place editing. It can be one of the following values:
CWnd::adjustBorder	Do not include scrollbar sizes in calculation.
CWnd::adjustOutside	Include scrollbar sizes in calculation.
Returns	Nothing is returned.

DeleteContents ■ 2.0 ■ 3.0

Description	This member is used to remove all the text contained within the edit view.
Syntax	public, virtual void DeleteContents();
Parameters	None.
Returns	Nothing is returned.
Example	See CDocument::DeleteContents

Dump

■ 2.0 ■ 3.0 ■ DO

Description This member is an MFC diagnostic function that is only compiled into the debug version of the application. This member is used to output the state of the CEditView object, and can be called directly by the programmer.

Syntax public, virtual void Dump(CDumpContext& dc) const;

Parameters

dc A streamable object that accepts the diagnostic text.

Returns Nothing is returned.

FindText

■ 2.0 ■ 3.0

Description This member will display the wait cursor and attempt to find the given text and set it as the current selection.

Syntax public, BOOL FindText(LPCTSTR lpszFind, BOOL bNext = TRUE, BOOL bCase = TRUE);

Parameters

lpszFind The string to find.

bNext If TRUE, then the search direction is from top to bottom. FALSE indicates the search direction is from bottom to top.

bCase If TRUE, then the case (upper or lower) of *lpszFind* must match exactly.

Returns TRUE if the text was found; otherwise FALSE.

GetBufferLength

■ 2.0 ■ 3.0

Description This member returns the length of text (in bytes) that is held in the edit control's buffer.

Syntax public, UINT GetBufferLength() const;

Parameters None.

Returns The length of text in bytes.

GetEditCtrl

■ 2.0 ■ 3.0

Description This member retrieves the edit control object that is associated with this view.

Syntax public, CEdit & GetEditCtrl() const;

Parameters None.

Returns A reference to the CEdit control.

GetPrinterFont ■ 2.0 ■ 3.0

Description This member is used to retrieve the font previously set by calling SetPrinterFont. If the printer font has not been previously set, then the font returned is the same as the display font. This font is selected into the device context when CEditView::OnPrint is called.

Syntax public, CFont * GetPrinterFont() const;

Parameters None.

Returns A pointer to the CFont object used for printing.

GetSelectedText ■ 2.0 ■ 3.0

Description This member retrieves the currently selected text within the edit view.

Syntax public, void GetSelectedText(CString & strResult) const;

Parameters

strResult A CString object that will receive the contents of the current selection.

Returns Nothing is returned.

InitializeReplace ■ 2.0 ■ 3.0 ■ UD

Description This member is used to find the first occurrence of the find string in a replace operation.

Syntax protected, BOOL InitializeReplace();

Parameters None.

Returns TRUE if the selection was found; otherwise FALSE.

LockBuffer ■ 2.0 ■ 3.0

Description This member is used to obtain a pointer to the edit view's text buffer. This member is used in conjunction with UnlockBuffer.

Syntax public, LPCTSTR LockBuffer() const;

Parameters None.

Returns A LPCTSTR to the contents of the text buffer.

OnBeginPrinting ■ 2.0 ■ 3.0

Description This member is called at the beginning of print or print preview to initialize any GDI resources needed for printing. This member is called after OnPreparePrinting.

Syntax protected, virtual void OnBeginPrinting(CDC * pDC, CPrintInfo * pInfo);

Parameters

pDC The print context to be used.

pInfo Contains information about the print job.

Returns Nothing is returned.

See Also CView::OnEndPrinting()

OnCreate

■ 2.0 ■ 3.0

Description This member is called after the creation of the edit view window but before the window is displayed.

Syntax protected, afx_msg int OnCreate(LPCREATESTRUCT lpcs);

Parameters

lpcs A pointer to a CREATESTRUCT that contains create-specific information.

Returns 0 to continue with creation, or non-zero to abort.

OnDestroy

■ 2.0 ■ 3.0 ■ UD

Description This member is invoked after the view window has been removed and before the edit view object is destroyed.

Syntax protected, afx_msg void OnDestroy();

Parameters None.

Returns Nothing is returned.

See Also CView::OnDestroy()

OnEditChange

■ 2.0 ■ 3.0 ■ UD

Description This member is called by the framework when the contents of the edit view have changed. By default, this member sets the document modified flag.

Syntax protected, afx_msg BOOL OnEditChange();

Parameters None.

Returns TRUE if the message was handled; otherwise FALSE to continue routing.

OnEditClear

■ 2.0 ■ 3.0 ■ UD

Description This member will delete the contents of the currently selected text from the view.

Syntax protected, afx_msg void OnEditClear();

Parameters None.

Returns Nothing is returned.

OnEditCopy

■ 2.0 ■ 3.0 ■ UD

Description This member is called to copy the contents of the current selection to the Clipboard.

Syntax protected, afx_msg void OnEditCopy();

Parameters None.

Returns Nothing is returned.

OnEditCut

■ 2.0 ■ 3.0 ■ UD

Description This member is used to copy the contents of the current selection to the Clipboard and to delete the current selection from the view.

Syntax protected, afx_msg void OnEditCut();

Parameters None.

Returns Nothing is returned.

OnEditFind

■ 2.0 ■ 3.0 ■ UD

Description This member is used to display the find dialog for the view. The find dialog allows the user several options when searching for a string of text. This member calls the OnEditFindReplace member.

Syntax protected, afx_msg void OnEditFind();

Parameters None.

Returns Nothing is returned.

OnEditFindReplace

■ 2.0 ■ 3.0 ■ UD

Description This member is used to display the find or the Find And Replace dialog for the view. The Find dialog allows the user several options when searching for a string of text.

Syntax protected, void OnEditFindReplace(BOOL bFindOnly);

Parameters

bFindOnly If TRUE, then only options for finding a string of text are displayed. Otherwise, all the find-and-replace options are available.

Returns Nothing is returned.

OnEditPaste

■ 2.0 ■ 3.0 ■ UD

Description This member is called to insert the text contents of the Clipboard at the current insertion point.

Syntax protected, afx_msg void OnEditPaste();
Parameters None.
Returns Nothing is returned.

OnEditRepeat

■ 2.0 ■ 3.0 ■ UD

Description This member is called to repeat the last find or replace operation.
Syntax protected, afx_msg void OnEditRepeat();
Parameters None.
Returns Nothing is returned.

OnEditReplace

■ 2.0 ■ 3.0 ■ UD

Description This member is called to display the Find And Replace dialog for the view. This member calls the OnEditFindReplace member with FALSE to display both the Find and Replace portions of the dialog.
Syntax protected, afx_msg void OnEditReplace();
Parameters None.
Returns Nothing is returned.

OnEditSelectAll

■ 2.0 ■ 3.0 ■ UD

Description This member is called to select the entire contents of the edit view buffer.
Syntax protected, afx_msg void OnEditSelectAll();
Parameters None.
Returns Nothing is returned.

OnEditUndo

■ 2.0 ■ 3.0 ■ UD

Description This member is called to undo the last edit operation.
Syntax protected, afx_msg void OnEditUndo();
Parameters None.
Returns Nothing is returned.

OnEndPrinting

■ 2.0 ■ 3.0 ■ UD

Description This member is called upon completion of a print or print preview job.
Syntax protected, virtual void OnEndPrinting(CDC * pDC, CPrintInfo * pInfo = NULL);

Parameters

pDC	The print context.
pInfo	Contains information about the print job.
Returns	Nothing is returned.
See Also	CEditView::OnBeginPrinting()

OnFindNext ■ 2.0 ■ 3.0

Description This member will attempt to repeat the last find operation. If the text is found, then the text is highlighted and the Find Next dialog is displayed.

Syntax protected, virtual void OnFindNext(LPCTSTR lpszFind, BOOL bNext, BOOL bCase);

Parameters

lpszFind	The string to find.
bNext	If TRUE, then the search direction goes from top to bottom; otherwise FALSE indicates a search direction of bottom to top.
bCase	If TRUE, then the case (upper or lower) of *lpszFind* must match exactly.
Returns	Nothing is returned.

OnFindReplaceCmd ■ 2.0 ■ 3.0 ■ UD

Description This member is invoked when the edit view receives a find or replace notification message, usually when the user selected the EDIT REPLACE menu option. The action that takes place is dependent on the current state of the Find/Replace dialog.

Syntax protected, afx_msg LRESULT OnFindReplaceCmd(WPARAM wParam, LPARAM lParam);

Parameters

wParam	Unused.
lParam	Contains information about the Find/Replace dialog.
Returns	Always returns zero.

OnPrepareDC ■ 2.0 ■ 3.0 ■ UD

Description This member is called before OnDraw and OnPrint to initialize the print context. By default, this member attempts to paginate to the given print page. If this fails (such as when the current page is greater than the number of pages in the view), then the print job will fail.

Syntax public, virtual void OnPrepareDC(CDC * pDC, CPrintInfo * pInfo);

Parameters

pDC The print context.

pInfo Contains information about the print job.

Returns Nothing is returned.

OnPreparePrinting ■ 2.0 ■ 3.0 ■ UD

Description This member is called before a print or print preview job begins. Override this member and call DoPreparePrinting to enable print and print preview.

Syntax protected, virtual BOOL OnPreparePrinting(CPrintInfo * pInfo);

Parameters

pInfo Contains information about the print job.

Returns TRUE to begin the print or print preview job; otherwise FALSE to abort.

OnPrint ■ 2.0 ■ 3.0 ■ UD

Description This member is called during a print or print preview job to print a page of information. The page to print is given by the **m_nCurpage** member of the *pInfo* variable. When OnPrint is called, the device context has already been initialized by calling OnPrepareDC.

Syntax protected, virtual void OnPrint(CDC * pDC, CPrintInfo * pInfo);

Parameters

pDC The print context.

pInfo Contains information about the print job.

Returns Nothing is returned.

OnReplaceAll ■ 2.0 ■ 3.0

Description This member is used to replace all of the occurrences of one text string with another. The framework calls this member from the Replace dialog box when the user clicks the Replace All button.

Syntax protected, virtual void OnReplaceAll(LPCTSTR lpszFind, LPCTSTR lpszReplace, BOOL bCase);

Parameters

lpszFind The string to find.

lpszReplace The string to use for replacement.

bCase If TRUE, then the case (upper or lower) of *lpszFind* must match exactly.

Returns Nothing is returned.

OnReplaceSel

■ 2.0 ■ 3.0

Description This member is used to replace the next occurrence of a string with the contents of another. This member is called by the framework in response to commands from the Replace dialog, such as when the user clicks the Replace button.

Syntax protected, virtual void OnReplaceSel(LPCTSTR lpszFind, BOOL bNext, BOOL bCase, LPCTSTR lpszReplace);

Parameters

lpszFind The string to find.

bNext If TRUE, then the search direction goes from top to bottom; otherwise FALSE indicates a search direction of bottom to top.

bCase If TRUE, then the case (upper or lower) of *lpszFind* must match exactly.

lpszReplace The string to use for replacement.

Returns Nothing is returned.

OnSetFont

■ 2.0 ■ 3.0 ■ UD

Description This member is called by the application framework when the view's window font has changed.

Syntax protected, afx_msg LRESULT OnSetFont(WPARAM wParam, LPARAM lParam);

Parameters

wParam The HFONT of the new font.

lParam Unused.

Returns Always returns zero.

OnTextNotFound

■ 2.0 ■ 3.0

Description This member is called by the framework when the results of a find or replace indicate that the text was not found within the view. By default, this member will produce a message beep.

Syntax protected, virtual void OnTextNotFound(LPCTSTR lpszFind);

Parameters

lpszFind The text that was not found.

Returns Nothing is returned.

OnUpdateEditUndo

■ 2.0 ■ 3.0 ■ UD

Description This member will enable the given interface object if the last edit action can be undone.

Syntax protected, afx_msg void OnUpdateEditUndo(CCmdUI * pCmdUI);

Parameters

pCmdUI A pointer to the user interface item to be enabled.

Returns Nothing is returned.

OnUpdateNeedClip ■ 2.0 ■ 3.0 ■ UD

Description This member is used to update the user interface object representing whether or not the user can use the Paste command.

Syntax protected, afx_msg void OnUpdateNeedClip(CCmdUI * pCmdUI);

Parameters

pCmdUI A pointer to the user interface item to update.

Returns Nothing is returned.

OnUpdateNeedFind ■ 2.0 ■ 3.0 ■ UD

Description This member is used to update the interface object representing whether or not the user can proceed with a find operation. This member will enable the interface object if there is text within the view and there is a current string to find.

Syntax protected, afx_msg void OnUpdateNeedFind(CCmdUI * pCmdUI);

Parameters

pCmdUI A pointer to the user interface item to update.

Returns Nothing is returned.

OnUpdateNeedSel ■ 2.0 ■ 3.0 ■ UD

Description This member will enable the given interface object if a current text selection exists in the view.

Syntax protected, afx_msg void OnUpdateNeedSel(CCmdUI * pCmdUI);

Parameters

pCmdUI A pointer to the user interface item to update.

Returns Nothing is returned.

OnUpdateNeedText ■ 2.0 ■ 3.0 ■ UD

Description This member will enable the given interface object if the view currently contains text.

Syntax protected, afx_msg void OnUpdateNeedText(CCmdUI * pCmdUI);

Parameters

pCmdUI A pointer to the user interface item to update.

Returns Nothing is returned.

PaginateTo

■ 2.0 ■ 3.0 ■ UD

Description This member is used to print a range of pages starting with the first page and ending with the page specified by the **m_nCurPage** member of *pInfo*.

Syntax protected, BOOL PaginateTo(CDC * pDC, CPrintInfo * pInfo);

Parameters

pDC The print context to be used.

pInfo Contains information about the print job.

Returns TRUE is successful; otherwise FALSE.

PreCreateWindow

■ 2.0 ■ 3.0 ■ UD

Description Override this member to modify the attributes of the CEditView before the window is created. This member can be used to set the initial size, position, and style of the view.

Syntax protected, virtual BOOL PreCreateWindow(CREATESTRUCT & cs);

Parameters

cs A reference to a CREATESTRUCT that will receive the modified attributes.

Returns TRUE to continue with creation of the window; FALSE to halt creation.

PrintInsideRect

■ 2.0 ■ 3.0

Description This member is used to print, into the given rectangle, a specific portion of the text within the edit view.

Syntax public, UINT PrintInsideRect(CDC * pDC, RECT & rectLayout, UINT nIndexStart, UINT nIndexStop);

Parameters

pDC The device context to print into.

rectLayout The bounding rectangle to print the selection into.

nIndexStart The index of the first character to be printed.

nIndexStop The desired index of the last character to be printed.

Returns The index of the first character that did not fit within *rectLayout*.

ReadFromArchive

■ 2.0 ■ 3.0

Description This member is used to read an amount of text from a file and place it into the current edit view.

Syntax public, void ReadFromArchive(CArchive & ar, UINT nLen);

Parameters

ar The archive to read from.

nLen	The length (in bytes) of text to read.
Returns	Nothing is returned.
See Also	CArchive()

SameAsSelected

■ 2.0 ■ 3.0

Description	This member is used to determine if the given text is the same as the current selection.
Syntax	protected, BOOL SameAsSelected(LPCTSTR lpszCompare, BOOL bCase);
Parameters	
lpszCompare	The text string to compare to the current selection.
bCase	If TRUE, then the case (upper or lower) of *lpszCompare* must match exactly.
Returns	TRUE if the current selection matches *lpszCompare*; otherwise FALSE.

Serialize

■ 2.0 ■ 3.0

Description	This member is used to save or load the contents of the view to the given archive. When saving, the length of the text is saved before the actual text. When loading, the length of the text is read before loading the text.
Syntax	public, virtual void Serialize(CArchive & ar);
Parameters	
ar	The archive that receives the contents of the edit view.
Returns	Nothing is returned.
See Also	CEditView:: WriteToArchive

SerializeRaw

■ 2.0 ■ 3.0

Description	This member is used to save or load only the text contents of the view to the given archive.
Syntax	public, void SerializeRaw(CArchive & ar);
Parameters	
ar	The archive that receives the contents of the edit view.
Returns	Nothing is returned.
See Also	CEditView:: WriteToArchive()

SetPrinterFont

■ 2.0 ■ 3.0

Description	This member is used to set the font that will be used when printing the edit view. By default, this font is selected into the print context during the OnPrint member.

Syntax public, void SetPrinterFont(CFont * pFont);

Parameters

pFont A pointer to the desired CFont object to use for printing.

Returns Nothing is returned.

SetTabStops ■ 2.0 ■ 3.0 ■ NM

Description This member sets the distance between tabs in the edit view. These tab stops will be used whenever a tab character is encountered in the text. By default, the view is updated after setting the tab stops.

Syntax public, void SetTabStops(int nTabStops);

Parameters

nTabStops The distance between tab stops in dialog units.

Returns Nothing is returned.

UnlockBuffer ■ 2.0 ■ 3.0

Description This member is used to release the internal buffer that was previously locked with LockBuffer.

Syntax public, void UnlockBuffer() const;

Parameters None.

Returns Nothing is returned.

WriteToArchive ■ 2.0 ■ 3.0 ■ UD

Description This member is used to save the text contents of the view to the given archive. This member is called from both the Serialize and SerializeRaw members.

Syntax public, void WriteToArchive(CArchive & ar);

Parameters

ar The archive that receives the contents of the view.

Returns Nothing is returned.

See Also CArchive()

The CFormView Class

The CFormView class allows for the creation of a view based on a dialog template. This allows you to easily add any dialog control (such as buttons, edit boxes, combo boxes, etc.) to your view. This is especially handy when creating a view that represents a question-and-answer form that the user fills with data.

When you first construct a CFormView, you pass it the resource ID of the dialog template you wish to use. This dialog template must have only the WS_CHILD style set. Then, when the new view is created, so are the dialog controls. You can access each control by using CWnd::GetDlgItem.

CFormView

■ 2.0 ■ 3.0

Description The constructor for the CFormView class.

Syntax protected, CFormView(LPCTSTR lpszTemplateName);
protected, CFormView(UINT nIDTemplate);

Parameters

lpszTemplateName The resource string identifying the dialog template used with this view.

nIDTemplate The resource ID identifying the dialog template used with this view.

Returns Nothing is returned.

AssertValid

■ 2.0 ■ 3.0 ■ DO

Description Determines whether the CFormView is in a valid state and if it is not, throws an assertion. This member is only compiled into the debug version of the application.

Syntax public, virtual void AssertValid() const;

Parameters None.

Returns Nothing is returned.

See Also CView::AssertValid()

Create

■ 2.0 ■ 3.0

Description This member is used to create the CFormView window and attach it to this object. Besides creating the view window, the dialog controls associated with the resource ID given in the CFormView constructor are created and initialized.

Syntax protected, virtual BOOL Create(LPCTSTR lpszClassName, LPCTSTR lpszWindowName, DWORD dwRequestedStyle, const RECT & rect, CWnd * pParentWnd, UINT nID, CCreateContext * pContext);

Parameters

lpszClassName Unused. Can be set to NULL.

lpszWindowName Unused. Can be set to NULL.

dwRequestedStyle The requested window style flags.

rect The initial size and position of the resultant window.

pParentWnd The parent window.

nID The child ID of the frame view window.

pContext — An optional pointer to a CCreateContext that will be passed to the CFormView::OnCreate method.

Returns — TRUE if successful; otherwise FALSE.

Dump

■ 2.0 ■ 3.0 ■ DO

Description — This member is an MFC diagnostic function that is only compiled into the debug version of the application. This member is used to output the state of the CFormView object, and can be called directly by the programmer.

Syntax — public, virtual void Dump(CDumpContext& dc) const;

Parameters

dc — A streamable object that accepts the diagnostic text.

Returns — Nothing is returned.

OnActivateFrame

■ 2.0 ■ 3.0

Description — This member is called when the form's frame is activated. If the frame is being deactivated, then the default behavior checks to see if the current focus window is one of the form's dialog controls. If it is, then the window handle is saved and used the next time the form receives focus.

Syntax — protected, virtual void OnActivateFrame(UINT nState, CFrameWnd* pFrameWnd);

Parameters

nState — The activation state of the frame. This can be any one of the following:

WA_ACTIVE — Frame activated by a method other than a mouse click.

WA_CLICKACTIVE — Frame activated by a mouse click.

WA_INACTIVE — Frame deactivated.

pFrameWnd — A pointer to the frame window.

Returns — Nothing is returned.

OnActivateView

■ 2.0 ■ 3.0

Description — This member is called when the view is activated or deactivated. If the view is being deactivated, then the default behavior checks to see if the current focus window is one of the form's dialog controls. If it is, then the window handle is saved and used the next time the form receives focus.

Syntax — protected, virtual void OnActivateView(BOOL bActivate, CView* pActivateView, CView* pDeactiveView);

Parameters

bActivate — TRUE indicates the form view is being activated.

pActivateView A pointer to the CView being activated.

pDeactiveView A pointer to the CView being deactivated.

Returns Nothing is returned.

OnCreate

■ 2.0 ■ 3.0

Description This member is called after the creation of the form view but before the window is displayed. This member initializes the *lpcs* parameter with a copy of the create structure used when the CFormView::Create member was called.

Syntax protected, afx_msg int OnCreate(LPCREATESTRUCT lpcs);

Parameters

lpcs A pointer to a CREATESTRUCT that contains create-specific information.

Returns 0 to continue with creation, or non-zero to abort.

OnDraw

■ 2.0 ■ 3.0

Description This member is called by the application framework when an image of the form view needs to be drawn. The given CDC object is used to represent the context in which the view should render itself. Note that by default, CFormViews do not support printing due to the dialog controls it may contain.

Syntax protected, virtual void OnDraw(CDC * pDC);

Parameters

pDC A pointer to a CDC object that represents the particular display context the view should render into.

Returns Nothing is returned.

OnInitialUpdate

■ 2.0 ■ 3.0

Description This member is invoked when the form view is initially displayed. The default behavior forces an UpdateData member to be called to display any data bound to the form's dialog controls.

Syntax public, virtual void OnInitialUpdate();

Parameters None.

Returns Nothing is returned.

OnSetFocus

■ 2.0 ■ 3.0

Description This member is invoked when the form receives the input focus. By default, the form view will attempt to set the focus to its last dialog control that had focus when the form was last deactivated.

Syntax protected, afx_msg void OnSetFocus(CWnd * pOldWnd);

Parameters

pOldWnd The window that lost focus.

Returns Nothing is returned.

PreTranslateMessage ■ 2.0 ■ 3.0

Description This member is used to intercept messages before they are dispatched. This member ensures that the frame messages are processed first so that they do not interfere with the dialog messages.

Syntax protected, virtual BOOL PreTranslateMessage(MSG * pMsg);

Parameters

pMsg The message to be pre-translated.

Returns Non-zero if the message was translated and should not be dispatched; otherwise 0 which will allow the message to be dispatched.

SaveFocusControl ■ 2.0 ■ 3.0

Description This member is used to save the dialog control that currently has focus. This member is used in conjunction with OnActivateFrame and OnActivateView.

Syntax protected, BOOL SaveFocusControl();

Parameters None.

Returns TRUE if the current focus window was a child window of the form view; otherwise FALSE.

The CListView Class

The CListView is derived from the CCtrlView class. This view manages a CListCtrl object that can display a list of information in various formats. As with all CCtrlView-based classes, the entire view is filled with a specific control. The base class handles all resizing of the control due to user interaction. In this case, the control is a CListCtrl which is described in greater detail in Chapter 9, *Windows Controls*.

CListView ■ 4.0

Description The constructor for the CListView class.

Syntax public, CListView();

Parameters None.

Returns Nothing is returned.

DrawItem

■ 4.0 ■ UD

Description This member is called whenever the display of an owner draw list view needs to be updated.

Syntax public, virtual void DrawItem(LPDRAWITEMSTRUCT lpDrawItemStruct);

Parameters

lpDrawItemStruct Specifies information about the aspect of the display that needs to be drawn. See the Windows SDK for more information on this structure.

Returns Nothing is returned.

GetListCtrl

■ 4.0

Description This member is used to retrieve the list view control that comprises this view.

Syntax public, CListCtrl & GetListCtrl() const;

Parameters None.

Returns A reference to the list view control contained in this view.

OnChildNotify

■ 4.0 ■ UD

Description This member can be overridden to receive notification messages from the list control.

Syntax protected, virtual BOOL OnChildNotify(UINT message, WPARAM wParam, LPARAM lParam, LRESULT* pResult);

Parameters

message Message.

wParam Message-specific data.

lParam Message-specific data.

pResult Address of the returned result code, dependent on the notification message.

Returns FALSE for unhandled messages, and TRUE for messages that were handled by the view.

OnNcDestroy

■ 4.0 ■ UD

Description This member is called when the non-client area of the list view is being destroyed. The default implementation takes this opportunity to remove any image lists associated with the list control before calling the base class CCtrlView::OnNcDestroy.

Syntax public,afx_msg void OnNcDestroy();

Parameters None.

Returns Nothing is returned.

PreCreateWindow ■ 4.0 ■ UD

Description Override this member to modify the attributes of the CListView before the window is created. This member can be used to set the initial size, position, and style of the view.

Syntax public, virtual BOOL PreCreateWindow(CREATESTRUCT & cs);

Parameters

cs A reference to a CREATESTRUCT that will receive the modified attributes.

Returns TRUE to continue with creation of the window; FALSE to halt creation.

RemoveImageList ■ 4.0 ■ UD

Description This member is used to remove a particular image from the list control's image list.

Syntax protected, void RemoveImageList(int nImageList);

Parameters

nImageList Specifies which list is to be removed. The value can be any one of the following:

LVSIL_NORMAL Image list that contains the large images.

LVSIL_SMALL Image list that contains the small images.

LVSIL_STATE Image list that contains the state images.

Returns Nothing is returned.

The CMultiDocTemplate Class

The CMultiDocTemplate is derived from the CDocTemplate object, and is used to manage multiple templates within an application. Applications that use multiple documents are said to have a Multiple Document Interface (or MDI for short). This object handles the various aspects of selecting the proper template when opening a document, as well as providing methods for iterating through the individual templates.

CMultiDocTemplate ■ 2.0 ■ 3.0

Description The constructor for the CMultiDocTemplate class.

Syntax public, CMultiDocTemplate(UINT nIDResource, CRuntimeClass* pDocClass, CRuntimeClass* pFrameClass, CRuntimeClass* pViewClass);

Parameters

nIdResource The ID of the resources to be used for this document type.

pDocClass A pointer to the run-time class of the document type.

pFrameClass A pointer to the run-time class of the frame type.

pViewClass A pointer to the run-time class of the view type.

Returns Nothing is returned.
See Also ~CMultiDocTemplate()

~CMultiDocTemplate ■ 2.0 ■ 3.0

Description The destructor for the CMultiDocTemplate class.
Syntax public, virtual ~CMultiDocTemplate();
Parameters None.
Returns Nothing is returned.
See Also CMultiDocTemplate()

AddDocument ■ 2.0 ■ 3.0

Description This member associates a document with the template. CMultiDocTemplate objects can manage one or more documents.
Syntax public, virtual void AddDocument(CDocument * pDoc);
Parameters
pDoc A pointer to the document to add.
Returns Nothing is returned.
See Also CMultiDocTemplate()

AssertValid ■ 2.0 ■ 3.0 ■ DO

Description Determines whether the CMultiDocTemplate is in a valid state and if it is not, throws an assertion. This member is only compiled into the debug version of the application.
Syntax public, virtual void AssertValid() const;
Parameters None.
Returns Nothing is returned.
See Also CWnd::AssertValid()

Dump ■ 2.0 ■ 3.0 ■ DO

Description This member is an MFC diagnostic function that is only compiled into the debug version of the application. This member is used to output the state of the CMultiDocTemplate object and can be called directly by the programmer.
Syntax public, virtual void Dump(CDumpContext& dc) const;
Parameters
dc A streamable object that accepts the diagnostic text.
Returns Nothing is returned.

GetFirstDocPosition ■ 2.0 ■ 3.0

Description Retrieves the POSITION of the first document associated with this template. This member is usually used in conjunction with GetNextDoc to iterate through all of the documents associated with this template.

Syntax public, virtual POSITION GetFirstDocPosition() const;

Parameters None.

Returns POSITION of the first associated document.

See Also CMultiDocTemplate()

Example See CDocTemplate::GetFirstDocPosition()

GetNextDoc ■ 2.0 ■ 3.0

Description This member is used to retrieve the next document associated with this template. This member should only be used after an initial call to GetFirstDocPosition.

Syntax public, virtual CDocument * GetNextDoc(POSITION & rPos) const;

Parameters

rPos The current reference document position.

Returns A pointer to the next document.

See Also CMultiDocTemplate()

Example See CDocTemplate::GetFirstDocPosition

OpenDocumentFile ■ 2.0 ■ 3.0

Description This member can either open an existing document file or create a new document for this template.

Syntax public, virtual CDocument * OpenDocumentFile(LPCTSTR lpszPathName, BOOL bMakeVisible = TRUE);

Parameters

lpszPathName The path name of the document file to open. If NULL, then a new CDocument will be created.

bMakeVisible If TRUE, then the window containing the document is made visible; otherwise it is not.

Returns A pointer to the new CDocument.

Example See CDocTemplate::OpenDocumentFile()

RemoveDocument ■ 2.0 ■ 3.0

Description This member is used to disassociate the document from the document template.

Syntax public, virtual void RemoveDocument(CDocument * pDoc);

Parameters

pDoc The document to remove.

Returns Nothing is returned.

SetDefaultTitle ■ 2.0 ■ 3.0

Description This member is used to set the title for the given document. The default title is created by accessing the resource strings associated with the document type.

Syntax public, virtual void SetDefaultTitle(CDocument * pDocument);

Parameters

pDocument The document whose title is to be set.

Returns Nothing is returned.

See Also CDocTemplate::GetDocString()

The CRichEditView Class

The CRichEditView is derived from the CCtrlView class. This view manages a CRichEditCtrl object that can display a richly formatted text (RTF) file. This view allows for the display, editing, saving, and loading of RTF files. See Chapter 9, *Windows Controls,* for a discussion of the CRichEditCtrl. See the samples included on the CD-ROM for an example of how to use rich edit views.

CRichEditView ■ 4.0

Description The constructor for the CRichEditView class. This member initializes the default format settings for the object.

Syntax public, CRichEditView();

Parameters None.

Returns Nothing is returned.

AdjustDialogPosition ■ 4.0

Description This member is used to move the given dialog so that it does not obscure the current selection (if possible). This member is a helper function and can be used on any dialog.

Syntax public, void AdjustDialogPosition(CDialog * pDlg);

Parameters

pDlg The dialog to adjust.

Returns Nothing is returned.

AssertValid

■ 4.0 ■ DO

Description Determines whether the CRichEditView is in a valid state and if it is not, throws an assertion. This member is only compiled into the debug version of the application.

Syntax public, virtual void AssertValid() const;

Parameters None.

Returns Nothing is returned.

CanPaste

■ 4.0

Description This member is used to determine whether or not the information on the Clipboard is of a format that can be pasted into the rich edit view.

Syntax public, BOOL CanPaste() const;

Parameters None.

Returns TRUE if the information can be pasted; otherwise FALSE.

DeleteContents

■ 4.0 ■ UD

Description This member is used to remove all the information contained within the rich edit control of the view. This member will also remove the contents of the undo buffer, which means this action cannot be reversed.

Syntax public, virtual void DeleteContents();

Parameters None.

Returns Nothing is returned.

Example See CDocument::DeleteContents()

Dump

■ 4.0 ■ DO

Description This member is an MFC diagnostic function that is only compiled into the debug version of the application. This member is used to output the state of the CRichEditView object and can be called directly by the programmer.

Syntax public, virtual void Dump(CDumpContext& dc) const;

Parameters

dc A streamable object that accepts the diagnostic text.

Returns Nothing is returned.

FindAndSelect

■ 4.0 ■ UD

Description This member is used to find the given text and make it the current selection if found. This member is called by the FindTextSimple member.

Syntax	public, long FindAndSelect(DWORD dwFlags, FINDTEXTEX & ft);
Parameters	
dwFlags	Contains the search flags and can be a combination of the following:
FT_MATCHCASE	The search is case sensitive.
FT_WHOLEWORD	Only match where the entire word is the same.
ft	A reference to a FINDTEXTEX structure that specifies the text to be searched and the range to search within and holds the results of the search.
Returns	The character index of the next match, otherwise -1.
See Also	CRichEditCtrl::FindText()

FindText ■ 4.0

Description	This member will display the wait cursor and attempt to find the given text and set it as the current selection. This member directly calls the FindTextSimple member.
Syntax	public, BOOL FindText(LPCTSTR lpszFind, BOOL bCase = TRUE, BOOL bWord = TRUE);
Parameters	
lpszFind	The string to find.
bCase	If TRUE, then the case (upper or lower) of *lpszFind* must match exactly.
bWord	If TRUE, then the text of *lpszFind* will only match if it is found as a whole word. In other words, *lpszFind* cannot be the prefix of any other text.
Returns	TRUE if the text was found; otherwise FALSE.

FindTextSimple ■ 4.0

Description	This member will attempt to find the given text and set it as the current selection. This member calls FindAndSelect to perform the actual selection.
Syntax	public, BOOL FindTextSimple(LPCTSTR lpszFind, BOOL bCase = TRUE, BOOL bWord = TRUE);
Parameters	
lpszFind	The string to find.
bCase	If TRUE, then the case (upper or lower) of *lpszFind* must match exactly.
bWord	If TRUE, then the text of *lpszFind* will only match if it is found as a whole word. In other words, *lpszFind* cannot be the prefix of any other text.
Returns	TRUE if the text was found; otherwise FALSE.

GetCharFormatSelection ■ 4.0

Description	This member retrieves the character format of the current selection.

Syntax public, CHARFORMAT & GetCharFormatSelection();

Parameters None.

Returns A CHARFORMAT structure that specifies the formatting attributes of the current selection.

GetDocument ■ 4.0

Description This member will return the associated CRichEditDoc document for this view. The CRichEditDoc is derived from the CDocument class and contains functionality for OLE manipulation.

Syntax public, CRichEditDoc * GetDocument() const;

Parameters None.

Returns The associated document.

Example See CView::GetDocument()

GetMargins ■ 4.0

Description This member will retrieve the margins used for printing the view.

Syntax public, CRect GetMargins() const;

Parameters None.

Returns A CRect specifying the print margins in MM_TWIPS.

GetPageRect ■ 4.0

Description This member is used to retrieve the page bounds used for printing the view.

Syntax public, CRect GetPageRect() const;

Parameters None.

Returns A CRect specifying the printing page size in MM_TWIPS.

GetPaperSize ■ 4.0

Description This member is used to retrieve the printing paper size.

Syntax public, CSize GetPaperSize() const;

Parameters None.

Returns A CSize specifying the paper size in MM_TWIPS.

GetParaFormatSelection ■ 4.0

Description This member is used to retrieve the paragraph formatting attributes of the current selection.

Syntax	public, PARAFORMAT & GetParaFormatSelection();
Parameters	None.
Returns	A PARAFORMAT structure specifying the attributes.

GetPrintRect ■ 4.0

Description	This member is used to retrieve the printing boundary within the current printing page.
Syntax	public, CRect GetPrintRect() const;
Parameters	None.
Returns	A CRect specifying the printing boundary in MM_TWIPS.

GetPrintWidth ■ 4.0

Description	This member is used to retrieve the width of the current printing area.
Syntax	public, int GetPrintWidth() const;
Parameters	None.
Returns	The width of the printing area in MM_TWIPS.

GetRichEditCtrl ■ 4.0

Description	This member retrieves the CRichEditCtrl associated with this view. This control can be accessed directly from this reference.
Syntax	public, CRichEditCtrl & GetRichEditCtrl() const;
Parameters	None.
Returns	The CRichEditCtrl associated with this view.

GetTextLength ■ 4.0

Description	This member will retrieve the length (in bytes) of the text stored within the view.
Syntax	public, long GetTextLength() const;
Parameters	None.
Returns	The length in bytes of the text in the view.

InsertFileAsObject ■ 4.0

Description	This member will insert the given file into the view.
Syntax	public, void InsertFileAsObject(LPCTSTR lpszFileName);

Parameters

lpszFileName — The name of the file to insert.

Returns — Nothing is returned.

IsRichEditFormat

■ 4.0

Description — This member is called to determine if the given Clipboard format is text or rich edit text.

Syntax — public, static BOOL AFX_CDECL IsRichEditFormat(CLIPFORMAT cf);

Parameters

cf — The Clipboard format to test.

Returns — TRUE if the format is text or rich edit text.

OnBeginPrinting

■ 4.0 ■ UD

Description — This member is called at the beginning of print or print preview to initialize any GDI resources needed for printing.

Syntax — protected, virtual void OnBeginPrinting(CDC * pDC, CPrintInfo * pInfo);

Parameters

pDC — The print context to be used.

pInfo — Contains information about the print job.

Returns — Nothing is returned.

OnBullet

■ 4.0 ■ UD

Description — This member is used to toggle the bulleting format for the currently selected text. If the current selection is already bulleted, then bulleting is removed; otherwise bulleting is applied.

Syntax — protected, afx_msg void OnBullet();

Parameters — None.

Returns — Nothing is returned.

OnCharBold

■ 4.0 ■ UD

Description — This member is used to set or clear the bold character effect for the current selection.

Syntax — protected, afx_msg void OnCharBold();

Parameters — None.

Returns — Nothing is returned.

OnCharEffect ■ 4.0

Description This member will either set or clear the given character formatting attribute on the current selection.

Syntax public, void OnCharEffect(DWORD dwMask, DWORD dwEffect);

Parameters

dwMask The mask that indicates which effects can be modified in the current selection. This value can be any of the character formatting masks, such as CFM_BOLD, CFM_ITALIC, etc. (See the Windows SDK for a complete list of masks.)

dwEffect The effects to apply or clear. This value can be any effect, such as CFE_BOLD, CFE_ITALIC, etc. (See the Windows SDK for a complete list of masks.)

Returns Nothing is returned.

OnCharItalic ■ 4.0 ■ UD

Description This member is used to set or clear the italic character effect on current selection.

Syntax protected, afx_msg void OnCharItalic();

Parameters None.

Returns Nothing is returned.

OnCharUnderline ■ 4.0 ■ UD

Description This member is used to set or clear the underlined character effect on current selection.

Syntax protected, afx_msg void OnCharUnderline();

Parameters None.

Returns Nothing is returned.

OnColorDefault ■ 4.0 ■ UD

Description This member sets the color of the current selection to the current default color.

Syntax protected, afx_msg void OnColorDefault();

Parameters None.

Returns Nothing is returned.

OnColorPick ■ 4.0 ■ UD

Description This member is used to specify the color to be applied to the current selection.

Syntax protected, afx_msg void OnColorPick(COLORREF cr);

Parameters

cr The new color of the current selection.

Returns Nothing is returned.

OnCreate ■ 4.0 ■ UD

Description This member is invoked after creation of the view window. After passing control to the base class CCtrlView::OnCreate, the rich edit control is initialized and the view is initialized to accept dropped files.

Syntax protected, afx_msg int OnCreate(LPCREATESTRUCT lpCreateStruct);

Parameters

lpCreateStruct A pointer to a CREATESTRUCT for the new view.

Returns 0 to proceed with the CRichEditView creation; otherwise a value of -1 will destroy the window.

See Also CView::OnCreate()

OnDestroy ■ 4.0 ■ UD

Description This member is invoked after the view window has been removed and before the view object is destroyed.

Syntax protected, afx_msg void OnDestroy();

Parameters None.

Returns Nothing is returned.

See Also CView::OnDestroy()

OnDevModeChange ■ 4.0 ■ UD

Description This member is called when there is a change in the given device mode settings. By default, this member will notify the view to make the necessary adjustments for changes in the printer.

Syntax protected, afx_msg void OnDevModeChange(LPTSTR lpDeviceName);

Parameters

lpDeviceName The name of the device whose settings have changed. A list of device names can be found in the WIN.INI file.

Returns Nothing is returned.

OnDropFiles ■ 4.0 ■ UD

Description This member is invoked when the user drags and drops a file into this view. By default, this member tries to insert the dropped file as an object.

Syntax protected, afx_msg void OnDropFiles(HDROP hDropInfo);

Parameters

hDropInfo A handle to information about the dropped files.

Returns Nothing is returned.

See Also CWnd::OnDropFiles, CRichEditView::InsertFileAsObject()

OnEditClear ■ 4.0 ■ UD

Description This member will delete any currently selected information from the rich edit control.

Syntax protected, afx_msg void OnEditClear();

Parameters None.

Returns Nothing is returned.

See Also CRichEditCtrl::Clear()

OnEditCopy ■ 4.0 ■ UD

Description This member will make a copy of the currently selected information and place it in the Clipboard.

Syntax protected, afx_msg void OnEditCopy();

Parameters None.

Returns Nothing is returned.

See Also CRichEditCtrl::Copy()

OnEditCut ■ 4.0 ■ UD

Description This member makes a copy of the currently selected information, places it into the Clipboard, then deletes the information from the view.

Syntax protected, afx_msg void OnEditCut();

Parameters None.

Returns Nothing is returned.

See Also CRichEditCtrl::Cut()

OnEditFind ■ 4.0 ■ UD

Description This member will invoke the Find dialog for the view.

Syntax protected, afx_msg void OnEditFind();

Parameters None.

Returns Nothing is returned.

OnEditFindReplace

■ 4.0 ■ UD

Description This member will invoke the Find or the Find and Replace dialog for the view.

Syntax protected, void OnEditFindReplace(BOOL bFindOnly);

Parameters

bFindOnly If TRUE, then only the find options will be available; otherwise both the find and replace options will be available.

Returns Nothing is returned.

OnEditPaste

■ 4.0 ■ UD

Description This member will paste the current contents of the Clipboard into the view at the current caret position.

Syntax protected, afx_msg void OnEditPaste();

Parameters None.

Returns Nothing is returned.

See Also CRichEditCtrl::Paste

OnEditPasteSpecial

■ 4.0 ■ UD

Description This member will paste the current contents of the Clipboard into the control at the current caret position and will display the Paste Special dialog.

Syntax protected, afx_msg void OnEditPasteSpecial();

Parameters None.

Returns Nothing is returned.

See Also CRichEditCtrl::PasteSpecial

OnEditRepeat

■ 4.0 ■ UD

Description This member will attempt to repeat the last find or replace operation.

Syntax protected, afx_msg void OnEditRepeat();

Parameters None.

Returns Nothing is returned.

OnEditReplace

■ 4.0 ■ UD

Description This member will invoke the Replace dialog for the view.

Syntax protected, afx_msg void OnEditReplace();

Parameters None.

Returns Nothing is returned.

See Also CView::OnEditFindReplace()

OnEditSelectAll

■ 4.0 ■ UD

Description This member will make the entire contents of the view the current selection.

Syntax protected, afx_msg void OnEditSelectAll();

Parameters None.

Returns Nothing is returned.

OnEditUndo

■ 4.0 ■ UD

Description This member will attempt to undo the last edit operation.

Syntax protected, afx_msg void OnEditUndo();

Parameters None.

Returns Nothing is returned.

See Also CRichEditCtrl::CanUndo()

OnEndPrinting

■ 4.0 ■ UD

Description This member is called upon completion of the print or print preview job.

Syntax public, virtual void OnEndPrinting(CDC * pDC, CPrintInfo * pInfo = NULL);

Parameters

pDC The print context.

pInfo Contains information about the print job.

Returns Nothing is returned.

See Also CRichEditView::OnBeginPrinting()

OnFindNext

■ 4.0

Description This member will attempt to repeat the last find operation. If the text is found, then the text is highlighted and the Find Next dialog is displayed.

Syntax protected, afx_msg void OnFindNext(LPCTSTR lpszFind, BOOL bNext, BOOL bCase, BOOL bWord);

Parameters

lpszFind The string to find.

bNext If TRUE, then the search direction goes from top to bottom; otherwise FALSE indicates a search direction of bottom to top.

bCase If TRUE, then the case (upper or lower) of *lpszFind* must match exactly.

bWord — If TRUE, then the text of *lpszFind* will only match if it is found as a whole word. In other words, *lpszFind* cannot be the prefix of any other text.

Returns — Nothing is returned.

OnFindReplaceCmd ■ 4.0 ■ UD

Description — This member is invoked when the rich edit view receives a find or replace notification message. The action that takes place is dependent on the current state of the find/replace dialog.

Syntax — protected, afx_msg LRESULT OnFindReplaceCmd(WPARAM wParam, LPARAM lParam);

Parameters

wParam — Unused.

lParam — Contains information about the find/replace dialog.

Returns — Always returns zero.

OnFormatFont ■ 4.0 ■ UD

Description — This member will set a new font for the current selection. To do this, the user is presented with the common font dialog.

Syntax — protected, afx_msg void OnFormatFont();

Parameters — None.

Returns — Nothing is returned.

OnInitialUpdate ■ 4.0

Description — This member is initially called after the view is attached to a document, but before the view is displayed. Override this member to perform one-time initialization of the view.

Syntax — public, virtual void OnInitialUpdate();

Parameters — None.

Returns — Nothing is returned.

See Also — CCtrlView::OnInitialUpdate()

OnKeyDown ■ 4.0 ■ UD

Description — This member is called to notify the view that a key has been pressed within the view. This notification is only for key combinations that do not have the ALT key pressed.

Syntax — protected, afx_msg void OnKeyDown(UINT nChar, UINT nRepCnt, UINT nFlags);

Parameters

nChar The virtual key code.

nRepCnt The number of times the key was repeatedly pressed.

nFlags Extra information about the state of the keyboard. See CWnd::OnKeyDown()

Returns Nothing is returned.

See Also CWnd::OnKeyDown()

OnParaAlign ■ 4.0

Description This member will set the paragraph alignment for the current selection.

Syntax public, void OnParaAlign(WORD wAlign);

Parameters

wAlign The new alignment. This can be one of the following:

PFA_CENTER The paragraph will be centered between the left and right margins.

PFA_LEFT The paragraph will be aligned to the left margin.

PFA_RIGHT The paragraph will be aligned to the right margin..

Returns Nothing is returned.

OnParaCenter ■ 4.0 ■ UD

Description This member will center the current paragraph selections between the left and right margins.

Syntax protected, afx_msg void OnParaCenter();

Parameters None.

Returns Nothing is returned.

OnParaLeft ■ 4.0 ■ UD

Description This member will align the current paragraph to the left margin.

Syntax protected, afx_msg void OnParaLeft();

Parameters None.

Returns Nothing is returned.

OnParaRight ■ 4.0 ■ UD

Description This member will align the current paragraph to the right margin.

Syntax protected, afx_msg void OnParaRight();

Parameters None.

Returns Nothing is returned.

OnPrepareDC

■ 4.0 ■ UD

Description This member is called before CView::OnDraw and CView::OnPrint to initialize the print context. By default, this member attempts to paginate to the given print page. If this fails, then the print job will fail.

Syntax public, virtual void OnPrepareDC(CDC * pDC, CPrintInfo * pInfo);

Parameters

pDC The print context.

pInfo Contains information about the print job.

Returns Nothing is returned.

OnPrint

■ 4.0 ■ UD

Description This member is called during a print or print preview job to print a page of information. The page to print is given by the **m_nCurpage** member of the *pInfo* variable. When OnPrint is called, the device context has already been initialized by calling OnPrepareDC. This member will call PrintPage.

Syntax public, virtual void OnPrint(CDC * pDC, CPrintInfo * pInfo);

Parameters

pDC The print context.

pInfo Contains information about the print job.

Returns Nothing is returned.

See Also CRichEditView::PrintPage()

OnPrinterChanged

■ 4.0

Description This member is invoked when the printer changes. By default, this member sets the paper size to the physical page size of the printer.

Syntax protected, virtual void OnPrinterChanged(const CDC & dcPrinter);

Parameters

dcPrinter A reference to a printer context for the new printer.

Returns Nothing is returned.

OnReplaceAll

■ 4.0

Description This member is used to replace all of the occurrences of one text string with another. The framework calls this member from the replace dialog box.

Syntax protected, virtual void OnReplaceAll(LPCTSTR lpszFind, LPCTSTR lpszReplace, BOOL bCase, BOOL bWord);

Parameters

lpszFind The string to find.

lpszReplace	The string to use for replacement.
bCase	If TRUE, then the case (upper or lower) of *lpszFind* must match exactly.
bWord	If TRUE, then the text of *lpszFind* will only match if it is found as a whole word. In other words, *lpszFind* cannot be the prefix of any other text.
Returns	Nothing is returned.

OnReplaceSel ■ 4.0

Description	This member is used to replace the next occurrence of a string with the contents of another. This member is called by the framework in response to commands from the replace dialog.
Syntax	protected, virtual void OnReplaceSel(LPCTSTR lpszFind, BOOL bNext, BOOL bCase, BOOL bWord, LPCTSTR lpszReplace);
Parameters	
lpszFind	The string to find.
bNext	If TRUE, then the search direction goes from top to bottom; otherwise FALSE indicates a search direction of bottom to top.
bCase	If TRUE, then the case (upper or lower) of *lpszFind* must match exactly.
bWord	If TRUE, then the text of *lpszFind* will only match if it is found as a whole word. In other words, *lpszFind* cannot be the prefix of any other text.
lpszReplace	The string to use for replacement.
Returns	Nothing is returned.

OnSelChange ■ 4.0 ■ UD

Description	This member is called by the framework when the current selection within the view has changed.
Syntax	protected, afx_msg void OnSelChange(NMHDR * pNMHDR, LRESULT * pResult);
Parameters	
pNMHDR	A pointer to a message notification structure.
pResult	A pointer to an LRESULT that contains the result of the operation.
Returns	Nothing is returned.

OnTextNotFound ■ 4.0

Description	This member is called by the framework when the results of a find or replace indicate that the text was not found within the view. By default, this member will produce a message beep using MB_ICONHAND.
Syntax	protected, virtual void OnTextNotFound(LPCTSTR lpszFind);

Parameters

lpszFind The text that was not found.

Returns Nothing is returned.

OnUpdateBullet

■ 4.0 ■ UD

Description This member is used to update the state of the bullet paragraph formatting user interface object, based upon the current selection.

Syntax protected, afx_msg void OnUpdateBullet(CCmdUI * pCmdUI);

Parameters

pCmdUI A pointer to the user interface item to update.

Returns Nothing is returned.

OnUpdateCharBold

■ 4.0 ■ UD

Description This member is used to update the state of the character bold formatting user interface object, based upon the current selection.

Syntax protected, afx_msg void OnUpdateCharBold(CCmdUI * pCmdUI);

Parameters

pCmdUI A pointer to the user interface item to update.

Returns Nothing is returned.

OnUpdateCharEffect

■ 4.0

Description This member is used to update the state of a user interface object representing the given formatting attribute, based upon the current selection.

Syntax public, void OnUpdateCharEffect(CCmdUI * pCmdUI, DWORD dwMask, DWORD dwEffect);

Parameters

pCmdUI A pointer to the user interface item to update.

dwMask The character formatting mask. See the Windows SDK for a complete list of formatting masks.

dwEffect The character formatting effect.

Returns Nothing is returned.

OnUpdateCharItalic

■ 4.0 ■ UD

Description This member is used to update the state of the character italic formatting user interface object, based upon the current selection.

Syntax protected, afx_msg void OnUpdateCharItalic(CCmdUI * pCmdUI);

Parameters

pCmdUI A pointer to the user interface item to update.

Returns Nothing is returned.

OnUpdateCharUnderline

■ 4.0 ■ UD

Description This member is used to update the state of the character underline formatting user interface object, based upon the current selection.

Syntax protected, afx_msg void OnUpdateCharUnderline(CCmdUI * pCmdUI);

Parameters

pCmdUI A pointer to the user interface item to update.

Returns Nothing is returned.

OnUpdateEditPasteSpecial

■ 4.0 ■ UD

Description This member is used to update the user interface object representing whether or not the user can use the Paste Special command.

Syntax protected, afx_msg void OnUpdateEditPasteSpecial(CCmdUI * pCmdUI);

Parameters

pCmdUI A pointer to the user interface item to update.

Returns Nothing is returned.

OnUpdateEditUndo

■ 4.0 ■ UD

Description This member will enable the given interface object if the last edit action can be undone.

Syntax protected, afx_msg void OnUpdateEditUndo(CCmdUI * pCmdUI);

Parameters

pCmdUI A pointer to the user interface object to enable.

Returns Nothing is returned.

OnUpdateNeedClip

■ 4.0 ■ UD

Description This member is used to update the user interface object representing whether or not the user can use the Paste command.

Syntax protected, afx_msg void OnUpdateNeedClip(CCmdUI * pCmdUI);

Parameters

pCmdUI A pointer to the user interface item to update.

Returns Nothing is returned.

OnUpdateNeedFind

■ 4.0 ■ UD

Description This member is used to update the interface object representing whether or not the user can proceed with a find operation. This member will enable the interface object if there is text within the view and there is a current string to find.

Syntax protected, afx_msg void OnUpdateNeedFind(CCmdUI * pCmdUI);

Parameters

pCmdUI A pointer to the user interface item to update.

Returns Nothing is returned.

OnUpdateNeedSel

■ 4.0 ■ UD

Description This member will enable the given interface object if a current selection exists in the view.

Syntax protected, afx_msg void OnUpdateNeedSel(CCmdUI * pCmdUI);

Parameters

pCmdUI A pointer to the user interface item to update.

Returns Nothing is returned.

OnUpdateNeedText

■ 4.0 ■ UD

Description This member will enable the given interface object if the view currently contains text.

Syntax protected, afx_msg void OnUpdateNeedText(CCmdUI * pCmdUI);

Parameters

pCmdUI A pointer to the user interface item to update.

Returns Nothing is returned.

OnUpdateParaAlign

■ 4.0 ■ UD

Description This member is used to enable and update the state of the given interface object to reflect the paragraph alignment of the current selection.

Syntax public, void OnUpdateParaAlign(CCmdUI * pCmdUI, WORD wAlign);

Parameters

pCmdUI A pointer to the user interface item to update.

wAlign The paragraph alignment format to update. This can be one of the following:

PFA_CENTER Update the command UI for the centered format.

PFA_LEFT Update the command UI for the left alignment format.

PFA_RIGHT Update the command UI for the right alignment format.

Returns Nothing is returned.

OnUpdateParaCenter

■ 4.0 ■ UD

Description This member is used to enable and update the state of the given interface object to reflect whether or not the paragraph format of the current selection is center aligned.

Syntax protected, afx_msg void OnUpdateParaCenter(CCmdUI * pCmdUI);

Parameters

pCmdUI A pointer to the user interface item to update.

Returns Nothing is returned.

OnUpdateParaLeft

■ 4.0 ■ UD

Description This member is used to enable and update the state of the given interface object to reflect whether or not the paragraph format of the current selection is left aligned.

Syntax protected, afx_msg void OnUpdateParaLeft(CCmdUI * pCmdUI);

Parameters

pCmdUI A pointer to the user interface item to update.

Returns Nothing is returned.

OnUpdateParaRight

■ 4.0 ■ UD

Description This member is used to enable and update the state of the given interface object to reflect whether or not the paragraph format of the current selection is right aligned.

Syntax protected, afx_msg void OnUpdateParaRight(CCmdUI * pCmdUI);

Parameters

pCmdUI A pointer to the user interface item to update.

Returns Nothing is returned.

PaginateTo

■ 4.0 ■ UD

Description This member is used to print a range of pages starting with the first page and ending with the page specified by the **m_nCurPage** member of *pInfo*.

Syntax protected, BOOL PaginateTo(CDC * pDC, CPrintInfo * pInfo);

Parameters

pDC The print context to be used.

pInfo Contains information about the print job.

Returns TRUE is successful; otherwise FALSE.

PreCreateWindow ■ 4.0 ■ UD

Description Override this member to modify the attributes of the CRichEditView before the window is created. This member can be used to set the initial size, position, and style of the view.

Syntax protected, virtual BOOL PreCreateWindow(CREATESTRUCT & cs);

Parameters

cs A reference to a CREATESTRUCT that will receive the modified attributes.

Returns TRUE to continue with creation of the window; FALSE to halt creation.

PrintInsideRect ■ 4.0

Description This member is used to render a specific portion of the text within the rich edit view into the given rectangle. This member is used in conjunction with CRichEditCtrl::DisplayBand.

Syntax public, long PrintInsideRect(CDC * pDC, RECT & rectLayout, long nIndexStart, long nIndexStop, BOOL bOutput);

Parameters

pDC The device context to print into.

rectLayout The bounding rectangle to print the selection into.

nIndexStart The index of the first character to be printed.

nIndexStop The desired index of the last character to be printed.

bOutput If TRUE, then the text is actually printed. If FALSE, then the selection should only be measured.

Returns The index of the first character that did not fit within *rectLayout*.

PrintPage ■ 4.0

Description This member is used to format a specific portion of the text within the rich edit view. This member is used in conjunction with CRichEditCtrl::DisplayBand.

Syntax public, long PrintPage(CDC * pDC, long nIndexStart, long nIndexStop);

Parameters

pDC The device context to print into.

nIndexStart The index of the first character to be printed.

nIndexStop The desired index of the last character to be printed.

Returns The index of the first character that did not fit on the page.

SameAsSelected

■ 4.0 ■ UD

Description This member is used to determine if the given text is the same as the current selection.

Syntax protected, BOOL SameAsSelected(LPCTSTR lpszCompare, BOOL bCase, BOOL bWord);

Parameters

lpszCompare The text string to compare to the current selection.

bCase If TRUE, then the case (upper or lower) of *lpszCompare* must match exactly.

bWord If TRUE, then the text of *lpszCompare* will only match if it is found as a whole word. In other words, *lpszCompare* cannot be the prefix of any other text.

Returns TRUE if the current selection matches *lpszCompare*; otherwise FALSE.

Serialize

■ 4.0 ■ UD

Description This member is used to save or load the contents of the view to the given archive. This member directly calls the CRichEditView::Stream member.

Syntax public, virtual void Serialize(CArchive & ar);

Parameters

ar The archive that receives the contents of the rich edit control.

Returns Nothing is returned.

SetCharFormat

■ 4.0

Description This member will set the character format attributes of the current text selection.

Syntax public, void SetCharFormat(CHARFORMAT cf);

Parameters

cf A CHARFORMAT specifying the formats for the current text selection.

Returns Nothing is returned.

SetMargins

■ 4.0

Description This member will set the margins used for printing the view.

Syntax public, void SetMargins(const CRect & rectMargin);

Parameters

rectMargin A CRect containing the new margins in MM_TWIPS.

Returns Nothing is returned.

SetPaperSize ■ 4.0

Description This member is used to set the printing paper size.

Syntax public, void SetPaperSize(CSize sizePaper);

Parameters

sizePaper A CSize specifying the new paper size in MM_TWIPS.

Returns Nothing is returned.

SetParaFormat ■ 4.0

Description This member is used to set the paragraph formatting attributes of the current selection.

Syntax public, void SetParaFormat(PARAFORMAT & pf);

Parameters

pf A PARAFORMAT structure specifying the new paragraph formatting attributes.

Returns Nothing is returned.

Stream ■ 4.0 ■ UD

Description This member is used to save or load information to or from an archive. This member directly calls the CRichEditCtrl::StreamIn and CRichEditCtrl::StreamOut members.

Syntax public, void Stream(CArchive & ar, BOOL bSelection);

Parameters

ar The archive used to save or load.

bSelection If TRUE, then only the current selection is used. Otherwise FALSE indicates the entire contents of the view.

Returns Nothing is returned.

TextNotFound ■ 4.0 ■ UD

Description This member is called when the specified text was not found during a find or replace operation. By default, this member resets the next find or replace to be a "first" find or replace and calls the OnTextNotFound member.

Syntax public, void TextNotFound(LPCTSTR lpszFind);

Parameters

lpszFind The text that was not found as a result of the find or replace operation.

Returns Nothing is returned.

WrapChanged ■ 4.0

Description This member is called to inform the view that the word wrap characteristics or the current printer settings have changed.

Syntax protected, virtual void WrapChanged();

Parameters None.

Returns Nothing is returned.

The CScrollView Class

The CScrollView is used to manage a virtual display area. This type of view is handy for views that require zooming or panning capabilities, or for representing data that is too big to fit on the screen. Much of the scroll bar interaction with the display area will be handled automatically if you derive from this object.

CScrollView ■ 2.0 ■ 3.0

Description The constructor for the CScrollView class.

Syntax protected, CScrollView();

Parameters None.

Returns Nothing is returned.

See Also ~CScrollView()

~CScrollView ■ 2.0 ■ 3.0

Description The destructor for the CScrollView class.

Syntax public, virtual ~CScrollView();

Parameters None.

Returns Nothing is returned.

See Also CScrollView()

AssertValid ■ 2.0 ■ 3.0 ■ DO

Description Determines whether the CScrollView is in a valid state and if it is not, throws an assertion. This member is only compiled into the debug version of the application.

Syntax public, virtual void AssertValid() const;

Parameters None.

Returns Nothing is returned.

See Also CView::AssertValid()

CalcWindowRect

■ 2.0 ■ 3.0 ■ UD

Description This member is called to determine the smallest rectangle necessary to enclose the CScrollView window that has the given size for its client area.

Syntax public, virtual void CalcWindowRect(LPRECT lpClientRect,UINT nAdjustType = adjustBorder);

Parameters

lpClientRect Contains the client rectangle size, and is filled with the calculated window rectangle.

nAdjustType Used for OLE in-place editing. It can be one of the following values:

CWnd::adjustBorder Do not include scrollbar sizes in calculation.

CWnd::adjustOutside Include scrollbar sizes in calculation.

Returns Nothing is returned.

CenterOnPoint

■ 2.0 ■ 3.0 ■ UD

Description This member is used to center the view display on a given point. This will force either horizontal or vertical scrolling to occur.

Syntax protected, void CenterOnPoint(CPoint ptCenter)

Parameters

ptCenter The point to center the view upon in client coordinates.

Returns Nothing is returned.

Dump

■ 2.0 ■ 3.0 ■ DO

Description This member is an MFC diagnostic function that is only compiled into the debug version of the application. This member is used to output the state of the CScrollView object and can be called directly by the programmer.

Syntax public, virtual void Dump(CDumpContext& dc) const;

Parameters

dc A streamable object that accepts the diagnostic text.

Returns Nothing is returned.

FillOutsideRect

■ 2.0 ■ 3.0

Description This member is used to paint the area outside of the scrolling area. This area appears as two small rectangles between the horizontal and vertical scroll bars. Call this member to avoid repainting the scrollbars themselves.

Syntax public, void FillOutsideRect(CDC * pDC, CBrush * pBrush);

Parameters

pDC The window device context.

pBrush The brush to use when filling the area to be painted.

Returns Nothing is returned.

GetDeviceScrollPosition ■ 2.0 ■ 3.0

Description This member will retrieve the horizontal and vertical scroll positions in device units.

Syntax public, CPoint GetDeviceScrollPosition() const;

Parameters None.

Returns A CPoint containing the horizontal postion in the **x** member and the vertical position in the **y** member.

See Also CScrollView::GetScrollPosition()

GetDeviceScrollSizes ■ 2.0 ■ 3.0

Description This member retrieves the current mapping mode and the various scrolling sizes in device units.

Syntax public, void GetDeviceScrollSizes(int & nMapMode, SIZE & sizeTotal, SIZE & sizePage, SIZE & sizeLine) const;

Parameters

nMapMode Receives the current view mapping mode. See the Windows SDK SetMapMode for a list of possible values.

sizeTotal The total size of the view in device units.

sizePage The amount of device units that represents a scrollbar page. A scrollbar page is the distance moved when the user clicks within the scrollbar track area.

sizeLine The amount of device units that represents a scrollbar line. A scrollbar line is the distance moved when the user clicks either the up or down arrow of the scrollbar.

Returns Nothing is returned.

GetScrollBarSizes ■ 2.0 ■ 3.0 ■ UD

Description This member will retrieve the device units of the width of the vertical scrollbar and the height of the horizontal scrollbar.

Syntax protected, void GetScrollBarSizes(CSize & sizeSb);

Parameters

sizeSb Receives the width of the vertical scrollbar in the **cx** member and the height of the horizontal bar in the **cy** member.

Returns Nothing is returned.

GetScrollBarState

■ 2.0 ■ 3.0 ■ UD

Description This member is used to retrieve the current state of the scrollbars without changing the state of the scrollbars.

Syntax protected, void GetScrollBarState(CSize sizeClient, CSize & needSb, CSize & sizeRange, CPoint & ptMove, BOOL bInsideClient);

Parameters

sizeClient The current size of the client area.

needSb Returns which scrollbars should be displayed. If the **x** member is non-zero, then a horizontal scrollbar needs to be shown. If the **y** member is used, then a vertical scrollbar needs to be shown.

sizeRange Returns the amount of room necessary to display the scrollbars.

ptMove Returns the device units that each scrollbar should be moved to.

bInsideClient If TRUE, then the size of the scrollbars is added to *sizeRange*.

Returns Nothing is returned.

GetScrollPosition

■ 2.0 ■ 3.0

Description This member will retrieve the horizontal and vertical scroll positions in logical units.

Syntax public, CPoint GetScrollPosition() const;

Parameters None.

Returns A CPoint containing the horizontal postion in the **x** member and the vertical position in the **y** member.

GetTotalSize

■ 2.0 ■ 3.0

Description This member retrieves the total size of the scroll view in logical coordinates.

Syntax public, CSize GetTotalSize() const;

Parameters None.

Returns The horizontal size in the **cx** member and the vertical size in the **cy** member.

GetTrueClientSize

■ 2.0 ■ 3.0 ■ UD

Description This member retrieves the client window size, including the size of the current scroll bars.

Syntax protected, BOOL GetTrueClientSize(CSize & size, CSize & sizeSb);

Parameters

size Receives the true client size.

sizeSb	Receives the size of the scrollbars.
Returns	TRUE if the client window can fit the scrollbars; otherwise FALSE.

OnDraw

■ 2.0 ■ 3.0 ■ UD

Description	This member is called by the application framework when an image of the scroll view needs to be drawn. The given CDC object is used to represent the context in which the view should render itself. There is no default implementation of this purely virtual member.
Syntax	protected, virtual void OnDraw(CDC * pDC) = 0;
Parameters	
pDC	A pointer to a CDC object that represents the particular display context the view should render into.
Returns	Nothing is returned.

OnHScroll

■ 2.0 ■ 3.0 ■ UD

Description	This member is invoked when a horizontal scroll event occurs in the view. The default behavior is to pass the event to the OnScroll member.
Syntax	public, afx_msg void OnHScroll(UINT nSBCode, UINT nPos, CScrollBar* pScrollBar);
Parameters	
nSBCode	The type of scroll action taking place. It can be any one of the following:
SB_ENDSCROLL	Bar scrolled to the end position.
SB_LEFT	Bar scrolled to far left.
SB_LINELEFT	Bar scrolled 1 unit (line) to the left.
SB_LINERIGHT	Bar scrolled 1 unit (line) to the right.
SB_PAGELEFT	Bar scrolled 1 page to the left.
SB_PAGERIGHT	Bar scrolled 1 page to the right.
SB_RIGHT	Bar scrolled to the far right.
SB_THUMBPOSITION	Bar scrolled to an absolute position (*nPos*) by moving the thumb bar.
SB_THUMBTRACK	Bar is scrolling and is currently at *nPos*. This occurs while user is moving the thumb bar.
nPos	The current scrollbar position for the SB_THUMBPOSITION and SB_THUMBTRACK codes; otherwise not used.
pScrollBar	The scrollbar control that sent notification. This parameter is NULL if the scrollbar belongs to the view.
Returns	Nothing is returned.

OnPrepareDC

■ 2.0 ■ 3.0 ■ UD

Description	This member is called before CScrollView::OnDraw and CView::OnPrint to initialize the print context. By default, this member shifts the context viewport to reflect the current scrolled position.
Syntax	public, virtual void OnPrepareDC(CDC * pDC, CPrintInfo * pInfo = NULL);
Parameters	
pDC	The print context.
pInfo	Contains information about the print job.
Returns	Nothing is returned.

OnScroll

■ 2.0 ■ 3.0 ■ UD

Description	This member is called to determine if the view can be scrolled to the new position.
Syntax	public, virtual BOOL OnScroll(UINT nScrollCode, UINT nPos, BOOL bDoScroll = TRUE);
Parameters	
nScrollCode	Contains the scroll code for the horizontal bar in the low order word and the scroll code for the vertical bar in the high order word. Each of these may be one of the following:
SB_BOTTOM	Scroll to bottom.
SB_LINEDOWN	Scrolls down one line.
SB_LINEUP	Scroll up one line.
SB_PAGEDOWN	Scroll one page down.
SB_PAGEUP	Scroll one page up.
SB_THUMBTRACK	The scrollbar is being moved to position specified in *nPos*.
SB_TOP	Scroll to Top.
nPos	If *nScrollCode* is SB_THUMBTRACK, then this specifies the tracking position; otherwise not used.
bDoScroll	If TRUE, then the view is scrolled to the new position if possible; otherwise FALSE will simply return whether or not the view could be scrolled.
Returns	TRUE if the view can be scrolled to the new position; otherwise FALSE.

OnScrollBy

■ 2.0 ■ 3.0 ■ UD

Description	This member is called when the user attempts to scroll beyond the current view size.
Syntax	public, virtual BOOL OnScrollBy(CSize sizeScroll, BOOL bDoScroll = TRUE);

Parameters

sizeScroll	The number of pixels scrolled.
bDoScroll	If TRUE, then the view will attempt to scroll; otherwise FALSE will not scroll the view.
Returns	TRUE if the view could scroll to the given position; otherwise FALSE.

OnSize

■ 2.0 ■ 3.0 ■ UD

Description	This member is called when the view has changed size. By default, this member adjusts the current scrollbars to reflect the new window size.
Syntax	public,afx_msg void OnSize(UINT nType, int cx, int cy);
Parameters	
nType	The type of resizing. It can be any one of the following:
SIZE_MAXHIDE	Popup windows receive this when some other window is maximized.
SIZE_MAXIMIZED	Window maximized.
SIZE_MAXSHOW	Popup windows receive this when some other window has been restored.
SIZE_MINIMIZED	Window minimized.
SIZE_RESTORED	Window resized, but not maximized or minimized.
cx	New width of the client area.
cy	New height of the client area.
Returns	Nothing is returned.

OnVScroll

■ 2.0 ■ 3.0 ■ UD

Description	This member is invoked when a vertical scroll event occurs in the view. The default behavior is to pass the event to the OnScroll member.
Syntax	public, afx_msg void OnVScroll(UINT nSBCode, UINT nPos, CScrollBar * pScrollBar);
Parameters	
nSBCode	The type of scroll action taking place. It can be any one of the following:
SB_ENDSCROLL	Bar scrolled to the end position.
SB_LEFT	Bar scrolled to far left.
SB_LINELEFT	Bar scrolled 1 unit (line) to the left.
SB_LINERIGHT	Bar scrolled 1 unit (line) to the right.
SB_PAGELEFT	Bar scrolled 1 page to the left.
SB_PAGERIGHT	Bar scrolled 1 page to the right.
SB_RIGHT	Bar scrolled to the far right.
SB_THUMBPOSITION	Bar scrolled to an absolute position (*nPos*) by moving the thumb bar.
SB_THUMBTRACK	Bar is scrolling and is currently at *nPos*. This occurs while user is moving the thumb bar.

nPos — The current scrollbar position for the SB_THUMBPOSITION and SB_THUMBTRACK codes; otherwise not used.

pScrollBar — The scrollbar control that sent notification. This parameter is NULL if the scrollbar belongs to the view.

Returns — Nothing is returned.

ResizeParentToFit ■ 2.0 ■ 3.0

Description — This member is used to force the size of the view's frame to be controlled by the size of the view.

Syntax — public, void ResizeParentToFit(BOOL bShrinkOnly = TRUE);

Parameters

bShrinkOnly — If TRUE, then the frame window can only shrink to fit the size of the view. If FALSE, then the frame will always be resized to the correct size to fit the view.

Returns — Nothing is returned.

ScrollToDevicePosition ■ 2.0 ■ 3.0 ■ UD

Description — This member scrolls the current view to the given device position, without any range checking.

Syntax — protected, void ScrollToDevicePosition(POINT ptDev);

Parameters

ptDev — The device positions to scroll. The **x** member contains the horizontal position and the **y** member contains the vertical postion.

Returns — Nothing is returned.

ScrollToPosition ■ 2.0 ■ 3.0

Description — This member scrolls the current view to the given logical coordinates. The coordinates are bounded by the maximum scroll positions.

Syntax — public, void ScrollToPosition(POINT pt);

Parameters

pt — The logical positions to scroll. The **x** member contains the horizontal position and the **y** member contains the vertical position.

Returns — Nothing is returned.

SetScaleToFitSize ■ 2.0 ■ 3.0

Description — This member is used to automatically shrink or stretch the view to the size of the window. With this option set, no scrollbars will be visible.

Syntax — public, void SetScaleToFitSize(SIZE sizeTotal);

Parameters

sizeTotal The scaled logical units. The horizontal units are stored in **cx**, and the vertical units are stored in **cy**.

Returns Nothing is returned.

SetScrollSizes

■ 2.0 ■ 3.0

Description This member is used to set the scrolling characteristics for the view and is usually called when the view is initialized or updated.

Syntax public, void SetScrollSizes(int nMapMode, SIZE sizeTotal, const SIZE & sizePage = sizeDefault, const SIZE & sizeLine = sizeDefault);

Parameters

nMapMode Determines the current view mapping mode. See the Windows SDK SetMapMode for a list of possible values.

sizeTotal The total size of the view in device units.

sizePage The amount of device units that represent a scrollbar page. A scrollbar page is the distance moved when the user clicks within the scrollbar track area.

sizeLine The amount of device units that represent a scrollbar line. A scrollbar line is the distance moved when the user clicks either the up or down arrow of the scrollbar.

Returns Nothing is returned.

UpdateBars

■ 2.0 ■ 3.0 ■ UD

Description This member is used to recalc the window layout and update the scrollbars to reflect the state of the view. This member is usually called when the size of the view has changed or the scrollbar size parameters have changed.

Syntax protected, void UpdateBars();

Parameters None.

Returns Nothing is returned.

The CSingleDocTemplate Class

This CSingleDocTemplate is derived from the CDocTemplate, and is used to manage only one document template. Applications that use this object are often referred to as having a Single Document Interface (SDI). SDI applications can only display one document at a time.

CSingleDocTemplate

■ 2.0 ■ 3.0

Description The constructor for the CSingleDocTemplate class.

Syntax public, CSingleDocTemplate(UINT nIDResource, CRuntimeClass* pDocClass, CRuntimeClass* pFrameClass, CRuntimeClass* pViewClass);

Parameters

nIDResource The resource ID of the menu and accelerators associated with the template.

pDocClass A pointer to the run-time class for the document type.

pFrameClass A pointer to the run-time class for the frame type.

pViewClass A pointer to the run-time class for the view type.

Returns Nothing is returned.

See Also ~CSingleDocTemplate()

~CSingleDocTemplate ■ 2.0 ■ 3.0

Description The destructor for the CSingleDocTemplate class.

Syntax public, virtual ~CSingleDocTemplate();

Parameters None.

Returns Nothing is returned.

See Also CSingleDocTemplate()

AddDocument ■ 2.0 ■ 3.0 ■ UD

Description This member associates a document with the template. Single document templates can have one and only one active document.

Syntax public, virtual void AddDocument(CDocument * pDoc);

Parameters

pDoc A pointer to the document.

Returns Nothing is returned.

AssertValid ■ 2.0 ■ 3.0 ■ DO

Description Determines whether the CSingleDocTemplate is in a valid state and if it is not, throws an assertion. This member is only compiled into the debug version of the application.

Syntax public, virtual void AssertValid() const;

Parameters None.

Returns Nothing is returned.

See Also CWnd::AssertValid()

Dump

■ 2.0 ■ 3.0 ■ DO

Description	This member is an MFC diagnostic function that is only compiled into the debug version of the application. This member is used to output the state of the CSingleDocTemplate object and can be called directly by the programmer.
Syntax	public, virtual void Dump(CDumpContext& dc) const;
Parameters	
dc	A streamable object that accepts the diagnostic text.
Returns	Nothing is returned.

GetFirstDocPosition

■ 2.0 ■ 3.0 ■ UD

Description	This member is used to return the position of the first document in the template. Note that the CSingleDocTemplate can only have one associated document.
Syntax	public, virtual POSITION GetFirstDocPosition() const;
Parameters	None.
Returns	A POSITION variable reference to the document associated with the template.
See Also	CMultiDocTemplate()
Example	See CDocTemplate::GetFirstDocPosition()

GetNextDoc

■ 2.0 ■ 3.0 ■ UD

Description	This member is used to retrieve the next document associated with the template. Note that the CSingleDocTemplate can only have 1 associated document.
Syntax	public, virtual CDocument * GetNextDoc(POSITION & rPos) const;
Parameters	
rPos	A POSITION referencing the document to retrieve.
Returns	A CDocument pointer if sucessful; otherwise NULL.
See Also	CMultiDocTemplate()
Example	See CDocTemplate::GetFirstDocPosition()

OpenDocumentFile

■ 2.0 ■ 3.0 ■ UD

Description	This member can either open an existing document file or create a new document from this template. Since the CSingleDocTemplate can only have one associated document, this member creates a new document or reinitializes the document if one currently exists.
Syntax	public, virtual CDocument * OpenDocumentFile(LPCTSTR lpszPathName, BOOL bMakeVisible = TRUE);

Parameters

lpszPathName The path name of the document file to open. If NULL, then a new CDocument will be created.

bMakeVisible If TRUE, then the window containing the document is made visible; otherwise it is not.

Returns A pointer to the new CDocument.

Example See CDocTemplate::OpenDocumentFile()

RemoveDocument ■ 2.0 ■ 3.0 ■ UD

Description This member is used to disassociate the document from the document template.

Syntax public, virtual void RemoveDocument(CDocument * pDoc);

Parameters

pDoc The document to remove.

Returns Nothing is returned.

SetDefaultTitle ■ 2.0 ■ 3.0 ■ UD

Description This member is used to set the title for the given document.

Syntax public, virtual void SetDefaultTitle(CDocument * pDocument);

Parameters

pDocument The document whose title is to be set.

Returns Nothing is returned.

The CTreeView Class

The CTreeView is derived from the CCtrlView class. This view manages a CTreeCtrl object that can display a hierarchical list of information. See Chapter 9, *Windows Controls,* for a discussion of the CTreeCtrl.

CTreeView ■ 2.0 ■ 3.0

Description The constructor for the CTreeView class.

Syntax public, CTreeView();

Parameters None.

Returns Nothing is returned.

GetTreeCtrl ■ 2.0 ■ 3.0

Description This member returns the tree control associated with this view.

Syntax	public, CTreeCtrl & GetTreeCtrl() const;
Parameters	None.
Returns	A reference to the tree control.

OnDestroy

■ 2.0 ■ 3.0 ■ UD

Description	This member is called to notify the view object that it is being destroyed. The default implementation removes the image lists associated with the tree control.
Syntax	public, afx_msg void OnDestroy();
Parameters	None.
Returns	Nothing is returned.

PreCreateWindow

■ 2.0 ■ 3.0 ■ UD

Description	Override this member to modify the attributes of the view before the window is created. This member can be used to set the initial size, position, and style of the view. The default implementation ensures that the common controls are initialized.
Syntax	public, virtual BOOL PreCreateWindow(CREATESTRUCT & cs);
Parameters	
cs	A reference to a CREATESTRUCT that will receive the modified attributes.
Returns	TRUE to continue with creation of the window; FALSE to halt creation.

RemoveImageList

■ 4.0 ■ UD

Description	This member is used to remove a particular image from the tree control's image list.
Syntax	protected, void RemoveImageList(int nImageList);
Parameters	
nImageList	Specifies which list is to be retrieved. The value can be any one of the following:
TVSIL_NORMAL	Image list that contains the unselected state images.
TVSIL_STATE	Image list that contains the selected state images.
Returns	Nothing is returned.

The CView Class

The CView class is the object responsible for displaying a representation of the document data. A view may be associated with only one document. Views are children of frame windows, the same frame window specified in the template associated with the document. If the frame has a splitter window, then multiple views can share the same frame. This class also has members helpful in implementing printing and print preview. See the samples included on the CD-ROM for examples of how to use views.

CView

■ 2.0 ■ 3.0

Description	The constructor for the CView class.
Syntax	protected, CView();
Parameters	None.
Returns	Nothing is returned.
See Also	~CView()

~CView

■ 2.0 ■ 3.0

Description	The destructor for the CView class. The default behavior is for the view to disassociate itself from the document.
Syntax	public, virtual ~CView();
Parameters	None.
Returns	Nothing is returned.

AssertValid

■ 2.0 ■ 3.0 ■ DO

Description	Determines whether the CView is in a valid state and if it is not, throws an assertion. This member is only compiled into the debug version of the application.
Syntax	public, virtual void AssertValid() const;
Parameters	None.
Returns	Nothing is returned.
See Also	CWnd::AssertValid()

CalcWindowRect

■ 2.0 ■ 3.0 ■ UD

Description	This member is called to determine the smallest rectangle necessary to enclose the CView window that has the given size for its client area.
Syntax	public, virtual void CalcWindowRect(LPRECT lpClientRect,UINT nAdjustType = adjustBorder);
Parameters	
lpClientRect	Contains the client rectangle size and is filled with the calculated window rectangle.
nAdjustType	Used for OLE in-place editing. It can be one of the following values:
CWnd::adjustBorder	Do not include scrollbar sizes in calculation.
CWnd::adjustOutside	Include scrollbar sizes in calculation.

Returns Nothing is returned.

DoPreparePrinting

■ 2.0 ■ 3.0

Description This member is used to prepare the device context for printing. This member handles if the print is for a print preview, or we are printing to a printer. For print preview, the current printer settings are used by passing the print dialog. For printing to a printer, the print dialog is displayed allowing the user to manipulate printer settings.

Syntax public, BOOL DoPreparePrinting(CPrintInfo * pInfo);

Parameters

pInfo A pointer to a CPrintInfo object that contains and receives parameters used for printing.

Returns Nothing is returned.

DoPrintPreview

■ 2.0 ■ 3.0 ■ UD

Description This member is called to invoke the application framework print preview mechanism. This member creates a new print preview window, a print preview toolbar, and forces the main application window to enter print preview mode.

Syntax public, BOOL DoPrintPreview(UINT nIDResource, CView * pPrintView, CRuntimeClass * pPreviewViewClass, CPrintPreviewState * pState);

Parameters

nIDResource The print preview toolbar resource ID.

pPrintView The view that is being previewed.

pPreviewViewClass A run-time class pointer to the object used for the actual print preview view.

pState A pointer to a CPrintPreviewState object that contains parameters used in the preview.

Returns Nothing is returned.

Dump

■ 2.0 ■ 3.0 ■ DO

Description This member is an MFC diagnostic function that is only compiled into the debug version of the application. This member is used to output the state of the CView object and can be called directly by the programmer.

Syntax public, virtual void Dump(CDumpContext& dc) const;

Parameters

dc A streamable object that accepts the diagnostic text.

Returns Nothing is returned.

GetDocument ■ 2.0 ■ 3.0

Description This member retrieves the document associated with the view.

Syntax public, CDocument * GetDocument() const;

Parameters None.

Returns A CDocument pointer to the associated document, or NULL if this view does not have an associated document.

Example The example below shows how to retrieve the view document. This particular example adds a string of data to the given CListBoxVDoc object.

```
CListBoxVDoc* CListBoxView::GetDocument()
{
        ASSERT(m_pDocument->IsKindOf(RUNTIME_CLASS(CListBoxVDoc)));
        return (CListBoxVDoc*)m_pDocument;
}

void CListBoxView::AddNewLBStringToDoc()
{
        CString strTemp;
        strTemp.Format("New String %d",GetListBoxCtrl().GetCount());
        GetDocument()->AddString(strTemp);
}
```

GetParentSplitter ■ 2.0 ■ 3.0 ■ UD

Description This member attempts to retrieve the splitter window for the given CWnd object. The splitter window should be the parent of the given window. To retrieve the splitter window for the view, simply pass **this** for the *pWnd* argument.

Syntax public, static CSplitterWnd * PASCAL GetParentSplitter(const CWnd * pWnd, BOOL bAnyState);

Parameters

pWnd The window whose parent is a splitter window.

bAnyState If TRUE, then the splitter window is returned if found. If FALSE, then NULL is returned if *pWnd* is in an iconic state.

Returns A pointer to the CWnd's splitter window if one exists; otherwise NULL.

GetScrollBarCtrl ■ 2.0 ■ 3.0 ■ UD

Description This member is used to return the given scrollbar control for the view. The scrollbar controls are children of the view's splitter window.

Syntax public, virtual CScrollBar * GetScrollBarCtrl(int nBar) const;

Parameters

nBar The ID of the scrollbar to retrieve. This may be one of the following:

SB_HORZ The horizontal scrollbar.

SB_VERT The vertical scrollbar.

Returns A pointer to the scrollbar control if one exists; otherwise NULL.

OnActivateFrame

■ 2.0 ■ 3.0

Description This member is called when the view's frame is activated. By default, this member does nothing.

Syntax protected, virtual void OnActivateFrame(UINT nState, CFrameWnd* pFrameWnd);

Parameters

nState The activation state of the frame. This can be any one of the following:

WA_ACTIVE Frame activated by a method other than a mouse click.

WA_CLICKACTIVE Frame activated by a mouse click.

WA_INACTIVE Frame deactivated.

pFrameWnd A pointer to the frame window.

Returns Nothing is returned.

OnActivateView

■ 2.0 ■ 3.0

Description This member is called when the view is activated or deactivated. By default, the view being activated will receive the focus.

Syntax protected, virtual void OnActivateView(BOOL bActivate, CView* pActivateView, CView* pDeactivateView);

Parameters

bActivate TRUE indicates the view is being activated.

pActivateView A pointer to the CView being activated.

pDeactiveView A pointer to the CView being deactivated.

Returns Nothing is returned.

OnBeginPrinting

■ 2.0 ■ 3.0

Description This member is called at the beginning of print or print preview to initialize any GDI resources needed for printing. This member is called after OnPreparePrinting.

Syntax protected, virtual void OnBeginPrinting(CDC * pDC, CPrintInfo * pInfo);

Parameters

pDC The print context to be used.

pInfo Contains information about the print job.

Returns Nothing is returned.

See Also CView::OnEndPrinting()

OnCmdMsg

■ 2.0 ■ 3.0 ■ UD

Description This member routes all command messages. First, it tries to route them to the view pane window. Next, if the command message is not handled, it is passed through the view's document.

Syntax protected, virtual BOOL OnCmdMsg(UINT nID, int nCode, void* pExtra, AFX_CMDHANDLERINFO* pHandlerInfo);

Parameters

nId Command ID.

nCode Notification code.

pExtra Dependent on *nCode*.

pHandlerInfo Typically NULL. If not NULL, then it is filled with handler information.

Returns TRUE if the command message is handled; otherwise FALSE.

OnCreate

■ 2.0 ■ 3.0 ■ UD

Description This member is invoked after creation of the view window. After passing control to the base class CWnd::OnCreate, the view is attached to its document (found in *lpCreateStruct*).

Syntax protected, afx_msg int OnCreate(LPCREATESTRUCT lpCreateStruct);

Parameters

lpCreateStruct A pointer to a CREATESTRUCT for the new view. This structure should hold a pointer to the view's document, but it may be NULL.

Returns 0 to proceed with the CView creation; otherwise a value of -1 will destroy the window.

See Also CWnd::OnCreate()

OnDestroy

■ 2.0 ■ 3.0 ■ UD

Description This member is invoked after the view window has been removed and before the view object is destroyed. By default, if this view is the current active view, then the view will deactivate itself.

Syntax protected, afx_msg void OnDestroy();

Parameters None.

Returns Nothing is returned.

See Also CWnd::OnDestroy()

OnDraw

■ 2.0 ■ 3.0

Description This member is called by the application framework when an image of the view needs to be drawn. The given CDC object is used to represent the context in which the view should render itself. There is no default implementation of this member.

Syntax protected, virtual void OnDraw(CDC * pDC) = 0;

Parameters

pDC A pointer to a CDC object that represents the particular display context the view should render into.

Returns Nothing is returned.

OnEndPrinting

■ 2.0 ■ 3.0

Description This member is called upon completion of the print or print preview job. By default this member does nothing, but it can be overridden to perform cleanup of resources allocated during CView::OnBeginPrinting.

Syntax protected, virtual void OnEndPrinting(CDC * pDC, CPrintInfo * pInfo);

Parameters

pDC The print context.

pInfo Contains information about the print job.

Returns Nothing is returned.

See Also CView::OnBeginPrinting()

OnEndPrintPreview

■ 2.0 ■ 3.0

Description This member is invoked after completion of a print preview session. By default, this member takes the main frame out of print preview mode and restores the application to its previous state. This member can be overridden to customize the switch from print preview mode or to retrieve information about the final print preview state.

Syntax protected, virtual void OnEndPrintPreview(CDC * pDC, CPrintInfo * pInfo, POINT point, CPreviewView * pView);

Parameters

pDC The print context.

pInfo Contains information about the print preview job.

point The last point on the page that was previewed.

pView A pointer to the view that was previewed.

Returns Nothing is returned.

OnFilePrint

■ 2.0 ■ 3.0 ■ UD

Description This member is called to print the view and contains the main print engine for the view. This member will call OnPreparePrinting, OnBeginPrinting, display the print status dialog, start the print document, loop through the pages and call OnPrint for each page, and clean up the print job by calling OnEndPrinting.

Syntax protected, afx_msg void OnFilePrint();

Parameters None.

Returns Nothing is returned.

See Also CView::OnPreparePrinting(), CView::OnBeginPrinting(), CView::OnPrint(), CView::OnEndPrinting()

OnFilePrintPreview ■ 2.0 ■ 3.0 ■ UD

Description This member is called to initiate a print preview session using this view. This member creates a new CPrintPreviewState object for the session, calls DoPrintPreview, then cleans up after the session has completed.

Syntax protected, afx_msg void OnFilePrintPreview();

Parameters None.

Returns Nothing is returned.

See Also CView::DoPrintPreview()

OnInitialUpdate ■ 2.0 ■ 3.0

Description This member is initially called after the view is attached to a document but before the view is displayed. The default implementation calls the CView::OnUpdate member with no hint information. Override this member to perform one-time initialization of the view.

Syntax public, virtual void OnInitialUpdate();

Parameters None.

Returns Nothing is returned.

See Also CView::OnUpdate()

OnMouseActivate ■ 2.0 ■ 3.0 ■ UD

Description This member is invoked when the user presses a mouse button while the cursor is within the view window. By default, this member passes the message to the base class CWnd::OnMouseActivate to determine if the view can be activated. If the view can be activated, then the view is either activated or reactivated.

Syntax protected, afx_msg int OnMouseActivate(CWnd * pDesktopWnd, UINT nHitTest, UINT message);

Parameters

pDesktopWnd A pointer to the top-level parent window of this view.

nHitTest	Specifies the location of the cursor when activation occurred.
message	The mouse message number.
Returns	Nothing is returned.

OnNextPaneCmd

■ 2.0 ■ 3.0 ■ UD

Description	This member is used to cycle the activation between multiple panes when the view has been split. This member will only work when the view has a splitter window.
Syntax	protected, afx_msg BOOL OnNextPaneCmd(UINT nID);
Parameters	
nID	The direction to cycle. This may be one of the following:
ID_NEXT_PANE	The next frame in succession will be activated.
ID_PREV_PANE	The previous frame in succession will be activated.
Returns	TRUE if successful; otherwise FALSE.

OnPaint

■ 2.0 ■ 3.0 ■ UD

Description	This member is called when a portion of the view needs to be repainted. By default, this member calls the default CWnd::OnPaint member. Override this member to display document information.
Syntax	protected, afx_msg void OnPaint();
Parameters	None.
Returns	Nothing is returned.

OnPrepareDC

■ 2.0 ■ 3.0

Description	This member is called before CView::OnDraw and CView::OnPrint to initialize the print context.
Syntax	public, virtual void OnPrepareDC(CDC * pDC, CPrintInfo * pInfo = NULL);
Parameters	
pDC	The print context.
pInfo	Contains information about the print job.
Returns	Nothing is returned.

OnPreparePrinting

■ 2.0 ■ 3.0

Description	This member is called before a print or print preview job. Override this member and call DoPreparePrinting to enable print and print preview.

Syntax protected, virtual BOOL OnPreparePrinting(CPrintInfo * pInfo);

Parameters

pInfo Contains information about the print job.

Returns TRUE to begin the print or print preview job; otherwise FALSE to abort.

OnPrint

■ 2.0 ■ 3.0

Description This member is called during a print or print preview job to print a page of information. The page to print is given by the **m_nCurpage** member of the *pInfo* variable. When OnPrint is called, the device context has already been initialized by calling OnPrepareDC.

Syntax protected, virtual void OnPrint(CDC * pDC, CPrintInfo * pInfo);

Parameters

pDC The print context.

pInfo Contains information about the print job.

Returns Nothing is returned.

OnSplitCmd

■ 2.0 ■ 3.0 ■ UD

Description This member is called when the view needs to be split by a user action. The view must have a splitter parent window for this member to split the view.

Syntax protected, afx_msg BOOL OnSplitCmd(UINT nID);

Parameters

nID Unused parameter.

Returns TRUE if the split was attempted or successful; otherwise FALSE.

OnUpdate

■ 2.0 ■ 3.0

Description This member is called when information in the document has changed, and the view should be updated to reflect this new information. By default, this member invalidates the entire view window forcing a repaint. Override this member and use the hint information to provide a more optimized update of the view information.

Syntax protected, virtual void OnUpdate(CView * pSender, LPARAM lHint, CObject * pHint);

Parameters

pSender The view that originated the update, or NULL to update all views.

lHint A programmer-supplied code indicating what document information has changed.

pHint A programmer-supplied object that can contain hint-specific information.

Returns Nothing is returned.

See Also CView::OnInitialUpdate()

Example The example below illustrates how to use the hint mechansim to update the display of a view.

```
// values for individual hints
const LPARAM    LBV_HINT_ADDNEW             = 1;
const LPARAM    LBV_HINT_REMOVE_STRING      = 2;

// class used to contain information about a specific hint
class CLBHint : public CObject
{
      DECLARE_DYNAMIC(CLBHint)
      public:
            CLBHint() {;}
            CString         m_strString;
};

void CListBoxView::OnUpdate(CView* pSender, LPARAM lHint, CObject* ⇒
                                pHint)
{
      CLBHint * pLBHint = NULL;
      // check to see if we have passed a valid hint object
      if( pHint && pHint->IsKindOf(RUNTIME_CLASS(CLBHint)) )
            pLBHint = (CLBHint*)pHint;

      // update the view dependent on the type of hint
      if( lHint == LBV_HINT_ADDNEW )
      {
            // display the last string added
            GetListBoxCtrl().AddString(LastStringInArray());
      }
      else if( lHint == LBV_HINT_REMOVE_STRING)
      {     // delete the item
            ASSERT(pLBHint);
            if(pLBHint)
            {
                  int nIdx = GetListBoxCtrl().FindStringExact(0,pLBHint-⇒
                                    >m_strString.GetBuffer(0));
                  if( nIdx != LB_ERR )
                        GetListBoxCtrl().DeleteString(nIdx);
            }
      }
}
```

OnUpdateNextPaneMenu

■ 2.0 ■ 3.0 ■ UD

Description This member is called to enable or disable moving activation to the next successive pane command interface for views with splitter windows.

Syntax protected, afx_msg void OnUpdateNextPaneMenu(CCmdUI * pCmdUI);

Parameters

pCmdUI A CCmdUI pointer representing the interface to enable or disable.

Returns Nothing is returned.

OnUpdateSplitCmd

■ 2.0 ■ 3.0 ■ UD

Description This member is called to enable or disable the split window command for this view.

Syntax protected, afx_msg void OnUpdateSplitCmd(CCmdUI * pCmdUI);

Parameters

pCmdUI A CCmdUI pointer representing the interface to enable or disable.

Returns Nothing is returned.

PostNcDestroy

■ 2.0 ■ 3.0 ■ UD

Description This member is called after the view window has been destroyed. By default, this member deletes the **this** object for the view.

Syntax protected, virtual void PostNcDestroy();

Parameters None.

Returns Nothing is returned.

PreCreateWindow

■ 2.0 ■ 3.0 ■ UD

Description Override this member to modify the attributes of the CView before the window is created. This member can be used to set the initial size, position, and style of the view.

Syntax protected, virtual BOOL PreCreateWindow(CREATESTRUCT & cs);

Parameters

cs A reference to a CREATESTRUCT that will receive the modified attributes.

Returns TRUE to continue with creation of the window; FALSE to halt creation.

7

FRAME WINDOWS

7 FRAME WINDOWS

Frame windows are among the most convenient sets of classes that MFC provides. Not only do they provide a simple encapsulation of their related Windows API functions, they deliver extended functionality that has become the standard in Windows applications. This richness in functionality can be seen in the frame window's document/view support, multiple document interface (MDI), status bars, and extensive control bar manipulation.

Table 7-1 summarizes the classes related to frame windows that are covered in this chapter.

Table 7-1 Chapter 7 class summary

Class Name	Description
CFrameWnd	Base class for all Frame Windows
CMDIFrameWnd	Frame class used for multi-document applications
CMDIChildWnd	Multiple document child window
CMiniFrameWnd	Frame window commonly used for toolbars

The CFrameWnd Class

The CFrameWnd class is the common base class for all frame objects. It provides the default behavior for a Single Document Interface (SDI) frame window, as well as control bars, views, and other child windows inside the frame. As can be seen in Figure 7-1, the CFrameWnd is used to contain and manage other windows.

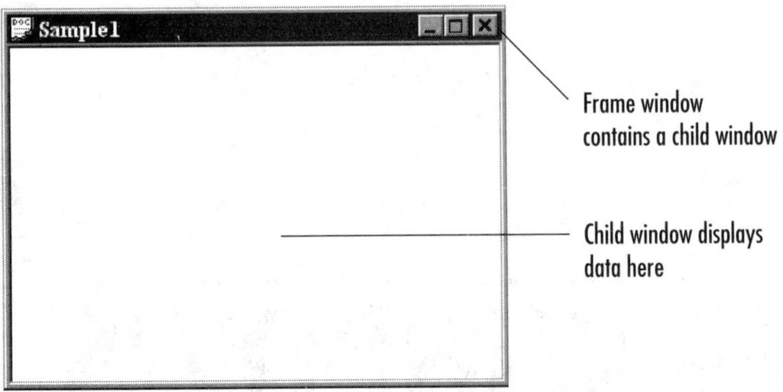

Figure 7-1 The CFrameWnd is used to contain other CWnd objects

CFrameWnd ■ 2.0 ■ 3.0

Description The constructor for the CFrameWnd class. This member initializes the internal member variables for the frame object. Also, MFC keeps track of the CFrameWnds created in the application by adding the new CFrameWnd to the CFrameWnd list stored in the AFX_THREAD_STATE structure.

Syntax public, CFrameWnd();

Parameters None.

Returns Nothing is returned.

See Also ~CFrameWnd(), LoadFrame(), AddFrameWnd()

~CFrameWnd ■ 2.0 ■ 3.0

Description The destructor for the CFrameWnd class. The main purpose of this member is to remove the CFrameWnd object from the frame list kept by MFC in the AFX_THREAD_STATE structure.

Syntax public, virtual ~CFrameWnd();

Parameters None.

Returns Nothing is returned.

See Also CFrameWnd()

ActivateFrame ■ 2.0 ■ 3.0

Description This member function will show the frame window (restore if it is currently iconic) and bring it to the top Z-order window position. It can also be used to display the window as the result of some user interaction or can be overridden to customize the default window activation behavior.

Syntax public, virtual void ActivateFrame(int nCmdShow = -1);

Parameters

nCmdShow The resulting show state of the frame window. If this value is -1, then the window will be restored if iconic (SW_RESTORE); otherwise SW_SHOWNORMAL is used. If the value is not -1, then the explicit value of *nCmdShow* will be used. See CWnd::ShowWindow for a list of values for this parameter.

Returns Nothing is returned.

See Also CWnd::ShowWindow()

Example The following example shows a function that can be invoked to activate the indicated frame. Note that when passing CFrameWnd objects, it is a good idea to assert the object's validity.

```
void ForceFrameActive(CFrameWnd *pFrameWnd)
{
	// check validity of frame
	ASSERT_VALID(pFrameWnd);

	...
}
```

AddControlBar

■ 2.0 ■ 3.0 ■ UD

Description This member will add a control bar to the list of control bars for this frame window. Once added, the control bar can be docked to the frame window. This member is called automatically through the CControlBar::OnCreate function.

Syntax public, void AddControlBar(CControlBar * pBar);

Parameters

pBar A pointer to the control bar that will be added.

Returns Nothing is returned.

AddFrameWnd

■ 2.0 ■ 3.0 ■ UD

Description This function will add the CFrameWnd object to the global list of frame windows. MFC keeps track of the CFrameWnds created in the application by adding the new CFrameWnd to the CFrameWnd list stored in the AFX_THREAD_STATE structure.

Syntax protected, void AddFrameWnd();

Parameters None.

Returns Nothing is returned.

See Also CFrameWnd()

Example Under normal circumstances, this member does not need to be called because it is invoked during the CFrameWnd constructor.

AssertValid

■ 2.0 ■ 3.0 ■ DO

Description Determines whether the CFrameWnd is in a valid state and if it is not, throws an assertion. The CFrameWnd implementation calls the base CWnd version and then checks to make sure that the currently active view is valid (if one exists).

Syntax public, virtual void AssertValid( ) const;

Parameters None.

Returns Nothing is returned.

See Also CWnd::AssertValid

Example See CFrameWnd::ActivateFrame

BeginModalState

■ 2.0 ■ 3.0

Description This member will disable all children of the CFrameWnd in order for it to enter the modal state. Each disabled window is saved and can be re-enabled by calling CFrameWnd::EndModalState.

Syntax public, virtual void BeginModalState();

Parameters None.

Returns Nothing is returned.

See Also CFrameWnd::EndModalState(), CFrameWnd::IsModalState()

BringToTop

■ 2.0 ■ 3.0 ■ UD

Description This member is used to display a frame window that is partially obscured by other windows, by moving it to the top of the window stack. The CFrameWnd will try to bring the last active popup window to the top or if none exists, then the CFrameWnd itself.

Syntax protected, void BringToTop(int nCmdShow);

Parameters

nCmdShow The Show value for the window, which must be a value that allows the window to be displayed. Only the following values are valid: SW_RESTORE, SW_SHOW, SW_SHOWMAXIMIZED, SW_SHOWNORMAL.

Returns Nothing is returned.

See Also CWnd::BringToTop(), CWnd::ShowWindow()

CanDock

■ 2.0 ■ 3.0 ■ UD

Description This function determines whether or not any of the control bars contained by the CFrameWnd can dock in the given rectangle (dock site). The CDockContext object calls this member.

Syntax public, DWORD CanDock(CRect rect, DWORD dwDockStyle, CDockBar** ppDockBar = NULL);

Parameters

rect The bounding rectangle that defines the docking site.

dwDockStyle Specifies the styles for the control bar that is a candidate for docking at this site. To dock, the control bar's styles must be compatible with the dock site's styles.

ppDockBar Optional reference to the control bar object that (if this parameter is supplied) is returned to the calling function.

Returns If successful, the DWORD style values of the control bar; otherwise 0.

CanEnterHelpMode

■ 2.0 ■ 3.0 ■ UD

Description This member function returns a value indicating whether or not the CFrameWnd has a context-sensitive help handler available.

Syntax public, BOOL CanEnterHelpMode();

Parameters None.

Returns TRUE if the frame has a handler for ID_CONTEXT_HELP and can load the help cursor from the application resources; otherwise FALSE.

Create

■ 2.0 ■ 3.0

Description This member is called after construction to create the actual frame window and attach it to this object.

Syntax public, BOOL Create(LPCTSTR lpszClassName, LPCTSTR lpszWindowName, DWORD dwStyle = WS_OVERLAPPEDWINDOW, const RECT & rect = rectDefault, CWnd * pParentWnd = NULL, LPCTSTR lpszMenuName = NULL, DWORD dwExStyle = 0, CCreateContext* pContext = NULL);

Parameters

lpszClassName Specifies the Windows class (or NULL to use default CFrameWnd class attributes). This name must have been previously registered using AfxRegisterWndClass or the Windows API call to RegisterClass.

lpszWindowName A NULL-terminated string that contains the title bar text.

dwStyle The window style attributes for the frame window. See CWnd::Create.

rect — The size and position of the new window (or use rectDefault for default window placement).

pParentWnd — The parent window of the frame. This value should be NULL for top level frame windows.

lpszMenuName — A NULL-terminated string that identifies the resource to be used as a menu for the CFrameWnd.

dwExStyle — Extended window style attributes.

pContext — An optional pointer to a CCreateContext object that will be passed to the CFrameWnd::OnCreate method.

Returns — Non-zero if the function is successful; zero otherwise

See Also — CWnd::Create()

CreateView ■ 4.0

Description — This member is used as a helper function for creating views that are not derived from the CView class. This member creates the object using the given context and sets the proper window borders. It is up to the calling function to make the view active or visible.

Syntax — public, CWnd * CreateView(CCreateContext* pContext, UINT nID = AFX_IDW_PANE_FIRST);

Parameters

pContext — Contains information regarding the view and document to be created.

nID — The view ID number.

Returns — A pointer to the new CWnd if successful; otherwise NULL.

DelayRecalcLayout ■ 2.0 ■ 3.0 ■ UD

Description — This member defers the recalculation of the frame layout until the next CFrameWnd::OnIdleUpdateCmdUI is called.

Syntax — public, void DelayRecalcLayout(BOOL bNotify = TRUE);

Parameters

bNotify — Whether or not to pass a notification to the OLE RecalcLayout hook process.

Returns — Nothing is returned.

DelayUpdateFrameMenu ■ 2.0 ■ 3.0 ■ UD

Description — This member will defer the update of the frame menu until the next time CFrameWnd::OnIdleUpdateCmdUI is called.

Syntax — public, virtual void DelayUpdateFrameMenu(HMENU hMenuAlt);

Parameters

hMenuAlt A handle to an alternate menu for the frame.

Returns Nothing is returned.

DelayUpdateFrameTitle

■ 2.0 ■ 3.0

Description This member will defer the update of the frame title until the next time CFrameWnd::OnIdleUpdateCmdUI is called.

Syntax public, void DelayUpdateFrameTitle();

Parameters None.

Returns Nothing is returned.

DestroyDockBars

■ 2.0 ■ 3.0 ■ UD

Description This member will remove and call the OnDestroy member of every docking bar associated with this frame. This member is automatically called from CFrameWnd::OnDestroy.

Syntax public, void DestroyDockBars();

Parameters None.

Returns Nothing is returned.

See Also CFrameWnd::OnDestroy()

DockControlBar

■ 2.0 ■ 3.0

Description This function will dock a specified control bar to the frame window. When a control bar is docked, it is attached to the given dock site and is no longer considered "floating".

Syntax public, void DockControlBar(CControlBar* pBar, UINT nDockBarID = 0,LPCRECT lpRect = NULL); public, void DockControlBar(CControlBar* pBar, CDockBar * pDockBar ,LPCRECT lpRect = NULL);

Parameters

pBar The control bar to dock.

nDockBarID Determines where the control bar is docked on the frame window. This may be 0 (for any side enabled for docking) or any of the following values:

AFX_IDW_DOCKBAR_BOTTOM Bottom side of the frame window.

AFX_IDW_DOCKBAR_LEFT Left side of the frame window.

AFX_IDW_DOCKBAR_RIGHT Right side of the frame window.

AFX_IDW_DOCKBAR_TOP Top side of the frame window.

pDockBar The destination dock bar.

lpRect The non-client area screen coordinates where the control bar will be docked within the dock site.

Returns Nothing is returned.

Example The following example illustrates how to create a new control bar and dock it to the frame window using DockControlBar.

```
CControlBar * CFrameApp::CreateNewBar(CFrameWnd * pFrameWnd)
{

        ASSERT_VALID(pFrameWnd);
        CDialogBar * pBar = NULL;

        if(pFrameWnd)
        {
                pBar = new CDialogBar();
                if( pBar- >Create(pFrameWnd,IDD_MYDIALOGBAR,⇒
                    CBRS_ALIGN_ANY,AFX_IDW_CONTROLBAR_LAST
-1) )
                {
                        pBar->EnableDocking(CBRS_ALIGN_TOP|CBRS_ALIGN_BOTTOM);
                        pFrameWnd->DockControlBar(pBar,AFX_IDW_DOCKBAR_TOP);
                        pBar->SetBarStyle(pBar->GetBarStyle()|CBRS_TOOLTIPS | ⇒
                                          CBRS_FLYBY);
                        pFrameWnd->RecalcLayout(TRUE);
                }
                else
                {
                        delete pBar;
                        pBar = NULL;
                }
        }

        return pBar;
}
```

Dump

■ 2.0 ■ 3.0 ■ DO

Description This member is an MFC diagnostic utility that is compiled only into the debug version of the application. The member is used to output the state of the object and can be called directly by the programmer.

Syntax public, virtual void Dump(CDumpContext & dc) const;

Parameters

dc A streamable object that accepts the diagnostic text.

Returns Nothing is returned.

See Also CObject::Dump()

EnableDocking

■ 2.0 ■ 3.0

Description This member allows docking of control bars to the frame window. This function is usually called once during the initialization of the frame window.

Syntax public, void EnableDocking(DWORD dwDockStyle);

Parameters

dwDockStyle Specifies allowable docking sites. This can be any of the following values:

CBRS_ALIGN_ANY Docking on any side of the frame window client area.

CBRS_ALIGN_BOTTOM Docking at the bottom of the frame window client area.

CBRS_ALIGN_LEFT Docking on the left side of the frame window client area.

CBRS_ALIGN_RIGHT Docking on the right side of the frame window client area.

CBRS_ALIGN_TOP Docking at the top of the frame window client area.

CBRS_FLOAT_MULTI Multiple floating control bars in one mini-frame window.

Returns Nothing is returned.

Example EnableDocking is usually called in the OnCreate function of the frame window to prepare it for docking. The sample below assumes that m_wndControlBar has already been initialized:

```
int CMainFrame::OnCreate(LPCREATESTRUCT lpCreateStruct)
{
        // Initialization of the m_wndControlBar
        ...
        m_wndControlBar.EnableDocking(CBRS_ALIGN_ANY);
        EnableDocking(CBRS_ALIGN_ANY);
        DockControlBar(&m_wndControlBar);
        ...
}
```

EndModalState

■ 2.0 ■ 3.0

Description This member function will re-enable the child windows disabled by calling CFrameWnd::BeginModalState.

Syntax public, virtual void EndModalState();

Parameters None.

Returns Nothing is returned.

See Also CFrameWnd::BeginModalState()

ExitHelpMode

■ 2.0 ■ 3.0 ■ UD

Description This member cancels the current application help session.

Syntax public, virtual void ExitHelpMode();

Parameters None.

Returns Nothing is returned.

FloatControlBar

■ 2.0 ■ 3.0

Description This member will take a docked control bar and allow it to "float" within the frame window. A "floating" control bar is a bar that can be moved to any position within the frame window client area (similar to a modeless dialog box).

Syntax public, void FloatControlBar(CControlBar* pBar, CPoint point, DWORD dwStyle = CBRS_ALIGN_TOP);

Parameters

pBar The control bar to "float."

point The new client coordinates of the floating control bar.

dwStyle The style bits to use for the floating control bar frame. (See CFrameWnd:: CreateFloatingFrame)

Returns Nothing is returned.

Example The following example illustrates how to use the FloatControlBar member:

```
void CMainFrame::OnViewFloatsamplebar()
{
	ASSERT_VALID(App()->m_pSampleBar);
	if( App()->m_pSampleBar )
		FloatControlBar(App()->m_pSampleBar,CPoint(100,100));
}
```

GetActiveDocument

■ 2.0 ■ 3.0

Description This member will retrieve the current active document contained in the CFrameWnd.

Syntax public, virtual CDocument* GetActiveDocument();

Parameters None.

Returns A pointer to the currently active CDocument or if there is no active document, then NULL.

See Also CFrameWnd::GetActiveView()

Example The following example uses GetActiveDocument to retrieve the current document's title text.

```
void CChildFrame::OnViewActivedocumenttitle()
{
	CString strMsg;
	CDocument * pDoc = GetActiveDocument();

	if( pDoc )
	{
		strMsg.Format("Active Doc Title: %s",(LPCSTR)pDoc->GetTitle());
		AfxMessageBox(strMsg,MB_ICONINFORMATION|MB_OK);
	}
	else // this should never be the case for this example
		AfxMessageBox("No Active document present.",MB_ICONINFORMATION|MB_OK);

}
```

GetActiveFrame

■ 2.0 ■ 3.0

Description This member will return the **this** value of the CFrameWnd. This behavior is overridden in the CMDIFrameWnd class.

Syntax public, virtual CFrameWnd* GetActiveFrame();

Parameters None.

Returns The **this** value of the CFrameWnd.

See Also CMDIFrameWnd::GetActiveFrame()

GetActiveView

■ 2.0 ■ 3.0

Description This member returns the currently active view (if any).

Syntax public, CView* GetActiveView() const;

Parameters None.

Returns A pointer to the currently active view or if none exists, NULL.

See Also CFrameWnd::SetActiveView()

GetControlBar

■ 2.0 ■ 3.0

Description This member will return the control bar associated with the given ID.

Syntax public, CControlBar* GetControlBar(UINT nID);

Parameters

nID The ID of the control bar to be returned. This is the child ID of the control bar window.

Returns A pointer to the control bar if successful; otherwise NULL.

GetDefaultAccelerator

■ 2.0 ■ 3.0 ■ UD

Description This member retrieves the default accelerators associated with the frame window. It does this by first trying to get the default accelerator for the active document. If there is no active document, then it returns the default accelerator for the frame window.

Syntax public, virtual HACCEL GetDefaultAccelerator();

Parameters None.

Returns The handle to the default accelerator or NULL if none exists.

See Also CFrameWnd::LoadAccelTable()

GetDockState

■ 2.0 ■ 3.0

Description This member fills a CDockState object with the size and position information of all the control bars associated with the frame window.

Syntax public, void GetDockState(CDockState& state) const;

Parameters

state An object that holds an array of control bar state information.

Returns Nothing is returned.

See Also CFrameWnd::SaveBarState()

GetIconWndClass

■ 2.0 ■ 3.0 ■ UD

Description This member can be used to register a new window class that has a different icon than the current frame window. This member is used internally when the frame resources are loaded to register the frame's icon.

Syntax protected, LPCTSTR GetIconWndClass(DWORD dwDefaultStyle, UINT nIDResource);

Parameters

dwDefaultStyle The default window styles for the window class.

nIDResource The ID of the resource that contains the new icon.

Returns The window class name associated with the new window class.

See Also CFrameWnd::LoadFrame()

GetMessageBar

■ 2.0 ■ 3.0

Description This member returns a pointer to the status bar window associated with the frame.

Syntax public, virtual CWnd* GetMessageBar();

Parameters None.

Returns A pointer to the frame's status bar window or NULL if none exists.

Example The following uses GetMessageBar to display message text with a time stamp.

```
void CChildFrame::SetMessageTextWithTime(CString strText)
{
	CWnd * pMsgBar = GetMessageBar();
	if( pMsgBar )
	{
		CString strMsg;
		strMsg = strText;
		strMsg += " [";
		CTime tmNow = CTime::GetCurrentTime();
		strMsg += tmNow.Format("%H:%M:%S");
```

```
            strMsg += "]";
            pMsgBar->SetWindowText(strMsg);
        }
}
```

GetMessageString

■ 2.0 ■ 3.0

Description This member loads a string from the application resources. This member also truncates the string at the first newline character ('\n'), which is helpful for retrieving just the text portion of a resource string that contains extra information appended to the end.

Syntax public, virtual void GetMessageString(UINT nID, CString& rMessage) const;

Parameters

nId The resource ID of the string to load.

rMessage The destination of the loaded string text.

Returns Nothing is returned.

See Also CFrameWnd:: OnSetMessageString()

InitialUpdateFrame

■ 2.0 ■ 3.0

Description This member is called to invoke all of the frame's descendant windows' OnInitialUpdate members. Also, if there are any views, then the primary view is made active. This function is primarily invoked by MFC in its built-in File Open and File New handlers.

Syntax public, void InitialUpdateFrame(CDocument* pDoc, BOOL bMakeVisible);

Parameters

pDoc The document that is associated with this frame.

bMakeVisible If TRUE, then the frame will be activated.

Returns Nothing is returned.

InModalState

■ 2.0 ■ 3.0

Description This member returns whether or not the frame is currently in a modal state.

Syntax public, BOOL InModalState() const;

Parameters None.

Returns TRUE if currently in a modal state; otherwise FALSE.

See Also CFrameWnd::BeginModalState(), CFrameWnd::EndModalState()

IsFrameWnd

■ 2.0 ■ 3.0 ■ UD

Description This function simply returns TRUE for this base class. This function is used to distinguish between frame and non-frame windows and is overridden from the CWnd base class to return TRUE.

Syntax public, virtual BOOL IsFrameWnd() const;

Parameters None.

Returns TRUE.

IsTracking

■ 2.0 ■ 3.0

Description This function returns whether or not the frame is tracking menu strings.

Syntax public, BOOL IsTracking() const;

Parameters None.

Returns TRUE if the frame is tracking; otherwise FALSE.

LoadAccelTable

■ 2.0 ■ 3.0

Description This member will load the specified accelerators from the application resources. A call to CFrameWnd::LoadFrame automatically calls this member to load the accelerators associated with the frame. A call to this member is helpful in loading an alternate accelerator set.

Syntax public, BOOL LoadAccelTable(LPCTSTR lpszResourceName);

Parameters

lpszResourceName The name of the accelerator resource.

Returns Non-zero if successful; otherwise 0.

See Also CFrameWnd::LoadFrame()

LoadBarState

■ 2.0 ■ 3.0

Description This member will load control bar information previously saved using CFrameWnd::SaveBarState from an initialization file. By calling this member, the control bars will be displayed at the position and configuration saved in the initialization file. This member is useful for returning an application desktop to a previously saved state.

Syntax public, void LoadBarState(LPCTSTR lpszProfileName);

Parameters

lpszProfileName The initialization file name.

Returns Nothing is returned.

See Also CFrameWnd::SaveBarState()

Example The following example illustrates how to load the control bar states from a previously saved initialization file. This should be done after the main frame for the application has been initialized.

```
BOOL CFrameApp::InitInstance()
{
     // Initialization of your application done here
     ...
     pMainFrame->LoadBarState("mfcsampframe");

     pMainFrame->ShowWindow(m_nCmdShow);
     pMainFrame->UpdateWindow();
     return TRUE;
}
```

LoadFrame ■ 2.0 ■ 3.0

Description This member is called after construction of the CFrameWnd to create the frame and load its resources. These resources include the icon, accelerators, and string tables associated with the frame. LoadFrame is a more convenient way to create frame windows, but more control can be had by calling CFrameWnd::Create() instead.

Syntax public, virtual BOOL LoadFrame(UINT nIDResource, DWORD dwDefaultStyle = WS_OVERLAPPEDWINDOW | FWS_ADDTOTITLE, CWnd* pParentWnd = NULL, CCreateContext* pContext = NULL);

Parameters

nIDResource The resource ID used to load frame resources. This same ID is used for the each of the resources mentioned above.

dwDefaultStyle The default frame window style. For automatic display of document titles, add the FWS_ADDTOTITLE style.

pParentWnd The parent of the frame.

pContext Pointer to a CCreateContext class.

Returns TRUE if successful; otherwise FALSE.

See Also CFrameWnd::Create()

NegotiateBorderSpace ■ 2.0 ■ 3.0

Description This member function implements OLE border space negotiation.

Syntax public, virtual BOOL NegotiateBorderSpace(UINT nBorderCmd, LPRECT lpRectBorder);

Parameters

nBorderCmd Border command. This can be any one of the following enumerations: **borderGet** = 1, **borderRequest** = 2, **borderSet** = 3.

lpRectBorder Destination of the border space.

Returns TRUE if a recalc layout is needed; otherwise FALSE.

NotifyFloatingWindows ■ 2.0 ■ 3.0 ■ UD

Description This member will update all the floating windows owned by the frame window. This is accomplished by sending a WM_FLOATSTATUS message.

Syntax public, void NotifyFloatingWindows(DWORD dwFlags);

Parameters

dwFlags Update flags passed to each floating window. This can be any of the following values:

FS_SHOW, FS_HIDE, FS_ACTIVATE, FS_DEACTIVATE, FS_ENABLE, FS_DISABLE, FS_SYNCACTIVE

Returns Nothing is returned.

OnActivate ■ 2.0 ■ 3.0 ■ UD

Description This member is called when the CFrameWnd is being activated or deactivated. First the base class CWnd::OnActivate is called; then any current views and floating windows associated with the frame are activated.

Syntax protected, afx_msg void OnActivate(UINT nState, CWnd* pWndOther, BOOL bMinimized);

Parameters

nState Whether or not the frame is activated or deactivated. It can be one of the following values:

WA_ACTIVE Frame activated by a method other than a mouse click.

WA_CLICKACTIVE Frame activated by a mouse click.

WA_INACTIVE Frame deactivated.

pWndOther Pointer to the newly activated or deactivated window. This may be NULL.

bMinimized If TRUE, then *pWndOther* is currently minimized.

Returns Nothing is returned.

See Also CFrameWnd::ActivateFrame()

OnActivateApp ■ 2.0 ■ 3.0 ■ UD ■ MO

Description This Macintosh-only member is called when the application is activated or deactivated. This allows recalculating of the frame window layout when the application is activated or deactivated.

Syntax protected, afx_msg void OnActivateApp(BOOL bActive, HTASK hTask);

Parameters

bActive	If TRUE, then the application is activated; otherwise deactivated.
hTask	Identifies the task of the CWnd being activated or deactivated. If *bActive* is TRUE, then *hTask* is the owner of the window being deactivated. Otherwise, *hTask* is the owner of the window being activated.
Returns	Nothing is returned.
See Also	CWnd::OnActivateApp()

OnActivateTopLevel

■ 2.0 ■ 3.0 ■ UD

Description	This member deactivates the current active view.
Syntax	protected, afx_msg LRESULT OnActivateTopLevel(WPARAM wParam, LPARAM lParam);
Parameters	
wParam	This parameter is only used for OLE support. This value specifies whether or not the window is active and minimized.
lParam	Not used.
Returns	Always returns an LRESULT of 0.

OnBarCheck

■ 2.0 ■ 3.0

Description	This member will display the control bar specified if it is not currently displayed.
Syntax	public, afx_msg BOOL OnBarCheck(UINT nID);
Parameters	
nID	The child ID of the control bar.
Returns	Nothing is returned.

OnClose

■ 2.0 ■ 3.0 ■ UD

Description	This member is called to close down the frame window. In response, the frame window determines if it can close and if so, destroys the frame window. Documents associated with this frame window will receive a CDocument::OnCloseDocument call.
Syntax	protected, afx_msg void OnClose();
Parameters	None.
Returns	Nothing is returned.
See Also	CDocument::OnCloseDocument()

OnCmdMsg

■ 2.0 ■ 3.0 ■ UD

Description This member routes all command messages. First, it tries to route them to the active view. Next, if the command message is not handled it is passed through the frame's base class CWnd::OnCmdMsg handler. And finally, if it is still not handled, it is passed to the application's CWinApp::OnCmdMsg handler.

Syntax public, virtual BOOL OnCmdMsg(UINT nID, int nCode, void* pExtra, AFX_CMDHANDLERINFO* pHandlerInfo);

Parameters

nID	Command ID.
nCode	Notification code.
pExtra	Dependent on *nCode*.
pHandlerInfo	Typically NULL. If not NULL, then it is filled with handler information.

Returns TRUE if the command message is handled; otherwise FALSE.

OnCommand

■ 2.0 ■ 3.0 ■ UD

Description This member routes command notifications from accelerators, controls, and menus. Before passing control to the base class CWnd::OnCommand, the frame window checks if the command is help related and if so, routes the proper help message.

Syntax protected, virtual BOOL OnCommand(WPARAM wParam, LPARAM lParam);

Parameters

wParam	Command ID of the accelerator, control, or menu.
lParam	This parameter depends on the source of the notification, as indicated below:
accelerator	Low-order = 0, Hi-order = 1
control	Low-order = control identifier, Hi-order = notification message
menu	Low-order = 0, Hi-order = 0

Returns TRUE if the message was processed; otherwise FALSE.

OnCommandHelp

■ 2.0 ■ 3.0 ■ UD

Description This member handles the help command invocation for the frame window.

Syntax protected, afx_msg LRESULT OnCommandHelp(WPARAM wParam, LPARAM lParam);

Parameters

wParam	Unused.

lParam Help context ID.

Returns An LRESULT that evaluates to TRUE if processed; otherwise FALSE.

See Also CWinApp::WinHelp()

OnContextHelp ■ 2.0 ■ 3.0

Description This member is invoked when the SHIFT+F1 key combination is pressed. The frame changes the cursor to the context help cursor and tracks its position while in context help mode.

Syntax public, afx_msg void OnContextHelp();

Parameters None.

Returns Nothing is returned.

OnCreate ■ 2.0 ■ 3.0 ■ UD

Description This member is invoked after creation of the frame window. After passing control to the base class CWnd::OnCreate, a new view is created and the layout of the frame window is recalculated.

Syntax protected, afx_msg int OnCreate(LPCREATESTRUCT lpCreateStruct);

Parameters

lpCreateStruct A pointer to a CREATESTRUCT for the new window.

Returns 0 to proceed with the CFrameWnd creation; otherwise a value of -1 will destroy the window.

See Also CWnd::OnCreate()

OnCreateClient ■ 2.0 ■ 3.0

Description The first time this member is called it creates the default view. This member can be overridden to customize the creation of frame child windows.

Syntax protected, virtual BOOL OnCreateClient(LPCREATESTRUCT lpcs, CCreateContext* pContext);

Parameters

lpcs A pointer to a CREATESTRUCT. The values provided are for informational purposes only. They can be modified by overriding CWnd::PreCreateWindow().

pContext A pointer to a CCreateContext structure that is for informational purposes only.

Returns TRUE if successful; otherwise FALSE.

OnCreateHelper

■ 2.0 ■ 3.0 ■ UD

Description This member is called by the CFrameWnd::OnCreate function. The helper first calls the base clase CWnd::OnCreate, next calls CFrameWnd::OnCreateClient, and finally initializes the frame by recalculating the layout.

Syntax protected, int OnCreateHelper(LPCREATESTRUCT lpcs, CCreateContext* pContext);

Parameters

lpcs A pointer to a CREATESTRUCT. The values provided are for informational purposes only. They can be modified by overriding the CWnd::PreCreateWindow.

pContext A pointer to a CCreateContext structure that is for informational purposes only.

Returns 0 to proceed with the CFrameWnd creation; otherwise a value of -1 will destroy the window.

OnDDEExecute

■ 2.0 ■ 3.0 ■ NM ■ UD

Description This member is invoked during a Dynamic Data Exchange (DDE) request to execute a command. First, the frame acknowledges the DDE request. Then it passes the request to the CWinApp::OnDDECommand member.

Syntax protected, afx_msg LRESULT OnDDEExecute(WPARAM wParam, LPARAM lParam);

Parameters

wParam HWND of the window sending the DDE execute.

lParam Contains DDE execute information. See ::UnpackDDElParam()

Returns Always returns an LRESULT of 0.

See Also CWinApp::OnDDECommand(), CFrameWnd::OnDDEInitiate(), CFrameWnd::OnDDETerminate()

OnDDEInitiate

■ 2.0 ■ 3.0 ■ NM ■ UD

Description This member is invoked when a DDE conversation is initiated. This function can either acknowledge the conversation or choose to ignore it.

Syntax protected, afx_msg LRESULT OnDDEInitiate(WPARAM wParam, LPARAM lParam);

Parameters

wParam HWND of the window initiating the DDE conversation.

lParam Contains DDE initiate information. This includes the destination atom in the LOWORD and the system topic in the HIWORD.

Returns	Always returns an LRESULT of 0.
See Also	CFrameWnd::OnDDEExecute(), CFrameWnd::OnDDETerminate()

OnDDETerminate ■ 2.0 ■ 3.0 ■ NM ■ UD

Description	This member is invoked to terminate a DDE conversation.
Syntax	protected, afx_msg LRESULT OnDDETerminate(WPARAM wParam, LPARAM lParam);
Parameters	
wParam	HWND of the other window in the conversation.
lParam	LPARAM value passed. Should be 0.
Returns	Always returns an LRESULT of 0.
See Also	CFrameWnd::OnDDEExecute(), CFrameWnd::OnDDEInitiate()

OnDestroy ■ 2.0 ■ 3.0 ■ UD

Description	This member is invoked when the frame is destroyed. First, the frame removes any associated control bars. Next, if the frame is the main window, it will close the help engine. Finally, the base classes' CWnd::OnDestroy is called, which will destroy the frame window and its children.
Syntax	protected, afx_msg void OnDestroy();
Parameters	None.
Returns	Nothing is returned.
See Also	CWnd::OnDestroy(), CFrameWnd::DestroyDockBars()

OnDropFiles ■ 2.0 ■ 3.0 ■ UD

Description	This member is only called if the frame window is a registered drop recipient. If so, then this function is invoked when the user releases the left mouse button during a file drag operation. The default implementation is to open the file dropped by calling the CWinApp:: OpenDocumentFile member.
Syntax	protected, afx_msg void OnDropFiles(HDROP hDropInfo);
Parameters	
hDropInfo	Handle to an internal data structure describing the dropped information. Access this information through the ::DragFinish, ::DragQueryFile, and ::DragQueryPoint functions.
Returns	Nothing is returned.
See Also	CWnd::OnDropFiles(), CWinApp::OpenDocumentFile()

Example The following illustrates how to interpret the name of the file that was dropped into the sample application. For default processing, this member should call the base class implementation of OnDropFiles.

```
void CMainFrame::OnDropFiles(HDROP hDropInfo)
{
      char sDropFileName[128];
      DragQueryFile(hDropInfo,0,sDropFileName,sizeof(sDropFileName));
      AfxMessageBox(sDropFileName,MB_ICONINFORMATION|MB_OK);
}
```

OnEnable ■ 2.0 ■ 3.0 ■ UD

Description This member is invoked when the enabled state of the frame has changed. When calling CFrameWnd::EnableWindow, this member is invoked before control returns but after the WM_DISABLED window style bit has been set. The default implementation causes modal dialogs to change state (by calling CFrameWnd::BeginModalState, CFrameWnd::EndModalState) and calls CFrameWnd::NotifyFloatingWindows with FS_ENABLE or FS_DISABLE.

Syntax protected, afx_msg void OnEnable(BOOL bEnable);

Parameters

bEnable If TRUE then the frame will be enabled for input.

Returns Nothing is returned.

OnEnterIdle ■ 2.0 ■ 3.0 ■ UD

Description This member is invoked by menus or modal dialogs that have entered the idle state. The idle state occurs when either the menu or the dialog have no more messages in their queues for processing. The default behavior of the frame is to set the message text for the current control (if one is currently specified).

Syntax protected, afx_msg void OnEnterIdle(UINT nWhy, CWnd* pWho);

Parameters

nWhy Determines why the idle state was entered. It can be one of the following:

MSGF_DIALOGBOX Dialog box entered idle state.

MSGF_MENU Menu entered idle state.

pWho A pointer to either the dialog or menu object specified by *nWhy*.

Returns Nothing is returned.

OnEraseBkgnd ■ 2.0 ■ 3.0 ■ UD

Description This member is invoked when the background of the frame needs to be erased to prepare it for painting. This is usually the result of a resize or when CWnd::InvalidateRect is called with TRUE for erasing the background. The default implementation of this function allows the active view to erase the background; else, if there is no active view, it passes control to the base class CWnd::OnEraseBkgnd.

Syntax protected, afx_msg BOOL OnEraseBkgnd(CDC* pDC);

Parameters

pDC A pointer to the device context for the frame.

Returns This member should return non-zero if the background was erased using a custom method; otherwise return 0 to use the default window erase.

See Also CWnd::OnEraseBkgnd()

OnHelp

■ 2.0 ■ 3.0 ■ UD

Description This member is invoked when a user triggers a help event (usually the F1 key). The default implementation calls the help engine with the current help context.

Syntax protected, afx_msg void OnHelp();

Parameters None.

Returns Nothing is returned.

OnHelpHitTest

■ 2.0 ■ 3.0 ■ UD

Description This member returns the help index ID of the current help topic. The help topic is determined by a user initiated action, such as clicking the mouse on an area of the frame.

Syntax protected, afx_msg LRESULT OnHelpHitTest(WPARAM wParam, LPARAM lParam);

Parameters

wParam Unused.

lParam Unused.

Returns The current help index ID; otherwise 0.

OnHScroll

■ 2.0 ■ 3.0 ■ UD

Description This member is invoked when a horizontal scroll event occurs in the frame window. The default behavior is to pass the event to the currently active view.

Syntax protected, afx_msg void OnHScroll(UINT nSBCode, UINT nPos, CScrollBar* pScrollBar);

Parameters

nSBCode The type of scroll action taking place. It can be any one of the following:

SB_ENDSCROLL	Bar scrolled to the end position.
SB_LEFT	Bar scrolled to far left.
SB_LINELEFT	Bar scrolled 1 unit (line) to the left.
SB_LINERIGHT	Bar scrolled 1 unit (line) to the right.
SB_PAGELEFT	Bar scrolled 1 page to the left.
SB_PAGERIGHT	Bar scrolled 1 page to the right.
SB_RIGHT	Bar scrolled to the far right.
SB_THUMBPOSITION	Bar scrolled to an absolute position (*nPos*) by moving the thumb bar.
SB_THUMBTRACK	Bar is scrolling and is currently at *nPos*. This occurs while user is moving the thumb bar.
nPos	The current scrollbar position for the SB_THUMBPOSITION and SB_THUMBTRACK codes; otherwise not used.
pScrollbar	The scrollbar control that sent notification. This parameter is NULL if the scrollbar belongs to the frame.
Returns	Nothing is returned.
See Also	CFrameWnd::OnVScroll()

OnIdleUpdateCmdUI ■ 2.0 ■ 3.0 ■ UD

Description This member is used to update the display of the frame during an idle state. The default implementation of this function checks to see which aspects of the display need updating. If necessary, it will update the menu and the frame title, recalculate the frame layout, and set the current message string. This member is mainly invoked when using OLE.

Syntax protected, afx_msg void OnIdleUpdateCmdUI();

Parameters None.

Returns Nothing is returned.

OnInitMenuPopup ■ 2.0 ■ 3.0 ■ UD

Description This member allows the frame window to modify a popup menu before it is displayed. This is useful is enabling/disabling menu options on the fly.

Syntax protected, afx_msg void OnInitMenuPopup(CMenu* pMenu, UINT nIndex, BOOL bSysMenu);

Parameters

pMenu	The pointer to the popup menu.
nIndex	Specifies the main menu index of the popup menu.
bSysMenu	If TRUE, then this menu is the system menu; otherwise FALSE. Note that the default implementation does no processing if this parameter is TRUE.
Returns	Nothing is returned.

OnMenuSelect

■ 2.0 ■ 3.0 ■ UD

Description This member is invoked when the user has selected a menu item.

Syntax protected, afx_msg void OnMenuSelect(UINT nItemID, UINT nFlags, HMENU hSysMenu);

Parameters

nItemID The menu item ID that was selected.

nFlags Contains information about the selected item. It can be one or more of the following:

MF_BITMAP Item is a bitmap.

MF_CHECKED Item is checked.

MF_DISABLED Item is disabled.

MF_GRAYED Item is dimmed.

MF_MOUSESELECT Item was selected with a mouse.

MF_OWNERDRAW Item is an owner-draw.

MF_POPUP Item contains a popup menu.

MF_SEPARATOR Item is a separator.

MF_SYSMENU Item is in the system menu specified by *hSysMenu*.

hSysMenu If *nFlags* is MF_SYSMENU, then this is a handle to the system menu; otherwise this value is not used.

Returns Nothing is returned.

OnNcActivate

■ 2.0 ■ 3.0 ■ UD

Description This member is invoked when the non-client area of the frame needs to be redrawn to indicate a change in the active state.

Syntax protected, afx_msg BOOL OnNcActivate(BOOL bActive);

Parameters

bActive If TRUE, then the frame is to be redrawn active; otherwise the frame should be inactive.

Returns Non-zero if default processing should continue; FALSE to prevent deactivation.

OnPaint

■ 2.0 ■ 3.0 ■ MO ■ UD

Description This member is overridden if compiling for the Macintosh. Basically, the default implementation paints areas that are possibly uncovered in the client area of the frame window.

Syntax protected, afx_msg void OnPaint();

Parameters None.

Returns Nothing is returned.

OnPaletteChanged

■ 4.0 ■ UD

Description This member is invoked when the current active window realizes a new palette, which effects a change in the system palette. This member allows the frame window to adjust for the new palette.

Syntax protected, afx_msg void OnPaletteChanged(CWnd * pFocusWnd);

Parameters

pFocusWnd The current focus window that effected the change in palettes.

Returns Nothing is returned.

OnPopMessageString

■ 2.0 ■ 3.0 ■ UD

Description This member is invoked when the frame receives a WM_POPMESSAGESTRING message. The default implementation will send a WM_SETMESSAGESTRING to set the message bar text, unless popped messages are disabled.

Syntax protected, afx_msg LRESULT OnPopMessageString(WPARAM wParam, LPARAM lParam);

Parameters

wParam The resource ID of the string, or 0 to use the string indicated by *lParam*.

lParam 0 if *wParam* is used; otherwise an LPCSTR to an explicit string.

Returns The resource ID of the previous message or 0 if the previous message was an explicit string stored in the *lParam*.

See Also CFrameWnd:: OnSetMessageString()

OnQueryEndSession

■ 2.0 ■ 3.0 ■ UD

Description This member is invoked when Windows is being exited or the current user is logged off using the ::ExitWindows API function. This member allows each application to save any information or stop the logging off process. To stop the logoff, the application should return FALSE.

Syntax protected, afx_msg BOOL OnQueryEndSession();

Parameters None.

Returns TRUE to continue the end session process; FALSE to stop the session from ending.

OnQueryNewPalette

■ 4.0 ■ UD

Description This member is invoked when the frame is about to become active and gives the frame the opportunity to realize a new palette.

Syntax protected, afx_msg BOOL OnQueryNewPalette();

Parameters None.

Returns TRUE if a new palette was realized; otherwise FALSE.

OnSetCursor

■ 2.0 ■ 3.0 ■ UD

Description This member is invoked when the cursor for the frame needs to be updated. The default implementation tests if the frame is in help mode and if so, sets the cursor to the default help cursor.

Syntax protected, afx_msg BOOL OnSetCursor(CWnd* pWnd, UINT nHitTest, UINT message);

Parameters

pWnd The window that contains the cursor.

nHitTest A hit test code that specifies the cursor's location.

message The mouse message number.

Returns 0 to stop processing the message; otherwise continue default message processing.

OnSetFocus

■ 2.0 ■ 3.0 ■ UD

Description This member is called after the frame has received input focus. The default behavior sets the focus to the active view (if any); otherwise it passes control to the base class CWnd::OnSetFocus.

Syntax protected, afx_msg void OnSetFocus(CWnd* pOldWnd);

Parameters

pOldWnd A temporary pointer to the window that lost focus.

Returns Nothing is returned.

OnSetMessageString

■ 2.0 ■ 3.0 ■ UD

Description This member is invoked when the frame receives a WM_SETMESSAGESTRING message. The default implementation will set the message bar text to the proper string.

Syntax protected, afx_msg LRESULT OnSetMessageString(WPARAM wParam, LPARAM lParam);

Parameters

wParam The resource ID of the string, or 0 to use the string indicated by *lParam*.

lParam 0 if *wParam* is used; otherwise an LPCSTR to an explicit string.

Returns The resource ID of the previous message or 0 if the previous message was an explicit string stored in the *lParam*.

See Also CFrameWnd:: GetMessageString()

OnSetPreviewMode

■ 2.0 ■ 3.0

Description This member is called to toggle the frame window into and out of print preview mode. The default implementation hides all control bars, menus, and the main window. It replaces these with the print preview view.

Syntax public, virtual void OnSetPreviewMode(BOOL bPreview, CPrintPreviewState* pState);

Parameters

bPreview TRUE will set the print preview mode; FALSE will disable the print preview mode.

pState A pointer to a CPrintPreviewState structure.

Returns Nothing is returned.

OnSize

■ 2.0 ■ 3.0 ■ UD

Description This member is invoked after the frame's size has changed. The default implementation calls the base class CWnd::OnSize member, then recalculates the frame layout.

Syntax protected, afx_msg void OnSize(UINT nType, int cx, int cy);

Parameters

nType The type of resizing. This value may be any one of the following:

SIZE_MAXHIDE Popup windows receive this when some other window is maximized.

SIZE_MAXIMIZED Window maximized.

SIZE_MAXSHOW Popup windows receive this when some other window has been restored.

SIZE_MINIMIZED Window minimized.

SIZE_RESTORE Window resized but not maximized or minimized.

cx New width of the client area.

cy New height of the client area.

Returns Nothing is returned.

OnSysCommand

■ 2.0 ■ 3.0 ■ UD

Description This member is invoked when an item from the control menu is selected or maximize and minimize are selected. The default implementation checks to see if the frame is in help mode and if so, sends a WM_COMMANDHELP message with the appropriate help context ID; otherwise processing is passed to the base class. CWnd::OnSysCommand.

Syntax protected, afx_msg void OnSysCommand(UINT nID, LONG lParam);

Parameters

nID The system command selected. See CWnd::OnSysCommand().

lParam If the item was selected with the mouse, then LOWORD = x-coord, HIWORD = y-coord; otherwise not used.

Returns Nothing is returned.

See Also CWnd::OnSysCommand()

OnToolTipText

■ 2.0 ■ 3.0 ■ UD

Description This member retrieves the tooltip text specified.

Syntax protected, afx_msg BOOL OnToolTipText(UINT nID, NMHDR* pNMHDR, LRESULT* pResult);

Parameters

nID Unused.

pNMHDR Pointer to an NMHDR structure that contains information about the tooltip and receives the text. This structure is internally cast to a TOOLTIPTEXT structure.

pResult Pointer to a result. Always filled with 0.

Returns TRUE.

OnUpdateContextHelp

■ 2.0 ■ 3.0 ■ UD

Description This member updates the state of the context help control bar button depending on whether or not the frame is in help mode.

Syntax protected, afx_msg void OnUpdateContextHelp(CCmdUI* pCmdUI);

Parameters

pCmdUI A pointer to a CCmdUI object that represents the context help interface.

Returns Nothing is returned.

OnUpdateControlBarMenu

■ 2.0 ■ 3.0 ■ UD

Description This member will update the command interface by setting the check on the interface item if the specified control bar is visible. An example of this is the check mark that MFC puts next to the TOOLBAR menu item when the toolbar is displayed.

Syntax public, afx_msg void OnUpdateControlBarMenu(CCmdUI* pCmdUI);

Parameters

pCmdUI A pointer to a CCmdUI object that represents the control bar.

Returns Nothing is returned.

OnUpdateFrameMenu

■ 2.0 ■ 3.0 ■ UD

Description This member sets the frame menu. If the given HMENU is NULL, then the frame attempts to use the default document menu. If the default document menu is NULL, then the menu associated with the frame is used.

Syntax public, virtual void OnUpdateFrameMenu(HMENU hMenuAlt);

Parameters

hMenuAlt Handle to the new frame menu.

Returns Nothing is returned.

OnUpdateFrameTitle

■ 2.0 ■ 3.0 ■ UD

Description This member is called to update the title bar of the frame window. This function will only work for frames that have the FWS_ADDTOTITLE style set.

Syntax public, virtual void OnUpdateFrameTitle(BOOL bAddToTitle);

Parameters

bAddToTitle TRUE will add the active document title to the current frame title. FALSE will use only the current frame title.

Returns Nothing is returned.

See Also CFrameWnd::UpdateFrameTitleForDocument()

OnUpdateKeyIndicator

■ 2.0 ■ 3.0 ■ UD

Description This member is invoked to update the status of the key indicators on the default status bar. These key indicators include CAPS, NUMLOCK, and SCROLLLOCK.

Syntax protected, afx_msg void OnUpdateKeyIndicator(CCmdUI* pCmdUI);

Parameters

pCmdUI A pointer to a CCmdUI object that represents the particular key indicator.

Returns Nothing is returned.

OnVScroll

■ 2.0 ■ 3.0 ■ UD

Description This member is invoked when the frame receives a vertical scroll event. The default processing will pass the scroll message to the current active view.

Syntax protected, afx_msg void OnVScroll(UINT nSBCode, UINT nPos, CScrollBar* pScrollBar);

Parameters

nSBCode	The type of scroll action taking place. It can be any one of the following:
SB_BOTTOM	Bar scrolled to bottom.
SB_ENDSCROLL	Bar scrolled to the end position.
SB_LINEDOWN	Bar scrolled 1 unit (line) down.
SB_LINEUP	Bar scrolled 1 unit (line) up.
SB_PAGEDOWN	Bar scrolled 1 page down.
SB_PAGEUP	Bar scrolled 1 page up.
SB_THUMBPOSITION	Bar scrolled to an absolute position (*nPos*) by moving the thumb bar.
SB_THUMBTRACK	Bar is scrolling and is currently at *nPos*. This occurs while user is moving the thumb bar.
SB_TOP	Bar scrolled to top.
nPos	The new thumb position.
pScrollbar	The scrollbar control that sent notification. This parameter is NULL if the scrollbar belongs to the frame.
Returns	Nothing is returned.

PostNcDestroy

■ 2.0 ■ 3.0 ■ UD

Description	This member is called internally to delete the CFrameWnd object that was allocated on the heap. Never delete a CFrameWnd object directly; it should be removed by calling DestroyWindow.
Syntax	protected, virtual void PostNcDestroy();
Parameters	None.
Returns	Nothing is returned.
See Also	CWnd::DestroyWindow()

PreCreateWindow

■ 2.0 ■ 3.0 ■ UD

Description	This member is called before the creation of the window. Window attributes such as size, position, and style bits may be set at this time.
Syntax	protected, virtual BOOL PreCreateWindow(CREATESTRUCT& cs);
Parameters	
cs	A reference to a CREATESTRUCT that can be filled in with specific window attributes.
Returns	TRUE.
See Also	CWnd::PreCreateWindow()

PreTranslateMessage

■ 2.0 ■ 3.0 ■ UD

Description	This member is used to intercept messages before they are dispatched. The default implementation attempts to translate the message using the accelerators for the frame.
Syntax	public, virtual BOOL PreTranslateMessage(MSG* pMsg);
Parameters	
pMsg	The message to be pre-translated.
Returns	Non-zero if the message was translated and should not be dispatched; otherwise 0 will allow the message to be dispatched.

ProcessHelpMsg

■ 2.0 ■ 3.0 ■ UD

Description	This member is used to dispatch only help-related messages.
Syntax	protected, BOOL ProcessHelpMsg(MSG& msg, DWORD* pContext);
Parameters	
msg	The message to process.
pContext	Returns an optional help context ID if the message is a mouse message.
Returns	FALSE to end help message processing; otherwise TRUE.

RecalcLayout

■ 2.0 ■ 3.0

Description	This member is called when the size of the frame window has changed or when control bars are displayed/hidden. This member can be overridden to customize the layout behavior of the frame window.
Syntax	public, virtual void RecalcLayout(BOOL bNotify = TRUE);
Parameters	
bNotify	If TRUE, then the active in-place item for the frame is notified about the layout change.
Returns	Nothing is returned.
Example	See CFrameWnd::DockControlBar()

ReDockControlBar

■ 4.0 ■ UD

Description	This function will reposition a currently docked control bar.
Syntax	public, void ReDockControlBar(CControlBar* pBar, CDockBar * pDockBar ,LPCRECT lpRect = NULL);
Parameters	
pBar	The control bar to dock.

pDockBar	The destination dock bar.
lpRect	The non-client area screen coordinates where the control bar will be docked.
Returns	Nothing is returned.

RemoveControlBar

■ 2.0 ■ 3.0 ■ UD

Description	This member is used to remove a control bar from the list of control bars for the frame. *Note:* After removing the control bar it is necessary to update the frame window and call CFrameWnd::RecalcLayout.
Syntax	public, void RemoveControlBar(CControlBar *pBar);
Parameters	
pBar	A pointer to the CControlBar to remove.
Returns	Nothing is returned.

RemoveFrameWnd

■ 2.0 ■ 3.0 ■ UD

Description	This member removes the frame window from the application global list of chained frame windows.
Syntax	protected, void RemoveFrameWnd();
Parameters	None.
Returns	Nothing is returned.
See Also	CFrameWnd::AddFrameWnd()

SaveBarState

■ 2.0 ■ 3.0

Description	This member will save control bar to an initialization file. This member is useful for returning an application desktop to a previously saved state.
Syntax	public, void SaveBarState(LPCTSTR lpszProfileName) const;
Parameters	
lpszProfileName	The initialization file name.
Returns	Nothing is returned.
See Also	CFrameWnd::LoadBarState()
Example	To always save the state of the application control bars, you can add SaveBarState to the application main frame's OnClose member or,as in the example application, in response to a menu selection.

```
void CMainFrame::OnViewSavebarstates()
{
     SaveBarState("mfcsampframe");
}
```

SetActiveView

■ 2.0 ■ 3.0

Description This member is used to set a new active view within the frame window. This is automatically invoked by the framework when the user selects a new view, but it may also be called explicitly within the application. The function first notifies the view that is losing activation, then notifies the view gaining activation.

Syntax public, void SetActiveView(CView* pViewNew, BOOL bNotify = TRUE);

Parameters

pViewNew A pointer to the view gaining activation.

bNotify If TRUE, then *pViewNew* will receive notification of the activation.

Returns Nothing is returned.

SetDockState

■ 2.0 ■ 3.0

Description This member is used to set up the frame and display the control bars defined in the CDockState structure. This member is automatically called after a call to CFrameWnd::LoadBarState but may be called directly by the application.

Syntax public, void SetDockState(const CDockState& state);

Parameters

state A reference to a CDockState structure that holds the display information.

Returns Nothing is returned.

See Also CFrameWnd::LoadBarState()

SetHelpCapture

■ 2.0 ■ 3.0 ■ UD

Description This member will set or release the context-sensitive help capture for the frame window.

Syntax protected, HWND SetHelpCapture(POINT point, BOOL* pbDescendant);

Parameters

point The current mouse position for help.

pbDescendant A pointer to a Boolean. This is filled in with TRUE if a descendant window of the frame is hit. This value can be NULL.

Returns HWND pointing to the window under *point*, or NULL.

SetMessageText

■ 2.0 ■ 3.0

Description This member will set the text in the default status bar pane (the default pane has an ID of 0).

Syntax	public, void SetMessageText(LPCTSTR lpszText); public, void SetMessageText(UINT nID);
Parameters	
lpszText	A NULL-terminated string containing the status text.
nID	The resource ID of the string containing the status text.
Returns	Nothing is returned.
See Also	CFrameWnd::GetMessageText()
Example	See CMDIFrameWnd:: MDICascade()

ShowControlBar ■ 2.0 ■ 3.0

Description	This member will display/hide the given control bar.
Syntax	public, void ShowControlBar(CControlBar* pBar, BOOL bShow, BOOL bDelay);
Parameters	
pBar	The control bar to display or hide depending on the value of *bShow*.
bShow	TRUE will display the control bar; FALSE will hide the control bar.
bDelay	TRUE will delay the display of the bar until the frame enters its idle state; FALSE will immediately update the frame window and call RecalcLayout.
Returns	Nothing is returned.

ShowOwnedWindows ■ 2.0 ■ 3.0

Description	This member will display or hide any descendant window of the frame.
Syntax	public, void ShowOwnedWindows(BOOL bShow);
Parameters	
bShow	TRUE will display descendants; FALSE will hide descendants.
Returns	Nothing is returned.

UpdateFrameTitleForDocument ■ 2.0 ■ 3.0 ■ UD

Description	This member will set the frame title. If the FWS_PREFIXTITLE style bit is set, the document title will be displayed before the frame title. Otherwise, the frame title is displayed before the document title.
Syntax	protected, void UpdateFrameTitleForDocument(LPCTSTR lpszDocName);
Parameters	
lpszDocName	The active document name. This value may be NULL.
Returns	Nothing is returned.
See Also	CFrameWnd::OnUpdateFrameTitle()

The CMDIFrameWnd Class

The CMDIFrameWnd class provides the functionality of a multiple document interface (MDI). The MDI frame manages a set of CMDIChildWnd objects and provides support for the MFC document/view architecture. Also, the MDI frame provides support for managing the standard MDI "Window" menu. See Chapter 6, *Documnent/View,* for more information about the multiple document interface architecture.

CMDIFRAMEWND ■ 2.0 ■ 3.0

Description The constructor for the CMDIFrameWnd class. This member initializes the internal member variables for the frame object. Also, MFC keeps track of all the CMDIFrameWnd (and CFrameWnd-derived classes) created in the application by adding the new CMDIFrameWnd class to the CFrameWnd list stored in the AFX_THREAD_STATE structure.

Syntax public, CMDIFrameWnd();

Parameters None.

Returns Nothing is returned.

ASSERTVALID ■ 2.0 ■ 3.0 ■ DO

Description Determines whether the CMDIFrameWnd is in a valid state and if it is not, throws an assertion.

Syntax public, virtual void AssertValid( ) const;

Parameters None.

Returns Nothing is returned.

See Also CFrameWnd::AssertValid()

CREATECLIENT ■ 2.0 ■ 3.0

Description This member is called to create the client area of the frame window. The client area is used to manage CMDIChildWnd objects. The default implementation sets window styles for the client window, then calls ::CreateWindowEx to create the client window. This member should be called if the base class CFrameWnd::OnCreate function is overridden.

Syntax public, virtual BOOL CreateClient(LPCREATESTRUCT lpCreateStruct, CMenu* pWindowMenu);

Parameters

lpCreateStruct A pointer to the CREATESTRUCT for the client window.

pWindowMenu A pointer to the client window menu.

Returns TRUE if the client window was created successfully; otherwise FALSE.

See Also CFrameWnd::OnCreate

DefWindowProc ■ 2.0 ■ 3.0 ■ UD

Description This member function calls the default message processing for the frame. Every message that is not handled by another procedure is routed through this function. The default for the CMDIFrameWnd is to pass the message to the Windows API function ::DefFrameProc.

Syntax protected, virtual LRESULT DefWindowProc(UINT nMsg, WPARAM wParam, LPARAM lParam);

Parameters

nMsg Window message.

wParam Message-specific information.

lParam Message-specific information.

Returns Nothing is returned.

See Also ::DefFrameProc()

DelayUpdateFrameMenu ■ 2.0 ■ 3.0 ■ UD

Description This member will defer the update of the frame menu until the application enters its next idle state.

Syntax public, virtual void DelayUpdateFrameMenu(HMENU hMenuAlt);

Parameters

hMenuAlt A handle to an alternate menu for the frame.

Returns Nothing is returned.

Dump ■ 2.0 ■ 3.0 ■ DO

Description This member is an MFC diagnostic utility that is compiled only into the debug version of the application. The member is used to output the state of the object and can be called directly by the programmer.

Syntax public, virtual void Dump() const;

Parameters None.

Returns Nothing is returned.

See Also CObject::Dump()

GetActiveFrame ■ 2.0 ■ 3.0 ■ UD

Description This member returns the currently active CMDIChildWnd, or in the absence of one it will return **this**.

Syntax public, virtual CFrameWnd* GetActiveFrame();

Parameters None.

Returns — The currently active CMDIChildWnd or **this** value of the CMDIFrameWnd if there is no currently active CMDIChildWnd.

GetWindowMenuPopup

■ 2.0 ■ 3.0

Description — This member is a convenience function that returns a handle to the typical "Windows" menu for MDI applications. Override this function if your application does not use the MFC standard menu IDs. The default implementation returns the menu that contains any IDs between AFX_IDM_WINDOW_FIRST and AFX_IDM_WINDOW_LAST.

Syntax — public, virtual HMENU GetWindowMenuPopup(HMENU hMenuBar);

Parameters

hMenuBar — The menu that contains the "Windows" sub-menu.

Returns — Handle to the "Windows" sub-menu if successful; otherwise NULL.

LoadFrame

■ 2.0 ■ 3.0 ■ UD

Description — This member is called after construction of the CMDIFrameWnd to create the frame and load its resources. These resources include the icon, accelerators, and string tables associated with the frame. The default implementation calls the base class CFrameWnd::LoadFrame, and saves the default frame menu to use when the CMDIFrameWnd has no active views displayed.

Syntax — public, virtual BOOL LoadFrame(UINT nIDResource, DWORD dwDefaultStyle = WS_OVERLAPPEDWINDOW | FWS_ADDTOTITLE, CWnd* pParentWnd = NULL, CCreateContext* pContext = NULL);

Parameters

nIDResource — The resource ID used to load frame resources. This same ID is used for the each of the resources mentioned above.

dwDefaultStyle — The default frame window style. For automatic display of document titles, add the FWS_ADDTOTITLE style.

pParentWnd — The parent of the frame.

pContext — Pointer to a CCreateContext object.

Returns — TRUE if successful; otherwise FALSE.

See Also — CFrameWnd::LoadFrame()

MDIActivate

■ 2.0 ■ 3.0

Description — This member is called to activate an MDI child window.

Syntax — public, void MDIActivate(CWnd* pWndActivate);

Parameters

pWndActivate The MDI child window to activate.

Returns Nothing is returned.

MDICascade

■ 2.0 ■ 3.0

Description This member arranges the MDI child window layout into a cascaded fashion. Cascaded windows are arranged so that each window's title bar is visible.

Syntax public, void MDICascade(); void MDICascade(int nType);

Parameters

nType If *nType* is MDITILE_SKIPDISABLED, then disabled child windows are not cascaded; otherwise all child windows are cascaded.

Returns Nothing is returned.

Example The following can be invoked to cascade the frame's child windows.

```
void CMainFrame::OnWindowCascade()

{
      MDICascade();
      SetMessageText("Cascaded Windows");
}
```

MDIGetActive

■ 2.0 ■ 3.0

Description This member retrieves the currently active MDI Child window.

Syntax public, CMDIChildWnd* MDIGetActive(BOOL* pbMaximized = NULL) const;

Parameters

pbMaximized An optional address of a Boolean that receives TRUE if the child window is maximized or FALSE if not maximized.

Returns Pointer to the active MDI Child window or NULL if none exists.

MDIIconArrange

■ 2.0 ■ 3.0

Description This member will arrange the icons of any minimized MDI child windows within the frame.

Syntax public, void MDIIconArrange();

Parameters None.

Returns Nothing is returned.

Example

```
void CMainFrame::OnWindowArrange()
{
      MDIIconArrange();
      SetMessageText("Arranged Icons for frame");
}
```

MDIMaximize ■ 2.0 ■ 3.0

Description This member is invoked to maximize the given MDI child window. When maximized, the child window is resized to fill the entire frame client window, the child title is added to the frame title, and the child's system menu and restore button are added to the frame menu bar.

Syntax public, void MDIMaximize(CWnd* pWnd);

Parameters

pWnd The MDI child window to maximize.

Returns Nothing is returned.

MDINext ■ 2.0 ■ 3.0

Description This member activates the next MDI child window in the window order. The currently active child window is deactivated and placed behind all other MDI child windows in the frame.

Syntax public, void MDINext();

Parameters None.

Returns Nothing is returned.

MDIRestore ■ 2.0 ■ 3.0

Description This member will restore a previously maximized or minimized MDI child window.

Syntax public, void MDIRestore(CWnd* pWnd);

Parameters

pWnd The MDI child window to restore.

Returns Nothing is returned.

MDISetMenu ■ 2.0 ■ 3.0

Description This member is used to replace the frame menu and the MDI "Windows" sub-menu on the menu bar. You should call DrawMenuBar after calling this function to update the menu appearance.

Syntax public, CMenu* MDISetMenu(CMenu* pFrameMenu, CMenu* pWindowMenu);

Parameters

pFrameMenu Pointer to a new frame menu or NULL for no change.

pWindowMenu Pointer to a new "Windows" sub-menu or NULL for no change.

Returns A pointer to the new frame menu or NULL if it was not changed.

MDITile

■ 2.0 ■ 3.0

Description This member function will tile all MDI child windows in the frame window by the given method.

Syntax public, void MDITile(); public, void MDITile(int nType);

Parameters

nType The tiling method to be used. It can be one of the following:

MDITILE_HORIZONTAL Child windows use maximum horizontal space from top to bottom.

MDITILE_SKIPDISABLED No disabled child windows will be tiled.

MDITILE_VERTICAL Child windows use maximum vertical space from left to right.

Returns Nothing is returned.

Example The following example simply adds a vertical tile callback to the sample program.

```
void CMainFrame::OnWindowTileVert()
{
	TileWindows(MDITILE_VERTICAL);
}

void CMainFrame::TileWindows(int nMethod)
{
	MDITile(nMethod);
	CString strMsg;
	switch(nMethod)
	{
		case MDITILE_HORIZONTAL:
			strMsg = "Tiled windows horizontally";
			break;
		case MDITILE_VERTICAL:
			strMsg = "Tiled windows vertically";
			break;
		default:
			strMsg = "Tiled windows";
			break;
	}
	SetMessageText(strMsg);
}
```

OnCmdMsg

■ 2.0 ■ 3.0 ■ UD

Description This member routes all command messages for the MDI frame window. First, it tries to route them to the active MDI child window. Next, if the command message is not handled, it is passed through the MDI frame's base class CFrameWnd::OnCmdMsg handler.

Syntax public, virtual BOOL OnCmdMsg(UINT nID, int nCode, void* pExtra, AFX_CMDHANDLERINFO* pHandlerInfo);

Parameters

nID Command ID.

nCode	Notification code.
pExtra	Dependent on *nCode*.
pHandlerInfo	Typically NULL. If not NULL, then it is filled with handler information.
Returns	TRUE if the command message is handled; otherwise FALSE.

OnCommand ■ 2.0 ■ 3.0 ■ UD

Description	This member routes command notifications from accelerators, controls, and menus. Before passing control to the base class CFrameWnd::OnCommand, the MDI frame window allows the active MDI child window to process the message first.
Syntax	protected, virtual BOOL OnCommand(WPARAM wParam, LPARAM lParam);
Parameters	
wParam	Command ID of the accelerator, control, or menu.
lParam	This parameter indicates one of the notification sources below:
accelerator	Low-order = 0, Hi-order = 1
control	Low-order = control identifier, Hi-order = notification message
menu	Low-order = 0, Hi-order = 0
Returns	TRUE if the message was processed; otherwise FALSE.

OnCommandHelp ■ 2.0 ■ 3.0 ■ UD

Description	This member handles the help command invocation for the MDI frame window. The MDI frame window first tries to route the message to the currently active MDI child window. If the child window does not process the message, then it is passed to the base class CFrameWnd::OnCommandHelp member.
Syntax	protected, afx_msg LRESULT OnCommandHelp(WPARAM wParam, LPARAM lParam);
Parameters	
wParam	Unused.
lParam	Help context ID.
Returns	TRUE if processed; otherwise FALSE.
See Also	CFrameWnd::OnCommandHelp(), CWinApp::WinHelp()

OnCreateClient ■ 2.0 ■ 3.0 ■ UD

Description	This member is used to create the default client window with the proper menu. This member can be overridden to customize the creation of the MDI client window.

Syntax public, virtual BOOL OnCreateClient(LPCREATESTRUCT lpcs, CCreateContext* pContext);

Parameters

lpcs A pointer to a CREATESTRUCT. The values provided are for informational purposes only. They can be modified by overriding the CWnd::PreCreateWindow.

pContext A pointer to a CCreateContext structure for informational purposes only.

Returns TRUE if successful; otherwise FALSE.

See Also CMDIFrameWnd:: CreateClient()

OnDestroy ■ 2.0 ■ 3.0 ■ UD

Description This member is invoked when the MDI frame is destroyed. First, the base class CFrameWnd::OnDestroy is called; then the default MDI client menu is restored.

Syntax protected, afx_msg void OnDestroy();

Parameters None.

Returns Nothing is returned.

See Also CFrameWnd::OnDestroy()

OnIdleUpdateCmdUI ■ 2.0 ■ 3.0 ■ UD

Description This member is used to update the display of the MDI frame during an idle state. The MDI frame first redraws the menu bar (if necessary) before passing control to the base class CFrameWnd::OnIdleUpdateCmdUI.

Syntax protected, afx_msg void OnIdleUpdateCmdUI();

Parameters None.

Returns Nothing is returned.

OnMDIWindowCmd ■ 2.0 ■ 3.0 ■ UD

Description This member is invoked when one of the MDI standard "Windows" menu options is selected. This member routes the menu selection to the proper Windows message.

Syntax protected, afx_msg BOOL OnMDIWindowCmd(UINT nID);

Parameters

nID The menu ID of the choice selected. This can be any one of the following:

ID_WINDOW_ARRANGE Arrange MDI child window icons.

ID_WINDOW_CASCADE Cascade MDI child windows.

ID_WINDOW_TILE_HORZ Tile MDI child windows horizontally.

ID_WINDOW_TILE_VERT Tile MDI child windows vertically.

Returns TRUE if menu selection was processed; otherwise FALSE.

OnSize

■ 2.0 ■ 3.0

Description This member is invoked after the MDI frame's size has changed. The default implementation recalculates the frame layout if the sizing is not the result of a SIZE_MINIMIZED operation.

Syntax protected, afx_msg void OnSize(UINT nType, int cx, int cy);

Parameters

nType	The type of resizing.
SIZE_MAXHIDE	Popup windows receive this when some other window is maximized.
SIZE_MAXIMIZED	Window maximized.
SIZE_MAXSHOW	Popup windows receive this when some other window has been restored.
SIZE_MINIMIZED	Window minimized.
SIZE_RESTORED	Window resized, but not maximized or minimized.
cx	New width of the client area. (Unused.)
cy	New height of the client area. (Unused.)

Returns Nothing is returned.

OnUpdateFrameMenu

■ 2.0 ■ 3.0 ■ UD

Description This member is used to change the appearance of the frame menu before it is displayed to the user. The default implementation is to allow the currently active child window to update the frame menu.

Syntax public, virtual void OnUpdateFrameMenu(HMENU hMenuAlt);

Parameters

hMenuAlt Handle to the frame menu.

Returns Nothing is returned.

OnUpdateFrameTitle

■ 2.0 ■ 3.0 ■ UD

Description This member is called to update the title bar of the frame window. This function will only work for frames that have the FWS_ADDTOTITLE style set. The default implementation adds the currently active document title to the frame title when the MDI child window is maximized.

Syntax public, virtual void OnUpdateFrameTitle(BOOL bAddToTitle);

Parameters

bAddToTitle TRUE will add the active document title to the current frame title. FALSE will use only the current frame title.

Returns Nothing is returned.

See Also CFrameWnd::UpdateFrameTitleForDocument()

OnUpdateMDIWindowCmd

■ 2.0 ■ 3.0 ■ UD

Description This member is invoked before the standard MDI "Windows" menu is displayed. If there is a currently active MDI child window, then the menu is enabled; otherwise it is disabled.

Syntax protected, afx_msg void OnUpdateMDIWindowCmd(CCmdUI* pCmdUI);

Parameters

pCmdUI A CCmdUI pointer representing the MDI child window menu choices.

Returns Nothing is returned.

PreCreateWindow

■ 2.0 ■ 3.0 ■ UD

Description This member is called before the creation of the MDI frame window. Window attributes such as size, position, and style bits may be set at this time.

Syntax public, virtual BOOL PreCreateWindow(CREATESTRUCT& cs);

Parameters

cs A reference to a CREATESTRUCT that can be filled in with specific window attributes.

Returns TRUE.

See Also CWnd::PreCreateWindow()

PreTranslateMessage

■ 2.0 ■ 3.0 ■ UD

Description This member is used to intercept messages before they are dispatched. The default implementation allows the current active MDI child window to pre-translate the message. If the child window does not process the message, then the frame attempts to translate the message into an accelerator.

Syntax public, virtual BOOL PreTranslateMessage(MSG* pMsg);

Parameters

pMsg The message to be pre-translated.

Returns Non-zero if the message was translated and should not be dispatched; otherwise 0 will allow the message to be dispatched.

The CMDIChildWnd Class

The CMDIChildWnd class implements the behavior of a multiple document child window. MDI child windows do not appear directly on the desktop; rather they appear inside of a CMDIFrameWnd. Each child does not have its own separate menu bar; rather it shares the menu kept on the MDI frame window.

CMDICHILDWND

■ 2.0 ■ 3.0

Description This member constructs an MDI child window.

Syntax public, CMDIChildWnd();

Parameters None.

Returns Nothing is returned.

ACTIVATEFRAME

■ 2.0 ■ 3.0 ■ UD

Description This member function will show the frame window (restore if it is currently iconic) and bring it to the top Z-order window position. It can also be used to display the window as the result of some user interaction or can be overridden to customize the default window activation behavior.

Syntax public, virtual void ActivateFrame(int nCmdShow = -1);

Parameters

nCmdShow The resulting show state of the frame window. If this value is -1, then the window will be restored if iconic (SW_RESTORE); otherwise SW_SHOWNORMAL is used. If the value is not -1, then the explicit value of *nCmdShow* will be used.

Returns Nothing is returned.

See Also CWnd::ShowWindow

Example See CFrameWnd::ActivateFrame()

ASSERTVALID

■ 2.0 ■ 3.0 ■ DO

Description Determines whether the CMDIChildWnd is in a valid state and if it is not, throws an assertion.

Syntax public, virtual void AssertValid( ) const;

Parameters None.

Returns Nothing is returned.

CREATE

■ 2.0 ■ 3.0

Description This member is called after construction to create the actual frame window and attach it to this CMDIChildWnd object.

Syntax public, BOOL Create(LPCTSTR lpszClassName, LPCTSTR lpszWindowName, DWORD dwStyle = WS_CHILD | WS_VISIBLE | WS_OVERLAPPEDWINDOW, const RECT & rect = rectDefault, CMDIFrameWnd * pParentWnd = NULL, CCreateContext* pContext = NULL);

Parameters

lpszClassName Specifies the Windows class (or NULL to use default CMDIChildWnd class attributes). If specified, this name must have been previously registered using AfxRegisterWndClass or the Windows API call to RegisterClass.

lpszWindowName A NULL-terminated string that contains the title bar text.

dwStyle The window style attributes for the window. The WS_CHILD attribute must be used. See CWnd::Create.

rect The size and position of the new window (or use rectDefault for default window placement).

pParentWnd The parent of the child window or NULL to specify the main application window.

pContext An optional pointer to a CCreateContext object that will be passed to the CFrameWnd::OnCreate method.

Returns Non-zero if the function is successful; zero otherwise.

See Also CWnd::Create()

DEFWINDOWPROC

■ 2.0 ■ 3.0 ■ UD

Description This member function calls the default message processing for the window. Every message that is not handled by another procedure is routed through this function. The default for the CMDIChildWnd is to pass the message to the Windows API function ::DefMDIChildProc.

Syntax protected, virtual LRESULT DefWindowProc(UINT nMsg, WPARAM wParam, LPARAM lParam);

Parameters

nMsg Window message.

wParam Message-specific information.

lParam Message-specific information.

Returns Nothing is returned.

See Also ::DefMDIChildProc()

DestroyWindow

■ 2.0 ■ 3.0 ■ UD

Description This member is used to destroy the window attached to the CMDIChildWnd object. The default implementation disables the automatic titling of the frame before it calls CMDIChildWnd::MDIDestroy.

Syntax public, virtual BOOL DestroyWindow();

Parameters None.

Returns Non-zero if the window was destroyed; otherwise 0.

Dump

■ 2.0 ■ 3.0 ■ DO

Description This member is an MFC diagnostic utility that is compiled only into the debug version of the application. The member is used to output the state of the object and can be called directly by the programmer.

Syntax public, virtual void Dump() const;

Parameters None.

Returns Nothing is returned.

See Also CObject::Dump()

GetMDIFrame

■ 2.0 ■ 3.0

Description This member retrieves the CMDIFrameWnd associated with this child window. Note that the parent of this child window is of type MDICLIENT, and it is the MDICLIENT's parent that is retrieved.

Syntax public, CMDIFrameWnd* GetMDIFrame();

Parameters None.

Returns Pointer to the CMDIFrameWnd.

GetMessageBar

■ 2.0 ■ 3.0 ■ UD

Description This member returns a pointer to the status bar window for the MDI child window.

Syntax protected, virtual CWnd* GetMessageBar();

Parameters None.

Returns A pointer to the MDI frame's status bar or NULL if none exists.

LoadFrame

■ 2.0 ■ 3.0 ■ UD

Description This member is used to create an MDI child window and load its associated resources. These resources include the child window's menu and icon.

Syntax public, virtual BOOL LoadFrame(UINT nIDResource, DWORD dwDefaultStyle, CWnd* pParentWnd, CCreateContext* pContext = NULL);

Parameters

nIDResource The resource ID used to load child window resources.

dwDefaultStyle The default frame window style. For automatic display of document titles, add the FWS_ADDTOTITLE style.

pParentWnd The parent of the frame.

pContext Pointer to a CCreateContext class.

Returns TRUE if successful; otherwise FALSE.

See Also CMDIChildWnd::Create()

MDIActivate ■ 2.0 ■ 3.0

Description This member is called to activate the MDI child window. If a call to CMDIFrameWnd::MDIActivate is made, the last active MDI child window is activated as well. This member allows you to bypass the activation of the last active child.

Syntax public, void MDIActivate();

Parameters None.

Returns Nothing is returned.

MDIDestroy ■ 2.0 ■ 3.0

Description This member is called by the CMDIChildWnd::DestroyWindow to destroy the MDI child window.

Syntax public, void MDIDestroy();

Parameters None.

Returns Nothing is returned.

MDIMaximize ■ 2.0 ■ 3.0

Description This member is invoked to maximize an MDI child window. When maximized, the child window is resized to fill the entire frame client window, the child title is added to the frame title, and the child's system menu and restore button are added to the frame menu bar.

Syntax public, void MDIMaximize();

Parameters None.

Returns Nothing is returned.

MDIRestore ■ 2.0 ■ 3.0

Description This member will restore the MDI child window if it was previously maximized or minimized.

Syntax public, void MDIRestore();

Parameters None.

Returns Nothing is returned.

OnCreate ■ 2.0 ■ 3.0 ■ UD

Description This member is invoked after creation of the MDI child window. The MDI child window implementation of this calls the base class CFrameWnd:: OnCreateHelper with the MDI window creation params.

Syntax protected, afx_msg int OnCreate(LPCREATESTRUCT lpCreateStruct);

Parameters

lpCreateStruct A pointer to a CREATESTRUCT for the new window.

Returns 0 to proceed with the CMDIChildWnd creation; otherwise a value of -1 will destroy the window.

See Also CWnd::OnCreate()

OnDestroy ■ 2.0 ■ 3.0 ■ UD

Description This member is invoked when the MDI child window is destroyed. This member first calls CMDIChildWnd:: UpdateClientEdge before passing control to the base class CFrameWnd::OnDestroy.

Syntax protected, afx_msg void OnDestroy();

Parameters None.

Returns Nothing is returned.

See Also CMDIChildWnd::UpdateClientEdge(), CFrameWnd::OnDestroy()

OnMDIActivate ■ 2.0 ■ 3.0 ■ UD

Description This member is called when a change in MDI child window activation occurs. This member will notify each window of the activation change, update the frame titles, and update the frame menus.

Syntax protected, afx_msg void OnMDIActivate(BOOL bActivate, CWnd* pActivateWnd, CWnd* pUnused);

Parameters

bActivate If TRUE, then the child window is being activated.

pActivateWnd A pointer to the window being activated.

pUnused Unused.

Returns Nothing is returned.

OnMouseActivate

■ 2.0 ■ 3.0 ■ UD

Description This member is called when the mouse is clicked in an inactive MDI child window. This member will pass control to CFrameWnd::OnMouseActivate and activate the child window if appropriate.

Syntax protected, afx_msg int OnMouseActivate(CWnd* pDesktopWnd, UINT nHitTest, UINT message);

Parameters

pDesktopWnd The top-level window associated with this MDI child window.

nHitTest A hit test code (see Windows API).

message The mouse message.

Returns One of the following values:

MA_ACTIVATE The MDIChildWnd was activated.

MA_ACTIVATEANDEAT The MDIChildWnd was activated and the mouse event was discarded.

MA_NOACTIVATE The MDIChildWnd was not activated.

MA_NOACTIVATEANDEAT The MDIChildWnd was not activated and the mouse event was discarded.

OnNcActivate

■ 2.0 ■ 3.0 ■ UD

Description This member is invoked when the non-client area needs to be changed to indicate an active or inactive state. This member bypasses the base class CFrameWnd::OnNcActivate and calls the CWnd::OnNcActivate.

Syntax protected, afx_msg BOOL OnNcActivate(BOOL bActive);

Parameters

bActive TRUE indicates the child window is being activated; FALSE indicates deactivation.

Returns Non-zero to proceed with default message processing; 0 to indicate that the request was handled.

OnNcCreate

■ 2.0 ■ 3.0 ■ UD

Description This member is called prior to window creation. This allows the child window to control the creation of the non-client area and to set the proper window style flags.

Syntax	protected, afx_msg BOOL OnNcCreate(LPCREATESTRUCT lpCreateStruct);
Parameters	
lpCreateStruct	A pointer to a CREATESTRUCT.
Returns	TRUE to continue processing; otherwise FALSE.

OnSize

■ 2.0 ■ 3.0 ■ UD

Description	This member is invoked after an MDI child window's size has changed. The default implementation recalculates the frame layout.
Syntax	protected, afx_msg void OnSize(UINT nType, int cx, int cy);
Parameters	
nType	The type of sizing event. The child window will not recalc the window layout if this is SIZE_MINIMIZED.
SIZE_MAXHIDE	Popup windows receive this when some other window is maximized.
SIZE_MAXIMIZED	Window maximized.
SIZE_MAXSHOW	Popup windows receive this when some other window has been restored.
SIZE_MINIMIZED	Window minimized.
SIZE_RESTORED	Window resized, but not maximized nor minimized.
cx	Unused.
cy	Unused.
Returns	Nothing is returned.

OnUpdateFrameMenu

■ 2.0 ■ 3.0 ■ UD

Description	This member is used to change the appearance of the frame menu before it is displayed to the user. The default implementation is to display the current document menu for this child window or the frame default menu if no document menu is found.
Syntax	public, virtual void OnUpdateFrameMenu(BOOL bActive, CWnd* pActivateWnd, HMENU hMenuAlt);
Parameters	
bActive	If TRUE and no menu specified by *hMenuAlt*, then the currently active document menu is used.
pActivateWnd	A pointer to the active window. If *bActive* is TRUE and no alternate menu is selected, then *pActivateWnd* should be **this**.
hMenuAlt	Handle to the frame menu.
Returns	Nothing is returned.

OnUpdateFrameTitle

■ 2.0 ■ 3.0 ■ UD

Description This member is called to update the title bar of the MDI child window. This function will only work for windows that have the FWS_ADDTOTITLE style set. The default implementation is to allow the parent MDI frame to set the title, then to append the child window number.

Syntax protected, virtual void OnUpdateFrameTitle(BOOL bAddToTitle);

Parameters

bAddToTitle TRUE will add the active document title to the current frame title. FALSE will use only the current frame title.

Returns Nothing is returned.

See Also CFrameWnd:: OnUpdateFrameTitle()

OnWindowPosChanging

■ 2.0 ■ 3.0 ■ UD

Description This member is invoked when the size, position, or Z-order of a child window is about to change. This allows the child window to adjust to the new MDI client area.

Syntax protected, afx_msg void
OnWindowPosChanging(LPWINDOWPOS lpWndPos);

Parameters

lpWndPos A pointer to a WINDOWPOS structure.

Returns Nothing is returned.

PreCreateWindow

■ 2.0 ■ 3.0 ■ UD

Description This member is called before the creation of a child window. Window attributes such as size, position, and style bits may be set at this time.

Syntax public, virtual BOOL PreCreateWindow(CREATESTRUCT& cs);

Parameters

cs A reference to a CREATESTRUCT that can be filled in with specific window attributes.

Returns TRUE.

See Also CWnd::PreCreateWindow()

Example The following example shows how you can manipulate the initial window size using this member.

```
BOOL CSampChildFrame::PreCreateWindow(CREATESTRUCT& cs)
{
      cs.cx = 200;    // window width always 200
      cs.cy = 100;    // window width always 100
      return CMDIChildWnd::PreCreateWindow(cs);
}
```

PreTranslateMessage

■ 2.0 ■ 3.0 ■ UD

Description This member is used to intercept messages before they are dispatched. The default implementation attempts to translate the message using the accelerators for the parent frame's menu.

Syntax public, virtual BOOL PreTranslateMessage(MSG* pMsg);

Parameters

pMsg The message to be pre-translated.

Returns Non-zero if the message was translated and should not be dispatched; otherwise 0 will allow the message to be dispatched.

UpdateClientEdge

■ 2.0 ■ 3.0 ■ UD

Description This member is used to adjust the window's client edge. This member is called as a maximize or a restore occurs.

Syntax protected, BOOL UpdateClientEdge(LPRECT lpRect = NULL);

Parameters

lpRect A pointer to the rectangle that will contain the new client area.

Returns TRUE if the client edge was adjusted; otherwise FALSE.

The CMiniFrameWnd Class

The CMiniFrameWnd class is a half-height frame window that is commonly used to contain floating control bars. The mini frame behaves much like the base frame class with only a couple of exceptions. It does not have minimize and maximize buttons in the non-client area and you only have to single-click on the system menu to dismiss the frame window.

CMiniFrameWnd

■ 2.0 ■ 3.0

Description This member constructs the mini frame window. It creates the bitmap used for the dismissal menu and also the small font used for the frame text.

Syntax public, CMiniFrameWnd();

Parameters None.

Returns Nothing is returned.

~CMiniFrameWnd

■ 2.0 ■ 3.0 ■ UD

Description This member destructs the CMiniFrameWnd object and calls DestroyWindow to remove the attached CWnd.

Syntax public, ~CMiniFrameWnd();

Parameters None.

Returns Nothing is returned.

CalcBorders

■ 2.0 ■ 3.0 ■ UD

Description This static member is called to determine the client rectangle using the given window styles. This member is used in determining the size of the display rectangle when dragging the mini frame window.

Syntax public, static void CalcBorders(LPRECT lpClientRect, DWORD dwStyle = WS_THICKFRAME | WS_CAPTION, DWORD dwExStyle = 0);

Parameters

lpClientRect Filled with the calculated window rectangle.

dwStyle The desired window styles used in calculating the border dimensions.

dwExStyle Extended window styles.

Returns Nothing is returned.

CalcWindowRect

■ 2.0 ■ 3.0 ■ UD

Description This member is called to determine the smallest rect necessary to enclose the CMiniFrameWnd window that has the given size for its client area.

Syntax public, virtual void CalcWindowRect(LPRECT lpClientRect,UINT nAdjustType = adjustBorder);

Parameters

lpClientRect Contains the client rectangle size and is filled with the calculated window rectangle.

nAdjustType Used for OLE in-place editing. It can be one of the following values:

CWnd::adjustBorder Do not include scrollbar sizes in calculation.

CWnd::adjustOutside Include scrollbar sizes in calculation.

Returns Nothing is returned.

Create

■ 2.0 ■ 3.0

Description This member is called after construction to create the actual mini frame window and attach it to this object.

Syntax public, BOOL Create(LPCTSTR lpszClassName, LPCTSTR lpszWindowName, DWORD dwStyle, const RECT & rect, CWnd * pParentWnd = NULL, UINT nID = 0);

Parameters

lpszClassName Specifies the Windows class (or NULL to use default window class).

lpszWindowName A NULL-terminated string that contains the title bar text.

dwStyle The window style attributes for the frame window. See CWnd::Create. It may also include the following styles:

MFS_4THICKFRAME The mini frame window cannot be resized.

MFS_ MOVEFRAME The mini frame window can be moved by clicking on any edge of the window and dragging.

MFS_SYNCACTIVE Synchronize the activation of the mini frame to the activation of its parent window.

MFS_THICKFRAME Allows resizing of the mini frame window.

rect The size and position of the new mini frame window.

pParentWnd The parent window of the frame.

nID The child ID of the mini frame window (if created as a child window); otherwise 0.

Returns Non-zero if the function is successful; zero otherwise

See Also CWnd::Create()

CreateEx

■ 4.0 ■ UD

Description This member is called after construction to create the actual mini frame window and attach it to this object. This version of the member allows the extended window styles attributes to be set.

Syntax public, BOOL Create(DWORD dwExStyle, LPCTSTR lpszClassName, LPCTSTR lpszWindowName, DWORD dwStyle, const RECT & rect, CWnd * pParentWnd = NULL , UINT nID = 0);

Parameters

dwExStyle The extended window style attributes for the frame window. See WINAPI reference for a list of WS_EX_ extended style attributes.

lpszClassName Specifies the Windows class (or NULL to use default window class).

lpszWindowName A null-terminated string that contains the title bar text.

dwStyle The window style attributes for the frame window. See CWnd::Create. It may also include the following styles:

MFS_4THICKFRAME The mini frame window cannot be resized.

MFS_ MOVEFRAME The mini frame window can be moved by clicking on any edge of the window and dragging.

MFS_SYNCACTIVE Synchronize the activation of the mini frame to the activation of its parent window.

MFS_THICKFRAME Allows resizing of the mini frame window.

rect The size and position of the new mini frame window.

pParentWnd The parent window of the frame.

nId The child ID of the mini frame window (if created as a child window); otherwise 0.

Returns Non-zero if the function is successful; zero otherwise

See Also CMiniFrameWnd::Create

INITIALIZE

■ 4.0 ■ UD

Description This static member is used for backward compatibility in setting the mini frame window's menu and small caption font. This member is called by the framework whenever a new mini frame window is constructed but only initializes these settings once.

Syntax public, static void AFX_CDECL Initialize();

Parameters None.

Returns Nothing is returned.

INVERTSYSMENU

■ 2.0 ■ 3.0 ■ UD

Description This member inverts the colors of the mini frame window's system menu. This is usually done in response to the user pressing the left mouse button on top of the system menu.

Syntax protected, void InvertSysMenu();

Parameters None.

Returns Nothing is returned.

ONFLOATSTATUS

■ 2.0 ■ 3.0 ■ UD

Description This member is called to set the status of the mini frame window to displayed, hidden, activated, or deactivated. This message is generated from the top-level frame windows that need their child window to reflect a new status.

Syntax public, afx_msg LRESULT OnFloatStatus(WPARAM wParam, LPARAM lParam);

Parameters

wParam Contains the new status. It can be any of the following:

FS_SHOW, FS_HIDE, FS_ACTIVATE, FS_DEACTIVATE,FS_ENABLE, FS_DISABLE, FS_SYNCACTIVE

lParam Unused.

Returns Returns a 1 if both *wParam* contains FS_SYNCACTIVE and the mini frame window has the MFS_SYNCACTIVE style flag set; otherwise this member returns 0 .

OnGetMinMaxInfo

■ 2.0 ■ 3.0 ■ UD

Description This member is used to determine the mini frame window's maximum size, maximized position, minimum tracking width and height, and maximum tracking width and height.

Syntax public, afx_msg void OnGetMinMaxInfo(MINMAXINFO* pMMI);

Parameters

pMMI A pointer to a MINMAXINFO object that holds the computed dimensions.

Returns Nothing is returned.

See Also CWnd::OnGetMinMaxInfo()

OnGetText

■ 2.0 ■ 3.0 ■ UD

Description This member is invoked when the caption text is requested.

Syntax public, afx_msg LRESULT OnGetText(WPARAM wParam, LPARAM lParam);

Parameters

wParam The maximum storage space (bytes) for the destination string specified by *lParam*.

lParam An LPCSTR that contains the destination storage for the mini frame window caption.

Returns The number of bytes copied into the string storage specified by *lParam*.

OnGetTextLength

■ 2.0 ■ 3.0 ■ UD

Description This member returns the length (in bytes) of the mini frame window's caption text.

Syntax public, afx_msg LRESULT OnGetTextLength(WPARAM wParam, LPARAM lParam);

Parameters

wParam Unused.

lParam Unused.

Returns The number of bytes needed to store the mini frame window's caption text.

OnLButtonUp

■ 2.0 ■ 3.0 ■ UD

Description This member is invoked when the left mouse button is released within the mini frame window. The mini frame tests the message to see if the system menu was hit and closes the window if necessary.

Syntax public, afx_msg void OnLButtonUp(UINT nFlags, CPoint pt);

Parameters

nFlags Contains virtual key codes. (Unused.)

pt Specifies the mouse coordinates relative to the upper left corner of the mini frame window.

Returns Nothing is returned.

OnMacintosh

■ 2.0 ■ 3.0 ■ UD ■ MO

Description This Macintosh-only member is used for Macintosh-specific messaging. The mini frame window uses this member to add any owner window's menu to the mini frame.

Syntax public, afx_msg LRESULT OnMacintosh(WPARAM wParam, LPARAM lParam);

Parameters

wParam Message-specific information.

lParam Message-specific information.

Returns Non-zero to continue processing the message or 0 if the message was handled.

OnMouseMove

■ 2.0 ■ 3.0 ■ UD

Description This member is invoked whenever the cursor moves within the mini frame window. The mini frame tracks the mouse movement to determine when the mini frame system menu needs to be tracked.

Syntax public, afx_msg void OnMouseMove(UINT nFlags, CPoint pt);

Parameters

nFlags Contains virtual key codes. (Unused.)

pt Specifies the mouse coordinates relative to the upper left corner of the mini frame window.

Returns Nothing is returned.

OnNcActivate

■ 2.0 ■ 3.0 ■ UD

Description This member is invoked when the non-client area of the mini frame needs to be redrawn to indicate a change in the active state.

Syntax public, afx_msg BOOL OnNcActivate(BOOL bActive);

Parameters

bActive If TRUE, then the frame is to be redrawn active; otherwise the frame should be inactive.

Returns Non-zero if default processing should continue. FALSE to prevent deactivation.

OnNcCalcSize

■ 2.0 ■ 3.0 ■ UD

Description This member is invoked when the size of the client area in the mini frame window needs to be recalculated.

Syntax public, afx_msg void OnNcCalcSize(BOOL bCalcValidRects, NCCALC-SIZE_PARAMS* lpParams);

Parameters

bCalcValidRects Unused.

lpParams A pointer to an NCCALCSIZE_PARAMS structure that contains useful sizing information about the windows scrollbars, borders, etc.

Returns Nothing is returned.

See Also CWnd::OnNcCalcSize()

OnNcCreate

■ 2.0 ■ 3.0 ■ UD

Description This member is called prior to window creation. This allows the mini frame window to control the creation of the non-client area and to set the proper window style flags.

Syntax public, afx_msg BOOL OnNcCreate(LPCREATESTRUCT lpCreateStruct);

Parameters

lpCreateStruct A pointer to a CREATESTRUCT.

Returns TRUE to continue processing; otherwise FALSE.

OnNcHitTest

■ 2.0 ■ 3.0 ■ UD

Description Whenever the mini frame window has been captured, this member is called to determine if a window object has been hit.

Syntax public, afx_msg UINT OnNcHitTest(CPoint point);

Parameters

point Screen coordinates of the current cursor position.

Returns A windows hit test enumeration type. See CWnd::OnNcHitText()

OnNcLButtonDown

■ 2.0 ■ 3.0 ■ UD

Description Whenever the user presses the left mouse button in the non-client area of the mini frame, this member is invoked. If the mini frame system menu is hit, then the system menu is inverted. Otherwise, processing is passed to the base class CFrameWnd::OnNcLButtonDown member.

Syntax public, afx_msg void OnNcLButtonDown(UINT nHitTest, CPoint pt);

Parameters

nHitTest A hit test code.

pt Screen coordinates of the current cursor position.

Returns Nothing is returned.

OnNcPaint ■ 2.0 ■ 3.0 ■ UD

Description This member is invoked whenever the non-client area of the mini frame window needs to be repainted.

Syntax public, afx_msg void OnNcPaint();

Parameters None.

Returns Nothing is returned.

OnQueryCenterWnd ■ 2.0 ■ 3.0 ■ UD

Description This member is called to determine which window to center against. If the mini frame window receives this request, it passes control to its parent window (which means you cannot center against a mini frame window).

Syntax public, afx_msg LRESULT OnQueryCenterWnd(WPARAM wParam, LPARAM lParam);

Parameters

wParam Unused.

lParam Unused.

Returns An HWND that is used to center against.

See Also CWnd::CenterWindow()

OnSetText ■ 2.0 ■ 3.0 ■ UD

Description This member is invoked to set and display the mini frame window caption text. This member can only be called by using ::SendMessage with WM_SETTEXT.

Syntax public, afx_msg LRESULT OnSetText(WPARAM wParam, LPARAM lParam);

Parameters

wParam Unused.

lParam An LPCSTR containing the new mini frame caption text.

Returns An LRESULT specifying TRUE if successfully completed; otherwise FALSE if an exception occurred.

OnSysCommand

■ 2.0 ■ 3.0 ■ UD

Description This member is called whenever an option is selected from the mini frame window control menu.

Syntax public, afx_msg void OnSysCommand(UINT nID, LPARAM lParam);

nID The system command selected. See CWnd::OnSysCommand().

lParam If the item was selected with the mouse, then LOWORD = x-coord, HIWORD = y-coord; otherwise not used.

Returns Nothing is returned.

See Also CWnd::OnSysCommand()

PreCreateWindow

■ 2.0 ■ 3.0 ■ UD

Description This member is called before the creation of the mini frame window. Window attributes such as size, position, and style bits may be set at this time.

Syntax protected, virtual BOOL PreCreateWindow(CREATESTRUCT& cs);

Parameters

cs A reference to a CREATESTRUCT that can be filled in with specific window attributes.

Returns TRUE.

See Also CWnd::PreCreateWindow

8

DIALOG BOXES

8

DIALOG BOXES

MFC provides several classes that support the display and manipulation of generic dialog boxes as well as the Windows common dialogs. The common dialogs are a group of dialogs supplied with Windows that provide often-used functionality, such as the *file open dialog,* the *color dialog,* and the *font dialog*. Providing these dialogs with Windows not only allows developers to use them without having to code them themselves, but also ensures a common interface to these features across applications.

MFC also provides classes that support the increasingly popular "tabbed" dialogs. A tabbed dialog is a dialog with multiple "tabs," or pages, each of which contains a group of controls. Typically, each tab represents a particular category of information. Having one dialog with multiple tabs that the user can choose from avoids the multi-level nested dialogs found in many applications. MFC, by the way, calls the tabbed dialog a "property sheet" and the tabs themselves "property pages". Beginning with MFC 4.0, the classes provided by MFC to implement property sheets and pages are simply wrappers around functionality provided by Windows 95, Windows NT 3.51, and Win32s 1.3. Before MFC version 4.0, MFC's implementation of tabbed dialogs was completely separate from the implementation in Windows 95. The MFC development team could not wait for Windows 95 to be released and therefore wrote their own. MFC 4.0 also provides an encapsulation of the "wizard" functionality provided by Windows 95, NT 3.51, and Win32s 1.3. Wizards are actually implemented as tabbed dialogs without drawing the tabs.

In addition to providing basic dialog functionality, MFC also includes a dialog data transfer and validation architecture called Dialog Data Exchange (DDX) and Validation (DDV). This architecture provides for the transfer of data between member variables and dialog controls as well as basic validation of that data. If the validation provided with MFC is not sufficient, advanced users can add their own custom transfer and validation routines. For more information on DDX and DDV, see Microsoft Technical Note 26.

All sample listings in this chapter can be found in the DlgSmpl sample program on the CD-ROM included with this book. DlgSmpl shows how to create and perform basic manipulations on the CDialog, CPropertySheet, and CPropertyPage objects as well as displaying each of the common dialogs.

The classes covered in this chapter are listed below in Table 8-1. The declarations of all of the functions contained in this chapter can be found in the MFC header files *afxwin.h* and *afxdlgs.h*.

Table 8-1 Chapter 8 class summary

Class Name	Description
CDialog	Encapsulates the Windows dialog object for displaying modal and modeless dialogs.
CPropertySheet	Together with the CPropertyPage object, implements "tabbed" dialogs.
CPropertyPage	Together with the CPropertySheet object, implements "tabbed" dialogs. Represents a "page" or set of items associated with a tab in a tabbed dialog.
CDataExchange	Aids in exchange of data between a dialog and object member variables.
CCommonDialog	Base class for individual common dialog classes.
CFileDialog	Encapsulates the Windows file open/save common dialog.
CColorDialog	Encapsulates the Windows color common dialog.
CFontDialog	Encapsulates the Windows font common dialog.
CPageSetupDialog	Encapsulates the Windows page setup common dialog (MFC 4.0+).
CPrintDialog	Encapsulates the Windows print common dialog.
CFindReplaceDialog	Encapsulates the Windows find/replace common dialog.

The CDialog Class

The CDialog class encapsulates the basic Windows dialog box. It is rarely used directly, but rather as a base class for other, more specific application-defined dialog classes. Visual C++'s ClassWizard will automatically create these dialog classes based on a selected dialog resource template.

Many of the Windows functions that one might associate with dialogs are not part of the CDialog object but are found in the CWnd class instead. This is actually a very revealing fact as it exposes the way in which these "dialog" functions really work. As an example, let's consider the Windows SDK function GetDlgItem. The usual use of this function is to retrieve the window handle (or, in MFC, a pointer to the CWnd object) associated with a specified dialog control. However, it can actually be used to retrieve any child window by its ID. The moral of this story is that most of the functions usually associated with the interaction of a dialog and its controls are really applicable to any window and its child windows.

CDialog ■ 2.0 ■ 3.0

Description The CDialog constructor comes in three different forms. The first form takes no parameters and should be used only to construct a dialog object that will be displayed as modeless. The other two forms are used to construct dialogs for modal display and differ only in the manner in which they accept the name of the dialog's resource template—one takes this parameter as an unsigned integer and the other takes it as a character string. Using the unsigned integer form is akin to using the MAKEINTRESOURCE macro in the Windows SDK.

Syntax public, CDialog(); public, CDialog(LPCSTR lpszTemplateName, CWnd* pParentWnd = NULL); public, CDialog(UINT nIDTemplate, CWnd *pParentWnd = NULL);

Parameters

lpszTemplateName Resource string of the dialog's resource template.

nIDTemplate Resource ID of the dialog's resource template.

pParentWnd Pointer to the window which will be used as the parent of the dialog. May be NULL or omitted, in which case the parent will be the application's main window.

Returns Nothing is returned.

See Also CDialog::~CDialog

~CDialog

■ 2.0 ■ 3.0

Description The CDialog destructor is called when a dialog object is destroyed. If the dialog's associated window has not been destroyed, the destructor will destroy it. If this occurs, MFC will output a warning (in debug mode only) explaining that the OnDestroy and PostNCDestroy member functions in the derived class will not be called. If you are using these functions in your CDialog-derived class, you should destroy the window yourself prior to destroying the CDialog object.

Syntax public, ~CDialog();

Parameters None.

Returns Nothing is returned.

See Also CDialog::CDialog

AssertValid

■ 2.0 ■ 3.0 ■ DO

Description The AssertValid function is a debug-only function that throws an assertion if the dialog object is considered "invalid." The dialog object is invalid if its associated window handle is not a valid window or if the dialog object cannot be found in MFC's permanent or temporary window mapping lists (these lists map window handles to MFC window objects). All of this validation is performed in the CWnd implementation of AssertValid. The CDialog implementation merely calls the CWnd implementation.

Syntax public, virtual void AssertValid() const;

Parameters None.

Returns Nothing is returned.

See Also CWnd::AssertValid, CDialog::Dump

Example

```
void CMyWnd::SomeFunc(CDialog *pDlg)
{
      pDlg->AssertValid(); // make sure passed dialog is valid
      .. // now we can safely use it
```

CheckAutoCenter ■ 2.0 ■ 3.0 ■ UD

Description This function is used by the framework to determine if the dialog should be centered on its parent window. The dialog is centered if it is a Windows common dialog or as long as the dialog's template does not include the DS_ABSALIGN style. Note that this function was not virtual before MFC version 4.0.

Syntax public, virtual BOOL CheckAutoCenter();

Parameters None.

Returns TRUE if the dialog should be centered on its parent; FALSE otherwise.

See Also CWnd::CenterWindow

Create ■ 2.0 ■ 3.0

Description The Create member function is used to display a modeless dialog. Note that in MFC, you do not have to worry about routing messages to a modeless dialog with IsDialogMessage—MFC automatically takes care of this for you. Although this function does some validity checking and setup, it is basically a wrapper around the CreateDialog SDK function.

Syntax public, BOOL Create(LPCTSTR lpszTemplateName, CWnd *pParentWnd = NULL);
public, BOOL Create(UINT nIDTemplate, CWnd *pParentWnd = NULL);

Parameters

lpszTemplateName Resource string of the dialog's resource template.

pParentWnd Pointer to the window which will be used as the parent of the dialog. May be NULL or omitted, in which case the parent will be the application's main window.

nIDTemplate Resource ID of the dialog's resource template.

Returns Non-zero if successful; zero otherwise.

See Also CDialog::CreateIndirect, CDialog::DoModal

Example

```
void CDlgSmplView::OnDialogsModelessdialog()
{
      // re-create dialog object each time we need to display it
      // MFC needs the object to be re-initialized each time
      m_pDialog = new CTestDlg(this,FALSE);
```

```
        m_pDialog->Create(IDD_TESTDIALOG,this);
}

// delete dialog object automatically when dialog window destroyed
void CTestDlg::OnDestroy()
{
        CDialog::OnDestroy();

        if (!m_bModal)
                delete this;
}
```

CreateIndirect

■ 2.0 ■ 3.0

Description The CreateIndirect member function is used to display a modeless dialog from a dialog template that has been loaded in memory in the form of a DialogBoxHeader structure. Note that in an MFC application, you do not have to worry about routing messages to a modeless dialog with IsDialogMessage—MFC automatically takes care of this for you.

Syntax public, BOOL CreateIndirect(const void* lpDialogTemplate, CWnd *pParentWnd = NULL);

Parameters

lpDialogTemplate A pointer to a DialogBoxHeader structure.

pParentWnd Pointer to the window that will be used as the parent of the dialog. May be NULL or omitted, in which case the parent will be the application's main window.

Returns Non-zero if successful; zero otherwise.

See Also CDialog::InitModalIndirect, CDialog::Create, CDialog::DoModal

DoModal

■ 2.0 ■ 3.0

Description Call the DoModal member function to display a dialog in modal form.

Syntax public, virtual int DoModal();

Parameters None.

Returns -1 if the dialog window could not be created; IDABORT if some other error occurs, or the value passed to EndDialog if successful. The value passed to EndDialog is most often IDCANCEL if the cancel button is pressed, or IDOK if the OK button is pressed.

See Also CDialog::Create, CDialog::CreateIndirect, CDialog::InitModalIndirect

Example

```
// displaying a modal dialog is as simple as creating the object
// and calling DoModal
void CDlgSmplView::OnDialogsModaldialog()
{
        CTestDlg dlg(this);
        dlg.DoModal();
}
```

DUMP

■ 2.0 ■ 3.0 ■ DO

Description The Dump function is a debug-only function that "dumps" various state information regarding the dialog object to a specified dump context.

Syntax public, virtual void Dump(CDumpContext& dc) const;

Parameters

dc A reference to the dump context to which the output should be sent. Usually this will be afxDump, which is a default dump context created by MFC. When debugging an MFC application, output sent to afxDump will appear in the debugger.

Returns Nothing is returned.

See Also CDialog::AssertValid

Example Example output from the Dump function.

```
// call to Dump
void CTestDlg::OnDump()
{
      // dump dialog data to debug context
      Dump(afxDump);
}

// output from Dump function
a CDialog at $12FB58

m_hWnd = 0x402C8 (permanent window)
caption = "Currency"
class name = "#32770"
rect = (L 282, T 272, R 742, B 496)
parent CWnd* = $5C1470
style = $94C800C0
m_lpDialogTemplate = 164
m_hDialogTemplate = 0x0
m_pParentWnd = $5C1470
m_nIDHelp = 0xA4
```

ENDDIALOG

■ 2.0 ■ 3.0

Description The EndDialog function is called to destroy a modal dialog. EndDialog will not destroy the dialog immediately but rather sets a flag to destroy it after the current message handler is complete. Delaying the destruction of the dialog in this manner allows the EndDialog function to be called at any point in any message handler. Note that EndDialog does not delete the CDialog object—it simply destroys the window associated with it. You will not usually need to explicitly call EndDialog to destroy a modal dialog—the default implementations of CDialog::OnOK and CDialog::OnCancel both call it.

Syntax public, void EndDialog(int nResult);

Parameters

nResult — An integer which will be returned by the DoModal function that was called to display the dialog.

Returns — Nothing is returned.

See Also — CDialog::DoModal, CDialog::OnOK, CDialog::OnCancel

Example

```
void CMyDlg::OnPerformOperation()
{ // handler which will perform a specified operation and then
  // dismiss the dialog

     DoStuff();
     EndDialog(TRUE);
}
```

GetDefID

■ 2.0 ■ 3.0

Description — The GetDefID member function is used to retrieve the ID of the current default push-button on the dialog.

Syntax — public, DWORD GetDefID() const;

Parameters — None.

Returns — 0 if no default button exists; otherwise the high word is DC_HASDEFID and the low word is the id of the default push-button.

See Also — CDialog::SetDefID

Example

```
// this handler will toggle the default button between the OK
// button and the Cancel button
void CMyDlg::OnToggleDefaultButton()
{
     if (GetDefID() == IDOK)
          SetDefID(IDCANCEL);
     else if (GetDefID() == IDCANCEL)
          SetDefID(IDOK);
}
```

GotoDlgCtrl

■ 2.0 ■ 3.0

Description — The GotoDlgCtrl function moves the focus to the specified control in the dialog. This is often used to set focus to a particular control when validation of the data in that control fails. It can also be useful for forcing the focus to a particular control depending on the user's actions when the default tab order is not sufficient.

Syntax — public, void GotoDlgCtrl(CWnd* pWndCtrl);

Parameters

pWndCtrl — Pointer to the control that should receive the input focus. The debug version of MFC will assert if the control is invalid.

Returns Nothing is returned.

See Also CDialog::NextDlgCtrl, CDialog::PrevDlgCtrl

Example

```
// constant definitions in header file
const int MoveCtrl_Prev = -1;
const int MoveCtrl_Next = -2;

// implementation
void CMyDialog::MoveFocus(int nCtrl)
{
     if (nCtrl == MoveCtrl_Prev)
          PrevDlgCtrl();
     else if (nCtrl == MoveCtrl_Next)
          NextDlgCtrl();
     else
     {
          CWnd *pWnd = GetDlgItem(nCtrl);
          if (pWnd)
               GotoDlgCtrl(pWnd);
     }
}
```

HandleInitDialog

–. ■ 4.0

Description Handler function for the WM_INITDIALOG message. HandleInitDialog first calls CDialog::PreInitDialog, then performs some OLE control initialization, then calls the default dialog procedure (which in turn ends up calling CDialog::OnInitDialog), and finally performs additional OLE control initialization.

Syntax protected, afx_msg LRESULT HandleInitDialog(WPARAM wParam, LPARAM lParam);

Parameters

wParam Contains the window handle of the control that will, by default, receive the input focus when the dialog is first displayed.

lParam A long data value that was passed to the dialog by a call to CreateDialogIndirectParam, CreateDialogParam, DialogBoxIndirectParam, or DialogBoxParam.

Returns FALSE if the focus has been set to a particular child control; TRUE otherwise.

See Also CDialog::PreInitDialog, CDialog::OnInitDialog

HandleSetFont

–. ■ 4.0

Description Handler function for the WM_SETFONT message. HandleSetFont first calls CDialog::OnSetFont and then calls the default dialog procedure. The WM_SETFONT message is sent to a window whenever its font is changed.

Syntax protected, afx_msg LRESULT HandleSetFont(WPARAM wParam, LPARAM lParam);

Parameters

wParam Contains the font handle of the new font for the window.

lParam TRUE if the window should redraw; FALSE otherwise.

Returns The result of a call to the default dialog procedure.

See Also CDialog::OnSetFont

InitModalIndirect

■ 2.0 ■ 3.0

Description The InitModalIndirect member function is used to initialize a dialog object with a dialog template that has been loaded in memory in the form of a DialogBoxHeader structure. As its name implies, you should use this function only for a dialog you are going to display in modal form using the DoModal function. To display a modeless dialog from a pre-loaded template, use the CreateIndirect function. Note that the second form of InitModalIndirect did not appear in MFC until version 4.0.

Syntax public, BOOL InitModalIndirect(HGLOBAL hDialogTemplate, CWnd *pParentWnd = NULL);
public, BOOL InitModalIndirect(LPCDLGTEMPLATE lpDialogTemplate, CWnd* pParentWnd = NULL);

Parameters

hDialogTemplate Global memory handle of memory containing dialog template. This template is in the form of a DLGTEMPLATE structure followed by data for each control in the dialog box.

lpDialogTemplate A pointer to memory containing a dialog template. This template is in the form of a DLGTEMPLATE structure followed by data for each control in the dialog box.

pParentWnd A pointer to the dialog's parent window.

Returns Non-zero if successful; zero otherwise.

See Also CDialog::CreateIndirect, CDialog::Create, CDialog::DoModal

MapDialogRect

■ 2.0 ■ 3.0

Description The MapDialogRect member function is used to convert coordinates from dialog box units to screen units (or pixels). Dialog box units are calculated based on the average height and width of the font used to draw text in the dialog box. This function is useful when you must manually align a particular control in the dialog.

Syntax public, void MapDialogRect(LPRECT lpRect) const;

Parameters

lpRect — Pointer to a rectangle containing the coordinates to convert. The dialog unit coordinates will be replaced with screen coordinates.

Returns — Nothing is returned.

Example — The following example uses MapDialogRect to align headings above columns in a list box with tab-separated columns. The list box calculates tab spacing in dialog units, which necessitates a unit conversion.

```
BOOL CPage5::OnInitDialog()
{
	CPropertyPage::OnInitDialog();

	// set a tab at 200 "dialog units"
	int nTab = 80;
	m_ctPeople.SetTabStops(1,&nTab);

	CRect rect,rectPeople,rectDialogUnits(0,0,nTab,20);

	// get client rect of "people" list box so we have
	// coordinate of left side of box
	m_ctPeople.GetWindowRect(rectPeople);
	ScreenToClient(rectPeople);

	// convert nTab dialog units to pixels using MapDialogRect
	// (don't care about other coordinates)
	MapDialogRect(rectDialogUnits);

	// move text header to correct location
	m_ctNumberText.GetWindowRect(rect);
	ScreenToClient(rect);
	rect.right = rect.right - rect.left + rectPeople.left +
		rectDialogUnits.right + 2;
	rect.left = rectPeople.left + rectDialogUnits.right + 2;
	m_ctNumberText.MoveWindow(rect);

	// add some choices
	m_ctPeople.AddString("Joe Smith\t555-4378");
	m_ctPeople.AddString("Jane Doe\t555-9883");
	m_ctPeople.AddString("Beth Jones\t555-8834");

	return TRUE;
}
```

NextDlgCtrl

■ 2.0 ■ 3.0

Description — The NextDlgCtrl function moves the focus to the next control in the dialog as determined by the tab order specified in the dialog template. If the focus is on the last control, the focus is moved to the first control in the dialog. Note that you would rarely need to use this function since Windows takes care of moving the focus when the user presses the tab key.

Syntax — public, void NextDlgCtrl() const;

Parameters — None.

Returns Nothing is returned.

See Also CDialog::PrevDlgCtrl, CDialog::GotoDlgCtrl

Example

```
// constant definitions in header file
const int MoveCtrl_Prev = -1;
const int MoveCtrl_Next = -2;

// implementation
void CMyDialog::MoveFocus(int nCtrl)
{
	if (nCtrl == MoveCtrl_Prev)
		PrevDlgCtrl();
	else if (nCtrl == MoveCtrl_Next)
		NextDlgCtrl();
	else
	{
		CWnd *pWnd = GetDlgItem(nCtrl);
		if (pWnd)
			GotoDlgCtrl(pWnd);
	}
}
```

OnCancel ■ 2.0 ■ 3.0

Description The OnCancel function is called when the user presses the Cancel button (or whatever button's ID is IDCANCEL). The base class implementation of this function destroys the dialog window by calling EndDialog with a parameter of IDCANCEL. Note that OnCancel is meant to be used only for modal dialogs. If you place a Cancel button on a modeless dialog, make sure you override this function and call DestroyWindow from within it—do not call the base class implementation.

Syntax protected, virtual void OnCancel();

Parameters None.

Returns Nothing is returned.

See Also CDialog::OnOK, CDialog::EndDialog, CWnd::DestroyWindow

Example

```
void CMyDialog::OnCancel()
{
	// clean up since user does not want to save
	CleanUpSomeStuff();

	// call base class which will end the dialog
	CDialog::OnCancel();
}
```

OnCmdMsg ■ 2.0 ■ 3.0 ■ UD

Description This function is called by the framework to route command messages. The CDialog implementation first checks to see if the command will be handled by the dialog itself (by searching the dialog's message map). If a handler is not found, the command is sent to the dialog's owner window. Finally, if the owner does not handle the command, it is routed to the application.

Syntax public, virtual BOOL OnCmdMsg(UINT nID, int nCode, void* pExtra, AFX_CMDHANDLERINFO* pHandlerInfo);

Parameters

nID	Identifies the command message.
nCode	Identifies the command notification code.
pExtra	Used according to the value of nCode.
pHandlerInfo	If not NULL, OnCmdMsg fills in the pHandlerInfo structure with the pTarget and pmf members of the CMDHANDLERINFO structure instead of dispatching the command. Typically, this parameter should be NULL. MFC passes a non-NULL value for this parameter to determine if a command would be handled without actually executing the command. This, in turn, is used to implement the default user-interface updating features of MFC.

Returns TRUE if the command is handled; FALSE if not.

See Also CWnd::OnCmdMsg, CCmdTarget::OnCmdMsg

Example See example for CCmdTarget::OnCmdMsg in Chapter 4, *Windows Messaging.*

OnCommandHelp ■ 2.0 ■ 3.0 ■ UD

Description Message map function that responds to the help command message. MFC invokes the Windows help engine with a context ID equal to the dialog's help ID (assigned using the SetHelpID function) plus the value of the HID_BASE_RESOURCE constant. If the dialog's help ID is zero, then the function does nothing. For more information regarding context sensitive help, please see Chapter 2, *The MFC Framework.*

Syntax protected, afx_msg LRESULT OnCommandHelp(WPARAM wParam, LPARAM lParam);

Parameters

wParam	Not used.
lParam	According to Microsoft, "the currently available help context." Basically this represents the help context ID that will be used unless you change it. If 0, then no help context has been determined yet. The default CDialog implementation of this handler will not change the context ID if one has already been determined by the framework (lParam <> 0).

Returns TRUE if the help engine was invoked; FALSE otherwise.

See Also CDialog::SetHelpID, Technical Note 28

OnCtlColor

■ 2.0 ■ 3.0 ■ UD

Description OnCtlColor is the message handler for the WM_CTLCOLOR message. It processes the message by first sending the message directly to the child control to which it applies. If the child handles it, it returns the result from the child. If the child does not handle the message, OnCtlColor calls the GrayCtlColor CWnd member function to determine which color should be used for the control.

Syntax protected, afx_msg HBRUSH OnCtlColor(CDC* pDC, CWnd* pWnd, UINT nCtlColor)

Parameters

pDC A pointer to the display context for the control to which the message pertains.

pWnd A pointer to the control window requesting the color.

nCtlColor One of the following values, specifying the control whose color is to be affected:

CTLCOLOR_BTN Button control.

CTLCOLOR_DLG Dialog box.

CTLCOLOR_EDIT Edit control.

CTLCOLOR_LIST BOX List box control.

CTLCOLOR_MSGBOX Message box.

CTLCOLOR_SCROLLBAR Scrollbar control.

CTLCOLOR_STATIC Static control.

Returns A handle to the brush that should be used for the background of the control.

See Also CWnd::GrayCtlColor, CWnd::SendChildNotifyLastMsg

OnHelpHitTest

■ 2.0 ■ 3.0 ■ UD

Description This function is used to determine the help context ID that should be passed to the Windows help engine when the user clicks at a particular location in the dialog while in SHIFT-F1 help mode. The default implementation always returns the dialog's help ID plus the value of the HID_BASE_RESOURCE constant (as long as the help ID is not zero). In order to implement real SHIFT-F1 help, you must override this handler.

Syntax protected, afx_msg LRESULT OnHelpHitTest(WPARAM wParam, LPARAM lParam)

Parameters

wParam Not used.

lParam The LOWORD contains the x-coordinate where the user clicked the left mouse button and the HIWORD contains the y-coordinate. You can use these coordinates to determine what the user clicked on and therefore what he or she is requesting help on. For more information regarding context-sensitive help, see Chapter 2, *The MFC Framework*.

Returns The help context ID which should be passed to the Windows help engine.

See Also CDialog::OnCommandHelp, CDialog::SetHelpID, Technical Note 28

OnInitDialog

■ 2.0 ■ 3.0

Description Called in response to the WM_INITDIALOG message. OnInitDialog is what MFC calls a "special message map" function. It is special because it always exists, unlike most MFC functions that are called in response to a Windows message, which are only present if declared in a message map. If you override this function, you should always call the base class implementation before doing anything else. The base implementation, among other things, takes care of dialog data exchange to initialize the dialog's controls.

Syntax public, virtual BOOL OnInitDialog();

Parameters None.

Returns You should return a non-zero value unless you have specifically set the focus to a control in the dialog. If you return non-zero, Windows will set the focus to the first control in the dialog.

Example

```
// use OnInitDialog to initialize list controls with choices
BOOL CTestDlg::OnInitDialog()
{
      CDialog::OnInitDialog();

      // list choices for combo box
      m_ctComboBox.AddString("Overnight");
      m_ctComboBox.AddString("Week");
      m_ctComboBox.AddString("Month");
      m_ctComboBox.SetCurSel(0);

      // list choices for list box
      m_ctListBox.AddString("Book");
      m_ctListBox.AddString("Magazine");
      m_ctListBox.AddString("Pamphlet");
      m_ctListBox.AddString("Newsletter");
      m_ctListBox.SetCurSel(1);

      return TRUE;
}
```

OnOK

■ 2.0 ■ 3.0

Description Called when the user presses the OK button (or whatever button's ID is IDOK). The base class implementation of this function performs data validation and exchange and then destroys the dialog window by calling

EndDialog with a parameter of IDOK. If you override this function, make sure to call the base class implementation in order to perform these tasks. Note that OnOK is meant to be used only for modal dialogs. If you place an OK button on a modeless dialog, make sure you override this function and call DestroyWindow from within it—do not call the base class implementation.

Syntax protected, virtual void OnOK();

Parameters None.

Returns Nothing is returned.

See Also CDialog::OnCancel, CDialog::EndDialog, CWnd::DestroyWindow

Example

```
void CMyDialog::OnOK()
{
      // get value of some edit boxes now that dialog is over
      m_ctEdit1.GetWindowText(m_strVal1);
      m_ctEdit2.GetWindowText(m_strVal2);

      // call base class version which will end the dialog
      CDialog::OnOK();
}
```

OnSetFont

■ 2.0 ■ 3.0

Description Called when the font for the dialog box changes (usually by a call to SetFont). Override this function if you want to do something whenever this occurs. The base class implementation of OnSetFont does absolutely nothing.

Syntax public, virtual void OnSetFont(CFont* pFont);

Parameters

pFont Pointer to the new font that will be used to draw text in the dialog box.

Returns Nothing.

See Also CWnd::SetFont

OnSysColorChange

■ 2.0 ■ 3.0 ■ UD ■ MO

Description A Macintosh-only function that is used to specify a solid brush (avoiding dithering) that will be used to paint the background of dialogs. This function is a message map handler for the Windows message WM_SYSCOLORCHANGE, which is called whenever the user changes a system color.

Syntax protected, afx_msg void OnSysColorChange();

Parameters None.

Returns Nothing is returned.

PostModal

■ 2.0 ■ 3.0 ■ UD

Description Cleans up after a dialog is displayed modally. It re-enables the dialog's parent window and removes the hook function installed by the PreModal function.

Syntax public, void PostModal();

Parameters None.

Returns Nothing is returned.

See Also CDialog::PreModal, CDialog::DoModal

PreInitDialog

–. ■ 4.0 ■ UD

Description The CDialog version of PreInitDialog does absolutely nothing. Several CDialog-derived classes override this function (particularly, dialogs associated with OLE).

Syntax protected, virtual void PreInitDialog();

Parameters None.

Returns Nothing is returned.

See Also CDialog::PostModal, CDialog::DoModal

PreModal

■ 2.0 ■ 3.0 ■ UD

Description Performs initialization before a dialog is displayed in modal form. It first disables the dialog's parent window and then installs a Windows hook function in order to monitor events while the dialog is being created.

Syntax public, HWND PreModal();

Parameters None.

Returns Window handle of dialog's parent.

See Also CDialog::PostModal, CDialog::DoModal

PreTranslateMessage

■ 2.0 ■ 3.0 ■ UD

Description The PreTranslateMessage is called by MFC to translate messages prior to dispatching them. You would rarely want to call this function directly, although you can override it if you want to implement some type of custom translation. The CDialog implementation simply returns the result of a call to IsDialogMessage unless the message is a non-input message (not a keyboard or mouse message) or the program is in context-sensitive help (SHIFT-F1) mode, in which case it returns FALSE.

Syntax public, virtual BOOL PreTranslateMessage(MSG* pMsg);

Parameters

pMsg A pointer to the message which should be translated.

Returns TRUE if the message is processed; FALSE otherwise.

See Also CWnd::PreTranslateMessage

PrevDlgCtrl

■ 2.0 ■ 3.0

Description The PrevDlgCtrl function moves the focus to the previous control in the dialog as determined by the tab order specified in the dialog template. If the focus is on the first control, the focus is moved to the last control in the dialog. Note that you would rarely need to use this function since Windows takes care of moving the focus when the user presses the tab key.

Syntax public, void PrevDlgCtrl() const;

Parameters None.

Returns Nothing is returned.

See Also CDialog::NextDlgCtrl, CDialog::GotoDlgCtrl

Example

```
// constant definitions in header file
const int MoveCtrl_Prev = -1;
const int MoveCtrl_Next = -2;

// implementation
void CMyDialog::MoveFocus(int nCtrl)
{
      if (nCtrl == MoveCtrl_Prev)
            PrevDlgCtrl();
      else if (nCtrl == MoveCtrl_Next)
            NextDlgCtrl();
      else
      {
            CWnd *pWnd = GetDlgItem(nCtrl);
            if (pWnd)
                  GotoDlgCtrl(pWnd);
      }
}
```

SetDefID

■ 2.0 ■ 3.0

Description The SetDefID member function tells MFC which push-button on the dialog should be the default button.

Syntax public, void SetDefID(UINT nID);

Parameters

nID Resource ID of the push-button control that should be made the default button.

Returns Nothing is returned.

See Also CDialog::GetDefID

Example

```
// this handler will toggle the default button between the OK
// button and the Cancel button
void CMyDlg::OnToggleDefaultButton()
{
     if (GetDefID() == IDOK)
          SetDefID(IDCANCEL);
     else if (GetDefID() == IDCANCEL)
          SetDefID(IDOK);
}
```

SetHelpID

■ 2.0 ■ 3.0

Description The SetHelpID member function tells MFC what help content ID should be passed to the Windows help system when the user clicks the help button on the dialog or presses the F1 key while the dialog is displayed.

Syntax public, void SetHelpID(UINT nIDR);

Parameters

nIDR Help ID to associate with this dialog. This ID will be passed to the help engine if the user clicks the help button on the dialog or presses the F1 key.

Returns Nothing.

Example

```
BOOL CMyDialog::OnInitDialog()
{
     // set the help ID
     SetHelpID(ID_MYDIALOG_HELP);
     ..
```

The CPropertySheet Class

The CPropertySheet class is MFC's tabbed dialog. The "sheet" holds the "pages", or tabs, which are covered in the next section of this chapter. The CPropertySheet class is not actually derived from CDialog, although it behaves in an almost identical fashion. To create a modal property sheet, you call DoModal. To create a modeless property sheet, you call Create. For modal property sheets, MFC creates four buttons on the sheet: OK, Cancel, Apply Now, and Help. No buttons are created for a modeless property sheet. If you want to add your own buttons (something that must be done in the modeless case), you should override the OnCreate message handler for the sheet (make sure you call the base implementation before doing your own stuff).

Of course, once you have a sheet you have to add some pages to it. The page is represented by the CPropertyPage object (which is derived from CDialog). This object is described in detail in the section after this one. Take special note of the styles that must exist on the template for a property page. MFC will complain if these styles do not exist. Depending on what you are doing, you may want to add the property pages to the sheet from the constructor for the sheet or from the location in the code at which the sheet object was created. In either case, make sure you destroy the pages once the sheet is destroyed. This is not done automatically. Again, you can do this from the destructor for the sheet or from the location at which you destroy the sheet.

As noted in the beginning of this chapter, MFC's developers implemented tabbed dialogs before they were introduced as part of the Windows 95 operating system (and Windows NT 3.51 and Win32s 1.3). In MFC version 4.0, Microsoft changed MFC to use the operating system-provided tabbed dialogs. Before version 4.0, MFC provided a complete implementation of tabbed dialogs by itself. The tabbed dialog implementation was originally available only in 32-bit MFC (version 3.0) but was later ported back into the 16-bit version beginning with version 2.51.

CPropertySheet ■ 2.51 ■ 3.0

Description Constructor that comes in three flavors; the first takes no parameters. If you use this version, you must later call CPropertySheet::Construct before trying to use the sheet. The second version takes the caption text as a string resource ID, and the final version takes the caption text as an actual string. This constructor does nothing but initialize data members of the class. Note that the first form of the constructor was not introduced until MFC 4.0.

Syntax

```
public, CPropertySheet();
public, CPropertySheet(UINT nIDCaption, CWnd* pParentWnd = NULL,
                       UINT iSelectPage = 0);
public, CPropertySheet(LPCTSTR pszCaption, CWnd* pParentWnd =
                       NULL, UINT iSelectPage = 0);
```

Parameters

nIDCaption Resource string ID of caption text.

pszCaption NULL-terminated string to be used as caption text.

pParentWnd Pointer to the window to use as a parent for the sheet or NULL.

iSelectPage Index of the property page that should be originally selected when the sheet is displayed.

Returns Nothing is returned.

See Also CPropertySheet::~CPropertySheet

~CPropertySheet ■ 2.51 ■ 3.0

Description Destructor that simply deletes the font used for the sheet.

Syntax public, virtual ~CPropertySheet();

Parameters None.

Returns Nothing is returned.

See Also CPropertySheet::CPropertySheet

AddPage

■ 2.51 ■ 3.0

Description Adds the specified property page to the property sheet. Pages added to a property sheet are not automatically deleted by the sheet when the sheet is destroyed, so make sure you do this yourself.

Syntax public, void AddPage(CPropertyPage* pPage);

Parameters

pPage A pointer to the property page that should be added to the sheet.

Returns Nothing is returned.

See Also CPropertySheet::RemovePage

Example

```
CTestSheet::CTestSheet(UINT nIDCaption, CWnd* pParentWnd,
                      UINT iSelectPage, BOOL bModal)
      :CPropertySheet(nIDCaption, pParentWnd, iSelectPage)
{
      // add property pages - remove in destructor
      AddPages();
      m_bModal = bModal;
}

void CTestSheet::AddPages()
{
      // add pages - don't need to store pointers to them - the
      // CPropertySheet will do this for us
      AddPage(new CPage1);
      AddPage(new CPage2);
      AddPage(new CPage3);
      AddPage(new CPage4);
      AddPage(new CPage5);
}
```

AssertValid

■ 2.51 ■ 3.0 ■ DO

Description Diagnostic function used to test the validity of a CPropertySheet object. The CPropertySheet version of this function calls the base CWnd version, checks to make sure that the number of pages it has is equal to the number of tabs contained in its associated tab control (which displays the tabs along the top of the dialog), and finally checks the validity of two internal arrays—one containing the pages in the sheet, and the other containing the tabs displayed across the top of the sheet.

Syntax public, virtual void AssertValid() const;

Parameters None.

Returns Nothing is returned.

See Also CPropertySheet::Dump

Example

```
void CMyWnd::SomeFunct(CPropertySheet *pSheet)
{
      pSheet->AssertValid(); // make sure passed sheet is valid
      .. // now we can safely use it
```

BuildPropPageArray

–. ■ 4.0 ■ UD

Description Internal MFC function which is called by CPropertySheet::DoModal and CPropertySheet::Create to create the sheet's pages. BuildPropPageArray loads the templates for each of the pages and creates an array of pointers to them. It also performs some special processing for the Macintosh platform. One very interesting thing that this function does is assert if any of the page's resource templates are extended dialog templates. The Windows property sheet API does not currently support extended templates as pages. A template is "extended" if it does any of the following: 1) Uses any of the extended dialog styles, 2) Has a help ID associated with any control in the dialog, 3) Has any control with an ID that is a DWORD, or 4) Applies weight, italic, or character set attributes to the dialog's font.

Syntax public, virtual void BuildPropPageArray();

Parameters None.

Returns Nothing is returned.

See Also CPropertySheet::DoModal, CPropertySheet::Create

CommonConstruct

■ 2.51 ■ 3.0 ■ UD

Description A simple helper function used by MFC in order to avoid duplicating initialization code for the two constructors for CPropertySheet. As such, it is called by both versions of the CPropertySheet constructor.

Syntax protected, void CommonConstruct(CWnd *pParent, UINT iSelectPage);

Parameters

pParent A pointer to the parent window for the CPropertySheet.

iSelectPage The index of the page that should be the initially active page.

Returns Nothing is returned.

See Also CPropertySheet::CPropertySheet

Construct

–. ■ 4.0

Description Call this function in order to initialize a property sheet that was created with the no-parameter version of the constructor. Construct simply associates a given caption, parent window, and initially active page with the sheet.

Syntax public, void Construct(UINT nIDCaption,CWnd *pParent, UINT iSelectPage); public, void Construct(LPCTSTR pszCaption,CWnd *pParent, UINT iSelectPage);

Parameters

nIDCaption Resource string ID of caption text.

pszCaption	NULL-terminated string to be used as caption text.
pParent	Pointer to the window to use as a parent for the sheet or NULL.
iSelectPage	Index of the property page that should be originally selected when the sheet is displayed.
Returns	Nothing is returned.
See Also	CPropertySheet::CPropertySheet

ContinueModal

–. ■ 4.0

Description Internal MFC function that is called by CPropertySheet::DoModal to determine if the "modal" loop associated with a modal dialog should continue. The CPropertySheet version first calls the base CWnd version, which returns TRUE if the CWnd member variable m_nFlags contains the WF_CONTINUEMODAL flag or FALSE if it does not. (This flag is set and cleared in many places within MFC.) Next, ContinueModal checks to see if the active page pointer is NULL and, if it is, ends the modal loop by returning FALSE.

Syntax public, virtual BOOL ContinueModal();

Parameters None.

Returns TRUE if the modal loop should continue; FALSE otherwise.

See Also CPropertySheet::DoModal, CWnd::RunModalLoop, CWnd::ContinueModal

Create

■ 2.51 ■ 3.0

Description Creates the property sheet in modeless form. Use CPropertySheet::DoModal() to create a modal property sheet. The property sheet is not really a dialog, so MFC basically creates a popup window when you call this function.

Syntax public, BOOL Create(CWnd* pParent = NULL, DWORD dwStyle = WS_SYSMENU | WS_POPUP | WS_CAPTION | DS_MODALFRAME | WS_VISIBLE, DWORD dwExStyle = DS_EX_DLGMODALFRAME);

Parameters

pParent	Pointer to the window that should be used as the parent for the sheet.
dwStyle	Window styles for the sheet. See the Windows API for a list of window styles.
dwExStyle	Extended window styles for the sheet. See the Windows API documentation for a list of extended window styles.
Returns	TRUE if the window was created; FALSE otherwise.
See Also	CPropertySheet::DoModal, CWnd::CreateEx

Example

```
void CDlgSmplView::OnPropertysheetsModelesspropertysheet()
{
	// re-create sheet object each time we need to display sheet
	// MFC needs the object to be re-initialized each time
	m_pSheet =new CTestSheet(IDD_TESTSHEETCAPTION,this,0,FALSE);
	m_pSheet->Create(this);
}

// delete the sheet object automatically when sheet is destroyed
void CTestSheet::OnDestroy()
{
	CPropertySheet::OnDestroy();

	if (!m_bModal)
		delete this;
}
```

DoModal

■ 2.51 ■ 3.0

Description Displays the property sheet in modal form. Use CPropertySheet::Create to create a modeless property sheet. Since the property sheet is not actually a dialog, MFC fakes dialog behavior by disabling the parent of the sheet and then establishing its own message loop to handle the dialog messages (just like what happens for a real dialog). Just like a normal dialog, EndDialog should be called to terminate a modal property sheet.

Syntax public, virtual int DoModal();

Parameters None.

Returns IDOK if the user pressed the OK button to terminate the dialog; IDCANCEL if the user pressed the cancel button or 0 if a failure occurred while creating the dialog.

See Also CPropertySheet::EndDialog, CPropertySheet::Create

Example

```
// create a property sheet object
CMyPropSheet sheet(IDD_MYSHEET,AfxGetMainWnd());

// display modal sheet
sheet.DoModal();

..
```

Dump

■ 2.51 ■ 3.0 ■ DO

Description A diagnostic function that outputs the current state of a CPropertySheet object to the specified dump context. The CPropertySheet version outputs the caption of the sheet, the number of pages, the current page, and the base CWnd information.

Syntax public, virtual void Dump(CDumpContext& dc) const;

Parameters

dc — A reference to the dump context to which the status information should be sent. Usually this will be the MFC default debug dump context *afxDump*. *afxDump* sends its output to the debugger and only exists in the debug build of MFC.

Returns — Nothing is returned.

See Also — CPropertySheet::AssertValid

Example — The following is an example of the output of the Dump function:

```
// call to Dump function
void CPage1::OnDumpsheet()
{
        // retrieve parent window (which we know is a CPropertySheet
        // since we are a CPropertyPage
        // and dump contents of object to debug context
        CPropertySheet *pSheet = (CPropertySheet *)GetParent();
        pSheet->Dump(afxDump);
}

// output from Dump call
a CPropertySheet at $63FC0C

m_hWnd = 0x0m_strCaption = Test Property Sheet
Number of Pages = 0
m_nCurPage = 0
```

EnableStackedTabs

■ 2.51 ■ 3.0

Description — Call this function to enable or disable the display of "stacked tabs." When enabled, MFC will display multiple rows of tabs when all of the tabs cannot fit on a single row. When disabled, MFC will display the tabs in a single row and allow the user to scroll through the tabs. Figure 8-1 shows an example of a non-stacked property sheet and a stacked property sheet.

Syntax — public, void EnableStackedTabs(BOOL bStacked);

Parameters

bStacked — TRUE if the tabs should be stacked; FALSE otherwise.

Returns — Nothing is returned.

Example

```
void CMySheet::OnInitDialog()
{
        // make MFC use one row of tabs that scrolls if needed
        EnableStackedTabs(FALSE);
        .. // other initialization
```

EndDialog

■ 2.51 ■ 3.0

Description — Call this function in order to terminate a property sheet that was displayed in modal form using the DoModal() function. This function is

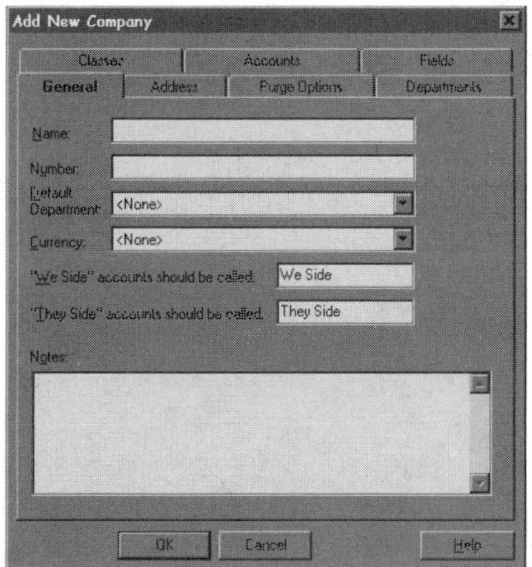

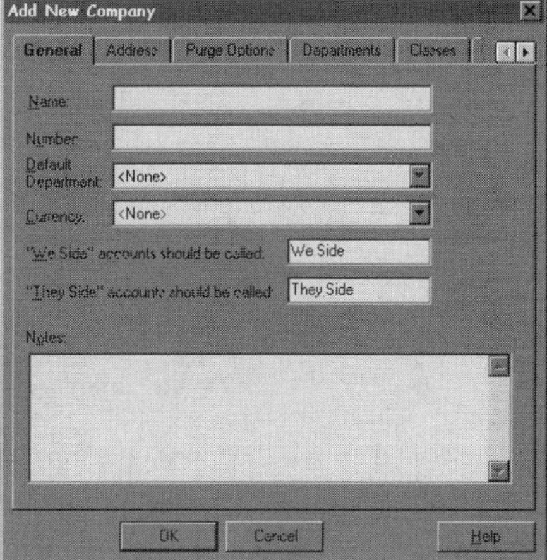

Figure 8-1 Stacked tabs vs. non-stacked tabs

called automatically by the default OnOK and OnCancel handlers. Because the CPropertySheet is really nothing but a popup window, EndDialog simply calls DestroyWindow to destroy the property sheet.

Syntax public, void EndDialog(int nEndID);

Parameters

nEndID The value that will be returned by the original call to DoModal.

Returns Nothing is returned.

See Also CPropertySheet::DoModal, CPropertySheet::OnOK, CPropertySheet::OnCancel

Example

```
void CMySheet::OnPerformOperation()
{ // handler which will perform a specified operation and then
  // dismiss the property sheet

     DoStuff();
     EndDialog(TRUE);
}
```

GetActiveIndex

–. ■ 4.0

Description Retrieves the index of the "active page." The active page is the page that is actually visible to the user.

Syntax protected, int GetActiveIndex() const;

Parameters None.

Returns The index of the currently active page.

See Also CPropertySheet::GetActivePage, CPropertySheet::GetPage, CPropertySheet::SetActivePage

Example

```
void CMySheet::UpdatePage()
{
      int nActivePage = GetActiveIndex();

      // if active page is 1 do something
      if (nActivePage == 1))
      {
            // do something to page
      }
      else if (nActivePage == 2)
      { // page 2 - do something different
            // do something to page
      }
}
```

GetActivePage

■ 2.51 ■ 3.0

Description Retrieves the "active page." The active page is the page that is actually visible to the user. Note that this function was not documented until MFC version 4.0.

Syntax protected, CPropertyPage *GetActivePage() const;

Parameters None.

Returns A pointer to the currently active page.

See Also CPropertySheet::GetActiveIndex, CPropertySheet::GetPage, CPropertySheet::SetActivePage

Example

```
void CMySheet::UpdatePage()
{
      CPropertyPage *pCurPage = GetActivePage();

      // determine type of current page
      if (pCurPage->IsKindOf(RUNTIME_CLASS(CMyPage1))
      {
            // do something to page
      }
      else
      { // page must be of type CMyPage2
            // do something to page
      }
}
```

GetPage

■ 2.51 ■ 3.0

Description Returns a pointer to a property page given the index of the page in the sheet. MFC does not validate the page index passed to it. The debug version will assert if the index is invalid due to an invalid array access.

Syntax public, CPropertyPage* GetPage(int nPage) const;

Parameters

nPage — The index of the page in the sheet. The index of a page is determined by when it was added by the AddPage function.

Returns — A pointer to the desired property page.

See Also — CPropertySheet::AddPage, CPropertySheet::RemovePage

Example

```
void CTestSheet::RemovePages()
{
     // remove however many pages there are in the sheet
     int nPageCount = GetPageCount();

     for (int nI = 0;nI < nPageCount;nI++)
          delete GetPage(nI);
}
```

GetPageCount

■ 2.51 ■ 3.0

Description — Returns the current number of pages in the sheet.

Syntax — public, int GetPageCount() const;

Parameters — None.

Returns — The number of pages in the sheet.

See Also — CPropertySheet::GetPage

Example — See CPropertySheet::GetPage

GetPageIndex

–. ■ 4.0

Description — Returns the index of a property page given a pointer to that page.

Syntax — public, int GetPageIndex(CPropertyPage *pPage) const;

Parameters

pPage — A pointer to the property page for which the index is desired.

Returns — The index of the page if found; otherwise -1.

See Also — CPropertySheet::GetPage, CPropertySheet::GetPageCount

Example

```
// set a particular page to active (the hard way)
void CMySheet::SetPageActive(CPropertyPage *pPage)
{
     int nPageIdx = GetPageIndex(pPage);
     SetActivePage(nPageIdx);
}
```

GotoControl

■ 2.51 ■ 3.0-3.2 ■ UD

Description — Used in conjunction with the FindNextControl function in order to implement the dialog control mnemonic keys. If the specified control is an enabled static text item, it skips ahead to the next control. This is the same behavior that one finds on a normal dialog. If the specified control (or the one skipped to) is a push button, MFC simulates a press of the button but does not give the button focus. By the way, it does this by literally highlighting the button, waiting a little bit, unhighlighting the button and then sending a BN_CLICKED message to simulate the button push. For all other control types, it sets the focus to the control. If the specified control is disabled, GotoControl searches for the next enabled control with the specified mnemonic. This function does not exist in MFC version 4.0 where the details of property sheet management are handled directly by the operating system.

Syntax protected, void GotoControl(HWND hWnd, TCHAR ch);

Parameters

hWnd The window handle of the control to go to.

ch The mnemonic character of the control. This is used to search for the next control that has the same mnemonic if the specified one is disabled.

Returns Nothing is returned.

See Also CPropertySheet::FindNextControl

GetTabControl

–. ■ 4.0

Description Returns a pointer to the Windows common tab control associated with the page. The tab control is what actually paints the tabs at the top of the sheet. This function did not appear until MFC version 4.0 because in earlier versions, the tab control was implemented internally by MFC. You may want to obtain a pointer to the tab control in order to control its behavior or appearance.

Syntax public, CTabCtrl *GetTabControl() const;

Parameters None.

Returns: A pointer to the tab control associated with the property sheet.

Example

```
// set the background color of the tab control to red
void CMySheet::MakeTabsRed()
{
      CTabCtrl *pTabs = GetTabControl();
      pTabs->SetBkColor(RGB(255,0,0));
}
```

HandleInitDialog

–. ■ 4.0 ■ UD

Description Message handler for the WM_INITDIALOG message. The CPropertySheet version does nothing but call the OnInitDialog member function.

Syntax public, afx_msg LRESULT HandleInitDialog(WPARAM wParam, LPARAM lParam);

Parameters

wParam	Not used.
lParam	Not used.
Returns	The result of a call to OnInitDialog.
See Also	CPropertySheet::OnInitDialog

OnClose

■ 2.51 ■ 3.0 ■ UD

Description	For modal property sheets, OnClose calls OnCancel to handle a close request in the same way as if the user had pressed the Cancel button. For modeless sheets, it simply calls the CWnd base implementation of OnClose which closes the sheet.
Syntax	protected, afx_msg void OnClose();
Parameters	None.
Returns	Nothing is returned.
See Also	CWnd::OnClose

OnCmdMsg

–. ■ 4.0 ■ UD

Description	Implements MFC's standard command routing scheme for property sheets. The CPropertySheet version first calls the base CWnd version. If the message is handled by the CWnd version, that is all that is done. If not, the command message is sent to the sheet's owner window. If the owner window does not handle the message, the message is sent to the current thread (usually, the application object).
Syntax	public, virtual BOOL OnCmdMsg(UINT nID, int nCode, void *pExtra, AFX_CMDHANDLERINFO *pHandlerInfo);
Parameters	
nID	The command ID.
nCode	The notification code.
pExtra	Points to data that is dependent on the value of the *nCode* parameter.
pHandlerInfo	If not NULL, OnCmdMsg fills in the pHandlerInfo structure with the pTarget and pmf members of the AFX_CMDHANDLERINFO structure instead of dispatching the command. Typically, this parameter should be NULL. MFC passes a non-NULL value to determine if a command would be handled without actually executing the command. This, in turn, is used to implement the default user-interface updating features of MFC. The AFX_CMDHANDLERINFO structure is defined in afxpriv.h.
Returns	Non-zero if the message is handled; otherwise 0.
See Also	CWnd::OnCmdMsg

OnCommand

–. ■ 4.0 ■ UD

Description Message handler for the WM_COMMAND message. The CPropertySheet version first calls the CWnd base class version, which routes the command message through the standard MFC routing scheme (see Chapter 4, *Windows Messaging*). It then checks to see whether the message is a button click and, if it is, stores the ID of the button in a CProperty sheet member variable (m_nModalResult).

Syntax public, virtual BOOL OnCommand(WPARAM wParam, LPARAM lParam);

Parameters

wParam The low-order word identifies the command ID of the menu item or control. The high-order word is the notification message, if the message is from a control. If the message is from an accelerator, the high-order word is 1. If the message is from a menu, the high-order word is 0.

lParam If the message is from a control, the window handle of the control; otherwise, zero.

Returns Non-zero if the message is processed; zero otherwise.

See Also CWnd::OnCommand

OnCommandHelp

■ 2.51 ■ 3.0 ■ UD

Description Message handler called in response to the WM_COMMANDHELP message that is sent when the Help button is pressed by the user. OnCommandHelp simply determines the active page and forwards the message to the page.

Syntax protected, afx_msg LRESULT OnCommandHelp(WPARAM wParam, LPARAM lParam);

Parameters

wParam The *wParam* associated with the WM_COMMANDHELP message. Simply passed on to the sheet.

lParam The *lParam* associated with the WM_COMMANDHELP message. Simply passed on to the sheet.

Returns The return code from the active page's WM_COMMANDHELP handler.

See Also CPropertyPage::OnCommandHelp

OnCtlColor

■ 2.51 ■ 3.0 ■ UD

Description Message handler for the WM_CTLCOLOR message. It processes the message by first sending the message directly to the child control to which it applies. If the child handles it, it returns the result from the child. If the child does not handle the message, it calls the GrayCtlColor CWnd member function to determine which color should be used for the control.

Syntax protected, afx_msg HBRUSH OnCtlColor(CDC* pDC, CWnd* pWnd, UINT nCtlColor)

Parameters

pDC A pointer to the display context for the control to which the message pertains.

pWnd A pointer to the control window requesting the color.

nCtlColor One of the following values indicating the affected control:

CTLCOLOR_BTN Button control.

CTLCOLOR_DLG Dialog box.

CTLCOLOR_EDIT Edit control.

CTLCOLOR_LIST BOX List box control.

CTLCOLOR_MSGBOX Message box.

CTLCOLOR_SCROLLBAR Scrollbar control.

CTLCOLOR_STATIC Static control.

Returns A handle to the brush that should be used for the background of the control.

See Also CWnd::GrayCtlColor, CWnd::SendChildNotifyLastMsg

OnInitDialog

–. ■ 4.0 ■ UD

Description Called by MFC in response to the WM_INITDIALOG message (from the CPropertySheet::HandleInitDialog message handler). The CPropertySheet version does several things regarding the layout and positioning of the sheet. It resizes the tab control, sets the "stacked" status of the tabs (stacked tabs or not), and centers the sheet on its parent window.

Syntax public, virtual BOOL OnInitDialog();

Parameters None.

Returns The result of a call to the default dialog procedure.

See Also CPropertySheet::EnableStackedTabs, CPropertySheet::GetTabControl, CPropertySheet::HandleInitDialog

OnNcCreate

–. ■ 4.0 ■ UD

Description Message handler for the WM_NCCREATE message. The CPropertySheet version disables the new Windows 95 help button in the caption bar. This is done because MFC does not support this help button. You can re-enable it in derived property sheets if you will support it yourself. The Windows 95 help button is enabled by including the WS_EX_CONTEXTHELP in the extended window style flags.

Syntax public, afx_msg BOOL OnNcCreate();

Parameters None.

Returns The result of a call to the default dialog procedure.

OnSetDefID

–. ■ 4.0 ■ UD

Description Message handler for the DM_SETDEFID message. This message is sent when the default button is being changed. MFC performs some validation to make sure that the requested button is valid. If it is not and the sheet is in "wizard" mode, it resets it to the first visible wizard button.

Syntax public, afx_msg LRESULT OnSetDefID(WPARAM wParam, LPARAM lParam);

Parameters

wParam ID of the new default button.

lParam Not used.

Returns The result of a call to the default dialog procedure (which always returns TRUE).

OnSysCommand

–. ■ 4.0 ■ UD

Description Message handler for the WM_SYSCOMMAND message. The CPropertySheet version converts the SC_CLOSE system menu command to a WM_CLOSE message. Otherwise, it simply calls the default dialog procedure.

Syntax public, afx_msg void OnSysCommand(UINT nID, LPARAM lParam);

Parameters

nID The ID of the system command being sent. For a list of possible values, see CWnd::OnSysCommand.

lParam Not used by this implementation. For a discussion of the general use of this parameter, see CWnd::OnSysCommand.

Returns Nothing is returned.

See Also CWnd::OnSysCommand

PressButton

–. ■ 4.0

Description Simulates the pressing of one of the property sheets buttons. Call this function if you want the sheet to behave as if a particular button were pressed.

Syntax public, BOOL PressButton(int nButton);

Parameters

nButton Indicates which button should be pressed. Can be one of the following values:

PSBTN_BACK	Presses the Back button.
PSBTN_NEXT	Presses the Next button.
PSBTN_FINISH	Presses the Finish button.
PSBTN_OK	Presses the OK button.
PSBTN_APPLYNOW	Presses the Apply Now button.
PSBTN_CANCEL	Presses the Cancel button.
PSBTN_HELP	Presses the Help button.

Returns Non-zero if successful; otherwise, zero.

Example

```
// press the  Next  button in a wizard to make the sheet go to the
// next step
pMySheet->PressButton(PSBTN_NEXT);
```

PreTranslateMessage

■ 2.51 ■ 3.0 ■ UD

Description Determines whether a message should be handled by the property sheet and, if so, how to handle it. It basically implements all of the behavior you would expect from a normal dialog: mnemonic keys, tabbing through controls, etc.

Syntax public, virtual BOOL PreTranslateMessage(MSG* pMsg);

Parameters

pMsg A pointer to the message structure containing the message to be translated.

Returns TRUE if the message was translated; FALSE otherwise.

See Also CPropertySheet::FindNextControl, CPropertySheet::GotoControl, CPropertySheet::ProcessChars, CPropertySheet::ProcessTab

RemovePage

■ 2.51 ■ 3.0

Description Call this function in order to remove a page from a property sheet. The debug version of MFC will assert if the specified page cannot be found. MFC takes care of any focus changes that are required by the removal of the page. Removing the page will destroy the window associated with the page but not the actual CPropertyPage object itself.

Syntax public, void RemovePage(int nPage);

public, void RemovePage(CPropertyPage *pPage);

Parameters

nPage The index of the page that should be removed from the sheet. The index of a page is determined by when it was added by the AddPage function.

pPage A pointer to the page that should be removed from the sheet.

Returns Nothing is returned.

See Also CPropertySheet::AddPage

Example See CPropertySheet::GetPage

SetActivePage

■ 2.51 ■ 3.0

Description Sets the specified page to be the active page. The active page is the page that the user can see and interact with. Note that the second version of this function did not exist until MFC version 4.0 and neither version was documented until 4.0. SetActivePage was not documented previous to version 4.0 because it could not be used by itself to actually set the active page. Previous to version 4.0, calling this function would set the selected page to be active, but the tab control on the sheet would not reflect the change.

Syntax public, BOOL SetActivePage(int nPage);
public, 4.0+, BOOL SetActivePage(CPropertyPage *pPage);

Parameters

nPage The index of the page to make the active page.

pPage A pointer to the page to make the active page.

Returns TRUE if the page is found and made active; FALSE otherwise.

See Also CPropertySheet::GetActivePage

SetFinishText

–. ■ 4.0

Description Sets the text of the Finish button in a wizard style property sheet. SetFinishText also hides the Back and Next buttons. Call this function if, when the user has finished the wizard, you want to hide the Back and Next buttons. Often, once the user has finished, a “this is what you have done” page is displayed before actually performing the results of the wizard.

Syntax public, void SetFinishText(LPCTSTR lpszText);

Parameters

lpszText A pointer to a NULL-terminated buffer containing the new text for the Finish button.

Returns Nothing is returned.

See Also CPropertySheet::SetWizardMode, CPropertySheet::SetWizardButtons

SetTitle

–. ■ 4.0

Description Sets the title of the property sheet. By default, the sheet is initially displayed with the caption specified in the constructor. Call this function if you want to change the title.

Syntax public, void SetTitle(LPCTSTR lpszTitle, UINT nStyle = 0);

Parameters

lpszTitle A pointer to a NULL-terminated buffer containing the new title.

nStyle	Zero or PSH_PROPTITLE in which case the specified title will be prefixed with the words "Properties for".
Returns	Nothing is returned.
See Also	CPropertySheet::CPropertySheet, CPropertySheet::Construct

SetWizardButtons

–. ■ 4.0

Description	Sets the state of the buttons on a wizard-style property sheet. Note that you should not call this function before the dialog is displayed (before DoModal or Create).
Syntax	public, void SetWizardButtons(DWORD dwFlags);
Parameters	
dwFlags	Indicates what should be done with the buttons. Can be a combination of the following values:
PSWIZB_BACK	Show the Back button.
PSWIZB_NEXT	Show the Next button.
PSWIZB_FINISH	Show the Finish button in an enabled state.
PSWIZB_DISABLEDFINISH	Show the Finish button in a disabled state.
Returns	Nothing is returned.
See Also	CPropertySheet::SetWizardMode, CPropertySheet::SetFinishText

SetWizardMode

–. ■ 4.0

Description	Makes the property sheet a "wizard." In this mode, the sheet does not display tabs and the user navigates between the pages using Back, Next, and Finish buttons.
Syntax	public, void SetWizardMode();
Parameters	None.
Returns	Nothing is returned.

The CPropertyPage Class

The CPropertyPage class implements a "tab" page on a tabbed dialog. CPropertyPage is derived from CDialog and, in fact, you define the format of a page by specifying a dialog resource template. This template must have the child style, a thin border, and a caption bar, and it must be disabled. Although Microsoft doesn't say so, you should also make it invisible. If you do not make it invisible, there are instances when, the first time the page is displayed, the user will see it displayed in the top corner of the parent sheet and then moved to the correct location. Beginning with MFC 4.0, the CPropertyPage object is a fairly shallow wrapper of the property page introduced with the Windows 95 operating system.

CPropertyPage

■ 2.51 ■ 3.0

Description Constructor that comes in three forms. The first form was introduced in MFC version 4.0 and takes no parameters. If you construct a property page using this constructor, you must later call one of the two forms of the member function Construct. The second version accepts the dialog template that should be used as a string, and the third version takes this parameter as an integer resource id. All three forms of the constructor do nothing but call the member function CommonConstruct.

Syntax public, CPropertyPage(); public, CPropertyPage(LPCTSTR lpszTemplateName, UINT nIDCaption = 0); public, CPropertyPage(UINT nIDTemplate, UINT nIDCaption = 0);

Parameters

lpszTemplateName Pointer to a NULL-terminated string buffer containing the name of the dialog template to be associated with the page.

nIDTemplate Integer resource ID of the dialog template to associate with the page.

nIDCaption String resource ID of the string that should be used as the caption for the page. If 0 or omitted, the caption is retrieved from the dialog template itself.

Returns Nothing is returned.

See Also CPropertyPage::CommonConstruct

~CPropertyPage

■ 2.51 ■ 3.0

Description The destructor for the property page does absolutely nothing.

Syntax public, ~CPropertyPage();

Parameters None.

Returns Nothing is returned.

AssertValid

■ 2.51 ■ 3.0 ■ UD ■ DO

Description A debug-only function that throws an assertion if the CPropertyPage object is considered "invalid." The property page implementation just calls the CDialog base implementation.

Syntax public, void AssertValid() const;

Parameters None.

Returns Nothing is returned.

See Also CDialog::AssertValid

Example

```
void CMyWnd::SomeFunct(CPropertyPage *pPage)
{
	pPage->AssertValid(); // make sure passed page is valid
	.. // now we can safely use it
```

CancelToClose

■ 2.51 ■ 3.0

Description You should call this function when a change has been made to the page from which it cannot be recovered. In versions of MFC previous to 4.0, the CPropertyPage::CancelToClose function simply calls the CancelToClose member function of the parent CPropertySheet object. In 4.0, it sends a PSM_CANCELTOCLOSE message to the parent sheet.

Syntax public, void CancelToClose();

Parameters None.

Returns Nothing is returned.

See Also CPropertySheet::CancelToClose

Example

```
void CPage3::OnChangeCanceltoclose()
{
      // contents of edit box changed and we can't reverse the
      // change so disable cancel button and change OK to "Close"
      CancelToClose();
}
```

CommonConstruct

■ 2.51 ■ 3.0 ■ UD

Description CommonConstruct is a utility function called by both versions of the CPropertyPage constructor. It saves the dialog template ID, loads the page caption, and initializes the page to the "unchanged" state.

Syntax protected, void CommonConstruct(LPCTSTR lpszTemplateName, UINT nIDCaption);

Parameters

lpszTemplateName The dialog template that should be associated with the page. The value of this parameter may be a pointer to a NULL-terminated string buffer containing the name of the template, or the value returned by MAKEINTRESOURCE for an integer ID template.

nIdCaption The resource ID of the string to use as the caption of the property sheet.

Returns: Nothing is returned.

See Also CPropertyPage::CPropertyPage

Construct

–. ■ 4.0

Description Call the construct function to associate the property page object with a given dialog template. You must call this function before displaying the parent sheet if you use the parameterless form of the CPropertyPage constructor.

Syntax public, void Construct(LPCTSTR lpszTemplateName, UINT nIDCaption = 0);
public, void Construct(UINT nIDTemplate, UINT nIDCaption = 0);

Parameters

lpszTemplateName	Pointer to a NULL-terminated string buffer containing the name of the dialog template to be associated with the page.
nIDTemplate	Integer resource ID of the dialog template to associate with the page.
nIDCaption	String resource ID of the string that should be used as the caption for the page. If 0 or omitted, the caption is retrieved from the dialog template itself.
Returns	Nothing is returned.
See Also	CPropertyPage, CPropertyPage::CommonConstruct

Dump

■ 2.5 ■ 3.0 ■ DO

Description Dump is a diagnostic function that outputs the current state of a CPropertyPage object to the specified dump context. The CPropertyPage version outputs the caption of the page, the "changed" state of the page, and the base CDialog information.

Syntax public, virtual void Dump(CDumpContext& dc) const;

Parameters

dc A reference to the dump context to which the status information should be sent. Usually this will be the MFC default debug dump context *afxDump*. *afxDump* sends its output to the debugger and only exists in the debug build of MFC.

Returns Nothing is returned.

See Also CPropertyPage::AssertValid

Example The following is an example of the output of the Dump function:

```
// call to Dump function
void CPage1::OnDumppage()
{
      // dump contents of CPage1 object to the debug context
      Dump(afxDump);
}

// output from Dump function
a CPropertyPage at $63FD14

m_hWnd = 0x0m_lpDialogTemplate = 130
m_hDialogTemplate = 0x0
m_pParentWnd = $0
m_nIDHelp = 0x0
m_strCaption = Dialog
m_bChanged = 0
```

EndDialog

■ 2.5 ■ 3.0 ■ UD ■ DO

Description This function is only present in the debug version of MFC and its only purpose is to ASSERT if it is called. You should never call EndDialog for a

	property page. All interaction should be through the parent CPropertySheet object.
Syntax	public, void EndDialog(int nEndID);
Parameters	
nEndID	Not used.
Returns	Nothing is returned.
See Also	CPropertySheet::EndDialog

OnApply

–. ■ 4.0

Description	Called when the user clicks the OK button or the Apply Now button. In either case, the user is indicating that the changes made should take effect. The default version simply calls CPropertyPage::OnOK.
Syntax	public, virtual BOOL OnApply();
Parameters	None.
Returns	Non-zero if applied; otherwise, zero.
See Also	CPropertySheet::OnCancel, CPropertyPage::OnOK

OnCancel

■ 2.51 ■ 3.0

Description	The default implementation of OnCancel before MFC version 4.0 simply sets the "changed" state of the page to FALSE. In MFC version 4.0, the default version does nothing. The framework calls the OnCancel function for the active page when the user presses the Cancel button on the property sheet. Override this function if you want to do anything else when the user presses the Cancel button on the property sheet.
Syntax	public, virtual void OnCancel();
Parameters	None.
Returns	Nothing is returned.
See Also	CPropertySheet::OnCancel, CPropertyPage::OnOK

OnCtlColor

■ 2.51 ■ 3.0 ■ UD

Description	Message handler for the WM_CTLCOLOR message. It processes the message by first sending the message directly to the child control to which it applies. If the child handles it, it returns the result from the child. If the child does not handle the message, it calls the GrayCtlColor CWnd member function to determine which color should be used for the control.
Syntax	protected, afx_msg HBRUSH OnCtlColor(CDC* pDC, CWnd* pWnd, UINT nCtlColor)

Parameters

pDC A pointer to the display context for the control to which the message pertains.

pWnd A pointer to the control window requesting the color.

nCtlColor One of the following values indicating the control to be affected:

CTLCOLOR_BTN Button control.

CTLCOLOR_DLG Dialog box.

CTLCOLOR_EDIT Edit control.

CTLCOLOR_LIST BOX List box control.

CTLCOLOR_MSGBOX Message box.

CTLCOLOR_SCROLLBAR Scrollbar control.

CTLCOLOR_STATIC Static control.

Returns A handle to the brush that should be used for the background of the control.

See Also CWnd::GrayCtlColor, CWnd::SendChildNotifyLastMsg

OnKillActive ■ 2.51 ■ 3.0

Description Called by MFC when the page is no longer the active page. The default implementation calls the UpdateData CWnd member function to retrieve and validate the data associated with the page. If data validation fails, OnKillActive returns FALSE and the page remains active.

Syntax public, virtual BOOL OnKillActive();

Parameters None.

Returns TRUE if it is OK to allow the page to become inactive; FALSE if the page should remain the active page.

See Also CWnd::UpdateData

Example

```
// perform custom validation for page data
BOOL CPage4::OnKillActive()
{
      CString strText;
      m_ctValid.GetWindowText(strText);
      if (strText != "Valid" && strText != "Invalid")
      {
            AfxMessageBox("Please enter Valid or Invalid.");
            m_ctValid.SetFocus();
            return FALSE;
      }
      return CPropertyPage::OnKillActive();
}
```

OnNotify

–. ■ 4.0

Description Handler for the WM_NOTIFY message. MFC uses this handler to parse property page notification messages and then call the appropriate handlers. For example, the PSN_APPLY notification is mapped to a call to the OnApply handler function. You can override this function if you want to change the way in which property page notifications are handled.

Syntax protected, virtual BOOL OnNotify(WPARAM wParam, LPARAM lParam, LRESULT *pResult);

Parameters

wParam The resource ID of the control sending the notification.

lParam A pointer to a NMHDR structure that describes the type of notification.

pResult A pointer to a long into which the result code of the notification is placed. The value returned depends on the type of notification.

Returns TRUE if the message is handled; FALSE otherwise.

See Also CWnd::OnNotify

OnOK

■ 2.51 ■ 3.0

Description In versions of MFC previous to 4.0, the default implementation of OnOK does nothing but set the "changed" state of the page to FALSE. In version 4.0, OnOK does nothing. OnOK is called by MFC when the user presses either the OK or Apply Now button on the property sheet.

Syntax public, virtual void OnOK();

Parameters None.

Returns Nothing is returned.

See Also CPropertySheet::OnOK, CPropertyPage::OnCancel

OnQueryCancel

–. ■ 4.0

Description Called by the framework when the Cancel button is pressed to determine whether the user is allowed to cancel. Override this function if you want to control whether the user can cancel the property sheet.

Syntax public, virtual BOOL OnQueryCancel();

Parameters None.

Returns TRUE if the page the user is allowed to Cancel; FALSE otherwise.

See Also CPropertyPage::OnCancel

OnReset

–. ■ 4.0

Description Called by MFC when the user presses the Cancel button. The default implementation simply calls the CPropertyPage::OnCancel function.

Syntax public, virtual void OnReset();

Parameters None.

Returns Nothing is returned.

See Also CPropertyPage::OnCancel

OnSetActive

■ 2.51 ■ 3.0

Description In versions of MFC previous to 4.0, if the property page window has not been created yet, OnSetActive creates the window; otherwise, it does nothing. MFC delays creation of the page's window until the first time it is made active. This makes initial display of the property sheet as fast as possible since MFC doesn't have to load all of the pages when the property sheet is initially displayed. In MFC version 4.0, OnSetActive simply calls CWnd::UpdateData to update the dialog's data.

Syntax public, virtual BOOL OnSetActive();

Parameters None.

Returns TRUE if the page was successfully set active or FALSE if creation of the page's window fails.

See Also CPropertyPage::OnKillActive

Example

```
BOOL CMyPage::OnSetActive()
{
      // do some special initialization

      return CPropertyPage::OnSetActive();
}
```

OnWizardBack

–. ■ 4.0

Description Called when the user presses the Back button in a wizard-style property sheet. Override this function if you want to do anything special when the Back button is pressed or if you want to prevent the user from moving backward in the wizard.

Syntax public, virtual LRESULT OnWizardBack();

Parameters None.

Returns Zero if the user is allowed to move back; -1 if not.

See Also CPropertyPage::OnWizardNext, CPropertyPage::OnWizardFinish

OnWizardFinish

–. ■ 4.0

Description	Called when the user presses the Finish button in a wizard-style property sheet. Override this function if you want to perform special operations when this occurs or if you want to control whether the user is allowed to finish the wizard.
Syntax	public, virtual BOOL OnWizardFinish();
Parameters	None.
Returns	TRUE if the user is allowed to finish or FALSE if not.
See Also	CPropertyPage::OnWizardBack, CPropertyPage::OnWizardNext

OnWizardNext

–. ■ 4.0

Description	Called when the user presses the Next button in a wizard-style property sheet. Override this function if you want to do anything special when the Next button is pressed or if you want to prevent the user from moving forward in the wizard.
Syntax	public, virtual LRESULT OnWizardNext();
Parameters	None.
Returns	Zero if the user is allowed to move forward; -1 if not.
See Also	CPropertyPage::OnWizardBack, CPropertyPage::OnWizardFinish

QuerySiblings

–. ■ 4.0

Description	Sends a message to each of the pages in the property sheet. If, along the way, any page returns a non-zero value in response to the message, subsequent pages are not sent the message.
Syntax	public, LRESULT QuerySiblings(WPARAM wParam, LPARAM lParam);
Parameters	
wParam	Any arbitrary information you want to send with the message.
lParam	Any arbitrary information you want to send with the message.
Returns	All property pages return zero from the message; otherwise, whatever value is returned from the page that returned a non-zero value.

SetModified

■ 2.51 ■ 3.0

Description	You should call SetModified to inform MFC of the "changed" state of the page. If the page is "dirty" (it has been changed in some way), call SetModified with a parameter of TRUE. If the page is clean, call

SetModified with a parameter of FALSE. MFC determines the state of the Apply Now, OK, and Cancel buttons depending on the "changed" state of each of the pages in a sheet. SetModified sets the state of the page as specified and then calls the PageChanged member of the CPropertySheet object to inform the sheet that a page's state has been changed.

Syntax public, void SetModified(BOOL bChanged = TRUE);

Parameters

bChanged TRUE if the page is dirty; FALSE if the page is clean.

Returns Nothing is returned.

See Also CPropertySheet::PageChanged

Example

```
void CPage2::OnChangeSetmodified()
{
	// page has changed - enable Apply Now button
	SetModified(TRUE);
}
```

The CDataExchange Class

The CDataExchange class is a very simple class used by MFC to facilitate the exchange of data between a CWnd-derived class and the window controls themselves. If you do any custom validation, you may also want to use the CDataExchange class. In actuality, most of the functions that aid in the transfer of this data, as well as the binding of controls to MFC control classes (CStatic, CEdit, etc.) are non-member functions. These functions are described in the next section of this chapter, "DDX/DDV Functions."

Whenever dialog control data needs to be exchanged or validated, MFC creates and initializes a CDataExchange object and passes it as a parameter to the DoDataExchange function of the parent window (usually a dialog). The contents of a typical DoDataExchange function are shown below in Listing 8-1. You can also perform your own validation with DoDataExchange either directly in the function or by creating your own DDV_ and DDX_ routines. The m_bSaveAndValidate member variable of the CDataExchange object specifies the direction of the exchange: TRUE indicates data is being retrieved from the dialog (and then validated); FALSE indicates data is being transferred to the dialog and controls are being bound to their respective MFC classes (CStatic, CEdit, etc.).

Listing 8-1 A Typical DoDataExchange Function

```
void CTestDlg::DoDataExchange(CDataExchange* pDX)
{
	CDialog::DoDataExchange(pDX);
	//{{AFX_DATA_MAP(CTestDlg)
	DDX_Control(pDX, IDC_LIST1, m_ctListBox);
	DDX_Control(pDX, IDC_COMBO1, m_ctComboBox);
	DDX_Control(pDX, IDC_CUSTOM, m_ctCustom);
	DDX_Check(pDX, IDC_CHECK1, m_bCheck);
	DDX_CBString(pDX, IDC_COMBO1, m_strComboSelect);
```

```
        DDX_LBString(pDX, IDC_LIST1, m_strListSelect);
        DDX_Text(pDX, IDC_EDIT1, m_nEditVal);
        DDV_MinMaxInt(pDX, m_nEditVal, 1, 10);
        DDX_Text(pDX, IDC_CUSTOM, m_strCustom);
        DDV_MaxChars(pDX, m_strCustom, 3);
        //}}AFX_DATA_MAP
}
```

CDataExchange

■ 2.0 ■ 3.0 ■ UD

Description Constructor that simply initializes its internal members with the parameters passed to it.

Syntax public, CDataExchange(CWnd* pDlgWnd, BOOL bSaveAndValidate)

Parameters

pDlgWnd Pointer to window containing controls for data exchange and validation. In most cases, this will be a dialog, although it does not have to be.

bSaveAndValidate TRUE if data is going to be retrieved from the dialog and validated; FALSE if data is being set in the dialog.

Returns Nothing is returned.

Fail

■ 2.0 ■ 3.0

Description Called by MFC's data validation routines when the data entered in a particular control fails the criteria established for that control. If you are using MSVC, you set the criteria via the ClassWizard. You can also manually establish the criteria by calling the appropriate validation routines (described in the next section) in the DoDataExchange function of your dialog or property page. When Fail is called, it sets the focus back to the control being validated and then throws an exception. If the control is an edit control, it also highlights the text in the control.

Syntax public, void Fail();

Parameters None.

Returns Nothing is returned.

See Also CDataExchange::PrepareCtrl, CDataExchange::PrepareEditCtrl

Example

```
void CTestDlg::DoDataExchange(CDataExchange* pDX)
{
      CDialog::DoDataExchange(pDX);
      //{{AFX_DATA_MAP(CTestDlg)
      DDX_Control(pDX, IDC_LIST1, m_ctListBox);
      DDX_Control(pDX, IDC_COMBO1, m_ctComboBox);
      DDX_Control(pDX, IDC_CUSTOM, m_ctCustom);
      DDX_Check(pDX, IDC_CHECK1, m_bCheck);
      DDX_CBString(pDX, IDC_COMBO1, m_strComboSelect);
      DDX_LBString(pDX, IDC_LIST1, m_strListSelect);
      DDX_Text(pDX, IDC_EDIT1, m_nEditVal);
```

continued on next page

continued from previous page

```
        DDV_MinMaxInt(pDX, m_nEditVal, 1, 10);
        DDX_Text(pDX, IDC_CUSTOM, m_strCustom);
        DDV_MaxChars(pDX, m_strCustom, 3);
        //}}AFX_DATA_MAP

        // do some custom validation
        if (pDX->m_bSaveAndValidate)
        {
                CString strText;

                // Get the edit box's text
                m_ctCustom.GetWindowText(strText);

                // Prepare edit control for validation
                pDX->PrepareEditCtrl(IDC_CUSTOM);
                if (strText != "Yes" && strText != "No")
                {
                        AfxMessageBox("Please enter Yes or No.");
                        pDX->Fail();
                }
        }
}
```

PrepareCtrl

■ 2.0 ■ 3.0

Description "Prepares" a non-edit control for exchange and validation. What it really does is retrieve the handle for the control and store it in a member. It does this so that later, when and if the Fail function is called, it can set focus back to the control.

Syntax public, HWND PrepareCtrl(int nIDC);

Parameters

nIDC The resource ID of the control.

Returns The window handle of the specified control.

See Also CDataExchange::PrepareEditCtrl, CDataExchange::Fail

Example

```
void CTestDlg::DoDataExchange(CDataExchange* pDX)
{
        CDialog::DoDataExchange(pDX);
        //{{AFX_DATA_MAP(CTestDlg)
        DDX_Control(pDX, IDC_LIST1, m_ctListBox);
        DDX_Control(pDX, IDC_COMBO1, m_ctComboBox);
        DDX_Control(pDX, IDC_CUSTOM, m_ctCustom);
        DDX_Check(pDX, IDC_CHECK1, m_bCheck);
        DDX_CBString(pDX, IDC_COMBO1, m_strComboSelect);
        DDX_LBString(pDX, IDC_LIST1, m_strListSelect);
        DDX_Text(pDX, IDC_EDIT1, m_nEditVal);
        DDV_MinMaxInt(pDX, m_nEditVal, 1, 10);
        DDX_Text(pDX, IDC_CUSTOM, m_strCustom);
        DDV_MaxChars(pDX, m_strCustom, 3);
        //}}AFX_DATA_MAP

        // do dome custom validation
        if (pDX->m_bSaveAndValidate)
```

```
        {
            CString strText;

            // get number of selections in list box
            int nNumSel = m_ctListBox.GetNumSel();

            // Prepare listbox control for validation
            pDX->PrepareCtrl(IDC_LIST1);
            if (nNumSel > 4)
            {
                AfxMessageBox("Please select only four. );
                pDX->Fail();
            }
        }
    }
```

PrepareEditCtrl

■ 2.0 ■ 3.0

Description "Prepares" an edit control for exchange and validation. What it really does is retrieve the handle for the control and store it in a member. It does this so that later, when and if the Fail function is called, it can set focus back to the control and highlight the text in the control.

Syntax public, HWND PrepareCtrl(int nIDC);

Parameters

nIDC The resource ID of the edit control.

Returns The window handle of the edit control.

See Also CDataExchange::PrepareCtrl, CDataExchange::Fail

Example

```
void CTestDlg::DoDataExchange(CDataExchange* pDX)
{
    CDialog::DoDataExchange(pDX);
    //{{AFX_DATA_MAP(CTestDlg)
    DDX_Control(pDX, IDC_LIST1, m_ctListBox);
    DDX_Control(pDX, IDC_COMBO1, m_ctComboBox);
    DDX_Control(pDX, IDC_CUSTOM, m_ctCustom);
    DDX_Check(pDX, IDC_CHECK1, m_bCheck);
    DDX_CBString(pDX, IDC_COMBO1, m_strComboSelect);
    DDX_LBString(pDX, IDC_LIST1, m_strListSelect);
    DDX_Text(pDX, IDC_EDIT1, m_nEditVal);
    DDV_MinMaxInt(pDX, m_nEditVal, 1, 10);
    DDX_Text(pDX, IDC_CUSTOM, m_strCustom);
    DDV_MaxChars(pDX, m_strCustom, 3);
    //}}AFX_DATA_MAP

    // do dome custom validation
    if (pDX->m_bSaveAndValidate)
    {
        CString strText;

        // Get the edit box's text
        m_ctCustom.GetWindowText(strText);

        // Prepare edit control for validation
```

continued on next page

continued from previous page

```
                pDX->PrepareEditCtrl(IDC_CUSTOM);
                if (strText != "Yes" && strText != "No")
                {
                     AfxMessageBox("Please enter Yes or No.");
                     pDX->Fail();
                }
           }
      }
```

DDX/DDV Functions

As stated earlier in this chapter, most of the work of data exchange and validation is actually accomplished by a series of non-object functions. Every one of the functions takes, as its first parameter, a pointer to the CDataExchange object associated with the validation. This begs the question: Why not make all of these functions members of the CDataExchange class? The most important reason is probably that it is easier to make your own exchange and validation routines if the functions are not member functions. If they were members, you would have to provide a class derived from CDataExchange in order to implement your own validation routines.

DDV_MaxChars ■ 2.0 ■ 3.0

Description Verifies that the given CString contains no more than the specified number of characters. If it has more than the specified number of characters, DDV_MaxChars calls the Fail member function of the given CDataExchange object.

Syntax public, void AFXAPI DDV_MaxChars(CDataExchange* pDX, CString const& value, int nChars);

Parameters

pDX A pointer to the data exchange object. The m_bSaveAndValidate member must be FALSE.

value A reference to the CString to validate.

nChars The maximum number of characters allowed.

Returns Nothing is returned.

Example

```
void CTestDlg::DoDataExchange(CDataExchange* pDX)
{
     CDialog::DoDataExchange(pDX);
     //{{AFX_DATA_MAP(CTestDlg)
     // only allow a maximum of 3 characters
     DDV_MaxChars(pDX, m_strCustom, 3);
     //}}AFX_DATA_MAP
```

DDV_MinMaxByte ■ 2.0 ■ 3.0

Description Verifies that the given BYTE value is within the specified range. If it is not, DDV_MinMaxByte calls the Fail member function of the given CDataExchange object.

Syntax public, void AFXAPI DDV_MinMaxByte(CDataExchange* pDX, BYTE value, BYTE minVal, BYTE maxVal);

Parameters

pDX A pointer to the data exchange object. The m_bSaveAndValidate member must be TRUE.

value The BYTE value to validate.

minVal The minimum allowable value.

maxVal The maximum allowable value.

Returns Nothing is returned.

Example

```
void CTestDlg::DoDataExchange(CDataExchange* pDX)
{
      CDialog::DoDataExchange(pDX);
      //{{AFX_DATA_MAP(CTestDlg)
      // only allow letters a - z
      DDV_MinMaxBYTE(pDX, m_strCustom, `a', `z');
      //}}AFX_DATA_MAP
```

DDV_MinMaxDouble

■ 2.0 ■ 3.0

Description Verifies that the given double value is within the specified range. If it is not, DDV_ MinMaxDouble calls the Fail member function of the given CDataExchange object.

Syntax public, void AFXAPI DDV_MinMaxDouble(CDataExchange* pDX, double const& value, double minVal, double maxVal);

Parameters

pDX A pointer to the data exchange object. The m_bSaveAndValidate member must be TRUE.

value The double value to validate.

minVal The minimum allowable value.

maxVal The maximum allowable value.

Returns Nothing is returned.

DDV_MinMaxDWord

■ 2.0 ■ 3.0

Description Verifies that the given DWORD value is within the specified range. If it is not, DDV_ MinMaxDWord calls the Fail member function of the given CDataExchange object.

Syntax public, void AFXAPI DDV_ MinMaxDWord(CDataExchange* pDX, DWORD value, DWORD minVal, DWORD maxVal);

Parameters

pDX A pointer to the data exchange object. The m_bSaveAndValidate member must be TRUE.

value	The DWORD value to validate.
minVal	The minimum allowable value.
maxVal	The maximum allowable value.
Returns	Nothing is returned.

DDV_MinMaxFloat ■ 2.0 ■ 3.0

Description Verifies that the given float value is within the specified range. If it is not, DDV_MinMaxFloat calls the Fail member function of the given CDataExchange object.

Syntax public, void AFXAPI DDV_MinMaxFloat(CDataExchange* pDX, float const& value, float minVal, float maxVal);

Parameters

pDX	A pointer to the data exchange object. The m_bSaveAndValidate member must be TRUE.
value	A reference to the float value to validate.
minVal	The minimum allowable value.
maxVal	The maximum allowable value.
Returns	Nothing is returned.

DDV_MinMaxInt ■ 2.0 ■ 3.0

Description Verifies that the given integer value is within the specified range. If it is not, DDV_ MinMaxInt calls the Fail member function of the given CDataExchange object.

Syntax public, void AFXAPI DDV_MinMaxInt(CDataExchange* pDX, int value, int minVal, int maxVal);

Parameters

pDX	A pointer to the data exchange object. The m_bSaveAndValidate member must be TRUE.
value	The integer value to validate.
minVal	The minimum allowable value.
maxVal	The maximum allowable value.
Returns	Nothing is returned.

DDV_MinMaxLong ■ 2.0 ■ 3.0

Description Verifies that the given long integer value is within the specified range. If it is not, DDV_ MinMaxLong calls the Fail member function of the given CDataExchange object.

Syntax	public, void AFXAPI DDV_ MinMaxLong(CDataExchange* pDX, long value, long minVal, long maxVal);
Parameters	
pDX	A pointer to the data exchange object. The m_bSaveAndValidate member must be TRUE.
value	The long integer value to validate.
minVal	The minimum allowable value.
maxVal	The maximum allowable value.
Returns	Nothing is returned.

DDV_MinMaxUInt ■ 2.0 ■ 3.0

Description	Verifies that the given unsigned integer value is within the specified range. If it is not, DDV_ MinMaxUInt calls the Fail member function of the given CDataExchange object.
Syntax	public, void AFXAPI DDV_ MinMaxUInt(CDataExchange* pDX, UINT value, UINT minVal, UINT maxVal);
Parameters	
pDX	A pointer to the data exchange object. The m_bSaveAndValidate member must be TRUE.
value	The unsigned integer value to validate.
minVal	The minimum allowable value.
maxVal	The maximum allowable value.
Returns	Nothing is returned.

DDX_CBIndex ■ 2.0 ■ 3.0

Description	Used to transfer data to/from a combo box. If data is being transferred to the combo box, then the current selection of the combo box will be set to the specified index. If data is being transferred from the combo box, the index of the current selections will be retrieved.
Syntax	public, void AFXAPI DDX_CBIndex(CDataExchange* pDX, int nIDC, int& index);
Parameters	
pDX	A pointer to the data exchange object. Check the m_bSaveAndValidate member to determine the direction of the exchange.
nIDC	The resource ID of the control with which exchange or validation is taking place.
index	A reference to an integer with which to perform the exchange.
Returns	Nothing is returned.
See Also	DDX_CBString, DDX_CBStringExact

DDX_CBString

■ 2.0 ■ 3.0

Description Used to transfer data to/from a combo box. If data is being transferred to the combo box, then the current selection of the combo box will be set to the specified string. MFC searches for the string using the FindString combo box function, so only a prefix match is required. If data is being transferred from the combo box, the given string will be filled with the text of the current selection.

Syntax public, void AFXAPI DDX_CBString(CDataExchange* pDX, int nIDC, CString& value);

Parameters

pDX A pointer to the data exchange object. Check the m_bSaveAndValidate member to determine the direction of the exchange.

nIDC The resource ID of the control with which exchange or validation is taking place.

value A reference to a CString with which to perform the exchange.

Returns Nothing is returned.

See Also DDX_CBStringExact, DDX_CBIndex

DDX_CBStringExact

■ 2.0 ■ 3.0

Description Used to transfer data to/from a combo box. If data is being transferred to the combo box, then the current selection of the combo box will be set to the specified string. MFC searches for the string using the FindStringExact list box function, so an exact match is required. If data is being transferred from the combo box, the given string will be filled with the text of the current selection.

Syntax public, void AFXAPI DDX_CBStringExact(CDataExchange* pDX, int nIDC, CString& value);

Parameters

pDX A pointer to the data exchange object. Check the m_bSaveAndValidate member to determine the direction of the exchange.

nIDC The resource ID of the control with which exchange or validation is taking place.

value A reference to a CString with which to perform the exchange.

Returns Nothing is returned.

See Also DDX_LBStringExact, DDX_CBIndex

DDX_CHECK

■ 2.0 ■ 3.0

Description Used to transfer data to/from a check box. A "checked" state is represented by a 1, an "unchecked" state is represented by a 0, and an indeterminate state is represented by the value 2.

Syntax public, void AFXAPI DDX_Check(CDataExchange* pDX, int nIDC, int& value);

Parameters

pDX A pointer to the data exchange object. Check the m_bSaveAndValidate member to determine the direction of the exchange.

nIDC The resource ID of the control with which exchange or validation is taking place.

value A reference to an integer with which to perform the exchange.

Returns Nothing is returned.

DDX_CONTROL

■ 2.0 ■ 3.0

Description Used to bind an MFC control object (CStatic, CEdit, CCombo box, etc.) to a window control. Once attached, the control can be accessed and manipulated via the class. MFC performs all data exchange in the default implementation of OnInitDialog. Therefore, any control bound using DDX_Control is bound before any actions need to be performed on the control.

Syntax public, void AFXAPI DDX_Control(CDataExchange* pDX, int nIDC, CWnd& rControl);

Parameters

pDX A pointer to the data exchange object. The m_bSaveAndValidate member must be FALSE.

nIDC The resource ID of the control to bind.

rControl A reference to an MFC control object that should be bound to the specified control.

Returns Nothing is returned.

DDX_LBINDEX

■ 2.0 ■ 3.0

Description Used to transfer data to/from a list box. If data is being transferred to the list box, then the current selection of the list box will be set to the specified index. If data is being transferred from the list box, the index of the current selections will be retrieved.

Syntax public, void AFXAPI DDX_LBIndex(CDataExchange* pDX, int nIDC, int& index);

Parameters

pDX	A pointer to the data exchange object. Check the m_bSaveAndValidate member to determine the direction of the exchange.
nIDC	The resource ID of the control with which exchange or validation is taking place.
index	A reference to an integer with which to perform the exchange.
Returns	Nothing is returned.
See Also	DDX_LBString, DDX_LBStringExact

DDX_LBString ■ 2.0 ■ 3.0

Description Used to transfer data to/from a list box. If data is being transferred to the list box, then the current selection of the list box will be set to the specified string. MFC searches for the string using the FindString list box function, so only a prefix match is required. If data is being transferred from the list box, the given string will be filled with the text of the current selection.

Syntax public, void AFXAPI DDX_LBString(CDataExchange* pDX, int nIDC, CString& value);

Parameters

pDX	A pointer to the data exchange object. Check the m_bSaveAndValidate member to determine the direction of the exchange.
nIDC	The resource ID of the control with which exchange or validation is taking place.
value	A reference to a CString with which to perform the exchange.
Returns	Nothing is returned.
See Also	DDX_LBStringExact, DDX_LBIndex

DDX_LBStringExact ■ 2.0 ■ 3.0

Description Used to transfer data to/from a list box. If data is being transferred to the list box, then the current selection of the list box will be set to the specified string. MFC searches for the string using the FindStringExact list box function, so an exact match is required. If data is being transferred from the list box, the given string will be filled with the text of the current selection.

Syntax public, void AFXAPI DDX_LBStringExact(CDataExchange* pDX, int nIDC, CString& value);

Parameters

pDX	A pointer to the data exchange object. Check the m_bSaveAndValidate member to determine the direction of the exchange.

nIDC	The resource ID of the control with which exchange or validation is taking place.
value	A reference to a CString with which to perform the exchange.
Returns	Nothing is returned.
See Also	DDX_LBString, DDX_LBIndex

DDX_Radio

■ 2.0 ■ 3.0

Description Used to transfer data to/from a radio button. A "checked" state is represented by a 1, an "unchecked" state is represented by a 0, and an indeterminate state is represented by the value 2.

Syntax public, void AFXAPI DDX_Radio(CDataExchange* pDX, int nIDC, int& value);

Parameters

pDX	A pointer to the data exchange object. Check the m_bSaveAndValidate member to determine the direction of the exchange.
nIDC	The resource ID of the control with which exchange or validation is taking place.
value	A reference to an integer with which to perform the exchange.
Returns	Nothing is returned.

DDX_Scroll

■ 2.0 ■ 3.0

Description Used to transfer data to/from a scrollbar. Depending on the direction of the exchange, the scroll position is retrieved/set to/from the specified integer variable.

Syntax public, void AFXAPI DDX_Scroll(CDataExchange* pDX, int nIDC, int& value);

Parameters

pDX	A pointer to the data exchange object. Check the m_bSaveAndValidate member to determine the direction of the exchange.
nIDC	The resource ID of the control with which exchange or validation is taking place.
value	A reference to an integer with which to perform the exchange.
Returns	Nothing is returned.

DDX_Text

■ 2.0 ■ 3.0

Description Used to exchange data with an edit box. It comes in several flavors that allow you to get and set data of almost any type. See the syntax section below for a list of all the different types.

Syntax

public, void AFXAPI DDX_Text(CDataExchange* pDX, int nIDC, BYTE& value);
public, void AFXAPI DDX_Text(CDataExchange* pDX, int nIDC, int& value);
public, void AFXAPI DDX_Text(CDataExchange* pDX, int nIDC, UINT& value);
public, void AFXAPI DDX_Text(CDataExchange* pDX, int nIDC, short & value);
public, void AFXAPI DDX_Text(CDataExchange* pDX, int nIDC, long& value);
public, void AFXAPI DDX_Text(CDataExchange* pDX, int nIDC, DWORD& value);
public, void AFXAPI DDX_Text(CDataExchange* pDX, int nIDC, CString& value);
public, void AFXAPI DDX_Text(CDataExchange* pDX, int nIDC, float& value);
public, void AFXAPI DDX_Text(CDataExchange* pDX, int nIDC, double& value);

Parameters

pDX A pointer to the data exchange object. Check the m_bSaveAndValidate member to determine the direction of the exchange.

nIDC The resource ID of the control with which exchange or validation is taking place.

value A reference to a member variable with which data will be exchanged.

Returns Nothing is returned.

The CCommonDialog Class

The CCommonDialog class was a completely undocumented class until MFC Version 4.0 which serves as the base class for all of MFC's common dialog implementation classes. It is a very simple class and probably exists more for conceptual beauty than anything else.

CCommonDialog ■ 2.0 ■ 3.0 ■ UD

Description Constructor that does nothing but call the base CDialog constructor with a template resource ID of 0.

Syntax public, CCommonDialog(CWnd* pParentWnd);

Parameters

pParentWnd A pointer to the dialog's parent window.

Returns Nothing is returned.

OnOK

■ 2.0 ■ 3.0 ■ UD

Description	Provided by CCommonDialog in order to stop EndDialog from being called. EndDialog should not be called to destroy a common dialog (which the base CDialog OnOK would do).
Syntax	public, virtual void OnOK();
Parameters	None.
Returns	Nothing is returned.
See Also	CCommonDialog::OnCancel

OnCancel

■ 2.0 ■ 3.0 ■ UD

Description	Provided by CCommonDialog in order to stop EndDialog from being called. EndDialog should not be called to destroy a common dialog (which the base CDialog OnCancel would do).
Syntax	protected, virtual void OnCancel();
Parameters	None.
Returns	Nothing is returned.
See Also	CCommonDialog::OnOK

The CFileDialog Class

The CFileDialog class is an encapsulation of the Windows file common dialog. With this class, displaying a basic file open dialog is trivial. You simply create a CFileDialog object and call DoModal. The class then provides several functions for retrieving the information entered by the user. If you want to customize the behavior of the dialog you can do one of two things: 1) modify the constructor's default parameters, or 2) modify the contents of the m_ofn member of the CFileDialog object. m_ofn is an OPENFILENAME structure that specifies exactly how the file open dialog should behave. For a description of the OPENFILENAME structure, see the Windows SDK documentation. The parameters to the constructor are, in general, more convenient but modifying the structure offers a wider degree of flexibility. Beginning with MFC version 4.0, the file open dialog can be created in the standard style or in the new Windows 95 Explorer style. Several functions were added in version 4.0 to support the new Explorer style file open dialog. Figure 8-2 depicts the file common dialog.

CFileDialog

■ 2.0 ■ 3.0

Description	Initializes the internal m_ofn (OPENFILENAME) structure with the values passed to the constructor as well as adding its own information. It then takes care of some ugly business by translating the | characters that

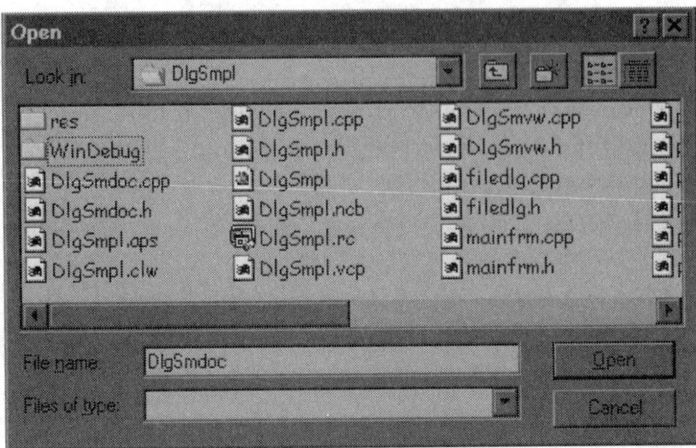

Figure 8-2 The Windows file common dialog

MFC uses to delineate the strings in the lpszFilter parameter into the '\0' characters that the common dialogs use.

Syntax public, CFileDialog(BOOL bOpenFileDialog, LPCTSTR lpszDefExt = NULL, LPCTSTR lpszFileName = NULL, DWORD dwFlags = OFN_HIDEREADONLY | OFN_OVERWRITEPROMPT, LPCTSTR lpszFilter = NULL, CWnd* pParentWnd = NULL);

Parameters

bOpenFileDialog TRUE if the file dialog should be an Open File dialog; FALSE if the dialog should be a Save dialog.

lpszDefExt The default file extension that, if the user does not specify one, will be appended to the file name. Can be NULL.

lpszFileName The default file name that will appear in the file name box when the dialog is initially displayed. Can be NULL.

dwFlags A series of flags that describe exactly how the file dialog should behave. These flags are the same flags that are used with the SDK OPENFILENAME structure. The CFileDialog has an OPENFILENAME structure as one of its members (m_ofn). This member is public, so you can also directly modify it in order to refine the file dialog's behavior.

lpszFilter A series of string pairs that describe what file types should be listed in the file types box on the dialog. The first string in each pair is a description of the file type and the second string is the file specification. An example of this parameter is shown below:

```
"Document Files (*.doc)|*.doc|Text Files (*.txt)|*.txt|All Files (*.*)|*.*||"
```

pParentWnd A pointer to the dialog's parent window.

Returns Nothing is returned.

Example See CFileDialog::DoModal

DoModal

■ 2.0 ■ 3.0

Description Displays the file dialog in modal form.

Syntax public, virtual int DoModal();

Parameters None.

Returns IDOK if the OK button was pressed, IDCANCEL if the Cancel button was pressed, or 0 if an error occurred. If an error occurs, you can use the CommDlgExtendedError SDK function to determine the exact error.

See Also ::CommDlgExtendedError

Example

```
// create the file dialog
CFileDialog fileDlg(TRUE,  exe , NULL, OFN_HIDEREADONLY |
     OFN_OVERWRITEPROMPT, "Programs (*.exe)|*.exe|All Files
     (*.*)|*.*||", pParentWnd);

// display the file dialog
fileDlg.DoModal();

// get all the file information we can
CString strExt = fileDlg.GetFileExt();
CString strName = fileDlg.GetFileName();
CString strTitle = fileDlg.GetFileTitle();
CString strPath = fileDlg.GetPathName();
```

Dump

■ 2.0 ■ 3.0 ■ DO

Description A debug-only function that "dumps" various state information regarding the CFileDialog object to a specified dump context.

Syntax public, virtual void Dump(CDumpContext& dc) const;

Parameters

dc A reference to the dump context to which the output should be sent. Usually this will be afxDump, which is a default dump context created by MFC. When debugging an MFC application, output sent to afxDump will appear in the debugger.

Returns Nothing is returned.

See Also CDialog::Dump

Example Example output from the Dump function.

```
// call to dump to output debug information
fileDlg.Dump(afxDump);

// output of Dump function
a CFileDialog at $63FB7C

m_hWnd = 0x0m_lpDialogTemplate = 0
m_hDialogTemplate = 0x0
m_pParentWnd = $0
m_nIDHelp = 0x7004
```

continued on next page

continued from previous page

```
File open dialog
m_ofn.hwndOwner = 0x0
m_ofn.nFilterIndex = 0
m_ofn.lpstrFile =
m_ofn.nMaxFile = 260
m_ofn.lpstrFileTitle =
m_ofn.nMaxFileTitle = 64
m_ofn.lpstrTitle = (NULL)
m_ofn.Flags = $80026
m_ofn.lpstrDefExt = (NULL)
m_ofn.nFileOffset = 0
m_ofn.nFileExtension = 0
m_ofn.lpstrFilter =
m_ofn.lpstrCustomFilter =
hook function set to standard MFC hook function
```

GetFileExt

■ 2.0 ■ 3.0

Description Retrieves the file extension of the selected file. If more than one file is selected, it returns the file extension of the first selected file.

Syntax public, CString GetFileExt() const;

Parameters None.

Returns The extension of the selected file.

See Also CFileDialog::GetFileName, CFileDialog::GetPathName, CFileDialog::GetFileTitle

Example See CFileDialog::DoModal

GetFileName

■ 2.0 ■ 3.0

Description Retrieves the name of the selected file. If more than one file is selected, it returns the name of the first selected file.

Syntax public, CString GetFileName() const;

Parameters None.

Returns The name of the selected file.

See Also CFileDialog::GetFile, CFileDialog::GetPathName, CFileDialog::GetFileTitle

Example See CFileDialog::DoModal

GetFileTitle

■ 2.0 ■ 3.0

Description Retrieves the title of the selected file. If more than one file is selected, it returns the title of the first selected file. The title of a file is its name and extension without path information.

Syntax public, CString GetFileTitle() const;

Parameters None.

Returns The title of the selected file.

See Also CFileDialog::GetFileName, CFileDialog::GetPathName, CFileDialog::GetFileExt

Example See CFileDialog::DoModal

GetFolderPath

–. ■ 4.0 ■ NM ■ UD

Description Retrieves the path to the folder currently open in the file dialog. This function is only valid while the dialog is displayed and only for dialogs with the OFN_EXPLORER style.

Syntax public, CString GetFolderPath() const;

Parameters None.

Returns The path name of the currently open folder.

Example See CFileDialog::HideControl

GetNextPathName

–. ■ 4.0

Description Retrieves the full path name of the next selected file in a multi-selection file dialog. You can allow multiple file selections by specifying the OFN_ALLOWMULTISELECT flag when you create the file common dialog. Use the CFileDialog::GetStartPosition member function to retrieve the position of the first filename and then call this function until the position is set to NULL. You should use this function to retrieve the filenames instead of parsing them yourself (from the lpstrFile member of the OPENFILENAME structure) because the format of this data is different depending on the operating system (Windows 3.1, Windows 95, etc.).

Syntax public, CString GetNextPathName(POSITION& pos) const;

Parameters

pos The position of the current path name. The start position should be retrieved from the CFileDialog::GetStartPosition function. GetNextPathName will then update this parameter each time it is called. When this parameter becomes NULL, no more path names exist.

Returns The path name of the next selected file.

See Also CFileDialog::GetStartPosition, CFileDialog::GetFileName, CFileDialog::GetFileExt, CFileDialog::GetFileTitle

Example

```
// create the file dialog
CFileDialog fileDlg(TRUE,  exe , NULL, OFN_HIDEREADONLY |
     OFN_OVERWRITEPROMPT | OFN_ALLOWMULTISELECT, "Programs
     (*.exe)|*.exe|All Files (*.*)|*.*||", pParentWnd);

// display the file dialog
fileDlg.DoModal();
```

continued on next page

continued from previous page

```
// get all selected paths
CStringArray straPaths;
POSITION pos = fileDlg.GetStartPosition();
while(pos)
      straPaths.Add(fileDlg.GetNextPathName(pos));
```

GetPathName

■ 2.0 ■ 3.0

Description Retrieves the full path name of the selected file. If more than one file is selected, it returns the path of the first selected file.

Syntax public, CString GetPathName() const;

Parameters None.

Returns The path name of the selected file.

See Also CFileDialog::GetFileName, CFileDialog::GetFileExt, CFileDialog::GetFileTitle

Example See CFileDialog::DoModal

GetReadOnlyPref

■ 2.0 ■ 3.0

Description Returns the state of the read-only check box on the file open dialog. The read-only check box is only displayed if the OFN_HIDEREADONLY is NOT specified when the dialog is created. Note that it is specified by default.

Syntax public, BOOL GetReadOnlyPref() const;

Parameters None.

Returns TRUE if the read-only check box is checked; FALSE otherwise.

GetStartPosition

–. ■ 4.0

Description Retrieves the position of the first path name in the list of selected path names in a multiple selection file dialog. Use this function in conjunction with the CFileDialog::GetNextPathName function to retrieve the selected path names in the file dialog.

Syntax public, POSITION GetStartPosition() const;

Parameters None.

Returns The position of the first path name. Pass this value to CFileDialog::GetNextPathName to retrieve the actual path name.

See Also CFileDialog::GetNextPathName

Example See CFileDialog::GetNextPathName

HideControl

–. ■ 4.0 ■ NM ■ UD

Description Hides the specified control in the file dialog. This function is valid only if the OFN_EXPLORER flag was set in the OPENFILENAME structure associated with the dialog. The OFN_EXPLORER flag makes the file dialog use the "new" Windows 95 Explorer look-and-feel. Note that unlike most of the CFileDialog member functions, you can call this function while the file dialog is visible.

Syntax public, void HideControl(int nID);

Parameters

nID The ID of the control to hide.

Returns Nothing is returned.

OnFileNameChange

–. ■ 4.0

Description Called when the user changes the current filename in the file dialog. The default version does nothing. This function is only called if the dialog has the OFN_EXPLORER style flag set.

Syntax protected, virtual void OnFileNameChange();

Parameters None.

Returns Nothing is returned.

Example See CFileDialog::HideControl

OnFileNameOK

■ 2.0 ■ 3.0

Description Called by the framework to validate a filename when the user presses the OK button. The default implementation performs basic filename validation. This is usually good enough. However, if you have application-specific validation that needs to be performed, override this function.

Syntax public, virtual BOOL OnFileNameOK();

Parameters None.

Returns TRUE if the filename is good; FALSE if the filename should be rejected.

OnFolderChange

–. ■ 4.0

Description Called when the user changes the current folder. Use the CFileDialog::GetFolderPath member function to retrieve the new folder name. This function is only valid if the file dialog has the OFN_EXPLORER style flag set.

Syntax	protected, virtual void OnFolderChange();
Parameters	None.
Returns	Nothing is returned.
Example	See CFileDialog::HideControl

OnInitDone

–. ■ 4.0

Description	Called when file dialog initialization is done. The default version simply calls the dialog parent window's CenterWindow function. Override this function if you need to do your own initialization after the file dialog is completely initialized. This function is only valid if the file dialog has the OFN_EXPLORER style flag set.
Syntax	protected, virtual void OnInitDone();
Parameters	None.
Returns	Nothing is returned.

OnNotify

–. ■ 4.0 ■ UD

Description	Handler for the WM_NOTIFY message. MFC uses this handler to dispatch several notification messages to their appropriate virtual member functions. Messages handled by this function include the CDN_INITDONE, CDN_SELCHANGE, CDN_FOLDERCHANGE, and CDN_SHAREVIOLATION, as well as several other messages. You should not need to override this function because not only does it simply call virtual member functions that you can implement but it also starts by calling the parent CCommonDialog version that will pump the messages through the message map.
Syntax	protected, virtual BOOL OnNotify();
Parameters	None.
Returns	TRUE if the message is processed; FALSE otherwise.

OnTypeChange

–. ■ 4.0

Description	Called when the user changes the current file type. This function is only valid if the file dialog has the OFN_EXPLORER style flag set.
Syntax	protected, virtual void OnTypeChange();
Parameters	None.
Returns	Nothing is returned.
Example	See CFileDialog::HideControl

OnLBSelChangedNotify

■ 2.0 ■ 3.0

Description Called by the framework whenever the selection changes in the filename list box. This function would normally be used to present file-specific details in a custom open file dialog template. Note that in the common file dialog on Windows 95 this function does not work because the files are no longer displayed in a list box.

Syntax public, virtual void OnLBSelChangedNotify(UINT nIDBox, UINT iCurSel, UINT nCode);

Parameters

nIDBox The resource ID of the list box in which the selection change occurred.

iCurSel The index of the affected item. See the description of the nCode parameter, below, for details.

nCode One of the following values:

CD_LBSELCHANGE iCurSel is the selected item in a single-selection list box.

CD_LBSELSUB iCurSel is no longer selected in a multiselection list box.

CD_LBSELADD iCurSel is selected in a multiselection list box.

CD_LBSELNOITEMS No selection exists in a multiselection list box.

Returns Nothing is returned.

Example

```
// function declaration
virtual void OnLBSelChangedNotify( UINT nIDBox, UINT iCurSel,
                                   UINT nCode);

// display special information whenever the file selected changes
void CSpecFileDlg::OnLBSelChangedNotify( UINT nIDBox,
                      UINT iCurSel, UINT nCode)
{
     if (nCode == CD_LBSELCHANGE)
          DoDisplaySpecialFileInfo();
}
```

OnShareViolation

■ 2.0 ■ 3.0

Description Called by the framework when the file selected by the user causes a share violation (the file is in use by another program). The default implementation simply returns OFN_SHAREWARN, which causes a warning dialog to be displayed. Override this function if you would like to change this behavior.

Syntax public, virtual UINT OnShareViolation(LPCTSTR lpszPathName);

Parameters

lpszPathName The full path name of the file on which the violation occurred.

Returns If you override this function, you should return one of the following values: OFN_SHAREFALLTHROUGH if the filename should be returned from the dialog box, or OFN_SHARENOWARN if no action should be taken, or OFN_SHAREWARN if the user should be warned about the violation.

SetControlText

–. ■ 4.0

Description Sets the text of a specified control in the file dialog to the specified string. This function is only valid if the file dialog was created with the OFN_EXPLORER style flag and should only be called while the file dialog is displayed.

Syntax public, void SetControlText(int nID, LPCSTR lpszText);

Parameters

nID ID of the control whose text should be set

lpszText A pointer to a NULL-terminated string containing the new text for the control.

Returns Nothing is returned.

Example See CFileDialog::HideControl

SetDefExt

–. ■ 4.0

Description Sets the current default file extension (type). This function is only valid if the file dialog was created with the OFN_EXPLORER style flag and should only be called while the file dialog is displayed.

Syntax public, void SetDefExt(LPCSTR lpszExt);

Parameters

lpszExt A pointer to a NULL-terminated string containing the new extension.

Returns Nothing is returned.

Example See CFileDialog::HideControl

SetTemplate

–. ■ 4.0

Description Helper function that allows you to easily specify an alternate template to be used for the file dialog. SetTemplate allows you to specify two different templates—the first one is used for the normal file dialog and the second one is used if the OFN_EXPLORER style flag is set.

Syntax public, void SetTemplate(UINT nWin3ID, UINT nWin4ID);
public, void SetTemplate(LPCTSTR lpWin3ID, LPCTSTR lpWin4ID);

Parameters

nWin3ID The resource ID of the template to use if the dialog does not have the OFN_EXPLORER style flag set.

Figure 8-3 The Windows common color dialog

nWin4ID	The resource ID of the template to use if the dialog does have the OFN_EXPLORER style flag set.
lpWin3ID	The name of the template resource to use if the dialog does not have the OFN_EXPLORER style flag set.
lpWin4ID	The name of the template resource to use if the dialog does have the OFN_EXPLORER style flag set.
Returns	Nothing is returned.
Example	See CFileDialog::HideControl

The CColorDialog Class

The CColorDialog class is an encapsulation of the Windows color common dialog. With this class, displaying a basic color dialog is easy. You simply create a CColorDialog object and call DoModal. The class then provides several functions for retrieving the information entered by the user. If you want to customize the behavior of the dialog you can do one of two things: 1) modify the constructor's default parameters, or 2) modify the contents of the m_cc member of the CColorDialog object. m_cc is a CHOOSECOLOR structure that specifies exactly how the color dialog should behave. For a complete description of the CHOOSECOLOR structure, see the Windows SDK Help. Modifying the CHOOSECOLOR structure offers greater flexibility than simply using the constructor; not all color dialog features can be manipulated via the constructor.

Figure 8-3 shows an example of the color common dialog.

CColorDialog

■ 2.0 ■ 3.0

Description Initializes the internal m_cc (CHOOSECOLOR) structure with the values passed to the constructor as well as adding its own information.

Syntax public, CColorDialog(COLORREF clrInit = 0, DWORD dwFlags = 0, CWnd* pParentWnd = NULL);

Parameters

clrInit The initial color selection when the dialog is displayed.

dwFlags A series of flags that describe the exact behavior of the dialog. These flags are the same ones used in the SDK structure CHOOSECOLOR (the Flags member of the structure).

pParentWnd A pointer to the dialog's parent window.

Returns Nothing is returned.

Example See CColorDialog::DoModal

DoModal

■ 2.0 ■ 3.0

Description Displays the color common dialog in modal form.

Syntax public, virtual int DoModal();

Parameters None.

Returns IDOK if the OK button was pressed, IDCANCEL if the Cancel button was pressed, or 0 if an error occurred. If an error occurs, you can use the CommDlgExtendedError SDK function to determine the exact error.

Example

```
// create the color dialog object
CColorDialog colorDlg(0,0,pParentWnd);

// since we didn't do it in the constructor, set the color to the
// initial color we want - red
colorDlg.SetCurrentColor(RGB(255,0,0));

// display the color dialog
if (colorDlg.DoModal() == IDOK)
{
      // get the selected color
      COLORREF crColor = dlg.GetColor();

      // get a pointer to the custom colors
      COLORREF *pCustomColors = colorDlg.GetSavedCustomColors();
      ..
}
```

Dump

■ 2.0 ■ 3.0 ■ DO

Description A debug-only function that "dumps" various state information regarding the CColorDialog object to a specified dump context.

Syntax public, virtual void Dump(CDumpContext& dc) const;

Parameters

dc A reference to the dump context to which the output should be sent. Usually this will be afxDump, which is a default dump context created by MFC. When debugging an MFC application, output sent to afxDump will appear in the debugger.

Returns Nothing is returned.

See Also CDialog::Dump;

Example Example output from the Dump function.

```
// call to Dump to output debug information
colorDlg.Dump(afxDump);

// output of Dump function
a CColorDialog at $63FCF8

m_hWnd = 0x0m_lpDialogTemplate = 0
m_hDialogTemplate = 0x0
m_pParentWnd = $0
m_nIDHelp = 0x7007
m_cc.hwndOwner = 0x0
m_cc.rgbResult = $0
m_cc.Flags = $10
m_cc.lpCustColors
          $FFFFFF
          $FFFFFF
          $FFFFFF
          $FFFFFF
          $FFFFFF
          $FFFFFF
          $FFFFFF
          $FFFFFF
          $FFFFFF
          $FFFFFF
          $FFFFFF
          $FFFFFF
          $FFFFFF
          $FFFFFF
          $FFFFFF
          $FFFFFF
hook function set to standard MFC hook function
```

GetColor ■ 2.0 ■ 3.0

Description Retrieves the RGB information for the color that is currently selected in the dialog.

Syntax public, COLORREF GetColor() const;

Parameters None.

Returns A COLORREF value that specifies the color's RGB information.

See Also CColorDialog::GetSavedCustomColors

Example See CFontDialog::DoModal

GetSavedCustomColors

■ 2.0 ■ 3.0

Description Retrieves the RGB information for the user-customizable colors. The color dialog allows the user to define up to sixteen custom colors. Note that this function is only valid after the call to DoModal returns IDOK. MFC stores these colors for the entire time an application is running, so each time the color dialog is invoked, the custom colors remain intact. If you want to save the colors for longer than this, you will have to do it yourself.

Syntax public, static COLORREF* PASCAL GetSavedCustomColors();

Parameters None.

Returns A pointer to an array of sixteen COLORREF values—one for each of the custom colors. Each member of this array is initialized to white so if the user has not specified all sixteen custom colors, those members in the array will contain RGB(255,255,255).

See Also CColorDialog::GetColor

Example See CFontDialog::DoModal

OnColorOK

■ 2.0 ■ 3.0

Description Called by the framework to verify that the selected color is valid. This function is called when the user attempts to dismiss the color dialog by pressing the OK button.

Syntax public, virtual BOOL OnColorOK();

Parameters None.

Returns Return 0 if the color is OK and the dialog can be dismissed. Returning non-zero will cause the dialog to remain displayed.

Example

```
BOOL CMyColorDlg::OnColorOK()
{
      COLORREF cr = GetColor();

      // only allow red and green to be selected
      if (cr != RGB(255,0,0) && cr != RGB(0,255,0))
      {
            // if red or green not selected, force red
            SetCurrentColor(RGB(255,0,0));
            return FALSE;
      }
      return TRUE;
}
```

OnCtlColor

■ 2.0 ■ 3.0 ■ UD

Description Message handler for the WM_CTLCOLOR message. The CColorDialog implementation simply returns the result of a call to the MFC default window procedure. This is done because the Windows common dialogs cannot handle dialogs with a colored background (gray, for example).

Syntax protected, afx_msg HBRUSH OnCtlColor(CDC* pDC, CWnd* pWnd, UINT nCtlColor)

Parameters

pDC A pointer to the display context for the control to which the message pertains.

pWnd A pointer to the control window requesting the color.

nCtlColor One of the following values specifying the control to be affected:

CTLCOLOR_BTN Button control.

CTLCOLOR_DLG Dialog box.

CTLCOLOR_EDIT Edit control.

CTLCOLOR_LIST BOX List box control.

CTLCOLOR_MSGBOX Message box.

CTLCOLOR_SCROLLBAR Scrollbar control.

CTLCOLOR_STATIC Static control.

Returns A handle to the brush that should be used for the background of the control.

See Also CWnd::Default

SetCurrentColor

■ 2.0 ■ 3.0

Description Sets the currently selected color in the dialog. You should only call this function after a call to DoModal.

Syntax public, void SetCurrentColor(COLORREF clr);

Parameters

clr The RGB value of the color that should be selected.

Returns Nothing is returned.

Example See CFontDialog::OnColorOK

The CFontDialog Class

The CFontDialog class is an encapsulation of the Windows font common dialog. With this class, displaying a basic font dialog is easy. You simply create a CFontDialog object and call DoModal. The class then provides several functions for retrieving the information entered by the user. If you want to customize the behavior of the dialog, you can do one of two things: 1) modify the constructor's default parameters, or 2) modify the contents of the m_cf member of the CFontDialog object. m_cf is a CHOOSEFONT structure that specifies exactly how the font dialog should behave. For a complete description of the CHOOSEFONT structure, see the Windows SDK Help. Modifying the CHOOSEFONT structure offers greater flexibility than simply using the constructor; not all font dialog features can be manipulated via the constructor.

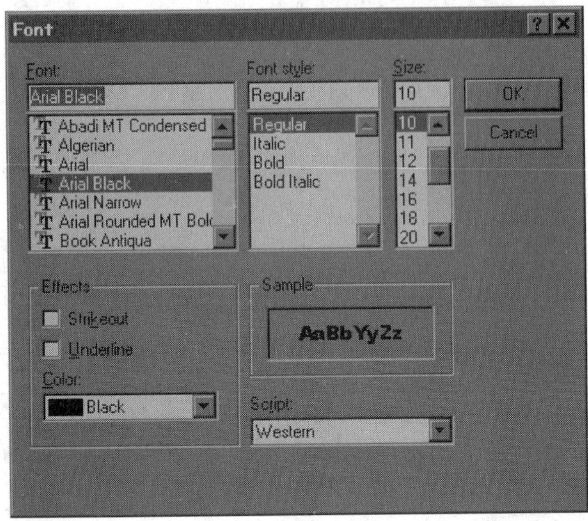

Figure 8-4 The Windows common font dialog

MFC version 4.0 added several functions to support the new rich edit common control. The font dialog can be initialized with and return back a CHARFORMAT structure that is used by the rich edit control to determine the current character attributes. Figure 8-4 shows an example of the font common dialog.

CFontDialog

■ 2.0 ■ 3.0

Description Initializes the internal m_cf (CHOOSEFONT) structure with the values passed to the constructor as well as adding its own information. Note that the second version of the constructor was introduced in version 4.0.

Syntax public, CFontDialog(LPLOGFONT lplfInitial = NULL, DWORD dwFlags = CF_EFFECTS | CF_SCREENFONTS, CDC* pdcPrinter = NULL, CWnd *pParentWnd); public, CFontDialog(const CHARFORMAT charFormat, DWORD dwFlags = CF_EFFECTS | CF_SCREENFONTS, CDC* pdcPrinter = NULL, CWnd *pParentWnd);

Parameters

lplfInitial A pointer to a LOGFONT structure that describes the font which should be initially selected when the dialog is displayed. Also, if this parameter is supplied, MFC will fill it with the selected font information when the dialog terminates (if the user presses OK).

dwFlags A series of flags that describe the exact behavior of the dialog. These flags are the same ones used in the SDK structure CHOOSEFONT (the Flags member of the structure).

pdcPrinter A pointer to a printer device context. If the flags specified in the dwFlags parameter include the capability to select printer fonts (CF_BOTH or

CF_PRINTERFONTS), this parameter should be a pointer to a device context for the printer on which the font will be printed.

pParentWnd A pointer to the dialog's parent window.

charFormat A reference to a CHARFORMAT structure that describes the font that should be initially selected when the dialog is displayed. The CHARFORMAT structure is used by the rich edit control to describe the character attributes. For more information about this structure, see the Windows SDK documentation.

Returns Nothing is returned.

Example See CFontDialog::DoModal

DoModal

■ 2.0 ■ 3.0

Description Displays the font common dialog in modal form.

Syntax public, virtual int DoModal();

Parameters None.

Returns IDOK if the OK button was pressed, IDCANCEL if the Cancel button was pressed, or 0 if an error occurred. If an error occurs, you can use the CommDlgExtendedError SDK function to determine the exact error.

Example

```
// create the font dialog object
CFontDialog fontDlg(NULL,CF_EFFECTS | CF_SCREENFONTS,NULL,pParentWnd);
LOGFONT logFont;

// display the dialog
fontDlg.DoModal();

COLORREF crFontColor = dlg.GetColor();

// retrieve font information - all at once
fontDlg.GetCurrentFont(&logFont);

// retrieve all the information about the font - one at a time
CString strFaceName = fontDlg.GetFaceName();
int nSize = fontDlg.GetSize();
CString strStyleName = fontDlg.GetStyleName();
int nWeight = fontDlg.GetWeight();
BOOL bBold = fontDlg.IsBold();
BOOL bItalic = fontDlg.IsItalic();
BOOL bStrikeOut = fontDlg.IsStrikeOut();
BOOL bUnderline = fontDlg.IsUnderline();
```

Dump

■ 2.0 ■ 3.0 ■ DO

Description A debug-only function that "dumps" various state information regarding the CFontDialog object to a specified dump context.

Syntax public, virtual void Dump(CDumpContext& dc) const;

Parameters

dc — A reference to the dump context to which the output should be sent. Usually this will be afxDump, which is a default dump context created by MFC. When debugging an MFC application, output sent to afxDump will appear in the debugger.

Returns — Nothing is returned.

See Also — CDialog::Dump;

Example — Example output from the Dump function.

```
// call to dump to output debug information
fontDlg.Dump(afxDump);

// output of Dump function
a CFontDialog at $63FBFC

m_hWnd = 0x0m_lpDialogTemplate = 0
m_hDialogTemplate = 0x0
m_pParentWnd = $0
m_nIDHelp = 0x7006
m_cf.hwndOwner = 0x0
m_cf.hDC = 0x0
m_cf.iPointSize = 0
m_cf.Flags = $109
m_cf.lpszStyle =
m_cf.nSizeMin = 0
m_cf.nSizeMax = 0
m_cf.nFontType = 0
m_cf.rgbColors = $0
hook function set to standard MFC hook function
```

FillInLogFont

–. ■ 4.0 ■ UD

Description — Used by MFC to fill in the internal CFontDialog LOGFONT structure member (m_lf) with the font attributes contained in a CHARFORMAT structure. You could also use this function yourself if you need to convert from a CHARFORMAT structure to a LOGFONT structure.

Syntax — public, DWORD FillInLogFont(CHARFORMAT &cf) const;

Parameters

cf — A reference to a CHARFORMAT structure that will be filled in with the current font attributes. For a complete description of the CHARFORMAT structure, see the Windows SDK documentation.

Returns — A DWORD containing the CHOOSEFONT flags derived from the CHARFORMAT structure.

See Also — CFontDialog::GetCharFormat

GetCharFormat

–. ■ 4.0

Description Retrieves the current font selections as a CHARFORMAT structure. The CHARFORMAT structure is used by the rich edit control to describe font attributes.

Syntax public, void GetCharFormat(CHARFORMAT &cf) const;

Parameters

cf A reference to a CHARFORMAT structure that will be filled in with the current font attributes. For a complete description of the CHARFORMAT structure, see the Windows SDK documentation.

Returns Nothing is returned.

See Also CFontDialog::FillInLogFont

GetColor

■ 2.0 ■ 3.0

Description Retrieves the color of the currently selected font.

Syntax public, COLORREF GetColor() const;

Parameters None.

Returns The RGB value for the color of the currently selected font.

Example See CFontDialog::DoModal

GetCurrentFont

■ 2.0 ■ 3.0

Description Fills a given LOGFONT structure with information regarding the currently selected font.

Syntax public, void GetCurrentFont(LPLOGFONT lplf);

Parameters

lplf A pointer to a LOGFONT structure that should be filled with the font information.

Returns Nothing is returned.

Example See CFontDialog::DoModal

GetFaceName

■ 2.0 ■ 3.0

Description Retrieves the face name of the currently selected font.

Syntax public, CString GetFaceName() const;

Parameters None.

Returns The face name of the currently selected font.

See Also CFontDialog::GetStyleName, CFontDialog::GetCurrentFont

Example See CFontDialog::DoModal

GetSize ■ 2.0 ■ 3.0

Description	Retrieves the point size of the currently selected font.
Syntax	public, int Getsize() const;
Parameters	None.
Returns	The point size of the currently selected font.
See Also	CFontDialog::GetWeight
Example	See CFontDialog::DoModal

GetStyleName ■ 2.0 ■ 3.0

Description	Retrieves the style name of the currently selected font.
Syntax	public, CString GetStyleName() const;
Parameters	None.
Returns	The style name of the currently selected font.
See Also	CFontDialog::GetFaceName, CFontDialog::GetCurrentFont
Example	See CFontDialog::DoModal

GetWeight ■ 2.0 ■ 3.0

Description	Retrieves the weight of the currently selected font.
Syntax	public, int GetWeight() const;
Parameters	None.
Returns	The weight of the currently selected font.
See Also	CFontDialog::GetSize;
Example	See CFontDialog::DoModal

IsBold ■ 2.0 ■ 3.0

Description	Determines whether the bold effect is enabled for the currently selected font.
Syntax	public, BOOL IsBold() const;
Parameters	None.
Returns	TRUE if the font is bold; FALSE otherwise.
See Also	CFontDialog::IsItalic, CFontDialog::IsUnderline, CFontDialog::IsStrikeOut;
Example	See CFontDialog::DoModal

IsItalic

■ 2.0 ■ 3.0

Description	Determines whether the italic effect is enabled for the currently selected font.
Syntax	public, BOOL IsItalic() const;
Parameters	None.
Returns	TRUE if the font is italic; FALSE otherwise.
See Also	CFontDialog::IsBold, CFontDialog::IsUnderline, CFontDialog::IsStrikeOut;

IsStrikeOut

■ 2.0 ■ 3.0

Description	Determines whether the strike-out effect is enabled for the currently selected font.
Syntax	public, BOOL IsStrikeOut() const;
Parameters	None.
Returns	TRUE if the font is strike-out; FALSE otherwise.
See Also	CFontDialog::IsItalic, CFontDialog::IsUnderline, CFontDialog::IsBold;
Example	See CFontDialog::DoModal

IsUnderline

■ 2.0 ■ 3.0

Description	Determines whether the underline effect is enabled for the currently selected font.
Syntax	public, BOOL IsUnderline() const;
Parameters	None.
Returns	TRUE if the font is underlined; FALSE otherwise.
See Also	CFontDialog::IsItalic, CFontDialog::IsBold, CFontDialog::IsStrikeOut;
Example	See CFontDialog::DoModal

The CPageSetupDialog Class

The CPageSetupDialog class is an encapsulation of the Windows page setup common dialog. The CPageSetupDialog class did not appear in MFC until version 4.0 and is not available on the Macintosh. The CPageSetupDialog class, along with its associated page setup common dialog, are designed to replace the print setup dialog. The page setup common dialog offers more control than the print setup dialog. With the CPageSetupDialog class, displaying a basic page setup dialog is easy. You simply create

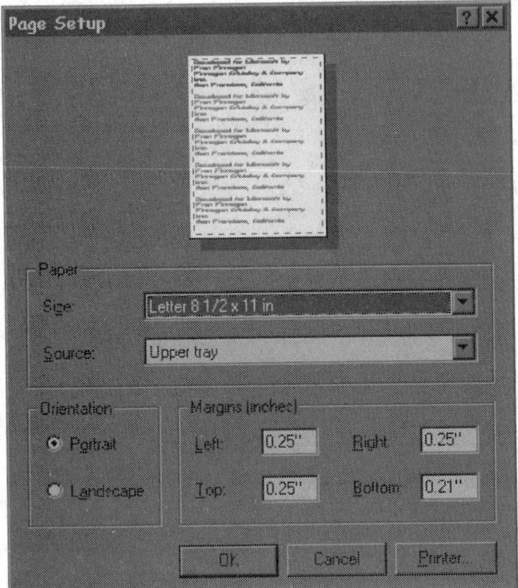

Figure 8-5 The Windows common page setup dialog

a CPageSetupDialog object and call DoModal. The class then provides several functions for retrieving the information entered by the user. If you want to customize the behavior of the dialog you can do one of two things: 1) modify the constructor's default parameters, or 2) modify the contents of the m_psd member of the CPageSetupDialog object. m_psd is a PAGESETUPDLG structure that specifies exactly how the print dialog should behave. For a complete description of the PAGESETUPDLG structure, see the Windows SDK documentation. Modifying the PAGESETUPDLG structure offers greater flexibility than simply using the constructor; not all page setup dialog features can be manipulated via the constructor.

Figure 8-5 shows an example of the page setup common dialog.

CPageSetupDialog

–. ■ 4.0 ■ NM

Description Constructor that initializes the CPageSetupDialog object's members.

Syntax public, CPageSetupDialog(DWORD dwFlags = PSD_MARGINS | PSD_INWININIINTLMEASURE, CWnd* pParentWnd = NULL);

Parameters

dwFlags A series of flags that describe the exact behavior of the dialog. These flags are the same ones used in the SDK structure PAGESETUPDLG (the Flags member of the structure).

pParentWnd A pointer to the dialog's parent window.

Returns Nothing is returned.

Example See CPageSetupDialog::DoModal

CreatePrinterDC

–. ■ 4.0 ■ NM

Description Creates a printer device context based on the parameters in the m_psd member of the print dialog. You can then use this device context to print with. Note that the dialog does not have to be displayed in order to use this feature.

Syntax public, HDC CreatePrinterDC();

Parameters None.

Returns A handle to the printer device context if successful or NULL if a failure occurred.

Example See CPageSetupDialog::DoModal

DoModal

–. ■ 4.0 ■ NM

Description Displays the page setup common dialog in modal form. After DoModal returns, you can use the functions provided by the CPageSetupDialog class to retrieve the user's selections.

Syntax public, virtual int DoModal();

Parameters None.

Returns IDOK if the OK button was pressed, IDCANCEL if the Cancel button was pressed, or 0 if an error occurred. If an error occurs, you can use the CommDlgExtendedError SDK function to determine the exact error.

Example

```
// create page setup dialog object
CPageSetupDialog psDlg(FALSE, = PSD_MARGINS | SD_INWININIINTLMEASURE
     , pParentWnd);

if (psDlg.DoModal() == IDOK)
{
     // get lots of info from dialog just for fun
     CString strDeviceName = psDlg.GetDeviceName();
     CString strDriverName = psDlg.GetDriverName();
     CString strPortName = psDlg.GetPortName();

     // get a printer DC based on user's selections
     HDC hPrintDc = psDlg.CreatePrinterDC();

     // get an object so we can be object-oriented
     CDC *pDc = CDC::FromHandle(hPrintDC);

     // do some printing here

     ::DeleteDC(hPrintDc);
}
```

DUMP

–. ■ 4.0 ■ NM ■ DO

Description Debug-only function that "dumps" various state information regarding the CPageSetupDialog object to a specified dump context.

Syntax public, virtual void Dump(CDumpContext& dc) const;

Parameters

dc A reference to the dump context to which the output should be sent. Usually this will be afxDump, which is a default dump context created by MFC. When debugging an MFC application, output sent to afxDump will appear in the debugger.

Returns Nothing is returned.

See Also CDialog::Dump;

Example Example output from the Dump function.

```
// call to dump to output debug information
pageSetupDlg.Dump(afxDump);

// output of Dump function
CPageSetupDialog at $64F76C

      m_hWnd = 0x0m_lpszTemplateName = 0
      m_hDialogTemplate = 0x0
      m_lpDialogTemplate = 0x0
      m_pParentWnd = $6610E0
      m_nIDHelp = 0x0
      m_psd.hwndOwner = 0x0
      m_psd.Flags = $42002
      m_psd.ptPaperSize = (0, 0)
      m_psd.rtMinMargin = (L 0, T 0, R 0, B 0)
      m_psd.rtMinMargin = (L 0, T 0, R 0, B 0)
      setup hook function set to standard MFC hook function
      print hook function set to non-standard hook function
```

GETDEVICENAME

–. ■ 4.0 ■ NM

Description Retrieves the name of the selected printer device.

Syntax public, CString GetDeviceName() const;

Parameters None.

Returns The name of the selected printer device.

See Also CPageSetupDialog::GetDriverName, CPageSetupDialog::GetPortName

Example See CPageSetupDialog::DoModal

GETDEVMODE

–. ■ 4.0 ■ NM

Description Retrieves device information for the currently selected printer device and initializes a DEVMODE structure with the information. You must later free this structure using the GlobalFree SDK function.

Syntax	public, LPDEVMODE GetDevMode() const;
Parameters	None.
Returns	A pointer to a DEVMODE structure containing the device information. For more information on the DEVMODE structure, see the Windows SDK Help.
Include File	afxdlgs.h

GetDriverName

–. ■ 4.0 ■ NM

Description	Retrieves the name of the selected printer driver.
Syntax	public, CString GetDriverName() const;
Parameters	None.
Returns	The name of the currently selected driver.
See Also	CPageSetupDialog::GetDeviceName, CPageSetupDialog::GetPortName
Example	See CPageSetupDialog::DoModal

GetMargins

–. ■ 4.0 ■ NM

Description	Retrieves the margins for the current printer. This function can retrieve both the current margins and the minimum allowable margins.
Syntax	public, void GetMargins(LPRECT lpRectMargins, LPRECT lpRectMinMargins) const;
Parameters	
lpRectMargins	A pointer to a RECT structure or a CRect object that will be filled with the coordinates (in 1/1000 inches or 1/100 mm) of the current margins.
lpRectMinMargins	A pointer to a RECT structure or a CRect object that will be filled with the coordinates (in 1/1000 inches or 1/100 mm) of the minimum allowable margins.
Returns	Nothing is returned.
Example	See CPageSetupDialog::DoModal

GetPaperSize

–. ■ 4.0 ■ NM

Description	Retrieves the selected paper size in 1/1000 inches or 1/100 mm.
Syntax	public, CSize GetPaperSize() const;
Parameters	None.
Returns	A CSize object containing the horizontal and vertical size of the selected paper (in 1/1000 inches or 1/100 mm).
Example	See CPageSetupDialog::DoModal

GetPortName

–. ■ 4.0 ■ NM

Description Retrieves the name of the currently selected printer port.

Syntax public, CString GetPortName() const;

Parameters None.

Returns The name of the currently selected printer port.

See Also CPageSetupDialog::GetDeviceName, CPageSetupDialog::GetDriverName

Example See CPageSetupDialog::DoModal

OnDrawPage

–. ■ 4.0 ■ NM

Description Called by MFC to paint the "sample" page on the page setup dialog. The default implementation depicts a page of text. If you would like to customize the drawing of the sample image, or of part of the sample image, override this function.

Syntax public, virtual UINT OnDrawPage(CDC *pDc, UINT nMessage, LPRECT lpRect);

Parameters

pDc A pointer to the device context on which to draw the page.

nMessage A constant that describes which part of the image should be drawn. Can be one of the following values:

WM_PSD_FULLPAGERECT The entire page.

WM_PSD_MINMARGINRECT The current minimum margins.

WM_PSD_MARGINRECT The current margins.

WM_PSD_GREEKTEXTRECT The contents of the page.

WM_PSD_ENVSTAMPRECT The area reserved for a postage stamp representation.

WM_PSD_YAFULLPAGERECT The area for a return address representation. This area extends to the edges of the sample page area.

lpRect A pointer to a RECT structure that contains the coordinates of the area needed to be drawn.

Returns Non-zero if handled; otherwise, zero.

See Also CPageSetupDialog::PreDrawPage

PaintHookProc

–. ■ 4.0 ■ UD ■ NM

Description Paint hook function installed by MFC to process page sample painting requests. This function is passed to the page setup common dialog in the lpfnPagePaintHook member of the PAGESETUPDLG structure. PaintHookProc parses the painting requests and then calls the CPageSetupDlg::PreDrawPage and/or CPageSetupDlg::OnDrawPage functions, as appropriate.

Syntax public, UINT CALLBACK PaintHookProc(HWND hWnd, UINT message, WPARAM wParam, LPARAM lParam)

Parameters

hWnd The window handle of the page setup dialog requesting painting.

message Indicates the type of painting required. See CPageSetupDialog::OnDrawPage for a list of valid values.

wParam If *message* is WM_PSD_PAGESETUPDLG, the LOWORD indicates the type of paper and the HIWORD indicates the orientation. See CPageSetupDialog::PreDrawPage for a list of valid values for these two parameters. For any other message, a device context handle to be used for painting.

lParam If *message* is WM_PSD_PAGESETUPDLG, a pointer to the page setup dialog that sent the message. For all other messages, a pointer to a RECT structure containing the coordinates of the rectangle to paint within.

Returns If the paint request (message parameter) is WM_PSD_PAGESETUPDLG, the return value from a call to PreDrawPage; otherwise the return value of a call to OnDrawPage.

See Also CPageSetupDialog::OnDrawPage, CPageSetupDialog::PreDrawPage

PreDrawPage

–. ■ 4.0 ■ NM

Description Called by MFC immediately before drawing the sample image on the page setup dialog. If you override this function and return a non-zero value, you must draw the entire image by overriding the OnDrawPage function.

Syntax public, virtual UINT PreDrawPage(WORD wPaper, WORD wFlags, LPPAGESETUPDLG lpPsd);

Parameters

wPaper Indicates the paper size. Can be any one of the following values:

DMPAPER_LETTER Letter, 8 1/2 by 11 inches.

DMPAPER_LEGAL Legal, 8 1/2 by 14 inches.

DMPAPER_A4 A4 Sheet, 210 by 297 millimeters.

DMPAPER_CSHEET C Sheet, 17 by 22 inches.

DMPAPER_DSHEET D Sheet, 22 by 34 inches.

DMPAPER_ESHEET E Sheet, 34 by 44 inches.

DMPAPER_LETTERSMALL Letter Small, 8 1/2 by 11 inches.

DMPAPER_TABLOID Tabloid, 11 by 17 inches.

DMPAPER_LEDGER Ledger, 17 by 11 inches.

DMPAPER_STATEMENT Statement, 5 1/2 by 8 1/2 inches.

DMPAPER_EXECUTIVE Executive, 7 1/4 by 10 1/2 inches.

DMPAPER_A3 A3 sheet, 297 by 420 millimeters.

DMPAPER_A4SMALL A4 small sheet, 210 by 297 millimeters.
DMPAPER_A5 A5 sheet, 148 by 210 millimeters.
DMPAPER_B4 B4 sheet, 250 by 354 millimeters.
DMPAPER_B5 B5 sheet, 182 by 257 millimeter paper.
DMPAPER_FOLIO Folio, 8 1/2 by 13 inch paper.
DMPAPER_QUARTO Quarto, 215 by 275 millimeter paper.
DMPAPER_10X14 10 by 14 inch sheet.
DMPAPER_11X17 11 by 17 inch sheet.
DMPAPER_NOTE Note, 8 1/2 by 11 inches.
DMPAPER_ENV_9 #9 Envelope, 3 7/8 by 8 7/8 inches.
DMPAPER_ENV_10 #10 Envelope, 4 1/8 by 9 1/2 inches.
DMPAPER_ENV_11 #11 Envelope, 4 1/2 by 10 3/8 inches.
DMPAPER_ENV_12 #12 Envelope, 4 3/4 by 11 inches.
DMPAPER_ENV_14 #14 Envelope, 5 by 11 1/2 inches.
DMPAPER_ENV_DL DL Envelope, 110 by 220 millimeters.
DMPAPER_ENV_C5 C5 Envelope, 162 by 229 millimeters.
DMPAPER_ENV_C3 C3 Envelope, 324 by 458 millimeters.
DMPAPER_ENV_C4 C4 Envelope, 229 by 324 millimeters.
DMPAPER_ENV_C6 C6 Envelope, 114 by 162 millimeters.
DMPAPER_ENV_C65 C65 Envelope, 114 by 229 millimeters.
DMPAPER_ENV_B4 B4 Envelope, 250 by 353 millimeters.
DMPAPER_ENV_B5 B5 Envelope, 176 by 250 millimeters.
DMPAPER_ENV_B6 B6 Envelope, 176 by 125 millimeters.
DMPAPER_ENV_ITALY Italy Envelope, 110 by 230 millimeters.
DMPAPER_ENV_MONARCH Monarch Envelope, 3 7/8 by 7 1/2 inches.
DMPAPER_ENV_PERSONAL 6 3/4 Envelope, 3 5/8 by 6 1/2 inches.
DMPAPER_FANFOLD_US US Std Fanfold, 14 7/8 by 11 inches.
DMPAPER_FANFOLD_STD_GERMAN German Std Fanfold, 8 1/2 by 12 inches.
DMPA PER_FANFOLD_LGL_GERMAN German Legal Fanfold, 8 1/2 by 13 inches.

wFlags Indicates the orientation of the paper or envelope and if the printer is dot matrix or if it is an HPPCL (Hewlett Packard Printer Control Language) printer. This parameter may be any one of the following values:

0x001 Paper, landscape mode, dot matrix.
0x003 Paper, landscape mode, HPPCL.
0x005 Paper, portrait mode, dot matrix.
0x007 Paper, portrait mode, HPPCL.
0x00b Envelope, landscape mode, HPPCL.

0x00d	Envelope, portrait mode, HPPCL.
0x019	Envelope, landscape mode, dot matrix.
0x01f	Envelope, portrait mode, dot matrix.
lpPsd	A pointer to a PAGESETUPDLG structure. For a complete description of this structure, see the Windows SDK documentation.
Returns	Non-zero if you handle the message (and therefore want to draw the image); otherwise, zero.
See Also	CPageSetupDialog::OnDrawPage

The CPrintDialog Class

The CPrintDialog class is an encapsulation of the Windows print common dialog. With this class, displaying a basic print dialog is easy. You simply create a CPrintDialog object and call DoModal. The class then provides several functions for retrieving the information entered by the user. If you want to customize the behavior of the dialog you can do one of two things: 1) modify the constructor's default parameters, or 2) modify the contents of the m_pd member of the CPrintDialog object. m_pd is a PRINTDLG structure that specifies exactly how the print dialog should behave. For a complete description of the PRINTDLG structure, see the Windows SDK Help. Modifying the PRINTDLG structure offers greater flexibility than simply using the constructor; not all print dialog features can be manipulated via the constructor.

Figure 8-6 shows an example of the print common dialog.

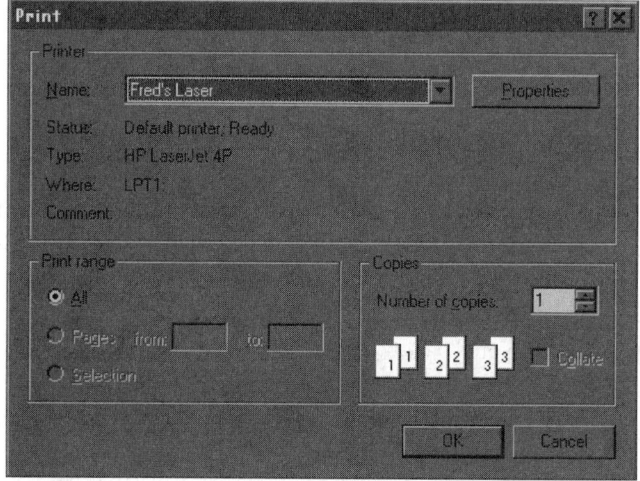

Figure 8-6 The Windows common print dialog

CPrintDialog ■ 2.0 ■ 3.0

Description Initializes the internal m_pd (PRINTDLG) structure with the values passed to the constructor as well as adding its own information.

Syntax public, CPrintDialog(BOOL bPrintSetupOnly,DWORD dwFlags = PD_ALLPAGES | PD_USEDEVMODECOPIES | PD_NOPAGENUMS | PD_HIDEPRINTOTFILE | PD_NOSELECTION, CWnd* pParentWnd = NULL);

Parameters

bPrintSetupOnly TRUE causes the print setup dialog to be displayed when DoModal is called. FALSE causes the print dialog to be displayed with a button to get to the print setup dialog.

dwFlags A series of flags that describe the exact behavior of the dialog. These flags are the same ones used in the SDK structure PRINTDLG (the Flags member of the structure).

pParentWnd A pointer to the dialog's parent window.

Returns Nothing is returned.

Example See CPrintDialog::DoModal

AttachOnSetup ■ 2.0 ■ 3.0 ■ UD

Description Utility function that MFC uses to exchange information (the m_pd structure) between the print setup dialog and the print dialog when the setup dialog is launched from the print dialog.

Syntax protected, virtual CPrintDialog* AttachOnSetup();

Parameters None.

Returns A pointer to the print setup dialog object.

CreatePrinterDC ■ 2.0 ■ 3.0

Description A very handy, maybe misplaced, function that will create a printer device context based on the parameters in the m_pd member of the print dialog. You can then use this device context to print with. Note that the dialog does not have to be displayed in order to use this feature.

Syntax public, HDC CreatePrinterDC();

Parameters None.

Returns A handle to the printer device context if successful or NULL if a failure occurred.

See Also CPrintDialog::GetDefaults, CPrintDialog::GetPrinterDC

Example See CPrintDialog::DoModal

DoModal

■ 2.0 ■ 3.0

Description Displays the print common dialog in modal form.

Syntax public, virtual int DoModal();

Parameters None.

Returns IDOK if the OK button was pressed, IDCANCEL if the Cancel button was pressed, or 0 if an error occurred. If an error occurs, you can use the CommDlgExtendedError SDK function to determine the exact error.

Example

```
// create print dialog object
CPrintDialog printDlg(FALSE,PD_ALLPAGES | PD_USEDEVMODECOPIES |
     PD_NOPAGENUMS | PD_HIDEPRINTOTFILE, pParentWnd);

if (printDlg.DoModal() == IDOK)
{
     // get lots of info from dialog just for fun
     int nCopies = printDlg.GetCopies();
     CString strDeviceName = printDlg.GetDeviceName();
     CString strDriverName = printDlg.GetDriverName();
     int nFromPage = printDlg.GetFromPage();
     CString strPortName = printDlg.GetPortName();
     int nToPage = printDlg.GetToPage();
     BOOL bPrintAll = printDlg.PrintAll();
     BOOL bPrintCollate = printDlg.PrintCollate();
     BOOL bPrintRange = printDlg.PrintRange();
     BOOL bPrintSel = printDlg.PrintSelection();

     // get a printer DC based on user's selections
     HDC hPrintDc = printDlg.GetPrinterDC();

     // get an object so we can be object-oriented
     CDC *pDc = CDC::FromHandle(hPrintDC);

     // do some printing here

     ::DeleteDC(hPrintDc);
}
```

Dump

■ 2.0 ■ 3.0 ■ DO

Description Debug-only function that "dumps" various state information regarding the CPrintDialog object to a specified dump context.

Syntax public, virtual void Dump(CDumpContext& dc) const;

Parameters

dc A reference to the dump context to which the output should be sent. Usually this will be afxDump, which is a default dump context created by MFC. When debugging an MFC application, output sent to afxDump will appear in the debugger.

Returns Nothing is returned.

See Also CDialog::Dump

Example Example output from the Dump function.

```
// call to dump to output debug information
colorDlg.Dump(afxDump);

// output of Dump function
a CPrintDialog at $63FCD4

m_hWnd = 0x0m_lpDialogTemplate = 0
m_hDialogTemplate = 0x0
m_pParentWnd = $0
m_nIDHelp = 0x7008
m_pd.hwndOwner = 0x0
m_pd.Flags = $14310C
m_pd.nFromPage = 0
m_pd.nToPage = 0
m_pd.nMinPage = 0
m_pd.nMaxPage = 0
m_pd.nCopies = 0
setup hook function set to standard MFC hook function
print hook function set to standard MFC hook function
```

GetCopies ■ 2.0 ■ 3.0

Description Retrieves the number of copies requested by the user.

Syntax public, int GetCopies() const;

Parameters None.

Returns The number of copies.

Example See CPrintDialog::DoModal

GetDefaults ■ 2.0 ■ 3.0

Description Like CreatePrinterDC, GetDefaults is actually a utility function that has nothing to do with the print dialog itself. It will retrieve the printer information for the current Windows default printer and fill the m_pd structure with the information.

Syntax public, BOOL GetDefaults();

Parameters None.

Returns Non-zero if the function is successful; 0 otherwise.

See Also CPrintDialog::CreatePrinterDC

GetDeviceName ■ 2.0 ■ 3.0

Description Retrieves the name of the selected printer device.

Syntax public, CString GetDeviceName() const;

Parameters None.

Returns	The name of the selected printer device.
See Also	CPrintDialog::GetDriverName, CPrintDialog::GetPortName
Example	See CPrintDialog::DoModal

GetDevMode ■ 2.0 ■ 3.0

Description	Retrieves device information for the currently selected printer device and initializes a DEVMODE structure with the information. You must later free this structure using the GlobalFree SDK function.
Syntax	public, LPDEVMODE GetDevMode() const;
Parameters	None.
Returns	A pointer to a DEVMODE structure containing the device information. For more information on the DEVMODE structure see the Windows SDK Help.

GetDriverName ■ 2.0 ■ 3.0

Description	Retrieves the name of the selected printer driver.
Syntax	public, CString GetDriverName() const;
Parameters	None.
Returns	The name of the currently selected driver.
See Also	CPrintDialog::GetDeviceName, CPrintDialog::GetPortName
Example	See CPrintDialog::DoModal

GetFromPage ■ 2.0 ■ 3.0

Description	Retrieves the number of the first page in a range of pages that should be printed.
Syntax	public, int GetFromPage() const;
Parameters	None.
Returns	The number of the first page to be printed.
See Also	CPrintDialog::GetToPage
Example	See CPrintDialog::DoModal

GetPortName ■ 2.0 ■ 3.0

Description	Retrieves the name of the currently selected printer port.
Syntax	public, CString GetPortName() const;
Parameters	None.
Returns	The name of the currently selected printer port.

See Also	CPrintDialog::GetDeviceName, CPrintDialog::GetDriverName
Example	See CPrintDialog::DoModal

GetPrinterDC ■ 2.0 ■ 3.0

Description	Retrieves a handle to the printer device context created by the print common dialog after it terminates. Remember that the common dialog only creates a DC if the PD_RETURNDC flag is set in the Flags member of the m_pd structure used by CPrintDialog. This function will ASSERT if this is not true.
Syntax	public, HDC GetPrinterDC() const;
Parameters	None.
Returns	A handle to the printer device context.
See Also	CPrintDialog::CreatePrinterDC
Example	See CPrintDialog::DoModal

GetToPage ■ 2.0 ■ 3.0

Description	Retrieves the number of the last page in a range of pages that should be printed.
Syntax	public, int GetToPage() const;
Parameters	None.
Returns	The number of the last page to be printed.
See Also	CPrintDialog::GetFromPage
Example	See CPrintDialog::DoModal

OnPrintSetup ■ 2.0 ■ 3.0 ■ UD

Description	Handler for the Print Setup button in the print dialog. It first calls AttachOnSetup to ensure that the print setup information is properly retrieved from the setup dialog (by sharing the m_pd member). Then it launches the print setup dialog.
Syntax	protected, afx_msg void OnPrintSetup();
Parameters	None.
Returns	Nothing is returned.

PrintAll ■ 2.0 ■ 3.0

Description	Retrieves the state of the Print All radio button on the print dialog.
Syntax	public, BOOL PrintAll() const;

Parameters None.
Returns TRUE if printing all pages; FALSE otherwise.
See Also CPrintDialog::PrintSelection, CPrintDialog::PrintRange
Example See CPrintDialog::DoModal

PrintCollate ■ 2.0 ■ 3.0

Description Retrieves the state of the collate check box on the print dialog.
Syntax public, BOOL PrintCollate() const;
Parameters None.
Returns TRUE if the pages should be collated; otherwise, FALSE.
Example See CPrintDialog::DoModal

PrintRange ■ 2.0 ■ 3.0

Description Retrieves the state of the Print Range radio button on the print dialog.
Syntax public, BOOL PrintRange() const;
Parameters None.
Returns TRUE if printing a range of pages; FALSE otherwise.
See Also CPrintDialog::PrintAll, CPrintDialog::PrintSelection
Example See CPrintDialog::DoModal

PrintSelection ■ 2.0 ■ 3.0

Description Retrieves the state of the Print Selection radio button on the print dialog.
Syntax public, BOOL PrintSelection() const;
Parameters None.
Returns TRUE if printing a selection; FALSE otherwise
See Also CPrintDialog::PrintAll, CPrintDialog::PrintRange
Example See CPrintDialog::DoModal

The CFindReplaceDialog Class

The CFindReplaceDialog class is an encapsulation of the Windows find/replace common dialog. With this class, displaying a basic find/replace dialog is trivial. You simply create a CFindReplaceDialog object and call Create. If you want to customize the behavior of the dialog you can do one of two things: 1) modify the constructor's default parameters, or 2) modify the contents of the m_fr member of the CFindReplaceDialog object. m_fr is a FINDREPLACE structure that specifies exactly how the find/replace dialog should behave. For a complete description of the FINDREPLACE structure, see the Windows SDK Help. To manipulate all aspects of the Find/Replace dialog behavior you will need to modify the FINDREPLACE structure; only a small subset is modifiable via the constructor.

Unfortunately, actually using the find/replace common dialog is a little more involved than the other common dialogs. In order to respond to the user's find/replace requests, you must register a special message using the Windows SDK function RegisterWindowMessage. After registering the message, you should create a message handler for it (using ON_REGISTERED_MESSAGE) in the dialog's parent window. An example of this procedure is shown below.

```
// parent window class declaration
class CDialogParent : public CWnd
{
    protected:
        afx_msg LONG LRESULT OnFindReplace(WPARAM wParam, LPARAM
          lParam);
        DECLARE_MESSAGE_MAP()
};

// parent window implementation file
static UINT WM_FINDREPLACE = ::RegisterWindowMessage(FINDMSGSTRING);

BEGIN_MESSAGE_MAP(CDialogParent, CWnd )
   //other message map entries here.
   ON_REGISTERED_MESSAGE( WM_FINDREPLACE, OnFindReplace )
END_MESSAGE_MAP
```

Make sure you use the provided string constant FINDMSGSTRING as the parameter to ::RegisterWindowMessage. Whenever the user requests a find/replace action, the find/replace dialog will send this message to the dialog's parent window. The first thing you will want to do in the message handler is call the CFindReplaceDialog member function GetNotifier, passing the lParam of the message as its parameter. This function will return a pointer to the dialog object that sent the message. Once you have this pointer, you can call the dialog's member functions to determine what command is being requested, as well as any search options that the user has specified. Of course, actually performing the search is your job.

CFindReplaceDialog ■ 2.0 ■ 3.0

Description	Initializes the dialog object's members.
Syntax	public, CFindReplaceDialog();
Parameters	None.
Returns	Nothing is returned.
Example	See CFindReplaceDialog::Create

CREATE

■ 2.0 ■ 3.0

Description Creates the find/replace dialog in modeless form. The dialog can be created as a find only dialog or a find/replace dialog.

Syntax public, BOOL Create(BOOL bFindDialogOnly, LPCTSTR lpszFindWhat, LPCTSTR lpszReplaceWith = NULL, DWORD dwFlags = FR_DOWN, CWnd* pParentWnd = NULL);

Parameters

bFindDialogOnly TRUE if the dialog should be a "find" only dialog; FALSE if the dialog should have full find/replace capabilities.

lpszFindWhat The default string to search for.

lpszReplaceWith The default string to replace found strings with.

dwFlags A series of flags that describe the exact behavior of the dialog. These flags are the same ones used in the SDK structure FINDREPLACE (the Flags member of the structure).

pParentWnd A pointer to the dialog's parent window. The parent window will receive the special find/replace registered message indicating a find or replace action has been requested.

Returns Non-zero if the dialog is successfully created; zero otherwise.

Example

```
// create find/replace dialog object
CFindReplaceDialog dlg;

// display the dialog in modeless form
dlg.Create(TRUE, ``'', NULL, FR_DOWN, pParentWnd);

// initialization of message map to handle messages from the
// dialog parent window class declaration
class CDialogParent : public CWnd
{
    protected:
        afx_msg LONG LRESULT OnFindReplace(WPARAM wParam, LPARAM
          lParam);
    DECLARE_MESSAGE_MAP()
};

// parent window implementation file
static UINT WM_FINDREPLACE =
     ::RegisterWindowMessage(FINDMSGSTRING);

BEGIN_MESSAGE_MAP(CDialogParent, CWnd )
   //other message map entries here.
   ON_REGISTERED_MESSAGE( WM_FINDREPLACE, OnFindReplace )
END_MESSAGE_MAP

// the message handler
void CDialogParent::OnFindReplace(UINT wParam, LONG lParam)
{
```

continued on next page

continued from previous page

```
        // get a pointer to the dialog that sent the message
        CFindReplaceDialog *pDlg;
        pDlg = CFindReplaceDialog::GetNotifier(lParam);

        // query some info from the dialog
        BOOL bIsFindNext = pDlg->FindNext();
        CString strFindText = pDlg->GetFindString();
        BOOL bTerm = pDlg->IsTerminating();
        BOOL bMatchCase = pDlg->MatchCase();
        BOOL bMatchWholeWord = pDlg->MatchWholeWord();
        BOOL bIsSearchDown = pDlb->SearchDown();
}
```

DUMP

■ 2.0 ■ 3.0 ■ DO

Description Debug-only function that "dumps" various state information regarding the CFindReplaceDialog object to a specified dump context.

Syntax public, virtual void Dump(CDumpContext& dc) const;

Parameters

dc A reference to the dump context to which the output should be sent. Usually this will be afxDump, which is a default dump context created by MFC. When debugging an MFC application, output sent to afxDump will appear in the debugger.

Returns Nothing is returned.

See Also CDialog::Dump

Example Example output from the Dump function.

```
// call to dump to output debug information
colorDlg.Dump(afxDump);

// output of Dump function
a CFindReplaceDialog at $63FBF4

m_hWnd = 0x0m_lpDialogTemplate = 0
m_hDialogTemplate = 0x0
m_pParentWnd = $0
m_nIDHelp = 0x0
m_fr.hwndOwner = 0x0
m_fr.Flags = $100
m_fr.lpstrFindWhat =
m_fr.lpstrReplaceWith = (NULL)
hook function set to standard MFC hook function
```

FINDNEXT

■ 2.0 ■ 3.0

Description Determines if the current find/replace command is Find Next. This function should be called in response to the special find/replace registered message. See the narrative at the beginning of this section for a description of this message.

Syntax public, BOOL FindNext() const;
Parameters None.
Returns TRUE if the command is Find Next; FALSE otherwise.
Example See CFindReplaceDialog::Create

GetFindString ■ 2.0 ■ 3.0

Description Retrieves the string that should be found.
Syntax public, CString GetFindString() const;
Parameters None.
Returns The string that should be found.
See Also CFindReplaceDialog::GetReplaceString
Example See CFindReplaceDialog::Create

GetNotifier ■ 2.0 ■ 3.0

Description You should call GetNotifier when responding to the special find/replace registered message in order to retrieve a pointer to the CFindReplaceDialog object that sent the message. From this pointer, then, you can call the dialog's member functions to determine the current find/replace command and options. See the narrative at the beginning of this section for a description of the special find/replace message.
Syntax public, static CFindReplaceDialog* PASCAL GetNotifier(LPARAM lParam);
Parameters
lParam The lParam passed to the message handler for the special find/replace registered message.
Returns A pointer to the CFindReplaceDialog object that sent the message.
Example See CFindReplaceDialog::Create

GetReplaceString ■ 2.0 ■ 3.0

Description Retrieves the string that should replace found strings.
Syntax public, CString GetReplaceString() const;
Parameters None.
Returns The string that should replace found strings.
See Also CFindReplaceDialog::GetFindString

IsTerminating ■ 2.0 ■ 3.0

Description Call the IsTerminating function to determine whether the user has requested that the find/replace dialog be terminated. This function should be called in response to the special find/replace registered message. See the narrative at the beginning of this section for a description of this message. If this function returns TRUE, you should call DestroyWindow for the dialog.

Syntax public, BOOL IsTerminating() const;

Parameters None.

Returns TRUE if the dialog is being terminated; FALSE otherwise.

Example See CFindReplaceDialog::Create

MatchCase ■ 2.0 ■ 3.0

Description Call the MatchCase function to determine whether the current find/replace command should be case-sensitive. This function should be called in response to the special find/replace registered message. See the narrative at the beginning of this section for a description of this message.

Syntax public, BOOL MatchCase() const;

Parameters None.

Returns TRUE if find should be case-sensitive; FALSE otherwise.

See Also CFindReplaceDialog::MatchWholeWord

Example See CFindReplaceDialog::Create

MatchWholeWord ■ 2.0 ■ 3.0

Description Call the MatchWholeWord function to determine whether the current find/replace command should be performed on whole words only. This function should be called in response to the special find/replace registered message. See the narrative at the beginning of this section for a description of this message.

Syntax public, BOOL MatchWholeWord() const;

Parameters None.

Returns TRUE if find should be on whole words only; FALSE otherwise.

See Also CFindReplaceDialog::MatchCase

Example See CFindReplaceDialog::Create

PostNcDestroy

■ 2.0 ■ 3.0 ■ UD

Description Called by the framework as part of the default implementation of OnNcDestroy (the message handler for WM_NCDESTROY). It is called after the window has been destroyed. The CFindReplaceDialog implementation deletes the dialog object itself.

Syntax protected, virtual void PostNcDestroy();

Parameters None.

Returns Nothing is returned.

See Also CWnd::PostNcDestroy, CWnd::OnNcDestroy

ReplaceAll

■ 2.0 ■ 3.0

Description Call the ReplaceAll function to determine whether the current find/replace command is Replace All. This function should be called in response to the special find/replace registered message. See the narrative at the beginning of this section for a description of this message.

Syntax public, BOOL ReplaceAll() const;

Parameters None.

Returns TRUE if the command is Replace All; FALSE otherwise.

See Also CFindReplaceDialog::ReplaceCurrent

ReplaceCurrent

■ 2.0 ■ 3.0

Description Call the ReplaceCurrent function to determine whether the current find/replace command is Replace Current. This function should be called in response to the special find/replace registered message. See the narrative at the beginning of this section for a description of this message.

Syntax public, BOOL ReplaceCurrent() const;

Parameters None.

Returns TRUE if the current command is Replace Current; FALSE otherwise.

SearchDown

■ 2.0 ■ 3.0

Description Call the SearchDown function to determine if the current find/replace search should be down or up. This function should be called in response to the special find/replace registered message. See the narrative at the beginning of this section for a description of this message.

Syntax	public, BOOL SearchDown() const;
Parameters	TRUE if search should be down; FALSE if search should be up.
Returns	Nothing is returned.
Example	See CFindReplaceDialog::Create

9

WINDOWS CONTROLS

9

WINDOWS CONTROLS

MFC provides many classes that encapsulate the standard Windows controls, such as list boxes, combo boxes, edit boxes, and buttons. All of these control classes are derived from the CWnd object, and behave exactly as any other CWnd object with the exceptions described below. Most of the time these objects will be used as controls in dialogs or form views, but they can easily be used as children of any CWnd-derived object. The window control class hierarchy can be seen in Figure 9-1.

The only control that deviates from the above hierarchy is the image list as shown in Figure 9-2. The image list control has no display capability, and is therefore not derived from the CWnd object.

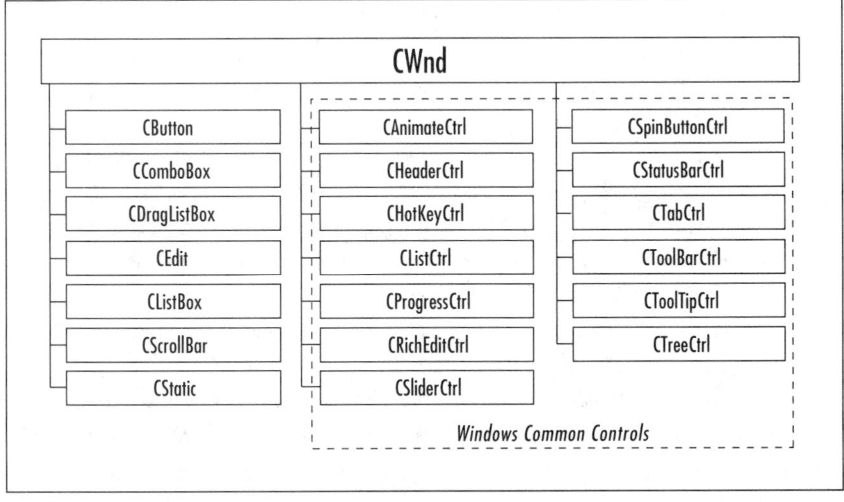

Figure 9-1 Window control hierarchy

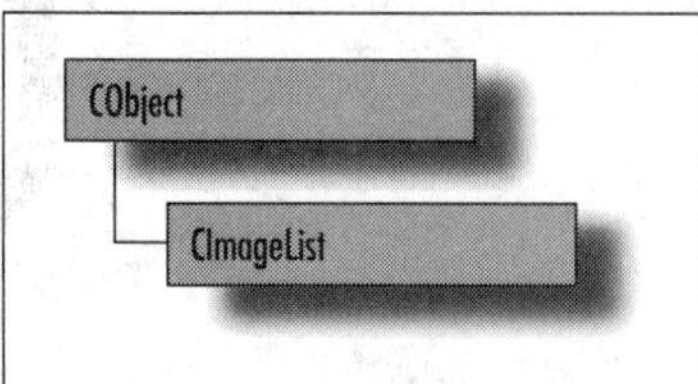

Figure 9-2 CImageList derivation hierarchy

As of MFC version 3.0, new Windows common control classes (see Table 9-1) are supported as well. This includes support for the ListView, TreeView, and ImageList controls. These new controls are a reflection of the new user interface in Windows 95 that was ported to the Windows NT and Win32(s) platforms.

Table 9-1 Chapter 9 class summary

Class Name	Description
CAnimateCtrl	Used to display and manipulate multimedia (*.AVI) files.
CButton	Encapsulates the button user-interface item.
CComboBox	Encapsulates the combo box control that allows selection of an item from a drop-down selection list.
CDragListBox	A list box-derived class that implements dragging and dropping of individual items.
CEdit	Control class that encapsulates entry of simple text.
CHeaderCtrl	Interface control that displays and manipulates a list of labeled columns.
CHotKeyCtrl	Manages a user-configurable key combination to perform specific application tasks.
CImageList	Encapsulates the manipulation of a list of images.
CListBox	Allows for the display and selection of a group of items using a list box control.
CListCtrl	Displays information in either iconic, small iconic, list, or report formats.
CProgressCtrl	Encapsulates the control that displays the completion status of a process.
CRichEditCtrl	The user-interface control that allows for the display and manipulation of rich text formatted documents.
CScrollBar	Encapsulates the scrollbar control that allows for a virtual display area within a window.
CSliderCtrl	Encapsulation of the interface control that allows the user to select a value or a range of values.
CSpinButtonCtrl	Class that encapsulates the spin button control that allows easy selection of a single value.
CStatic	Control class that allows display, but not user entry, of text.
CStatusBarCtrl	The control class that encapsulates a programmer-defined status window that can be associated with other windows.
CTabCtrl	Encapsulates the multi-row tab control that allows the user to select from various tabbed "pages" of information.
CToolBarCtrl	Class that encapsulates the toolbar control that allows for a graphical representation of user-selectable actions.
CToolTipCtrl	Control that can be associated with other windows to display a brief "tip" message in response to user actions.
CTreeCtrl	A class that encapsulates a hierarchical list of information, where the display of parent/child relationship between items is desired.

CAnimateCtrl

The CAnimateCtrl is a control that encapsulates the display and manipulation of multimedia (*.AVI) files. This control makes it very easy to load, play, pause, and move around the frames in the multimedia clip. Only 256- and 16-color animations that are uncompressed or compressed using the REL8 format are supported by the control. The example program that is associated with this section can be found in the Chapter 9 directory (under CAnimate) on the CD-ROM.

CAnimateCtrl ■ 3.0

Description This is the constructor for the animation control. The real initialization of this object is done in the Create member function.

Syntax public, CAnimateCtrl();

Parameters None.

Returns Nothing is returned.

See Also CAnimateCtrl::Create(), ~CAnimateCtrl()

~CAnimateCtrl ■ 3.0 ■ UD

Description Destroys the animation control.

Syntax public, virtual ~CAnimateCtrl();

Parameters None.

Returns Nothing is returned.

See Also CAnimateCtrl()

Close ■ 3.0

Description Stops execution and frees memory from any currently loaded animation.

Syntax public, BOOL Close();

Parameters None.

Returns TRUE if successful; otherwise FALSE.

See Also CAnimateCtrl::Open()

Create ■ 3.0

Description After construction, call to create the animation control and attach it to this object.

Syntax public, BOOL Create(DWORD dwStyle, const RECT & rect, Cwnd * pParentWnd, UINT nID);

Parameters

dwStyle	Styles used for this control. The allowable styles can be found in the Windows API documentation.
rect	Indicates the control's position and size in terms of its parent's client coordinates.
pParentWnd	Parent window of control.
nID	The child ID of this control. Must be unique among its siblings.
Returns	TRUE if creation successful; otherwise FALSE.

OPEN

■ 3.0

Description Opens an animation from a file located on disk, an AVI resource file, or from a resource ID. This function should be called after the Create function.

Syntax public, BOOL Open(LPCTSTR lpszFileName);
public, BOOL Open(UINT nID);

Parameters

lpszFileName	Name of the *.AVI file located on disk, or the name of an AVI resource. If this parameter is NULL then any current clip is closed.
nID	ID of an AVI resource.
Returns	TRUE if successful; otherwise FALSE.
See Also	CAnimateCtrl::Create()
Example	The following code illustrates how to load an AVI file into the control.

```
BOOL  CAnimTestDlg::OpenAVIFile(CAnimateCtrl * pAnimCtrl)
{
      ASSERT_VALID(pAnimCtrl);
      BOOL bSuccess = FALSE;

      if( pAnimCtrl )
      {
            CFileDialog dlgOpen(TRUE,"*.avi",NULL,OFN_HIDEREADONLY |
            OFN_OVERWRITEPROMPT,"Animation Files (*.avi) | *.avi",this);
            bSuccess = (dlgOpen.DoModal()==IDOK);
            if( bSuccess  )
            {
                    bSuccess = pAnimCtrl->Open(dlgOpen.GetPathName());
                    if( !bSuccess )
                    {
                    CString strMsg;
                    strMsg.Format("Error opening File [%s]",dlgOpen.GetPathName());
                    AfxMessageBox(strMsg);
                    }
}
      }

      return bSuccess;
}
```

PLAY ■ 3.0

Description This function will start displaying the animation. The entire animation can be played, or only a portion. This call should be made after the animation has been loaded using the Open method, unless the style ACS_AUTOPLAY was used in the call to Create.

Syntax public, BOOL Play(UINT nFrom, UINT nTo, UINT nRep);

Parameters

nFrom The beginning frame of the portion of the animation that should be played, or 0 for the very first frame in the clip.

nTo The ending frame to be played, or -1 (OxFFFF) for the last frame of the clip.

nRep The number of times to repeat the selection specified by nFrom, nTo.

Returns TRUE if successful; otherwise FALSE. Note that a separate thread is used for playing the clip, and this method will most likely return before the clip has fully displayed.

See Also CAnimateCtrl::Play()

SEEK ■ 3.0

Description Displays a single frame within the currently loaded animation.

Syntax public, BOOL Seek(UINT nTo);

Parameters

nTo The frame number that should be displayed.

Returns TRUE if successful; otherwise FALSE.

See Also CAnimateCtrl::Open()

STOP ■ 3.0

Description Stops the display of a currently running animation.

Syntax public, BOOL Stop();

Parameters None.

Returns TRUE if successful; otherwise FALSE.

See Also CAnimateCtrl::Play()

CButton

The CButton object encapsulates one of the most fundamental Windows controls, the button. A button can be a push button, a radio button, or a check box. There are several general rules to keep in mind when choosing which type of button to use. A push button is generally used to initiate an action, such as displaying a dialog or starting a process. Radio buttons are generally used to present multiple, exclusive choices to a user. Mainly, the radio buttons are used when only one (1) choice among multiple choices makes sense. The check box is intended to allow multiple, non-exclusive options to be selected. A three-state check box may also be used when a choice may be indeterminate, such as indicating that *some* of the selected items in a list box have a particular characteristic.

CBUTTON ■ 2.0 ■ 3.0

Description This is the constructor for the button control. The real initialization of this object is done in the Create member function.

Syntax public, CButton();

Parameters None.

Returns Nothing is returned.

See Also CButton::Create()

~CBUTTON ■ 2.0 ■ 3.0 ■ UD

Description Destroys the button control object.

Syntax public, virtual ~CButton();

Parameters None.

Returns Nothing is returned.

See Also CButton()

CREATE ■ 2.0 ■ 3.0

Description After construction, call this member to create the button control and attach it to this object.

Syntax public, BOOL Create(LPCTSTR lpszCaption,DWORD dwStyle, const RECT & rect, CWnd* pParentWnd, UINT nID);

Parameters

lpszCaption The text that will be displayed in the button.

dwStyle A combination of valid window or button styles. The allowable styles can be found in the Windows API documentation.

rect Indicates the control's position and size in terms of its parent's client coordinates.

pParentWnd Parent window of control.

nID The child ID of this control. Must be unique among its siblings.

Returns TRUE if successful; otherwise FALSE.

See Also CButton()

DrawItem

■ 2.0 ■ 3.0

Description This virtual function is called whenever an owner-draw CButton object needs to be displayed or updated. It is passed a pointer to a DrawItemStruct that contains various information on how the control is to be drawn.

Syntax public, virtual void DrawItem(LPDRAWITEMSTRUCT lpDrawItemStruct);

Parameters

lpDrawItemStruct Contains parameters for drawing the item. See Windows API documentation for a description of this structure.

Returns Nothing is returned.

See Also CWnd::DrawItem()

GetBitmap

■ 3.0

Description Retrieves the handle to the bitmap associated with the button. A bitmap can be displayed on the button face by using the CButton::SetBitmap member function.

Syntax public, HBITMAP GetBitmap() const;

Parameters None.

Returns A handle to the associated bitmap, or NULL if no bitmap is associated with the button.

See Also CButton::SetBitmap

GetButtonStyle

■ 2.0 ■ 3.0

Description This function retrieves the window styles of the button. Note, only the styles prefixed by BS_ are returned by this function. (For example, BS_AUTOCHECKBOX). The styles for the button were previously set by the CButton::Create() or CButton::SetButtonStyle() functions.

Syntax public, UINT GetButtonStyle() const;

Parameters None.

Returns The styles used to create the button. Mask individual styles against the return value to determine if the style is in use.

See Also CButton::Create(), CButton::SetButtonStyle()

GetCheck

■ 2.0 ■ 3.0

Description This function will return the check state of a button. This is only valid for radio buttons and check boxes.

Syntax public, int GetCheck() const;

Parameters None.

Returns The return value can be any of the following:

0 The button is not checked (or radio button is not selected).

1 The button is checked (or radio button is selected).

2 The button is indeterminate (only for 3-state buttons).

See Also CButton::SetCheck(),CButton::GetState()

GetCursor ■ 3.0

Description Retrieves the handle to the cursor image associated with the button. A cursor image can be displayed on the face of the button by using the CButton::SetCursor member function.

Syntax public, HCURSOR GetCursor();

Parameters None.

Returns A handle to the associated cursor, or NULL if no cursor is associated with the button.

See Also CButton::SetCursor()

GetIcon ■ 3.0

Description Retrieves the handle to the icon associated with the button. An icon can be displayed on the button face by using the CButton::SetIcon member function.

Syntax public, HICON GetIcon() const;

Parameters None.

Returns A handle to the associated icon, or NULL if no icon is associated with the button.

See Also CButton::SetIcon

GetState ■ 2.0 ■ 3.0

Description Retrieves state information about the button including whether it is checked (only for radio buttons and check boxes), if the button is highlighted, and if it has input focus.

Syntax public, UINT GetState() const;

Parameters None.

Returns The state of the button. To determine the individual characteristics, use the following bit masks against the returned value:

0x0003 Using this mask on the result will determine the checked status of the button (this only applies to radio buttons and check boxes). If the result is

	equal to 0, then the button is unchecked. If the result is equal to 1, then the button is checked. If the button is a 3-state check box, then a value of 2 will indicate the indeterminate state.
0x0004	This mask determines the highlight state of the button. If the result is 0, then the button is not highlighted.
0x0008	This mask determines the focus state of the control. If the result is 0, then the control does not have the input focus.

See Also CButton::SetState()

OnChildNotify

■ 2.0 ■ 3.0 ■ UD

Description This function is called by the CButton's parent whenever a notification applies to this control. This function should never be called directly, but can be overridden for owner-draw buttons.

Syntax protected, virtual BOOL OnChildNotify(UINT, WPARAM, LPARAM, LRESULT *);

Parameters

UINT	Notification message.
WPARAM	Message-specific data.
LPARAM	Message-specific data.
*LRESULT**	Address of returned result code, dependent on notification message.

Returns The default implementation returns FALSE for every message except WM_DRAWITEM in which case CButton::DrawItem() is invoked. This only happens in the case of an owner-draw button.

See Also CWnd::OnChildNotify(), CButton::DrawItem()

SetBitmap

■ 3.0

Description This member allows for the display of a bitmap on the face of the button for classes derived from CButton. This function is only useful for buttons that have the BS_BITMAP style. By default, the bitmap is centered both horizontally and vertically. This can be modified by using a combination of the following styles: BS_BOTTOM, BS_CENTER, BS_LEFT, BS_RIGHT, BS_TOP, BS_VCENTER.

Syntax public, HBITMAP SetBitmap(HBITMAP hBitmap);

Parameters

hBitmap	A handle to the new bitmap.

Returns A handle to the previously associated bitmap, or NULL if no bitmap was associated with the button.

See Also CButton::GetBitmap

SetButtonStyle

■ 2.0 ■ 3.0

Description Sets new styles for a button control. These styles may be any combination of button-specific styles that start with BS_.

Syntax public, void SetButtonStyle(UINT nStyle, BOOL bRedraw = TRUE);

Parameters

nStyle Combination of button-specific styles that start with BS_.

bRedraw TRUE causes an immediate redraw of the control (default); FALSE will defer the updating of the control until it becomes invalidated.

Returns Nothing is returned.

See Also CButton::GetButtonStyle()

SetCheck

■ 2.0 ■ 3.0

Description This function will set the check state of a button. This is only valid for radio buttons and check boxes.

Syntax public, void SetCheck(int nCheck);

Parameters

nCheck The new check state of the button. This parameter can be any of the following values:

0 The button will be unchecked (or unselected for radio buttons).

1 The button will be checked (or selected for radio buttons).

2 The button state will be indeterminate (only for 3-state buttons).

Returns Nothing is returned.

See Also CButton::GetCheck(), CButton::GetState()

SetCursor

■ 3.0

Description This member allows for the display of a cursor image on the face of the button for classes derived from CButton. This function is only useful for buttons that have the BS_BITMAP style. By default, the cursor image is centered both horizontally and vertically. This can be modified by using a combination of the following styles: BS_BOTTOM, BS_CENTER, BS_LEFT, BS_RIGHT, BS_TOP, BS_VCENTER.

Syntax public, HCURSOR SetCursor(HCURSOR hCursor);

Parameters

hBitmap A handle to the new cursor image.

Returns A handle to the previously associated cursor image, or NULL if no cursor image was associated with the button.

See Also CButton::GetCursor

SetIcon

■ 3.0

Description This allows for the display of an icon on the face of the button. This function is only useful for buttons that have the BS_ICON style. By default, the icon is centered both horizontally and vertically. This can be modified by using a combination of the following styles: BS_BOTTOM, BS_CENTER, BS_LEFT, BS_RIGHT, BS_TOP, BS_VCENTER.

Syntax public, HICON SetIcon(HICON hIcon);

Parameters

hBitmap A handle to the new icon.

Returns A handle to the previously associated icon, or NULL if no icon was associated with the button.

See Also CButton::GetIcon

SetState

■ 2.0 ■ 3.0

Description This method controls the highlight state of a button.

Syntax public, void SetState(BOOL bHighlight);

Parameters

bHighlight TRUE will cause the button to be highlighted; FALSE will remove any highlighting.

Returns Nothing is returned.

See Also CButton::GetState()

CComboBox

The CComboBox object encapsulates the Windows combo box control. The combo box control is mainly used for two purposes. One use of the combo box is to display a list of choices in a very small space so as not to clutter the parent window. The second use is to present a list of predefined choices for easy selection, yet to allow users to enter a choice of their own.

Either way, the combo box control is really the combination of an edit box and a list box. The edit box is positioned above the list box, and displays or allows the user to edit the current selection. The list box portion resides below the edit box, and allows the user to choose among predefined choices. The example program that is associated with this section can be found in the CCombo directory on the CD-ROM.

CComboBox

■ 2.0 ■ 3.0

Description This is the constructor for the combo box control. The real initialization of this object is done in the Create member function.

Syntax public, CComboBox();

Parameters None.

Returns Nothing is returned.

See Also CComboBox::Create()

~CComboBox

■ 2.0 ■ 3.0 ■ UD

Description Destroys the combo box object.

Syntax public, virtual ~CComboBox();

Parameters None.

Returns Nothing is returned.

See Also CComboBox:CComboBox()

AddString

■ 2.0 ■ 3.0

Description This function appends a string to the items currently in the combo box. If the combo box has the CBS_SORT style, then the string is inserted in its sorted position.

Syntax public, int AddString(LPCTSTR lpszString);

Parameters

lpszString A null-terminated string that contains the text to be added.

Returns A value greater than or equal to zero indicating the position of the string that was added. Otherwise the return value will be CB_ERR or CB_ERRSPACE.

See Also CComboBox::InsertString(), CComboBox::CompareItem()

Example The following code shows how to use this function to add text entries into the combo box.

```
void CComboDlg::OnLoadtext()
{
      CString strText;

      m_ComboCtl.ResetContent();
      for(int nI=0;nI<100;nI++)
      {
      strText.Format("Entry %d",nI);
      m_ComboCtl.AddString(strText);
      }
      m_ComboCtl.SetCurSel(0);
}
```

Clear

■ 2.0 ■ 3.0

Description This function will delete the selected text from the edit box portion of the combo box.

Syntax public, void Clear();

Parameters None.

Returns Nothing is returned.

See Also CComboBox::Cut(), CComboBox::Copy()

CompareItem

■ 2.0 ■ 3.0

Description This function allows a programmer to override the default system sorting algorithm by determining the relative value of items in the control. This function must be overridden for owner-draw controls. Typically, the programmer will use the information supplied in *lpCompareItemStruct* to determine a relative sort "value" for the two given items. Windows will handle calling this member for each sort "pair."

Syntax public, virtual int CompareItem(LPCOMPAREITEMSTRUCT lpCompareItemStruct);

Parameters

lpCompareItemStruct Structure containing indices of the items to be compared. See the Windows API documentation.

Returns The return value has three values:

-1	Item 1 appears before item 2.
0	Item 1 and item 2 are of equal value.
1	Item 1 appears after item 2.

See Also CWnd::OnCompareItem(), CComboBox::AddString()

Copy

■ 2.0 ■ 3.0

Description This function will copy to the Clipboard the selected text from the edit box portion of the combo box. This data will be available on the in CF_TEXT format.

Syntax public, void Copy();

Parameters None.

Returns Nothing is returned.

See Also CComboBox::Cut(), CComboBox::Clear(), CComboBox::Paste()

Create

■ 2.0 ■ 3.0

Description After construction, call this member to create the combo box control and attach it to this object.

Syntax public, BOOL Create(DWORD dwStyle, const RECT & rect, Cwnd * pParentWnd, UINT nID);

Parameters

dwStyle A combination of valid window or combo box styles. The allowable styles can be found in the Windows API documentation.

rect Indicates the control's position and size in terms of its parent's client coordinates.

pParentWnd Parent window of control.

nID The child ID of this control. Must be unique among its siblings.

Returns TRUE if successful; otherwise FALSE.

See Also CComboBox::CComboBox()

CUT ■ 2.0 ■ 3.0

Description This function will copy to the Clipboard the selected text from the edit box portion of the combo box, then remove the selection. This data will be available on the Clipboard in CF_TEXT format.

Syntax public, void Cut();

Parameters None.

Returns Nothing is returned.

See Also CComboBox::Copy(), CComboBox::Clear(), CComboBox::Paste()

DELETEITEM ■ 2.0 ■ 3.0

Description This function can be overridden to receive notification from the framework when an item is removed from the control.

Syntax public, virtual void DeleteItem(LPDELETEITEMSTRUCT lpDeleteItemStruct);

Parameters

lpDeleteItemStruct Structure containing information about the item to be removed.

Returns Nothing is returned.

See Also CWnd::OnDeleteItem(), CWnd::DeleteString()

DELETESTRING ■ 2.0 ■ 3.0

Description Removes the specified item from the combo box.

Syntax public, int DeleteString(UINT nIndex)

Parameters

nIndex The index of the item to be removed. This value can be from 0 to GetCount()-1.

Returns If successful, then the return value is the number of remaining items; otherwise CB_ERR.

DIR

■ 2.0 ■ 3.0

Description This function will load the combo box with a list of files or directories.

Syntax public, int Dir(UINT attr, LPCTSTR lpszWildCard);

Parameters

attr This value specifies which items will be loaded into the combo box. It can be any combination of the following values:

DDL_ARCHIVE Archived files.

DDL_DIRECTORY The parameter lpszWildCard indicates a directory.

DDL_DRIVES Load all drives that match lpszWildCard.

DDL_EXCLUSIVE If this flag is set, only files of the specified type are listed. Otherwise, files of the specified type are listed in addition to "normal" files.

DDL_HIDDEN Hidden files.

DDL_READWRITE Files that can be read from or written to.

DDL_READONLY Files that cannot be written to.

DDL_SYSTEM System files.

lpszWildCard A NULL-terminated string that specifies which files will be loaded. This string can contain wildcards (such as "*.*").

Returns If successful, then the index of the last inserted item; otherwise CB_ERR or CB_ERRSPACE.

Example The following code loads the given combo box with the contents of the current directory.

```
void CComboDlg::OnLoaddir()
{
        m_ComboCtl.ResetContent();
        m_ComboCtl.Dir(DDL_READWRITE|DDL_READONLY,"*.*");
        m_ComboCtl.SetCurSel(0);
}
```

DRAWITEM

■ 2.0 ■ 3.0

Description This overridable function is called whenever a visual aspect of an owner-draw combo box has changed. This function must be overridden for owner-draw controls.

Syntax public, virtual void DrawItem(LPDRAWITEMSTRUCT lpDrawItemStruct);

Parameters

lpDrawItemStruct Structure specifying information useful in carrying out the drawing of the item.

Returns Nothing is returned.

See Also CWnd::OnDrawItem()

FindString

■ 2.0 ■ 3.0

Description This function will attempt to find the first item that contains the supplied string (case-insensitive).

Syntax public, int FindString(int nStartAfter, LPCTSTR lpszString) const;

Parameters

nStartAfter The first index of the item where the search should begin. This value can range from 0 to GetCount()-1, or can be -1 to search the entire contents of the combo box.

lpszString A NULL-terminated string that is to be searched for within the combo box items. This string will match an item if it is a prefix of the item.

Returns The index of the matching item, or CB_ERR if not found.

See Also CComboBox::FindStringExact()

FindStringExact

■ 2.0 ■ 3.0

Description This function will attempt to find an exact whole-word match (case-sensitive) between the supplied string, and any of the combo box items.

Syntax public, int FindStringExact(int nIndexStart,LPCTSTR lpszFind) const;

Parameters

nIndexStart The first index of the item where the search should begin. This value can range from 0 to GetCount()-1, or can be -1 to search the entire contents of the combo box.

lpszFind A NULL-terminated string that is to be searched for within the combo box items.

Returns The index of the matching item, or CB_ERR if not found.

See Also CComboBox::FindString()

GetCount

■ 2.0 ■ 3.0

Description This function is used to retrieve the number of items in the list box portion of the combo box.

Syntax public, int GetCount() const;

Parameters None.

Returns The number of items in the combo box, or CB_ERR.

GetCurSel

■ 2.0 ■ 3.0

Description This function is used to retrieve the currently selected item index from the list box portion of the combo box.

Syntax public, int GetCurSel() const;

Parameters	None.
Returns	The index of the currently selected item, or CB_ERR if there is an error or no item is selected. Note that this index is zero-based (the first entry having an index of 0, the second having an index of 1,....).
See Also	CComboBox::SetCurSel()
Example	See CComboBox::GetItemData()

GetDroppedControlRect ■ 2.0 ■ 3.0

Description	This function retrieves the screen coordinates of the list box portion of the combo box.
Syntax	public, void GetDroppedControlRect(LPRECT lprect) const;
Parameters	
lprect	The address of the RECT structure that will receive the screen coordinates.
Returns	Nothing is returned.

GetDroppedState ■ 2.0 ■ 3.0

Description	This functions returns whether the list box portion of the combo box is currently displayed (dropped down).
Syntax	public, BOOL GetDroppedState() const;
Parameters	None.
Returns	Non-zero if the list box portion is currently displayed; otherwise FALSE.
See Also	CComboBox::ShowDropDown()

GetDroppedWidth ■ 3.0

Description	Returns the minimum allowable width for the list box portion of the combo box. The actual width is the greater of the combo box width and the minimum allowable width.
Syntax	public, int GetDroppedWidth() const;
Parameters	None.
Returns	The minimum allowable width for the list box portion of the combo box.
See Also	CComboBox::SetDroppedWidth()

GetEditSel ■ 2.0 ■ 3.0

Description	This function retrieves the starting and ending positions of text that are selected in the edit control portion of the combo box.
Syntax	public, DWORD GetEditSel() const;

Parameters None.

Returns A DWORD that contains the first selected character position in the low-order word, and the first nonselected character in the high-order word. If an error occurs or the combo box has no edit control, the return value is CB_ERR.

See Also CComboBox::SetEditSel()

GetExtendedUI ■ 2.0 ■ 3.0

Description Returns the current state of the combo box user interface, either standard or extended.

Syntax public, BOOL GetExtendedUI() const;

Parameters None.

Returns 0 if the current user interface is standard; non-zero if extended.

See Also CComboBox::SetExtendedUI()

GetHorizontalExtent ■ 3.0

Description Returns the width by which the list box portion of the combo box can be scrolled horizontally. This is only valid if the list box portion has a horizontal scrollbar.

Syntax public, UINT GetHorizontalExtent() const;

Parameters None.

Returns The width in pixels that the list box portion of the combo box can be scrolled horizontally.

See Also CComboBox::SetHorizontalExtent()

GetItemData ■ 2.0 ■ 3.0

Description This function retrieves a DWORD value that has been associated with an item in the combo box. This value should be set by the CComboBox::SetItemData() member. The item data is usually used to associate an ID or value to a string in the combo box.

Syntax public, DWORD GetItemData(int nIndex) const;

Parameters

nIndex Index of the item whose data is to be retrieved.

Returns 32-bit associated data value; otherwise CB_ERR.

See Also CComboBox::SetItemData(), CComboBox::GetItemDataPtr(), CComboBox::SetItemDataPtr()

Example The following example illustrates how to retrieve the item data of the currently selected item.

```
DWORD CComboDlg::GetCurSelItemData(CComboBox * pCombo)
{
        ASSERT_VALID(pCombo);
        int nIdx;
        DWORD dwData = 0;

        if( pCombo )
        {
                nIdx = pCombo->GetCurSel();
                if (nIdx == CB_ERR)
                dwData = (DWORD)-1;
                else
                dwData = pCombo->GetItemData(nIdx);
        }
        return dwData;
}
```

GetItemDataPtr

■ 2.0 ■ 3.0

Description This function retrieves a (void *) pointer that has been associated with an item in the combo box. This value should be set by the CComboBox::SetItemDataPtr() member.

Syntax public, void * GetItemDataPtr(int nIndex) const;

Parameters

nIndex Index of the item whose data is to be retrieved.

Returns A void * associated with the item; otherwise CB_ERR.

See Also CComboBox::SetItemDataPtr(), CComboBox::GetItemData(), CComboBox::SetItemData()

GetItemHeight

■ 2.0 ■ 3.0

Description Retrieves the height in pixels of an item in the combo box.

Syntax public, int GetItemHeight(int nIndex) const;

Parameters

nIndex Index of the item whose height is to be retrieved. An index of -1 indicates the edit portion of the control. If the control does not have the CBS_OWNERDRAWVARIABLE style, then any index value other than -1 indicates the uniform height of items in the list box portion. Otherwise, indices from 0 to GetCount()-1 indicate the height of individual items.

Returns The height of the item in pixels, or CB_ERR.

See Also CComboBox::SetItemHeight()

GetLBText

■ 2.0 ■ 3.0

Description This function retrieves the text of the list box entry at the given index.

Syntax	public, int GetLBText(int nIndex,CString & rString) const;
Parameters	
nIndex	The index of the entry in the list box portion of the combo box.
rString	The destination for the text.
Returns	Non-zero if successful; otherwise CB_ERR.
See Also	CComboBox::GetLBTextLen()

GetLBTextLen ■ 2.0 ■ 3.0

Description	This function retrieves the length of the text of the entry at the given index.
Syntax	public, int GetLBTextLen(int nIndex) const;
Parameters	
nIndex	The index of the entry in the list box portion of the combo box.
Returns	The length (in bytes) of the text. This value does not include the terminating NULL character.
See Also	CComboBox::GetLBText(), CComboBox::GetItemHeight()

GetLocale ■ 2.0 ■ 3.0

Description	This function retrieves the locale identifier that determines how strings in the combo box are treated.
Syntax	public, LCID GetLocale() const;
Parameters	None.
Returns	The locale identifier.
See Also	CComboBox::SetLocale(), ::GetSystemDefaultLCID()

GetTopIndex ■ 3.0

Description	Retrieves the index of the topmost visible item in the combo box.
Syntax	public, int GetTopIndex() const;
Parameters	None.
Returns	The zero-based index of the topmost visible item in the combo box.
See Also	CComboBox::SetTopIndex()

InitStorage ■ 3.0

Description	Call this member before loading a large number of items into the combo box to optimize memory allocation time. Normally, when individual

items are added to the combo box, a memory allocation occurs. This member can be called to optimize performance by allocating memory for many items at once, rather than individually. Note that Windows 95 is limited to 32,767 items, but the memory that they use is only limited by the available system memory.

Syntax public, int InitStorage(int nItems, UINT nBytes);

Parameters

nItems The number of items that will be added to the combo box.

nBytes The number of bytes per item that is necessary to store the item string entry.

Returns If successful, the maximum number of items that can be stored before a memory allocation occurs. Otherwise CB_ERR if the requested amount of memory was not available.

InsertString ■ 2.0 ■ 3.0

Description This function will insert a new item at the given index, moving down the current item at that position and any other items below it. Inserting a string in this manner will override any sorting options if the CBS_SORT style is set.

Syntax public, int InsertString(int nIndex, LPCTSTR lpszString);

Parameters

nIndex The index where the new string should reside.

lpszString A NULL-terminated string that will be inserted into the combo box.

Returns If successful, then the index of the newly inserted item; otherwise CB_ERR or CB_ERRSPACE.

See Also CComboBox::AddString()

LimitText ■ 2.0 ■ 3.0

Description This function is used to limit the length of text in bytes that the user can type into the edit control portion of the combo box. Note, the combo box must have the CBS_DROPDOWNLIST style for this function to return successfully.

Syntax public, BOOL LimitText(int nMaxChars);

Parameters

nMaxChars Maximum number of bytes that can be entered. If zero, then the limit is 65,535.

Returns Non-zero if successful, or CB_ERR.

MeasureItem

■ 2.0 ■ 3.0

Description This function, only valid for an owner-draw combo box, can be overridden to supply the operating system with information regarding the dimensions of the list box portion of the control. This function is called only once unless the CBS_OWNERDRAWVARIABLE style is set, then it is called once for each item in the control. This function must be overridden for owner-draw controls.

Syntax public, virtual void MeasureItem(LPMEASUREITEMSTRUCT lpMeasureItemStruct);

Parameters

lpMeasureItemStruct A pointer to a structure containing information on the control, current item, and width and height information. This structure should be filled with the appropriate dimensions.

Returns Nothing is returned.

See Also CWnd::OnMeasureItem()

OnChildNotify

■ 2.0 ■ 3.0 ■ UD

Description This function can be overridden to receive notification messages from the parent control. The default implementation of this function interprets and executes other virtual notification member functions (such as interpreting WM_DRAWITEM to execute CComboBox::DrawItem()).

Syntax protected, virtual BOOL OnChildNotify(UINT, WPARAM, LPARAM, LRESULT*);

Parameters

UINT Message.

WPARAM Message-specific data.

LPARAM Message-specific data.

*LRESULT** Address of returned result code, dependent on Notification message.

Returns The default implementation returns FALSE for every unhandled message, and TRUE for messages that were handled by the control.

Returns Nothing is returned.

See Also CWnd::OnChildNotify()

Paste

■ 2.0 ■ 3.0

Description This function will copy the contents of the Clipboard (if in CF_TEXT format) into the edit control portion of the combo box, at the current cursor position.

Syntax public, void Paste();
Parameters None.
Returns Nothing is returned.
See Also CComboBox::Copy(), CComboBox::Cut()

ResetContent ■ 2.0 ■ 3.0

Description Removes all items from the combo box.
Syntax public, void ResetContent();
Parameters None.
Returns Nothing is returned.
Example See CComboBox::Dir()

SelectString ■ 2.0 ■ 3.0

Description This function will select the first item in the list box that contains the supplied text (case-insensitive), and update the edit portion of the combo box.
Syntax public, int SelectString(int nStartAfter, LPCTSTR lpszString);
Parameters
nStartAfter The first index of the item where the search should begin. This value can range from 0 to GetCount()-1, or can be -1 to search the entire contents of the combo box.
lpszString A NULL-terminated string that is to be searched for within the combo box items. This string will match an item if it is a prefix of the item.
Returns The index of the matching item, or CB_ERR if not found.
See Also CComboBox::FindString(), CComboBox::FindStringExact()

SetCurSel ■ 2.0 ■ 3.0

Description This function is used to set the currently selected item in the list box portion of the combo box, and update the edit box portion with the new selection. If the item is not in view, the item is scrolled into view.
Syntax public, int SetCurSel(int nSelect);
Parameters
nSelect Zero-based index of the string to select from the list box portion of the combo box. The valid values for this parameter range from 0 to CComboBox::GetCount()-1, or -1 to clear any current selections.
Returns The index of the item selected, or CB_ERR.

SetEditSel

■ 2.0 ■ 3.0

Description This function sets the highlighted selection in the edit control portion of the combo box. Note, the combo box must have the CBS_DROPDOWNLIST style for this function to return successfully.

Syntax public, BOOL SetEditSel(int nStartChar, int nEndChar);

Parameters

nStartChar The first selected character, or -1 to remove the current selection.

nEndChar The last selected position, or -1 to select from nStartChar to the last character in the control.

Returns Non-zero if successful; otherwise CB_ERR.

SetExtendedUI

■ 2.0 ■ 3.0

Description This function will set either the default user interface for the combo box, or the extended user interface if the control has either the CBS_DROPDOWNLIST or CBS_DROPDOWN styles. The extended user interface has the following properties:

Scrolling in the edit box portion is disabled when the item list is not visible.

The down arrow key (instead of the F4 function key) displays the item list.

Clicking the edit box portion with the mouse displays the item list if the control has the CBS_DROPDOWNLIST style.

Syntax public, int SetExtendedUI(BOOL bExtended = TRUE);

Parameters

bExtended TRUE if the extended user interface (described above) is to be used; otherwise FALSE for the default user interface.

Returns CB_OKAY if successful; otherwise CB_ERR.

See Also CComboBox::GetExtendedUI()

SetHorizontalExtent

■ 3.0

Description Sets the width by which the list box portion of the combo box can be scrolled horizontally. If this value is greater than the width of the list box then the horizontal scrollbar is displayed; otherwise the horizontal scrollbar is hidden.

Syntax public, void SetHorizontalExtent(UINT nExtent);

Parameters

nExtent The total width in pixels that the list box portion of the combo box can be scrolled horizontally.

Returns Nothing is returned.

See Also CComboBox::GetHorizontalExtent()

SetItemData

■ 2.0 ■ 3.0

Description This function sets a DWORD value that is associated with an item in the combo box. This value can be retrieved through the CComboBox::GetItemData() member. The item data is usually used to associate an ID or value to a string in the combo box.

Syntax public, int SetItemData(int nIndex, DWORD dwItemData);

Parameters

nIndex Index of the item whose data is to be set.

dwItemData 32-bit value associated with the given index.

Returns Non-zero if successful; otherwise CB_ERR.

See Also CComboBox::GetItemData(), CComboBox::GetItemDataPtr(), CComboBox::SetItemDataPtr()

SetItemDataPtr

■ 2.0 ■ 3.0

Description This function sets a (void *) pointer that is associated with an item in the combo box. This pointer can be retrieved through the CComboBox::GetItemDataPtr() member.

Syntax public, int SetItemDataPtr(int nIndex, void * pData);

Parameters

nIndex Index of the item whose data is to be set.

pData A void * that is to be associated with the given item.

Returns Non-zero if successful; otherwise CB_ERR.

See Also CComboBox::GetItemDataPtr(), CComboBox::GetItemData(), CComboBox::SetItemData()

SetItemHeight

■ 2.0 ■ 3.0

Description This function serves the dual purpose of setting either the height of the edit box portion of the control, or the height of the items in the list box portion. If the control does not have the CBS_OWNERDRAWVARIABLE style flag set, then all of the list box items will have the same height.

Syntax public, int SetItemHeight(int nIndex,UINT cyItemHeight);

Parameters

nIndex Index of the item that will be affected by the new height. An index of -1 indicates the edit portion of the control. If the control does not have the CBS_OWNERDRAWVARIABLE style, then any index value other than -1 indicates all items in the list box portion of the control. Otherwise, indices from 0 to GetCount()-1 inidicate individual items.

cyItemHeight The height in pixels of the item indicated by *nIndex*.

Returns CB_OKAY if successful; otherwise CB_ERR.

SetLocale ■ 2.0 ■ 3.0

Description This function sets the locale identifier that determines how strings in the combo box are treated.

Syntax public, LCID SetLocale(LCID nNewLocale);

Parameters

nNewLocale The new locale identifier.

Returns The previous locale identifier.

See Also CComboBox::GetLocale(), ::GetSystemDefaultLCID()

SetTopIndex ■ 3.0

Description Sets the specified item as the topmost visible item in the list box portion of the combo box. The item is guaranteed to be displayed, but may not be the actual topmost item if the maximum vertical scroll range has been reached.

Syntax public, int SetTopIndex(int nIndex);

Parameters

nIndex The index of the item that should be scrolled into view.

Returns Zero if successful; otherwise CB_ERR.

See Also CComboBox::SetTopIndex()

ShowDropDown ■ 2.0 ■ 3.0

Description This function will display or hide the list box portion of the combo box. This only applies to combo boxes with the CBS_DROPDOWNLIST or CBS_DROPDOWN styles.

Syntax public, void ShowDropDown(BOOL bShowIt = TRUE);

Parameters

bShowIt TRUE if the list box potion is to be displayed (dropped down); FALSE to hide the list box.

Returns Nothing is returned.

See Also CComboBox::GetDroppedState()

CDragListBox

The CDragListBox provides all the functionality of a standard list box, but adds the capability of letting the user reorder the items contained in the control. This is done by dragging and dropping items into their new locations. Note that you can replace any existing CListBox object with this object as long as you have removed the LBS_SORT and LBS_MULTIPLESEL styles.

CDragListBox ■ 4.0

Description This is the constructor for the control.

Syntax public, CDragListBox();

Parameters None.

Returns Nothing is returned.

See Also CListBox::Create(), ~CDragListBox()

~CDragListBox ■ 4.0, UD

Description Destroys the control.

Syntax public, virtual ~CDragListBox();

Parameters None.

Returns Nothing is returned.

See Also CDragListBox()

BeginDrag ■ 4.0

Description This member is called to initiate a dragging session for the control. Override this virtual member to provide custom dragging behavior.

Syntax public, virtual BOOL BeginDrag(CPoint pt);

Parameters

pt Coordinates of the item to be dragged.

Returns TRUE is dragging is allowed; otherwise FALSE.

CancelDrag ■ 4.0

Description This member is called when a drag session has been cancelled. Override this virtual member to provide custom dragging behavior.

Syntax public, virtual void CancelDrag(CPoint pt);

Parameters

pt Coordinates of the item that was dragged.

Returns Nothing is returned.

Dragging ■ 4.0

Description This member is called during a drag operation for the control. Override this virtual member to provide custom dragging behavior.

Syntax public, virtual UINT Dragging(CPoint pt);

Parameters

pt New coordinates of the item being dragged.

Returns The resource ID of the cursor to be displayed. The default value is DL_MOVECURSOR, but it can also be a user-supplied cursor ID or one of the following:

DL_COPYCURSOR	Indicates a copy operation.
DL_MOVECURSOR	Indicates an item move operation.
DL_STOPCURSOR	Indicates an invalid drop site.

DrawInsert ■ 4.0

Description This member is called to draw the insertion point for the item being dragged. Override this virtual member to provide a custom insertion indicator.

Syntax public, virtual void DrawInsert(int nItem);

Parameters

nItem Index of the item where the insertion point should be displayed.

Returns Nothing is returned.

DrawSingle ■ 4.0 ■ UD

Description This member is called to draw a line indicating the insertion point. This member first clears the last insertion line, then draws the new one. Internally, this is called fromCDragListBox:: DrawInsert().

Syntax public, void DrawSingle(int nIndex);

Parameters

nIndex The index of the new insertion point.

Returns Nothing is returned.

See Also CDragListBox::DrawInsert()

Dropped ■ 4.0

Description This member is called when an item has been dropped to a new location in the control. Override this virtual member to provide custom dragging behavior.

Syntax public, virtual void Dropped(int nSrcIndex, CPoint pt);

Parameters

nSrcIndex The index of the dropped item.

pt Coordinates of the drop site.

Returns Nothing is returned.

ItemFromPt

■ 4.0

Description This member is called to retrieve the index of the list box entry at the given point.

Syntax public, int ItemFromPt(CPoint pt, BOOL bAutoScroll = TRUE) const;

Parameters

pt Coordinates of the item to be dragged.

BAutoScroll TRUE if scrolling is enabled; otherwise FALSE for no scrolling.

Returns Index of the item.

OnChildNotify

■ 4.0 ■ UD

Description This member is invoked when it receives notification messages from the control's parent. This member intercepts these messages and calls the appropriate member function.

Syntax protected, virtual BOOL OnChildNotify(UINT, WPARAM, LPARAM, LRESULT *);

Parameters

UINT Notification message.

WPARAM Message-specific data.

LPARAM Message-specific data.

*LRESULT** Address of returned result code, dependent on notification message.

Returns TRUE if the notification message was handled; otherwise FALSE to continue processing the message.

PreSubclassWindow

■ 4.0 ■ UD

Description This member is called to allow the object to perform any object-specific subclassing before Windows subclassing occurs. The CDragListBox uses this member to assert that the proper window styles are set and to create the draw list window.

Syntax public, virtual void PreSubclassWindow();

Parameters None.

Returns Nothing is returned.

See Also CWnd::PreSubclassWindow()

CEdit

The CEdit control is used when a string of text needs to be displayed or input into the system. A single line of text or an entire document may be input/displayed by using this control. One of the benefits of using this control is that the control will automatically handle text cut, copy, and paste operations. The associated example files for this section can be found in the CEdit directory on the CD-ROM.

CEdit

■ 2.0 ■ 3.0

Description This is the constructor for the edit control. The real initialization of this object is done in the Create member function.

Syntax public, CEdit();

Parameters None.

Returns Nothing is returned.

See Also CEdit::Create(),~CEdit()

~CEdit

■ 2.0 ■ 3.0 ■ UD

Description Destroys the edit control object.

Syntax public, virtual ~CEdit();

Parameters None.

Returns Nothing is returned.

See Also CEdit()

CanUndo

■ 2.0 ■ 3.0

Description This function determines if the last edit operation can be undone. This includes pasting of text, as well as typed text.

Syntax public, BOOL CanUndo() const;

Parameters None.

Returns TRUE if the operation can be undone; otherwise FALSE.

See Also CEdit::EmptyUndoBuffer()

CharFromPos

■ 3.0

Description This Windows 95-specific member returns the closest line and character indices of a given point within the CEdit control.

Syntax public, int CharFromPos(CPoint pt) const;

Parameters

pt An x,y point within the CEdit control.

Returns The line index in the hi-order WORD and the character index in the low-order WORD.

Clear ■ 2.0 ■ 3.0

Description This function will delete the selected text from the edit control.

Syntax public, void Clear();

Parameters None.

Returns Nothing is returned.

See Also CEdit::Cut(), CEdit::Copy()

Copy ■ 2.0 ■ 3.0

Description This function will copy to the Clipboard the selected text from the edit control. This data will be available on the Clipboard in CF_TEXT format.

Syntax public, void Copy();

Parameters None.

Returns Nothing is returned.

See Also CEdit::Cut(),CEdit::Clear(),CEdit::Paste()

Create ■ 2.0 ■ 3.0

Description After construction, call this member to create the edit control and attach it to this object.

Syntax public, BOOL Create(DWORD dwStyle, const RECT & rect, Cwnd * pParentWnd, UINT nID);

Parameters

dwStyle Styles used for this control. The allowable styles can be found in the Windows API documentation.

rect Indicates the control's position and size in terms of its parent's client coordinates.

pParentWnd Parent window of control.

nID The child ID of this control. Must be unique among its siblings.

Returns TRUE if creation successful; otherwise FALSE.

Cut ■ 2.0 ■ 3.0

Description This function will copy to the Clipboard the selected text from the edit control. This data will be available on the Clipboard in CF_TEXT format.

Syntax public, void Cut();

Parameters None.

Returns Nothing is returned.

See Also CEdit::Copy(),CEdit::Clear(),CEdit::Paste()

Example The following sample illustrates how to use this member function. Although it is not necessary to check for a current text selection, it is a good idea to disable your method for cutting the selection when there is nothing selected.

```
void CCEditDlg::OnCut()
{
     if( !HasCurrentTextSelection(m_EditCtl) )
          return;

     // cut the selection contents to the Clipboard
     m_EditCtl.Cut();
}
```

EmptyUndoBuffer ■ 2.0 ■ 3.0

Description This function will reset the contents of the undo buffer, and disallow a call to undo any previous edit. This function is automatically called by the CEdit::SetHandle() and the CWnd::SetWindowText() functions.

Syntax public, void EmptyUndoBuffer();

Parameters None.

Returns Nothing is returned.

See Also CEdit::CanUndo()

FmtLines ■ 2.0 ■ 3.0

Description This function determines if soft line breaks are to be used in a multi-line edit control. A soft line break consists of two carriage return characters and one line feed character. These characters are usually inserted into the text due to wordwrapping. The use of soft line breaks only affects text that is retrieved from the edit control, but does not change the display of the text.

Syntax public, BOOL FmtLines(BOOL bAddEOL);

Parameters

bAddEOL TRUE will allow the control to use soft line breaks; FALSE will not.

Returns Non-zero if the control had to switch formatting; otherwise 0.

GetFirstVisibleLine ■ 2.0 ■ 3.0

Description This function returns the index of the first visible line in a multi-line edit control.

Syntax public, int GetFirstVisibleLine() const;

Parameters None.

Returns The index of the first visible line in a multi-line edit control, or 0 for single line edit controls.

See Also CEdit::GetLine()

GetHandle ■ 2.0 ■ 3.0

Description This function returns a memory handle that contains the contents of a multi-line edit control. To use this function, the edit control must have the DS_LOCALEDIT style.

Syntax public, HLOCAL GetHandle() const;

Parameters None.

Returns Memory handle to the contents of the control; otherwise NULL. If the control does not have the DS_LOCALEDIT style, then the returned value may not be NULL, but cannot be used.

See Also CEdit::SetHandle()

GetLimitText ■ 3.0

Description This Windows 95-specific member retrieves the maximum amount of text that the control can accept.

Syntax public, UINT GetLimitText() const;

Parameters None.

Returns The maximum amount of text, in bytes, that the control can contain.

See Also CEdit::SetLimitText()

GetLine ■ 2.0 ■ 3.0

Description This function retrieves a line of text from the control, at the specified index.

Syntax public, int GetLine(int nIndex, LPTSTR lpszBuffer) const;
public, int GetLine(int nIndex, LPTSTR lpszBuffer, int nMaxLength) const;

Parameters

nIndex The index of the line to retrieve. This number should be between 0 and GetLineCount()-1.

lpszBuffer The destination address for the retrieved text. For the first version of this member, the first word in the buffer should contain the size (in bytes) of the buffer.

nMaxLength The size of the buffer in bytes.

Returns The actual number of bytes copied.

See Also CEdit::GetFirstVisibleLine()

GetLineCount

■ 2.0 ■ 3.0

Description This function returns the number of text lines in a multi-line edit control.

Syntax public, int GetLineCount() const;

Parameters None.

Returns The number of lines in the control. If the control contains no text, then a value of 1 is returned.

See Also CEdit::GetLine()

GetMargins

■ 3.0

Description This Windows 95-specific member retrieves the left and right margins of the edit control.

Syntax public, DWORD GetMargins() const;

Parameters None.

Returns The low-order WORD contains the left margin in pixels, and the high-order word contains the right margin in pixels.

See Also CEdit::SetMargins()

GetModify

■ 2.0 ■ 3.0

Description This function determines if the contents of an edit contol have been changed. This function is useful in determining if user parameters have changed value.

Syntax public, BOOL GetModify() const;

Parameters None.

Returns Non-zero if the contents of the control have been changed; otherwise 0.

See Also CEdit::SetModify()

GetPasswordChar

■ 2.0 ■ 3.0

Description This function retrieves the character used to mask password edit controls.

Syntax public, TCHAR GetPasswordChar() const;

Parameters None.

Returns The character used for masking, or NULL if no password character has been set.

See Also CEdit::SetPasswordChar()

GetRect

■ 2.0 ■ 3.0

Description This function retrieves the formatting rectangle of multiline edit controls. This formatting rectangle is independent of the size of the control, but by default it fills the entire control on creation.

Syntax public, void GetRect(LPRECT lpRect) const;

Parameters

lpRect Address of a rectangle that will contain the text formatting coordinates.

Returns Nothing is returned.

See Also CEdit::SetRect(), CEdit::SetRectNP()

GetSel

■ 2.0 ■ 3.0

Description This function will return the starting and ending positions of the currently highlighted text selection within the control.

Syntax public, DWORD GetSel(void) const;
public, void GetSel(int& nStartChar, int& nEndChar) const;

Parameters

nStartChar Will be filled with the value of the first selected character position within the control.

nEndChar Will be filled with the value of the first non-selected character position after the highlighted selection within the control.

Returns The first version of this member returns a value whose low-order word contains nStartChar and high-order word contains nEndChar. The second version of this member returns nothing.

Example The following example illustrates how to determine the current selection for the list box. In this example, the function will return TRUE if there is a current selection; otherwise it will return FALSE.

```
BOOL CCEditDlg::HasCurrentTextSelection(CEdit & editBox)
{
      // check for a current selection
      int nStartPos, nEndPos;
      editBox.GetSel(nStartPos,nEndPos);
      if( nStartPos == nEndPos )
      {
            AfxMessageBox("No Current Text Selection");
            return FALSE;
      }
      // return TRUE if there was a text selection
      return TRUE;
}
```

LimitText

■ 2.0 ■ 3.0

Description This function will set an upper limit on the number of bytes that can be used to enter text into the control.

Syntax public, void LimitText(int nChars = 0);

Parameters

nChars The number of characters (in bytes) that can be entered into the control. A value of 0 will set the limit to the maximum value of UINT_MAX bytes.

Returns Nothing is returned.

LineFromChar

■ 2.0 ■ 3.0

Description This function will translate a character position within the text buffer of a multi-line edit control, and return the line index. This index can then be used to call CEdit::GetLine().

Syntax public, int LineFromChar(int nIndex = -1) const;

Parameters

nIndex The index of the character whose line index is desired. A value of -1 indicates the line that has the current caret postion.

Returns The index of the line containing the character position, or if *nIndex* = -1 and text is highlighted, then the line index of the first selected character.

See Also CEdit::GetLine()

LineIndex

■ 2.0 ■ 3.0

Description This function translates the line index into a character index in a multi-line edit control. The character index is the number of characters from the beginning of the edit control to the specified line.

Syntax public, int LineIndex(int nLine = -1) const;

Parameters

nLine Index of the line whose character position is to be retrieved. A value of -1 indicates the current line position (the line containing the caret).

Returns If successful, the character position of the line; otherwise -1.

See Also CEdit::LineFromChar(), CEdit::GetLine()

LineLength

■ 2.0 ■ 3.0

Description This function retrieves the length of the specified line (in bytes). This function may be used on both single and multi-line edit controls.

Syntax public, int LineLength(int nLine = -1) const;

Parameters

nLine The line whose length is desired. A value of -1 indicates the current line (the line containing the caret). This parameter is ignored for single line edit controls.

Returns The length in bytes of the specified line.

See Also CEdit::GetLine()

LineScroll ■ 2.0 ■ 3.0

Description This function will scroll a multi-line edit control both vertically and horizontally.

Syntax public, void LineScroll(int nLines, int nChars = 0);

Parameters

nLines The number of lines to scroll vertically. Note that the edit control will stop scrolling when it has reached the last line of text in the control.

nChars The number of characters to scroll horizontally. This parameter has no effect if the ES_CENTER or ES_RIGHT styles are set.

Returns Nothing is returned.

Paste ■ 2.0 ■ 3.0

Description This function will copy the contents of the Clipboard (if in CF_TEXT format) into the edit control, at the current caret position.

Syntax public, void Paste();

Parameters None.

Returns Nothing is returned.

See Also CEdit::Copy(),CEdit::Cut()

PosFromChar ■ 3.0

Description This Windows 95-specific member will return the coordinate of the given character within the edit control. The coordinate indicates the upper-left corner of the character cell.

Syntax public, CPoint PosFromChar(UINT nChar) const;

Parameters

nChar The zero-based index of the character whose position is to be returned. If this value is greater than the number of characters within the control, then the position returned will be that of the character just past the end of the current contents.

Returns A point indicating the upper-left coordinate of the given character's cell.

See Also CEdit::CharFromPos()

ReplaceSel

■ 2.0 ■ 3.0

Description This function will replace any currently selected text within the control with the supplied text. If the control has no current selection, then the text is inserted at the current caret position.

Syntax public, void ReplaceSel(LPCTSTR lpszNewText);

Parameters

lpszNewText A NULL-terminated string containing the text to insert.

Returns Nothing is returned.

See Also CWnd::SetWindowText()

SetHandle

■ 2.0 ■ 3.0

Description This function supplies a new buffer to a multi-line edit control. Before this function is invoked, the current buffer should be obtained by calling CEdit::GetHandle() and should be set free by calling the Windows function LocalFree().

Syntax public, void SetHandle(HLOCAL hBuffer);

Parameters

hBuffer A handle to a new buffer that can be filled with text. The text should be NULL-terminated, or the first byte should be set to 0.

Returns Nothing is returned.

See Also CEdit::GetHandle()

SetLimitText

■ 3.0

Description This Windows 95-specific member sets the maximum amount of text that the user can enter into the control, but does not affect the amount of text that is set using ::SetWindowText().

Syntax public, void SetLimitText(UINT nMax);

Parameters

nMax The maximum amount of text the user is allowed to enter, in bytes.

Returns Nothing is returned.

See Also CEdit::GetLimitText()

SetMargins

■ 3.0

Description This Windows 95-specific member sets the left and right margins of the edit control.

Syntax public, void SetMargins(UINT nLeft, UINT nRight);

Parameters

nLeft The left margin for the control, in pixels.

NRight The right margin for the control, in pixels.

Returns Nothing is returned.

See Also CEdit::GetMargins()

SetModify ■ 2.0 ■ 3.0

Description This function sets the modified state of an edit control.

Syntax public, void SetModify(BOOL bModified = TRUE);

Parameters

bModified The state to which the control should be set. TRUE indicates that the control has been modified; FALSE clears the modification flag.

Returns Nothing is returned.

See Also CEdit::GetModify()

SetPasswordChar ■ 2.0 ■ 3.0

Description This function will allow a password mask character to be applied to a single line edit control. This mask character will be used to replace any text displayed in the edit control.

Syntax public, void SetPasswordChar(TCHAR ch);

Parameters

ch Character mask, or 0 to remove any previous password character.

Returns Nothing is returned.

See Also CEdit::GetPasswordChar()

SetReadOnly ■ 2.0 ■ 3.0

Description This function toggles the edit state of the control between read-only and editable.

Syntax public, BOOL SetReadOnly(BOOL bReadOnly = TRUE);

Parameters

bReadOnly A value of TRUE disallows editing of the controls contents; FALSE allows editing.

Returns TRUE if successful; otherwise FALSE.

SetRect

■ 2.0 ■ 3.0

Description This function sets the formatting rectangle of multiline edit controls. This formatting rectangle is independent of the size of the control, but by default it fills the entire control on creation.

Syntax public, void SetRect(LPCRECT lpRect);

Parameters

lpRect Address of a rectangle that defines the formatting rectangle coordinates.

Returns Nothing is returned.

See Also CEdit::SetRectNP(), CEdit::GetRect()

SetRectNP

■ 2.0 ■ 3.0

Description This function sets the formatting rectangle of multiline edit controls without redrawing the control. This formatting rectangle is independent of the size of the control, but by default it fills the entire control on creation.

Syntax public, void SetRectNP(LPCRECT lpRect);

Parameters

lpRect Address of a rectangle that defines the formatting rectangle coordinates.

Returns Nothing is returned.

See Also CEdit::SetRect(), CEdit::GetRect()

SetSel

■ 2.0 ■ 3.0

Description This function selects a range of characters within the control.

Syntax public, void SetSel(DWORD dwSelection, BOOL bNoScroll = FALSE);
public, void SetSel(int nStartChar, int nEndChar, BOOL bNoScroll = FALSE);

Parameters

dwSelection Contains the starting character index in the low-order word, and the ending character index in the high-order word. A starting index of 0 and an ending index of -1 will select all text within the control. A starting index of -1 removes any current selection.

bNoScroll FALSE will scroll the caret into view; TRUE will not.

nStartChar Contains the starting character index.

nEndChar Contains the ending character index. A starting index of 0 and an ending index of -1 will select all text within the control. A starting index of -1 removes any current selection.

Returns Nothing is returned.

See Also CEdit::GetSel()

SetTabStops

■ 2.0 ■ 3.0 ■ NM

Description This function sets the tab stops in a multi-line edit control to varying positions. These tab stops will be used whenever a tab character is encountered in the edit control text. This function does not automatically update the edit control. The first version of this member sets the tab stops in a multi-line edit control to the uniform default positions of 32 dialog units. Note, this method is not available when compiling for the Macintosh.

Syntax public, void SetTabStops(); BOOL SetTabStops(const int& cxEachStop);
public, BOOL SetTabStops(int nTabStops, LPINT rgTabStops);

Parameters

cxEachStop A tab stop will be set at every *cxTabStop* dialog unit.

nTabStops The number of tab stops (unsigned integers) contained in rgTabStops. This value must be greater than 1.

rgTabStops An array of *nTabStops* unsigned integers that represent dialog unit values for individual tab stops.

Returns Non-zero if successful; otherwise 0.

See Also CEdit::GetTabStops()

Example The following code illustrates how to set tab stops for the control.

```
void CCEditDlg::InitializeEditBox(CEdit * pEdit)
{
      ASSERT_VALID(pEdit);
      int nTabArray[4] = {10,20,35,50};

      if( pEdit )
      {
            pEdit->SetTabStops(4,nTabArray);
            pEdit->SetWindowText("A\tB\tC\tD");
      }
}
```

Undo

■ 2.0 ■ 3.0

Description This function will undo the last edit operation. The undo function qualifies as an edit operation and can also be "undone".

Syntax public, BOOL Undo();

Parameters None.

Returns A single line edit control will always return TRUE. A multi-line edit control will return TRUE if successful; otherwise FALSE.

See Also CEdit::CanUndo(), CEdit::EmptyUndoBuffer()

CHeaderCtrl

The header control displays a list of labeled columns. These columns can be selected or resized by using the mouse or keyboard. The main use of a header control is to provide a simple interface for another control or a graphic display area. One example would be to use the header control to represent the column widths in a CListCtrl. Whenever a column in the header is resized, the notification messages generated would allow for resizing of the list control's columns. This would be useful for implementing a spreadsheet-type display of information. The example program that is associated with this section can be found in the CHeader directory on the CD-ROM.

CHeaderCtrl ■ 3.0

Description This is the constructor for the header control. The real initialization of this object is done in the Create member function.

Syntax public, CHeaderCtrl();

Parameters None.

Returns Nothing is returned.

See Also CHeaderCtrl::Create()

~CHeaderCtrl ■ 3.0 ■ UD

Description Destroys the header control object.

Syntax public, virtual ~CHeaderCtrl();

Parameters None.

Returns Nothing is returned.

See Also CHeaderCtrl()

Create ■ 3.0

Description After construction, call this member to create the header control and attach it to this object.

Syntax public, BOOL Create(DWORD dwStyle, const RECT & rect, Cwnd * pParentWnd, UINT nID);

Parameters

dwStyle Styles used for this control. The allowable styles can be found in the Windows API documentation.

rect Indicates the control's position and size in terms of its parent's client coordinates.

pParentWnd Parent window of control.

nID	The child ID of this control. Must be unique among its siblings.
Returns	TRUE if creation successful; otherwise FALSE.

DeleteItem ■ 3.0

Description	This function removes an item from the header control.
Syntax	public, BOOL DeleteItem(int nPos);
Parameters	
nPos	Index position of the item to be removed. This value can range from 0 to GetItemCount()-1.
Returns	TRUE if successful; otherwise FALSE.
See Also	CHeaderCtrl::InsertItem()

DrawItem ■ 3.0

Description	This virtual function is called whenever an owner-draw CHeaderCtrl object needs to be displayed or updated. It is passed a pointer to a DrawItemStruct that contains information on how the object is to be drawn.
Syntax	public, virtual void DrawItem(LPDRAWITEMSTRUCT lpDrawItemStruct);
Parameters	
lpDrawItemStruct	Contains parameters for drawing the item. See Windows API documentation for a description of this structure.
Returns	Nothing is returned.
See Also	CWnd::DrawItem()

GetItem ■ 3.0

Description	This function retrieves the item at the specified index.
Syntax	public, BOOL GetItem(int nPos, HD_ITEM* pHeaderItem);
Parameters	
nPos	The position of the item to be retrieved. This value can range from 0 to GetItemCount()-1.
pHeaderItem	Pointer to an HD_ITEM structure that will receive the item. The structure's mask flags must be filled in with the item data that is to be retrieved.
Returns	TRUE if successful; otherwise FALSE.
See Also	CHeaderCtrl::SetItem()

Example The following example illustrates the use of this function by setting the text of each item in the control to a new value.

```
void CCHeaderDlg::ChangeItemText(CHeaderCtrl * pHeader)
{
	ASSERT_VALID(pHeader);

	int nNumItems = pHeader->GetItemCount();
	HD_ITEM item;
	char sTemp[32];
	int nRet;

	// make sure we request text information to be retrieved
	item.mask = HDI_TEXT;
	item.pszText = sTemp;
	item.cchTextMax = sizeof(sTemp)-1;

	for(int nI=0;nI<nNumItems;nI++)
	{
		if( pHeader->GetItem(nI,&item) )
		{
				sprintf(sTemp,"Order %d",nI);
				item.pszText = sTemp;
				item.cchTextMax = strlen(sTemp);
				nRet = pHeader->SetItem(nI,&item);
				ASSERT(nRet!=-1);
		}
	}
}
```

GetItemCount ■ 3.0

Description This function retrieves the number of items in the header control.

Syntax public, int GetItemCount() const;

Parameters None.

Returns The number of items in the control if successful; otherwise -1.

Example See CHeaderCtrl::GetItem()

InsertItem ■ 3.0

Description This function inserts a new item into the header control.

Syntax public, int InsertItem(int nPos, HD_ITEM* phdi);

Parameters

nPos Index where the item is to be inserted. This value can range from 0 to GetItemCount()-1.

Phdi Pointer to an HD_ITEM structure that contains the item attributes. This structure's mask flags must be filled in to indicate which attributes are valid.

Returns Index of the newly inserted item; otherwise -1.

See Also CHeaderCtrl::GetItem()

Example The following code shows how to insert items into the header control.

```
void CCHeaderDlg::InitializeHeaderControl(CHeaderCtrl * pHeader)
{
      HD_ITEM    item;
      char sTemp[64];
      int nRet;

      ASSERT_VALID(pHeader);

      for(int nI=0;nI<5;nI++)
      {
            sprintf(sTemp,"Item First %d",nI);
            item.pszText = sTemp;
            item.cchTextMax = strlen(sTemp);
            item.cxy = 80;
            item.fmt = HDF_CENTER|HDF_STRING;
            item.mask = HDI_TEXT|HDI_WIDTH|HDI_FORMAT;
            nRet = pHeader->InsertItem(nI,&item);
            ASSERT(nRet!=-1);
      }
}
```

LAYOUT ■ 3.0

Description This function retrieves size and position information about the header control.

Syntax public, BOOL Layout(HD_LAYOUT* pHeaderLayout);

Parameters

pHeaderLayout Address of an HD_LAYOUT structure that will receive the size and position information.

Returns TRUE if successful; otherwise FALSE.

ONCHILDNOTIFY ■ 3.0 ■ UD

Description This function is called by the CHeaderCtrl's parent whenever a notification applies to this control. This function should never be called directly, but can be overridden for owner-draw controls.

Syntax protected, virtual BOOL OnChildNotify(UINT, WPARAM, LPARAM, LRESULT *);

Parameters

UINT Notification message.

WPARAM Message-specific Data.

LPARAM Message-specific Data.

*LRESULT** Address of returned result code, dependent on notification message.

Returns The default implementation returns FALSE for every message except WM_DRAWITEM in which case CHeaderCrl::DrawItem() is invoked. This only happens in the case of an owner-draw control.

See Also CWnd::OnChildNotify(), CHeaderCtrl::DrawItem()

SetItem ■ 3.0

Description This function modifies attributes of a particular item in the header control.

Syntax public, BOOL SetItem(int nPos, HD_ITEM* pHeaderItem);

Parameters

nPos Index of the item to be modified. This value can range from 0 to GetItemCount()-1.

pHeaderItem Pointer to an HD_ITEM structure that contains the new attributes. This structure's mask flags must be filled in to indicate which attributes are to be modified.

Returns TRUE if successful; otherwise FALSE.

See Also CHeaderCtrl::GetItem(), CHeaderCtrl::InsertItem()

Example See CHeaderCtrl::GetItem()

CHotKeyCtrl

The CHotKeyCtrl allows the user to enter a key combination that the application can use to perform specific tasks. Any invalid key combinations, such as those hard-coded into the application, can be masked from the control so that they will not be duplicated. To actually set up the action that the hot key will perform, the programmer must register the hot key with the system by using the WM_SETHOTKEY window message. Note that this control is only available under Windows 95 and WinNT 3.51 and later.

CHotKeyCtrl ■ 3.0

Description This is the constructor for the hot key control. The real initialization of this object is done in the Create member function.

Syntax public, CHotKeyCtrl();

Parameters None.

Returns Nothing is returned.

See Also CHotKeyCtrl::Create()

~CHotKeyCtrl ■ 3.0

Description Destroys the hot key control object.

Syntax public, virtual ~CHotKeyCtrl();

Parameters None.
Returns Nothing is returned.
See Also CHotKeyCtrl()

CREATE ■ 3.0

Description After construction, call this member to create the hot key control and attach it to this object.

Syntax public, BOOL Create(DWORD dwStyle, const RECT & rect, Cwnd * pParentWnd, UINT nID);

Parameters

dwStyle Styles used for this control. The allowable styles can be found in the Windows API documentation.

rect Indicates the control's position and size in terms of its parent's client coordinates.

pParentWnd A pointer to the parent window of this control.

nID The child ID of this control. Must be unique among its siblings.

Returns TRUE if creation successful; otherwise FALSE.

GETHOTKEY ■ 3.0

Description Reterieves the currently set hot key combination.

Syntax public, DWORD GetHotKey();
public, void GetHotKey(WORD &wVirtualKeyCode, WORD &wModifiers);

Parameters

wVirtualKeyCode Address to store the virtual key code.

wModifiers Address to store the hot key modifiers.

Returns The first version of this member returns a DWORD; the low-order word contains the virtual key code, and the high-order word contains the key modifiers. The second version of this member returns nothing.

See Also CHotKeyCtrl::SetHotKey()

SETHOTKEY ■ 3.0

Description Sets the hot key combination for the control.

Syntax public, void SetHotKey(WORD wVirtualKeyCode, WORD wModifiers);

Parameters

wVirtualKeyCode The virtual key code of the hot key.

wModifiers Keys that are used in combination with the hot key. Valid values are

HOTKEYF_ALT	ALT key
HOTKEYF_CONTROL	CTRL key
HOTKEYF_EXT	Extended key
HOTKEYF_SHIFT	SHIFT key
Returns	Nothing is returned.
See Also	CHotKeyCtrl::GetHotKey()

SetRules ■ 3.0

Description This function sets the rules that specify invalid hot key configurations. This function is useful to eliminate duplicate keys.

Syntax public, void SetRules(WORD wInvalidComb, WORD wModifiers);

Parameters

wInvalidComb Specifies the invalid key combinations. This can be a combination of the following:

HKCOMB_A	ALT
HKCOMB_C	CTRL
HKCOMB_CA	CTRL+ALT
HKCOMB_NONE	unmodified keys
HKCOMB_S	SHIFT
HKCOMB_SA	SHIFT+ALT
HKCOMB_SC	SHIFT+CTRL
HKCOMB_SCA	SHIFT+CTRL+ALT

wModifiers Specifies the key combination to use in the event the user enters an invalid combination.

Returns Nothing is returned.

CImageList

The image list represents a convenient and efficient way to manage multiple bitmaps or icons in an application. Basically, the image list maintains one large bitmap that consists of many uniformly sized sub-images. These sub-images can be retrieved or displayed through the control's interface. This image list control is also used in conjunction with many of the common controls, to provide a simple way to associate images with items. The example program that is associated with this section can be found in the CImgList directory on the CD-ROM.

CImageList ■ 3.0

Description This is the constructor for the image list control. The real initialization of this object is done in the Create member function.

Syntax public, CImageList();

Parameters None.

Returns Nothing is returned.

See Also CImageList::Create()

~CImageList ■ 3.0 ■ UD

Description Destroys the image list control object.

Syntax public, virtual ~CImageList();

Parameters None.

Returns Nothing is returned.

See Also CImageList()

operator HIMAGELIST() ■ 4.0

Description Casts the object to its internal HIMAGELIST handle. This is a convenient way to use the object with other members or functions that require the HIMAGELIST handle. Otherwise, you would always have to use CImageList::GetSafeHandle() to retrieve the HIMAGELIST.

Syntax public, operator HIMAGELIST() const;

Add ■ 3.0

Description This function adds a new bitmap into the image list.

Syntax public, int Add(CBitmap* pbmImage, CBitmap* pbmMask);
public, int Add(CBitmap* pbmImage, COLORREF crMask);
public, int Add(HICON hIcon);

Parameters

pbmImage Pointer to the bitmap image to add.

pbmMask Pointer to a mask for the bitmap image, or NULL for no mask.

crMask A color used to generate a mask for *pbmImage*. Usually this color is the background color of *pbmImage* so that the image may be painted transparently.

hIcon Handle to the icon that will be added.

Returns The index of the first new image; otherwise -1 if an error occurred.

See Also CImageList::Remove()

Example The following illustrates how to create and add an icon into the image list:

```
CImageList * CCImgListDlg::CreateNewList(void)
{
	CImageList * pNewImgList = new CImageList();

	try
	{
```

continued on next page

continued from previous page

```
            // initialize the image list to contain our image
            if( !pNewImgList->Create(32,32,FALSE,1,1) )
                        AfxThrowUserException();

            // load the application's icon into the list
            // as a sample image
            HICON hAppIcon = AfxGetApp()->LoadIcon(IDR_MAINFRAME);
            ASSERT(hAppIcon);
            if( !hAppIcon || pNewImgList->Add(hAppIcon)==-1 )
                        AfxThrowUserException();
        }
        catch(...)
        {
            ASSERT(FALSE);
            delete pNewImgList;
            pNewImgList = NULL;
        }
        return pNewImgList;
    }
```

Attach ■ 3.0

Description This function sets the internal **m_hImageList** variable to the supplied HIMAGELIST. It is up to the caller to free any currently attached HIMAGELIST.

Syntax public, BOOL Attach(HIMAGELIST hImageList);

Parameters

hImageList The new HIMAGELIST to associate with this object.

Returns TRUE if successful; otherwise FALSE.

See Also CImageList::Detach()

BeginDrag ■ 3.0

Description This function is called to initiate a dragging session using one of the images in the image list. A temporary image list is created to combine the current cursor and the specified image.

Syntax public, BOOL BeginDrag(int nImage, CPoint ptHotSpot);

Parameters

nImage The index of the image that will be used to drag.

ptHotSpot The coordinates, relative to the upper left of the specified image, of the drag hotspot. This allows the caller to synch a point on the image with the hotspot of the cursor.

Returns TRUE if successful; otherwise FALSE.

See Also CImageList::EndDrag(), CImageList::DragMove()

Create ■ 3.0

Description	After construction, call this member to create the image list control and attach it to this object. The first version of this member creates the image list from a bitmap resource. The second version of this member merges two image lists.

Syntax	public, BOOL Create(int cx, int cy, BOOL bMask, int nInitial, int nGrow);
	public, BOOL Create(UINT nBitmapID, int cx, int nGrow, COLORREF crMask);
	public, BOOL Create(LPCTSTR lpszBitmapID, int cx, int nGrow, COLORREF crMask);
	public, BOOL Create(CImageList& imageList1, int nImage1, CImageList& imageList2, int nImage2, int dx, int dy);

Parameters	
cx	Width of each sub-image in pixels.
cy	Height of each sub-image in pixels.
bMask	If TRUE, then the image contains a mask image.
nInitial	The number of initial images the list will contain. This value is used to pre-allocate memory for all images instead of individually allocating memory for each image as it is added to the list.
nGrow	The number of images the list will grow when the list is resized.
nBitmapID	The number of resource IDs associated with this list.
lpszBitmapID	A string containing the resource IDs of the images.
cx	Width of each sub-image in pixels.
crMask	If TRUE, then the list contains two bitmaps, one of which is a mask. If FALSE, then the image list contains only 1 bitmap.
imageList1	The first image list to merge.
nImage1	Number of images in *imageList1*.
imageList2	The second image list to merge.
nImage2	The number of images in *imageList2*.
dx	Width of each sub-image in pixels.
dy	Height of each sub-image in pixels.
Returns	TRUE if successful; otherwise FALSE.
Example	See CImageList::Add()

DeleteImageList ■ 3.0

Description	This member function will detach and destroy the current HIMAGELIST.
Syntax	public, BOOL DeleteImageList();
Parameters	None.

Returns TRUE if the image list was destroyed; FALSE if there is no current HIMAGELIST or an error occurred.

DeleteTempMap ■ 3.0

Description This function removes any temporary CImageList objects that were created by calls to CImageList::FromHandle(). This function does not affect the state of the attached HIMAGELIST handles.

Syntax public, static void PASCAL DeleteTempMap();

Parameters None.

Returns Nothing is returned.

See Also CImageList::FromHandle (),CImageList::FromHandlePermanent()

Detach ■ 3.0

Description This function removes any previously attached HIMAGELIST from the object. It is up to the caller to free (delete) any detached HIMAGELIST.

Syntax public, HIMAGELIST Detach();

Parameters None.

Returns The handle to any previously attached HIMAGELIST.

See Also CImageList::Attach()

DragEnter ■ 3.0

Description This function locks updates to the specified window during a drag operation, until the CImageList::DragLeave() member is called. This member is declared **static** so that it may be called without knowledge of the particular CImageList that is used for dragging.

Syntax public, static BOOL PASCAL DragEnter(CWnd* pWndLock, CPoint point);

Parameters

pWndLock Pointer to the window to lock.

point Position of the drag image, relative to the upper left corner of *pWndLock* .

Returns TRUE if successful; otherwise FALSE.

See Also CImageList::DragLeave(), CImageList::DragShowNolock()

DragLeave ■ 3.0

Description This function unlocks the specified window so that it can be updated. This function is usually called after a call to CImageList::DragEnter().This member is declared **static** so that it may be called without knowledge of the particular CImageList that is used for dragging.

Syntax	public, static PASCAL BOOL DragLeave(CWnd* pWndLock);
Parameters	
pWndLock	Pointer to the window to unlock.
Returns	TRUE if successful; otherwise FALSE.
See Also	CImageList::DragEnter(), CImageList::DragShowNolock()

DragMove ■ 3.0

Description	This function moves the drag image to a new location. This call should be made after a call to CImageList::BeginDrag(), usually during a CWnd::OnMouseMove() message to update the drag image to the new mouse location.
Syntax	public, static BOOL PASCAL DragMove(CPoint pt);
Parameters	
pt	Screen coordinates of new image location.
Returns	TRUE if successful; otherwise FALSE.
See Also	CImageList::BeginDrag(), CImageList::EndDrag()

DragShowNolock ■ 3.0

Description	This function allows the drag image to be displayed or hidden, regardless of whether the window is locked for dragging. The CImageList::DragEnter() member locks updates to a window during a drag operation.
Syntax	public, static BOOL PASCAL DragShowNolock(BOOL bShow);
Parameters	
bShow	TRUE to display the drag image; FALSE to hide.
Returns	TRUE if successful; otherwise FALSE.
See Also	CImageList::DragEnter()

Draw ■ 3.0

Description	This function will draw the specified image into the given device context.
Syntax	public, BOOL Draw(CDC* pDC, int nImage, POINT pt, UINT nStyle);
Parameters	
pDC	Pointer to a device context.
nImage	The index of the image that will be drawn.
pt	The point where the image will be drawn within the device context.
nStyle	How the image will be drawn. This can be any one of the following:

ILD_NORMAL Use the image list background if available; otherwise use the mask for the image.

ILD_TRANSPARENT Use the image mask to draw the image transparently.

ILD_BLEND50 Use the system highlight color to indicate the image is selected. Only valid for images with masks.

ILD_BLEND25 Use the system highlight color to indicate the image has focus. Only valid for images with masks.

ILD_OVERLAYMASK Use another image as an overlay mask for this image. The index of the overlay image is combined with this flag by using the INDEXTOOVERLAYMASK macro. See CImagelist::SetOverlayImage()

Returns TRUE if successful; otherwise FALSE.

Example The following example shows how to draw an image from an image list. In this example, the first image is drawn onto a dialog using several different drawing styles.

```
void CCImgListDlg::OnPaint()
{
      if (IsIconic())
      {
            CPaintDC dc(this); // device context for painting

            SendMessage(WM_ICONERASEBKGND, (WPARAM) dc.GetSafeHdc(), 0);

            // Center icon in client rectangle
            int cxIcon = GetSystemMetrics(SM_CXICON);
            int cyIcon = GetSystemMetrics(SM_CYICON);
            CRect rect;
            GetClientRect(&rect);
            int x = (rect.Width() - cxIcon + 1) / 2;
            int y = (rect.Height() - cyIcon + 1) / 2;

            // Draw the icon
            dc.DrawIcon(x, y, m_hIcon);
      }
      else
      {
            // if we have an image list, then draw its first image
            // using various styles
            if(m_pImageList)
            {
                        CPaintDC dc(this); // device context for painting
                        IMAGEINFO info;
                        m_pImageList->GetImageInfo(0,&info);

                  CRect rImage(info.rcImage);
                  m_pImageList-
>Draw(&dc,0,CPoint(rImage.Width(),rImage.Height()),ILD_NORMAL);
            m_pImageList-
>Draw(&dc,0,CPoint(rImage.Width()*2,rImage.Height()),ILD_TRANSPARENT);
            m_pImageList-
>Draw(&dc,0,CPoint(rImage.Width()*3,rImage.Height()),ILD_BLEND50 );
            m_pImageList-
>Draw(&dc,0,CPoint(rImage.Width()*4,rImage.Height()),ILD_BLEND25);
            }
      }
```

EndDrag

■ 3.0

Description This function ends a drag session and cleans up any temporary items created. This call should be made after a call to CImageList::BeginDrag().

Syntax public, static void PASCAL EndDrag();

Parameters None.

Returns Nothing is returned.

See Also CImageList::BeginDrag(), CImageList::DragMove()

ExtractIcon

■ 3.0

Description This function will create an HICON using the image and mask at the specified index.

Syntax public, HICON ExtractIcon(int nImage);

Parameters

nImage The index of the image that will be used to create the icon.

Returns The handle of the new icon; otherwise NULL.

FromHandle

■ 3.0

Description This static class function will return a CImageList object from a valid HIMAGELIST handle. If no CImageList is currently attached to the handle, then a temporary CImageList is created and attached to the handle. The temporary CImageList is only valid until the next window message is processed, or a call is made to CImageList::DeleteTempMap.

Syntax public, static CImageList* PASCAL FromHandle(HIMAGELIST hImageList);

Parameters

hImageList Handle to a valid image list.

Returns A pointer to a previously currently attached CImageList object, or a pointer to a temporary CImageList object.

See Also CImageList::FromHandlePermanent(), CImageList::DeleteTempMap()

FromHandlePermanent

■ 3.0

Description This static member function returns the CImageList object that is attached to the given HIMAGELIST.

Syntax public, static CImageList* PASCAL FromHandlePermanent(HIMAGELIST hImageList);

Parameters

hImageList Handle to a valid image list.

Returns A pointer to the attached CImageList object; if no CImageList is attached then the return value is NULL.

See Also CImageList::FromHandle()

GetBkColor ■ 3.0

Description This function retrieves the current background color used to paint images.

Syntax public, COLORREF GetBkColor() const;

Parameters None.

Returns The current background color. A value of CLR_NONE indicates the images are drawn transparently using the mask.

See Also CImageList::SetBkColor()

GetDragImage ■ 3.0

Description Retrieves the current drag image and drag position information.

Syntax public, static CImageList* PASCAL GetDragImage(LPPOINT lpPoint, LPPOINT lpPointHotSpot);

Parameters

lpPoint Address of a POINT structure that receives the screen coordinates of the current drag position.

lpPointHotSpot Address of a POINT structure that receives the current drag image hotspot. This point is relative to the current drag position.

Returns A pointer to the temporary drag image list if successful; otherwise NULL.

See Also CImageList::SetDragCursorImage()

GetImageCount ■ 3.0

Description This function returns the number of images in the image list.

Syntax public, int GetImageCount() const;

Parameters None.

Returns The number of images.

GetImageInfo ■ 3.0

Description This function retrieves the attributes of the specified image.

Syntax public, BOOL GetImageInfo(int nImage, IMAGEINFO* pImageInfo) const;

Parameters

nImage — The index of the image in the list. This value can range from 0 to GetImageCount()-1.

pImageInfo — The address of an IMAGEINFO structure that will receive the information on the specified image.

Returns — TRUE if successful; otherwise FALSE.

See Also — CImageList::GetImageCount()

Example — The following example shows how to iterate through the images in the list and retrieve the image info on each one. See also CImageList::Draw()

```
void CCImgListDlg::IterateThroughImages(CImageList * pImageList)
{
	ASSERT_VALID(pImageList);

	int nNumImages = pImageList->GetImageCount();
	IMAGEINFO info;

	for(int nI=0;nI<nNumImages;nI++)
	{
		if( pImageList->GetImageInfo(nI,&info) )
		{
			// do something with info
		}
	}
}
```

GetSafeHandle ■ 3.0

Description — This function retrieves the HIMAGELIST handle contained in the object.

Syntax — public, HIMAGELIST GetSafeHandle() const;

Parameters — None.

Returns — Returns the m_hImageList member, or NULL.

Read ■ 3.0

Description — This function will read the contents of an image list from an archive.

Syntax — public, BOOL Read(CArchive* pArchive);

Parameters

pArchive — Archive that contains image list information.

Returns — TRUE if successful; otherwise FALSE.

See Also — CImageList::Write()

Remove ■ 3.0

Description — This function removes an image from the image list.

Syntax public, BOOL Remove(int nImage);

Parameters

nImage The index of the image to remove from the list.

Returns TRUE if successful; otherwise FALSE.

See Also CImageList::Add(), CImageList::Replace()

REPLACE ■ 3.0

Description Replaces an existing image in the list with a new bitmap or icon.

Syntax public, BOOL Replace(int nImage, CBitmap* pbmImage, CBitmap* pbmMask);
public, int Replace(int nImage, HICON hIcon);

Parameters

nImage The index of the image that will be replaced.

pbmImage Pointer to the new bitmap image.

pbmMask Pointer to a mask for the new bitmap image, or NULL for no mask.

hIcon Pointer to the new icon.

Returns TRUE if successful; otherwise FALSE.

See Also CImageList::Add(), CImageList::Remove()

SETBKCOLOR ■ 3.0

Description This function sets the background color that will be used when painting images.

Syntax public, COLORREF SetBkColor(COLORREF cr);

Parameters

cr The new background color, or CLR_NONE to transparently paint images using the mask.

Returns The previous background color.

See Also CImageList::GetBkColor()

SETDRAGCURSORIMAGE ■ 3.0

Description This function combines the current drag image with the new image specified. Note that the cursor will be re-combined with the image unless a call to CWnd::ShowCursor() is made to hide the cursor. Otherwise, the resulting image may contain two images of the system cursor.

Syntax public, BOOL SetDragCursorImage(int nDrag, CPoint ptHotSpot);

Parameters

nDrag Index of a new image to combine with the current drag image.

ptHotSpot	New hot spot of the combined image.
Returns	TRUE if successful; otherwise FALSE.
See Also	CImageList::GetDragImage(), CImageList::BeginDrag(),CImageList::EndDrag(), CImageList::DragMove()

SetOverlayImage ■ 3.0

Description	Fills one of four available positions with the index of an image that can be used as overlay images. An overlay image can be drawn transparently on top of another image by using the CImageList::Draw() member.
Syntax	public, BOOL SetOverlayImage(int nImage, int nOverlay);
Parameters	
nImage	The index of the image that will be used as an overlay image.
nOverlay	The position of the overlay image. This value can only range from 1 to 4.
Returns	TRUE if successful; otherwise FALSE.
See Also	CImageList::Draw()

Write ■ 3.0

Description	This function will write the current contents of the image list to an archive. This information can be retrieved later by using the CImageList::Read() member.
Syntax	public, BOOL Write(CArchive* pArchive);
Parameters	
pArchive	Archive that will receive the image list information.
Returns	TRUE if successful; otherwise FALSE.
See Also	CImageList::Read()

CListBox

The CListBox object is the MFC encapsulation of a Windows list box. It provides the interfaces necessary to display and manipulate a columned list of items and can support single or multiple selections. The CListBox can be retrieved from an existing dialog or can be created from within another window object. When used in conjunction with an existing dialog template, the Visual C++ ClassWizard can automatically create a CListBox member and attach it to the list box dialog item. The example program that is associated with this section can be found in the CLBoxSamp directory on the CD-ROM.

CListBox ■ 2.0 ■ 3.0

Description	This is the constructor for the list box control. The real initialization of this object is done in the Create member function.

Syntax public, CListBox();
Parameters None.
Returns Nothing is returned.
See Also CListBox::Create()

~CListBox

■ 2.0 ■ 3.0 ■ UD

Description Destroys the list box object.
Syntax public, virtual ~CListBox();
Parameters None.
Returns Nothing is returned.
See Also CListBox: CListBox()

AddString

■ 2.0 ■ 3.0

Description This function appends a string to the items currently in the list box. If the list box has the LBS_SORT style, then the string is inserted in its sorted position.

Syntax public, int AddString(LPCTSTR lpszString);

Parameters

lpszString A NULL-terminated string that contains the text to be added.

Returns A value greater than or equal to zero indicating the position of the string that was added. Otherwise the return will be LB_ERR or LB_ERRSPACE.

See Also CListBox::InsertString(), CListBox::CompareItem()

Example The following example shows how to add a string of text and user data to the list box.

```
int CCustListBox::AddStringAndData(LPCSTR sStr, DWORD dwData)
{
        // this member will set both the text and user data of a new entry
        int nIdx;

        nIdx = AddString(sStr);
        ASSERT(nIdx!=LB_ERR);
        SetItemData(nIdx,dwData);
        return nIdx;
}
```

CharToItem

■ 3.0

Description Override this member function to perform custom selection of items in response to a WM_CHARTOITEM message sent from the list box. This member is only called for non-empty, owner-draw list boxes that do not have the LBS_HASSTRINGS style flag set. A typical use of this member is to provide custom selection of list box entries using the keyboard.

Syntax public, virtual int CharToItem(UINT nKey, UINT nIndex);

Parameters

nKey The ANSI character code of the key hit by the user.

nIndex The current list box caret position.

Returns By default, this member returns -1 to perform the default list box processing. When overriding this member, return -2 to indicate no processing needs to be done (unused key typed). A return index value of 0 or greater indicates that the default action for *nKey* should be peformed on the item at the return index.

See Also CListBox::VKeyToItem()

CompareItem ■ 2.0 ■ 3.0

Description This function allows overriding of the default system sorting algorithm by determining the relative value of items in the control. This function must be overridden for owner-draw controls.

Syntax public, virtual int CompareItem(LPCOMPAREITEMSTRUCT lpCompareItemStruct);

Parameters

lpCompareItemStruct Structure containing indices of the items to be compared.

Returns The return value has three values:

- -1 Item 1 appears before item 2.
- 0 Item 1 and item 2 are of equal value.
- 1 Item 1 appears after item 2.

See Also CWnd::OnCompareItem(), CListBox::AddString()

Create ■ 2.0 ■ 3.0

Description After construction, call this member to create the list box control and attach it to this object.

Syntax public, BOOL Create(DWORD dwStyle, const RECT & rect, Cwnd * pParentWnd, UINT nID);

Parameters

dwStyle A combination of valid window or list box styles. The allowable styles can be found in the Windows API documentation.

rect Indicates the control's position and size in terms of its parent's client coordinates.

pParentWnd Parent window of control.

nID The child ID of this control. Must be unique among its siblings.

Returns TRUE if successful; otherwise FALSE.

See Also CListBox:: CListBox()

DeleteItem

■ 2.0 ■ 3.0

Description This function can be overridden to receive notification when an item is removed from the control.

Syntax public, virtual void DeleteItem(LPDELETEITEMSTRUCT lpDeleteItemStruct);

Parameters

lpDeleteItemStruct Structure containing information about the item to be removed.

Returns Nothing is returned.

See Also CWnd::OnDeleteItem(), CWnd::DeleteString()

DeleteString

■ 2.0 ■ 3.0

Description Removes the specified item from the list box.

Syntax public, int DeleteString(UINT nIndex);

Parameters

nIndex The index of the item to be removed. This value can be from 0 to GetCount()-1.

Returns If successful, then the return value is the number of remaining items; otherwise LB_ERR.

Example The following example shows how to delete the currently selected string from a single selection list box.

```
void CCLBoxSampDlg::OnDelete()
{
        int nSelId = m_ListCtrl.GetCurSel();
        if( nSelId != LB_ERR )
                m_ListCtrl.DeleteString(nSelId);
}
```

Dir

■ 2.0 ■ 3.0

Description This function will load the list box with a list of files or directories.

Syntax public, int Dir(UINT attr, LPCTSTR lpszWildCard);

Parameters

attr This value specifies which items will be loaded into the list box. It can be any combination of the following values:

DDL_ARCHIVE Archived files.

DDL_DIRECTORY The parameter *lpszWildCard* indicates a directory.

DDL_DRIVES Load all drives that match *lpszWildCard*.

DDL_EXCLUSIVE If this flag is set, only files of the specified type are listed. Otherwise, files of the specified type are listed in addition to "normal" files.

DDL_HIDDEN Hidden files.

DDL_READWRITE	Files that can be read from or written to.
DDL_READONLY	Files that cannot be written to.
DDL_SYSTEM	System files.
lpszWildCard	A NULL-terminated string that specifies a path for the files that will be loaded. This string can contain wildcards (such as "*.*").
Returns	If successful, then the index of the last inserted item; otherwise LB_ERR or LB_ERRSPACE.

DrawItem ■ 2.0 ■ 3.0

Description This overridable function is called whenever a visual aspect of an owner-draw list box has changed. This function must be overridden for owner-draw controls.

Syntax public, virtual void DrawItem(LPDRAWITEMSTRUCT lpDrawItemStruct);

Parameters

lpDrawItemStruct Structure specifying information useful in carrying out the drawing of the item.

Returns Nothing is returned.

See Also CWnd::OnDrawItem()

FindString ■ 2.0 ■ 3.0

Description This function will attempt to find the first item that contains the supplied string (case-insensitive).

Syntax public, int FindString(int nStartAfter, LPCTSTR lpszString) const;

Parameters

nStartAfter The first index of the item where the search should begin. This value can range from 0 to GetCount()-1, or can be -1 to search the entire contents of the list box.

lpszFind A NULL-terminated string that is to be searched for within the list box. This string will match an item if it is a prefix of the item.

Returns The index of the matching item, or LB_ERR if not found.

See Also CListBox::FindStringExact(), CListBox::SelectString()

FindStringExact ■ 2.0 ■ 3.0

Description This function will attempt to find an exact whole-word match (case-insensitive) between the supplied string, and any of the list box items.

Syntax public, int FindStringExact(int nIndexStart,LPCTSTR lpszFind) const;

Parameters

nIndexStart	The first index of the item where the search should begin. This value can range from 0 to GetCount()-1, or can be -1 to search the entire contents of the list box.
lpszFind	A NULL-terminated string that is to be searched for within the combo box items.

Returns The index of the matching item, or LB_ERR if not found.

See Also CListBox::FindString(),CListBox::SelectString()

GetAnchorIndex ■ 2.0 ■ 3.0

Description This function retrieves the current anchor in a contiguous selection range for multi-select list boxes using extended selection. The anchor is defined as the starting index from which a selection extends.

Syntax public, int GetAnchorIndex() const;

Parameters None.

Returns The index of the current anchor item; otherwise LB_ERR.

See Also CListBox::SetAnchorIndex()

GetCaretIndex ■ 2.0 ■ 3.0

Description This function retrieves the item index that has the current focus in a multi-select list box.

Syntax public, int GetCaretIndex() const;

Parameters None.

Returns The index of the current focus item, or the currently selected item in a single selection list box.

See Also CListBox::SetCaretIndex()

GetCount ■ 2.0 ■ 3.0

Description This function is used to retrieve the number of items in the list box.

Syntax public, int GetCount() const;

Parameters None.

Returns The number of items in the list box, or LB_ERR.

GetCurSel ■ 2.0 ■ 3.0

Description This function is used to retrieve the currently selected item index from a single selection list box.

Syntax public, int GetCurSel() const;

Parameters None.

Returns The index of the currently selected item. A value of LB_ERR indicates there is an error, no item is selected, or the list box is multi-select. Note that this index is zero-based (the first entry having an index of 0, the second having an index of 1,....).

See Also CListBox::SetCurSel()

Example See CListBox::DeleteString()

GetHorizontalExtent ■2.0 ■3.0

Description Determines the number of pixels that a list box may be scrolled horizontally. This value is determined by the CListBox::SetHorizontalExtent() member. By default, this member will return 0 pixels.

Syntax public, int GetHorizontalExtent() const;

Parameters None.

Returns The number of pixels that the list box can scroll horizontally.

See Also CListBox::SetHorizontalExtent()

GetItemData ■2.0 ■3.0

Description This function retrieves a DWORD value that has been associated with an item in the list box. This value should be set by the CListBox::SetItemData() member. The item data is usually used to associate an ID or value to a string in the list box.

Syntax public, DWORD GetItemData(int nIndex) const;

Parameters

nIndex Index of the item whose data is to be retrieved.

Returns 32-bit associated data value; otherwise LB_ERR.

See Also CListBox::SetItemData(), CListBox::GetItemDataPtr(), CListBox::SetItemDataPtr()

Example The following example illustrates how to use this member for retrieving the item data of the currently selected item.

```
DWORD CCustListBox::GetCurSelItemData(void)
{
     // this member will return the user data for the current selection
     int nIdx = GetCurSel();
     if( nIdx == LB_ERR )
          return 0;

           return GetItemData(nIdx);
}
```

GetItemDataPtr

■ 2.0 ■ 3.0

Description This function retrieves a (void *) pointer that has been associated with an item in the list box. This value should be set by the CListBox::SetItemDataPtr() member.

Syntax public, void * GetItemDataPtr(int nIndex) const;

Parameters

nIndex Index of the item whose data is to be retrieved.

Returns A void * associated with the item; otherwise LB_ERR.

See Also CListBox::SetItemDataPtr(), CListBox::GetItemData(), CListBox::SetItemData()

GetItemHeight

■ 2.0 ■ 3.0

Description Retrieves the height in pixels of an item in the list box.

Syntax public, int GetItemHeight(int nIndex) const;

Parameters

nIndex Index of the item whose height is to be retrieved. If the control does not have the LBS_OWNERDRAWVARIABLE style, then any index value other than 0 indicates the uniform height of items in the list box portion. Otherwise, indices from 0 to GetCount()-1 indicate individual items.

Returns The height of the item in pixels, or LB_ERR.

See Also CListBox::SetItemHeight()

GetItemRect

■ 2.0 ■ 3.0

Description This function retrieves the list box client coordinates of an item's bounding rectangle. Note that the item must be currently visible.

Syntax public, int GetItemRect(int nIndex, LPRECT lpRect) const;

Parameters

nIndex Index of the item.

lpRect Address where the item's client coordinates will be placed.

Returns LB_ERR if an error occurs; otherwise success.

GetLocale

■ 2.0 ■ 3.0

Description This function retrieves the locale identifier that determines how strings in the list box are treated.

Syntax public, LCID GetLocale() const;

Parameters None.

Returns The locale identifier.

See Also CListBox::SetLocale(), ::GetSystemDefaultLCID()

GetSel ■ 2.0 ■ 3.0

Description This function retrieves the selection state of an individual item in the list box.

Syntax public, int GetSel(int nIndex) const;

Parameters

nIndex Index of list box item.

Returns Non-zero if the item is currently selected; otherwise FALSE.

See Also CListBox::SetSel()

GetSelCount ■ 2.0 ■ 3.0

Description This function returns the number of selected items in a multi-select list box.

Syntax public, int GetSelCount() const;

Parameters None.

Returns The number of selected items, or LB_ERR for a single selection list box.

See Also CListBox::GetSelItems()

GetSelItems ■ 2.0 ■ 3.0

Description This function returns an array of selected item indices for multi-select list boxes.

Syntax public, int GetSelItems(int nMaxItems, LPINT rgIndex) const;

Parameters

nMaxItems The number of indices that can be stored in *rgIndex*.

rgIndex User-allocated storage for the selection indices.

Returns The number of indices written to *rgIndex*, or LB_ERR for single selection list boxes.

See Also CListBox::GetSelCount()

GetText ■ 2.0 ■ 3.0

Description This function retrieves the text of the list box item at the given index.

Syntax public, int GetText(int nIndex, LPTSTR lpszBuffer) const;
public, void GetText(int nIndex, CString& rString) const;

Parameters

nIndex Index of the item.

lpszBuffer Address of buffer to contain the item text. This buffer must have sufficient space to contain the item text.

rString	Destination buffer for the item text.
Returns	The length in bytes of the string; otherwise LB_ERR if an error occurs.
See Also	CListBox::GetTextLen()

GetTextLen ■ 2.0 ■ 3.0

Description	This function retrieves the length of the text of the item at the given index.
Syntax	public, int GetTextLen(int nIndex) const;
Parameters	
nIndex	Index of the item.
Returns	The byte size of the item's text excluding the NULL-terminating character, or LB_ERR if an error occurs.
See Also	CListBox::GetText()

GetTopIndex ■ 2.0 ■ 3.0

Description	Returns the index of the first visible item in the list box.
Syntax	public, int GetTopIndex() const;
Parameters	None.
Returns	The index of the first visible item.
See Also	CListBox::SetTopIndex()

InitStorage ■ 3.0

Description	Call this member before loading a large number of items into the list box to optimize memory allocation time. Normally, when individual items are added to the list box, a memory allocation occurs. This member can be called to optimize performance by allocating memory for many items at once, rather than individually. Note that Windows 95 is limited to 32,767 items, but the memory that they use is only limited by the available system memory.
Syntax	public, int InitStorage(int nItems, UINT nBytes);
Parameters	
nItems	The number of items that will be added to the list box.
nBytes	The number of bytes per item that is necessary to store the item string entry.
Returns	If successful, the maximum number of items that can be stored before a memory allocation occurs. Otherwise LB_ERR if the requested amount of memory was not available.

InsertString ■ 2.0 ■ 3.0

Description	This function will insert a new item at the given index, moving down the current item at that position and any other items below it. Inserting a string in this manner will override any sorting options if the LBS_SORT style is set.
Syntax	public, int InsertString(int nIndex, LPCTSTR lpszString);
Parameters	
nIndex	The index where the new string should reside.
lpszString	A NULL-terminated string that will be inserted into the list box.
Returns	If successful, then the index of the newly inserted item; otherwise LB_ERR or LB_ERRSPACE.
See Also	CListBox::AddString()

ItemFromPoint ■ 3.0

Description	Determines the list box item closest to the point specified.
Syntax	UINT ItemFromPoint(CPoint pt, BOOL& bOutside) const;
Parameters	
pt	The coordinates indicating the position in question, relative to the list box's upper left corner.
bOutside	A reference to a Boolean. This value is set to TRUE if *pt* is outside the list box's client area; otherwise FALSE indicates that *pt* is located within the list box.
Returns	The index of the item nearest to the given coordinates.

MeasureItem ■ 2.0 ■ 3.0

Description	This function, only valid for an owner-draw list box, can be overridden to supply the operating system with information regarding the dimensions of the list box. This function is called only once unless the LBS_OWNERDRAWVARIABLE style is set; then it is called once for each item in the control. This function must be overridden for owner-draw controls.
Syntax	public, virtual void MeasureItem(LPMEASUREITEMSTRUCT lpMeasureItemStruct);
Parameters	
lpMeasureItemStruct	A pointer to a structure containing information on the control, current item, and width and height information. This structure should be filled with the appropriate dimensions.
Returns	Nothing is returned.
See Also	CWnd::OnMeasureItem()

OnChildNotify

■ 2.0 ■ 3.0 ■ UD

Description	This function can be overridden to receive notification messages from the parent control. The default implementation of this function interprets and executes other virtual notification member functions (such as interpreting WM_DRAWITEM to execute CListBox::DrawItem()).
Syntax	protected, virtual BOOL OnChildNotify(UINT, WPARAM, LPARAM, LRESULT*);
Parameters	
UINT	Message.
WPARAM	Message-specific data.
LPARAM	Message-specific data.
*LRESULT**	Address of returned result code, dependent on notification message.
Returns	The default implementation returns FALSE for every unhandled message, and TRUE for messages that were handled by the control.
Returns	Nothing is returned.
See Also	CWnd::OnChildNotify()

ResetContent

■ 2.0 ■ 3.0

Description	This function will remove all items from the list box.
Syntax	public, void ResetContent();
Parameters	None.
Returns	Nothing is returned.
Example	See CListBox::AddString()

SelectString

■ 2.0 ■ 3.0

Description	This function will find and select the first item that matches the supplied string (case-insensitive) or that contains the specified string as a prefix. The selected item will also be scrolled into view. This function is only available to single selection list boxes.
Syntax	public, int SelectString(int nStartAfter, LPCTSTR lpszItem);
Parameters	
nStartAfter	Index to begin search from, or -1 to search entire list.
lpszItem	A NULL-terminated string that is to be searched for within the list box. This string will also match an item if it is a prefix of the item.
Returns	The index of the selected item, or LB_ERR if not found.
See Also	CListBox::FindString(), CListBox::FindStringExact()

SelItemRange ■ 2.0 ■ 3.0

Description This function selects or de-selects a range of items within the list box.

Syntax public, int SelItemRange(BOOL bSelect, int nFirstItem, int nLastItem);

Parameters

bSelect TRUE will select the range; FALSE will remove any selection on the range.

nFirstItem Index of first item in range.

nLastItem Index of the last item in range.

Returns LB_ERR if an error occurs; otherwise success.

See Also CListBox::SetSel()

SetAnchorIndex ■ 2.0 ■ 3.0

Description This function sets the first item in a contiguous selection range for multi-select list boxes using extended selection.

Syntax public, void SetAnchorIndex(int nIndex);

Parameters

nIndex Index of list box item.

Returns Nothing is returned.

See Also CListBox::GetAnchorIndex()

SetCaretIndex ■ 2.0 ■ 3.0

Description This function sets the current focus to a specific item in a multi-select list box.

Syntax public, int SetCaretIndex(int nIndex, BOOL bScroll = TRUE);

Parameters

nIndex Index of the item to receive focus.

bScroll If TRUE, then the item is scrolled into view until it is at least partially visible. If FALSE, then the item is scrolled into view so that it is fully visible.

Returns LB_ERR if an error occurs; otherwise success.

See Also CListBox::SetCaretIndex()

SetColumnWidth ■ 2.0 ■ 3.0

Description This function sets the width in pixels of all columns in a list box with the LBS_MULTICOLUMN style.

Syntax public, void SetColumnWidth(int cxWidth);

Parameters

cxWidth The width in pixels of columns in the list box.

Returns Nothing is returned.

SetCurSel

■ 2.0 ■ 3.0

Description This function is used to set the currently selected item in a single selection list box. If the item is not in view, the item is scrolled into view.

Syntax public, int SetCurSel(int nSelect);

Parameters

nSelect Zero-based index of the string to select from the list box. The valid values for this parameter range from 0 to CListBox::GetCount()-1, or -1 to clear any current selections.

Returns The index of the item selected, or LB_ERR.

SetHorizontalExtent

■ 2.0 ■ 3.0

Description This member sets the number of horizontal pixels that the list box can be scrolled. Note that even though the WS_HSCROLL style is set for the list box, the scrollbar will not appear unless the horizontal extent has been set to a value greater than the width of the list box.

Syntax public, void SetHorizontalExtent(int cxExtent);

Parameters

cxExtent Determines the horizontal width in pixels that the list box may be scrolled.

Returns Nothing is returned.

See Also CListBox::GetHorizontalExtent()

SetItemData

■ 2.0 ■ 3.0

Description This function sets a DWORD value that is associated with an item in the list box. This value can be retrieved through the CListBox::GetItemData() member. The item data is usually used to associate an ID or value to a string in the list box.

Syntax public, int SetItemData(int nIndex, DWORD dwItemData);

Parameters

nIndex Index of the item whose data is to be set.

dwItemData 32-bit value associated with the given index.

Returns Non-zero if successful; otherwise LB_ERR.

See Also CListBox::GetItemData(), CListBox::GetItemDataPtr(), CListBox::SetItemDataPtr()

Example See CListBox::AddString()

SetItemDataPtr

■ 2.0 ■ 3.0

Description This function sets a (void *) pointer that is associated with an item in the list box. This pointer can be retrieved through the CListBox::GetItemDataPtr() member.

Syntax public, int SetItemDataPtr(int nIndex, void * pData);

Parameters

nIndex Index of the item whose data is to be set.

pData A void * that is to be associated with the given item.

Returns Non-zero if successful; otherwise LB_ERR.

See Also CListBox::GetItemDataPtr(), CListBox::GetItemData(), CListBox::SetItemData()

SetItemHeight

■ 2.0 ■ 3.0

Description This function sets the height of items in the list box. If the control does not have the LBS_OWNERDRAWVARIABLE style flag set, then all of the list box items will have the same height.

Syntax public, int SetItemHeight(int nIndex,UINT cyItemHeight);

Parameters

nIndex Index of the item that will be affected by the new height. If the control does not have the LBS_OWNERDRAWVARIABLE style, then any index value other than 0 indicates all items in the list box. Otherwise, indices from 0 to GetCount()-1 inidicate individual items.

cyItemHeight The height in pixels of the item indicated by *nIndex*.

Returns LB_ERR if an error occurs; otherwise success.

See Also CListBox::GetItemHeight()

SetLocale

■ 2.0 ■ 3.0

Description This function sets the locale identifier that determines how strings in the list box are treated.

Syntax public, LCID SetLocale(LCID nNewLocale);

Parameters

nNewLocale The new locale identifier.

Returns The previous locale identifier.

See Also CListBox::GetLocale(), ::GetSystemDefaultLCID()

SetSel

■ 2.0 ■ 3.0

Description This function sets the selection state of an individual item in a multi-select list box.

Syntax public, int SetSel(int nIndex, BOOL bSelect = TRUE);

Parameters

nIndex Index of list box item.

bSelect TRUE will select the item; FALSE will remove any selection from the item.

Returns LB_ERR if an error occurs; otherwise success.

See Also CListBox::GetSel()

SetTabStops

■ 2.0 ■ 3.0

Description This function sets the tab stops in a list box to varying positions. This will only affect list boxes that have the LBS_USETABSTOPS style. These tab stops will be used whenever a tab character is encountered in the "item's" text.

Syntax public, BOOL SetTabStops(int nTabStops, LPINT rgTabStops);

Parameters

nTabStops The number of tab stops (unsigned integers) contained in rgTabStops. This value must be greater than 1.

rgTabStops An array of *nTabStops* unsigned integers that represent dialog unit values for individual tab stops.

Returns Non-zero if successful; otherwise 0.

SetTabStops

■ 2.0 ■ 3.0

Description This function sets the tab stops in the list box to the uniform default position of 2 dialog units. This will only affect list boxes that have the LBS_USETABSTOPS style.

Syntax public, void SetTabStops();

Parameters None.

Returns Non-zero if successful; otherwise 0.

SetTabStops

■ 2.0 ■ 3.0

Description This function sets the tab stops in a list box to uniform positions. This will only affect list boxes that have the LBS_USETABSTOPS style.

Syntax public, BOOL SetTabStops(const int& cxEachStop);

Parameters

cxEachStop A tab stop will be set at every *cxEachbStop* dialog unit.

Returns Non-zero if successful; otherwise 0.

SetTopIndex

■ 2.0 ■ 3.0

Description This function sets the first visible item in the list box, scrolling the contents if necessary. If the maximum scroll range of the list box is reached, then the item will be visible but not necessarily the first visible item.

Syntax public, int SetTopIndex(int nIndex);

Parameters

nIndex Indexed position of the item.

Returns LB_ERR if an error occurs; otherwise success.

See Also CListBox::GetTopIndex()

VKeyToItem

■ 3.0

Description Override this member function to perform custom selection of items in response to a WM_VKEYTOITEM message sent from the list box. This member is only called for non-empty list boxes that do have the LBS_WANTKEYBOARDINPUT style flag set.

Syntax public, virtual int VKeyToItem(UINT nKey, UINT nIndex);

Parameters

nKey The virtual-key code of the key hit by the user.

nIndex The current list box caret position.

Returns By default, this member returns -1 to process the key with the default behavior. When overriding this member, return -2 to indicate no processing needs to be done (unused key typed). A return index value of 0 or greater indicates that the default action for *nKey* should be peformed on the item at the return index.

See Also CListBox::CharToItem()

CListCtrl

The CListCtrl is a powerful control, capable of displaying information in icon view, small icon view, list view, or report view. The icon view displays items with a supplied icon that indicates the item state (selected, not selected, has focus, drop target, etc.), and each icon can be relocated anywhere within the control's display space. The small icon view displays a small icon and a text label that can also be relocated within the control's display space. The list view is a non-relocatable, columned version of the small icon view. And finally, the report view is a vertical list with multiple columns that contain various information about the items. The report view can also display sub-item information: extra information associated with each item and displayed to the right of the item's data. The example program that is associated with this section can be found in the CListCtrl directory on the CD-ROM.

CListCtrl

■ 3.0

Description This is the constructor for the list control. The real initialization of this object is done in the Create member function.

Syntax public, CListCtrl();

Parameters None.

Returns Nothing is returned.

See Also CListCtrl::Create()

~CListCtrl

■ 3.0 ■ UD

Description Destroys the list control object.

Syntax public, virtual ~CListCtrl();

Parameters None.

Returns Nothing is returned.

See Also CListCtrl()

Arrange

■ 3.0

Description This function determines how the items in the control will be arranged.

Syntax public, BOOL Arrange(UINT nCode);

Parameters

nCode A code specifying the arrangement type combined with optional sorting parameters.

LVA_ALIGNBOTTOM Items will be arranged along the bottom of the control.

LVA_ALIGNLEFT Items will be arranged along the left of the control.

LVA_ALIGNRIGHT Items will be arranged along the right of the control.

LVA_ALIGNTOP Items will be arranged along the top of the control.

LVA_DEFAULT Items will be arranged using the current arrangement method.

LVA_SNAPTOGRID Icons will be snapped to the nearest grid position.

LVA_SORTASCENDING Items will be sorted by ascending text label.

LVA_SORTDESCENDING Items will be sorted by descending text label.

Returns TRUE if successful; otherwise FALSE.

Create

■ 3.0

Description After construction, call this member to create the list control and attach it to this object.

Syntax	public, BOOL Create(DWORD dwStyle, const RECT & rect, Cwnd * pParentWnd, UINT nID);
Parameters	
dwStyle	A combination of valid window or list control styles. The allowable styles can be found in the Windows API documentation.
rect	Indicates the control's position and size in terms of its parent's client coordinates.
pParentWnd	Parent window of control.
nID	The child ID of this control. Must be unique among its siblings.
Returns	TRUE if successful; otherwise FALSE.
See Also	CListCtrl:: CListCtrl()

CreateDragImage ■ 3.0

Description	This function will create a drag list image for a specific item.
Syntax	public, CImageList* CreateDragImage(int nItem, LPPOINT lpPoint);
Parameters	
nItem	The index of the item.
lpPoint	A pointer to a POINT structure that receives the client coordinates of the upper left corner of the image.
Returns	If successful, a pointer to the new drag image list; otherwise NULL.

DeleteAllItems ■ 3.0

Description	This function removes all items from the control.
Syntax	public, BOOL DeleteAllItems();
Parameters	None.
Returns	TRUE if successful; otherwise FALSE.
See Also	CListCtrl::DeleteItem()

DeleteColumn ■ 3.0

Description	This function removes an existing column from the control.
Syntax	public, BOOL DeleteColumn(int nCol);
Parameters	
nCol	The index of the column that is to be removed.
Returns	TRUE if successful; otherwise FALSE.
See Also	CListCtrl::InsertColumn()

DeleteItem ■ 3.0

Description This function removes an item from the control.

Syntax public, BOOL DeleteItem(int nItem);

Parameters

nItem Index of the item to remove.

Returns TRUE if successful; otherwise FALSE.

See Also CListCtrl::DeleteAllItems(), CListCtrl::InsertItem()

Example The following example shows how to delete the selected items in the control.

```
void CCListCtlDlg::OnDel()
{
	// check to see if any are selected
	if( m_ListCtrl.GetSelectedCount() == 0 )
	{
		AfxMessageBox("No items selected.");
		return;
	}

	// delete all selected items
	LV_ITEM item;
	int nIdx;

	memset(&item,0,sizeof(item));
	item.mask = LVIF_STATE;
	item.stateMask = LVIS_SELECTED;
	for(nIdx=m_ListCtrl.GetItemCount();nIdx>=0;nIdx--)
	{
		item.iItem = nIdx;
		m_ListCtrl.GetItem(&item);
		if( item.state == LVIS_SELECTED )
			m_ListCtrl.DeleteItem(nIdx);
	}
}
```

DrawItem ■ 3.0

Description This virtual function is called whenever an owner-draw CListCtrl object needs to be displayed or updated. It is passed a DrawItemStruct that contains various information on how the control is to be drawn.

Syntax public, virtual void DrawItem(LPDRAWITEMSTRUCT lpDrawItemStruct);

Parameters

lpDrawItemStruct Contains parameters for drawing the item. See Windows API documentation for a description of this structure.

Returns Nothing is returned.

See Also CWnd::DrawItem()

EditLabel ■ 3.0

Description This function retrieves the edit control used to edit the item label, and initiates user editing of the label (by giving focus to the edit control). The control must have the LVS_EDITLABELS style set.

Syntax public, CEdit* EditLabel(int nItem);

Parameters

nItem The index of the item.

Returns A pointer to the edit control if successful; otherwise NULL.

See Also CListCtrl::EnsureVisible()

EnsureVisible ■ 3.0

Description This function will scroll a list item into view, if necessary, to make it visible within the control.

Syntax public, BOOL EnsureVisible(int nItem, BOOL bPartialOK);

Parameters

nItem The index of the item that should be visible.

bPartialOK TRUE if the item does not have to be fully visible; otherwise FALSE.

Returns TRUE if successful; otherwise FALSE.

See Also CListCtrl::SetTopIndex(), CListCtrl::Scroll()

FindItem ■ 3.0

Description This function searches for an item in the list that matches the given attributes.

Syntax public, int FindItem(LV_FINDINFO* pFindInfo, int nStart = -1) const;

Parameters

pFindInfo A pointer to an LV_FINDINFO structure that contains attributes to search for.

nStart The index to begin the search from.

Returns If successful, then the index of the item. If the item is not found, then -1.

GetBkColor ■ 3.0

Description This function retrieves the current background color of the control.

Syntax public, COLORREF GetBkColor() const;

Parameters None.

Returns A COLORREF value specifying the current background color.

See Also CListCtrl::SetBkColor()

GetCallbackMask ■ 3.0

Description This function retrieves the callback mask for the control. The callback mask is used to determine whether the control maintains all state information about the items in the control, or the user will track the information.

Syntax public, UINT GetCallbackMask() const;

Parameters None.

Returns The current callback mask. By default, the control will handle all item states and this callback mask is 0. A non-zero mask indicates that the application rather than the control will handle the given states.

See Also CListCtrl::SetCallbackMask()

GetColumn ■ 3.0

Description This function retrieves the display characteristics of a column in the control.

Syntax public, BOOL GetColumn(int nCol, LV_COLUMN* pColumn) const;

Parameters

nCol The index of the column.

pColumn A pointer to an LV_COLUMN structure that will contain the column display attributes. Note that the **mask** member of the structure indicates which attributes are to be retrieved. If the LVCF_TEXT mask is used, then the **pszText** and **cchTextMax** members must also be initialized.

Returns TRUE if successful; otherwise FALSE.

See Also CListCtrl::SetColumn()

GetColumnWidth ■ 3.0

Description This function retrieves the width of a particular column when the control is in either list or report view.

Syntax public, int GetColumnWidth(int nCol) const;

Parameters

nCol The index of the column.

Returns The width of the column (in pixels).

See Also CListCtrl::SetColumnWidth()

GetCountPerPage ■ 3.0

Description This function returns the number of items that fit vertically within the control pane. This function is only valid when the control is in list or report view.

Syntax	public, int GetCountPerPage() const;
Parameters	None.
Returns	The number of items.

GetEditControl ■ 3.0

Description	This function returns a pointer to the CEdit control used to edit an item's label. This member does not initiate user-editing of the label. See CListCtrl::EditLabel().
Syntax	public, CEdit* GetEditControl() const;
Parameters	None.
Returns	The pointer to the CEdit if successful; otherwise NULL.
See Also	CListCtrl::EditLabel()

GetImageList ■ 3.0

Description	This function retrieves one of the three image lists contained in the control.
Syntax	public, CImageList* GetImageList(int nImageList) const;
Parameters	
nImageList	Specifies which list is to be retrieved. The value can be any one of the following:
LVSIL_NORMAL	Image list that contains the large images.
LVSIL_SMALL	Image list that contains the small images.
LVSIL_STATE	Image list that contains the state images.
Returns	The specified image list.
See Also	CListCtrl::SetImageList()

GetItem ■ 3.0

Description	This function retrieves an item from the control.
Syntax	public, BOOL GetItem(LV_ITEM* pItem) const;
Parameters	
pItem	A pointer to an LV_ITEM structure that will contain the retrieved item. The item to be retrieved is specified by the **iItem** member of the LV_ITEM structure.
Returns	TRUE if successful; otherwise FALSE.
See Also	CListCtrl::SetItem(), CListCtrl::GetNextItem()
Example	See CListCtrl::DeleteItem()

GetItemCount ■ 3.0

Description This function retrieves the number of items in the control.

Syntax public, int GetItemCount() const;

Parameters None.

Returns The number of items in the control.

See Also CListCtrl::GetItem()

Example See CListCtrl::DeleteItem()

GetItemData ■ 3.0

Description This function retrieves the lParam member of the LV_ITEM structure associated with the given item.

Syntax public, DWORD GetItemData(int nItem) const;

Parameters

nItem The index of the item to retrieve.

Returns The lParam associated with the given item.

See Also CListCtrl::GetItem()

GetItemPosition ■ 3.0

Description This function will retrieve a particular item's position within the control.

Syntax public, BOOL GetItemPosition(int nItem, LPPOINT lpPoint) const;

Parameters

nItem The index of the item.

lpPoint A pointer to a POINT structure that will receive the position in client coordinates.

Returns TRUE if successful; otherwise FALSE.

See Also CListCtrl::SetItemPosition()

GetItemRect ■ 3.0

Description This function retrieves the control's client coordinates of an item's bounding rectangle. Note that the item must be currently visible.

Syntax public, BOOL GetItemRect(int nItem, LPRECT lpRect, UINT nCode) const;

Parameters

nItem The index of the item.

lpRect A pointer to a RECT that will receive the client coordinates.

nCode	Indicates which part of the item. It can be any one of the following values:
LVIR_BOUNDS	Indicates the bounds of the entire item.
LVIR_ICON	Indicates the bounds of the icon.
LVIR_LABEL	Indicates the bounds of the item text.
Returns	TRUE if successful; otherwise FALSE.
See Also	CListCtrl::GetViewRect()

GetItemState ■ 3.0

Description	This function retrieves the state bits of the specified item.
Syntax	public, UINT GetItemState(int nItem, UINT nMask) const;
Parameters	
nItem	Index of the item.
nMask	The mask used to determine which state bits are to be retrieved.
Returns	The requested state bits of the item. This value can be a combination of the following: LVIS_CUT, LVIS_DROPHILIGHTED, LVIS_FOCUSED, LVIS_SELECTED.
See Also	CListCtrl::SetItemState()

GetItemText ■ 3.0

Description	This function retrieves the specified text from an item, or its associated sub-item.
Syntax	public, int GetItemText(int nItem, int nSubItem, LPTSTR lpszText, int nLen) const; public, CString GetItemText(int nItem, int nSubItem) const;
Parameters	
nItem	The index of the item.
nSubItem	The index of the sub-item whose text is to be retrieved. If the item's label is to be retrieved, then this value should be 0. Otherwise, the label for the sub-item is retrieved.
lpszText	Address of the buffer that will receive the item text.
nLen	The length of the text buffer specified by *lpszText*.
Returns	The first version of this member returns the length of the retrieved text (in bytes). The second version returns CString containing the retrieved text.
See Also	CListCtrl::SetItemText()

GetNextItem ■ 3.0

Description	This function retrieves the item that matches the specified criteria (the next item in the given order).

Syntax public, int GetNextItem(int nItem, int nFlags) const;

Parameters

nItem The index of the item that the search will begin from. A value of -1 will start at the beginning of the control. The item specified by *nItem* is excluded from the search.

nFlags The flags specify which items will meet the search criteria, and can be any one of the following values:

LVNI_ABOVE	Retrieves the first item above *nItem*.
LVNI_ALL	Retrieves the next item by index.
LVNI_BELOW	Retrieves the first item below *nItem*.
LVNI_PREVIOUS	Retrieves the previous item by index.
LVNI_TOLEFT	Retrieves the next item to the left of *nItem*.
LVNI_TORIGHT	Retrieves the next item to the right of *nItem*.

Returns The index of the next item that matches the criteria; otherwise -1.

See Also CListCtrl::GetItem()

GetOrigin ■ 3.0

Description This function retrieves the current view origin coordinates.

Syntax public, BOOL GetOrigin(LPPOINT lpPoint) const;

Parameters

lpPoint The address of a POINT structure that will receive the view origin coordinates.

Returns TRUE if successful; otherwise FALSE.

GetSelectedCount ■ 3.0

Description This function returns the number of selected items in the control.

Syntax public, UINT GetSelectedCount() const;

Parameters None.

Returns The number of items selected.

See Also CListCtrl::GetItemCount()

Example See CListCtrl::DeleteItem()

GetStringWidth ■ 3.0

Description This function determines the minimum column width necessary to display the entire string passed.

Syntax public, int GetStringWidth(LPCTSTR lpsz) const;

Parameters

lpsz The string to be displayed.

Returns The minimum column width (in pixels) necessary to display *lpsz*.

GetTextBkColor ■ 3.0

Description This function returns the background color used when text is displayed within the control.

Syntax public, COLORREF GetTextBkColor() const;

Parameters None.

Returns A COLORREF specifying the background color used when displaying text within the control.

See Also CListCtrl::SetTextBkColor()

GetTextColor ■ 3.0

Description This function returns the color used to display text within the control.

Syntax public, COLORREF GetTextColor() const;

Parameters None.

Returns A COLORREF specifying the color used to display text within the control.

See Also CListCtrl::SetTextColor()

GetTopIndex ■ 3.0

Description Returns the index of the first visible item in the control.

Syntax public, int GetTopIndex() const;

Parameters None.

Returns The index of the first visible item.

GetViewRect ■ 3.0

Description This function returns the bounding rectangle of all items in the control when in either icon or small icon view.

Syntax public, BOOL GetViewRect(LPRECT lpRect) const;

Parameters

lpRect Address of a RECT structure that will receive the bounding rectangle coordinates.

Returns TRUE if successful; otherwise FALSE.

See Also CListCtrl::GetItemRect()

HitTest ■ 3.0

Description This function determines which item in the control is at a certain position.

Syntax
public, int HitTest(LV_HITTESTINFO* pHitTestInfo) const;
public, int HitTest(CPoint pt, UINT* pFlags = NULL) const;

Parameters

pHitTestInfo A pointer to an LV_HITTESTINFO structure that contains position information and receives flags about the results of the hit test.

pt The point of the hit.

pFlags The address where extra hit-specific flags will be stored.

Returns The index of the item at the specified position, or -1 if no item qualified.

InsertColumn ■ 3.0

Description This function inserts a new column into the control.

Syntax
public, int InsertColumn(int nCol, const LV_COLUMN* pColumn);
public, int InsertColumn(int nCol, LPCTSTR lpszColumnHeading,
int nFormat = LVCFMT_LEFT, int nWidth = -1, int nSubItem = -1);

Parameters

nCol The index of the new column.

pColumn A pointer to an LV_COLUMN structure that contains the column attributes.

lpszColumnHeading A pointer to a string containing the new column's heading.

nFormat The column alignment. This can be any one of the following:
LVCFMT_LEFT, LVCFMT_RIGHT, or LVCFMT_CENTER

nWidth The new column width in pixels, or -1 to specify no width.

nSubItem The index of the sub-item associated with the column, or -1 to specify no sub-item.

Returns If successful, the index of the new column; otherwise -1.

See Also CListCtrl::DeleteColumn()

Example See CListCtrl::InsertItem()

InsertItem ■ 3.0

Description This function inserts a new item into the control.

Syntax
public, int InsertItem(const LV_ITEM* pItem);
public, int InsertItem(int nItem, LPCTSTR lpszItem);
public, int InsertItem(int nItem, LPCTSTR lpszItem, int nImage);

Parameters

pItem A pointer to an LV_ITEM structure that describes the new item.

nItem The index where the item should be inserted.

lpszItem A pointer to a string containing the new item's label.

nImage The index of the new item's image, or I_IMAGECALLBACK if the item is a callback item.

Returns The index of the new item if the operation is successful; otherwise -1.

See Also CListCtrl::DeleteItem()

Example The following shows how to insert items into the list control.

```
void CCListCtlDlg::InitializeList(CListCtrl & listCtrl)
{
      char sLabel[64];
      LV_COLUMN column;
      LV_ITEM item;
      int nRet;

      listCtrl.SetBkColor(RGB(255,255,232));

      sprintf(sLabel,"Column 1");
      column.mask = LVCF_TEXT|LVCF_WIDTH;
      column.pszText = sLabel;
      column.cchTextMax = strlen(sLabel);
      column.cx = 150;
         nRet = listCtrl.InsertColumn(0,&column);
         ASSERT(nRet!=-1);

         memset(&item,0,sizeof(item));
         for(int nI=0;nI<50;nI++)
         {
                  sprintf(sLabel,"Item number %d",nI);
                  item.pszText = sLabel;
                  item.cchTextMax = strlen(sLabel);
                  item.iItem = 0;
                  item.lParam = nI;
                  item.mask = LVIF_TEXT|LVIF_PARAM;
                  nRet = listCtrl.InsertItem(&item);
                  ASSERT(nRet!=-1);
      }
}
```

OnChildNotify ■ 3.0 ■ UD

Description This function is called by the CListCtrl's parent whenever a notification applies to this control. This function should never be called directly, but can be overridden for owner-draw buttons.

Syntax protected, virtual BOOL OnChildNotify(UINT, WPARAM, LPARAM, LRESULT*);

Parameters

UINT Notification message.

WPARAM Message-specific data.

LPARAM Message-specific data.

*LRESULT** Address of returned result code, dependent on notification message.

Returns The default implementation returns FALSE for every unhandled message, and TRUE for messages that were handled by the control.

OnNcDestroy ■ 3.0 ■ UD

Description The default implementation of this protected member function is used to remove any current image lists from the control.

Syntax protected, afx_msg void OnNcDestroy();

Parameters None.

Returns Nothing is returned.

See Also CListCtrl::RemoveImageList()

RedrawItems ■ 3.0

Description This function repaints a range of items in the control.

Syntax public, BOOL RedrawItems(int nFirst, int nLast);

Parameters

nFirst The index of the first item to be redrawn.

nLast The index of the last item to be redrawn.

Returns TRUE if successful; otherwise FALSE.

See Also CListCtrl::Update()

RemoveImageList ■ 3.0 ■ UD

Description This protected member function will release any of the three image lists used by the control. If the control has the LVS_SHAREIMAGELISTS style set, then the actual information stored in the image list will not be destroyed; otherwise all memory and resources associated with the list will be released.

Syntax protected, void RemoveImageList(int nImageList);

Parameters

nImageList Specifies which list is to be removed. The value can be any one of the following:

LVSIL_NORMAL Image list that contains the large images.

LVSIL_SMALL Image list that contains the small images.

LVSIL_STATE Image list that contains the state images.

Returns Nothing is returned.

See Also CListCtrl::OnNcDestroy()

SCROLL ■ 3.0

Description This function will scroll the control either vertically, horizontally, or both.

Syntax public, BOOL Scroll(CSize size);

Parameters

size The amount of distance vertically and horizontally to scroll the control. The horizontal distance is specified by **cx** and is in pixels. Vertical scrolling is only peformed in increments of the item height, so the actual distance scrolled in pixels is **cy** multiplied by the item height. Both distances can be negative values.

Returns TRUE if successful; otherwise FALSE.

See Also CListCtrl::EnsureVisible(), CListCtrl::SetTopIndex()

SETBKCOLOR ■ 3.0

Description This function sets the current background color of the control.

Syntax public, BOOL SetBkColor(COLORREF cr);

Parameters

cr A value specifying the new background color (the RGB macro can be used to build a color from its component red, green, and blue values).

Returns TRUE if successful; otherwise FALSE.

See Also CListCtrl::GetBkColor()

Example See CListCtrl::InsertItem()

SETCALLBACKMASK ■ 3.0

Description This function sets the callback mask for the control. The callback mask is used to determine whether the control maintains all state information about the items in the control, or if the user will track the information. If the callback mask is supplied by the application, then it is the reponsibility of the application to supply state information to the control.

Syntax public, BOOL SetCallbackMask(UINT nMask);

Parameters

nMask The new callback mask.

Returns TRUE if successful; otherwise FALSE.

See Also CListCtrl::GetCallbackMask()

SETCOLUMN ■ 3.0

Description This function sets the display characteristics of a column in the control.

Syntax	public, BOOL SetColumn(int nCol, const LV_COLUMN* pColumn);
Parameters	
nCol	The index of the column.
pColumn	A pointer to an LV_COLUMN structure that contains the new column display attributes. Note that the **mask** member of the structure indicates which attributes are to be set.
Returns	TRUE if successful; otherwise FALSE.
See Also	CListCtrl::GetColumn()

SetColumnWidth ■ 3.0

Description	This function specifies the width of a particular column when the control is in either list or report view
Syntax	public, BOOL SetColumnWidth(int nCol, int cx);
Parameters	
nCol	The index of the column if in report view; otherwise this value should be -1.
cx	The width of the column.
Returns	TRUE if successful; otherwise FALSE.
See Also	CListCtrl::GetColumnWidth()

SetImageList ■ 3.0

Description	This function sets the image lists used to display items in the control.
Syntax	public, CImageList* SetImageList(CImageList* pImageList, int nImageList);
Parameters	
pImageList	The new image list.
nImageList	Specifies which list is to be set. The value can be any one of the following:
LVSIL_NORMAL	Image list that contains the large images.
LVSIL_SMALL	Image list that contains the small images.
LVSIL_STATE	Image list that contains the state images.
Returns	The previously set image list (if any).
See Also	CListCtrl::GetImageList()

SetItem ■ 3.0

Description	This function sets the attributes of an item in the control. The specific item is designated by the **iItem** and **iSubItem** members of the LV_ITEM structure passed to this function.

Syntax public, BOOL SetItem(const LV_ITEM* pItem);
public, BOOL SetItem(int nItem, int nSubItem, UINT nMask, LPCTSTR lpszItem, int nImage, UINT nState, UINT nStateMask, LPARAM lParam);

Parameters

pItem A pointer to an LV_ITEM structure that contains the attributes that will affect the item. It is necessary to specify which attributes are to be updated by the **mask** member of the LV_ITEM structure.

nItem The index of the item whose attributes are to be set.

nSubItem The index of the sub-item whose attributes are to be set.

nMask The mask flags that determine which attributes are to be set.

lpszItem The new text label for the item.

nImage The new image index for the item.

nState The new state values for the item.

nStateMask The state mask flags that determine which state attributes are to be set.

lParam Item-specific data.

Returns TRUE if successful; otherwise FALSE.

See Also CListCtrl::GetItem()

SetItemCount ■ 3.0

Description This function is used to optimize performance of the control when adding large numbers of items. It basically allows the control to reallocate its internal storage buffers once, rather than every time an item is added.

Syntax public, void SetItemCount(int nItems);

Parameters

nItems The total number of items that the control will contain.

Returns Nothing is returned.

See Also CListCtrl::GetItemCount()

SetItemData ■ 3.0

Description Sets the item-specific data stored with each item. The item-specific data is used by the programmer to store a generic 32-bit value.

Syntax public, BOOL SetItemData(int nItem, DWORD dwData);

Parameters

nItem The index of the item whose data is to be set.

dwData The 32-bit that will be associated with the item.

Returns TRUE if successful; otherwise 0.

SetItemPosition ■ 3.0

Description This function will move a particular item to a position within the view, provided the control does not have the LVS_NOITEMDATA style and the control is in the icon or small icon view. The control will be automatically arranged after the function call if the LVS_AUTOARRANGE style is set.

Syntax public, BOOL SetItemPosition(int nItem, POINT pt);

Parameters

nItem The index of the item.

pt The client coordinates of the new position.

Returns TRUE if successful; otherwise FALSE.

See Also CListCtrl::GetItemPosition()

SetItemState ■ 3.0

Description This function sets the state bits on the specified item.

Syntax public, BOOL SetItemState(int nItem, LV_ITEM* pItem);
public, BOOL SetItemState(int nItem, UINT nState, UINT nMask);

Parameters

nItem Index of the item.

pItem Address of an LV_ITEM structure whose **stateMask** and **state** members contain the new state bits that will be set.

nState The new state bits for the item. Valid states include: LVIS_CUT, LVIS_DROPHILIGHTED, LVIS_FOCUSED, LVIS_SELECTED.

nMask The mask used to determine which bits in *nState* are actually valid.

Returns TRUE if successful; otherwise FALSE.

See Also CListCtrl::GetItemState()

SetItemText ■ 3.0

Description This function sets the specified item text.

Syntax public, BOOL SetItemText(int nItem, int nSubItem, LPCTSTR lpszText);

Parameters

nItem The index of the item.

nSubItem The index of the sub-item whose text is to be set. If the item's label is to be set, then this value should be 0.

lpszText Address of the buffer that contains the new text.

Returns TRUE if sucessful; otherwise FALSE.

See Also CListCtrl::GetItemText()

SetTextBkColor ■ 3.0

Description This function sets the background color used when text is displayed within the control.

Syntax public, BOOL SetTextBkColor(COLORREF cr);

Parameters

cr The new background color that will be used to display text.

Returns TRUE if successful; otherwise FALSE.

See Also CListCtrl::GetTextBkColor()

SetTextColor ■ 3.0

Description This function sets the color used to display text within the control.

Syntax public, BOOL SetTextColor(COLORREF cr);

Parameters

cr The new color that will be used to display text.

Returns TRUE if successful; otherwise FALSE.

See Also CListCtrl::GetTextColor()

SortItems ■ 3.0

Description This function will sort the items in the control using a user-supplied comparison function.

Syntax public, BOOL SortItems(PFNLVCOMPARE pfnCompare, DWORD dwData);

Parameters

pfnCompare The address of the user-supplied comparison function. The declaration of this function is of the form:

```
int CALLBACK CompareFunc(LPARAM lParam1,LPARAM lParam2,LPARAM lParamSort);
```

dwData A user-defined data value that will be passed into the comparison function.

Returns TRUE if successful; otherwise FALSE.

Update ■ 3.0

Description This function forces the control to repaint a specific item.

Syntax public, BOOL Update(int nItem);

Parameters

nItem	Index of the item to be repainted.
Returns	TRUE if successful; otherwise FALSE.
See Also	CListCtrl::RedrawItems()

CProgressCtrl

The CProgressCtrl is used to display the amount of a process that has been completed (or the amount that is left to do) during a lengthy operation. This type of control has been used effectively in many different types of applications in the past, and is now a standard operating system control. The example program that is associated with this section can be found in the CProgress directory on the CD-ROM.

CProgressCtrl ■ 3.0

Description	This is the constructor for the progress bar control. The real initialization of this object is done in the Create member function.
Syntax	public, CProgressCtrl();
Parameters	None.
Returns	Nothing is returned.
See Also	CProgressCtrl::Create(), ~ CProgressCtrl()

~CProgressCtrl ■ 3.0 ■ UD

Description	Destroys the progress bar control.
Syntax	public, virtual ~ CProgressCtrl();
Parameters	None.
Returns	Nothing is returned.
See Also	CProgressCtrl()

Create ■ 3.0

Description	After construction, call this member to create the progress bar control and attach it to this object.
Syntax	public, BOOL Create(DWORD dwStyle, const RECT & rect, Cwnd * pParentWnd, UINT nID);
Parameters	
dwStyle	Styles used for this control. The allowable styles can be found in the Windows API documentation.
rect	Indicates the control's position and size in terms of its parent's client coordinates.

pParentWnd	Parent window of control.
nID	The child ID of this control. Must be unique among its siblings.
Returns	TRUE if creation successful; otherwise FALSE.

OffsetPos ■ 3.0

Description	This function advances the position of the bar by the relative amount given.
Syntax	public, int OffsetPos(int nPos);
Parameters	
nPos	Amount to increase the bar's current position.
Returns	The previous bar position.

SetPos ■ 3.0

Description	This function sets the current bar position of the control.
Syntax	public, int SetPos(int nPos);
Parameters	
nPos	The new bar position.
Returns	The previous bar position.

SetRange ■ 3.0

Description	This function sets the lower and upper bounds for the control.
Syntax	public, void SetRange(int nLower, int nUpper);
Parameters	
nLower	The lower bound of the control.
nUpper	The upper bound of the control.
Returns	Nothing is returned.
See Also	CProgressCtrl::SetPos()
Example	The following shows how to set the range of the progress control.

```
void CCProgressDlg::InitializeProgCtrl(CProgressCtrl & progCtrl)
{
	progCtrl.SetRange(100,900);
	progCtrl.SetStep(50);
}
```

SetStep ■ 3.0

Description	This function specifies the increment that the bar will advance when the CProgressCtrl::StepIt() function is used.

Syntax public, int SetStep(int nStep);

Parameters

nStep The amount to advance the bar's current position each time CProgressCtrl::StepIt() is called.

Returns The previous step increment.

See Also CProgressCtrl::StepIt()

Example See CProgressCtrl::SetRange()

StepIt ■ 3.0

Description This function advances the current bar position by the current step increment.

Syntax public, int StepIt();

Parameters None.

Returns The previous bar position.

See Also CProgressCtrl::SetStep()

Example The following illustrates how to step the control in response to a timer message:

```
void CCProgressDlg::OnTimer(UINT nIDEvent)
{
	m_ProgCtrl.StepIt();
	CDialog::OnTimer(nIDEvent);
}
```

CRichEditCtrl

The CRichEditCtrl class encapsulates an edit control with extended formatting capabilities. The control handles a variety of text and paragraph formatting, such as mutiple fonts, colored text, text alignment, and embeddable OLE objects. Also, the control supports a simple stream interface to allow for saving and loading of rich text format (RTF) files.

CRichEditCtrl ■ 4.0

Description This is the constructor for the rich edit control. The real initialization of this object is done in the Create member function.

Syntax public, CRichEditCtrl();

Parameters None.

Returns Nothing is returned.

See Also CRichEditCtrl::Create(), ~ CRichEditCtrl()

~CRichEditCtrl ■ 4.0 ■ UD

Description	Destroys the rich edit control.
Syntax	public, ~ CRichEditCtrl();
Parameters	None.
Returns	Nothing is returned.
See Also	CRichEditCtrl();

CanPaste ■ 4.0

Description	This member determines if the contents of the Clipboard can be pasted into this control.
Syntax	public, BOOL CanPaste(UINT nFormat = 0) const;
Parameters	
nFormat	The particular Clipboard format to test, or 0 to test for any acceptable format. This value can be any predefined Clipboard format, or any format registered with the Clipboard.
Returns	TRUE if successful; otherwise FALSE.

CanUndo ■ 4.0

Description	This member determines if the last editing operation can be undone using the CRichEditCtrl::Undo() member.
Syntax	public, BOOL CanUndo() const;
Parameters	None.
Returns	TRUE if successful; otherwise FALSE.
See Also	CRichEditCtrl::Undo(),CRichEditCtrl::EmptyUndoBuffer()

Clear ■ 4.0

Description	This member will delete any currently selected information from the rich edit control. The information is not saved on the Clipboard like the CRichEditCtrl::Cut() member; however the operation can be undone by calling the CRichEditCtrl::Undo() member.
Syntax	public, void Clear();
Parameters	None.
Returns	Nothing is returned.

COPY ■ 4.0

Description This member will make a copy of the currently selected information and place it in the Clipboard. This information is then available for pasting into the control or any other window capable of accepting the Clipboard information.

Syntax public, void Copy();

Parameters None.

Returns Nothing is returned.

CREATE ■ 4.0

Description After construction, call this member to create the rich edit control and attach it to this object.

Syntax public, BOOL Create(DWORD dwStyle, const RECT & rect, Cwnd * pParentWnd, UINT nID);

Parameters

dwStyle Styles used for this control. The allowable styles can be found in the Windows API documentation.

rect Indicates the control's position and size in terms of its parent's client coordinates.

pParentWnd Parent window of control.

nID The child ID of this control. Must be unique among its siblings.

Returns TRUE if creation successful; otherwise FALSE.

CUT ■ 4.0

Description This member makes a copy of the currently selected information, places it into the Clipboard, then deletes the information from the control. This operation is reversible by calling the CRichEditCtrl::Undo() member.

Syntax public, void Cut();

Parameters None.

Returns Nothing is returned.

DISPLAYBAND ■ 4.0

Description This member will render a portion of the rich edit control to the device specified by a previous call to CRichEditCtrl::FormatRange(). This function is useful for rendering the contents of the control to another device like a printer.

Syntax public, BOOL DisplayBand(LPRECT pDisplayRect);

Parameters

pDisplayRect The portion of the control to render.

Returns TRUE if successful; otherwise FALSE.

EmptyUndoBuffer ■ 4.0

Description This member will release the contents of the rich edit control's internal undo buffer. After calling this member, no previous edits to the control can be undone by calling the CRichEditCtrl::Undo() member.

Syntax public, void EmptyUndoBuffer();

Parameters None.

Returns Nothing is returned.

FindText ■ 4.0

Description This member is used to find a string of text within the control.

Syntax public, long FindText(DWORD dwFlags, FINDTEXTEX* pFindText) const;

Parameters

dwFlags Contains the search flags, and can be a combination of the following:

FT_MATCHCASE The search is case-sensitive.

FT_WHOLEWORD Only match where the entire word is the same.

pFindText A pointer to a FINDTEXTEX structure that specifies the text to be searched, and the range to search within, and holds the results of the search.

Returns The character index of the next match; otherwise -1.

FormatRange ■ 4.0

Description This member is used to format a range of text within the control for a supplied device context. After this member is called, a call to CRichEditCtrl::DisplayBand should be used to output the text to the device context. If the text is to be rendered to multiple devices, then you should call this member with *pfr* = NULL to free the internal cached display data between switching device contexts.

Syntax public, long FormatRange(FORMATRANGE* pfr, BOOL bDisplay = TRUE);

Parameters

pfr A pointer to a FORMATRANGE structure that contains information about the new device context, and the text range to format. If NULL, then the internal cached display information is freed.

bDisplay	TRUE will render the text; FALSE will simply measure the text.
Returns	The index of the first character that did not fit within the range specified. This value is useful when making multiple calls to this member.
See Also	CRichEditCtrl::DisplayBand()

GetCharPos ■ 4.0

Description	This member will return the location within the control of the character specified.
Syntax	public, CPoint GetCharPos(long lChar) const;
Parameters	
lChar	The index of the character.
Returns	A CPoint structure specifying the upper-left corner position of the character.

GetDefaultCharFormat ■ 4.0

Description	This member retrieves the current default character formatting attributes.
Syntax	public, DWORD GetDefaultCharFormat(CHARFORMAT & cf) const;
Parameters	
cf	A reference to a CHARFORMAT object that will receive the formatting information.
Returns	The *dwMask* member of the CHARFORMAT structure returned. This mask specifies which attributes are valid within the structure.

GetEventMask ■ 4.0

Description	This member retrieves the event mask for the rich edit control. The event mask specifies which events are passed to the parent window of the control.
Syntax	public, long GetEventMask() const;
Parameters	None.
Returns	The current event mask for the control.

GetFirstVisibleLine ■ 4.0

Description	This member will retrieve the index of the first line that is visible within the control.
Syntax	public, int GetFirstVisibleLine() const;
Parameters	None.
Returns	The index of the first visible line.

GetLimitText ■ 4.0

Description This member retrieves the current limit (in bytes) of the amount of text that the user can enter into the control.

Syntax public, long GetLimitText() const;

Parameters None.

Returns The current text limit in bytes.

GetLine ■ 4.0

Description This member retrieves the text from the line specified, into the given buffer.

Syntax public, int GetLine(int nIndex, LPTSTR lpszBuffer) const;
public, int GetLine(int nIndex, LPTSTR lpszBuffer, int nMaxLength) const;

Parameters

nIndex Index of the line of text to retrieve.

lpszBuffer A buffer that will receive the contents of the text line. The size of the buffer must be stored in the first word of storage pointed to by the buffer.

nMaxLength The length (in bytes) of the buffer pointed to by *lpszBuffer*.

Returns The actual number of characters copied into *lpszBuffer*.

GetLineCount ■ 4.0

Description This member retrieves the current number of text lines in the control.

Syntax public, int GetLineCount() const;

Parameters None.

Returns The number of lines of text.

GetModify ■ 4.0

Description This member returns whether or not the contents of the edit control have changed since creation, or the last call to CRichEditCtrl::SetModify(). This function is useful in determining whether or not the contents of the control should be processed or saved.

Syntax public, BOOL GetModify() const;

Parameters None.

Returns TRUE if the contents have changed; otherwise FALSE.

See Also CRichEditCtrl::SetModify()

GetParaFormat ■ 4.0

Description This member retrieves the formatting attributes of the currently selected paragraph. If multiple paragraphs are selected, then the attributes represent those of the first paragraph selected. The return value specifies which attributes are consistent across all selected paragraphs.

Syntax public, DWORD GetParaFormat(PARAFORMAT &pf) const;

Parameters

pf A reference to a PARAFORMAT structure that will receive the formatting attributes.

Returns The *dwMask* member of the PARAFORMAT struct, which specifies those attributes that are consistent across all selected paragraphs.

GetRect ■ 4.0

Description This member retrieves the current formatting rectangle of the rich edit control. Like CEdit controls, this formatting rectangle is independent of the actual control window rectangle.

Syntax public, void GetRect(LPRECT lpRect) const;

Parameters

lpRect A pointer to a RECT structure that will receive the coordinates of the formatting rectangle.

Returns Nothing is returned.

See Also CRichEditCtrl::SetRect()

GetSel ■ 4.0

Description This member retrieves the starting and ending character positions of the current text selection within the control.

Syntax public, void GetSel(long & nStartChar, long & nEndChar) const;
public, void GetSel(CHARRANGE &cr) const;

Parameters

nStartChar The character index of the selection starting position.

nEndChar The character index of the selection ending position.

cr A reference to a CHARRANGE structure that holds the range minimum and maximum indices.

Returns Nothing is returned.

GetSelectionCharFormat ■ 4.0

Description This member retrieves the character attributes found in the current text selection. The return value specifies those attributes that are consistent within the selection.

Syntax public, DWORD GetSelectionCharFormat(CHARFORMAT &cf) const;

Parameters

cf A reference to a CHARFORMAT structure that receives the character attributes.

Returns The *dwMask* member of the CHARFORMAT structure that specifies attributes that are consistent within the selection.

GetSelectionType ■ 4.0

Description This member returns the types of information in the current selection.

Syntax public, WORD GetSelectionType() const;

Parameters None.

Returns A value representing the contents of the current selection. This value may be a combination of the following values:

SEL_EMPTY No current selection.

SEL_MULTICHAR More than one character contained in selection.

SEL_MULTIOBJECT More than one OLE object contained in selection.

SEL_OBJECT One or more OLE items contained in selection.

SEL_TEXT The current selection contains text.

GetSelText ■ 4.0

Description This member will retrieve the currently selected text.

Syntax public, CString GetSelText() const;

Parameters None.

Returns A CString object containing the text in the current selection.

GetSelText ■ 4.0

Description This member will retrieve the currently selected text.

Syntax public, long GetSelText(LPSTR lpBuf) const;

Parameters

lpBuf A buffer to hold the retrieved text. This buffer must have enough space allocated to hold the text selection.

Returns The number of characters actually copied (not including the null character) into the destination buffer *lpBuf*.

GetTextLength

■ 4.0

Description This member will retrieve the length (in bytes) of the text within the control.

Syntax public, long GetTextLength() const;

Parameters None.

Returns The length in bytes of the text in the control.

HideSelection

■ 4.0

Description This member will display or hide the current selection.

Syntax public, void HideSelection(BOOL bHide, BOOL bPerm);

Parameters

bHide TRUE will hide the selection; FALSE will display the selection.

bPerm TRUE will make the change in visibility permanent and change the ECO_NOHIDESEL style; FALSE will not make the style changes.

Returns Nothing is returned.

LimitText

■ 4.0

Description This member will limit the amount of text that a user can enter into the control.

Syntax public, void LimitText(long nChars = 0);

Parameters

nChars The maximum number of characters that the control will accept, or 0 to accept UINT_MAX number of characters.

Returns Nothing is returned.

LineFromChar

■ 4.0

Description This member will retrieve the index of the line that contains the specified character index.

Syntax public, long LineFromChar(long nIndex) const;

Parameters

nIndex The character index, or -1 to indicate the line with the caret.

Returns The zero-based line index of the character specified by *nIndex*.

LineIndex ■ 4.0

Description This member will retrieve the character index of the line specified.

Syntax public, int LineIndex(int nLine = -1) const;

Parameters

nLine The index of the line requested, or -1 to indicate the line with the caret.

Returns The character index of the line requested, or -1 if *nLine* is outside the range of lines in the control.

LineLength ■ 4.0

Description This member will retrieve the length of text in the specified line.

Syntax public, int LineLength(int nLine = -1) const;

Parameters

nLine The index of the line requested, or -1 to indicate the line with the caret.

Returns The length in bytes of the line specified by *nLine*.

LineScroll ■ 4.0

Description This member will scroll the control to a specified position. This member has no effect on controls created with the ES_RIGHT or ES_CENTER attributes.

Syntax public, void LineScroll(int nLines, int nChars = 0);

Parameters

nLines The number of lines to scroll vertically.

nChars The number of characters to scroll horizontally.

Returns Nothing is returned.

Paste ■ 4.0

Description This member will paste the current contents of the Clipboard into the control at the current caret position.

Syntax public, void Paste();

Parameters None.

Returns Nothing is returned.

PasteSpecial ■ 4.0

Description This member will paste the current contents of the Clipboard into the control at the current caret position, using the specified characteristics.

Syntax public, void PasteSpecial(UINT nClipFormat, DWORD dvAspect = 0, HMETAFILE hMF = 0);

Parameters

nClipFormat A specific Clipboard format to paste.

dvAspect Device aspect for the Clipboard data.

hMF Handle to the metafile containing the icon view of the information to be pasted, or NULL for no icon.

Returns Nothing is returned.

ReplaceSel ■ 4.0

Description This member will replace the contents of the current selection with the given text. To replace the entire text contents of the control, use SetWindowText.

Syntax public, void ReplaceSel(LPCTSTR lpszNewText);

Parameters

lpszNewText A pointer to a NULL-terminated string containing the replacement text.

Returns Nothing is returned.

RequestResize ■ 4.0

Description This member will send resize notifications to its parent control. This is useful in supporting rich edit controls that are as large as the objects that they contain, or “bottomless” rich edit controls.

Syntax public, void RequestResize();

Parameters None.

Returns Nothing is returned.

Send32s ■ 4.0 ■ UD

Description This member is used to send messages when the rich edit control is executed in a Win32s environment. This member is used internally for Win32s compatibility.

Syntax public, LRESULT Send32s(UINT nMsg, WPARAM wParam, LPARAM lParam) const;

Parameters

nMsg Message to send.

wParam Message-specific data.

lParam Message-specific data.

Returns A message-specific result.

SetBackgroundColor ■ 4.0

Description This member is used to set the color of the control's background.

Syntax public, COLORREF SetBackgroundColor(BOOL bSysColor, COLORREF cr);

Parameters

bSysColor If TRUE, then the background is set to the default system color used for all windows. If FALSE, then the color is set to *cr*.

cr A COLORREF containing the new background color.

Returns The previous control background color.

SetDefaultCharFormat ■ 4.0

Description This member sets the default character formatting attributes.

Syntax public, BOOL SetDefaultCharFormat(CHARFORMAT &cf);

Parameters

cf The new default formatting attributes. Only the attributes specified by the *dwMask* member of *cf* are applied.

Returns TRUE if successful; otherwise FALSE.

SetEventMask ■ 4.0

Description This member specifies which event notifications are sent to the parent of this control.

Syntax public, DWORD SetEventMask(DWORD dwEventMask);

Parameters

dwEventMask Contains the notification messages to be sent to the parent of this control.

Returns The previous event mask settings.

SetModifiy ■ 4.0

Description Sets or clears the control's modification flag. This flag is used to determine if the contents of the control have changed.

Syntax public, void SetModify(BOOL bModified = TRUE);

Parameters

bModified TRUE indicates the contents of the control have been modified; FALSE indicates that the contents have not changed.

Returns Nothing is returned.

SetOptions ■ 4.0

Description This member sets various options for the control.

Syntax public, void SetOptions(WORD wOp, DWORD dwFlags);

Parameters

wOp Specifies how to apply the options specified by *dwFlags*. This can be one of the following values:

ECOOP_AND Keep only the options that are specified by *dwFlags*.

ECOOP_OR Keep the current options and those specified by *dwFlags*.

ECOOP_SET Set the options to those specified by dwFlags.

ECOOP_XOR Keep only the current options that are not specified by *dwFlags*.

dwFlags The rich edit control options to set. This can be a combination of the following:

ECO_AUTOHSCROLL Hitting the ENTER key on the last line causes the control to scroll up one page.

ECO_AUTOVSCROLL The ENTER key automatically scrolls back to the first position in the next line. Also, the control automatically scrolls text to the right by 10 characters when the user types a character at the end of the line.

ECO_AUTOWORDSELECTION A double-click selects a whole word.

ECO_NOHIDESEL If specified, then the control always inverts the current text selection no matter if the control has focus. This is contrary to the default control behavior of removing the highlighted text when the control loses focus.

ECO_READONLY The control does not accept user input.

ECO_SAVESEL Keeps the current selection when the control loses focus. The default behavior is to select all text when the control receives focus.

ECO_VERTICAL Displays text and objects in a vertical direction. Used for international applications.

ECO_WANTRETURN Allows the ENTER key to be pressed within the rich edit control, instead of notifying the parent window of a default button event.

Returns Nothing is returned.

SetParaFormat ■ 4.0

Description This member sets the paragraph formatting attributes for the current text selection.

Syntax public, BOOL SetParaFormat(PARAFORMAT &pf);

Parameters

pf A reference to a PARAFORMAT structure containing the atttributes to set. Only the attributes specified by the *dwMask* member of *pf* are applied.

Returns TRUE if successful; otherwise FALSE.

SetReadOnly

■ 4.0

Description This member will allow or disallow user edits to the control.

Syntax public, BOOL SetReadOnly(BOOL bReadOnly = TRUE);

Parameters

bReadOnly TRUE will disallow user edits; FALSE will allow the user to modify the control's contents.

Returns TRUE if successful; otherwise FALSE.

SetRect

■ 4.0

Description This member sets the formatting rectangle for the control. Note that the formatting rectangle is independent of the size of the rich edit control window.

Syntax public, void SetRect(LPCRECT lpRect);

Parameters

lpRect A pointer to a RECT structure containing the new size of the formatting rectangle.

Returns Nothing is returned.

SetSel

■ 4.0

Description This member sets the currently selected text to the specified character range.

Syntax public, void SetSel(long nStartChar, long nEndChar);
public, void SetSel(CHARRANGE &cr);

Parameters

nStartChar The starting character position of the new selection.

nEndChar The ending character position of the new selection.

cr A CHARRANGE structure specifying the starting and ending character positions of the new selection.

Returns Nothing is returned.

SetSelectionCharFormat

■ 4.0

Description This member sets the formatting attributes of the currently selected text.

Syntax public, BOOL SetSelectionCharFormat(CHARFORMAT &cf);

Parameters

cf A reference to a CHARFORMAT structure containing the new formatting attributes. Only the attributes specified by the *dwMask* member of *cf* are applied.

Returns TRUE if successful; otherwise FALSE.

SetTargetDevice ■ 4.0

Description This member sets a device context to be used as the output device for WYSIWYG display of the control's contents.

Syntax public, BOOL SetTargetDevice(HDC hDC, long lLineWidth);
public, BOOL SetTargetDevice(CDC &dc, long lLineWidth);

Parameters

hDC A handle to the new device context.

lLineWidth The line width used in formatting of the control's text.

dc The new device context.

Returns TRUE if successful; otherwise FALSE.

SetWordCharFormat ■ 4.0

Description This member sets the character formatting attributes of the currently selected word.

Syntax public, BOOL SetWordCharFormat(CHARFORMAT & cf);

Parameters

cf A reference to a CHARFORMAT structure containing the new formatting attributes. Only the attributes specified by the *dwMask* member of *cf* are applied.

Returns TRUE if successful; otherwise FALSE.

StreamIn ■ 4.0

Description This member allows the control to accept input from an input stream.

Syntax public, long StreamIn(int nFormat, EDITSTREAM &es);

Parameters

nFormat Specifies the allowable input data formats.

es An EDITSTREAM structure describing the input stream.

Returns The number of characters actually read from the input stream.

StreamOut ■ 4.0

Description This member saves the information in the control to the given output stream.

Syntax public, long StreamOut(int nFormat, EDITSTREAM &es);

Parameters

nFormat The data format for output. This value can be one of the following:

SF_TEXT Outputs text only.

SF_RTF	Outputs text and formatting only.
SF_RTFNOOBJS	Outputs text and formatting, replacing any contained OLE object with spaces.
SF_TEXTIZED	Outputs text and formatting, replacing any contained OLE objects with textual representations.
es	An EDITSTREAM structure describing the output stream.
Returns	The number of characters written to the output stream.

UNDO ■ 4.0

Description	This member will undo the last edit operation performed in the control.
Syntax	public, BOOL Undo();
Parameters	None.
Returns	TRUE if successful; otherwise FALSE.

CScrollBar

The scrollbar control is used to provide an interface to a virtual display space. The MFC encapsulation allows the user full access to the standard Windows scrollbar API.

CSCROLLBAR ■ 2.0 ■ 3.0

Description	This is the constructor for the scrollbar control. The real initialization of this object is done in the Create member function.
Syntax	public, CScrollBar();
Parameters	None.
Returns	Nothing is returned.
See Also	CScrollBar::Create()

~CSCROLLBAR ■ 2.0 ■ 3.0 ■ UD

Description	Destroys the scrollbar object.
Syntax	public, virtual ~CScrollBar();
Parameters	None.
Returns	Nothing is returned.
See Also	CScrollBar()

CREATE ■ 2.0 ■ 3.0

Description	After construction, call this member to create the scrollbar window and attach it to this object.

Syntax public, BOOL Create(DWORD dwStyle, const RECT & rect, CWnd* pParentWnd, UINT nID);

Parameters

dwStyle A combination of valid window or scrollbar styles. The allowable styles can be found in the Windows API documentation.

rect Indicates the control's position and size in terms of its parent's client coordinates.

pParentWnd Parent window of control.

nID The child ID of this control. Must be unique among its siblings.

Returns TRUE if successful; otherwise FALSE.

See Also CScrollBar()

EnableScrollBar ■ 2.0 ■ 3.0

Description This function will enable or disable various parts of the scrollbar.

Syntax public, BOOL EnableScrollBar(UINT nArrowFlags = ESB_ENABLE_BOTH);

Parameters

nArrowFlags Specifies which sides of the scrollbar are enabled or disabled. This value can be one of the following:

ESB_ENABLE_BOTH	Enables both arrows.
ESB_DISABLE_LTUP	Disables the left/up arrow.
ESB_DISABLE_RTDN	Disables the right/down arrow.
ESB_DISABLE_BOTH	Disables both arrows.

Returns TRUE if successful; FALSE if the arrows already exist in the specified state or if an error occurred.

GetScrollInfo ■ 3.0

Description Retrieves the 32-bit scrolling information contained in the SCROLLINFO struct that describes such things as the minimum and maximum scrolling positions, the page size, and the current thumb tracking position.

Syntax public, BOOL GetScrollInfo(LPSCROLLINFO lpScrollInfo, UINT nMask = SIF_ALL);

Parameters

lpScrollInfo A pointer to a SCROLLINFO structure containing the scrolling information. See the Windows API documentation.

nMask Specifies the scroll information to retrieve. This can be any combination of the following: SIF_ALL, SIF_PAGE, SIF_POS, SIF_RANGE, SIF_TRACKPOS.

Returns TRUE if successful; otherwise FALSE.

See Also CScrollBar::SetScrollInfo()

GetScrollLimit ■ 3.0

Description Retrieves the maximum scrolling position.

Syntax public, int GetScrollLimit();

Parameters None.

Returns The maximum scrolling value if successful; otherwise 0.

GetScrollPos ■ 2.0 ■ 3.0

Description This function retrieves the current position of the scrollbar.

Syntax public, int GetScrollPos() const;

Parameters None.

Returns The current position of the scrollbar. This value is depends on the current scrollbar range.

See Also CScrollBar::SetScrollPos(), CScrollBar::GetScrollRange()

GetScrollRange ■ 2.0 ■ 3.0

Description This function will return the current scrollbar range.

Syntax public, void GetScrollRange(LPINT lpMinPos, LPINT lpMaxPos) const;

Parameters

lpMinPos Address of an integer that will receive the minimum scrollbar position.

lpMaxPos Address of an integer that will receive the maximum scrollbar position.

Returns Nothing is returned.

See Also CScrollBar::SetScrollRange()

SetScrollInfo ■ 3.0

Description Sets the 32-bit scrolling information contained in the SCROLLINFO struct that describes such things as the minimum and maximum scrolling positions, the page size, and the current thumb tracking position.

Syntax public, BOOL SetScrollInfo(LPSCROLLINFO lpScrollInfo, BOOL bRedraw = TRUE);

Parameters

lpScrollInfo A pointer to a SCROLLINFO structure containing the new scrolling information. See the Windows API documentation.

bRedraw TRUE will force the scrollbar to repaint. FALSE will not force a repaint.

Returns TRUE if successful; otherwise FALSE.

See Also CScrollBar::GetScrollInfo()

SetScrollPos ■ 2.0 ■ 3.0

Description This function sets the current position of the scrollbar.

Syntax public, int SetScrollPos(int nPos, BOOL bRedraw = TRUE);

Parameters

nPos The new position.

bRedraw TRUE will automatically redraw the scrollbar to reflect the new position; FALSE will not update the scrollbar display.

Returns If successful, the previous scrollbar position; otherwise 0.

See Also CScrollBar::GetScrollPos()

SetScrollRange ■ 2.0 ■ 3.0

Description This function will set the scrollbar range.

Syntax public, void SetScrollRange(int nMinPos, int nMaxPos, BOOL bRedraw = TRUE);

Parameters

nMinPos The new minimum scrollbar position.

nMaxPos The new maximum scrollbar position.

bRedraw TRUE will automatically redraw the scrollbar to reflect the new range; FALSE will not update the scrollbar display.

Returns Nothing is returned.

See Also CScrollBar::GetScrollRange()

ShowScrollBar ■ 2.0 ■ 3.0

Description This function will can either hide or display the scrollbar.

Syntax public, void ShowScrollBar(BOOL bShow = TRUE);

Parameters

bShow If TRUE, then the scrollbar is displayed. FALSE will hide the scrollbar.

Returns Nothing is returned.

CSliderCtrl

The CSliderCtrl allows the user to select a value from a range of values by dragging a slider. A typical example is a volume control where a particular volume level can be selected from a range of levels. The control also supports the use of tick marks that give a visual indication of the discrete levels within the slider range. The example program that is associated with this section can be found in the CSlider directory on the CD-ROM.

CSliderCtrl ■ 3.0

Description This is the constructor for the slider control. The real initialization of this object is done in the Create member function.

Syntax public, CSliderCtrl();

Parameters None.

Returns Nothing is returned.

See Also CSliderCtrl::Create(), ~ CSliderCtrl()

~CSliderCtrl ■ 3.0 ■ UD

Description Destroys the slider control.

Syntax public, virtual ~CSliderCtrl();

Parameters None.

Returns Nothing is returned.

See Also CSliderCtrl()

ClearSel ■ 3.0

Description This function clears any current selection in the control.

Syntax public, void ClearSel(BOOL bRedraw = FALSE);

Parameters

bRedraw If TRUE, then the slider is redrawn to update the display. If FALSE, then the slider display is not updated.

Returns Nothing is returned.

See Also CSliderCtrl::SetSelection()

ClearTics ■ 3.0

Description This function removes all current tick marks from the control.

Syntax public, void ClearTics(BOOL bRedraw = FALSE);

Parameters

bRedraw If TRUE, then the slider is redrawn to update the display. If FALSE, then the slider display is not updated.

Returns Nothing is returned.

See Also CSliderCtrl::SetTic()

CREATE ■ 3.0

Description After construction, call this member to create the slider control and attach it to this object.

Syntax public, BOOL Create(DWORD dwStyle, const RECT & rect, Cwnd * pParentWnd, UINT nID);

Parameters

dwStyle Styles used for this control. The allowable styles can be found in the Windows API documentation.

rect Indicates the control's position and size in terms of its parent's client coordinates.

pParentWnd Parent window of control.

nID The child ID of this control. Must be unique among its siblings.

Returns TRUE if creation successful; otherwise FALSE.

GETCHANNELRECT ■ 3.0

Description This function retrieves the rectangle containing the client coordinates of the slider channel. The slider channel is that area that ranges from the minimum to the maximum slider position, and contains the highlight of the current selection.

Syntax public, void GetChannelRect(LPRECT lprc) const;

Parameters

lprc Address of the RECT structure that will receive the client coordinates of the channel.

Returns Nothing is returned.

GETLINESIZE ■ 3.0

Description This function retrieves the number of units that make up a line. A line determines the lowest resolution that the slider can move.

Syntax public, int GetLineSize() const;

Parameters None.

Returns The number of units per line.

See Also CSliderCtrl::SetLineSize(), CSliderCtrl::GetPageSize()

GETNUMTICS ■ 3.0

Description This function retrieves the number of tick marks that the slider is currently displaying.

Syntax public, UINT GetNumTics() const;

Parameters	None.
Returns	The current number of tick marks.
See Also	CSliderCtrl::SetTic()

GetPageSize ■ 3.0

Description	This function retrieves the number of units that make up the page size for the control. The page size is the number of units the slider moves when it receives a TB_PAGEUP or TB_PAGEDOWN notification.
Syntax	public, int GetPageSize() const;
Parameters	None.
Returns	The current number of units per page.
See Also	CSliderCtrl::SetPageSize()

GetPos ■ 3.0

Description	This function will retrieve the current position of the slider thumb.
Syntax	public, int GetPos() const;
Parameters	None.
Returns	The current position of the slider.
See Also	CSliderCtrl::SetPos()

GetRange ■ 3.0

Description	This function retrieves both the minimum and maximum ranges of the slider.
Syntax	public, void GetRange(int& nMin, int& nMax) const;
Parameters	
nMin	Reference to the integer that will receive the current minimum range value.
nMax	Reference to the integer that will receive the current maximum range value.
Returns	Nothing is returned.
See Also	CSliderCtrl::SetRange()

GetRangeMax ■ 3.0

Description	This function returns the maximum unit position of the slider.
Syntax	public, int GetRangeMax() const;
Parameters	None.

Returns	The current maximum position.
See Also	CSliderCtrl::GetRange(), CSliderCtrl::GetRangeMin(), CSliderCtrl::SetRangeMax()

GetRangeMin ■ 3.0

Description	This function returns the minimum unit position of the slider.
Syntax	public, int GetRangeMin() const;
Parameters	None.
Returns	The current minimum position.
See Also	CSliderCtrl::GetRange(), CSliderCtrl::GetRangeMax(), CSliderCtrl::SetRangeMin ()

GetSelection ■ 3.0

Description	This function returns the current selected range of the control. A range may be selected in a slider control by using CSliderCtrl::SetSelection().
Syntax	public, void GetSelection(int& nMin, int& nMax) const;
Parameters	
nMin	A reference to an integer that will receive the new minimum selection position.
nMax	A reference to an integer that will receive the new maximum selection position.
Returns	Nothing is returned.
See Also	CSliderCtrl::SetSelection(), CSliderCtrl::ClearSel()

GetThumbRect ■ 3.0

Description	This function retrieves a rectangle containing the client coordinates of the slider thumb. The thumb is the handle that is used to move the slider control.
Syntax	public, void GetThumbRect(LPRECT lprc) const;
Parameters	
lprc	Address of the RECT structure that will receive the client coordinates of the slider thumb.
Returns	Nothing is returned.

GetTic ■ 3.0

Description	This function returns the unit position of the specified tick mark.
Syntax	public, int GetTic(int nTic) const;

Parameters

nTic The index of the tick mark. This value can range from 0 to GetNumTics().

Returns The position of the specified tick mark, or -1 if an error occurs.

See Also CSliderCtrl::SetTic()

GetTicArray ■ 3.0

Description This function returns an array of the current tick mark positions within the control's range.

Syntax public, DWORD* GetTicArray() const;

Parameters None.

Returns The array of tick mark positions. The array points to GetNumTics() marks.

See Also CSliderCtrl::GetNumTics()

GetTicPos ■ 3.0

Description This function returns the client coordinates of the specified tick mark.

Syntax public, int GetTicPos(int nTic) const;

Parameters

nTic The index of the tick mark. This value can range from 0 to GetNumTics().

Returns The position of the tick mark in client coordinates.

SetLineSize ■ 3.0

Description This function sets the number of units that make up a line. A line determines the lowest resolution that the slider can move.

Syntax public, int SetLineSize(int nSize);

Parameters

nSize The new number of units per line.

Returns The previous line size.

See Also CSliderCtrl::GetLineSize(), CSliderCtrl::SetPageSize()

SetPageSize ■ 3.0

Description This function sets the number of units that make up the page size for the control. The page size is the number of units the slider moves when it receives a TB_PAGEUP or TB_PAGEDOWN notification.

Syntax public, int SetPageSize(int nSize);

Parameters

nSize The new number of units per page.

Returns The previous number of units per page.

See Also CSliderCtrl::GetPageSize()

Example See CSliderCtrl::SetRange()

SetPos

■ 3.0

Description This function will set the current position of the slider thumb.

Syntax public, void SetPos(int nPos);

Parameters

nPos The new slider thumb position.

Returns Nothing is returned.

See Also CSliderCtrl::GetPos()

SetRange

■ 3.0

Description This function sets both the minimum and maximum unit positions of the slider.

Syntax public, void SetRange(int nMin, int nMax, BOOL bRedraw = FALSE);

Parameters

nMin The new minimum slider position.

nMax The new maximum slider position.

bRedraw If TRUE, then the slider is redrawn to display the new range. If FALSE, then the slider display is not updated.

Returns Nothing is returned.

See Also CSliderCtrl::GetRange()

Example The following shows an example of how to initialize a typical slider control.

```
void CCSliderDlg::SetUpSlider(CSliderCtrl * pSlider)
{
	ASSERT_VALID(pSlider);

	// set the slider to move between
	// the values 0 and 100
	pSlider->SetRange(0,100);

	pSlider->SetPageSize(10);

	pSlider->SetTicFreq(5);
}
```

SetRangeMax

■ 3.0

Description This function sets the maximum unit position of the slider.

Syntax public, void SetRangeMax(int nMax, BOOL bRedraw = FALSE);

Parameters

nMax The new maximum range value.

bRedraw If TRUE, then the slider is redrawn to display the new range. If FALSE, then the slider display is not updated.

Returns Nothing is returned.

See Also CSliderCtrl::SetRange(), CSliderCtrl::SetRangeMin()

SetRangeMin

■ 3.0

Description This function sets the minimum unit position of the slider.

Syntax public, void SetRangeMin(int nMin, BOOL bRedraw = FALSE);

Parameters

nMin The new minimum range value.

bRedraw If TRUE, then the slider is redrawn to display the new range. If FALSE, then the slider display is not updated.

Returns Nothing is returned.

See Also CSliderCtrl::SetRange(), CSliderCtrl::SetRangeMax()

SetSelection

■ 3.0

Description This function sets the selected range of the control. The selected portion of the control is displayed as a highlighted bar within the slider, bracketed by triangles next to the corresponding tick marks.

Syntax public, void SetSelection(int nMin, int nMax);

Parameters

nMin The new minimum selected position.

nMax The new maximum selected position.

Returns Nothing is returned.

See Also CSliderCtrl::GetSelection(), CSliderCtrl::ClearSel()

SetTic

■ 3.0

Description This function sets a new tick mark at the specified position.

Syntax public, BOOL SetTic(int nTic);

Parameters

nTic The position where the new tick mark will be placed.

Returns TRUE if successful; otherwise FALSE.

See Also CSliderCtrl::GetTic()

SetTicFreq ■ 3.0

Description This function sets the uniform frequency at which tick marks will appear in the control. This function is only valid if the control has the TBS_AUTOTICKS style.

Syntax public, void SetTicFreq(int nFreq);

Parameters

nFreq The number of positions between tick marks.

Returns Nothing is returned.

See Also CSliderCtrl::SetTic()

Example See CSliderCtrl::SetRange()

VerifyPos ■ 3.0

Description This function is called to verify that the slider is within the current minimum and maximum positions.

Syntax public, void VerifyPos();

Parameters None.

Returns Nothing is returned.

See Also CSliderCtrl::GetRange()

CSpinButtonCtrl

The CSpinButtonCtrl is useful when an interface is needed that allows a value to be incremented or decremented. The actual spin control is usually paired with a buddy control (usually a CEdit) that is used to display the new value. The example program that is associated with this section can be found in the CSpin directory on the CD-ROM.

CSpinButtonCtrl ■ 3.0

Description This is the constructor for the spin button control. The real initialization of this object is done in the Create member function.

Syntax public, CSpinButtonCtrl();

Parameters None.

Returns Nothing is returned.

See Also CSpinButtonCtrl::Create(), ~ CSpinButtonCtrl()

~CSpinButtonCtrl

■ 3.0 ■ UD

Description Destroys the spin button control.

Syntax public, virtual ~CSpinButtonCtrl();

Parameters None.

Returns Nothing is returned.

See Also CSpinButtonCtrl()

Create

■ 3.0

Description After construction, call this member to create the spin button control and attach it to this object.

Syntax public, BOOL Create(DWORD dwStyle, const RECT & rect, Cwnd * pParentWnd, UINT nID);

Parameters

dwStyle Styles used for this control. The allowable styles can be found in the Windows API documentation.

rect Indicates the control's position and size in terms of its parent's client coordinates.

pParentWnd Parent window of control.

nID The child ID of this control. Must be unique among its siblings.

Returns TRUE if creation successful; otherwise FALSE.

GetAccel

■ 3.0

Description This function retrieves the acceleration information for the spin control. The acceleration consists of a value increment that will increase or decrease the longer the spin control is pressed.

Syntax public, UINT GetAccel(int nAccel, UDACCEL* pAccel) const;

Parameters

nAccel The number of UDACCEL structures specified by *pAccel.*

pAccel A pointer to a buffer of UDACCEL structures that will receive the current accelerator structures.

Returns The actual number of accelerator structures retrieved.

See Also CSpinButtonCtrl::SetAccel()

GetBase ■ 3.0

Description This function retrieves the base unit for the spin control.

Syntax public, UINT GetBase() const;

Parameters None.

Returns The previous base for the control. This value can be either 10 for decimal or 16 for hexadecimal.

See Also CSpinButtonCtrl::SetBase()

GetBuddy ■ 3.0

Description This function retrieves the window that is paired with the spin control. This buddy window is constantly updated with the values from the spin control.

Syntax public, CWnd * GetBuddy() const;

Parameters None.

Returns The current buddy window.

See Also CSpinButtonCtrl::SetBuddy()

GetPos ■ 3.0

Description This function retrieves the current position of the spin control.

Syntax public, int GetPos() const;

Parameters None.

Returns The low-order word contains the current position. The high-order word will be non-zero if an error occurs.

See Also CSpinButtonCtrl::SetPos()

GetRange ■ 3.0

Description This function returns the lower and upper limits of the spin control.

Syntax public, DWORD GetRange() const;
public, void GetRange(int& nLower, int nUpper) const;

Parameters None.

nLower A reference to an integer that will receive the current lower range limit.

nUpper A reference to an integer that will receive the current upper range limit.

Returns The first version of this member function returns a DWORD. The low-order word contains the upper limit, and the high-order word contains the lower limit. The second version of this member function returns nothing.

See Also CSpinButtonCtrl::SetRange()

Example See CSpinButtonCtrl::SetBuddy

SetAccel ■ 3.0

Description This function sets the acceleration for the spin control. The acceleration consists of a value increment that will increase or decrease the longer the spin control is pressed.

Syntax public, BOOL SetAccel(int nAccel, UDACCEL* pAccel);

Parameters

nAccel The number of UDACCEL structures specified by *pAccel*.

pAccel A pointer to a number of UDACCEL structures that contain various times and spin increments. Note that these structures should be sorted by the **nSec** member.

Returns TRUE if successful; otherwise FALSE.

See Also CSpinButtonCtrl::GetAccel()

SetBase ■ 3.0

Description This function sets the base unit for the spin control.

Syntax public, int SetBase(int nBase);

Parameters

nBase The new base unit for the control. This value can be either 10 for decimal or 16 for hexadecimal.

Returns The previous base for the control.

See Also CSpinButtonCtrl::GetBase()

SetBuddy ■ 3.0

Description This function sets the window that will be paired with the spin control. This buddy window be updated with the values from the spin control.

Syntax public, CWnd * SetBuddy(CWnd* pWndBuddy);

Parameters

pWndBuddy The new window that will be paired with the spin control.

Returns The previous buddy window.

See Also CSpinButtonCtrl::GetBuddy()

Example The following code illustrates the use of a buddy control.

```
BOOL CCSpinDlg::OnInitDialog()
{
      CDialog::OnInitDialog();
```

continued on next page

continued from previous page

```
        CenterWindow();

        // Add "About..." menu item to system menu.

        // IDM_ABOUTBOX must be in the system command range.
        ASSERT((IDM_ABOUTBOX & 0xFFF0) == IDM_ABOUTBOX);
        ASSERT(IDM_ABOUTBOX < 0xF000);

        CMenu* pSysMenu = GetSystemMenu(FALSE);
        CString strAboutMenu;
        strAboutMenu.LoadString(IDS_ABOUTBOX);
        if (!strAboutMenu.IsEmpty())
        {
            pSysMenu->AppendMenu(MF_SEPARATOR);
            pSysMenu->AppendMenu(MF_STRING, IDM_ABOUTBOX, strAboutMenu);
        }

        m_SpinCtl.SetBuddy(&m_BuddyCtl);
        m_SpinCtl.SetRange(0,200);
        m_SpinCtl.SetPos(0);
        m_SpinCtl.SetPos(0);
        DWORD dwRange = m_SpinCtl.GetRange();
        CString strMsg;
        int nLow = LOWORD(dwRange);
        int nHigh = HIWORD(dwRange);
        strMsg.Format("Low: %d  High: %d",nLow,nHigh);
        AfxMessageBox(strMsg);
        return TRUE;  // return TRUE  unless you set the focus to a control
}
```

SetPos ■ 3.0

Description This function sets a new position for the spin control.

Syntax public, int SetPos(int nPos);

Parameters

nPos The new position. This value must be in the range set for the control.

Returns The previous position.

See Also CSpinButtonCtrl::GetPos()

Example See CSpinButtonCtrl::SetBuddy()

SetRange ■ 3.0

Description This function sets the valid lower and upper limits of the spin control.

Syntax public, void SetRange(int nLower, int nUpper);

Parameters

nLower The new lower bound of the spin control.

nUpper The new upper bound of the spin control.

Returns Nothing is returned.

See Also CSpinButtonCtrl::GetRange()

Example See CSpinButtonCtrl::SetBuddy()

CStatic

The CStatic object is an encapsulation of the standard static text control. Either text or an icon can be displayed by this control.

CStatic ■ 2.0 ■ 3.0

Description This is the constructor for the static text control. The real initialization of this object is done in the Create member function.

Syntax public, CStatic();

Parameters None.

Returns Nothing is returned.

See Also CStatic::Create()

~CStatic ■ 2.0 ■ 3.0 ■ UD

Description Destroys the static text control object.

Syntax public, virtual ~CStatic();

Parameters None.

Returns Nothing is returned.

See Also CStatic()

Create ■ 2.0 ■ 3.0

Description After construction, call this member to create the static text control and attach it to this object.

Syntax public, BOOL Create(LPCTSTR lpszCaption,DWORD dwStyle, const RECT & rect, CWnd* pParentWnd, UINT nID = 0);

Parameters

lpszCaption The text that will be displayed in the control.

dwStyle A combination of valid window or static text styles. The allowable styles can be found in the Windows API documentation.

rect Indicates the control's position and size in terms of its parent's client coordinates.

pParentWnd Parent window of control.

nID The child ID of this control. Must be unique among its siblings.

Returns TRUE if successful; otherwise FALSE.

See Also CStatic()

GetBitmap ■ 4.0

Description This Windows 95-specific member retrieves the bitmap that is associated with this CStatic object.

Syntax public, HBITMAP GetBitmap() const;

Parameters None.

Returns The handle of the associated bitmap, or NULL if no bitmap is associated.

See Also CStatic::SetBitmap()

GetCursor ■ 4.0

Description This Windows 95-specific member retrieves the cursor image that is associated with this CStatic object.

Syntax public, HCURSOR GetCursor();

Parameters None.

Returns The handle of the associated cursor image, or NULL if there is no associated cursor image.

See Also CStatic::SetCursor()

GetEnhMetafile ■ 4.0

Description This Windows 95-specific member retrieves the enhanced metafile that is associated with this CStatic object.

Syntax public, HENHMETAFILE GetEnhMetafile() const;

Parameters None.

Returns The handle of the associated enhanced metafile, or NULL if there is no associated enhanced metafile.

See Also CStatic::SetEnhMetafile()

GetIcon ■ 2.0 ■ 3.0

Description This function retrieves the current icon displayed in a static text control that has the SS_ICON style.

Syntax public, HICON GetIcon() const;

Parameters None.

Returns The handle of the current icon, or NULL if an error occurred.

See Also CStatic::SetIcon()

SetBitmap ■ 4.0

Description This Windows 95-specific member sets the bitmap that is displayed in the CStatic window. To use this feature, the SS_BITMAP style flag must be set. By default, the bitmap is displayed in the upper-left corner of the CStatic window. This can be modified by using the SS_CENTERIMAGE style flag.

Syntax public, HBITMAP SetBitmap(HBITMAP hBitmap);

Parameters

hBitmap A handle to the new bitmap image.

Returns The handle of the previously associated bitmap, or NULL if no bitmap was previously associated.

See Also CStatic::GetBitmap()

SetCursor ■ 4.0

Description This Windows 95-specific member sets the cursor image that is displayed in the CStatic window. To use this feature, the SS_ICON style flag must be set. By default, the bitmap is displayed in the upper-left corner of the CStatic window. This can be modified by using the SS_CENTERIMAGE style flag.

Syntax public, HCURSOR SetCursor(HCURSOR hCursor);

Parameters

hBitmap A handle to the new cursor image.

Returns The handle of the previously associated cursor image, or NULL if no cursor image was previously associated.

See Also CStatic::GetCursor()

SetEnhMetafile ■ 4.0

Description This Windows 95-specific member sets the enhanced metafile image that is displayed in the CStatic window. To use this feature, the SS_ENHMETAFILE style flag must be set. The enhanced metafile is always scaled to the current size of the CStatic window.

Syntax public, HENHMETAFILE SetEnhMetafile(HENHMETAFILE hMetaFile);

Parameters

hMetaFile A handle to the new enhanced metafile.

Returns The handle of the previously associated enhanced metafile, or NULL if no enhanced metafile was previously associated.

See Also CStatic::GetEnhMetafile()

SetIcon ■ 2.0 ■ 3.0

Description This function sets a new icon to be displayed in a static text control that has the SS_ICON style.

Syntax public, HICON SetIcon(HICON hIcon);

Parameters

hIcon Handle of the new icon.

Returns The handle of the previous icon displayed in the control, or NULL if an error occurred.

See Also CStatic::GetIcon()

CStatusBarCtrl

The CStatusBarCtrl is similar to the CStatusBar object, but contains much more functionality. This control can have dynamically set panes, and each pane has independent display attributes.

CStatusBarCtrl ■ 3.0

Description This is the constructor for the status bar control. The real initialization of this object is done in the Create member function.

Syntax public, CStatusBarCtrl();

Parameters None.

Returns Nothing is returned.

See Also CStatusBarCtrl::Create(), ~ CStatusBarCtrl()

~CStatusBarCtrl ■ 3.0 ■ UD

Description Destroys the status bar control.

Syntax public, virtual ~CStatusBarCtrl();

Parameters None.

Returns Nothing is returned.

See Also CStatusBarCtrl()

Create ■ 3.0

Description After construction, call this member to create the status bar control and attach it to this object.

Syntax public, BOOL Create(DWORD dwStyle, const RECT & rect, CWnd * pParentWnd, UINT nID);

Parameters

dwStyle Styles used for this control. The allowable styles can be found in the Windows API documentation.

rect Indicates the control's position and size in terms of its parent's client coordinates.

pParentWnd Parent window of control.

nID The child ID of this control. Must be unique among its siblings.

Returns TRUE if creation successful; otherwise FALSE.

DrawItem ■ 3.0

Description This virtual function is called whenever an owner-draw status bar object needs to be displayed or updated. It is passed a DrawItemStruct that contains various information on how the control is to be drawn.

Syntax public, virtual void DrawItem(LPDRAWITEMSTRUCT lpDrawItemStruct);

Parameters

lpDrawItemStruct Contains parameters for drawing the item. See Windows API for a description of this structure.

Returns Nothing is returned.

See Also CWnd::DrawItem()

GetBorders ■ 3.0

Description This functions retrieves the current horizontal, vertical, and spacing borders in the control.

Syntax public, BOOL GetBorders(int* pBorders) const;
public, BOOL GetBorders(int& nHorz, int& nVert, int& nSpacing);

Parameters

pBorders This is the address of an integer array that will receive the three integer borders. The first integer contains the width of the horizontal border, the second integer contains the width of the vertical border, and the third integer contains the width of the border between panes. A value of -1 in any of these elements indicates that the default width will be used.

nHorz A reference to an integer that will receive the width of the horizontal border.

nVert A reference to an integer that will receive the width of the vertical border.

nSpacing A reference to an integer that will receive the width of the border between panes.

Returns TRUE if successful; otherwise FALSE.

GetParts ■ 3.0

Description This function retrieves the current number of panes (parts) in the status bar, and their size.

Syntax public, int GetParts(int nParts, int* pParts) const;

Parameters

nParts The number of parts allocated by *pParts*.

pParts An array of integers that will receive the right edge coordinate of each part in the control.

Returns The actual number of parts in the control, or 0 if an error occurs.

See Also CStatusBarCtrl::SetParts()

GetRect ■ 3.0

Description This function retrieves the bounding rectangle of a pane in the control.

Syntax public, BOOL GetRect(int nPane, LPRECT lpRect);

Parameters

nPane The pane whose bounding rectangle is to be retrieved.

lpRect Address of a RECT structure that will receive the bounding rectangle.

Returns TRUE if successful; otherwise FALSE.

See Also CStatusBarCtrl::GetParts()

GetText ■ 3.0

Description This function retrieves the current text from a pane in the status bar.

Syntax public, int GetText(LPCTSTR lpszText, int nPane, int* pType = NULL) const;
public,CString GetText(int nPane, int* pType = NULL) const;

Parameters

lpszText A NULL-terminated string buffer that will receive the current text.

nPane The pane whose text is to be retrieved.

pType A pointer to an integer which will receive the display flags for the pane. This value can be any one of the following:

0 The text is sunken into the status bar.

SBT_NOBORDERS The text will have no borders.

SBT_OWNERDRAW The text is drawn by the parent window.

SBT_POPOUT The text appears raised above the status bar.

Returns The first version of this member returns the length in bytes of the text copied. The second version returns a CString containing the retrieved text.

See Also CStatusBarCtrl ::GetTextLength(), CStatusBarCtrl::SetText()

GetTextLength ■ 3.0

Description	This function returns the length of text stored in the specified pane, and the text display type.
Syntax	public, int GetTextLength(int nPane, int* pType = NULL) const;
Parameters	
nPane	The pane whose text length is to be retrieved.
pType	A pointer to an integer which will receive the display flags for the pane. This value can be any one of the following:
0	The text is sunken into the status bar.
SBT_NOBORDERS	The text will have no borders.
SBT_OWNERDRAW	The text is drawn by the parent window.
SBT_POPOUT	The text appears raised above the status bar.
Returns	The length in bytes of the text stored in the specified pane.
See Also	CStatusBarCtrl::GetText()

OnChildNotify ■ 3.0 ■ UD

Description	This function is called by the status bar's parent whenever a notification applies to this control. This function should never be called directly, but can be overridden for owner-draw controls.
Syntax	protected, virtual BOOL OnChildNotify(UINT, WPARAM, LPARAM, LRESULT *);
Parameters	
UINT	Notification message.
WPARAM	Message-specific data.
LPARAM	Message-specific data.
LRESULT*	Address of returned result code, dependent on notification message.
Returns	The default implementation returns FALSE for every unhandled message, and TRUE for messages that were handled by the control.
See Also	CWnd::OnChildNotify(), CStatusBarCtrl::DrawItem()

SetMinHeight ■ 3.0

Description	This function sets the minimum height (in pixels) of the status bar's drawing area.
Syntax	public, void SetMinHeight(int nMin);
Parameters	
nMin	The new minimum height in pixels.
Returns	Nothing is returned.
See Also	CStatusBarCtrl::GetHeight()

SetParts

■ 3.0

Description This function sets the number of panes (parts) in a status bar, and their size.

Syntax public, BOOL SetParts(int nParts, int* pWidths);

Parameters

nParts The new number of panes in the control.

pWidths A pointer to an array of integers specifying the right edge of each pane in client coordinates. An edge value of -1 indicates the edge will be the same as the right edge of the control.

Returns TRUE if successful; otherwise FALSE.

See Also CStatusBarCtrl::GetParts()

SetSimple

■ 3.0

Description This function sets whether the control displays simple text, or uses the settings passed by the CStatusBarCtrl::SetParts() member.

Syntax public, BOOL SetSimple(BOOL bSimple = TRUE);

Parameters

bSimple A value of true displays simple text; FALSE uses current display settings.

Returns TRUE if successful; otherwise FALSE.

See Also CStatusBarCtrl::SetParts()

SetText

■ 3.0

Description This function sets the text in a pane of the status bar.

Syntax public, BOOL SetText(LPCTSTR lpszText, int nPane, int nType);

Parameters

lpszText A NULL-terminated string containing the new text. For controls with the SBT_OWNERDRAW style, this member represents a 32-bit value that is passed to the control.

nPane The destination pane.

nType Determines how the text will be displayed in the pane. It can be any one of the following values:

0 The text is sunken into the status bar.

SBT_NOBORDERS The text will have no borders.

SBT_OWNERDRAW The text is drawn by the parent window.

SBT_POPOUT The text appears raised above the status bar.

Returns TRUE if successful; otherwise FALSE.

See Also CStatusBarCtrl::GetText()

CTabCtrl

The CTabCtrl is useful for displaying multiple pages of information in the same display area. The tabs themselves can be stacked, or contain multiple rows. Also, the tabs can be displayed as rows of buttons. It is important to note that the CTabCtrl is not the same as the CPropertySheetDlg discussed in Chapter 8, *Dialog Boxes*. Rather, the CPropertySheet contains a CTabCtrl and uses it to manage multiple "pages" on one dialog. The CTabCtrl contains all the functionality in the actual tab buttons themselves, and manages the user's interaction with them. In this regard, the CTabCtrl is very similar to a CHeaderCtrl. The example program that is associated with this section can be found in the CTabCtrl directory on the CD-ROM.

CTabCtrl ■ 3.0

Description This is the constructor for the tab control. The real initialization of this object is done in the Create member function.

Syntax public, CTabCtrl();

Parameters None.

Returns Nothing is returned.

See Also CTabCtrl::Create(), ~ CTabCtrl()

~CTabCtrl ■ 3.0 ■ UD

Description Destroys the tab control.

Syntax public, virtual ~CTabCtrl();

Parameters None.

Returns Nothing is returned.

See Also CTabCtrl()

AdjustRect ■ 3.0

Description This function will either calculate the display area of the control (given the size of the window rectangle) or it will calculate the window rectangle (for a given display area size). The display area is the area under the tabs that correspond to the tab "page." The window rectangle is the bounding rectangle for the entire control.

Syntax public, void AdjustRect(BOOL bLarger, LPRECT lpRect);

Parameters

bLarger If TRUE, then the window rectangle is calculated (the larger rectangle). If FALSE, then the display rectangle is computed.

lpRect If *bLarger* is TRUE, then this address contains the display rectangle and will receive the corresponding window rectangle. If *bLarger* is FALSE, then this address contains the window rectangle and will receive the corresponding display rectangle.

Returns Nothing is returned.

CREATE ■ 3.0 ■ UD

Description After construction, call this member to create the tab control and attach it to this object.

Syntax public, BOOL Create(DWORD dwStyle, const RECT & rect, Cwnd * pParentWnd, UINT nID);

Parameters

dwStyle Styles used for this control. The allowable styles can be found in the Windows API documentation.

rect Indicates the control's position and size in terms of its parent's client coordinates.

pParentWnd Parent window of control.

nID The child ID of this control. Must be unique among its siblings.

Returns TRUE if creation successful; otherwise FALSE.

DELETEALLITEMS ■ 3.0

Description This function removes all tabs from the control.

Syntax public, BOOL DeleteAllItems();

Parameters None.

Returns TRUE if successful; otherwise FALSE.

See Also CTabCtrl::DeleteItem()

DELETEITEM ■ 3.0

Description This function removes the tab at the specified index from the control.

Syntax public, BOOL DeleteItem(int nItem);

Parameters

nItem The index of the tab that should be removed from the control.

Returns TRUE if successful; otherwise FALSE.

See Also CTabCtrl::InsertItem()

DRAWITEM ■ 3.0

Description This virtual function is called whenever an owner-draw CTabCtrl object needs to be displayed or updated. It is passed a DrawItemStruct that contains various information on how the control is to be drawn.

Syntax	public, virtual void DrawItem(LPDRAWITEMSTRUCT lpDrawItemStruct);
Parameters	
lpDrawItemStruct	Contains parameters for drawing the item. See Windows API documentation for a description of this structure.
Returns	Nothing is returned.
See Also	CWnd::DrawItem()

GetCurFocus ■ 3.0

Description	This function will retrieve the index of the tab with the current focus.
Syntax	public, int GetCurFocus() const;
Parameters	None.
Returns	The index of the tab with the current focus.
See Also	CTabCtrl::GetCurSel()

GetCurSel ■ 3.0

Description	This function is used to retrieve the currently selected tab index.
Syntax	public, int GetCurSel() const;
Parameters	None.
Returns	The index of the currently selected tab. Note that this index is zero-based (the first tab having an index of 0, the second having an index of 1,...).
See Also	CTabCtrl::SetCurSel()

GetImageList ■ 3.0

Description	This function retrieves the image list that is associated with the tab control.
Syntax	public, CImageList* GetImageList() const;
Parameters	None.
Returns	The associated image list.
See Also	CTabCtrl::SetImageList()

GetItem ■ 3.0

Description	This function retrieves the item at the specified index. In this case, the item represents the actual tab and its attributes.
Syntax	public, BOOL GetItem(int nItem, TC_ITEM* pTabCtrlItem) const;

Parameters

nItem The position of the item to be retrieved. This value can range from 0 to GetItemCount()-1.

pTabCtrlItem Pointer to a TC_ITEM structure that will receive the item. The structure's masks must be filled in with the item data that is to be retrieved.

Returns TRUE if successful; otherwise FALSE.

See Also CTabCtrl::SetItem()

GetItemCount ■ 3.0

Description This function retrieves the number of items (tabs) in the tab control.

Syntax public, int GetItemCount() const;

Parameters None.

Returns The number of items in the control if successful; otherwise -1.

Example The following example queries information about the tab control:

```
void CCTabCtrlDlg::CheckTabCtrl(CTabCtrl * pTabs)
{
     ASSERT_VALID(pTabs);

     int nRows = m_TabCtrl.GetRowCount();
     int nItems = m_TabCtrl.GetItemCount();
     CString strText;
     strText.Format("%d rows   %d items",nRows,nItems);
     AfxMessageBox(strText);
}
```

GetItemRect ■ 3.0

Description This function retrieves the client coordinates of an tab's bounding rectangle.

Syntax public, BOOL GetItemRect(int nItem, LPRECT lpRect) const;

Parameters

nItem The index of the tab.

lpRect A pointer to a RECT that will receive the coordinates.

Returns TRUE if successful; otherwise FALSE.

GetRowCount ■ 3.0

Description This function retrieves the current number of tab rows in the control.

Syntax public, int GetRowCount() const;

Parameters None.

Returns The current number of rows in the control. If the control does not have the TCS_MULTILINE style, this function will return 1.

Example See CTabCtrl::GetItemCount()

GetTooltips ■ 3.0

Description This function returns the tooltip control that is associated with this control.

Syntax public, CToolTipCtrl* GetTooltips();

Parameters None.

Returns A pointer to the tooltip control, or NULL if there is no current association.

See Also CTabCtrl::SetTooltips()

HitTest ■ 3.0

Description This function will calculate which tab, if any, resides at the specified location.

Syntax public, int HitTest(TC_HITTESTINFO* pHitTestInfo) const;

Parameters

pHitTestInfo A pointer to a TC_HITTESTINFO structure that contains location information and returns the results of the hit test.

Returns The index of the tab that corresponds to the hit test location, or -1 if no tab qualifies.

InsertItem ■ 3.0

Description This function will insert a new tab item into the control at the specified index.

Syntax public, BOOL InsertItem(int nItem, TC_ITEM* pTabCtrlItem);

Parameters

nItem The index where the tab should be inserted into the control.

pTabCtrlItem A pointer to a TC_ITEM structure that contains information about the tab item. Note that the **mask** attribute of the structure should be set to indicate the information that is valid.

Returns The index of the new tab if successful; otherwise -1.

See Also CTabCtrl::DeleteItem()

Example The following illustrates the additon of items to the tab control.

```
void CCTabCtrlDlg::InitializeTabCtrl(CTabCtrl * pTabs)
{
     ASSERT_VALID(pTabs);

     // TODO: Add extra initialization here
     TC_ITEM item;
     char sText[64];

     for(int nI=0;nI<10;nI++)
     {
```

continued on next page

continued from previous page

```
                        sprintf(sText,"Tab %d",nI);
                        item.pszText = sText;
                        item.cchTextMax = strlen(sText);
                        item.mask = TCIF_TEXT;
                        pTabs->InsertItem(0,&item);
                }
        }
```

OnChildNotify ■ 3.0 ■ UD

Description This function is called by the CTabCtrl's parent whenever a notification applies to this control. This function should never be called directly, but can be overridden for owner-draw controls.

Syntax protected, virtual BOOL OnChildNotify(UINT, WPARAM, LPARAM, LRESULT *);

Parameters

UINT Notification message.

WPARAM Message-specific data.

LPARAM Message-specific data.

*LRESULT** Address of returned result code, dependent on notification message.

Returns The default implementation returns FALSE for every unhandled message, and TRUE for messages that were handled by the control.

See Also CWnd::OnChildNotify(), CTabCtrl::DrawItem()

OnDestroy ■ 3.0 ■ UD

Description The default implementation of this protected member function is used to remove any current image list from the control.

Syntax protected, afx_msg void OnDestroy();

Parameters None.

Returns Nothing is returned.

See Also CTabCtrl::RemoveImage()

RemoveImage ■ 3.0

Description This function will remove an image from the associated image list.

Syntax public, void RemoveImage(int nImage);

Parameters

nImage Index of the image to remove.

Returns Nothing is returned.

See Also CTabCtrl::GetImageList()

SetCurSel ■ 3.0

Description This function is used to select a tab in the control.

Syntax public, int SetCurSel(int nItem);

Parameters

nItem The index of the tab to be selected.

Returns The index of the previously selected tab, or -1 if no tab was previously selected.

See Also CTabCtrl::GetCurSel()

SetImageList ■ 3.0

Description This function associates an image list with the control.

Syntax public, CImageList* SetImageList(CImageList* pImageList);

Parameters

pImageList A pointer to a new image list control.

Returns A pointer to the previous image list control, or NULL.

See Also CTabCtrl::GetImageList()

SetItem ■ 3.0

Description This function modifies attributes of a current item.

Syntax public, BOOL SetItem(int nItem, TC_ITEM* pTabCtrlItem);

Parameters

nItem Index of the item to be modified. This value can range from 0 to GetItemCount()-1.

pTabCtrlItem Pointer to a TC_ITEM structure that contains the new attributes. This structure's masks must be filled in to indicate which attributes are to be modified.

Returns TRUE if successful; otherwise FALSE.

See Also CTabCtrl::GetItem(), CTabCtrl::InsertItem()

SetItemSize ■ 3.0

Description This function sets the physical dimensions of all the tabs in the control.

Syntax public, CSize SetItemSize(CSize size);

Parameters

size The new width and height of the tabs, in pixels.

Returns The previous tab dimensions.

See Also CTabCtrl::SetPadding()

SetPadding ■ 3.0

Description This function sets the amount of padding between the tab's label (icon and text) and the tab borders.

Syntax public, void SetPadding(CSize size);

Parameters

size The new width and height of the padding, in pixels.

Returns The previous tab padding.

See Also CTabCtrl::SetItemSize()

SetTooltips ■ 3.0

Description This function will asssociate a tooltip control with the tab control.

Syntax public, void SetTooltips(CToolTipCtrl* pWndTip);

Parameters

pWndTip The new tooltip control.

Returns Nothing is returned.

See Also CTabCtrl::GetTooltips()

CToolBarCtrl

This control is a much more functional version of the original MFC CToolBar object (See Chapter 10, *Menus and Control Bars*). This object supports multiple rows of buttons, and can be resized dynamically. Also, a CToolTipCtrl object can be associated with the control to display help information on each button.

CToolBarCtrl ■ 3.0

Description This is the constructor for the toolbar control. The real initialization of this object is done in the Create member function.

Syntax public, CToolBarCtrl();

Parameters None.

Returns Nothing is returned.

See Also CToolBarCtrl::Create(), ~ CToolBarCtrl()

~CToolBarCtrl ■ 3.0 ■ UD

Description Destroys the toolbar control.

Syntax public, virtual ~CToolBarCtrl();

Parameters None.

Returns Nothing is returned.

See Also CToolBarCtrl()

AddBitmap ■ 3.0

Description This function will add a bitmap to the toolbar. This bitmap can consist of one or more sub images.

Syntax public, int AddBitmap(int nNumButtons, UINT nBitmapID);
public, int AddBitmap(int nNumButtons, CBitmap* pBitmap);

Parameters

nNumButtons The number of sub images in the bitmap.

nBitmapID The resource ID of the bitmap.

pBitmap A pointer to a bitmap object that contains the images.

Returns If successful, the index of the first new image; otherwise -1.

AddButtons ■ 3.0

Description This function will add an array of buttons into the toolbar.

Syntax public, BOOL AddButtons(int nNumButtons, LPTBBUTTON lpButtons);

Parameters

nNumButtons The number of buttons contained in *lpButtons*.

lpButtons An array of TBBUTTON structures that describes the buttons to be added.

Returns TRUE if successful; otherwise FALSE.

See Also CToolBarCtrl::InsertButton()

AddString ■ 3.0

Description This function will add a new string into the toolbar's internal string list. This string can be used as button text when adding buttons into the toolbar.

Syntax public, int AddString(UINT nStringID);

Parameters

nStringID The resource ID of the string to be added.

Returns If successful, the index of the new string added; otherwise -1.

See Also CToolBarCtrl::AddStrings() ,CToolBarCtrl ::InsertButton(), CToolBarCtrl::AddButtons()

AddStrings ■ 3.0

Description This function will add new strings into the toolbar's internal string list. These strings can be used as button text when adding buttons into the toolbar.

Syntax public, int AddStrings(LPCTSTR lpszStrings);

Parameters

lpszStrings A pointer to a list of NULL-terminated strings that will be added into the internal list. The last string in the list should be terminated with two NULL characters (or the last string should be empty).

Returns If successful, the first index of the new strings added; otherwise -1.

See Also CToolBarCtrl::AddString(), CToolBarCtrl ::InsertButton(), CToolBarCtrl::AddButtons()

AutoSize ■ 3.0

Description This function will automatically resize the toolbar to display new settings.

Syntax public, void AutoSize();

Parameters None.

Returns Nothing is returned.

CheckButton ■ 3.0

Description This function will check or uncheck the specified button.

Syntax public, BOOL CheckButton(int nID, BOOL bCheck = TRUE);

Parameters

nID The command ID of the button.

bCheck TRUE will check the button; FALSE will uncheck the button.

Returns TRUE if successful; otherwise FALSE.

See Also CToolBarCtrl::SetState()

CommandToIndex ■ 3.0

Description This function will translate a command ID into a button index.

Syntax public, UINT CommandToIndex(UINT nID) const;

Parameters

nID Command ID of the button whose index is desired.

Returns The index of the specified button.

Create ■ 3.0

Description After construction, call this member to create the toolbar and attach it to this object.

Syntax public, BOOL Create(DWORD dwStyle, const RECT & rect, CWnd * pParentWnd, UINT nID);

Parameters

dwStyle Styles used for this control. The allowable styles can be found in the Windows API documentation.

rect Indicates the control's position and size in terms of its parent's client coordinates.

pParentWnd Parent window of control.

nID The child ID of this control. Must be unique among its siblings.

Returns TRUE if creation successful; otherwise FALSE.

Customize ■ 3.0

Description This function will display the Customize Toolbar dialog to allow customization of this toolbar. To customize the toolbar, the toolbar must have been created with the CCS_ADJUSTABLE style, and the toolbar's parent window must handle the customization messages.

Syntax public, void Customize();

Parameters None.

Returns Nothing is returned.

DeleteButton ■ 3.0

Description This function will remove the button at the specified index.

Syntax public, BOOL DeleteButton(int nIndex);

Parameters

nIndex The index of the button that will be removed.

Returns TRUE if successful; otherwise FALSE.

EnableButton ■ 3.0

Description This function will enable or disable the specified button.

Syntax public, BOOL EnableButton(int nID, BOOL bEnable = TRUE);

Parameters

nID The command ID of the button.

bEnable TRUE will enable the button for input; FALSE will disable the button.

Returns TRUE if successful; otherwise FALSE.

See Also CToolBarCtrl::SetState()

GetBitmapFlags ■ 3.0

Description This function retrieves the bitmap flags that indicate what types of bitmaps are supported.

Syntax public, UINT GetBitmapFlags() const;

Parameters None.

Returns The current bitmap flags. This value can be TBBF_LARGE if large bitmaps are supported, or 0 if not.

See Also CToolBarCtrl::SetBitmapSize()

GetButton ■ 3.0

Description This function retrieves information about the given button.

Syntax public, BOOL GetButton(int nIndex, LPTBBUTTON lpButton) const;

Parameters

nIndex The index of the button.

lpButton A pointer to a TBBUTTON structure that will receive the button information.

Returns TRUE if successful; otherwise FALSE.

See Also CToolBarCtrl::GetButtonCount()

GetButtonCount ■ 3.0

Description This function retrieves the number of buttons in the toolbar.

Syntax public, int GetButtonCount() const;

Parameters None.

Returns The number of buttons in the toolbar.

GetItemRect ■ 3.0

Description This function retrieves the bounding rectangle of the specified button.

Syntax public, BOOL GetItemRect(int nIndex, LPRECT lpRect) const;

Parameters

nIndex The index of the button.

lpRect A pointer to a RECT structure that will receive the coordinates.

Returns TRUE if successful; otherwise FALSE.

GetRows ■ 3.0

Description This function will retrieve the number of rows of buttons in the toolbar.

Syntax public, int GetRows() const;

Parameters None.

Returns The current number of rows, or 1 for toolbars with the TBSTYLE_WRAPABLE style.

See Also CToolBarCtrl::SetRows()

GetState

■ 3.0

Description This function retrieves the current state of a button on the toolbar.

Syntax public, int GetState(int nID) const;

Parameters

nID The index of the button.

Returns Returns the button state flags if successful; otherwise -1. These flags can be a combination of the following:

TBSTATE_CHECKED	The button will be checked (for buttons with the TBSTYLE_CHECK style).
TBSTATE_ENABLED	The button is enabled for user input.
TBSTATE_HIDDEN	The button is hidden and not displayed.
TBSTATE_INDETERMINATE	The button is in the indeterminate grayed state.
TBSTATE_PRESSED	The button is pressed.
TBSTATE_WRAP	When used in conjunction with the TBSTATE_ENABLED state, a separator is inserted after the button.

See Also CToolBarCtrl::IsButtonChecked(), CToolBarCtrl::IsButtonEnabled(), CToolBarCtrl::IsButtonHidden(), CToolBarCtrl::IsButtonIndeterminate(), CToolBarCtrl::IsButtonPressed()

GetToolTips

■ 3.0

Description This function returns the tooltip control that is associated with this control.

Syntax public, CToolTipCtrl* GetToolTips() const;

Parameters None.

Returns A pointer to the tooltip control, or NULL if there is no current association.

HideButton

■ 3.0

Description This function will hide or display the specified button.

Syntax public, BOOL HideButton(int nID, BOOL bHide = TRUE);

Parameters

nID The command ID of the button.

bHide TRUE will hide the button; FALSE will display the button.

Returns TRUE if successful; otherwise FALSE.

See Also CToolBarCtrl::SetState()

INDETERMINATE

■ 3.0

Description This function sets or removes the indeterminate state of the specified button.

Syntax public, BOOL Indeterminate(int nID, BOOL bIndeterminate = TRUE);

Parameters

nID The command ID of the button.

bIndeterminate TRUE will set the gray indeterminate state; FALSE will remove the indeterminate state.

Returns TRUE if successful; otherwise FALSE.

See Also CToolBarCtrl::SetState()

INSERTBUTTON

■ 3.0

Description This function will insert a button into the toolbar at the specified location.

Syntax public, BOOL InsertButton(int nIndex, LPTBBUTTON lpButton);

Parameters

nIndex The desired index of the inserted button.

lpButtons A pointer to a TBBUTTON structure that describes the button to be inserted.

Returns TRUE if successful; otherwise FALSE.

See Also CToolBarCtrl::AddButtons()

ISBUTTONCHECKED

■ 3.0

Description This function determines whether or not the specified button is checked.

Syntax public, BOOL IsButtonChecked(int nID) const;

Parameters

nId The command ID of the button.

Returns TRUE if the button is checked; otherwise FALSE.

See Also CToolBarCtrl::GetState()

ISBUTTONENABLED

■ 3.0

Description This function determines whether or not the specified button is enabled.

Syntax public, BOOL IsButtonEnabled(int nID) const;

Parameters

nId The command ID of the button.

Returns TRUE if the button is enabled; otherwise FALSE.

See Also CToolBarCtrl::GetState()

IsButtonHidden

■ 3.0

Description This function determines whether or not the specified button is hidden.

Syntax public, BOOL IsButtonHidden(int nID) const;

Parameters

nID The command ID of the button.

Returns TRUE if the button is hidden; otherwise FALSE.

See Also CToolBarCtrl::GetState()

IsButtonIndeterminate

■ 3.0

Description This function determines whether or not the specified button is in the indeterminate state.

Syntax public, BOOL IsButtonIndeterminate(int nID) const;

Parameters

nID The command ID of the button.

Returns TRUE if the button is indeterminate; otherwise FALSE.

See Also CToolBarCtrl::GetState()

IsButtonPressed

■ 3.0

Description This function determines whether or not the specified button is pressed.

Syntax public, BOOL IsButtonPressed(int nID) const;

Parameters

nID The command ID of the button.

Returns TRUE if the button is pressed; otherwise FALSE.

See Also CToolBarCtrl::GetState()

OnCreate

■ 3.0 ■ UD

Description This protected function is overridden to set the default button structure size to be the size of the TBBUTTON structure (for future compatibility). Override this function as a convenient place to set a custom button structure size.

Syntax protected, afx_msg int OnCreate(LPCREATESTRUCT lpCreateStruct);

Parameters

lpCreateStruct A pointer to a CREATESTRUCT structure. See the Windows API help for a description of this structure.

Returns 0 for success; otherwise -1.

See Also CWnd::OnCreate()

PressButton

■ 3.0

Description	This function will press or release the specified button.
Syntax	public, BOOL PressButton(int nID, BOOL bPress = TRUE);
Parameters	
nID	The command ID of the button.
bPress	TRUE will press the button; FALSE will release the button.
Returns	TRUE if successful; otherwise FALSE.
See Also	CToolBarCtrl::SetState()

RestoreState

■ 3.0

Description	This function will restore the state of the toolbar from the system registry.
Syntax	public, void RestoreState(HKEY hKeyRoot, LPCTSTR lpszSubKey, LPCTSTR lpszValueName);
Parameters	
hKeyRoot	This parameter specifies which root key the state information will be retrieved from. It can specify a predefined keyword such as: HKEY_CLASSES_ROOT HKEY_CURRENT_USER HKEY_LOCAL_MACHINE HKEY_USERS
lpszSubKey	The name of the registry subkey, or NULL.
lpszValueName	The name of the toolbar state value that contains the state information.
Returns	Nothing is returned.
See Also	CToolBarCtrl::SaveState()

SaveState

■ 3.0

Description	This function will save the current toolbar state in the system registry for later retrieval.
Syntax	public, void SaveState(HKEY hKeyRoot, LPCTSTR lpszSubKey, LPCTSTR lpszValueName);
Parameters	
hKeyRoot	This parameter specifies which root key the state information will be saved under. It can specify a predefined keyword such as: HKEY_CLASSES_ROOT HKEY_CURRENT_USER HKEY_LOCAL_MACHINE HKEY_USERS

lpszSubKey The name of the registry subkey, or NULL.

lpszValueName The name that the toolbar state value will be saved under. If this name currently exists it will be overwritten; if it does not currently exist it will be created.

Returns Nothing is returned.

See Also CToolBarCtrl::RestoreState()

SetBitmapSize ■ 3.0

Description This function is called before buttons are added, to set the dimensions of the bitmapped images that will be displayed on the buttons. The default dimensions are 16 pixels in width by 15 pixels in height.

Syntax public, BOOL SetBitmapSize(CSize size);

Parameters

size The dimensions, in pixels, of the bitmaps.

Returns TRUE if successful; otherwise FALSE.

See Also CToolBarCtrl::SetButtonSize()

SetButtonSize ■ 3.0

Description This function is called before buttons are added, to set the dimensions of the buttons. The default dimensions are 24 pixels in width by 22 pixels in height.

Syntax public, BOOL SetButtonSize(CSize size);

Parameters

size The dimensions, in pixels, of the buttons to be added.

Returns TRUE if successful; otherwise FALSE.

See Also CToolBarCtrl::SetBitmapSize()

SetButtonStructSize ■ 3.0

Description This function allows the programmer to store extra information on a per button basis within the control. This is done by using this function to set the size of the button structure. The programmer can derive a class from TBBUTTON, or include TBBUTTON as the first member in a user-defined structure.

Syntax public, void SetButtonStructSize(int nSize);

Parameters

nSize The size in bytes of the new structure.

Returns Nothing is returned.

SetCmdID ■ 3.0

Description This function will set the command ID that will be sent to the owner window when a particular button is pressed.

Syntax public, BOOL SetCmdID(int nIndex, UINT nID);

Parameters

nIndex Index of the button whose command ID is to be set.

nID The command ID.

Returns TRUE if successful; FALSE otherwise.

SetOwner ■ 3.0

Description This function sets the window that will receive notification messages from the control.

Syntax public, void SetOwner(CWnd* pWnd);

Parameters

pWnd A pointer to the window that will receive toolbar notification messages.

Returns Nothing is returned.

SetRows ■ 3.0

Description This function will set the number of rows of buttons in the toolbar. It is only valid for toolbars with the TBSTYLE_WRAPABLE style.

Syntax public, void SetRows(int nRows, BOOL bLarger, LPRECT lpRect);

Parameters

nRows The requested number of rows.

bLarger If *nRows* cannot be obtained, then if this parameter is TRUE more rows are used; if FALSE then fewer rows are used.

lpRect Address of the RECT structure that will receive the new bounding rectangle of the toolbar.

Returns Nothing is returned.

See Also CToolBarCtrl::GetRows()

SetState ■ 3.0

Description This function sets the state of a button on the toolbar.

Syntax public, BOOL SetState(int nID, UINT nState);

Parameters

nID The command ID of the button whose state is to be set.

nState	State flags specifying the new state of the button. This value can be a combination of the following:
TBSTATE_CHECKED	The button will be checked (for buttons with the TBSTYLE_CHECK style).
TBSTATE_ENABLED	The button is enabled for user input.
TBSTATE_HIDDEN	The button is hidden and not displayed.
TBSTATE_INDETERMINATE	The button is in the indeterminate grayed state.
TBSTATE_PRESSED	The button is pressed.
TBSTATE_WRAP	When used in conjunction with the TBSTATE_ENABLED state, a separator is inserted after the button.
Returns	TRUE if successful; otherwise FALSE.
See Also	CToolBarCtrl::GetState()

SetToolTips

■ 3.0

Description	This function will asssociate a tooltip control with the toolbar control.
Syntax	public, void SetToolTips(CToolTipCtrl* pWndTip);
Parameters	
pWndTip	The new tooltip control.
Returns	Nothing is returned.
See Also	CToolBarCtrl::GetToolTips()

CToolTipCtrl

The CToolTipCtrl object is used to display help text when the mouse moves over an area within a window. This area is usually another control, like a CToolBarCtrl or a CTabCtrl.

CToolTipCtrl

■ 3.0

Description	This is the constructor for the tooltip control. The real initialization of this object is done in the Create member function.
Syntax	public, CToolTipCtrl();
Parameters	None.
Returns	Nothing is returned.
See Also	CToolTipCtrl::Create(), ~ CToolTipCtrl()

~CToolTipCtrl

■ 3.0 ■ UD

Description	Destroys the tooltip control.
Syntax	public, virtual ~CToolTipCtrl();

Parameters None.

Returns Nothing is returned.

See Also CToolTipCtrl()

ACTIVATE ■ 3.0

Description This function will enable or disable a tooltip's automatic display.

Syntax public, void Activate(BOOL bActivate);

Parameters

bActivate If TRUE, then the tooltips will be displayed when invoked. A value of FALSE will not display the tooltips when invoked.

Returns Nothing is returned.

ADDTOOL ■ 3.0

Description This function will add a new tooltip to the control.

Syntax public, BOOL AddTool(CWnd* pWnd, UINT nIDText, LPCRECT lpRectTool = NULL, UINT nIDTool = 0);
public, BOOL AddTool(CWnd* pWnd, LPCTSTR lpszText = LPSTR_TEXTCALLBACK, LPCRECT lpRectTool = NULL, UINT nIDTool = 0);

Parameters

pWnd The window that will contain the new tool.

nIDText The resource ID of the text string used.

lpRectTool A pointer to a RECT structure specifying the tool's bounding rectangle in *pWnd* client coordinates.

nIDTool The ID of the new tool.

lpszText The tooltip text, or LPSTR_TEXTCALLBACK to post notification messages to the *pWnd* window when the text is needed.

Returns TRUE if successful; otherwise FALSE.

See Also CToolTipCtrl::DelTool()

CREATE ■ 3.0

Description After construction, call this member to create the tooltip control and attach it to this object.

Syntax public, BOOL Create(CWnd* pParentWnd, DWORD dwStyle = 0);

Parameters

pParentWnd A pointer to the parent of the control.

dwStyle The window style attributes.

Returns TRUE if successful; otherwise FALSE.

DelTool

■ 3.0

Description This function will remove the specified tooltip.

Syntax public, void DelTool(CWnd* pWnd, UINT nIDTool = 0);

Parameters

pWnd The window that contains the tooltip.

nIDTool The ID of the tooltip.

Returns Nothing is returned.

See Also CToolTipCtrl::AddTool()

FillInToolInfo

■ 3.0 ■ UD

Description This function will fill a TOOLINFO structure with the proper values based on the tool ID. If *nIDTool* is 0, then the **uId** member of the structure uses the window handle of *pWnd* to keep track of the tool (and the **hWnd** member contains the parent of *pWnd*, and the TTF_IDISHWND flag is set to indicate this condition).

Syntax public, void FillInToolInfo(TOOLINFO& ti, CWnd* pWnd, UINT nIDTool) const;

Parameters

ti A reference to the TOOLINFO structure that is to be filled in.

pWnd The window that contains the tool.

nIDTool The ID of the tool.

Returns Nothing is returned.

GetText

■ 3.0

Description This function will retrieve the tooltip text from the specified window.

Syntax public, void GetText(CString& str, CWnd* pWnd, UINT nIDTool = 0);

Parameters

str This string will receive the retrieved text.

pWnd A pointer to the window that contains the tooltip.

nIDTool The tool ID.

Returns Nothing is returned.

GetToolCount

■ 3.0

Description This function retrieves the number of tooltips contained in the control.

Syntax public, int GetToolCount() const;

Parameters None.

Returns The number of tooltips in the control.

GetToolInfo ■ 3.0

Description This function is used to retrieve the characteristics of a specific tooltip.

Syntax public, BOOL GetToolInfo(CToolInfo& ToolInfo, CWnd* pWnd, UINT nIDTool = 0) const;

Parameters

ToolInfo A CToolInfo reference that will receive the tool's attributes.

pWnd A pointer to the window that contains the tooltip.

nIDTool The tool ID.

Returns TRUE if successful; otherwise FALSE.

See Also CToolTipCtrl::GetText()

HitTest ■ 3.0

Description This function determines which item in the control is at a certain position.

Syntax public, BOOL HitTest(CWnd* pWnd, CPoint pt, LPTOOLINFO lpToolInfo) const;

Parameters

pWnd The window that contains the tool.

pt The screen coordinate of the position to be tested.

lpToolInfo A pointer to a TOOLINFO structure that will receive information on the tool that was hit.

Returns TRUE if a valid tool was found to contain the point; otherwise FALSE.

OnAddTool ■ 3.0 ■ UD

Description This member is called by the framework whenever a tool is registered with the control.

Syntax public, afx_msg LRESULT OnAddTool(WPARAM wParam, LPARAM lParam);

Parameters

wParam Should always be set to zero.

lParam Contains a pointer to a TOOLINFO structure.

Returns An LRESULT indicating TRUE if successful; otherwise FALSE.

OnDisableModal ■ 3.0 ■ UD

Description This member is called by the framework to disable the tooltip control.

Syntax public, afx_msg LRESULT OnDisableModal(WPARAM, LPARAM);

Parameters

WPARAM Unused.

LPARAM Unused.

Returns Always returns FALSE.

OnWindowFromPoint ■ 3.0 ■ UD

Description This member is called to retrieve the window handle from a screen coordinate. This member is supplied so that the tooltips will work properly with combo boxes.

Syntax public, afx_msg LRESULT OnWindowFromPoint(WPARAM, LPARAM lParam);

Parameters

lParam Contains a pointer to a POINT structure indicating the position.

Returns An LRESULT indicating the HWND handle is successful; otherwise 0.

RelayEvent ■ 3.0

Description This function passes a mouse event to the tooltip control. This function should be called within the application whenever a mouse message is encountered to ensure proper display of the tooltips.

Syntax public, void RelayEvent(LPMSG lpMsg);

Parameters

lpMsg A pointer to the MSG structure for the particular mouse message.

Returns Nothing is returned.

SetDelayTime ■ 3.0

Description This function will set the delay time that the cursor must remain within a tool's boundary before the tip is displayed.

Syntax public, void SetDelayTime(UINT nDelay);

Parameters

nDelay The new delay time (in milliseconds).

Returns Nothing is returned.

SetToolInfo ■ 3.0

Description This function is used to set characteristics of a specific tooltip.

Syntax public, void SetToolInfo(LPTOOLINFO lpToolInfo);

Parameters

lpToolInfo A pointer to a TOOLINFO structure that contains the new attributes.

Returns Nothing is returned.

See Also CToolTipCtrl::GetToolInfo()

SetToolRect ■ 3.0

Description Sets the bounding rectangle for a tool.

Syntax public, void SetToolRect(CWnd* pWnd, UINT nIDTool, LPCRECT lpRect);

Parameters

pWnd A pointer to the window that contains the tool.

nIDTool The ID of the tool.

lpRect The new bounding rectangle for the tool.

Returns Nothing is returned.

UpdateTipText ■ 3.0

Description This function will change the text of a tooltip.

Syntax public, void UpdateTipText(LPCTSTR lpszText, CWnd* pWnd, UINT nIDTool = 0);
public, void UpdateTipText(UINT nIDText, CWnd* pWnd, UINT nIDTool = 0);

Parameters

lpszText A pointer to a new NULL-terminated text string for the tip.

pWnd A pointer to the window that contains the tool.

nIDTool The ID of the tool.

nIDText The string resource ID of the new text for the tip.

Returns Nothing is returned.

CTreeCtrl

The CTreeCtrl is used to display hierarchical data. For example, directories that contain files can be displayed as parent items and their children. The parent items can be expanded or collapsed to show or hide their children.

Included on the CD-ROM companion disk is a sample program that illustrates how to use the tree control. The example shows how to derive your own tree control from the MFC CTreeCtrl, and override its default behavior. The particular coding example shows how to encapsulate the tree items into node objects, which is a convenient metaphor when using an expandable tree. Please refer to the TreeNode directory on the companion disk for examples from this section.

CTreeCtrl ■ 3.0

Description	This is the constructor for the tree control. The real initialization of this object is done in the Create member function.
Syntax	public, CTreeCtrl();
Parameters	None.
Returns	Nothing is returned.
See Also	CTreeCtrl::Create()

~CTreeCtrl ■ 3.0 ■ UD

Description	Destroys the tree control object.
Syntax	public, virtual ~CTreeCtrl();
Parameters	None.
Returns	Nothing is returned.
See Also	CTreeCtrl()

Create ■ 3.0

Description	After construction, call this member to create the tree control and attach it to this object.
Syntax	public, BOOL Create(DWORD dwStyle, const RECT & rect, Cwnd * pParentWnd, UINT nID);
Parameters	
dwStyle	A combination of valid window or tree control styles. The allowable styles can be found in the Windows API documentation.
rect	Indicates the control's position and size in terms of its parent's client coordinates.
pParentWnd	Parent window of control.
nID	The child ID of this control. Must be unique among its siblings.
Returns	Nothing is returned.
See Also	CTreeCtrl:: CTreeCtrl()

CreateDragImage

■ 3.0

Description This function will create a drag image for a specific tree item.

Syntax public, CImageList* CreateDragImage(HTREEITEM hItem);

Parameters

hItem Item whose image is to be created.

Returns If successful, a new image list containing the drag image; otherwise NULL.

DeleteAllItems

■ 3.0

Description This function removes all items from the control.

Syntax public, BOOL DeleteAllItems();

Parameters None.

Returns TRUE if successful; otherwise FALSE.

See Also CTreeCtrl::DeleteItem()

DeleteItem

■ 3.0

Description This function removes a tree item from the control.

Syntax public, BOOL DeleteItem(HTREEITEM hItem);

Parameters

hItem The item to remove from the control.

Returns TRUE if successful; otherwise FALSE.

See Also CTreeCtrl::DeleteAllItems()

EditLabel

■ 3.0

Description This function will initiate in-place editing of the specified item label.

Syntax public, CEdit* EditLabel(HTREEITEM hItem);

Parameters

hItem The item whose label is to be edited.

Returns If successful, a pointer to the edit control used to edit the label; otherwise NULL.

See Also CTreeCtrl::GetEditControl()

EnsureVisible

■ 3.0

Description This function will scroll the view if necessary to make the given item visible within the control.

Syntax public, BOOL EnsureVisible(HTREEITEM hItem);

Parameters

hItem The item to make visible.

Returns TRUE if successful; otherwise FALSE.

See Also CTreeCtrl::GetFirstVisibleItem()

EXPAND ■ 3.0

Description This function will expand or collapse the specified item. This function will not affect items that have no children.

Syntax public, BOOL Expand(HTREEITEM hItem, UINT nCode);

Parameters

hItem The item to expand.

nCode The expansion code. It can be any one of the following:

TVE_COLLAPSE The item will collapse.

TVE_COLLAPSERESET The item will collapse and its children will be removed.

TVE_EXPAND The item will be expanded.

TVE_TOGGLE Will expand the item if it is currently collapsed, and collapse the item if it is currently expanded.

GETCHILDITEM ■ 3.0

Description This function retrieves the first child of the specified item.

Syntax public, HTREEITEM GetChildItem(HTREEITEM hItem) const;

Parameters

hItem Handle to the parent item.

Returns If successful, the HTREEITEM of the first child; otherwise NULL.

See Also CTreeCtrl::GetNextSiblingItem(), CTreeCtrl::GetNextItem()

GETCOUNT ■ 3.0

Description This function is used to retrieve the number of items in the tree control.

Syntax public, UINT GetCount() const;

Parameters None.

Returns The number of items in the control.

See Also CTreeCtrl::GetVisibleCount()

GETDROPHIGHLIGHTITEM ■ 3.0

Description This function will retrieve the current item that is the target of a drop operation.

Syntax	public, HTREEITEM GetDropHighlightItem() const;
Parameters	None.
Returns	If successful, the HTREEITEM of the drop target item; otherwise NULL.

GetEditControl ■ 3.0

Description	This function will return the edit control used to modify the item's label. This control will only be available when the user is editing a current label.
Syntax	public, CEdit* GetEditControl() const;
Parameters	None.
Returns	A pointer to the edit control.
See Also	CTreeCtrl::EditLabel()

GetFirstVisibleItem ■ 3.0

Description	This function will retrieve the first item that is visible in the tree control.
Syntax	public, HTREEITEM GetFirstVisibleItem() const;
Parameters	None.
Returns	If successful, the HTREEITEM of the first visible item; otherwise NULL.
See Also	CTreeCtrl::EnsureVisible()

GetImageList ■ 3.0

Description	This function retrieves one of the two image lists contained in the control. Images from the TVSIL_STATE list are used to display an item when it is selected, and images from the TVSIL_NORMAL list are used to display items that are not selected.
Syntax	public, CImageList* GetImageList(int nImageList) const;
Parameters	
nImageList	Specifies which list is to be retrieved. The value can be either of the following:
TVSIL_NORMAL	Image list that contains the unselected state images.
TVSIL_STATE	Image list that contains the selected state images.
Returns	The specified image list.
See Also	CTreeCtrl::SetImageList()

GetIndent ■ 3.0

Description	This function retrieves the number of pixels child items are indented from their parents.
Syntax	public, UINT GetIndent()const;

Parameters	None.
Returns	The indent width in pixels.
See Also	CTreeCtrl::SetIndent()

GetItem ■ 3.0

Description	This function will retrieve the settings for the specified item in the control.
Syntax	public, BOOL GetItem(TV_ITEM* pItem) const;
Parameters	
pItem	A pointer to a TV_ITEM structure that will receive the attributes of the specified item. Note that the **hItem** member of the structure contains the item to be retrieved. Also, only the values specified by the **mask** member will be retrieved.
Returns	TRUE if successful; otherwise FALSE.
See Also	CTreeCtrl::SetItem()

GetItemData ■ 3.0

Description	Retrieves the 32-bit programmer-defined data associated with the given item.
Syntax	public, DWORD GetItemData(HTREEITEM hItem) const;
Parameters	
hItem	Handle to the tree item whose value is to be retrieved.
Returns	32-bit programmer-defined data associated with the given item.

GetItemImage ■ 3.0

Description	Retrieves the image indices associated with the given item. Each item has two associated images: one to indicate the item is selected, and another to indicate the item is not selected. This member does not return the actual images; rather, it returns indices into the CTreeCtrl's image list.
Syntax	public, BOOL GetItemImage(HTREEITEM hItem, int& nImage, int& nSelectedImage) const;
Parameters	
hItem	Handle to the tree item whose image is to be retrieved.
nImage	A reference to an integer that will contain the index of the image indicating the item is not selected.
nSelectedImage	A reference to an integer that will contain the index of the image indicating the item is selected.
Returns	TRUE if successful; otherwise FALSE.

GetItemRect ■ 3.0

Description Retrieves the bounding rectangle of the given item, in relation to the upper-left corner of the CTreeCtrl window.

Syntax public, BOOL GetItemRect(HTREEITEM hItem, LPRECT lpRect, BOOL bTextOnly) const;

Parameters

hItem Handle to the tree item whose bounding rect is to be retrieved.

lpRect A pointer to a RECT structure that will receive the coordinates of the item's bounding rectangle. This structure is only filled if the given item is visible.

bTextOnly TRUE indicates that the requested bounding rectangle should be limited to the item text label only; otherwise FALSE indicates the entire item's bounding rectangle.

Returns TRUE if successful and the item was visible; otherwise FALSE.

GetItemState ■ 3.0

Description Retrieves the state of the given item.

Syntax public, UINT GetItemState(HTREEITEM hItem, UINT nStateMask) const;

Parameters

hItem Handle to the tree item whose state is to be retrieved.

nStateMask The state mask that indicates the state bits to be retrieved.

Returns A UINT containing the item state bits.

GetItemText ■ 3.0

Description Retrieves the text label of the given item.

Syntax public, CString GetItemText(HTREEITEM hItem) const;

Parameters

hItem Handle to the tree item whose text is to be retrieved.

Returns A CString object containing the desired item's text label.

GetNextItem ■ 3.0

Description This function will attempt to retrieve the next item in the control that matches the given relationship to the specified item.

Syntax public, HTREEITEM GetNextItem(HTREEITEM hItem, UINT nCode) const;

Parameters

hItem The handle of a tree item to start the search from.

nCode	The relationship between the item searched for and the one specified by *hItem*. This can by any one of the following values:
TVGN_CARET	The currently selected item (*hItem* is ignored).
TVGN_CHILD	The first child of root of the tree (*hItem* is ignored).
TVGN_DROPHILITE	The drag drop target item (*hItem* is ignored).
TVGN_FIRSTVISIBLE	The first item that is visible in the control (*hItem* is ignored).
TVGN_NEXT	The next sibling of *hItem*.
TVGN_NEXTVISIBLE	The next item (after *hItem)* that is visible.
TVGN_PARENT	The parent of *hItem*.
TVGN_PREVIOUS	The previous sibling of *hItem*.
TVGN_PREVIOUSVISIBLE	The previous item (before *hItem)* that is visible.
TVGN_ROOT	The first child of the root that contains *hItem*.
Returns	If successful, the HTREEITEM identifying the specified item; otherwise NULL.
See Also	CTreeCtrl::GetChildItem()

GetNextSiblingItem ■ 3.0

Description This function will retrieve the next item that has the same parent as the specified item.

Syntax public, HTREEITEM GetNextSiblingItem(HTREEITEM hItem) const;

Parameters

hItem Handle to the current sibling item.

Returns If successful, the HTREEITEM of the next sibling item; otherwise NULL.

See Also CTreeCtrl::GetNextItem()

GetNextVisibleItem ■ 3.0

Description This function will retrieve the next item that is visible in the tree control.

Syntax public, HTREEITEM GetNextVisibleItem(HTREEITEM hItem) const;

Parameters

hItem Handle to the current visible item.

Returns If successful, the HTREEITEM of the next visible item; otherwise NULL.

See Also CTreeCtrl::GetFirstVisibleItem(), CTreeCtrl::EnsureVisible()

GetParentItem ■ 3.0

Description This function will retrieve the parent of the specified item.

Syntax public, HTREEITEM GetParentItem(HTREEITEM hItem) const;

Parameters

hItem Handle to the current child item.

Returns If successful, the HTREEITEM of the parent item; otherwise NULL.

GetPrevSiblingItem ■ 3.0

Description This function will retrieve the previous item that has the same parent as the specified item.

Syntax public, HTREEITEM GetPrevSiblingItem(HTREEITEM hItem) const;

Parameters

hItem Handle to the current sibling item.

Returns If successful, the HTREEITEM of the previous sibling item; otherwise NULL.

See Also CTreeCtrl::GetNextItem()

GetPrevVisibleItem ■ 3.0

Description This function will retrieve the previous item that is visible in the tree control.

Syntax public, HTREEITEM GetPrevVisibleItem(HTREEITEM hItem) const;

Parameters

hItem Handle to the current visible item.

Returns If successful, the HTREEITEM of the previous visible item; otherwise NULL.

See Also CTreeCtrl::GetFirstVisibleItem(), CTreeCtrl::EnsureVisible()

GetRootItem ■ 3.0

Description This function will retrieve the tree control's first root item.

Syntax public, HTREEITEM GetRootItem() const;

Parameters None.

Returns If successful, the HTREEITEM of the first root item; otherwise NULL.

GetSelectedItem ■ 3.0

Description This function will retrieve the currently selected item in the control.

Syntax public, HTREEITEM GetSelectedItem() const;

Parameters None.

Returns If successful, the HTREEITEM of the currently selected item; otherwise NULL.

GetVisibleCount ■ 3.0

Description This function returns the number of items that are currently visible within the control window.

Syntax public, UINT GetVisibleCount() const;

Parameters None.

Returns The number of items currently visible.

See Also CTreeCtrl::GetCount()

HitTest ■ 3.0

Description This function will retrieve the item that meets the given location criteria.

Syntax public, HTREEITEM HitTest(CPoint pt, UINT* pFlags = NULL) const;
public, HTREEITEM HitTest(TV_HITTESTINFO* pHitTestInfo) const;

Parameters

pt The hit point (usually a mouse click), in client coordinates.

pFlags The address of an integer that will receive the results of the hit test. This value can be any one of the following:

TVHT_ABOVE The given point was above the client area.

TVHT_BELOW The given point was below the client area.

TVHT_NOWHERE The given point was in the client area but past the last item in the list.

TVHT_ONITEM The given point was on the bitmap or label of an item.

TVHT_ONITEMBUTTON The given point was on the button of an item.

TVHT_ONITEMICON The given point was on the bitmap of an item.

TVHT_ONITEMINDENT The given point was in the indented area of an item.

TVHT_ONITEMLABEL The given point was on the label of an item.

TVHT_ONITEMRIGHT The given point was in the area to the right of an item (past the label).

TVHT_ONITEMSTATEICON The given point was on the state icon (for user-defined states).

TVHT_TOLEFT The given point was to the right of the client area.

TVHT_TORIGHT The given point was to the left of the client area.

pHitTestInfo A pointer to a TV_HITTESTINFO that specifies the point of the hit test, and receives flags specifying the results of the hit test.

Returns If successful, then the HTREEITEM of the item occupied by the given position; otherwise NULL.

InsertItem ■ 3.0

Description This function inserts a new tree item into the control.

Syntax
public, HTREEITEM InsertItem(LPTV_INSERTSTRUCT lpInsertStruct);
public, HTREEITEM InsertItem(UINT nMask, LPCTSTR lpszItem, int nImage, int nSelectedImage, UINT nState, UINT nStateMask, LPARAM lParam, HTREEITEM hParent, HTREEITEM hInsertAfter);
public, HTREEITEM InsertItem(LPCTSTR lpszItem, HTREEITEM hParent = TVI_ROOT, HTREEITEM hInsertAfter = TVI_LAST);
public, HTREEITEM InsertItem(LPCTSTR lpszItem, int nImage, int nSelectedImage, HTREEITEM hParent = TVI_ROOT, HTREEITEM hInsertAfter = TVI_LAST);

Parameters

lpInsertStruct A pointer to a TV_INSERTSTRUCT that contains the attributes of the new item. Note that the **hInsertAfter** and **hParent** members specify the location of the inserted item.

nMask Mask flag that indicates which attributes are to be set.

lpszItem A string containing the item's label text.

nImage Index indicating which image is to be used for displaying the item when it is not selected. This is an index into the CTreeCtrl's image list.

nSelectedImage Index indicating which image is to be used for displaying the item when it is selected. This is an index into the CTreeCtrl's image list.

nState The item state flags.

nStateMask Mask flag indicating which of the *nState* bits are to be set.

lParam 32-bit programmer supplied data that is to be associated with this item.

hParent A handle to a parent item (which would make this item the child item), or NULL for no parent.

hInsertAfter A handle to the tree item after which this item will be placed.

Returns If successful, the HTREEITEM of the newly inserted item; otherwise NULL.

See Also CTreeCtrl::DeleteItem()

OnDestroy ■ 3.0

Description The default implementation of this member function is used to remove any current image lists from the control.

Syntax public, afx_msg void OnDestroy();

Parameters None.

Returns Nothing is returned.

See Also CTreeCtrl::RemoveImageList()

RemoveImageList ■ 3.0, UD

Description This protected member function will release either of the two image lists used by the control.

Syntax protected, void RemoveImageList(int nImageList);

Parameters

nImageList Specifies which list is to be removed. The value can be either of the following:

TVSIL_NORMAL Image list that contains the unselected state images.

TVSIL_STATE Image list that contains the selected state images.

Returns Nothing is returned.

See Also CTreeCtrl::OnDestroy()

SELECT ■ 3.0

Description This function will select the given item as the current focus item, the target of a drop operation, or as the first visible item in the control.

Syntax public, HTREEITEM Select(HTREEITEM hItem, UINT nCode);

Parameters

hItem The item to select.

nCode The method by which to select the item. It can be any one of the following:

TVGN_CARET The item will have the current input focus.

TVGN_DROPHILITE The item will be selected as the target of a drop operation.

TVGN_FIRSTVISIBLE The item will be made the first visible item, and selected as the current input focus.

Returns Non-zero if successful; otherwise 0.

See Also CTreeCtrl::SelectItem(),CTreeCtrl::SelectDropTarget()

SELECTDROPTARGET ■ 3.0

Description This function will select the given item as the target of a drop operation.

Syntax public, HTREEITEM SelectDropTarget(HTREEITEM hItem);

Parameters

hItem The item to select as the drop target.

Returns Non-zero if successful; otherwise 0.

See Also CTreeCtrl::Select()

SELECTITEM ■ 3.0

Description This function will select the given item in the control.

Syntax public, HTREEITEM SelectItem(HTREEITEM hItem);

Parameters

hItem The item to select.

Returns Non-zero if successful; otherwise 0.

See Also CTreeCtrl::Select()

SetImageList ■ 3.0

Description This function sets one of the two image lists contained in the control. Images from the TVSIL_STATE list are used to display an item when it is selected, and images from the TVSIL_NORMAL list are used to display items that are not selected.

Syntax public, CImageList* SetImageList(CImageList* pImageList, int nImageList);

Parameters

pImageList The new image list.

nImageList Specifies which list is to be set. The value can be one of the following:

TVSIL_NORMAL Image list that contains the unselected state images.

TVSIL_STATE Image list that contains the selected state images.

Returns The previously set image list (if any).

See Also CTreeCtrl::GetImageList()

SetIndent ■ 3.0

Description This function sets the number of pixels that child items are indented from their parents.

Syntax public, BOOL SetIndent(UINT nIndent);

Parameters

nIndent The indent width in pixels.

Returns TRUE if successful; otherwise FALSE.

See Also CTreeCtrl::GetIndent()

SetItem ■ 3.0

Description This function will modify the settings of the specified item in the control.

Syntax public, BOOL SetItem(TV_ITEM* pItem);
public, BOOL SetItem(HTREEITEM hItem, UINT nMask, LPCTSTR lpszItem, int nImage, int nSelectedImage, UINT nState, UINT nStateMask, LPARAM lParam);

Parameters

pItem A pointer to a TV_ITEM structure that contains the new attributes of the specified item. Note that the **hItem** member of the structure contains the item to be modified. Also, only the values specified by the **mask** member will be modified.

hItem A handle to the item whose attributes are to be set.
nMask Mask flag that indicates which attributes are to be set.
lpszItem A string containing the item's label text.
nImage Index indicating which image is to be used for displaying the item when it is not selected. This is an index into the CTreeCtrl's image list.
nSelectedImage Index indicating which image is to be used for displaying the item when it is selected. This is an index into the CTreeCtrl's image list.
nState The item state flags.
nStateMask Mask flag indicating which of the *nState* bits are to be set.
lParam 32-bit programmer supplied data that is to be associated with this item.
Returns TRUE if successful; otherwise FALSE.
See Also CTreeCtrl::GetItem()

SetItemData ■ 3.0

Description Sets the 32-bit programmer-defined data that is to be associated with the given item.
Syntax public, BOOL SetItemData(HTREEITEM hItem, DWORD dwData);
Parameters
hItem Handle to the tree item whose data value is to be set.
dwData 32-bit programmer-defined data value.
Returns TRUE if successful; otherwise FALSE.

SetItemImage ■ 3.0

Description Sets the image indices associated with the given item. Each item has two associated images: one to indicate the item is selected, and another to indicate the item is not selected. The indices refer to the images contained in the CTreeCtrl's image list.
Syntax public, BOOL SetItemImage(HTREEITEM hItem, int nImage, int nSelectedImage);
Parameters
hItem Handle to the tree item whose image is to be set.
nImage Index of the image indicating the item is not selected.
nSelectedImage Index of the image indicating the item is selected.
Returns TRUE if successful; otherwise FALSE.

SetItemState ■ 3.0

Description Sets the state of the given item.

Syntax public, BOOL SetItemState(HTREEITEM hItem, UINT nState, UINT nStateMask);

Parameters

hItem Handle to the tree item whose state is to be set.

nState The new state flags.

nStateMask The state mask that indicates which of the bits in *nState* are to be set.

Returns TRUE if successful; otherwise FALSE.

SetItemText ■ 3.0

Description Sets the text label of the given item.

Syntax public, BOOL SetItemText(HTREEITEM hItem, LPCTSTR lpszItem);

Parameters

hItem Handle to the tree item whose text is to be set.

lpszItem A string containing the new label text for the given item.

Returns TRUE if successful; otherwise FALSE.

SortChildren ■ 3.0

Description This function will initiate item sorting of the children of the given tree item. The sort is based upon the item label text.

Syntax public, BOOL SortChildren(HTREEITEM hItem);

Parameters

hItem The parent item whose children are to be sorted.

Returns TRUE if successful; otherwise FALSE.

See Also CTreeCtrl::SortChildrenCB()

SortChildrenCB ■ 3.0

Description This function will initiate a user-supplied sorting function.

Syntax public, BOOL SortChildrenCB(LPTV_SORTCB pSort);

Parameters

pSort A pointer to a TV_SORTCB structure.

```
typedef struct _TV_SORTCB { tvscb
     HTREEITEM    hParent;        // handle of parent item
     PFNTVCOMPARE lpfnCompare;
     LPARAM       lParam;         // application-defined 32-bit value
} TV_SORTCB;
```

Returns TRUE if successful; otherwise FALSE.

See Also CTreeCtrl::SortChildren()

10

MENUS AND CONTROL BARS

10

MENUS AND CONTROL BARS

Despite the large number of helper classes and functions in MFC—the collection classes and debugging macros for example—the primary focus of the Microsoft engineers has always been making it easier for programmers to develop user-friendly Windows interfaces for their applications. The greatest effort has been made in presenting a clean, object-oriented abstraction of the Windows API and in hiding from the programmer some of the more obscure, clumsy aspects of writing Windows programs the old-fashioned way. The majority of interface classes in MFC, falling into this abstraction category, address these objectives.

There is another category of classes, however, that is concerned with what the user sees rather than with what the programmer does. The goal of this group of classes is to provide implementations of the latest, cutting-edge interface elements, like the Windows 95 common controls discussed in Chapter 9, *Windows Controls,* or the property pages and sheets discussed in Chapter 8, *Dialog Boxes*. In this chapter, we will be discussing the CMenu class, a member of the abstraction group of interface classes, and the CControlBar-related classes, members of this second group. The list of classes covered in this chapter is summarized in Table 10-1 below:

Table 10-1 Chapter 10 class summary

Class Name	Description
CMenu	Wrapper class for a menu.
CControlBar	Base class for dockable user interface window objects.
CStatusBar	MFC status bar class, uses underlying common control.
CToolBar	MFC toolbar class, uses underlying common control.
CDialogBar	Modeless dialog control bar.

About the Program

On the companion CD-ROM is a sample application that covers usage examples of the menu and control bar classes discussed in this chapter. The purpose of this program is to show how these interface classes are typically incorporated in an MFC program rather than to show the full breadth of capability of their functionality.

The CMenu Class

The CMenu class is possibly one of the classes used least frequently by MFC programmers. This is because the MFC framework, specifically the CCmdUI command interface updating and the CDocument/CView architecture, encapsulates so much of the Windows menu functionality that the programmer rarely needs to use a CMenu class directly. In its menu implementation, however, MFC uses the CMenu class liberally, so an understanding of it is valuable. The Enable and SetText members of the CCmdUI class actually call CMenu members when the interface object is a menu. Furthermore, code within the CDocument class ensures that when a document is loaded, the menu resource for the document is loaded from the resource file. Whenever a view is activated, the application's menu bar is set to this menu. In making this functionality happen, MFC calls many of the CMenu class members. Although MFC, in general, takes care of creating and destroying menus, of enabling and disabling menu items, the programmer can also perform these tasks through the members of the CMenu class. One general note, however: Whenever you call a CMenu member that affects the appearance of the menu of a window, you should call the DrawMenuBar member of the appropriate CWnd object to tell Windows to redraw the menu bar so that the changes may be seen.

The one case in which the CMenu class is typically used directly by the programmer is in the implementation of popup menus. This is a fairly straightforward process. The programmer needs to instantiate a CMenu object, call the CreatePopupMenu member to create the popup menu, add menu items to the menu, using AppendMenu or a similar member, and then finally call TrackPopupMenu to execute the popup menu. The destructor of the CMenu class will automatically destroy the menu.

CMenu Class Reference

CMenu ■ 2.0 ■ 3.0

Description Constructor for the CMenu object, initializes the m_hMenu member that stores the handle to the menu.

Syntax public, CMenu();

Parameters None.

Returns Nothing is returned.

See Also CMenu::~CMenu

Example

```
CMenu* pMenu;

pMenu = new CMenu(); // create menu, call constructor

// do something with menu

delete pMenu; // delete menu, call destructor
```

~CMenu

■ 2.0 ■ 3.0 ■ UD

Description Destructor for the CMenu object, destroys the menu if necessary.

Syntax public, virtual ~CMenu();

Parameters None.

Returns Nothing is returned.

See Also CMenu::CMenu

Example See CMenu::CMenu

AppendMenu

■ 2.0 ■ 3.0

Description Appends a menu item or popup menu to the menu. This member wraps the ::AppendMenu Windows SDK function. The version which takes a bitmap appends MF_BITMAP to the flags and passes the bitmap handle as the menu item. If there is an owning window, CWnd::DrawMenuBar should be called to update the appearance of the menu. See the Windows SDK documentation for more information about ::AppendMenu.

Syntax public, BOOL AppendMenu(UINT nFlags, UINT nIDNewItem = 0,LPCT-STR lpszNewItem = NULL); BOOL AppendMenu(UINT nFlags, UINT nIDNewItem, const CBitmap* pBmp);

Parameters

nFlags Flags for new menu item or popup menu; see the Windows SDK documentation for details.

nIDNewItem Command ID for new menu item or popup menu handle, if the MF_POPUP flag is used; see the Windows SDK documentation for details.

lpszNewItem Text of the menu item when using the MF_STRING flag, handle to bitmap when using the MF_BITMAP flag; see the Windows SDK documentation for details.

pBmp Pointer to CBitmap object to use for the menu item.

Returns TRUE if successful; FALSE otherwise.

See Also CMenu::DeleteMenu, CMenu::RemoveMenu, CMenu::InsertMenu

Example

```
void CMyWnd::OnRButtonDown(UINT nFlags, CPoint point)
{
	CMenu menu;

	menu.CreatePopupMenu();
	menu.AppendMenu(MF_STRING,ID_POPUP_COPY, &Copy );
	menu.AppendMenu(MF_STRING,ID_POPUP_PASTE, &Paste );
	menu.InsertMenu(0,MF_STRING,ID_POPUP_CUT, Cu&t );

	menu.TrackMenuPopup(TPM_CENTERALIGN,point.x,point.y,this);
}
```

AssertValid

■ 2.0 ■ 3.0 ■ DO

Description Validation function for CMenu object. Ensures that the m_hMenu member is not NULL and that it is actually a handle to a menu. For more information about diagnostics, see Chapter 15, *Debugging and Exception Handling*.

Syntax public, virtual void AssertValid() const;

Parameters None.

Returns Nothing is returned.

See Also CMenu::Dump

Example See CMenu::CreateMenu

Attach

■ 2.0 ■ 3.0

Description Sets the m_hMenu member and adds the menu handle to MFC's permanent map. Attach is used to associate an already-existing HMENU handle to a CMenu object. This member can be used to encapsulate an HMENU handle that has been created outside of MFC in a CMenu object.

Syntax public, BOOL Attach(HMENU hMenu);

Parameters

hMenu Handle to menu.

Returns TRUE if successful; FALSE otherwise.

See Also CMenu::Detach

Example

```
CMenu* CMyApp::CreateMenu(HMENU hMenu)
{
	CMenu* pMenu = new CMenu();

	if ( !pMenu->Attach(hMenu) )
	{
		delete pMenu;
		pMenu = NULL;
	}

	return pMenu;
}
```

CheckMenuItem

■ 2.0 ■ 3.0

Description Puts a check mark next to a menu item. This member wraps the ::CheckMenuItem Windows SDK function. See the Windows SDK documentation for more information.

Syntax public, UINT CheckMenuItem(UINT nIDCheckItem, UINT nCheck);

Parameters

nIDCheckItem The menu item to be checked or unchecked—either the command ID for the menu or the zero-based position of the menu item, depending upon the value of *nCheck*.

nCheck Indicates whether to check or uncheck the menu item (MF_CHECKED or MF_UNCHECKED) and how the menu item is specified (MF_BYCOMMAND or MF_BYPOSITION).

Returns The previous check status, MF_CHECKED or MF_UNCHECKED, or -1 if the menu item does not exist.

See Also CMenu::CheckMenuRadioItem

Example

```
// check menu item
menu.CheckMenuItem(ID_MYCOMMAND,MF_BYCOMMAND | MF_CHECKED);

// uncheck menu item (ID_MYCOMMAND is first menu item in the menu)
menu.CheckMenuItem(0,MF_BYPOSITION | MF_UNCHECKED);
```

CheckMenuRadioItem

■ 2.0 ■ 3.0 ■ NM

Description Checks a menu item, using a bullet bitmap instead of a check bitmap, and unchecks all other items in the range. This creates radio button type behavior. This member wraps the ::CheckMenuRadioItem Windows SDK function. See the Windows SDK documentation for more information.

Syntax public, BOOL CheckMenuRadioItem(UINT nIDFirst, UINT nIDLast, UINT nIDItem, UINT nFlags);

Parameters

nIDFirst First menu item in the range, either the command ID for the menu or the position of the menu item, depending upon the value of *nFlags*.

nIDLast Last menu item in the range, either the command ID for the menu or the position of the menu item, depending upon the value of *nFlags*.

nIDItem Menu item to check, either the command ID for the menu or the position of the menu item, depending upon the value of *nFlags*.

nFlags MF_BYCOMMAND or MF_BYPOSITION, indicating how the menu items are specified.

Returns TRUE if successful; FALSE otherwise.

See Also CMenu::CheckMenuItem

Example

```
menu.CheckMenuRadioItem(0,4,2,MF_BYPOSITION);
```

CreateMenu ■ 2.0 ■ 3.0

Description Creates a menu and attaches the menu handle to the CMenu object. This member wraps the ::CreateMenu Windows SDK function. See the Windows SDK documentation for more information.

Syntax public, BOOL CreateMenu();

Parameters None.

Returns TRUE if successful; FALSE otherwise.

See Also CMenu::CreatePopupMenu, CMenu::DestroyMenu

Example

```
CMenu menu;

menu.CreateMenu();
menu.AssertValid(); // ASSERT if menu creation failed
```

CreatePopupMenu ■ 2.0 ■ 3.0

Description Creates a popup menu and attaches the menu handle to the CMenu object. This member wraps the ::CreatePopupMenu Windows SDK function. See the Windows SDK documentation for more information.

Syntax public, BOOL CreatePopupMenu();

Parameters None.

Returns TRUE if successful; FALSE otherwise.

See Also CMenu::CreateMenu, CMenu::DestroyMenu

Example See CMenu::AppendMenu

DeleteMenu ■ 2.0 ■ 3.0

Description Deletes a menu item from the menu. If the specified item is a popup menu, it is destroyed. If there is an owning window, CWnd::DrawMenuBar should be called to update the appearance of the menu. This member wraps the ::DeleteMenu Windows SDK function. See the Windows SDK documentation for more information.

Syntax public, BOOL DeleteMenu(UINT nPosition, UINT nFlags);

Parameters

nPosition Zero-based index of menu item to delete; can be a popup menu.

nFlags MF_BYCOMMAND or MF_BYPOSITION, indicating how the menu item is specified.

Returns TRUE if successful; FALSE otherwise.

See Also CMenu::AppendMenu, CMenu::InsertMenu, CMenu::RemoveMenu

Example

```
BOOL DeleteLastMenu(CMenu* pMenu)
{
     UINT nLast;
     UINT nID;

     nLast = pMenu->GetMenuItemCount();
     nID = pMenu->GetMenuItemID(nLast);
     return pMenu->DeleteMenu(nID,MF_BYCOMMAND);
}
```

DeleteTempMap ■ 2.0 ■ 3.0

Description Deletes all temporary CMenu objects. This member is called during MFC's idle-processing to clean up on-the-fly CMenu objects created. DeleteTempMap rarely needs to be called by the programmer directly.

Syntax public, static void PASCAL DeleteTempMap();

Parameters None.

Returns Nothing is returned.

See Also CHandleMap class

DestroyMenu ■ 2.0 ■ 3.0

Description Detaches the menu handle from the CMenu object and destroys it. DestroyMenu is called by the destructor of the CMenu object. It does not need to be called by the programmer. This member wraps the ::DestroyMenu Windows SDK function. See the Windows SDK documentation for more information.

Syntax public, BOOL DestroyMenu();

Parameters None.

Returns TRUE if successful; FALSE otherwise.

See Also CMenu::CreateMenu, CMenu::CreatePopupMenu, CMenu::~CMenu

Detach ■ 2.0 ■ 3.0

Description Sets the m_hMenu to NULL and removes the menu handle from MFC's permanent map. Detach is called by DestroyMenu. The programmer should call this member to prevent the menu from being destroyed when the CMenu object is destroyed.

Syntax public, HMENU Detach();

Parameters None.

Returns The menu handle.

See Also CMenu::Attach

Example

```
HMENU CreateHMENU()
{
      CMenu menu;

      menu.CreateMenu(); // create HMENU and attach it to CMenu object

      // detach so that destructor will not destroy HMENU generated
      return menu.Detach();
}
```

DrawItem

■ 2.0 ■ 3.0

Description Draws an owner-draw menu item. This member should be overridden for owner-draw menus. The default does nothing. DrawItem is called by CWnd::OnDrawItem of the owning window.

Syntax public, virtual void DrawItem(LPDRAWITEMSTRUCT lpDrawItemStruct);

Parameters

lpDrawItemStruct Pointer to DRAWITEMSTRUCT structure; see the Windows SDK documentation for more information.

Returns Nothing is returned.

See Also CMenu::MeasureItem, CWnd::OnDrawItem

Example

```
void CMyMenu::DrawItem(LPDRAWITEMSTRUCT lpDrawItemStruct)
{
      CDC  dc;
      dc.Attach(lpDrawItemStruct->hDC);

      switch ( lpDrawItemStruct->itemID )
      {
            case ID_COMMAND1:
                  // draw command 1
                  break;
            case ID_COMMAND2:
                  // draw command 2
                  break;
            case ID_COMMAND3:
                  // draw command 3
                  break;
      }

      dc.Detach();
}
```

Dump

■ 2.0 ■ 3.0 ■ DO

Description Dumps the contents of the CMenu object. For more information about diagnostics, see Chapter 15, *Debugging and Exception Handling*.

Syntax public, virtual void Dump(CDumpContext& dc) const;

Parameters

dc Dump context.

Returns Nothing is returned.

See Also CMenu::AssertValid

Example

```
CMyWnd::Dump(CDumpContext& dc)
{
	CWnd::Dump(dc); // dump CWnd object

	m_Menu.Dump(dc); // dump CMenu data member
}
```

EnableMenuItem

■ 2.0 ■ 3.0

Description Enables or disables a menu item. This member wraps the ::EnableMenuItem Windows SDK function. See the Windows SDK documentation for more information.

Syntax public, UINT EnableMenuItem(UINT nIDEnableItem, UINT nEnable);

Parameters

nIDEnableItem The menu item to be enabled or disabled; either the command ID for the menu or the position of the menu item, depending upon the value of nEnable.

nEnable Indicates whether to enable or disable the menu item (MF_DISABLED, MF_ENABLED or MF_GRAYED) and how the menu item is specified (MF_BYCOMMAND or MF_BYPOSITION).

Returns The previous enable status, MF_DISABLED, MF_ENABLED, or MF_GRAYED, or -1 if the menu item does not exist.

See Also CMenu::CheckMenuItem, CMenu::CheckMenuRadioItem

Example

```
menu.EnableMenuItem(3,MF_ENABLED | MF_BYPOSITION);
```

FromHandle

■ 2.0 ■ 3.0

Description Returns a CMenu object associated with the menu handle. FromHandle will look in MFC's permanent map first, then the temporary map, then, if necessary, create a temporary CMenu object and add the menu handle to the temporary map. The temporary CMenu object is destroyed during idle processing.

Syntax public, static CMenu* PASCAL FromHandle(HMENU hMenu);

Parameters

hMenu Menu handle.

Returns Pointer to CMenu object, may be temporary.

See Also CMenu::FromHandlePermanent

Example

```
CMenu* CMyWnd::MyGetMenu(BOOL bPermanentOnly)
{
     HMENU hMenu;

     hMenu = ::GetMenu(m_hWnd); // get HMENU through SDK call
     if ( hMenu == NULL )
          AfxMessageBox("No menu for window!);

     if ( bPermanentOnly )
          return CMenu::FromHandlePermanent(hMenu);

     return CMenu::FromHandle(hMenu);
}
```

FromHandlePermanent ■ 2.0 ■ 3.0

Description Returns a CMenu object associated with the menu handle. FromHandlePermanent will only look in MFC's permanent map and will not create a temporary handle.

Syntax public, static CMenu* PASCAL CMenu::FromHandlePermanent(HMENU hMenu);

Parameters

hMenu Menu handle.

Returns Pointer to CMenu object.

See Also CMenu::FromHandle

Example See CMenu::FromHandle

GetMenuContextHelpId ■ 2.0 ■ 3.0 ■ NM

Description Gets the context help ID for the menu. This member wraps the ::GetMenuContextHelpId Windows SDK function. See the Windows SDK documentation for more information.

Syntax public, DWORD GetMenuContextHelpId() const;

Parameters None.

Returns Context help ID.

See Also CMenu::SetMenuContextHelpId

GetMenuItemCount ■ 2.0 ■ 3.0

Description Gets the number of items in the menu. This member wraps the ::GetMenuItemCount Windows SDK function. See the Windows SDK documentation for more information.

Syntax public, UINT GetMenuItemCount() const;

Parameters None.

Returns The number of menu items; -1 if there is an error.

Example See CMenu::DeleteMenu

GetMenuItemId

■ 2.0 ■ 3.0

Description Gets the command ID for the menu item, based on a zero-based position. This member wraps the ::GetMenuItemId Windows SDK function. See the Windows SDK documentation for more information.

Syntax public, UINT GetMenuItemID(int nPos) const;

Parameters

nPos Position of menu item.

Returns Command ID of the menu item, 0 if the item is a separator, -1 if the item is a popup menu.

Example See CMenu::DeleteMenu

GetMenuState

■ 2.0 ■ 3.0

Description Gets the state of the menu item. This member wraps the ::GetMenuState Windows SDK function. See the Windows SDK documentation for more information.

Syntax public, UINT GetMenuState(UINT nID, UINT nFlags) const;

Parameters

nID Menu item.

nFlags MF_BYCOMMAND or MF_BYPOSITION, indicating how the menu item is specified.

Returns State of the menu item; see the Windows SDK documentation for more information.

See Also CMenu::SetMenuState

Example

```
void ToggleMenuItems(CMenu* pMenu)
{
      UINT nCount = pMenu->GetMenuItemCount();
      UINT nI;

      for (nI = 0;nI < nCount;nI++)
      {
            if ( pMenu->GetMenuState(nI,MF_BYPOSITION) | MF_CHECKED )
               pMenu->CheckMenuItem(nI,MF_BYPOSITION | MF_UNCHECKED);
            else
               pMenu->CheckMenuItem(nI,MF_BYPOSITION | MF_CHECKED);
      }
}
```

GetMenuString

■ 2.0 ■ 3.0

Description Gets the text of the menu item. This member wraps the ::GetMenuString Windows SDK function. See the Windows SDK documentation for more information.

Syntax public, int GetMenuString(UINT nIDItem, LPTSTR lpString, int nMaxCount,UINT nFlags) const; int GetMenuString(UINT nIDItem, CString& rString, UINT nFlags) const;

Parameters

nIDItem Menu item.

lpString Pointer to character buffer.

nMaxCount Maximum number of characters to retrieve.

rString Reference to string to be used.

nFlags MF_BYCOMMAND or MF_BYPOSITION, indicating how the menu item is specified.

Returns Number of characters copied.

See Also CMenu::SetMenuString

Example

```
void ShowMenuText(CMenu* pMenu,UINT nID)
{
	CString str;

	pMenu->GetMenuString(nID,str,MF_BYCOMMAND);
	AfxMessageBox(str);
}
```

GetSafeHmenu

■ 2.0 ■ 3.0

Description Gets the m_hMenu member of the CMenu object. GetSafeHmenu first checks to make sure that the this pointer is not NULL.

Syntax public, HMENU GetSafeHmenu() const;

Parameters None.

Returns Menu handle; NULL if invalid CMenu object.

See Also CMenu::operator HMENU

GetSubMenu

■ 2.0 ■ 3.0

Description Gets a CMenu object associated with a popup menu of the menu. This member wraps the ::GetSubMenu Windows SDK function. See the Windows SDK documentation for more information.

Syntax public, CMenu* GetSubMenu(int nPos) const;

Parameters

nPos Position of the popup menu.

Returns Pointer to CMenu object associated with popup menu; may be temporary.

Example

```
void DestroyPopup(CMenu* pMenu,int nPos)
{
     CMenu* pPopup;

     pPopup = pMenu->GetSubMenu(nPos);
     delete pPopup; // will destroy HMENU
}
```

InsertMenu

■ 2.0 ■ 3.0

Description Inserts a menu item or popup menu into the menu. This member wraps the ::InsertMenu Windows SDK function. The version which takes a bitmap appends MF_BITMAP to the flags and passes the bitmap handle as the menu item. If there is an owning window, CWnd::DrawMenuBar should be called to update the appearance of the menu. See the Windows SDK documentation for more information.

Syntax public, BOOL InsertMenu(UINT nPosition, UINT nFlags, UINT nIDNewItem = 0,LPCTSTR lpszNewItem = NULL);
BOOL InsertMenu(UINT nPosition, UINT nFlags, UINT nIDNewItem, const CBitmap* pBmp);

Parameters

nPosition Zero-based position in the menu indicating where to insert the menu item or popup menu.

nFlags Flags for menu item or popup menu; see the Windows SDK for details.

nIDNewItem Command ID for new menu item or popup menu handle if the MF_POPUP flag is used; see the Windows SDK documentation for details.

lpszNewItem Text of the menu item when using the MF_STRING flag, handle to bitmap when using the MF_BITMAP flag; see the Windows SDK for details.

pBmp Pointer to CBitmap object to use for the menu item.

Returns TRUE if successful; FALSE otherwise.

See Also CMenu::DeleteMenu, CMenu::AppendMenu, CMenu::RemoveMenu

Example See CMenu::AppendMenu

LoadMenu

■ 2.0 ■ 3.0

Description Loads a menu resource. This member wraps the ::LoadMenu Windows SDK function. See the Windows SDK documentation for more information.

Syntax public, BOOL LoadMenu(LPCTSTR lpszResourceName);
BOOL LoadMenu(UINT nIDResource);

Parameters

lpszResourceName Resource name.

nIDResource Resource ID.

Returns TRUE if successful; FALSE otherwise.

See Also CMenu::LoadMenuIndirect

Example

```
CMenu menu;

if ( !menu.LoadMenu(IDR_MYMENU) )
     AfxMessageBox("Menu failed to load! );
```

LoadMenuIndirect ■ 2.0 ■ 3.0

Description Loads a menu resource directly from a menu template. This member wraps the ::LoadMenuIndirect Windows SDK function. See the Windows SDK documentation for more information.

Syntax public, BOOL LoadMenuIndirect(const void* lpMenuTemplate);

Parameters

lpMenuTemplate Pointer to menu template.

Returns TRUE if successful; FALSE otherwise.

See Also CMenu::LoadMenu

MeasureItem ■ 2.0 ■ 3.0

Description Measures an owner-draw menu item. This member should be overridden for owner-draw menus. The default does nothing. MeasureItem is called by CWnd::OnMeasureItem of the owning window.

Syntax public, virtual void MeasureItem(LPMEASUREITEMSTRUCT lpMeasureItemStruct);

Parameters

lpMeasureItemStruct Pointer to MEASUREITEMSTRUCT structure; see the Windows SDK documentation for more information.

Returns Nothing is returned.

See Also CMenu::DrawItem, CWnd::OnMeasureItem

Example

```
void CMyMenu::MeasureItem(LPMEASUREITEMSTRUCT lpMeasureItemStruct)
{
     int nIndex;

     nIndex = lpMeasureItemStruct->itemData; // item data gives index

     // widths and heights of menus stored in array data members
     lpMeasureItemStruct->itemWidth = m_Widths[nIndex];
     lpMeasureItemstruct->itemHeight = m_Heights[nIndex];
}
```

ModifyMenu

■ 2.0 ■ 3.0

Description Modifies a menu item or popup menu of the menu. This member wraps the ::ModifyMenu Windows SDK function. The version that takes a bitmap appends MF_BITMAP to the flags and passes the bitmap handle as the menu item. If there is an owning window, CWnd::DrawMenuBar should be called to update the appearance of the menu. See the Windows SDK documentation for more information.

Syntax public, BOOL ModifyMenu(UINT nPosition, UINT nFlags, UINT nIDNewItem = 0,LPCTSTR lpszNewItem = NULL); BOOL ModifyMenu(UINT nPosition, UINT nFlags, UINT nIDNewItem, const CBitmap* pBmp);

Parameters

nPosition Zero-based position in the menu indicating which menu item or popup menu to modify.

nFlags Flags for menu item or popup menu; see the Windows SDK for details.

nIDNewItem Command ID for new menu item or popup menu handle, if the MF_POPUP flag is used; see the Windows SDK documentation for details.

lpszNewItem Text of the menu item when using the MF_STRING flag, handle to bitmap when using the MF_BITMAP flag; see the Windows SDK for details.

pBmp Pointer to CBitmap object to use for the menu item.

Returns TRUE if successful; FALSE otherwise.

See Also CMenu::InsertMenu, CMenu::AppendMenu, CMenu::DeleteMenu

operator HMENU

■ 2.0 ■ 3.0

Description Type-casting operator to convert the CMenu object to an HMENU menu handle.

Syntax public, operator HMENU() const;

Parameters None.

Returns m_hMenu menu handle.

See Also CMenu::GetSafeHmenu

RemoveMenu

■ 2.0 ■ 3.0

Description Deletes a menu item from the menu. If the specified item is a popup menu, the menu handle is not destroyed. If there is an owning window, CWnd::DrawMenuBar should be called to update the appearance of the menu. This member wraps the ::RemoveMenu Windows SDK function. See the Windows SDK documentation for more information.

Syntax public, BOOL RemoveMenu(UINT nPosition, UINT nFlags);

Parameters

nPosition The menu item to be deleted; either the command ID for the menu or the position of the menu item, depending upon the value of *nFlags*. If the menu item refers to a popup menu, RemoveMenu does not destroy the menu handle.

nFlags MF_BYCOMMAND or MF_BYPOSITION, indicating how the menu item is specified.

Returns TRUE if successful; FALSE otherwise.

See Also CMenu::AppendMenu, CMenu::InsertMenu, CMenu::DeleteMenu

SetMenuContextHelpId ■ 2.0 ■ 3.0 ■ NM

Description Sets the context help ID for the menu. This member wraps the ::SetMenuContextHelpId Windows SDK function. See the Windows SDK documentation for more information.

Syntax public, BOOL SetMenuContextHelpId(DWORD dwContextHelpId);

Parameters

dwContextHelpId Context help ID.

Returns TRUE if successful; FALSE otherwise.

See Also CMenu::GetMenuContextHelpId

SetMenuItemBitmaps ■ 2.0 ■ 3.0

Description Sets the checked and unchecked bitmaps to use for a menu item. This member wraps the ::SetMenuItemBitmaps Windows SDK function. SetMenuItemBitmaps retrieves the HBITMAP handles from the CBitmap objects and passes them to the SDK function. See the Windows SDK documentation for more information.

Syntax public, BOOL SetMenuItemBitmaps(UINT nPosition, UINT nFlags, const CBitmap* pBmpUnchecked, const CBitmap* pBmpChecked);

Parameters

nPosition The menu item, either the command ID for the menu or the position of the menu item, depending upon the value of *nFlags*.

nFlags MF_BYCOMMAND or MF_BYPOSITION, indicating how the menu item is specified.

pBmpUnchecked Pointer to the bitmap to use when the menu item is unchecked.

pBmpChecked Pointer to the bitmap to use when the menu item is checked.

Returns TRUE if successful; FALSE otherwise.

See Also CMenu::CheckMenuItem

TrackPopupMenu

■ 2.0 ■ 3.0

Description Executes a popup menu. TrackPopupMenu displays the popup menu and goes into a modal loop, waiting for the user to choose a menu item or cancel the menu. This member wraps the ::TrackPopupMenu Windows SDK function. See the Windows SDK documentation for more information.

Syntax public, BOOL TrackPopupMenu(UINT nFlags, int x, int y, CWnd* pWnd, LPCRECT lpRect = 0);

Parameters

nFlags Flags for tracking the popup menu; see the Windows SDK documentation for details.

x x position of popup menu.

y y position of popup menu.

pWnd Pointer to CWnd object that owns the popup menu; see the Windows SDK documentation for details.

lpRect Bounding rectangle for popup menu; see the Windows SDK documentation for details.

Returns TRUE if successful; FALSE otherwise.

Example See CMenu::AppendMenu

The CControlBar Class

The CControlBar class serves as a virtual base class for all MFC control bars. Control bars are child windows that contain either HWND-based or non-HWND-based user interface elements. The three control bar types supplied by MFC are the status bar, a collection of status panes that contain informative text for the user; the toolbar, a collection of bitmap buttons that generate commands when pressed and which generally map to menu commands; and the dialog bar, a modeless dialog box implemented as a child window in a frame window typically used to add interactive controls to a document's view. These three kinds of control bars not only exist in almost all of Microsoft's applications, even the Visual C++ IDE itself, but also exist in the vast majority of new applications being distributed today.

The interface elements of control bars are updated through the idle-processing version of the CCmdUI command interface mechanism discussed in Chapter 4, *Windows Messaging*. A control bar is either statically positioned to one of four sides of its parent frame window or dynamically "dockable," meaning that it can either float in its own frame window or be docked to one of the sides of its parent frame window. Actually, of the three types of control bars provided by MFC, only the toolbar and dialog bar can become "dockable."

When a control bar is "dockable," MFC uses an internal, fourth type of control bar, the CDockBar, to serve as the controlling parent of the control bar. The programmer first must specify which of the four sides of the parent frame can serve as a docking

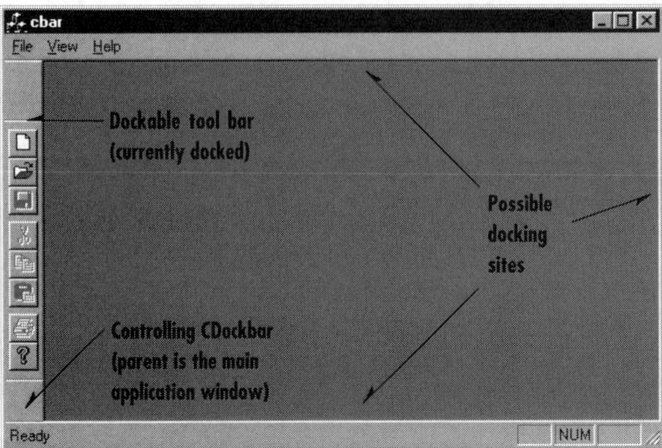

Figure 10-1 Docked toolbar

station for control bars by calling the CFrameWnd::EnableDocking member function. This creates a CDockBar object for each docking side. The programmer than calls CControlBar::EnableDocking to specify on which sides of the frame window the particular control bar can be docked. Finally, CFrameWnd::DockControlBar is called to position the control bar in its default docking position. "Dockable" control bars must start out docked.

The user can alter the position of a "dockable" control bar by dragging it to another side or double-clicking on it to toggle its floating state. When the control bar becomes a floating one, its controlling CDockBar parent changes from the one located on the parent frame window to one located on a dynamically created floating CMiniFrameWnd frame window. Because "dockable" control bars can change their orientation from left side to right side, from horizontal to vertical, there is a lot of MFC internal code to implement a dynamic calculation of the layout of its elements. Figures 10-1 and 10-2 show examples of a toolbar both in a docked and floating state.

Another one of the major features of control bars, whether they are "dockable" or not, is the ability to resize their parent frame windows so that the resultant client area of the frame window is the same size as if the control bars were not present. For example, say that a frame window containing a status bar positioned at the bottom of the window is sized such that its horizontal and vertical dimensions are 600 and 400 pixels respectively. Normally, if the height of the status bar is 20 pixels, only 380 pixels would be left vertically for the client area of the frame window (typically taken up by the child CView object). Instead, MFC sends a WM_SIZEPARENT message to all of the child windows of a frame window whenever its size changes. This allows the child window, the control bar in this case, to enlarge the frame window to keep the client area the same, 600 x 400 in the case above. Actually, this feature is available for any child window that handles the WM_SIZEPARENT message. Of all of MFC, however, the control bars are the only objects that handle this message.

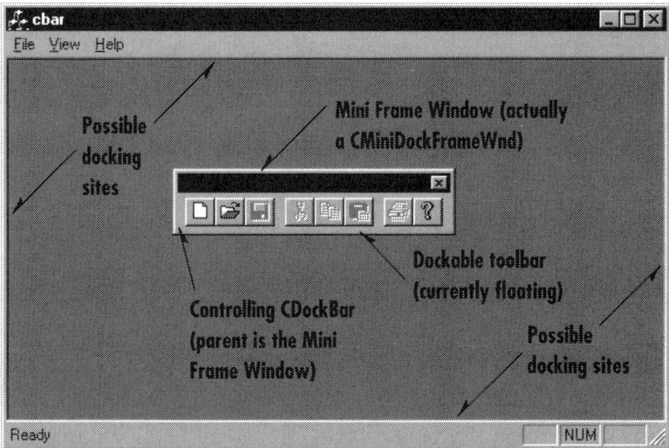

Figure 10-2 Floating toolbar

With MFC 4.0, there is a major change in the underlying implementation of the status bar and toolbar control bars. This is because, in MFC 4.0 or greater, the Windows 95 common controls are supported. This includes the status bar and toolbar controls encapsulated by the CStatusBarCtrl and CToolBarCtrl classes. These classes are discussed in Chapter 9, *Windows Controls*. The CStatusBar and CToolBar classes remain for backwards-compatibility reasons. One final note—most of the members of the control bar classes are not called directly by the programmer. They contain a lot of implementation code. So, instead of looking at individual examples of member usage, the reader is encouraged to take a look at the sample control bar-based applications that are included on the companion CD-ROM, including the sample application written specifically for this chapter.

CControlBar Class Members

CControlBar ■ 2.0 ■ 3.0

Description Constructor for the CControlBar object; initializes the members of the CControlBar object. The constructor is protected because CControlBar is a virtual base class; it is not possible to construct a CControlBar object externally. The programmer must construct an object derived from CControlBar.

Syntax protected, CControlBar();

Parameters None.

Returns Nothing is returned.

See Also CControlBar::~CControlBar

~CControlBar

■ 2.0 ■ 3.0 ■ UD

Description Destructor for the CControlBar object; destroys the window and deletes the elements allocated for the control bar.

Syntax public, virtual ~CControlBar();

Parameters None.

Returns Nothing is returned.

See Also CControlBar::CControlBar, CControlBar::AllocElements

AllocElements

■ 2.0 ■ 3.0 ■ UD

Description Allocates the elements used by the control bar. This generic allocation function is used by CControlBar-derived objects to allocate their specific elements. The memory allocated is freed by the destructor. This function is rarely called by the programmer directly.

Syntax public, BOOL AllocElements(int nElements, int cbElement);

Parameters

nElements Number of elements.

cbElement Byte size of each element.

Returns TRUE if successful; FALSE otherwise.

See Also CControlBar::~CControlBar

AssertValid

■ 2.0 ■ 3.0 ■ DO

Description Validates the CControlBar object. For more information on diagnostics, see Chapter 15, *Debugging and Exception Handling*.

Syntax public, virtual void AssertValid() const;

Parameters None.

Returns Nothing is returned.

See Also CControlBar::Dump

Example

```
void CMyView::AssertValid()
{
      CView::AssertValid(); // view valid?

      m_ControlBar.AssertValid(); // child control bar valid?
}
```

CalcDynamicLayout

■ 2.0 ■ 3.0

Description Calculates the dynamic size of the control bar. Dynamic control bars are control bars that change appearance depending upon whether or not they

	are docking and/or whether or not they are docked horizontally or vertically on the parent frame window. CalcDynamicLayout is called by the framework when repositioning the control bar. The programmer should override this member for CControlBar-derived classes to perform custom dynamic layout calculation. The default calls CalcFixedLayout.
Syntax	public, virtual CSize CalcDynamicLayout(int nLength, DWORD nMode);
Parameters	
nLength	Desired length, either horizontal or vertical, depending upon *nMode*.
nMode	Bitwise-OR combination of the following values:
LM_STRETCH	Indicates that the control bar should be stretched to the size of the parent frame window.
LM_HORZ	Indicates that the control bar is horizontal; vertical otherwise.
LM_MRUWIDTH	Indicates that the most recently used width should be used instead of the nLength parameter.
LM_LENGTHY	Indicates that the nLength parameter is a vertical parameter, horizontal otherwise.
LM_HORZDOC	Indicates that the control bar will be horizontally docked.
LM_VERTDOC	Indicates that the control bar will be vertically docked.
LM_COMMIT	Indicates that the current width should be saved as the most recently used.
Returns	Calculated size of the control bar.
See Also	CControlBar::CalcFixedLayout

CalcFixedLayout ■ 2.0 ■ 3.0

Description	Calculates the fixed size of the control bar. The programmer should override this member for CControlBar-derived classes to perform custom fixed layout calculation.
Syntax	public, virtual CSize CalcFixedLayout(BOOL bStretch, BOOL bHorz);
Parameters	
bStretch	Indicates whether or not the control bar should be stretched to the size of the parent frame window.
bHorz	Indicates whether or not the control bar is horizontal.
Returns	Calculated size of the control bar.
See Also	CControlBar::CalcDynamicLayout

CalcInsideRect ■ 2.0 ■ 3.0 ■ UD

Description	Adjusts the client rectangle of the control bar to account for the borders.
Syntax	public, void CalcInsideRect(CRect& rect, BOOL bHorz) const;

Parameters

rect	Rectangle to adjust; should be set first to the client area of the control bar.
bHorz	Indicates whether or not the control bar is horizontal.
Returns	Nothing is returned.
See Also	CControlBar::CalcFixedLayout

CheckMonochrome ■ MO ■ 3.0 ■ UD

Description Checks to see if the Macintosh application is running on a monochrome monitor. This member is called internally by MFC to determine if control bar elements should be drawn using monochrome colors.

Syntax public, BOOL CheckMonochrome();

Parameters None.

Returns TRUE if running on a monochrome monitor; FALSE otherwise.

DelayShow ■ 2.0 ■ 3.0 ■ UD

Description Shows or hides the control bar. MFC does not show or hide a control bar directly. Instead, an internal state flag of the control bar, set by DelayShow, is checked during idle-processing to determine if the control bar's visibility needs to be changed.

Syntax public, virtual void DelayShow(BOOL bShow);

Parameters

bShow	TRUE to show the control bar; FALSE to hide the control bar.
Returns	Nothing is returned.
See Also	CControlBar::OnIdleUpdateCmdUI, CControlBar::RecalcDelayShow, CControlBar::IsVisible

DestroyWindow ■ 2.0 ■ 3.0 ■ UD

Description Destroys the control bar. Overridden from the CWnd class, DestroyWindow either destroys the docking frame if the control bar is floating or destroys the control bar itself.

Syntax public, virtual BOOL DestroyWindow();

Parameters None.

Returns TRUE if successful; FALSE otherwise.

See Also CWnd::DestroyWindow

DoPaint

■ 2.0 ■ 3.0 ■ UD

Description Draws the control bar elements. This member is called in response to the WM_PAINT message. The programmer should override this member for CControlBar-derived classes to perform custom painting. The default draws the borders of the control bar.

Syntax public, virtual void DoPaint(CDC* pDC);

Parameters

pDC Pointer to DC to use for painting.

Returns Nothing is returned.

See Also CControlBar::OnPaint, CControlBar::DrawBorders

DrawBorders

■ 2.0 ■ 3.0 ■ UD

Description Draws the borders of the control bar.

Syntax public, void DrawBorders(CDC* pDC, CRect& rect);

Parameters

pDC Pointer to DC to use for painting.

rect Bounding rectangle to draw in, usually the client rectangle.

Returns Nothing is returned.

See Also CControlBar::DoPaint

Dump

■ 2.0 ■ 3.0 ■ DO

Description Dumps the contents of the CControlBar object. For more information about diagnostics see Chapter 15, *Debugging and Exception Handling*.

Syntax public, virtual void Dump(CDumpContext& dc) const;

Parameters

dc Dump context.

Returns Nothing is returned.

See Also CControlBar::AssertValid

Example

```
void CMyView::Dump(CDumpContext& dc)
{
     CView::Dump(dc); // dump contents of view

     m_ControlBar.Dump(dc); // dump contents of child control bar
}
```

EnableDocking

■ 2.0 ■ 3.0

Description Allows the control bar to be docked or floated. If the programmer does not call both this function, CFrameWnd::EnableDocking, and CFrameWnd::DockControlBar for the control bar, the control bar will remain stationary for the entire duration of the application.

Syntax public, void EnableDocking(DWORD dwDockStyle);

Parameters

dwDockStyle Indicates the docking style, one or more of the following values:.

CBRS_ALIGN_TOP Allows docking on the top of the parent frame window.

CBRS_ALIGN_LEFT Allows docking on the left of the parent frame window.

CBRS_ALIGN_BOTTOM Allows docking on the bottom of the parent frame window.

CBRS_ALIGN_RIGHT Allows docking on the right of the parent frame window.

CBRS_ALIGN_ANY Allows docking on any side of the parent frame window.

CBRS_FLOAT_MULTI Allows more than one control bar to float in the same window.

Returns Nothing is returned.

See Also CFrameWnd::EnableDocking, CFrameWnd::DockControlBar

Example

```
static UINT indicators[] =
{
          ID_SEPARATOR,           // status line indicator
          ID_INDICATOR_CAPS,
          ID_INDICATOR_NUM,
          ID_INDICATOR_SCRL,
};

int CMainFrame::OnCreate(LPCREATESTRUCT lpCreateStruct)
{
          if (CMDIFrameWnd::OnCreate(lpCreateStruct) == -1)
               return -1;

          if (!m_wndToolBar.Create(this) ||
               !m_wndToolBar.LoadToolBar(IDR_MAINFRAME))
          {
               TRACE0("Failed to create toolbar\n");
               return -1;      // fail to create
          }

          if (!m_wndStatusBar.Create(this) ||
               !m_wndStatusBar.SetIndicators(indicators,
               sizeof(indicators)/sizeof(UINT)))
          {
               TRACE0("Failed to create status bar\n");
               return -1;      // fail to create
          }

          m_wndToolBar.SetBarStyle(m_wndToolBar.GetBarStyle() |
               CBRS_TOOLTIPS | CBRS_FLYBY | CBRS_SIZE_DYNAMIC);

          m_wndToolBar.EnableDocking(CBRS_ALIGN_ANY);
```

```
            EnableDocking(CBRS_ALIGN_ANY);
            DockControlBar(&m_wndToolBar);

            return 0;
}
```

EraseNonClient

■ 2.0 ■ 3.0 ■ UD

Description Erases the non-client area of the control bar. This is an internal function called by MFC.

Syntax public, void EraseNonClient();

Parameters None.

Returns Nothing is returned.

GetBarInfo

■ 2.0 ■ 3.0 ■ UD

Description Called by the framework to get the current state of the control bar. GetBarInfo is used when serializing the appearance of the parent frame window and all of its control bars.

Syntax public, void GetBarInfo(CControlBarInfo* pInfo);

Parameters

pInfo Pointer to CControlBarInfo object containing the information about the control bar.

Returns Nothing is returned.

See Also CFrameWnd::GetDockState, CFrameWnd::SaveBarState, CFrameWnd::LoadBarState

GetBarStyle

■ 2.0 ■ 3.0

Description Gets the control bar specific styles for the control bar.

Syntax public, DWORD GetBarStyle();

Parameters None.

Returns Control bar styles; see SetBarStyle for details.

See Also CControlBar::SetBarStyle

Example

```
BOOL HasBorder(CControlBar* pBar,BOOL bForce)
{
      DWORD dwStyle;
      BOOL bHasBorder = FALSE;

      dwStyle = pBar->GetBarStyle();
      if ( dwStyle & CBRS_BORDER_TOP || dwStyle & CBRS_BORDER_BOTTOM ||
           dwStyle & CBRS_BORDER_LEFT || dwStyle & CBRS_BORDER_RIGHT )
           bHasBorder = TRUE;
```

continued on next page

continued from previous page

```
        if ( !bHasBorder && bForce )
            pBar->SetBarStyle(dwStyle | CBRS_BORDER_TOP |
            CBRS_BORDER_BOTTOM | CBRS_BORDER_LEFT | CBRS_BORDER_RIGHT);

        return bHasBorder;
}
```

GetCount

■ 2.0 ■ 3.0

Description Gets the number of control bar elements, set by calling AllocElements.

Syntax public, int GetCount() const;

Parameters None.

Returns Number of elements.

See Also CControlBar::AllocElements

GetDockingFrame

■ 2.0 ■ 3.0

Description Gets the parent frame window.

Syntax public, CFrameWnd* GetDockingFrame() const;

Parameters None.

Returns Parent frame window.

IsDockBar

■ 2.0 ■ 3.0 ■ UD

Description Determines if the CControlBar-derived object is a CDockBar object. This is an internal function called by MFC.

Syntax public, virtual BOOL IsDockBar() const;

Parameters None.

Returns TRUE if the CControlBar-derived object is a CDockBar object; FALSE otherwise.

IsFloating

■ 2.0 ■ 3.0

Description Determines if the control bar is currently floating.

Syntax public, BOOL IsFloating() const;

Parameters None.

Returns TRUE if the control bar is floating; FALSE otherwise.

See Also CControlBar::EnableDocking

IsVisible

■ 2.0 ■ 3.0 ■ UD

Description Determines if the control bar is visible. Rather than just checking for the WS_VISIBLE style, IsVisible also checks the internal state flag to determine if the control bar is about to become visible.

Syntax public, virtual BOOL IsVisible() const;

Parameters None.

Returns TRUE if visible; FALSE otherwise.

See Also CControlBar::DelayShow, CControlBar::RecalcDelayShow

OnBarStyleChange

■ 2.0 ■ 3.0 ■ UD

Description Virtual function called by the framework when the control bar style changes.

Syntax public, virtual void OnBarStyleChange(DWORD dwOldStyle, DWORD dwNewStyle);

Parameters

dwOldStyle Old styles; see SetBarStyle for values.

dwNewStyle New styles; see SetBarStyle for values.

Returns Nothing is returned.

See Also CControlBar::GetBarStyle, CControlBar::SetBarStyle

OnCreate

■ 2.0 ■ 3.0 ■ UD

Description Handler for the WM_CREATE message. OnCreate creates the control bar, enables tooltips if desired, and adds the control bar to the parent frame window.

Syntax public, afx_msg int OnCreate(LPCREATESTRUCT lpcs);

Parameters

lpcs Pointer to the CREATESTRUCT window creation structure; see the Windows SDK documentation for details.

Returns 0 if the control bar is created successfully; -1 causes the control bar to be destroyed.

OnCtlColor

■ 2.0 ■ 3.0 ■ UD

Description Handler for the WM_CTLCOLOR message. OnCtlColor sets the background to gray and text to black for the child window elements of the control bar.

Syntax public, afx_msg HBRUSH OnCtlColor(CDC* pDC, CWnd* pWnd, UINT nCtlColor);

Parameters

pDC	Pointer to DC for the child window.
pWnd	Pointer to child window.
nCtlColor	Type of control; see CWnd::OnCtlColor for details.
Returns	Handle to background brush.
See Also	CWnd::OnCtlColor

OnDestroy ■ 2.0 ■ 3.0 ■ UD

Description	Handler for the WM_DESTROY message. OnDestroy removes the control bar from the parent frame window.
Syntax	public, afx_msg void OnDestroy();
Parameters	None.
Returns	Nothing is returned.
See Also	CWnd::OnDestroy

OnEraseBkgnd ■ MO ■ 3.0 ■ UD

Description	Handler for the WM_ERASEBKGND message. OnEraseBkgnd paints the background white on the Macintosh.
Syntax	public, afx_msg BOOL OnEraseBkgnd(CDC* pDC);
Parameters	
pDC	Pointer to DC for the control bar.
Returns	TRUE if the background is erased; FALSE otherwise.
See Also	CWnd::OnEraseBkgnd

OnHelpHitTest ■ 2.0 ■ 3.0 ■ UD

Description	Handler for the MFC-specific WM_HELPHITTEST message. OnHelpHitTest returns the help context ID for the appropriate control bar element.
Syntax	public, afx_msg LRESULT OnHelpHitTest(WPARAM wParam, LPARAM lParam);
Parameters	
wParam	x-axis device coordinate for mouse position.
lParam	y-axis device coordinate for mouse position.
Returns	Help context ID.

OnIdleUpdateCmdUI

■ 2.0 ■ 3.0 ■ UD

Description Handler for the MFC-specific WM_IDLEUPDATECMDUI message. OnIdleUpdateCmdUI performs idle-processing by hiding or showing the control bar if necessary and calling OnUpdateCmdUI to update the command interfaces of the control bar elements. The programmer can call OnIdleUpdateCmdUI directly in order to update the control bar immediately (without waiting for idle-processing).

Syntax public, afx_msg LRESULT OnIdleUpdateCmdUI(WPARAM wParam, LPARAM lParam);

Parameters

wParam Passed to OnUpdateCmdUI as bDisableIfNoHandle parameter; see OnUpdateCmdUI for details.

lParam Unused.

Returns 0 if handled; -1 otherwise.

See Also CControlBar::OnUpdateCmdUI

OnInitialUpdate

■ 2.0 ■ 3.0 ■ UD

Description Handler for the MFC-specific WM_INITIALUPDATE message. OnInitialUpdate calls OnIdleUpdateCmdUI to update the command interfaces of the control bar elements before the control bar is displayed.

Syntax public, afx_msg void OnInitialUpdate();

Parameters None.

Returns Nothing is returned.

See Also CControlBar::OnIdleUpdateCmdUI

OnLButtonDblClk

■ 2.0 ■ 3.0 ■ UD

Description Handler for the WM_LBUTTONDBLCLK message. OnLButtonDblClk toggles the docking state of the control bar if the click point is in an empty area of the control bar and the control bar is docking-enabled.

Syntax public, afx_msg void OnLButtonDblClk(UINT nFlags, CPoint pt);

Parameters

nFlags Message flags; see CWnd::OnLButtonDblClk for details.

pt Device coordinates of mouse.

Returns Nothing is returned.

See Also CWnd::OnLButtonDblClk

OnLButtonDown

■ 2.0 ■ 3.0 ■ UD

Description Handler for the WM_LBUTTONDOWN message. OnLButtonDown starts the dragging process of the control bar if the click point is in an empty area of the control bar and the control bar is docking-enabled. MFC captures the mouse until the drag process is complete.

Syntax public, afx_msg void OnLButtonDown(UINT nFlags, CPoint pt);

Parameters

nFlags Message flags; see CWnd::OnLButtonDown for details.

pt Device coordinates of mouse.

Returns Nothing is returned.

See Also CWnd::OnLButtonDown

OnMacintosh

■ MO ■ 3.0 ■ UD

Description Handler for the MFC-specific WM_MACINTOSH message.

Syntax public, afx_msg LRESULT OnMacintosh(WPARAM wParam, LPARAM lParam);

Parameters

wParam Word parameter.

lParam Long parameter.

Returns 1 if handled; 0 otherwise.

OnMouseActivate

■ 2.0 ■ 3.0 ■ UD

Description Handler for the WM_MOUSEACTIVATE message. OnMouseActivate activates the parent frame window when the control bar is floating.

Syntax public, afx_msg int OnMouseActivate(CWnd* pDesktopWnd, UINT nHitTest, UINT nMsg);

Parameters

pDesktopWnd Pointer to the top-level parent window.

nHitTest Indicates which area of the window the cursor was over; see CWnd::OnMouseActivate for details.

nMsg Indicates the mouse message; see CWnd::OnMouseActivate for details.

Returns Indicates whether or not the window should be activated; see CWnd::OnMouseActivate for details.

See Also CWnd::OnMouseActivate

OnMove

■ MO ■ 3.0 ■ UD

Description Handler for the WM_MOVE message, only handled for the Macintosh. OnMove calls OnReposition, another Macintosh-only member.

Syntax public, afx_msg void OnMove(int x, int y);

Parameters

x New x-axis device coordinate of cursor.

y New y-axis device coordinate of cursor.

Returns Nothing is returned.

See Also CControlBar::OnReposition, CWnd::OnMove

OnPaint

■ 2.0 ■ 3.0 ■ UD

Description Handler for the WM_PAINT message. OnPaint creates a paint DC and calls DoPaint if the IsVisible member returns TRUE. The programmer should override DoPaint instead of OnPaint in order to perform custom painting for CControlBar-derived classes.

Syntax public, afx_msg void OnPaint();

Parameters None.

Returns Nothing is returned.

See Also CControlBar::DoPaint, CControlBar::IsVisible

OnReposition

■ MO ■ 3.0 ■ UD

Description Redraws the control bar if the monochrome status of the display has changed. This is a Macintosh-only member.

Syntax public, void OnReposition();

Parameters None.

Returns Nothing is returned.

See Also CControlBar::OnMove

OnSize

■ MO ■ 3.0 ■ UD

Description Handler for the WM_SIZE message, only handled for the Macintosh. OnSize calls OnReposition, another Macintosh-only member.

Syntax public, afx_msg void OnSize(UINT nType, int cx, int cy);

Parameters

nType Type of resizing; see CWnd::OnSize for more details.

cx New horizontal size.

cy New vertical size.

Returns Nothing is returned.

See Also CControlBar::OnReposition, CWnd::OnSize

OnSizeParent

■ 2.0 ■ 3.0 ■ UD

Description Handler for the MFC-specific WM_SIZEPARENT message. Whenever the size of a parent frame window changes, WM_SIZEPARENT messages are sent to each child window. This gives the child windows an opportunity to enlarge the client area of the parent frame window so that the resultant remaining size will be the original client size once space has been allocated to draw the child windows. All control bars handle this message and adjust the parent frame window accordingly. With MFC 3.0 and greater, MFC tries to use the Win32 DeferWindowPos function to speed the resizing process.

Syntax public, afx_msg LRESULT OnSizeParent(WPARAM wParam, LPARAM lParam);

Parameters

wParam Word parameter, unused.

lParam Pointer to AFX_SIZEPARENTPARAMS structure; see CFrameWnd for details.

Returns 0 if handled.

See Also CWnd::RepositionBars

OnSysColorChange

■ MO ■ 3.0 ■ UD

Description Handler for the WM_SYSCOLORCHANGE message, only handled for the Macintosh. OnSysColorChange sets the monochrome flag for the control bar by calling CheckMonochrome.

Syntax public, afx_msg void OnSysColorChange();

Parameters None.

Returns Nothing is returned.

See Also CControlBar::CheckMonochrome

OnTimer

■ 2.0 ■ 3.0 ■ UD

Description Handler for the WM_TIMER message. MFC control bars use two timers in implementing tooltips and fly-by status bar text. Fly-by status bar text is the feature that synchronizes the text of the status bar with whatever control bar control the user is currently over. This allows the user to receive status bar help without having to first select the control (usually a toolbar button). One timer is used to detect a pause over the control. This timer is set to 300 milliseconds. If there is no mouse action over the control bar for this time period, tooltips and/or fly-by status bar text begin to display. The second timer, set to 200 milliseconds, is used to determine if the tooltips and/or fly-by status bar text needs to be removed. This happens if the user has moved off the particular control bar element.

Syntax public, afx_msg void OnTimer(UINT nIDEvent);

Parameters

nIDEvent Indicates which timer triggered the message.

Returns Nothing is returned.

See Also CWnd::OnTimer, CControlBar::SetStatusText, CControlBar::PreTranslateMessage, CControlBar::ResetTimer

OnUpdateCmdUI

■ 2.0 ■ 3.0

Description Pure virtual member that must be overridden by CControlBar-derived classes. This member is called by the framework during idle-processing, allowing the control bar to update the interface of its control bar elements. For more information about CCmdUI-based interface updating, see Chapter 4, *Windows Messaging*.

Syntax public, virtual void OnUpdateCmdUI(CFrameWnd* pTarget, BOOL bDisableIfNoHndler) = 0;

Parameters

pTarget Pointer to main window of the application.

bDisableIfNoHndler Indicates whether or not each interface element should be disabled if no handler for that element exists.

Returns Nothing is returned.

See Also CCmdUI class

OnWindowPosChanging

■ 2.0 ■ 3.0 ■ UD

Description Handler for the WM_WINDOWPOSCHANGING message. OnWindowPosChanging invalidates the border areas of the control bar, forcing them to be repainted when the control bar is resized.

Syntax public, afx_msg void OnWindowPosChanging(LPWINDOWPOS lpWndPos);

Parameters

lpWndPos WINDOWPOS structure; see CWnd::OnWindowPosChanging for more details.

Returns Nothing is returned.

See Also CWnd::OnWindowPosChanging

PostNcDestroy

■ 2.0 ■ 3.0 ■ UD

Description Called by OnNcDestroy, handler of the WM_NCDESTROY message, as the last chance opportunity for clean up after the window is destroyed. OnNcDestroy deletes the CControlBar object if the m_bAutoDelete member is TRUE.

Syntax public, virtual void PostNcDestroy();

Parameters None.

Returns Nothing is returned.

See Also CWnd::OnNcDestroy

PreCreateWindow

■ 2.0 ■ 3.0 ■ UD

Description Called before the control bar window is actually created. PreCreateWindow forces the control bar to have the WS_CLIPSIBLINGS style. Also, it performs border style conversions when running on Windows 95 unless the CBRS_BORDER_3D style is set.

Syntax public, virtual BOOL PreCreateWindow(CREATESTRUCT& cs);

Parameters

cs Create structure; see CWnd::PreCreateWindow for more details.

Returns TRUE if the window should be created; FALSE otherwise.

See Also CWnd::PreCreateWindow

PreTranslateMessage

■ 2.0 ■ 3.0 ■ UD

Description Called by the framework before a message for the control bar is translated and dispatched. PreTranslateMessage pre-processes mouse messages in updating tooltips and fly-by status bar text.

Syntax public, virtual BOOL PreTranslateMessage(MSG* pMsg);

Parameters

pMsg Pointer to MSG message structure; see CWnd::PreTranslateMessage for more details.

Returns TRUE if the message was processed fully and should not be dispatched; FALSE if the message should be dispatched.

See Also CWnd::PreTranslateMessage

RecalcDelayShow

■ 2.0 ■ 3.0 ■ UD

Description Called by OnSizeParent while resizing the control bar. The purpose of this member is to account for the fact that control bars are not shown or made hidden directly. Instead, the internal state flag of the control bar is set and the change is made during idle-processing.

Syntax	public, virtual DWORD RecalcDelayShow(AFX_SIZEPARENTPARAMS* lpLayout);
Parameters	
lpLayout	Pointer to AFX_SIZEPARENTPARAMS structure; see CWnd::RepositionBars for more details.
Returns	The effective styles of the control bar.
See Also	CControlBar::OnSizeParent, CControlBar::DelayShow

ResetTimer

■ 2.0 ■ 3.0 ■ UD

Description	Called by the control bar to reset the two timers used to implement tooltips and fly-by status bar text. ResetTimer will destroy both timers and only the one specified in nEvent is recreated.
Syntax	public, void ResetTimer(UINT nEvent, UINT nTime);
Parameters	
nEvent	Timer to create.
nTime	Time interval of timer, in milliseconds.
Returns	Nothing is returned.
See Also	CControlBar::OnTimer

SetBarInfo

■ 2.0 ■ 3.0 ■ UD

Description	Called by the framework to set the current state of the control bar. SetBarInfo is used when serializing the appearance of the parent frame window and all of its control bars.
Syntax	public, void SetBarInfo(CControlBarInfo* pInfo, CFrameWnd* pFrameWnd);
Parameters	
pInfo	Pointer to CControlBarInfo object containing the information about the control bar.
pFrameWnd	Pointer to parent frame window.
Returns	Nothing is returned.
See Also	CFrameWnd::GetDockState, CFrameWnd::SaveBarState, CFrameWnd::LoadBarState, CFrameWnd::SetDockState

SetBarStyle

■ 2.0 ■ 3.0

Description	Sets the control bar styles. SetBarStyle also enables tooltips if the CBRS_TOOLTIPS style is included and calls OnBarStyleChange, allowing control bars to adjust their appearances.
Syntax	public, void SetBarStyle(DWORD dwStyle);

Parameters

dwStyle	Bitwise-OR combination of control bar styles, one or more of the following:
CBRS_ALIGN_TOP	Control bar can be aligned at the top of the parent frame window.
CBRS_ALIGN_LEFT	Control bar can be aligned at the left of the parent frame window.
CBRS_ALIGN_BOTTOM	Control bar can be aligned at the bottom of the parent frame window.
CBRS_ALIGN_RIGHT	Control bar can be aligned at the right of the parent frame window.
CBRS_ALIGN_ANY	Control bar can be aligned at any side of the parent frame window.
CBRS_BORDER_TOP	Draws a border at the top of the control bar.
CBRS_BORDER_LEFT	Draws a border at the left of the control bar.
CBRS_BORDER_BOTTOM	Draws a border at the bottom of the control bar.
CBRS_BORDER_RIGHT	Draws a border at the right of the control bar.
CBRS_FLOAT_MULTI	Allows more than one control bar to be floated in a parent frame window.
CBRS_TOOLTIPS	Enables tooltips.
CBRS_FLYBY	Enables fly-by status bar text.
Returns	Nothing is returned.
See Also	CControlBar::OnBarStyleChange, CControlBar::GetBarStyle
Example	See CControlBar::GetBarStyle

SetStatusText ■ 3.0 ■ UD

Description	Sets the text for the tooltips and/or the fly-by status bar text. This member is called internally by MFC.
Syntax	public, virtual BOOL SetStatusText(int nHit);
Parameters	
nHit	Control bar element.
Returns	TRUE if successful; FALSE otherwise.
See Also	CControlBar::OnTimer, CControlBar::PreTranslateMessage

WindowProc ■ 2.0 ■ 3.0 ■ UD

Description Default window procedure for control bars. Dispatched messages for control bars get sent here first. The following messages are sent to be processed by the parent frame window if they are not handled by the control bar: WM_NOTIFY, WM_COMMAND, WM_DRAWITEM, WM_MEASUREITEM, WM_DELETEITEM, WM_COMPAREITEM, WM_VKEYTOITEM, and WM_CHARTOITEM. Prior to MFC 4.0, these messages were always sent to the parent frame window for processing. As a result, command handlers at the control bar level would never work by default. This is no longer the case.

Syntax public, virtual LRESULT WindowProc(UINT nMsg, WPARAM wParam, LPARAM lParam);

Parameters

nMsg Message.

wParam Word parameter.

lParam Long parameter.

Returns Return-code for message.

See Also CWnd::WindowProc

The CStatusBar Class

The CStatusBar class is used to implement status bars. A status bar is a control bar that has non-HWND-based pane elements used for displaying text. Derived versions of CStatusBar can be implemented that allow for the display of content other than text (bitmaps or progress controls, for example). The typical AppWizard-generated application includes a CStatusBar member for the main frame window. MFC uses this status bar to display text for commands in the first pane as the user traverses the application's menu. Generally speaking, there are three major uses of status bar panes: providing help (i.e., display text for menu commands), indicating toggled states (i.e., Scroll Lock), and showing the user what's happening during a long process (i.e., "Loading file..."). For more information about status bars, see Chapter 9, *Windows Controls*.

CStatusBar Class Members

CStatusBar ■ 2.0 ■ 3.0

Description Constructor for the CStatusBar object; initializes data members.

Syntax public, CStatusBar();

Parameters None.

Returns Nothing is returned.

See Also CStatusBar::~CStatusBar

~CStatusBar ■ 2.0 ■ 3.0 ■ UD

Description Destructor for the CStatusBar object; frees memory allocated for status bar elements.

Syntax public, virtual ~CStatusBar();

Parameters None.

Returns Nothing is returned.

See Also CStatusBar::CStatusBar

_GetPanePtr

■ 2.0 ■ 3.0 ■ UD

Description Gets pointer to internal pane information for a particular pane. The CStatusBar class has other members for setting and getting the internal values stored in this structure. This member does not need to be called by the programmer.

Syntax protected, AFX_STATUSPANE* _GetPanePtr(int nIndex) const;

Parameters

nIndex Zero-based index of which status bar pane to retrieve.

Returns Pointer to the AFX_STATUSPANE structure:

```
struct AFX_STATUSPANE

{
   UINT    nID;      // IDC of indicator: 0 => normal text area
   int     cxText;        // width of string area in pixels
   UINT   nStyle;         // style flags (SBPS_*)
   UINT   nFlags;         // state flags (SBPF_*)
   CString strText;  // text in the pane
};
```

See Also CStatusBar::SetPaneInfo, CStatusBar::GetPaneInfo

AllocElements

■ 2.0 ■ 3.0 ■ UD

Description Destroys old status bar elements and allocates new ones, called internally by MFC when specifying new status bar elements. CControlBar::AllocElements is used to perform the actual memory allocation.

Syntax public, BOOL AllocElements(int nElements, int cbElement);

Parameters

nElements Number of elements.

cbElement Size of each element, always size of AFX_STATUSPANE structure.

Returns TRUE if successful; FALSE otherwise.

See Also CControlBar::AllocElements

AssertValid

■ 2.0 ■ 3.0 ■ DO

Description Validates the CStatusBar object. For more information about diagnostics, see Chapter 15, *Debugging and Exception Handling*.

Syntax public, virtual void AssertValid() const;

Parameters None.

Returns Nothing is returned.

See Also CStatusBar::Dump

Example

```
void CMyFrame::AssertValid()
{
      CFrameWnd::AssertValid(); // frame valid?

      m_StatusBar.AssertValid(); // child status bar valid?
}
```

CalcFixedLayout

■ 2.0 ■ 3.0 ■ UD

Description Calculates the fixed size of the status bar.

Syntax public, virtual CSize CalcFixedLayout(BOOL bStretch, BOOL bHorz);

Parameters

bStretch Indicates whether or not the status bar should be stretched to the size of the parent frame window.

bHorz Indicates whether or not the control bar is horizontal.

Returns Calculated size of the control bar.

See Also CControlBar::CalcFixedLayout

CalcInsideRect

■ 2.0 ■ 3.0 ■ UD

Description Adjusts the client rectangle of the status bar to account for the borders and the size grip, if present.

Syntax public, void CalcInsideRect(CRect& rect, BOOL bHorz) const;

Parameters

rect Rectangle to adjust; should be set first to the client area of the status bar.

bHorz Indicates whether or not the status bar is horizontal.

Returns Nothing is returned.

See Also CControlBar::CalcInsideRect

CommandToIndex

■ 2.0 ■ 3.0

Description Gets the index of the status bar pane with a particular command ID. This command ID is set by calling SetIndicators.

Syntax public, int CommandToIndex(UINT nIDFind) const;

Parameters

nIDFind Command ID to find.

Returns Zero-based index indicating the particular status bar pane.

See Also CStatusBar::SetIndicators, CStatusBar::GetItemID

Example

```
void CMyStatusBar::GetPaneInfo(UINT nCommand,UINT& nStyle,int& cxWidth)
{
      int nIndex;

      nIndex = CommandToIndex(nCommand);
      GetPaneInfo(nIndex,nCommand,nStyle,cxWidth);
}
```

Create

■ 2.0 ■ 3.0

Description Creates the status bar. By default, a status bar is given the AFX_IDW_STATUS_BAR child window ID. This is how the MFC framework knows which child window of the frame window is the status bar, so that it can set the status bar text when the user is selecting menu commands or during fly-by status bar text updating.

Syntax public, BOOL Create(CWnd* pParentWnd, DWORD dwStyle = WS_CHILD | WS_VISIBLE | CBRS_BOTTOM, UINT nID = AFX_IDW_STATUS_BAR);

Parameters

pParentWnd Pointer to parent window.

dwStyle Window and control bar styles; see CWnd::Create and CControlBar::SetBarStyle for more details.

nID Child window ID.

Returns TRUE if successful; FALSE otherwise.

See Also CWnd::Create, CControlBar::SetBarStyle

Example See CControlBar::EnableDocking

DrawItem

■ 2.0 ■ 3.0

Description Asserts if called. This is because CStatusBar-derived classes must be used for owner-draw status bars. This function exists only to give a warning to the programmer to derive a class and implement DrawItem whenever using owner-draw panes. DrawItem will be called by the MFC framework in response to a WM_DRAWITEM message sent by the underlying status bar common control whenever it attempts to draw a owner-draw status bar pane. The programmer should be aware that background of the pane is drawn first before the WM_DRAWITEM message is sent.

Syntax public, virtual void DrawItem(LPDRAWITEMSTRUCT lpDrawItemStruct);

Parameters

lpDrawItemStruct Pointer to DRAWITEMSTRUCT structure; see Windows SDK documentation for more details.

Returns Nothing is returned.

DUMP

■ 2.0 ■ 3.0 ■ DO

Description Dumps the contents of the CStatusBar object. For more information about diagnostics, see Chapter 15, *Debugging and Exception Handling*.

Syntax public, virtual void Dump(CDumpContext& dc) const;

Parameters

dc Dump context.

Returns Nothing is returned.

See Also CStatusBar::AssertValid

Example

```
void CMyFrame::Dump(CDumpContext& dc)
{
     CFrameWnd::Dump(dc); // dump frame contents

     m_StatusBar.Dump(dc); // dump child status bar contents
}
```

ENABLEDOCKING

■ 2.0 ■ 3.0 ■ DO

Description Asserts if called. This is because status bars do not support docking and floating. Status bars are always fixed to the top or bottom of the parent frame window. This member only exists in the debug version of MFC.

Syntax public, void EnableDocking(DWORD dwDockStyle);

Parameters N/A.

Returns Nothing is returned.

See Also CControlBar::EnableDocking

GETITEMID

■ 2.0 ■ 3.0

Description Gets the command ID for a particular status bar pane.

Syntax public, UINT GetItemID(int nIndex) const;

Parameters

nIndex Zero-based index indicating the particular status bar pane.

Returns Command ID for the status bar pane.

See Also CStatusBar::SetPaneInfo, CStatusBar::CommandToIndex

Example

```
UINT nCommandID;

nCommandID = pBar->GetItemID(4); // get command ID for fifth pane
```

GetItemRect

■ 2.0 ■ 3.0

Description Gets the bounding rectangle for a particular status bar pane.

Syntax public, void GetItemRect(int nIndex, LPRECT lpRect) const;

Parameters

nIndex Zero-based index indicating the particular status bar pane.

lpRect Pointer of the rectangle structure to fill.

Returns Nothing is returned.

See Also CStatusBar::SetPaneInfo, CStatusBar::GetPaneInfo

Example

```
CRect rect;
pBar->GetItemRect(2,&rect); // get bounding rectangle for third pane
```

GetPaneInfo

■ 2.0 ■ 3.0

Description Gets additional pane information for a particular status bar pane.

Syntax public, void GetPaneInfo(int nIndex, UINT& nID, UINT& nStyle, int& cxWidth) const;

Parameters

nIndex Zero-based index indicating the particular status bar pane.

nID Command ID for the pane.

nStyle Style of the pane; see SetPaneInfo for more details.

cxWidth Width of the pane.

Returns Nothing is returned.

See Also CStatusBar::SetPaneInfo, CStatusBar::CommandToIndex, CStatusBar::GetItemID, CStatusBar::GetPaneStyle, CStatusBar::SetPaneStyle

Example See CStatusBar::CommandToIndex

GetPaneStyle

■ 2.0 ■ 3.0

Description Gets the style for a particular status bar pane.

Syntax public, UINT GetPaneStyle(int nIndex) const;

Parameters

nIndex Zero-based index indicating the particular status bar pane.

Returns Style of pane; see SetPaneInfo for more details.

See Also CStatusBar::SetPaneStyle, CStatusBar::SetPaneInfo, CStatusBar::GetPaneInfo

GetPaneText

■ 2.0 ■ 3.0

Description Gets the text for a particular status bar pane.

Syntax public, CString GetPaneText(int nIndex) const;

Parameters

nIndex Zero-based index indicating the particular status bar pane.

Returns Pane text.

See Also CStatusBar::SetPaneText

GetStatusBarCtrl

■ 4.0

Description Type-casts CStatusBar object to the Windows 95 common control CStatusBarCtrl class.

Syntax public, CStatusBarCtrl& GetStatusBarCtrl() const;

Parameters None.

Returns Reference to CStatusBarCtrl object.

See Also CStatusBarCtrl class

OnBarStyleChange

■ 2.0 ■ 3.0 ■ UD

Description Recalculates non-client area for the status bar when the border style changes.

Syntax public, virtual void OnBarStyleChange(DWORD dwOldStyle, DWORD dwNewStyle);

Parameters

dwOldStyle Old styles; see CControlBar::SetBarStyle for values.

dwNewStyle New styles; see CControlBar::SetBarStyle for values.

Returns Nothing is returned.

See Also CControlBar::GetBarStyle, CControlBar::SetBarStyle

OnChildNotify

■ 2.0 ■ 3.0 ■ UD

Description Allows status bar to handle owner-draw message sent as a notification message to the status bar's parent.

Syntax protected, virtual BOOL OnChildNotify(UINT message, WPARAM, LPARAM, LRESULT*);

Parameters

message Notification message to process.

Returns TRUE if the message is processed; FALSE otherwise.

See Also CWnd::OnChildNotify

OnGetText

■ 2.0 ■ 3.0 ■ UD

Description Gets the text of the status bar pane with 0 as the command ID (AppWizard makes pane 0 this pane by default). This is the handler for the WM_GETTEXT message.

Syntax protected, afx_msg LRESULT OnGetText(WPARAM wParam, LPARAM lParam);

Parameters

wParam Maximum number of bytes to copy.

lParam Pointer to character buffer to fill.

Returns Number of bytes copied.

See Also CStatusBar::OnSetText

OnGetTextLength

■ 2.0 ■ 3.0 ■ UD

Description Gets the text length of the status bar pane with 0 as the command ID (AppWizard makes pane 0 this pane by default). This is the handler for the WM_GETTEXTLENGTH message.

Syntax protected, afx_msg LRESULT OnGetTextLength(WPARAM wParam, LPARAM lParam);

Parameters

wParam Ignored.

lParam Ignored.

Returns Length of text; does not include the NULL terminator.

See Also CStatusBar::OnGetText, CStatusBar::OnSetText

OnNcCalcSize

■ 2.0 ■ 3.0 ■ UD

Description Handler for WM_NCCALCSIZE message. Calculates the border size.

Syntax protected, afx_msg void OnNcCalcSize(BOOL, NCCALCSIZE_PARAMS* lpncsp);

Parameters

lpncsp Pointer to NCCALCSIZE_PARAMS structure; see CWnd::OnNcCalcSize.

Returns Nothing is returned.

See Also CWnd::OnNcCalcSize

OnNcHitTest

■ 2.0 ■ 3.0 ■ UD

Description Hander for WM_NCHITTEXT message. Forces hit test to be HTCLIENT, unless default returns HTBOTTOMRIGHT.

Syntax	protected, afx_msg UINT OnNcHitTest(CPoint);
Parameters	Ignored.
Returns	Hit test.
See Also	CWnd::OnNcHitTest

OnNcPaint ■ 2.0 ■ 3.0 ■ UD

Description	Handler for WM_NCPAINT message; erases the non-client area.
Syntax	protected, afx_msg void OnNcPaint();
Parameters	None.
Returns	Nothing is returned.
See Also	CWnd::OnNcPaint

OnPaint ■ 2.0 ■ 3.0 ■ UD

Description	Handler for WM_PAINT message; calls UpdateAllPanes to notify the underlying status bar control of the contents of the status bar.
Syntax	public, afx_msg void OnPaint();
Parameters	None.
Returns	Nothing is returned.
See Also	CStatusBar::UpdateAllPanes

OnSetMinHeight ■ 4.0 ■ UD

Description	Handler for SB_SETMINHEIGHT status bar control message. Sets the internal member used to track the minimum height for the status bar.
Syntax	protected, afx_msg LRESULT OnSetMinHeight(WPARAM wParam, LPARAM lParam);
Parameters	
wParam	New minimum height.
lParam	Ignored.
Returns	Non-zero if handled; 0 otherwise.
See Also	CStatusBarCtrl class

OnSetText ■ 2.0 ■ 3.0 ■ UD

Description	Sets the text of the status bar pane with 0 as the command ID (AppWizard makes pane 0 this pane by default). This is the handler for the WM_SETTEXT message.
Syntax	protected, afx_msg LRESULT OnSetText(WPARAM wParam, LPARAM lParam);

Parameters

wParam	Ignored.
lParam	Pointer to character buffer with new text.
Returns	TRUE if successful; FALSE otherwise.
See Also	CStatusBar::OnGetText

OnSize

■ 2.0 ■ 3.0 ■ UD

Description	Handler for WM_SIZE message. OnSize calls UpdateAllPanes to adjust the pane rectangles.
Syntax	protected, afx_msg void OnSize(UINT nType, int cx, int cy);
Parameters	
nType	Sizing type; see CWnd::OnSize for more details.
cx	New horizontal size.
cy	New vertical size.
Returns	Nothing is returned.
See Also	CControlBar::OnSize, CWnd::OnSize

OnUpdateCmdUI

■ 2.0 ■ 3.0 ■ UD

Description	Called by the framework during idle-processing, allowing the status bar to update the interface of its status bar elements. OnUpdateCmdUI creates a CStatusCmdUI (derived from CCmdUI) object for each pane and calls DoUpdate. For more information about CCmdUI-based interface updating, see Chapter 4, *Windows Messaging.*
Syntax	public, virtual void OnUpdateCmdUI(CFrameWnd* pTarget, BOOL bDisableIfNoHndler) = 0;
Parameters	
pTarget	Pointer to main window of the application.
bDisableIfNoHndler	Indicates whether or not each interface element should be disabled if no handler for that element exists.
Returns	Nothing is returned.
See Also	CCmdUI class, CCmdUI::DoUpdate

OnWindowPosChanging

■ 2.0 ■ 3.0 ■ UD

Description	Handler for the WM_WINDOWPOSCHANGING message. OnWindowPosChanging temporarily changes the border styles, preventing CControlBar::OnWindowPosChanging from invalidating the border area because it is not necessary.

Syntax protected, afx_msg void OnWindowPosChanging(LPWINDOWPOS lpWndPos);

Parameters

lpWndPos WINDOWPOS structure; see CWnd::OnWindowPosChanging for more details.

Returns Nothing is returned.

See Also CWnd::OnWindowPosChanging, CControlBar::OnWindowPosChanging

PreCreateWindow

■ 2.0 ■ 3.0 ■ UD

Description Called before the status bar window is actually created. PreCreateWindow removes any border styles when running on Windows 95 because in this case the underlying common control provides the borders in the client area of the control.

Syntax public, virtual BOOL PreCreateWindow(CREATESTRUCT& cs);

Parameters

cs Create structure; see CWnd::PreCreateWindow for more details.

Returns TRUE if the window should be created; FALSE otherwise.

See Also CWnd::PreCreateWindow, CControlBar::PreCreateWindow

SetIndicators

■ 2.0 ■ 3.0

Description Sets the pane indicators for the status bar. SetIndicators is called to specify the command IDs and number of the status bar panes. For each pane, a resource string given by the pane ID is loaded, specifying the default text for the pane. The size of the pane is specified by calculating the text extent based upon the font used for the status bar.

Syntax public, BOOL SetIndicators(const UINT* lpIDArray, int nIDCount);

Parameters

lpIDArray Pointer to array of UINTs, specifying the command IDs for the status bar panes.

nIDCount Number of panes; should be same as the number of elements in the lpIDArray array.

Returns TRUE if successful; FALSE otherwise.

See Also CStatusBar::GetPaneInfo, CStatusBar::SetPaneInfo, CStatusBar::CommandToIndex

Example See CControlBar::EnableDocking

SetPaneInfo

■ 2.0 ■ 3.0

Description Sets additional pane information for a particular status bar pane.

Syntax public, void SetPaneInfo(int nIndex, UINT nID, UINT nStyle, int cxWidth);

Parameters

nIndex Zero-based index indicating the particular status bar pane.

nID Command ID for the pane.

nStyle Style of the pane; one or more of the following values:

SBPS_NOBORDERS No border.

SBPS_POPOUT Popout border.

SBPS_DISABLED Disabled pane, no text is drawn; this is set automatically by the OnUpdateCmdUI processing.

SBPS_STRETCH Stretch pane to take remaining space; only one per status bar allowed.

SBPS_NORMAL Default pane.

cxWidth Width of the pane.

Returns Nothing is returned.

See Also CStatusBar::GetPaneInfo, CStatusBar::CommandToIndex, CStatusBar::GetItemID, CStatusBar::GetPaneStyle, CStatusBar::SetPaneStyle

Example

```
pBar->SetPaneInfo(0,ID_SEPARATOR,SBPS_POPOUT | SBPS_STRETCH,10);
```

SetPaneStyle

■ 2.0 ■ 3.0

Description Sets the style for a particular status bar pane.

Syntax public, void SetPaneStyle(int nIndex, UINT nStyle);

Parameters

nIndex Zero-based index indicating the particular status bar pane.

nStyle Style of the pane; see SetPaneInfo for more details.

Returns Nothing is returned.

See Also CStatusBar::GetPaneStyle, CStatusBar::SetPaneInfo, CStatusBar::GetPaneInfo

SetPaneText

■ 2.0 ■ 3.0

Description Sets the text for a particular status bar pane.

Syntax public, BOOL SetPaneText(int nIndex, LPCTSTR lpszNewText, BOOL bUpdate = TRUE);

Parameters

nIndex Zero-based index indicating the particular status bar pane.

lpszNewText	New pane text.
bUpdate	TRUE if the status bar should be updated now; FALSE otherwise.
Returns	TRUE if successful; FALSE otherwise.
See Also	CStatusBar::GetPaneText

UpdateAllPanes

■ 4.0 ■ UD

Description	Updates the appearance of the status bar by notifying the underlying Windows 95 status bar control. This member is called throughout the CStatusBar class in order to affect the actual appearance of the status bar. This implementation, present since MFC 4.0, replaces the previous detailed implementation necessary before the Windows 95 status bar control.
Syntax	protected, void UpdateAllPanes(BOOL bUpdateRects, BOOL bUpdateText);
Parameters	
bUpdateRects	Update pane rectangles.
bUpdateText	Update pane text.
Returns	Nothing is returned.
See Also	CStatusBarCtrl class

The CToolBar Class

The CToolBar class is used for implementing toolbars. A toolbar consists of a single bitmap that contains a number of adjacent images that serve as buttons when displayed in the application. The programmer can programmatically specify separators that are inserted between these buttons on the toolbar. Rather than providing three bitmaps for each button (indicating normal, depressed, and disabled states), Windows will affect the display of these buttons accordingly using a dithering algorithm. Obviously, this removes a lot of work otherwise necessary for the programmer. The buttons on the toolbar represent commands that can be generated by the user and handled by the application. Typically, they map to menu commands. The programmer can enable tooltips and fly-by help for these commands of the toolbar. For more information on the toolbar common control, see Chapter 9, *Window Controls*.

CToolBar Class Members

CToolBar

■ 2.0 ■ 3.0

Description	Constructor for CToolBar object; initializes the data members.
Syntax	public, CToolBar();
Parameters	None.
Returns	Nothing is returned.
See Also	CToolBar::~CToolBar

~CToolBar

■ 2.0 ■ 3.0 ■ UD

Description Destructor for CToolBar object; performs object clean-up.

Syntax public, virtual ~CToolBar();

Parameters None.

Returns Nothing is returned.

See Also CToolBar::CToolBar

_GetButton

■ 2.0 ■ 3.0 ■ UD

Description Gets the information for a particular button on the toolbar. This member is called internally by MFC; there are other members (GetButtonInfo and GetButtonText) that should be called by the programmer to retrieve this information.

Syntax protected, void _GetButton(int nIndex, TBBUTTON* pButton) const;

Parameters

nIndex Zero-based index specifying the desired button.

pButton Pointer to TBBUTTON structure containing button information to be filled; see the CToolBarCtrl for details on this structure.

Returns Nothing is returned.

See Also CToolBar::_SetButton, CToolBarCtrl class, CToolBar::GetButtonInfo, CToolBar::GetButtonText, CToolBar::SetButtonInfo, CToolBar::SetButtonText

_SetButton

■ 2.0 ■ 3.0 ■ UD

Description Sets information for a particular button on the toolbar. This member is called internally by MFC; there are other members (SetButtonInfo and SetButtonText) that should be called by the programmer to set this information.

Syntax protected, void _SetButton(int nIndex, TBBUTTON* pButton);

Parameters

nIndex Zero-based index specifing the desired button.

pButton Pointer to TBBUTTON structure containing button information; see the CToolBalCtrl for details on this structure.

Returns Nothing is returned.

See Also CToolBar::_GetButton, CToolBarCtrl class, CToolBar::GetButtonInfo, CToolBar::GetButtonText, CToolBar::SetButtonInfo, CToolBar::SetButtonText

AddReplaceBitmap

■ 2.0 ■ 3.0 ■ UD

Description Adds or replaces bitmap used for toolbar. This member is called internally by MFC; the programmer should use SetBitmap to set this information.

Syntax public, BOOL AddReplaceBitmap(HBITMAP hbmImageWell);

Parameters

hbmImageWell Handle to bitmap.

Returns TRUE if successful; FALSE otherwise.

See Also CToolBar::LoadBitmap, CToolBar::SetBitmap

AssertValid

■ 2.0 ■ 3.0 ■ DO

Description Validates the CToolBar object. For more information about diagnostics, see Chapter 15, *Debugging and Exception Handling.*

Syntax public, virtual void AssertValid() const;

Parameters None.

Returns Nothing is returned.

See Also CToolBar::Dump

Example

```
void CMyFrame::AssertValid()
{
     CFrameWnd::AssertValid(); // frame valid?

     m_ToolBar.AssertValid(); // child toolbar valid?
}
```

CalcDynamicLayout

■ 2.0 ■ 3.0 ■ UD

Description Calculates the dynamic size of the toolbar. CalcDynamicLayout is called by the framework when repositioning the toolbar. The programmer should override this member for CControlBar-derived classes to perform custom dynamic layout calculation. The default calls CalcFixedLayout.

Syntax public, virtual CSize CalcDynamicLayout(int nLength, DWORD nMode);

Parameters

nLength Desired length, either horizontal or vertical, depending upon nMode.

nMode Bitwise-OR combination layout values; see CControlBar::CalcDynamicLayout.

Returns Calculated size of the toolbar.

See Also CToolBar::CalcFixedLayout, CToolBar::CalcLayout, CControlBar::CalcFixedLayout

CalcFixedLayout

■ 2.0 ■ 3.0 ■ UD

Description Calculates the fixed size of the toolbar.

Syntax public, virtual CSize CalcFixedLayout(BOOL bStretch, BOOL bHorz);

Parameters

bStretch Indicates whether or not the control bar should be stretched to the size of the parent frame window.

bHorz Indicates whether or not the toolbar is horizontal.

Returns Calculated size of the toolbar.

See Also CToolBar::CalcDynamicLayout, CToolBar::CalcLayout, CControlBar::CalcFixedLayout

CalcLayout

■ 2.0 ■ 3.0 ■ UD

Description Helper function called by CalcDynamicLayout and CalcFixedLayout to calculate the layout of the toolbar. This member is called internally by MFC.

Syntax protected, CSize CalcLayout(DWORD nMode, int nLength = -1);

Parameters

nMode Layout mode; see CControlBar::CalcDynamicLayout for more details.

nLength Length; see CControlBar::CalcDynamicLayout for more details.

Returns Calculated size of the toolbar.

See Also CToolBar::CalcDynamicLayout, CToolBar::CalcFixedLayout

CalcSize

■ 2.0 ■ 3.0 ■ UD

Description Helper function called to calculate the layout size of the toolbar. This member is called internally by MFC.

Syntax protected, CSize CalcSize(TBBUTTON* pData, int nCount);

Parameters

pData Pointer to array of TBBUTTON structures.

nCount Number of buttons.

Returns Calculated size of the toolbar.

See Also CToolBar::CalcDynamicLayout, CToolBar::CalcFixedLayout

CommandToIndex

■ 2.0 ■ 3.0

Description Gets the index of the control bar button with a particular command ID. This command ID is set by calling SetButtons.

Syntax public, int CommandToIndex(UINT nIDFind) const;

Parameters

nIDFind Command ID to find.

Returns Zero-based index indicating the particular control bar button.

See Also CToolBar::SetButtons, CToolBar::GetItemID

Example

```
void CMyToolbar::GetButtonInfo(UINT nCommand,UINT& nStyle,int& iImage)
{
	int nIndex;

	nIndex = CommandToIndex(nCommand);
	GetButtonInfo(nIndex,nCommand,nStyle,iImage);
}
```

CREATE

■ 2.0 ■ 3.0

Description Creates the toolbar. By default, a toolbar is given the AFX_IDW_TOOLBAR child window ID. This is how the MFC framework knows which child window of the frame window is the toolbar.

Syntax public, BOOL Create(CWnd* pParentWnd, DWORD dwStyle = WS_CHILD | WS_VISIBLE | CBRS_TOP, UINT nID = AFX_IDW_TOOLBAR);

Parameters

pParentWnd Pointer to parent window.

dwStyle Window and control bar styles; see CWnd::Create and CControlBar::SetBarStyle for more details.

nID Child window ID.

Returns TRUE if successful; FALSE otherwise.

See Also CWnd::Create, CControlBar::SetBarStyle

Example See CControlBar::EnableDocking

DUMP

■ 2.0 ■ 3.0 ■ DO

Description Dumps the contents of the CToolBar object. For more information about diagnostics see Chapter 15, *Debugging and Exception Handling*.

Syntax public, virtual void Dump(CDumpContext& dc) const;

Parameters

dc Dump context.

Returns Nothing is returned.

See Also CToolBar::AssertValid

Example

```
void CMyFrame::Dump(CDumpContext& dc)
{
	CFrameWnd::Dump(dc); // dump frame contents

	m_Toolbar.Dump(dc); // dump child toolbar contents
}
```

GetButtonInfo

■ 2.0 ■ 3.0

Description Gets information for a particular toolbar button.

Syntax public, void GetButtonInfo(int nIndex, UINT& nID, UINT& nStyle, int& iImage) const;

Parameters

nIndex Zero-based index indicating the particular toolbar button.

nID Command ID for the pane.

nStyle Style of the button; see SetButtonStyle for more details.

iImage Zero-based index of image within the toolbar bitmap—indicates pixel width of separator if *nIndex* refers to a separator.

Returns Nothing is returned.

See Also CToolBar::SetButtonInfo, CToolBar::GetButtonStyle, CToolBar::SetButtonStyle

Example See CToolBar::CommandToIndex

GetButtonStyle

■ 2.0 ■ 3.0

Description Gets the style for a particular toolbar button.

Syntax public, UINT GetButtonStyle(int nIndex) const;

Parameters

nIndex Zero-based index indicating the particular toolbar button.

Returns Button style; see SetButtonStyle for more details.

See Also CToolBar::SetButtonStyle, CToolBar::GetButtonInfo, CToolBar::SetButtonInfo

Example

```
DWORD dwStyle;

dwStyle = pBar->GetButtonStyle(0); // button style of first button
```

GetButtonText

■ 2.0 ■ 3.0

Description Gets the text for a particular toolbar button. The text is specified by a string resource whose ID is the same as the command ID.

Syntax public, void GetButtonText(int nIndex, CString& rString) const;
public, CString GetButtonText(int nIndex) const;

Parameters

nIndex Zero-based index indicating the particular toolbar button.

rString Reference to CString to fill.

Returns Button text, for second syntax.

See Also CToolBar::SetButtonText, CToolBar::SetButtons

GetItemID

■ 2.0 ■ 3.0

Description Gets command ID for a particular toolbar button. This is set by calling SetButtons.

Syntax public, UINT GetItemID(int nIndex) const;

Parameters

nIndex Zero-based index indicating the particular toolbar button.

Returns Command ID for button.

See Also CToolBar::SetButtons

Example

```
UINT nCommandID;

nCommandID = pBar->GetItemID(3); // command ID for fourth button
```

GetItemRect

■ 2.0 ■ 3.0

Description Gets the bounding rectangle of a particular toolbar button.

Syntax public, virtual void GetItemRect(int nIndex, LPRECT lpRect) const;

Parameters

nIndex Zero-based index indicating the particular toolbar button.

lpRect Pointer to rectangle to fill.

Returns Nothing is returned.

See Also CToolBar::SetButtons

GetToolBarCtrl

■ 2.0 ■ 3.0

Description Typecasts CToolBar object to reference to a CToolBarCtrl class.

Syntax public, CToolBarCtrl& GetToolBarCtrl() const;

Parameters None.

Returns Reference to CToolBarCtrl object.

See Also CToolBarCtrl class

LoadBitmap

■ 2.0 ■ 3.0

Description Loads the bitmap for the toolbar from the current resource file as specified by resource name or resource ID.

Syntax public,BOOL LoadBitmap(LPCTSTR lpszResourceName);
BOOL LoadBitmap(UINT nIDResource);

Parameters

lpszResourceName Resource name.

nIDResource Resource ID.

Returns	TRUE if successful; FALSE otherwise.
See Also	CToolBar::SetBitmap, CToolBar::LoadToolBar

LoadToolBar ■ 4.0

Description	Loads information for the toolbar, including the bitmap, from the current resource file as specified by resource name or resource ID. With Visual C++ 4.0 and above, there is now a toolbar resource type. Programmers using this new resource type should call LoadToolBar instead of LoadBitmap.
Syntax	public, BOOL LoadToolBar(LPCTSTR lpszResourceName); BOOL LoadToolBar(UINT nIDResource);
Parameters	
lpszResourceName	Resource name.
nIDResource	Resource ID.
Returns	TRUE if successful; FALSE otherwise.
See Also	CToolBar::LoadBitmap, CToolBar::SetBitmap
Example	See CControlBar::EnableDocking

OnBarStyleChange ■ 2.0 ■ 3.0 ■ UD

Description	Recalculates non-client area for the toolbar when the border style changes. OnBarStyleChange also enforces that certain incompatible toolbar styles are not present.
Syntax	public, virtual void OnBarStyleChange(DWORD dwOldStyle, DWORD dwNewStyle);
Parameters	
dwOldStyle	Old styles; see CControlBar::SetBarStyle for values.
dwNewStyle	New styles; see CControlBar::SetBarStyle for values.
Returns	Nothing is returned.
See Also	CControlBar::GetBarStyle, CControlBar::SetBarStyle

OnEraseBkgnd ■ 2.0 ■ 3.0 ■ UD

Description	Handler for the WM_ERASEBKGND message
Syntax	protected, afx_msg BOOL OnEraseBkgnd(CDC* pDC);
Parameters	
pDC	Pointer to DC for the control bar.
Returns	TRUE if the background is erased: FALSE otherwise.
See Also	CWnd::OnEraseBkgnd

OnNcCalcSize

■ 2.0 ■ 3.0 ■ UD

Description Handler for WM_NCCALCSIZE message. OnNcCalcSize calculates the border size.

Syntax protected, afx_msg void OnNcCalcSize(BOOL, NCCALCSIZE_PARAMS* lpncsp);

Parameters

lpncsp Pointer to NCCALCSIZE_PARAMS structure; see CWnd::OnNcCalcSize.

Returns Nothing is returned.

See Also CWnd::OnNcCalcSize

OnNcCreate

■ 2.0 ■ 3.0 ■ UD

Description Handler for WM_NCCREATE message. OnNcCreate sets the owner of the toolbar.

Syntax protected, afx_msg BOOL OnNcCreate(LPCREATESTRUCT lpCreateStruct);

Parameters

lpCreateStruct Pointer to CREATESTRUCT structure; see CWnd::OnNcCreate for more details.

Returns TRUE if the non-client area is created; FALSE otherwise.

See Also CWnd::OnNcCreate

OnNcHitTest

■ 2.0 ■ 3.0 ■ UD

Description Handler for WM_NCHITTEST message. Forces hit test to be HTCLIENT.

Syntax protected, afx_msg UINT OnNcHitTest(CPoint);

Parameters Ignored.

Returns Hit test.

See Also CWnd::OnNcHitTest

OnNcPaint

■ 2.0 ■ 3.0 ■ UD

Description Handler for WM_NCPAINT message; erases the non-client area.

Syntax protected, afx_msg void OnNcPaint();

Parameters None.

Returns Nothing is returned.

See Also CWnd::OnNcPaint

OnPaint

■ 2.0 ■ 3.0 ■ UD

Description Handler for WM_PAINT message. OnPaint calculates the layout of the toolbar, if needed. The layout of the toolbar is not calculated initially until the toolbar receives its first WM_PAINT message. The actual painting of the toolbar is done by the underlying Windows 95 toolbar control.

Syntax protected, afx_msg void OnPaint();

Parameters None.

Returns Nothing is returned.

See Also CWnd::OnPaint

OnSetBitmapSize

■ 4.0 ■ UD

Description Handler for the TB_SETBITMAPSIZE toolbar message. OnSetBitmapSize sets the CToolBar internal data member used to store the bitmap size.

Syntax protected, afx_msg LRESULT OnSetBitmapSize(WPARAM, LPARAM lParam);

Parameters

lParam Bitmap size.

Returns Result-code for message.

See Also CToolBarCtrl class

OnSetButtonSize

4.0 ■ UD

Description Handler for the TB_SETBUTTONSIZE toolbar message. OnSetButtonSize sets the CToolBar internal data member used to store the button size.

Syntax protected, afx_msg LRESULT OnSetButtonSize(WPARAM, LPARAM lParam);

Parameters

lParam Button size.

Returns Result-code for message.

See Also CToolBarCtrl class

OnSysColorChange

■ 2.0 ■ 3.0 ■ UD

Description Handler for WM_SYSCOLORCHANGE message. OnSysColorChange regenerates the toolbar bitmap to reflect the new system colors.

Syntax protected, afx_msg void OnSysColorChange();

Parameters None.

Returns Nothing is returned.

See Also CWnd::OnSysColorChange

OnToolHitTest

■ 3.0 ■ UD

Description Called to determine which toolbar button the cursor is currently over. This member is called when implementing tooltips.

Syntax public, virtual int OnToolHitTest(CPoint point, TOOLINFO* pTI) const;

Parameters

point Position of cursor in device coordinates.

pTI Pointer to TOOLINFO structure; see CWnd::OnToolHitTest for more details.

Returns Command ID of the button; -1 if cursor is over no buttons.

See Also CWnd::OnToolHitTest, CWnd::EnableToolTips

OnUpdateCmdUI

■ 2.0 ■ 3.0 ■ UD

Description Called by the framework during idle-processing, allowing the toolbar to update the interface of its toolbar elements. OnUpdateCmdUI creates a CToolCmdUI (derived from CCmdUI) object for each button and calls DoUpdate. For more information about CCmdUI-based interface updating, see Chapter 4, *Windows Messaging.*

Syntax public, virtual void OnUpdateCmdUI(CFrameWnd* pTarget, BOOL bDisableIfNoHndler) = 0;

Parameters

pTarget Pointer to main window of the application.

bDisableIfNoHndler Indicates whether or not each interface element should be disabled if no handler for that element exists.

Returns Nothing is returned.

See Also CCmdUI class, CCmdUI::DoUpdate

OnWindowPosChanging

■ 2.0 ■ 3.0 ■ UD

Description Handler for the WM_WINDOWPOSCHANGING message. OnWindowPosChanging temporarily changes the border styles, preventing CControlBar::OnWindowPosChanging from invalidating the border area because it is not necessary.

Syntax protected, afx_msg void OnWindowPosChanging(LPWINDOWPOS lpWndPos);

Parameters

lpWndPos WINDOWPOS structure; see CWnd::OnWindowPosChanging for more details.

Returns Nothing is returned.

See Also CWnd::OnWindowPosChanging, CControlBar::OnWindowPosChanging

SetBitmap

■ 2.0 ■ 3.0

Description Sets the bitmap of the toolbar to a new bitmap

Syntax public, BOOL SetBitmap(HBITMAP hbmImageWell);

Parameters

hbmImageWell Handle to bitmap.

Returns TRUE if successful; FALSE otherwise.

See Also CToolBar::AddReplaceBitmap

SetButtonInfo

■ 2.0 ■ 3.0

Description Sets information for a particular toolbar button.

Syntax public, void SetButtonInfo(int nIndex, UINT nID, UINT nStyle, int iImage);

Parameters

nIndex Zero-based index indicating the particular toolbar button.

nID Command ID for the pane.

nStyle Style of the button; see SetButtonStyle for more details.

iImage Zero-based index of image within the toolbar bitmap—indicates pixel width of separator if *nIndex* refers to a separator.

Returns Nothing is returned.

See Also CToolBar::GetButtonInfo, CToolBar::GetButtonStyle, CToolBar::SetButtonStyle

SetButtons

■ 2.0 ■ 3.0

Description Sets the command IDs for the buttons of the toolbar.

Syntax public, BOOL SetButtons(const UINT* lpIDArray, int nIDCount);

Parameters

lpIDArray Pointer to array of UINTs specifying the command IDs for the buttons of the toolbar.

nIDCount Number of toolbar buttons.

Returns TRUE if successful; FALSE otherwise.

See Also CToolBar::GetButtonInfo, CToolBar::SetButtonInfo, CToolBar::CommandToIndex

SetButtonStyle

■ 2.0 ■ 3.0

Description Sets the style of a particular toolbar button.

Syntax public, void SetButtonStyle(int nIndex, UINT nStyle);

Parameters

nIndex	Zero-based index indicating the particular toolbar button.
nStyle	One of the following values:
TBBS_NORMAL	Pushbutton.
TBBS_SEPARATOR	Separator.
TBBS_CHECKBOX	Check-box button.
TBBS_GROUP	Start of pushbutton group.
TBBS_CHECKGROUP	Start of check-box group.
Returns	Nothing is returned.
See Also	CToolBar::GetButtonInfo, CToolBar::SetButtonInfo, CToolBar::GetButtonStyle

SetButtonText

■ 2.0 ■ 3.0

Description	Sets the text of a particular toolbar button.
Syntax	public, BOOL SetButtonText(int nIndex, LPCTSTR lpszText);
Parameters	
nIndex	Zero-based index indicating the particular toolbar button.
lpszText	Button text.
Returns	TRUE if successful; FALSE otherwise.
See Also	CToolBar::GetButtonText

SetHeight

■ 2.0 ■ 3.0

Description	Sets the height of the toolbar; can be different than the bitmap height.
Syntax	public, void SetHeight(int cyHeight);
Parameters	
cyHeight	Height of toolbar.
Returns	Nothing is returned.

SetOwner

■ 2.0 ■ 3.0 ■ UD

Description	Sets the owner of the toolbar.
Syntax	public, void SetOwner(CWnd* pOwnerWnd);
Parameters	
pOwnerWnd	Pointer to owner of toolbar.
Returns	Nothing is returned.
See Also	CWnd::SetOwner

SetSizes

■ 2.0 ■ 3.0

Description Sets the button and image sizes of the toolbar. Call this member for toolbars that depart from the Windows standard, meaning that they have different button and image sizes.

Syntax public, void SetSizes(SIZE sizeButton, SIZE sizeImage);

Parameters

sizeButton Button size.

sizeImage Image size.

Returns Nothing is returned.

SizeToolBar

■ 2.0 ■ 3.0 ■ UD

Description Helper function for calculating the layout of the toolbar.

Syntax protected, void SizeToolBar(TBBUTTON* pData, int nCount, int nLength, BOOL bVert = FALSE);

Parameters

pData Pointer to button information array.

nCount Number of buttons.

nLength Length layout value.

bVert TRUE if toolbar is vertical; FALSE otherwise.

Returns Nothing is returned.

See Also CToolBar::CalcDynamicLayout, CToolBar::CalcFixedLayout

WrapToolBar

■ 2.0 ■ 3.0 ■ UD

Description Helper function for calculating the layout of the toolbar.

Syntax protected, int WrapToolBar(TBBUTTON* pData, int nCount, int nWidth);

Parameters

pData Pointer to button information array.

nCount Number of buttons.

nWidth Width layout value.

Returns Resultant size.

See Also CToolBar::CalcDynamicLayout, CToolBar::CalcFixedLayout

The CDialogBar Class

The CDialogBar class implements a dialog bar. A dialog bar is a modeless dialog implemented as a child window of a frame window. The programmer creates a dialog template, using AppStudio, and then creates a dialog bar to attach to a frame window. Much of the support for dialog bars in MFC 4.0 is now located at the CWnd level; see Chapter 5, *The MFC Window*, for more details.

CDialogBar Class Members

CDialogBar

■ 2.0 ■ 3.0

Description	Constructor for CDialogBar object; initializes data members.
Syntax	public, CDialogBar();
Parameters	None.
Returns	Nothing is returned.
See Also	CDialogBar::~CDialogBar

~CDialogBar

■ 2.0 ■ 3.0 ■ UD

Description	Destructor for CDialogBar object; performs clean-up for the object.
Syntax	public, virtual ~CDialogBar();
Parameters	None.
Returns	Nothing is returned.
See Also	CDialogBar::CDialogBar

CalcFixedLayout

■ 2.0 ■ 3.0 ■ UD

Description	Calculates the fixed size of the dialog bar.
Syntax	public, virtual CSize CalcFixedLayout(BOOL bStretch, BOOL bHorz);
Parameters	
bStretch	Indicates whether or not the dialog bar should be stretched to the size of the parent frame window.
bHorz	Indicates whether or not the dialog bar is horizontal.
Returns	Calculated size of the dialog bar.
See Also	CControlBar::CalcFixedLayout

Create

■ 2.0 ■ 3.0

Description Creates a dialog bar.

Syntax public, BOOL Create(CWnd* pParentWnd, LPCTSTR lpszTemplateName, UINT nStyle, UINT nID); BOOL Create(CWnd* pParentWnd, UINT nIDTemplate,UINT nStyle, UINT nID);

Parameters

pParentWnd Pointer to parent window.

lpszTemplateName Template name.

nIDTemplate Template ID.

nStyle Window and dialog bar styles; see CWnd::Create and CControlBar::SetBarStyle.

nID ID for child window.

Returns TRUE if successful; FALSE otherwise.

See Also CWnd::Create

Example

```
int CCbarView::OnCreate(LPCREATESTRUCT lpCreateStruct)
{
      if (CView::OnCreate(lpCreateStruct) == -1)
            return -1;

      if ( !m_DialogBar.Create(GetParentFrame(),IDD_DIALOGBAR, CBRS_RIGHT,1))
            return -1;

      m_DialogBar.SetBarStyle(m_DialogBar.GetBarStyle() |
            CBRS_TOOLTIPS | CBRS_FLYBY | CBRS_SIZE_DYNAMIC);
      m_DialogBar.EnableDocking(CBRS_ALIGN_ANY);
      GetParentFrame()->EnableDocking(CBRS_ALIGN_ANY);
      GetParentFrame()->DockControlBar(&m_DialogBar);

      return 0;
}
```

HandleInitDialog

■ 2.0 ■ 3.0 ■ UD

Description Helper function for creating a dialog bar.

Syntax protected, afx_msg LRESULT HandleInitDialog(WPARAM, LPARAM);

Parameters Ignored.

Returns TRUE to continue creating; FALSE otherwise.

See Also CDialogBar::Create

OnUpdateCmdUI

■ 2.0 ■ 3.0 ■ UD

Description Called by the framework during idle-processing, allowing the dialog bar to update the interface of its dialog bar elements. OnUpdateCmdUI calls

CWnd:: UpdateDialogControls to update the dialog controls. For more information about CCmdUI-based interface updating, see Chapter 4, *Windows Messaging*.

Syntax public, virtual void OnUpdateCmdUI(CFrameWnd* pTarget, BOOL bDisableIfNoHndler) = 0;

Parameters

pTarget Pointer to main window of the application.

bDisableIfNoHndler Indicates whether or not each interface element should be disabled if no handler for that element exists.

Returns Nothing is returned.

See Also CCmdUI class, CCmdUI::DoUpdate

SetOccDialogInfo ■ 2.0 ■ 3.0 ■ UD

Description OLE control container helper function. This is an internal MFC function and does not need to be called by the programmer directly.

Syntax protected, virtual BOOL SetOccDialogInfo(_AFX_OCC_DIALOG_INFO* pOccDialogInfo);

Parameters

pOccDialogInfo Pointer to internal OLE control container structure.

Returns TRUE if successful; FALSE otherwise.

11

DEVICE CONTEXTS

11

DEVICE CONTEXTS

The device context is the interface, provided by Windows, between an application and a logical display device, such as a monitor or printer. MFC provides a series of classes, beginning with the CDC class, which encapsulate the concept of a device context. The classes provided by MFC for device context manipulation are "shallow." That is, although they do provide some additional functionality, for the most part they simply wrap and organize the device context functionality provided by the Windows SDK.

One interesting capability that MFC does provide in its device context classes is the ability to actually use two device contexts within the same CDC class: one for input and one for output. MFC directs input queries (GetXXX functions) to one of the device contexts (the "attribute" context) and output requests to another device context (the "output" device context). In most cases, these two device contexts are actually the same. One example of where they are different is MFC's print preview function. In this case, the attribute device context is the printer and the output device context is the screen. This allows MFC to simulate the printer on the screen, providing the "print preview" effect. When MFC requests information about the device from the CDC object, the requests are routed to the printer. Therefore, if MFC needs to know the resolution of the device or the extents of a text string on the device, the printer device context supplies that information. However, when MFC actually draws the text, it is sent to the screen device context. In this way, MFC can output text and graphics to the screen and have them rendered as if it were the printer. Once the two device contexts are associated with the CDC object, all of this is handled automatically.

This chapter describes many functions that are not available in 16-bit Windows. Most of these functions are associated with more advanced graphical operations, such as Bézier splines and paths. A Bézier spline is simply a curve defined by two end points and two "control" points. The curve is drawn between the two end points through the two control points. You may be familiar with a drawing program which allows you to draw these curves and then allows you to re-form the curve by moving the control points. A "path" is simply a collection of figures (lines, curves, etc.). The benefit of using paths is that you can describe a very complex shape by piecing its components together—maybe a few lines, some curves, a bit of text. Once the path is described, you can treat it as a single entity—outline it with a specified pen, fill it with a specified brush, or turn it into a region so you can use any of the Windows region operations.

MFC actually provides five distinct classes to aid in the manipulation of device contexts. The CDC class provides for the vast majority of functionality and serves as the base class for the other four. The CClientDC class encapsulates a device context for the client area of a specified window. The CWindowDC class encapsulates a device context for the entire drawing area of a window. The CPaintDC encapsulates the device context passed to the application with a WM_PAINT message. Finally, the CMetaFileDC class encapsulates a metafile. Table 11-1, below, summarizes the classes discussed in this chapter. The declarations of all of the functions contained in this chapter can be found in the MFC header file *afxwin.h*.

A sample program called GDISMPL, which shows how to use many of the functions documented in this chapter, is included on the CD-ROM packaged with this book. GDISMPL demonstrates how to draw and manipulate various simple GDI objects and how to work with MFC's various device context objects. GDI objects are covered in Chapter 12, *The MFC GDI*. GDISMPL is a Visual C++ 4.0 (32-bit) project.

Table 11-1 Chapter 11 class summary

Class Name	Description
CDC	Encapsulates the Windows device context.
CPaintDC	Same as CDC except it encapsulates the BeginPaint and EndPaint functions used in response to the WM_PAINT message.
CClientDC	Encapsulates a device context for the client area of a window.
CWindowDC	Encapsulates a device context for the entire area of a window.
CMetaFileDC	Encapsulates a device context for a metafile.

The CDC Class

The CDC class encapsulates the Windows device context. As mentioned earlier, the CDC class is a very shallow class. In fact, most of its member functions are actually inline wrapper functions. For more information regarding MFC's implementation of device context classes, see the introduction at the beginning of this chapter.

CDC

■ 2.0 ■ 3.0

Description The constructor for the CDC class. The constructor does nothing of any real interest.

Syntax public, CDC();

Parameters None.

Returns Nothing is returned.

See Also ~CDC

~CDC

■ 2.0 ■ 3.0 ■ UD

Description The destructor for the CDC class. If the CDC object still has a device context attached to it, it is detached and deleted.

Syntax public, ~CDC( );

Parameters None.

Returns Nothing is returned.

See Also CDC

AbortDoc

■ 2.0 ■ 3.0

Description AbortDoc terminates the current print job and erases everything written to the print DC since the last call to StartDoc. AbortDoc is an inline wrapper for the AbortDoc SDK function. AbortDoc uses the CDC output DC. It will assert in debug mode if the output device context handle is NULL.

Syntax public, int AbortDoc();

Parameters None.

Returns A value greater than or equal to 0 if the function was successful; otherwise a negative error value. Possible error values are listed below:

SP_ERROR A general error occurred.

SP_OUTOFDISK There is not enough disk space to spool the print job.

SP_OUTOFMEMORY There is not enough memory to spool the print job.

SP_USERABORT The user canceled the print job from the Print Manager.

See Also CDC::StartDoc()

Example

```
..
CString strText = "This is a test message";
DOCINFO docInfo;
docInfo.cbSize = sizeof(DOCINFO);
docInfo.lpszDocName = "Test Print";
docInfo.lpszOutput = NULL;// printing to printer, not file
dc.StartDoc(&docInfo);    // begin print job
if (!dc.TextOut(5,20,strText))
     dc.AbortDoc();       // an error occurred printing the text, abort
else
     dc.EndDoc();    // successful completion of print job
```

AbortPath

■ 3.0 ■ NM

Description AbortPath closes and discards the currently open path. A path is opened by calling the BeginPath function. For more information regarding paths, see the BeginPath function.

Syntax public, BOOL AbortPath();

Parameters None.

Returns Non-zero if the function is successful; 0 otherwise.

See Also CDC::BeginPath, CDC::EndPath

Example

```
..
dc.BeginPath();
dc.MoveTo(1,1);
dc.LineTo(20,27);
dc.Rectangle(100,100,200,200);

BOOL bContinue = ShouldContinuePath();

if (bContinue)
{ // close the path and fill it
      dc.EndPath();
      dc.FillPath();
}
else
      dc.AbortPath(); // abort the path
```

AddMetaFileComment

■ 2.0 ■ 3.0 ■ NM

Description Call AddMetaFileComment to add any arbitrary comment to a metafile. The official line is that the comment should begin with an application identifier and should not contain position data. The latter is suggested because one metafile can be embedded in another metafile, in which case the position data specified may be incorrect. AddMetaFileComment is an inline wrapper for the GdiComment SDK function.

AddMetaFileComment uses the CDC output DC. It will assert in debug mode if the output device context handle is NULL.

Syntax public, BOOL AddMetaFileComment(UINT nDataSize, const BYTE *pCommentData);

Parameters

nDataSize The length of the comment buffer in bytes.

pCommentData Pointer to the comment buffer.

Returns Non-zero if the function is successful; otherwise 0.

See Also CMetafileDC::CreateEnhanced, ::GdiComment

Example

```
void CMyWnd::DrawToMetaDc(CMetaFileDC *pDc)
{
      CString strComment = "The following is a rectangle";
      pDc->AddMetaFileComment(strComment.GetLength(),strComment);
      pDc->Rectangle(1,1,100,100);
}
```

AngleArc

■ 2.0 ■ 3.0 ■ NM

Description This function draws a line segment from the current position to the beginning of the specified arc starting point and then draws a circular arc from

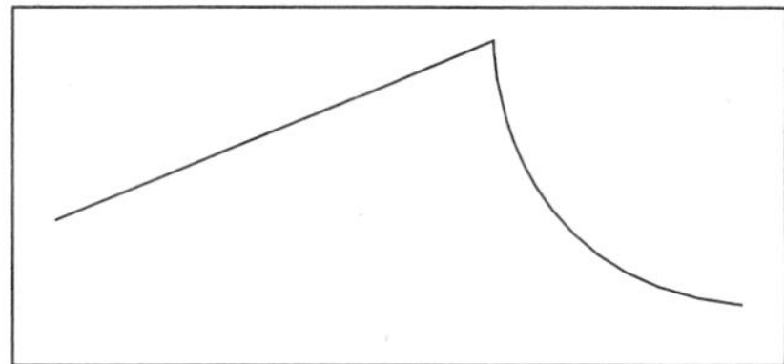

Figure 11-1 Sample output of AngleArc

the specified starting point to the specified ending point. All drawing is done with the current pen and, since the arc is not necessarily a closed figure, it is not filled. The arc is drawn along the perimeter of a circle with the given radius and center point and sweeps from the specified starting angle, measured counterclockwise in degrees from the x-axis, for the number of degrees specified in the given sweep angle. If the specified sweep angle is greater than 360 degrees, the arc is drawn multiple times. The arc is drawn in the current arc drawing direction. This value can be set using the CDC::SetArcDirection function. The default is counterclockwise. Figure 11-1 depicts a sample output from this function.

Syntax — public, BOOL AngleArc(int x, int y, int nRadius, float fStartAngle, float fSweepAngle);

Parameters

x — The x coordinate, in logical units, of the center of the circle describing the arc.

y — The y coordinate, in logical units of the center of the circle describing the arc.

nRadius — The radius, in logical units, of the circle describing the arc.

fStartAngle — The angle, in degrees, counterclockwise from the x-axis at which the arc should begin.

fSweepAngle — The angle, in degrees, through which the arc should be swept.

Returns — Non-zero if the function is successful; 0 otherwise.

See Also — CDC::Arc, CDC::ArcTo

Example

```
..
// draw a half-circle arc with center 150,150 and radius 100
// also, line segement will be drawn from 150,150 to 250,150
dc.MoveTo(150,150);
dc.AngleArc(150,150,100,0,180);
```

ARC

■ 2.0 ■ 3.0

Description — Draws an elliptical arc as specified by the given bounding rectangle and starting and ending points. The arc drawn is a portion of the ellipse

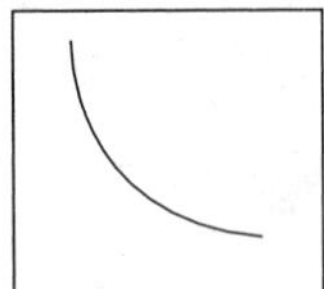

Figure 11-2
Sample output of Arc

defined by the given bounding rectangle. Note that the starting and ending points do not have to lie on the arc. The arc will begin at the point where a ray drawn from the center of the bounding rectangle to the specified starting point intersects the ellipse defined by the same bounding rectangle. The end point is similarly defined. The width and height of the bounding rectangle must be greater than 2 logical units and less than 32,767 logical units. If the starting point and the ending point are the same, a complete ellipse will be drawn. The arc is drawn in the current arc drawing direction. This value can be set using the CDC::SetArcDirection function. The default is counterclockwise. Figure 11-2 shows a sample output of the Arc function.

Syntax

public, BOOL Arc(int x1, int y1, int x2, int y2, int x3, int y3, int x4, int y4);
public, BOOL Arc(LPCRECT lpRect, POINT ptStart, POINT ptEnd);

Parameters

x1 — The x coordinate, in logical units, of the upper-left corner of the bounding rectangle describing the arc.

y1 — The y coordinate, in logical units, of the upper-left corner of the bounding rectangle describing the arc.

x2 — The x coordinate, in logical units, of the lower-right corner of the bounding rectangle describing the arc.

y2 — The y coordinate, in logical units, of the lower-right corner of the bounding rectangle describing the arc.

x3 — The x coordinate, in logical units, of the starting point of the arc. This point does not have to lie directly on the arc.

y3 — The y coordinate, in logical units, of the starting point of the arc. This point does not have to lie directly on the arc.

x4 — The x coordinate, in logical units, of the ending point of the arc. This point does not have to lie directly on the arc.

y4 — The y coordinate, in logical units, of the ending point of the arc. This point does not have to lie directly on the arc.

lpRect — A pointer to a CRect or tagRECT that describes the bounding rectangle that contains the arc.

ptStart — A CPoint object or POINT structure containing the starting point of the arc. This point does not have to lie directly on the arc.

ptEnd — A CPoint object or POINT structure containing the ending point of the arc. This point does not have to lie directly on the arc.

Returns — Non-zero if the function is successful; 0 otherwise.

See Also — CDC::AngleArc, CDC::ArcTo

Example

```
..
// draw half-ellipse arc
dc.Arc(0,0,300,200,150,0,150,200);

// or draw this way
CRect rect(0,0,300,200);
CPoint ptStart(150,0), ptEnd(150,200);
dc.Arc(rect,ptStart,ptEnd);
```

ArcTo

■ 2.0 ■ 3.0 ■ NM

Description — Draws an elliptical arc as specified by the given bounding rectangle and starting and ending points. This function is very similar to the CDC::Arc function except that it also draws a line segment from the current position to the beginning of the arc and, assuming an error does not occur, it moves the current position to the end of the arc. As with the CDC::Arc function, the arc drawn is a portion of the ellipse defined by the given bounding rectangle. Note that the starting and ending points do not have to lie on the arc. The arc will begin at the point where a ray drawn from the center of the bounding rectangle to the specified starting point intersects the ellipse defined by the same bounding rectangle. The end point is similarly defined. The width and height of the bounding rectangle must be greater than 2 logical units and less than 32,767 logical units. If the starting point and the ending point are the same, a complete ellipse will be drawn. Figure 11-3 shows a sample output from the ArcTo function.

Syntax — public, BOOL ArcTo(int x1, int y1, int x2, int y2, int x3, int y3, int x4, int y4); public, BOOL ArcTo(LPCRECT lpRect, POINT ptStart, POINT ptEnd);

Parameters

x1 — The x coordinate, in logical units, of the upper-left corner of the bounding rectangle describing the arc.

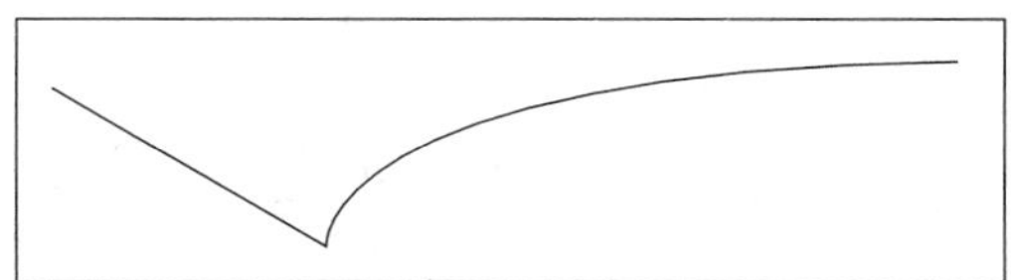

Figure 11-3 Sample output of ArcTo

y1	The y coordinate, in logical units, of the upper-left corner of the bounding rectangle describing the arc.
x2	The x coordinate, in logical units, of the lower-right corner of the bounding rectangle describing the arc.
y2	The y coordinate, in logical units, of the lower-right corner of the bounding rectangle describing the arc.
x3	The x coordinate, in logical units, of the starting point of the arc. This point does not have to lie directly on the arc. See the discussion above for more information about where the arc actually begins and ends.
y3	The y coordinate, in logical units, of the starting point of the arc. This point does not have to lie directly on the arc.
x4	The x coordinate, in logical units, of the ending point of the arc. This point does not have to lie directly on the arc.
y4	The y coordinate, in logical units, of the ending point of the arc. This point does not have to lie directly on the arc.
lpRect	A pointer to a CRect or tagRECT that describes the bounding rectangle that describes the arc.
ptStart	A CPoint object or POINT structure containing the starting point of the arc. This point does not have to lie directly on the arc. See the discussion above for more information about where the arc actually begins and ends.
ptEnd	A CPoint object or POINT structure containing the ending point of the arc. This point does not have to lie directly on the arc.

Returns Non-zero if the function is successful; 0 otherwise.

See Also CDC::AngleArc, CDC::Arc

Example

```
..
// draw half-ellipse arc with line segment
// line segment will be from 100,100 to approximately 150,0
dc.SetArcDirection(AD_CLOCKWISE);
dc.MoveTo(100,100);
dc.ArcTo(0,0,300,200,150,0,150,200);
```

AssertValid ■ 2.0 ■ 3.0 ■ DO

Description Tests the validity of the CDC object. The CDC version of AssertValid does nothing but call the CObject::AssertValid function.

Syntax public, virtual void AssertValid() const;

Parameters None.

Returns Nothing is returned.

See Also CObject::AssertValid()

Example

```
void CMyWnd::SomeDrawFunc(CDC *pDc)
{
     pDc->AssertValid(); // make sure passed object is valid
     ..
```

Attach

■ 2.0 ■ 3.0

Description Attach will associate a CDC object with a pre-existing device context. You can then use the CDC object to manipulate the device context. Use the Detach function to "detach" the device context from the CDC object when you are done using it. Normally, you would use the CDC object to create the device context directly. Attach is useful when, for example, you are passed a device context (an HDC) from Windows or another piece of software.

Syntax public, BOOL Attach(HDC hDC);

Parameters

hDC A handle to the device context to associate with the CDC object.

Returns Non-zero if the function is successful; 0 otherwise.

See Also CDC::Detach

Example

```
void CMyWnd::SomeDrawFunc(HDC hDc)
{
        CDC dc;

        // attach hDc to CDC object so we can be object-oriented
        dc.Attach(hDc);

        // do some drawing in the dc
        dc.Rectangle(1,1,20,25);

        // when done, detach the device context handle
        dc.Detach();
}
```

BeginPath

■ 3.0 ■ NM

Description BeginPath begins a path "bracket" on the output DC associated with the CDC object. For a general discussion of paths, see the introduction to this chapter. BeginPath is an inline wrapper for the BeginPath SDK function. It will assert in debug mode if the output device context handle is NULL. Once BeginPath is called, you can call the GDI functions AngleArc, PolyBezierTo, Arc, PolyDraw, ArcTo, Polygon, Chord, Polyline, CloseFigure, PolylineTo, Ellipse, PolyPolygon, ExtTextOut, PolyPolyline, LineTo, Rectangle, MoveToEx, RoundRec, Pie, TextOut, and PolyBezier to define the points in the path. Call EndPath to close the path bracket and select it into the device context.

Syntax public, BOOL BeginPath();

Parameters None.

Returns Non-zero if the function is successful; 0 otherwise.

See Also CDC::EndPath, CDC::FillPath, CDC::CreateFromPath, CDC::SelectClipPath, CDC::StrokeAndFillPath, CDC::StrokePath, CDC::WidenPath, ::BeginPath

Example

```
...
dc.BeginPath();
dc.MoveTo(1,1);
dc.LineTo(20,27);
dc.Rectangle(100,100,200,200);
dc.EndPath();
dc.FillPath();
```

BitBlt

■ 2.0 ■ 3.0

Description BitBlt copies a bitmap from a specified source device context to the device context attached to the CDC object. If the logical coordinate mappings in effect for each of the device contexts are not the same, BitBlt may call StretchBlt to copy the bitmap (StretchBlt will stretch or compress the bitmap as necessary). The BitBlt function is considerably faster if the client or window area into which the bitmap is being copied is byte-aligned. You can force a window or client area to be byte-aligned by specifying the CS_BYTEALIGNWINDOW or CS_BYTEALIGNCLIENT styles when registering a window class. Note that MFC does not force either of these styles for its window classes, so you will have to do this yourself if you need optimal BitBlts. If the source or pattern bitmap involved in the BitBlt does not have the same color format as the destination, it is converted to the destination bitmap's color format. If the bitmap is converted from monochrome to color, this function sets on bits (1) to the destination device context's current background color and off bits (0) to the current foreground color. If the bitmap is converted from color to monochrome, BitBlt sets pixels that match the destination device context's current background color to white and all other pixels to black.

Syntax public, BOOL BitBlt(int x, int y, int nWidth, int nHeight, CDC* pSrcDC, int xSrc, int ySrc, DWORD dwRop);

Parameters

x The x coordinate of the upper-left corner of the destination rectangle (in logical units).

y The y coordinate of the upper-left corner of the destination rectangle (in logical units).

nWidth The width of the bitmap to copy (in logical units). This does not have to be the full width of the bitmap in the source device context.

nHeight The height of the bitmap to copy (in logical units). This does not have to be the full height of the bitmap in the source device context.

pSrcDC A pointer to the source device context in which the bitmap to copy is currently selected. If the raster operation specified by the *dwRop* parameter does not require a source bitmap, this should be NULL.

xSrc The x coordinate of the upper-left corner of the source rectangle (in logical units).

ySrc	The y coordinate of the upper-left corner of the source rectangle (in logical units).
dwRop	The raster operation to use when copying the bitmap. A raster operation describes how the Windows GDI should combine the color information of the source bitmap, the destination bitmap, and the current brush. This parameter may be any one of the following common raster operation codes. There are many other, more obscure codes. For more information about raster operation codes, see the Windows SDK documentation.
BLACKNESS	Turns all output black.
DSTINVERT	Inverts the destination bitmap.
MERGECOPY	Combines the pattern and the source bitmap using the Boolean AND operator.
MERGEPAINT	Combines the inverted source bitmap with the destination bitmap using the Boolean OR operator.
NOTSRCCOPY	Copies the inverted source bitmap to the destination.
NOTSRCERASE	Inverts the result of combining the destination and source bitmaps using the Boolean OR operator.
PATCOPY	Copies the pattern to the destination bitmap.
PATINVERT	Combines the destination bitmap with the pattern using the Boolean XOR operator.
PATPAINT	Combines the inverted source bitmap with the pattern using the Boolean OR operator. Combines the result of this operation with the destination bitmap using the Boolean OR operator.
SRCAND	Combines pixels of the destination and source bitmaps using the Boolean AND operator.
SRCCOPY	Copies the source bitmap to the destination bitmap.
SRCERASE	Inverts the desination bitmap and combines the result with the source bitmap using the Boolean AND operator.
SRCINVERT	Combines pixels of the destination and source bitmaps using the Boolean XOR operator.
SRCPAINT	Combines pixels of the destination and source bitmaps using the Boolean OR operator.
WHITENESS	Turns all output white.
Returns	Non-zero if the function is successful; 0 otherwise
See Also	CDC::StretchBlt, CDC::MaskBlt, CDC::PlgBlt, CDC::PatBlt, ::BitBlt

Example

```
void CMyWnd::DrawBitmap(CDC *pDc)
{
      CDC memDc;
      CBitmap bmp;
      BITMAP bitmap, *pOldBmp;

      // create a memory dc to use as the source dc
```

continued on next page

continued from previous page

```
        dc.CreateCompatibleDC(pDc);

        // load the bitmap and obtain its dimensions
        bmp.LoadBitmap(IDB_TESTBMP);
        bmp.GetObject(sizeof(BITMAP),&bitmap);
        pOldBmp = dc.SelectObject(&bmp);

        // simply copy the bitmap
        dc.BltBlt(0,0,bitmap.bmWidth,bitmap.bmHeight,&memDc,0,0,SRCCOPY);

        // clean up
        memDc.SelectObject(pOldBmp);
        memDc.DeleteDC();
}
```

Chord

■ 2.0 ■ 3.0 ■ NM

Description

Draws a chord outlined with the current pen and filled with the current brush. A chord is the area bounded by the intersection of an ellipse and a line segment called a "secant." Figure 11-4, below, illustrates a chord.

Syntax

public, BOOL Chord(int x1, int y1, int x2, int y2, int x3, int y3, int x4, int y4); public, BOOL Chord(LPCRECT lpRect, POINT ptStart, POINT ptEnd);

Parameters

x1 The x coordinate of the upper-left corner of the bounding rectangle of the ellipse used to draw the chord.

y1 The y coordinate of the upper-left corner of the bounding rectangle of the ellipse used to draw the chord.

x2 The x coordinate of the lower-right corner of the bounding rectangle of the ellipse used to draw the chord.

y2 The y coordinate of the lower-right corner of the bounding rectangle of the ellipse used to draw the chord.

x3 The x coordinate of the starting point of the chord. This is the x coordinate of one of the endpoints of the secant.

y3 The y coordinate of the starting point of the chord. This is the y coordinate of one of the endpoints of the secant.

x4 The x coordinate (in logical coordinates) of the ending point of the chord. This is the x coordinate of one of the endpoints of the secant.

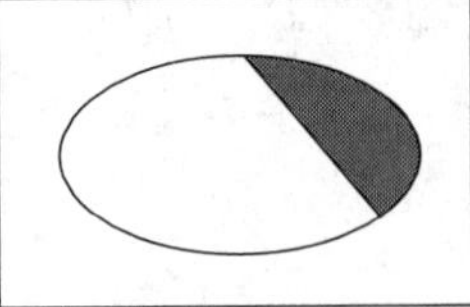

Figure 11-4 Sample output of Chord

y4 The y coordinate (in logical coordinates) of the ending point of the chord. This is the y coordinate of one of the endpoints of the secant.

lpRect A pointer to a RECT structure or a CRect object that defines the bounding rectangle of the ellipse used to draw the chord. The coordinates of the rectangle should be in logical coordinates.

ptStart A POINT structure or CPoint object that represents the starting point of the chord or, in other words, one of the endpoints of the secant. The point specified should be in logical coordinates.

ptEnd A POINT structure or CPoint object that represents the ending point of the chord or, in other words, one of the endpoints of the secant. The point specified should be in logical coordinates.

Returns Non-zero if the function is successful; 0 otherwise.

See Also CDC::AngleArc, CDC::Arc, CDC::ArcTo, CDC::Pie, ::Chord

Example

```
CClientDC dc(pWnd);
dc.Chord(1,1,100,200,50,1,50,200); // draws a half-ellipse

// or draw this way
CRect rect(1,1,100,200);
CPoint ptStart(50,1);
CPoint ptEnd(50,200);
dc.Chord(rect,ptStart,ptEnd);
```

CloseFigure

■ 3.0 ■ NM

Description Closes a figure in the current path bracket. The figure is closed by drawing a line from the current position to the starting point of the figure. The current join style is used to join the line drawn with the other lines of the figure. If LineTo were used instead of CloseFigure, end caps would be used instead. This function will fail if there is not a currently open path bracket. A figure in a path is open unless it is closed with this fuction. Once a figure in a path bracket is closed, the next GDI drawing function called begins a new figure.

Syntax public, BOOL CloseFigure();

Parameters None.

Returns Non-zero if the function is successful; 0 otherwise.

See Also CDC::BeginPath, CDC::EndPath, CDC::LineTo, ::CloseFigure

Example

```
CClientDC dc(pWnd);
dc.BeginPath();
dc.MoveTo(1,1); // start figure
dc.LineTo(132,100);
dc.LineTo(100,100);
dc.CloseFigure();    // close figure
dc.MoveTo(200,210); // start new figure
dc.LineTo(300,300);
dc.EndPath();
..
```

CreateCompatibleDC ■ 2.0 ■ 3.0

Description Creates a memory device context that is compatible with the specified device context. This is necessary if you are going to paint bitmaps to a display. It can also be handy if you want to perform a lot of drawing, but want to display it in an instantaneous manner. You can do this by performing the drawing into a memory device context and then copying the contents to a screen device context. Note that you must create a bitmap of the correct size and select it into the memory device context before trying to draw into it. By default, a memory device context contains a one pixel by one pixel monochrome bitmap.

Syntax public, virtual BOOL CreateCompatibleDC(CDC* pDC);

Parameters

pDC A pointer to the device context to which the created device context should be compatible

Returns Non-zero if the function is successful; 0 otherwise

See Also CDC::CreateDC, CBitmap::CreateCompatibleBitmap, ::CreateCompatibleDC

Example

```
void CMyWnd::DrawBitmap(CDC *pDc)
{
	CDC memDc;
	CBitmap bmp;
	BITMAP bitmap, *pOldBmp;

	// create a memory dc to use as the source dc
	dc.CreateCompatibleDC(pDc);

	// load the bitmap and obtain its dimensions
	bmp.LoadBitmap(IDB_TESTBMP);
	bmp.GetObject(sizeof(BITMAP),&bitmap);
	pOldBmp = dc.SelectObject(&bmp);

	// simply copy the bitmap
	dc.BltBlt(0,0,bitmap.bmWidth,bitmap.bmHeight,&memDc,0,0,SRCCOPY);

	// clean up
	memDc.SelectObject(pOldBmp);
	memDc.DeleteDC();
}
```

CreateDC ■ 2.0 ■ 3.0

Description Creates a device context for a specified device.

Syntax public, virtual BOOL CreateDC(LPCTSTR lpszDriverName, LPCTSTR lpszDeviceName, LPCTSTR lpszOutput, const void* lpInitData);

Parameters

lpszDriverName — Points to a NULL-terminated string that contains the filename of the device driver without the extension. Win32-based applications should set this parameter to NULL as it is no longer used. In Win32, the device name is used to determine the driver. One exception to this is that you can pass "DISPLAY" to obtain a device context for the display.

lpszDeviceName — Points to a NULL-terminated string that contains the name of the device for which a device context is to be created. For a printer, this name is the name displayed by the Print Manager.

lpszOutput — Points to a NULL-terminated string that specifies the output filename or port name. In Win32-based applications, this parameter should be NULL. In this case, output can be directed to a specified file when the CDC::StartDoc function is called (by filling in the *lpszOutput* member of the DOCINFO structure).

lpInitData — A pointer to a DEVMODE structure that contains specific initialization data for the device. If you want the device to be initialized to the default setup specified by the user in the Windows Control Panel, this parameter should be NULL. You can retrieve this structure, filled in with the current defaults by using the ::ExtDeviceMode function in 16-bit Windows and the ::DocumentProperties function in Win32.

Returns — Non-zero if the function is successful; 0 otherwise.

See Also — CDC::CreateIC, CDC::DeleteDC, ::CreateDC, ::ExtDeviceMode, ::DocumentProperties

Example

```
CDC dc;

// create the dc for a printer
if (!dc.CreateDC(NULL,"Panasonic XL24",NULL,NULL))
     AfxMessageBox("Error creating dc");
else
{
     // print some stuff to dc
     CString strMsg("Some text");
     dc.TextOut(5,5,strMsg);
}

// delete the dc we created - optional since destructor would do it
// for us
dc.DeleteDC();
```

CreateIC

■ 2.0 ■ 3.0

Description — Creates an information context for the specified device. An information context can be used to retrieve information about a device but it can not be used for output to the device. An "information" context is created significantly faster and with much less overhead than a normal device context. For this reason, if you only require information about the device, use this function.

Syntax public, BOOL CreateIC(LPCTSTR lpszDriverName, LPCTSTR lpszDeviceName, LPCTSTR lpszOutput, const void* lpInitData);

Parameters

lpszDriverName Points to a NULL-terminated string that contains the filename of the device driver without the extension. Win32-based applications should set this parameter to NULL as it is no longer used. One exception to this is that you can pass "DISPLAY" to obtain a device context for the display.

lpszDeviceName Points to a NULL-terminated string that contains the name of the device for which an information context is to be created. For a printer, this name is the name displayed by the Print Manager.

lpszOutput Points to a NULL-terminated string that specifies the output filename or port name. In Win32-based applications, this parameter should be NULL. In this case, output can be directed to a specified file when the CDC::StartDoc function is called (by filling in the lpszOutput member of the DOCINFO structure).

lpInitData A pointer to a DEVMODE structure that contains specific initialization data for the device. If you want the device to be initialized to the default setup specified by the user in the Windows Control Panel, this parameter should be NULL. You can retrieve this structure, filled in with the current defaults by using the ::ExtDeviceMode function in 16-bit Windows and the ::DocumentProperties function in Win32.

Returns Non-zero if the function is successful; 0 otherwise

See Also CDC::CreateDC, CDC::DeleteDC, ::CreateDC, ::ExtDeviceMode, ::DocumentProperties

Example

```
CDC dc;

// if just using for device info, faster to user CreateIC than CreateDC
dc.CreateIC(NULL,"Panasonic XL24",NULL,NULL);

// get some info
CString strMsg("Test message");
CSize textSize = dc.GetTextExtent(strMsg);

// delete the dc we created - optional since destructor would do it
// for us
dc.DeleteDC();
```

DeleteDC ■ 2.0 ■ 3.0

Description Detaches and deletes the device context currently attached to the CDC object. Typically, the device context being deleted was created by a call to CDC::CreateDC, CDC::CreateIC, or CDC::CreateCompatibleDC. Do not call this function for a device context obtained using the CDC::GetDC function. Device contexts obtained in this manner should be released using the CDC::ReleaseDC function. Note that you will normally not need to call this function since the CDC destructor does it for you. If you want to use the same CDC object for multiple device contexts, however, you will need to call this function between each use. Make sure that there are no GDI objects currently selected into the device context before deleting the device context.

Syntax public, BOOL DeleteDC( );

Parameters None.

Returns Non-zero if the function is successful; 0 otherwise.

See Also CDC::CDC, CDC::CreateDC, CDC::CreateIC, CDC::CreateCompatibleDC, CWnd::GetDC, CWnd::ReleaseDC, ::DeleteDC

Example See CDC::CreateDC

DeleteTempMap

■ 2.0 ■ 3.0

Description DeleteTempMap is called automatically by MFC during its idle-time processing (from CWinApp::OnIdle) to delete any temporary CDC objects that were created using the CDC::FromHandle function. Using this method allows the developer to retrieve a CDC object for a given device context handle without worrying about destroying it. Also, MFC uses the CDC map to ensure that only one CDC object is allocated for a given HDC. If one has already been allocated when you call FromHandle, MFC simply returns a pointer to the CDC object already allocated. Because MFC destroys any temporary CDC objects during its idle loop, you must not store a CDC pointer returned by FromHandle for later use. If the idle loop is entered, your pointer will be invalid.

Syntax public, static void PASCAL DeleteTempMap( );

Parameters None.

Returns Nothing is returned.

See Also CDC::Detach, CDC::FromHandle, CWinApp::OnIdle

Detach

■ 2.0 ■ 3.0

Description Detach removes the CDC's association with its device context. This association is most likely created using the CDC::Attach function. Detach will detach the output DC from the CDC object and set both the output DC and attribute DC handles to NULL. Detach does not destroy the device context itself. If you detach the device context handle from the CDC objext, you will probably want to call the SDK function ::DeleteDC to destroy the device context.

Syntax public, HDC Detach( );

Parameters None.

Returns The handle of the device context being detached.

See Also CDC::Attach

Example

```
void CMyWnd::SomeDrawFunc(HDC hDc)
{
	CDC dc;

	// attach hDc to CDC object so we can be object-oriented
	dc.Attach(hDc);

	// do some drawing in the dc
	dc.Rectangle(1,1,20,25);

	// when done, detach the device context handle
	dc.Detach();
}
```

DPtoHIMETRIC

■ 2.0 ■ 3.0

Description Converts coordinates from device coordinates to HIMETRIC coordinates. HIMETRIC coordinates are used by OLE, so whenever you need to pass coordinates to OLE or interpret coordinates from OLE you will need to convert them to/from HIMETRIC. If the current mapping mode of the device context is a contained mode (e.g., MM_LOENGLISH, MM_HIENGLISH, MM_LOMETRIC or MM_HIMETRIC), then the conversion is based on the number of pixels in the physical inch. If the current mapping mode is one of the other modes (e.g., MM_TEXT), then the conversion is based on the number of pixels in the logical inch.

Syntax public, void DPtoHIMETRIC(LPSIZE lpSize) const;

Parameters

lpSize A pointer to a SIZE structure or a CSize object that contains the coordinates to convert.

Returns Nothing is returned.

See Also CDC::DPtoLP, CDC::LPtoDP, CDC::HIMETRICtoLP, CDC::HIMETRICtoDP, CDC::LPtoHIMETRIC

Example

```
...
// create an enhanced-format metafile
CClientDC dc(pWnd);
CMetaFileDC dcMeta;
CRect rect;

// calculate the rectangle for the metafile - must be in HIMETRIC units
pWnd->GetClientRect(rect);
CSize tempSize;
tempSize.cx = rect.TopLeft().x;
tempSize.cy = rect.TopLeft().y;
DPtoHIMETRIC(tempSize);
rect.TopLeft().x = tempSize.cx;
rect.TopLeft().y = tempSize.cy;
tempSize.cx = rect.BottomRight().x;
tempSize.cy = rect.BottomRight().y;
```

```
DPtoHIMETRIC(tempSize);
rect.BottomRight().x = tempSize =.cx;
rect.BottomRight().y = tempSize.cy;

dcMeta.CreateEnhanced(&dc,"testmeta",rect,"Test App\0Picture\0\0");

// do some drawing
dcMeta.Rectangle(1,1,100,100);
dcMeta.MoveTo(50,50);
dcMete.LineTo(75,100);

// close the metafile
HENHMETAFILE hMeta = dcMeta.CloseEnhanced();

// use the handle for whatever - could use for ::CopyMetaFile

// when done, delete the metafile
::DeleteEnhMetaFile(hMeta);
..
```

DPtoLP

■ 2.0 ■ 3.0

Description Converts coordinates from device coordinates to logical coordinates. Conversion to logical coordinates depends on the current mapping mode of the device context, the current window and viewport origins and extents, and the current world transformation that is in effect. See the description of the CDC::SetMapMode function for more information regarding mapping modes. See the description of the CDC::LPtoDP function for the equation used to convert between device coordinates and logical coordinates.

Syntax public, void DPtoLP(LPPOINT lpPoints, int nCount = 1) const;
public, void DPtoLP(LPRECT lpRect) const;
public, void DPtoLP(LPSIZE lpSize) const;

Parameters

lpPoints A pointer to an array of POINT structure or CPoint objects to be converted.

nCount The number of points to be converted.

lpRect A pointer to a RECT structure or a CRect object to be converted.

lpSize A pointer to a SIZE structure or a CSize object to be converted.

Returns Nothing is returned.

See Also CDC::DPtoHIMETRIC, CDC::LPtoDP, CDC::HIMETRICtoLP, CDC::HIMETRICtoDP, CDC::LPtoHIMETRIC

Example

```
CClientDC dc(pWnd);
CRect rc;
CPoint pt;

// set mapping mode to MM_ANISOTROPIC (logical with no constraints)
dc.SetMapMode(MM_ANISOTROPIC);
```

continued on next page

continued from previous page

```
// get client rectangle of window and use as window coordinates
pWnd->GetClientRect(rc);
dc.SetWindowOrg(rc.left,rc.top);
dc.SetWindowExt(rc.right,rc.bottom);

// create mapping such that no matter what the window size, always have
// 100 x 100 grid
dc.SetViewportOrg(0,0);
dc.SetViewportExt(100,100);

// convert an arbitrary point to logical coordinates - if client area of
// window were 600 x 500 logical point would be 120, 100
CPoint devPoint(20,20);
dc.DPtoLP(&devPoint,1);

// convert a rectangle
CRect rect(20,20,100,100);
dc.DPtoLP(rect);

// convert an arbitrary point to device coordinates - if client area of
// window were 600 x 500 device point would be 20, 20
CPoint logPoint(120, 100);
dc.LPtoDP(&logPoint,1);

..
```

DRAW3DRECT

■ 2.0 ■ 3.0

Description Draws a rectangle with a 3-dimensional effect. Draw3dRect does this by drawing the left and top sides of the rectangle with a specified color and the right and bottom sides with a different specified color. Using varying shades of the same color (e.g., white and dark gray) yields a shadow effect.

Syntax public, void Draw3dRect(LPCRECT lpRect, COLORREF clrTopLeft, COLORREF clrBottomRight);
public, void Draw3dRect(int x, int y, int cx, int cy, COLORREF clrTopLeft, COLORREF clrBottomRight);

Parameters

lpRect A pointer to a RECT structure or a CRect object containing the coordinates of the rectangle to draw (in logical coordinates).

clrTopLeft The color to use to outline the left and top sides of the rectangle.

clrBottomRight The color to use to outline the right and bottom sides of the rectangle.

x The x coordinate of the upper-left corner of the rectangle to draw (in logical coordinates).

y The y coordinate of the upper-right corner of the rectangle to draw (in logical coordinates).

cx The width of the rectangle to draw (in logical coordinates).

cy The height of the rectangle to draw (in logical coordinates).

Returns Nothing is returned.

Example

```
CRect rect(10,10,100,200);

// outline rect using dark and light gray
CClientDC dc(pWnd);
dc.Draw3dRect(rect,RGB(50,50,50),RGB(200,200,200));

// draw another one using second form
dc.Draw3dRect(150,10,250,200, RGB(50,50,50),RGB(200,200,200));
```

DrawDragRect

■ 2.0 ■ 3.0

Description Aids in the drawing of a filled rectangle that is being dragged or sized. DrawDragRect does this in a very efficient manner so that a flicker effect is avoided.

Syntax public, void DrawDragRect(LPCRECT lpRect, SIZE size,LPCRECT lpRectLast, SIZE sizeLast, Cbrush* pBrush = NULL, CBrush* pBrushLast = NULL);

Parameters

lpRect Pointer to a RECT structure or a CRect object containing the coordinates of the current rectangle (in logical coordinates).

size Size of the rectangle pointed to by *lpRect* (in logical units).

lpRectLast Pointer to a RECT structure or a CRect object containing the coordinates of the last rectangle drawn with this function (in logical coordinates).

sizeLast Size of the last rectangle pointed to the *lpRectLast.*

pBrush Pointer to the brush to be used to draw the current rectangle.

pBrushLast Pointer to the brush that was used to draw the last rectangle.

Returns Nothing is returned.

DrawEdge

■ 4.0 ■ NM

Description Draws a rectangle with edges of a specified type and style. Use this function to draw various types of "3D" rectangles.

Syntax public, int DrawEdge(LPRECT lpRect, UINT nEdge, UINT nFlags);

Parameters

lpRect A pointer to a RECT structure or a CRect object containing the coordinates of the rectangle to draw (in logical units)

nEdge The type of inner and outer edge to draw. Should be a combination of one flag from each of the groups listed below:

Inner Edge Flags:

BDR_RAISEDINNER Raised inner edge.

BDR_SUNKENINNER Sunken inner edge.

Outer Edge Flags:

BDR_RAISEDOUTER Raised outer edge.

BDR_SUNKENOUTER Sunken outer edge.

You can OR the flags together yourself, or you can use one of the predefined macros listed below:

EDGE_BUMP BDR_RAISEDOUTER and BDR_SUNKENINNER.

EDGE_ETCHED BDR_SUNKENOUTER and BDR_RAISEDINNER.

EDGE_RAISED BDR_RAISEDOUTER and BDR_RAISEDINNER.

EDGE_SUNKEN BDR_SUNKENOUTER and BDR_SUNKENINNER.

nFlags Specifies what part of the specified rectangle to draw. Can be one of the following values:

BF_RECT Entire rectangle.

BF_LEFT Left side of rectangle.

BF_BOTTOM Bottom of rectangle.

BF_RIGHT Right side of rectangle.

BF_TOP Top of rectangle.

BF_TOPLEFT Top and left side of rectangle.

BF_TOPRIGHT Top and right side of rectangle.

BF_BOTTOMLEFT Bottom and left side of rectangle.

BF_BOTTOMRIGHT Bottom and right side of rectangle.

BF_DIAGONAL_ENDBOTTOMLEFT Diagonal border. The starting point is the top-right corner of the rectangle and the end point is the bottom-left corner of the rectangle.

BF_DIAGONAL_ENDBOTTOMRIGHT Diagonal border. The starting point is the top-left corner of the rectangle and the end point is the bottom-right corner of the rectangle.

BF_DIAGONAL_ENDTOPLEFT Diagonal border. The starting point is the bottom-right corner of the rectangle and the end point is the top-left corner of the rectangle.

BF_DIAGONAL_ENDTOPRIGHT Diagonal border. The starting point is the bottom-left corner of the rectangle and the end point is the top-right corner of the rectangle.

Returns Non-zero if successful; otherwise, zero.

Example

```
...
CClientDC dc(pWnd);
CRect rect(10,10,200,300);

// draw a sunken rectangle
dc.DrawEdge(rect, EDGE_SUNKEN, BF_RECT);
```

DrawEscape

■ 2.0 ■ 3.0 ■ NM

Description Provides a method to talk to a device driver directly. The DrawEscape function passes the specified data directly to the device driver associated with the device context. This allows an application to access features of a device driver which are not directly supported by the Windows GDI.

Syntax public, int DrawEscape(int nEscape, int nInputSize, LPCSTR lpszInputData);

Parameters

nEscape The escape function to perform (defined by device driver).

nInputSize The size of the data buffer pointed to by *lpszInputData.*

lpszInputData A pointer to a buffer of data which will be passed to the device driver.

Returns Greater than zero if successful or, in the case of the QUERYESCSUPPORT draw escape, if the escape is supported; zero if the escape specified with the QUERYESCSUPPORT draw escape is not supported, or less than zero if an error occurred.

See Also CDC::Escape, ::DrawEscape

DrawFocusRect

■ 2.0 ■ 3.0

Description Draws a rectangle "in the style that indicates focus." The rectangle drawn is XORed on, so calling this function again with the same rectangle will erase the rectangle from the previous call. Note that the rectangle drawn cannot be scrolled with one of the device context scrolling routines. If you must scroll the area containing the rectangle, erase it and, after scrolling, draw it at the new location.

Syntax public, void DrawFocusRect(LPCRECT lpRect);

Parameters

lpRect A pointer to a RECT structure or a CRect object containing the coordinates (in logical coordinates) of the rectangle to draw.

Returns Nothing is returned.

See Also CDC::FrameRect, ::DrawFocusRect

Example

```
CRect rect(10,10,100,200);

// draw a focus rect
CClientDC dc(pWnd);
dc.DrawFocusRect(rect);

// do something else

// erase the focus rect
dc.DrawFocusRect(rect);
```

DrawFrameControl

–. ■ 4.0 ■ NM

Description Draws one of the Windows controls in a given state. For example, you can use this function to draw a check box or a scrollbar.

Syntax public, BOOL DrawFrameControl(LPRECT lpRect, UINT nType, UINT nState);

Parameters

lpRect A pointer to a RECT structure or a CRect object containing the coordinates (in logical coordinates) of the control to draw.

nType The type of control to draw. Can be one of the following values:

DFC_BUTTON Standard button.

DFC_CAPTION Title bar.

DFC_MENU Menu.

DFC_SCROLL Scrollbar.

nState This parameter indicates the state of the control as well as more specific type information. It can be a combination of one of the state flags listed below and one of the type flags listed below. Also, if you want DrawFrameControl to adjust the specified rectangle to exclude the surrounding edge of a push button, OR in the DFCS_ADJUSTRECT flag.

State Flags:

DFCS_CHECKED Button is checked.

DFCS_FLAT Button has a flat border.

DFCS_INACTIVE Button is inactive (grayed).

DFCS_MONO Button has a monochrome border.

DFCS_PUSHED Button is pushed.

Type Flags:

For the DFC_BUTTON style:

DFCS_BUTTON3STATE Three-state button.

DFCS_BUTTONCHECK Check box.

DFCS_BUTTONPUSH Push button.

DFCS_BUTTONRADIO Radio button.

DFCS_BUTTONRADIOIMAGE Image for radio button (nonsquare needs image).

DFCS_BUTTONRADIOMASK Mask for radio button (nonsquare needs mask).

For the DFC_CAPTION:

DFCS_CAPTIONCLOSE Close button.

DFCS_CAPTIONHELP Help button.

DFCS_CAPTIONMAX Maximize button.

DFCS_CAPTIONMIN Minimize button.

DFCS_CAPTIONRESTORE Restore button.

For the DFC_MENU:

DFCS_MENUARROW Submenu arrow.

DFCS_MENUBULLET Bullet.

DFCS_MENUCHECK Check mark.

For the DFC_SCROLL:

DFCS_SCROLLCOMBOBOX Combo box scrollbar.

DFCS_SCROLLDOWN Down arrow of scrollbar.

DFCS_SCROLLLEFT Left arrow of scrollbar.

DFCS_SCROLLRIGHT Right arrow of scrollbar.

DFCS_SCROLLSIZEGRIP Size grip in bottom-right corner of window.

DFCS_SCROLLUP Up arrow of scrollbar.

Returns -zero if successful; otherwise, zero.

Example

```
...
CClientDc dc(pWnd);
CRect rect(5,5,30,15);

// draw a disabled push button
dc.DrawFrameControl(rect,DFC_BUTTON,DFCS_BUTTONPUSH|DFCS_INACTIVE);
```

DrawIcon

■ 2.0 ■ 3.0

Description Draws an icon at a specified location.

Syntax public, BOOL DrawIcon(int x, int y, HICON hIcon); public, BOOL DrawIcon(POINT point, HICON hIcon);

Parameters

x The x coordinate of the top-left corner of the icon (in logical coordinates).

y The y coordinate of the top-left corner of the icon (in logical coordinates).

hIcon The handle of the icon to draw. MFC does not have an object that represents an icon, so a handle must be used.

point A POINT structure or CPoint object containing the coordinates at which the icon should be displayed (in logical coordinates).

Returns Non-zero if the fuction is successful; otherwise, zero.

See Also CWinApp::LoadIcon, CWinApp::LoadStandardIcon, CWinApp::LoadOEMIcon, ::DrawIcon

Example

```
void CMyWin::SomeFunc(CDC *pDc)
{
      HICON hIcon;
      hIcon = AfxGetApp()->LoadIcon(IDI_SOMEICON);
      pDc->DrawIcon(50,50,hIcon);
      ..
}
```

DRAWSTATE

–. ■ 4.0 ■ NM

Description

Draws an image that may be a bitmap, icon, text, or custom image and applies a specified visual effect that indicates state. You can use this function, for example, to draw a toolbar button and then make it look disabled. Note that this function is only available in Windows versions 4.0 and up and is not available on the Macintosh.

Syntax

public, BOOL DrawState(CPoint pt, CSize size, HBITMAP hBitmap, UINT nFlags, HBRUSH hBrush = NULL);
public, BOOL DrawState(CPoint pt, CSize size, CBitmap *pBitmap, UINT nFlags, CBrush *pBrush = NULL);
public, BOOL DrawState(CPoint pt, CSize size, HICON hIcon, UINT nFlags, HBRUSH hBrush = NULL);
public, BOOL DrawState(CPoint pt, CSize size, HICON hIcon, UINT nFlags, CBrush *pBrush = NULL);
public, BOOL DrawState(CPoint pt, CSize size, LPCTSTR lpszText, UINT nFlags, BOOL bPrefixText = TRUE, int nTextLen = 0, HBRUSH *hBrush = NULL);
public, BOOL DrawState(CPoint pt, CSize size, LPCTSTR lpszText, UINT nFlags, BOOL bPrefixText = TRUE, int nTextLen = 0, CBrush *pBrush = NULL);
public, BOOL DrawState(CPoint pt, CSize size, DRAWSTATEPROC lpDrawProc, LPARAM lData, UINT nFlags, HBRUSH hBrush = NULL);
public, BOOL DrawState(CPoint pt, CSize size, DRAWSTATEPROC lpDrawProc, LPARAM lData, UINT nFlags, CBrush * pBrush = NULL);

Parameters

pt — A POINT structure or CPoint object containing the coordinates where the image should be drawn.

size — The size of the image.

hBitmap — A handle to the bitmap image that is to be drawn.

nFlags — A series of flags that indicate the type of image to be drawn and the effect that should be applied. This parameter should be a combination of one flag from the first list below and one flag from the second list below. Note that MFC will automatically OR in the type flag (since it knows the type based on the version of the function that you use), so you could just pass a style flag.

Image Type Flags:

DST_BITMAP — The image is a bitmap.

DST_COMPLEX — The image is application defined. To render the image, DrawState calls the callback function specified by the lpDrawProc parameter.

DST_ICON — The image is an icon.

DST_PREFIXTEXT	The image is text that may contain an accelerator mnemonic. DrawState interprets the ampersand (&) prefix character as a directive to underscore the character that follows.
DST_TEXT	The image is text.

Image State Flags:

DSS_DEFAULT	Makes the image bold.
DSS_DISABLED	Embosses the image.
DSS_MONO	Draws the image using the brush specified by the *hBrush* or *pBrush* parameter.
DSS_NORMAL	Draws the image without making any changes.
DSS_UNION	Dithers the image.

hBrush	For the DSS_MONO state, contains a handle to the brush that will be used to draw the image. For all other states this parameter is ignored and can be left off.
pBitmap	A pointer to a CBitmap object that represents the bitmap image that is to be drawn.
pBrush	For the DSS_MONO state, contains a pointer to the brush that will be used to draw the image. For all other states this parameter is ignored and can be left off.
hIcon	A handle to the icon image that is to be drawn.
lpszText	A pointer to a NULL-terminated buffer containing the text string to be drawn.
bPrefixText	This parameter should be TRUE if the specified text may contain the prefix character & and you want the & to translate to underscoring the following character. Otherwise, set this parameter to FALSE.
nTextLen	The length of the text pointed to by *lpszText*.
lpDrawProc	A pointer to a DRAWSTATEPROC custom drawing procedure. MFC will call this procedure to actually draw the image. For more information about DRAWSTATEPROC, see the Windows SDK documentation.
lData	User-defined data that will be passed to the drawing procedure pointed to by *lpDrawProc*.

Returns Non-zero if successful; otherwise, zero.

Example

```
...
CClientDC dc(pWnd);
CBitmap bmp;
CPoint pt(5,5);
CSize size(20,20);

bmp.LoadBitmap(IDB_MYBITMAP);

// draw the bitmap in a disabled (grayed) state
dc.DrawState(pt, size, &bmp, DSS_DISABLED);
```

DrawText

■ 2.0 ■ 3.0

Description Draws formatted text using the current font and text and background colors. Formatting can include alignment, tab expansion, and word wrap. If you do not need any special formatting, you can use the CDC::TextOut function which is faster. Unless the DT_NOCLIP flag is specified, this function clips the text to the specified rectangle. If the TA_UPDATECP flag has been set using the CDC::SetTextAlign function, all text alignment flags specified are ignored and the text is output begining at the current position instead. Note that the second version of this function became available in MFC Version 4.0.

Syntax public, virtual int DrawText(LPCTSTR lpszString, int nCount, LPRECT lpRect, UINT nFormat);
public, int DrawText(CString &strText, LPRECT lpRect, UINT nFormat);

Parameters

lpszString A pointer to the text to be drawn. If the *nCount* parameter is -1, the string must be NULL-terminated.

nCount The number of characters in the string pointed to by *lpszString*. If *lpszString* points to a NULL-terminated string this parameter may be -1, in which case DrawText calculates the length of the string.

lpRect A pointer to the rectangle into which the text will be drawn. The coordinates specified should be in logical units.

nFormat One or more flags describing the formatting of the text. If the DT_TABSTOP flag is specified, the DT_CALCRECT, DT_EXTERNALLEADING, DT_INTERNAL, DT_NOCLIP, and DT_NOPREFIX flags cannot be used. Valid formatting flags are listed below:

DT_BOTTOM If the DT_SINGLELINE flag is specified, the text will be bottom-aligned.

DT_CALCRECT Causes DrawText to determine the width and height of the rectangle required to draw the text without actually drawing it. If there are multiple lines of text, DrawText will use the width of the rectangle pointed to by lpRect and extend the base of the rectangle to bound the last line of text. If there is only one line of text, DrawText will modify the right side of the rectangle so that it bounds the last character in the line.

DT_CENTER Centers the text horizontally.

DT_EXPANDTABS Expands tab characters. The default number of characters per tab is eight.

DT_EXTERNALLEADING Includes the font's external leading in the line height. Normally, external leading is not included in the height of a line of text.

DT_LEFT Left-aligns the text.

DT_NOCLIP Draws the text without clipping. DrawText is somewhat faster when this flag is used.

DT_NOPREFIX	Turns off processing of prefix characters. Normally, DrawText interprets the ampersand (&) mnemonic-prefix character as a directive to underscore the character that follows, and the two-ampersand (&&) mnemonic-prefix characters as a directive to print a single ampersand. By specifying DT_NOPREFIX this processing is turned off.
DT_RIGHT	Right-aligns the text.
DT_SINGLELINE	Specifies single line only. Carriage returns and linefeeds do not break the line.
DT_TABSTOP	Sets tab stops. The high-order byte of *nFormat* is the number of characters for each tab. The default number of characters per tab is eight.
DT_TOP	If the DT_SINGLELINE flag is specified, top-aligns the text.
DT_VCENTER	If the DT_SINGLELINE flag is specified, vertically centers the text.
DT_WORDBREAK	Specifies word-breaking. Lines are automatically broken between words if a word would extend past the edge of the rectangle specified by *lpRect*. This flag is ignored if the TA_UPDATECP has been set using the CDC::SetTextAlign function.

&strText A reference to the CString containing the text to be drawn.

Returns The height of the drawn text.

See Also CDC::TextOut, CDC::ExtTextOut, CDC::TabbedTextOut, CDC::SetTextColor, CDC::SetTextAlign, ::DrawText

Example

```
..
CClientDC dc(pWnd);
RECT rect(10,10,300,25);
CString strTestMsg = "This is a text";
dc.DrawText(strTestMst,-1,rect,DT_SINGLELINE|DT_VCENTER|DT_LEFT);
..
```

DUMP

■ 2.0 ■ 3.0 ■ DO

Description Dump is a diagnostic function which outputs the current state of a CDC object to the specified dump context.

Syntax public, virtual void Dump(CDumpContext& dc) const;

Parameters

dc A reference to the dump context to which the status information should be sent. Usually this will be the MFC default debug dump context *afxDump*. *afxDump* sends its output to the debugger and only exists in the debug build of MFC.

Returns Nothing is returned.

See Also CObject::Dump, CDumpContext, afxDump

Figure 11-5 Sample output of Ellipse

Example

```
// call to dump function
CDC dc;
dc.Dump(afxDump);

// output from call
a CDC at $64F810
m_hDC = 0x0
m_hAttribDC = 0x0
m_bPrinting = 0
```

ELLIPSE

■ 2.0 ■ 3.0

Description Draws an ellipse outlined with the current pen and filled with the current brush. The center of the ellipse is the center of the specified bounding rectangle. A sample of an ellipse is shown in Figure 11-5.

Syntax public, BOOL Ellipse(int x1, int y1, int x2, int y2);
public, BOOL Ellipse(LPCRECT lpRect);

Parameters

x1	The x coordinate of the upper-left corner of the bounding rectangle (in logical units).
y1	The y coordinate of the upper-left corner of the bounding rectangle (in logical units).
y1	The x coordinate of the lower-right corner of the bounding rectangle (in logical units).
y2	The y coordinate of the lower-right corner of the bounding rectangle (in logical units).
lpRect	A pointer to the RECT structure or a CRect object containing the coordinates, in logical units, of the bounding rectangle of the ellipse.

Returns Nothing is returned.

See Also CDC::Arc, CDC::Chord, ::Ellipse

Example

```
...
CClientDC dc(pWnd);
CPen pen(PS_SOLID,1,RGB(255,0,0)), *pOldPen;
CBrush brush(RBG(0,255,0)), *pOldBrush;

// draw a red-outlined, blue-filled ellipse
pOldPen = dc.SelectObject(&pen);
```

```
pOldBrush = dc.SelectObject(&brush);
dc.Ellipse(1,1,200,100);

// select old GDI objects back
dc.SelectObject(pOldPen);
dc.SelectObject(pOldBrush);
..
```

EndDoc

■ 2.0 ■ 3.0

Description Ends the current document that was started with the CDC::StartDoc function. This function should be called immediately after finishing a successful print job. If the print job is being spooled using Print Manager, the job will be sent to the printer after this function is called.

Syntax public, int EndDoc( );

Parameters None.

Returns Greater than or equal to zero if successful; otherwise, one of the following values:

SP_ERROR General error.

SP_OUTOFDISK Not enough disk space is currently available for spooling, and no more space will become available.

SP_OUTOFMEMORY There is not enough memory available for spooling.

SP_USERABORT The user ended the job through the Print Manager.

See Also CDC::StartDoc, CDC::AbortDoc, CDC::Escape

Example

```
..
CString strTestMsg = "Test Print Message";
DOCINFO docInfo;
docInfo.cbSize = sizeof(DOCINFO);
docInfo.lpszDocName = "Test Document";
docInfo.lpszOutput = NULL;
printDc.StartDoc(&docInfo);
printDc.TextOut(5,20,strTestMsg);
printDc.EndDoc();
..
```

EndPage

■ 2.0 ■ 3.0

Description Ends the current page when printing. Normally, this would instruct the printer driver to advance to the next page. Unfortunately, calling EndPage and the corresponding CDC::StartPage functions perform different operations depending on what version of Windows you are running. EndPage advances to the next page on all platforms; however, the state of the device context after the call varies. On Windows 3.x, the device context is returned to its default state. Objects are selected out of the device context and the mapping mode is set back to the default. On Windows 95 this is not done when EndPage is called but it is done when CDC::StartPage is called. On Windows NT (begining with version 3.5), the device context is not reset in either case.

Syntax public, int EndPage( );

Parameters None.

Returns Greater than or equal to zero if successful; otherwise, one of the following values:

SP_ERROR General error.

SP_OUTOFDISK Not enough disk space is currently available for spooling, and no more space will become available.

SP_OUTOFMEMORY There is not enough memory available for spooling.

SP_USERABORT The user ended the job through the Print Manager.

SP_APPABORT Job was ended because the application's abort function returned 0.

See Also CDC::StartPage, ::EndPage

Example

```
..
CString strTestMsg = "Test Print Message";
DOCINFO docInfo;
docInfo.cbSize = sizeof(DOCINFO);
docInfo.lpszDocName = "Test Document";
docInfo.lpszOutput = NULL;
printDc.StartDoc(&docInfo);

// print message on page 1
printDc.StartPage();
printDc.TextOut(5,20,strTestMsg);
printDc.EndPage();

// print message on page 2
printDc.StartPage();
printDc.TextOut(5,20,strTestMsg);
printDc.EndPage();

printDc.EndDoc();
..
```

EndPath ■ 3.0 ■ NM

Description Ends the current path bracket (begun with the CDC::BeginPath function) and selects the path into the device context. The path can then be manipulated (filled, outlined, etc.).

Syntax public, BOOL EndPath( );

Parameters None.

Returns Greater than zero if successful; otherwise, 0. If 0 is returned, you can call ::GetLastError to retrieve a more descriptive error code, which may be one of the following values: ERROR_CAN_NOT_COMPLETE, ERROR_INVALID_PARAMETER.

See Also CDC::BeginPath, ::EndPath

Example

```
..
dc.BeginPath();
dc.MoveTo(1,1);
dc.LineTo(20,27);
dc.Rectangle(100,100,200,200);
dc.EndPath();
dc.FillPath();
```

EnumObjects

■ 2.0 ■ 3.0

Description Enumerates the pens or brushes available in the device context. For each pen or brush, EnumObjects calls a specified callback procedure and passes it information regarding the pen or brush. If pens are being enumerated, the data passed to the callback function is a LOGPEN structure. If brushes are being enumerated, the data passed is a LOGBRUSH structure. The process of enumeration continues until all pens or brushes have been enumerated or the callback function returns zero.

Syntax public int EnumObjects(int nObjectType, int (CALLBACK * lpfn)(LPVOID, LPARAM), LPARAM lpData);

Parameters

nObjectType The type of object to enumerate. Can be OBJ_BRUSH or OBJ_PEN.

lpfn A pointer to the callback function which will be invoked for each pen or brush.

lpData User-defined data which will be passed to the callback procedure.

Returns The last value returned by the specified callback function. Since the callback function is defined by the developer, the meaning of this value is user-defined.

See Also ::EnumObjects

Example

```
...
CClientDC dc(pWnd);

// enumerate brushes available in DC - pass address of our dc object
// just in case enumeration function wants it (remember - a callback
// function can not be a non-static object member function)
dc.EnumObjects(OBJ_BRUSH,myCallback,&dc);

// call back definition
int myCallback(LPVOID lpObj, LPARAM lpData)
{
      // parse out Parameters
      CDC *pDc = (CDC *)lpData;
      LOGBRUSH *pLogBrush = (LOGBRUSH *)lpObj;

}
```

ESCAPE

■ 2.0 ■ 3.0

Description Allows an application to send commands to a device that is not directly supported by Windows. The first version of Escape should be used for sending driver-defined escape codes to the device. The second version of Escape should be used for sending escape commands which are defined by Windows. In the Win32 API, many escape commands have been replaced by specific functions. The following are several functions which replace escape commands:

AbortDoc Terminates a print job. Replaces the ABORTDOC escape.

EndDoc Ends a print job. Replaces the ENDDOC escape.

EndPage Ends a page. Replaces the NEWFRAME escape. Unlike the NEWFRAME escape, this function is always called after printing a page.

SetAbortProc Sets the abort function for a print job. Replaces the SETABORTPROC escape.

StartDoc Starts a print job. Replaces the STARTDOC escape.

StartPage Prepares the printer driver to receive data.

In addition to providing several new commands, the Win32 API also provides several new flags for use with the CDC::GetDeviceCaps function which also replace escape commands. A list of these new flags is shown below:

PHYSICALHEIGHT Height, in pixels, of the physical page. Replaces the GETPHYSPAGESIZE escape.

PHYSICALOFFSETX Offset in the x direction, in pixels, from the upper-left corner of the physical page where the actual printing or drawing begins. Replaces the GETPRINTINGOFFSET escape.

PHYSICALOFFSETY Offset in the y direction, in pixels, from the upper-left corner of the physical page where the actual printing or drawing begins. Replaces the GETPRINTINGOFFSET escape.

PHYSICALWIDTH Width, in pixels, of the physical page. Replaces the GETPHYSPAGESIZE escape.

SCALINGFACTORX Scaling factor for the x-axis of a printer. Replaces the GETSCALINGFACTOR escape.

SCALINGFACTORY Scaling factor for the y-axis of a printer. Replaces the GETSCALINGFACTOR escape.

The following escape commands are supported in Win32 only for backward compatibility with 16-bit windows: ABORTDOC, ENDDOC, GETPHYSPAGESIZE, GETPRINTINGOFFSET, GETSCALINGFACTOR, NEWFRAME, NEXTBAND, PASSTHROUGH, SETABORTPROC, and STARTDOC. Note that the second version of the function, shown below, is not available on the Macintosh version of MFC.

Syntax public, virtual int Escape(int nEscape, int nCount, LPCSTR lpszInData, LPVOID lpOutData); public, int Escape(int nEscape, int nInputSize, LPCSTR lpszInputData, int nOutputSize, LPSTR lpszOutputData);

Parameters

nEscape The escape command to send to the device.

nCount The size (in bytes) of the buffer pointed to by the *lpszInData* parameter.

lpszInData Points to the input data structure required for the escape specified by *nEscape.*

lpOutData Points to the output data structure which will receive the results of the escape. If the specified escape does not produce output data, this parameter should be NULL.

nInputSize The size (in bytes) of the buffer pointed to by the *lpszInputData* parameter.

lpszInputData Points to the input data structure required for the escape specified by *nEscape.*

nOutputSize The size (in bytes) of the buffer pointed to by the *lpszOutputData* parameter.

lpszOutputData Points to the output data structure that will receive the results of the escape. If the specified escape does not produce output data, this parameter should be NULL.

Returns Positive if the function is successful or in the case of the QUERYESCSUPPORT escape, if the escape is supported. Zero is returned if the QUERYESCSUPPORT escape is used and the specified escape is not implemented. A negative value is returned if an error occurs. The following are common error values:

SP_ERROR A general error occurred.

SP_OUTOFDISK Not enough disk space is currently available for spooling, and no more space will become available.

SP_OUTOFMEMORY Not enough memory is available for spooling.

SP_USERABORT User ended the job through the Print Manager.

See Also CDC::StartDoc, CDC::EndDoc, CDC::AbortDoc, CDC::StartPage, CDC::EndPage, CDC::SetAbortProc, CDC::GetDeviceCaps, ::Escape, ::ExtEscape

ExcludeClipRect ■ 2.0 ■ 3.0

Description Creates a new clipping region by removing the specified rectangle from the current clipping region. In effect, this will prevent drawing within the specified rectangle.

Syntax public, int ExcludeClipRect(int x1, int y1, int x2, int y2); public, int ExcludeClipRect(LPCRECT lpRect);

Parameters

x1	The x coordinate of the upper-left corner of the rectangle to exclude (in logical coordinates).
y1	The y coordinate of the upper-left corner of the rectangle to exclude (in logical coordinates).
x2	The x coordinate of the lower-right corner of the rectangle to exclude (in logical coordinates).
y2	The y coordinate of the lower-right corner of the rectangle to exclude (in logical coordinates).
lpRect	A pointer to a RECT structure or a CRect object defining the rectangle, in logical coordinates, to exclude.
Returns	The type of the new clipping region. It can be any one of the following values:
COMPLEXREGION	Region has overlapping borders.
NULLREGION	Region is empty.
SIMPLEREGION	Region has no overlapping borders.
ERROR	No region was created.
See Also	CDC::ExcludeUpdateRgn, ::ExcludeClipRect

Example

```
...
CClientDC dc(pWnd);
CRect rect(100,100,500,500);

// create a "whole" in the clipping region
dc.ExcludeClipRect(rect);

// this rectangle will be clipped so that only half of it will be
// visible (400,400 to 500,500)
dc.Rectangle(400,400,600,600);
```

ExcludeUpdateRgn ■ 2.0 ■ 3.0

Description	Excludes the current update region from the current clipping region. The update region of a specified window is the area of that window that is currently flagged for repainting (it has been invalidated). Calling ExcludeUpdateRgn prevents any drawing from taking place in this area.
Syntax	public, int ExcludeUpdateRgn(CWnd* pWnd);
Parameters	
pWnd	A pointer to the window in which the update region should be excluded.
Returns	The type of region which was excluded. It can be any one of the following values:
COMPLEXREGION	Region has overlapping borders.
NULLREGION	Region is empty.

SIMPLEREGION	Region has no overlapping borders.
ERROR	No region was created.

See Also CDC::ExcludeClipRect, ::ExcludeUpdateRgn

EXTFLOODFILL

■ 2.0 ■ 3.0 ■ NM

Description Fills an area containing a specified point and bounded by a specified color or filled with a specified color, with the current brush. Filling begins at the specified point and continues in all directions until the color boundary is reached. If the FLOODFILLBORDER style is used, the color boundary is defined by one color. Filling continues outward from the specified point in all directions until the specified color is reached. If the FLOODFILLSURFACE style is specified, the area containing the specified start point is assumed to be of one color and filling continues outward from the specified start point in all directions until any color other that the specified one is reached.

Syntax public, BOOL ExtFloodFill(int x, int y, COLORREF crColor, UINT nFillType);

Parameters

x The x coordinate (in logical units) of the point where filling should begin.

y The y coordinate (in logical units) of the point where filling should begin.

crColor The RGB value of the color that bounds the area to be filled (if the FLOODFILLBORDER style is specified) or the color of the area to be filled (if the FLOODFILLSURFACE style is specified).

nFillType The type of filling to be performed. Must be one of the following values:

FLOODFILLBORDER The fill area is bounded by the color specified by *crColor*. Using this style causes ExtFloodFill to behave exactly as CDC::FloodFill.

FLOODFILLSURFACE The fill area is defined by the color specified by *crColor*. Filling continues outward in all directions as long as the specified color is encountered. This style allows for the filling of areas that are bounded by several different colors but are themselves uniform in color.

Returns Non-zero if successful; otherwise, zero.

See Also CDC::FloodFill, ::ExtFloodFill

Example

```
...
CClientDC dc(pWnd);
CPen *pOldPen, pen(PS_SOLID,1,RGB(255,0,0));
CBrush *pOldBrush, brush(RGB(0,0,255));

pOldPen = dc.SelectObject(&pen);
pOldBrush = dc.SelectObject(&brush);

// draw a red rectangle
dc.Rectangle(100,100,400,200);
```

continued on next page

continued from previous page

```
// fill the rectangle with blue
dc.ExtFloodFill(117,153,RGB(255,0,0),FLOODFILLBORDER);

// clean up
dc.SelectObject(pOldPen);
dc.SelectObject(pOldBrush);
```

ExtTextOut

■ 2.0 ■ 3.0

Description Outputs text at a specified location and optionally clips the text to a given rectangle. This function will also optionally fill the output area, defined by the specified output rectangle, with the current background color of the device context. By default, ExtTextOut outputs the text at a user-defined location. Optionally, you can use the CDC::SetTextAlign function with the TA_UPDATECP option to force ExtTextOut to output the text beginning at the current position. In this case, the *x* and *y* parameters to ExtTextOut are ignored and if the function is successful, ExtTextOut updates the current position. The current position is updated to the end of the previous line of text or to the position specified by the last element of the array pointed to by the *lpDxWidths* parameter, whichever is greater. Note that the second version of this function became available beginning with MFC Version 4.0.

Syntax public, virtual BOOL ExtTextOut(int x, int y, UINT nOptions, LPCRECT lpRect, LPCTSTR lpszString, UINT nCount, LPINT lpDxWidths);
public, BOOL ExtTextOut(int x, int y, UINT nOptions, LPCRECT lpRect, const CString &strText, LPINT lpDxWidths);

Parameters

x	The x coordinate (in logical units) where the text output should begin.
y	The y coordinate (in logical units) where the text output should begin.
nOptions	Zero, one, or both of the following flags:
ETO_CLIPPED	The text should be clipped to the rectangle pointed to by *lpRect*.
ETO_OPAQUE	The current background color should fill the rectangle pointed to by *lpRect*.
lpRect	A pointer to a RECT structure or a CRect object that describes the rectangle that may optionally be used for clipping the text or may be painted with the current background color. This parameter may be NULL if clipping and filling are not necessary.
lpszString	A pointer to a character buffer containing the text to output.
nCount	The length of the string pointed to by *lpszString*.
lpDxWidths	Points to an array of values that indicate the distance between origins of adjacent character cells. For example, lpDxWidths[i] logical units will separate the origins of character cell i and character cell i + 1. This para-

meter may be NULL, in which case ExtTextOut uses the default spacing between characters.

strText A reference to a CString object which contains the text to draw.

Returns Nothing is returned.

See Also CDC::TextOut, CDC::TabbedTextOut, CDC::DrawText, CDC::SetTextAlign, ::ExtTextOut

Example

```
...
CClientDC dc(pWnd);
CRect rect(1,1,100,30);
CString strText("Test Message");

// draw the text and fill the specified rectangle with the current brush
dc.ExtTextOut(5,20,ETO_OPAQUE, rect, strText);
```

FillPath

■ 3.0 ■ NM

Description FillPath closes any open figures in the current path and fills the path's interior using the current brush and polygon-filling mode. After the interior of the path is filled, the path is deselected from the device context.

Syntax public, BOOL FillPath( );

Parameters None.

Returns Non-zero if the function is successful; 0 otherwise. If 0 is returned, you can call ::GetLastError to retrieve a more descriptive error code, which may be one of the following values: ERROR_CAN_NOT_COMPLETE, ERROR_INVALID_PARAMETER, ERROR_NOT_ENOUGH_MEMORY.

See Also CDC::BeginPath, CDC::EndPath, CDC::SetPolyFillMode, CDC::StrokeAndFillPath, CDC::StrokePath, ::FillPath

Example

```
...
CClientDC dc(pWnd);
CBrush *pOldBrush, brush(RGB(0,0,255));

// make a little path
dc.BeginPath();
dc.MoveTo(10,10);
dc.LineTo(100,50);
dc.LineTo(120,75);
dc.EndPath();

// close the triangular path and fill it with the blue brush
pOldBrush = dc.SelectObject(&brush);
dc.FillPath();

// clean up
dc.SelectObject(pOldBrush);
```

FillRect

■ 2.0 ■ 3.0

Description Fills the specified rectangle with the specified brush. The rectangle is filled including the left and top borders but excluding the right and bottom borders. The rectangle must be normalized; otherwise the rectangle will not be filled. A rectangle is normalized if the top is less than the bottom and the left is less than the right.

Syntax public, void FillRect(LPCRECT lpRect, CBrush* pBrush);

Parameters

lpRect A pointer to a RECT structure or a CRect object containing the coordinates (in logical coordinates) of the rectangle to fill.

pBrush A pointer to the brush to be used to fill the rectangle.

Returns Nothing is returned.

See Also CDC::FillSolidRect

Example

```
..
CClientDC dc(pWnd);
CBrush brush(RBG(100,100,100));
CRect rect(1,1,100,100);
dc.FillRect(rect,&brush);
..
```

FillRgn

■ 2.0 ■ 3.0

Description Fills the specified region with the specified brush. The region is not outlined.

Syntax public, BOOL FillRgn(CRgn* pRgn, CBrush* pBrush);

Parameters

pRgn A pointer to the region to be filled.

pBrush A pointer to the brush to use to fill the region.

Returns Non-zero if successful; otherwise 0.

See Also CDC::FrameRgn, CDC::PaintRgn, CBrush::CreateSolidBrush, CBrush::CreateHatchBrush, CBrush::CreatePatternBrush, CBrush::CreateDIBPatternBrush

Example

```
..
CClientDC dc(pWnd);
CBrush brush(RGB(0,0,0));
CRgn rgn;
rgn.CreateRectRgn(1,1,100,100);
dc.FillRgn(&rgn,&brush);
..
```

FillSolidRect

■ 2.0 ■ 3.0

Description Fills a specified rectangle by setting the background color to the specified color and then calling the SDK function ::ExtTextOut using the ETO_OPAQUE attribute and an empty text string. This is the fastest way to draw a solid color rectangle.

Syntax public, void FillSolidRect(int x, int y, int cx, int cy, COLORREF clr);
public, void FillSolidRect(LPCRECT lpRect, COLORREF clr);

Parameters

x The x coordinate (in logical coordinates) of the upper-left corner of the rectangle to fill.

y The y coordinate (in logical coordinates) of the upper-left corner of the rectangle to fill.

cx The width (in logical units) of the rectangle to fill.

cy The height (in logical units) of the rectangle to fill.

clr The RGB color with which to fill the rectangle.

lpRect A pointer to a RECT structure or a CRect object containing the position and size of the rectangle to fill.

Returns Nothing is returned.

See Also CDC::FillRect

Example

```
..
CClientDC dc(pWnd);
dc.FillSolidRect(1,1,100,100,RGB(255,0,0));

// or fill like this
CRect rect(1,1,100,100);
dc.FillSolidRect(rect,RGB(255,0,0));
..
```

FlattenPath

■ 3.0 ■ NM

Description Converts any curves contained in the path currently selected into the device context into line segments. This can be useful if you want to retrieve the path using the CDC::GetPath function but do not want to handle curves.

Syntax public, BOOL FlattenPath( );

Parameters None.

Returns Non-zero if successful; otherwise, 0.

See Also CDC::WidenPath

Example

```
...
CClientDC dc(pWnd);
CPoints curvePts[7] = {CPoint(10,10), CPoint(40,17), CPoint(50,22),
          CPoint(55,27), CPoint(42,35), CPoint(37,32), CPoint(30,22)};

// make a path with curves
dc.BeginPath();
dc.PolyBezier(curvePts,7);
dc.EndPath();

// flatten the path before getting it because we don't like curves
dc.FlattenPath();

int nCount = dc.GetPath(NULL,NULL,0); // determine buffer size needed
CPoint *pts = new CPoint[nCount];
BYTE *types = new BYTE[nCount];

// now get the path
dc.GetPath(pts,types,nCount);

// do something with the flattened path

// clean up
delete pts;
delete types;
```

FloodFill

■ 2.0 ■ 3.0 ■ NM

Description Fills an area containing a specified point and bounded by a specified color with the current brush. Filling begins at the specified point and continues in all directions until the color boundary is reached.

Syntax public, BOOL FloodFill(int x, int y, COLORREF crColor);

Parameters

x The x coordinate (in logical units) of the point where filling should begin.

y The y coordinate (in logical units) of the point where filling should begin.

crColor The RGB value of the color which bounds the area to be filled.

Returns Non-zero if successful; otherwise, zero.

See Also CDC::ExtFloodFill, ::FloodFill

Example

```
...
CClientDC dc(pWnd);
CPen *pOldPen, pen(PS_SOLID,1,RGB(255,0,0));
CBrush *pOldBrush, brush(RGB(0,0,255));

pOldPen = dc.SelectObject(&pen);
pOldBrush = dc.SelectObject(&brush);

// draw a red rectangle
dc.Rectangle(100,100,400,200);

// fill the rectangle with blue
```

```
dc.FloodFill(117,153,RGB(255,0,0));

// clean up
dc.SelectObject(pOldPen);
dc.SelectObject(pOldBrush);
```

FRAMERECT

■ 2.0 ■ 3.0

Description Outlines the specified rectangle using the specified brush. The outline, or frame, is always one logical unit thick. The outline created is the same as what would be created using the CDC::Rectangle function with a pen that is one logical unit thick. This function will not frame the specified rectangle if that rectangle is not normalized. A rectangle is normalized if the top is less than the bottom and the left is less than the right.

Syntax public, void FrameRect(LPCRECT lpRect, CBrush* pBrush);

Parameters

lpRect A pointer to a RECT structure or a CRect object that defines the rectangle to frame. The coordinates specified should be in logical units.

pBrush A pointer to the brush which will be used to frame the rectangle.

Returns Nothing is returned.

See Also CDC::Rectangle, CDC::FillRect, ::FrameRect

Example

```
...
CClientDC dc(pWnd);
CRect rect(1,1,200,100);
CBrush brush(RGB(0,0,255));

// frame the rectangle using the blue brush
dc.FrameRect(rect,&brush);
```

FRAMERGN

■ 2.0 ■ 3.0

Description Outlines the specified region with the specified brush.

Syntax public, BOOL FrameRgn(CRgn* pRgn, CBrush* pBrush, int nWidth, int nHeight);

Parameters

pRgn A pointer to the region to be framed using the specified brush.

pBrush A pointer to the brush to use to frame the region.

nWidth The horizontal width of the stroke used to frame the region. This will be the width of the frame on vertical edges of the region. This parameter should be in device units unless the program is running under Windows 3.0 or earlier, in which case it should be in logical units.

nHeight The vertical height of the stroke used to frame the region. This will be the height of the frame on horizontal edges of the region. This parameter should be in device units unless the program is running under Windows 3.0 or earlier, in which case it should be in logical units.

Returns Non-zero if successful; otherwise, zero.

See Also CDC::FillRgn, CDC::PaintRgn, ::FrameRgn

Example

```
...
CRgn rgn;
CClientDC dc(pWnd);
CBrush solidBrush(RGB(255,0,0)), *pOldBrush;

pOldBrush = dc.SelectObject(&solidBrush);
rgn.CreateRectRgn(1,1,150,100);

// outline the region with the red brush
dc.FrameRgn(&rgn,&solidBrush,1,1);

// clean up
dc.SelectObject(pOldBrush);
...
```

FromHandle ■ 2.0 ■ 3.0

Description Returns a pointer to a CDC given a Windows device context handle. If MFC does not already have a permanent CDC associated with the specified handle, it creates a temporary one and attaches it to the handle. Temporary CDC objects are automatically destroyed during idle-time processing so you can only depend on the validity of the CDC returned by FromHandle until your application enters its idle loop which can occur any time you return control to Windows (i.e., returning from a message map).

Syntax public, static CDC* PASCAL FromHandle(HDC hDC);

Parameters

hDC A handle to the Windows device context object for which a CDC should be returned.

Returns A pointer to a CDC which may be temporary.

See Also CDC::DeleteTempMap

Example

```
void CMyWnd::SomeDrawFunc(HDC hDc)
{
      // get a possibly temporary CDC
      CDC *pTempDc = CDC::FromHandle(hDC);
      pTempDc->Rectangle(1,1,50,50);
}
```

GetArcDirection ■ 2.0 ■ 3.0 ■ NM

Description Retrieves the current arc direction. Both arcs and rectangles are drawn in the direction indicated by the current arc direction.

Syntax public, int GetArcDirection( ) const;

Parameters None.

Returns If the function is successful, the current arc direction which may be AD_COUNTERCLOCKWISE or AD_CLOCKWISE. If unsuccessful, zero.

See Also CDC::SetArcDirection, ::GetArcDirection

Example

```
...
CClientDC dc(pWnd);

// get the default arc direction
int nArcDir = dc.GetArcDirection();
```

GetAspectRatioFilter ■ 2.0 ■ 3.0

Description Retrieves the current aspect-ratio filter. The aspect ratio is the ratio formed by a device's pixel width and height. Information about a device's aspect ratio is used in the creation, selection, and display of fonts. Windows provides a special filter, the aspect-ratio filter, to select fonts designed for a particular device from all of the available fonts. The filter uses the aspect ratio specified by the CDC::SetMapperFlags member function.

Syntax public, CSize GetAspectRatioFilter( ) const;

Parameters None.

Returns A CSize object containing the aspect ratio used by the current aspect ratio filter.

See Also CDC::SetMapperFlags, ::GetAspectRatioFilter, ::GetAspectRatioFilterEx

Example

```
...
CClientDC dc(pWnd);

// get current aspect ratio
Csize size = dc.GetAspectRatioFilter();
```

GetBkColor ■ 2.0 ■ 3.0

Description Retrieves the RGB value of the current background color for the device context. If the background mode is OPAQUE, the system uses the background color to fill the gaps in styled lines, the gaps between hatched lines in brushes, and the background in character cells. The system also uses the background color when converting bitmaps between color and monochrome device contexts. When a monochrome bitmap is converted to color, all bits that are on (1) are set to the current background color.

Syntax public, COLORREF GetBkColor( ) const;

Parameters None.

Returns The RGB value of the current background color.

See Also CDC::SetBkColor, CDC::GetBkMode, CDC::SetBkMode, ::GetBkColor

Example

```
...
CClientDC dc(pWnd);

// get default background color
COLORREF cr = dc.GetBkColor();
```

GetBkMode

■ 2.0 ■ 3.0

Description Retrieves the current background mode. The background mode defines whether the system repaints the background with the current background color when drawing text, hatched brushes, or any pen style that is not a solid line.

Syntax public, int GetBkMode( ) const;

Parameters None.

Returns The current background mode that may be TRANSPARENT, indicating that the background will not be touched, or OPAQUE, indicating that the background will be painted with the current background color.

See Also CDC::SetBkMode, CDC::GetBkColor, CDC::SetBkColor, ::GetBkMode

Example

```
...
CClientDC dc(pWnd);
int nMode = dc.GetBkMode(); // retrieve default background mode
...
```

GetBoundsRect

■ 2.0 ■ 3.0 ■ NM

Description Retrieves the current accumulated bounding rectangle for the device context and optionally clears the bounding rectangle. The bounding rectangle is accumulated by ORing (union) the bounding rectangle of anything drawn to the device content with the current bounding rectangle for the device context.

Syntax public, UINT GetBoundsRect(LPRECT lpRectBounds, UINT flags);

Parameters

lpRectBounds A pointer to a RECT structure or a CRect object into which the bounding rectangle will be placed. The coordinates of the rectangle are in logical units.

flags Can be zero or a combination of the following flags:

DCB_RESET Clears the bounding rectangle after it is returned.

DCB_WINDOWMGR Retrieves the Windows bounding rectangle instead of the application's.

Returns If successful, the current state of the bounding rectangle; otherwise zero. The current state is expressed as a combination of the following values:

DCB_ACCUMULATE Bounding rectangle accumulation is occurring.

DCB_RESET The bounding rectangle is empty.

DCB_SET The bounding rectangle is not empty.

DCB_ENABLE Bounding accumulation is on.

DCB_DISABLE Bounding accumulation is off.

See Also CDC::SetBoundsRect, ::GetBoundsRect

GetBrushOrg

■ 2.0 ■ 3.0

Description Retrieves the current brush origin. The default brush origin for a device context is 0,0. Because a brush is represented by an eight pixel by eight pixel bitmap, both the x and y coordinates of the brush origin can range from zero to seven. When a drawing operation requires a brush, Windows maps the upper-left corner of the brush bitmap (0,0) to the point in the client area of the destination window specified by the current brush origin. For example, if the current brush origin is set to (3,1) Windows will map the upper-left corner of the brush bitmap (0,0) with the point (3,1) in the client area of the Window in which it is drawing.

Syntax public, CPoint GetBrushOrg( ) const;

Parameters None.

Returns A CPoint object containing the coordinates of the current brush origin in device units

See Also CDC::SetBrushOrg, ::GetBrushOrg, ::GetBrushOrgEx

Example

```
...
CClientDC dc(pWnd);

// get default brush origin (0,0)
CPoint ptOrg = dc.GetBrushOrg();
```

GetCharABCWidths

■ 2.0 ■ 3.0

Description Retrieves the widths of a specified range of characters from the current TrueType font. The widths retrieved are in logical units. This function will fail if the current font in the device context is not a TrueType font. For non-TrueType fonts, use the CDC::GetCharWidth function. The TrueType rasterizer provides "ABC" character spacing after a specific point size has been selected for the font. "A" spacing refers to the distance that is added to the current position before placing the glyph; "B" spacing refers to the width of the black part of the glyph; and "C" spacing refers to the distance added to the current position to account for the white space to the right of the glyph. The total advanced width is given by A + B + C. If a negative "A" or "C" width is retrieved for a character, that character includes underhangs or overhangs. For characters outside the range of the current font, this GetCharABCWidths returns the widths of the default character. Note that the second form of this function is not available on the Macintosh.

Syntax public, BOOL GetCharABCWidths(UINT nFirstChar, UINT nLastChar, LPABC lpabc) const;
public, BOOL GetCharABCWidths(UINT nFirstChar, UINT nLastChar, LPABCFLOAT lpABCF) const;

Parameters

nFirstChar The first character in the range of characters for which "ABC" widths are desired.

nLastChar The last character in the range of characters for which "ABC" widths are desired.

lpabc A pointer to an array of ABC structures that will be filled with the requested widths. The integer members of the ABC structure are described below:

abcA The "A" spacing of the character. The "A" spacing is the distance to add to the current position before drawing the character glyph.

abcB The "B" spacing of the character. The "B" spacing is the width of the drawn portion of the character glyph.

abcC The "C" spacing of the character. The "C" spacing is the distance to add to the current position to provide white space to the right of the character glyph.

lpABCF A pointer to an array of ABCFLOAT structures that will be filled with the requested widths. The float members of the ABCFLOAT structure are described below:

abcfA The "A" spacing of the character. The "A" spacing is the distance to add to the current position before drawing the character glyph.

abcfB The "B" spacing of the character. The "B" spacing is the width of the drawn portion of the character glyph.

abcfC The "C" spacing of the character. The "C" spacing is the distance to add to the current position to provide white space to the right of the character glyph.

Returns Non-zero if successful; otherwise, zero.

See Also CDC::GetCharWidth, ::GetCharABCWidths

Example

```
...
CClientDC dc(pWnd);
CFont *pOldFont;

// assuming pFont is a TrueType font
pOldFont = dc.SelectObject(pFont);

// get abc widths for some characters
```

```
ABC widths[5];
dc.GetCharABCWidths('a','e',widths);

// clean up
dc.SelectObject(pOldFont);
```

GetCharWidth

■ 2.0 ■ 3.0

Description Retrieves the widths of a specified range of characters from the current font. The widths retrieved are in logical units. For characters outside the range of the current font, GetCharWidths returns the widths of the default character. Note that this function uses the attribute device context associated with the CDC object. To force the use of the output device context, use the CDC::GetOutputCharWidth function. Note that the second form of the function is not available on the Macintosh.

Syntax public, BOOL GetCharWidth(UINT nFirstChar, UINT nLastChar, LPINT lpBuffer) const;
public, BOOL GetCharWidth(UINT nFirstChar, UINT nLastChar, float* lpFloatBuffer) const;

Parameters

nFirstChar The first character in the range of characters for which a width is desired.

nLastChar The last character in the range of characters for which a width is desired.

lpBuffer A pointer to an array of unsigned integers that will be filled with the widths of the specified range of characters.

lpFloatBuffer A pointer to an array of floats that will be filled with the widths of the specified range of characters.

Returns Non-zero if successful; otherwise, zero.

See Also CDC::GetOutputCharWidth, CDC::GetCharABCWidths, ::GetCharWidth, ::GetCharWidthFloat, ::GetCharWidth32

Example

```
...
CClientDC dc(pWnd);

// get character widths for some characters
int widths[5];
dc.GetCharWidth('a','e',widths);
```

GetClipBox

■ 2.0 ■ 3.0

Description Retrieves the bounding rectangle of the current clipping region. The bounding rectangle is the smallest rectangle that can completely contain the clipping region.

Syntax public, virtual int GetClipBox(LPRECT lpRect) const;

Parameters

lpRect A pointer to a RECT structure or a CRect object that will be filled with the coordinates of the bounding rectangle.

Returns The clipping region's type. It can be one of the following values:

COMPLEXREGION Clipping region has overlapping borders.

NULLREGION Clipping region is empty.

SIMPLEREGION Clipping region has no overlapping borders.

ERROR Device context is not valid.

See Also CDC::SelectClipRgn, ::GetClipBox

Example

```
...
CClientDC dc(pWnd);
CRect clipBox;

// get initial clipping region (entire client area)
dc.GetClipBox(clipBox);
```

GetColorAdjustment ■ 3.0 ■ NM

Description Retrieves the color adjustment values in use for the device context. The color adjustment values are used to adjust the input color of the source bitmap for calls to the CDC::StretchBlt member function when HALFTONE mode is set.

Syntax public, BOOL GetColorAdjustment(LPCOLORADJUSTMENT lpColorAdjust) const;

Parameters

lpColorAdjust A pointer to a COLORADJUSTMENT structure. For a complete description of this structure, see the Windows SDK documentation.

Returns Non-zero if successful; otherwise, zero.

See Also CDC::SetColorAdjustment, CDC::StretchBlt, CDC::SetStretchBltMode, ::StretchDIBits

GetCurrentBitmap ■ 2.0 ■ 3.0

Description Retrieves a pointer to the currently selected bitmap. The bitmap object returned may be temporary. Temporary objects are automatically deleted by MFC as part of its idle time processing so you should not use the object returned by this function once you have given control back to Windows (after the current message has been processed).

Syntax public, CBitmap* GetCurrentBitmap( ) const;

Parameters None.

Returns A pointer to the current bitmap.

See Also CDC::SelectObject, ::GetCurrentObject

GetCurrentBrush ■ 2.0 ■ 3.0

Description Retrieves a pointer to the currently selected brush. The brush object returned may be temporary. Temporary objects are automatically deleted by MFC as part of its idle time processing so you should not use the object returned by this function once you have given control back to Windows (after the current message has been processed).

Syntax public, CBrush* GetCurrentBrush( ) const;

Parameters None.

Returns A pointer to the current brush.

See Also CDC::SelectObject, ::GetCurrentObject

Example

```
...
CClientDC dc(pWnd);

// get pointer to default brush
CBrush *pBrush = dc.GetCurrentBrush();
```

GetCurrentFont ■ 2.0 ■ 3.0

Description Retrieves a pointer to the currently selected font. The font object returned may be temporary. Temporary objects are automatically deleted by MFC as part of its idle time processing so you should not use the object returned by this function once you have given control back to Windows (after the current message has been processed).

Syntax public, CFont* GetCurrentFont( ) const;

Parameters None.

Returns A pointer to the current font.

See Also CDC::SelectObject, ::GetCurrentObject

Example

```
...
CClientDC dc(pWnd);

// get pointer to default system font
CFont *pFont = dc.GetCurrentFont();
```

GetCurrentPalette ■ 2.0 ■ 3.0

Description Retrieves a pointer to the currently selected palette. The palette object returned may be temporary. Temporary objects are automatically deleted by MFC as part of its idle time processing so you should not use the object returned by this function once you have given control back to Windows (after the current message has been processed).

Syntax public, CPalette* GetCurrentPalette( ) const;

Parameters None.

Returns A pointer to the current palette.

See Also CDC::SelectObject, ::GetCurrentObject

Example

```
...
CClientDC dc(pWnd);

// get pointer to default palette
CPalette *pPal = dc.GetCurrentPalette();
```

GetCurrentPen

■ 2.0 ■ 3.0

Description Retrieves a pointer to the currently selected pen. The pen object returned may be temporary. Temporary objects are automatically deleted by MFC as part of its idle time processing so you should not use the object returned by this function once you have given control back to Windows (after the current message has been processed).

Syntax public, CPen* GetCurrentPen( ) const;

Parameters None.

Returns A pointer to the current pen.

See Also CDC::SelectObject, ::GetCurrentObject

Example

```
...
CClientDC dc(pWnd);

// get pointer to default pen
CPen *pPen = dc.GetCurrentPen();
```

GetCurrentPosition

■ 2.0 ■ 3.0

Description Retrieves the current drawing position in logical coordinates.

Syntax public, CPoint GetCurrentPosition( ) const;

Parameters None.

Returns A CPoint object containing the coordinates of the current position (in logical units).

See Also CDC::MoveTo, ::GetCurrentPosition, ::GetCurrentPositionEx

Example

```
...
CClientDC dc(pWnd);

dc.MoveTo(1,5);
dc.LineTo(22,35);
...
CPoint ptCurPos = dc.GetCurrentPosition(); // ptCurPos = 22,35
```

GetDeviceCaps

■ 2.0 ■ 3.0

Description	Queries the device associated with the device context for various information regarding the capabilities of the device.
Syntax	public, int GetDeviceCaps(int nIndex) const;
Parameters	
nIndex	The capability to be queried. The following table lists the device capability values on the left and the possible return values for that query on the right:
DRIVERVERSION	The device driver version.
TECHNOLOGY	Device technology. It can be one of the following values:
DT_PLOTTER	Vector plotter.
DT_RASDISPLAY	Raster display.
DT_RASPRINTER	Raster printer.
DT_RASCAMERA	Raster camera.
DT_CHARSTREAM	Character stream.
DT_METAFILE	Metafile.
DT_DISPFILE	Display file.
HORZSIZE	Width, in millimeters, of the physical screen.
VERTSIZE	Height, in millimeters, of the physical screen.
HORZRES	Width, in pixels, of the screen.
VERTRES	Height, in raster lines, of the screen.
LOGPIXELSX	Number of pixels per logical inch along the screen width.
LOGPIXELSY	Number of pixels per logical inch along the screen height.
BITSPIXEL	Number of adjacent color bits for each pixel.
PLANES	Number of color planes.
NUMBRUSHES	Number of device-specific brushes.
NUMPENS	Number of device-specific pens.
NUMFONTS	Number of device-specific fonts.
NUMCOLORS	Number of entries in the device's color table.
ASPECTX	Relative width of a device pixel used for line drawing.
ASPECTY	Relative height of a device pixel used for line drawing.
ASPECTXY	Diagonal width of the device pixel used for line drawing.
PDEVICESIZE	Reserved.
CLIPCAPS	Flag that indicates the clipping capabilities of the device. If the device can clip to a rectangle, it is 1. Otherwise, it is 0.
SIZEPALETTE	Number of entries in the system palette. This index is valid only if the device driver sets the RC_PALETTE bit in the RASTERCAPS index and is available only if the driver is compatible with Windows version 3.0 or later.

NUMRESERVED	Number of reserved entries in the system palette. This index is valid only if the device driver sets the RC_PALETTE bit in the RASTERCAPS index and is available only if the driver is compatible with Windows version 3.0 or later.
COLORRES	Actual color resolution of the device, in bits per pixel. This index is valid only if the device driver sets the RC_PALETTE bit in the RASTERCAPS index and is available only if the driver is compatible with Windows version 3.0 or later.
PHYSICALWIDTH	For printing devices: the physical width, in device units.
PHYSICALHEIGHT	For printing devices: the physical height, in device units.
PHYSICALOFFSETX	For printing devices: the physical printable area horizontal margin.
PHYSICALOFFSETY	For printing devices: the physical printable area vertical margin.
SCALINGFACTORX	For printing devices: the scaling factor along the horizontal axis.
SCALINGFACTORY	For printing devices: the scaling factor along the vertical axis.
VREFRESH	Windows NT only: For display devices: the current vertical refresh rate of the device, in cycles per second (Hz).
DESKTOPHORZRES	Windows NT only: Width, in pixels, of the virtual desktop. This value may be larger than HORZRES if the device supports a virtual desktop or multiple displays.
DESKTOPVERTRES	Windows NT only: Height, in pixels, of the virtual desktop. This value may be larger than VERTRES if the device supports a virtual desktop or multiple displays.
BLTALIGNMENT	Windows NT only: Preferred horizontal drawing alignment, expressed as a multiple of pixels. For best drawing performance, windows should be horizontally aligned to a multiple of this value. A value of zero indicates that the device is accelerated, and any alignment may be used.
RASTERCAPS	Value that indicates the raster capabilities of the device.
RC_BANDING	Requires banding support.
RC_BITBLT	Capable of transferring bitmaps.
RC_BITMAP64	Capable of supporting bitmaps larger than 64K.
RC_DI_BITMAP	Capable of supporting the SetDIBits and GetDIBits functions.
RC_DIBTODEV	Capable of supporting the SetDIBitsToDevice function.
RC_FLOODFILL	Capable of performing flood fills.
RC_GDI20_OUTPUT	Capable of supporting features of Windows 2.0.
RC_PALETTE	Specifies a palette-based device.
RC_SCALING	Capable of scaling.
RC_STRETCHDIB	Capable of performing the StretchDIBits function.
CURVECAPS	Value that indicates the curve capabilities of the device.
CC_NONE	Device does not support curves.
CC_CIRCLES	Device can draw circles.

CC_PIE	Device can draw pie wedges.
CC_CHORD	Device can draw chord arcs.
CC_ELLIPSES	Device can draw ellipses.
CC_WIDE	Device can draw wide borders.
CC_STYLED	Device can draw styled borders.
CC_WIDESTYLED	Device can draw borders that are wide and styled.
CC_INTERIORS	Device can draw interiors.
CC_ROUNDRECT	Device can draw rounded rectangles.
LINECAPS	Value that indicates the line capabilities of the device.
LC_NONE	Device does not support lines.
LC_POLYLINE	Device can draw a polyline.
LC_MARKER	Device can draw a marker.
LC_POLYMARKER	Device can draw multiple markers.
LC_WIDE	Device can draw wide lines.
LC_STYLED	Device can draw styled lines.
LC_WIDESTYLED	Device can draw lines that are wide and styled.
LC_INTERIORS	Device can draw interiors.
POLYGONALCAPS	Value that indicates the polygon capabilities of the device.
PC_NONE	Device does not support polygons.
PC_POLYGON	Device can draw alternate-fill polygons.
PC_RECTANGLE	Device can draw rectangles.
PC_WINDPOLYGON	Device can draw winding-fill polygons.
PC_SCANLINE	Device can draw a single scanline.
PC_WIDE	Device can draw wide borders.
PC_STYLED	Device can draw styled borders.
PC_WIDESTYLED	Device can draw borders that are wide and styled.
PC_INTERIORS	Device can draw interiors.
TEXTCAPS	Value that indicates the text capabilities of the device.
TC_OP_CHARACTER	Device is capable of character output precision.
TC_OP_STROKE	Device is capable of stroke output precision.
TC_CP_STROKE	Device is capable of stroke clip precision.
TC_CR_90	Device is capable of 90-degree character rotation.
TC_CR_ANY	Device is capable of any character rotation.
TC_SF_X_YINDEP	Device can scale independently in the x- and y-directions.
TC_SA_DOUBLE	Device is capable of doubled character for scaling.
TC_SA_INTEGER	Device uses integer multiples only for character scaling.
TC_SA_CONTIN	Device uses any multiples for exact character scaling.
TC_EA_DOUBLE	Device can draw double-weight characters.

TC_IA_ABLE	Device can italicize.
TC_UA_ABLE	Device can underline.
TC_SO_ABLE	Device can draw strikeouts.
TC_RA_ABLE	Device can draw raster fonts.
TC_VA_ABLE	Device can draw vector fonts.
TC_RESERVED	Reserved; must be zero.
TC_SCROLLBLT	Device can scroll using a bit-block transfer.

Returns The return value depends on what capability was queried. See the Parameters section for possible return values.

See Also ::GetDeviceCaps, ::DeviceCapabilities

Example

```
...
CClientDC dc(pWnd);

// get the horizontal resolution of the screen (probably 640, 800, or
// 1024)
int nHorzRes = dc.GetDeviceCaps(HORZRES);
```

GetFontData ■ 2.0 ■ 3.0

Description Retrieves font-metric information from a TrueType font file. The information to retrieve is identified by specifying an offset into the font file and the length of the information to return. This function will fail if the font identified is not a TrueType font.

Syntax public, DWORD GetFontData(DWORD dwTable, DWORD dwOffset, LPVOID lpData, DWORD cbData) const;

Parameters

dwTable The name of the metric table to be returned. This parameter can be one of the metric tables documented in the TrueType Font Files specification published by Microsoft Corporation. If this parameter is 0, the information is retrieved starting at the beginning of the font file.

dwOffset The offset from the beginning of the table at which to begin retrieving information. If this parameter is 0, the information is retrieved starting at the beginning of the table specified by the *dwTable* parameter. If this value is greater than or equal to the size of the table, GetFontData returns 0.

lpData Points to a buffer that will be filled with the font information. This parameter can be NULL, in which case GetFontData will return the size of the buffer required, in bytes.

cbData The size of the buffer pointed to by *lpData.* If this parameter is 0, GetFontData returns the size of the data specified in the *dwTable* parameter.

Returns If *lpData* is NULL, the number of bytes required to hold the font information requested. Otherwise, if the function is successful, it returns the number of bytes copied to *lpData.* If the function fails, it returns zero.

See Also CDC::GetOutlineTextMetrics, ::GetFontData

GetGlyphOutline

■ 2.0 ■ 3.0 ■ NM

Description Retrieves the outline or bitmap for a character in the current TrueType font. If the current font is not a TrueType font, this function will fail. Note that the glyph outline returned by this function is for a grid-fitted glyph. A grid-fitted glyph is a glyph that has been modified so that its bitmapped image conforms, as closely as possible, to the original design of the glyph. If an application needs an unmodified glyph outline, it can request the glyph outline for a character in a font whose size is equal to the font's em unit. The value for a font's em unit is stored in the otmEMSquare member of the OUTLINETEXTMETRIC structure.

Syntax public, DWORD GetGlyphOutline(UINT nChar, UINT nFormat, LPGLYPHMETRICS lpgm, DWORD cbBuffer, LPVOID lpBuffer, const MAT2 * lpmat2) const;

Parameters

nChar The character for which the outline information should be retrieved

nFormat The format in which GetGlyphOutline should return the requested information. This parameter may be GGO_BITMAP, GGO_NATIVE, or zero. If this parameter is zero, GetGlyphOutline fills the GLYPHMETRICS structure pointed to by *lpgm* but does not retrieve any glyph outline information. If GGO_BITMAP is specified, the function retrieves the glyph bitmap. In this case, the buffer pointed to by *lpBuffer* contains a 1-bit-per-pixel bitmap whose rows start on doubleword boundaries. If GGO_NATIVE is specified, the function retrieves the curve data points in the rasterizer's native format, using device units. When this value is specified, any transformation specified in lpmat2 is ignored. The native format is a series of contours, each defined by a TTPOLYGONHEADER structure followed by as many TTPOLYCURVE structures as are required to describe it. For more information regarding these structures, see the Window SDK documentation.

lpgm A pointer to a GLYPHMETRICS structure which will be filled with information describing the placement of the glyph in the character cell. For a description of the GLYPHMETRICS structure, see the Windows SDK documentation.

cbBuffer The size of the buffer, in bytes, pointed to by the *lpBuffer* parameter. If this parameter is zero, GetGlyphOutline will return the number of bytes necessary to hold the requested information but will not actually retrieve the information.

lpBuffer A pointer to a buffer which will be filled with the requested glyph information. If this parameter is NULL, GetGlyphOutline will return the number of bytes necessary to hold the requested information but will not actually retrieve the information.

lpmat2	Points to a MAT2 structure that contains a transformation matrix for the character. This parameter cannot be NULL, even when the GGO_NATIVE value is specified for nFormat (in which case it is ignored). In this case, simply pass a pointer to an empty MAT2 structure. For more information regarding the MAT2 structure, see the Windows SDK documentation.
Returns	If *lpBuffer* is NULL or *cbBuffer* is zero, the size of the buffer (in bytes) required to hold the requested information. Otherwise, if the function is successful, it returns a positive value. If it fails, it returns -1.
See Also	CDC::GetOutlineTextMetrics, ::GetGlyphOutline

GetHalftoneBrush ■ 3.0 ■ UD

Description	A utility function used by MFC to create halftone brushes. This function creates only one brush and then, when called, attaches a temporary CBrush object to the halftone brush and returns it. Since the halftone brush for a given device context is always the same, this function aids in efficient resource management.
Syntax	public, static CBrush * PASCAL GetHalftoneBrush();
Parameters	None.
Returns	A CBrush object attached to a halftone brush for the device context.
See Also	CBrush::CreateHalftoneBrush

GetKerningPairs ■ 2.0 ■ 3.0 ■ NM

Description	Retrieves the character-kerning pairs for the current font.
Syntax	public, int GetKerningPairs(int nPairs, LPKERNINGPAIR lpkrnpair) const;
Parameters	
nPairs	The number of KERNINGPAIR structures in the array pointed to by *lpkrnpair*.
lpkrnpair	A pointer to an array of KERNINGPAIR structures that will be filled with the kerning pairs for the current font. This parameter can be NULL, in which case GetKerningPairs returns the total number of kerning pairs in the font. For a description of the KERNINGPAIR structure, see the Windows SDK documentation.
Returns	If the *lpkrnpair* parameter is NULL, the total number of kerning pairs in the font. Otherwise, if the function is successful it returns the number of kerning pairs copied to the supplied buffer. If the function fails, it returns zero.
See Also	::GetKerningPairs

Example

```
...
CClientDC dc(pWnd);

// first determine the buffer size we need
int nSize = dc.GetKerningPairs(0,NULL);

LPKERNINGPAIR pairs = new KERNINGPAIR[nSize];

// now get the pairs
dc.GetKerningPairs(nSize,pairs);

// do something with them

// clean up
delete pairs;
```

GetMapMode

■ 2.0 ■ 3.0

Description Retrieves the current mapping mode for the device context. The mapping mode controls how coordinates are mapped from the device to a logical coordinate space and vice versa.

Syntax public, int GetMapMode( ) const;

Parameters None.

Returns One of the following mapping mode constants:

MM_ANISOTROPIC Logical units are mapped to arbitrary units with arbitrarily scaled axes. The SetWindowExtEx and SetViewportExtEx functions can be used to specify the units, orientation, and scaling that should be used.

MM_HIENGLISH Each logical unit is mapped to 0.001 inch. Positive x is to the right; positive y is up.

MM_HIMETRIC Each logical unit is mapped to 0.01 millimeter. Positive x is to the right; positive y is up.

MM_ISOTROPIC Logical units are mapped to arbitrary units with equally scaled axes. One unit along the x-axis is equal to one unit along the y-axis. The SetWindowExtEx and SetViewportExtEx functions can be used to specify the units and the orientation of the axes that should be used. The Windows GDI makes adjustments as necessary to ensure the x and y units remain the same size.

MM_LOENGLISH Each logical unit is mapped to 0.01 inch. Positive x is to the right; positive y is up.

MM_LOMETRIC Each logical unit is mapped to 0.1 millimeter. Positive x is to the right; positive y is up.

MM_TEXT Each logical unit is mapped to one device pixel. Positive x is to the right; positive y is down. In effect, no mapping is done.

MM_TWIPS Each logical unit is mapped to one-twentieth of a printer's point (1/1440 inch, also called a "twip"). Positive x is to the right; positive y is up.

See Also CDC::SetMapMode, CDC::DPtoLP, CDC::LPtoDP, CDC::SetWindowOrg, CDC::SetWindowExt, CDC::SetViewportOrg, CDC::SetViewportExt, ::GetMapMode

Example

```
...
CClientDC dc(pWnd);

// get the default mapping mode (MM_TEXT)
int nMapMode = dc.GetMapMode();
```

GetMiterLimit ■ 3.0 ■ NM

Description Retrieves the current miter limit for the device context. The miter limit is used when drawing geometric lines that have miter joins.

Syntax public, float GetMiterLimit( ) const;

Parameters None.

Returns The current miter limit.

See Also CDC::SetMiterLimit, CPen::CreatePen, ::GetMiterLimit

Example

```
CClientDC dc(pWnd);

// get the default miter limit (10)
float fMiter = dc.GetMiterLimit();
```

GetNearestColor ■ 2.0 ■ 3.0

Description Returns an RGB color value representing the closest color to a specified color that can be represented by the device associated with the device context.

Syntax public, COLORREF GetNearestColor(COLORREF crColor) const;

Parameters

crColor The color for which a closest match should be found.

Returns The RGB color value of the closest color to the specified color that can be represented by the device. Use the SDK functions ::GetRValue, ::GetGValue, and ::GetBValue to retrieve the individual red, green, and blue intensity values.

See Also CPalette::GetNearestPaletteIndex, ::GetNearestColor, ::GetRValue, ::GetGValue, ::GetBValue

Example

```
...
CClientDC dc(pWnd);

// get the closest color to our red that the device can do (on VGA this
// would probably be bright red, RGB(255,0,0)
COLORREF crClosest = dc.GetNearestColor(RGB(210,10,10));
```

GetOutlineTextMetrics ■ 2.0 ■ 3.0

Description Retrieves metric information for the current TrueType font. If the current font is not a TrueType font, this function will fail.

Syntax public, UINT GetOutlineTextMetrics(UINT cbData, LPOUTLINETEXTMETRIC lpotm) const;

Parameters

cbData The size of the buffer pointed to by *lpotm*.

lpotm A pointer to an OUTLINETEXTMETRIC structure that will be filled with the metric information. If this parameter is NULL, GetOutlineTextMetrics returns the size of the buffer required to hold the necessary information. This is required because the last four members of the OUTLINETEXTMETRIC structure involve strings which may be of any length. For a detailed description of the OUTLINETEXTMETRIC structure, see the Window SDK documentation.

Returns If the *lpotm* parameter is NULL, the number of bytes required to hold the metric information. Otherwise, non-zero if successful and zero if the function fails.

See Also CDC::GetTextMetrics, ::GetOutlineTextMetrics, ::GetTextMetrics

Example

```
...
CClientDC dc(pWnd);

// assuming pFont is a TrueType font
CFont *pOldFont = dc.SelectFont(pFont);

// first find out size of buffer required
int nSize = dc.GetOutlineTextMetrics(0,NULL);

// now allocate the space and get the metric info
LPOUTLINETEXTMETRIC pMetrics = (LPOUTLINETEXTMETRIC)new char[nSize];
dc.GetOutlineTextMetrics(nSize,pMetrics);

// use metrics for something

// clean up
delete pMetrics;
```

GetOutputCharWidth ■ 2.0 ■ 3.0

Description Retrieves the widths of a specified range of characters from the current font. The widths retrieved are in logical units. For characters outside the range of the current font, GetCharWidths returns the widths of the default character. Note that this function uses the output device context associated with the CDC object. To force the use of the attribute device context, use the CDC::GetCharWidth function. Note that the second version of the function was done away with beginning with MFC Version 4.0.

Syntax
public, BOOL GetOutputCharWidth(UINT nFirstChar, UINT nLastChar, LPINT lpBuffer) const;
public, BOOL GetOutputCharWidth(UINT nFirstChar, UINT nLastChar, float* lpFloatBuffer) const;

Parameters

nFirstChar The first character in the range of characters for which a width is desired.

nLastChar The last character in the range of characters for which a width is desired.

lpBuffer A pointer to an array of unsigned integers which will be filled with the widths of the specified range of characters. Usually, integer values will provide enough accuracy. If you require the highest degree of accuracy, use the floating point version of GetOutputCharWidth.

lpFloatBuffer A pointer to an array of floats which will be filled with the widths of the specified range of characters.

Returns Non-zero if successful; otherwise, zero.

See Also CDC::GetCharWidth, CDC::GetCharABCWidths, ::GetCharWidth, ::GetCharWidthFloat, ::GetCharWidth32

Example

```
...
CClientDC dc(pWnd);

// get character widths for some characters using the output dc
int widths[5];
dc.GetOutputCharWidth(`a','e',widths);
```

GetOutputTabbedTextExtent ■ 2.0 ■ 3.0

Description Calculates the height and width (in logical units) of the specified string using the current font. If the string contains tab characters, they are expanded according to the specified tab stop positions. This function uses the output device context associated with the CDC object. To use the attribute device context, use the CDC::GetTabbedTextExtent function. Note that, because of kerning, the sum of the extents of the characters in a string may not be the same as the extent of the string itself.

Syntax
public, CSize GetOutputTabbedTextExtent(LPCTSTR lpszString, int nCount, int nTabPositions, LPINT lpnTabStopPositions) const;
public, 4.0+, CSize GetOutputTabbedTextExtent(const CString &strText, int nTabPositions, LPINT lpnTabStopPositions) const;

Parameters

lpszString A pointer to the text string to calculate the dimensions of.

nCount The number of characters in the string pointed to by *lpszString*.

nTabPositions The number of tab positions specified in the *lpnTabStopPositions* array. If this parameter is zero and *lpnTabStopPositions* is NULL, a default tab width of eight average characters is used. If this parameter is one, *lpnTabStopPositions* should point to a single value which will be used as

	the spacing between tabs. If this parameter is greater than one, *lpnTabStopPositions* should point to an array of *nTabStop* tab positions.
lpnTabStopPositions	A pointer to an array of integers specifying where, in logical units, tab stops should be placed. The values specified must be sorted in increasing order. See the *nTabPositions* parameter for a complete description of the uses of this parameter.
strText	A reference to a CString object containing the text string to calculate the dimensions of.
Returns	A CSize object containing the height and width of the tabbed text.
See Also	CDC::GetTabbedTextExtent, CDC::GetTextExtent, CDC::GetOutputTextExtent, ::GetTabbedTextExtent
Example	See CDC::GetTabbedTextExtent

GetOutputTextExtent ■ 2.0 ■ 3.0

Description	Calculates the height and width (in logical units) of the specified string using the current font. This function will not expand tab characters in the string. Use the CDC::GetOutputTabbedTextExtent function if tabs need to be expanded. This function uses the output device context associated with the CDC object. To use the attribute device context, use the CDC::GetTextExtent function. Note that, because of kerning, the sum of the extents of the characters in a string may not be the same as the extent of the string itself.
Syntax	public, CSize GetOutputTextExtent(LPCTSTR lpszString, int nCount) const; public, 4.0+, CSize GetOutputTextExtent(CString &strText) const;
Parameters	
lpszString	A pointer to the text string for which the dimensions should be computed.
nCount	The length of the string (in bytes) pointed to by the *lpszString* parameter.
strText	A reference to a CString object containing the string for which the dimensions should be computed.
Returns	A CSize object containing the dimensions (in logical units) of the string.
See Also	CDC::GetTextExtent, CDC::GetOutputTabbedTextExtent, ::GetTextExtent
Example	See CDC::GetTextExtent

GetOutputTextMetrics ■ 2.0 ■ 3.0

Description	Retrieves metric information for the current font of the output device context associated with the CDC object.
Syntax	public, BOOL GetOutputTextMetrics(LPTEXTMETRIC lpMetrics) const;

Parameters

lpMetrics — A pointer to a TEXTMETRIC structure that will be filled with the metric information for the current font. For a complete description of the TEXTMETRIC structure, see the Windows SDK documentation.

Returns — Non-zero if successful; otherwise, zero.

See Also — CDC::GetTextMetrics, CDC::GetOutlineTextMetrics, ::GetTextMetrics

Example — See CDC::GetTextMetrics

GetPath

■ 3.0 ■ NM

Description — Retrieves the points that make up the path currently selected into the device context. These points represent the line endpoints and curve control points that compose the path. A closed path bracket must currently be selected into the device context or this function will fail. The points returned by this function are in logical coordinates. Since the path is stored internally in device coordinates, the points are converted at the time this function is called (using the current mapping mode and device context state).

Syntax — public, int GetPath(LPPOINT lpPoints, LPBYTE lpTypes, int nCount) const;

Parameters

lpPoints — Points to an array of POINT structures or CPoint objects that will be filled with the points defining the path. These points may be line endpoints or curve control points. If the *nCount* parameter is zero, this parameter may be NULL.

lpTypes — A pointer to an array of bytes that will be filled with values describing how each of the points in the *lpPoints* array should be interpreted. This parameter may be NULL if the *nCount* parameter is zero. Each byte in this array may be one of the following values:

PT_MOVETO — The corresponding point in *lpPoints* starts a disjoint figure.

PT_LINETO — The previous point and the corresponding point in *lpPoints* are the endpoints of a line.

PT_BEZIERTO — The corresponding point in *lpPoints* is a control point or ending point for a Bézier curve. This value always occurs in consecutive sets of three. The point immediately preceding the set of three is the starting point of the curve. The first two points with the PT_BEZIERTO designation are the control points and the final point with the PT_BEZIERTO designation is the end point. This flag may be combined with the PT_CLOSEFIGURE flag which indicates that the figure is automatically closed after this curve is drawn. The figure is closed by drawing a line from the this curve to the point corresponding to the last PT_MOVETO.

Returns If an error occurs, -1. If -1 is returned (indicating an error), you may call the ::GetLastError SDK function for more information. GetLastError can return one of the following error values: ERROR_CAN_NOT_COMPLETE, ERROR_INVALID_PARAMETER, or ERROR_BUFFER_OVERFLOW. If the *nCount* parameter is zero, the number of points in the path; otherwise, the number of points actually copied to the *lpPoints* buffer.

Example

```
...
CClientDC dc(pWnd);
CPoints curvePts[7] = {CPoint(10,10), CPoint(40,17), CPoint(50,22),
          CPoint(55,27), CPoint(42,35), CPoint(37,32), CPoint(30,22)};

// make a path with curves
dc.BeginPath();
dc.PolyBezier(curvePts,7);
dc.EndPath();

// flatten the path before getting it because we don't like curves
dc.FlattenPath();

int nCount = dc.GetPath(NULL,NULL,0); // determine buffer size needed
CPoint *pts = new CPoint[nCount];
BYTE *types = new BYTE[nCount];

// now get the path
dc.GetPath(pts,types,nCount);

// do something with the flattened path

// clean up
delete pts;
delete types;
```

GetPixel

■ 2.0 ■ 3.0

Description Retrieves the RGB color value of a specified pixel in the device context. The point specified must be within the current clipping region for the device context.

Syntax public, COLORREF GetPixel(int x, int y) const; public, COLORREF GetPixel(POINT point) const;

Parameters

x The x coordinate (in logical coordinates) of the point whose color value should be retrieved.

y The y coordinate (in logical coordinates) of the point whose color value should be retrieved.

point A POINT structure or a CPoint object containing the coordinates (in logical coordinates) of the point whose color value should be retrieved.

Returns The RGB color value of the specified pixel.

See Also CDC::SetPixel, CDC::SetPixelV, ::GetPixel

Example

```
...
CClientDC dc(pWnd);
COLORREF crOld;

// turn green pixels red and red pixels blue along a horizontal line
for (int nX = 0;nX < 200;nX++)
{
      crOld = dc.GetPixel(nX,10);
      if (crOld == RGB(0,255,0))
             dc.SetPixelV(nX,10,RGB(255,0,0));
      else if (crOld == RGB(255,0,0))
             dc.SetPixelV(nX,10,RGB(0,0,255));
}
```

GetPolyFillMode

■ 2.0 ■ 3.0

Description Retrieves the current polygon fill mode that can be ALTERNATE or WINDING. See Figure 11-10 for an example of both an ALTERNATE filled polygon and a WINDING filled polygon.

Syntax public, int GetPolyFillMode( ) const;

Parameters None.

Returns The current polygon fill mode: ALTERNATE or WINDING. A value of ALTERNATE means Windows fills the area between odd and even numbered sides on a per scan line basis (it draws a horizontal line between the odd side and the even side). WINDING means that Windows considers the direction in which each line segment of the polyline is drawn. It does this by drawing an imaginary line from each enclosed area in the polygon to outside of the figure. Each time this imaginary line crosses a line segment which was drawn in a clockwise direction, a count is incremented. Each time the imaginary line crosses a line segment which was drawn in a counterclockwise direction, the count is decremented. If, after this process, the count is non-zero, the enclosed area from which the imaginary line began is filled.

See Also CDC::SetPolyFillMode, ::GetPolyFillMode

Example

```
void CMyWnd::DrawPolygon(CDC *pDc)
{
      int nMode = pDc->GetPolyFillMode(); // store old mode
      CPoint pts[5] = {CPoint(100,140), CPoint(230,10), CPoint(10,10),
                CPoint(231,300), CPoint(50,50)};
      pDc->SetPolyFillMode(ALTERNATE); // set mode to ALTERNATE
      pDc->Polygon(pts,5);
      pDc->SetPolyFillMode(nMode); // restore to old mode
}
```

GetROP2

■ 2.0 ■ 3.0

Description	Retrieves the current raster operation code (or drawing mode). The drawing mode specifies how the colors of the pen and the interior of filled objects are combined with the color already on the display surface. As the name implies, the drawing mode is for raster devices only and does not apply to vector devices. Drawing modes are binary raster-operation codes representing all possible Boolean combinations of two variables, using the binary operators AND, OR, and XOR (exclusive OR), and the unary operator, NOT.
Syntax	public, int GetROP2( ) const;
Parameters	None.
Returns	The current raster operation code (or drawing mode). This may be any one of the following values:
R2_BLACK	Pixel is always black.
R2_WHITE	Pixel is always white.
R2_NOP	Pixel remains unchanged.
R2_NOT	Pixel is the inverse of the screen color.
R2_COPYPEN	Pixel is the pen color.
R2_NOTCOPYPEN	Pixel is the inverse of the pen color.
R2_MERGEPENNOT	Pixel is a combination of the pen color and the inverse of the screen color.
R2_MASKPENNOT	Pixel is a combination of the colors common to both the pen and the inverse of the screen.
R2_MERGENOTPEN	Pixel is a combination of the screen color and the inverse of the pen color.
R2_MASKNOTPEN	Pixel is a combination of the colors common to both the screen and the inverse of the pen.
R2_MERGEPEN	Pixel is a combination of the pen color and the screen color.
R2_NOTMERGEPEN	Pixel is the inverse of the R2_MERGEPEN color.
R2_MASKPEN	Pixel is a combination of the colors common to both the pen and the screen.
R2_NOTMASKPEN	Pixel is the inverse of the R2_MASKPEN color.
R2_XORPEN	Pixel is a combination of the colors that are in the pen or in the screen, but not in both.
R2_NOTXORPEN	Pixel is the inverse of the R2_XORPEN color.
See Also	CDC:::SetROP2, ::GetROP2

Example

```
...
CClientDC dc(pWnd);

// get default raster op
int nROP = dc.GetROP2();
```

GetSafeHdc

■ 2.0 ■ 3.0

Description Returns the Windows device context handle currently attached to the CDC. This function is called "safe" because it will work even if called with a NULL CDC pointer. See the example below for an example of this. This is done in order to allow NULL as a valid value which requires no special handling. This is similar to the C++ language specification which allows a pointer passed to the delete operator to be NULL.

Syntax HDC GetSafeHdc( ) const;

Parameters None.

Returns The Windows device context handle currently attached to the CDC object

Example

```
HDC hDc;
CClientDC dc(pWnd);
hDc = dc.GetSafeHdc();
// use hDc for something (like passing to a function which requires
// an hDc and not a CDC object
```

GetStretchBltMode

■ 2.0 ■ 3.0

Description Retrieves the current bitmap-stretching mode. The stretching mode defines how color data is added to or removed from bitmaps that are stretched or compressed using the StretchBlt function.

Syntax public, int GetStretchBltMode( ) const;

Parameters None.

Returns If the function fails, zero. Otherwise, the current stretching mode, which may be STRETCH_ANDSCANS, STRETCH_ORSCANS, or STRETCH_DELETESCANS. The first two modes are typically used to preserve foreground pixels in monochrome bitmaps. The STRETCH_DELETESCANS mode is typically used to preserve color in color bitmaps. When compressing a bitmap, STRETCH_ANDSCANS will cause pixels of the bitmap to be combined using an AND operation. STRETCH_ORSCANS will cause pixels of the bitmap to be combined using an OR operation. STRETCH_DELETESCANS will cause pixels to be discarded without combining them.

See Also CDC::SetStretchBltMode, CDC::StretchBlt, ::GetStretchBltMode

Example

```
...
CClientDC dc(pWnd);

// get the default stretch blt mode
int nMode = dc.GetStretchBltMode();
```

GetTabbedTextExtent ■ 2.0 ■ 3.0

Description Calculates the height and width (in logical units) of the specified string using the current font. If the string contains tab characters, they are expanded according to the specified tab stop positions. This function uses the attribute device context associated with the CDC object. To use the output device context, use the CDC::GetOutputTabbedTextExtent function. Note that, because of kerning, the sum of the extents of the characters in a string may not be the same as the extent of the string itself.

Syntax public, CSize GetTabbedTextExtent(LPCTSTR lpszString, int nCount, int nTabPositions, LPINT lpnTabStopPositions) const; public, 4.0+, CSize GetTabbedTextExtent(CString &strText, int nTabPositions, LPINT lpnTabStopPositions) const;

Parameters

lpszString A pointer to the text string to calculate the dimensions of.

nCount The number of characters in the string pointed to by *lpszString*.

nTabPositions The number of tab positions specified in the *lpnTabStopPositions* array. If this parameter is zero and *lpnTabStopPositions* is NULL, a default tab width of eight average characters is used. If this parameter is one, *lpnTabStopPositions* should point to a single value which will be used as the spacing between tabs. If this parameter is greater than one, *lpnTabStopPositions* should point to an array of *nTabStop* tab positions.

lpnTabStopPositions A pointer to an array of integers specifying where, in logical units, tab stops should be placed. The values specified must be sorted in increasing order. See the *nTabPositions* parameter for a complete description of the uses of this parameter.

strText A reference to a CString object containing the text string to calculate the dimensions of.

Returns A CSize object containing the height and width of the tabbed text.

See Also CDC::GetOutputTabbedTextExtent, CDC::GetTextExtent, CDC::GetOutputTextExtent, ::GetTabbedTextExtent

Example

```
...
CClientDC dc(pWnd);
int nTabs[3] = {50,100,160};
CString strTabbedText("Make\tModel\tColor\tPrice");

// get the dimensions of our test string
CSize size = dc.GetTabbedTextExtent( strTabbedText, 3, nTabs);
```

GetTextAlign

■ 2.0 ■ 3.0

Description	Retrieves the current text alignment flags. The text alignment flags control how the CDC::TextOut and CDC::ExtTextOut function align text as well as whether or not they use the current position or the user-specified position.
Syntax	public, UINT GetTextAlign( ) const;
Parameters	None.
Returns	The current state of the text alignment flags. Can be a combination of the following:
TA_BASELINE	The reference point is on the base line of the text.
TA_BOTTOM	The reference point is on the bottom edge of the bounding rectangle.
TA_TOP	The reference point is on the top edge of the bounding rectangle.
TA_CENTER	The reference point is aligned horizontally with the center of the bounding rectangle.
TA_LEFT	The reference point is on the left edge of the bounding rectangle.
TA_RIGHT	The reference point is on the right edge of the bounding rectangle.
TA_RTLREADING	Windows 95 only: If the font is Hebrew or Arabic, the text is laid out in right to left reading order, as opposed to the default left to right order.
TA_NOUPDATECP	The current position is not updated after each text output call.
TA_UPDATECP	The current position is updated after each text output call.
VTA_BASELINE	Used in place of TA_BASELINE for fonts which have a vertical default base line (e.g., Kanji). The reference point is on the base line of the text.
VTA_CENTER	Used in place of TA_CENTER for fonts which have a vertical default base line (e.g., Kanji). The reference point is aligned vertically with the center of the bounding rectangle.
See Also	CDC::SetTextAlign, CDC::TextOut, CDC::ExtTextOut, ::GetTextAlign

Example

```
CClientDC dc(pWnd);

// get the default text alignment
UINT uAlign = dc.GetTextAlign();
```

GetTextCharacterExtra

■ 2.0 ■ 3.0

Description	Retrieves the current intercharacter spacing. The intercharacter spacing defines the extra space, in logical units along the base line, that the TextOut or ExtTextOut functions add to each character as a line is written. The default intercharacter spacing is zero.
Syntax	public, int GetTextCharacterExtra( ) const;
Parameters	None.
Returns	The amount of intercharacter spacing, in logical units.

See Also CDC::SetTextCharacterExtra, ::GetTextCharacterExtra

Example

```
CClientDC dc(pWnd);

// get the default extra space (0)
int nExtra = dc.GetTextCharacterExtra();
```

GetTextColor ■ 2.0 ■ 3.0

Description Retrieves the current text color. The text color is the color used to draw text using any of the GDI text output functions.

Syntax public, COLORREF GetTextColor( ) const;

Parameters None.

Returns The RGB color value for the current text color.

See Also CDC::SetTextColor, CDC::TextOut, CDC::ExtTextOut, CDC::TabbedTextOut, CDC::DrawText, ::GetTextColor

Example

```
...
CClientDC dc(pWnd);

// get the default text color (black)
COLORREF cr = dc.GetTextColor();
```

GetTextExtent ■ 2.0 ■ 3.0

Description Calculates the height and width (in logical units) of the specified string using the current font. This function will not expand tab characters in the string. Use the CDC::GetOutputTabbedTextExtent function if tabs need to be expanded. This function uses the attribute device context associated with the CDC object. To use the output device context, use the CDC::GetOutputTextExtent function. Note that, because of kerning, the sum of the extents of the characters in a string may not be the same as the extent of the string itself.

Syntax public, CSize GetTextExtent(LPCTSTR lpszString, int nCount) const;
public, 4.0+, CSize GetTextExtent(CString &strText) const;

Parameters

lpszString A pointer to the text string for which the dimensions should be computed.

nCount The length of the string (in bytes) pointed to by the *lpszString* parameter.

strText A reference to a CString object that contains the text string for which the dimensions should be computed.

Returns A CSize object containing the dimensions (in logical units) of the string.

See Also CDC::GetOutputTextExtent, CDC::GetOutputTabbedTextExtent, ::GetTextExtent

Example

```
...
CClientDC dc(pWnd);
CString strText("Test String");

// get the dimensions of our string
CSize size = dc.GetTextExtent(strText);

// or could call like this
size = dc.GetTextExtent("Test String", 11);
```

GetTextFace

■ 2.0 ■ 3.0

Description Retrieves the typeface name for the current font as a NULL-terminated string.

Syntax public, int GetTextFace(int nCount, LPTSTR lpszFaceName) const;
public, int GetTextFace(CString &strFaceName) const;

Parameters

nCount The size of the buffer pointed to by the *lpszFaceName* parameter. If the typeface name is larger than the buffer supplied, the name will be truncated.

lpszFaceName A pointer to the buffer into which the typeface name will be placed.

strFaceName A reference to a CString into which the typeface name will be placed.

Returns The number of bytes, not including the terminating NULL character, copied to the buffer.

See Also CDC::GetTextMetrics, ::GetTextFace

Example

```
...
CClientDC dc(pWnd);

// get the type face name of the default font
CString strFaceName;
dc.GetTextFace(strFaceName);

// or could do like this
char sFaceName[30];
dc.GetTextFace(sFaceName,30);
```

GetTextMetrics

■ 2.0 ■ 3.0

Description Retrieves metric information about the current font. Note that this function uses the attribute device context associated with the CDC object.

Syntax public, BOOL GetTextMetrics(LPTEXTMETRIC lpMetrics) const;

Parameters

lpMetrics A pointer to a TEXTMETRIC structure that will be filled with metric information for the current font. For more information about the TEXTMETRIC structure, see the Windows SDK documentation.

Returns Non-zero if the function is successful; otherwise, zero.

See Also CDC::GetTextAlign, CDC::GetOutputTextMetrics, CDC::GetTextExtent, CDC::GetTextFace, ::GetTextMetrics

Example

```
...
CClientDC dc(pWnd);

// get the metrics info for the default font
TEXTMETRIC metrics;
dc.GetTextMetrics(&metrics);
```

GetViewportExt ■ 2.0 ■ 3.0

Description Retrieves the current x and y extents of the viewport in device coordinates. The viewport origin and extents, together with the window origin and extents, determine how coordinates are mapped between device coordinates and logical coordinates. See the CDC::DPtoLP and CDC::LPtoDP functions for a discussion regarding these mappings.

Syntax public, CSize GetViewportExt( ) const;

Parameters None.

Returns A CSize object containing the x and y extents of the viewport in device units.

See Also CDC::GetViewportOrg, CDC::GetWindowExt, CDC::GetWindowOrg, CDC::DPtoLP, CDC::LPtoDP, ::GetViewportExt, ::GetViewportExtEx

Example

```
...
CClientDC dc(pWnd);
CRect rc;

// get client area
pWnd->GetClientRect(rc);

// set up one-to-one logical mapping
dc.SetMapMode(MM_ANISOTROPIC);
dc.SetWindowOrg(0,0);
dc.SetWindowExt(rc.right,rc.bottom);
dc.SetViewportOrg(0,0);
dc.SetViewportExt(rc.right,rc.bottom);

// draw some stuff

// sometime later - we need the viewport extents and origin
CSize extents = dc.GetViewportExt(); // extents = rc.right, rc.bottom
CSize org = dc.GetViewportOrg(); // org = 0,0
```

GetViewportOrg ■ 2.0 ■ 3.0

Description Retrieves the current x and y origin of the viewport in device coordinates. The viewport origin and extents, together with the window origin and extents, determine how coordinates are mapped between device

	coordinates and logical coordinates. See the CDC::DPtoLP and CDC::LPtoDP functions for a discussion regarding these mappings.
Syntax	public, CPoint GetViewportOrg( ) const;
Parameters	None.
Returns	A CPoint object containing the current coordinates of the viewport origin, in device units.
See Also	CDC::GetViewportExt, CDC::GetWindowExt, CDC::GetWindowOrg, CDC::DPtoLP, CDC::LPtoDP, ::GetViewportOrg, ::GetViewportOrgEx
Example	See CDC::GetViewportExt

GetWindow ■ 2.0 ■ 3.0

Description	Retrieves a pointer to the window with the specified relationship to this window.
Syntax	public, CWnd* GetWindow(UINT nRelation) const;
Parameters	
nRelation	A flag which indicates the type of window desired. Can be one of the following values:
GW_CHILD	Identifies the CWnd first child window.
GW_HWNDFIRST	If CWnd is a child window, returns the first sibling window. Otherwise, it returns the first top-level window in the list.
GW_HWNDLAST	If CWnd is a child window, returns the last sibling window. Otherwise, it returns the last top-level window in the list.
GW_HWNDNEXT	Returns the next window on the window manager's list.
GW_HWNDPREV	Returns the previous window on the window manager's list.
GW_OWNER	Identifies the CWnd.
Returns	A pointer to the specified window, if successful; otherwise, NULL.
See Also	CDC::GetWindowOrg, CDC::GetViewportOrg, CDC::GetViewPortExt, CDC::DPtoLP, CDC::LPtoDP, ::GetWindowExt, ::GetWindowExtEx

GetWindowExt ■ 2.0 ■ 3.0

Description	Retrieves the current x and y extents of the window in device coordinates. The window origin and extents, together with the viewport origin and extents, determine how coordinates are mapped between device coordinates and logical coordinates. See the CDC::DPtoLP and CDC::LPtoDP function for a discusion regarding these mappings.
Syntax	public, CSize GetWindowExt( ) const;
Parameters	None.
Returns	A CSize object containing the x and y extents of the window in device units.

See Also CDC::GetWindowOrg, CDC::GetViewportOrg, CDC::GetViewPortExt, CDC::DPtoLP, CDC::LPtoDP, ::GetWindowExt, ::GetWindowExtEx

Example

```
...
CClientDC dc(pWnd);
CRect rc;

// get client area
pWnd->GetClientRect(rc);

// set up one-to-one logical mapping
dc.SetMapMode(MM_ANISOTROPIC);
dc.SetWindowOrg(0,0);
dc.SetWindowExt(rc.right,rc.bottom);
dc.SetViewportOrg(0,0);
dc.SetViewportExt(rc.right,rc.bottom);

// draw some stuff

// sometime later - we need the window extents and origin
CSize extents = dc.GetWindowExt(); // extents = rc.right, rc.bottom
CSize org = dc.GetWindowOrg(); // org = 0,0
```

GetWindowOrg

■ 2.0 ■ 3.0

Description Retrieves the current x and y origin of the window in device coordinates. The window origin and extents, together with the viewport origin and extents, determine how coordinates are mapped between device coordinates and logical coordinates. See the CDC::DPtoLP and CDC::LPtoDP functions for a discussion regarding these mappings.

Syntax public, CPoint GetWindowOrg( ) const;

Parameters None.

Returns A CPoint object containing the current coordinates of the window origin, in device units.

See Also CDC::GetWindowExt, CDC::GetViewportExt, CDC::GetViewportOrg, CDC::DPtoLP, CDC::LPtoDP, ::GetWindowOrg, ::GetWindowOrgEx

Example See CDC::GetWindowExt

GrayString

■ 2.0 ■ 3.0

Description Draws gray (dimmed) text at a specified location. The text is grayed by drawing it into a memory bitmap, graying the bitmap using the specified brush, and then copying the bitmap to the screen. If the *lpfnOutput* parameter is NULL, GrayString uses the TextOut function to draw the text using the current font. In this case, the *lpData* parameter should be a pointer to the string of text to output. If the string is in a form that TextOut can not handle (i.e., already in bitmap form), you must supply a callback function to output the text.

Syntax public, virtual BOOL GrayString(CBrush* pBrush, BOOL (CALLBACK * lpfnOutput)(HDC, LPARAM, int), LPARAM lpData, int nCount, int x, int y, int nWidth, int nHeight);

Parameters

pBrush A pointer to the brush to use for dimming.

lpfnOutput A pointer to a callback function which will draw the text. If this parameter is NULL, GrayString uses the CDC::TextOut function to draw the text and the *lpData* parameter should point to the text string to be drawn.

lpData A pointer to the data representing the string to be drawn. If the *lpfnOutput* parameter is NULL, this parameter should point to a text string. This parameter is passed to the function specified by the *lpfnOutput* parameter, if provided.

nCount The size, in bytes, of the data buffer pointed to by *lpData*.

x The x coordinate (in logical units) of the upper-left corner of the rectangle which bounds the text.

y The y coordinate (in logical units) of the upper-left corner of the rectangle which bounds the text.

nWidth The width of the rectangle which bounds the text. If *nWidth* is zero and *lpData* points to a text string, GrayString will calculate the width.

nHeight The height of the rectangle that bounds the text. If *nHeight* is zero and *lpData* points to a text string, GrayString will calculate the height.

Returns Non-zero if the string is drawn; zero if either the TextOut function or the application-supplied output function returned zero or if there was insufficient memory to create a memory bitmap for dimming.

See Also CDC::TextOut, ::GrayString

OPERATOR HDC

–. ■ 4.0

Description Cast operator that converts the CDC object to an HDC (device context handle). This operator allows you to pass a CDC object to any function that requires an HDC. This would, of course, include any call to an SDK device context function.

Syntax public, operator HDC() const;

Parameters None.

Returns The HDC associated with the CDC object.

Example

```
...
CClientDC dc(pWnd);

// call an SDK function requiring an HDC
::SetBkColor(dc,RGB(255,0,0));
```

HIMETRICToDP

■ 2.0 ■ 3.0

Description Converts coordinates from HIMETRIC coordinates to device coordinates. HIMETRIC coordinates are used by OLE, so whenever you need to pass coordinates from OLE or interpret coordinates from OLE you will need to convert them to/from HIMETRIC. If the current mapping mode of the device context is a contained mode (e.g., MM_LOENGLISH, MM_HIENGLISH, MM_LOMETRIC or MM_HIMETRIC), then the conversion is based on the number of pixels in the physical inch. If the current mapping mode is one of the other modes (e.g., MM_TEXT), then the conversion is based on the number of pixels in the logical inch.

Syntax public, void HIMETRICtoDP(LPSIZE lpSize) const;

Parameters

lpSize A pointer to a SIZE structure or CSize object that contains the coordinates to convert.

Returns Nothing is returned.

See Also CDC::DPtoHIMETRIC, CDC::LPtoHIMETRIC, CDC::HIMETRICtoLP

HIMETRICToLP

■ 2.0 ■ 3.0

Description Converts coordinates from HIMETRIC coordinates to logical coordinates. HIMETRIC coordinates are used by OLE, so whenever you need to pass coordinates from OLE or interpret coordinates from OLE you will need to convert them to/from HIMETRIC. This function is really a simple convenience function which first converts the coordinates from HIMETRIC to device (see CDC::HIMETRICtoDP) and then converts the device coordinates to logical coordinates (see CDC::DPtoLP).

Syntax public, void HIMETRICtoLP(LPSIZE lpSize) const;

Parameters

lpSize A pointer to a SIZE structure or CSize object which contains the coordinates to convert.

Returns Nothing is returned.

See Also CDC::DPtoHIMETRIC, CDC::LPtoHIMETRIC, CDC::HIMETRICtoDP, CDC::DPtoLP

IntersectClipRect

■ 2.0 ■ 3.0

Description Forms a new clipping region by intersecting the specified rectangle with the current clipping region. Windows clips all output to the current clipping region.

Syntax public, virtual int IntersectClipRect(int x1, int y1, int x2, int y2);
public, virtual int IntersectClipRect(LPCRECT lpRect);

Parameters

x1 The x coordinate, in logical units, of the upper-left corner of the rectangle to intersect with the current clipping region.

y1 The y coordinate, in logical units, of the upper-left corner of the rectangle to intersect with the current clipping region.

x2 The x coordinate, in logical units, of the lower-right corner of the rectangle to intersect with the current clipping region.

y2 The y coordinate, in logical units, of the lower-right corner of the rectangle to intersect with the current clipping region.

lpRect A pointer to a RECT structure or a CRect object containing the rectangle to intersect with the current clipping region.

Returns The new clipping region's type. It can be one of the following values:

COMPLEXREGION The new clipping region has overlapping borders.

NULLREGION The new clipping region is empty.

SIMPLEREGION The new clipping region has no overlapping borders.

ERROR Device context is not valid.

See Also ::IntersectClipRect

Example

```
...
CClientDC dc(pWnd);
CRect rect(100,100,500,400);

// intersect rectangle with current clipping region (entire client area)
// new clipping region will be our rectangle - all drawing will be
// clipped to this area
dc.IntersectClipRect(rect);

// now do it again - new clipping region will be the intersection of this
// rectangle and the last one (300,200,500,400)
dc.IntersectClipRect(300,200,600,600);
```

InvertRect ■ 2.0 ■ 3.0

Description Inverts the contents of the specified rectangle. Inversion is a logical NOT operation which flips the bits of each pixel. Calling InvertRect twice with the same rectangle restores the display to its previous colors.

Syntax public, void InvertRect(LPCRECT lpRect);

Parameters

lpRect A pointer to a RECT structure or a CRect object defining the area to be inverted.

Returns Nothing is returned.

See Also CDC::InvertRgn, CDC::FillRect, ::InvertRect

Example

```
...
CClientDC dc(pWnd);

// invert a retangle on the screen
CRect rect(1,1,100,200);
dc.InvertRect(rect);
```

InvertRgn ■ 2.0 ■ 3.0

Description Inverts the contents of the specified region. Inversion is a logical NOT operation which flips the bits of each pixel. Calling InvertRgn twice with the same region restores the display to its previous colors. See the CRgn class description in Chapter 12, *The MFC GDI*, for a discussion about regions.

Syntax public, BOOL InvertRgn(CRgn* pRgn);

Parameters

pRgn A pointer to the region whose contents will be inverted.

Returns Non-zero if successful; otherwise, zero.

See Also CDC::PaintRgn, CDC::FillRgn, CDC::InvertRect, ::InvertRgn

Example

```
...
CClientDC dc(pWnd);

// make a triangular region
CPoint pts[3] = {CPoint(10,20), CPoint(100,40), CPoint(50,50)};
CRgn rgn;
rgn.CreatePolygonRgn(pts,3,ALTERNATE);

// invert pixels in the triangle region created above
dc.InvertRgn(&rgn);
```

IsPrinting ■ 2.0 ■ 3.0

Description Determines whether the device context is currently printing.

Syntax public, BOOL IsPrinting( ) const;

Parameters None.

Returns Non-zero if the device context is printing; otherwise, zero.

Example

```
void CMyWnd::SomePaintFunction(CDC *pDc)
{
     CPen *pOldPen;

     if (pDc->IsPrinting())
     { // if printing, do everything in black and white (just to be
       // safe
         CPen blackPen(PS_SOLID,2,RGB(0,0,0));
         pOldPen = dc.SelectObject(&blackPen);
         dc.Rectangle(1,1,500,500);
```

continued on next page

continued from previous page

```
        }
        else
        { // painting to screen - do color
            CPen redPen(PS_SOLID,2,RGB(255,0,0));
            pOldPen = dc.SelectObject(&redPen);
            dc.Rectangle(1,1,500,500);
        }

        // clean up
        dc.SelectObject(pOldPen);
}
```

LineTo

■ 2.0 ■ 3.0

Description Draws a line from the current position to the specified position using the current pen. The line is actually drawn up to, but not including, the specified end point.

Syntax public, BOOL LineTo(int x, int y);
public, BOOL LineTo(POINT point);

Parameters

x The x coordinate, in logical units, of the line end point.

y The y coordinate, in logical units, of the line end point.

point A POINT structure or CPoint object which contains the line end point in logical coordinates.

Returns Non-zero if the function is successful; otherwise, zero.

See Also CDC::MoveTo, ::LineTo

Example

```
...
CClientDC dc(pWnd);

// draw a few lines
dc.MoveTo(1,1);
dc.LineTo(10,12);
dc.LineTo(100,132);
```

LPtoDP

■ 2.0 ■ 3.0

Description Converts coordinates from logical coordinates to device coordinates. Conversion to device coordinates depends on the current mapping mode of the device context, the current window and viewport origins and extents, and the current world transformation that is in effect. See the description of the CDC::SetMapMode function for more information regarding mapping modes. The formulas used for converting logical coordinates to device coordinates are as follows:

Dx = ((Lx—WOx) * VEx / WEx) + VOx

Dy = ((Ly—WOy) * VEy / WEy) + VOy

where:

Dx x value in device units.

Lx x value in logical units.

WOx window x origin.

VOx viewport x origin.

WEx window x-extent.

VEx viewport x-extent.

Dy y value in device units.

Ly y value in logical units.

WOy window y origin.

VOy viewport y origin.

WEy window y-extent.

VEy viewport y-extent.

Syntax public, void LPtoDP(LPPOINT lpPoints, int nCount = 1) const;
public, void LPtoDP(LPRECT lpRect) const;
public, void LPtoDP(LPSIZE lpSize) const;

Parameters

lpPoints A pointer to an array of POINT structure or CPoint objects to be converted.

nCount The number of points to be converted.

lpRect A pointer to a RECTANGLE structure or a CRect object to be converted.

lpSize A pointer to a SIZE structure or a CSize object ot be converted.

Returns Nothing is returned.

See Also CDC::DPtoHIMETRIC, CDC::LPtoDP, CDC::HIMETRICtoLP, CDC::HIMETRICtoDP, CDC::LPtoHIMETRIC

Example

```
..
CClientDC dc(pWnd);
CRect rc;
CPoint pt;

// set mapping mode to MM_ANISOTROPIC (logical with no constraints)
dc.SetMapMode(MM_ANISOTROPIC);

// get client rectangle of window and use as window coordinates
pWnd->GetClientRect(rc);
dc.SetWindowOrg(rc.left,rc.top);
dc.SetWindowExt(rc.right,rc.bottom);

// create mapping such that no matter what the window size, always have
// 100 x 100 grid
dc.SetViewportOrg(0,0);
dc.SetViewportExt(100,100);

// convert an arbitrary point to logical coordinates - if client area of
// window were 600 x 500 logical point would be 120, 100
```

continued on next page

continued from previous page

```
CPoint devPoint(20,20);
dc.DPtoLP(&devPoint,1);

// convert an arbitrary point to device coordinates - if client area of
// window were 600 x 500 device point would be 20, 20
CPoint logPoint(120, 100);
dc.LPtoDP(&logPoint,1);

..
```

LPtoHIMETRIC

■ 2.0 ■ 3.0

Description Converts coordinates from logical coordinates to HIMETRIC coordinates. HIMETRIC coordinates are used by OLE, so whenever you need to pass coordinates from OLE or interpret coordinates from OLE you will need to convert them to/from HIMETRIC. This function is really a simple convenience function which first converts the coordinates from logical to device units (see CDC::LPtoDP) and then converts the device coordinates to HIMETRIC coordinates (see CDC::DPtoHIMETRIC).

Syntax public, void LPtoHIMETRIC(LPSIZE lpSize) const;

Parameters

lpSize A pointer to a SIZE structure or CSize object that contains the coordinates to convert.

Returns Nothing is returned.

See Also CDC::HIMETRICtoLP, CDC::DPtoHIMETRIC, CDC::HIMETRICtoDP, CDC::LPtoDP

MaskBlt

■ 2.0 ■ 3.0 ■ NM

Description Combines the color data for the source and destination bitmaps using the specified mask and raster operation. A value of 1 in the mask bitmap indicates that the foreground raster operation code specified by the *dwRop* parameter should be used at that location. A value of 0 in the mask indicates that the background raster operation code specified by the *dwRop* parameter should be applied at that location. If the raster operations require a source, the mask rectangle must cover the source rectangle. If the color formats of the source, pattern, and destination bitmaps are different, this function converts the pattern or source format, or both, to match the destination format. The mask bitmap is optional. If it is not supplied, MaskBlt behaves exactly like BitBlt, using the foreground raster operation code. This function may fail for any of the following reasons:

- If the specified raster operation codes require a source and the mask bitmap does not completely cover the source rectangle.
- If the specified raster operation codes do not require a source and the mask bitmap does not completely cover the destination rectangle.

- If a rotation or shear transformation is in effect for the source device context.
- If the mask bitmap is not a monochrome bitmap.
- If an enhanced metafile is being recorded and the source device context identifies an enhanced-metafile device context.

Syntax public, BOOL MaskBlt(int x, int y, int nWidth, int nHeight, CDC* pSrcDC, int xSrc, int ySrc, CBitmap& maskBitmap, int xMask, int yMask, DWORD dwRop);

Parameters

x	The x coordinate, in logical units, of the upper-left corner of the destination rectangle.
y	The y coordinate, in logical units, of the upper-left corner of the destination rectangle.
nWidth	The width, in logical units, of the destination rectangle and the source bitmap.
nHeight	The height, in logical units, of the destination rectangle and the source bitmap.
pSrcDC	A pointer to the source device context (which contains the source bitmap).
xSrc	The x coordinate, in logical units, of the upper-left corner of the source bitmap.
ySrc	The x coordinate, in logical units, of the upper-left corner of the source bitmap.
maskBitmap	A reference to the mask bitmap. If this parameter references a NULL bitmap, MaskBlt acts just like BitBlt.
xMask	A horizontal offset into the mask bitmap.
yMask	A vertical offset into the mask bitmap.
dwRop	The foreground and background raster operation codes that are used to control the combination of the source bitmap, destination bitmap, and mask bitmap. The background raster operation code is stored in the high byte of the high word of this value. The foreground raster operation code is stored in the low byte of the high word of this value. The low word of this value is ignored, and should be zero. Use the MAKEROP4 macro to create the value for this parameter.

Returns Non-zero if successful; otherwise, zero.

See Also CDC::BitBlt, CDC::PlgBlt, CDC::StretchBlt, ::MaskBlt

Example

```
void CMyWnd::DrawMaskedBitmap(CDC *pDc)
{
	CDC memDc;
	CBitmap bmp,maskBmp;
	BITMAP bitmap, *pOldBmp;
```

continued on next page

continued from previous page

```
        // create a memory dc to use as the source dc
        dc.CreateCompatibleDC(pDc);

        // load the bitmap and obtain its dimensions
        bmp.LoadBitmap(IDB_TESTBMP);
        bmp.GetBitmap(&bitmap);
        pOldBmp = dc.SelectObject(&bmp);

        // get mask bitmap
        bmp.LoadBitmap(IDB_MASKBMP);

        // copy the bitmap to the destination
        dc.MaskBlt(50,50,bitmap.bmWidth,bitmap.bmHeight,&memDc,0,0
                   &maskBmp,0,0,MAKEROP4(SRCCOPY,SRCAND));

        // clean up
        memDc.SelectObject(pOldBmp);
        memDc.DeleteDC();
}
```

MoveTo

■ 2.0 ■ 3.0

Description Moves the current position to the specified coordinates.

Syntax public, CPoint MoveTo(int x, int y); public, CPoint MoveTo(POINT point);

Parameters

x The x coordinate, in logical units, of the new position.

y The y coordinate, in logical units, of the new position.

point A POINT structure or CPoint object containing the coordinate, in logical units, of the new position.

Returns The previous position.

See Also CDC::GetCurrentPosition, CDC::LineTo, ::MoveTo

Example

```
...
CClientDC dc(pWnd);

// draw a few lines
dc.MoveTo(1,1);
dc.LineTo(10,12);
dc.LineTo(100,132);

dc.MoveTo(200,220);
dc.LineTo(250,250);
```

OffsetClipRgn

■ 2.0 ■ 3.0

Description Moves the current clipping region by a specified amount horizontally and vertically.

Syntax public, int OffsetClipRgn(int x, int y); public, int OffsetClipRgn(SIZE size);

Parameters

x — The amount (in logical units) by which the region should be shifted horizontally. A negative value will shift the region to the left and a positive value will shift it to the right.

y — The amount (in logical units) by which the region should be shifted vertically. A negative value will shift the region up and a positive value will shift it down.

size — A SIZE structure or CSize object contains the amounts, in logical units, by which the current region should be shifted.

Returns — The new region's type. It can be any of the following values:

COMPLEXREGION — The clipping region has overlapping borders.

NULLREGION — The clipping region is empty.

SIMPLEREGION — The clipping region has no overlapping borders.

ERROR — The device context is not valid.

See Also — CDC::SelectClipRgn, CDC::IntersectClipRgn, ::OffsetClipRgn

Example

```
...
CClientDC dc(pWnd);
CRect rect(100,100,500,400);

// intersect rectangle with current clipping region (entire client area)
// new clipping region will be our rectangle - all drawing will be
// clipped to this area
dc.IntersectClipRect(rect);

// now shift the clipping rect - new one will be 200,150,600,450
dc.OffsetClipRgn(100,50);
```

OffsetViewportOrg ■ 2.0 ■ 3.0

Description — Moves the current viewport origin by the specified amounts in the horizontal and vertical directions. The specified offsets are added to the current origin. The viewport origin and extents, together with the window origin and extents, determine how coordinates are mapped between device coordinates and logical coordinates. See the CDC::DPtoLP and CDC::LPtoDP functions for a discussion regarding these mappings.

Syntax — public, virtual CPoint OffsetViewportOrg(int nXOffset, int nYOffset);

Parameters

nXOffset — The number of device units to add to the x coordinate of the viewport origin.

nYOffset — The number of device units to add to the y coordinate of the viewport origin.

Returns — A CPoint object containing the old viewport origin.

See Also — CDC::GetViewportOrg, CDC::SetViewportOrg, CDC::OffsetWindowOrg, ::OffsetViewportOrg, ::OffsetViewportOrgEx

Example

```
..
CClientDC dc(pWnd);
CRect rc;
CPoint pt;

// set mapping mode to MM_ANISOTROPIC (logical with no constraints)
dc.SetMapMode(MM_ANISOTROPIC);

// get client rectangle of window and use as window coordinates
pWnd->GetClientRect(rc);
dc.SetWindowOrg(rc.left,rc.top);
dc.SetWindowExt(rc.right,rc.bottom);

// create mapping such that no matter what the window size, always have
// 100 x 100 grid
dc.SetViewportOrg(0,0);
dc.SetViewportExt(100,100);

// convert an arbitrary point to device coordinates - if client area of
// window were 600 x 500 device point would be 20, 20
CPoint logPoint(120, 100);
dc.LPtoDP(&logPoint,1);

// now offset the window org
dc.OffsetViewportOrg(-10,0);

// convert an arbitrary point to device coordinates - if client area of
// window were 600 x 500 device point would be 30, 20
CPoint logPoint(120, 100);
dc.LPtoDP(&logPoint,1);
```

OffsetWindowOrg ■ 2.0 ■ 3.0

Description Moves the current window origin by the specified amounts in the horizontal and vertical directions. The specified offsets are added to the current origin. The window origin and extents, together with the viewport origin and extents, determine how coordinates are mapped between device coordinates and logical coordinates. See the CDC::DPtoLP and CDC::LPtoDP functions for a discussion regarding these mappings.

Syntax public, CPoint OffsetWindowOrg(int nXOffset, int nYOffset);

Parameters

nXOffset The number of device units to add to the x coordinate of the window origin.

nYOffset The number of device units to add to the y coordinate of the window origin.

Returns A CPoint object containing the old window origin.

See Also CDC::GetWindowOrg, CDC::SetWindowOrg, CDC::OffsetViewportOrg, ::OffsetWindowOrg, ::OffsetWindowOrgEx

Example

```
..
CClientDC dc(pWnd);
CRect rc;
CPoint pt;
```

```
// set mapping mode to MM_ANISOTROPIC (logical with no constraints)
dc.SetMapMode(MM_ANISOTROPIC);

// get client rectangle of window and use as window coordinates
pWnd->GetClientRect(rc);
dc.SetWindowOrg(rc.left,rc.top);
dc.SetWindowExt(rc.right,rc.bottom);

// create mapping such that no matter what the window size, always have
// 100 x 100 grid
dc.SetViewportOrg(0,0);
dc.SetViewportExt(100,100);

// convert an arbitrary point to device coordinates - if client area of
// window were 600 x 500 device point would be 20, 20
CPoint logPoint(120, 100);
dc.LPtoDP(&logPoint,1);

// now offset the window org
dc.OffsetWindowOrg(-10,0);

// convert an arbitrary point to device coordinates - if client area of
// window were 600 x 500 device point would be 10, 20
CPoint logPoint(120, 100);
dc.LPtoDP(&logPoint,1);
```

PaintRgn ■ 2.0 ■ 3.0

Description Fills the specified region using the current brush.

Syntax public, BOOL PaintRgn(CRgn* pRgn);

Parameters

pRgn A pointer to the region to be filled. The region's coordinates should be in logical units.

Returns Non-zero if successful; otherwise, zero.

See Also CDC::FillRgn, ::PaintRgn

Example

```
..
CRgn rgn;
CClientDC dc(pWnd);
CBrush solidBrush(RGB(255,0,0)), *pOldBrush;

pOldBrush = dc.SelectObject(&solidBrush);
rgn.CreateRectRgn(1,1,150,100);
dc.PaintRgn(&rgn);
dc.SelectObject(pOldBrush);
..
```

PatBlt ■ 2.0 ■ 3.0

Description Paints a pattern to a specified rectangle on the device. The pattern is a combination of the current brush and the pattern already on the device.

The current brush and pattern are combined according to a specified raster operation code.

Syntax public, BOOL PatBlt(int x, int y, int nWidth, int nHeight, DWORD dwRop);

Parameters

x	The x coordinate, in logical units, of the upper-left corner of the rectangle that will be filled with the pattern.
y	The y coordinate, in logical units, of the upper-left corner of the rectangle that will be filled with the pattern.
nWidth	The width of the rectangle that will be filled with the pattern.
nHeight	The height, in logical units, of the rectangle that will be filled with the pattern.
dwRop	The raster operation code that will control how the brush and pattern are combined. This parameter can be one of the following codes:
PATCOPY	Copies pattern to destination bitmap.
PATINVERT	Combines destination bitmap with pattern using the Boolean XOR operator.
DSTINVERT	Inverts the destination bitmap.
BLACKNESS	Turns all output black.
WHITENESS	Turns all output white.
PATPAINT	Paints the destination bitmap.

Returns Non-zero if successful; otherwise, zero.

See Also ::PatBlt

Example

```
...
CClientDC dc(pWnd);

// invert the contents of a section of the window
dc.PatBlt(100,100,200,100,DSTINVERT);
```

PIE

■ 2.0 ■ 3.0

Description Draws a pie-shaped wedge by drawing an elliptical arc as specified by the given bounding rectangle and starting and ending points and then drawing two lines from the center of the bounding rectangle to each end of the arc. The arc drawn is a portion of the ellipse defined by the given bounding rectangle. Note that the starting and ending points do not have to lie on the arc. The arc will begin at the point where a ray drawn from the center of the bounding rectangle to the specified starting point intersects the ellipse defined by the same bounding rectangle. The end point is similarly defined. The width and height of the bounding rectangle must be greater than 2 logical units and less than 32,767 logical units. If the starting point and the ending point are the same, a complete ellipse will be drawn with a single line drawn from the center of the bounding rectangle

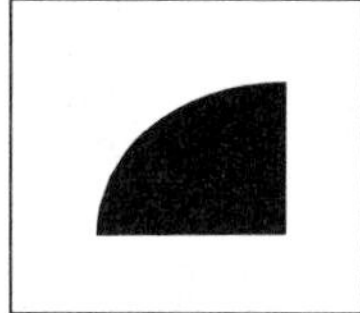

Figure 11-6
Sample output
of Pie

to the ending point of the arc. The arc is drawn in the current arc drawing direction. This value can be set using the CDC::SetArcDirection function. The default is counterclockwise. Figure 11-6 shows a sample output from the Pie function.

Syntax

public, BOOL Pie(int x1, int y1, int x2, int y2, int x3, int y3, int x4, int y4);
public, BOOL Pie(LPCRECT lpRect, POINT ptStart, POINT ptEnd);

Parameters

x1 — The x coordinate, in logical units, of the upper-left corner of the bounding rectangle of the arc.

y1 — The y coordinate, in logical units, of the upper-left corner of the bounding rectangle of the arc.

x2 — The x coordinate, in logical units, of the lower-right corner of the bounding rectangle of the arc.

y2 — The y coordinate, in logical units, of the lower-right corner of the bounding rectangle of the arc.

x3 — The x coordinate, in logical units, of the starting point of the arc. This point does not have to lie on the arc.

y3 — The y coordinate, in logical units, of the starting point of the arc. This point does not have to lie on the arc.

x4 — The x coordinate, in logical units, of the ending point of the arc. This point does not have to lie on the arc.

y4 — The y coordinate, in logical units, of the ending point of the arc. This point does not have to lie on the arc.

lpRect — A pointer to a RECT structure or a CRect object containing the coordinates, in logical units, of the bounding rectangle of the arc.

ptStart — A POINT structure or CPoint object containing the coordinates, in logical units, of the starting point of the arc. This point does not have to lie on the arc.

ptEnd — A POINT structure or CPoint object containing the coordinates, in logical units, of the ending point of the arc. This point does not have to lie on the arc.

Returns

Non-zero if successful; otherwise, zero.

See Also CDC::Chord, CDC::Arc, CDC::ArcTo, ::Pie

Example

```
...
CClientDC dc(pWnd);

// draw a half-circle pie
// draw half-ellipse arc
dc.Pie(0,0,300,200,150,0,150,200);
```

PlayMetaFile

■ 2.0 ■ 3.0

Description Plays the specified metafile on the device context associated with the CDC object. The first version plays a normal metafile. The second version plays an enhanced metafile. Enhanced metafiles allow for much more flexibility. The picture defined by an enhanced metafile is mapped from the rectangle defined in the metafile to the rectangle specified by the call to PlayMetaFile. This mapping includes any transforms that are currently defined for the device context. PlayMetaFile preserves the state of the device context. That is, the device context is restored to the state it was in before the call to PlayMetaFile. An enhanced metafile may have a palette associated with it. You can retrieve the palette using the ::GetEnhMetaFilePaletteEntries function. Note that the second version of this function is not available on the Macintosh.

Syntax public, BOOL PlayMetaFile(HMETAFILE hMF);
public, BOOL PlayMetaFile(HENHMETAFILE hEnhMetaFile, LPCRECT lpBounds);

Parameters

hMF A handle to the metafile to play.

hEnhMetaFile A handle to the enhanced metafile to play.

lpBounds A pointer to a RECT structure or a CRect object containing the coordinates, in logical units, of the rectangle used to display the picture described by the enhanced metafile.

Returns Non-zero if successful; otherwise, zero.

See Also ::GetMetaFile, ::GetEnhMetaFile, ::GetEnhMetaFileHeader, ::GetEnhMetaFilePaletteEntries, ::SetWorldTransform, ::PlayMetaFile, ::PlayEnhMetaFile

Example

```
...
CClientDC dc(pWnd);

HMETAFILE hMeta = ::GetMetaFile("MyMeta");
if (hMeta)
{
      dc.PlayMetaFile(hMeta);
      ::DeleteMetaFile(hMeta);
}
```

PlgBlt

■ 2.0 ■ 3.0 ■ NM

Description Copies a rectangular source bitmap to a destination parallelogram, optionally masking the color data in the process. If a valid mask bitmap is provided, a value of one in the mask indicates that the source pixel color should be copied to the destination. A value of zero in the mask indicates that the destination pixel color is not to be changed. This function can fail for any one of the following reasons:

- If a rotation or shear transform is active on the source device context (scaling, translation, and reflection transformations are allowed).
- If the mask bitmap is not a monochrome bitmap.
- If an enhanced metafile is being recorded and the source device context identifies an enhanced-metafile device context.
- If the source and destination device contexts represent incompatible devices.

PlgBlt transforms destination coordinates according to the destination device context and source coordinates according to the source device context. If the destination and source rectangles do not have the same color format, PlgBlt converts the source rectangle to match the destination rectangle.

Syntax public, BOOL PlgBlt(LPPOINT lpPoint, CDC* pSrcDC, int xSrc, int ySrc, int nWidth, int nHeight, Cbitmap& maskBitmap, int xMask, int yMask);

Parameters

lpPoint Points to an array of three points in logical space that identify three of the four corners of the destination parallelogram. The upper-left corner of the source rectangle is mapped to the first point in this array, the upper-right corner to the second point in this array, and the lower-left corner to the third point. The lower-right corner of the source rectangle is mapped to the implicit fourth point in the parallelogram.

pSrcDC A pointer to the source device context which contains the bitmap to copy.

xSrc The x coordinate, in logical units, of the upper-left corner of the source bitmap.

ySrc The y coordinate, in logical units, of the upper-left corner of the source bitmap.

nWidth The width, in logical units, of the source bitmap.

nHeight The height, in logical units, of the source bitmap.

maskBitmap A reference to a mask bitmap that is used to mask the colors of the source bitmap. This bitmap is optional. If the mask bitmap is smaller than the source and destination rectangles, PlgBlt replicates the mask pattern as necessary.

xMask A horizontal offset into the mask bitmap specified by the *maskBitmap* parameter.

yMask A vertical offset into the mask bitmap specified by the *maskBitmap* parameter.

Returns Non-zero if successful; otherwise, zero.

See Also CDC::BitBlt, CDC::MaskBlt, CDC::StretchBlt, ::PlgBlt

Example

```
void CMyWnd::DrawSkewedBitmap(CDC *pDc)
{
        CDC memDc;
        CBitmap bmp,maskBmp;
        BITMAP bitmap, *pOldBmp;

        // create a memory dc to use as the source dc
        dc.CreateCompatibleDC(pDc);

        // load the bitmap and obtain its dimensions
        bmp.LoadBitmap(IDB_TESTBMP);
        bmp.GetBitmap(&bitmap);
        pOldBmp = dc.SelectObject(&bmp);

        // get mask bitmap
        bmp.LoadBitmap(IDB_MASKBMP);

        // make destination parallelogram points
        CPoint pts[3];
        pts[1] = CPoint(100,100);
        pts[2].y = 100;
        pts[2].x = 100 + bitmap.bmWidth;
        pts[3].x = 50;
        pts[3].y = 100 + bitmap.bmHeight;

        // copy the bitmap to the parallelogram
        dc.PlgBlt(pts,&memDc, bitmap.bmWidth, bitmap.bmHeight, &maskBmp, ,0,0);

        // clean up
        memDc.SelectObject(pOldBmp);
        memDc.DeleteDC();
}
```

PolyBezier

■ 2.0 ■ 3.0 ■ NM

Description Draws Bézier splines using the current pen. Each spline is defined by using two endpoints and two control points. The first spline is drawn from the first point specified to the fourth point by using the second and third points as control points. Each subsequent spline in the sequence needs three more points: The end point of the previous spline is used as the starting point, the next two points in the sequence are the control points, and the third is the end point. This function does not use the current position. The CDC::PolyBezierTo function performs the same function as PolyBezier but it uses the current position. Figure 11-7 shows a sample output from the PolyBezier function.

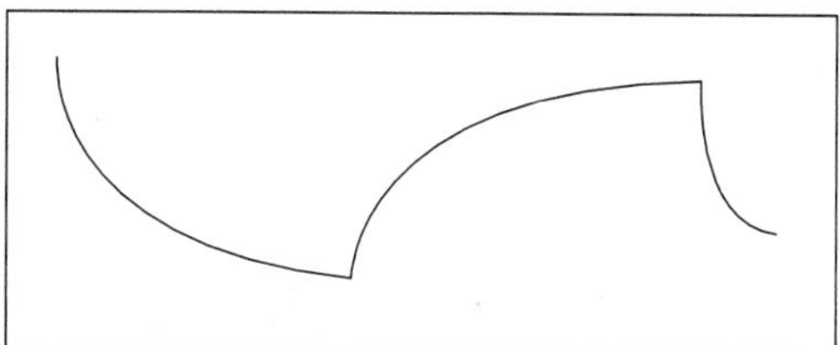

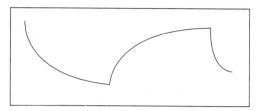

Figure 11-7 Sample output of PolyBezier

Syntax public, BOOL PolyBezier(const POINT* lpPoints, int nCount);

Parameters

lpPoints A pointer to an array of points which define the Bézier splines. The first spline requires four points—two endpoints and two control points. Each additional spline requires only three points, since the end point of the previous spline is used as the starting point of the new spline.

nCount The number of points in the array pointed to by *lpPoints.*

Returns Non-zero if successful; otherwise, zero.

See Also CDC::PolyBezierTo, ::PolyBezier

Example

```
...
CClientDC dc(pWnd);
CPoints curvePts[7] = {CPoint(10,10), CPoint(40,17), CPoint(50,22),
          CPoint(55,27), CPoint(42,35), CPoint(37,32), CPoint(30,22)};

// draw a couple curves
dc.PolyBezier(curvePts,7);
```

PolyBezierTo

■ 2.0 ■ 3.0 ■ NM

Description Draws Bézier splines using the current pen. Each spline is defined by using two endpoints and two control points. The first spline is drawn from the current position to the third point specified by using the first and second points as control points. Each subsequent spline in the sequence needs three more points: The end point of the previous spline is used as the starting point, the next two points in the sequence are the control points, and the third is the end point. This function is similar to the CDC::PolyBezier function except that it uses the current position as the starting point of the first spline and it updates the current position to the end point of the last spline. See Figure 11-7 for a sample Bézier curve output.

Syntax public, BOOL PolyBezierTo(const POINT* lpPoints, int nCount);

Parameters

lpPoints A pointer to an array of points that define the Bézier splines. Each spline requires three points—two control points and an end point.

nCount The number of points in the array pointed to by *lpPoints.*

Returns Non-zero if successful; otherwise, zero.

See Also CDC::PolyBezier, ::PolyBezierTo

Example

```
...
CClientDC dc(pWnd);
CPoints curvePts[6] = {CPoint(10,10), CPoint(40,17), CPoint(50,22),
          CPoint(55,27), CPoint(42,35), CPoint(37,32), CPoint(30,22)};

// draw a couple curves
dc.MoveTo(5,5);
dc.PolyBezierTo(curvePts,6);
```

POLYDRAW

■ 2.0 ■ 3.0 ■ NM

Description Draws a series of line segments and Bézier splines. This function basically replaces a series of calls to the CDC::MoveTo, CDC::LineTo, and CDC::PolyBezierTo functions. All lines and curves are drawn using the current pen and no filling takes place, even for closed figures. PolyDraw sets the current position to the last specified point when it is finished.

Syntax public, BOOL PolyDraw(const POINT* lpPoints, const BYTE* lpTypes, int nCount);

Parameters

lpPoints A pointer to an array of points that define the line segments and splines. The meaning of each point is given by the corresponding entry in the *lpTypes* array.

lpTypes Points to an array of bytes. Each byte describes how the corresponding point in the *lpPoints* array should be used. Possible values for each byte are given below:

PT_MOVETO The corresponding point starts a disjoint figure. The current position is moved to the specified position.

PT_LINETO A line is to be drawn from the current position to this point, which becomes the new current position. This style can be combined with the PT_CLOSEFIGURE style that indicates that the figure should be closed after the line is drawn. The figure is closed by drawing a line from this point to the most recent PT_MOVETO or MoveTo point.

PT_BEZIERTO This point is a control point or ending point for a Bézier spline. This type always occurs in sets of three. The current position defines the starting point for the spline. The first two PT_BEZIERTO points are the control points, and the third PT_BEZIERTO point is the ending point. The ending point becomes the new current position. If there are not three consecutive PT_BEZIERTO points, an error occurs. This style can be combined with the PT_CLOSEFIGURE style that indicates that the figure should be closed and the line is drawn. The figure is closed by drawing a line from this point to the most recent PT_MOVETO or MoveTo point.

nCount The number of entries in the *lpPoints* array and the *lpTypes* array.

Figure 11-8 Sample output of Polygon

Returns Non-zero if successful; otherwise, zero.

See Also CDC::MoveTo, CDC::LineTo, CDC::PolyBezierTo, ::PolyDraw

Example

```
...
CClientDC dc(pWnd);
CPoints pts[7] = {CPoint(1,1), CPoint(10,10), CPoint(30,20),
            CPoint(50,25), CPoint(60,30), CPoint(70,35), CPoint(10,10)};
BYTE types[7] = {PT_MOVETO, PT_LINETO, PT_LINETO, PT_BEZIERTO,
                PT_BEZIERTO, PT_BEZIERTO, PT_LINETO};

// draw a line from 1,1 to 10,10 then from 10,10 to 30,20, then a curve
// from 30,20 to 70,35 through 50,25 and 60,30 and finally a line from
// 70,35 to 10,10
dc.PolyDraw(pts,types,7);
```

POLYGON

■ 2.0 ■ 3.0

Description Draws a closed polygon outlined with the current pen and filled with the current brush. The polygon is closed automatically, if necessary, by drawing a line from the last point specified back to the first point. The figure is filled according to the current polygon fill mode, which can be set using the CDC::SetPolyFillMode function. Figure 11-8 shows an example output from the Polygon function.

Syntax public, BOOL Polygon(LPPOINT lpPoints, int nCount);

Parameters

lpPoints A pointer to an array of POINT structures or CPoint objects which define the polygon. All coordinates should be in logical units.

nCount The number of points in the array pointed to by the *lpPoints* parameter.

Returns Non-zero if successful; otherwise, zero.

See Also CDC::SetPolyFillMode, CDC::GetPolyFillMode, CDC::Polyline, ::Polygon

Example

```
...
CClientDC dc(pWnd);
CPoints pts[3] = {CPoint(10,20), CPoint(25,30), CPoint(15,40)};

// draw a triangle
dc.Polygon(pts,3);
```

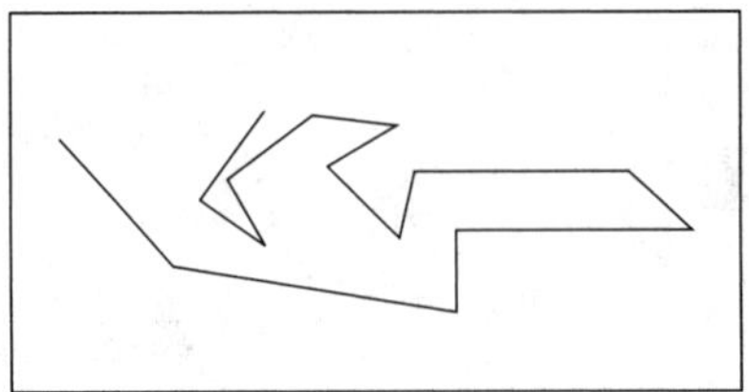

Figure 11-9 Sample output of Polyline

POLYLINE

■ 2.0 ■ 3.0

Description Draws a series of line segments using the current pen. The current position is not affected by this function. See the CDC::PolylineTo function if you want the current position to be updated. A sample output of the Polyline function is shown in Figure 11-9.

Syntax public, BOOL Polyline(LPPOINT lpPoints, int nCount);

Parameters

lpPoints A pointer to an array of POINT structures or CPoint objects which define the line segments to be drawn. All coordinates should be in logical units.

nCount The number of points in the array pointed to by the *lpPoints* parameter.

Returns Non-zero if successful; otherwise, zero.

See Also CDC::Polygon, CDC::PolylineTo, ::Polyline

Example

```
...
CClientDC dc(pWnd);
CPoints pts[3] = {CPoint(10,20), CPoint(25,30), CPoint(15,40)};

// draw a couple of line segments
dc.Polyline(pts,3);
```

POLYLINETO

■ 2.0 ■ 3.0 ■ NM

Description Draws a series of line segments using the current pen. PolylineTo updates the current position to the last point specified. Also, the first line drawn by this function is from the current position to the first point specified.

Syntax public, BOOL PolylineTo(const POINT* lpPoints, int nCount);

Parameters

lpPoints A pointer to an array of POINT structures or CPoint objects which define the line segments to be drawn. All coordinates should be in logical units.

nCount The number of points in the array pointed to by the *lpPoints* parameter.

Returns Non-zero if successful; otherwise, zero.

See Also CDC::Polyline, CDC::Polygon, ::PolylineTo

Example

```
...
CClientDC dc(pWnd);
CPoints pts[3] = {CPoint(10,20), CPoint(25,30), CPoint(15,40)};

// draw a few line segments (first one from 1,1 to 10,20)
dc.MoveTo(1,1);
dc.PolylineTo(pts,3);
```

PolyPolygon

■ 2.0 ■ 3.0 ■ NM

Description Draws a series of polygons. Each polygon is outlined using the current pen and filled using the current brush. You must close each polygon manually, as this function will not automatically close the polygons. Each polygon drawn is filled according to the current polygon fill mode which can be set using the CDC::SetPolyFillMode function. If you are drawing a series of polygons, this function is faster that a series of calls to the CDC::Polygon function. If you are drawing a single polygon, use the CDC::Polygon function.

Syntax public, BOOL PolyPolygon(LPPOINT lpPoints, LPINT lpPolyCounts, int nCount);

Parameters

lpPoints A pointer to an array of POINT structures or CPoint objects which define the polygons. All coordinates should be in logical units.

lpPolyCounts A pointer to an array of integers, each specifying the number of points in one of the polygons.

nCount The number of polygons to be drawn.

Returns Non-zero if successful; otherwise, zero.

See Also CDC::PolyPolyline, CDC::Polygon, CDC::SetPolyFillMode, CDC::GetPolyFillMode, ::PolyPolygon

Example

```
...
CClientDC dc(pWnd);
CPoints pts[8] = {CPoint(20,20), CPoint(30,30), CPoint(25,40),
                  CPoint(20,20), CPoint(100,100), CPoint(140,130),
                  CPoint(120,150), CPoint(100,100)};
DWORD dwCounts[2] = {4,4};

// draw a couple of triangles (note each triangle closed manually)
dc.PolyPolygon(pts,dwCounts,2);
```

PolyPolyline

■ 2.0 ■ 3.0 ■ NM

Description Draws a series of polylines using the current pen. If you are drawing a series of polylines, this function is faster that a series of calls to the CDC::Polyline function. If you are drawing a single polyline, use the CDC::Polyline function.

Syntax public, BOOL PolyPolyline(const POINT* lpPoints, const DWORD* lpPolyPoints, int nCount);

Parameters

lpPoints A pointer to an array of POINT structures or CPoint objects that define the polylines. All coordinates should be in logical units.

lpPolyCounts A pointer to an array of integers, each specifying the number of points in one of the polylines.

nCount The number of polylines to be drawn.

Returns Non-zero if successful; otherwise, zero.

See Also CDC::PolyPolygon, CDC::Polyline, CDC::SetPolyFillMode, CDC::GetPolyFillMode, ::PolyPolyline

Example

```
...
CClientDC dc(pWnd);
CPoints pts[6] = {CPoint(20,20), CPoint(30,30), CPoint(25,40),
                 CPoint(100,100), CPoint(140,130), CPoint(120,150)};
DWORD dwCounts[2] = {3,3};

// draw a couple of stick figures
dc.PolyPolyline(pts,dwCounts,2);
```

PtVisible ■ 2.0 ■ 3.0

Description Determines whether a given point is within the current clipping region for the device context.

Syntax public, virtual BOOL PtVisible(int x, int y) const; public, virtual BOOL PtVisible(POINT point) const;

Parameters

x The x coordinate, in logical units, of the point to check.

y The y coordinate, in logical units, of the point to check.

point A POINT structure or CPoint object containing the coordinate, in logical units, of the point to check.

Returns Non-zero if the specified point is with the clipping region; otherwise, zero.

See Also CDC::RectVisible, ::PtVisible

Example

```
...
CClientDC dc(pWnd);

// set up a clipping area
CRect rectClip(100,100,200,400);
dc.IntersectClipRect(rectClip);

CPoint pt1(150,150), pt2(225,100);
BOOL bVis1 = dc.PtVisible(pt1); // bVis1 = TRUE
BOOL bVis2 = dc.PtVisible(pt2); // bVis2 = FALSE
```

RealizePalette

■ 2.0 ■ 3.0

Description Maps entries from the current logical palette to the system palette. RealizePalette is used to manage the various color requirements of running applications and the possibly limited availability of those colors. For example, many displays can only show a maximum of 256 colors simultaneously. However, the sum total of the colors needed by multiple applications may be greater that 256. When a window has the input focus and calls RealizePalette, Windows ensures that the window will display all the requested colors, up to the maximum number simultaneously available on the screen. Windows will also display colors not found in the window's palette by matching them to available colors. In addition, Windows matches the colors requested by inactive windows that call RealizePalette as closely as possible to the available colors. This prevents, to the greatest extent possible, any undesirable changes in the colors displayed in inactive windows.

Syntax public, UINT RealizePalette( );

Parameters None.

Returns The number of entries in the logical palette that were mapped to different entries in the system palette. This represents the number of entries that RealizePalette remapped to accommodate changes in the system palette since the logical palette was last realized.

See Also CDC::SelectPalette, ::RealizePalette

Example

```
void CMyWnd::SomeDrawFunc(CPalette &pal, CDC *pDc)
{
     CPalette *pOldPal = pDc->SelectPalette(&pal,FALSE);

     // realize our palette making our window the one whose colors
     // will be most closely matched with what we want
     pDc->RealizePalette();

     // do some fancy high-color drawing
...
}
```

Rectangle

■ 2.0 ■ 3.0

Description Draws a rectangle outlined with the current pen and filled with the current brush. The rectangle drawn does not include the right and bottom edges.

Syntax public, BOOL Rectangle(int x1, int y1, int x2, int y2); public, BOOL Rectangle(LPCRECT lpRect);

Parameters

x1 The x coordinate, in logical units, of the upper-left corner of the rectangle.

y1 The y coordinate, in logical units, of the upper-left corner of the rectangle.

x2 The x coordinate, in logical units, of the lower-right corner of the rectangle.

y2 The y coordinate, in logical units, of the lower-right corner of the rectangle.

lpRect A pointer to a RECT structure or a CRect object containing the coordinates, in logical units, of the rectangle.

Returns Non-zero if successful; otherwise, zero.

See Also CDC::RoundRect, ::Rectangle

Example

```
...
CClientDC dc(pWnd);

// draw a rectangle
dc.Rectangle(1,1,300,100);

// draw another one
CRect rect(100,200,150,225);
dc.Rectangle(rect);
```

RECTVISIBLE ■ 2.0 ■ 3.0

Description Determines whether any part of a specified rectangle is within the current clipping region.

Syntax public, virtual BOOL RectVisible(LPCRECT lpRect) const;

Parameters

lpRect A pointer to a RECT structure or a CRect object containing the rectangle, in logical coordinates.

Returns Non-zero if any part of the rectangle is within the current clipping region; otherwise, zero.

See Also CDC::PtVisible, ::RectVisible

Example

```
...
CClientDC dc(pWnd);

// set up a clipping area
CRect rectClip(100,100,200,400);
dc.IntersectClipRect(rectClip);

CRect rect1(175,300,240,350), rect2(205,150,300,400);
BOOL bVis1 = dc.RectVisible(rect1); // bVis1 = TRUE
BOOL bVis2 = dc.RectVisible(rect2); // bVis2 = FALSE
```

RELEASEATTRIBDC ■ 2.0 ■ 3.0

Description Sets the attribute device context associated with the CDC object to NULL. Note that the attribute device context is never “attached” to the CDC object, so it is not detached by this function.

Syntax public, virtual void ReleaseAttribDC( );

Parameters None.

Returns Nothing is returned.

See Also CDC::SetAttribDC, CDC::SetOutputDC, CDC::ReleaseOutputDC

ReleaseOutputDC

■ 2.0 ■ 3.0

Description Sets the output device context associated with the CDC object to NULL. Do not call this function if the output device context is attached to the CDC object. Call the CDC::Detach function to detach an output device context that has been attached to the CDC object.

Syntax public, virtual void ReleaseOutputDC( );

Parameters None.

Returns Nothing is returned.

See Also CDC::ReleaseAttribDC, CDC::SetOutputDC, CDC::SetAttribDC

ResetDC

■ 2.0 ■ 3.0

Description Resets the state of the attribute device context to that specified by the given DEVMODE structure. You must select all non-stock objects out of the device context prior to calling this function. Also, you cannot use this function to change the driver name, device name, or output port associated with the device context. This function is often used to respond to the WM_DEVMODECHANGE message which indicates that the user has changed the settings for the device associated with the device context.

Syntax public, BOOL ResetDC(const DEVMODE* lpDevMode);

Parameters

lpDevMode A pointer to a DEVMODE structure containing the new device information. For more information regarding this structure, see the Windows SDK documentation.

Returns Non-zero if successful; otherwise, zero.

See Also ::ResetDC

RestoreDC

■ 2.0 ■ 3.0

Description Restores the device context to a state previously saved using the CDC::SaveDC function. You may save the state of a device context many times. The state information is stored on a stack. Because of this, if you call RestoreDC to restore the device state to anything other than that which was last saved, the interim saves are lost.

Syntax public, virtual BOOL RestoreDC(int nSavedDC);

Parameters

nSavedDC — An integer that identifies the state information to restore. This integer is returned from a call to the CDC::SaveDC function. This parameter can be -1, in which case the last save is restored.

Returns — Non-zero if successful; otherwise, zero.

See Also — CDC::SaveDC, ::RestoreDC

Example

```
...
CClientDC dc(pWnd);

// do some dc setup here

// save the dc state
dc.SaveDC();

// do some more dc setup stuff here

// restore dc back to state when saved
dc.RestoreDC(-1);
```

RoundRect

■ 2.0 ■ 3.0

Description — Draws a rectangle with rounded corners. The rectangle is outlined using the current pen and filled with the current brush.

Syntax — public, BOOL RoundRect(int x1, int y1, int x2, int y2, int x3, int y3);
public, BOOL RoundRect(LPCRECT lpRect, POINT point);

Parameters

x1 — The x coordinate, in logical units, of the upper-left corner of the rectangle.

y1 — The y coordinate, in logical units, of the upper-left corner of the rectangle.

x2 — The x coordinate, in logical units, of the lower-right corner of the rectangle.

y2 — The y coordinate, in logical units, of the lower-right corner of the rectangle.

x3 — The width, in logical units, of the ellipse used to draw the rounded corners.

y3 — The height, in logical units, of the ellipse used to draw the rounded corners.

lpRect — A pointer to a RECT structure or a CRect object containing the coordinates, in logical units, of the rectangle.

point — A POINT structure or a CPoint object containing the width and height, in logical units, of the ellipse used to draw the rounded corners.

Returns — Non-zero if successful; otherwise, zero.

See Also — CDC::Rectangle, ::RoundRect

Example

```
...
CClientDC dc(pWnd);

// draw a rectangle with rounded corners
dc.RoundRect(10,10,200,100,20,10);
```

```
// or draw one like this
CRect rect(10,10,200,100);
CPoint ptEllipse(20,10);
dc.RoundRect(rect,ptEllipse);
```

SaveDC

■ 2.0 ■ 3.0

Description Saves the current state of the device context. This state can then be later restored using the CDC::RestoreDC function. The saved information is placed on a stack maintained by Windows. You may call SaveDC any number of times. This function can be useful if you are doing a lot of graphics manipulation and do not want to have to re-setup the DC many times. For example, if you are changing mapping modes and coordinates, it can be easier to save each setup if you will need to re-use them.

Syntax public, virtual int SaveDC( );

Parameters None.

Returns If the function is successful, an integer representing the saved context information. This integer can then be used with the CDC::RestoreDC function. If the function fails, the return value is zero.

See Also CDC::RestoreDC, ::SaveDC

Example

```
...
CClientDC dc(pWnd);

// do some dc setup here

// save the dc state
dc.SaveDC();

// do some more dc setup stuff here

// restore dc back to state when saved
dc.RestoreDC(-1);
```

ScaleViewportExt

■ 2.0 ■ 3.0

Description Scales the current viewport extents according to the specified fractions. The viewport origin and extents, together with the window origin and extents, determine how coordinates are mapped between device coordinates and logical coordinates. See the CDC::DPtoLP and CDC::LPtoDP functions for a discussion regarding these mappings.

Syntax public, virtual CSize ScaleViewportExt(int xNum, int xDenom, int yNum, int yDenom);

Parameters

xNum The amount by which to multiply the horizontal viewport extent.

xDenom The amount by which to divide the result of multiplying the horizontal extent by *xNum*.

yNum — The amount by which to multiply the vertical viewport extent.

yDenom — The amount by which to divide the result of multiplying the vertical extent by *yNum*.

Returns — A CSize object containing the old viewport extents.

See Also — CDC::ScaleWindowExt, CDC::GetViewportExt, CDC::SetViewportExt, ::ScaleViewportExt

Example

```
...
CClientDC dc(pWnd);
CRect rc;

// get client area
pWnd->GetClientRect(rc);

// set up one-to-one logical mapping
dc.SetMapMode(MM_ANISOTROPIC);
dc.SetWindowOrg(0,0);
dc.SetWindowExt(rc.right,rc.bottom);
dc.SetViewportOrg(0,0);
dc.SetViewportExt(rc.right,rc.bottom);

// draw some stuff

// scale viewport to twice normal - everything drawn will shrink by a
// factor of 4
dc.ScaleViewportExt(2,1,2,1);
```

ScaleWindowExt ■ 2.0 ■ 3.0

Description — Scales the current window extents according to the specified fractions. The window origin and extents, together with the viewport origin and extents, determine how coordinates are mapped between device coordinates and logical coordinates. See the CDC::DPtoLP and CDC::LPtoDP functions for a discussion regarding these mappings.

Syntax — public, virtual CSize ScaleWindowExt(int xNum, int xDenom, int yNum, int yDenom);

Parameters

xNum — The amount by which to multiply the horizontal window extent.

xDenom — The amount by which to divide the result of multiplying the horizontal extent by *xNum*.

yNum — The amount by which to multiply the vertical window extent.

yDenom — The amount by which to divide the result of multiplying the vertical extent by *yNum*.

Returns — A CSize containing the old window extents.

See Also — CDC::ScaleViewportExt, CDC::GetWindowExt, CDC::SetWindowExt, ::ScaleWindowExt

Example

```
...
CClientDC dc(pWnd);
CRect rc;

// get client area
pWnd->GetClientRect(rc);

// set up one-to-one logical mapping
dc.SetMapMode(MM_ANISOTROPIC);
dc.SetWindowOrg(0,0);
dc.SetWindowExt(rc.right,rc.bottom);
dc.SetViewportOrg(0,0);
dc.SetViewportExt(rc.right,rc.bottom);

// draw some stuff

// scale window to twice normal - everything drawn will expand by a
// factor of 4
dc.ScaleWindowExt(2,1,2,1);
```

ScrollDC

■ 2.0 ■ 3.0

Description Scrolls the contents of a specified rectangle within the device context. If you need to scroll the entire client area of a window, use the CWnd::ScrollWindow function instead.

Syntax public, BOOL ScrollDC(int dx, int dy, LPCRECT lpRectScroll, LPCRECT lpRectClip, CRgn* pRgnUpdate, LPRECT lpRectUpdate);

Parameters

dx The number of device units to scroll horizontally. Negative values will scroll left; positive values will scroll right.

dy The number of device units to scroll vertically. Negative values will scroll up; positive values will scroll down.

lpRectScroll A pointer to a RECT structure or a CRect object containing the coordinates, in device units, of the rectangle that should be scrolled.

lpRectClip A pointer to a RECT structure or a CRect object containing the coordinates, in device units, of the clipping rectangle. Only areas within both the scrolling rectangle and the clipping rectangle will be scrolled.

pRgnUpdate A pointer to a CRgn object which, if supplied, will be initialized to the region uncovered by the scrolling process. Windows does not automatically invalidate this area, so you may want to use this parameter in a call to CWnd::InvalidateRgn. The CRgn object supplied must already contain a valid region handle. If this parameter and the *lpRectUpdate* parameter are NULL, the update region is not calculated.

lpRectUpdate A pointer to a RECT structure or a CRect object that will be filled with the coordinates of the bounding rectangle of the update region (the region uncovered by the scrolling process). If this parameter is NULL, the bounding rectangle is not calculated.

Returns Non-zero if successful; otherwise, zero.

See Also CWnd::ScrollWindow, CWnd::InvalidateRgn, ::ScrollDC

Example

```
...
CClientDC dc(pWnd);
CRect rectScrollArea(100,100,300,300),rectUpdate;

// scroll the area inside our rectangle up 10 pixels
dc.ScrollDC( 0,-10,rectScrollArea,rectScrollArea,NULL,rectUpdate);

// invalidate the uncovered area
dc.InvalidateRect(rectUpdate);
```

SelectClipPath

■ 3.0 ■ NM

Description Creates a new clipping region by combining the current path with the current clipping region. The manner in which the two are combined can also be specified. This function will fail if the device context does not contain a closed path.

Syntax public, BOOL SelectClipPath(int nMode);

Parameters

nMode Describes how the path should be combined with the current clipping region. Can be one of the following values:

RGN_AND The new clipping region includes the intersection (overlapping areas) of the current clipping region and the current path.

RGN_COPY The new clipping region is the current path.

RGN_DIFF The new clipping region includes the areas of the current clipping region with those of the current path excluded.

RGN_OR The new clipping region includes the union (combined areas) of the current clipping region and the current path.

RGN_XOR The new clipping region includes the union of the current clipping region and the current path but without the overlapping areas.

Returns Non-zero if successful; otherwise, zero. If the return value is zero, you can call the ::GetLastError function for more information. ::GetLastError may return one of the following values: ERROR_CAN_NOT_COMPLETE, ERROR_INVALID_PARAMETER, or ERROR_NOT_ENOUGH_MEMORY.

See Also CDC::BeginPath, CDC::EndPath, ::SelectClipPath

Example

```
...
CClientDC dc(pWnd);

// make a triangular path
```

```
dc.BeginPath();
dc.MoveTo(10,20);
dc.LineTo(100,40);
dc.LineTo(50,50);
dc.CloseFigure();
dc.EndPath();

// make the triangle the clipping region - after this, all drawing will
// be clipped to the inside of this triangle
dc.SelectClipPath(RGN_COPY);
```

SelectClipRgn

■ 2.0 ■ 3.0

Description Sets the clipping region of the device context to a specified region or combines the specified region with the current region. The first version of this function is the same as the second version with the *nMode* parameter set to RGN_COPY. Note that the second version of this function is not available on the Macintosh.

Syntax public, int SelectClipRgn(CRgn* pRgn);
public, int SelectClipRgn(CRgn* pRgn, int nMode);

Parameters

pRgn A pointer to the region to use as the new clipping region or to combine with the current region. For the first version of SelectClipRgn and the second version with *nMode* equal to RGN_COPY, this parameter can be NULL. In this case, the clipping region is set to the entire client area of the window.

nMode Describes how the specified region should be combined with the current clipping region. Can be any of the following values:

RGN_AND The new clipping region combines the overlapping areas of the current clipping region and the specified region.

RGN_COPY The new clipping region is a copy of the specified region.

RGN_DIFF The new clipping region combines the areas of the current clipping region with those areas excluded from the specified region.

RGN_OR The new clipping region combines the current clipping region and the specified region.

RGN_XOR The new clipping region combines the current clipping region and the specified region but excludes any overlapping areas.

Returns The new clipping region's type. It can be any of the following values:

COMPLEXREGION New clipping region has overlapping borders.

NULLREGION New clipping region is empty.

SIMPLEREGION New clipping region has no overlapping borders.

ERROR Device context or region is not valid.

See Also CDC::SelectClipPath, ::SelectRgn, ::ExtSelectRgn

Example

```
...
CClientDC dc(pWnd);

// make a triangular region
CPoint pts[3] = {CPoint(10,20), CPoint(100,40), CPoint(50,50)};
CRgn rgn;
rgn.CreatePolygonRgn(pts,3,ALTERNATE);

// make the triangle the clipping region - after this, all drawing will
// be clipped to the inside of this triangle
dc.SelectClipRgn(&rgn);
```

SelectGdiObject ■ 2.0 ■ 3.0 ■ UD

Description A simple utility function that wraps the SDK ::SelectObject function. This function is used internally by MFC to implement the more specific CDC::SelectObject functions.

Syntax protected, static CGdiObject* PASCAL SelectGdiObject(HDC hDC, HGDIOBJ hObj);

Parameters

hDC A handle to the device context into which the specified object should be selected.

hObj A handle to the GDI object to select into the device context.

Returns A pointer to a CGdiObject which represents the object previously selected into the device context. This pointer is created using the CDC::FromHandle function and, as such, may be temporary.

See Also CDC::SelectObject, ::SelectObject

SelectObject ■ 2.0 ■ 3.0

Description A series of type-safe overloaded functions which select various types of GDI objects into the device context. Once you select an object into the device context, you must select it back out of the device context before the device context is destroyed. The last version of SelectObject selects a clipping region into the device context by calling the CDC::SelectClipRgn function. This differs from the other four which are basically type-safe wrappers of the ::SelectObject SDK function. Note that a bitmap can only be selected into a memory device context and that the bitmap must either be monochrome or compatible with the color format of the memory device context.

Syntax
public, CPen* SelectObject(CPen* pPen);
public, CBrush* SelectObject(CBrush* pBrush);
public, virtual CFont* SelectObject(CFont* pFont);
public, CBitmap* SelectObject(CBitmap* pBitmap);
public, int SelectObject(CRgn* pRgn);

Parameters

pPen	A pointer to the pen to be selected into the device context.
pBrush	A pointer to the brush to be selected into the device context.
pFont	A pointer to the font to be selected into the device context.
pBitmap	A pointer to the bitmap to be selected into the device context.
pRgn	A pointer to the region to be selected into the device context.
Returns	For the first four versions of the function, a pointer to the previously selected object of the same type as that which is selected. For example, if you select a pen into the device context, this function returns the pen that was previously selected into the device context. The pointer returned is created using the CDC::FromHandle function and, as such, may be temporary. The version of SelectObject that selects a clipping region returns an integer indicating the type of the region. It can be any one of the following values:
COMPLEXREGION	The new clipping region has overlapping borders.
NULLREGION	The new clipping region is empty.
SIMPLEREGION	The new clipping region has no overlapping borders.
ERROR	Device context or region is not valid.
See Also	CDC::SelectGdiObject, CDC::FromHandle, CDC::SelectPalette, CDC::SelectClipRgn, ::SelectObject

Example

```
...
CClientDC dc(pWnd);
CPen *pOldPen, pen(PS_SOLID,1,RGB(255,0,0));

// select red pen for rectangle drawing
pOldPen = dc.SelectObject(&pen);

// draw something
dc.Rectangle(1,1,100,200);

// clean up
dc.SelectObject(pOldPen);
```

SelectPalette

■ 2.0 ■ 3.0

Description	Selects the specified palette into the device context (makes it the current palette). As long as the device contexts refer to the same physical device, you can select the same logical palette into more than one device context at the same time. Note, however, that changes made to the logical palette will affect all associated device contexts.
Syntax	public, CPalette* SelectPalette(CPalette* pPalette, BOOL bForceBackground);

Parameters

pPalette	A pointer to the logical palette to be selected into the device context.

bForceBackground If non-zero, the palette is forced to be a background-only palette. In this case, the palette is always treated as a background palette even when the associated window has the input focus. If this parameter is zero, the palette is a foreground palette when its associated window has the input focus and a background palette when the window does not have the input focus. Windows maps logical palettes differently when they are the foreground palette.

Returns A pointer to the previously selected logical palette. This pointer is created using the CDC::FromHandle function and, as such, may be temporary. If an error occurs, the function returns NULL.

See Also CDC::RealizePalette, ::SelectPalette

Example

```
...
CClientDC dc(pWnd);
CPalette pal;

// creat a palette
pal.CreateHalftonePalette();

// select it
CPalette *pOldPal = dc.SelectPalette(&pal);

// realize palette and draw some stuff

// clean up
dc.SelectPalette(pOldPal);
```

SelectStockObject ■ 2.0 ■ 3.0

Description Selects one of the Windows stock objects into the device context.

Syntax public, virtual CGdiObject* SelectStockObject(int nIndex);

Parameters

nIndex An integer that defines which stock object to select. Values for this parameter are listed below:

BLACK_BRUSH	Black brush.
DKGRAY_BRUSH	Dark gray brush.
GRAY_BRUSH	Gray brush.
HOLLOW_BRUSH	Hollow brush (same as NULL_BRUSH).
LTGRAY_BRUSH	Light gray brush.
NULL_BRUSH	Null brush (same as HOLLOW_BRUSH).
WHITE_BRUSH	White brush.
BLACK_PEN	Black pen.
NULL_PEN	Null pen.
WHITE_PEN	White pen. ANSI_FIXED_FONTANSI fixed-pitch system font.
ANSI_VAR_FONT	ANSI variable-pitch system font.

DEVICE_DEFAULT_FONT Device-dependent font (NT only).

DEVICE_GUI_FONT Default font for user interface objects such as menus and dialog boxes. (Windows 95 only).

OEM_FIXED_FONT OEM-dependent fixed-pitch font.

SYSTEM_FONT The system font used by default, to draw menus, dialog-box controls, and other text. In Windows versions 3.0 and later, the system font is proportional width; earlier versions of Windows use a fixed-width system font.

SYSTEM_FIXED_FONT The fixed-pitch system font used in Windows prior to version 3.0. This object is available for compatibility with earlier versions of Windows.

DEFAULT_PALETTE Default color palette which consists of the 20 static colors in the system palette.

Returns A pointer to the previously selected object. Depending on the stock object select, this may be a pointer to a CPen, CBrush, CFont, or CPalette.

See Also CGdiObject::GetObject,CDC::SelectObject, ::GetStockObject

Example

```
void CMyWnd::DrawWhiteRectangle(CDC *pDc)
{
      CRectangle rect(1,1,10,10);
      CBrush *pOldBrush;
      pOldBrush = pDc->SelectStockObject(WHITE_BRUSH);
      pDc->Rectangle(rect);
      pDc->SelectObject(pOldBrush);
}
```

SetAbortProc ■ 2.0 ■ 3.0

Description Installs an abort procedure that will be called by Print Manager if the user attempts to cancel a print job during spooling or if the system runs out of disk space for spooling. This function must be called prior to the call to CDC::StartDoc that begins the print job. If you do not set an abort procedure, the user will not be able to cancel printing during spooling. If the spooler runs out of disk space and no abort procedure is registered, the print job will fail.

Syntax public, int SetAbortProc(BOOL (CALLBACK EXPORT* lpfn)(HDC hDc, int nCode));

Parameters

lpfn A pointer to the function to install as the abort procedure. This function should return non-zero if the print job should continue or zero if the print job should be aborted. The two parameters to this callback function are described below:

hDc The device context that is printing.

nCode Zero if no error occured or SP_OUTOFDISK if the Print Manager is currently out of space but expects that more space will become available if the application waits. If *nCode* is SP_OUTOFDISK, the application does not have to abort the print job. If it does not, it must yield to the Print Manager by calling the PeekMessage or GetMessage Windows function.

Returns The outcome of the SetAbortProc function. Can be one of the following values:

SP_ERROR General error.

SP_OUTOFDISK Not enough disk space is currently available for spooling, and no more space will become available.

SP_OUTOFMEMORY Not enough memory is available for spooling.

SP_USERABORT User ended the job through the Print Manager.

See Also CDC::AbortDoc, ::SetAbortProc

SetArcDirection ■ 2.0 ■ 3.0 ■ NM

Description Sets the current arc direction. Windows draws arcs and rectangles in the direction indicated by the current arc direction. The default direction for a device context is counterclockwise. Functions that use the current arc direction include CDC::Arc, CDC::ArcTo, CDC::Chord, CDC::Ellipse, CDC::Pie, CDC::Rectangle, and CDC::RoundRect.

Syntax public, int SetArcDirection(int nArcDirection);

Parameters

nArcDirection The direction in which arcs and rectangles should be draw. Can be AD_CLOCKWISE or AD_COUNTERCLOCKWISE.

Returns The previous arc direction.

See Also CDC::GetArcDirection

Example

```
...
CClientDC dc(pWnd);

// set arc direction to clockwise
int nOldDir = dc.SetArcDirection(AD_CLOCKWISE);

// draw half-ellipse arc in a clockwise direction
dc.Arc(0,0,300,200,150,0,150,200);

// clean up
dc.SetArcDirection(nOldDir);
```

SetAttribDC ■ 2.0 ■ 3.0

Description Sets the attribute device context to the specified device context. The device context is not attached to the CDC object.

Syntax public, virtual void SetAttribDC(HDC hDC);

Parameters

hDC The handle of the device context to be associated with the CDC object as the attribute device context.

Returns Nothing is returned.

See Also CDC::SetOutputDC, CDC::ReleaseAttribDC, CDC::ReleaseOutputDC

SetBkColor ■ 2.0 ■ 3.0

Description Sets the current background color of the device context to the specified RGB color value. If the specified color can not be supported on the device, the nearest color is used. If the current background mode is OPAQUE (see CDC::SetBkMode), Windows uses the current background color to fill the gaps in lines, the gaps between hatches in brushes, and the background of text.

Syntax public, virtual COLORREF SetBkColor(COLORREF crColor);

Parameters

crColor The RGB value of the new background color.

Returns The RGB value of the previous background color. If an error occurs, the return value is 0x80000000.

See Also CDC::GetBkColor, CDC::SetBkMode

Example

```
void CMyWnd::OutputSomeText(CDC *pDc)
{
	COLORREF crOld = pDc->SetTextColor(RGB(255,0,0)); // red text
	int nOldMode = pDc->SetBkMode(OPAQUE); // colored background
	COLORREF crOldBk = pDc->SetTextColor(RGB(0,0,255); // green bg
	CString strTestText = "Christmas Text.";

	// output message with green background and red text
	pDc->TextOut(10,50,strTestText);

	// clean up
	pDc->SetBkMode(nOldMode);
	pDc->SetTextColor(crOld);
	pDc->SetBkColor(crOld);
}
```

SetBkMode ■ 2.0 ■ 3.0

Description Sets the current background mode. The background mode defines whether the system repaints the background with the current background color when drawing text, hatched brushes, or any pen style that is not a solid line.

Syntax public, int SetBkMode(int nBkMode);

Parameters

nBkMode The new background mode. This parameter can be TRANSPARENT, indicating that the background will not be touched, or OPAQUE, indicating that the background will be painted with the current background color.

Returns The previous background mode.

See Also CDC::GetBkMode, CDC::GetBkColor, CDC::SetBkColor, ::SetBkMode

Example

```
void CMyWnd::OutputSomeText(CDC *pDc)
{
	COLORREF crOld = pDc->SetTextColor(RGB(255,0,0)); // red text
	int nOldMode = pDc->SetBkMode(OPAQUE); // colored background
	COLORREF crOldBk = pDc->SetTextColor(RGB(0,0,255); // green bg
	CString strTestText = "Christmas Text.";

	// output message with green background and red text
	pDc->TextOut(10,50,strTestText);

	// clean up
	pDc->SetBkMode(nOldMode);
	pDc->SetTextColor(crOld);
	pDc->SetBkColor(crOld);
}
```

SetBoundsRect

■ 2.0 ■ 3.0 ■ NM

Description Controls the accumulation of bounding-rectangle information for the specified device context. Windows can optionally maintain a bounding rectangle for all drawing operations. This rectangle can be queried and reset by an application using this function.

Syntax public, UINT SetBoundsRect(LPCRECT lpRectBounds, UINT flags);

Parameters

lpRectBounds A pointer to a RECT structure or a CRect object containing the rectangle, in logical coordinates, to be used when setting the bounding rectangle.

flags A set of flags which determines how bounding rectangle accumulation will be affected. Can be a combination of the following values:

DCB_ACCUMULATE Adds the specified rectangle to the bounding rectangle. If you use both the DCB_RESET flag and the DCB_ACCUMULATE flag, the bounding rectangle will be set to the specified rectangle.

DCB_DISABLE Turns off boundary accumulation.

DCB_ENABLE Turns on boundary accumulation, which is disabled by default.

DCB_RESET Clears the bounding rectangle.

Returns The current state of bounding rectangle accumulation. This value is a combination of the same flags described with the *flags* parameter above.

See Also CDC::GetBoundsRect, ::SetBoundsRect

SetBrushOrg

■ 2.0 ■ 3.0

Description Sets the current brush origin. The default brush origin for a device context is 0,0. Because a brush is represented by an eight pixel by eight pixel bitmap, both the x and y coordinates of the brush origin can range from zero to seven. When a drawing operation requires a brush, Windows maps the upper-left corner of the brush bitmap (0,0) to the point in the client area of the destination window specified by the current brush origin. For example, if the current brush origin is set to (3,1) Windows will map the upper-left corner of the brush bitmap (0,0) with the point (3,1) in the client area of the window in which it is drawing. To change the origin of a brush, first call the CGdiObject::UnrealizeObject function for the CBrush object, call SetBrushOrg, and then call the CDC::SelectObject member function to select the brush into the device context.

Syntax public, CPoint SetBrushOrg(int x, int y); public, CPoint SetBrushOrg(POINT point);

Parameters

x The x coordinate, in device units, of the new brush origin. This parameter can range from zero to seven.

y The y coordinate, in device units, of the new brush origin. This parameter can range from zero to seven.

point A POINT structure or CPoint object containing the coordinates, in device units, of the new brush origin.

Returns A CPoint object containing the previous brush origin, in device units.

See Also CDC::GetBrushOrg, CDC::SelectObject, CGdiObject::UnrealizeObject, ::SetBrushOrg

SetColorAdjustment ■ 2.0 ■ 3.0 ■ NM

Description Sets the color adjustment values to use for the device context. The color adjustment values are used to adjust the input color of the source bitmap for calls to the CDC::StretchBlt member function when HALFTONE mode is set.

Syntax public, BOOL SetColorAdjustment(const COLORADJUSTMENT* lpColorAdjust);

Parameters

lpColorAdjust A pointer to a COLORADJUSTMENT structure. For a complete description of this structure, see the Windows SDK documentation.

Returns Non-zero if successful; otherwise, zero.

See Also CDC::GetColorAdjustment, CDC::SetStretchBltMode, CDC::StretchBlt, ::StretchDIBits

SetMapMode ■ 2.0 ■ 3.0

Description Sets the current coordinate mapping mode. The mapping mode controls how coordinates are mapped from the device to a logical coordinate space and vice versa.

Syntax public, virtual int SetMapMode(int nMapMode);

Parameters

nMapMode The new mapping mode as specified by one of the following constants:

MM_ANISOTROPIC Logical units are mapped to arbitrary units with arbitrarily scaled axes. The SetWindowExtEx and SetViewportExtEx functions can be used to specify the units, orientation, and scaling that should be used.

MM_HIENGLISH Each logical unit is mapped to 0.001 inch. Positive x is to the right; positive y is up.

MM_HIMETRIC Each logical unit is mapped to 0.01 millimeter. Positive x is to the right; positive y is up.

MM_ISOTROPIC Logical units are mapped to arbitrary units with equally scaled axes. One unit along the x-axis is equal to one unit along the y-axis. The SetWindowExtEx and SetViewportExtEx functions can be used to specify the units and the orientation of the axes that should be used.The Windows GDI makes adjustments as necessary to ensure the x and y units remain the same size.

MM_LOENGLISH Each logical unit is mapped to 0.01 inch. Positive x is to the right; positive y is up.

MM_LOMETRIC Each logical unit is mapped to 0.1 millimeter. Positive x is to the right; positive y is up.

MM_TEXT Each logical unit is mapped to one device pixel. Positive x is to the right; positive y is down. In effect, no mapping is done.

MM_TWIPS Each logical unit is mapped to one twentieth of a printer's point (1/1440 inch, also called a "twip"). Positive x is to the right; positive y is up.

Returns The previous coordinate mapping mode.

See Also CDC::GetMapMode, CDC::DPtoLP, CDC::LPtoDP, CDC::SetWindowOrg, CDC::SetWindowExt, CDC::SetViewportOrg, CDC::SetViewportExt, ::SetMapMode

Example

```
..
CClientDC dc(pWnd);
CRect rc;
CPoint pt;

// set mapping mode to MM_ANISOTROPIC (logical with no constraints)
dc.SetMapMode(MM_ANISOTROPIC);

// get client rectangle of window and use as window coordinates
pWnd->GetClientRect(rc);
dc.SetWindowOrg(rc.left,rc.top);
dc.SetWindowExt(rc.right,rc.bottom);

// create mapping such that no matter what the window size, always have
// 100 x 100 grid
dc.SetViewportOrg(0,0);
dc.SetViewportExt(100,100);
```

```
// convert an arbitrary point to logical coordinates - if client area of
// window were 600 x 500 logical point would be 120, 100
CPoint devPoint(20,20);
dc.DPtoLP(&devPoint,1);

// convert an arbitrary point to device coordinates - if client area of
// window were 600 x 500 device point would be 20, 20
CPoint logPoint(120, 100);
dc.LPtoDP(&logPoint,1);

..
```

SetMapperFlags

■ 2.0 ■ 3.0

Description Determines what method the Windows font mapper uses when it converts a logical font to a physical font. SetMapperFlags controls whether the font mapper will only choose a font that exactly matches the aspect ratio of the device associated with the device context. Typically, if you are using TrueType fonts, this is not necessary because TrueType fonts can be scaled accurately. If you are using a bitmap font, the font may become unreadable if it is scaled to a different aspect ratio.

Syntax public, DWORD SetMapperFlags(DWORD dwFlag);

Parameters

dwFlag If this parameter is ASPECT_FILTERING, the font mapper attempts to match a font's aspect height and width to the device. If no matching font is found, the mapper chooses a new aspect ratio and then retrieves a font that matches the new ratio. If you do not want the mapper to filter font selection based on aspect ratio, set this parameter to zero.

Returns The previous value of the font mapper flag.

See Also ::SetMapperFlags

Example

```
...
CClientDC dc(pWnd);

DWORD dwOldMapping = dc.SetMapperFlags(ASPECT_FILTERING);

// do some font work

// clean up
dc.SetMapperFlags(dwOldMapping);
```

SetMiterLimit

■ 3.0 ■ NM

Description Sets the limit for the length of miter joins for the device context associated with the CDC object. The miter length is the distance from the intersection of the line walls on the inside of a join to the intersection of the line walls on the outside of a join. The miter limit is the maximum allowed ratio of the miter length to the line width. The default miter limit is 10.0. Windows uses the miter limit when drawing geometric lines that have miter joins.

Syntax public, BOOL SetMiterLimit(float fMiterLimit);

Parameters

fMiterLimit The new miter limit.

Returns Non-zero if successful; otherwise, zero.

See Also CDC::GetMiterLimit

Example

```
...
CClientDC dc(pWnd);

// set miter limit before drawing some connecting lines
dc.SetMiterLimit(20);

// draw some mitered lines
LOGBRUSH logBrush = {BS_SOLID,RGB(0,255,0),0};
CPen *pOldPen, miterPen(PS_GEOMETRIC|PS_SOLID|PS_JOIN_MITER,1,
                        &logBrush,);

pOldPen = dc.SelectObject(&miterPen);

dc.MoveTo(1,1);
dc.LineTo(10,20);
dc.LineTo(25,35);

// clean up
dc.SelectObject(pOldPen);
```

SetOutputDC ■ 2.0 ■ 3.0

Description Sets the output device context associated with the CDC object. Do not call this function if the CDC object is attached to a device context. This function simply associates the device context with the CDC object—it does not attach to the device context.

Syntax public, virtual void SetOutputDC(HDC hDC);

Parameters

hDC A handle of the device context to associate with the CDC object as its output device context.

Returns Nothing is returned.

See Also CDC::SetAttribDC, CDC::ReleaseOutputDC, CDC::ReleaseAttribDC

SetPixel ■ 2.0 ■ 3.0

Description Sets a specified pixel to the specified color. The actual color assigned to the pixel may vary from that specified if the color specified can not be represented by the device. In this case, the closest representable color is used. SetPixel returns the actual color used. If you do not require this information, you should use the CDC::SetPixelV function which is faster but does not retrieve the actual color used (which is what makes it faster).

Syntax public, COLORREF SetPixel(int x, int y, COLORREF crColor);
public, COLORREF SetPixel(POINT point, COLORREF crColor);

Parameters

x The x coordinate, in logical units, of the pixel whose color value should be set.

y The y coordinate, in logical units, of the pixel whose color value should be set.

crColor The RBG color value to which the pixel should be set.

point A POINT structure or a CPoint object that contains the coordinates, in logical units, of the pixel to set.

Returns The RGB value of the actual color used. This value may not be the same as the color requested.

See Also CDC::SetPixelV, CDC::GetPixel, ::SetPixel, ::SetPixelV

Example

```
...
CClientDC dc(pWnd);

// draw a horizontal red line, 1 pixel at a time
for (int nX = 10;nX < 30;nX++)
     dc.SetPixel(nX,20,RGB(255,0,0));
```

SetPixelV

■ 2.0 ■ 3.0 ■ NM

Description Sets a specified pixel to the specified color. The actual color assigned to the pixel may vary from that specified if the color specified can not be represented by the device. In this case, the closest representable color is used. SetPixelV is faster than its counterpart, CDC::SetPixel because it does not return the actual color used for the pixel.

Syntax public, BOOL SetPixelV(int x, int y, COLORREF crColor);
public, BOOL SetPixelV(POINT point, COLORREF crColor);

Parameters

x The x coordinate, in logical units, of the pixel whose color value should be set.

y The y coordinate, in logical units, of the pixel whose color value should be set.

crColor The RGB color value to which the pixel should be set.

point A POINT structure or a CPoint object which contains the coordinates, in logical units, of the pixel to set.

Returns Non-zero if successful; otherwise, zero

See Also CDC::SetPixel, CDC::GetPixel, ::SetPixel, ::SetPixelV

Figure 11-10 ALTERNATE vs. WINDING Polygon filling

Example

```
...
CClientDC dc(pWnd);

// draw a horizontal red line, 1 pixel at a time
for (int nX = 10;nX < 30;nX++)
     dc.SetPixelV(nX,20,RGB(255,0,0));
```

SetPolyFillMode

■ 2.0 ■ 3.0

Description Sets the current polygon filling mode. The polygon filling mode can be either ALTERNATE or WINDING. ALTERNATE means that Windows fills the area between odd and even numbered sides on a per scanline basis (it draws a horizontal line between the odd side and the even side). WINDING means that Windows considers the direction in which each line segment of the polyline is drawn. It does this by drawing an imaginary line from each enclosed area in the polygon to outside of the figure. Each time this imaginary line crosses a line segment which was drawn in a clockwise direction, a count is incremented. Each time the imaginary line crosses a line segment which was drawn in a counterclockwise direction, the count is decremented. If, after this process, the count is non-zero, the enclosed area from which the imaginary line began is filled. Figure 11-10 shows an example of both the ALTERNATE and WINDING polygon modes.

Syntax public, int SetPolyFillMode(int nPolyFillMode);

Parameters

nPolyFillMode The new polygon fill mode; ALTERNATE or WINDING.

Returns The previous polygon fill mode.

See Also CDC::GetPolyFillMode, ::SetPolyFillMode

Example

```
void CMyWnd::DrawPolygon(CDC *pDc)
{
     int nMode = pDc->GetPolyFillMode(); // store old mode
     CPoint pts[5] = {CPoint(100,140), CPoint(230,10), CPoint(10,10),
             CPoint(231,300), CPoint(50,50)};
```

```
        pDc->SetPolyFillMode(ALTERNATE); // set mode to ALTERNATE
        pDc->Polygon(pts,5);
        pDc->SetPolyFillMode(nMode); // restore to old mode
}
```

SetROP2

■ 2.0 ■ 3.0

Description Sets the current raster operation code (or drawing mode). The drawing mode specifies how the colors of the pen and the interior of filled objects are combined with the color already on the display surface. As the name implies, the drawing mode is for raster devices only and does not apply to vector devices. Drawing modes are binary raster-operation codes representing all possible Boolean combinations of two variables, using the binary operators AND, OR, and XOR (exclusive OR), and the unary operator, NOT.

Syntax public, int SetROP2(int nDrawMode);

Parameters

nDrawMode The new raster operation code. See the description of CDC::GetROP2 for a list of valid values.

Returns The previous raster operation code.

See Also CDC::GetROP2, ::SetROP2

Example

```
...
CClientDC dc(pWnd);
CPen pen(PS_SOLID,1,RGB(255,0,0)), *pOldPen;

pOldPen = dc.SelectObject(&pen);
int nOldROP = dc.SetROP2(R2_XORPEN);

// draw a rectangle - it will be Xor'd on
dc.Rectangle(1,1,100,200);

// do some other stuff

// erase the rectangle - since we are Xor'ing, drawing the rectangle
// again will erase it
dc.Rectangle(1,1,100,200);

// clean up
dc.SelectObject(pOldPen);
dc.SetROP2(nOldROP);
```

SetStretchBltMode

■ 2.0 ■ 3.0

Description Sets the current bitmap-stretching mode. The stretching mode defines how color data is added to or removed from bitmaps that are stretched or compressed using the StretchBlt function.

Syntax public, int SetStretchBltMode(int nStretchMode);

Parameters

nStretchMode The new stretching mode. This parameter can be STRETCH_ANDSCANS, STRETCH_ORSCANS, or STRETCH_DELETESCANS. STRETCH_ANDSCANS uses the AND operator to combine eliminated lines with remaining lines. This tends to preserve black pixels over colored or white pixels. STRETCH_ORSCANS uses the OR operator to combine eliminated lines with remaining lines. This tends to preserve colored or white pixels over black pixels. STRETCH_DELETESCANS deletes any eliminated lines. The first two modes are typically used to preserve foreground pixels in monochrome bitmaps. The STRETCH_DELETESCANS mode is typically used to preserve color in color bitmaps.

Returns The previous stretching mode.

See Also CDC::GetStretchBltMode, CDC::StretchBlt, ::SetStretchBltMode

Example

```
void CMyWnd::StretchAndCompressBitmap(CDC *pDc)
{
	CDC memDc;
	CBitmap bmp;
	int nOldMode;
	BITMAP bitmap, *pOldBmp;

	// create a memory dc to use as the source dc
	dc.CreateCompatibleDC(pDc);

	// load the bitmap and obtain its dimensions
	bmp.LoadBitmap(IDB_TESTBMP);
	bmp.GetObject(sizeof(BITMAP),&bitmap);
	pOldBmp = dc.SelectObject(&bmp);

	// best mode for color bitmaps
	nOldMode = dc.SetStretchBltMode(STRETCH_DELETESCANS);

	// stretch bitmap to twice its size
	dc.StretchBlt(0,0,bitmap.bmWidth*2,bitmap.bmHeight*2,
		&memDc,0,0,bitmap.bmWidth,bitmap.bmHeight,SRCCOPY);

	// clean up
	dc.SetStretchBltMode(nOldMode);
	memDc.SelectObject(pOldBmp);
	memDc.DeleteDC();
}
```

SetTextAlign ■ 2.0 ■ 3.0

Description Sets the current text alignment flags. The text alignment flags control how the CDC::TextOut and CDC::ExtTextOut functions align text as well as whether or not they use the current position or the user-specified position.

Syntax public, UINT SetTextAlign(UINT nFlags);

Parameters

nFlags The new text alignment flags. Can be a combination of the following values:

TA_BASELINE	The reference point is on the base line of the text.
TA_BOTTOM	The reference point is on the bottom edge of the bounding rectangle.
TA_TOP	The reference point is on the top edge of the bounding rectangle.
TA_CENTER	The reference point is aligned horizontally with the center of the bounding rectangle.
TA_LEFT	The reference point is on the left edge of the bounding rectangle.
TA_RIGHT	The reference point is on the right edge of the bounding rectangle.
TA_RTLREADING	Windows 95 only: If the font is Hebrew or Arabic, the text is laid out in right to left reading order, as opposed to the default left to right order.
TA_NOUPDATECP	The current position is not updated after each text output call.
TA_UPDATECP	The current position is updated after each text output call.
VTA_BASELINE	Used in place of TA_BASELINE for fonts that have a vertical default base line (e.g. Kanji). The reference point is on the base line of the text.
VTA_CENTER	Used in place of TA_CENTER for fonts that have a vertical default base line (e.g. Kanji). The reference point is aligned vertically with the center of the bounding rectangle.

Returns The previous text alignment flags.

See Also CDC::GetTextAlign, CDC::TextOut, CDC::ExtTextOut, ::SetTextAlign

Example

```
...
CClientDC dc(pWnd);
CString strText("Test Output String");
CRect rect(1,1,100,100);

// output the string at the top left of the box
dc.SetTextAlign(TA_LEFT|TA_TOP);
dc.ExtTextOut(5,5,ETO_CLIPPED,strText,rect,NULL);

// now output the same string at the bottom right of the box
dc.SetTextAlign(TA_RIGHT|TA_BOTTOM);
dc.ExtTextOut(100,100,ETO_CLIPPED,strText,rect,NULL);
```

SetTextCharacterExtra ■ 2.0 ■ 3.0

Description Sets the current intercharacter spacing. The intercharacter spacing defines the extra space, in logical units along the base line, that the TextOut or ExtTextOut functions add to each character as a line is written. The default intercharacter spacing is zero.

Syntax public, int SetTextCharacterExtra(int nCharExtra);

Parameters

nCharExtra The new amount of intercharacter spacing, in logical units.

Returns The previous amount of intercharater spacing.

See Also CDC::GetTextCharacterExtra, ::SetTextCharacterExtra

Example

```
...
CClientDC dc(pWnd);
CString strText(``Test Message");

// output the text normally
dc.TextOut(5,5,strText);

// now output like this ``T e s t  M e s s a g e"
dc.SetTextCharacterExtra(10);
dc.TextOut(5,20,strText);
```

SetTextColor ■ 2.0 ■ 3.0

Description Sets the current text color. The text color is the color used to draw text using any of the GDI text output functions.

Syntax public, virtual COLORREF SetTextColor(COLORREF crColor);

Parameters

crColor The RGB color value for the new text color.

Returns The previous text color as an RGB color value.

See Also CDC::GetTextColor, CDC::TextOut, CDC::ExtTextOut, CDC::TabbedTextOut, CDC::DrawText, ::SetTextColor

Example

```
void CMyWnd::OutputSomeText(CDC *pDc)
{
	COLORREF crOld = pDc->SetTextColor(RBG(255,0,0)); // red text
	int nOldMode = pDc->SetBkMode(TRANSPARENT); // transparent text
	CString strTestText = "This is a test message.";

	pDc->TextOut(10,50,strTestText); // output a message

	// clean up
	pDc->SetBkMode(nOldMode);
	pDc->SetTextColor(crOld);
}
```

SetTextJustification ■ 2.0 ■ 3.0 ■ NM

Description Adds space to the break characters in a string. You can use the GetTextMetrics member function to retrieve a particular font's break character, which is usually the space character. After the SetTextJustification function is called, a call to a text-output function, such as TextOut, distributes the specified extra space evenly among the specified number of break characters. The CDC::GetTextExtent function is typically used with SetTextJustification. GetTextExtent computes the width of a given line before alignment. You can determine how much space to specify in the nBreakExtra parameter by subtracting the value returned by GetTextExtent from the width of the string after alignment. The

SetTextJustification function can be used to align a line that contains multiple text strings in different fonts. In this case, the line must be created piecemeal by aligning and writing each string separately. Because rounding errors can occur during alignment, Windows keeps a running error term that defines the current error. When aligning a line that contains multiple strings, GetTextExtent automatically uses this error term when it computes the extent of the next string. This allows the text-output function to blend the error into the new string. After each line has been aligned, this error term must be cleared to prevent it from being incorporated into the next line. The term can be cleared by calling SetTextJustification with nBreakExtra set to zero.

Syntax public, int SetTextJustification(int nBreakExtra, int nBreakCount);

Parameters

nBreakExtra The amount of extra space to add to the break characters. If the current mapping mode is not MM_TEXT, SetTextJustification converts the value according to the current mapping mode and rounds to the nearest device unit.

nBreakCount The number of break characters over which to distribute the extra space.

Returns If the function is successful, one; otherwise, zero.

See Also CDC::GetTextExtent, CDC::GetTextMetrics, CDC::TextOut, ::SetTextJustification

Example

```
...
CClientDC dc(pWnd);
CString strMessage("Test Message");

// output message normally
dc.TextOut(5,5,strMessage);

// now output the message spread out like this "T e s t  M e s s a g e"
dc.SetTextJustification(8,1);
dc.TextOut(5,20,strMessage);
```

SetViewportExt

■ 2.0 ■ 3.0

Description Sets the horizontal and vertical extents of the viewport. The viewport origin and extents, together with the window origin and extents, determine how coordinates are mapped between device coordinates and logical coordinates. See the CDC::DPtoLP and CDC::LPtoDP functions for a discussion regarding these mappings. Calls to this function are ignored for the MM_HIENGLISH, MM_LOMETRIC, MM_HIMETRIC, MM_TEXT, MM_LOENGLISH, and MM_TWIPS mapping modes.
If the MM_ISOTROPIC mode is set, you should call the SetWindowExt member function before you call SetViewportExt because Windows automatically makes adjustments to the values specified in order to maintain the correct aspect ratio.

Syntax public, virtual CSize SetViewportExt(int x, int y);
public, CSize SetViewportExt(SIZE size);

Parameters

x The horizontal extent of the viewport, in device units.

y The vertical extent of the viewport, in device units.

size A SIZE structure or a CSize object that contains the new viewport extents, in device units.

Returns A CPoint object containing the previous viewport extents.

See Also CDC::GetViewportExt, CDC::SetWindowExt, CDC::SetViewportOrg, CDC::DPtoLP, CDC::LPtoDP, ::SetViewportExt

Example See CDC::GetViewportExt

SetViewportOrg ■ 2.0 ■ 3.0

Description Sets the origin of the viewport. The viewport origin and extents, together with the window origin and extents, determine how coordinates are mapped between device coordinates and logical coordinates. See the CDC::DPtoLP and CDC::LPtoDP functions for a discussion regarding these mappings.

Syntax public, virtual CPoint SetViewportOrg(int x, int y);
public, virtual CPoint SetViewportOrg(POINT point);

Parameters

x The x coordinate, in device units, of the new viewport origin.

y The y coordinate, in device units, of the new viewport origin.

point A POINT structure or a CPoint object that contains the new viewport origin, in device units.

Returns A CPoint object containing the previous viewport origin.

See Also CDC::GetViewportOrg, CDC::SetWindowOrg, CDC::SetViewportExt, CDC::DPtoLP, CDC::LPtoDP, ::SetViewportOrg

Example See CDC::GetViewportExt

SetWindowExt ■ 2.0 ■ 3.0

Description Sets the horizontal and vertical extents of the window. The window origin and extents, together with the viewport origin and extents, determine how coordinates are mapped between device coordinates and logical coordinates. See the CDC::DPtoLP and CDC::LPtoDP functions for a discussion regarding these mappings. Calls to this function are ignored for the MM_HIENGLISH, MM_LOMETRIC, MM_HIMETRIC, MM_TEXT, MM_LOENGLISH, and MM_TWIPS mapping modes. If the MM_ISOTROPIC mode is set, you should call the SetWindowExt member function before you call SetViewportExt because Windows automatically makes adjustments to the values specified in order to maintain the correct aspect ratio.

Syntax public, virtual CSize SetWindowExt(int cx, int cy);
public, virtual CSize SetWindowExt(SIZE size);

Parameters

cx The horizontal extent of the window, in device units.

cy The vertical extent of the window, in device units.

size A SIZE structure or a CSize object which contains the new window extents, in device units.

Returns A CPoint object containing the previous window extents.

See Also CDC::GetWindowExt, CDC::SetViewportExt, CDC::SetWindowOrg, CDC::DPtoLP, CDC::LPtoDP, ::SetWindowExt

Example See CDC::GetWindowExt

SetWindowOrg ■ 2.0 ■ 3.0

Description Sets the origin of the window. The window origin and extents, together with the viewport origin and extents, determine how coordinates are mapped between device coordinates and logical coordinates. See the CDC::DPtoLP and CDC::LPtoDP functions for a discussion regarding these mappings.

Syntax public, CPoint SetWindowOrg(int x, int y);
public, CPoint SetWindowOrg(POINT point);

Parameters

x The x coordinate, in device units, of the new window origin.

y The y coordinate, in device units, of the new window origin.

point A POINT structure or a CPoint object that contains the new window origin, in device units.

Returns A CPoint object containing the previous window origin.

See Also CDC::GetWindowOrg, CDC::SetViewportOrg, CDC::SetWindowExt, CDC::DPtoLP, CDC::LPtoDP, ::SetWindowOrg

Example See CDC::GetWindowExt

StartDoc ■ 2.0 ■ 3.0

Description Informs the device driver that a new print job is starting and that all subsequent StartPage and EndPage calls should be spooled under the same job until an EndDoc call occurs. This ensures that documents longer than one page will not be interspersed with other jobs. You should not use this function inside a metafile. For Windows versions 3.1 and later, the

StartDoc function replaces the STARTDOC printer escape. When running under Windows version 3.0, this function simply sends a STARTDOC printer escape. The second version of this function is provided strictly for Windows 3.0 compatibility and should not be used.

Syntax

public, int StartDoc(LPDOCINFO lpDocInfo);
public, int StartDoc(LPCTSTR lpszDocName);

Parameters

lpDocInfo A pointer to a DOCINFO structure. The members of the DOCINFO structure are described below:

cbSize The size, in bytes, of the DOCINFO structure.

lpszDocName Points to a NULL-terminated string that specifies the name of the document being printed.

lpszOutput Points to a NULL-terminated string that specifies the name of an output file. If this pointer is NULL, the output will be sent to the device identified by the device context (usually a printer).

lpszDatatype On Windows 95 only, points to a NULL-terminated string that specifies the type of data used to record the print job.

fwType On Windows 95 only, specifies additional information about the print job. Can be zero or DI_APPBANDING if the application will use banding. For optimal performance during printing, banding applications should specify DI_APPBANDING.

lpszDocName A pointer to a document name string.

Returns A positive value if the function is successful; otherwise, zero.

See Also CDC::EndDoc, CDC::AbortDoc, CDC::Escape, ::StartDoc

Example

```
..
CString strTestMsg = ``Test Print Message";
DOCINFO docInfo;
docInfo.cbSize = sizeof(DOCINFO);
docInfo.lpszDocName = ``Test Document";
docInfo.lpszOutput = NULL;
printDc.StartDoc(&docInfo);

// print message on page 1
printDc.StartPage();
printDc.TextOut(5,20,strTestMsg);
printDc.EndPage();

// print message on page 2
printDc.StartPage();
printDc.TextOut(5,20,strTestMsg);
printDc.EndPage();

printDc.EndDoc();
..
```

StartPage

■ 2.0 ■ 3.0

Description Prepares the device driver to accept data. This function replaces the NEWFRAME and BANDINFO escapes. Note that Windows disables the CDC::ResetDC function between calls to CDC::StartPage and CDC::EndPage. When running under Windows 3.0 or earlier, this function does nothing.

Syntax public, int StartPage( );

Parameters None.

Returns If successful, a value greater than zero; if the function fails, a value equal to or less than zero.

See Also CDC::EndPage, CDC::Escape, ::StartPage

Example See CDC::StartDoc

StretchBlt

■ 2.0 ■ 3.0

Description Copies a bitmap from a specified source device context to the device context attached to the CDC object, stretching or compressing the bitmap as necessary. The manner in which the bitmap is stretched or compressed is controlled by the current bitmap stretching mode (which you can set using the CDC::SetStretchBltMode function). If the source or pattern bitmap involved in the BitBlt does not have the same color format as the destination, it is converted to the destination bitmap's color format. If the bitmap is converted from monochrome to color, this function sets on bits (1) to the destination device context's current background color and off bits (0) to the current foreground color. If the bitmap is converted from color to monochrome, StretchBlt sets pixels that match the destination device context's current background color to white and all other pixels to black. You can use StretchBlt to create mirror images of bitmaps, either horizontally, vertically, or both, by specifying widths and/or heights which differ in sign.

Syntax public, BOOL StretchBlt(int x, int y, int nWidth, int nHeight, CDC* pSrcDC, int xSrc, int ySrc, int nSrcWidth, int nSrcHeight, DWORD dwRop);

Parameters

x The x coordinate, in logical units, of the upper-left corner of the destination rectangle.

y The y coordinate, in logical units, of the upper-left corner of the destination rectangle.

nWidth The width, in logical units, of the destination rectangle.

nHeight — The height, in logical units, of the destination rectangle.

pSrcDC — A pointer to the source device context which contains the source bitmap.

xSrc — The x coordinate, in logical units, of the upper-left corner of the source rectangle.

ySrc — The y coordinate, in logical units, of the upper-left corner of the source rectangle.

nSrcWidth — The width, in logical units, of the source rectangle.

nSrcHeight — The height, in logical units, of the source rectangle.

dwRop — The raster operation to use when copying the bitmap. A raster operation describes how the Windows GDI should combine the color information of the source bitmap, the destination bitmap, and the current brush. For more information about raster operation codes, see the Windows SDK documentation. For a list of common raster operation codes, see the CDC::BitBlt function.

Returns Non-zero if successful; otherwise, zero.

See Also CDC::BitBlt, CDC::MaskBlt, CDC::PlgBlt, CDC::PatBlt, ::StretchBlt

Example

```
void CMyWnd::StretchAndCompressBitmap(CDC *pDc)
{
      CDC memDc;
      CBitmap bmp;
      int nOldMode;
      BITMAP bitmap, *pOldBmp;

      // create a memory dc to use as the source dc
      dc.CreateCompatibleDC(pDc);

      // load the bitmap and obtain its dimensions
      bmp.LoadBitmap(IDB_TESTBMP);
      bmp.GetObject(sizeof(BITMAP),&bitmap);
      pOldBmp = dc.SelectObject(&bmp);

      // best mode for color bitmaps
      nOldMode = dc.SetStretchBltMode(STRETCH_DELETESCANS);

      // stretch bitmap to twice its size
      dc.StretchBlt(0,0,bitmap.bmWidth*2,bitmap.bmHeight*2,
                  &memDc,0,0,bitmap.bmWidth,bitmap.bmHeight,SRCCOPY);

      // compress bitmap to half its size
      dc.StretchBlt(500,0,bitmap.bmWidth/2,bitmap.bmHeight/2,
                  &memDc,0,0,bitmap.bmWidth,bitmap.bmHeight,SRCCOPY);

      // clean up
      dc.SetStretchBltMode(nOldMode);
      memDc.SelectObject(pOldBmp);
      memDc.DeleteDC();
}
```

StrokeAndFillPath

■ 3.0 ■ NM

Description Outlines the current path with the current pen and fills it with the current brush. This function automatically closes any open figures in the path. The device context must contain a closed path or this function will fail.

Syntax public, BOOL StrokeAndFillPath( );

Parameters None.

Returns Non-zero if successful; otherwise, zero.

See Also CDC::BeginPath, CDC::EndPath, CDC::StrokePath, CDC::FillPath, ::StrokeAndFillPath

Example

```
...
CClientDC dc(pWnd);
CPen *pOldPen,pen(PS_SOLID,1,RGB(255,0,0));
CBrush *pOldBrush,brush(RGB(0,255,0));
CPoint pts[3] = {CPoint(10,20),CPoint(100,60),CPoint(50,100)};

// create a triangular path
dc.BeginPath();
dc.Polygon(pts,3);
dc.EndPath();

// stroke the path with a red pen and fill it with a green brush
pOldPen = dc.SelectPen(&pen);
pOldBrush = dc.SelectBrush(&brush);
dc.StrokeAndFillPath();

// clean up
dc.SelectPen(pOldPen);
dc.SelectBrush(pOldBrush);
```

StrokePath

■ 3.0 ■ NM

Description Outlines the current path using the current pen. The device context must contain a closed path or this function will fail.

Syntax public, BOOL StrokePath( );

Parameters None.

Returns Non-zero if successful; otherwise, zero.

See Also CDC::BeginPath, CDC::EndPath, CDC::StokeAndFillPath, CDC::FillPath, ::StrokePath

Example

```
...
CClientDC dc(pWnd);
CPen *pOldPen,pen(PS_SOLID,1,RGB(255,0,0));
CPoint pts[3] = {CPoint(10,20),CPoint(100,60),CPoint(50,100)};
```

continued on next page

continued from previous page

```
// create a triangular path
dc.BeginPath();
dc.Polygon(pts,3);
dc.EndPath();

// stroke the path with a red pen
pOldPen = dc.SelectPen(&pen);
dc.StrokePath();

// clean up
dc.SelectPen(pOldPen);
```

TabbedTextOut ■ 2.0 ■ 3.0

Description Outputs a specified text string at a specified location. The text is drawn using the current text color and, if the current background mode is OPAQUE, the background is filled with the current background color. Any tabs encountered in the text are expanded as specified. By default, TabbedTextOut outputs the text at a user-defined location. Optionally, you can use the CDC::SetTextAlign function with the TA_UPDATECP option to force TabbedTextOut to output the text beginning at the current position. In this case, the *x* and *y* parameters to TabbedTextOut are ignored and, if the function is successful, TabbedTextOut updates the current position. The interpretation of the location specified by the *x* and *y* parameters depends on the current text-alignment mode.

Syntax public, virtual CSize TabbedTextOut(int x, int y, LPCTSTR lpszString, int nCount, int nTabPositions, LPINT lpnTabStopPositions, int nTabOrigin); public, virtual CSize TabbedTextOut(int x, int y, const CString &strString, int nTabPositions, LPINT lpnTabStopPositions, int nTabOrigin);

Parameters

x The x coordinate, in logical units, of the starting point of the text.

y The y coordinate, in logical units, of the starting point of the text.

lpszString A pointer to the text string to output.

nCount The number of characters in the string pointed to by *lpszString*.

nTabPositions The number of tab positions specified in the *lpnTabStopPositions* array. If this parameter is zero and *lpnTabStopPositions* is NULL, a default tab width of eight average characters is used. If this parameter is one, *lpnTabStopPositions* should point to a single value which will be used as the spacing between tabs. If this parameter is greater than one, *lpnTabStopPositions* should point to an array of *nTabStop* tab positions.

lpnTabStopPositions A pointer to an array of integers specifying where, in logical units, tab stops should be placed. The values specified must be sorted in increasing order. See the *nTabPositions* parameter for a complete description of the uses of this parameter.

nTabOrigin The x coordinate, in logical units, of the origin from which the tabs will be expanded. Using this parameter allows you to call TabbedTextOut several times for the same line using a different text starting point but maintaining the same tabs.

strString A reference to a CString object containing the text string to output.

Returns A CSize object containing the dimensions of the string in logical units.

See Also CDC::TextOut, CDC::GetTabbedTextExtent, ::TabbedTextOut

Example

```
...
CClientDC dc(pWnd);
int nTabs[3] = {40,100,150};
CString strText("Make\tModel\tColor\tPrice");

dc.TabbedTextOut(5,10,strText,3,nTabs,5);
```

TextOut ■ 2.0 ■ 3.0

Description Outputs a specified text string at a specified location. The text is drawn using the current text color and, if the current background mode is OPAQUE, the background is filled with the current background color. By default, TextOut outputs the text at a user-defined location. Optionally, you can use the CDC::SetTextAlign function with the TA_UPDATECP option to force TextOut to output the text beginning at the current position. In this case, the *x* and *y* parameters to TextOut are ignored and, if the function is successful, TextOut updates the current position. The interpretation of the location specified by the *x* and *y* parameters depends on the current text-alignment mode.

Syntax public, virtual BOOL TextOut(int x, int y, LPCTSTR lpszString, int nCount);
public, BOOL TextOut(int x, int y, const CString& str);

Parameters

x The x coordinate, in logical units, where the text should begin.

y The y coordinate, in logical units, where the text should begin.

lpszString A pointer to the text string to output.

nCount The number of characters in the string pointed to by the *lpszString* parameter.

str A reference to a CString object containing the text string to output.

Returns Non-zero if successful; otherwise, zero.

See Also CDC::ExtTextOut, CDC::DrawText, CDC::SetTextColor, CDC::SetBkMode, CDC::SetBkColor, ::TextOut

Example

```
void CMyWnd::OutputSomeText(CDC *pDc)
{
      COLORREF crOld = pDc->SetTextColor(RBG(255,0,0)); // red text
      int nOldMode = pDc->SetBkMode(TRANSPARENT); // transparent text
```

continued on next page

continued from previous page

```
        CString strTestText = "This is a test message.";

        pDc->TextOut(10,50,strTestText); // output a message

        // clean up
        pDc->SetBkMode(nOldMode);
        pDc->SetTextColor(crOld);
}
```

UpdateColors

■ 2.0 ■ 3.0

Description Updates the colors in the client area of the window associated with the device context by matching the colors of the pixels in the window with the colors in the current system palette on a pixel by pixel basis. When the system palette changes, you can use this process instead of repainting the client area of the window. Updating the colors instead of repainting can be considerably faster, although each call to this function can result in some loss of color accuracy.

Syntax public, void UpdateColors( );

Parameters None.

Returns Nothing is returned.

See Also CDC::RealizePalette, ::UpdateColors

WidenPath

■ 3.0 ■ NM

Description Redefines the current path as the area that would be painted if the path were outlined using the current pen. This function is successful only if the current pen is a geometric pen created by the second version of CPen::CreatePen function, or if the pen is created with the first version of CPen::CreatePen and has a width, in device units, of greater than 1. The device context must contain a closed path. Any Bézier curves in the path are converted to sequences of straight lines approximating the widened curves.

Syntax public, BOOL WidenPath( );

Parameters None.

Returns Non-zero if the fuction was successful; otherwise, zero.

See Also CDC::BeginPath, CDC::EndPath, CDC::SetMiterLimit, CDC::FlattenPath, ::WidenPath

Example

```
CClientDC dc(pWnd);
CPen *pOldPen,pen(PS_SOLID,10,RGB(255,0,0));
CPoint pts[3] = {CPoint(10,20),CPoint(100,60),CPoint(50,100)};

// create a triangular path
dc.BeginPath();
dc.Polygon(pts,3);
```

```
dc.EndPath();

// widen the path to the area that would be covered by the path if it
// stroked with the thick (10 pixels) pen
pOldPen = dc.SelectPen(&pen);
dc.WidenPath();

// clean up
dc.SelectPen(pOldPen);
```

The CPaintDC Class

The CPaintDC class encapsulates a device context that is to be used when processing a WM_PAINT message. The CPaintDC class is derived from the CDC class and provides no additional functionality over the CDC class except that it automatically retrieves a device context in its constructor using the SDK ::BeginPaint function and destroys it in its destructor using the ::EndPaint function.

CPaintDC ■ 2.0 ■ 3.0

Description The constructor for the CPaintDC class. CPaintDC calls the SDK function ::BeginPaint to retrieve a device context for painting. This call also fills in the m_ps PAINTSTRUCT member of the CPaintDC object. You should only create a CPaintDC object while responding to a WM_PAINT message from Windows (in MFC, this is usually in your OnPaint handler function). CPaintDC will throw a resource exception if this procedure fails. Remember that under 16-bit Windows, there are only five display contexts available for all Windows applications, so this procedure could easily fail if many applications are running simultaneously.

Syntax public, CPaintDC(CWnd *pWnd);

Parameters

pWnd A pointer to the CWnd object for which a paint device context is required.

Returns Nothing is returned.

See Also ~CPaintDC(), ::BeginPaint

~CPaintDC ■ 2.0 ■ 3.0 ■ UD

Description The CPaintDC destructor. The destructor releases the paint device context obtained in the constructor by calling the SDK ::EndPaint function and then detaches the device context from the CPaintDC object.

Syntax public, virtual ~CPaintDC();

Parameters None.

Returns Nothing is returned.

See Also CPaintDC(), ::EndPaint

AssertValid

■ 2.0 ■ 3.0 ■ DO

Description AssertValid is a diagnostic function used to test the validity of a CPaintDC object. The CPaintDC version of this function first calls the CDC version and then asserts the window passed to the constructor is a valid window by calling the SDK function ::IsWindow.

Syntax public, virtual void AssertValid() const;

Parameters None.

Returns Nothing is returned.

See Also CDC::AssertValid(), ::IsWindow

Example

```
void CMyWnd::SomeFunct(CPaintDC &dcPaint)
{
      dcPaint.AssertValid(); // make sure passed dc is valid
      .. // now we can safely use it
```

Dump

■ 2.0 ■ 3.0 ■ DO

Description Dump is a diagnostic function that outputs the current state of the CPaintDC object to the specified dump context. The CPaintDC version calls the CDC version and then dumps the window associated with the object (which was passed to the constructor) and the values of the members of the PAINTSTRUCT member variable, m_ps.

Syntax public, virtual void Dump(CDumpContext& dc) const;

Parameters

dc A reference to the dump context to which the status information should be sent. Usually this will be the MFC default debug dump context *afxDump*. *afxDump* sends its output to the debugger and only exists in the debug build of MFC.

Returns Nothing is returned.

See Also CDC::Dump, CDumpContext, afxDump

The CClientDC Class

The CClientDC class encapsulates a device context for the client area of a window. The CClientDC is derived from the CDC class and provides no additional functionality over the CDC class except that it automatically creates the device context for a specified window in its constructor and destroys it in its destructor.

CClientDC

■ 2.0 ■ 3.0

Description The constructor for the CClientDC class. CClientDC calls the SDK function ::GetDC to get a device context for the client area of a specified window. CClientDC will throw a resource exception if this procedure fails. Remember that under 16-bit Windows, there are only five display contexts available for all Windows applications, so this procedure could easily fail if many applications are running simultaneously.

Syntax public, CClientDC(CWnd *pWnd);

Parameters

pWnd A pointer to a CWnd object for which a device context should be created.

Returns Nothing is returned.

See Also ~CClientDC, ::GetDC, ::ReleaseDC

~CClientDC ■ 2.0 ■ 3.0 ■ UD

Description The destructor for the CClientDC class. The destructor detaches the device context associated with the CClientDC object and releases it by calling the SDK function ::ReleaseDC.

Syntax public, virtual ~CClientDC();

Parameters None.

Returns Nothing is returned.

See Also CClientDC, ::ReleaseDC

AssertValid ■ 2.0 ■ 3.0 ■ DO

Description AssertValid is a diagnostic function used to test the validity of a CClientDC object. The CClientDC version of this function first calls the CDC version and then asserts that the window passed to the constructor is a valid window by calling the SDK function ::IsWindow.

Syntax public, virtual void AssertValid() const;

Parameters None.

Returns Nothing is returned.

See Also CDC::AssertValid(), ::IsWindow

Example

```
void CMyWnd::SomeFunct(CClientDC &dcClient)
{
     dcClient.AssertValid(); // make sure passed dc is valid
     .. // now we can safely use it
```

Dump ■ 2.0 ■ 3.0 ■ DO

Description Dump is a diagnostic function that outputs the current state of the CClientDC object to the specified dump context. The CClientDC version calls the CDC version and then dumps the window associated with the object (which was passed to the constructor).

Syntax public, virtual void Dump(CDumpContext& dc) const;

Parameters

dc A reference to the dump context to which the status information should be sent. Usually this will be the MFC default debug dump context *afxDump*. *afxDump* sends its output to the debugger and only exists in the debug build of MFC.

Returns Nothing is returned.

See Also CDC::Dump, CDumpContext, afxDump

Example

```
// call to dump function
CClientDC dc(pWnd);
dc.Dump(afxDump);

// output from dump call
a CClientDC at $64F80C
m_hDC = 0x5FE
m_hAttribDC = 0x5FE
m_bPrinting = 0
m_hWnd = 0xA74
```

The CWindowDC Class

The CWindowDC class encapsulates a device context for the entire area of a window. The CWindowDC class is derived from the CDC class and provides no additional functionality over the CDC class except that it automatically creates the device context for a specified window in its constructor and destroys it in its destructor.

CWindowDC ■ 2.0 ■ 3.0

Description The contructor for the CWindowDC class. CWindowDC calls the SDK function ::GetDC to get a device context for the entire area of a specified window. CWindowDC will throw a resource exception if this procedure fails. Remember that under 16-bit Windows, there are only five display contexts available for all Windows applications, so this procedure could easily fail if many applications are running simultaneously.

Scope public

Syntax CWindowDC();

Parameters None.

Returns Nothing is returned.

See Also ~CWindowDC, ::GetDC

~CWindowDC ■ 2.0 ■ 3.0

Description The destructor for the CWindowDC class. The destructor detaches the device context associated with the CWindowDC object and releases it by calling the SDK function ::ReleaseDC.

Scope	public
Syntax	~CWindowDC();
Parameters	None.
Returns	Nothing is returned.
See Also	CWindowDC, ::ReleaseDC

AssertValid

■ 2.0 ■ 3.0

Description AssertValid is a diagnostic function used to test the validity of a CWindowDC object. The CWindowDC version of this function first calls the CDC version and then asserts that the window passed to the constructor is a valid window by calling the SDK function ::IsWindow.

Scope public, debug only

Syntax virtual void AssertValid() const;

Parameters None.

Returns Nothing is returned.

See Also CObject::AssertValid()

Example

```
void CMyWnd::SomeFunct(CWindowDC &dwWin)
{
	dcWin.AssertValid(); // make sure passed dc is valid
	.. // now we can safely use it
```

Dump

■ 2.0 ■ 3.0

Description Dump is a diagnostic function that outputs the current state of a CWindowDC object to the specified dump context.

Scope public, debug only

Syntax virtual void Dump(CDumpContext& dc) const;

Parameters

dc A reference to the dump context to which the status information should be sent. Usually this will be the MFC default debug dump context *afxDump*. *afxDump* sends its output to the debugger and only exists in the debug build of MFC.

Returns Nothing is returned.

See Also CDC::Dump, CDumpContext, afxDump

Example

```
// call to dump function
CWindowDC dc(pWnd);
dc.Dump(afxDump);

// output from dump call
a CWindowDC at $64F80C
```

continued on next page

continued from previous page

```
m_hDC = 0x5FE
m_hAttribDC = 0x5FE
m_bPrinting = 0
m_hWnd = 0xA74
```

The CMetaFileDC Class

The CMetaFileDC encapsulates a metafile device context. The CMetaFileDC consists of several functions for the creation of metafiles along with several overrides of CDC functions that provide special processing specific to metafiles. Normally, only output GDI functions are valid for a metafile device context. This makes sense because you can't query a metafile for display attributes. (It is simply a recording of the functions you call.) MFC, through the use of the attribute device context, allows you to use non-output functions as well. You can do this by first creating a metafile using one of the CMetaFileDC creation functions (which sets the output device context to the metafile device context). Next, you create a device context which can be used for non-output (attribute) GDI calls. This device context would very likely be a printer or the screen. You then call the CMetaFileDC::SetAttribDC function to assign the device context to the CMetaFileDC object. From then on, MFC will route all output GDI functions to the metafile device context and all non-output calls to the attribute device context. Most of the overrides found in the CMetaFileDC object exist specifically to handle this special situation.

CMetaFileDC ■ 2.0 ■ 3.0

Description The constructor for the CMetaFileDC class. CMetaFileDC does absolutely nothing. You must call CMetaFileDC::Create or CMetaFileDC::CreateEnhanced to create a metafile and attach it to the CMetaFileDC object before using the object.

Syntax public, CMetaFileDC();

Parameters None.

Returns Nothing is returned.

See Also ~CMetaFile

~CMetaFileDC ■ 2.0 ■ 3.0

Description The destructor for the CMetaFileDC class. If an open metafile is still associated with the CMetaFileDC object it is deleted using the ::DeleteMetaFile SDK function. The debug version of MFC will output a warning message about this fact.

Syntax public, virtual ~CMetaFileDC()

Parameters None.

Returns Nothing is returned.

See Also CMetaFileDC, ::DeleteMetaFile

AdjustCP

■ 2.0 ■ 3.0 ■ UD

Description An internal MFC function that shifts the horizontal location of the current position on the attribute device context, if one exists. MFC calls this function in order to keep the attribute device context in sync with the output device context.

Syntax protected, void AdjustCP(int cx);

Parameters

cx The amount by which the x coordinate of the current position should be shifted.

Returns Nothing is returned.

Close

■ 2.0 ■ 3.0

Description Closes the metafile device context and creates a Windows metafile handle that can be used to play the metafile using the CDC::PlayMetaFile function. The Windows metafile handle can also be used to manipulate the metafile with Windows metafile functions. After you are done using the metafile handle, you should delete it using the Windows SDK function ::DeleteMetaFile.

Syntax public, HMETAFILE Close( );

Parameters None.

Returns A handle to the Windows metafile

See Also CMetaFileDC::CloseEnhanced, CDC::PlayMetaFile, ::CloseMetaFile, ::DeleteMetaFile

Example

```
// create a metafile
CMetaFileDC dcMeta;
dcMeta.Create("testmeta");

// do some drawing
dcMeta.Rectangle(1,1,100,100);
dcMeta.MoveTo(50,50);
dcMete.LineTo(75,100);

// close the metafile
HMETAFILE hMeta = dcMeta.Close();

// use the handle for whatever - could use for ::CopyMetaFile

// when done, delete the metafile
::DeleteMetaFile(hMeta);
..
```

CloseEnhanced

■ 2.0 ■ 3.0 ■ NM

Description Closes the enhanced-format metafile device context and creates an enhanced-format metafile handle that can be used to play the metafile using the CDC::PlayEnhMetaFile function. The enhanced-format metafile handle can also be used to manipulate the metafile with Windows metafile functions. After you are done using the metafile handle, you should delete it using the Windows SDK function ::DeleteEnhMetaFile.

Syntax public, HENHMETAFILE CloseEnhanced( );

Parameters None.

Returns A handle to the enhanced-format metafile.

See Also CMetaFileDC::CloseEnhanced, CDC::PlayMetaFile, ::CloseMetaFile, ::DeleteMetaFile

Example

```
..
// create an enhanced-format metafile
CClientDC dc(pWnd);
CMetaFileDC dcMeta;
CRect rect;

// calculate the rectangle for the metafile - must be in HIMETRIC units
pWnd->GetClientRect(rect);
CSize tempSize;
tempSize.cx = rect.TopLeft().x;
tempSize.cy = rect.TopLeft().y;
DPtoHIMETRIC(tempSize);
rect.TopLeft().x = tempSize.cx;
rect.TopLeft().y = tempSize.cy;
tempSize.cx = rect.BottomRight().x;
tempSize.cy = rect.BottomRight().y;
DPtoHIMETRIC(tempSize);
rect.BottomRight().x = tempSize =.cx;
rect.BottomRight().y = tempSize.cy;

dcMeta.CreateEnhanced(&dc,"testmeta",rect," Test App\0Picture\0\0");

// do some drawing
dcMeta.Rectangle(1,1,100,100);
dcMeta.MoveTo(50,50);
dcMete.LineTo(75,100);

// close the metafile
HENHMETAFILE hMeta = dcMeta.CloseEnhanced();

// use the handle for whatever - could use for ::CopyMetaFile

// when done, delete the metafile
::DeleteEnhMetaFile(hMeta);
..
```

CREATE

■ 2.0 ■ 3.0

Description Create creates a Windows metafile device context and attaches it to the CMetaFileDC object.

Syntax public, BOOL Create(LPCTSTR lpszFilename = NULL);

Parameters

lpszFilename If the metafile should be stored on disk, the parameter points to the name of the file. If this parameter is NULL, the metafile will be memory-based.

Returns Non-zero if successful; otherwise, zero.

See Also CMetaFileDC::CreateEnhanced, ::CreateMetafile

Example

```
// create a metafile
CMetaFileDC dcMeta;
dcMeta.Create("testmeta");

// do some drawing
dcMeta.Rectangle(1,1,100,100);
dcMeta.MoveTo(50,50);
dcMete.LineTo(75,100);

// close the metafile
HMETAFILE hMeta = dcMeta.Close();

// use the handle for whatever - could use for ::CopyMetaFile

// when done, delete the metafile
::DeleteMetaFile(hMeta);
..
```

CREATEENHANCED

■ 2.0 ■ 3.0 ■ NM

Description Creates an enhanced-format metafile device context and attaches it to the CMetaFileDC object.

Syntax public, BOOL CreateEnhanced(CDC* pDCRef, LPCTSTR lpszFileName, LPCRECT lpBounds, LPCTSTR lpszDescription);

Parameters

pDCRef A pointer to the reference device context. If this parameter is NULL, the current device context is used.

lpszFileName If the metafile should be stored on disk, the parameter points to the name of the file. If this parameter is NULL, the metafile will be memory-based.

lpBounds Pointer to a RECT structure or a CRect object that contains the dimensions of the picture to be stored in the enhanced-format metafile, in HIMETRIC units. The left coordinate must be less than the right and the top coordinate must be less than the bottom. This parameter can be NULL, in which case Windows calculates the smallest rectangle necessary to contain the picture drawn.

lpszDescripion Pointer to a NULL-terminated string that specifies the name of the application that created the picture and the picture's title. The string should contain a NULL character between the application name and the picture title and should end with two NULL characters (e.g., "Application\0Picture Title\0\0").

Returns Non-zero if successful; otherwise, zero.

See Also CMetaFileDC::Create, ::CreateEnhMetaFile

Example

```
..
// create an enhanced-format metafile
CClientDC dc(pWnd);
CMetaFileDC dcMeta;
CRect rect;

// calculate the rectangle for the metafile - must be in HIMETRIC units
pWnd->GetClientRect(rect);
CSize tempSize;
tempSize.cx = rect.TopLeft().x;
tempSize.cy = rect.TopLeft().y;
DPtoHIMETRIC(tempSize);
rect.TopLeft().x = tempSize.cx;
rect.TopLeft().y = tempSize.cy;
tempSize.cx = rect.BottomRight().x;
tempSize.cy = rect.BottomRight().y;
DPtoHIMETRIC(tempSize);
rect.BottomRight().x = tempSize =.cx;
rect.BottomRight().y = tempSize.cy;


dcMeta.CreateEnhanced(&dc,"testmeta",rect,"Test App\0Picture\0\0");

// do some drawing
dcMeta.Rectangle(1,1,100,100);
dcMeta.MoveTo(50,50);
dcMete.LineTo(75,100);

// close the metafile
HENHMETAFILE hMeta = dcMeta.CloseEnhanced();

// use the handle for whatever - could use for ::CopyMetaFile

// when done, delete the metafile
::DeleteEnhMetaFile(hMeta);
..
```

DrawText

■ 2.0 ■ 3.0 ■ UD

Description Draws formatted text using the current font and text and background colors. Formatting can include alignment, tab expansion, and wordwrap. If you do not need any special formatting, you can use the CDC::TextOut function which is faster. Unless the DT_NOCLIP flag is specified, this function clips the text to the specified rectangle. If the TA_UPDATECP flag has been set using the CDC::SetTextAlign function, all text alignment flags specified are ignored and the text is output beginning at the current position instead. Note that this function updates not only the current position of the output device context but also that of the attribute device context.

Syntax public, virtual int DrawText(LPCTSTR lpszString, int nCount, LPRECT lpRect, UINT nFormat);

Parameters

lpszString A pointer to the text to be drawn. If the *nCount* parameter is -1, the string must be NULL-terminated.

nCount The number of characters in the string pointed to by *lpszString*. If *lpszString* points to a NULL-terminated string this parameter may be -1, in which case DrawText calculates the length of the string.

lpRect A pointer to the rectangle into which the text will be drawn. The coordinates specified should be in logical units.

nFormat One or more flags describing the formatting of the text. If the DT_TABSTOP flag is specified, the DT_CALCRECT, DT_EXTERNALLEADING, DT_INTERNAL, DT_NOCLIP, and DT_NOPREFIX cannot be used. Valid formatting flags are listed below:

DT_BOTTOM If the DT_SINGLELINE flag is specified, the text will be bottom-aligned.

DT_CALCRECT Causes DrawText to determine the width and height of the rectangle required to draw the text without actually drawing it. If there are multiple lines of text, DrawText will use the width of the rectangle pointed to by lpRect and extend the base of the rectangle to bound the last line of text. If there is only one line of text, DrawText will modify the right side of the rectangle so that it bounds the last character in the line.

DT_CENTER Centers the text horizontally.

DT_EXPANDTABS Expands tab characters. The default number of characters per tab is eight.

DT_EXTERNALLEADING Includes the font's external leading in the line height. Normally, external leading is not included in the height of a line of text.

DT_LEFT Left-aligns the text.

DT_NOCLIP Draws the text without clipping. DrawText is somewhat faster when this flag is used.

DT_NOPREFIX Turns off processing of prefix characters. Normally, DrawText interprets the ampersand (&) mnemonic-prefix character as a directive to underscore the character that follows, and the two-ampersand (&&) mnemonic-prefix characters as a directive to print a single ampersand. By specifying DT_NOPREFIX this processing is turned off.

DT_RIGHT Right-aligns the text

DT_SINGLELINE Specifies single line only. Carriage returns and linefeeds do not break the line.

DT_TABSTOP	Sets tab stops. The high-order byte of *nFormat* is the number of characters for each tab. The default number of characters per tab is eight.
DT_TOP	If the DT_SINGLELINE flag is specified, top-aligns the text.
DT_VCENTER	If the DT_SINGLELINE flag is specified, vertically centers the text.
DT_WORDBREAK	Specifies word-breaking. Lines are automatically broken between words if a word would extend past the edge of the rectangle specified by *lpRect*. This flag is ignored if the TA_UPDATECP has been set using the CDC::SetTextAlign function.

Returns The height of the drawn text.

See Also CDC::TextOut , CDC::ExtTextOut, CDC::TabbedTextOut, CDC::SetTextColor, CDC::SetTextAlign, ::DrawText

Example See CDC::DrawText

Escape

■ 2.0 ■ 3.0 ■ UD

Description An override of the CDC::Escape function that first sends the specified escape to the output device context and then passes only selective escapes to the attribute device contest. Only the following escapes are actually passed through:

BANDINFO	GETPRINTINGOFFSET	SETALLJUSTVALUES
DRAFTMODE	GETSCALEINGFACTOR	SETBACKGROUNDCOLOR
ENABLEDUPLEX	GETSETPAPERBINS	SETCHARSET
ENABLEPAIRKERNING	GETSETPAPERMETRICS	SETCOLORTABLE
ENABLERELATIVEWIDTHS	GETSETPRINTORIENT	SETCOPYCOUNT
ENUMPAPERBINS	GETTECHNOLOGY	SETKERNTRACK
FLUSHOUTPUT	GETTEXTENDEDTEXTMETRICS	SETLINECAP
GETCOLORTABLE	GETTRACKKERNTABLE	SETLINEJOIN
GETEXTENTTABLE	GETVECTORBRUSHSIZE	SETMITERLIMIT
GETPAIRKERNTABLE	NEXTBAND	SETSCREENANGLE
GETPENWIDTH	QUERYESCSUPPORT	SETSPREAD
GETPHYSPAGESIZE	SELECTPAPERSOURCE	

Syntax

```
public, virtual int Escape( int nEscape, int nCount, LPCSTR lpszInData,
LPVOID lpOutData );
public, int ExtEscape( int nEscape, int nInputSize, LPCSTR
lpszInputData, int nOutputSize, LPSTR lpszOutputData );
```

Parameters

nEscape	The escape command to send to the device.
nCount	The size (in bytes) of the buffer pointed to by the *lpszInData* parameter.
lpszInData	Points to the input data structure required for the escape specified by *nEscape*.

lpOutData	Points to the output data structure which will receive the results of the escape. If the specified escape does not produce output data, this parameter should be NULL.
nInputSize	The size (in bytes) of the buffer pointed to by the *lpszInputData* parameter.
lpszInputData	Points to the input data structure required for the escape specified by *nEscape*.
nOutputSize	The size (in bytes) of the buffer pointed to by the *lpszOutputData* parameter.
lpszOutputData	Points to the output data structure that will receive the results of the escape. If the specified escape does not produce output data, this parameter should be NULL.

Returns Positive if the function is successful or in the case of the QUERYESCSUPPORT escape, if the escape is supported. Zero is returned if the QUERYESCSUPPORT escape is used and the specified escape is not implemented. A negative value is returned if an error occurs. The following are common error values:

SP_ERROR	A general error occurred.
SP_OUTOFDISK	Not enough disk space is currently available for spooling, and no more space will become available.
SP_OUTOFMEMORY	Not enough memory is available for spooling.
SP_USERABORT	User ended the job through the Print Manager.

See Also CDC::StartDoc, CDC::EndDoc, CDC::AbortDoc, CDC::StartPage, CDC::EndPage, CDC::SetAbortProc, CDC::GetDeviceCaps, ::Escape, ::ExtEscape

Example See CDC::Escape

ExtTextOut

■ 2.0 ■ 3.0 ■ UD

Description Outputs text at a specified location and optionally clips the text to a given rectangle. This function will also optionally fill the output area of the text with the current background color of the device context. By default, ExtTextOut outputs the text at a user-defined location. Optionally, you can use the CDC::SetTextAlign function with the TA_UPDATECP option to force ExtTextOut to output the text beginning at the current position. In this case, the *x* and *y* parameters to ExtTextOut are ignored and if the function is successful, ExtTextOut updates the current position. The current position is updated to the end of the previous line of text or to the position specified by the last element of the array pointed to by the *lpDxWidths* parameter, whichever is greater. Note that this function updates the current position of both the output and attribute device contexts.

Syntax public, virtual BOOL ExtTextOut(int x, int y, UINT nOptions, LPCRECT lpRect, LPCTSTR lpszString, UINT nCount, LPINT lpDxWidths);

public, virtual BOOL ExtTextOut(int x, int y, UINT nOptions, LPCRECT lpRect, const Cstring &str, LPINT lpDxWidths);

Parameters

x	The x coordinate (in logical units) where the text output should begin.
y	The y coordinate (in logical units) where the text output should begin.
nOptions	Zero, one, or both of the following flags:
ETO_CLIPPED	The text should be clipped to the rectangle pointed to by *lpRect*.
ETO_OPAQUE	The current background color should fill the rectangle pointed to by *lpRect*.
lpRect	A pointer to a RECT structure or a CRect object that describes the rectangle that may optionally be used for clipping the text or may be painted with the current background color. This parameter may be NULL if clipping and filling are not necessary.
lpszString	A pointer to a character buffer containing the text to output.
nCount	The length of the string pointed to by *lpszString*.
str	A Cstring containing the text to draw.
lpDxWidths	Points to an array of values that indicate the distance between origins of adjacent character cells. For example, lpDxWidths[i] logical units will separate the origins of character cell i and character cell i + 1. This parameter may be NULL, in which case ExtTextOut uses the default spacing between characters.

Returns Non-zero if successful; othersize, zero.

See Also CDC::TextOut, CDC::TabbedTextOut, CDC::DrawText, CDC::SetTextAlign, ::ExtTextOut

Example See CDC::ExtTextOut

GetClipBox

■ 2.0 ■ 3.0 ■ UD

Description Retrieves the bounding rectangle of the current clipping region defined in the attribute device context. The bounding rectangle is the smallest rectangle that can completely contain the clipping region.

Syntax public, virtual int GetClipBox(LPRECT lpRect) const;

Parameters

lpRect	A pointer to a RECT structure or a CRect object that will be filled with the coordinates of the bounding rectangle.

Returns The clipping region's type. It can be one of the following values:

COMPLEXREGION	Clipping region has overlapping borders.
NULLREGION	Clipping region is empty.
SIMPLEREGION	Clipping region has no overlapping borders.

ERROR	Device context is not valid.
See Also	CDC::SelectClipRgn, ::GetClipBox
Example	See CDC::GetClipBox

OffsetViewportOrg

■ 2.0 ■ 3.0 ■ UD

Description Moves the current viewport origin by the specified amounts in the horizontal and vertical directions. The specified offsets are added to the current origin. The viewport origin and extents, together with the window origin and extents, determine how coordinates are mapped between device coordinates and logical coordinates. See the CDC::DPtoLP and CDC::LPtoDP functions for a discussion regarding these mappings. The viewport origin is adjusted on both the output device context and the attribute device context.

Syntax public, virtual CPoint OffsetViewportOrg(int nXOffset, int nYOffset);

Parameters

nXOffset	The number of device units to add to the x coordinate of the viewport origin.
nYOffset	The number of device units to add to the y coordinate of the viewport origin.

Returns A CPoint object containing the old viewport origin.

See Also CDC::GetViewportOrg, CDC::SetViewportOrg, CDC::OffsetWindowOrg, ::OffsetViewportOrg, ::OffsetViewportOrgEx

Example See CDC::OffsetViewportOrg

PtVisible

■ 2.0 ■ 3.0 ■ UD

Description Determines whether a given point is within the current clipping region for the attribute device context.

Syntax public, virtual BOOL PtVisible(int x, int y) const;
public, BOOL PtVisible(POINT point) const;

Parameters

x	The x coordinate, in logical units, of the point to check.
y	The y coordinate, in logical units, of the point to check.
point	A POINT structure or CPoint object containing the coordinate, in logical units, of the point to check.

Returns Non-zero if the specified point is with the clipping region; otherwise, zero.

See Also CDC::RectVisible, ::PtVisible

Example See CDC::PtVisible

RectVisible

■ 2.0 ■ 3.0 ■ UD

Description Rectangles are considered visible at all times for a metafile. Therefore, this function always returns TRUE. This function exists in order to override the RectVisible function present at the CDC level. Otherwise, calls to RectVisible for a metafile dc would end up calling the CDC implementation.

Syntax public, virtual BOOL RectVisible(LPCRECT lpRect) const;

Parameters

lpRect The rectangle to check for visibility.

Returns TRUE.

See Also CMetaFileDC::PtVisible, CDC::RectVisible, ::RectVisible

Example See CDC::RectVisible

ReleaseOutputDC

■ 2.0 ■ 3.0 ■ UD

Description This function exists simply to override the CDC version and prevent release of the output device context. You should close the metafile to accomplish this. The debug version of MFC will output a message warning you about this fact.

Syntax protected, virtual void ReleaseOutputDC( );

Parameters None.

Returns Nothing is returned.

See Also CDC::ReleaseAttribDC, CDC::SetOutputDC, CDC::SetAttribDC

ScaleViewportExt

■ 2.0 ■ 3.0 ■ UD

Description Scales the current viewport extents according to the specified fractions. The viewport origin and extents, together with the window origin and extents, determine how coordinates are mapped between device coordinates and logical coordinates. See the CDC::DPtoLP and CDC::LPtoDP functions for a discussion regarding these mappings. This function scales the viewport extents on both the output and attribute device contexts.

Syntax public, virtual CSize ScaleViewportExt(int xNum, int xDenom, int yNum, int yDenom);

Parameters

xNum The amount by which to multiply the horizontal viewport extent.

xDenom The amount by which to divide the result of multiplying the horizontal extent by *xNum*.

yNum The amount by which to multiply the vertical viewport extent.

yDenom The amount by which to divide the result of multiplying the vertical extent by *yNum*.

Returns A CSize object containing the old viewport extents.

See Also CDC::ScaleWindowExt, CDC::GetViewportExt, CDC::SetViewportExt, ::ScaleViewportExt

Example See CDC::ScaleViewportExt

SetAttribDC

■ 2.0 ■ 3.0 ■ UD

Description Sets the attribute device context to the specified device context. The device context is not attached to the CDC object. This version, which is an override of the CDC version, prevents setting the attribute device context to the same device context as the output device context (because the output device context is a metafile).

Syntax public, virtual void SetAttribDC(HDC hDC);

Parameters

hDC The handle of the device context to be associated with the CDC object as the attribute device context.

Returns Nothing is returned.

See Also CMetaFileDC::SetOutputDC, CMetaFileDC::ReleaseAttribDC, CMetaFileDC::ReleaseOutputDC

SetOutputDC

■ 2.0 ■ 3.0 ■ UD

Description This function exists simply to override the CDC version and prevent setting of the output device context. You should create a metafile to accomplish this. The debug version of MFC will output a message warning you about this fact.

Syntax protected, virtual void SetOutputDC(HDC hDC);

Parameters

hDC A handle of the device context to associated with the CDC object as its output device context.

Returns Nothing is returned.

See Also CMetaFileDC::SetAttribDC, CMetaFileDC::ReleaseOutputDC, CMetaFileDC::ReleaseAttribDC

SetViewportExt

■ 2.0 ■ 3.0 ■ UD

Description Sets the horizontal and vertical extents of the viewport on both the output device context and the attribute device context. The viewport origin and extents, together with the window origin and extents, determine how coordinates are mapped between device coordinates and logical coordinates. See the CDC::DPtoLP and CDC::LPtoDP functions for a discussion regarding these mappings. Calls to this function are ignored for the MM_HIENGLISH, MM_LOMETRIC, MM_HIMETRIC, MM_TEXT, MM_LOENGLISH, and MM_TWIPS mapping modes. If the MM_ISOTROPIC mode is set, you should call the SetWindowExt member function before you call SetViewportExt because Windows automatically makes adjustments to the values specified in order to maintain the correct aspect ratio.

Syntax public, virtual CSize SetViewportExt(int x, int y);
public, virtual CSize SetViewportExt(SIZE size);

Parameters

x The horizontal extent of the viewport, in device units.

y The vertical extent of the viewport, in device units.

size A SIZE structure or a CSize object which contains the new viewport extents, in device units.

Returns A CSize object containing the previous viewport extents.

See Also CDC::GetViewportExt, CMetaFileDC::SetWindowExt, CMetaFileDC::SetViewportOrg, CDC::DPtoLP, CDC::LPtoDP, ::SetViewportExt

Example See CDC::SetViewportExt

SetViewportOrg ■ 2.0 ■ 3.0 ■ UD

Description Sets the origin of the viewport on both the output device context and the attribute device context. The viewport origin and extents, together with the window origin and extents, determine how coordinates are mapped between device coordinates and logical coordinates. See the CDC::DPtoLP and CDC::LPtoDP functions for a discussion regarding these mappings.

Syntax public, virtual CPoint SetViewportOrg(int x, int y); public, virtual CPoint SetViewportOrg(POINT point);

Parameters

x The x coordinate, in device units, of the new viewport origin.

y The y coordinate, in device units, of the new viewport origin.

point A POINT structure or a CPoint object that contains the new viewport origin, in device units.

Returns A CPoint object containing the previous viewport origin.

See Also CDC::GetViewportOrg, CMetaFileDC::SetWindowOrg, CMetaFileDC::SetViewportExt, CDC::DPtoLP, CDC::LPtoDP, ::SetViewportOrg

Example See CDC::SetViewportOrg

TabbedTextOut

■ 2.0 ■ 3.0 ■ UD

Description Outputs a specified text string at a specified location. The text is drawn using the current text color and, if the current background mode is OPAQUE, the background is filled with the current background color. Any tabs encountered in the text are expanded as specified. By default, TabbedTextOut outputs the text at a user-defined location. Optionally, you can use the CDC::SetTextAlign function with the TA_UPDATECP option to force TabbedTextOut to output the text beginning at the current position. In this case, the *x* and *y* parameters to TabbedTextOut are ignored and, if the function is successful, TabbedTextOut updates the current position. This function updates the current position of both the output and the attribute device contexts. The interpretation of the location specified by the *x* and *y* parameters depends on the current text-alignment mode.

Syntax public, virtual CSize TabbedTextOut(int x, int y, LPCTSTR lpszString, int nCount, int nTabPositions, LPINT lpnTabStopPositions, int nTabOrigin); public, CSize TabbedTextOut(int x, int y, const CString &str, int nCount, int nTabPositions, LPINT lpnTabStopPositions, int nTabOrigin);

Parameters

x The x coordinate, in logical units, of the starting point of the text.

y The y coordinate, in logical units, of the starting point of the text.

lpszString A pointer to the text string to output.

nCount The number of characters in the string pointed to by *lpszString*.

nTabPositions The number of tab positions specified in the *lpnTabStopPositions* array. If this parameter is zero and *lpnTabStopPositions* is NULL, a default tab width of eight average characters is used. If this parameter is one, *lpnTabStopPositions* should point to a single value which will be used as the spacing between tabs. If this parameter is greater than one, *lpnTabStopPositions* should point to an array of *nTabStop* tab positions.

lpnTabStopPositions A pointer to an array of integers specifying where, in logical units, tab stops should be placed. The values specified must be sorted in increasing order. See the *nTabPositions* parameter for a complete description of the uses of this parameter.

nTabOrigin The x coordinate, in logical units, of the origin from which the tabs will be expanded. Using this parameter allows you to call TabbedTextOut several times for the same line using a different text starting point but maintaining the same tabs.

Str A CString containing the text to output.

Returns A CSize object containing the dimensions of the string in logical units.

See Also CDC::TextOut, CDC::GetTabbedTextExtent, ::TabbedTextOut

Example See CDC::TabbedTextOut

TextOut

■ 2.0 ■ 3.0 ■ UD

Description Outputs a specified text string at a specified location. The text is drawn using the current text color and, if the current background mode is OPAQUE, the background is filled with the current background color. By default, TextOut outputs the text at a user-defined location. Optionally, you can use the CDC::SetTextAlign function with the TA_UPDATECP option to force TextOut to output the text beginning at the current position. In this case, the *x* and *y* parameters to TextOut are ignored and, if the function is successful, TextOut updates the current position. This function will update the current position of both the output device context and the attribute device context. The interpretation of the location specified by the *x* and *y* parameters depends on the current text-alignment mode.

Syntax public, virtual BOOL TextOut(int x, int y, LPCTSTR lpszString, int nCount); public, BOOL TextOut(int x, int y, const CString& str);

Parameters

x The x coordinate, in logical units, where the text should begin.

y The y coordinate, in logical units, where the text should begin.

lpszString A pointer to the text string to output.

nCount The number of characters in the string pointed to by the *lpszString* parameter.

str A reference to a CString object containing the text string to output.

Returns Non-zero if successful; otherwise, zero.

See Also CMetaFileDC::ExtTextOut, CMetaFileDC::DrawText, CDC::SetTextColor, CDC::SetBkMode, CDC::SetBkColor, ::TextOut

Example See CDC::TextOut

12

THE MFC GDI

12

THE MFC GDI

The classes provided by MFC for GDI manipulation are very much like their related device context classes—very shallow. This is not a reference to the vanity of these classes, of course, but rather to the fact that many of the member functions of these classes are simple, inline wrappers for their Windows SDK counterparts. MFC does provide a good number of enhancements, mostly by way of convenience functions. Also, as it does elsewhere, MFC provides good error checking to aid in the debug process. For example, unlike with the SDK, if you use a brush whose object handle is NULL, you will know right away.

The MFC GDI provides classes that wrap each of the Windows GDI objects. These include the CPen, CBrush, CBitmap, CPalette, CRgn, and CFont classes. All of these classes are derived from a common parent, the CGdiObject class, which provides functions shared by each of the classes. In addition, MFC provides classes that wrap the basic Windows structures, POINT (CPoint class), SIZE (CSize class), and RECT (CRect class). The classes presented in this chapter are summarized in Table 12-1 below. The declarations of all of the functions contained in this chapter can be found in the MFC header file *afxwin.h*.

A sample program called GDISMPL, which shows how to use many of the functions documented in this chapter, is included on the CD-ROM packaged with this book. GDISMPL demonstrates how to draw and manipulate various simple GDI objects. It also shows how to work with MFC's various device context objects. Device contexts are covered in Chapter 11, *Device Contexts*. GDISMPL is a Visual C++ 4.0 (32-bit) project.

Table 12-1 Chapter 12 class summary

Class Name	Description
CBitmap	Encapsulates the Windows GDI bitmap used for performing raster graphics operations.
CBrush	Encapsulates the Windows GDI brush used for filling graphical objects.
CFont	Encapsulates the Windows GDI font used to represent text characterstics.
CPalette	Encapsulates the Windows GDI palette used for color mapping.

continued on next page

continued from previous page

Class Name	Description
CPen	Encapsulates the Windows GDI pen used for drawing and outlining graphical objects.
CPoint	Encapsulates the Windows POINT structure and provides basic point manipulation routines.
CRect	Encapsulates the Windows RECT structure and provides basic rectangle manipulation routines.
CRgn	Encapsulates the Windows GDI region used for describing arbitrary spacial areas.
CSize	Encapsulates the Windows SIZE structure and provides basic size manipulation routines.

The CPoint Class

The CPoint class is a very basic class that wraps the Windows POINT structure. The class adds no data members. Because of this, all MFC functions that require a point as a parameter will accept a CPoint object or the POINT structure. What the CPoint object does provide is a group of operator functions that aid in the manipulation of points—adding an offset to a point, subtracting two points, etc.

CPOINT ■ 2.0 ■ 3.0

Description The constructor for the CPoint class. The constructor does nothing of any real interest.

Syntax

public, CPoint();
public, CPoint(int x, int y);
public, CPoint(POINT pt);
public, CPoint(SIZE size);
public, CPoint(DWORD dwCoord);

Parameters

x The initial value for the x coordinate of the point.

y The initial value for the y coordinate of the point.

pt A POINT structure or a CPoint object that will be used to initialize the point.

size A SIZE structure or a CSize object that will be used to initialize the point. The x coordinate of the point will be initialized to the cx member of the size structure or object and the y coordinate of the point will be initialized to the cy member of the size structure or object.

dwCoord The x coordinate will be initialized to the LOWORD of this parameter and the y coordinate of the point will be initialized to the HIWORD of this parameter.

Returns Nothing is returned.

Example See CPoint::Offset

Offset

■ 2.0 ■ 3.0

Description This function adds separate values to the x and y coordinates of a point. These values may be specified independently or as a CPoint or CSize object.

Syntax public, void Offset(int xOffset, int yOffset);
public, void Offset(POINT point);
public, void Offset(SIZE size);

Parameters

xOffset The amount by which to offset the x coordinate of the point.

yOffset The amount by which to offset the y coordinate of the point.

point The amount by which to offset the point as specified by the x and y members of the specified CPoint object. You may pass a CPoint object or a POINT structure for this parameter.

size The amount by which to offset the point as specified by the cx and cy members of the specified CSize object. You may pass a CSize object or a SIZE structure for this parameter.

Returns Nothing is returned.

See Also CPoint::operator +=, CPoint::operator -=

Example

```
CPoint point(5,5); // initialize point to x=5, y=5
point.Offset(4,3); // adds 4 to x coordinate and 3 to the y coordinate
```

Operator !=

■ 2.0 ■ 3.0

Description Compares two points for inequality.

Syntax public, BOOL operator !=(POINT point) const;

Parameters

point The point to compare with this point. You may pass a CPoint object or a POINT structure for this parameter.

Returns TRUE if the two points are not equal; FALSE if they are equal.

See Also CPoint::operator ==

Example

```
void CMyClass::OnLButtonDown(CWnd *pWnd,int nFlags,CPoint point)
{
     static CPoint oldPoint(0,0);
     if (oldPoint != point)
     {
          // position change since last left button down message
     }
     oldPoint = point;
}
```

OPERATOR +

■ 2.0 ■ 3.0

Description Adds a CSize object or another CPoint object to the point. The resultant point is the original point with x and y members offset by the cx and cy members, respectively, of the CSize object or the x and y members of the CPoint object. Alternatively, the third version of this function adds this point to a specified rectangle and returns the rectangle offset by the x and y values of this point.

Syntax
public, CPoint operator +(SIZE size) const;
public, 4.0+, CPoint operator +(POINT point) const;
public, 4.0+, CRect operator +(const RECT* lpRect) const;

Parameters

size The size that should be added to the point. You may pass a CSize object or a SIZE structure for this parameter.

point The point that should be added to this point. You may pass a CPoint object or a POINT structure for this parameter.

lpRect The rectangle to which this point should be added. You may pass a CRect object or a pointer to a RECT structure for this parameter.

Returns A point whose contents represent the sum of the original point and the specified size or point or a rectangle offset by the contents of this point.

See Also CPoint::operator +=, CPoint::operator -, CSize::operator +

Example

```
CPoint origPoint(5,5), anotherPoint(5,5), newPoint;
CSize size(3,4);

newPoint = origPoint + size; // new point set to 8,9
newPoint = origPoint + anotherPoint; // new point set to 10,10
```

OPERATOR +=

■ 2.0 ■ 3.0

Description Adds a CSize object or CPoint object to the point and assigns the resultant point to this point object. The resultant point is the original point with x and y members offset by the cx and cy members, respectively, of the CSize object or the x and y members of the CPoint object.

Syntax
public, void operator +=(SIZE size);
public, 4.0+, void operator +=(POINT point);

Parameters

size The size that should be added to the point. You may pass a CSize object or a SIZE structure for this parameter.

point The point that should be added to this point. You may pass a CPoint object or a POINT structure for this parameter.

Returns Nothing is returned.

See Also CPoint::operator +, CPoint::operator -=

Example

```
CPoint point(5,5), anotherPoint(5,5);
CSize size(3,4);

point += size; // point now set to 8,9
point += anotherPoint; // point now set to 13,14
```

OPERATOR -

■ 2.0 ■ 3.0

Description

The first form of this function subtracts one point from another, yielding a CSize object representing the differences in the x and y coordinates of the two points. The second version of this function subtracts a CSize object from the CPoint object, yielding another CPoint object whose x and y coordinates are offset by the cx and cy coordinates of the CSize object. The third version of this operator subtracts this CPoint object from a specified rectangle, yielding a rectangle negatively offset by the x and y members of this CPoint object. The final version of this operator is the unary minus operator. It negates the point (for example 3,4 turns into -3,-4).

Syntax

public, CSize operator -(POINT point) const;
public, CPoint operator -(SIZE size) const;
public, 4.0+, CRect operator -(const RECT* lpRect) const;
public, CPoint operator -( ) const;

Parameters

point — The point to be subtracted from this point. You may pass a CPoint object or a POINT structure for this parameter.

size — The size to be subtracted from this point. You may pass a CSize object or a SIZE structure for this parameter.

lpRect — The rectangle from which this point should be subtracted. You may pass a CRect object or a pointer to a RECT structure for this parameter.

Returns

The first form of the function returns a CSize object whose coordinates represent the differences between the coordinates of this point and the specified point. The second form of the function returns a CPoint object whose coordinates represent the original point object (this point object) offset by the sizes given in the specified CSize object. The third form returns a rectangle that is the supplied rectangle negatively offset by the x and y members of this CPoint object. The final version of this operator returns the point negated.

See Also

CPoint::operator -=, CPoint::operator +

Example

```
CPoint origPoint(10,9), anotherPoint(2,1), newPoint;
CSize size(3,4);

newPoint = origPoint - size; // new point set to 7,5
size = newPoint - anotherPoint; // size set to 5,4
```

OPERATOR -=

■ 2.0 ■ 3.0

Description This function subtracts a specified size or point from the point and assigns the resultant point to this point. The x and y coordinates of the point are offset by the cx and cy members of the specified CSize object or the x and y members of the specified point.

Syntax public, void operator -=(SIZE size);
public, 4.0+, void operator -+(POINT point);

Parameters

size The size to be subtracted from this point. You may pass a CSize object or a SIZE structure for this parameter.

point The point to be subtracted from this point. You may pass a CPoint object or a POINT structure for this parameter.

Returns Nothing is returned.

See Also CPoint::operator -, CPoint::operator +=

Example

```
CPoint point(5,5),anotherPoint(1,1);
CSize size(3,4);

point -= size; // point now set to 2,1
point -+ anotherPoint; // point now set to 1,0
```

OPERATOR ==

■ 2.0 ■ 3.0

Description Compares this point and another point for equality.

Syntax public, BOOL operator ==(POINT point) const;

Parameters

point The point to compare with this point. You may pass a CPoint object or a POINT structure for this parameter.

Returns TRUE if the two points are equavalent; FALSE if they are not.

See Also CPoint::operator !=

Example

```
void CMyClass::OnLButtonDown(CWnd *pWnd,int nFlags,CPoint point)
{
      static CPoint oldPoint(0,0);
      if (oldPoint == point)
      {
            // position is the same since last left button down message
      }
      oldPoint = point;
}
```

The CRect Class

The CRect class is a very basic class that wraps the Windows RECT structure. The class adds no data members. Because of this, most MFC functions that require a RECT or pointer to a RECT as a parameter will accept a CRect object or RECT structure. What the CRect object does provide is a group of operator functions which aid in the manipulation of rectangles.

CRect

■ 2.0 ■ 3.0

Description The constructor for the CRect class. The constructor does nothing of any real interest. It comes in many forms that allow you to initialize the rectangle's coordinates.

Syntax
public, CRect();
public, CRect(int l, int t, int r, int b);
public, CRect(const RECT &srcRect);
public, CRect(LPCRECT lpSrcRect);
public, CRect(POINT point, SIZE size);
public, 4.0+, CRect(POINT topLeft, POINT bottomRight);

Parameters

l	The x coordinate of the upper-left corner of the rectangle.
t	The y coordinate of the upper-left corner of the rectangle.
r	The x coordinate of the lower-right corner of the rectangle.
b	The y coordinate of the lower-right corner of the rectangle.
srcRect	A reference to a RECT structure or CRect object that will be used to initialize this CRect object.
lpSrcRect	A pointer to a RECT structure or a CRect object that will be used to initialize this CRect object.
point	A point representing the upper-left corner of the rectangle.
size	The size of the rectangle.
topLeft	A point representing the upper-left corner of the rectangle.
bottomRight	A point representing the lower-right corner of the rectangle.

Returns Nothing is returned.

BottomRight

■ 2.0 ■ 3.0

Description Returns a reference to the bottom-right corner point of the rectangle.

Syntax
public, CPoint& BottomRight( );
public, 4.0+ const CPoint& BottomRight() const;

Parameters None.

Returns A reference to the CPoint representing the bottom-right corner of the rectangle.

See Also CRect::TopLeft

Example

```
CRect rect(2,3,4,5);
CPoint br = rect.BottomRight; // br set to 4,5
```

CenterPoint

–. ■ 4.0

Description Calculates the center point of the rectangle. The center point is defined as follows: x = left + (right-left)/2, y = top + (bottom-top)/2.

Syntax public, CPoint CenterPoint( ) const;

Parameters None.

Returns A CPoint representing the center point of the rectangle.

See Also CRect::TopLeft, CRect::BottomRight

Example

```
CRect rect(0,0,10,20);
CPoint center = rect.CenterPoint(); // center set to 5,10
```

CopyRect

■ 2.0 ■ 3.0

Description Copies the specified rectangle to the CRect object.

Syntax public, void CopyRect(LPCRECT lpSrcRect);

Parameters

lpSrcRect A pointer to a RECT structure or a CRect object (because of LPCRECT operator) whose contents will be copied to the CRect object.

Returns Nothing is returned.

See Also CRect::operator =

Example

```
CRect rect(2,3,4,5), copiedRect;
copiedRect.CopyRect(rect); // copiedRect set to 2,3,4,5
```

DeflateRect

–. ■ 4.0

Description Inflates or deflates the rectangle by the specified horizontal and vertical amounts. If the specified amounts are negative, the rectangle is inflated. If the specified amounts are positive, the rectangle is deflated. The specified horizontal amount is added to the left side of the rectangle and subtracted from the right side, causing the total width to increase or decrease (depending on the sign of the specified amount) by two times the specified amount. The same holds true for the height. This behavior is exactly opposite to that of the CRect::InflateRect function.

Syntax public, void DeflateRect(int x, int y);
public, void DeflateRect(SIZE size);
public, void DeflateRect(LPCRECT lpRect);
public, void DeflateRect(int l, int t, int r, int b);

Parameters

x Half the amount by which the width should be increased or decreased. A negative value will cause the width to be increased. This function will add x to the left side of the rectangle and subtract x from the right side.

y Half the amount by which the height should be increased or decreased. A negative value will cause the height to be increased. This function will add y to the top of the rectangle and subtract y from the bottom.

size Specifies the amounts by which the rectangle should be adjusted. The cx member of the CSize object corresponds to the x parameter described above and the cy member of the CSize object corresponds to the y parameter described above.

lpRect A pointer to a RECT structure or a CRect object that specifies the amount by that each side should be inflated. The value *lpRect*->TopLeft().x is added to the left side of the rectangle, the value *lpRect*->TopLeft().y is added to the top of the rectangle, the value *lpRect*->BottomRight().x is subtracted from the right side of the rectangle, and the value *lpRect*->BottomRight().y is subtracted from the bottom of the rectangle.

l The amount to add to the left side of the rectangle.

t The amount to add to the top side of the rectangle.

r The amount to subtract from the right side of the rectangle.

b The amount to subtract from the bottom side of the rectangle.

Returns Nothing is returned.

See Also CRect::InflateRect, ::InflateRect

Example

```
CRect rect(2,3,4,5);
rect.DeflateRect(1,2); // rect now set to 1,1,5,7
```

EqualRect

■ 2.0 ■ 3.0

Description Determines whether this CRect object is equal to a specified rectangle.

Syntax public, BOOL EqualRect(LPCRECT lpRect) const;

Parameters

lpRect A pointer to a RECT structure or a CRect object (because of the LPCRECT operator) whose contents are to be compared with the CRect object.

Returns TRUE if the CRect object is equal to the specified rectangle; FALSE otherwise.

See Also CRect::operator ==, ::EqualRect

Example

```
void SomeFunc(CRect rect1, CRect rect2)
{
      ..
      if (rect1.EqualRect(rect2))
      {
            // rectangles are equal
      }
      else
      ..
}
```

HEIGHT

■ 2.0 ■ 3.0

Description Returns the height of the rectangle as given by BottomRight().y—TopLeft().y. Note that if TopLeft().y is greater than BottomRight().y, the result will be negative. The CRect object does not force the bottom to be greater than the top.

Syntax public, int Height( ) const;

Parameters None.

Returns The height of the rectangle.

See Also CRect::Width

Example

```
CRect rect(2,3,4,5);
int nHeight = rect.Height(); // nHeight = 2
```

INFLATERECT

■ 2.0 ■ 3.0

Description Inflates or deflates the rectangle by the specified horizontal and vertical amounts. If the specified amounts are positive, the rectangle is inflated. If the specified amounts are negative, the rectangle is deflated. (This is the opposite of the behavior of the DeflateRect function). The specified horizontal amount is subtracted from the left side of the rectangle and added to the right side, causing the total width to increase or decrease (depending on the sign of the specified amount) by two times the specified amount. The same holds true for the height.

Syntax

public, void InflateRect(int x, int y);
public, void InflateRect(SIZE size);
public, 4.0+, void InflateRect(LPCRECT lpRect);
public, 4.0+, void InflateRect(int l, int t, int r, int b);

Parameters

x Half the amount by which the width should be increased or decreased. A negative value will cause the width to be decreased. This function will subtract x from the left side of the rectangle and add x to the right side.

y Half the amount by which the height should be increased or decreased. A negative value will cause the height to be decreased. This function will subtract y from the top of the rectangle and add y to the bottom.

size Specifies the amounts by which the rectangle should be adjusted. The cx member of the CSize object corresponds to the x parameter described above and the cy member of the CSize object corresponds to the y parameter described above.

lpRect A pointer to a RECT structure or a CRect object that specifies the amount by which each side should be inflated. The value *lpRect*->TopLeft().x is subtracted from the left side of the rectangle, the value *lpRect*->TopLeft().y is subtracted from the top of the rectangle, the value *lpRect*->BottomRight().x is added to the right side of the rectangle, and the value *lpRect*->BottomRight().y is added to the bottom of the rectangle.

l The amount to subtract from the left side of the rectangle.

t The amount to subtract from the top side of the rectangle.

r The amount to add to the right side of the rectangle.

b The amount to add to the bottom side of the rectangle.

Returns Nothing is returned.

See Also CRect::DeflateRect, ::InflateRect

Example

```
CRect rect(2,3,4,5);
rect.InflateRect(1,2); // rect now set to 1,1,5,7

// or do it this way
rect.InflateRect(1,2,3,4); // rect now set to 0,-1,8,11
```

IntersectRect

■ 2.0 ■ 3.0

Description Sets the CRect object to the intersection of two other rectangles. The intersection of two rectangles is the area where the two rectangles overlap, which is always a rectangle itself. In order for this function to work, both rectangles passed as parameters must be normalized—that is, the top must be less than the bottom and the left must be less than the right. Figure 12-1, below, is an example of the intersection of two rectangles.

Syntax public, BOOL IntersectRect(LPCRECT lpRect1, LPCRECT lpRect2);

Parameters

lpRect1 A pointer to a RECT structure or a CRect object (because of the LPCRECT operator).

lpRect2 A pointer to a RECT structure or a CRect object (because of the LPCRECT operator).

Returns TRUE if the two rectangles intersect; FALSE if the intersection is empty.

See Also CRect::operator &, CRect::operator &=, ::IntersectRect

Example

```
CRect rect1(1,1,5,5), rect2(3,3,7,7);
CRect insRect;
insRect.IntersectRect(rect1,rect2); // sets insRect to 3,3,5,5
```

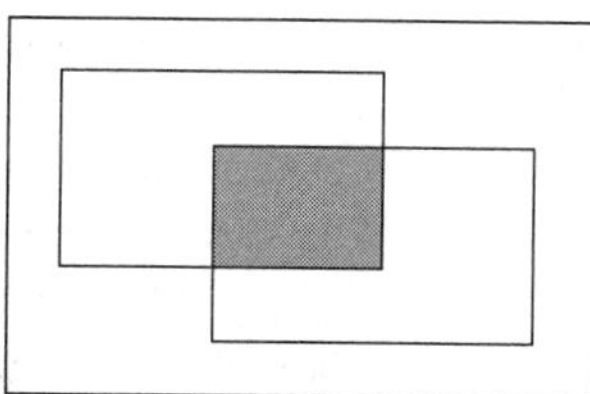

Figure 12-1 Intersection of two rectangles

IsRectEmpty

■ 2.0 ■ 3.0

Description Determines whether the CRect object represents an empty rectangle. A rectangle is empty if either its width or height are zero or negative. Note that this does not mean that the coordinates of the rectangle are themselves zero (a NULL rectangle). IsRectEmpty is a wrapper for the SDK function ::IsRectEmpty.

Syntax public, BOOL IsRectEmpty( ) const;

Parameters None.

Returns TRUE if the rectangle is empty; FALSE otherwise.

See Also CRect::IsRectNull, ::IsRectEmpty

Example

```
void DrawRect(CDC *pDc, CRect rect)
{
	if (!rect.IsRectEmpty())
		pDc->Rectangle(rect); // draw rectangle if not empty
}
```

IsRectNull

■ 2.0 ■ 3.0

Description Determines whether all coordinates of the CRect are zero (left,top,right,bottom). IsRectNull is a wrapper for the SDK function ::IsRectNull.

Syntax public, BOOL IsRectNull() const;

Parameters None.

Returns TRUE if the CRect object represents a NULL rectangle; FALSE otherwise.

See Also CRect::IsRectEmpty, ::IsRectNull

Example

```
void DrawRect(CDC *pDc, CRect rect)
{
	if (!rect.IsRectNull())
		pDc->Rectangle(rect); // draw rectangle if not null
}
```

MulDiv

–. ■ 4.0

Description Muliplies and divides the coordinates of the rectangle by the specified amounts and returns the resulting, scaled rectangle. To determine the resultant rectangle, each coordinate of this rectangle is first multiplied by the specified amount and then the result of that multiplication is divided by the specified amount.

Syntax public, CRect MulDiv(int nMultiplier, int nDivisor) const;

Parameters

nMultiplier The amount by which each coordinate of the rectangle will be multiplied.

nDivisor The amount by which the result of multiplying each coordinate by *nMultiplier* will be divided.

Returns A CRect object containing the rectangle scaled by the specified amounts.

See Also ::MulDiv

Example

```
CRect rect(5,6,2,3);
CRect scaledRect = rect.MulDiv(2,3); // rect now set to 3,4,1,2
```

NormalizeRect

■ 2.0 ■ 3.0

Description Ensures that the top of the rectangle is less than the bottom and the left is less than the right by swapping them if necessary. Several operations performed on rectangles (e.g., IntersectRect) require the rectangle to be normalized in this fashion.

Syntax public, void NormalizeRect( );

Parameters None.

Returns Nothing is returned.

Example

```
CRect rect(5,6,2,3);
rect.NormalizeRect(); // rect now set to 2,3,5,6
```

OffsetRect

■ 2.0 ■ 3.0

Description Moves a rectangle by a specified amount in the horizontal and/or vertical direction. Negative values move the rectangle to the left and the top. Positive values move the rectangle to the right and the bottom.

Syntax public, void OffsetRect(int x, int y);
public, void OffsetRect(POINT point);
public, void OffsetRect(SIZE size);

Parameters

x The amount by which the rectangle should be moved horizontally. A negative value will move the rectangle to the left. A positive value will move it to the right.

y The amount by which the rectangle should be moved vertically. Depending on the current coordinate mapping mode, a positive value will move the rectangle up or down. For example, if the mapping mode is MM_TEXT, a positive value will move the rectangle down. If the mapping mode is MM_HIENGLISH, a positive value will move the rectangle up. If the mapping mode is MM_ANISOTROPIC or MM_ISOTROPIC, the direction in which the rectangle will move depends on the current viewport and window origin and extents.

point A POINT structure or a CPoint object containing the amounts by which the rectangle should be moved. The x member of the point corresponds to the x parameter described above and the y member of the point corresponds to the y parameter described above.

size A SIZE structure or a CSize object containing the amounts by which the rectangle should be moved. The cx member of the size corresponds to the x parameter described above and the cy member of size corresponds to the y parameter described above.

Returns Nothing is returned.

See Also CRect::operator +=, CRect::operator +, ::OffsetRect

OPERATOR != ■ 2.0 ■ 3.0

Description Determines whether a specified rectangle is not equal to the CRect object. Two rectangles are equal if both the upper-left and lower-right coordinates are equal.

Syntax public, BOOL operator !=(const RECT& rect) const;

Parameters

rect A reference to the rectangle to be compared with the CRect. This parameter may be a RECT structure or a CRect object.

Returns TRUE if the CRect is not equal to the specified rectangle; FALSE otherwise.

See Also CRect::EqualRect, CRect::operator ==

Example

```
void SomeFunc(CRect rect1, CRect rect2)
{
        ..
        if (rect1 != rect2)
        {
                // rectangles are NOT equal
        }
        else
        ..
}
```

OPERATOR & ■ 2.0 ■ 3.0

Description Returns a rectangle representing the intersection of the CRect object with a specified rectangle. The intersection of two rectangles is the area where the two rectangles overlap, which is always a rectangle itself. In order for this operator to work, both rectangles must be normalized—that is, the top must be less than the bottom and the left must be less than the right.

Syntax public, CRect operator &(const RECT& rect2) const;

Parameters

rect2 A reference to a RECT structure or CRect object to intersect with the CRect object.

Returns A CRect object representing the intersection of the CRect object and the specified rectangle.

See Also CRect::IntersectRect, ::IntersectRect, CRect::operator &=

Example

```
CRect rect1(1,1,5,5), rect2(3,3,7,7);
CRect insRect;
insRect = rect1 & rect2; // sets insRect to 3,3,5,5
```

OPERATOR &=

■ 2.0 ■ 3.0

Description Sets the CRect object to the rectangle representing the intersection of the CRect object with a specified rectangle. The intersection of two rectangles is the area where the two rectangles overlap, which is always a rectangle itself. In order for this operator to work, both rectangles must be normalized—that is, the top must be less than the bottom and the left must be less than the right.

Syntax public, void operator &=(const RECT& rect);

Parameters

rect A reference to a RECT structure or CRect object to intersect with the CRect object.

Returns Nothing is returned.

See Also CRect::operator &, CRect::IntersectRect, ::IntersectRect

Example

```
CRect rect1(1,1,5,5), rect2(3,3,7,7);
CRect insRect;
rect1 &= rect2; // sets rect1 to 3,3,5,5
```

OPERATOR +

■ 2.0 ■ 3.0

Description Returns a rectangle that represents the CRect object moved by a specified amount in the horizontal and vertical directions. Negative values move the rectangle to the left and the top. Positive values move the rectangle to the right and the bottom. The first version of the operator offsets the rectangle based on the x and y values of a point. The second version offsets each of the rectangle's coordinates by its corresponding coordinate in a another, specified rectangle. Finally, the third version of the operator offsets the rectangle based on the cx and cy values of a size.

Syntax public, CRect operator +(POINT point) const;
public, 4.0+, CRect operator +(LPCRECT lpRect) const;
public, 4.0+, CRect operator +(SIZE size) const;

Parameters

point A POINT structure or a CPoint object containing the amounts by which the rectangle should be moved. The x member of the point specifies the amount the rectangle should be moved horizontally. A negative value will move the rectangle to the left and a positive value will move it to the right. The y member of the point specifies the amount the rectangle

	should be moved vertically. In most coordinate mapping modes, a negative value will move the rectangle up and a positive value will move the rectangle down.
lpRect	A CRect object or a pointer to a RECT structure whose coordinates will be added to the corresponding coordinates of this rectangle.
size	A SIZE structure or a CSize object containing the amounts by which the rectangle should be moved. The cx member of the point specifies the amount the rectangle should be moved horizontally. A negative value will move the rectangle to the left and a positive value will move it to the right. The cy member of the point specifies the amount the rectangle should be moved vertically. In most coordinate mapping modes, a negative value will move the rectangle up and a positive value will move the rectangle down.
Returns	A CRect object representing the CRect object moved by the specified amounts
See Also	CRect::OffsetRect, CRect::operator -, CRect::operator+=, CRect::operator -=
Example	

```
CRect rect1(1,1,5,5), offsetRect;
CPoint point(5,6);
offsetRect = rect1 + point; // sets offsetRect to 6,7,10,11
```

OPERATOR +=

■ 2.0 ■ 3.0

Description	Sets the CRect to its current contents moved by a specified amount in the horizontal and vertical directions. Negative values move the rectangle to the left and the top. Positive values move the rectangle to the right and the bottom.

Syntax	public, void operator +=(POINT point) const;
	public, void operator +=(SIZE size) const;
	public, void operator +=(LPCRECTlpRect) const;

Parameters	
point	A POINT structure or a CPoint object containing the amounts by which the rectangle should be moved. The x member of the point specifies the amount the rectangle should be moved horizontally. A negative value will move the rectangle to the left and a positive value will move it to the right. The y member of the point specifies the amount the rectangle should be moved vertically. In most coordinate mapping modes, a negative value will move the rectangle up and a positive value will move the rectangle down.
size	A SIZE structure or a CSize object containing the amounts by which the rectangle should be moved. The cx member of the point specifies the amount the rectangle should be moved horizontally. A negative value will move the rectangle to the left and a positive value will move it to the

right. The cy member of the point specifies the amount the rectangle should be moved vertically. In most coordinate mapping modes, a negative value will move the rectangle up and a positive value will move the rectangle down.

lpRect — A CRect object or a pointer to a RECT structure whose coordinates will be added to the corresponding coordinates of this rectangle.

Returns — Nothing is returned.

See Also — CRect::OffsetRect, CRect::operator +, CRect::operator -=, CRect::operator -, ::OffsetRect

Example

```
CRect rect1(1,1,5,5);
CPoint point(5,6);
rect1 += point; // sets rect1 to 6,7,10,11
```

OPERATOR -

■ 2.0 ■ 3.0

Description — Returns a rectangle that represents the CRect object moved by a specified amount in the horizontal and vertical directions. Negative values move the rectangle to the right and the bottom. Positive values move the rectangle to the left and the top. The first version of the operator offsets the rectangle based on the x and y values of a point. The second version offsets each of the rectangle's coordinates by its corresponding coordinate in a another specified rectangle. Finally, the third version of the operator offsets the rectangle based on the cx and cy values of a size. Note that the second and third versions of this function did not become available until MFC Version 4.0.

Syntax — public, CRect operator -(POINT point) const;
public, CRect operator -(LPCRECT lpRect) const;
public, CRect operator -(SIZE size) const;

Parameters

point — A POINT structure or a CPoint object containing the amounts by which the rectangle should be moved. The x member of the point specifies the amount the rectangle should be moved horizontally. A negative value will move the rectangle to the right and a positive value will move it to the left. The y member of the point specifies the amount the rectangle should be moved vertically. In most coordinate mapping modes, a negative value will move the rectangle down and a positive value will move the rectangle up.

lpRect — A CRect object or a pointer to a RECT structure whose coordinates will be subtracted from the corresponding coordinates of this rectangle.

size — A SIZE structure or a CSize object containing the amounts by which the rectangle should be moved. The cx member of the point specifies the amount the rectangle should be moved horizontally. A negative value will move the rectangle to the right and a positive value will move it to the left. The cy member of the point specifies the amount the rectangle should be moved vertically. In most coordinate mapping modes, a negative value will move the rectangle down and a positive value will move the rectangle up.

Returns A CRect object representing the CRect object moved by the specified amounts.

See Also CRect::OffsetRect, CRect::operator +, CRect::operator+=, CRect::operator -=

Example

```
CRect rect1(3,2,5,5), offsetRect;
CPoint point(2,1);
offsetRect = rect1 - point; // sets offsetRect to 1,1,3,4
```

OPERATOR -=

■ 2.0 ■ 3.0

Description Sets the CRect to its current contents moved by a specified amount in the horizontal and vertical directions. Negative values move the rectangle to the right and the bottom. Positive values move the rectangle to the left and the top. Note that the second and third version of this function did not become available until MFC Version 4.0.

Syntax

public, void operator -=(POINT point) const;
public, void operator -=(SIZE size) const;
public, void operator -=(LPCRECT lpRect) const;

Parameters

point A POINT structure or a CPoint object containing the amounts by which the rectangle should be moved. The x member of the point specifies the amount the rectangle should be moved horizontally. A negative value will move the rectangle to the right and a positive value will move it to the left. The y member of the point specifies the amount the rectangle should be moved vertically. In most coordinate mapping modes, a negative value will move the rectangle down and a positive value will move the rectangle up.

size A SIZE structure or a CSize object containing the amounts by which the rectangle should be moved. The cx member of the point specifies the amount the rectangle should be moved horizontally. A negative value will move the rectangle to the right and a positive value will move it to the left. The cy member of the point specifies the amount the rectangle should be moved vertically. In most coordinate mapping modes, a negative value will move the rectangle down and a positive value will move the rectangle up.

lpRect A CRect object or a pointer to a RECT structure whose coordinates will be subtracted from the corresponding coordinates of this rectangle.

Returns Nothing is returned.

See Also CRect::OffsetRect, CRect::operator +, CRect::operator+=, CRect::operator -

Example

```
CRect rect1(3,2,5,5);
CPoint point(2,1);
rect1 -= point; // sets rect1 to 1,1,3,4
```

OPERATOR =

■ 2.0 ■ 3.0

Description Copies the contents of the specified rectangle to the CRect object.

Syntax public, void operator =(const RECT& srcRect);

Parameters

srcRect A reference to the RECT structure or CRect object to be copied to the CRect.

Returns Nothing is returned.

See Also CRect::SetRect, ::CopyRect

Example

```
CRect rect1(3,2,5,5), newRect;
newRect = rect1; // sets newRect to 3,2,5,5
```

OPERATOR ==

■ 2.0 ■ 3.0

Description Determines whether the CRect is equivalent to the specified rectangle. Two rectangles are equivalent if they have the same upper left and lower right coordinates.

Syntax public, BOOL operator ==(const RECT& rect) const;

Parameters

rect A reference to a RECT structure or a CRect object to compare with the CRect.

Returns TRUE if the CRect is equal to the specified rectangle; FALSE otherwise.

See Also CRect::EqualRect, ::EqualRect

Example

```
..
if (checkRect == desiredRect)
{
     // rectangles are equal
}
else
..
```

OPERATOR |

■ 2.0 ■ 3.0

Description Returns a CRect object that represents the union of the CRect object with a specified rectangle. The union of two rectangles is the smallest rectangle that contains the two rectangles. In order for this operator to work, both rectangles must be normalized—that is, the top must be less than

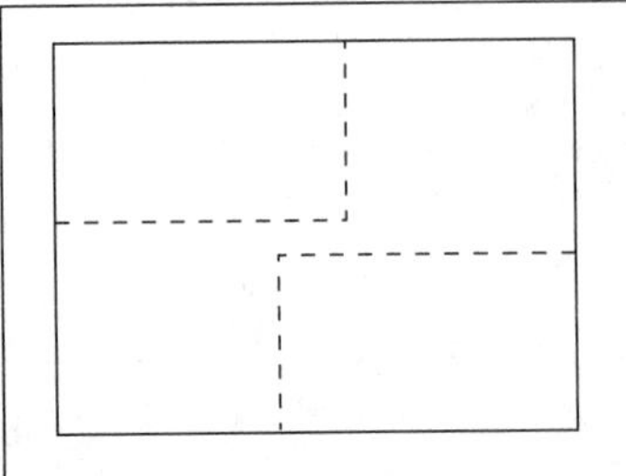

Figure 12-2 Union of two rectangles

the bottom and the left must be less than the right. Figure 12-2 is an example of the union of two rectangles.

Syntax public, CRect operator |(const RECT& rect) const;

Parameters

rect A reference to a RECT structure or a CRect object to union with the CRect object.

Returns A CRect that represents the union of the CRect object with the specified rectangle.

See Also CRect::UnionRect, CRect::operator |=, ::UnionRect

Example

```
CRect rect1(1,1,5,5), rect2(3,3,7,7);
CRect unionRect;
unionRect = rect1 | rect2; // sets unionRect to 1,1,7,7
```

OPERATOR |=

■ 2.0 ■ 3.0

Description Sets the CRect object to the union of the CRect object with a specified rectangle. The union of two rectangles is the smallest rectangle that contains the two rectangles. In order for this operator to work, both rectangles must be normalized—that is, the top must be less than the bottom and the left must be less than the right.

Syntax public, void operator |=(const RECT& rect);

Parameters

rect A reference to a RECT structure or a CRect object to union with the CRect object.

Returns Nothing is returned.

See Also CRect::UnionRect, CRect::operator |, ::UnionRect

Example

```
CRect rect1(1,1,5,5), rect2(3,3,7,7);
rect1 |= rect2; // sets rect1 to 1,1,7,7
```

OPERATOR LPCRECT

■ 2.0 ■ 3.0

Description A cast operator that converts the CRect object into a const RECT far *. This function is useful when passing CRect objects to normal SDK functions that work with the RECT structure.

Syntax public, operator LPCRECT( ) const;

Parameters None.

Returns A LPCRECT (which is a macro for const RECT far *) which points to the contents of the CRect object. The contents of the CRect object are identical to the SDK RECT structure.

See Also CRect::operator LPRECT

Example

```
CRect rect1(1,1,5,5), rect2(3,3,7,7);
CRect insRect;

// SDK IntersectRect function declared as IntersectRect(LPRECT lpRect,
// CONST RECT *pRect1, CONST RECT *pRect2)
::IntersectRect(insRect,rect1,rect2); // works because of cast operators
```

OPERATOR LPRECT

■ 2.0 ■ 3.0

Description A cast operator that converts the CRect object into a RECT far *. This function is useful when passing CRect objects to normal SDK functions which work with the RECT structure.

Syntax public, operator LPRECT( );

Parameters None.

Returns A LPRECT (which is a macro for RECT far *) that points to the contents of the CRect object. The contents of the CRect object are identical to the SDK RECT structure.

See Also CRect::operator LPCRECT

Example

```
CRect rect1(1,1,5,5), rect2(3,3,7,7);
CRect insRect;

// SDK IntersectRect function declared as
// IntersectRect(LPRECT lpRect, CONST RECT *pRect1,CONST RECT *pRect2)
::IntersectRect(insRect,rect1,rect2); // works because of cast operators
```

PTINRECT

■ 2.0 ■ 3.0

Description Determines whether the specified point lies within the bounds of the CRect. A point lies within the rectangle if it is within all four sides or if it lies on the left or top side (but not the bottom or right sides). In order for this operator to work, both rectangles must be normalized—that is, the top must be less than the bottom and the left must be less than the right.

Syntax public, BOOL PtInRect(POINT point) const;

Parameters

point The point that should be checked for inclusion.

Returns TRUE if the point is within the CRect; FALSE otherwise.

See Also ::PointInRect

Example

```
void CMyClass::OnLButtonDown(,,CPoint point)
{
      CRect screenRect(20,20,100,100); // area of interest on screen
      if (screenRect.PtInRect(point))
      {
            // user pressed mouse button in area of interest - do
            // something
      }
      ..
}
```

SetRect ■ 2.0 ■ 3.0

Description Sets the contents of the CRect to the specified coordinates. Note that the second version of this function did not become available until MFC Version 4.0

Syntax public, void SetRect(int x1, int y1, int x2, int y2);
public, void SetRect(POINT topLeft, POINT bottomRight);

Parameters

x1 The x coordinate of the upper-left corner of the rectangle.

y1 The y coordinate of the upper-left corner of the rectangle.

x2 The x coordinate of the lower-right corner of the rectangle.

y2 The y coordinate of the lower-right corner of the rectangle.

topLeft A CPoint object or a POINT structure containing the new upper-left corner of the rectangle.

bottomRight A CPoint object or a POINT structure containing the new lower-right corner of the rectangle.

Returns Nothing is returned.

See Also CRect::CRect, CRect::SetRectEmpty, ::SetRect

Example

```
CRect rect;
CPoint pt1(1,1), pt2(10,10);

rect.SetRect(1,1,100,100); // first form
rect.SetRect(pt1,pt2);     // second form
```

SetRectEmpty

■ 2.0 ■ 3.0

Description Sets the coordinates of the rectangle to 0,0,0,0. Note that this not only creates an empty rectangle but a NULL one as well.

Syntax public, void SetRectEmpty( );

Parameters None.

Returns Nothing is returned.

See Also CRect::SetRect, ::SetRectEmpty

Example

```
CRect rect1;
rect1.SetRectEmpty(); // initializes rectangle to 0,0,0,0 (NULL)
```

Size

■ 2.0 ■ 3.0

Description Calculates the width and height of the rectangle and returns them as a CSize object. The width is the right x coordinate minus the left x coordinate. The height is the lower y coordinate minus the upper y coordinate. Either of these values can be negative if the rectangle is not normalized.

Syntax public, CSize Size( ) const;

Parameters None.

Returns A CSize object whose cx member represents the width of the rectangle and whose cy member represents the height of the rectangle.

See Also CRect::Width, CRect::Height

Example

```
CRect rect1(1,1,5,7);
CSize size;
size = rect1.Size(); // size set to 4,6
```

SubtractRect

■ 2.0 ■ 3.0

Description Subtracts one rectangle from another and assigns the result to the CRect object. This function will only subtract the rectangles if they intersect completely in at least one direction. In other words, at least one side of one of the rectangles must be completely contained in the other rectangle. If they intersect completely in only one direction, only that direction will be subtracted. See Figure 12-3 for further explanation.

Syntax public, BOOL SubtractRect(LPCRECT lpRectSrc1, LPCRECT lpRectSrc2);

Parameters

lpRectSrc1 The source rectangle from which the other source rectangle will be subtracted.

lpRectSrc2 The source rectangle that will be subtracted from the first source rectangle.

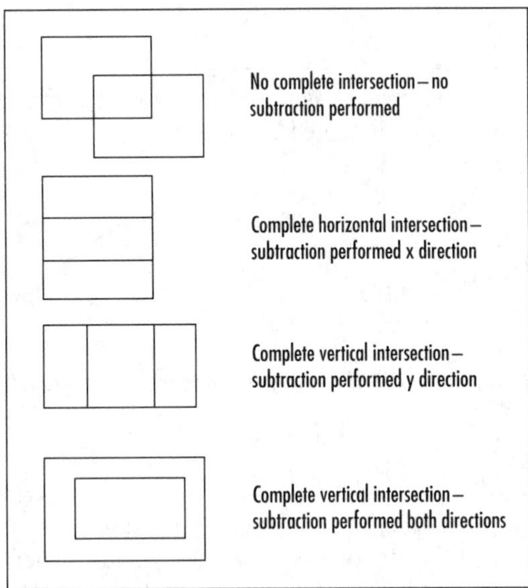

Figure 12-3 SubtractRect intersection scenarios

Returns TRUE if the function is successful; FALSE otherwise.

See Also CRect::IntersectRect, CRect::UnionRect, ::SubtractRect

Example

```
CRect rect1(50,50,200,200), rect2(100,100,150,150),
            rect3(100,175,150,250), rect4(25,100,75,150);
CRect subRect;

// subRect = 50,50,150,150 (completely intersect x & y)
subRect.SubtractRect(rect1,rect2);

// subRect = 50,50,150,200 (completely intersect x only)
subRect.SubtractRect(rect1,rect3);

// subRect = 50,50,200,150 (completely intersect y only)
subRect.SubtractRect(rect1,rect4);
```

TopLeft

■ 2.0 ■ 3.0

Description Returns a reference to the CPoint object representing the rectangle's top-left corner. Note that the second version of this function did not become available until MFC Version 4.0.

Syntax public, CPoint& TopLeft( );
public, const CPoint& TopLeft() const;

Parameters None.

Returns A reference to the CPoint object representing the rectangle's top-left corner.

See Also CRect::BottomRight

Example

```
CRect rect1(1,1,5,5);
CPoint ptTopLeft;
ptTopLeft = rect1.TopLeft(); // assigns 1,1 to ptTopLeft
```

UnionRect

■ 2.0 ■ 3.0

Description Sets the CRect object to the union of two specified rectangles. The union of two rectangles is the smallest rectangle that contains the two rectangles. In order for this operator to work, both rectangles must be normalized—that is, the top must be less than the bottom and the left must be less than the right.

Syntax public, BOOL UnionRect(LPCRECT lpRect1, LPCRECT lpRect2);

Parameters

lpRect1 A source rectangle that will be unioned with a second source rectangle. This parameter may be a pointer to a RECT structure or a CRect object (because of the LPCRECT operator).

lpRect2 A source rectangle that will be unioned with a second source rectangle. This parameter may be a pointer to a RECT structure or a CRect object (because of the LPCRECT operator).

Returns Non-zero if the function is successful; zero otherwise.

See Also CRect::operator |, CRect::operator |=, ::UnionRect

Example

```
CRect rect1(1,1,5,5), rect2(3,3,7,7);
CRect unionRect;
unionRect.UnionRect(rect1, rect2); // sets unionRect to 1,1,7,7
```

Width

■ 2.0 ■ 3.0

Description Returns the width of the rectangle as given by BottomRight().x—TopLeft().x. Note that if TopLeft().x is greater than BottomRight().x, the result will be negative. The CRect object does not force the bottom to be greater than the top.

Syntax public, int Width( ) const;

Parameters None.

Returns The width of the rectangle.

See Also CRect::Height

Example

```
CRect rect(2,3,4,5);
int nWidth = rect.Width(); // nWidth = 2
```

The CSize Class

The CSize class is a very basic class that wraps the Windows SIZE structure. The class adds no data members. Because of this, most MFC functions that require a SIZE or pointer to a SIZE as a parameter will accept a CSize object or SIZE structure. Like its partners, CPoint and CRect, CSize provides a group of operator functions that aid in the manipulation of sizes.

CSize ■ 2.0 ■ 3.0

Description The constructor for the CSize class. The constructor does nothing of any real interest.

Syntax
public, CSize();
public, CSize(int cx,int cy);
public, CSize(SIZE size);
public, CSize(POINT pt);
public, CSize(DWORD dwSize);

Parameters

cx The initial value for the cx component of the size.

cy The initial value for the cy component of the size.

size A SIZE structure or a CSize object that will be used to initialize the size.

pt A POINT structure or a CPoint object that will be used to initialize the size. The cx component of the size will be initialized to the x member of the point structure or object and the cy component of the size will be initialized to the y member of the point structure or object.

dwSize The cx component will be initialized to the LOWORD of this parameter and the cy component of the size will be initialized to the HIWORD of this parameter.

Returns Nothing is returned.

Example See CSize::operator !=

OPERATOR != ■ 2.0 ■ 3.0

Description Determines whether two sizes are not equal.

Syntax public, BOOL operator !=(SIZE size) const;

Parameters

size A size to compare to the CSize object. This parameter can be a SIZE structure or a CSize object.

Returns Non-zero if the sizes are not equal; otherwise, zero.

See Also CSize::operator =

Example

```
CSize size1(3,5), size2(5,6);
if (size1 != size2)
{
     // sizes not equal
}
else
..
```

OPERATOR +

■ 2.0 ■ 3.0

Description Adds a CSize object to another size, a point, or a rectangle. This operator adds the cx member of the CSize object to the specified size, point or rectangle horizontal coordinate and adds the cy member of the CSize object to the specified size, point, or rectangle vertical coordinate.

Syntax public, CSize operator +(SIZE size) const;
public, 4.0+, CPoint operator +(POINT point) const;
public, 4.0+, CRect operator +(const RECT* lpRect) const;

Parameters

size The size that should be added to this CSize object to determine the resultant size. You may pass a CSize object or a SIZE structure for this parameter.

point The point that should be added to this CSize object to determine the resultant point. You may pass a CPoint object or a POINT structure for this parameter.

lpRect The rectangle that should be added to this CSize object to determine the resultant rectangle. You may pass a CRect object or a pointer to a RECT structure for this parameter.

Returns A CSize, CPoint, or CRect object offset by this CSize object.

See Also CSize::operator +=, CSize::operator -, CRect::operator +, CPoint::operator +

Example

```
CSize size1(3,5), size2(5,6);
CPoint pt(10,12);
CRect rect(1,1,20,25);

CSize totalSize = size1 + size2; // totalSize = 8,11
CPoint newPoint = size1 + pt; // newPoint = 13,17
CRect newRect = size1 + rect; // newRect = 4,6,23,30
```

OPERATOR +=

■ 2.0 ■ 3.0

Description Adds a specified size to the CSize object.

Syntax public, void operator +=(SIZE size);

Parameters

size The size to add to the CSize object. This parameter may be a SIZE structure or a CSize object.

Returns Nothing is returned.

See Also CSize::operator +, CSize::operator -=

Example

```
CSize size1(3,5), size2(5,6);
size1 += size2; // size1 = 8,11
```

OPERATOR -

■ 2.0 ■ 3.0

Description Negates a size object or subtracts one size from another and returns the result as a CSize object or subtracts a size from a point and returns the result as a CPoint object or subtracts a size from a rectangle and returns the result as a CRect object. Note that the final two versions of this function were introduced with MFC Version 4.0.

Syntax
public, CSize operator -() const;
public, CSize operator -(SIZE size) const;
public, CPoint operator -(POINT point) const;
public, CRect operator -(LPRECT lpRect) const;

Parameters

size The size to subtract from the CSize object. This parameter may be a SIZE structure or a CSize object

point The point from which this CSize object should be subtracted. You may pass a CPoint object or a POINT structure for this parameter.

lpRect The rectangle from which this CSize object should be subtracted. You may pass a CRect object or a pointer to a RECT structure for this parameter.

Returns A CSize, CPoint, or CRect object offset by this CSize object.

See Also CSize::operator -=, CSize::operator +, CPoint::operator -, CRect::operator -

Example

```
CSize size1(3,5), size2(5,6);
CSize diffSize = size2 Ñ size1; // diffsize = 2,1
```

OPERATOR -=

■ 2.0 ■ 3.0

Description Subtracts a specified size from the CSize object and assigns the result to this object.

Syntax public, void operator -=(SIZE size);

Parameters

size The size to subtract from the CSize object. This parameter may be a SIZE structure or a CSize object.

Returns Nothing is returned.

See Also CSize::operator -, CSize::operator +=

Example

```
CSize size1(3,5), size2(5,6);
size2 -= size1; // size2 = 2,1
```

OPERATOR ==

■ 2.0 ■ 3.0

Description Determines whether two sizes are equal.

Syntax public, BOOL operator ==(SIZE size) const;

Parameters

size A size to compare to the CSize object. This parameter can be a SIZE structure or a CSize object.

Returns Non-zero if the sizes are equal; otherwise, zero.

See Also CSize::operator !=

Example

```
CSize size1(3,5), size2(3,5);
if (size1 == size2)
{
     // sizes are equal
}
else
..
```

The CGdiObject Class

The CGdiObject class serves as the parent class for all of the MFC GDI classes that are discussed later in this chapter. You should never create a CGdiObject class directly. It exists simply to provide several functions that are applicable across all of the GDI objects. Interestingly, the developers of MFC also place a couple of functions in the CGdiObject class that are not applicable to all of its children but rather only some of them—a decision many would disagree with, but nevertheless, the way it is. Because the developer should never use the CGdiObject class directly, all examples given for this class will use the CBrush object, which is derived from CGdiObject.

CGDIOBJECT

■ 2.0 ■ 3.0

Description The constructor for the CGdiObject class. The constructor does nothing of any real interest.

Syntax public, CGdiObject();

Parameters None.

Returns Nothing is returned.

See Also ~CGdiObject

Example See CGdiObject::AssertValid

~CGDIOBJECT

■ 2.0 ■ 3.0 ■ UD

Description The destructor for the CGdiObject class. If the CGdiObject object still has a drawing object attached to it, it is detached and deleted.

Syntax public, ~CGdiObject( );

Parameters None.

Returns Nothing is returned.

See Also CGdiObject()

AssertValid

■ 2.0 ■ 3.0 ■ DO

Description Determines whether the CGdiObject is in a valid state and if it is not, throws an assertion. The CGdiObject implementation calls the base CObject version and then performs the following check: If the associated Windows GDI object handle is non-NULL and the operating system on which the program is running is not Win32s, then it checks to make sure the handle represents a valid object by calling the SDK function ::GetObjectType. MFC does not perform this check on Win32s because the ::GetObjectType function is not supported on that platform.

Syntax public, virtual void AssertValid( ) const;

Parameters None.

Returns Nothing is returned.

See Also CObject::AssertValid

Example

```
void SomeDrawFunc(CDC *pDc, CBrush *pBrush)
{
      CRect rect(5,5,10,10);
      pBrush->AssertValid(); // check to make sure brush is valid
      before using it
      pDc->FillRect(rect,pBrush);
      ..
}
```

Attach

■ 2.0 ■ 3.0

Description Associates the CGdiObject with a specified Windows GDI object. Once attached to a Windows GDI object, the CGdiObject can be used to manipulate the object to which it is attached. This function is useful if you are given a Windows GDI object handle and would like to manipulate it in an object-oriented fashion. If you create a GDI object directly using one of CGdiObject's child classes, you will not need to use this function.

Syntax public, BOOL Attach(HGDIOBJ hObject);

Parameters

hObject A handle to a Windows GDI object, such as an HPEN, HBRUSH, HBITMAP, HFONT, HPALETTE, or HRGN.

Returns None-zero if the function is successful; otherwise, zero.

See Also CGdiObject::Detach

Example

```
void CMyWnd::SomeDrawFunc(HBRUSH hBrush)
{
```

```
        CBrush brush;
        CClientDC dc(this);
        CRect rect(5,5,10,10);
        brush.Attach(hBrush);
        dc.FillRect(rect,&brush); // use newly attached brush object
        brush.Detach();           // detach object from HBRUSH - could
                                  // just let destructor do it if you wanted to
        ..
}
```

CreateStockObject

■ 2.0 ■ 3.0

Description Associates the CGdiObject with a specified Windows stock GDI object. Windows provides many commonly used pens, brushes, and fonts as "stock" objects. If you need an object that is contained in Windows' list of stock objects, it is always more efficient to use the Windows stock object instead of creating a new object. This function is an example of how MFC will let you get yourself into trouble on occasion. Because you never use the CGdiObject directly, you will be calling this function from a derived class; for example, the CPen. It is up to you to make sure you never try to call this function with a stock brush request from the CPen object. Note that it is not necessary to destroy (using DeleteObject) an object created using this function but you can if you want to (which allows you to destroy a CGdiObject in all cases, without worrying about whether it is a stock object or not).

Syntax public, BOOL CreateStockObject(int nIndex);

Parameters

nIndex One of the stock object constants defined by Windows and listed below:

BLACK_BRUSH Black brush.

DKGRAY_BRUSH Dark gray brush.

GRAY_BRUSH Gray brush.

HOLLOW_BRUSH Hollow brush (same as NULL_BRUSH).

LTGRAY_BRUSH Light gray brush.

NULL_BRUSH Null brush (same as HOLLOW_BRUSH).

WHITE_BRUSH White brush.

BLACK_PEN Black pen.

NULL_PEN Null pen.

WHITE_PEN White pen.

ANSI_FIXED_FONT ANSI fixed-pitch system font.

ANSI_VAR_FONT ANSI variable-pitch system font.

DEVICE_DEFAULT_FONT Device-dependent font (NT only).

DEVICE_GUI_FONT Default font for user interface objects such as menus and dialog boxes. (Windows 95 only).

OEM_FIXED_FONT OEM-dependent fixed-pitch font.

SYSTEM_FONT The system font used by default, to draw menus, dialog-box controls, and other text. In Windows versions 3.0 and later, the system font is proportional width; earlier versions of Windows use a fixed-width system font.

SYSTEM_FIXED_FONT The fixed-pitch system font used in Windows prior to version 3.0. This object is available for compatibility with earlier versions of Windows.

DEFAULT_PALETTE Default color palette that consists of the 20 static colors in the system palette.

Returns Non-zero if the function is successful; otherwise, zero.

See Also ::GetStockObject

Example

```
void CMyWnd::DrawWhiteRectangle(CDC *pDc)
{
      CRectangle rect(1,1,10,10);
      CBrush brush, *pOldBrush;
      brush.CreateStockObject(WHITE_BRUSH);
      pOldBrush = pDc->SelectObject(&brush);
      pDc->Rectangle(rect);
      pDc->SelectObject(pOldBrush);
}
```

DeleteObject

■ 2.0 ■ 3.0

Description Destroys the Windows GDI object currently associated with the CGdiObject. The CGdiObject itself is not destroyed. You should not destroy a GDI object that is currently selected into a device context. Select the object out of the device context before calling DeleteObject.

Syntax public, BOOL DeleteObject( );

Parameters None.

Returns Non-zero if the object is deleted; zero if an error occurs.

See Also CGdiObject::Detach

Example

```
void CMyWnd::DrawRectangles(CDC *pDc)
{
      CRectangle rect(1,1,10,10);
      CBrush brush, *pOldBrush;

      // draw a red rectangle
      brush.CreateSolidBrush(RGB(255,0,0));
      pOldBrush = pDc->SelectObject(&brush);
      pDc->Rectangle(rect);
      pDc->SelectObject(pOldBrush);   // select object out of dc and
                                      // delete the object
      brush.DeleteObject();           // so we can re-use the CBrush
                                      // for another rect

      // draw blue rectangle
      brush.CreateSolidBrush(RGB(0,0,255));
      pOldBrush = pDc->SelectObject(&brush);
      pDc->Rectangle(rect);
      pDc->SelectObject(pOldBrush);
}
```

DeleteTempMap

■ 2.0 ■ 3.0

Description Deletes any temporary CGdiObjects created using the CGdiObject::FromHandle function. MFC automatically calls this function as part of its idle-time processing (in the CWinApp idle handler). The Windows GDI objects associated with the temporary CGdiObjects are detached from the CGdiObjects before the CGdiObjects are deleted. The Windows GDI objects are not destroyed. This function is an MFC utility function that you would rarely want to call yourself.

Syntax public, static void PASCAL DeleteTempMap( );

Parameters None.

Returns Nothing is returned.

See Also CGdiObject::Detach, CGdiObject::FromHandle, CWinApp::OnIdle

Detach

■ 2.0 ■ 3.0

Description Detaches the currently associated Windows GDI object from the CGdiObject.

Syntax public, HGDIOBJ Detach( );

Parameters None.

Returns If the function is successful, it returns a handle to the Window GDI object that was detached. If no GDI object was attached to the CGdiObject, NULL is returned.

See Also CGdiObject::Attach

Example See CGdiObject::Attach

Dump

■ 2.0 ■ 3.0 ■ DO

Description Outputs diagnostic information about the current state of the CGdiObject. For the CGdiObject this information is simply the handle of the Windows GDI object currently attached to it.

Syntax public, virtual void Dump(CDumpContext& dc) const;

Parameters

dc A reference to the dump context to which the status information should be sent. Usually this will be the MFC default debug dump context *afxDump*. *afxDump* sends its output to the debugger and only exists in the debug build of MFC.

Returns Nothing is returned.

See Also CObject::Dump

Example

```
// call to dump function
CGdiObject tempGdiObj;
tempGdiObj.Dump(afxDump);

// output from dump function
a CGdiObject at $64F818
m_hObject = 0x0
```

FromHandle

■ 2.0 ■ 3.0

Description Returns a pointer to a CGdiObject given a Windows GDI object handle. If MFC does not already have a permanent CGdiObject associated with the specified handle, it creates a temporary one and attaches it to the handle. Temporary CGdiObjects are automatically destroyed during idle-time processing so you can only depend on the validity of the CGdiObject returned by FromHandle until your application enters its idle loop, which can occur any time you return control to Windows (i.e., returning from a message map).

Syntax public, static CGdiObject* PASCAL FromHandle(HGDIOBJ hObject);

Parameters

hObject A handle to the Windows GDI object for which a CGdiObject should be returned.

Returns A pointer to a CGdiObject, which may be temporary.

See Also CGdiObject::DeleteTempMap

Example

```
void CMyWnd::SomeDrawFunc(HBRUSH hBrush)
{
      // get possibly temporary brush
      CBrush *pTempBrush = CBrush::FromHandle(hBrush);
      CClientDC dc(this);
      CRect rect(1,1,50,50);
      dc.FillRect(rect,pTempBrush);
}
```

GetObject

■ 2.0 ■ 3.0

Description Retrieves information about the Windows GDI object currently attached to the CGdiObject. Unfortunately, MFC does not provide type-safe versions of this function for each of the CGdiObject child classes, so you must ensure that you pass the correct parameters depending on the type of object. The object types and their respective buffer structures are listed below in the parameters section. Although this function still exists in MFC 4.0, Microsoft added a specific function for each type of object (e.g., GetBitmap and GetBrush). These more specific functions are type-safe and are therefore preferable to the GetObject function itself.

Syntax public, int GetObject(int nCount, LPVOID lpObject) const;

Parameters

nCount The maximum number of bytes to copy to the specified buffer. Typically, this would be the sizeof() whatever object is pointed to by the buffer parameter.

lpObject A pointer to the buffer into which the object information will be placed. The table below shows the type of buffer you should specify for each of the GDI object classes.

CPen LOGPEN for normal pens, EXTLOGPEN for extended pens.

CBrush LOGBRUSH.

CFont LOGFONT.

CBitmap BITMAP.

CPalette WORD specifying the number of entries in the logical palette. To retrieve the actual palette entries, use CPalette::GetPaletteEntries.

CRgn Not supported.

Returns If successful, the number of bytes copied to the buffer; otherwise, zero.

See Also ::GetObject

Example

```
void CMyWnd::GetObjectInformation(CBrush *pBrush)
{
      LOGBRUSH logBrush;
      // fills logBrush with info about pBrush - our brush
      // see CBrush::CBrush for a description of the LOGBRUSH structure
      // which is retrieved
      pBrush->GetObject(sizeof(LOGBRUSH),&logBrush);

}
```

GetObjectType

–. ■ 4.0

Description Retrieves the type of object currently attached to the CGdiObject.

Syntax public, int GetObjectType() const;

Parameters None.

Returns If successful, the type of object attached to the CGdiObject. Can be one of the following values:

OBJ_BITMAP Bitmap.

OBJ_BRUSH Brush.

OBJ_FONT Font.

OBJ_PAL Palette.

OBJ_PEN Pen.

OBJ_EXTPEN Extended pen.

OBJ_REGION Region.

OBJ_DC	Device context.
OBJ_MEMDC	Memory device context.
OBJ_METAFILE	Metafile.
OBJ_METADC	Metafile device context.
OBJ_ENHMETAFILE	Enhanced metafile.
OBJ_ENHMETADC	Enhanced metafile device context.

See Also CGdiObject::GetObject

GetSafeHandle ■ 2.0 ■ 3.0

Description Returns the Windows GDI object handle currently attached to the CGdiObject. This function is called "safe" because it will work even if called with a NULL CGdiObject pointer. See the example below for an example of this. This is done in order to allow NULL as a valid value that requires no special handling. This is similar to the C++ language specification that allows a pointer passed to the delete operator to be NULL.

Syntax public, HGDIOBJ GetSafeHandle( ) const;

Parameters None.

Returns The Windows GDI object handle currently attached to the CGdiObject.

Example

```
HBRUSH hBrush;
CBrush brush, *pBrush = NULL;
brush.CreateSolidBrush(RGB(100,100,100));
hBrush = (HBRUSH)brush.GetSafeHandle();
// use hbrush for something
hBrush = (HBRUSH)pBrush->GetSafeHandle();
// set hBrush to NULL instead of bombing
```

operator HGDIOBJ –. ■ 4.0

Description Cast operator that converts the CGdiObject object to a HGIDOBJ (GDI object handle). This operator allows you to pass a CGdiObject object wherever an HGDIOBJ is required—such as for an SDK function involving GDI objects.

Syntax public, operator HGDIOBJ() const;

Parameters None.

Returns The HGDIOBJ associated with the CGdiObject object.

UnrealizeObject ■ 2.0 ■ 3.0

Description Resets the origin of a CBrush object or resets a CPalette object. Unfortunately, MFC provides this function at the CGdiObject level instead of the CBrush and CPalette levels so you must make sure that you use it only for CGdiObjects that are actually brushes or palettes. Unrealizing a brush means that Windows will reset its origin the next time the brush is selected into a device context. Unrealizing a palette means that Windows will treat the palette as if it had never been realized using the RealizePalette function. This, in turn, means that Windows will fully remap the palette the next time RealizePalette is called for the palette. There are several do's and don'ts, listed below, regarding this function:

1. Do not call UnrealizeObject for anything other than a CBrush or a CPalette.
2. Do not call UnrealizeObject for a Windows stock object.
3. Do not call UnrealizeObject for any object currently selected into a device context.
4. You must call UnrealizeObject whenever you call CDC::SetBrushOrigin.

Syntax public, BOOL UnrealizeObject( );

Parameters None.

Returns Non-zero if the function is successful; otherwise zero.

See Also CDC::SetBrushOrg, CDC::RealizePalette

Example

```
void CMyWnd::SomeDrawFunc(CDC *pDc)
{
      CBrush brush;
      CBitmap bmp;

      bmp.LoadBitmap(IDB_SOMEBITMAP);
      brush.CreatePatternBrush(&bmp);
      pDc->SetBrushOrg(3,3);
      brush.UnrealizeObject();
      pOldBrush = pDc->SelectObject(&brush);
      .. // draw something
}
```

The CPen Class

The CPen class is MFC's encapsulation of the Windows GDI pen object, represented by an HPEN. The CPen object provides very little in the way of functionality. It simply encapsulates the creation of pens.

CPen

■ 2.0 ■ 3.0

Description The constructor for the CPen class. The first version of the constructor does nothing. If you construct a CPen in this way, you must later attach the CPen object to a pen or call one of the create functions to create the pen. The second version of the constructor creates one of the standard pen types and is available in all versions of MFC. The last version of the constructor creates an extended pen and is not available in 16-bit MFC or the Macintosh version. The final two versions of the constructor will throw an exception (of type CResourceException) if the pen cannot be created. If you use either of these two, make sure you handle the exception. If you do not want to deal with exceptions, use the first version of the constructor and then use one of the create functions to actually create the pen object. For more information about pen styles and types, see the descriptions for the CPen create functions below.

Syntax

public, CPen( );
public, CPen(int nPenStyle, int nWidth, COLORREF crColor) throw(CResourceException);
public, CPen(int nPenStyle, int nWidth, const LOGBRUSH* pLogBrush, int nStyleCount = 0, const DWORD* lpStyle = NULL) throw(CResourceException);

Parameters

nPenStyle For the standard pen constructor, any of the following values:

PS_SOLID Solid pen.

PS_DASH Dashed pen. Valid only when the pen width is one.

PS_DOT Dotted pen. Valid only when the pen width is one.

PS_DASHDOT Alternating dashes and dots. Valid only when the pen width is one.

PS_DASHDOTDOT Alternating dashes and double dots. Valid only when the pen width is one.

PS_NULL Null pen.

PS_INSIDEFRAME For objects that involve a frame, or bounding rectangle (e.g., Rectangle, Ellipse, Pie), this creates a pen that draws inside the frame. This means that even if you choose a thick pen (for example, five pixels wide), the entire stroke of the pen will be inside the defined frame. Normally, the pen's width would be centered on the frame.

PS_ALTERNATE Pen that sets every other pixel. This style is only valid for the extended version of the constructor and is only applicable to cosmetic pens (those with a style of PS_COSMETIC).

PS_USERSTYLE Pen that uses a styling array supplied by the user. This style is valid only for the extended version of the constructor. For the extended version of the CPen constructor, this parameter actually specifies a combination of type, style, end cap, and join attributes. This parameter should be a bitwise OR'ing of these values. The style values are those given above. The type can be either PS_GEOMETRIC or PS_COSMETIC. A geometric pen can be of any thickness and can have any of the styles of a logical brush. A cosmetic pen is always one solid color and one pixel wide. Cosmetic pens are generally faster than geometric pens. The end cap can be one of three values: PS_ENDCAP_ROUND for round end caps, PS_ENDCAP_SQUARE for square end caps, and PS_ENDCAP_FLAT for end caps that are flat. Finally, the join attribute can be one of three values: PS_JOIN_BEVEL for beveled joins, PS_JOIN_ROUND for round joins, or PS_JOIN_MITER for joins that are mitered when they are within the current miter limit set by the ::SetMiterLimit function. If the PS_JOIN_MITER attribute is specified and a join is not within the current miter limit, the join is beveled instead.

nWidth The thickness of the pen. For the standard pen version of the constructor this value is in logical units; however, if it is zero, then the pen's width is one pixel, regardless of mapping mode. For the extended version of the constructor, if the pen style is PS_GEOMETRIC, this value is in logical units. If the pen style is PS_COSMETIC, this value should always be set to one.

crColor The RGB color value for the pen.

pLogBrush A pointer to a LOGBRUSH structure. If the pen style is PS_COSMETIC, then only the lbColor member of the structure is used. The lbStyle member should be set to BS_SOLID. If the pen style is PS_GEOMETRIC, all members of the LOGBRUSH structure are used to create the pen.

nStyleCount If the pen style is PS_USERSTYLE, this parameter specifies the number of styles pointed to by the lpStyle parameter. If the pen style is not PS_USERSTYLE, this parameter should be set to zero.

lpStyle If the pen style is PS_USERSTYLE, this parameter points to an array of doubleword values specifying the lengths of the dashes and spaces in the pen. The first value specifies the length of the first dash in a user-defined style, the second value specifies the length of the first space, and so on. If the pen style is not PS_USERSTYLE, this parameter should be set to NULL.

Returns Nothing is returned.

See Also CPen::~CPen, CPen::CreatePen, CPen::CreatePenIndirect

Example

```
CClientDC dc(pWnd);
CPen solidPen(PS_SOLID,1,RGB(255,0,0));

LOGBRUSH logBrush;
logBrush.lbStyle = BS_HATCHED;
logBrush.lbColor = RGB(0,0,200);
logBrush.lbHatch = HS_CROSS;
CPen extPen(PS_GEOMETRIC,5,&logBrush);

CPen *pOldPen = dc.SelectObject(&solidPen);
dc.Rectangle(1,1,100,100);

dc.SelectObject(&extPen);
dc.Rectangle(50,50,200,225);

dc.SelectObject(pOldPen);
```

~CPEN

■ 2.0 ■ 3.0 ■ UD

Description Destructor for the CPen class.

Syntax public, virtual ~CPen();

Parameters None.

Returns Nothing is returned.

See Also CPen::CPen

CREATEPEN

■ 2.0 ■ 3.0

Description The first version of CreatePen creates one of the standard pen types and is available in all versions of MFC. The second version of CreatePen creates an extended pen and is not available in 16-bit MFC or the Macintosh version.

Syntax public, BOOL CreatePen(int nPenStyle, int nWidth, COLORREF crColor); public, BOOL CreatePen(int nPenStyle, int nWidth, const LOGBRUSH* pLogBrush, int nStyleCount = 0, const DWORD* lpStyle = NULL);

Parameters

nPenStyle For creating a standard pen, any of the following values:

PS_SOLID Solid pen.

PS_DASH Dashed pen. Valid only when the pen width is one.

PS_DOT Dotted pen. Valid only when the pen width is one.

PS_DASHDOT Alternating dashes and dots. Valid only when the pen width is one.

PS_DASHDOTDOT Alternating dashes and double dots. Valid only when the pen width is one.

PS_NULL Null pen.

PS_INSIDEFRAME For objects that involve a frame, or bounding rectangle (e.g., Rectangle, Ellipse, Pie), this creates a pen which draws inside the frame. This means that even if you choose a thick pen (for example, five pixels wide), the entire stroke of the pen will be inside the defined frame. Normally, the pen's width would be centered on the frame.

PS_ALTERNATE Pen that sets every other pixel. This style is only valid for extended pens and is only applicable to cosmetic pens (those with a style of PS_COSMETIC).

PS_USERSTYLE Pen that uses a styling array supplied by the user. This style is valid only for extended pens. For creating an extended pen, this parameter actually specified a combination of type, style, end cap, and join attributes. This parameter should be a bitwise OR'ing of these values. The style values are those given above. The type can be either PS_GEOMETRIC or PS_COSMETIC. The end cap can be one of three values: PS_ENDCAP_ROUND for round end caps, PS_ENDCAP_SQUARE for square end caps, and PS_ENDCAP_FLAT for end caps that are flat. Finally, the join attribute can be one of three values: PS_JOIN_BEVEL for beveled joins, PS_JOIN_ROUND for round joins, or PS_JOIN_MITER for joins that are mitered when they are within the current miter limit set by the ::SetMiterLimit function. If the PS_JOIN_MITER attribute is specified and a join is not within the current miter limit, the join is beveled instead.

nWidth The thickness of the pen. For standard pens, this value is in logical units; however, if it is zero, then the pen's width is one pixel, regardless of mapping mode. For extended pens, if the pen style is PS_GEOMETRIC, this value is in logical units. If the pen style is PS_COSMETIC, this value should always be set to one.

crColor The RGB color value for the pen.

pLogBrush A pointer to a LOGBRUSH structure. If the pen style is PS_COSMETIC, then only the lbColor member of the structure is used. The lbStyle member should be set to BS_SOLID. If the pen style is PS_GEOMETRIC, all members of the LOGBRUSH structure are used to create the pen.

nStyleCount If the pen style is PS_USERSTYLE, this parameter specifies the number of styles pointed to by the lpStyle parameter. If the pen style is not PS_USERSTYLE, this parameter should be set to zero.

lpStyle If the pen style is PS_USERSTYLE, this parameter points to an array of doubleword values specifying the lengths of the dashes and spaces in the pen. The first value specifies the length of the first dash in a user-defined style, the second value specifies the length of the first space, and so on. If the pen style is not PS_USERSTYLE, this parameter should be set to NULL.

Returns Non-zero if the pen is successfuly created; otherwise, zero.

See Also CPen::CPen, CPen:CreatePenIndirect, ::CreatePen, ::ExtCreatePen

Example

```
CClientDC dc(pWnd);
CPen solidPen, extPen, *pOldPen;

solidPen.CreatePen(PS_SOLID,1,RGB(255,0,0));

LOGBRUSH logBrush;
logBrush.lbStyle = BS_HATCHED;
logBrush.lbColor = RGB(0,0,200);
logBrush.lbHatch = HS_CROSS;
extPen.CreatePen(PS_GEOMETRIC,5,&logBrush);

pOldPen = dc.SelectObject(&solidPen);
dc.Rectangle(1,1,100,100);

dc.SelectObject(&extPen);
dc.Rectangle(50,50,200,225);

dc.SelectObject(pOldPen);
```

CreatePenIndirect ■ 2.0 ■ 3.0

Description Creates a pen from the specifications provided in the specified LOGPEN structure. You cannot create a pen with an extended style using this method. Use CreatePen to create a pen with an extended style.

Syntax public, BOOL CreatePenIndirect(LPLOGPEN lpLogPen);

Parameters

lpLogPen A pointer to a LOGPEN structure. The members of the LOGPEN structure are described below:

lopnStyle – Specifies the style of the pen. Can be one of the following values:

PS_SOLID	Solid pen.
PS_DASH	Dashed pen.
PS_DOT	Dotted pen.
PS_DASHDOT	Pen with alternating dashes and dots.
PS_DASHDOTDOT	Pen with alternating dashes and double dots.
PS_NULL	Invisible pen.
PS_INSIDEFRAME	Solid pen that, when used with a GDI function involving a bounding rectangle (e.g., Rectangle, Ellipse, etc.), always stays within the bounding rectangle. This effectively means that the dimensions of the object being drawn are reduced so that it always fits within the bounding rectangle, regardless of the thickness of the pen.

lopnWidth – A POINT structure that specifies the width of the pen. The width should be specified in the x member of the POINT structure. The y member is not used. If the width value is zero, a width of one pixel is used regardless of the current device context mapping mode.

lopnColor – Specifies the color of the pen. This value should be created using the RGB macro.

Returns Non-zero if the function is successful; otherwise, zero.

See Also CPen::CPen, CPen::CreatePen, ::CreatePenIndirect

Example

```
CClientDC dc(pWnd);
CPen pen, *pOldPen;
LOGPEN logPen;

logPen.lopnStyle = PS_DASHDOT;
logPen.lopnWidth = 3;
logPen.lopnColor = RGB(20,20,20);
pen.CreatePenIndirect(&logPen);

pOldPen = dc.SelectObject(&pen);
dc.Rectangle(1,1,100,100);

dc.SelectObject(pOldPen);
```

DUMP

■ 2.0 ■ 3.0 ■ DO

Description
Outputs diagnostic information about the current state of the CPen object. For the CPen class this information includes the handle of the Windows GDI pen currently attached to it, and the style, thickness, and color of the pen.

Syntax
public, virtual void Dump(CDumpContext& dc) const;

Parameters

dc
A reference to the dump context to which the status information should be sent. Usually this will be the MFC default debug dump context *afxDump*. *afxDump* sends its output to the debugger and only exists in the debug build of MFC.

Returns
Nothing is returned.

See Also
CGdiObject::Dump

Example

```
// call to dump function
CPen pen;
pen.Dump(afxDump);

// output from dump function
a CPen at $64F910
m_hObject = 0x1142
lgpn.lopnStyle = 0x0
lgpn.lopnWidth.x (width) = 1
lgpn.lopnColor = $FF
```

FROMHANDLE

■ 2.0 ■ 3.0

Description
Returns a pointer to a CPen given a Windows GDI pen handle. If MFC does not already have a permanent CPen associated with the specified handle, it creates a temporary one and attaches it to the handle. Temporary CPens are automatically destroyed during idle-time processing so you can only depend on the validity of the CPen returned by FromHandle until your application enters its idle loop, which can occur any time you return control to Windows (i.e., returning from a message map).

Syntax
public, static CPen* PASCAL FromHandle(HPEN hPen);

Parameters

hPen
A handle to the Windows GDI pen for which a CPen should be returned.

Returns
A pointer to a CPen, which may be temporary.

See Also
CGdiObject::FromHandle, CGdiObject::DeleteTempMap

Example

```
void CMyWnd::SomeDrawFunc(HPEN hPen)
{
      // get possibly temporary pen
      CPen *pTempPen = CPen::FromHandle(hPen);
      CClientDC dc(this);
      CPen *pOldPen = dc.SelectObject(pTempPen);
      dc.Rectangle(10,10,50,50);
      dc.SelectObject(pOldPen);
      // don't need to delete the pointer returned by FromHandle
}
```

GetExtLogPen

–. ■ 4.0 ■ NM

Description Fills an EXTLOGPEN SDK structure with information regarding the extended pen associated with the CPen object. Extended pens are those created using the third form of the constructor or the second form of CPen::CreatePen. In versions of MFC before 4.0, use the CGdiObject::GetObject function to perform this task.

Syntax public, int GetExtLogPen(EXTLOGPEN* pLogPen);

Parameters A pointer to a EXTLOGPEN structure that will be filled with information about the pen. For more information about the EXTLOGPEN structure, see the Windows SDK documentation.

Returns Non-zero if successful; otherwise, zero.

See Also CGdiObject::GetObject

Example

```
...
CClientDC dc(pWnd);
CPen extPen;

// create an extended pen
LOGBRUSH logBrush;
logBrush.lbStyle = BS_HATCHED;
logBrush.lbColor = RGB(0,0,200);
logBrush.lbHatch = HS_CROSS;
extPen.CreatePen(PS_GEOMETRIC,5,&logBrush);

// get info about pen
EXTLOGPEN extLogPen;
pen.GetExtLogPen(&extLogPen);
```

GetLogPen

–. ■ 4.0

Description Fills a LOGPEN SDK structure with information regarding the pen associated with the CPen object. In versions of MFC before 4.0, use the CGdiObject::GetObject function to perform this task.

Syntax public, int GetLogPen(LOGPEN* pLogPen);

Parameters A pointer to a LOGPEN structure that will be filled with information about the pen. For a description of this structure see the CPen::CreatePenIndirect function.

Returns Non-zero if successful; otherwise, zero.

See Also CGdiObject::GetObject

Example

```
...
CClientDC dc(pWnd);
CPen pen(PS_SOLID,2,RGB(100,120,100));

// get info about pen
LOGPEN logPen;
pen.GetLogPen(&logPen);
```

OPERATOR HPEN

–. ■ 4.0

Description Cast operator that converts the CPen object to an HPEN (pen handle). This operator allows you to pass a CPen object wherever an HPEN is required—such as for an SDK function involving pens.

Syntax public, operator HPEN() const;

Parameters None.

Returns The HPEN associated with the CPen object.

Example

```
...
CClientDC dc(pWnd);
CPen pen(PS_SOLID,2,RGB(100,120,100));

// use SDK function for some unknown reason
::SelectObject(dc,pen);
```

The CBrush Class

The CBrush class is MFC's encapsulation of the Windows GDI brush object, represented by an HBRUSH. The CBrush object provides very little in the way of functionality. It simply encapsulates the creation of brushes.

CBRUSH

■ 2.0 ■ 3.0

Description The constructor for the CBrush class. The first version of the constructor does nothing. If you use this version, you must use one of the CBrush creation functions or attach a brush to the CBrush object before using it. The second version of the constructor creates a solid brush in the same fashion as the CBrush::CreateSolidBrush function. The third version of the constructor creates a hatched brush of the specified style and color in the same manner as CBrush::CreateHatchBrush. The final version of the constructor creates a pattern brush using the specified bitmap in the same manner as CBrush::CreatePatternBrush. All of the constructors except the first version may throw a resource exception if any part of the brush creation process fails. If you do not want to handle exceptions, use the first version of the constructor and create the brush with one of the CBrush creation functions.

Syntax

```
public, CBrush( );
public, CBrush( COLORREF crColor ) throw( CResourceException );
public, CBrush( int nIndex, COLORREF crColor ) throw(
CResourceException );
public, CBrush( CBitmap* pBitmap ) throw( CResourceException );
```

Parameters

crColor	An RGB color value created using the RGB macro. The brush will be created using this color.
nIndex	A hatch style value. This parameter can be any of the following values:
HS_BDIAGONAL	Downward hatch (left to right) at 45 degrees.
HS_CROSS	Horizontal and vertical crosshatch.
HS_DIAGCROSS	Crosshatch at 45 degrees.
HS_FDIAGONAL	Upward hatch (left to right) at 45 degrees.
HS_HORIZONTAL	Horizontal hatch.
HS_VERTICAL	Vertical hatch.
pBitmap	A pointer to a CBitmap object representing the pattern bitmap to use for the brush. This bitmap must be at least 8 pixels by 8 pixels. It can be larger, but in Windows 95 only the upper-left 8x8 block will be used. This bitmap can not be a DIB section (created using ::CreateDIBSection). If the specified bitmap is a monochrome bitmap, the bits that are on (1) will use the current background color and bits that are off (0) will use the current text color.

Returns Nothing is returned.

See Also CBrush::CBrush, CBrush::CreateSolidBrush, CBrush::CreateHatchBrush, CBrush::CreatePatternBrush

~CBrush ■ 2.0 ■ 3.0 ■ UD

Description Destructor for the CBrush class.

Syntax public, virtual ~CBrush();

Parameters None.

Returns Nothing is returned.

See Also CBrush::CBrush

CreateBrushIndirect ■ 2.0 ■ 3.0

Description Creates a brush from the specifications provided in the specified LOGBRUSH structure.

Syntax public, BOOL CreateBrushIndirect(LPLOGBRUSH lpLogBrush);

Parameters

lpLogBrush	A pointer to a LOGBRUSH structure. The LOGBRUSH structure members should be initialized as specified below:

lbStyle – Specifies the style of the brush. Can be one of the following values:

BS_DIBPATTERN	Brush is a pattern brush with the pattern defined by a device-independent bitmap. The lbHatch LOGBRUSH member should contain a handle to a global memory block containing the packed device-independent bitmap specification.
BS_DIBPATTERN8X8	Same as BS_DIBPATTERN. This define is included as a reminder that in Windows 95, pattern bitmaps larger than 8x8 pixels are not supported. If you specify a bitmap larger than this, Windows 95 will only use the upper-left 8x8 pixels.
BS_DIBPATTERNPT	Brush is a pattern brush with the pattern defined by a device-independent bitmap. The lbHatch LOGBRUSH member should contain a pointer to a packed device-independent bitmap specification.
BS_HATCHED	Hatched brush.
BS_HOLLOW	Hollow brush.
BS_NULL	Same as BS_HOLLOW.
BS_PATTERN	Pattern brush defined by a device-dependent bitmap. The lbHatch LOGBRUSH member should contain an HBITMAP for the pattern bitmap.
BS_PATTERN8X8	Same as BS_PATTERN.
BS_SOLID	Solid brush.

lbColor – For BS_DIBPATTERN or BS_DIBPATTERNBT style brushes, the low-order word of lbColor specifies whether the bmiColors[] members of the BITMAPINFO structure defining the DIB contain explicit RGB values or indices into the current logical palette. If explicit values are used, this parameter should be DIB_RGB_COLORS. If indices are used, this member should be DIB_PAL_COLORS. If the style of the brush is BS_HOLLOW, BS_NULL, or BS_PATTERN, this member is ignored. For all other brush styles, this member contains the RGB color value for the brush.

lbHatch – If the style of the brush is BS_DIBPATTERN, this member should contain the global memory handle of a block of memory containing the DIB description. If the style of the brush is BS_DIBPATTERNPT, this member should contain a pointer to a DIB description. If the style of the brush is BS_PATTERN, lbHatch should contain a handle to the pattern bitmap. If the brush style is BS_HOLLOW, BS_NULL, or BS_SOLID, lbHatch is ignored. Finally, if the brush style is BS_HATCHED, this member is, as its name implies, a hatch style. Valid hatch styles are given below:

HS_BDIAGONAL	A 45-degree upward, left-to-right hatch.
HS_CROSS	Horizontal and vertical crosshatch.
HS_DIAGCROSS	45-degree crosshatch.

HS_FDIAGONAL	A 45-degree downward, left-to-right hatch.
HS_HORIZONTAL	Horizontal hatch.
HS_VERTICAL	Vertical hatch.

Returns Non-zero if the function is successful; otherwise, zero.

See Also CBrush::CBrush, CBrush::CreateSolidBrush, CBrush::CreateHatchBrush, CBrush::CreatePatternBrush, CBrush::CreateDIBPatternBrush

Example

```
CClientDC dc(pWnd);
CBrush brush;
LOGBRUSH logBrush;

logBrush.lbStyle = BS_HATCHED;
logBrush.lbColor = RGB(100,135,234);
logBrush.lbHatch = HS_VERTICAL;
brush.CreateBrushIndirect(&logBrush);

CRect rect(1,1,50,50);
dc.FillRect(rect,&brush);
```

CreateDIBPatternBrush ■ 3.0

Description Creates a pattern brush given a device-independent bitmap. Windows fills areas painted with the brush by repeatedly copying the pattern bitmap into the area painted by the brush.

Syntax public, BOOL CreateDIBPatternBrush(HGLOBAL hPackedDIB, UINT nUsage);
public, BOOL CreateDIBPatternBrush(const void* lpPackedDIB, UINT nUsage);

Parameters

hPackedDIB A handle to a global memory block containing a packed device-independent bitmap that is made up of a BITMAPINFO structure immediately followed by an array of bytes defining the pixels of the bitmap.

nUsage Determines whether the bmiColors[] fields of the BITMAPINFO data structure specified in the DIB contain explicit RGB values or indices into the current logical palette. This parameter should be DIB_RGB_COLORS if the values provided are RGB colors or DIB_PAL_COLORS if the values are indices into the current palette. For the second version of CreateDIBPatternBrush, you may also specify DIB_PAL_INDICES which indicates that no table is provided. In this case, the bitmap itself contains indices into the current logical palette. This final option is not allowed on Win32s.

lpPackedDIB A pointer to a block of memory containing a packed device-independent bitmap that is made up of a BITMAPINFO structure immediately followed by an array of bytes defining the pixels of the bitmap.

Returns Non-zero if the function is successful; otherwise, zero.

See Also CBrush::CBrush, CBrush::CreateSolidBrush, CBrush::CreateHatchBrush, CBrush::CreatePatternBrush, ::CreateDIBPatternBrush, ::CreateDIBPatternBrushPt

Example

```
..
CClientDC dc(pWnd);

brush.CreateDIBPatternBrush(hBitmap); // hBitmap handle to DIB

CRect rect(1,1,50,50);
dc.FillRect(rect,&brush);
```

CreateHatchBrush

■ 2.0 ■ 3.0

Description Creates a hatched brush with the specified hatch style and color and attaches it to the CBrush object.

Syntax public, BOOL CreateHatchBrush(int nIndex, COLORREF crColor);

Parameters

nIndex A hatch style. See CBrush::CreateBrushIndirect for a list of valid styles.

crColor An RGB color value. You can create this value using the RGB macro.

Returns Non-zero if the function is successful; otherwise, zero.

See Also CBrush::CBrush, CBrush::CreateSolidBrush, CBrush::CreateDIBPatternBrush, CBrush::CreatePatternBrush, ::CreateHatchBrush

Example

```
CClientDC dc(pWnd);
CBrush brush;

brush.CreateHatchBrush(HS_VERTICAL,RGB(100,50,75);

CRect rect(1,1,50,50);
dc.FillRect(rect,&brush);
```

CreatePatternBrush

■ 2.0 ■ 3.0

Description Creates a pattern brush based on the specified pattern bitmap and attaches it to the CBrush object. Note that the pattern brush simply uses the specified bitmap—it does not take ownership of it. You can create several pattern brushes from the same bitmap and destroying the brushes will not affect the bitmap.

Syntax public, BOOL CreatePatternBrush(CBitmap* pBitmap);

Parameters

pBitmap A pointer to a device-dependent pattern bitmap. Pattern bitmaps should be 8x8 pixels. You can specify a larger bitmap, but Windows 95 and Windows 3.x will only use the upper-left 8x8 pixels. If the specified bitmap is a monochrome bitmap, pixels set to one will be drawn using the current background color and pixels set to zero will be drawn using the current text color.

Returns Non-zero if the function is successful; otherwise, zero.

See Also CBrush::CBrush, CBrush::CreateSolidBrush, CBrush::CreateDIBPatternBrush, CBrush::CreateHatchBrush, ::CreatePatternBrush

Example

```
CClientDC dc(pWnd);
CBitmap bmp;
CBrush brush;

bmp.LoadBitmap(IDB_PATTERNBMP);
brush.CreatePatternBrush(&bmp);

CRect rect(1,1,50,50);
dc.FillRect(rect,&brush);
```

CreateSolidBrush ■ 2.0 ■ 3.0

Description Creates a brush using the specified solid color and attaches it to the CBrush object.

Syntax public, BOOL CreateSolidBrush(COLORREF crColor);

Parameters

crColor An RGB color value for the brush. This value can be created using the RGB macro.

Returns Non-zero if the function is successful; otherwise, zero.

See Also CBrush::CBrush, CBrush::CreateHatchBrush, CBrush::CreateDIBPatternBrush, CBrush::CreatePatternBrush, ::CreateSolidBrush

Example

```
CClientDC dc(pWnd);
CBrush brush;

brush.CreateSolidBrush(RGB(100,50,75));

CRect rect(1,1,50,50);
dc.FillRect(rect,&brush);
```

CreateSysColorBrush –. ■ 4.0

Description Creates a brush that has the color of one of the 21 specified system elements such as the active caption bar, menu area, etc.

Syntax public, BOOL CreateSysColorBrush(int nIndex);

Parameters

nIndex An index that indicates which system element should be used for the brush. Can be one of the following values:

COLOR_3DDKSHADOW Dark shadow for three-dimensional display elements (Windows 95 only).

COLOR_3DFACE Face color for three-dimensional display elements (Windows 95 only).

COLOR_3DHILIGHT Highlight color for three-dimensional display elements (Windows 95 only).

COLOR_3DLIGHT Light color for three-dimensional display elements (Windows 95 only).

COLOR_3DSHADOW Shadow color for three-dimensional display elements (Windows 95 only).

COLOR_ACTIVEBORDER Active window border.

COLOR_ACTIVECAPTION Active window caption.

COLOR_APPWORKSPACE Background color of multiple document interface applications.

COLOR_BACKGROUND Desktop.

COLOR_BTNFACE Face shading on push buttons (Windows NT only).

COLOR_BTNHILIGHT Highlight color for buttons (same as COLOR_3DHILIGHT) (Windows 95 only).

COLOR_BTNSHADOW Edge shading on push buttons.

COLOR_BTNTEXT Text on push buttons.

COLOR_CAPTIONTEXT Text in caption, size box, and scrollbar arrow box.

COLOR_GRAYTEXT Grayed (disabled) text. This color is set to 0 if the current display driver does not support a solid gray color.

COLOR_HIGHLIGHT Item(s) selected in a control.

COLOR_HIGHLIGHTTEXT Text of item(s) selected in a control.

COLOR_INACTIVEBORDER Inactive window border.

COLOR_INACTIVECAPTION Inactive window caption.

COLOR_INACTIVECAPTIONTEXT Color of text in an inactive caption.

COLOR_INFOBK Background color for tooltip controls (Windows 95 only).

COLOR_INFOTEXT Text color for tooltip controls (Windows 95 only).

COLOR_MENU Menu background.

COLOR_MENUTEXT Text in menus (Windows NT only).

COLOR_SCROLLBAR Scrollbar gray area.

COLOR_WINDOW Window background.

COLOR_WINDOWFRAME Window frame.

COLOR_WINDOWTEXT Text in windows.

Returns Non-zero if the function is successful; otherwise, zero.

See Also ::GetSysColorBrush, ::GetSysColor

Example

```
CClientDC dc(pWnd);
CBrush brush;

// create a brush with the same color as the system's caption text color
brush.CreateSysColorBrush(COLOR_CAPTIONTEXT);
```

DUMP

■ 2.0 ■ 3.0 ■ DO

Description Outputs diagnostic information about the current state of the CBrush object. For the CBrush class this information includes the handle of the Windows GDI brush currently attached to it, as well as the style and color of the brush.

Syntax public, virtual void Dump(CDumpContext& dc) const;

Parameters

dc A reference to the dump context to which the status information should be sent. Usually this will be the MFC default debug dump context *afxDump*. *afxDump* sends its output to the debugger and only exists in the debug build of MFC.

Returns Nothing is returned.

See Also CGdiObject::Dump

Example

```
// call to dump function
CBrush brush;
brush.Dump(afxDump);

// output from dump function
a CBrush at $64F910
m_hObject = 0x100A
lb.lbStyle = 0x0
lb.lbHatch = 0
lb.lbColor = $FF
```

FROMHANDLE

■ 2.0 ■ 3.0

Description Returns a pointer to a CBrush given a Windows GDI brush handle. If MFC does not already have a permanent CBrush associated with the specified handle, it creates a temporary one and attaches it to the handle. Temporary CBrushes are automatically destroyed during idle-time processing so you can only depend on the validity of the CBrush returned by FromHandle until your application enters its idle loop, which can occur any time you return control to Windows (i.e., returning from a message map).

Syntax public, static CBrush* PASCAL FromHandle(HBRUSH hBrush);

Parameters

hBrush A handle to the Windows GDI brush for which a CBrush should be returned.

Returns A pointer to a CBrush that may be temporary.

See Also CGdiObject::FromHandle, CGdiObject::DeleteTempMap

Example

```
void CMyWnd::SomeDrawFunc(HBRUSH hBrush)
{
      // get possibly temporary brush
```

```
        CBrush *pTempBrush = CBrush::FromHandle(hBrush);
        CClientDC dc(this);
        CRect rect(1,1,100,100);
        dc.FillRect(rect,pTempBrush);
        // don't need to delete the pointer returned by FromHandle
}
```

GetLogBrush

–. ■ 4.0

Description Fills a LOGBRUSH SDK structure with information regarding the brush associated with the CBrush object. In versions of MFC before 4.0, use the CGdiObject::GetObject function to perform this task.

Syntax public, int GetLogBrush(LOGBRUSH* pLogBrush);

Parameters

pLogBrush A pointer to a LOGBRUSH structure that will be filled with information about the brush. For a description of this structure see the CBrush::CreateBrushIndirect function.

Returns Non-zero if successful; otherwise, zero.

See Also CGdiObject::GetObject

Example

```
...
CClientDC dc(pWnd);
CBrush brush(RGB(10,10,20));

// get info about brush
LOGBRUSH logBrush;
brush.GetLogBrush(&logBrush);
```

operator HBRUSH

–. ■ 4.0

Description Cast operator that converts the CBrush object to a HBRUSH (brush handle). This operator allows you to pass a CBrush object wherever an HBRUSH is required—such as for an SDK function involving brushes.

Syntax public, operator HBRUSH() const;

Parameters None.

Returns The HBRUSH associated with the CBrush object.

Example

```
// define polygon points (triangle in this case)
CPoint pts[3] = {CPoint(1,1), CPoint(5,9), CPoint(20,8)};
CRgn rgn;
CClientDC dc(pWnd);
CBrush brush(RGB(255,0,0,0));

rgn.CreatePolygonRgn(pts,sizeof(pts),ALTERNATE);

// pass brush to SDK function needing an HBRUSH
::FillRgn(dc,rgn,brush);
```

The CBitmap Class

The CBitmap class is MFC's encapsulation of the Windows GDI bitmap object, represented by an HBITMAP. The CBitmap object provides functions for loading and creating device-dependent bitmaps as well as functions that aid in the manipulation of the bitmap's bits.

CBitmap ■ 2.0 ■ 3.0

Description The constructor for the CBitmap class. CBitmap does nothing of real interest.

Syntax public, CBitmap();

Parameters None.

Returns Nothing is returned.

See Also CBitmap::~CBitmap

~CBitmap ■ 2.0 ■ 3.0 ■ UD

Description The destructor for the CBitmap class.

Syntax public, virtual ~CBitmap();

Parameters None.

Returns Nothing is returned.

See Also CBitmap::CBitmap

CreateBitmap ■ 2.0 ■ 3.0

Description Creates a bitmap of a specified size and color format and optionally initializes the bitmap to a specified bit pattern. Once created, the bitmap must be selected into a memory device context in order to be manipulated. Remember that in Windows, a bitmap cannot be copied directly to a device context (and therefore, can not be directly displayed). You must first select it into a memory device context that is compatible with the desired device context and then copy the bitmap from the memory device context to the device context using one of the Blt functions like BitBlt. Although CreateBitmap can be used to create any type of bitmap, as a practical matter you should only use it to create monochrome bitmaps. Using a color bitmap created with CreateBitmap is slower than using a color bitmap created using CreateCompatibleBitmap because CreateCompatibleBitmap ensures the bitmap's compatibility with a given device context ahead of time. If you use CreateBitmap, Windows must verify compatibility every time the bitmap is selected into a device context. Also note that if the bitmap is monochrome, bits set to one will be drawn using the current background color of the device context into which the bitmap is selected. Similarly, bits set to zero will be drawn using the current text color.

Syntax public, BOOL CreateBitmap(int nWidth, int nHeight, UINT nPlanes, UINT nBitcount, const void* lpBits);

Parameters

nWidth The width, in pixels, of the bitmap. If the *nWidth* or *nHeight* parameter is zero, CreateBitmap creates a one pixel by one pixel monochrome bitmap.

nHeight The height, in pixels, of the bitmap. If the *nWidth* or *nHeight* parameter is zero, CreateBitmap creates a one pixel by one pixel monochrome bitmap.

nPlanes The number of color planes in the bitmap. For a monochrome bitmap, this parameter should be one. For a color bitmap, either this parameter or the *nBitCount* parameter should be one.

nBitcount The number of bits per pixel. For a monochrome bitmap, this value should be one. For a color bitmap, either the *nPlanes* or this parameter should be one.

lpBits A pointer to a buffer containing the initial bit pattern for the bitmap. This parameter may be NULL, in which case the bitmap is left uninitialized. For more information about the format of the buffer pointed to by this parameter, see the description of the BITMAP structure in the CBitmap::CreateBitmapIndirect function.

Returns Non-zero if successful; otherwise, zero.

See Also CBitmap::CreateBitmapIndirect, CBitmap::CreateCompatibleBitmap, CBitmap::CreateDiscardableBitmap, ::CreateBitmap

Example

```
CBitmap bmp;

// create a monochrome, random bit pattern bitmap
char *pBits = new char[100];        // uninitialized, so filled with
                                    // random data

bmp.CreateBitmap(50,16,1,1,pBits);
...
```

CreateBitmapIndirect

■ 2.0 ■ 3.0

Description Creates a device-dependent bitmap of the type, size, and color format described by the given BITMAP stucture. Once created, the bitmap must be selected into a memory device context in order to be manipulated. Remember that in Windows, a bitmap cannot be copied directly to a device context (and therefore, can not be directly displayed). You must first select it into a memory device context that is compatible with the desired device context and then copy the bitmap from the memory device context to the device context using one of the Blt functions like BitBlt. Although CreateBitmapIndirect can be used to create any type of bitmap, as a practical matter you should only use it to create monochrome bitmaps. Using a color bitmap created with CreateBitmapIndirect is slower than using a color bitmap created using CreateCompatibleBitmap because CreateCompatibleBitmap ensures the bitmaps compatibility with a given device context ahead of time. If you use CreateBitmap, Windows must verify compatibility every time the bitmap is selected into a device context. Also note that if the bitmap is monochrome, bits set to one will be drawn using the current background color of the device context into which the bitmap is selected. Similarly, bits set to zero will be drawn using the current text color.

Syntax public, BOOL CreateBitmapIndirect(LPBITMAP lpBitmap);

Parameters

lpBitmap A pointer to a BITMAP structure that describes the characteristics of the bitmap. The members of the BITMAP structure are described below:

bmType – The bitmap type. For logical bitmaps the member should be zero.

bmWidth – The width of the bitmap in pixels.

bmHeight – The height of the bitmap in pixels.

bmWidthBytes – The number of bytes in each raster line. This parameter must be an even value since the Window GDI assumes that the bit values of a bitmap form an array of 2-byte integer values. In other words, bmWidthBytes * 8 must be the next multiple of 16 greater than or equal to the value obtained when the bmWidth member is multiplied by the bmBitsPixel member.

bmPlanes – The number of color planes in the bitmap.

bmBitsPixel – The number of bits required to describe the color value of a single pixel.

bmBits – A pointer to a buffer containing the bit pattern for the bitmap.

Returns Non-zero if successful; otherwise, zero.

See Also CBitmap::CreateBitmap, CBitmap::CreateCompatibleBitmap, CBitmap::CreateDiscardableBitmap, ::CreateBitmapIndirect

CreateCompatibleBitmap ■ 2.0 ■ 3.0

Description Creates a bitmap of the specified size that is guaranteed to be compatible with the color format of the specified device context. You can then manipulate the bitmap by selecting into any memory device context that is compatible with the specified device context. If the specified device context is a memory device context, then the bitmap created has the same color format as the bitmap currently selected into the specified memory device context. For this reason, be careful when using memory device contexts. If the eventual destination of the bitmap is a hardware device context, you should create all memory device contexts used to manipulate the bitmap using CDC::CreateCompatibleDC which will ensure that the memory device context's color format is the same as the specified hardware device context.

Syntax public, BOOL CreateCompatibleBitmap(CDC* pDC, int nWidth, int nHeight);

Parameters

pDC A pointer to the device context from which the color format should be copied.

nWidth The desired width of the bitmap. If the *nWidth* or *nHeight* parameter is zero, CreateCompatibleBitmap creates a one pixel by one pixel monochrome bitmap.

nHeight The desired height of the bitmap. If the *nWidth* or *nHeight* parameter is zero, CreateCompatibleBitmap creates a one pixel by one pixel monochrome bitmap.

Returns Non-zero if successful; otherwise, zero.

See Also CBitmap::CreateBitmap, CBitmap::CreateBitmapIndirect, CBitmap::CreateDiscardableBitmap, ::CreateCompatibleBitmap

CreateDiscardableBitmap ■ 2.0 ■ 3.0

Description Performs the same function as the CreateCompatibleBitmap function, described above. The only difference between the bitmap created using this function and that created using the CreateCompatibleBitmap function is that the bitmap created by this function can be discarded by Windows at any time that it is not currently selected into a device context. If it is selected into a device context, Windows will not discard it. Windows may discard the bitmap if it is running low on memory or resources. If the bitmap is discarded, selecting it into a device context will fail.

Syntax public, BOOL CreateDiscardableBitmap(CDC* pDC, int nWidth, int nHeight);

Parameters

pDC A pointer to the device context whose color format should be copied.

nWidth The desired width of the bitmap. If the *nWidth* or *nHeight* parameter is zero, CreateDiscardableBitmap creates a one pixel by one pixel monochrome bitmap.

nHeight The desired height of the bitmap. If the *nWidth* or *nHeight* parameter is zero, CreateDiscardableBitmap creates a one pixel by one pixel monochrome bitmap.

Returns Non-zero if successful; otherwise, zero.

See Also CBitmap::CreateBitmap, CBitmap::CreateBitmapIndirect, CBitmap::CreateCompatibleBitmap, ::CreateDiscardableBitmap

DUMP

■ 2.0 ■ 3.0 ■ DO

Description Outputs diagnostic information about the current state of the CBitmap object. For the CBitmap class this information includes the handle of the Windows GDI bitmap currently attached to it, as well as the size, type, and color depth of the bitmap.

Syntax public, virtual void Dump(CDumpContext& dc) const;

Parameters

dc A reference to the dump context to which the status information should be sent. Usually this will be the MFC default debug dump context *afxDump*. *afxDump* sends its output to the debugger and only exists in the debug build of MFC.

Returns Nothing is returned.

See Also CGdiObject::Dump

Example

```
// call to dump function
CBitmap bmp;
bmp.LoadBitmap(IDB_TESTBMP);
bmp.Dump(afxDump);

// output from dump function
a CBitmap at $64F910
m_hObject = 0x0
```

FROMHANDLE

■ 2.0 ■ 3.0

Description Returns a pointer to a CBitmap given a Windows GDI bitmap handle. If MFC does not already have a permanent CBitmap associated with the specified handle, it creates a temporary one and attaches it to the handle. Temporary CBitmaps are automatically destroyed during idle-time processing so you can only depend on the validity of the CBitmap returned by FromHandle until your application enters its idle loop, which can occur any time you return control to Windows (i.e., returning from a message map).

Syntax public, static CBitmap* PASCAL FromHandle(HBITMAP hBitmap);

Parameters

hBitmap A handle to the Windows GDI bitmap for which a CBitmap should be returned.

Returns A pointer to a CBitmap, which may be temporary.

See Also CGdiObject::FromHandle, CGdiObject::DeleteTempMap

Example

```
void CMyWnd::SomeDrawFunc(HBITMAP hBmp)
{
        // get possibly temporary bitmap
        CBitmap *pTempBmp = CBitmap::FromHandle(hBmp);
```

```
        CClientDC dc(this);
        CDC memDC;
        memDC.CreateCompatibleDC(&dc);
        CBitmap *pOldBmp = memDC.SelectObject(pTempBmp);
        dc.BitBlt(0,0,100,100,&memDC,0,0,SRCCOPY);
        memDC.SelectObject(pOldBmp);
        // don't need to delete the pointer returned by FromHandle
}
```

GetBitmap

–. ■ 4.0

Description Fills a specified SDK bitmap structure with information regarding the CBitmap objects' associated bitmap. In versions of MFC before 4.0, use the CGdiObject::GetObject function to perform this task.

Syntax public, int GetBitmap(BITMAP* pBitmap);

Parameters

pBitmap A pointer to a BITMAP structure that will be filled with information about the bitmap. For more information about the BITMAP structure, see the CBitmap::CreateBitmapIndirect function.

Returns Non-zero if successful; otherwise, zero.

See Also CGdiObject::GetObject

Example

```
void CMyWnd::DrawBitmap(CDC *pDc)
{
        CDC memDc;
        CBitmap bmp;
        BITMAP bitmap, *pOldBmp;

        // create a memory dc to use as the source dc
        dc.CreateCompatibleDC(pDc);

        // load the bitmap and obtain its dimensions
        bmp.LoadBitmap(IDB_TESTBMP);
        bmp.GetBitmap(&bitmap);
        pOldBmp = dc.SelectObject(&bmp);

        // simply copy the bitmap
        dc.BltBlt(0,0,bitmap.bmWidth,bitmap.bmHeight,&memDc,0,0,SRCCOPY);

        // clean up
        memDc.SelectObject(pOldBmp);
        memDc.DeleteDC();
}
```

GetBitmapBits

■ 2.0 ■ 3.0

Description Fills a given buffer with the bit pattern of the bitmap. Bit patterns are always an even number of bytes, as is each scanline in the bitmap. You can use the CGdiObject::GetObject function to determine the necessary size for the bit pattern buffer.

Syntax public, DWORD GetBitmapBits(DWORD dwCount, LPVOID lpBits) const;

Parameters

dwCount The maximum number of bytes to copy to the supplied buffer. The value for this parameter can be determined by using the CGdiObject::GetObject function for the bitmap.

lpBits A pointer to a memory buffer into which the bit pattern will be copied.

Returns The actual number of bytes in the bit pattern if successful; otherwise, zero.

See Also CBitmap::SetBitmapBits, ::GetBitmapBits

Example

```
CBitmap bmp;
bmp.LoadBitmap(IDB_TESTBMP);

// get the required buffer size
BITMAP bitmap;
bmp.GetObject(sizeof(BITMAP),&bitmap);
DWORD dwSizeNeeded = bitmap.bmWidthBytes * bitmap.bmHeight;

// get the bits
char *pBitBuffer = new char[dwSizeNeeded];
bmp.GetBitmapBits(dwSizeNeeded,pBitBuffer);

// do something with bits

delete pBitBuffer;
..
```

GetBitmapDimension ■ 2.0 ■ 3.0

Description Retrieves the dimensions of the bitmap as set by SetBitmapDimension. This function, together with its counterpart, CBitmap::SetBitmapDimension is simply a developer convenience function. Windows does not use the specified dimensions. The Windows documention says the dimensions should be in 0.1 millimeter units. However, because Windows doesn't use the dimensions at all, the units can be any that you prefer.

Syntax public, CSize GetBitmapDimension( ) const;

Parameters None.

Returns A CSize object containing the width and height of the bitmap as specified by the SetBitmapDimension function. If the dimensions have not been set using this function, the dimensions returned are zero.

See Also CBitmap::SetBitmapDimension, ::GetBitmapDimension, ::GetBitmapDimensionEx

Example

```
CBitmap bmp;
bmp.LoadBitmap(IDB_TESTBMP);
bmp.SetBitmapDimension(100,300);

..

// sometime later..
CSize = bmp.GetBitmapDimension();
..
```

OPERATOR HBITMAP

–. ■ 4.0

Description Cast operator that converts the CBitmap object to an HBITMAP (bitmap handle). This operator allows you to pass a CBitmap object wherever an HBITMAP is required—such as for an SDK function involving bitmaps.

Syntax public, operator HBITMAP() const;

Parameters None.

Returns The HBITMAP associated with the CBitmap object.

Example

```
...
void SomeFunc(CBitmap *pBmp)
{
// use SDK function - for some unknown reason
CSize size;
::GetBitmapDimensionEx(*pBmp,size);
...
}
```

LOADBITMAP

■ 2.0 ■ 3.0

Description Loads a named bitmap resource from the program's executable file and attaches it to the CBitmap object. If the specified bitmap does not exist or there is not enough memory to load the bitmap, this function will fail.

Syntax public, BOOL LoadBitmap(LPCTSTR lpszResourceName);
public, BOOL LoadBitmap(UINT nIDResource);

Parameters

lpszResourceName A pointer to a NULL-terminated string containing the name of the bitmap resource to load.

nIDResource An integer ID that identifies the bitmap resource to load. This version of LoadBitmap uses the SDK MAKEINTRESOURCE macro to load the bitmap.

Returns Non-zero if the function is successful; otherwise, zero.

See Also CBitmap::LoadOEMBitmap, ::LoadBitmap

Example

```
CBitmap bmp;
bmp.LoadBitmap(IDB_TESTBMP);
```

LoadMappedBitmap

–. ■ 4.0

Description Loads a named bitmap resource from the program's executable file and attaches it to the CBitmap object. If the specified bitmap does not exist or there is not enough memory to load the bitmap, this function will fail.

Syntax public, BOOL LoadMappedBitmap(UINT nIDBitmap, UINT nFlags = 0, LPCOLORMAP lpColorMap = NULL, int nMapSize = 0);

Parameters

nIDBitmap An integer ID that identifies the bitmap resource to load.

nFlags Zero or CMB_MASKED, in which case the specified bitmap is treated as a mask bitmap.

lpColorMap Points to an array of COLORMAP structures. This parameter can be NULL, in which case a series of default system color maps are used. The members of the COLORMAP structure are shown below:

COLORREF from–The color to change from.

COLORREF to–The color to change to.

nMapSize The number of color maps pointed to by *lpColorMap*.

Returns Non-zero if the function is successful; otherwise, zero.

See Also CBitmap::LoadBitmap, CBitmap::LoadOEMBitmap, ::CreateMappedBitmap

Example

```
CBitmap bmp;
COLORMAP clrMap = {RGB(255,0,0),RGB(0,255,0)};

// load a bitmap changing red pixels to green
bmp.LoadMappedBitmap(IDB_TESTBMP,&clrMap,1);
```

LoadOEMBitmap

■ 2.0 ■ 3.0 ■ NM

Description Loads a pre-defined Windows bitmap resource and attaches it to the CBitmap object.

Syntax public, BOOL LoadOEMBitmap(UINT nIDBitmap);

Parameters

nIDBitmap The integer identifier of the pre-defined bitmap to load. Possible values for this parameter are listed below. Bitmap IDs beginning with OBM_OLD represent bitmaps used in Windows version 3.0 and earlier. Note that in order to use these constants, you must define the OEMRESOURCE constant before including windows.h.

OBM_BTNCORNERS	OBM_OLD_RESTORE
OBM_BTSIZE	OBM_OLD_RGARROW
OBM_CHECK	OBM_OLD_UPARROW
OBM_CHECKBOXES	OBM_OLD_ZOOM

OBM_CLOSE	OBM_REDUCE
OBM_COMBO	OBM_REDUCED
OBM_DNARROW	OBM_RESTORE
OBM_DNARROWD	OBM_RESTORED
OBM_DNARROWI	OBM_RGARROW
OBM_LFARROW	OBM_RGARROWD
OBM_LFARROWD	OBM_RGARROWI
OBM_LFARROWI	OBM_SIZE
OBM_MNARROW	OBM_UPARROW
OBM_OLD_CLOSE	OBM_UPARROWD
OBM_OLD_DNARROW	OBM_UPARROWI
OBM_OLD_LFARROW	OBM_ZOOM
OBM_OLD_REDUCE	OBM_ZOOMD

Returns Non-zero if the function is successful; otherwise, zero.

See Also CBitmap::LoadBitmap, ::LoadBitmap

Example

```
#define OEMRESOURCE
#include "windows.h"
..
CBitmap bmp;
bmp.LoadOEMBitmap(OBM_LFARROW); // load left-pointing array bitmap
```

SetBitmapBits

■ 2.0 ■ 3.0

Description Sets the bit pattern of the bitmap to the supplied bit pattern.

Syntax public, DWORD SetBitmapBits(DWORD dwCount, const void* lpBits);

Parameters

dwCount The number of bytes in the supplied bit pattern.

lpBits A pointer to a memory buffer containing the new bit pattern.

Returns The actual number of bytes used or zero if the function fails.

See Also CBitmap::GetBitmapBits, ::SetBitmapBits, ::SetDIBits

Example

```
CBitmap bmp;
bmp.LoadBitmap(IDB_TESTBMP);

// get the required buffer size
BITMAP bitmap;
bmp.GetObject(sizeof(BITMAP),&bitmap);
DWORD dwSizeNeeded = bitmap.bmWidthBytes * bitmap.bmHeight;

// get the bits
char *pBitBuffer = new char[dwSizeNeeded];

// fill pBitBuffer with the desired bit pattern
```

continued on next page

continued from previous page

```
bmp.SetBitmapBits(dwSizeNeeded,pBitBuffer);

delete pBitBuffer;
..
```

SetBitmapDimension

■ 2.0 ■ 3.0

Description Sets the dimensions of the bitmap. The dimensions specified are not used by Windows. Once the dimensions have been set, they can be later retrieved using the GetBitmapDimension function. The Windows documentation states that the dimensions are in 0.1 millimeter units. However, since the specified dimensions are not used by the system, they can be in any desired units.

Syntax public, CSize SetBitmapDimension(int nWidth, int nHeight);

Parameters

nWidth The width of the bitmap.

nHeight The height of the bitmap.

Returns A CSize object containing the previous dimensions of the bitmap.

See Also CBitmap::GetBitmapDimension, ::SetBitmapDimension, ::SetBitmapDimensionEx

Example

```
CBitmap bmp;
bmp.LoadBitmap(IDB_TESTBMP);
bmp.SetBitmapDimension(100,300);

..

// sometime later..
CSize = bmp.GetBitmapDimension();
..
```

The CPalette Class

The CPalette class is MFC's encapsulation of the Windows GDI palette object, represented by an HPALETTE. The CPalette object provides functions for creating and manipulating palettes. The CPalette object does not provide any functionality that is not available in the Windows SDK; it simply provides an object-oriented interface to that functionality.

CPalette

■ 2.0 ■ 3.0

Description The constructor for the CPalette class. CPalette does nothing of real interest. You must call CreatePalette, CreateHalftonePalette, or FromHandle to associate a logical palette with the CPalette object.

Syntax public, CPalette();

Parameters None.

Returns Nothing is returned.

See Also CPalette::~CPalette

~CPalette ■ 2.0 ■ 3.0 ■ UD

Description The destructor for the CPalette class.

Syntax public, virtual ~CPalette();

Parameters None.

Returns Nothing is returned.

See Also CPalette::CPalette

AnimatePalette ■ 2.0 ■ 3.0 ■ NM

Description Replaces specified color entries in the logical palette and, if the palette is associated with the active window, immediately maps the changes into the system palette. This causes the contents of the active window to reflect the color changes immediately. This function only replaces color values for entries with the PC_RESERVED flag set.

Syntax public, void AnimatePalette(UINT nStartIndex, UINT nNumEntries, LPPALETTEENTRY lpPaletteColors);

Parameters

nStartIndex Index of first palette entry to replace.

nNumEntries Number of palette entries to replace.

lpPaletteColors A pointer to a series of *nNumEntries* PALETTEENTRY structures. The members of the PALETTEENTRY structure are described below:

peRed–The red intensity value of the palette entry (0-255).

peGreen–The green intensity value of the palette entry (0-255).

peBlue–The blue intensity value of the palette entry (0-255).

peFlags–Specifies how the palette entry will be used. Can be zero or one of the following values:

PC_EXPLICIT The low-order word of the logical palette entry designates a hardware palette index. This flag allows the application to show the contents of the display device palette.

PC_NOCOLLAPSE The color should be placed in an unused entry in the system palette instead of being matched to an existing color in the system palette. If there are no unused entries in the system palette, the color is matched normally. Once this color is in the system palette, colors in other logical palettes can be matched to this color.

PC_RESERVED The logical palette entry should be used for palette animation. This flag prevents other windows from matching colors to the palette entry since the color frequently changes. If an unused system-palette entry is available, the color is placed in that entry. Otherwise, the color is not available for animation.

Returns Nothing is returned.

See Also ::AnimatePalette

Example

```
void CMyWnd::CreateUglyFlashingEffect(CPalette *pCurrentPalette)
{
        int nI;
        PALETTEENTRY entries1[10], entries2[10];
        PALETTEENTRY palWhiteEntry = {255,255,255,PC_RESERVED};
        PALETTEENTRY palBlackEntry = {0,0,0,PC_RESERVED};

        // initialize entry arrays
        for (nI = 0;nI < 10;nI++)
        {
                entries1[nI] = palWhiteEntry;
                entries2[nI] = palBlackEntry;
        }

        // animate palette back and forth
        for (nI = 0;nI < 1000;nI++)
        {
                pCurrentPalette->AnimatePalette(0,10,entries1);
                pCurrentPalette->AnimatePalette(0,10,entries2);
        }
}
```

CreateHalftonePalette ■ 2.0 ■ 3.0 ■ NM

Description Creates a halftone palette for the specified device context. This palette can then be realized for the device context. A halftone palette should be created and realized when the stretching mode for a device context is set to HALFTONE. This should be done prior to using the StretchBlt or StretchDIBits functions. When performing a StretchBlt or StretchDIBits, a stretch mode of HALFTONE causes Windows to map pixels from the source rectangle into blocks of pixels in the destination rectangle with the average color over the destination block of pixels approximating the color of the source pixels.

Syntax public, BOOL CreateHalftonePalette(CDC* pDC);

Parameters

pDC A pointer to the device context for which the halftone palette should be created.

Returns Non-zero if the palette is created; zero if the function fails.

See Also CPalette::CreatePalette, CDC::StretchBlt, CDC::StretchDIBits, CDC::SetStretchBltMode, CDC::RealizePalette, ::CreateHalftonePalette

Example

```
..
CClientDC dc(pWnd);
CPalette pal;
pal.CreateHalftonePalette(&dc);
..
```

CreatePalette

■ 2.0 ■ 3.0

Description Creates a logical palette as described by the given LOGPALETTE structure. In order to use this palette, it must be selected and realized into a device context using the CDC::SelectPalette and CDC::RealizePalette functions.

Syntax public, BOOL CreatePalette(LPLOGPALETTE lpLogPalette);

Parameters

lpLogPalette A pointer to a LOGPALETTE structure that defines the palette. The members of the LOGPALETTE structure are described below:

palVersion–The version of the LOGPALETTE structure. The current version is 0x300.

palNumEntries–The number of entries in the palette.

palPalEntry–An array of PALETTEENTRY structures that define each entry in the palette. For a description of the PALETTENTRY structure, see CPalette::AnimatePalette.

Returns Non-zero if the palette is created; zero if the function fails.

See Also CPalette::CreateHalftonePalette, CPalette::AnimatePalette, ::CreatePalette

Example

```
void CMyPalette::CreateShadesOfGrayPalette()
{
     // allocate LOGPALETTE structure with room for 200
     // PALETTEENTRYs -(the one in the LOGPALETTE plus 199 more
     LOGPALETTE *pLogPal = new char[sizeof(LOGPALETTE +
                     sizeof(PALETTEENTRY) * 199];
     PALETTEENTRY palEntry = {0,0,0,0};
     pLogPal->palVersion = 0x300;
     pLogPal->palNumEntries = 3;

     // initialize palette entry array to shades of gray
     for (nI = 0;nI < 200;nI++)
     {
          pLogPal->palPalEntry[nI].peRed = nI;
          pLogPal->palPalEntry[nI].peGreen = nI;
          pLogPal->palPalEntry[nI].peBlue = nI;
     }

     CreatePalette(pLogPal);
     delete pLogPal
}
```

FromHandle

■ 2.0 ■ 3.0

Description Returns a pointer to a CPalette given a Windows GDI palette handle. If MFC does not already have a permanent CPalette associated with the specified handle, it creates a temporary one and attaches it to the handle. Temporary CPalettes are automatically destroyed during idle-time processing so you can only depend on the validity of the CPalette returned by FromHandle until your application enters its idle loop, which can occur any time you return control to Windows (i.e., returning from a message map).

Syntax public, static CPalette* PASCAL FromHandle(HPALETTE hPal);

Parameters

hPal A handle to the Windows GDI palette for which a CPalette should be returned.

Returns A pointer to a CPalette that may be temporary.

See Also CGdiObject::FromHandle, CGdiObject::DeleteTempMap

Example

```
void CMyWnd::SomeDrawFunc(HPALETTE hPal)
{
	// get possibly temporary palette
	CPalette *pPalette = CPalette::FromHandle(hPal);
	CClientDC dc(this);
	CPalette *pOldPal = dc.SelectPalette(pPalette,FALSE);
	dc.RealizePalette(pPalette);
	..
	dc.SelectPalette(pOldPal);
	// don't need to delete the pointer returned by FromHandle
}
```

GetEntryCount

–. ■ 4.0

Description Returns the number of entries in the logical palette associated with the CPalette object.

Syntax public, int GetEntryCount();

Parameters None.

Returns The number of entries in the logical palette.

Example

```
...
CPalette pal;
CClientDC dc(pWnd);

pal.CreateHalftonePalette(&dc);

// get number of entries in halftone palette
int nNumEntries = pal.GetEntryCount();
```

GetNearestPaletteIndex ■ 2.0 ■ 3.0

Description Retrieves the index of the logical palette entry whose color most closely matches a specified color. Note that if any of the entries in the logical palette were created with the PC_EXPLICIT flag, the return value will be undefined.

Syntax public, UINT GetNearestPaletteIndex(COLORREF crColor) const;

Parameters

crColor The color for which the palette index of the nearest color should be found.

Returns The index of the closest color if successful; otherwise CLR_INVALID.

See Also CPalette::GetPaletteEntries, CDC::GetNearestColor, ::GetNearestPaletteIndex

GetPaletteEntries ■ 2.0 ■ 3.0

Description Retrieves a specified range of color entries from the logical palette associated with the CPalette object.

Syntax public, UINT GetPaletteEntries(UINT nStartIndex, UINT nNumEntries, LPPALETTEENTRY lpPaletteColors) const;

Parameters

nStartIndex The first entry in the logical palette that should be retrieved.

nNumEntries The number of entries to retrieve from the logical palette.

lpPaletteColors A pointer to an array of *nNumEntries* PALETTEENTRY structures into which the requested palette entries will be placed. For a description of the PALETTEENTRY structure, see CPalette::AnimatePalette.

Returns The number of entries copied if successful; otherwise zero.

See Also CPalette::SetPaletteEntries, ::GetPaletteEntries

Example

```
void CMyWnd::ChangePalette(CPalette *pCurrentPal)
{
     PALETTEENTRY palEntry;

     // get the third palette entry and set its red intensity to 255
     pCurrentPal->GetPaletteEntries(2,1,&palEntry);
     palEntry.peRed = 255;
     pCurrentPal->SetPaletteEntries(2,1,&palEntry);
}
```

operator HPALETTE –. ■ 4.0

Description Cast operator that converts the CPalette object to an HPALETTE (palette handle). This operator allows you to pass a CPalette object wherever an HPALETTE is required—such as for an SDK function involving palettes.

Syntax public, operator HPALETTE() const;

Parameters None.

Returns The HPALETTE associated with the CPalette object.

Example

```
...
CClientDC dc(pWnd);

// pass to SDK function needing an HPALETTE
::RealizePalette(dc,palette,FALSE);
```

ResizePalette ■ 2.0 ■ 3.0

Description Resizes the palette to the specified number of entries. If the specified number of entries is less than the number currently in the logical palette, the remaining entries are left unchanged. If the specified number of entries is greater than the number currently in the logical palette, the excess entries are initialized to black, with flags set to zero.

Syntax public, BOOL ResizePalette(UINT nNumEntries);

Parameters

nNumEntries The new number of entries in the logical palette.

Returns Non-zero if the function was successful; otherwise, zero.

See Also ::ResizePalette

Example

```
CPalette pal;

// allocate LOGPALETTE structure with room for three PALETTEENTRYs -
// (the one in the LOGPALETTE plus two more
LOGPALETTE *pLogPal = new char[sizeof(LOGPALETTE + sizeof(PALETTEENTRY) * 2];
PALETTEENTRY palEntry = {255,0,0,0};
pLogPal->palVersion = 0x300;
pLogPal->palNumEntries = 3;
pLogPal->palPalEntry[0] = palEntry; // red
palEntry.peRed = 0;
palEntry.peGreen = 255;
pLogPal->palPalEntry[1] = palEntry; // green
palEntry.peGreen = 0;
palEntry.peBlue = 255;
pLogPal->palPalEntry[2] = palEntry; // blue

pal.CreatePalette(pLogPal);

// use palette for something

// later on, increase palette size so we can add another color
pal.ResizePalette(4);

// add additional color
palEntry.peRed = 255;
palEntry.peGreen = 255;
palEntry.peBlue = 255;
```

```
pal.SetPaletteEntries(3,1,&palEntry);  // add white

// use new palette

delete pLogPal;
```

SetPaletteEntries ■ 2.0 ■ 3.0

Description Sets a specified range of palette entries in the logical palette.

Syntax public, UINT SetPaletteEntries(UINT nStartIndex, UINT nNumEntries, LPPALETTEENTRY lpPaletteColors);

Parameters

nStartIndex The first palette entry that should be set.

nNumEntries The number of palette entries to be set.

lpPaletteColors A pointer to an array of *nNumEntries* PALETTEENTRY structure describing the new palette entries. For a description of the PALETTEENTRY structure, see CPalette::AnimatePalette.

Returns The number of palette entries actually set, if successful; otherwise, zero.

See Also CPalette::GetPaletteEntries, ::SetPaletteEntries

Example See the examples under CPalette::GetPaletteEntries and CPalette::ResizePalette

The CRgn Class

The CRgn class is MFC's encapsulation of the Windows GDI region object, represented by an HRGN. Regions represent one or more areas (shapes) that may then be manipulated as one. The CRegion object provides functions for creating and manipulating regions. The CRgn object does not provide any functionality that is not available in the Windows SDK; it simply provides an object-oriented interface to that functionality.

CRgn ■ 2.0 ■ 3.0

Description The contructor for the CRgn class. CRgn does nothing of real interest.

Syntax public, CRgn();

Parameters None.

Returns Nothing is returned.

See Also CRgn::~CRgn

~CRgn ■ 2.0 ■ 3.0 ■ UD

Description The destructor for the CRgn class.

Syntax public, virtual ~CRgn();

Parameters None.

Returns Nothing is returned.

See Also CRgn::CRgn

COMBINERGN

■ 2.0 ■ 3.0

Description Combines two regions in a specified manner. The resulting region replaces the region currently associated with the CRgn object. Note that this function assumes that there already is a GDI region associated with the CRgn object. The debug version of CombineRgn will assert if this is not true. This requirement occurs because CRgn::CombineRgn is a simple wrapping of the SDK ::CombineRgn function that requires an HRGN in which to place the resulting, combined region. Finally, you can use this function to copy one region to another but it is simpler to use CopyRgn for that task.

Syntax public, int CombineRgn(CRgn* pRgn1, CRgn* pRgn2, int nCombineMode);

Parameters

pRgn1	A pointer to one of the regions to be combined.
pRgn2	A pointer to one of the regions to be combined.
nCombineMode	A constant that describes how the two regions should be combined. Can be one of the following values:
RGN_AND	Create the intersection of the two combined regions.
RGN_COPY	Creates a copy of *pRgn1*.
RGN_DIFF	Combines the parts of *pRgn1* that are not part of *pRgn2*.
RGN_OR	Creates the union of the two combined regions.
RGN_XOR	Creates the union of the two combined regions except for any overlapping areas.

Returns One of the following values:

NULLREGION	The combined region is empty.
SIMPLEREGION	The combined region is a single rectangle.
COMPLEXREGION	The combined region is more than a single rectangle.
ERROR	No region was created.

See Also CRegion::CopyRgn, ::CombineRgn

Example

```
CRgn rgn1, rgn2, combinedRgn;
rgn1.CreateRectRgn(1,1,100,100);
rgn2.CreateRectRgn(200,225,350,621);
combinedRgn.CreateRectRgn(1,1,2,2); // fake region - must have one
combinedRgn.CombineRgn(&rgn1,&rgn2,RGN_OR)
```

CopyRgn

■ 2.0 ■ 3.0

Description Copies the specified region to the region associated with the CRgn object. This function is actually implemented by a call to CRgn::CombineRgn using the RGN_COPY specifier. Note that this function assumes that there already is a GDI region associated with the CRgn object. The debug version of CopyRgn will assert if this is not true. This requirement occurs because CRgn::CopyRgn is a simple wrapping of the SDK ::CombineRgn function which requires an HRGN in which to place the resulting copied region.

Syntax public, int CopyRgn(CRgn* pRgnSrc);

Parameters

pRgnSrc A pointer to the region to be copied.

Returns One of the following values:

NULLREGION The copied region is empty.

SIMPLEREGION The copied region is a single rectangle.

COMPLEXREGION The copied region is more than a single rectangle.

ERROR No region was created.

See Also CRgn::CombineRgn

Example

```
CRgn origRgn, copyRgn;
origRgn.CreateRectRgn(1,1,100,100);
copyRgn.CreateRectRgn(1,1,2,2); // fake region - must have one

// same as CombineRgn(&origRgn,&origRng,RGN_COPY);
copyRgn.CopyRgn(&origRgn);
```

CreateEllipticRgn

■ 2.0 ■ 3.0

Description Creates an elliptical region described by a given bounding rectangle and attaches the region to the CRgn object. The bounding rectangle defines the size, shape, and orientation of the region in the following manner: The long sides of the rectangle define the length of the ellipse's major axis; the short sides define the length of the ellipse's minor axis; the center of the rectangle defines the intersection of the major and minor axes.

Syntax public, BOOL CreateEllipticRgn(int x1, int y1, int x2, int y2);

Parameters

x1 The x coordinate of the upper-left corner of the bounding rectangle (in logical units).

y1 The y coordinate of the upper-left corner of the bounding rectangle (in logical units).

x2 The x coordinate of the lower-right corner of the bounding rectangle (in logical units).

y2 The y coordinate of the lower-right corner of the bounding rectangle (in logical units).

Returns Non-zero if the region is successfuly created; otherwise, zero.

See Also CRgn::CreateEllipticRgnIndirect, ::CreateEllipticRgn

Example

```
CRgn rgn;
rgn.CreateEllipticRgn(100,100,400,200);
```

CreateEllipticRgnIndirect ■ 2.0 ■ 3.0

Description Creates an elliptical region described by a given bounding rectangle (given as a pointer to a RECT structure) and attaches the region to the CRgn object. The bounding rectangle defines the size, shape, and orientation of the region in the following manner: The long sides of the rectangle define the length of the ellipse's major axis; the short sides define the length of the ellipse's minor axis; the center of the rectangle defines the intersection of the major and minor axes.

Syntax public, BOOL CreateEllipticRgnIndirect(LPCRECT lpRect);

Parameters

lpRect A pointer to a RECT structure or a CRect object that defines the bounding rectangle of the ellipse.

Returns Non-zero if the region is successfuly created; otherwise, zero.

See Also CRgn::CreateEllipticRgn, ::CreateEllipticRgnIndirect

Example

```
CRgn rgn;
CRect rect(100,100,400,200);
rgn.CreateEllipticRgnIndirect(rect);
```

CreateFromData ■ 2.0 ■ 3.0 ■ NM

Description Creates a GDI region directly from a set of specified region data and attaches that region to the CRgn object.

Syntax public, BOOL CreateFromData(const XFORM* lpXForm, int nCount, const RGNDATA* pRgnData);

Parameters

lpXForm A pointer to an XFORM structure that describes the transformation to apply to the region data. If this parameter is NULL, no transformation is performed (the identity transformation). For a discussion on transforms and a definition of the XFORM structure, see ::SetWorldTransform.

nCount The size of the specified region data buffer.

pRgnData A pointer to an RGNDATA structure that describes the region. An RGNDATA structure is made up of the following members:

rdh–An RGNDATAHEADER structure with the following members:

dwSize–The size of the header (sizeof (RGNDATAHEADER)).

iType–The type of region (must be RDH_RECTANGLES).

nCount–The number of rectangles that make up the region.

nRgnSize–The size of the buffer required to hold the RECT structures that describe the region. This parameter can be zero if the size is not known.

rcBound–The bounding rectangle of the region.

Buffer–A memory buffer containing the rectangles (in RECT structure format) that make up the region.

Returns Non-zero if the region was created; otherwise, zero.

See Also CRgn::GetRegionData, ::ExtCreateRegion

Example

```
// Create a buffer for the region data - the "-1" is because RGNDATA
// has a 1 byte place-holder for the rectangle data
int nSizeNeeded = sizeof(RGNDATA) + sizeof(RECT) * 2 - 1;
REGIONDATA *pRgnData = (RGNDATA *)new char[nSizeNeeded];

// initialize region data
pRgnData->rdh.dwSize = sizeof(RGNDATAHEADER);
pRgnData->rdh.iType = RDH_RECTANGLES; // mandatory value
pRgnData->nCount = 2; // two rectangles is region
pRgnData->nRgnSize = sizeof(RECT) * 2;
RECT rect1 = {1,1,100,100};
RECT rect2 = {100,100,200,200};
memcpy(pRgnData->Buffer,&rect1,sizeof(RECT));
memcpy(pRgnData->Buffer + sizeof(RECT),&rect2,sizeof(RECT));

// finally, create the region with no transform
CRgn;
rgn.CreateFromData(NULL,nSizeNeeded,pRgnData);
delete pRgnData;
```

CreateFromPath

■ 2.0 ■ 3.0 ■ NM

Description Creates a region from the currently selected path in the specified device context and attaches the region to the CRgn object. This function will fail if the specified device context does not contain a closed path. After this function is executed, Windows will discard the path from the device context.

Syntax public, BOOL CreateFromPath(CDC* pDC);

Parameters

pDC A pointer to the device context containing the closed path on which to base the region.

Returns Non-zero if the function is successful; otherwise, zero.

See Also CDC::BeginPath, CDC::EndPath

Example

```
..
CRgn rgn;
CClientDC dc(pWnd);

dc.BeginPath();
dc.Rectangle(1,1,100,100);
dc.EndPath();

// create region from path (just a rectangle in this case)
rgn.CreateFromPath(&dc);
```

CreatePolygonRgn

■ 2.0 ■ 3.0

Description Creates a polygon-shaped region and attaches the region to the CRgn object. The polygon will be closed by Windows, if necessary.

Syntax public, BOOL CreatePolygonRgn(LPPOINT lpPoints, int nCount, int nPolyFillMode);

Parameters

lpPoints A pointer to an array of points that describe the polygon.

nCount The number of points pointed to by *lpPoints*.

nPolyFillMode The fill mode for the polygon. This parameter can be ALTERNATE or WINDING. A value of ALTERNATE causes Windows to fill the area between odd and even numbered sides on a per scanline basis (it draws a horizontal line between the odd side and the even side). WINDING causes Windows to consider the direction in which each line segment of the polyline is drawn. It does this by drawing an imaginary line from each enclosed area in the polygon to outside of the figure. Each time this imaginary line crosses a line segment that was drawn in a clockwise direction, a count is incremented. Each time the imaginary line crosses a line segment that was drawn in a counterclockwise direction, the count is decremented. If, after this process, the count is non-zero, the enclosed area from which the imaginary line began is filled. An example of each of the filling modes is given below in Figure 12-4.

Figure 12-4 ALTERNATE versus WINDING polygon filling

Returns Non-zero if successful; othersize, zero.

See Also CRgn::CreatePolyPolygonRgn, ::CreatePolygonRgn

Example

```
// define polygon points (triangle in this case)
CPoint pts[3] = {CPoint(1,1), CPoint(5,9), CPoint(20,8)};
CRgn rgn;
rgn.CreatePolygonRgn(pts,sizeof(pts),ALTERNATE);
```

CreatePolyPolygonRgn

■ 2.0 ■ 3.0 ■ NM

Description Creates a region made up of multiple polygons and attaches the region to the CRgn object. Each polygon specified is assumed to be a closed polygon. The polygons may overlap.

Syntax public, BOOL CreatePolyPolygonRgn(LPPOINT lpPoints, LPINT lpPolyCounts, int nCount, int nPolyFillMode);

Parameters

lpPoints A pointer to the series of POINT structures that describe the polygons.

lpPolyCounts A pointer to an array of integers representing the number of points in each polygon.

nCount The number of polygons.

nPolyFillMode The fill mode for the polygon. This parameter can be ALTERNATE or WINDING. A value of ALTERNATE causes Windows to fill the area between odd and even numbered sides on a per scanline basis. (It draws a horizontal line between the odd side and the even side.) WINDING causes Windows to consider the direction in which each line segment of the polyline is drawn. It does this by drawing an imaginary line from each enclosed area in the polygon to outside of the figure. Each time this imaginary line crosses a line segment that was drawn in a clockwise direction, a count is incremented. Each time the imaginary line crosses a line segment that was drawn in a scanline direction, the count is decremented. If, after this process, the count is non-zero, the enclosed area from which the imaginary line began is filled.

Returns Non-zero if the function is successful; otherwise, zero.

See Also CRgn::CreatePolygonRgn, ::CreatePolyPolygonRgn

Example

```
// define polygon points (2 triangles in this case)
// must close them manually
CPoint pts[8] = {CPoint(1,1), CPoint(5,9), CPoint(20,8), CPoint(1,1),
      CPoint(100,121), CPoint(91,91), CPoint(110,118), CPoint(100,121)};
int counts[2] = {4,4};
CRgn rgn;
rgn.CreatePolyPolygonRgn(pts,counts,sizeof(counts),ALTERNATE);
```

CreateRectRgn

■ 2.0 ■ 3.0

Description Creates a rectangular region and attaches the region to the CRgn object. The bottom and right edges of the rectangle are not included in the region.

Syntax public, BOOL CreateRectRgn(int x1, int y1, int x2, int y2);

Parameters

x1 The x coordinate of the upper-left corner of the rectangle (logical units).

y1 The y coordinate of the upper-left corner of the rectangle (logical units).

x2 The x coordinate of the lower-right corner of the rectangle (logical units).

y2 The y coordinate of the lower-right corner of the rectangle (logical units).

Returns Non-zero if the function is successful; otherwise, zero.

See Also CRgn::CreateRectRgnIndirect, CRgn::CreateRoundRectRgn, CRgn::SetRectRegion, ::CreateRectRgn

Example

```
CRgn rgn;
CRect rect(1,1,100,100);
rgn.CreateRectRgn(rect);
```

CreateRectRgnIndirect ■ 2.0 ■ 3.0

Description Creates a rectangular region given a pointer to a RECT structure and attaches the region to the CRgn object. The bottom and right edges of the rectangle are not included in the region.

Syntax public, BOOL CreateRectRgnIndirect(LPCRECT lpRect);

Parameters

lpRect A pointer to the RECT structure or a CRect object that contains the region's coordinates.

Returns Non-zero if the function is successful; otherwise, zero.

See Also CRgn::CreateRectRgn, CRgn::CreateRoundRectRgn, ::CreateRectRgnIndirect

Example

```
CRgn rgn;
CRect rect(1,1,100,100);
rgn.CreateRectRgnIndirect(rect);
```

CreateRoundRectRgn ■ 2.0 ■ 3.0

Description Creates a rectangular region with rounded corners and attaches the region to the CRgn object. The bottom and right edges of the rectangle are not included in the region.

Syntax public, BOOL CreateRoundRectRgn(int x1, int y1, int x2, int y2, int x3, int y3);

Parameters

x1 The x coordinate of the upper-left corner of the rectangle (logical units).

y1 The y coordinate of the upper-left corner of the rectangle (logical units).

x2 The x coordinate of the lower-right corner of the rectangle (logical units).

y2 The y coordinate of the lower-right corner of the rectangle (logical units).

x3 The width of the ellipse used to create the rounded corners. Together with the *y3* parameter, this parameter controls the degree to which the corner will be rounded (how far back on the rectangle's sides the curve will begin). Larger values of *x3* and *y3* will yield more rounded corners. Usually, you will want the width and height of the ellipse used to draw the corners to be of the same ratio as the width and height of the rectangle itself.

y3 The height of the ellipse used to create the rounded corners. Together with the *x3* parameter, this parameter controls the degree to which the corner will be rounded (how far back on the rectangle's sides the curve will begin). Larger values of *x3* and *y3* will yield more rounded corners. Usually, you will want the width and height of the ellipse used to draw the corners to be of the same ratio as the width and height of the rectangle itself.

Returns Non-zero if the function is successful; otherwise, zero.

See Also CRgn::CreateRectRgn, CRgn::CreateRectRgnIndirect, ::CreateRoundRectRgn

Example

```
CRgn rgn;
rgn.CreateRoundRectRgn(1,1,100,100,5,5);
```

EqualRgn ■ 2.0 ■ 3.0

Description Determines whether the specified region is equivalent to the CRgn object.

Syntax public, BOOL EqualRgn(CRgn* pRgn) const;

Parameters

pRgn A pointer to the region to be compared with the CRgn object.

Returns Non-zero if the regions are equal; zero if the regions are not equal.

See Also ::EqualRgn

Example

```
CRgn rgn1,rgn2,rgn3;
rgn1.CreateRectRgn(1,1,100,100);
rgn2.CreateRectRgn(1,1,100,100);
rgn3.CreateRectRgn(1,1,100,101);

if (rgn1.EqualRgn(&rgn2)) // this one succeeds
{
..
}

if (rgn1.EqualRgn(&rgn3)) // this one doesn't succeed
{
..
}
```

FromHandle ■ 2.0 ■ 3.0

Description Returns a pointer to a CRgn given a Windows GDI region handle. If MFC does not already have a permanent CRgn associated with the specified handle, it creates a temporary one and attaches it to the handle. Temporary CRgns are automatically destroyed during idle-time processing so you can only depend on the validity of the CRgn returned by FromHandle until your application enters its idle loop, which can occur any time you return control to Windows (i.e., returning from a message map).

Syntax public, static CRgn* PASCAL FromHandle(HRGN hRgn);

Parameters

hRgn A handle to the Windows GDI region for which a CRgn should be returned.

Returns A pointer to a CRgn that may be temporary.

See Also CGdiObject::FromHandle, CGdiObject::DeleteTempMap

Example

```
void CMyWnd::SomeDrawFunc(HRGN hRng)
{
	// get possibly temporary region
	CRgn *pTempRgn = CRgn::FromHandle(hRgn);
	CClientDC dc(this);
	CBrush brush(RGB(100,100,100));
	dc.FrameRgn(pGrn,&brush,2,2);
}
```

GetRegionData

■ 2.0 ■ 3.0 ■ NM

Description Retrieves the data representing the region or the amount of space required in order to store that data.

Syntax public, int GetRegionData(LPRGNDATA lpRgnData, int nCount) const;

Parameters

lpRgnData A pointer to a RGNDATA structure that will receive the region data. If this parameter is NULL, GetRegionData will calculate and return the size of the buffer required to hold the data but will not return the data itself.

nCount The size of the buffer pointed to by *lpRgnData*.

Returns If *lpRgnData* is NULL, the size of the buffer required to hold the region data. Otherwise, non-zero indicates the function was successful and zero indicates that it failed.

See Also CRgn::CreateFromData, ::GetRegionData

Example

```
void CMyFunc(CRgn *pRgn)
{
	int nSizeNeeded = pRgn->GetRegionData(NULL,0);
	REGIONDATA *pRgnData = (REGIONDATA *)new char[nSizeNeeded];
	pRgn->GetRegionData(pRgnData,nSizeNeeded);
	.. // use region data
	delete pRgnData;
}
```

GetRgnBox

■ 2.0 ■ 3.0

Description Retrieves the bounding rectangle of the region. The bounding rectangle of the region is the smallest rectangle that can completely contain the region.

Syntax public, int GetRgnBox(LPRECT lpRect) const;

Parameters

lpRect A pointer to RECT structure or a CRect object that will receive the bounding rectangle coordinates.

Returns One of the following values:

COMPLEXREGION The region has overlapping borders.

NULLREGION The region is empty.

SIMPLEREGION The region has no overlapping borders.

ERROR The CRgn object does not specify a valid region.

See Also ::GetRgnBox

Example

```
// define polygon points (triangle in this case)
CPoint pts[3] = {CPoint(1,1), CPoint(5,9), CPoint(20,8)};
CRgn rgn;
rgn.CreatePolygonRgn(pts,sizeof(pts),ALTERNATE);

CRect rect;
rgn.GetRgnBox(rect); // rect = 1,1,20,9
```

operator HRGN

–. ■ 4.0

Description Cast operator that converts the CRgn object to a HRGN (region handle). This operator allows you to pass a CRgn object wherever an HRGN is required—such as for an SDK function involving regions.

Syntax public, operator HRGN() const;

Parameters None.

Returns The HRGN associated with the CRgn object.

Example

```
// define polygon points (triangle in this case)
CPoint pts[3] = {CPoint(1,1), CPoint(5,9), CPoint(20,8)};
CRgn rgn;
CClientDC dc(pWnd);
CBrush brush(RGB(255,0,0,0));

rgn.CreatePolygonRgn(pts,sizeof(pts),ALTERNATE);

// pass to SDK function needing an HRGN
::FillRgn(dc,rgn,brush);
```

OffsetRgn

■ 2.0 ■ 3.0

Description Moves the region by the specified amounts in the horizontal and vertical directions. Remember that the coordinates of a region must be between -32767 and +32767 so be careful not to exceed these limits when shifting the region.

Syntax public, int OffsetRgn(int x, int y);
public, int OffsetRgn(POINT point);

Parameters

x	The amount by which to horizontally shift the region.
y	The amount by which to vertically shift the region.
point	The amount by which to shift the region in the x and y directions.

Returns One of the following values describing the region:

COMPLEXREGION	The region has overlapping borders.
NULLREGION	The region is empty.
SIMPLEREGION	The region has no overlapping borders.
ERROR	The region handle is not valid.

See Also ::OffsetRgn

Example

```
// define polygon points (triangle in this case)
CPoint pts[3] = {CPoint(1,1), CPoint(5,9), CPoint(20,8)};
CRgn rgn;
rgn.CreatePolygonRgn(pts,sizeof(pts),ALTERNATE);

rgn.OffsetRgn(2,3); // region points now 3,4 7,12 22,11
```

PtInRegion

■ 2.0 ■ 3.0

Description Determines whether a given point is within the bounds of the region.

Syntax public, BOOL PtInRegion(int x, int y) const;
public, BOOL PtInRegion(POINT point) const;

Parameters

x	The x coordinate of the point to check.
y	The y coordinate of the point to check.
point	The point to check as either a POINT structure or a CPoint object.

Returns Non-zero if the point is within the region or zero if it is not.

See Also ::PtInRegion

Example

```
void CSomeWnd::OnLButtonDown(UINT uFlags, CPoint pt)
{
      // define polygon points (triangle in this case)
      CPoint pts[3] = {CPoint(1,1), CPoint(5,9), CPoint(20,8)};
      CRgn rgn;
      rgn.CreatePolygonRgn(pts,sizeof(pts),ALTERNATE);
```

```
        // see if button pressed within triangle
        if (rgn.PtInRegion(pt))
        {
            .. // do something
        }
}
```

RectInRegion

■ 2.0 ■ 3.0

Description Determines whether any part of a specified rectangle lies within the bounds of the region.

Syntax public, BOOL RectInRegion(LPCRECT lpRect) const;

Parameters

lpRect A pointer to the RECT structure or the CRect object to check for inclusion.

Returns Non-zero if any part of the rectangle is within the region; otherwise, zero.

See Also ::RectInRegion

Example

```
void CSomeWnd::OnMouseMove(UINT uFlags, CPoint pt)
{
        // define polygon points (triangle in this case)
        CPoint pts[3] = {CPoint(1,1), CPoint(5,9), CPoint(20,8)};
        CRgn rgn;
        rgn.CreatePolygonRgn(pts,sizeof(pts),ALTERNATE);

        // user is dragging rectangle, original left button down point
        // is in m_ptButtonDown;
        // see dragged rectangle intersects with triangle
        CRect rect(m_ptButtonDown.x, m_ptButtonDown.y,pt.x,pt.y);
        if (rgn.RectInRegion(rect))
        {
            .. // do something
        }
}
```

SetRectRegion

■ 2.0 ■ 3.0

Description Sets the region to be the specified rectangle. Note that this function, unlike CRgn::CreateRectRgn, does not create a new region. It assumes that the CRgn object already contains a valid GDI region and then sets that region to be the given rectangle. Using this function is faster than using CRgn::CreateRectRgn because it does not have to allocate memory for the region.

Syntax public, void SetRectRgn(int x1, int y1, int x2, int y2);
public, void SetRectRgn(LPCRECT lpRect);

Parameters

x1 The x coordinate of the upper-left corner of the rectangle (logical units).

y1 The y coordinate of the upper-left corner of the rectangle (logical units).

x2 The x coordinate of the lower-right corner of the rectangle (logical units).

y2 The y coordinate of the lower-right corner of the rectangle (logical units).

lpRect A pointer to a RECT structure or a CRect object describing the rectangle.

Returns Nothing is returned.

See Also CRgn::CreateRectRgn, ::SetRectRegion

Example

```
CRgn rectRgn;

// first time, must use create
rectRgn.CreateRgn(1,1,100,100);

.. // do something with original region

// now we can just use set to change the region which is faster than
// using create again
rectRgn.SetRectRgn(201,201,300,300);

.. // do something with new region
```

The CFont Class

The CFont class is MFC's encapsulation of the Windows GDI font object, represented by an HFONT. The CFont object provides very little in the way of functionality. It simply encapsulates the creation of fonts.

CFont ■ 2.0 ■ 3.0

Description The constructor for the CFont class. It does nothing. You must call one of the font creation member functions, such as CreateFont, before using the font object.

Syntax public, CFont( );

Parameters None.

Returns Nothing is returned.

See Also CFont::~ CFont, CFont::CreateFont, CFont::CreateFontIndirect, CFont::CreatePointFont, CFont::CreatePointFontIndirect

~CFont ■ 2.0 ■ 3.0 ■ UD

Description Destructor for the CFont class.

Syntax public, virtual ~CFont();

Parameters None.

Returns Nothing is returned.

See Also CFont::CFont

CreateFont ■ 2.0 ■ 3.0

Description Creates a font with the specified characteristics and attaches it to the CFont object.

Syntax public, BOOL CreateFont(int nHeight, int nWidth, int nEscapement, int nOrientation, int nWeight, BYTE bItalic, BYTE bUnderline, BYTE bStrikeOut, BYTE nCharSet, BYTE nOutPrecision, BYTE nClipPrecision, BYTE nQuality, BYTE nPitchAndFamily, LPCTSTR lpszFacename);

Parameters

nHeight Specifies the desired height of the font, in logical units. If *nHeight* is greater than zero, it is converted to device units and matched with the cell height of the available fonts. If *nHeight* is zero, a "reasonable" default size is selected by the system. If *nHeight* is less than zero, it is converted to device units and the absolute values are then matched with the cell height of the available fonts.

nWidth Specifies the average character width, in logical units. If this parameter is zero, the system will choose a width based on the value of *nHeight* and the aspect ratio of the device.

nEscapement The angle, in tenths of degrees relative to the bottom of the page, of each line of text written in the font—usually zero.

nOrientation The angle, in tenths of degrees relative to the bottom of the page, of each character's baseline—usually zero.

nWeight The weight of the font. This parameter should be in the range of 0 to 1000. 400 is considered "normal" and 700 is considered bold. If this parameter is zero, a default weight is used.

bItalic If TRUE, the font is italic.

bUnderline If TRUE, the font is underlined.

bStrikeOut If TRUE, the font is a strikeout font.

nCharSet Specifies the character set. Can be a system-dependent value, or one of the following predefined values:

ANSI_CHARSET	DEFAULT_CHARSET
OEM_CHARSET	SHIFTJIS_CHARSET
SYMBOL_CHARSET	UNICODE_CHARSET

nOutPrecision The output precision. Output precision specifies how closely the text output must match the height, width, orientation, escapement, and pitch that are requested. Can be one of the following values:

OUT_CHARACTER_PRECIS	OUT_DEVICE_PRECIS
OUT_DEFAULT_PRECIS	OUT_TT_PRECIS
OUT_STRING_PRECIS	OUT_RASTER_PRECIS
OUT_STROKE_PRECIS	

nClipPrecision The clipping precision that defines how characters that fall partially outside the clipping region will be clipped. Can be one of the following values:

	CLIP_CHARACTER_PRECIS	CLIP_MASK	CLIP_TT_ALWAYS
	CLIP_DEFAULT_PRECIS	CLIP_ENCAPSULATE	
	CLIP_STROKE_PRECIS	CLIP_LH_ANGLES	

nQuality The output quality that defines how carefully the GDI should attempt to match the logical font's attributes to those of the actual physical font. This parameter can be one of the following values:

DEFAULT_QUALITY Appearance of the font does not matter.

DRAFT_QUALITY Appearance of the font is less important than when PROOF_QUALITY is used. For GDI fonts, scaling is enabled, which means that more font sizes are available, but the quality may be lower. Bold, italic, underline, and strikeout fonts are created if necessary.

PROOF_QUALITY Character quality of the font is more important than exact matching of the logical-font attributes. For GDI fonts, scaling is disabled and the font closest in size is chosen. Although the chosen font size may not be mapped exactly when PROOF_QUALITY is used, the quality of the font is high and there is no distortion of appearance. Bold, italic, underline, and strikeout fonts are created if necessary.

nPitchAndFamily Specifies the pitch and family of the font. Can be a combination of one value from each of the following lists:

Pitch Flags: DEFAULT_PITCH, FIXED_PITCH, VARIABLE_PITCH

Familty Flags:

FF_DECORATIVE Novelty fonts.

FF_DONTCARE Don't care.

FF_MODERN Fonts with constant stroke width (fixed-pitch), with or without serifs. Fixed-pitch fonts are usually modern.

FF_ROMAN Fonts with variable stroke width (proportionally spaced) and with serifs.

FF_SCRIPT Fonts designed to look like handwriting.

FF_SWISS Fonts with variable stroke width (proportionally spaced) and without serifs.

lpszFacename Points to a NULL-terminated string that specifies the typeface of the font. This buffer should never be longer that 32 characters. If this parameter is NULL, a default typeface is selected.

Returns Non-zero if the font is successfully created; otherwise, zero.

See Also CFont:CreateFontIndirect, CFont::CreatePointFont, CFont::CreatePointFontIndirect, ::CreateFont

Example

```
CClientDC dc(pWnd);
CFont font, *pOldFont;

font.CreateFont(14,0,0,0,400,FALSE,FALSE,FALSE,ANSI_CHARSET,
     OUT_DEFAULT_PRECIS,CLIP_DEFAULT_PRECIS,DEFAULT_QUALITY,
     VARIABLE_PITCH|FF_ROMAN,"Time New Roman");

// draw some text
pOldFont = dc.SelectObject(&font);
```

```
dc.TextOut(5,20,"Test My Font",12);

// clean up
dc.SelectObject(pOldFont);
```

CreateFontIndirect ■ 2.0 ■ 3.0

Description Creates a font from the specifications provided in the specified LOGFONT structure.

Syntax public, BOOL CreateFontIndirect(const LPLOGFONT lpLogFont);

Parameters

lpLogFont A pointer to a LOGFONT structure. The members of the LOGFONT structure are described below:

lfHeight–The height of the font in logical units. If lfHeight is greater than zero, it is converted into device units and matched with the cell height of the available fonts. If it is zero, a "reasonable" default size is selected. If it is less than zero, it is converted into device units and the absolute value is matched with the character height of the available fonts.

lfWidth –Specifies the average character width, in logical units. If this parameter is zero, the system will choose a width based on the value of *lfHeight* and the aspect ratio of the device.

lfEscapement–The angle, in tenths of degrees relative to the bottom of the page, of each line of text written in the font—usually zero.

lfOrientation–The angle, in tenths of degrees relative to the bottom of the page, of each character's baseline—usually zero.

lfWeight–The weight of the font. This parameter should be in the range of 0 to 1000. 400 is considered "normal" and 700 is considered bold. If this parameter is zero, a default weight is used.

lfItalic–Specifies an italic font if set to TRUE.

lfUnderline–Specifies an underlined font if set to TRUE.

lfStrikeOut–Specifies a strikeout font if set to TRUE.

lfCharSet–Specifies the character set. Can be a system-dependent OEM character set or one of the following predefined values:

ANSI_CHARSET	UNICODE_CHARSET
OEM_CHARSET	DEFAULT_CHARSET
SYMBOL_CHARSET	SHIFTJIS_CHARSET

lfOutPrecision–The output precision. Output precision specifies how closely the text output must match the height, width, orientation, escapement, and pitch that are requested. Can be one of the following values:

OUT_CHARACTER_PRECIS	OUT_DEVICE_PRECIS
OUT_DEFAULT_PRECIS	OUT_TT_PRECIS
OUT_STRING_PRECIS	OUT_RASTER_PRECIS
OUT_STROKE_PRECIS	

lfClipPrecision–The clipping precision that defines how characters that fall partially outside the clipping region will be clipped. Can be one of the following values:

CLIP_CHARACTER_PRECIS	CLIP_ENCAPSULATE
CLIP_DEFAULT_PRECIS	CLIP_LH_ANGLES
CLIP_STROKE_PRECIS	CLIP_TT_ALWAYS
CLIP_MASK	

lfQuality–The output quality that defines how carefully the GDI should attempt to match the logical font's attributes to those of the actual physical font. This parameter can be one of the following values:

DEFAULT_QUALITY Appearance of the font does not matter.

DRAFT_QUALITY Appearance of the font is less important than when PROOF_QUALITY is used. For GDI fonts, scaling is enabled, which means that more font sizes are available, but the quality may be lower. Bold, italic, underline, and strikeout fonts are created if necessary.

PROOF_QUALITY Character quality of the font is more important than exact matching of the logical-font attributes. For GDI fonts, scaling is disabled and the font closest in size is chosen. Although the chosen font size may not be mapped exactly when PROOF_QUALITY is used, the quality of the font is high and there is no distortion of appearance. Bold, italic, underline, and strikeout fonts are created if necessary.

lfPitchAndFamily–Specifies the pitch and family of the font. Can be a combination of one value from each of the following lists:

Pitch Flags: DEFAULT_PITCH, FIXED_PITCH, VARIABLE_PITCH

Family Flags:

FF_DECORATIVE Novelty fonts.

FF_DONTCARE Don't care.

FF_MODERN Fonts with constant stroke width (fixed-pitch), with or without serifs. Fixed-pitch fonts are usually modern.

FF_ROMAN Fonts with variable stroke width (proportionally spaced) and with serifs.

FF_SCRIPT Fonts designed to look like handwriting.

FF_SWISS Fonts with variable stroke width (proportionally spaced) and without serifs.

lfFaceName–Points to a NULL-terminated string that specifies the typeface of the font. This buffer should never be longer that 32 characters. If this parameter is NULL, a default typeface is selected.

Returns Non-zero if the function is successful; otherwise, zero.

See Also CFont::CreateFont, ::CreateFontIndirect

Example

```
CClientDC dc(pWnd);
CFont font,*pOldFont;

// create the font
LOGFONT logFont;
memset(&logfont,0,sizeof(LOGFONT));
logfont.lfHeight = 14;
logfont.lfWeight = FW_NORMAL;
logfont.lfPitchAndFamily = VARIABLE_PITCH | FF_SWISS;
lstrcpy(logfont.lfFaceName,"MS Sans Serif");
font.CreateFontIndirect(&logfont);

pOldFont = dc.SelectObject(&font);
dc.TextOut(5,20,"Test My Font",12);

// clean up
dc.SelectObject(pOldFont);
```

CreatePointFont

–. ■ 4.0

Description Provides a simple way to create a basic font of a specified point size. This function is very convenient because you do not have to specify the plethora of information required for the other font creation functions.

Syntax public, BOOL CreatePointFont(int nPointSize, LPCTSTR lpszFaceName, CDC *pDC = NULL);

Parameters

nPointSize The size of the desired font in tenths of a point.

lpszFaceName The typeface name of the desired font.

pDC A pointer to the device context that will be used to convert the specified point size into logical units. This parameter can be NULL, in which case a default screen device context will be used.

Returns Non-zero if the font is successfully created; otherwise, zero.

See Also CFont:CreatePointFontIndirect, CFont::CreateFont, CFont::CreateFontIndirect,

Example

```
CClientDC dc(pWnd);
CFont font, *pOldFont;

// create a 12-point font
font.CreatePointFont(120,"Time New Roman",&dc);

// draw some text
pOldFont = dc.SelectObject(&font);
dc.TextOut(5,20,"Test My Font",12);

// clean up
dc.SelectObject(pOldFont);
```

CreatePointFontIndirect

–. ■ 4.0

Description Creates a font in the same manner as CreateFontIndirect except that the specified font height should be in tenths of a point instead of logical units. This function automatically converts the requested point size into logical units using the supplied device context or a default screen device context.

Syntax public, BOOL CreatePointFontIndirect(const LOGFONT* pLogFont, CDC *pDC = NULL);

Parameters

lpLogFont A pointer to a LOGFONT structure that describes the desired font. For a complete description of this structure, see CFont::CreateFontIndirect. This structure should be filled in in the same manner as with the CreateFontIndirect function except that the lfHeight member should contain the font's desired point size, in tenths of a point, instead of in logical units.

pDC A pointer to the device context that will be used to convert the specified point size into logical units. This parameter can be NULL, in which case a default screen device context will be used.

Returns Non-zero if the font is successfully created; otherwise, zero.

See Also CFont::CreatePointFont, CFont::CreateFontIndirect

Example See CFont::CreateFontIndirect

Dump

■ 2.0 ■ 3.0 ■ DO

Description Outputs diagnostic information about the current state of the CFont object. For the CFont class this information includes the handle of the Windows GDI font currently attached to it, and the contents of the LOGFONT structure associated with the font.

Syntax public, virtual void Dump(CDumpContext& dc) const;

Parameters

dc A reference to the dump context to which the status information should be sent. Usually this will be the MFC default debug dump context *afxDump*. *afxDump* sends its output to the debugger and only exists in the debug build of MFC.

Returns Nothing is returned.

See Also CGdiObject::Dump

Example

```
// call to dump function
CFont font;
font.Dump(afxDump);

// output from dump function
a CFont at $64F818
```

```
m_hObject = 0xD10
lf.lfHeight = -16
lf.lfWidth = 0
lf.lfEscapement = 0
lf.lfOrientation = 0
lf.lfWeight = 0
lf.lfItalic = 0
lf.lfUnderline = 0
lf.lfStrikeOut = 0
lf.lfCharSet = 1
lf.lfOutPrecision = 0
lf.lfClipPrecision = 0
lf.lfQuality = 0
lf.lfPitchAndFamily = 0
lf.lfFaceName = MS Sans Serif
```

FromHandle

■ 2.0 ■ 3.0

Description Returns a pointer to a CFont given a Windows GDI font handle. If MFC does not already have a permanent CFont associated with the specified handle, it creates a temporary one and attaches it to the handle. Temporary CFonts are automatically destroyed during idle-time processing so you can only depend on the validity of the CFont returned by FromHandle until your application enters its idle loop, which can occur any time you return control to Windows (i.e., returning from a message map).

Syntax public, static CFont* PASCAL FromHandle(HFONT hFont);

Parameters

hFont A handle to the Windows GDI font for which a CFont should be returned.

Returns A pointer to a CFont, which may be temporary.

See Also CGdiObject::FromHandle, CGdiObject::DeleteTempMap

Example

```
void CMyWnd::SomeDrawFunc(HFONT hFont)
{
      // get possibly temporary font
      CFont *pTempFont = CFont::FromHandle(hFont);
      CClientDC dc(this);
      CFont *pOldFont = dc.SelectObject(pTempFont);
      dc.TextOut(5,10,"Hello",5);
      dc.SelectObject(pOldFont);
      // don't need to delete the pointer returned by FromHandle
}
```

GetLogFont

–. ■ 4.0

Description Fills a LOGFONT SDK structure with information regarding the font associated with the CFont object. In versions of MFC before 4.0, use the CGdiObject::GetObject function to perform this task.

Syntax public, int GetLogFont(LOGFONT* pLogFont);

Parameters

pLogFont A pointer to a LOGFONT structure that will be filled with information about the font. For a description of this structure see the CFont::CreateFontIndirect function.

Returns Non-zero if successful; otherwise, zero.

See Also CGdiObject::GetObject

Example

```
...
CClientDC dc(pWnd);
CPen font;

font.CreateFont(14,0,0,0,400,FALSE,FALSE,FALSE,ANSI_CHARSET,
      OUT_DEFAULT_PRECIS,CLIP_DEFAULT_PRECIS,DEFAULT_QUALITY,
      VARIABLE_PITCH|FF_ROMAN,"Time New Roman");

// get info about font
LOGFONT logFont;
font.GetLogFont(&logFont);
```

operator HFONT

–. ■ 4.0

Description Cast operator that converts the CFont object to an HFONT (font handle). This operator allows you to pass a CFont object wherever an HFONT is required—such as for an SDK function involving fonts.

Syntax public, operator HFONT() const;

Parameters None.

Returns The HFONT associated with the CFont object.

Example

```
...
CClientDC dc(pWnd);
CFont font;

font.CreateFont(14,0,0,0,400,FALSE,FALSE,FALSE,ANSI_CHARSET,
      OUT_DEFAULT_PRECIS,CLIP_DEFAULT_PRECIS,DEFAULT_QUALITY,
      VARIABLE_PITCH|FF_ROMAN,"Time New Roman");

// use SDK function for some unknown reason
::SelectObject(dc,font);
```

13

COLLECTION CLASSES

13

COLLECTION CLASSES

Data structures such as arrays, lists, and similar objects are key elements of all but the very simplest programs. Most programmers cut their coding teeth on such topics as linked lists and multidimensional arrays. With the advent of C++, data structures have been encapsulated by abstract classes that do much of the grunt work and bit-twiddling. MFC, like many class hierarchies, includes such worker bee classes with the framework. These classes, known as the Collection Classes, have proven to be indispensable to the MFC programmer. Functionally, they consist of arrays, lists, and maps, including the CString class—a special type of character array—and have become perhaps the most frequently used of all the classes of MFC.

Whereas the average programmer is quite familiar with the nature and purpose of arrays, and maybe even such things as doubly-linked lists, a few of the provided objects, such as maps, are more esoteric. Maps are a great way to store data and can be keyed by a certain value, a look-up for quickly retrieving the information later. An implementation of an address book, which keys entries by each letter of the alphabet, is a good example of a map.

The collection classes can be grouped into two general categories: non-template-based and template-based. This chapter will deal with the non-template-based classes first. Prior to MFC 3.0, all collection classes were non-template-based, mainly because the Visual C++ compiler up to that point did not support C++ templates. As a result, there are a good number of very similar classes that differ only in the data types being stored. The approach in documenting these classes will be to discuss the characteristics of a group of classes as a whole (for example, all array classes), list the members of one class in detail, and simply give examples, noting any gotchas, for the other classes in the same "family."

With MFC 3.0+, the collection classes also come in template-based versions. For the programmer unfamiliar with C++ templates in general, there are many excellent books that cover the subject. Space limits prohibit a proper treatment of this feature of the language here. The key advantage of the template-based collection classes is that, by their nature, they allow the programmer to determine the actual data types being stored with each usage. The programmer is no longer confined by the small number of primitive types implemented by the non-template-based collection classes. In Table 13-1 below, there is a summary of the classes covered in this chapter:

Table 13-1 Chapter 13 class summary

Class Name	Description
CByteArray	Array of bytes
CWordArray	Array of WORDs
CDWordArray	Array of DWORDs
CUIntArray	Array of UINTs
CPtrArray	Array of pointers
CObArray	Array of CObject-based objects
CStringArray	Array of CString objects
CPtrList	List of pointers
CObList	List of CObject-based objects
CStringList	List of CString objects
CMapWordToOb	Map of WORDs to CObject-based objects
CMapWordToPtr	Map of WORDs to pointers
CMapPtrToWord	Map of pointers to WORDs
CMapPtrToPtr	Map of pointers to pointers
CMapStringToPtr	Map of CString objects to pointers
CMapStringToOb	Map of CString objects to CObject-based objects
CMapStringToString	Map of CString objects to CString objects
CString	MFC string class (dynamic array of CHARs)
CArray	Template-based array class
CList	Template-based list class
CMap	Template-based map class

About the Program

This chapter also introduces a sample application used to track courses, students, and professors at a university. This program is used in the following chapter as well as a source of illustrative examples of the MFC issues discussed. It is essentially a data entry program that allows the user to enter information for all the students and professors at a school, and then enter the courses offered for a particular semester, as well as the syllabus for each course. The user can then assign students and a professor to a class, saving and loading the data to and from a file. The program uses various kinds of collection classes to store the data objects and the relationships between them. There are four major data objects: CBook, CStudent, CProfessor, and CCourse. There is also a global CCourseData that holds the collections of courses, students, and professors. The full source code for this program can be found on the companion CD-ROM.

Arrays

The array classes of MFC store a dynamically changing amount of homogeneous data in a contiguous block of memory. There are classes for storing BYTEs, WORDs, DWORDs, UINTs, CStrings, void pointers, and pointers to CObjects. The CString class, which stores an array of characters, will be discussed later in this chapter. Each class has four data members:

- a pointer to the data (m_pData).
- the number of elements in use (m_nSize).
- the number of allocated elements (m_nMaxSize).
- the minimum number of new elements to be added when the array needs to grow (m_nGrowBy).

For performance reasons, when creating new elements, the array allocates memory as BYTEs and then type-casts, regardless of the actual data type being stored, by-passing in all cases any calls to a generic C++ constructor. When the size of the array increases, a new contiguous block of memory is allocated and the contents of the old array are copied with a call to the memcpy function. For this reason, it is valuable to increase the m_nGrowBy member when adding a large number of elements sequentially to avoid a new memory allocation and copy with each new element. When the size of the array decreases, the member m_nSize is changed appropriately but the excess memory is not released explictly at that time. The array destructor, however, releases all outstanding allocated memory. Although MFC performs housekeeping for all memory the array allocates, for arrays that store pointers (CPtrArray and CObArray) it is the programmer's responsibility to delete the pointers themselves.

The elements of the array are accessed through a zero-based index. Because the size of the array is stored as an integer, the maximum number of elements is the value of the UINT_MAX constant, but could be less, depending upon the size of the data type being stored. In order to avoid using huge pointers, the amount of memory allocated for the array is limited to 64K for the 16-bit versions of MFC. In Debug mode, the array will assert if an attempt is made to exceed either of these limits. An often overlooked fact is that, as the array is resized, an index of a particular element can change. This is because when you remove an element in the middle of the array, all indices above the removed element are shifted down by one. One of the most common mistakes made with the Collection Classes is to treat the array index as if it were actually a key, always referring to the same element. For example, the following code, in Listing 13-1, written to delete elements from a CPtrArray, will produce undesired results, actually causing a memory leak:

Listing 13-1 Incorrect usage of index

```
void CMyDoc::DeleteElements()
{
      int nI;
      CMyObject* pObj;

      for (nI = 0;nI < m_MyPtrArray.GetSize();nI++)
      {
            pObj = (CMyObject*)m_MyPtrArray.GetAt(nI);
            m_MyPtrArray.RemoveAt(nI);
            delete pObj;
      }
}
```

The problem with this code is that the member RemoveAt shrinks the array, causing the indices of all elements above the element being removed to be reduced by one. Because of this fact, the deletion process as written above will skip over every other element in the array. To see why this is true, follow the for loop through two iterations. The first time through, nI equals 0, meaning that element 0 is deleted and removed. The side effect is that element 1 now becomes element 0. The second time through, nI equals 1, meaning that what was element 2 is deleted and removed, and what was initially element 1 is completely skipped.

A correct way of rewriting this function, as shown in Listing 13-2, is to wait until after deleting each element before removing all of the elements from the array at once:

Listing 13-2 Correct DeleteElements function

```
void CMyDoc::DeleteElements()
{
      int nI;
      CMyObject* pObj;

      for (nI = 0;nI < m_MyPtrArray.GetSize();nI++)
      {
            pObj = (CMyObject*)m_MyPtrArray.GetAt(nI);
            delete pObj;
      }
      m_MyPtrArray.RemoveAll();
}
```

A more sophisticated way of making the DeleteElements function work correctly would be to iterate through the elements of the array in inverse order, going from index m_nSize–1 to index 0. This way, a call to RemoveAt will not change the indices of any remaining elements.

CByteArray

The CByteArray class stores an array of BYTEs. BYTEs are usually used to store data flags, so a typical use of a CByteArray is to store a series of flagged values.

CByteArray Class Reference

CByteArray

■ 2.0 ■ 3.0

Description The constructor for the CByteArray class. CByteArray initializes the members of the array class.

Syntax public, CByteArray();

Parameters None.

Returns Nothing is returned.

See Also CByteArray::~CByteArray

~CByteArray

■ 2.0 ■ 3.0

Description Destructor deletes all memory allocated.

Syntax public, ~CByteArray();

Parameters None.

Returns Nothing is returned.

See Also CByteArray::CByteArray

Add

■ 2.0 ■ 3.0

Description Add appends an element to the end of the array.

Syntax public, int Add(BYTE newElement);

Parameters

newElement Value of the element to be added.

Returns The index of the added element.

Example

```
CByteArray x;
BYTE y;

y =10;
x.Add(y);
```

AssertValid

■ 2.0 ■ 3.0 ■ DO

Description This function validates the current state of the object, causing an assertion if object is invalid. For more information about debugging, see Chapter 15, *Debugging and Exception Handling.*

Syntax public, void AssertValid() const;

Parameters None.

Returns Nothing is returned.

Dump

■ 2.0 ■ 3.0 ■ DO

Description Dump dumps diagnostics information on the current state of the object. For more information about debugging, see Chapter 15, *Debugging and Exception Handling*.

Syntax public, void Dump(CDumpContext& dc) const;

Parameters

dc Dump context for diagnostics.

Returns Nothing is returned.

ElementAt

■ 2.0 ■ 3.0

Description ElementAt returns an element of the array. This value can be used as either an l-value or an r-value of an expression. Primarily, though, ElementAt is used to produce an l-value of an expression because GetAt produces only r-values.

Syntax public, BYTE& ElementAt(int nIndex);

Parameters

nIndex Zero-based index of the element of the array.

Returns Reference to the actual element of the array specified by the index.

See Also CByteArray::GetAt, CByteArray::operator[]

Example

```
CByteArray x;
BYTE y;

x.SetSize(10);
y = 10;
x.ElementAt(3) = y;
```

FreeExtra

■ 2.0 ■ 3.0

Description FreeExtra releases any memory allocated for elements not currently used. This function should be used after calls to RemoveAt() or RemoveAll(). This function actually creates a new array of m_nSize size and copies the used data from the old array before deleting it.

Syntax public, void FreeExtra();

Parameters None.

Returns Nothing is returned.

See Also CByteArray::RemoveAt, CByteArray::RemoveAll

GetAt

■ 2.0 ■ 3.0

Description GetAt retrieves an element of the array. The returned value can only be an r-value of an expression.

Syntax public, BYTE GetAt(int nIndex) const;

Parameters

nIndex Zero-based index of the element of the array.

Returns Value of the element of the array specified by the index.

See Also CByteArray::SetAt, CByteArray::ElementAt, CByteArray::operator[]

Example

```
CByteArray x;
BYTE y;

x.Add(10);
y = x.GetAt(0);
```

GetSize

■ 2.0 ■ 3.0

Description GetSize returns the m_nSize data member, the number of elements in the array. This function is typically used to find the bounds when iterating through the elements of the array.

Syntax public, int GetSize() const;

Parameters None.

Returns Number of elements in the array.

See Also CByteArray::SetSize, CByteArray::GetUpperBound

Example

```
CByteArray x;
int nI;
BYTE y;

for (nI = 0;nI < x.GetSize();nI++)
     y = x[nI];
```

GetUpperBound

■ 2.0 ■ 3.0

Description GetUpperBound returns the upper index of the array, the index of the last element, equal to one less than the total number of elements returned by GetSize.

Syntax public, int GetUpperBound() const;

Parameters None.

Returns Upper index of the array (m_nSize–1).

See Also CByteArray::SetSize, CByteArray::GetSize

INSERTAT

■ 2.0 ■ 3.0

Description InsertAt inserts elements into the array at a certain position. Can be used also to insert one CByteArray into another.

Syntax public, void InsertAt(int nIndex, BYTE newElement, int nCount = 1); void InsertAt(int nStartIndex, CByteArray* pNewArray);

Parameters

nIndex Index where to insert the element.

newElement Value of element.

nCount Number of new identical elements to add.

nStartIndex Index where to insert the elements of the copied array.

pNewArray Array to insert.

Returns Nothing is returned.

Example

```
CByteArray x;
BYTE y;

y = 10;
x.InsertAt(3,y,10);
```

OPERATOR[]

■ 2.0 ■ 3.0

Description This operator provides access to an element in the array; index is zero-based. Returned value can be used either as an l-value or an r-value in an expression. The version returning a BYTE calls GetAt. The version returning a BYTE reference calls ElementAt. The compiler will determine which one to use depending upon the context of its usage (whether or not it is used as an l-value or an r-value).

Syntax public, BYTE operator[](int nIndex) const; BYTE& operator[](int nIndex);

Parameters

nIndex Index of the element in the array.

Returns Either the value of the element of the array or a reference to the actual element specified by the index.

See Also CByteArray::GetAt, CByteArray::ElementAt

Example

```
CByteArray x;
int nI;

x.SetSize(10);
for (nI = 0;nI < x.GetSize();nI++)
     x[nI] = 5;
```

RemoveAll

■ 2.0 ■ 3.0

Description RemoveAll removes all elements of the array—the memory allocated for the array is not freed until a call to FreeExtra() or the object is destroyed.

Syntax public, void RemoveAll();

Parameters None.

Returns Nothing is returned.

See Also CByteArray::FreeExtra, CByteArray::RemoveAt

RemoveAt

■ 2.0 ■ 3.0

Description RemoveAt removes elements from the array. The memory allocated for the element is not freed. Indices for elements above the element removed will decrease by one.

Syntax public, void RemoveAt(int nIndex, int nCount = 1);

Parameters

nIndex Index of element to be removed.

nCount Number of elements to remove.

Returns Nothing is returned.

See Also CByteArray::RemoveAll

Example

```
CByteArray x;
int nI;

// iterate backwards so that indexes remain the same
for (nI = x.GetUpperBound();nI >= 0;nI--)
     x.RemoveAt(nI);
```

Serialize

■ 2.0 ■ 3.0

Description Serializes current state of the array, copying the contents of the array to a CArchive, which in turn saves and loads the information to and from a file. See Chapter 14, *Files and Serialization*, for a discussion of serialization.

Syntax public, void Serialize(CArchive& ar);

Parameters

ar Archive context for serialization.

Returns Nothing is returned.

SetAt

■ 2.0 ■ 3.0

Description SetAt sets an element of the array. The index must be a valid one.

Syntax public, void SetAt(int nIndex, BYTE newElement);

Parameters

nIndex — Index of the element of the array to be set.

newElement — Value of element.

Returns — Nothing is returned.

See Also — CByteArray::GetAt, CByteArray::operator[]

SetAtGrow

■ 2.0 ■ 3.0

Description — SetAtGrow sets an element of the array, growing the array if necessary.

Syntax — public, void SetAtGrow(int nIndex, BYTE newElement);

Parameters

nIndex — Index of the element of the array.

newElement — Value of the element.

Returns — Nothing is returned.

See Also — CByteArray::SetAt

SetSize

■ 2.0 ■ 3.0

Description — SetSize sets the number of elements of the array, allocating or de-allocating memory if necessary. The nGrowBy parameter specifies the minimum number of elements created if the array needs to grow.

Syntax — public, void SetSize(int nNewSize, int nGrowBy = -1);

Parameters

nNewSize — New number of elements.

nGrowBy — Number of extra elements to create.

Returns — Nothing is returned.

See Also — CByteArray::GetSize, CByteArray::GetUpperBound

Example

```
CByteArray x;
x.SetSize(30,10); // set size initially to 30, grow by 10 thereafter
```

CWordArray

The CWordArray class stores an array of WORDs. The Courses application uses a CWordArray (m_HeldOn, member of the CCourse object) to store the days of the week a course is held on. A different word value corresponds to a particular day of the week (0 = Sunday, 1 = Monday, etc.). When displaying information for a course, the application lists the days of the week in a CListBox and then uses the CWordArray to determine which elements of the CListBox to select, as shown in Listing 13-3 below:

Listing 13-3 CWordArray example

```
static char BASED_CODE sDays[7][20] =
{"Sunday","Monday","Tuesday","Wednesday","Thursday",
"Friday","Saturday"};

void CCourseDlg::ListHeldOn()
{
        CListBox* pListBox = (CListBox*)GetDlgItem(IDC_HELDON);
        int nI;

        pListBox->ResetContent();
        for (nI = 0;nI < 7;nI++)
               pListBox->AddString(sDays[nI]);

        for (nI = 0;nI < m_pCourse->m_HeldOn.GetSize();nI++)
               pListBox->SetSel(m_pCourse->m_HeldOn[nI],TRUE);
}
```

CDWordArray

The CDWordArray class stores an array of DWORDs. The Courses application uses a CDWordArray (m_Students, member of the CCourse object) to store which students have registered for a particular course. The values reference the global CPtrArray object that stores the students themselves. When displaying information for the course, the application lists all of the students in a CListBox, then uses the CDWordArray to determine which students to select, as shown in Listing 13-4 below:

Listing 13-4 CDWordArray example

```
void CCourseDlg::ListStudents()
{
   CStudent* pStudent;
   int nI,nJ,nWhich;
   CListBox* pListBox = (CListBox*)GetDlgItem(IDC_STUDENTS);
   CString strName;
   BOOL bSelect;

   pListBox->ResetContent();
   for (nI = 0;nI < App()->Data()->m_Students.GetSize();nI++)
   {
          pStudent = (CStudent*)App()->Data()->m_Students[nI];
          strName = pStudent->m_strLastName + ", " +
             pStudent->m_strFirstName + " " + pStudent->m_cMiddleInitial;
          nWhich = pListBox->AddString(strName);
          pListBox->SetItemData(nWhich,nI);

          bSelect = FALSE;
          for (nJ = 0;nJ < m_pCourse->m_Students.GetSize();nJ++)
          {
                 if ( m_pCourse->m_Students[nJ] == (DWORD)nI )
                 {
```

continued on next page

continued from previous page

```
                        bSelect = TRUE;
                        break;
                    }
                }
                if ( bSelect )
                    pListBox->SetSel(nWhich,TRUE);
        }
    }
```

CUIntArray

The CUIntArray class stores an array of UINTs (unsigned integers; values from 0 to the value of the UINT_MAX constant). The Courses application does not use a CUIntArray; however, using it is no different than using any of the other array classes.

CPtrArray

The CPtrArray class stores an array of void pointers, and thus can be used to manage any sort of data. It is the programmer's responsibility to delete these pointers before the array is destroyed (unless these pointers are stored separately as well, in which case the pointers can be deleted afterwards as appropriate). Typically, the class that instantiates the array contains code (usually in the destructor or in a member function called by the destructor) for removing and deleting each pointer. One of the most frequent mistakes made by the beginner MFC programmer is to remove elements from a CPtrArray without deleting them, thus causing a memory leak. The Courses application uses a CPtrArray (m_Students, member of the global CCourseData object) to store the students. When listing the students into a CListBox, the program iterates through each student, composing a string by combining the first name, last name, and middle initial of the student and then adding them to the CListBox, as shown in Listing 13-5 below:

Listing 13-5 CPtrArray example

```
void CStudentsDlg::ListStudents()
{
    CStudent* pStudent;
    int nI,nWhich;
    CListBox* pListBox = (CListBox*)GetDlgItem(IDC_STUDENTS);
    CString strName;

    pListBox->ResetContent();
    for (nI = 0;nI < App()->Data()->m_Students.GetSize();nI++)
    {
        pStudent = (CStudent*)App()->Data()->m_Students[nI];
        strName = pStudent->m_strLastName + ", " +
        pStudent->m_strFirstName + " " + pStudent->m_cMiddleInitial;
        nWhich = pListBox->AddString(strName);
        pListBox->SetItemData(nWhich,nI);
    }

    OnSelchangeStudents();
}
```

CObArray

The CObArray stores an array of pointers to CObject-derived objects. It is the programmer's responsibility to delete these pointers. The two major advantages of using a CObArray instead of a CPtrArray when storing pointers to CObject-derived objects are

- You do not need to type-cast when calling CObject-level functions for elements of the array.
- The CObArray automatically serializes each element of the array when the array itself is serialized. See Chapter 14, *Files and Serialization,* for a discussion of serialization.

The Courses application uses a CObArray (m_Courses, member of the global CCourseData object) for storing the courses. Below, in Listing 13-6, is the code the program uses to properly remove a course from its CObArray.

Listing 13-6 CObArray example

```
void CCoursesDlg::OnRemove()
{
        CListBox* pListBox = (CListBox*)GetDlgItem(IDC_COURSES);
        CCourse* pCourse;
        int nWhich,nCourse;

        if ( (nWhich = pListBox->GetCurSel()) != LB_ERR )
        {
                nCourse = pListBox->GetItemData(nWhich);
                pCourse = (CCourse*)App()->Data()->m_Courses[nCourse];
                delete pCourse;
                App()->Data()->m_Courses.RemoveAt(nCourse);
                ListCourses();
        }
}
```

CStringArray

The CStringArray stores an array of CStrings. The array actually stores only a copy of the characters passed in whenever a CString is added. This means that it is not necessary to delete the CString when it is removed from the array or to delete all CStrings before the array is destroyed because the copies are automatically deleted when the array is destroyed. Note that the constructor and destructor for CString are not called for performance reasons; the CStrings stored in the array are created as BYTEs and then typecasted to CStrings. Serializing CStrings stored in a CStringArray is easy because the array will automatically serialize each element, not requiring the programmer to serialize each separately. See Chapter 14, *Files and Serialization,* for a discussion of serialization.

Lists

The list classes of MFC store data of a particular data type in a doubly-linked list of nodes. There are classes for storing void pointers, pointers to CObjects, and CStrings. Each class has six data members:

- a pointer to the head node in the list (m_pNodeHead).
- a pointer to the tail node in the list (m_pNodeTail).
- the number of nodes in the list (m_nCount).
- a pointer to the allocated but unused nodes (m_pNodeFree).
- a pointer to the blocks of nodes allocated (m_pBlocks).
- the number of nodes to create at a time (m_nBlockSize).

Because the number of nodes in the list is stored as an integer, the maximum number of nodes is the value of the INT_MAX constant. In Debug mode, the list will assert if an attempt is made to exceed this limit. Nodes are not necessarily allocated one at a time. They are allocated in blocks of m_nBlockSize size by a structure known in MFC parlance as a plex. The m_nBlockSize data member is set at construction time; the default value is 10. A node consists of pointers to the next and previous nodes and the data itself, the data type of which depends upon the list (a void pointer for CPtrList, a pointer to a CObject for CObList, or a CString from CStringList). For the CPtrList and the CObList, it is the programmer's responsibility to delete the data pointer of each node; the list takes care of deleting the nodes themselves.

Plexes, consisting of a contiguous array of nodes and a pointer to the next plex, are singly chained together by the list to keep track of all allocated nodes. The nodes within a given plex do not necessarily have to be chained with each other. A node of one plex can be chained with any other nodes in any other plex. This relationship can be seen in Figure 13-1.

While elements of an array are accessed by index, the data in nodes of a list are accessed by position. The POSITION construct, which is a typedef for a void pointer, denotes the position in the list. This pointer is actually a pointer to the node itself. The real question, then, is how to determine the position of a particular node. The answer is that there are member functions for determining the "position" of the first and last nodes, and member functions for stepping from these two nodes to all the other nodes. There also is a member function that will determine the "position" of a node based on an index, which is actually the number of nodes past the first node in the chain.

When a node is freed, the nodes previous and next to it then become chained together. The freed node gets added to the singly-chained list of nodes that have been allocated but are unused (tracked by the m_pNodeFree member), to be used again when needed. The plexes themselves (and the nodes within them) are not deleted until the list is destroyed or until a call is made to the RemoveAll member function. A new plex is created automatically when a new node is to be used but there are no more free nodes left.

CPtrList

The CPtrList class stores a list of pointers. It is the programmer's responsibility to delete these pointers.

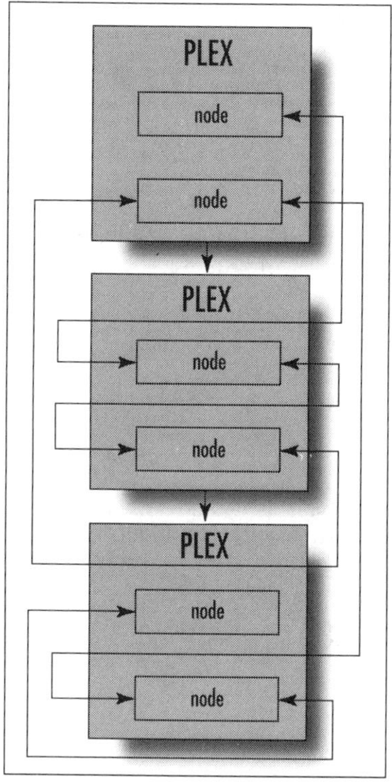

Figure 13-1 Singly chained plexes and doubly linked Nodes

CPtrList Class Reference

CPtrList

■ 2.0 ■ 3.0

Description The constructor for the CPtrList class. CPtrList initializes the members of the list class.

Syntax public, CPtrList(int nBlockSize = 10);

Parameters

nBlockSize Number of nodes to create at a time.

Returns Nothing is returned.

See Also CPtrList::~CPtrList

~CPtrList

■ 2.0 ■ 3.0

Description Destructor frees all nodes by calling RemoveAll.

Syntax public, ~CPtrList();

Parameters None.

Returns Nothing is returned.

See Also CPtrList::RemoveAll

ADDHEAD

■ 2.0 ■ 3.0

Description AddHead adds a node before what was the first (head) node of the list. The new node becomes the head. It can also be used to chain lists together by passing a pointer to another list.

Syntax public, POSITION AddHead(void* newElement);
void AddHead(CPtrList* pNewList);

Parameters

newElement Pointer to the data for the new node.

pNewList Pointer to the new list to add.

Returns The first version returns the position (the pointer) of the new node.

See Also CPtrList::AddTail

Example

```
CPtrList list;
void* pX;
void* pY;

pY = list.GetAt(list.AddHead(pX));
```

ADDTAIL

■ 2.0 ■ 3.0

Description AddTail adds a node after what was the last (tail) node of the list. The new node becomes the tail. It can also be used to chain lists together by passing a pointer to another list.

Syntax public, POSITION AddTail(void* newElement);
void AddTail(CPtrList* pNewList);

Parameters

newElement Pointer to the data for the new node.

pNewList Pointer to the new list to add.

Returns The position (the pointer) of the new node.

See Also CPtrList::AddHead

Example

```
CPtrList list1;
CPtrList list2;

list1.AddTail(&list2);
```

ASSERTVALID

■ 2.0 ■ 3.0 ■ DO

Description Validation function for CPtrList, will assert if object is invalid. For more information about debugging, see Chapter 15, *Debugging and Exception Handling*.

Syntax public, void AssertValid() const;

Parameters None.

Returns Nothing is returned.

See Also CPtrList::Dump

DUMP

■ 2.0 ■ 3.0 ■ DO

Description Dump dumps diagnostics information on the current state of the object. For more information about debugging, see Chapter 15, *Debugging and Exception Handling.*

Syntax public, void Dump(CDumpContext& dc) const;

Parameters

dc Dump context for diagnostics.

Returns Nothing is returned.

See Also CPtrList::AssertValid

FIND

■ 2.0 ■ 3.0

Description Find tries to find the position of a node based upon search criteria.

Syntax public, POSITION Find(void* searchValue, POSITION startAfter = NULL) const;

Parameters

searchValue Pointer to data of node to be found.

startAfter Position of starting node in the search.

Returns Position of desired node; NULL if not found.

See Also CPtrList::FindIndex

Example

```
CPtrList list;
POSITION pos;
void* pOb;

pos = list.Find(pOb);
if ( pos != NULL )
     AfxMessageBox("Object found!");
```

FINDINDEX

■ 2.0 ■ 3.0

Description FindIndex finds the position of a node based upon the specified index.

Syntax public, POSITION FindIndex(int nIndex) const;

Parameters

nIndex Zero-based index of the desired node; should equal the number of nodes past the head node.

Returns The position of the desired node; NULL if not found.

See Also CPtrList::Find

Example

```
CPtrList list;
void* pOb;
POSITION pos;

pos = list.FindIndex(list.GetCount() Ñ 1);
// get last element of list, not necessarily tail
if ( pos != NULL )
     pOb = list.GetAt(pos);
```

FreeNode

■ 2.0 ■ 3.0 ■ UD

Description FreeNode frees a node, which then becomes added to the pool of available nodes. The previous node and next node are then chained together. No memory is freed until a call to RemoveAll().

Syntax protected, void FreeNode(CNode* pNode);

Parameters

pNode Pointer to node to be freed.

Returns Nothing is returned.

See Also CPtrList::NewNode

GetAt

■ 2.0 ■ 3.0

Description GetAt returns the data of a node, based upon the position specified. Value can be either an l-value or and r-value of an expression. The compiler will determine which of the two versions of GetAt to use depending upon the context of its usage (whether or not it is used as an l-value or an r-value).

Syntax public, void*& GetAt(POSITION position);
void* GetAt(POSITION position) const;

Parameters

position Position of desired node.

Returns Pointer or pointer reference to the data of the desired node.

See Also CPtrList::SetAt

Example

```
CPtrList list;
void* pOb;

pOb = list.GetAt(list.GetHeadPosition()); // get head object
```

GetCount

■ 2.0 ■ 3.0

Description GetCount returns the number of nodes in the list.

Syntax public,int GetCount() const;

Parameters None.

Returns Returns the number of nodes in the list (m_nCount).

See Also CPtrList::IsEmpty

GetHead

■ 2.0 ■ 3.0

Description GetHead returns the data of the first (head) node in the list. Value can be either an l-value or and r-value of an expression. The compiler will determine which of the two versions of GetHead to use depending upon the context of its usage (whether or not it is used as an l-value or an r-value).

Syntax public,void*& GetHead(); void* GetHead() const;

Parameters None.

Returns Pointer or pointer reference to the data of the first (head) node in the list.

See Also CPtrList::GetTail

GetHeadPosition

■ 2.0 ■ 3.0

Description GetHeadPosition returns the position (pointer) of the first (head) node in the list.

Syntax public, POSITION GetHeadPosition() const;

Parameters None.

Returns The position (pointer) of the first (head) node in the list.

See Also CPtrList::GetTailPosition, CPtrList::GetNext, CPtrList::GetPrev

Example

```
CPtrList list;
POSITION pos;
void* pOb;

pos = list.GetHeadPosition();
while ( pos != NULL )
        pOb = list.GetNext(pos); // iterate through list elements
```

GetNext

■ 2.0 ■ 3.0

Description GetNext gets the next node in the list, based upon the position specified. Value can be either an l-value or and r-value of an expression. The compiler will determine which of the two versions of GetNext to use depending upon the context of its usage (whether or not it is used as an l-value or an r-value).

Syntax public,void*& GetNext(POSITION& rPosition);
void* GetNext(POSITION& rPosition) const;

Parameters

rPosition Position of current node.

Returns Pointer or pointer reference to the data of the next node.

See Also CPtrList::GetHeadPosition, CPtrList::GetTailPosition, CPtrList::GetPrev

GetPrev

■ 2.0 ■ 3.0

Description GetPrev gets the previous node in the list, based upon the position specified. Value can be either an l-value or and r-value of an expression. The compiler will determine which of the two versions of GetPrev to use depending upon the context of its usage (whether or not it is used as an l-value or an r-value).

Syntax public,void*& GetPrev(POSITION& rPosition);
void* GetPrev(POSITION& rPosition) const;

Parameters

rPosition Position of current node.

Returns Pointer or pointer reference to the data of the previous node.

See Also CPtrList::GetHeadPosition, CPtrList::GetTailPosition, CPtrList::GetNext

Example

```
CPtrList list;
POSITION pos;
void* pOb;

pos = list.GetTailPosition();
while ( pos != NULL )
      pOb = list.GetPrev(pos);
```

GetTail

■ 2.0 ■ 3.0

Description GetTail returns the data of the last (tail) node of the list. Value can be either an l-value or and r-value of an expression. The compiler will determine which of the two versions of GetTail to use depending upon the context of its usage (whether or not it is used as an l-value or an r-value).

Syntax public,void*& GetTail(); void* GetTail() const;

Parameters None.

Returns Pointer or pointer reference to the data of the last (tail) node in the list.

See Also CPtrList::GetHead

Example

```
CPtrList list;
void* pOb;

pOb = list.GetTail(); // tail of list
```

GetTailPosition

■ 2.0 ■ 3.0

Description GetTailPosition returns the position (pointer) of the last (tail) node in the list.

Syntax public,POSITION GetTailPosition() const;

Parameters None.

Returns The position (pointer) of the last (tail) node in the list.

See Also CPtrList::GetHeadPosition, CPtrList::GetNext, CPtrList::GetPrev

InsertAfter

■ 2.0 ■ 3.0

Description InsertAfter inserts a node after a given position.

Syntax public,POSITION InsertAfter(POSITION rPosition,void* newElement);

Parameters

rPosition Desired position.

newElement Pointer to data for new node.

Returns The position (pointer) of the new node.

See Also CPtrList::InsertBefore

Example

```
CPtrList list;
POSITION pos;
void* pOb;

pos = list.GetHeadPosition();
list.InsertAfter(pos,pOb); // insert after head of list
```

InsertBefore

■ 2.0 ■ 3.0

Description InsertBefore inserts a node before a given position.

Syntax public, POSITION InsertBefore(POSITION position, void* newElement);

Parameters

position Desired position.

newElement Pointer to data for new node.

Returns The position (pointer) of the new node.

See Also CPtrList::InsertAfter

Example

```
CPtrList list;
POSITION pos;
void* pOb;

pos = list.GetTailPosition();
list.InsertBefore(pos,pOb); // insert before tail of list
```

IsEmpty

■ 2.0 ■ 3.0

Description	IsEmpty determines whether there are no nodes in the list.
Syntax	public,BOOL IsEmpty() const;
Parameters	None.
Returns	TRUE if the list is empty; FALSE otherwise.
See Also	CPtrList::GetCount

NewNode

■ 2.0 ■ 3.0 ■ UD

Description	NewNode is called to generate a new node. This function will create new plexes when needed. The number of nodes in a plex is determined by the m_nBlockSize data member set when the list is constructed. When there are no more free nodes, NewNode will create another plex. This function is called internally by MFC.
Syntax	protected,CNode* NewNode(CNode* pPrev,CNode* pNext);
Parameters	
pPrev	Pointer to node previous to the new node.
pNext	Pointer to next node from the new node.
Returns	Pointer to the new node.
See Also	CPtrList::FreeNode

RemoveAll

■ 2.0 ■ 3.0

Description	RemoveAll removes all nodes from the list. Also, all plexes (containers for nodes) are deleted, freeing all memory currently allocated. This function is called during destruction to clean up the object, but can be called by the programmer at any time.
Syntax	public,void RemoveAll();
Parameters	None.
Returns	Nothing is returned.
See Also	CPtrList::RemoveAt

RemoveAt

■ 2.0 ■ 3.0

Description	RemoveAt removes a node from the list, based upon the position specified. Nodes to either side of the node removed will thereafter be chained together.
Syntax	public,void RemoveAt(POSITION position);

Parameters

position Position of desired node.

Returns Nothing is returned.

See Also CPtrList::RemoveAll

Example

```
CPtrList list;

list.RemoveAt(list.GetTailPosition()); // same as RemoveTail()
```

RemoveHead

■ 2.0 ■ 3.0

Description RemoveHead removes the first (head) node of the list. The next node then becomes the head. Do not call this function on an empty list.

Syntax public,void* RemoveHead();

Parameters None.

Returns Pointer to the data of what was the first (head) node in the list.

See Also CPtrList::RemoveTail

RemoveTail

■ 2.0 ■ 3.0

Description RemoveTail removes the last (tail) node of the list. The previous node then becomes the tail. Do not call this function on an empty list.

Syntax public,void* RemoveTail();

Parameters None.

Returns Pointer to the data of what was the last (tail) node in the list.

See Also CPtrList::RemoveHead

SetAt

■ 2.0 ■ 3.0

Description SetAt sets the data of a specified node, based upon the position specified.

Syntax public,void SetAt(POSITION pos, void* newElement);

Parameters

pos Position of desired node.

newElement Pointer to the new data for desired node.

Returns Nothing is returned.

See Also CPtrList::GetAt

Example

```
CPtrList list;
void* pOb;

// changes the value of the head element of the list
list.SetAt(list.GetHeadPosition(),pOb);
```

CObList

The CObList class stores a list of pointers to CObject-derived objects. It is the programmer's responsibility to delete these pointers before the list is destroyed. The two major advantages of using a CObList instead of a CPtrList when storing pointers to CObject-derived objects are

- You do not need to type-cast when calling CObject-level functions for elements of the array.
- CObList automatically serializes each element of the list when the list itself is serialized. See Chapter 14, *Files and Serialization*, for a discussion of serialization.

The Courses application uses a CObList (m_Syllabus, member of the CCourse object) to store the books for a course. Listing 13-7 shows code used by the application to list the books for a course in a CListBox:

Listing 13-7 CObList example

```
void CCourseDlg::ListBooks()
{
        POSITION pos,current;
        CBook* pBook;
        int nWhich;
        CListBox* pListBox = (CListBox*)GetDlgItem(IDC_BOOKS);

        pListBox->ResetContent();
        pos = m_pCourse->m_Syllabus.GetHeadPosition();
        while ( pos != NULL )
        {
                current = pos;
                pBook = (CBook*)m_pCourse->m_Syllabus.GetNext(pos);
                nWhich = pListBox->AddString(pBook->m_strTitle);
                pListBox->SetItemData(nWhich,(DWORD)current);
        }

        OnSelchangeBooks();
}
```

Listing 13-8 shows how the CCourse object deletes the books upon destruction.

Listing 13-8 Deleting CObList elements

```
CCourse::~CCourse()
{
        POSITION pos;
        CBook* pBook;

        pos = m_Syllabus.GetHeadPosition();
        while ( pos != NULL )
        {
                pBook = (CBook*)m_Syllabus.GetNext(pos);
                delete pBook;
        }
}
```

CStringList

The CStringList class stores a list of CStrings. The list stores a copy of the data passed in, so the programmer does not have to worry about deleting the data of each node. A CStringList class is not used by the CCourses application, but its usage is no different than that of a CObList, other than not having to delete the members of the list.

Maps

The map classes of MFC store data of a particular data type in a singly-linked list of nodes which can be referenced directly by keys of a particular data type. There are classes for storing pointers to CObjects keyed by WORDs, void pointers keyed by WORDs, WORDs keyed by void pointers, void pointers keyed by void pointers, void pointers keyed by CStrings, pointers to CObjects keyed by CStrings, and CStrings keyed by CStrings. This is summarized by Table 13-2 below.

Table 13-2 Map classes

Map Class	Key Data Type	Stored Data Type
CMapWordToPtr	WORD	void*
CMapPtrToWord	void*	WORD
CMapPtrToPtr	void*	void*
CMapWordToOb	WORD	CObject*
CMapStringToPtr	CString	void*
CMapStringToOb	CString	CObject*
CMapStringToString	CString	CString

Note that MFC map classes are named such that the key data type appears first and the data type appears second.

Each map class has six data members:

- a pointer to the hash table (m_pHashTable).
- the size of the hash table (m_nHashTableSize).
- the number of nodes in the map (m_nCount).
- a pointer to allocated but unused nodes (m_pFreeList).
- a pointer to the blocks of nodes allocated (m_pBlocks).
- the number of nodes to create at a time (m_nBlockSize).

The implementation of the map classes is very similar to the implementation of the list classes. For maps, nodes are represented by an internal CAssoc structure. The CAssoc structure consists of a pointer to the next CAssoc, a hash value (indicating into which bin of the hash table this CAssoc belongs), a key, and the data. The data types of the key and the data depend upon the particular map class.

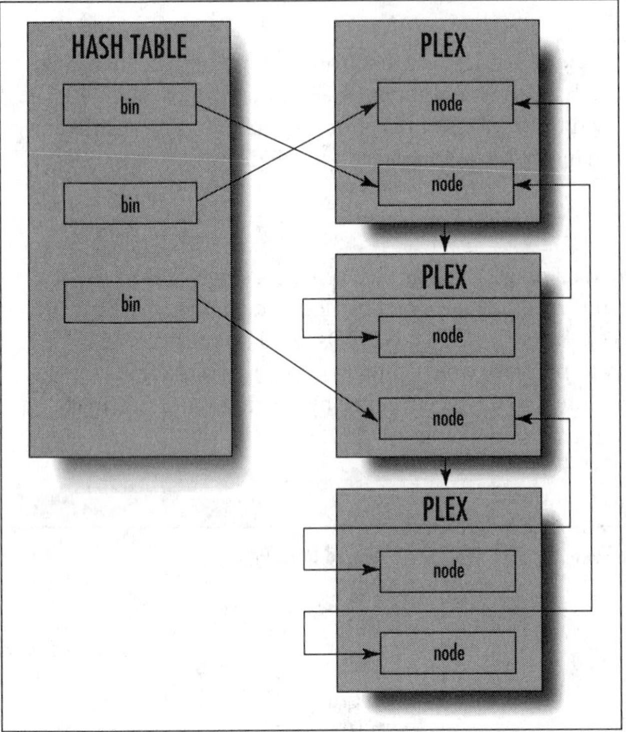

Figure 13-2 The hash table, plexes, and nodes of a map

The big difference between a map and a list is the presence of a hash table. Recall that in a list, the nodes are arbitrarily distributed. When you want to find a particular node, you have no choice but to start at one of the ends and iterate until you find the one you want. With significantly large lists, this process can become quite slow. What a hash table does essentially is separate the nodes into different bins. The key for each node, normally determined by some algorithmic process, indicates to which bin the node belongs. When a programmer wants to access the data of a particular node, the key and the hash table are used in conjunction to determine a starting point for the search. This instantly eliminates the large majority of nodes which are in the map.

The hash table is simply a list of pointers to nodes. These are the starting nodes for each bin. A hash value is used to determine which of these pointers should be used to start the search. The MFC map classes use a very slick method of determining the hash value for a key which works for most primitive types, but not CStrings. In the cases where a CString is used as a key, there is a slightly different method. The hash table structure is wholly different from the plexes that perform the memory allocation for the nodes. The relationship among the hash table, plexes, and nodes for a map can be seen in Figure 13-2.

CMapWordToOb

The CMapWordToOb class stores pointers to CObject-based classes keyed by WORDs.

CMapWordToOb Class Reference

CMapWordToOb ■ 2.0 ■ 3.0

Description The constructor for the CMapWordToOb class. CMapWordToOb initializes the members of the map class.

Syntax public,CMapWordToOb(int nBlockSize = 10);

Parameters

nBlockSize Number of nodes to create at a time.

Returns Nothing is returned.

See Also CMapWordToOb::~CMapWordToOb

~CMapWordToOb ■ 2.0 ■ 3.0

Description Destructor frees all nodes by calling RemoveAll().

Syntax public,~CMapWordToOb();

Parameters None.

Returns Nothing is returned.

See Also CMapWordToOb::RemoveAll

AssertValid ■ 2.0 ■ 3.0 ■ DO

Description Validation function for CMapWordToOb, will assert if object is invalid. For more information about debugging, see Chapter 15, *Debugging and Exception Handling*.

Syntax public,void AssertValid() const;

Parameters None.

Returns Nothing is returned.

See Also CMapWordToOb::Dump

Dump ■ 2.0 ■ 3.0 ■ DO

Description Dump dumps diagnostics information on the current state of the object. For more information about debugging, see Chapter 15, *Debugging and Exception Handling*.

Syntax public, void Dump(CDumpContext& dc) const;

Parameters

dc — Dump context for diagnostics.

Returns — Nothing is returned.

See Also — CMapWordToOb::AssertValid

FreeAssoc ■ 2.0 ■ 3.0 ■ UD

Description — FreeAssoc frees a node. The node then becomes part of the pool of available nodes. The previous node and next node are then chained together. No memory is freed until RemoveAll() is called. This function is called internally by MFC when RemoveKey() is called.

Syntax — protected,void FreeAssoc(CAssoc* pAssoc);

Parameters

pAssoc — Pointer to node to be freed.

Returns — Nothing is returned.

See Also — CMapWordToOb::NewAssoc

GetAssocAt ■ 2.0 ■ 3.0 ■ UD

Description — GetAssocAt gets the node from the hash table by its key. This function is called internally by MFC when trying to access an element of the map.

Syntax — protected,CAssoc* GetAssocAt(WORD key,UINT& nHash) const;

Parameters

key — Key of node.

nHash — Hash value to determine which bin to start the search.

Returns — The pointer to the node.

See Also — CMapWordToOb::Lookup, CMapWordToOb::operator[]

GetCount ■ 2.0 ■ 3.0

Description — GetCount determines the number of nodes in the map. Because the map classes have no method to access elements by index, there is little need to find the bounds of the map.

Syntax — public,int GetCount() const;

Parameters — None.

Returns — The number of nodes in the map (m_nCount).

See Also — CMapWordToOb::IsEmpty

Example

```
CMapWortToOb map;
int nCount;

nCount = map.GetCount();
```

GetHashTableSize

■ 2.0 ■ 3.0

Description GetHashTableSize returns the number of bins (pointers to nodes) in the hash table. The default size is 17. This function would be used in the implementation of a derived map class that provided a different hashing scheme than what is provided by the base class.

Syntax public,UINT GetHashTableSize() const;

Parameters None.

Returns The size of the hash table.

See Also CMapWordToOb::InitHashTable

GetNextAssoc

■ 2.0 ■ 3.0

Description GetNextAssoc returns the position of the next node of the map with a given key, based upon the position specified.

Syntax public,void GetNextAssoc(POSITION& rNextPosition, WORD& rKey, CObject*& rValue) const;

Parameters

rNextPosition Position of next node.

rKey Key of node.

rValue Data of node.

Returns Nothing is returned.

See Also CMapWordToOb::GetStartPosition

Example

```
CMapWordToOb map;
POSITION pos;
WORD wKey = 10;

pos = map.GetStartPosition();
while ( pos != NULL )
     GetNextAssoc(pos,wKey,pOb); // retrieve all objects keyed by 10
```

GetStartPosition

■ 2.0 ■ 3.0

Description GetStartPosition returns the position of the first node of the map, used in order to iterate through each node in the map. This function is called regardless of which key will actually be searched for.

Syntax public,POSITION GetStartPosition() const;

Parameters None.

Returns The position (pointer) of the first node in the map.

See Also CMapWordToOb::GetNextAssoc

Example

```
CMapWordToOb map;
POSITION pos;

pos = map.GetStartPosition();
if ( pos == NULL )
     AfxMessageBox("The Map is Empty!");
```

HashKey

■ 2.0 ■ 3.0

Description HashKey determines the hash value for a given key. It is called internally by MFC to retrieve the hash value for the key, which indicates in which bin the keyed associations are stored. This function would be called by the programmer, mostly, in derived map classes implementing an enhanced hashing scheme.

Syntax public,UINT HashKey(WORD key) const;

Parameters

key Key.

Returns Hash value.

InitHashTable

■ 2.0 ■ 3.0

Description InitHashTable initializes the hash table. This function is called internally by MFC. It would be called by the programmer when deriving from the base class when implementing a custom hashing scheme.

Syntax public,void InitHashTable(UINT hashSize, BOOL bAllocNow = TRUE);

Parameters

hashSize Number of bins in hash table.

bAllocNow TRUE if the hash table should be allocated immediately; FALSE otherwise.

Returns Nothing is returned.

See Also CMapWordToOb::GetHashTableSize

IsEmpty

■ 2.0 ■ 3.0

Description IsEmpty determines whether or not the map is empty.

Syntax public,BOOL IsEmpty() const;

Parameters None.

Returns TRUE if the map is empty; FALSE otherwise.

See Also CMapWordToOb::GetCount

Example

```
CMapWordToOb map;

if ( map.IsEmpty() )
     AfxMessageBox("The Map is Empty!");
```

LOOKUP

■ 2.0 ■ 3.0

Description Lookup looks up a node by its key and determines its data. This is the primary method of finding elements in a map.

Syntax public,BOOL Lookup(WORD key,CObject*& rValue) const:

Parameters

key Key for node.

rValue Data for node.

Returns TRUE if the node was found; FALSE otherwise.

See Also CMapWordToOb::operator[], CMapWordToOb::GetAssocAt

Example

```
CMapWordToOb map;
CObject* pOb;
WORD wKey = 10;

if ( !map.Lookup(wKey,pOb) )
     AfxMessageBox("Object not found!");
```

NEWASSOC

■ 2.0 ■ 3.0 ■ UD

Description NewAssoc is called to generate a new node. This function will create new plexes when needed. It is called internally by MFC.

Syntax protected, CAssoc* NewAssoc();

Parameters None.

Returns The new node.

See Also CMapWordToOb::FreeAssoc

OPERATOR[]

■ 2.0 ■ 3.0

Description The operator[] function accesses a node by its key. This function is equivalent to SetAt().

Syntax public,CObject*& operator[](WORD key);

Parameters

key Key for node.

Returns The data for the node.

See Also CMapWordToOb::Lookup, CMapWordToOb::GetAssocAt, CMapWordToOb::SetAt

Example

```
CMapWordToOb map;
CObject* pOb;
WORD wKey = 10;

map[10] = pOb; // add object to map, keyed by 10
```

RemoveAll

■ 2.0 ■ 3.0

Description RemoveAll removes all nodes from the map; it also deletes all memory allocated.

Syntax public,void RemoveAll();

Parameters None.

Returns Nothing is returned.

See Also CMapWordToOb::RemoveKey, CMapWordToOb::~CMapWordToOb

RemoveKey

■ 2.0 ■ 3.0

Description RemoveKey removes a node determined by its key. No memory is freed until RemoveAll() is called.

Syntax public, BOOL RemoveKey(WORD key);

Parameters

key Key of node to be removed.

Returns TRUE if node is found and removed; FALSE otherwise.

See Also CMapWordToOb::RemoveAll

Example

```
CMapWordToOb map;
WORD wKey = 10;

while ( map.RemoveKey(wKey) ); // removes all elements keyed by 10
```

Serialize

■ 2.0 ■ 3.0

Description Serializes current state of the map, copying the contents of the map to a CArchive, which in turn, saves and loads the information to and from a file. See Chapter 14, *Files and Serialization,* for a discussion of serialization.

Syntax public,void Serialize(CArchive& ar);

Parameters

ar Archive.

Returns Nothing is returned.

SetAt

■ 2.0 ■ 3.0

Description SetAt adds a new node.

Syntax public,void SetAt(WORD key,CObject* newValue);

Parameters

key Key for new node.

newValue Pointer to data for new node.

Returns Nothing is returned.

Example

```
CMapWordToOb map;
WORD wKey = 10;
CObject* pOb;

map.SetAt(wKey,pOb); // add object, keyed by 10
```

CMapWordToPtr

The CMapWordToPtr class stores pointers keyed by WORDs.

CMapPtrToWord

The CMapPtrToWord class stores WORDs keyed by pointers.

CMapPtrToPtr

The CMapPtrToPtr class stores pointers keyed by pointers.

CMapStringToPtr

The CMapStringToPtr class stores pointers keyed by CStrings.

CMapStringToOb

The CMapStringToOb class stores pointers to CObject-based classes keyed by CStrings.

CMapStringToString

The CMapStringToString class stores CStrings keyed by CStrings.

CString

The CString class of MFC stores a dynamically changing number of characters in a contiguous block of memory. Throughout MFC, CStrings can be used interchangeably with traditional C character arrays. Whenever there is a function that takes a const char* as a parameter, there is almost invariably a version that takes a CString instead. This is particularly true for the functions of MFC that are wrappers of the Windows API. The CString class consists largely of members for getting and setting the character array, including many overloaded operators for treating the CString class as if it were a primitive data type.

In versions of MFC prior to MFC 4.0, the CString class has three data members:

- a pointer to the data (m_pchData, zero terminated).
- the number of characters in use (m_nDataLength, does not include the terminating NULL).
- the number of characters allocated (m_nAllocLength, does not include the terminating NULL).

In versions of MFC starting with MFC 4.0, this implementation was changed in order to support reference counting. There is now just one data member, m_pchData. This is misleading, however. When the m_pchData buffer is first created, by the AllocBuffer member, 12 bytes (the size of the CStringData structure) are allocated just before the memory pointed to by m_pchData. This extra memory is used for a CStringData structure, a helper class that contains the following three data members:

- reference count (nRefs, -1 means that no referencing is allowed; 0 means that the string buffer is no longer shared and can now be deleted; >1 means string buffer is shared).
- the number of characters in use (nDataLength; does not include the terminating NULL).
- the number of characters allocated (nAllocLength; does not include the terminating NULL, nor does it include the memory used by the CStringData structure).

In MFC 4.0, reference counting for CStrings was added. When a CString is created as a copy of another CString (either when the string is constructed or through the use of the assignment operator), the CString buffer points to the characters of the source string, instead of actually copying them. Each time a CString buffer is shared in this way, the reference counter is incremented. Each time a CString is destructed that is sharing a buffer, the reference counter is decremented. Only when this reference counter equals 0 is the buffer actually deleted. When the value of a CString created as a reference changes, the reference is removed and the entire string is copied into a newly allocated buffer. The programmer can use the LockBuffer and UnlockBuffer functions to disable or enable the CString reference counting feature. Reference counting for CStrings is a powerful feature, greatly enhancing performance whenever calling functions which have CStrings as parameters, and greatly reducing the memory needed to store identical string values.

Because the number of characters allocated is stored as an integer, the maximum number of characters in a string is the value of the INT_MAX-1 constant, leaving the last character for the terminating NULL. In Debug mode, the string will assert if an attempt is made to exceed this limit. The string will also assert if an attempt is made to access a character by an invalid index. The implementation of a CString is very similar to the implementation of the array classes. When the size of the string needs to grow, a new array of characters is created and the characters from the old array are copied with a call to the memcpy function. If the string is shrunk, the characters allocated but no longer in use will stay around until the class is destroyed or until a call to Empty is made.

The CString class includes a type-cast operator for converting a CString to a const char*. This makes the CString class interchangeable with a C character array when the contents of the string do not need to change. Sometimes, this operator needs to be called explictly—for example, with the use of a sprintf call:

```
sprintf(sBuf,"The string value is %s",(const char*)str);
```

One of the major hurdles a programmer encounters when using the CString class as a parameter of a function is what to do when the contents of the string do need to change (e.g., the parameter is of type char*, not const char*). The correct solution involves calls to the GetBuffer, ReleaseBuffer, and GetBufferSetLength member functions, as shown in Listing 13-9 below:

Listing 13-9 Setting the contents of a CString

```
void CopyBuffer(CString& str,char* sSource)
{
	char* pBuf;
	nLength = strlen(sSource);

	pBuf = str.GetBuffer(nLength); // allocate nLength characters
	strcpy(pBuf,sSource);
	str.ReleaseBuffer();
}
```

One of the most convenient features of the CString class is the ability to chain together many CStrings with ordinary character buffers and characters in a single assignment statement. This is because the overloaded addition and concatenation operators return a CString, which allows the continuous formation of the string. For example, the following is a valid way of assigning a value to the CString str1:

str1 = str2 + " and " + str3 + '.' + str4; // CString + LPCSTR + CString + char + CString

The only constraint, caused by the data types of the specific operators overloaded, is that the programmer must alternate the parameters so that a CString appears at least as every other operand. If this poses an inconvenience, another alternative (available only in MFC 3.0+) is the Format() method, which provides the CString equivalent of a sprintf function:

str1.Format("%s and %s.%s",(const char*)str2,(const char*)str3,(const char*)str4);

The Courses application uses string concatenation in many places. One example, shown in Listing 13-10, is when listing professors in a CListBox:

Listing 13-10 CString operator + example

```
void CProfessorsDlg::ListProfessors()
{
	CProfessor* pProfessor;
	int nI,nWhich;
	CListBox* pListBox = (CListBox*)GetDlgItem(IDC_PROFESSORS);
	CString strName;

	pListBox->ResetContent();
	for (nI = 0;nI < App()->Data()->m_Professors.GetSize();nI++)
	{
		pProfessor = App()->Data()->m_Professors[nI];
		strName = pProfessor->m_strLastName + ", " +
		pProfessor->m_strFirstName + " " + pProfessor->m_cMiddleInitial;
		nWhich = pListBox->AddString(strName);
		pListBox->SetItemData(nWhich,nI);
	}

	OnSelchangeProfessors();
}
```

CString Class Reference

CString

■ 2.0 ■ 3.0

Description Constructor initializes members of the object. It also will optionally set the value of the string based on the specified value. For MFC 4.0+, the copy constructor (the second version listed below) will create a reference if the source string's buffer is not locked.

Syntax public,CString(); CString(const CString& stringSrc); CString(TCHAR ch, int nRepeat = 1); CString(LPCSTR lpsz); CString(LPCWSTR lpsz); CString(LPCTSTR lpch, int nLength); CString(const unsigned char* psz);

Parameters

stringSrc Source string for copy constructor version.

ch Initializing character.

nRepeat Number of characters to initialize string to.

lpsz Initializing character buffer, NULL-terminated.

lpch Initializing character buffer, not NULL-terminated.

nLength Length of character buffer.

psz Initializing character buffer, NULL-terminated.

Returns Nothing is returned.

See Also CString::~CString

Example

```
CString str("Hello World");
```

~CString

■ 2.0 ■ 3.0

Description Destructor empties the string and deletes all allocated memory.

Syntax public,~CString()

Parameters None.

Returns Nothing is returned.

See Also CString::CString

AllocBeforeWrite

■ 4.0 ■ UD

Description AllocBeforeWrite is a reference counting helper function used internally by MFC. AllocBeforeWrite is called to see if a reference exists. If so, the reference is removed and a new buffer is allocated. AllocBeforeWrite is called in situations right before the string buffer is assigned a completely new value (from within CString::operator=, for example). In contrast, in situations where the string buffer is only being modified (from within CString::SetAt, for example), CopyBeforeWrite is called instead.

Syntax protected, void AllocBeforeWrite(int nLen);

Parameters

nLen Length of buffer to allocate.

Returns Nothing is returned.

See Also CString::CopyBeforeWrite

AllocBuffer ■ 2.0 ■ 3.0

Description AllocBuffer allocates the buffer for the characters of the string. This function is used internally by MFC.

Syntax protected, void AllocBuffer(int nLen);

Parameters

nLen Number of characters to allocate.

Returns Nothing is returned.

AllocCopy ■ 2.0 ■ 3.0

Description AllocCopy copies the contents of a string to another string. This function is used internally by MFC.

Syntax protected, void AllocCopy(CString& dest, int nCopyLen, int nCopyIndex, int nExtraLen) const;

Parameters

dest Destination string.

nCopyLen Number of characters to copy.

nCopyIndex Starting position for copy.

nExtraLen Number of extra characters to allocate.

Returns Nothing is returned.

AllocSysString ■ 2.0 ■ 3.0

Description AllocSysString allocates an OLE BSTR. A BSTR is a character array that is not terminated by a 0. Instead the two bytes before the array are used to store the length.

Syntax public,BSTR AllocSysString() const;

Parameters None.

Returns BSTR allocated.

See Also CString::SetSysString

AnsiToOem

■ 2.0 ■ 3.0

Description AnsiToOem converts all characters in the string from the ANSI to OEM character sets.

Syntax public, void AnsiToOem();

Parameters None.

Returns Nothing is returned.

See Also CString::OemToAnsi

AssignCopy

■ 2.0 ■ 3.0

Description AssignCopy copies the contents of a character array into the string. This is an internal function called by MFC.

Syntax protected, void AssignCopy(int nSrcLen, LPCTSTR lpszSrcData);

Parameters

nSrcLen Number of characters to copy.

lpszSrcData Characters to copy.

Returns Nothing is returned.

Collate

■ 2.0 ■ 3.0

Description Collate compares the string with a character array, using the run-time function _tcscoll which takes into account locale-specific sorting.

Syntax public, int Collate(LPCTSTR lpsz) const;

Parameters

lpsz Character array to compare.

Returns 0 if the strings are identical, -1 if psz is greater than the string, 1 if the string is greater.

See Also CString::Compare, CString::CompareNoCase

Example

```
CString str1, str2;

if ( str1.Collate(str2) == 0 )
     AfxMessageBox("Strings Match!");
```

Compare

■ 2.0 ■ 3.0

Description Compare compares the string with another character array. The comparison is case-sensitive. Unlike Collate, Compare does not take into account locale-specific sorting.

Syntax public, int Compare(LPCTSTR lpsz) const;

Parameters

lpsz Character array to compare.

Returns 0 if the strings are identical, , < 0 if lpsz is greater than the string, > 0 if the string is greater than lpsz.

See Also CString::CompareNoCase, CString::Collate

Example

```
CString str1("HELLO");
CString str2("hello");
int nRet;

nRet = str1.Compare(str2); // should be > 0
```

CompareNoCase

■ 2.0 ■ 3.0

Description CompareNoCase compares the string with another character array. The comparison is case-insensitive.

Syntax public, int CompareNoCase(LPCTSTR lpsz) const;

Parameters

lpsz Character array to compare.

Returns 0 if the strings are identical, < 0 if lpsz is greater than the string, > 0 if the string is greater than lpsz.

See Also CString::Compare, CString::Collate

Example

```
CString str1("HELLO");
CString str2("hello");
int nRet;

nRet = str1.CompareNoCase(str2); // should equal 0
```

ConcatCopy

■ 2.0 ■ 3.0

Description ConcatCopy concatenates two separate character arrays, storing the result in the string. This is an internal function called by MFC.

Syntax protected, void ConcatCopy(int nSrc1Len, LPCTSTR lpszSrc1Data, int nSrc2Len, LPCTSTR lpszSrc2Data);

Parameters

nSrc1Len Length of first array.

lpszSrc1Data First array.

nSrc2Len Length of second array.

lpszSrc2Data Second array.

Returns Nothing is returned.

ConcatInPlace

■ 2.0 ■ 3.0

Description ConcatInPlace concatenates a character array with the string itself (i.e., the string is replaced by its concatenation with the character array). This is an internal function called by MFC.

Syntax protected, void ConcatInPlace(int nSrcLen, LPCTSTR lpszSrcData);

Parameters

nSrcLen Length of source array.

lpszSrcData Source array.

Returns Nothing is returned.

CopyBeforeWrite

■ 4.0 ■ UD

Description CopyBeforeWrite is a reference counting helper function used internally by MFC. CopyBeforeWrite is called to see if a reference exists. If so, the reference is removed, a new buffer is allocated, and the previously referenced string is copied into the new buffer. AllocBeforeWrite is called in situations right before the string buffer is assigned a completely new value (from within CString::operator=, for example). In contrast, in situations where the string buffer is only being modified (from within CString::SetAt, for example), CopyBeforeWrite is called instead.

Syntax protected, void CopyBeforeWrite();

Parameters None.

Returns Nothing is returned.

See Also CString::AllocBeforeWrite

Empty

■ 2.0 ■ 3.0

Description Empty empties the string, deleting all allocated memory.

Syntax public, void Empty();

Parameters None.

Returns Nothing is returned.

Find

■ 2.0 ■ 3.0

Description Find returns the position of the the first instance of a character or substring in the string. Find performs a forward search.

Syntax public,int Find(TCHAR ch) const; int Find(LPCTSTR lpszSub) const; *(new with MFC 4.0)*

Parameters

ch Character to find.

lpszSub	Substring to find.
Returns	Position of character, -1 if character not found.
See Also	CString::ReverseFind
Example	

```
CString str("Hello\tWorld");
int nTab;

nTab = str.Find('\t');
str = str.Right(str.GetLength() -  nTab - 1); // strip left of tab
```

FindOneOf

■ 2.0 ■ 3.0

Description	FindOneOf finds the first instance of any of a string of specified characters in a character array.
Syntax	public, int FindOneOf(LPCTSTR lpszCharSet) const;
Parameters	
lpszCharSet	Array of characters to search for.
Returns	Position of first character found, -1 if no characters are found.

Format

■ 3.0

Description	Format is the sprintf function for the string. With MFC 4.0, there are now two versions of Format, one that takes the format string as a LPCTSTR, the other taking the format string as a string resource ID. Each version, in turn, calls the new FormatV function to do the actual formatting. FormatV predetermines how large to make the buffer, then calls sprintf. In MFC 3.x, it is the Format function itself that calls sprintf.
Syntax	public, void AFX_CDECL Format(LPCTSTR lpszFormat, ...); void AFX_CDECL Format(UINT nFormatID, ...); *(new with MFC 4.0)*
Parameters	
lpszFormat	Format string to be passed to sprintf.
nFormatID	String resource ID for format string to be passed to sprintf.
Returns	Nothing is returned.
See Also	CString::FormatV
Example	

```
CString str;
CString str2("Testing");

str.Format("%s %i times",(const char*)str2,5);
```

FormatMessage

■ 4.0 ■ NM

Description	FormatMessage is a wrapper function for the ::FormatMessage Windows API function. See the Windows SDK documentation for more details.

Syntax public, void AFX_CDECL FormatMessage(LPCTSTR lpszFormat, ...);
void AFX_CDECL FormatMessage(UINT nFormatID, ...);

Parameters

lpszFormat Format string to be passed to sprintf.

nFormatID String resource ID for format string to be passed to sprintf.

Returns Nothing is returned.

FormatV ■ 4.0

Description FormatV is called by Format to perform the actual string formatting. FormatV predetermines how large to make the buffer, then calls sprintf.

Syntax protected, void FormatV(LPCTSTR lpszFormat, va_list argList);

Parameters

lpszFormat Format string to be passed to sprintf.

argList Argument list originally passed to Format.

Returns Nothing is returned.

See Also CString::Format

FreeExtra ■ 4.0

Description FreeExtra frees any memory allocated by the string but not currently used.

Syntax public, void FreeExtra();

Parameters None.

Returns Nothing is returned.

GetAllocLength ■ 2.0 ■ 3.0

Description GetAllocLength returns the number of characters allocated for the string. This can be different from the number of used characters for the string. This function is very useful when the CString is used to hold non NULL-terminating character buffers.

Syntax public, int GetAllocLength() const;

Parameters None.

Returns The number of allocated characters (m_nAllocLength).

GetAt ■ 2.0 ■ 3.0

Description GetAt accesses a character in the string by a zero-based index. This function is functionally equivalent to the operator[]() function.

Syntax public, TCHAR GetAt(int nIndex) const;

Parameters

nIndex Index for character array.

Returns The desired character.

See Also CString::operator[]

Example

```
CString str("Test");
char cChar;

cChar = str.GetAt(3);
```

GetBuffer ■ 2.0 ■ 3.0

Description GetBuffer returns the actual data pointer of the string. The buffer will be pre-allocated to the size desired. Use this function when you need a non-const character pointer.

Syntax public, LPTSTR GetBuffer(int nMinBufLength);

Parameters

nMinBufLength Minimum buffer length. You do not need to account for the NULL terminator. If this is greater than the current allocation size, the buffer will grow; otherwise there is no impact. You need to call ReleaseBuffer only if you change the contents of the buffer.

Returns Pointer to character array.

See Also CString::ReleaseBuffer, CString::GetBufferSetLength

Example

```
char sBuf[200] = "A text example";
CString str;
char* pBuf;

pBuf = str.GetBuffer(200);
strcpy(pBuf,sBuf);
str.ReleaseBuffer(-1);
```

GetBufferSetLength ■ 2.0 ■ 3.0

Description GetBufferSetLength returns the actual data pointer of the string. The buffer will be pre-allocated to the size desired. GetBufferSetLength should be used when the exact size is known. If the new length is less than the current length, the string will truncate. You do not need to call ReleaseBuffer after this function is called, regardless of whether the contents change.

Syntax public, LPTSTR GetBufferSetLength(int nNewLength);

Parameters

nNewLength Exact length of the buffer to allocate.

Returns Pointer to character array.

See Also CString::GetBuffer

Example

```
CString str("Short string");
char* sBuf[200];

strcpy(sBuf,str.GetBufferSetLength(5)); // sBuf will equal "Short"
```

GetData

■ 4.0

Description GetData is an inline function called internally by MFC that takes the m_pchData data member and subtracts from it the size of the CStringData structure, returning a pointer to the CStringData structure for the string.

Syntax protected, CStringData* GetData() const;

Parameters None.

Returns Pointer to CStringData structure.

GetLength

■ 2.0 ■ 3.0

Description GetLength returns the length of the data in the string. It does not include the terminating NULL.

Syntax public, int GetLength() const;

Parameters None.

Returns The length of the string (m_nDataLength).

See Also CString::IsEmpty

Init

■ 2.0 ■ 3.0

Description Init initializes the character array. This is an internal function called by MFC.

Syntax protected, void Init();

Parameters None.

Returns Nothing is returned.

IsEmpty

■ 2.0 ■ 3.0

Description IsEmpty determines if the string is empty.

Syntax public, BOOL IsEmpty() const;

Parameters None.

Returns TRUE if the string is empty; FALSE otherwise.

See Also CString::GetLength

Left

■ 2.0 ■ 3.0

Description Left extracts a subset of the string beginning from the left.

Syntax public, CString Left(int nCount) const;

Parameters

nCount Number of characters from the left to extract.

Returns Desired subset.

See Also CString::Mid, CString::Right

Example

```
CString str("Left Middle Right");
CString str2;

str2 = str.Left(4); // str2 equals "Left"
```

LoadString

■ 2.0 ■ 3.0

Description LoadString loads a string resource and sets the contents of the string. Note that the limit of a string resource is 255 characters.

Syntax public, BOOL LoadString(UINT nID);

Parameters

nID String resource ID.

Returns TRUE if string resource loaded successfully; FALSE otherwise.

LockBuffer

■ 4.0

Description LockBuffer sets the reference counter of the string to -1, preventing it from being referenced by any other CString. Call UnlockBuffer to unlock the buffer and allow string referencing.

Syntax public, LPTSTR LockBuffer();

Parameters None.

Returns Pointer to the character buffer.

See Also CString::UnlockBuffer

MakeLower

■ 2.0 ■ 3.0

Description MakeLower makes all the characters in the string lowercase.

Syntax public, void MakeLower();

Parameters None.

Returns Nothing is returned.

See Also CString::MakeUpper

MakeReverse

■ 2.0 ■ 3.0

Description MakeReverse reverses the order of the characters in the string.

Syntax public, void MakeReverse();

Parameters None.

Returns Nothing is returned.

MakeUpper

■ 2.0 ■ 3.0

Description MakeUpper makes all the characters in the string uppercase.

Syntax public, void MakeUpper();

Parameters None.

Returns Nothing is returned.

See Also CString::MakeLower

Mid

■ 2.0 ■ 3.0

Description Mid extracts a subset of the string.

Syntax public, CString Mid(int nFirst, int nCount) const;
CString Mid(int nFirst) const;

Parameters

nFirst First character to extract.

nCount Number of characters to extract.

Returns Desired subset of the string, if *nCount* is not specifed; the remainder of the string is included.

See Also CString::Left, CString::Right

Example

```
CString str("Left Middle Right");
CString str2;

str2 = str.Mid(6,6); // str2 equals "Middle"
```

OemToAnsi

■ 2.0 ■ 3.0

Description OemToAnsi converts all characters in the string from the OEM to ANSI character sets.

Syntax public, void OemToAnsi();

Parameters None.

Returns Nothing is returned.

See Also CString::AnsiToOem

OPERATOR +

■ 2.0 ■ 3.0

Description The addition operator adds (concatenates) characters to a string. You can use this operator sequentially in one assignment operation as long as a CString appears as at least every other operand. These are actually friend functions to the CString class, not members themselves. This is so these functions can access the character buffer directly, for performance reasons.

Syntax public, friend CString AFXAPI operator+(const CString& string1,const CString& string2);
friend CString AFXAPI operator+(const CString& string, TCHAR ch);
friend CString AFXAPI operator+(TCHAR ch, const CString& string);
friend CString AFXAPI operator+(const CString& string, LPCTSTR lpsz);
friend CString AFXAPI operator+(LPCTSTR lpsz, const CString& string);
friend CString AFXAPI operator+(const CString& string, char ch); *(UNICODE only)*
friend CString AFXAPI operator+(char ch, const CString& string); *(UNICODE only)*

Parameters

string1 String 1 to add.

string2 String 2 to add.

string String to add.

ch Character to add.

lpsz NULL-terminated character buffer to add.

Returns New string created.

See Also CString::operator +=

Example

```
CString str1("One");
CString str2("Two");
CString str3;

str3 = str1 + " and " + str2;
```

OPERATOR +=

■ 2.0 ■ 3.0

Description The concatenation operator concatenates the string and stores the result in the original string.

Syntax public, const CString& operator+=(const CString& string);
const CString& operator+=(TCHAR ch);
const CString& operator+=(char ch); *(UNICODE only)*
const CString& operator+=(LPCTSTR lpsz);

Parameters

string String to concatenate.

ch Character to concatenate.

lpsz NULL-terminated character buffer to concatenate.

Returns Reference to new string created.

See Also operator + (friend of CString)

Example

```
CString str1("One");
CString str2(" and Two");

str1 += str2; // now equals "One and Two"
```

OPERATOR << ■ 2.0 ■ 3.0

Description Output string operator, archives string. See Chapter 14, *Files and Serialization,* for a discussion of serialization. This function is actually a friend to the CString class, in order to access the character buffer directly.

Syntax public, friend CArchive& AFXAPI operator <<(CArchive& ar, const CString& string);

Parameters

ar Archive context.

string String to archive.

Returns Reference to archive.

See Also operator >> (friend of CString)

OPERATOR = ■ 2.0 ■ 3.0

Description The assignment operator sets the contents of the string.

Syntax public, const CString& operator=(const CString& stringSrc);
const CString& operator=(TCHAR ch);
const CString& operator=(char ch); *(UNICODE only)*
const CString& operator=(LPCSTR lpsz);
const CString& operator=(LPCWSTR lpsz);
const CString& operator=(const unsigned char* psz);

Parameters

stringSrc New value for string.

ch New character for string.

lpsz New character buffer (null-terminated) for string.

Returns Reference to string created.

Example

```
CString str1("Test");
CString str2;

str2 = str1;
```

OPERATOR >>

■ 2.0 ■ 3.0

Description Input string operator, loads string from archive. See Chapter 14, *Files and Serialization,* for a discussion of serialization. This function is actually a friend to the CString class, in order to access the character buffer directly.

Syntax public, friend CArchive& AFXAPI operator >>(CArchive& ar, CString& string);

Parameters

ar Archive context.

string String to archive.

Returns Reference to archive.

See Also operator >> (friend of CString)

OPERATOR LPCTSTR

■ 2.0 ■ 3.0

Description The operator LPCTSTR function converts a CString to a LPCTSTR; can be called implicitly by the compiler or explicitly by the programmer.

Syntax public, operator LPCTSTR() const;

Parameters None.

Returns Data of type LPCTSTR.

Example

```
CString str("Test");
CString str2;

str2.Format("%s",(LPCTSTR)str);
```

OPERATOR[]

■ 2.0 ■ 3.0

Description The operator[] operator accesses a character in the string by a zero-based index. This operator is equivalent to the GetAt() function.

Syntax public, TCHAR operator[](int nIndex) const;

Parameters

nIndex Index for character array.

Returns The desired character.

See Also CString::GetAt

RELEASE

■ 4.0

Description Release is an internal function called by MFC to decrement the reference count for the string. Release will delete the buffer if the reference count becomes equal to zero.

Syntax protected, void Release(); static void PASCAL Release(CStringData* pData);

Parameters

pData Pointer to CStringData structure for string reference to decrement.

Returns Nothing is returned.

ReleaseBuffer

■ 2.0 ■ 3.0

Description ReleaseBuffer releases the buffer returned by GetBuffer. It will add a NULL terminator to the character buffer.

Syntax public, void ReleaseBuffer(int nNewLength = -1);

Parameters

nNewLength New length of the buffer; if -1, string assumes buffer is terminating with a 0.

Returns Nothing is returned.

See Also CString::GetBuffer

ReverseFind

■ 2.0 ■ 3.0

Description ReverseFind returns the position of the the first instance of a character in the string; reverse search.

Syntax public, int ReverseFind(TCHAR ch) const;

Parameters

ch Character to find.

Returns Position of character; -1 if character not found.

See Also CString::Find

Right

■ 2.0 ■ 3.0

Description Right extracts a subset of the string beginning from the right.

Syntax public, CString Right(int nCount) const;

Parameters

nCount Number of characters from the right to extract.

Returns Desired subset.

See Also CString::Mid, CString::Left

Example

```
CString str("Left Middle Right");
CString str2;

str2 = str.Right(5); // str2 equals "Right"
```

SafeStrlen

■ 2.0 ■ 3.0

Description	SafeStrlen safely determines the length of the string. This is an internal function called by MFC.
Syntax	protected, static int PASCAL SafeStrlen(LPCTSTR lpsz);
Parameters	
lpsz	Pointer to array.
Returns	Length of the string; terminating 0 is ignored.

SetAt

■ 2.0 ■ 3.0

Description	SetAt sets the value of a character in the string, specified by a zero-based index.
Syntax	public, void SetAt(int nIndex, TCHAR ch);
Parameters	
nIndex	Index for character array.
ch	Value of the character.
Returns	Nothing is returned.
See Also	CString::GetAt

SetSysString

■ 2.0 ■ 3.0

Description	SetSysString sets the value of the BSTR created by AllocSysString.
Syntax	public, BSTR SetSysString(BSTR* pbstr) const;
Parameters	
pbstr	System string.
Returns	The BSTR set.
See Also	CString::AllocSysString

SpanExcluding

■ 2.0 ■ 3.0

Description	SpanExcluding returns a subset of the string, starting with the first character of the string and ending with the character one before any of the characters specified in the lpszCharSet string. If no characters in the lpszCharSet string are found, the returned string is empty.
Syntax	public, CString SpanExcluding(LPCTSTR lpszCharSet) const;
Parameters	
lpszCharSet	Search string.
Returns	Desired subset.

See Also CString::SpanIncluding

Example

```
void ParseString(CString& str)
{
        // parse tab or comma-delimited string
        CString strTemp = str;
        CString strParse;
        while ( !strTemp.IsEmpty() )
        {
                strParse = strTemp.SpanExcluding("\t,");
                if ( strParse.IsEmpty() )
                        strTemp.Empty();
                else
                {
                        // do something with parse

                        // prepare for next parse
                        strTemp = strTemp.Right(strTemp.GetLength() -
                                        strParse.GetLength() - 1);
                }
        }
}
```

SpanIncluding ■ 2.0 ■ 3.0

Description SpanIncluding returns a subset of the string, starting with the first character of the string and ending with the last character that is one of the characters specified in the lpszCharSet string. If the first character of the string is not in the lpszCharSet string, the returned string is empty.

Syntax public, CString SpanIncluding(LPCTSTR lpszCharSet) const;

Parameters

lpszCharSet Search string.

Returns Desired subset.

See Also CString::SpanExcluding

Example

```
CString str = "11235813";
CString str2 = str.SpanIncluding("12345");
// str2 = "11235"
```

TrimLeft ■ 4.0

Description TrimLeft removes leading space, tab, and "\n" characters from the string.

Syntax public, void TrimLeft();

Parameters None.

Returns Nothing is returned.

See Also CString::TrimRight

TrimRight

■ 4.0

Description	TrimRight removes trailing space, tab, and "\n" characters from the string.
Syntax	public, void TrimRight();
Parameters	None.
Returns	Nothing is returned.
See Also	CString::TrimLeft

UnlockBuffer

■ 4.0

Description	UnlockBuffer sets the reference counter of the string to 1, allowing it to be referenced by any other CString. Calling UnlockBuffer unlocks the buffer previously locked by calling LockBuffer.
Syntax	public, void UnlockBuffer();
Parameters	None.
Returns	Nothing is returned.
See Also	CString::LockBuffer

Template-based Collection Classes

The template-based collection classes of MFC consist of CArray, CList, and CMap classes. The implementation and interface for these classes are almost identical to their non-template based brethren. The only difference is that when instantiating a collection object, the programmer also is specifying the data types involved. Every time a collection object of a different type is used, the compiler will create a copy of the implementation code for the actual data types. This is the basic principle behind all C++ templates.

The Courses application uses a template-based array (m_Professors, member of the global CCourseData object) to store the professors. Here is its declaration:

```
CArray<CProfessor*,CProfessor*> m_Professors;
```

The major advantage in this case is the absence of a need to type-cast the stored elements to a pointer to a CProfessor object. For example, here, in Listing 13-11, is the code used to list the professors in a CListBox.

Listing 13-11 Template example

```
void CProfessorsDlg::ListProfessors()
{
        CProfessor* pProfessor;
        int nI,nWhich;
        CListBox* pListBox = (CListBox*)GetDlgItem(IDC_PROFESSORS);
        CString strName;
```

continued on next page

continued from previous page

```
        pListBox->ResetContent();
        for (nI = 0;nI < App()->Data()->m_Professors.GetSize();nI++)
        {
            pProfessor = App()->Data()->m_Professors[nI];
            strName = pProfessor->m_strLastName + ", " +
            pProfessor->m_strFirstName + " " + pProfessor->m_cMiddleInitial;
            nWhich = pListBox->AddString(strName);
            pListBox->SetItemData(nWhich,nI);
        }

    OnSelchangeProfessors();
}
```

14

FILES AND SERIALIZATION

14

FILES AND SERIALIZATION

In general, users want the information generated and presented in an application stored and made available for future sessions. This is, after all, one of the primary purposes of files in the first place. Files created by an application hold information in either ASCII or binary format that can be retrieved later whenever desired. From an object-oriented point of view, this idea is represented by the concept of object persistence. An object is persistent if the data it maintains can survive separate instantiations. There is no built-in feature of the C++ language to support this; it must be implemented by the programmer.

MFC comes to the rescue by providing for object persistence at the CObject level through serialization, the process of archiving information contained in objects to permanent storage and then retrieving it, dynamically creating objects as necessary. MFC also supplies general-purpose file classes that provide a thin-layer abstraction of the C run-time I/O functions, including, as a bonus, the CMemFile class for temporary files stored in memory. We will continue using the Courses application from Chapter 13, *Collection Classes*, as a source for examples.

We'll be taking a look at the relatively straightforward file classes first before tackling the more difficult subject of object serialization. The major advantages of the MFC file classes are as follows:

- MFC-based exception handling with each call to an I/O member function.
- Encapsulation of the file (or stream) handle.
- Assembly code implementation for file seeks and locks for efficiency and more accurate failure codes.
- Members for reading and writing data greater than 64K-1 bytes (only necessary for 16-bit programming).

The classes discussed in this chapter are summarized in Table 14-1, below:

Table 14-1 Chapter 14 class summary

Class Name	Description
CFileStatus	Structure for retrieving information on DOS files.
CFile	MFC class for DOS file handle.
CStdioFile	Special file class for handling standard C buffered I/O streams.
CMemFile	Special file class for handling memory-mapped files.
CArchive	Class used to serialize objects to and from files.

The CFileStatus Class

The CFileStatus class is a structure, entirely comprised of data members, used to encapsulate the DOS-level information of a file. It is used by the CFile::GetStatus() member function when retrieving information about a file. Table 14-2 lists the members of this class.

Table 14-2 CFileStatus member variables

Member	Description
m_atime	Last access date/time of file.
m_attribute	Attribute flag containing OR-ed CFile::Attribute values.
m_ctime	Creation date/time for file.
m_mtime	Last modification date/time for file.
m_padding	Structure padding.
m_size	Logical size of file (in bytes).
m_szFullName	Absolute path name.

The CFile Class

The CFile class is essentially a wrapper class for a file handle. Most of its members consist of calls to standard I/O C run-time functions. The m_hFile member variable, which stores the file handle, is a public member accessible at any time.

Getting File Information

To get information about a file or to find out if a file exists, use the GetStatus() member function. As shown in Listing 14-1, before loading course information, the Courses application first checks to see if the file exists:

Listing 14-1 Use of GetStatus function

```
BOOL CMainFrame::FileExists(CString& strPath)
{
   CFileStatus status;
   BOOL bFileExists = TRUE;

   if ( !CFile::GetStatus(strPath,status) ) // static member
     bFileExists = FALSE;

   return bFileExists;
}
```

Opening Files

A file can be opened either in the constructor or through a call to the Open member function. The CFile class specifies enumerated values to denote the different sharing and access modes used when opening the file. The different possibilities are shown in Table 14-3 below. One access flag and one sharing flag must be included. The Open member function optionally takes a CFileException class that it will use instead of throwing an exception in case of errors.

Table 14-3 CFile open flags

Flag	Meaning
CFile::modeCreate	Creates a new file. If a file exists, its contents are erased.
CFile::modeNoInherit	Child processes will not be able to use this file.
CFile::modeRead	Opens the file for read-only.
CFile::modeReadWrite	Opens the file for read/write.
CFile::modeWrite	Opens the file for write-only.
CFile::shareCompat	Opens file in compatibility mode.
CFile::shareDenyNone	No sharing restrictions.
CFile::shareDenyRead	Denies read access to other processes.
CFile::shareDenyWrite	Denies write access to other processes.
CFile::shareExclusive	Denies any access by other processes.
CFile::typeBinary	Opens file in binary mode.
CFile::typeText	Opens file in text mode.

Reading from Files

To read data from a file that has been opened, use either the Read or ReadHuge member functions. ReadHuge should be used in 16-bit applications to read more than 64K-1 bytes worth of data. For backward compatibility purposes, 32-bit versions of MFC keep this function, mapping it simply to a call to Read. Listing 14-2 gives an example of how Read and ReadHuge might be used.

Listing 14-2 Reading from files

```
BOOL ReadData(CFile& file,void* pBuf,DWORD dwCount)
{
   BOOL bReadEnough = FALSE;

   if ( dwCount > 65535 )
      bReadEnough = ( file.ReadHuge(pBuf,dwCount) == dwCount );
   else
      bReadEnough = ( file.Read(pBuf,(UINT)dwCount) == dwCount );

   return bReadEnough;
}
```

Writing to Files

To write data to a file that has been opened, use either the Write or WriteHuge member functions. WriteHuge should be used in 16-bit applications to write more than 64K-1 bytes worth of data. For backward compatibility purposes, 32-bit versions of MFC keep this function, mapping it simply to a call to Write. Listing 14-3 gives an example of how Write and WriteHuge might be used.

Listing 14-3 Writing to files

```
void WriteData(CFile& file,void* pBuf,DWORD dwCount)
{
   if ( dwCount > 65535 )
      file.WriteHuge(pBuf,dwCount);
   else
      file.Write(pBuf,(UINT)dwCount);
}
```

Closing Files

The CFile destructor automatically closes an opened file as long as the m_hFile file handle was not passed in during construction. This is because MFC assumes that a file handle passed in belongs to another CFile object or some other external module as well and could have a lifetime beyond that of the particular CFile object. To close a file explicitly, the programmer should call the Close member function. The Abort member can be called to close a file without the possibility of throwing an exception.

CFile Class Reference

CFile

■ 2.0 ■ 3.0

Description The constructor for the CFile class. CFile initializes the members of the class, optionally calling the Open member function to open a particular file.

Syntax public, CFile();
CFile(int hFile);
CFile(LPCTSTR pszFileName, UINT nOpenFlags);

Parameters	
hFile	Passed-in file handle.
pszFileName	Path of file to open.
nOpenFlags	Sharing and access mode flags for file to be opened.
Returns	Nothing is returned.
See Also	CFile::~CFile

~CFile

■ 2.0 ■ 3.0

Description	Destructor calls Close when the m_hFile file handle is not passed in.
Syntax	public, virtual ~CFile();
Parameters	None.
Returns	Nothing is returned.
See Also	CFile::CFile

Abort

■ 2.0 ■ 3.0

Description	Abort closes a file, does not throw exceptions and can be called with an unopened file.
Syntax	public, virtual void Abort();
Parameters	None.
Returns	Nothing is returned.
See Also	CFile::Close

Example

```
void AbortIO(CFile* pFile)
{
	AfxMessageBox("File I/O error has occurred!");

#ifdef _DEBUG
	pFile->Dump(afxDump);
#endif
	pFile->Abort(); // close file, throw no exceptions
}
```

AssertValid

■ 2.0 ■ 3.0 ■ DO

Description	Validates the CFile object. For more information on diagnostics, see Chapter 15, *Debugging and Exception Handling*.
Syntax	public, virtual void AssertValid() const;
Parameters	None.
Returns	Nothing is returned.
See Also	CFile::Dump

Example

```
void WriteString(CFile* pFile,char* sBuf,int nCount)
{
      pFile->AssertValid(); // valid file?

      pFile->Write(sBuf,nCount);
      TRACE0("String written to file.\n");
}
```

Close

■ 2.0 ■ 3.0

Description Close closes the file, called automatically by the destructor when the m_hFile file handle is not passed in.

Syntax public, virtual void Close();

Parameters None.

Returns Nothing is returned.

See Also CFile::Abort

Example See CFile::Open

Dump

■ 2.0 ■ 3.0 ■ DO

Description Diagnostics function outputs the value of the file handle. For more information about debugging, see Chapter 15, *Debugging and Exception Handling*.

Syntax public, virtual void Dump(CDumpContext& dc) const;

Parameters

dc Dump context.

Returns Nothing is returned.

See Also CFile::AssertValid

Example See CFile::Abort

Duplicate

■ 2.0 ■ 3.0

Description Duplicate creates a new CFile object that references the same file.

Syntax public, virtual CFile* Duplicate() const;

Parameters None.

Returns Pointer to new CFile object that must be deleted by the programmer.

See Also CFile::CFile

Flush

■ 2.0 ■ 3.0

Description Flush causes all bytes in the write buffer to be written to the file.

Syntax public, virtual void Flush();

Parameters None.

Returns Nothing is returned.

Example

```
void AddSignatureBytes(CFile* pFile)
{
     pFile->Flush(); // flush all bytes to file, first

     pFile->SeekToEnd(); // seek to end of file
     pFile->Write("MYFILE",6);
}
```

GetFileName

■ 4.0

Description GetFileName retrieves the file name for the file. The file name for C:\files\katie.txt, for example, is katie.txt.

Syntax public, virtual CString GetFileName() const;

Parameters None.

Returns File name for the file.

See Also CFile::GetFilePath, CFile::GetFileTitle

GetFilePath

■ 4.0

Description GetFilePath retrieves the full path name for the file. The full path name for C:\files\katie.txt, for example, is C:\files\katie.txt.

Syntax public, virtual CString GetFilePath() const;

Parameters None.

Returns Full path name for the file.

See Also CFile::GetFileName, CFile::GetFileTitle

GetFileTitle

■ 4.0

Description GetFileTitle retrieves the title for the file. The title for C:\files\katie.txt, for example, is katie.

Syntax public, virtual CString GetFileTitle() const;

Parameters None.

Returns Title for the file.

See Also CFile::GetFileName, CFile::GetFilePath

GetLength

■ 2.0 ■ 3.0

Description GetLength returns the length of the file.

Syntax public, virtual DWORD GetLength() const;

Parameters None.

Returns The length of the file in bytes.

See Also CFile::SetLength

Example

```
BOOL CheckSignatureBytes(CFile* pFile)
{
        BOOL bOK = TRUE;
        DWORD dwEnd;
        CString str;

        // get length of file
        dwEnd = pFile->GetLength();

        // seek to signature position
        pFile->Seek(dwEnd - 6,CFile::begin);

        // read 6 bytes into a CString buffer
        str.ReleaseBuffer(pFile->Read(str.GetBuffer (6),6));

        return ( str.Compare("MYFILE") == 0 );
}
```

GetPosition

■ 2.0 ■ 3.0

Description GetPosition returns the current position of the file pointer. This position can be saved and used in subsequent calls to Seek().

Syntax public, virtual DWORD GetPosition() const;

Parameters None.

Returns Position of file pointer.

See Also CFile::Seek

Example

```
CFile file;
DWORD dwPos;

dwPos = file.GetPosition();
file.Seek(dwPos);
```

GetStatus

■ 2.0 ■ 3.0

Description GetStatus fills in a CFileStatus structure for a particular file; can be used also to test if a file exists. The non-static version is used with an already-opened file.

Syntax public, BOOL GetStatus(CFileStatus& rStatus) const;
static BOOL PASCAL GetStatus(LPCTSTR pszFileName, CFileStatus& rStatus);

Parameters

rStatus CFileStatus structure to be filled in.

pszFileName Path of file.

Returns TRUE if successful; FALSE if file does not exist.

See Also CFile::SetStatus

Example

```
BOOL FileExists(LPCTSTR pszFileName)
{
     CFileStatus status;

     return CFile::GetStatus(pszFileName,status);
}
```

LockRange

■ 2.0 ■ 3.0

Description LockRange locks a range of bytes of a file. This feature can only be used in Windows 3.x in conjunction with SHARE.EXE (Windows for Workgroups, Windows 95, and Windows NT do not require SHARE.EXE).

Syntax public, virtual void LockRange(DWORD dwPos, DWORD dwCount);

Parameters

dwPos Starting position.

dwCount Number of bytes to lock.

Returns Nothing is returned.

See Also CFile::UnlockRange

Example

```
CFile file;
DWORD dwPos;

dwPos = file.GetPosition();
file.LockRange(dwPos,100); // lock 100 bytes from current position
```

Open

■ 2.0 ■ 3.0

Description Open opens a file.

Syntax public, virtual BOOL Open(LPCTSTR pszFileName, UINT nOpenFlags, CFileException* pError = NULL);

Parameters

pszFileName Path of file.

nOpenFlags Open flags.

pError CFileException object to use in case of errors.

Returns TRUE if successful; FALSE otherwise.

See Also CFile::Close

Example

```
void CMainFrame::OnFileSave()
{
	CFileDialog dlg(FALSE);
	CString strFile;
	CFile file;

	if ( dlg.DoModal() == IDOK )
	{
		strFile = dlg.GetPathName();
		if ( file.Open(strFile,CFile::modeCreate |
			CFile::modeWrite | CFile::shareDenyNone) )
		{
			CArchive saveArchive(&file, CArchive::store |
						CArchive::bNoFlushOnDelete);
			App()->Data()->Serialize(saveArchive);
			saveArchive.Close();
			file.Close();
		}
	}
}
```

OPERATOR HFILE

■ 4.0

Description Type-casting operator to convert the CFile object to an HFILE menu handle.

Syntax public, operator HFILE() const;

Parameters None.

Returns m_hFile handle.

READ

■ 2.0 ■ 3.0

Description Read reads a specific number of bytes from the file and adjusts the file pointer.

Syntax public, virtual UINT Read(void * lpBuf,UINT nCount);

Parameters

lpBuf Buffer to read to.

nCount Number of bytes to read.

Returns The number of bytes read—can be less than nCount if the end of the file has been reached.

See Also CFile::ReadHuge

Example See CFile::GetLength

READHUGE

■ 2.0 ■ 3.0

Description ReadHuge reads more than 64K-1 bytes of data from a file. The 32-bit versions of MFC maps this function to a call to Read.

Syntax public, DWORD ReadHuge(void * lpBuffer, DWORD dwCount);

Parameters

lpBuffer Buffer to read to.

dwCount Number of bytes to read.

Returns Number of bytes read.

See Also CFile::Read

Remove ■ 2.0 ■ 3.0

Description Remove deletes a file.

Syntax public, static void PASCAL Remove(LPCTSTR pszFileName);

Parameters

pszFileName File to delete.

Returns Nothing is returned.

Rename ■ 2.0 ■ 3.0

Description Rename renames a file.

Syntax public, static void PASCAL Rename(LPCTSTR pszOldName, LPCTSTR pszNewName);

Parameters

pszOldName Old file name.

pszNewName New file name.

Returns Nothing is returned.

Example

```
CFile::Rename("myfile.new","myfle.old");
```

Seek ■ 2.0 ■ 3.0

Description Seek moves the file pointer to a specific position.

Syntax public, virtual LONG Seek(LONG lOff, UINT nFrom);

Parameters

lOff Number of bytes to move.

nFrom One of the following enum values:

CFile::begin (from the beginning of the file).
CFile::current (from the current position in the file).
CFile::end (from the end of file).

Returns The new position of the file pointer.

See Also CFile::SeekToBegin, CFile::SeekToEnd

Example See CFile::GetLength

SeekToBegin

■ 2.0 ■ 3.0

Description SeekToBegin moves the file pointer to the beginning of the file.

Syntax public, void SeekToBegin();

Parameters None.

Returns Nothing is returned.

See Also CFile::Seek, CFile::SeekToEnd

SeekToEnd

■ 2.0 ■ 3.0

Description SeekToEnd moves the file pointer to the end of the file.

Syntax public, DWORD SeekToEnd();

Parameters None.

Returns New position of file pointer.

See Also CFile::Seek, CFile::SeekToBegin

Example See Flush

SetFilePath

■ 4.0

Description SetFilePath sets the full path name for the file. SetFilePath will not rename or move a file. Instead, it just sets the value of the m_strFileName data member.

Syntax public, virtual void SetFilePath(LPCTSTR lpszNewName);

Parameters

lpszNewName New full path name for the file.

Returns Nothing is returned.

See Also CFile::GetFilePath

SetLength

■ 2.0 ■ 3.0

Description SetLength sets the length of the file. If the specified length is greater than the current length of the file, the file will grow as needed. If the length is less than the current length, the file will shrink as needed.

Syntax public, virtual void SetLength(DWORD dwNewLen);

Parameters

dwNewLen New length.

Returns Nothing is returned.

See Also CFile::GetLength

SetStatus

■ 2.0 ■ 3.0

Description SetStatus sets the DOS-level information for a file.

Syntax public, static void PASCAL SetStatus(LPCTSTR pszFileName, const CFileStatus& status);

Parameters

pszFileName Path of file.

status CFileStatus structure to set.

Returns Nothing is returned.

See Also CFile::GetStatus

UnlockRange

■ 2.0 ■ 3.0

Description UnlockRange unlocks a range of bytes of a file. This feature can only be used in Windows 3.x in conjunction with SHARE.EXE (Windows for Workgroups, Windows 95, and Windows NT do not require SHARE.EXE).

Syntax public, virtual void UnlockRange(DWORD dwPos,DWORD dwCount);

Parameters

dwPos Starting position.

dwCount Number of bytes to unlock.

Returns Nothing is returned.

See Also CFile::LockRange

Example

```
CFile file;
DWORD dwPos;

dwPos = file.GetPosition();
file.UnlockRange(dwPos,100); // unlock 100 bytes from current position
```

Write

■ 2.0 ■ 3.0

Description Write writes a specific number of bytes to the file.

Syntax public, virtual void Write(const void * lpBuf, UINT nCount);

Parameters

lpBuf Buffer to write from.

nCount Number of bytes to write.

Returns Nothing is returned.

See Also CFile::WriteHuge

Example See CFile::Flush

WriteHuge ■ 2.0 ■ 3.0

Description WriteHuge writes more than 64K-1 bytes of data to a file. The 32-bit versions of MFC maps this function to a call to Write.

Syntax public, void WriteHuge(const void * lpBuffer,DWORD dwCount);

Parameters

lpBuffer Buffer to write from.

dwCount Number of bytes to write.

Returns Nothing is returned.

See Also CFile::Write

CStdioFile

The CStdioFile class is for standard C buffered I/O streams. This class redefines only the necessary CFile-inherited virtual member functions. Whereas the CFile class uses the _dos class of run-time functions (e.g., _dos_open, _dos_read, _dos_write), CStdioFile uses the _f class of functions (e.g., _fopen, _fread, _fwrite). The m_pStream member variable holds the handle to the open stream. The m_hFile member variable inherited from CFile is equal to the equivalent file handle. The Duplicate, LockRange, and UnlockRange member functions are unsupported. If they are called, a CNotSupportedException is generated.

CStdioFile Class Reference

CStdioFile ■ 2.0 ■ 3.0

Description The constructor for the CStdioFile class. CStdioFile initializes the members of the class, optionally calling the Open member function to open a particular file.

Syntax public, CStdioFile();
CStdioFile(FILE* pOpenStream);
CStdioFile(LPCTSTR pszFileName, UINT nOpenFlags);

Parameters

pOpenStream Passed-in file stream.

pszFileName Path of file to open.

nOpenFlags Sharing and access mode flags for file to be opened.

Returns Nothing is returned.

See Also CStdioFile::~CStdioFile

~CStdioFile ■ 2.0 ■ 3.0

Description Destructor calls Close when the m_pStream stream handle is not passed in.

Syntax public, virtual ~CStdioFile();
Parameters None.
Returns Nothing is returned.
See Also CStdioFile::CStdioFile

ABORT ■ 2.0 ■ 3.0

Description The CStdioFile implementation of Abort closes a file—does not throw exceptions and can be called with an unopened file.
Syntax public, virtual void Abort();
Parameters None.
Returns Nothing is returned.
See Also CStdioFile::Close
Example See CFile::Abort

CLOSE ■ 2.0 ■ 3.0

Description The CStdioFile implementation of Close closes the file, called automatically by the destructor when the m_hFile file handle is not passed in.
Syntax public, virtual void Close();
Parameters None.
Returns Nothing is returned.
See Also CStdioFile::Abort
Example See CFile::Close

DUMP ■ 2.0 ■ 3.0 ■ DO

Description Diagnostics function outputs the value of the stream handle. For more information about diagnostics, see Chapter 15, *Debugging and Exception Handling*.
Syntax public, virtual void Dump(CDumpContext& dc) const;
Parameters
dc Dump context.
Returns Nothing is returned.
Example See CFile::Dump

DUPLICATE ■ 2.0 ■ 3.0

Description The CStdioFile implementation of Duplicate is an unsupported function that will generate a CNotSupportedException if called.

Syntax public, virtual CFile* Duplicate() const;

Parameters None.

Returns N/A.

See Also CNotSupportedException

FLUSH

■ 2.0 ■ 3.0

Description The CStdioFile implementation of Flush causes all bytes in the write buffer to be written to the file.

Syntax public, virtual void Flush();

Parameters None.

Returns Nothing is returned.

Example See CFile::Flush

GETPOSITION

■ 2.0 ■ 3.0

Description The CStdioFile implementation of GetPosition returns the current position of the file pointer. This position can be saved and used in subsequent calls to Seek.

Syntax public, virtual DWORD GetPosition() const;

Parameters None.

Returns Position of file pointer.

See Also CStdioFile::Seek

Example See CFile::GetPosition

LOCKRANGE

■ 2.0 ■ 3.0

Description The CStdioFile implementation of LockRange is an unsupported function that will generate a CNotSupportedException if called.

Syntax public, virtual void LockRange(DWORD dwPos, DWORD dwCount);

Parameters N/A.

Returns Nothing is returned.

See Also CNotSupportedException

OPEN

■ 2.0 ■ 3.0

Description The CStdioFile implementation of Open opens a file.

Syntax public, virtual BOOL Open(LPCTSTR pszFileName, UINT nOpenFlags, CFileException* pError = NULL);

Parameters

pszFileName Path of file.

nOpenFlags Open flags.

pError CFileException object to use in case of errors.

Returns TRUE if successful; FALSE otherwise.

See Also CStdioFile::Close

Example See CFile::Open

READ ■ 2.0 ■ 3.0

Description The CStdioFile implementation of Read reads a specific number of bytes from the file and adjusts the file pointer.

Syntax public, virtual UINT Read(void * lpBuf,UINT nCount);

Parameters

lpBuf Buffer to read to.

nCount Number of bytes to read.

Returns The number of bytes read can be less than *nCount* if the end of the file has been reached.

See Also CFile::ReadHuge

Example See CFile::Read

READSTRING ■ 2.0 ■ 3.0

Description ReadString reads a string of data. Reading is terminated by a carriage return—line feed pair.

Syntax public, virtual LPTSTR ReadString(LPTSTR lpsz, UINT nMax);
BOOL ReadString(CString& rString);

Parameters

lpsz Buffer in which to store the string.

nMax Maximum number of characters to read.

rString Reference of string to use to store the string.

Returns Pointer to string buffer.

See Also CStdioFile::WriteString

SEEK ■ 2.0 ■ 3.0

Description The CStdioFile implementation of Seek moves the file pointer to a specific position.

Syntax public, virtual LONG Seek(LONG lOff, UINT nFrom);

Parameters

lOff Number of bytes to move.

nFrom One of the following enum values:
CFile::begin (from the beginning of the file).
CFile::current (from the current position in the file).
CFile::end (from the end of file).

Returns The new position of the file pointer.

See Also CFile::SeekToBegin, CFile::SeekToEnd

Example See CFile::Seek

UnlockRange ■ 2.0 ■ 3.0

Description The CStdioFile implementation of UnlockRange is an unsupported function that will generate a CNotSupportedException if called.

Syntax public, virtual void UnlockRange(DWORD dwPos, DWORD dwCount);

Parameters N/A.

Returns Nothing is returned.

See Also CNotSupportedException

Write ■ 2.0 ■ 3.0

Description The CStdioFile implementation of Write writes a specific number of bytes to the file.

Syntax public, virtual void Write(const void * lpBuf, UINT nCount);

Parameters

lpBuf Buffer to write from.

nCount Number of bytes to write.

Returns Nothing is returned.

See Also CFile::WriteHuge

Example See CFile::Write

WriteString ■ 2.0 ■ 3.0

Description WriteString writes a string of data; the terminating '\0' is not written.

Syntax public, virtual void WriteString(LPCTSTR lpsz);

Parameters

lpsz String to write.

Returns Nothing is returned.

See Also CStdioFile::ReadString

CMemFile

The CMemFile class supports files in memory. This is especially useful for transferring serialized objects in memory. The m_hFile member is not used. Instead, the m_lpBuffer member variable points to the memory allocated for the file. The Duplicate, LockRange, and UnlockRange member functions are unsupported. If they are called, a CNotSupportedException is generated.

CMemFile Class Reference

CMemFile ■ 2.0 ■ 3.0

Description	The constructor for the CMemFile class. The second version is used to tell MFC to use an external memory buffer as opposed to one the CMemFile object would ordinarily create internally.
Syntax	public, CMemFile(UINT nGrowBytes = 1024); CMemFile(BYTE* lpBuffer, UINT nBufferSize, UINT nGrowBytes = 0);
Parameters	
nGrowBytes	The number of bytes to allocate at a time.
lpBuffer	Pointer to buffer to use.
nBufferSize	Size of buffer to use.
Returns	Nothing is returned.
See Also	CMemFile::~CMemFile, CMemFile::Attach

~CMemFile ■ 2.0 ■ 3.0

Description	The destructor closes the file, meaning that all memory allocated is freed.
Syntax	public, virtual ~CMemFile();
Parameters	None.
Returns	Nothing is returned.
See Also	CMemFile::CMemFile

Abort ■ 2.0 ■ 3.0

Description	The CMemFile implementation of Abort closes a file, does not throw exceptions, and can be called with an unopened file.
Syntax	public, virtual void Abort();
Parameters	None.
Returns	Nothing is returned.
See Also	CMemFile::Close
Example	See CFile::Abort

ALLOC

■ 2.0 ■ 3.0

Description Alloc is an internal function used for allocating memory for the file.

Syntax protected, virtual BYTE * Alloc(DWORD nBytes);

Parameters

nByte Number of bytes to allocate.

Returns Pointer to bytes allocated.

See Also CMemFile::Realloc

ASSERTVALID

■ 2.0 ■ 3.0 ■ DO

Description Validates the CMemFile object. For more information on diagnostics, see Chapter 15, *Debugging and Exception Handling.*

Syntax public, virtual void AssertValid() const;

Parameters None.

Returns Nothing is returned.

See Also CMemFile::Dump

Example See CFile::AssertValid

ATTACH

■ 4.0

Description Attach allows the programmer to specify the memory buffer to use for the file.

Syntax public, void Attach(BYTE* lpBuffer, UINT nBufferSize, UINT nGrowBytes = 0);

Parameters

nGrowBytes The number of bytes to allocate at a time.

lpBuffer Pointer to buffer to use.

nBufferSize Size of buffer to use.

Returns Nothing is returned.

See Also CMemFile::CMemFile

CLOSE

■ 2.0 ■ 3.0

Description The CMemFile implementation of Close closes the file, and is called automatically by the destructor when the m_hFile file handle is not passed in.

Syntax public, virtual void Close();

Parameters None.

Returns Nothing is returned.

See Also CMemFile::Abort

Example See CFile::Close

DETACH

■ 2.0 ■ 3.0

Description Detach returns a pointer to the memory used for the file and closes it. You need to call Attach to re-open the file.

Syntax public, BYTE* Detach();

Parameters None.

Returns Pointer to the memory used for the file.

See Also CMemFile::Attach

DUMP

■ 2.0 ■ 3.0 ■ DO

Description Diagnostics function outputs the statistics of the memory file. For more information about debugging, see Chapter 15, *Debugging and Exception Handling*.

Syntax public, virtual void Dump(CDumpContext& dc) const;

Parameters

dc Dump context.

Returns Nothing is returned.

See Also CMemFile::AssertValid

Example See CFile::Dump

DUPLICATE

■ 2.0 ■ 3.0

Description The CMemFile implementation of Duplicate is an unsupported function that will generate a CNotSupportedException if called.

Syntax public, virtual CFile* Duplicate() const;

Parameters None.

Returns N/A.

See Also CNotSupportedException

FLUSH

■ 2.0 ■ 3.0

Description The CMemFile implementation of Flush causes all bytes in the write buffer to be written to the file.

Syntax public, virtual void Flush();

Parameters None.

Returns Nothing is returned.

Example See CFile::Flush

FREE

■ 2.0 ■ 3.0

Description Free is an internal function used to free allocated memory.

Syntax protected, virtual void Free(BYTE * lpMem);

Parameters

lpMem Pointer to memory to be freed.

Returns Nothing is returned.

See Also CMemFile::Alloc, CMemFile::Realloc

GETPOSITION

■ 2.0 ■ 3.0

Description The CMemFile implementation of GetPosition returns the current position of the file pointer. This position can be saved and used in subsequent calls to Seek.

Syntax public, virtual DWORD GetPosition() const;

Parameters None.

Returns Position of file pointer.

See Also CMemFile::Seek

Example See CFile::GetPosition

GETSTATUS

■ 2.0 ■ 3.0

Description The CMemFile implementation of this virtual function returns an empty CFileStatus structure.

Syntax public, BOOL GetStatus(CFileStatus& rStatus) const;

Parameters

rStatus CFileStatus structure.

Returns TRUE if successful; FALSE otherwise.

GROWFILE

■ 2.0 ■ 3.0

Description GrowFile is an internal function used to grow the file. The smallest amount of new memory allocated is determined by the *nGrowBytes* parameter passed in to the constructor.

Syntax protected, virtual void GrowFile(DWORD dwNewLen);

Parameters

dwNewLen New length.

Returns Nothing is returned.

See Also CMemFile::CMemFile

LockRange ■ 2.0 ■ 3.0

Description The CMemFile implementation of LockRange is an unsupported function that will generate a CNotSupportedException if called.

Syntax public, virtual void LockRange(DWORD dwPos, DWORD dwCount);

Parameters N/A.

Returns Nothing is returned.

See Also CNotSupportedException

Memcpy ■ 2.0 ■ 3.0

Description Memcpy is an internal function used for copying memory in the file.

Syntax protected, virtual BYTE * Memcpy(BYTE * lpMemTarget, const BYTE * lpMemSource, UINT nBytes);

Parameters

lpMemTarget Target of memory copy.

lpMemSource Source of memory copy.

nBytes Number of bytes to copy.

Returns Pointer to target of memory copied.

Read ■ 2.0 ■ 3.0

Description The CMemFile implementation of Read reads a specific number of bytes from the file and adjusts the file pointer.

Syntax public, virtual UINT Read(void * lpBuf,UINT nCount);

Parameters

lpBuf Buffer to read to.

nCount Number of bytes to read.

Returns The number of bytes read — can be less than *nCount* if the end of the file has been reached.

See Also CFile::ReadHuge

Example See CFile::Read

Realloc ■ 2.0 ■ 3.0

Description Realloc is an internal function used for reallocating memory for the file.

Syntax protected, virtual BYTE * Realloc(BYTE * lpMem, DWORD nBytes);

Parameters

lpMem Pointer to memory to reallocate.

nBytes Number of bytes to reallocate.
Returns Pointer to bytes reallocated.
See Also CMemFile::Alloc

SEEK ■ 2.0 ■ 3.0

Description The CMemFile implementation of Seek moves the file pointer to a specific position.
Syntax public, virtual LONG Seek(LONG lOff, UINT nFrom);
Parameters
lOff Number of bytes to move.
nFrom One of the following enum values:
CFile::begin (from the beginning of the file).
CFile::current (from the current position in the file).
CFile::end (from the end of file).
Returns The new position of the file pointer.
See Also CFile::SeekToBegin, CFile::SeekToEnd
Example See CFile::Seek

SETLENGTH ■ 2.0 ■ 3.0

Description The CMemFile implementation of SetLength sets the length of the file, allocating memory if necessary.
Syntax public, virtual void SetLength(DWORD dwNewLen);
Parameters
dwNewLen New length.
Returns Nothing is returned.

UNLOCKRANGE ■ 2.0 ■ 3.0

Description The CMemFile implementation of UnlockRange is an unsupported function that will generate a CNotSupportedException if called.
Syntax public, virtual void UnlockRange(DWORD dwPos, DWORD dwCount);
Parameters N/A.
Returns Nothing is returned.
See Also CNotSupportedException

WRITE ■ 2.0 ■ 3.0

Description The CMemFile implementation of Write writes a specific number of bytes to the file.

Syntax	public, virtual void Write(const void * lpBuf, UINT nCount);
Parameters	
lpBuf	Buffer to write from.
nCount	Number of bytes to write.
Returns	Nothing is returned.
See Also	CFile::WriteHuge
Example	See CFile::Write

Serialization

Serialization in MFC involves the cooperation of many different classes. First of all, the CFile class (or a class derived from CFile) takes care of all of the actual I/O (reading and writing to permanent storage). Secondly, the CArchive class creates an archive context by which objects are serialized in an optimized and coherent manner. Finally, the CObject-derived classes themselves implement a Serialize member that specifies which data is to be stored for each object. It is typical that a given implementation of Serialize for an object causes subsequent calls to the Serialize members of other objects. The five-step serialization process is outlined below:

- Open a file to store/retrieve the information by using a CFile-derived object
- Create an archive context by using a CArchive-derived object
- Calls to the Serialize members of all objects to be archived
- Close the archive context
- Close the file

There are a few restrictions for the CFile-based object used for serialization, mainly that it must be opened in a mode consistent with the archive's mode (i.e. if the archive is storing, the file needs to be opened in write mode; if the archive is loading, the file needs to be opened in read mode). It can be used to store other information before or after the archiving of the objects. This is handy, for example, if the programmer wishes to provide special versioning or security access. The same file can also be used to store multiple archive contexts; this is potentially useful for 16-bit applications because a given archive context cannot support archiving more than 32,766 objects. Because archives are buffered, it is important to make sure all data archived has actually been written out before attempting to store information after an archive context. This is done by calling the Flush member function of the CArchive object.

CObject-derived classes exchange data with the archive either through the use of insertion (<<) and extraction (>>) operators or directly by calling the ReadObject or WriteObject members of the CArchive class. The insertion and extraction operators map to call ReadObject and WriteObject respectively, which in turn eventually call the Serialize member of the object. Only CObject-derived classes that have the DECLARE_SERIAL and IMPLEMENT_SERIAL macros defined can be serialized. For

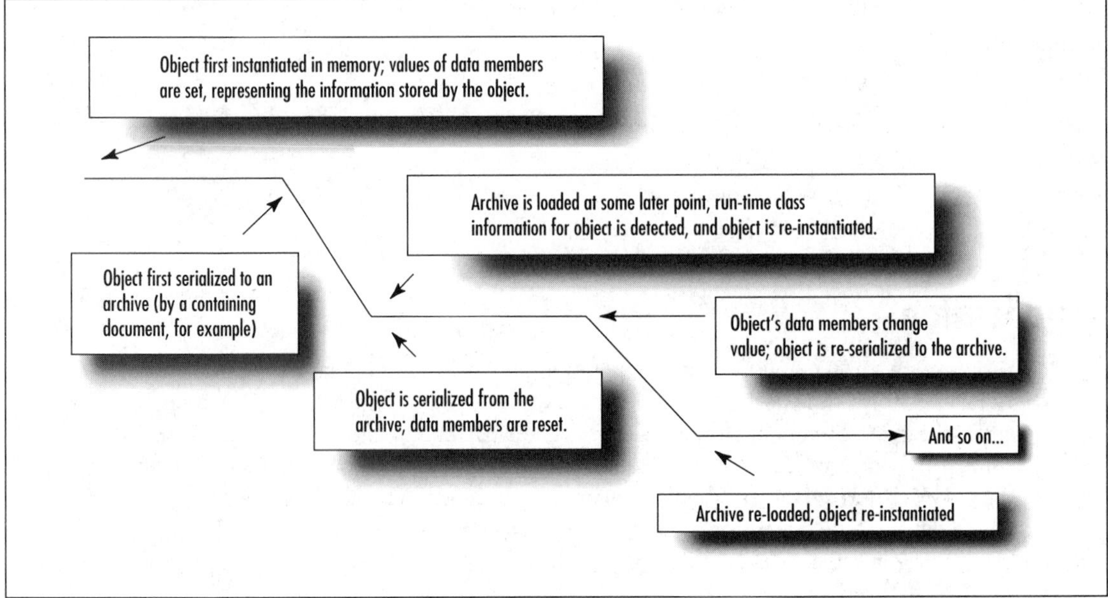

Figure 14-1 Persistence of a CObject-based object's information

primitive types (BYTE, WORD, DWORD, LONG, float, double, and the CString class), the CArchive class includes implementations that directly store and load the actual data. Figure 14-1 illustrates the persistence of information stored in a CObject-based object.

The CArchive class maintains a buffered stream for the information that is being serialized. The archive adds class information (the CRuntimeClass structure as well as a versioning schema number to indicate different implementations of the same class) to objects written out so that they can be identified and reconstructed when the archive is loaded. It keeps track of which objects have been written out, preventing redundant serialization and marking null objects. An example of how to create and execute an archive can be seen by taking a look at the MFC code for opening and saving a document. Listing 14-4 shows the archiving portions of the CDocument::OnOpenDocument function. The archive is created in a loading mode, the document's Serialize member is called, and the archive is closed. External to this process, the actual file is opened and then closed.

Listing 14-4 Opening a document

```
BOOL CDocument::OnOpenDocument(LPCTSTR lpszPathName)
{
      // pre-archive code..., creates and opens pFile CFile object

      CArchive loadArchive(pFile, CArchive::load |
                              CArchive::bNoFlushOnDelete);
      loadArchive.m_pDocument = this;
```

```
        loadArchive.m_bForceFlat = FALSE;
        TRY
        {
            CWaitCursor wait;
            if (pFile->GetLength() != 0)
                Serialize(loadArchive);     // load me
            loadArchive.Close();
            ReleaseFile(pFile, FALSE);
        }
        CATCH_ALL(e)
        {
            ReleaseFile(pFile, TRUE);
            DeleteContents();   // remove failed contents

            TRY
            {
                ReportSaveLoadException(lpszPathName, e,
                      FALSE, AFX_IDP_FAILED_TO_OPEN_DOC);
            }
            END_TRY
            DELETE_EXCEPTION(e);
            return FALSE;
        }
        END_CATCH_ALL

        // post-archive code...

        return TRUE;
}
```

Listing 14-5 shows the archiving portions of the CDocument::OnSaveDocument function. The archive is created in a storing mode, the document's Serialize member is called, and the archive is closed. External to this process, the actual file is opened and then closed.

Listing 14-5 Saving a document

```
BOOL CDocument::OnSaveDocument(const char* pszPathName)
{
      // pre-archive code..., creates and opens pFile CFile object

      CArchive saveArchive(pFile, CArchive::store |
                                  CArchive::bNoFlushOnDelete);
      saveArchive.m_pDocument = this;
      saveArchive.m_bForceFlat = FALSE;
      TRY
      {
            CWaitCursor wait;
            Serialize(saveArchive);      // save me
            saveArchive.Close();
            ReleaseFile(pFile, FALSE);
      }
      CATCH_ALL(e)
      {
            ReleaseFile(pFile, TRUE);

            TRY
            {
```

continued on next page

continued from previous page

```
                ReportSaveLoadException(lpszPathName, e,
                     TRUE, AFX_IDP_FAILED_TO_SAVE_DOC);
          }
          END_TRY
          DELETE_EXCEPTION(e);
          return FALSE;
     }
     END_CATCH_ALL

     // post-archive code

     return TRUE;
}
```

Because the Courses application is dialog-based, not document-based, it cannot use this built-in mechanism. Listing 14-6, below, shows how the Courses application saves and loads its data. The code is more simplistic, but the principles mentioned above in regards to document saving and loading are the same.

Listing 14-6 Saving and loading course information

```
void CMainFrame::OnFileSave()
{
     CFileDialog dlg(FALSE);
     CString strFile;
     CFile file;

     if ( dlg.DoModal() == IDOK )
     {
          strFile = dlg.GetPathName();
          if ( file.Open(strFile,CFile::modeCreate | CFile::modeWrite |
                    CFile::shareDenyNone) )
          {
               CArchive saveArchive(&file, CArchive::store |
                                   CArchive::bNoFlushOnDelete);
               App()->Data()->Serialize(saveArchive);
               saveArchive.Close();
               file.Close();
          }
     }
}

void CMainFrame::OnFileLoad()
{
     CFileDialog dlg(TRUE);
     CString strFile;
     CFile file;

     if ( dlg.DoModal() == IDOK )
     {
          strFile = dlg.GetPathName();
          if ( !FileExists(strFile) )
               return;

          if ( file.Open(strFile,CFile::modeRead | CFile::shareDenyNone) )
          {
               App()->Data()->DeleteData(); // delete data first
```

```
                CArchive loadArchive(&file,CArchive::load |
                                   CArchive::bNoFlushOnDelete);
                App()->Data()->Serialize(loadArchive);
                loadArchive.Close();
                file.Close();
            }
        }
    }
```

Writing Serialize functions for your CObject-derived classes is a fairly straightforward process. First, you need to check whether or not the archive is storing or loading. Then, conditionally, you need to write out or read in each data member of your class. Usually this is done through the use of the insertion or extraction operators. Alternatively, the CArchive::Read or CArchive::Write functions can be called to read from or write to the archive directly. If your data member is a CObject-derived class, call the Serialize function of that class, passing in the archive that was passed to you. In order to get a feel for how to do this, take a look at Listing 14-7, below, which contains various Serialize implementations found in the Courses application:

Listing 14-7 Serialization of Courses application objects

```
void CBook::Serialize(CArchive& ar)
{
    if ( ar.IsStoring() )
    {
        ar << m_strTitle;
        ar << m_strAuthor;
        ar << (WORD)m_bRequired;
    }
    else
    {
        ar >> m_strTitle;
        ar >> m_strAuthor;
        ar >> (WORD&)m_bRequired;
    }
}

void CCourse::Serialize(CArchive& ar)
{
    if ( ar.IsStoring() )
    {
        ar << m_strDepartment;
        ar << m_strTitle;
        ar << m_strDescription;
        ar << m_strRoom;
        ar << m_dCredits;
        ar << (DWORD)m_nProfessor;
    }
    else
    {
        ar >> m_strDepartment;
        ar >> m_strTitle;
        ar >> m_strDescription;
        ar >> m_strRoom;
        ar >> m_dCredits;
        ar >> (DWORD&)m_nProfessor;
```

continued on next page

continued from previous page

```
        }

        m_HeldOn.Serialize(ar);
        m_Syllabus.Serialize(ar);
        m_Students.Serialize(ar);
}

void CStudent::Serialize(CArchive& ar)
{
        if ( ar.IsStoring() )
        {
                ar << m_strFirstName;
                ar << m_strLastName;
                ar << (WORD)m_cMiddleInitial;
                ar << m_strSSN;
                ar << m_strAddress;
                ar << m_strCity;
                ar << m_strState;
                ar << m_strZip;
                ar << (WORD)m_nYear;
        }
        else
        {
                ar >> m_strFirstName;
                ar >> m_strLastName;
                ar >> (WORD&)m_cMiddleInitial;
                ar >> m_strSSN;
                ar >> m_strAddress;
                ar >> m_strCity;
                ar >> m_strState;
                ar >> m_strZip;
                ar >> (WORD&)m_nYear;
        }
}

void CProfessor::Serialize(CArchive& ar)
{
        if ( ar.IsStoring() )
        {
                ar << m_strFirstName;
                ar << m_strLastName;
                ar << (WORD)m_cMiddleInitial;
                ar << m_strSSN;
                ar << m_strAddress;
                ar << m_strCity;
                ar << m_strState;
                ar << m_strZip;
                ar << (WORD)m_nLevel;
        }
        else
        {
                ar >> m_strFirstName;
                ar >> m_strLastName;
                ar >> (WORD&)m_cMiddleInitial;
                ar >> m_strSSN;
                ar >> m_strAddress;
                ar >> m_strCity;
```

```
            ar >> m_strState;
            ar >> m_strZip;
            ar >> (WORD&)m_nLevel;
        }
}

void CCourseData::Serialize(CArchive& ar)
{
        CStudent* pStudent;
        CProfessor* pProfessor;
        int nI;

        CObject::Serialize(ar);

        if ( ar.IsStoring() )
        {
                ar << (WORD)m_Students.GetSize();
                for (nI = 0;nI < m_Students.GetSize();nI++)
                {
                        pStudent = (CStudent*)m_Students[nI];
                        ar << pStudent;
                }
        }
        else
        {
                WORD wSize;
                ar >> wSize;
                m_Students.SetSize(wSize);
                for (nI = 0;nI < m_Students.GetSize();nI++)
                {
                        ar >> pStudent;
                        m_Students.SetAt(nI,pStudent);
                }
        }

        if ( ar.IsStoring() )
        {
                ar << (WORD)m_Professors.GetSize();
                for (nI = 0;nI < m_Professors.GetSize();nI++)
                {
                        pProfessor = m_Professors[nI];
                        ar << pProfessor;
                }
        }
        else
        {
                WORD wSize;
                ar >> wSize;
                m_Professors.SetSize(wSize);
                for (nI = 0;nI < m_Professors.GetSize();nI++)
                {
                        ar >> pProfessor;
                        m_Professors.SetAt(nI,pProfessor);
                }
        }

        m_Courses.Serialize(ar);
}
```

CArchive Class Reference

CArchive

■ 2.0 ■ 3.0

Description The constructor for the CArchive class. CArchive initializes the members of the archive class, including the buffer used in conjunction with the CFile-derived class to be stored or retrieved.

Syntax public, CArchive(CFile* pFile, UINT nMode, int nBufSize = 4096, void * lpBuf = NULL);

Parameters

pFile File to use.

nMode Mode of archive, one of the following.

CArchive::store–archive is storing.

CArchive::load–archive is loading.

CArchive::bNoFlushOnDelete–Flush will not automatically be called when archive is destructed; you must call Close explictly instead.

CArchive:: bNoByteSwap–archive will not swap bytes when storing or loading primitive values; only applicable for the Macintosh (new to MFC 4.0).

nBufSize Buffer size for archive; lpBuf–buffer to use for archive.

Returns Nothing is returned.

See Also CArchive::~CArchive

Example See Listings 14-5 and 14-6

~CArchive

■ 2.0 ■ 3.0

Description Destructor for class, optionally automatically calls Close().

Syntax public, ~CArchive();

Parameters None.

Returns Nothing is returned.

See Also CArchive::CArchive

Example See Listings 14-5 and 14-6

Abort

■ 2.0 ■ 3.0

Description Abort closes the archive without flushing the archive buffer.

Syntax public, void Abort();

Parameters None.

Returns Nothing is returned.

See Also CArchive::Close, CArchive::Flush

Close

■ 2.0

Description Close calls Flush(), flushing the archive buffer, and closes the archive, preventing any future archive operations. You must close the file separately.

Syntax public, void Close();

Parameters None.

Returns Nothing is returned.

See Also CArchive::Abort, CArchive::Flush

Example See Listings 14-5 and 14-6

FillBuffer

■ 2.0 ■ 3.0 ■ UD

Description FillBuffer fills the internal archive buffer.

Syntax public, void FillBuffer(UINT nBytesNeeded);

Parameters

nBytesNeeded Number of bytes to fill.

Returns Nothing is returned.

Flush

■ 2.0 ■ 3.0

Description Flush flushes all bytes in the archive buffer, writing them out to the file.

Syntax public, void Flush();

Parameters None.

Returns Nothing is returned.

GetFile

■ 2.0 ■ 3.0

Description GetFile returns the CFile-derived object involved in the archive. Flush should be called first before doing anything with this file.

Syntax public, CFile* GetFile() const;

Parameters None.

Returns Pointer to CFile-derived object involved in the archive.

GetObjectSchema

■ 4.0

Description GetObjectSchema retrieves the schema value (the data member, m_nObjectSchema) for the CObject-derived object just read from the archive. This function should only be called once per serialized CObject-derived object and only when the archive is loading. GetObjectSchema resets m_nObjectSchema to (UINT)-1 to prevent further calling by the same object.

Syntax public, UINT GetObjectSchema();

Parameters None.

Returns Schema value for the last CObject-derived object read from the archive. The value is (UINT)-1 when the schema value is unknown.

See Also CArchive::SetObjectSchema

IsBufferEmpty ■ 2.0 ■ 3.0

Description IsBufferEmpty determines if the archive buffer is empty; only needed when using the CSocketFile class.

Syntax public, BOOL IsBufferEmpty() const;

Parameters None.

Returns TRUE if buffer is empty; FALSE otherwise.

IsByteSwapping ■ 4.0 ■ UD

Description IsByteSwapping determines if the archive has byte-swapping enabled. When byte-swapping is disabled, the archive will not swap bytes when storing or loading primitive values. This option is only applicable for the Macintosh.

Syntax public, BOOL IsByteSwapping() const;

Parameters None.

Returns TRUE if byte-swapping is enabled; FALSE otherwise.

IsLoading ■ 2.0 ■ 3.0

Description IsLoading determines if the archive is loading.

Syntax public, BOOL IsLoading() const;

Parameters None.

Returns TRUE if the archive is loading; FALSE otherwise.

See Also CArchive::IsStoring

IsStoring ■ 2.0 ■ 3.0

Description IsStoring determines if the archive is storing.

Syntax public, BOOL IsStoring() const;

Parameters None.

Returns TRUE if the archive is storing; FALSE otherwise.

See Also CArchive::IsLoading

OPERATOR<< ■ 2.0 ■ 3.0

Description The different versions of the insertion operator are used to write data of specific primitive types to the archive. Only portable types are included.

Syntax

```
public, CArchive& operator<<(BYTE by);
    CArchive& operator<<(WORD w);
    CArchive& operator<<(LONG l);
    CArchive& operator<<(DWORD dw);
    CArchive& operator<<(float f);
    CArchive& operator<<(double d);
    CArchive& operator<<(int i); (new to MFC 4.0)
    CArchive& operator<<(short w); (new to MFC 4.0)
    CArchive& operator<<(char ch); (new to MFC 4.0)
    CArchive& operator<<(unsigned u); (new to MFC 4.0)
```

Parameters

by	BYTE to be archived.
w	WORD (or short) to be archived.
l	LONG to be archived.
dw	DWORD to be archived.
f	float to be archived.
d	double to be archived.
i	int to be archived.
ch	char to be archived.
u	unsigned to be archived.

Returns Reference to archive; used to chain insertion operations together in one statement.

See Also CArchive::operator>>

Example See Listing 14-7

OPERATOR>> ■ 2.0 ■ 3.0

Description The different versions of the extraction operator are used to read data of specific primitive types from the archive. Only portable types are provided.

Syntax

```
public, CArchive& operator>>(BYTE by);
        CArchive& operator>>(WORD w);
        CArchive& operator>>(LONG l);
        CArchive& operator>>(DWORD dw);
        CArchive& operator>>(float f);
        CArchive& operator>>(double d);
        CArchive& operator>>(int& i);
        CArchive& operator>>(short& w);
```

CArchive& operator>>(char& ch);
CArchive& operator>>(unsigned& u);

Parameters

by	BYTE to be read from archive.
w	WORD (or short) to be read from archive.
l	LONG to be read from archive.
dw	DWORD to be read from archive.
f	float to be read from archive.
d	double to be read from archive.
i	int to be read from archive.
ch	char to be read from archive.
u	unsigned to be read from archive.

Returns Reference to archive; used to chain extraction operations together in one statement.

See Also CArchive::operator<<

Example See Listing 14-7

MapObject ■ 4.0

Description MapObject adds a CObject-derived object to the internal map of classes kept by the archive in order to maintain pointer references when storing and loading objects. This happens automatically when ReadObject or WriteObject is called, so the programmer typically would only call MapObject for CObject-derived objects not actually serialized to the archive.

Syntax public, void MapObject(const CObject* pOb);

Parameters

pOb Pointer to CObject-derived object to map.

Returns Nothing is returned.

Read ■ 2.0 ■ 3.0

Description Read is a buffered read from the archive; will call Read for the file involved. Use this function when there is no explicit archiving function for the data you need to read in.

Syntax public, UINT Read(void * lpBuf,UINT nMax);

Parameters

lpBuf Buffer to read to.

nMax Number of bytes to read.

Returns Number of bytes read.

See Also CArchive::Write

ReadClass

■ 4.0

Description ReadClass loads a CRuntimeClass object, holding run-time type information for some class, previously stored by calling WriteClass. ReadClass is called automatically by ReadObject when the archive is determining which type of object to load next.

Syntax
```
public, CRuntimeClass* ReadClass(const CRuntimeClass*
        pClassRefRequested = NULL,
        UINT* pSchema = NULL, DWORD* pObTag = NULL);
```

Parameters

pClassRefRequested Pointer to CRuntimeClass structure expected. If pClassRefRequested is not NULL and the loaded CRuntimeClass structure represents a class not derived from the class represented by pClassRefRequested, a CArchiveException is generated.

pSchema Pointer to UINT value used to store the schema value of the CRuntimeClass loaded. This pointer can be NULL if this information is not desired.

pObTag Pointer to DWORD value used to store the unique object tag of the CRuntimeClass loaded. This pointer can be NULL if this information is not desired.

Returns Pointer to CRuntimeClass loaded.

See Also CArchive::WriteClass, CArchive::SerializeClass, CArchive::ReadObject

ReadObject

■ 2.0 ■ 3.0

Description ReadObject dynamically creates an object loaded from the archive and calls its Serialize member. Each definition of the IMPLEMENT_SERIAL defines an extraction operator for the class that calls ReadObject with the appropriate CRuntimeClass object. The programmer will rarely need to call this function directly.

Syntax
```
public, CObject* ReadObject(const CRuntimeClass* pClass);
```

Parameters

pClass Run-time class information.

Returns Pointer to the object created.

See Also CArchive::WriteObject

ReadString

■ 4.0

Description ReadString loads ASCII data from the archive, terminating when a carriage return/ line feed pair is reached. A NULL character (\0) is then appended to the end of the string. This method differs from the way a

CString is typically archived in that the length of the string is not stored in the file.

Syntax public, LPTSTR ReadString(LPTSTR lpsz, UINT nMax);
BOOL ReadString(CString& rString);

Parameters

lpsz Pointer to buffer used to hold string.

nMax Size of the buffer passed in. nMax-1 equals the maximum number of characters that can be read.

rString Reference to CString used to hold string.

Returns Pointer to buffer used; NULL if there was an error. The second version returns TRUE if successful; FALSE otherwise.

See Also CArchive::WriteString

SerializeClass ■ 4.0

Description SerializeClass is a simple helper function that calls ReadClass if the archive is loaded or WriteClass if the archive is storing.

Syntax public, void SerializeClass(const CRuntimeClass* pClassRef);

Parameters

pClassRef Pointer to CRuntimeClass structure to serialize.

Returns Nothing is returned.

See Also CArchive::ReadClass, CArchive::WriteClass

SetLoadParams ■ 4.0

Description SetLoadParams sets the incremental grow size of an internal array used by MFC while archiving objects. This allows the programmer to tweak the serialization performance when loading a lot of objects.

Syntax public, void SetLoadParams(UINT nGrowBy = 1024);

Parameters

nGrowBy Number of elements to grow the array by.

Returns Nothing is returned.

See Also CArchive::SetStoreParams

SetObjectSchema ■ 4.0

Description SetObjectSchema sets the schema value (the data member, m_nObjectSchema) of the last CObject-derived object loaded. A subsequent call to GetObjectSchema will return this value. This is an advanced function that allows the programmer to force a particular schema of an object to be used.

Syntax public, void SetObjectSchema(UINT nSchema);

Parameters

nSchema Schema value to set.

Returns Nothing is returned.

See Also CArchive::GetObjectSchema

SetStoreParams ■ 4.0

Description SetStoreParams sets the hash size and block size of an internal map used by MFC while archiving objects. This allows the programmer to tweak the serialization performance when storing a lot of objects.

Syntax public, void SetStoreParams(UINT nHashSize = 2053, UINT nBlockSize = 128);

Parameters

nHashSize Hash size to use.

nBlockSize Block size to use

Returns Nothing is returned.

See Also CArchive::SetLoadParams

Write ■ 2.0 ■ 3.0

Description Write is a buffered write to the archive; will call Write for the file involved. Use this function when there is no explicit archiving function for the data you need to write.

Syntax public, void Write(const void FAR* lpBuf, UINT nMax);

Parameters

lpBuf Buffer to write from.

nMax Number of bytes to write.

Returns Nothing is returned.

See Also CArchive::Read

WriteClass ■ 4.0

Description WriteClass stores a CRuntimeClass object, holding run-time type information for some class. WriteClass is called automatically by WriteObject right before the Serialize member of the associated CObject-derived class is called.

Syntax public, void WriteClass(const CRuntimeClass* pClassRef);

Parameters

pClassRef Pointer to CRuntimeClass structure to write.

Returns Nothing is returned.

See Also CArchive::ReadClass, CArchive::SerializeClass, CArchive::WriteObject

WriteObject

■ 2.0 ■ 3.0

Description WriteObject writes class information for each object and calls its Serialize member. The programmer will rarely need to call this function directly.

Syntax public, void WriteObject(const CObject* pOb);

Parameters

pOb Object to be written.

Returns Nothing is returned.

See Also CArchive::ReadObject

WriteString

■ 4.0

Description WriteString stores ASCII data in the archive, terminating when the NULL (\0) character is found. Be aware that a carriage return/line feed pair, required by ReadString, is not written; just the contents of the character buffer are stored.

Syntax public, void WriteString(LPCTSTR lpsz);

Parameters

lpsz Pointer to character buffer to write.

Returns Nothing is returned.

See Also CArchive::ReadString

15

DEBUGGING AND EXCEPTION HANDLING

15

DEBUGGING AND EXCEPTION HANDLING

Despite the programmer's best efforts, rarely is code written without some errors in the beginning. Much of the programmer's time is spent trying to figure out what went wrong. This can involve using third-party diagnostic programs for postmortem analysis, running in the compiler's debugging environment to inspect variables or the call stack, or even mucking around at the assembly code level.

Each year, newer and more advanced tools arrive at the programmer's desktop, always striving to make the debugging process easier. Notwithstanding these efforts, there will invariably be limits as to what can be done outside of the source code itself. MFC, in an attempt to help the programmer from the "inside," has built within it many features to prevent errors from happening in the first place or, if they do occur, to either handle them as appropriate or provide as much information as possible regarding their nature and cause.

The MFC philosophy of error prevention and detection is comprised of four general principles: Verifying assumptions made during coding, object validation and inspection when needed, checking for memory corruption and leaks, and exception handling for unavoidable errors or failures beyond the scope of the source code of the application. Of these four, all but exception handling are typically done only in the debug build of your application. This is simply because the overhead required to implement these procedures becomes unnecessary and unwanted in streamlined release builds.

When writing a MFC application, the programmer is greatly encouraged to extend upon MFC's debugging facilities by incorporating these features into all new code and classes written. This point cannot be stressed too much by the authors of this book.

We feel very strongly that the key to good MFC programming is to take advantage of these services and build upon them at all times when appropriate. As a side note, with MFC 4.0, the implementation of many of these techniques was moved into the C run-time library so that non-MFC programmers could benefit as well. As a conclusion to this book, this chapter will discuss these techniques and give examples of their proper usage.

Asserting

One of the first things that stands out to someone looking at the code of MFC is the prolific usage of the ASSERT macro. As of MFC 4.0, there are more than 3700 calls to this macro. Listing 15-1 shows a few examples:

Listing 15-1 MFC ASSERT examples

```
BOOL CWnd::Attach(HWND hWndNew)
{
        ASSERT(m_hWnd == NULL);         // only attach once, detach on destroy
        // other code...

        return TRUE;
}

void CString::AllocBuffer(int nLen)
{
        ASSERT(nLen >= 0);
        ASSERT(nLen <= INT_MAX-1);      // max size (enough room for 1 extra)
        // other code...
}

void CDocument::AddView(CView* pView)
{
        // other code...
        ASSERT(pView->m_pDocument == NULL); // must not be already attached
        ASSERT(m_viewList.Find(pView, NULL) == NULL);    // must not be in list
        // other code...
}
```

ASSERT tests the Boolean value of an expression, the purpose being to validate the assumptions currently in effect for the surrounding code. When ASSERT is used, the expression should evaluate to non-zero ("TRUE") under normal circumstances. The code below the assertion relies upon the assumptions made in this expression. If the expression evaluates to non-zero, nothing happens. If the expression evaluates to zero, a dialog box appears, interrupting the flow of the program, similar to the one in Figure 15-1.

Clicking on the Abort button of this dialog box exits the application. Clicking on the Ignore button ignores the assertion and returns to the execution of the program. This is a very dangerous thing to do, usually leading to a subsequent unrecoverable application error (UAE). Clicking on the Retry button causes the application to break into the debugger, allowing the programmer to diagnose what caused the failed assertion. Prior to MFC 4.0, this dialog box was implemented by MFC itself. With MFC 4.0, this functionality was moved to the C run-time library and accessed by calling _CrtDbgReport.

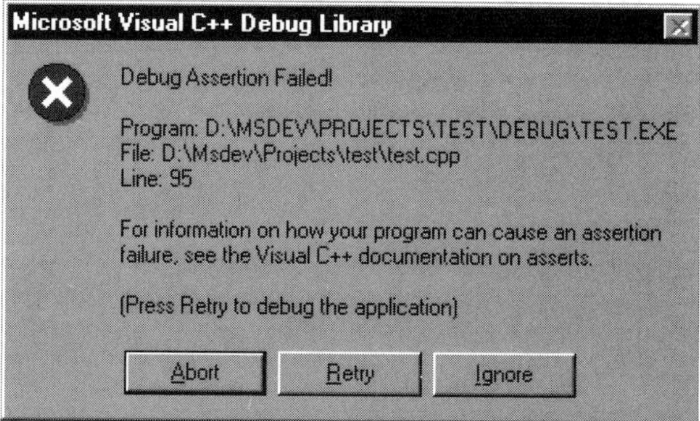

Figure 15-1 The MFC assertion dialog box

A lot of the time in MFC, there are comments in the general vicinity of an assertion giving the programmer some idea as to what went wrong. For example, here is a usage of ASSERT found in the CFrameWnd function for docking a toolbar:

```
ASSERT(pDockBar != NULL);
// assert fails when initial CBRS_ of bar does not
// match available docking sites, as set by EnableDocking()
```

Often, there are places in the MFC code where ASSERT(FALSE) appears, always causing a failed assertion. This indicates either that the programmer called an obsolete or unsupported function or that the flow of program execution reached an erroneous branch. The ASSERT macro is also used extensively to check for the presence of NULL pointers.

In general, the assertions in MFC are life-savers for the programmer. They help point out fundamental errors immediately during development that otherwise would go undetected or produce indeterminate behavior. Assertions also prevent bad parameters from being passed to lower-level API functions. In this way, they behave as a buffer between the source code and the operating system, and as a result cause far fewer UAEs in the application during the early stages of development.

The expression found in an ASSERT macro is not evaluated in the release build of an application. This is one of the facts most commonly overlooked by programmers new to MFC. The macro is set up, however, so that it can be placed anywhere a normal statement can be, both in debug and release builds. Under debug mode, ASSERT(f) expands to:

```
do
{
   if (!(f) && AfxAssertFailedLine(THIS_FILE, __LINE__))
         AfxDebugBreak();
} while (0)
```

The somewhat unusual appearance of the do/while loop in this circumstance ensures that the ASSERT macro must be terminated by a semi-colon. A compile-time error is produced without it. Under release mode, ASSERT(f) expands to:

```
((void)0)
```

The expression is then optimized away.

The AfxAssertFailedLine function is where the assertion dialog box is created and processed. It is also where the line of execution is when the programmer clicks on the Retry button and breaks into the debugger. The AfxDebugBreak function is what actually causes the break and can be used by the programmer as well. On i386-based platforms, AfxDebugBreak expands to _asm { int 3 }, causing a break in the debugger at the source code level. Otherwise, the Win32 API DebugBreak function is called, causing a break in the debugger at the kernel level that is less helpful most of the time.

The VERIFY macro behaves identically to the ASSERT macro except that the expression is evaluated both in debug and release builds. This allows the programmer to execute a statement and assert its returned value at the same time. For example, the following code:

```
pWnd = GetParent();
ASSERT(pWnd);
```

can be replaced with:

```
VERIFY(pWnd = GetParent);
```

MFC also includes several macros based on the ASSERT macro that perform specific commonly made assertions. ASSERT_KINDOF asserts that a pointer is of a particular class type by calling the CObject::IsKindOf function. ASSERT_POINTER asserts that a pointer is not NULL and points to a valid address. ASSERT_NULL_OR_POINTER asserts that a pointer is either NULL or points to a valid address. Examples of these special assertions are as follows:

```
ASSERT_KINDOF(CMyWnd, pWnd);
ASSERT_POINTER(m_pWnd);
ASSERT_NULL_OR_POINTER(pWnd);
```

Object Validation and Inspection

In Chapter 2, *The MFC Framework*, the CObject::AssertValid and CObject::Dump functions were discussed briefly. These functions are used in conjunction with other MFC debugging facilities to perform CObject-based validation and inspection only in debug builds of an application. When deriving classes from CObject, the programmer can override these members in order to provide specific handling for each new class. Although this is certainly not required, it is the best way to extend the fail-safe nature of MFC into your own application code.

The purpose of AssertValid is to perform assertions on any assumptions made in considering a particular object valid. Calling the AssertValid function of an object is often refered to as either asserting the validity of the object or validating the object. Typically, the implementation of an AssertValid function involves first calling the base class version of AssertValid and then using the ASSERT macro to check the values of the object's data members. As an example, Listing 15-2 shows the AssertValid function for the CObList class:

Listing 15-2 Example of AssertValid implementation

```
void CObList::AssertValid() const
{
	CObject::AssertValid();

	if (m_nCount == 0)
	{
		// empty list
		ASSERT(m_pNodeHead == NULL);
		ASSERT(m_pNodeTail == NULL);
	}
	else
	{
		// non-empty list
		ASSERT(AfxIsValidAddress(m_pNodeHead, sizeof(CNode)));
		ASSERT(AfxIsValidAddress(m_pNodeTail, sizeof(CNode)));
	}
}
```

MFC includes an ASSERT_VALID macro for providing a safe way of testing the validity of an object. ASSERT_VALID expands to a call to AfxAssertValidObject. First, if the object pointer is NULL, if the VTable pointer for the object is corrupt, or if the memory block for the object is invalid, AfxAssertValidObject simulates a failed assertion. Finally, if the object pointer is indeed valid, the AssertValid member is called. Often, an AssertValid function includes usages of the ASSERT_VALID macro to test the validity of contained data member objects. The CDocument::AssertValid function is shown in Listing 15-3.

Listing 15-3 Using the ASSERT_VALID macro in an AssertValid function

```
void CDocument::AssertValid() const
{
	CObject::AssertValid();

	POSITION pos = GetFirstViewPosition();
	while (pos != NULL)
	{
		CView* pView = GetNextView(pos);
		ASSERT_VALID(pView);
	}
}
```

The purpose of the Dump function is to output the values of the data members of an object in human-readable form to a dump context, encapsulated by the CDumpContext class. There is a default CDumpContext object, accessed by the afxDump global, that outputs the text to the debugger's Output window. The Dump function allows the programmer to programmatically inspect the contents of an object without having to break into the debugger. The CDumpContext class has overloaded versions of the operator << function that allows it to behave like a stream class for most primitive data types. There is also a version of the operator << function that calls the Dump function for a given CObject-derived object. The typical implementation of the Dump function involves calling the base class version of the Dump function and then using the dump context parameter to output the value of each data member. In order to maintain proper formatting, each Dump function should end with output of the newline character. Listing 15-4 shows some examples of the Dump function, one from MFC and one from a potential CPerson class derived from CObject.

Listing 15-4 Dump function examples

```
void CBitmapButton::Dump(CDumpContext& dc) const
{
      CButton::Dump(dc);

      dc << "m_bitmap = " << (UINT)m_bitmap.m_hObject;
      dc << "\nm_bitmapSel = " << (UINT)m_bitmapSel.m_hObject;
      dc << "\nm_bitmapFocus = " << (UINT)m_bitmapFocus.m_hObject;
      dc << "\nm_bitmapDisabled = " << (UINT)m_bitmapDisabled.m_hObject;

      dc << "\n";
}

void CPerson::Dump(CDumpContext& dc) const
{
      CObject::Dump(dc);

      dc << "First name = " << m_strFirstName;
      dc << "\nLast name = " << m_strLastName;
      dc << "\nAddress = " << m_strAddress;
      dc << "\nPhone Number = " << m_strPhoneNumber;
      dc << "\nAge = " << m_nAge;
      dc << "\nMarital Status = " << m_cMarried;

      dc << "\n";
}
```

Unlike the AssertValid function, MFC conditionally calls the Dump function of data members within a Dump function for an object. The CDumpContext class supports both deep and shallow dumps through the use of the GetDepth and SetDepth members. By default, the depth value of the dump context is set to 0, indicating a shallow dump. When this value is greater than 0, the CObject-derived data members of the object should be dumped as well. This is especially useful for the MFC collection classes. Listing 15-5 shows the Dump function for the CObArray class.

Listing 15-5 Non-shallow Dump example

```
void CObArray::Dump(CDumpContext& dc) const
{
     CObject::Dump(dc);

     dc << "with " << m_nSize << " elements";
     if (dc.GetDepth() > 0)
     {
     for (int i = 0; i < m_nSize; i++)
     dc << "\n\t[" << i << "] = " << m_pData[i];
     }

     dc << "\n";
}
```

The output of a dump context can go either to the Output window of the debugger or a file. When writing the output, the CDumpContext class will either call the AfxOutputDebugString function or use a pointer to a CFile object passed in during construction to write out the text. AfxOutputDebugString expands to a call to the C run-time library function _RPT0 for debug builds and expands to the Win32 API OutputDebugString function for release builds. As mentioned above, the default dump context, accessed by the afxDump global variable, goes to the Output window of the debugger. The AfxDump function can be used to dump an object to this default dump context. The implementation of this function is very straightforward, as shown in Listing 15-6.

Listing 15-6 The AfxDump function

```
void AFXAPI AfxDump(const CObject* pOb)
{
     afxDump << pOb;
}
```

The CDumpContext class will not output anything unless tracing has been enabled for the debugging environment. The programmer can enable tracing by using the TRACER.EXE program that comes with the Visual C++ product. Running this program produces this screen, shown in Figure 15-2.

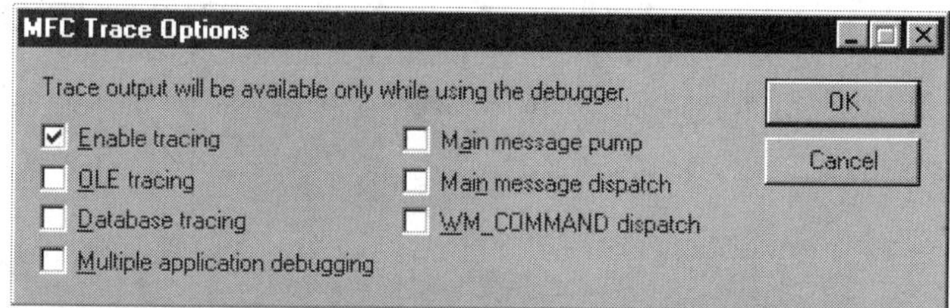

Figure 15-2 The TRACER.EXE program

This program modifies the tracing flags kept in the AFX.INI file in the \MFC\SRC directory. The programmer can set these flags to fine-tune the tracing output produced by MFC during debug builds. The afxTraceEnabled global variable specifies whether or not tracing output has been enabled at all. The afxTraceFlags global variable specifies which of the tracing options have been set. Tracing can be enabled for OLE operations, ODBC or DAO operations, message pumping and dispatch, and command message dispatch individually or in different combinations. If multiple application tracing is enabled, the application name is appended to each output text. To enable object dumping, there is no specific flag to be set—tracing itself just needs to be enabled. MFC periodically checks for these flags and conditionally uses the TRACE macro.

The TRACE macro is used to format text in a print-like fashion and send it to the default dump context, the Output window of the debugger. The TRACE macro calls the AfxTrace function, that in turn uses the _vstprintf function to format the text and then outputs it to afxDump. Here are some examples of TRACE macro usage:

```
TRACE(``Error code: %I\n",m_nCode);
TRACE(``Day: %i, Month: %i",tDate.GetDay(),tDate.GetMonth());
```

There are also versions of the TRACE macro that enforce a certain number of parameters. TRACE0 allows no other parameters other than the format string. The TRACE1, TRACE2, and TRACE3 macros require one, two, and three additional parameters respectively.

Detecting Memory Corruption and Leaks

In debug builds of an application, MFC monitors all memory allocations. When a debug build of an application exits, MFC performs a check of the memory allocated and reports any leakage to the Output window of the debugger. MFC uses the CMemoryState class to implement this feature. CMemoryState is used to perform a checkpoint of the current memory state and calculate the difference between two memory states and report the statistics. MFC creates a CMemoryState object when the application loads, performs a checkpoint by calling the CheckPoint function, then creates another CMemoryState object when the application terminates, calling the CheckPoint function to perform a second checkpoint, and calls the Difference function of a third CMemoryState object to determine if the memory states are different (if memory was allocated, but not deleted). The DumpStatistics function is then called to report the leakage. Every object dumped was allocated by the application but not deleted before the application terminated. Listing 15-7 is an example of this leakage report.

Listing 15-7 Memory leak report

```
Detected memory leaks!
Dumping objects ->
C:\Msdev\Projects\test\test.cpp(156) : {151} normal block at 0x00650EAC, 24 bytes long.
 Data: <                > CD CD CD CD CD CD CD CD CD CD CD CD CD CD CD CD
C:\Msdev\Projects\test\test.cpp(155) : {150} client block at 0x006523D0, subtype 0, 20 bytes
long.
a CObject object at $006523D0, 20 bytes long
Object dump complete.
```

A client block is a block allocated for CObject-derived classes. A normal block is for all other memory allocations. The numbers between the curly braces refer to a reference number for the allocation. When an application begins, the first memory request is given an allocation number of 1, the second is given an allocation number of 2, and so forth. When a CObject-derived class is leaked, the Dump function for this object is called.

There are many ways of determining where memory leaks occur and why. The first thing to do is add a #define new DEBUG_NEW line at the top of each implementation file. This causes the file name and line number for each memory allocation to be kept so that this information can be included when reporting leaks, as shown in the report above. Unfortunately, this does not tell when the offending memory allocation was made, but instead just where. The AfxSetAllocStop function addresses this issue. Calling this function with a particular allocation number tells MFC to break into the debugger when this allocation is made. This is a very powerful tool when trying to nail down each leaked memory allocation. The programmer can also set up a callback function to be called for each memory allocation by calling the AfxSetAllocHook function. Prior to MFC 4.0, this functionality was implemented entirely in MFC. In MFC 4.0 and above, however, much of this code was moved to the C run-time library.

The programmer, at any time, can also perform a memory check by calling AfxCheckMemory. This function tests for heap corruption. Listing 15-8 shows an example of heap corruption and what is reported from a call to AfxCheckMemory.

Listing 15-8 Memory corruption example

```
void CTestApp::OnFileCorruptheap()
{
        // Allocate client block CObject-derived object
        CTestObject* pObject = new CTestObject();

        // Allocate normal block structure
        CTestStruct* pStruct = new CTestStruct();

        // reference invalid client block memory
        *((char*)pObject - 1) = 'X';

        // reference invalid normal block memory
        *((char*)pStruct + sizeof(CTestStruct) + 1) = 'X';

        // perform memory check
        AfxCheckMemory();
}
```

```
memory check error at 0x00651E6D = 0x58, should be 0xFD.
DAMAGE: after Normal block (#145) at 0x00651E54.
Normal allocated at file C:\Msdev\Projects\test\test.cpp(163).
Normal located at 0x00651E54 is 24 bytes long.
memory check error at 0x0065136B = 0x58, should be 0xFD.
DAMAGE: before Client block (#144) at 0x0065136C.
Client allocated at file C:\Msdev\Projects\test\test.cpp(162).
Client located at 0x0065136C is 20 bytes long.
```

Similar to the memory leak report, client blocks refer to blocks allocated for CObject-derived objects and normal blocks refer to all other allocations. The numbers in parentheses following the '#' character refer to the memory allocation numbers for the blocks. If the #define new DEBUG_NEW line does not appear in the implementation file of the memory allocations, the file names and line numbers do not appear on this report.

Exception Handling

Of all the MFC techniques for catching programmer errors, exception handling is by far the most important. As mentioned in the beginning of the chapter, it is the only mechanism also present in the release build of an application. Furthermore, it not only handles programmer errors that can be debugged and fixed, but also it addresses unavoidable errors arising from I/O-type problems and system resource limitations (e.g., low-memory conditions). Exception handling is actually a principle inherent in the C++ language itself. Space prohibits an in-depth discussion of this very significant feature of the language. Instead, the general MFC implementation of exception handling as well as the CException-derived classes will be described.

Prior to Visual C++ 2.0, the Microsoft compiler did not support C++ exceptions. As a result, MFC implemented the TRY/THROW/CATCH concept through macros that took advantage of the C run-time library setjmp and longjmp functions. There were several limitations to this setup, the primary one being that the programmer could only throw exceptions derived from the CException class. When the compiler did support C++ exceptions, MFC was changed such that the TRY/THROW/CATCH macros now map to the try/catch/throw C++ keywords.

Programmers creating new applications are encouraged to use the C++ keywords: They produce slightly smaller code and accept thrown exceptions of any data type. The MFC macros are supported, yet they still can only be used with CException-derived exception objects. The major differences between the MFC macros and the C++ keywords are as follows:

- The MFC macros automatically delete the CException-derived exception handled by a CATCH block. The C++ keywords do not. When MFC throws an exception, a CException-derived object is dynamically created and the pointer to this object is what is thrown. This means that if the CException-derived object is caught by the C++ keyword catch, this object must be deleted by the programmer.
- The catch syntax is different. The C++ keyword syntax is catch(CException* e) whereas the MFC macro syntax is CATCH(CException, e).
- The CATCH and the AND_CATCH macros both map to the catch keyword. No distinction needs to be made. Moreover, the END_CATCH macro maps to nothing; it is not needed.
- Both the THROW and the THROW_LAST macros map to the throw keyword. The THROW macro, however, is used to throw a new exception whereas the THROW_LAST macro is used to re-throw the current exception.

CException-based classes are used by MFC to throw and catch internal exceptions. The programmer is free to use these classes as well. Table 15-1 lists these classes and describes the context in which they should be used.

Table 15-1 MFC exceptions

Exception Class	Meaning
CException	Base class for exceptions.
CSimpleException	Generic exception.
CNotSupportedException	Not-supported feature was requested.
CMemoryException	Out-of-memory exception.
CArchiveException	Error while serializing objects.
CFileException	Error during file I/O.
CResourceException	Resource not found or unable to be loaded.
CUserException	User-specified exception.

The AfxThrow... functions, discussed in Chapter 2, *The MFC Framework*, can be used to throw these exceptions automatically. A good example of proper MFC exception handling can be seen in the CArchive::ReadString function, shown in Listing 15-9 below:

Listing 15-9 MFC exception handling

```
LPTSTR CArchive::ReadString(LPTSTR lpsz, UINT nMax)
{
      ASSERT(AfxIsValidAddress(lpsz, (nMax+1) * sizeof(TCHAR)));

      _TUCHAR ch;
      UINT nRead = 0;

      TRY
      {
      // read string here
      }
      CATCH(CArchiveException, e)
      {
            if (e->m_cause == CArchiveException::endOfFile)
            {
                  DELETE_EXCEPTION(e);
                  if (nRead == 0)
                        return NULL;
            }
            else
            {
                  THROW_LAST();
            }
      }
      END_CATCH

      lpsz[nRead] = '\0';
      return lpsz;
}
```

APPENDIX

MFC CROSS-REFERENCE CLASS HIERARCHY

Classes are grouped by function and by parent class. Derivations are shown by arrows.

MFC Base Class

Class	Chapter
CObject	chapter 2

Support Classes

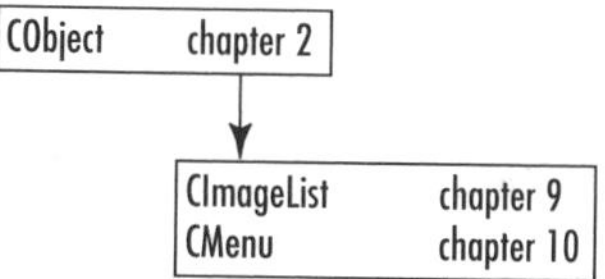

Class	Chapter
CArchive	chapter 14
CCmdUI	chapter 4
CCommandLineInfo	chapter 3
CCreateContext	chapter 5
CDataExchange	chapter 8
CDumpContext	chapter 15
CFileStatus	chapter 14
CPoint	chapter 12
CRect	chapter 12
CRuntmeClass	chapter 2
CSize	chapter 12
CString	chapter 13

Command Targets

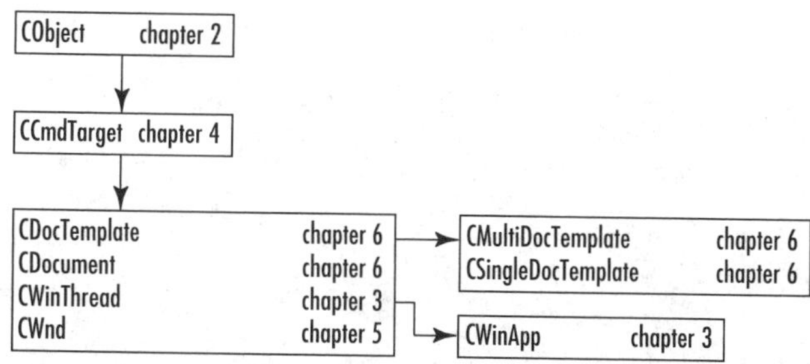

Exceptions

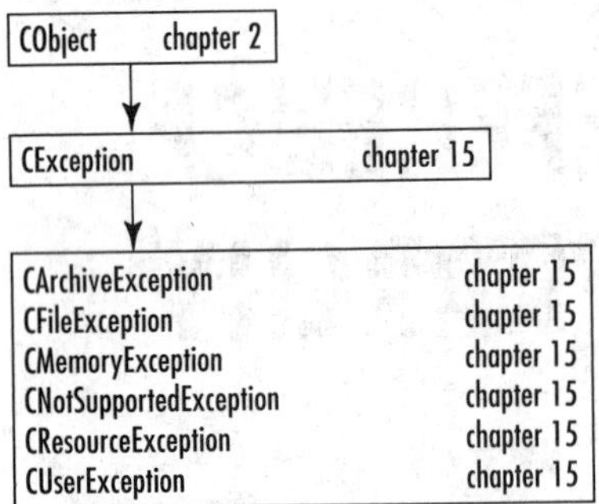

Windows

Miscellaneous

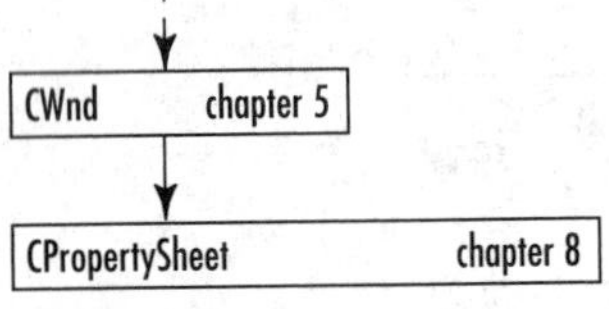

Frame Windows

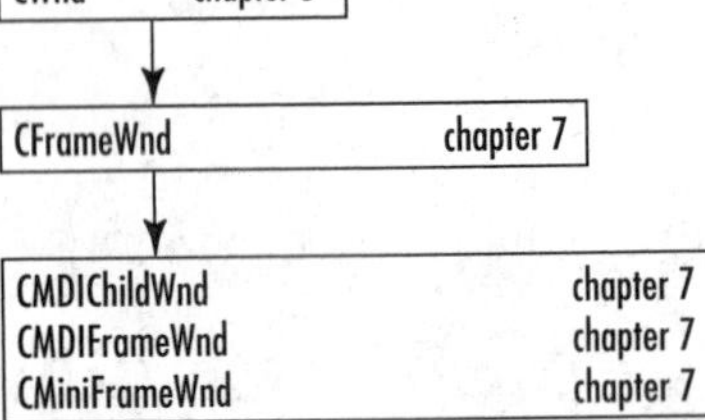

Control Bars

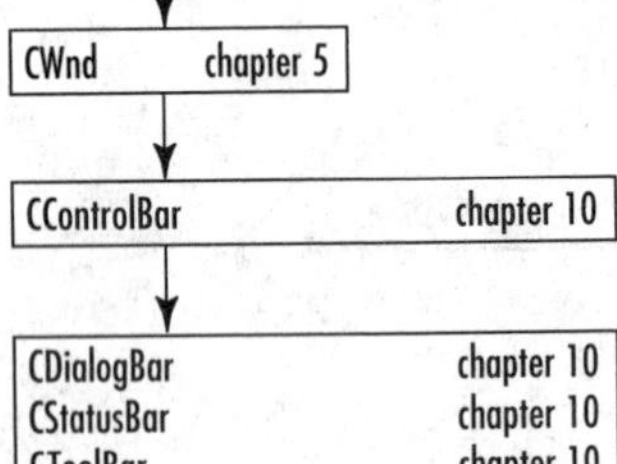

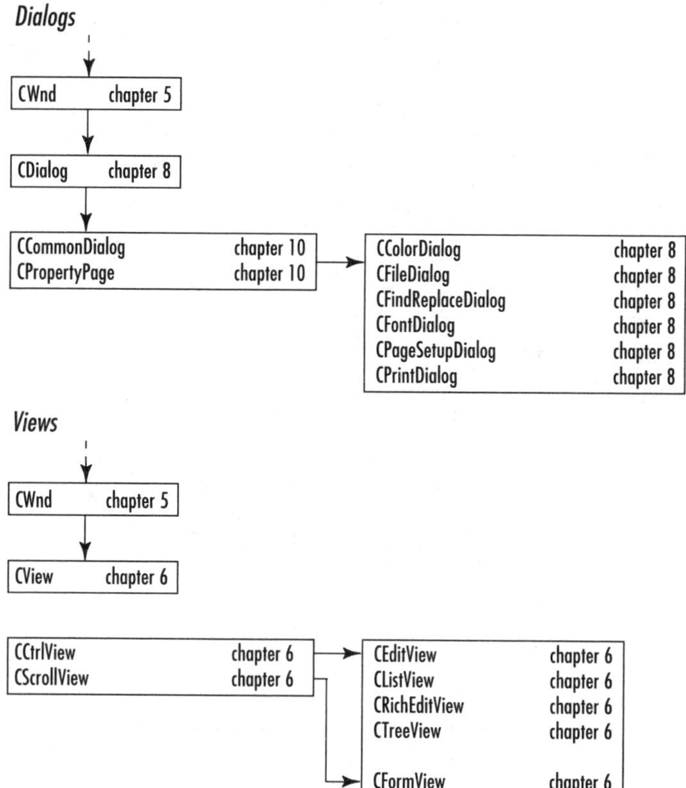
Dialogs
CWnd chapter 5
CDialog chapter 8
CCommonDialog chapter 10
CPropertyPage chapter 10
CColorDialog chapter 8
CFileDialog chapter 8
CFindReplaceDialog chapter 8
CFontDialog chapter 8
CPageSetupDialog chapter 8
CPrintDialog chapter 8
Views
CWnd chapter 5
CView chapter 6
CCtrlView chapter 6
CScrollView chapter 6
CEditView chapter 6
CListView chapter 6
CRichEditView chapter 6
CTreeView chapter 6
CFormView chapter 6

Window Controls

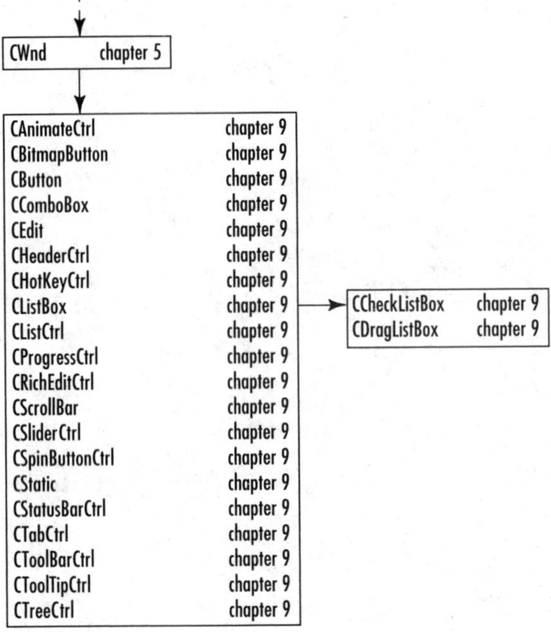
CWnd chapter 5
CAnimateCtrl chapter 9
CBitmapButton chapter 9
CButton chapter 9
CComboBox chapter 9
CEdit chapter 9
CHeaderCtrl chapter 9
CHotKeyCtrl chapter 9
CListBox chapter 9
CListCtrl chapter 9
CProgressCtrl chapter 9
CRichEditCtrl chapter 9
CScrollBar chapter 9
CSliderCtrl chapter 9
CSpinButtonCtrl chapter 9
CStatic chapter 9
CStatusBarCtrl chapter 9
CTabCtrl chapter 9
CToolBarCtrl chapter 9
CToolTipCtrl chapter 9
CTreeCtrl chapter 9
CCheckListBox chapter 9
CDragListBox chapter 9

Files

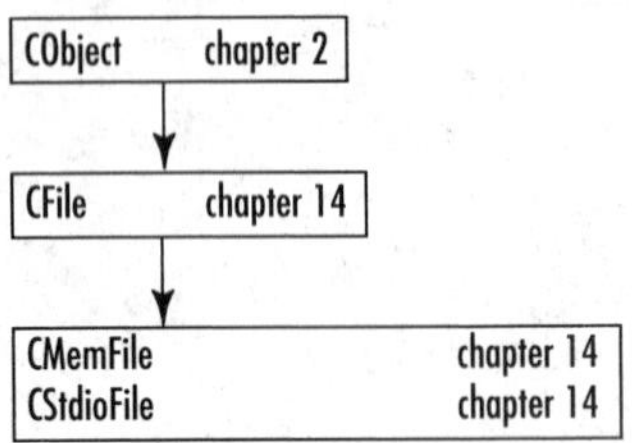
CObject chapter 2
CFile chapter 14
CMemFile chapter 14
CStdioFile chapter 14

Device Context and GDI Classes

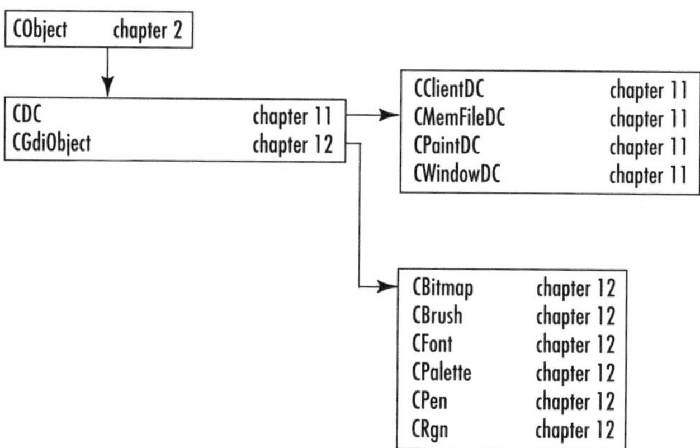

Collection Classes

Arrays

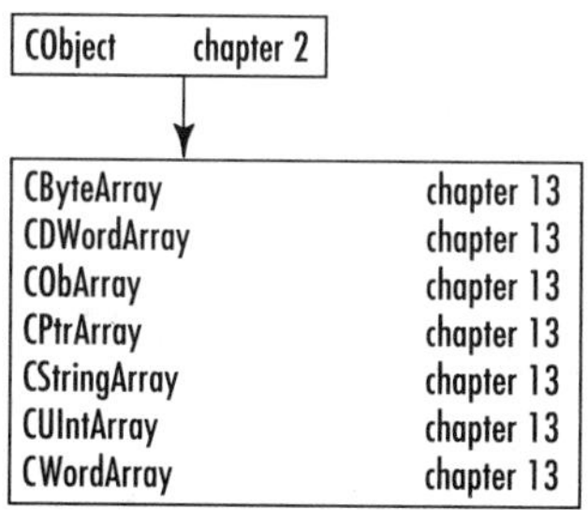

Lists

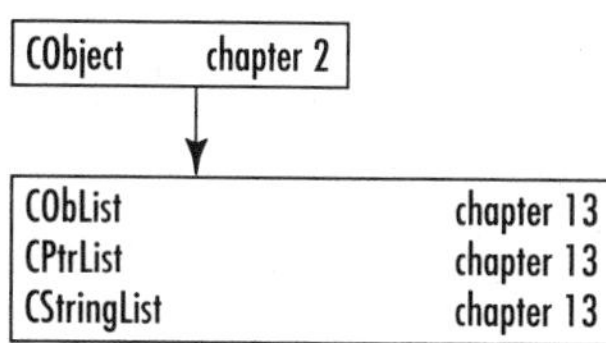

Maps

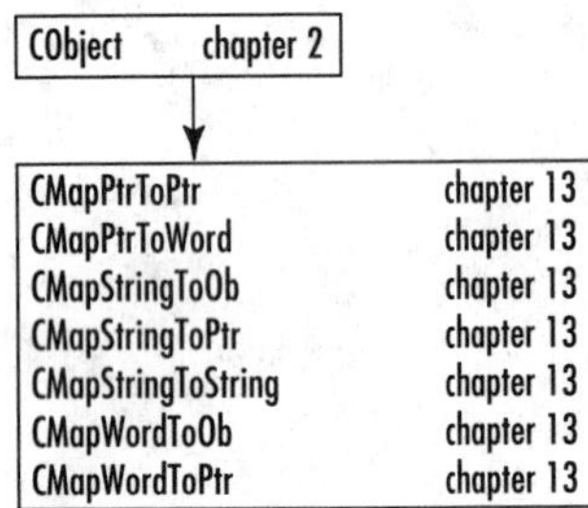
CObject chapter 2
CMapPtrToPtr chapter 13
CMapPtrToWord chapter 13
CMapStringToOb chapter 13
CMapStringToPtr chapter 13
CMapStringToString chapter 13
CMapWordToOb chapter 13
CMapWordToPtr chapter 13

Template-Based Classes

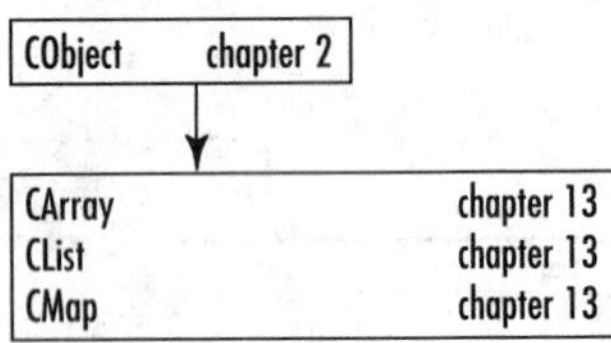
CObject chapter 2
CArray chapter 13
CList chapter 13
CMap chapter 13

Index

A

B

C

T

U

V

W

NOTES

NOTES

NOTES

NOTES

NOTES

NOTES

NOTES

NOTES

NOTES

NOTES

NOTES

ENVIRONMENTAL AWARENESS

Books have a substantial influence on the destruction of the forests of the Earth. For example, it takes 17 trees to produce one ton of paper. A first printing of 30,000 copies of a typical 480-page book consumes 108,000 pounds of paper, which will require 918 trees!

Waite Group Press™ is against the clear-cutting of forests and supports reforestation of the Pacific Northwest of the United States and Canada, where most of this paper comes from. As a publisher with several hundred thousand books sold each year, we feel an obligation to give back to the planet. We will therefore support organizations which seek to preserve the forests of planet Earth.

This is a legal agreement between you, the end user and purchaser, and The Waite Group®, Inc., and the authors of the programs contained in the disk. By opening the sealed disk package, you are agreeing to be bound by the terms of this Agreement. If you do not agree with the terms of this Agreement, promptly return the unopened disk package and the accompanying items (including the related book and other written material) to the place you obtained them for a refund.

SOFTWARE LICENSE

1. The Waite Group, Inc. grants you the right to use one copy of the enclosed software programs (the programs) on a single computer system (whether a single CPU, part of a licensed network, or a terminal connected to a single CPU). Each concurrent user of the program must have exclusive use of the related Waite Group, Inc. written materials.

2. The program, including the copyrights in each program, is owned by the respective author and the copyright in the entire work is owned by The Waite Group, Inc. and they are therefore protected under the copyright laws of the United States and other nations, under international treaties. You may make only one copy of the disk containing the programs exclusively for backup or archival purposes, or you may transfer the programs to one hard disk drive, using the original for backup or archival purposes. You may make no other copies of the programs, and you may make no copies of all or any part of the related Waite Group, Inc. written materials.

3. You may not rent or lease the programs, but you may transfer ownership of the programs and related written materials (including any and all updates and earlier versions) if you keep no copies of either, and if you make sure the transferee agrees to the terms of this license.

4. You may not decompile, reverse engineer, disassemble, copy, create a derivative work, or otherwise use the programs except as stated in this Agreement.

GOVERNING LAW

This Agreement is governed by the laws of the State of California.

LIMITED WARRANTY

The following warranties shall be effective for 90 days from the date of purchase: (i) The Waite Group, Inc. warrants the enclosed disk to be free of defects in materials and workmanship under normal use; and (ii) The Waite Group, Inc. warrants that the programs, unless modified by the purchaser, will substantially perform the functions described in the documentation provided by The Waite Group, Inc. when operated on the designated hardware and operating system. The Waite Group, Inc. does not warrant that the programs will meet purchaser's requirements or that operation of a program will be uninterrupted or error-free. The program warranty does not cover any program that has been altered or changed in any way by anyone other than The Waite Group, Inc. The Waite Group, Inc. is not responsible for problems caused by changes in the operating characteristics of computer hardware or computer operating systems that are made after the release of the programs, nor for problems in the interaction of the programs with each other or other software.

THESE WARRANTIES ARE EXCLUSIVE AND IN LIEU OF ALL OTHER WARRANTIES OF MERCHANTABILITY OR FITNESS FOR A PARTICULAR PURPOSE OR OF ANY OTHER WARRANTY, WHETHER EXPRESS OR IMPLIED.

EXCLUSIVE REMEDY

The Waite Group, Inc. will replace any defective disk without charge if the defective disk is returned to The Waite Group, Inc. within 90 days from date of purchase.

This is Purchaser's sole and exclusive remedy for any breach of warranty or claim for contract, tort, or damages.

LIMITATION OF LIABILITY

THE WAITE GROUP, INC. AND THE AUTHORS OF THE PROGRAMS SHALL NOT IN ANY CASE BE LIABLE FOR SPECIAL, INCIDENTAL, CONSEQUENTIAL, INDIRECT, OR OTHER SIMILAR DAMAGES ARISING FROM ANY BREACH OF THESE WARRANTIES EVEN IF THE WAITE GROUP, INC. OR ITS AGENT HAS BEEN ADVISED OF THE POSSIBILITY OF SUCH DAMAGES.

THE LIABILITY FOR DAMAGES OF THE WAITE GROUP, INC. AND THE AUTHORS OF THE PROGRAMS UNDER THIS AGREEMENT SHALL IN NO EVENT EXCEED THE PURCHASE PRICE PAID.

COMPLETE AGREEMENT

This Agreement constitutes the complete agreement between The Waite Group, Inc. and the authors of the programs, and you, the purchaser.

Some states do not allow the exclusion or limitation of implied warranties or liability for incidental or consequential damages, so the above exclusions or limitations may not apply to you. This limited warranty gives you specific legal rights; you may have others, which vary from state to state.

SATISFACTION REPORT CARD

Please fill out this card if you wish to know of future updates to *Microsoft Foundation Class 4 Bible*, or to receive our catalog.

First Name: _______________ **Last Name:** _______________

Street Address: _______________

City: _______________ **State:** _______________ **Zip:** _______________

E-mail Address _______________

Daytime Telephone: ( ) _______________

Date product was acquired: Month Day Year Your Occupation:

Overall, how would you rate *Microsoft Foundation Class 4 Bible*?

- ☐ Excellent ☐ Very Good ☐ Good
- ☐ Fair ☐ Below Average ☐ Poor

What did you like MOST about this book? _______________

What did you like LEAST about this book? _______________

Please describe any problems you may have encountered with installing or using the disk: _______________

How did you use this book (problem-solver, tutorial, reference...)? _______________

What is your level of computer expertise?

- ☐ New ☐ Dabbler ☐ Hacker
- ☐ Power User ☐ Programmer ☐ Experienced Professional

What computer languages are you familiar with? _______________

Please describe your computer hardware:

Computer _______________ Hard disk _______________

5.25" disk drives _______________ 3.5" disk drives _______________

Video card _______________ Monitor _______________

Printer _______________ Peripherals _______________

Sound Board _______________ CD ROM _______________

Where did you buy this book?

- ☐ Bookstore (name): _______________
- ☐ Discount store (name): _______________
- ☐ Computer store (name): _______________
- ☐ Catalog (name): _______________
- ☐ Direct from WGP ☐ Other _______________

What price did you pay for this book? _______________

What influenced your purchase of this book?

- ☐ Recommendation ☐ Advertisement
- ☐ Magazine review ☐ Store display
- ☐ Mailing ☐ Book's format
- ☐ Reputation of Waite Group Press ☐ Other

How many computer books do you buy each year? _______________

How many other Waite Group books do you own? _______________

What is your favorite Waite Group book? _______________

Is there any program or subject you would like to see Waite Group Press cover in a similar approach? _______________

Additional comments? _______________

Please send to: **Waite Group Press**
200 Tamal Plaza
Corte Madera, CA 94925

☐ **Check here for a free Waite Group catalog**

SATISFACTION CARD

BEFORE YOU OPEN THE DISK OR CD-ROM PACKAGE ON THE FACING PAGE, CAREFULLY READ THE LICENSE AGREEMENT.

Opening this package indicates that you agree to abide by the license agreement found in the back of this book. If you do not agree with it, promptly return the unopened disk package (including the related book) to the place you obtained them for a refund.